lonely planet

Europe

Kerry Walker, Kate Armstrong, Mark Baker,
Joel Balsam, Cristian Bonetto, Marc Di Duca,
Peter Dragicevich, Mark Eveleigh, Kata Fári,
Anthony Ham, Paula Hotti, Anna Kaminski,
Catherine Le Nevez, James March, Vesna Maric,
Virginia Maxwell, Owen Morton, Anja Mutić,
Isabella Noble, Leonid Ragozin, Anna Richards,
Helena Smith, Joana Taborda, Brana Vladisavljevic,
Luke Waterson, Nicola Williams,
Barbara Woolsey, Angelo Zinna

CONTENTS

Gullfoss (p601), Iceland

Roman Forum (p654), Rome, Italy

Paris (p384), France

Burek (p46)

Toolkit

Storybook

FLORIAN AUGUSTIN/SHUTTERSTOCK

Eisriesenwelt ice caves (p89), Austria

EUROPE
THE JOURNEY BEGINS HERE

My heart beats Europe. For me, childhood holidays each year meant ticking off a new country or island, and I would cry when our plane landed back in London. Two years of post-graduation travels around Europe with a 1960s bubble caravan in tow forged a profound love of this continent, with its insanely rich mix of languages, landscapes, food and culture. As I strayed further into Europe as a Lonely Planet author, the countries I explored touched deeper still. I lived for seven years in Germany's Black Forest. I spent stints working in France, Switzerland, Corfu and Spain. These places shaped me. Today, I still get a thrill when I pick up a map of Greece, my finger alighting on a never-heard-of island, or board a train curling high into the Alps, with all the wonder of the day yet to come.

My favourite experience
is delving deep into the frozen chambers of Eisriesenwelt ice caves (p89) in Werfen before striking out on a sky-high hike in Austria's Tennengebirge.

Kerry Walker

𝕏 *@kerryawalker*

Kerry wrote the Plan Your Trip, Toolkit and History chapters, and curated the Austria chapter.

WHO GOES WHERE

Our writers and experts choose the places which, for them, define Europe.

Nafplio (p540) is my Greek magnet. I love wandering through the alleyways to evoke aspects of the past. The crowds don't detract from Nafplio's soul: the bougainvillea-enshrouded Venetian houses, the maze of pedestrian lanes and the generosity of its locals.

Kate Armstrong
katearmstrongtravelwriter.com
Kate curated the Greece chapter.

My favourite place in Prague is the **Charles Bridge** (p285). I love to wander the old town's closed-in, cobbled streets and then emerge onto the open bridge – hopefully on a sunny day.

Mark Baker
markbakerprague.com
Mark curated the Czechia, Romania and Slovenia chapters.

I love to wander around the Ottoman-era stone alleyways in **Berat** (p62), snapping photos as the light strikes its cherished windows.

Joel Balsam
@*joelbalsam*
Joel curated the Albania chapter.

Naples (p694) is a visceral, esoteric place, littered with contradiction, magic and a raw energy. As elegant and erudite as it is coarse and gritty, Napoli has almost 3000 years of tales to tell – in its ghostly catacombs, gilded royal palaces and beautiful hilltop vistas.

Cristian Bonetto
@*cristian_alessandro_bonetto*
Cristian curated the Italy chapter.

STREETFLASH/SHUTTERSTOCK

RATNAKORN PIYASIRISOROST/GETTY IMAGES

CHANOOK PHOTOGRAPHY/SHUTTERSTOCK

KYLE LITTLE/GETTY IMAGES

A blend of 20th-century history, compelling museums, windswept beaches and filling Baltic food make the capital of the north, **Gdańsk** (p889), my favourite place in Poland. It's a city I never grow tired of returning to.

Marc Di Duca
@marcdiduca
Marc curated the Poland chapter.

Montenegro claimed a special place in my heart the first time I crossed the border from Croatia and took a drive around the astonishingly beautiful **Bay of Kotor** (p793). The same thrill hits me each time I return.

Peter Dragicevich
@peterdragnz
Peter curated the Montenegro chapter.

My favourite experience is pausing halfway across the sage-green **Liberty Bridge** (p575) to marvel at Budapest's incredible beauty.

Kata Fári
@kata.fari
Kata curated the Hungary chapter.

My perfect day in North Macedonia centres on **Lake Ohrid** (p834), in the timeworn villages that feel far from the clamour of the modern world. I love mornings in Trpejca, a seafood lunch in Ohrid town, and an afternoon and evening in Vevčani, truly the medieval Balkans the world forgot.

Anthony Ham
𝕏 @AnthonyHamWrite
Anthony curated the Denmark, Finland, Iceland, Kosovo, North Macedonia, Norway and Sweden chapters.

For nearly 20 years, the Curonian Spit has been one of my happy places: I've come back to Nida, time and again to walk in solitude along pine-scented forest trails and up the **Parnidis Dune** (p763) to recapture the silence that's missing from my daily life.

Anna Kaminski
@anna.cohen.kaminski
Anna wrote the From Baguettes to Vodka essay and curated the Lithuania chapter.

My favourite experience is the **Slea Head Drive** (p631), a journey through millennia of history along spectacular, edge-of-the-world coastline, ending in an inviting, music-filled Dingle pub.

Catherine Le Nevez

lonelyplanet.com/authors/catherine-le-nevez
Catherine curated the Ireland chapter.

A romantic collection of widescreen valleys, chocolate-box villages and stately homes, the **Peak District** (p194) is my favourite place to get lost for a while. The wind-sculpted hills of the Hope Valley are the most spectacular stretch.

James March

⊙ *@jmarchtravel*
James curated the Britain chapter.

My favourite place is Sarajevo, where the Ottoman quarter of **Baščaršija** (p152) and the medley of historic architecture is coupled with great food and warm and wonderful locals.

Vesna Maric

⊙ *@vesnamarx*
Vesna curated the Bosnia & Hercegovina chapter.

There's nowhere quite like **İstanbul** (p1144). Whether it be the remnants of a grand Byzantine-era palace or a backstreet tea garden with a Bosphorus view, serendipitous encounters make every visit magical.

Virginia Maxwell

⊙ *@maxwellvirginia*
Virginia curated the Türkiye chapter.

A cloudburst erupted just as I reached the top of the stairs of the **Candle of Gratitude** (p781). Then a beautiful rainbow appeared in the sky, stretching across the river from Moldova to Ukraine.

Owen Morton

⊙ *@owenmortonmanul*
Owen curated the Moldova chapter.

I love driving along the backroads of **Hvar Island** (p265) and exploring the unsung spots of the island's interior, with its olive groves, fields of aromatic herbs and half-abandoned stone hamlets.

Anja Mutić

⊙ *@everthenomad*
Anja curated the Croatia chapter.

Few places feel as magical for me as the **Costa de la Luz** (p1080) in Andalucía. It's something to do with the crisp natural light beaming across wild blonde beaches and wandering through the whitewashed streets of ancient, buzzing towns.

Isabella Noble

@ *@isabellamnoble*
Isabella curated the Spain chapter.

Lyon (p413) is wonderfully close to the Alps – a city for people who secretly hate cities. My perfect day in summer is spent hiking in the mountains; in winter I swap my hiking boots for skis. Come evening, you'll find me enjoying the city buzz, in a gourmet restaurant or wine bar.

Anna Richards

𝕏 *@annahrichards*
Anna curated the France chapter.

My favourite place in Portugal is **Alqueva Lake** (p927). I love swimming in its warm river beaches, walking amongst its surrounding villages and capturing the clear starry skies above me.

Joana Taborda

@ *@cityodes*
Joana curated the Portugal chapter.

Walking aimlessly around the old town of **Sofia** (p230) is one of my favourite pastimes in Bulgaria. Everything is outdoors in good weather – and the weather is good most of the time.

Leonid Ragozin

𝕏 *@leonidragozin*
Leonid curated the Belarus, Bulgaria, Latvia, Russia and Ukraine chapters.

I was blown away by **Museum Sint-Janshospitaal** (p130) in Bruges. Contemporary works inspired by the hospital's founding principles have been woven into the collection. They speak of compassion and care, and their dialogue with the historic collection is fascinating.

Helena Smith

@ *@helenasmithpix*
Helena curated the Belgium & Luxembourg chapter.

In **Ðerdap National Park** (p979), it's as if the Danube casts a spell on all those who enter the formidable Iron Gates – even the name evokes a fantasy world.

Brana Vladisavljevic

lonelyplanet.com/authors/brana-vladisavljevic
Brana curated the Serbia chapter.

FROM LEFT: KLICIAR IVAN/SHUTTERSTOCK, IAN KALBERMATTEN FOR LONELY PLANET

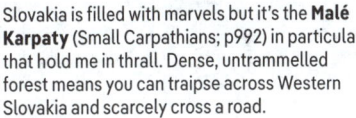

Slovakia is filled with marvels but it's the **Malé Karpaty** (Small Carpathians; p992) in particular that hold me in thrall. Dense, untrammelled forest means you can traipse across Western Slovakia and scarcely cross a road.

Luke Waterson

lukeandhiswords.com
Luke curated the Slovakia chapter.

My favourite experience is crunching over crevasses with crampons, roped to a guide, on the mammoth **Aletsch Glacier** (p1130) – it will be gone by 2100. The rumbling of water flowing deep beneath your feet is an emotive song to the glacier's immensity and fragility.

Nicola Williams

🔘 *@tripalong*
Nicola curated the Switzerland chapter.

FROM LEFT: RICHARD SEMIK/SHUTTERSTOCK, REGINA M ART/SHUTTERSTOCK

I loved hopping on a train from Den Haag to **Gouda** (p816) for the traditional cheese market. I loved the entire smorgasbord of Dutch snacks and fresh seafood. The perfect market keepsake was snapping a photo of my one-year-old sitting on stacked round cheese blocks.

Barbara Woolsey

🔘 *@xo.babxi*
Barbara curated the Germany and Netherlands chapters.

The remote island of **Ruhnu** sits in the middle of the Baltic Sea, far from mainland Estonia. It feels like a different world, with obscure stories echoing through its forests, such as that of the Ruhnu bear, an animal that appeared out of nowhere a decade ago and hasn't been seen since.

Angelo Zinna

🔘 *@angelo_zinna*
Angelo curated the Estonia chapter.

Lofoten Islands, Norway
Arctic isles for peaks, beaches and wilderness (p856)

Abisko, Sweden
Sámi culture, northern lights and midnight sun (p1109)

Prague, Czechia
Castles, medieval streets and beer halls (p280)

Vienna, Austria
Imperial palaces, coffeehouses and galleries (p78)

Bački Monoštor, Serbia
Time-lost village in the 'Amazon of Europe' (p977)

London, Britain
Pubs, palaces, art and glorious food (p172)

Bath, Britain
Roman baths, Georgian grandeur and tea rooms (p186)

500 km
250 miles

ICELAND
REYKJAVÍK

IRELAND
DUBLIN
NORTHERN IRELAND
BELFAST
SCOTLAND
EDINBURGH
BRITAIN

Tromsø
Abisko
Lofoten Islands

NORWAY
OSLO
North Sea
SWEDEN
STOCKHOLM
Baltic Sea
DENMARK
COPENHAGEN

FINLAND
HELSINKI
TALLINN
ESTONIA
RIGA
LATVIA
LITHUANIA
VILNIUS
MINSK
BELARUS

RUSSIA
MOSCOW

İstanbul, Türkiye
Grand bazaars, mosques and palaces (p1144)

Mycenae, Greece
Legends and ancient history in the Peloponnese (p542)

Florence, Italy
A feast of Renaissance art in Tuscany (p683)

Lake Bohinj, Slovenia
Jewel-like alpine lake and water sports (p1015)

Granada, Spain
Moorish Alhambra palace and Sierra Nevada views (p1081)

Paris, France
City of love, culture and joie de vivre (p384)

Gruyères, Switzerland
Chocolate-box villages, forested peaks and cheese (p1122)

ART IN FOCUS

From Old Masters in lavish former palaces to on-the-pulse galleries and post-industrial factories emblazoned with street art, Europe's culture-crammed towns and cities enthral with world-class collections and newfound creativity. No matter how often you visit, you'll never see it all, so tailor your visit wisely. Beyond the canvas, seek out the places that inspired the paintbrush: from Munch's Oslo to Matisse's Nice.

Advance Bookings

Many of Europe's big-hitter galleries and museums have online bookings, sometimes with dedicated time slots. Snag tickets ahead to skip the queue. Plan to arrive early.

Art Pilgrimages

For creativity in one-artist doses, head to Barcelona (Gaudí, Picasso, Miró); Nice (Chagall, Matisse); Amsterdam (Rembrandt, Van Gogh); Bern (Klee); Vienna (Klimt); Brussels (Magritte) and Oslo (Munch).

Free Visits

Lots of museums and galleries (especially state-run ones) offer free admission on certain days of the month or week. Check websites ahead to time your visit well.

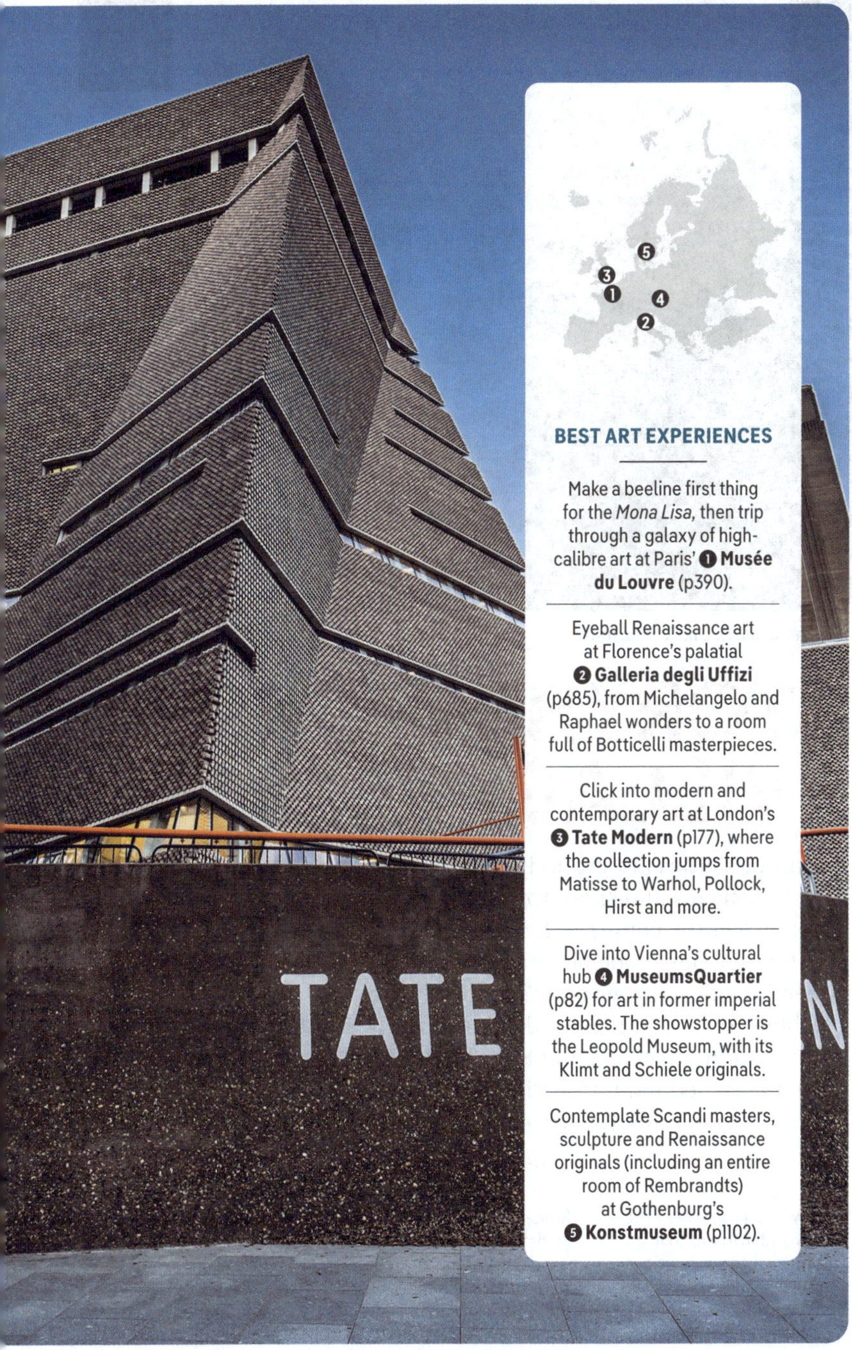

BEST ART EXPERIENCES

Make a beeline first thing for the *Mona Lisa*, then trip through a galaxy of high-calibre art at Paris' ❶ **Musée du Louvre** (p390).

Eyeball Renaissance art at Florence's palatial ❷ **Galleria degli Uffizi** (p685), from Michelangelo and Raphael wonders to a room full of Botticelli masterpieces.

Click into modern and contemporary art at London's ❸ **Tate Modern** (p177), where the collection jumps from Matisse to Warhol, Pollock, Hirst and more.

Dive into Vienna's cultural hub ❹ **MuseumsQuartier** (p82) for art in former imperial stables. The showstopper is the Leopold Museum, with its Klimt and Schiele originals.

Contemplate Scandi masters, sculpture and Renaissance originals (including an entire room of Rembrandts) at Gothenburg's ❺ **Konstmuseum** (p1102).

Bellagio (p671), Lake Como, Italy

STORYBOOK VILLAGES

Europe's cities are grand indeed, but it's in the villages and small towns where you really feel the country's heartbeat. From Italy's honey-stone beauties pinned to steep hillsides, to Germany's crooked lanes, cobblestones and medieval gables freshly minted for a fairy tale, and Slovakia's folksy, castle-crowned mountain villages, daily life plays out on a quieter, less-crowded scale.

Visiting Tips

Many popular villages have fallen victim to overtourism, so turn your gaze instead to unsung beauties one valley, mountain or beach over, or visit in low season.

Village-Thick Regions

Road-trip *pueblos blancos* in Andalucía (Spain), medieval *bastides* in Dordogne (France), Britain's pretty Cotswolds, the hill towns of Tuscany (Italy), and *aldeias históricas* in Alentejo (Portugal).

BEST VILLAGE EXPERIENCES

Live the Cotswolds country dream in ❶ **Bibury** (p187), with its honey-stone cottages, lanes and old-school tearooms by the River Coln.

Tune into Hungarian folk culture admiring medieval thatched-roof houses with carved wooden porches in fort-topped ❷ **Hollókő** (p587).

Fall for the charm of ❸ **Bellagio** (p671) on Lake Como, with its bobbing boats, steep staircases, red-roofed houses and cypress groves.

Watch horseshoe and fishing-net makers at work in ❹ **Bački Monoštor** (p977) in Serbia's Gornje Podunavlje, dubbed the 'Amazon of Europe'.

Float in a hot-air balloon above the 'fairy chimney' rock formations and cave dwellings at ❺ **Göreme** (p1160) in Cappadocia, Türkiye.

TASTE OF THE LAND

While Googling the nearest top-ranking restaurant is all well and good, there's nothing like tastings at the source. From spices to truffles, smoked fish to cheese and wine, folding a food experience into your European travels gives you a genuine flavour of each country and gets you that bit closer to its heart (by way of the stomach!).

Market Mornings

Rise early to hit a market and engage with local life, from Provence's headily fragrant *marchés* to Türkiye's spice-laden bazaars and Scandinavia's briny fish markets.

Food Tours

One way to really slip under the skin of Europe's cities is with a food tour or cookery class. The local tourist board should be able to point you in the right direction.

Wine Trails

Regions where cellars doors fling open for tours and tastings include the Loire Valley and Bordeaux in France, Portugal's Douro Valley, Tokaj in Hungary and Slovakia, and Spain's La Rioja.

BEST FOOD EXPERIENCES

Visit the village of Gruyères to see one of Switzerland's top cheeses being made over a wood fire at rustic **❶ Fromagerie d'Alpage de Moléson** (p1122).

Enjoy Sicilian street theatre at Catania's **❷ La Pescheria** (p709), where fishmongers gut and locals snap up prawns, clams, mussels and sea urchins.

Fill bags with dried fruits, nuts, honey and spices, pistachio-laced baklava and Turkish delight at İstanbul's fragrant **❸ Spice Bazaar** (p1147).

Try a classic smørrebrød of smoked herring on rye bread with chives and raw egg yolk from the smokehouses of **❹ Bornholm** (p320), Denmark.

Gorge on white truffles from **❺ Istria** (p258), Croatia. The prized tuber grows underground in dense forests and is sniffed out by specially trained dogs.

DREAMY SHORES

Pick up a map of Europe and you'll quickly lose yourself in its labyrinth of inlets and islands, fjords and beaches. From the tiny cliff-wrapped coves and pine-scented islands of the Med to the wild, storm-bashed beaches of Scandinavia, Iceland's dramatic black sands to snow-frosted Arctic shores visited by whales and lit by northern lights, there's a beach and island for every mood and moment. Swim, sunbathe, hike, surf, dive – the possibilities are boundless.

When to Go

To avoid the tourist crush at popular spots, sidestep peak months like July and August. Shoulder seasons (spring and early autumn) mean better deals and quieter sands.

Surf's Up

Ride the Atlantic's high rollers, from the cliff-rimmed, dune-fringed, surf-pounded shores of Portugal's Costa Vicentina to wave-smashed Newquay (pictured; p183) in Cornwall. Winter is best.

Island-Hopping

Greece, Italy, Spain and Croatia are obvious faves, with ferries breezing over to idyllic beaches. Also seek out the wild isles of Scotland and Scandinavia's Baltic beauties.

BEST BEACH & ISLAND EXPERIENCES

Go straight to beach heaven in ❶ **Ksamil** (p65) on the Albanian Riviera, where cliff-wrapped sands slide into the jewel-like Ionian Sea.

Squeeze into designer bathing togs to flaunt it like a silver-screen legend on the glamorous sands of France's ❷ **St-Tropez** (p429).

Take a *gület* (traditional wooden yacht) cruise along Türkiye's Turquoise Coast to ❸ **Ölüdeniz** (p1159), a lovely spit of sandy beach with a sheltered lagoon.

Dig your toes into flour-white sands on the dune-flanked, surf-whipped beaches of ❹ **Formentera** (p1071), which are some of Spain's finest.

Find the Arctic dream on Norway's ❺ **Lofoten Islands** (p856), where spiky granite peaks punch above creamy sands and sapphire-blue waters.

CHRISTIAN WITTMANN/SHUTTERSTOCK

Butrint (p65), Albania

ANCIENT HISTORY

For anyone who cares about the rituals of past civilisations, Europe's ancient history is gripping stuff. Experience it firsthand at Neolithic stone circles, prehistoric caves dancing with paintings, and Ancient Greek citadels. In southern Europe, you can trip back 2000 years exploring Roman amphitheatres, temples, baths and mosaic-filled halls.

Cave Art

Cave walls across Europe give a fascinating insight into early cultures. Top billing goes to Grotte Chauvet 2 in France's Gorges de l'Ardèche and Spain's 18,500-year-old Altamira.

Standing Stones

The ring forts, hill forts, dolmens and stone circles of Great Britain are your backstage pass to prehistory. Fabulous examples include 5000-year-old Stonehenge and Heart of Neolithic Orkney.

BEST ANCIENT HISTORY EXPERIENCES

Trip over Roman cobbles at the haunting ruins of Italy's ❶ **Pompeii** (p699), buried beneath volcanic ash of Mt Vesuvius in 79 CE.

Splash in thermal waters like the Romans in Britain's ❷ **Bath** (p186), with its temple to the goddess Sulis Minerva.

Channel the spirit of Ancient Greece at ❸ **Mycenae** (p542), home of legendary King Agamemnon during the Trojan War.

Follow in the footsteps of Ancient Greeks and Romans as you explore the romantic ruins of ❹ **Butrint** (p65) in Albania.

Marvel at the remarkably intact city of ❺ **Ephesus** (p1156) in Türkiye, with its hillside theatre and mosaic-filled Roman houses.

PALATIAL SPLENDOUR

Romantically ruined medieval forts astride hilltops; grand riverside châteaux; lavish, art-stuffed royal palaces; or Moorish marvels – Europe's castles and palaces were built to cement the legacy of whoever held the reins of power at the time of their construction. Visit them for a deep dive into the continent's fascinating and tumultuous history.

BEST CASTLE & PALACE EXPERIENCES

Saunter around the gardens and dazzling Hall of Mirrors at Paris' ❶ **Château de Versailles** (p396), built for Louis XIV, the Roi Soleil (Sun King).

Immerse yourself in the opulent world of sultans, courtiers and beautiful concubines in the Ottoman wonder of İstanbul's ❷ **Topkapı Palace** (p1147).

Trace 700 years of imperial Habsburg rule at Vienna's spectacular ❸ **Hofburg** (p80), where white Lipizzaner stallions dance and crown jewels glitter.

Roam ornate residences, courtyards and gardens at Granada's spellbinding ❹ **Alhambra** (p1081), the Moorish fort and palace at the foot of the Sierra Nevada.

Immerse yourself in millennia-spanning history exploring the palaces, museums, galleries and basilica of ❺ **Prague Castle** (p280), high above the Vltava River.

Set in Stone

Castle fans should zoom in on Wales for romantic ruins and Spain's Moorish Andalucía (Palacios Nazaríes, Granada, pictured; p1081). Regions like France's châteaux-laden Loire Valley come up trumps for palaces.

Comfy Footwear

Swap high heels and flip-flops for sturdy, comfortable shoes to trot around cobbled courtyards worn smooth over centuries and tiptoe softly through chandelier-lit halls.

Castle Sleeps

Act out your wildest childhood fantasies and get the royal treatment by spending the night in one of Europe's castles. See *castlestostay.com* for inspiration.

MOVING MOUNTAINS

Whether you're puffing up an alpine pass at daybreak, glacier hiking in the shadow of Mt Blanc, bedding down in a *rifugio* in the rosy-hued Dolomites, tearing down snowy slopes in the Pyrenees or going off-piste into the wilds of the Albanian Alps, Europe's mountains will move you in more ways than one. From the loch-laced munros of the Scottish Highlands to the icy Arctic, there are peaks ripe for outdoor adventure.

Alternative East

The Alps get all the love, but edging east are sky-high regions with fewer crowds, from Slovenia's Julian Alps to the wild Albanian Alps (pictured; p68) and craggy peaks of Galičica in North Macedonia.

Scandi Heights

Geographically, the higher you go, the wilder things get. From Norway's rock-rippled Lofoten Islands (pictured; p856) to whale-watching in Akureyri, Iceland, the Arctic casts its own spell.

Hut to Hut

Blaze to the heart of the mountains by hiking from hut to hut. France, Switzerland, Austria, Italy, Germany, Spain and Norway have well-developed hut networks.

BEST MOUNTAIN EXPERIENCES

Lace up boots to stride along trails and over gorge-spanning bridges in the wild limestone peaks of Spain's ❶ **Parque Nacional Picos de Europa** (p1060).

Summit ❷ **Aiguille du Midi** (p409), towering above France's Mont Blanc massif, to hike past glaciers and spurs, seracs and shimmering ice fields.

Take a walk on the wild side on the cross-range ❸ **Tatranská Magistrala** (p999) trail in Slovakia's High Tatras, keeping an alert eye out for brown bears.

Gasp at the jewel-like ❹ **Lake Bohinj** (p1015) in Slovenia's rugged Julian Alps, where you can swim, kayak and stand-up paddleboard in peak-gazing wonder.

Marvel at the dazzling midnight sun or northern lights flashing in night skies from the ❺ **Aurora Sky Station** (p1109) atop Mt Nuolja in Arctic Sweden.

COUNTRIES

Find the places that tick all your boxes.

Netherlands

CYCLING, CANALS AND DUTCH COURAGE

Progressive and easy-going, the Netherlands extends a warm welcome with its cutting-edge food and design scenes and tinkling bicycles. Great Dutch Masters have left their mark on Amsterdam, a capital of art, 17th-century canals and candlelit brown cafes. Go further to discover windmills, tulip fields, exquisite Maastricht and pulsing port of Rotterdam.

Belgium & Luxembourg

GABLED BUILDINGS AND OFFBEAT CHARM

Eccentric little Belgium has canal-woven cities built by medieval guilds, rollicking beer halls, comic strips and chocolate galore. Brussels and Bruges are heart-stealers. Beyond, castle-topped Ghent, coastal Ostend and Antwerp (for diamonds and Rubens) beguile. Pocket-sized Luxembourg has a capital famed for banking and a UNESCO-listed old town.

Portugal

A LAND SHAPED BY THE ATLANTIC

Portugal's popularity has sky-rocketed in recent years. This Atlantic-facing nation enthrals, from hill-crowned Lisbon to riverside Porto with its port-wine cellars. Fields of oak, olive and vines ripple south to rural Alentejo's whitewashed medieval towns and the Algarve's wave-beaten shores. The welcome is genuine, the food fantastic.

Netherlands
p803

Belgium & Luxembourg
p112

Germany
p453

Austria
p75

Switzerland
p1115

France
p378

Italy
p644

Portugal
p898

Spain
p1023

Italy
p644

Spain

A SOULFUL, SUNNY, FIESTA-LOVING LAND

Sunny, party-mad Spain is one of Europe's most entrancing lands. Dive in to discover cities that fizz with culture, cutting-edge art, Moorish palaces and tapas bars. The outdoors is just as compelling, winging you from ancient hilltop villages to the trail-laced Pyrenees, the wild Atlantic coast to the Med's pine-rimmed coves.

Italy

EUROPE'S CULTURAL AND CULINARY PARADISE

Cinematic natural landscapes, limelight-stealing art and architecture, a passion for food and wine – la dolce vita is real. Rome, Florence and Venice are as incredible as you imagine, but there's more. From Tuscany's medieval hill towns to Sicily's beaches and volcanoes, and the icy northern Alps, Italy has everything that makes Europe great.

Germany

**TRANQUIL LANDSCAPES
AND FESTIVE TRADITIONS**

Germany often surprises. Live-wire capital Berlin's hard-hitting history, colossal art and all-night parties are just for starters. Beyond, a spectacularly diverse land whisks you from medieval, maritime Hamburg to baroque beauty Dresden; Bavaria's fantasy castles, Alps and rollicking beer halls; and the Black Forest's misty woodlands and fairy-tale villages.

France

**WINE, CHEESE AND WILDLY
VARIED SCENERY**

From the Côte d'Azur's cliff-wrapped glamour to the snow-frosted French Alps, Provence's heady lavender fields to the Loire's fairy-tale châteaux, France's mystique is irresistible. Paris' cultural showstoppers like the Eiffel Tower, Notre-Dame and the Louvre are just an amuse-bouche for a country of ravishing landscapes and sensational food and wine.

Greece

THE PLACE FOR EPIC ADVENTURES

Greece has been a colossal force in European history. From Athens to Delphi and Olympia, its status is legendary. Looking at its piercing-blue skies, island-sprinkled seas, rugged mountains and silver-green olive groves, you can still picture the places immortalised in Homeric myth. It's the land of heroes, where people eat like gods.

Austria

WHERE CULTURE HITS THE HEIGHTS

Austria is a whirl of culture, history and pinch-yourself beautiful landscapes. Mozart symphonies echo through grand concert halls and the majesty of the Habsburg Empire still glitters in the baroque palaces and coffee houses of Vienna, Innsbruck and Salzburg. Beyond, the vine-ribbed Danube and outdoor adventures in the Alps await.

Switzerland

**ALPINE TRADITION, OUTDOOR ACTION
AND URBAN FUN**

Small but perfectly formed Switzerland is the Alpine dream. Cue chocolate-box villages with cinematic mountain backdrops, epic rail journeys skimming past glacier-frosted peaks, thundering falls, and art-rich cities on the shores of glassy blue lakes. This quadrilingual land wings you from ritzy ski resort St Moritz to palms and piazzas of Ticino.

Türkiye

WHERE EUROPE AND ASIA MEET

From the ravishing Aegean and Mediterranean coasts to ebullient cities like İstanbul, with its minaret-pierced skyline and spice-scented bazaars, Türkiye is an irresistible mix of culture and adventure, old and new. Rewind time in mountain villages, soar over Cappadocia's fairy chimneys by hot-air balloon and explore ancient ruined cities like Troy.

Iceland

THE WILD POWER OF NATURE

Rumbling with volcanic activity, Iceland is a country of wild enchantment. Crashing waterfalls, glinting glaciers, hissing geysers, black-sand beaches and lava fields give it a dawn-of-creation feel. Kick off in cool capital Reykjavík, then go beyond for adventures from northern-lights gazing to hot-spring bathing, mountain trekking and whale-watching.

Ireland

ANCIENT HISTORY, SPELLBINDING SCENERY AND SPIRITED CULTURE

This small island on Europe's fringes swirls in saintly legend. Its misty mountains, valleys and wild Atlantic coastline reveal a history reaching back to the pre-Celts. Roam this vividly green land to find ancient monastic sites, brightly painted villages, fire-warmed pubs, folk music and culture-laden cities with the friendliest of welcomes.

Britain

AN ANCIENT AND INSPIRING ISLAND

Little Britain has a huge personality. History, royal heritage, art, culture, food, natural beauty, humour and eccentricity – it's all right here on this island in the North Atlantic. From London's cultural big-hitters to the Cotswolds' fetching gold-stone villages and Scotland's epic wilderness – this country is a one-off.

Latvia

DUNES AND BALTIC FORESTS

Forest and lakes in blue and green, pine-hemmed, dune-flanked beaches rippling down to the Baltic – Latvia's real charm lies outdoors. But first, kick off in Rīga, a vibrant, elegant capital that quietly captivates with a mix of medieval and art nouveau. Go beyond for rural landscapes, rolling hills, baroque palaces and lively port cities.

Norway

LANDSCAPES, ARTS, ACTIVITIES AND ARCHITECTURE

Nature went all out in Norway, a dramatic land shaped by fjords, forests and glaciers. Expect off-the-charts beauty, whether snowshoeing in the Arctic underneath the northern lights, boating past a rainbow-kissed waterfall or hiking into the wilds. Culture enthrals too, from Viking heritage to Sámi spirit and Oslo's stash of Munch art.

Iceland
p593

Denmark

VIKINGS, HYGGE, CASTLES AND CULTURE

Fairy tales were born in Denmark. And you can see why touring the country's pretty-as-can-be villages, castles and island-sprinkled coastline shaped by the North and Baltic Seas. Creative Copenhagen is the springboard for a country of hygge cafes, Viking museums, on-the-pulse design stores and restaurants dishing up New Nordic cuisine.

Ireland
p613

Britain
p167

Lithuania

UNSPOILED NATURE MEETS MILLENNIAL HISTORY

The biggest Baltic state is a stunner, with an outdoors that whisks you off the beaten track exploring lake-splashed forests, white-sand beaches and dune-rippled coastlines. Lithuania's creativity pulses in Kaunas, with its interwar architecture, and baroque Vilnius. Quiet roads unravel through gentle countryside to time-lost villages and country manors.

Sweden

FUTURISTIC CITIES, PLACID ARCHIPELAGOS AND THE ARCTIC

Nature calls the shots in Sweden. Even in capital Stockholm, with its progressive art, design, food and fashion scenes, the outdoors beckons. Beyond, uncover archipelagos for island-hopping, Baltic beaches, medieval walled cities and Viking rune stones. Up north, Lappland's vast Arctic landscapes are lit by northern lights and infused with Sámi spirit.

Finland

SCENERY, DESIGN AND FASCINATING CULTURE

Finland moves to its own Nordic beat, with extremes of light and landscape – from culture-rammed, design-minded capital Helsinki to the frozen wilds of Lapland where reindeer roam and northern lights rave. This is a country of forests, lakes and islands, but also of quirks – from nude saunas to Santa sparkle.

Estonia

A CULTURAL CROSSROADS

Ping-ponged between empires through history, Estonia is culturally unique. Putting its turbulent past behind it, this nation keeps a tight grip on tradition while cantering into the future. Begin in Tallinn's UNESCO-stamped, medieval Old Town, then go deeper, exploring forested national parks, rural villages and islands that dot the Baltic coast.

Russia

THE WORLD'S LARGEST COUNTRY AT WAR

Russia was still visitable after 2014 when it annexed Crimea, thus starting its war against Ukraine that was a low-intensity conflict initially. But the full-scale aggression it launched in February 2022 turned this huge and fascinating country, diverse in every respect, into a no-go zone, at least for the nationals of major Western countries.

Finland
p357

Norway
p843

Sweden
p1088

Estonia
p335

Russia
p961

Latvia
p732

Lithuania
p751

Denmark
p304

Belarus
p106

Poland
p869

Ukraine
p1169

Belarus

EUROPE'S ODDEST POLITY

Since president Aleksandr Lukashenko came to power in 1994, Belarus has been one of Europe's political oddities. Although Lukashenko makes attempts to distance himself from Russia's war in Ukraine, Belarus remains under Western sanctions for its role in the war as well as previous ones for mass human-rights violations.

Poland

A WARM, WELCOMING AND RESILIENT NATION

Poland has been shaped but not defined by its long history of war and invaders. With its irrepressible spirit, this Slavic nation captivates in cultured, old-meets-new cities like Warsaw and Kraków. Beyond are northern beaches and southern mountains, plus towns and cities sprinkled with ruined castles and medieval churches to explore.

Ukraine

A COUNTRY UNDER BRUTAL ATTACK

All of Ukraine was an active war zone at the time of writing, ever since Russia unleashed an all-out invasion of this country in February 2022. Almost seven million people left Ukraine due the war by the spring of 2025 – 17% of the country's pre-war population, most of them women and children.

Czechia

BREATHTAKING CASTLES AND EVEN BETTER BEER

The fall of communism in 1989 gave Czechia a new zest for life. You'll be smitten by its historical architecture, beer halls and youthful spirit. Prague's castle-crowned Old Town is a medieval knockout, but venture beyond to discover regal spa towns and the fantasy castles and palaces of Bohemia and Moravia.

Slovakia

MAJESTIC MOUNTAINS, CASTLES AND MEDIEVAL MARVELS

Unsung and folklore-spun, Slovakia feels refreshingly crowd-free and authentic, whether you're exploring Bratislava's medieval and baroque architecture or dipping into the forested hills beyond. Nature is the country's highlight, from the High Tatras' jagged peaks to gorge-riven national parks and the primeval beech forests of the Carpathians.

Hungary

STUNNING ARCHITECTURE AND THERMAL SPAS

Little Hungary punches above its weight culturally. Here, imperial history and art nouveau architecture intertwine. Perched on the Danube, Budapest is a history-laden hit, with its mighty medieval castle, steamy thermal baths and treasure-crammed museums. Stray further to find vineyards, tradition-steeped villages, birdlife-rich lakes and the moody Great Plain.

Croatia

LIVING UP TO THE HYPE

Game of Thrones put Croatia on the world map, and about time. Roman, Venetian, Austro-Hungarian and Italian occupiers shaped the country culturally. Beyond pristine medieval towns, you'll be amazed by the topaz waters and islands of the Adriatic coast, primevally pretty forested national parks, mountains, rivers, lakes and falls.

Slovenia

RELAXING TOWNS AND PRISTINE NATURE

Slovenia packs an insane amount of beauty into a tiny land – from the lofty Julian Alps to cathedral-like caves, deep forests, jewel-like lakes and rivers, and the compact Adriatic coastline. Start in castle-topped cultural magnet Ljubljana, then dive into the outdoors, whether hiking, biking, rafting, canyoning, caving or skiing.

Bosnia & Hercegovina

RICH HISTORY, WILD NATURE, WARM WELCOME

Though still scarred by the devastating war of the 1990s, Bosnia is emerging as a Balkan beauty. Mountain-buckled national parks, crashing waterfalls and bargain skiing lure you into its wild backyard, while Sarajevo and Mostar impress with Ottoman architecture, street cafes, grill restaurants and flourishing arts scenes.

Montenegro

MOUNTAINS, COAST AND ANCIENT TOWNS

Small Montenegro has a ludicrous amount of beauty for a country of its size. Its Adriatic coast punches high with the stunning Bay of Kotor, where mountains dip to the bluest of seas, walled towns and pink-pebble beaches. History is everywhere, from Illyrian ruins to Roman mosaics, Byzantine frescoes, Venetian palaces and Ottoman mosques.

Moldova

UNDERGROUND WINE LABYRINTHS AND SOVIET MEMORABILIA

Squished between Romania and Ukraine, former Soviet republic Moldova has charms unsung. With its upbeat bars and restaurants, vibrant capital Chişinău is a launchpad for deeper forays into the country, from limestone tunnels sheltering wineries to the ridge-top cave monastery of Orheiul Vechi and fairy-tale fortress of Soroca.

Romania

RURAL CHARM, UNSPOILT NATURE, ENERGETIC CITIES

Wild, wonderful Romania is one of Europe's last great unknowns. To travel here is to be surprised, whether you're touring rapidly evolving cities like Braşov, Sibiu and Bucharest, venturing to time-lost villages and UNESCO-listed painted monasteries, hiking in bear territory in the Carpathians, or feeling the medieval mystery of Transylvania.

Bulgaria

ANCIENT MONUMENTS, GREAT OUTDOORS, BEACHES GALORE

Bulgaria begins with its relaxed capital Sofia, tripping through millennia in monuments – from the Romans to communism. Beyond, remote and rugged mountains where you can hike and ski, history-rammed cities like Plovdiv and Veliko Târnovo, hilltop Orthodox monasteries and the beautiful Black Sea coast invite exploration.

Serbia

DIVERSITY OFF THE BEATEN PATH

From Ottoman and Habsburg rule to the fall of socialism, Serbia's turbulent past has been shaped by its location at Europe's crossroads. Spirited festivals and Yugoslav arts give this Balkan country unique cultural edge. The outdoors is equally diverse, skipping from sunflower fields to river gorges, karst caves and the Dinaric Alps.

Kosovo

A YOUNG AND BEAUTIFUL NATION

History is in the making in Kosovo. Europe's newest nation is packed with Ottoman history, remote, trail-laced mountains and UNESCO-listed medieval Orthodox monasteries. A youthful spirit prevails as traditional society is sent swinging into the 21st century. Go now while it is still largely undiscovered.

Albania

MYSTERIOUS NO LONGER

Since the fall of communism, Albania is slowly but surely getting its moment to shine. Besides the coastal allure of dreamy beaches pummelled by the turquoise-blue Ionian Sea, this warmly welcoming country has cities pulsing with newfound cool, Ottoman architecture, Roman and Greek ruins, and trails weaving high into the Albanian Alps.

North Macedonia

WILD NATURE, ANCIENT HISTORY

Often at the crossroads of history, this little-known Balkan beauty is flavoured by Greek, Roman and Ottoman legacies. Travel here still feels like an offbeat adventure, from the shores of mysterious Lake Ohrid to Orthodox monasteries, dramatic mountains and Ottoman old towns. Superb food and wine are the clincher.

29

ARCADY/SHUTTERSTOCK

Vienna (p78), Austria

ITINERARIES

First-Time Europe

Allow: 18 days **Distance**: 2288km

This is the big one: a grand tour of some of Europe's finest cities, whisking you from vivacious British capital London to regal Vienna in Austria by rail. Palaces, castles, blockbuster sights, art-rammed museums, phenomenal food – three weeks barely touches the surface. Dodge high season for fewer crowds.

❶ LONDON ⏱ 3 DAYS

London (p172) is calling. Britain's timeless capital is an overload of epic museums, palaces, regal parks, and rave-worthy food and nightlife. The Tower of London, Big Ben, St Paul's Cathedral, Shakespeare's Globe – this city on the Thames has the lot.

🚗 *Detour: Head to seaside* **Brighton** *(p179) for an Indian-style pleasure palace, fish and chips, and breezy walks on the pier.*

❷ PARIS ⏱ 3 DAYS

There's nothing like rocking up in the French capital (p384) for that wow-I'm-in-Europe feeling. Glimpse the *Mona Lisa* at the Louvre, walk the steep streets of Sacré-Cœur at sunrise, get a gargoyle's-eye view of Gothic Notre-Dame and see the Eiffel Tower twinkle by night. Magic.

🚗 *Detour: Tour the Hall of Mirrors and formal gardens at majestic* **Versailles** *(p396), Louis XIV's palace to out-pomp them all.*

❸ AMSTERDAM ⏱ 3 DAYS

The art theme continues in **Amsterdam** (p808), a laid-back city of bridge-laced canals, step-gabled buildings, fountain-splashed parks and mellow brown cafes – best explored on foot or by bicycle or cruise. Feast on works by Van Gogh, Vermeer and Rembrandt in the Rijksmuseum.

🚗 *Detour: It's tulip time. At* **Keukenhof Gardens** *(p818), seven million bulbs bloom from mid-March to mid-May.*

FROM LEFT: BRESTER IRINA/SHUTTERSTOCK, OLIVEROUGE 3/SHUTTERSTOCK, ARTUR BOGACKI/SHUTTERSTOCK

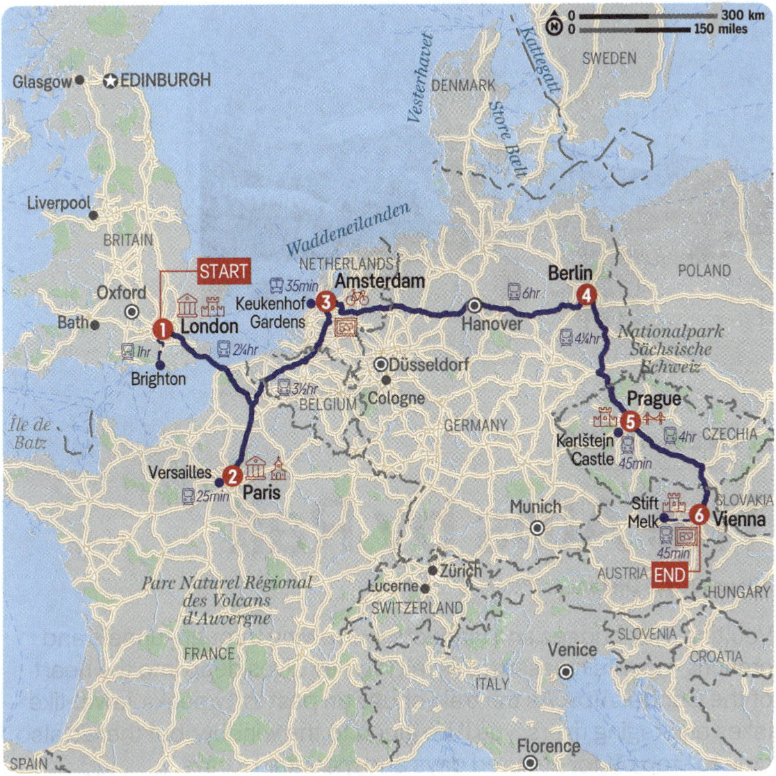

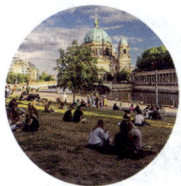

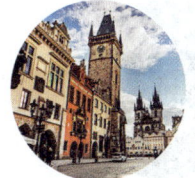

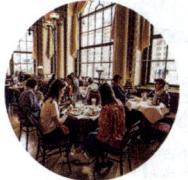

4 BERLIN 3 DAYS

Next, travel to free-spirited, party-mad **Berlin** (p458), where you can see the remains of the communist-era wall and the street art now festooning it. The German capital is the cultural mother lode, with art and history on every stately bend – from the triumphal Brandenburger Tor to Museumsinsel (pictured), where five grand galleries take you from Egyptian mummies to Monet.

5 PRAGUE 3 DAYS

Czechia's capital (p280) shakes up old and new. High above the Vltava River, Prague Castle hogs the limelight with its palaces, treasure-filled galleries and Gothic St Vitus Cathedral. Wander over resplendent Charles Bridge and roam the streets and squares of medieval Staré Město.

Detour: *Be wowed by 14th-century **Karlštejn Castle** (p288) – its riot of turrets and towers is pure fantasy.*

6 VIENNA 3 DAYS

HQ of an empire for 600 years, the Austrian capital (p78) thrills with opulent Habsburg palaces, sculpture-strewn parks, chandelier-lit coffeehouses and concert halls reverberating to Strauss waltzes. Art is everywhere, from the MuseumsQuartier to Klimt's famous *The Kiss* at Schloss Belvedere.

Detour: *Baroque **Stift Melk** (p83), Austria's finest abbey, rises high above the Danube in the Wachau Valley.*

FROM LEFT: KAVALENKAU/SHUTTERSTOCK, CAVAN-IMAGES/SHUTTERSTOCK, GIANNIS PAPANIKOS/SHUTTERSTOCK

Kitzbühel (p98), Austria

ITINERARIES

The Alps by Rail

Allow: 10 days **Distance**: 986km

Vaulting over bridges and viaducts, burrowing through tunnels and cresting mountain passes, this rail journey dives deep into the heart of the Central Alps. As the train chugs on past lofty peaks, jewel-like lakes and raging rivers, you'll be glued to the window, but there's also time to stop off for cultured days and mountain forays.

❶ MUNICH ⏱ 2 DAYS

The Alps hover tantalisingly on the horizon on clear days in Bavaria's graceful capital (p485). Before hopping on the train, kick off your trip with a blowout of baroque palaces, high-calibre art, landscaped gardens and rollicking beer halls where it's Oktoberfest 365 days of the year. For starters, visit the palatial Residenz, Schloss Nymphenburg and the Pinakothek galleries (Alte Pinakothek pictured).

❷ KITZBÜHEL ⏱ 1 DAY

You'll be riveted by the views on the crazily scenic ride south to **Kitzbühel** (p98) in the Austrian Alps, as you breeze past cow-nibbled pastures, timber huts and sky-high peaks. With ski slopes of Olympic legend and hiking trails with killer views of Wilder Kaiser, the mountains take centre stage here regardless of season.

❸ INNSBRUCK ⏱ 2 DAYS

It's another wonderfully scenic ride south to Tyrol's petite capital (p95), where the ragged limestone turrets of the Nordkette Alps punch high. Urban slides into outdoors in Innsbruck, with peak-gazing, Habsburg palaces and Swarovski sparkle. Zaha Hadid's space-age funicular lifts you up to impressive heights for alpine hiking, biking and skiing in minutes.

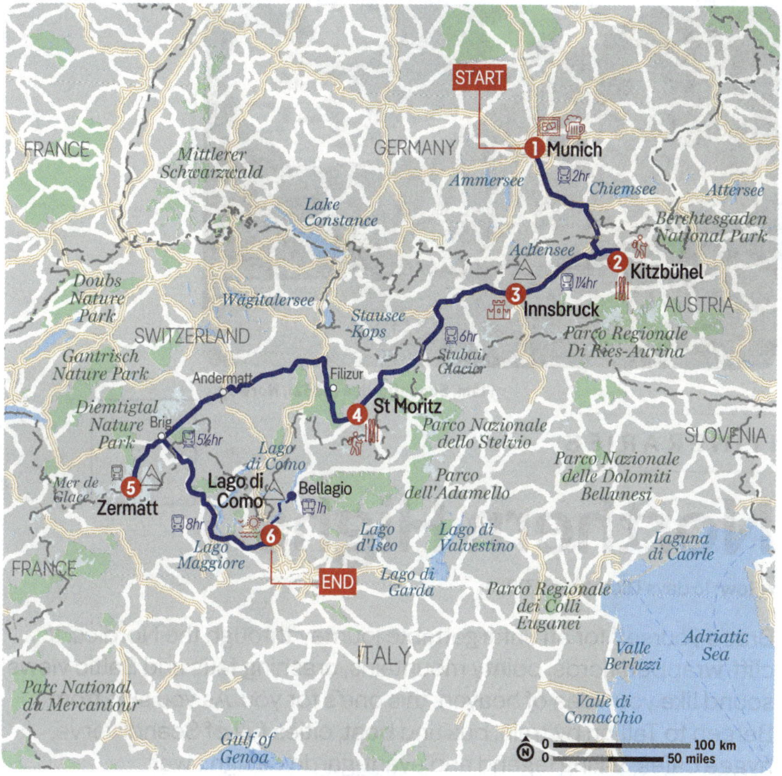

The map shows a route from Munich to the END point in Italy, with labeled stops:

- **START** — ① Munich — 🚂 2hr
- ② Kitzbühel — 🚂 1¼hr
- ③ Innsbruck — 🚂 6hr
- ④ St Moritz
- ⑤ Zermatt — 🚂 5½hr / 🚂 8hr
- ⑥ Bellagio — 🚂 1hr — **END**

Map locations: FRANCE, GERMANY, AUSTRIA, SWITZERLAND, ITALY, SLOVENIA, Mittlerer Schwarzwald, Lake Constance, Ammersee, Chiemsee, Attersee, Berchtesgaden National Park, Doubs Nature Park, Wägitalersee, Stauseе Kops, Achensee, Stubai Glacier, Parco Regionale Di Ries-Aurina, Gantrisch Nature Park, Andermatt, Filisur, Parco Nazionale dello Stelvio, Parco Nazionale delle Dolomiti Bellunesi, Diemtigtal Nature Park, Brig, Lago di Como, Parco dell'Adamello, Laguna di Caorle, Mer de Glace, Lago di Como, Lago d'Iseo, Lago di Valvestino, Zermatt, Lago Maggiore, Lago di Garda, Parco Regionale dei Colli Euganei, Adriatic Sea, Parc National du Mercantour, Valle Berluzzi, Valle di Comacchio, Gulf of Genoa

Scale: 0 — 100 km / 0 — 50 miles

④ ST MORITZ ⏱ 1 DAY

Ritzy **St Moritz** (p1131) in the ravishing Upper Engadine is Switzerland's cradle of alpine tourism, drawing the rich and royal to the slopes since 1864. The resort raises pulses still today, with its combination of luxe hotels, lake views and towering mountains with sensational skiing and hiking. Or ramp up thrills further on the Olympic Bob Run.

⑤ ZERMATT ⏱ 2 DAYS

Soaring mountains, foaming rivers and gorge-leaping viaducts wow on the journey aboard the narrow-gauge *Glacier Express* west to **Zermatt** (p1128) in Valais. The train ride traverses 91 tunnels and 291 bridges. You'll never forget the moment you first clap eyes on the 4478m-high Matterhorn (pictured), the fang-shaped mountain that's a backdrop for terrific skiing and hiking.

⑥ LAGO DI COMO ⏱ 2 DAYS

The ride into Italy takes in glacier-capped peaks and startlingly blue lakes. Cross the border to Domodossola and swing east to Como (pictured), a fetching town on **Lago di Como** (p670) that looks up to the Alps. Ride a vintage funicular to the hill village of Brunate for heart-racing views.

➳ *Detour:* Head north to **Bellagio** (p671), with its cobbled alleys, elegant villas, cypress groves and oleanders.

Flåm, Sognefjorden (p852), Norway

ITINERARIES

Northern Highs

Allow: 16 days **Distance:** 2310km

Brace yourself for an unforgettable journey through the Nordics. If cliff-wrapped fjords, pointy mountains, crashing falls and Baltic views sound like your idea of heaven, this one's for you. As you skip from Bergen to Tallinn by train, bus and boat, cities full of Scandi verve, hygge cafes, Viking legend and avant-garde design await.

① BERGEN & FJORDS ⏱ 3 DAYS

Begin with a hit of Nordic beauty in **Bergen** (p849), rimmed by hills and fjords. Tune into Hanseatic League history in Bryggen district (pictured), with its chocolate-box houses. Take a boat from Bergen along the cliff-rimmed Sognefjorden, Norway's deepest fjord, to Flåm to ride the world's steepest railway. From Flåm, it's a fjord-skimming bus ride east to Oslo.

② OSLO ⏱ 3 DAYS

Next up is **Oslo** (p846), Norway's capital wedged between mountains and fjords. Fizzing with culture, Oslo entices with its neoclassical Royal Palace, glacier-shaped, Snøhetta-designed Opera House, and a feast of museums and galleries including the striking Munch Museum (pictured) and the mammoth Nasjonalmuseet, where you can eyeball Munch's *The Scream*.

③ COPENHAGEN ⏱ 3 DAYS

Danish capital **Copenhagen** (p308) is the hipster of the Nordic block. The regal Christiansborg Slot, the roller-coasters of Tivoli Gardens and the heavyweight Nationalmuseet are just the icing on the cake. Wander canals, bike the waterfront and hop between cocktail bars and restaurants playing up New Nordic flavours.

⚓ ***Detour:*** *Day-trip to* **Roskilde** *(p317) to see the royal tombs in its cathedral and the Viking Ship Museum.*

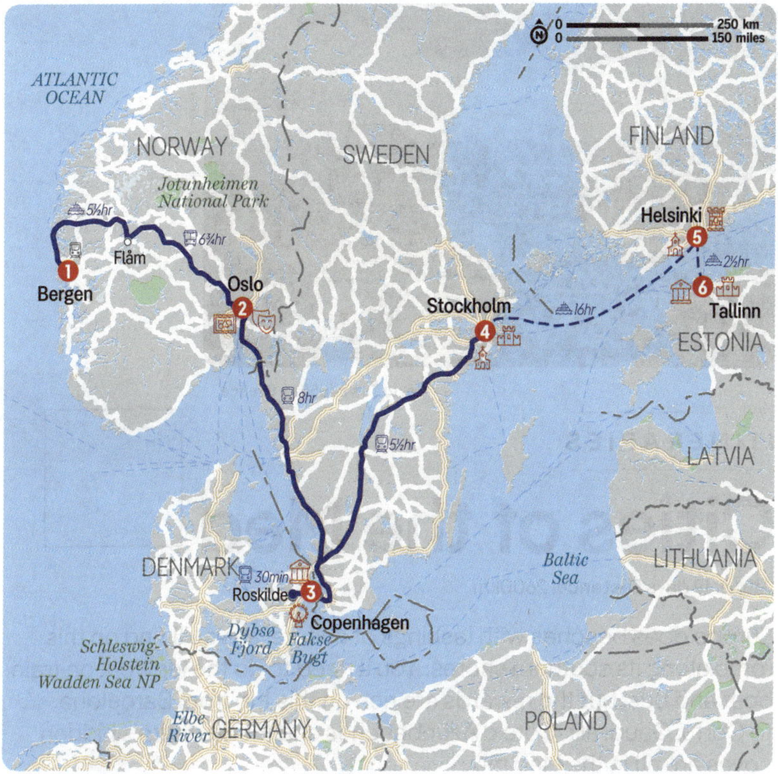

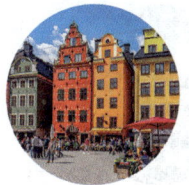

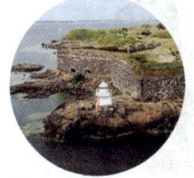

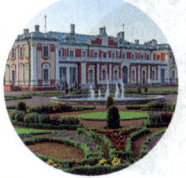

4

STOCKHOLM 3 DAYS

Take the train to gorgeous **Stockholm** (p1092). Spilling across 14 islands, Sweden's capital grabs you with Baltic breezes and Viking spirit. Rewind time roaming Gamla Stan, with its cobbled lanes, gabled houses, baroque cathedral and Kungliga Slottet (Royal Palace), before island-hopping or hitting the ABBA museum. In between, find time for smorgasbords and saunas.

5

HELSINKI 2 DAYS

From Stockholm, take an overnight cruise across the brilliantly blue Baltic to **Helsinki** (p360). Shaped by inlets and islands, the Finnish capital moves to its own design-driven beat. Besides cultural draws like the neoclassical Tuomiokirkko cathedral, Suomenlinna island fortress (pictured) and the Architecture & Design Museum, factor in time for market trips and sauna steams.

6

TALLINN 2 DAYS

Wind up your spin of the Baltic by taking the ferry from Helsinki to **Tallinn** (p338), Estonia's charismatic capital. The UNESCO World Heritage-listed Old Town is a cinematic jumble of turrets, church spires, winding streets, hidden courtyards, taverns and cafes. Get a breath of fresh air at Kadriorg Park, then explore its baroque palace and twinset of art museums (Kadriorg Art Museum pictured).

FROM LEFT: MISTERVLAD/SHUTTERSTOCK, MAISICON/SHUTTERSTOCK, TRABANTOS/SHUTTERSTOCK

EGUCHI NAOHIRO/SHUTTERSTOCK

Corfu Town (p553), Greece

ITINERARIES

Cities of the Med

Allow: 19 days **Distance**: 2600km

Europe does beaches with lashings of culture, as you'll find on this romp along its southern shores. You'll need to do the legwork on train, boat and bus, but the rewards are rich on this trip from Barcelona to Corfu. Gaudí art, Côte d'Azur beaches and Montenegro's hidden coves are all in the Med mix.

① BARCELONA ⏱ 3 DAYS

Kick off with a shot of culture by the sea in fiesta-mad Catalan capital, **Barcelona** (p1043). Devote time to biggies like tree-lined boulevard La Rambla and the tapas joints of Mercat de la Boqueria (pictured), Gaudí's fantastical La Sagrada Família and galleries spotlighting Miró and Picasso. For chill time and sunsets, make for *chiringuitos* (beach bars) on the city's golden sands.

② NICE & CÔTE D'AZUR ⏱ 4 DAYS

Swing northeast by train, crossing the border into France, then beach-hopping along the Côte d'Azur to **Nice** (p425) with its palm-lined seafront and alley-woven Old Town rammed with markets, boutiques and bars.

〰️ **Detour**: *Take the twisty coastal corniches to rock-top, honey-stone village of Èze (p428) for castle ruin, cactus-garden rambles and entrancing coastal views.*

③ NAPLES ⏱ 3 DAYS

From Nice, take the train south to **Naples** (p694) for Italy in overdrive. Mt Vesuvius smoulders on the horizon, Vespas splutter through streets and the country's best pizzas fly out of wood-fired ovens. Discover baroque churches and Renaissance piazzas.

〰️ **Detour**: *Boat over to dreamy Capri (p698), explore ill-fated Pompeii (p699) or clamber up the staircases of Sorrento (p702) on the Amalfi Coast.*

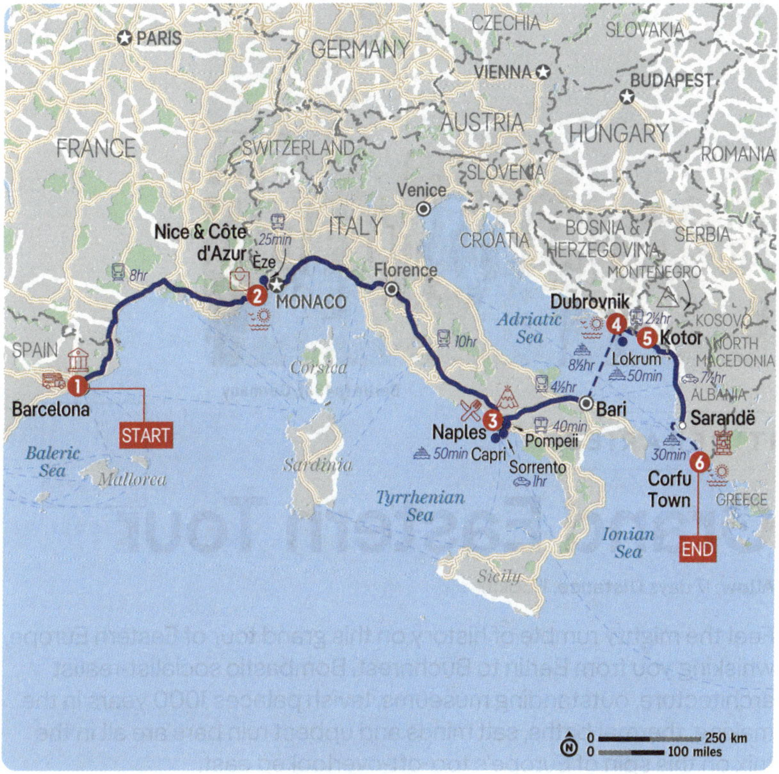

Map labels:

PARIS

GERMANY

CZECHIA

SLOVAKIA

VIENNA

BUDAPEST

FRANCE

SWITZERLAND

AUSTRIA

HUNGARY

ROMANIA

SLOVENIA

Venice

Nice & Côte d'Azur — 25min — Èze

ITALY

CROATIA

BOSNIA & HERZEGOVINA

SERBIA

MONTENEGRO

KOSOVO

8hr

MONACO

Florence

Dubrovnik

Adriatic Sea

Kotor

NORTH MACEDONIA

SPAIN

10hr

Corsica

8½hr

Lokrum — 50min

ALBANIA

7¾hr

1 Barcelona

4½hr

Bari

Sarandë

START

Balearic Sea

Mallorca

Naples **3**

40min
Pompeii

50min Capri

Sorrento
1hr

Sardinia

Tyrrhenian Sea

Ionian Sea

30min

Corfu Town **6**

GREECE

END

Sicily

2 MONACO

4 Dubrovnik · 2½hr · 5 Kotor

0 — 250 km
0 — 100 miles

4

DUBROVNIK ⏲ 3 DAYS

Catch a train to Bari and cross the Adriatic by ferry to Croatian beauty **Dubrovnik** (p266). Ramble along the fortified city walls for mesmerising views across terracotta-roofed baroque buildings. Swim and enjoy sundowners on Banje beach.

🔺 **Detour:** *For a more peaceful feel, hop over to the nearby forested island of **Lokrum** (p270). Its medieval Benedictine monastery is magnificent.*

5

KOTOR ⏲ 3 DAYS

Bus it south through mountainous, cove-riddled Montenegro. Base yourself in the walled town of **Kotor** (p793) in the pinch-yourself pretty, UNESCO-protected bay of the same name. A tangle of cobbled alleys, museums, churches, cafe-rimmed squares and Venetian palaces awaits. By night, the city walls snaking up Mt Lovćen glow gold.

6

CORFU TOWN ⏲ 3 DAYS

Hire your own wheels to breeze south through the white, crescent-shaped beaches of Albania, stopping in Sarandë, where you can take the ferry across to Corfu in Greece's Ionian Islands. With its maze of Venetian streets, pavement cafes and historic forts, **Corfu Town** (p553) is a charismatic springboard for exploring the island's pine-flanked beaches, mountain villages and coves.

Berlin (p458), Germany

ITINERARIES

Grand Eastern Tour

Allow: 17 days **Distance**: 1930km

Feel the mighty rumble of history on this grand tour of Eastern Europe, whisking you from Berlin to Bucharest. Bombastic socialist-realist architecture, outstanding museums, lavish palaces 1000 years in the making, thermal baths, salt mines and upbeat ruin bars are all in the mix on this spin of Europe's too-oft-overlooked east.

① BERLIN ⏱ 3 DAYS

Begin in **Berlin** (p458), Germany's wildly creative capital. Once a city divided, it now crackles with music, art, food and nightlife. Big-hitter sights abound. High on any list should be the Brandenburger Tor triumphal arch, eye-popping street art on the former Berlin Wall at the East Side Gallery, the cultural treasures of Museums-insel and Daniel Libeskind's thunderbolt Jewish Museum (pictured).

② WARSAW ⏱ 2 DAYS

Cross the former Iron Curtain to Poland's capital **Warsaw** (p872), a city that's survived all that history could throw at it and was meticulously restored after WWII. Factor in visits to the opulent red-brick Royal Castle, the Soviet-era monolith Palace of Culture & Science with skyline views from its 30th-floor terrace, and the millennium-spanning POLIN Museum of the History of Polish Jews.

③ KRAKÓW ⏱ 3 DAYS

Miraculously spared destruction in WWII, the royal capital of **Kraków** (p878) pairs medieval looks with student-fuelled fun. Top billing goes to the ancient market square (Rynek Główny; pictured), Gothic St Mary's Basilica and Schindler's Factory. In the backstreets, pin down lost bars for craft cocktails.

🚗 **Detour**: *Squeeze in a day trip to* **Wieliczka Salt Mine** *(p883), with its underground chapel carved entirely from salt.*

FROM LEFT: WORLDWIDE/SHUTTERSTOCK, LOMB/SHUTTERSTOCK, , TOLOBALAGUER.COM/SHUTTERSTOCK

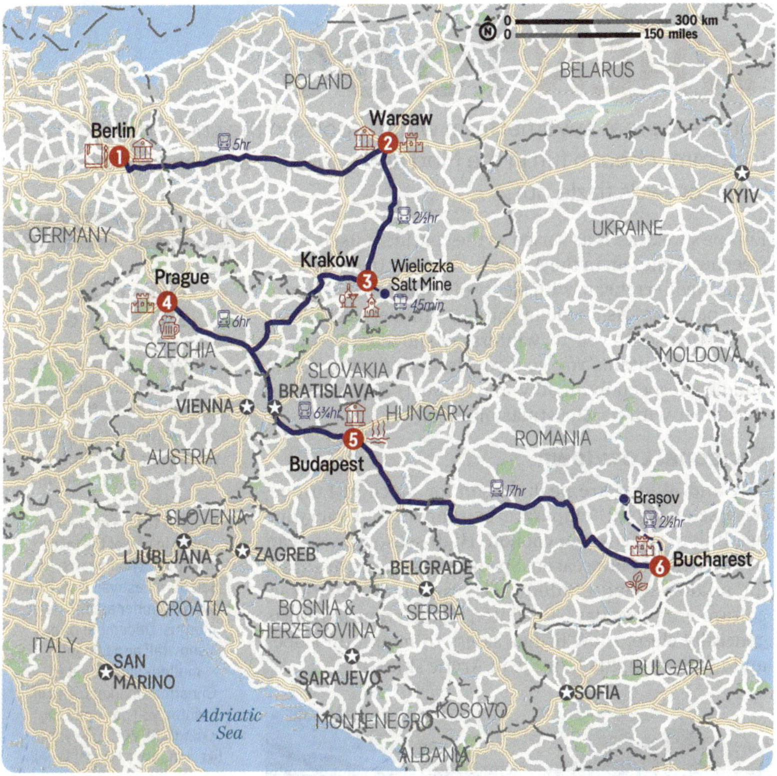

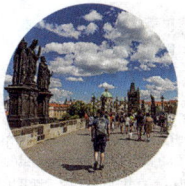

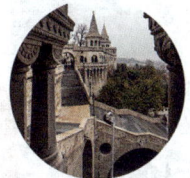

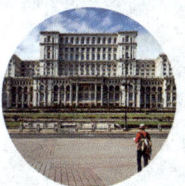

4

PRAGUE ⏱ 3 DAYS

Take a train into Czechia to reach **Prague** (p280), which ramps up the romance tenfold. The fairy-tale Prague Castle is unmissable. Wander over 14th-century Charles Bridge (pictured), atmospherically lit at dawn and dusk, revel in the medieval beauty of the Old Town Square and explore the Prague Jewish Museum's synagogues and cemeteries. Days round out in Bohemian beer halls.

5

BUDAPEST ⏱ 3 DAYS

Moving back east, **Budapest** (p570) beckons. The Hungarian capital's showstopper, Castle Hill (pictured), towers above the Danube with its monuments breezing through 2000 years of history. Allow time for Old Masters at the Renaissance-style Museum of Fine Arts, relaxing in the mineral-rich waters of posh bathhouses, and big nights out in quirky ruin bars.

6

BUCHAREST ⏱ 3 DAYS

Board the night train from Budapest to Romania's capital. **Bucharest** (p938) waited a long time for its place in the sun. Its museums, Orthodox churches, elegant parks, coffeehouses and grand 19th-century villas are fantastic, while the Palace of Parliament (pictured) is a tribute to dictatorial megalomania.

Detour*: Tag on an extra day to head north to Transylvania's* ***Brașov*** *(p944) for castles and Dracula tales.*

FROM LEFT: LEGACY1995/SHUTTERSTOCK, MARCOS CAMPOS/SHUTTERSTOCK, ANNA KUZKINA/SHUTTERSTOCK

WHEN TO GO

Europe is great anytime: from winter sports in the snow-dusted Alps to summer beach fun in the Med and shoulder-season city breaks when crowds fizzle out.

Europe's weather is as varied as the continent itself, from freezing climes up in the Arctic to roasting temperatures in the Mediterranean, with plenty of unpredictable weather in between. As a rule of thumb, summers get hotter the further south you go, winters get snowier the higher into the mountains you go. Crowds swell during school holidays (especially in July and August) and briefly in December with its Christmas markets.

Seasonal Lowdown

July and August are peak season for much of Europe, with schools out, temperatures soaring and everyone heading to the coast to cool off. High-season prices can be twice that of low season. Spring and autumn are great for mild weather, outdoor activities and crowd-free, culture-crammed days. In winter, Mediterranean resorts generally close, snow brings skiers to mountain slopes and northern lights twinkle in Arctic skies.

FROM LEFT: AARONCHENPSZ/SHUTTERSTOCK, MARCIN JUCHA/SHUTTERSTOCK.

Swiss Alps (p1127), Switzerland

⊛ I LIVE HERE

MAGICAL SALZBURG

Hildegard Strohmeyer is a city and hiking guide in Salzburg. *hildastroh.com*

I love living in Salzburg year-round. In spring, don't miss the magnolia blossom on Makartplatz. Come in summer to hike in the Alps, swim in one of the lakes near the city and catch the Salzburg Festival. October and November are the quiet months. December brings snowfall and romantic, mulled-wine-scented Christmas markets. And in winter, you can combine skiing with cultural events like January's Mozart Week.

MOUNTAIN WEATHER

Sunny in the mountains? Perhaps, but the weather can change at the drop of a hat, bringing fog, sleet, snow, storm – you name it – even in summer. Check forecasts locally before setting out. Or check the handy website *mountain-forecast.com.*

Weather through the Year: London

JANUARY	**FEBRUARY**	**MARCH**	**APRIL**	**MAY**	**JUNE**
Avg. daytime max: **7–8°C**	Avg. daytime max: **7–9°C**	Avg. daytime max: **10–11°C**	Avg. daytime max: **13–14°C**	Avg. daytime max: **16–18°C**	Avg. daytime max: **18–21°C**
Days of rainfall: **11–17**	Days of rainfall: **9–13**	Days of rainfall: **10–15**	Days of rainfall: **9–12**	Days of rainfall: **9–12**	Days of rainfall: **8–11**

SUMMER HEAT

In recent years, Mediterranean countries like Spain, Italy and Greece have notched record summer highs, with temperatures hitting up to 40°C in July and August. To prevent sunstroke, avoid the midday sun, apply high-factor sunscreen and drink at least 2L of water a day.

Carnivals & Crowd-Pullers

Carnaval de Nice (p428)
On the Côte d'Azur, France's biggest carnival erupts in a riot of colour, music and mayhem, with flower parades, floats, performers, giant paper-mâché figures and fireworks galore.
February

Festa de São João (p911)
Porto's biggest street party brings plenty of music and feasting, and folks going around whacking each other with plastic hammers just before the fireworks go off.
June

Festes de La Mercè (p1047)
Barcelona's post-summer extravaganza is riotous fun, with *castells* (human towers), *gegants* (papier-mâché giants) and *correfocs* (fire-running).
September

Guy Fawkes Night (p171)
Britain's skies fill with fireworks in commemoration of a failed attempt to blow up parliament back in 1605. It's also known as Bonfire Night; Lewes hosts a banger. **November**

Music, Maestro

Mozartwoche (p77) Salzburg celebrates Mozart's birthday with Mozart Week, an 11-day music extravaganza featuring world-renowned orchestras, conductors and soloists.
January–February

Arena di Verona Opera Festival (p673) Thousands of opera lovers pour into Verona's pink marble Roman Arena on the city's Piazza Brà for a feast of opera from Verdi to Puccini.
June–September

Fête de la Musique (p392) France pulls out all the music stops for this mammoth countrywide bash on summer solstice. Free concerts bring joy to streets, squares, parks and châteaux. **June**

Athens Epidaurus Festival (p543) The ancient theatre at Epidavros and Odeon of Herodes Atticus are the headline venues of Athens' annual cultural shindig, featuring music, dance, theatre and more. **June–August**

WINTER SNOW

From roughly November, flakes fall in the Alps, Dolomites, Pyrenees and the Arctic climes of Scandinavia. From December to March snow is pretty much guaranteed, especially above the 2000m mark. For snow reports, visit *snow-forecast.com*.

JULY	**AUGUST**	**SEPTEMBER**	**OCTOBER**	**NOVEMBER**	**DECEMBER**
Avg. daytime max: **20–23°C**	Avg. daytime max: **19–23°C**	Avg. daytime max: **16–20°C**	Avg. daytime max: **13–16°C**	Avg. daytime max: **9–11°C**	Avg. daytime max: **7–9°C**
Days of rainfall: **8–12**	Days of rainfall: **8–13**	Days of rainfall: **9–14**	Days of rainfall: **11–17**	Days of rainfall: **10–16**	Days of rainfall: **10–16**

FROM LEFT: MINISERIES/GETTY IMAGES, UBER BILDER/ALAMY

GET PREPARED FOR EUROPE

Useful things to load in your bag, your ears and your brain.

Clothes

Rain jacket The further north you go, the more likely it is to rain. A waterproof jacket is essential.

Swimwear Pack your swimming gear and a quick-drying towel for beaches, lakes, rivers and saunas.

Casual clothes T-shirts and shorts are fine for most restaurants, cafes and bars in summer.

Smarter dress Shirts, trousers and dresses are encouraged for posher hotels, restaurants and theatres.

Footwear Bring solid shoes for cobbles in historic city centres, and walking boots for hikes.

Layers Layering up is key for the great outdoors. You'll want thermal gear, gloves and a hat for cold climes.

Manners

Civilities remain important. Say 'please' and 'thank you' in the local lingo – a lot!

To get someone's attention, saying 'excuse me' or 'sorry' is traditional.

Queuing is sacrosanct. Attempts to 'queue jump' will result in tuts and stares.

On public transport, refrain from eating food or loudly using your phone; use headphones.

Wrap Modest dress is required for visiting churches and mosques. Bring a cover-up shawl, scarf or wrap.

📖 READ

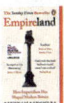

Empireland
(Sathnam Sanghera; 2021) Award-winning deep dive into the British Empire's legacy.

The World of Yesterday
(Stefan Zweig; 1942) Zweig's moving memoir as a Jew in exile is set against the rise of Nazi power.

La Bella Figura
(Beppe Severgnini; 2006) Inside guide to how Italian minds tick – a hilarious primer for visiting the country.

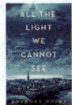

All the Light We Cannot See
(Anthony Doerr; 2014) A touching novel about a blind French girl during WWII.

How to say 'Hello'

Albanian
Tungjatjeta (toon-dya-*tye*-ta)

Bosnian
Zdravo (*zdra*-vo)

Bulgarian
Здравейте (zdra-*vey*-te)

Croatian
Dobar dan (do-bar dan)

Czech
Ahoj (*uh*-hoy)

Danish
Goddag (go-da)

Dutch
Dag/Hallo (dakh/ha-loh)

Estonian
Tere (te-re)

Finnish
Hei (hay)

French
Bonjour (bon-zhoor)

German
Servus (ser-vus)

Greek
Γειά σας (ya-sas)

Hungarian
Jó napot (yoh nah-pot)

Icelandic
Halló (ha-loh)

Italian
Ciao (chao)

Latvian
Sveiks (svayks)

Lithuanian
Sveiki (svay-ki)

Macedonian
Здраво (zdra-vo)

Montenegrin
Zdravo (zdra-vo)

Norwegian
Goddag (goo-dahg)

Polish
Cześć (cheshch)

Portuguese
Olá (o-laa)

Romanian
Bună ziua (*boo*-nuh *zee*-wa)

Serbian
Zdravo/Здраво (zdra-vo)

Slovene
Zdravo (zdra-vo)

Spanish
Hola (o-la)

Swedish
Hej (hey)

Turkish
Merhaba (mer-ha-ba)

📺 WATCH

The Third Man (Carol Reed; 1949; pictured) Classic film noir set in shadowy, postwar Vienna.

La Dolce Vita (Federico Fellini; 1960) Marcello Mastroianni and Anita Ekberg frolicking in Rome's Trevi Fountain.

Trainspotting (Danny Boyle; 1996) Landmark dark comedy set in Edinburgh that delves into the city's underbelly of drug addiction.

Moulin Rouge! (Baz Luhrmann; 2001) All the glitz, glamour and passion of Paris come to the fore in this romantic musical drama.

The Way (Emilio Estevez; 2010) A grieving father follows in the footsteps of his late son by trekking the Camino de Santiago.

🎧 LISTEN

Abbey Road (The Beatles; 1969) One of the best chart-topping albums from one of the greatest-ever British rock bands.

Eine kleine Nachtmusik, K 525 (Wolfgang Amadeus Mozart; 1787) The most uplifting composition for a chamber ensemble.

Mariza canta Amália (Mariza; 2020) Portuguese fado singer Mariza pays tribute to Amália Rodrigues' (the genre's diva) best songs.

Resonate (Papooz; 2024) Cult Paris-based duo, Ulysse Cottin and Armand Penicaut, elevate spirits with their upbeat mix of French folk, pop and rock.

Fish and chips, Britain

THE **FOOD** SCENE

Eating out in Europe is a delight, whether you're scoffing street food, shooting high for Michelin stars or finding ingredients at the source.

Diving into Europe's food scene is your pass to the continent's soul. Whether you're sampling farm-fresh pecorino, wine and olives at a remote Italian *agriturismo* (farm-stay accommodation), pinning down the perfect bistro in the backstreets of Paris, devouring posh cakes in a coffeehouse in Vienna, touring Madrid by tapas, or enjoying meze at a beachfront taverna in Greece – each plate delivers a generous dollop of culture. Embrace brunch and the lazy lunch.

An overall boom in regional, seasonal and organic ingredients and sustainable sourcing means quality is up big-time. Plant-based, farm-to-fork and nose-to-tail dining are having a moment, as are ingredient-led menus geared towards vegans and vegetarians. Slow Food is the watch word – small producers and zero food miles. New-wave chefs are riffing on local ingredients, bringing in foraged flavours and pairing tasting menus with natural and biodynamic wines. Food festivals are playing up everything from asparagus to truffles and farmers' markets rich in picnic fixings.

To Market!

You can't beat a food market for a bite to eat on the hoof. From the crack-of-dawn fish markets of Scandinavia where the day's catch is hauled in, to the bountiful farmers' markets of Provence, London's world-on-a-plate Borough Market to Barcelona's tapas-rammed Mercat de la Boqueria, markets deliver heaps of local flavour. Bring along your own and fill it with whatever is

---

Best European Dishes

FISH AND CHIPS
Battered fish served with chips, often doused in salt and vinegar, is a British fave.

RAGÙ ALLA BOLOGNESE
Rich sauce made with *soffritto*, minced meat and red wine.

PAELLA
Spain's national dish of saffron-infused rice, vegetables, chicken and seafood.

MOUSSAKA
Greek classic: layers of potato, aubergine and minced meat topped with a creamy sauce.

seasonal – from mountain cheeses to truffles, Arctic cloudberries to ripe beef tomatoes. An early start usually means fewer crowds and richer pickings, plus time to hang out at street-food stalls and cafes after a morning shop.

Coffeehouse Culture

Coffee is social glue in many European countries and an integral part of daily life. From the elbow-jostling bazaars of İstanbul, where you can slurp thick *türk kahve* (Turkish coffee) with baklava and fortune telling on the side, to the fancy cakes and palatial backdrops of Vienna's *Kaffeehäuser* and Budapest's *kávéházak*, coffeehouses deliver a decadent shot of culture for small change. Italy with its espresso bars, France with its boulevard cafes for people-watching and patisserie, Greece with its *kafenía* for ice-cold frappés and backgammon – all invite you to relax, chat, read and watch the world go by.

Through the Grapevine

No drink in Europe ignites such passion as wine, and a winery tour and tasting is a cultural deep-dive. Wineries range from France's grand châteaux to family-run affairs in Greece with open doors and ancient grape-growing traditions. Many countries

pair wine with season-spun food in rustic settings – from *osterie* in Italy, with succinct menus and a relaxed vibe, to stone-walled *adegas* (wine cellars) in Portugal. In Swiss Ticino, *grotti* (rustic inns) match merlot reds with dishes like beef braised in red wine on tree-shaded terraces. In Austria, *Heurigen* (wine taverns) are identified by a green wreath and pair wines with hearty grub like roast pork and pickled vegetables.

FESTIVALS TO FEAST AT

CioccolaTò *(turismotorino.org; February; pictured)* Turin's mammoth chocolate fest brings joy to the sun-deprived days of winter.

Nemea Wine Festival *(p542; nemeawineland.com; September)* Nemea in the Peloponnese pops a cork celebrating the local *agiorgitiko* grape with tastings and concerts.

Oktoberfest *(p489; oktoberfest.de; September/October)* Munich rolls out the barrel with foaming wheat beer and a feast of pork knuckles, sausages and sauerkraut.

Budapest Wine Festival *(p571; aborfesztival. hu; September)* A glamorous wine festival full of tastings and Danube sunsets at the Royal Palace in Budapest.

Feira da Castanha *(cm-marvao.pt; November)* The hill town of Marvão in the Alentejo goes all out for chestnuts, with street food, cooking demos, new wine and music.

WIENER SCHNITZEL	FONDUE	GOULASH	BACALHAU À BRÁS	MOULES ET FRITES
Breaded veal cutlet, often as big as a boot and fried to golden perfection, is Vienna's signature.	An alpine feast of gooey melted cheese and toasted bread.	Hearty Hungarian beef soup with lashings of onions, garlic and paprika.	Portuguese codfish with potato sticks, scrambled eggs, olives and parsley.	Belgian-style steamed mussels served with fries and mayonnaise.

Specialities

Cheap Eats

Francesinha Multi-layered meat sandwich covered in melted cheese and a rich sauce, typical for Porto, Portugal.

Ćevapčići Serbia's small kebabs, made with minced beef, lamb or pork.

Kiluvõileib Estonian sprat sandwich served on dark rye bread with a hard-boiled egg.

Plăcintă Moldova's flaky pastry treat stuffed with cheese, meat, potatoes or herbs.

Lakror Doughy Albanian pie usually stuffed with spinach, sometimes also cheese, leeks or meat.

Tarte flambée Light, thin-crust Alsatian pizza topped with crème fraîche, onions and lardons.

Sweet Treats

Apfelstrudel Austrian classic with sugar-dusted layers of flaky pastry, diced apple and cinnamon.

Cream tea British scones with strawberry jam and clotted cream.

Cannoli Sicily's crisp, fried shells filled with sweetened ricotta and candied fruit, chocolate or pistachios.

Kiluvõileib

Churros Spain's sugary fried dough sticks, dunked in thick chocolate sauce.

Gaufres Crunchy, fluffy Belgian waffles served with chocolate, whipped cream or icing sugar.

Street Food

Socca A crispy galette from Nice made from chickpea flour, olive oil and water.

Lángos Hungary's disc-shaped deep-fried flatbread topped with sour cream and cheese.

Käsekrainer This fat, cheese-filled sausage is a popular beer-mopping snack in Austria.

Cornish pasty Turnover-shaped pastry filled with beef, potato, swede and onion, beloved in Britain.

Burek Flaky pastry with meat or cheese, found across the Balkans.

MEALS OF A LIFETIME

Auberge Sauvage (p400) Set in a medieval presbytery, this Michelin-starred haven near Mont St-Michel makes local produce and foraged delicacies shine.

Tasca Zé dos Cornos (p907) Good old-fashioned Portuguese homecooking is the deal at this family-run *tasca* (tavern) in the heart of Lisbon.

Obauer (p90) The Obauer brothers elevate regional ingredients to epic heights at this two-Michelin-starred restaurant in the Austrian Alps.

Casa Perbellini (p672) Giancarlo Perbellini walks the culinary high-wire at this three-star Michelin stunner in Verona.

Paul Ainsworth at No 6 (p182) Michelin-starred restaurant in Padstow, Cornwall, where Paul Ainsworth works magic at the stove.

THE YEAR IN FOOD

SPRING

Spring brings produce like lamb, asparagus, artichokes, leeks, spring greens, wild garlic (pictured) and onions, samphire, rhubarb and the first potatoes to the table. Sweet breads studded with dried fruit usher in Easter.

SUMMER

Abundant fruit and veg, from sweet peas to tomatoes. Cherries, figs, strawberries, raspberries, peaches and lemons are in season. Try crab (pictured), lobster, mussels and sardines on the coast.

AUTUMN

Look out for wild mushrooms, game, pumpkin, chestnuts, truffles (pictured) and slow-cooked stews on menus. Apples come into their own in juice, cider, pies and crumbles. Sample new wine as grape harvests get underway.

WINTER

Menus big up roast meats, root vegetables and hearty stews. As snow falls, fondue and raclette provide comfort food in the Alps. Mulled wine (pictured) and spiced cookies come to Christmas markets.

EKATERINA POKROVSKY/SHUTTERSTOCK

HOW TO... Travel Europe on a Budget

With a little forward planning, travelling Europe on a budget is a breeze. Many of the best moments are free, and even high culture doesn't have to cost the earth.

Know your Seasons

You can save a mint by dodging high season. Cities and beaches get swamped during school holidays (especially July and August), when flights and room rates skyrocket. Christmas often sees another spike in crowds and costs. Choose spring or autumn instead.

Cast your Net Wider

Everyone wants to see Venice and Santorini, but equally compelling, quieter and cheaper alternatives abound. Consider less touristed destinations. We're talking Montenegro instead of Mallorca, Albania instead of Amalfi. A sense of adventure often pays off handsomely.

Arrive Cheaply

Budget airlines zip around Europe's skies. You can bag terrific deals if you travel outside high season and book well ahead. The more flexible you can be on dates, the better (flights are often cheaper midweek). The same goes for train tickets (p48).

Walk this Way

Many European cities are walkable and a joy to explore on foot. If you do use public transport, look out for money-saving passes (24-hour tickets, for instance). Some destinations, including Luxembourg and Belgrade, have free public transport.

Snag Meal Deals

Bakeries and supermarkets are ideal for grabbing a snack for lunch or picnic ingredients. Fixed-price lunches tend to be best value in restaurants, often costing a fraction of an evening meal. Avoid eating in touristed hot spots as this can jack up the price.

Save on Sightseeing

London's big-hitter museums give free entry to their permanent collections. Elsewhere, museums and galleries have free or reduced-admission days per month or one evening per week. **Sandemans New Europe** (*neweuropetours.eu*) runs free city walking tours across Europe, including Amsterdam, Berlin and Florence.

GUEST-PASS HEAVEN

Many countries in Central Europe (Germany, France, Austria and Switzerland, for instance) provide free guest passes, tourist cards or welcome cards when you stay overnight in a town, city or mountain resort. The benefits of these vary wildly, but most cover public transport, and many will throw in admission to local sights; activities such as guided walking tours; and entry to lidos in summer or cross-country skiing and snowshoeing in winter. Some will even cover the odd cable-car ride. It's really worth doing your homework on the places that offer these as they can seriously slash the overall cost of your trip.

47

Lake Geneva, Lausanne (p1121), Switzerland

TRIP PLANNER

ON THE RAILS

With a little advance planning, Europe really is your oyster by rail. Given the continent's diminutive proportions, trains often zip from one astonishing city to the next in a matter of hours, cracking open phenomenal views of country, coast and mountain. Read on for our tips on planning, booking and saving.

Planning your Train Journey

BOOKING TICKETS

Long-distance and high-speed trains can often be booked between four and six months ahead. The cheapest tickets sell out in a flash. Booking early can save you up to 70% on standard fares, but exchanges and refunds are generally excluded. Some tickets are loaded in blocks, prioritising major routes.

Eurostar (*eurostar.com*) releases tickets six to eight months in advance; get the app to see when sales go live and to grab the best deals. Also sign up for **Rail Europe** (*raileurope.com*) ticket availability notifications to be at the front of the booking queue. Travelling midweek and off-peak is often quieter and cheaper; flexibility is the key. If tickets to one station have sold out, try another nearby. Extra charges can apply on fast and international trains, where you may need to reserve a seat at peak times.

THE NIGHT TRAIN

If you fancy going to bed in Budapest, Rome or Vienna and waking up in Bucharest, Palermo (Sicily) or Berlin, consider hopping on one of Europe's night train services. These include the **ÖBB Nightjet** and **EuroNight** (*nightjet.com*) trains, linking 25 European cities, the **InterCity Notte** (*trenitalia.com*) connecting major Italian cities, France's **Intercités de Nuit** (*sncf-connect.com*), and the **European Sleeper** (*europeansleeper. eu*) from Brussels, heading east to Prague and south to Venice.

The **European Rail Timetable** *(europeanrailtimetable.eu)* is an invaluable resource for planning a trip, with all train schedules, supplements, reservations information and maps.

Comprehensive, reliable and eco-minded, **The Man in Seat 61** *(seat61.com)* should also be a first port of call when planning a long-distance rail trip through Europe. Mark Smith's website has incredibly helpful, detailed information on everything from tickets to times, fares, passes, changing stations and travelling with bikes, and will help you plan even the trickiest route from A to B.

If you prefer a paper guide, **Europe by Rail** (Nicky Gardner and Susanne Kries; 2024) is very useful for route planning.

Overnight trains usually offer a choice between reclining seats or pricier private sleeping cabins, and have a dining car or snacks available. Tickets can usually be booked up to six months in advance. For all night routes at a glance, visit the **Eurail** *(eurail.com)* website.

RAIL PASSES

If you plan on travelling a lot by train, a rail pass is a no-brainer, but do your homework, comparing point-to-point prices beforehand to make sure you're getting the best deal.

Europe-wide passes include **Interrail** *(interrail.eu),* with a Global Pass offering European residents unlimited rail travel through 33 European countries. Passes are valid for four, five or seven days in a month; 10 or 15 days in two months. Or opt for a One Country pass, valid for a month. The equivalent for non-European residents are **Eurail** *(eurail.com)* passes, yielding the same benefits. Many countries have their own money-saving passes, offering hefty discounts on tickets, including Germany's BahnCard, Switzerland's Half-Fare Card and Austria's ÖBB Vorteilscard.

Interrail pass

RASMUS LINDKVIST/SHUTTERSTOCK

FIVE EPIC RAIL RIDES

Glacier Express (p1129) Right up there with the best of Switzerland's rail routes is this 290km ride linking Zermatt and St Moritz. It's an Alpine feast of mountains, lakes, tunnels, bridges and gorge-skipping viaducts.

Linha do Douro (p914) Trundling from Porto to Pocinho near the Spanish border, this 160km retro railway unzips the romance of Portugal's river-woven Douro Valley, taking in steep terraced vineyards, tiny villages, historic quintas (wineries) and riveting views.

Belgrade–Bar Railway Winging you from Serbia to Montenegro over rugged, mountainous terrain, this 476km ride is a stunner. It burrows through 254 tunnels and leaps over 435 bridges, commanding sensational views of Balkan landscapes.

West Highland Line (p216) Scotland turns up the drama to max on this 330km, single-track railway, unravelling moody moors, lochs and misty munros en route from Glasgow to Oban or Mallaig. Loch Lomond, wild Rannoch Moor and the 21-arch Glenfinnan Viaduct of Harry Potter fame are standouts.

Bergen Railway (p852) Linking Oslo to Bergen, this 496km, seven-hour ride delivers knockout Norwegian landscapes with cliff-wrapped fjords and glacier-frosted mountains. The highlight is Hardangervidda, a wild plateau home to reindeer, musk ox and elk.

FROM LEFT: MARCOS CAMPOS/SHUTTERSTOCK, ZEDSPIDER/SHUTTERSTOCK

Santiago de Compostela (p1061), Spain

THE OUTDOORS

Europe's outdoors is truly great: from hiking to cloud-shredding mountain peaks to kayaking along emerald rivers and surfing monstrous Atlantic waves.

For a continent of its size, Europe packs in an impressive amount of outdoor adventures – from hiking in the hut-dotted peaks of the Alps, to freewheeling past vineyards on the banks of the Danube. And if you're craving bigger thrills, you can dial up the action sea-kayaking to hidden islands, white-water rafting on fast-flowing rivers or swooshing down the slopes on skis as the winter snows drift in.

Walking & Hiking

Europe is heaven on earth for hikers. Central Europe's glacier-topped Alps, the rugged Carpathians in Eastern Europe and Spain's jagged Picos de Europa beckon with multiday, hut-to-hut treks. If you're up for a challenge, France's glacier-grazing Tour du Mont Blanc, Spain's pilgrim magnet of Camino de Santiago, Scotland's munro-skimming West Highland Way, Slovakia's cross-range Tatranská Magistrala, and Albania's Balkan beauty Valbonë Pass are up there with the continent's finest hikes. That's before you've even set foot on Norway's fjord-riven Lofoten Islands, trekked through Crete's Samaria Gorge, or hoofed it along Portugal's Rota Vicentina.

Cicerone (*cicerone.co.uk*) publishes well-researched walking guides, while **Kompass** (*kompass.de*) produces reliable maps. Handy apps include **AllTrails** (*alltrails.com*). For walking holidays in Europe, check out **Ramble Worldwide** (*rambleworldwide. co.uk*), **Headwater** (*headwater.com*) and **Macs Adventure** (*macsadventure.com*).

Adrenaline Sports

BOBSLEDDING
For a minute in the life of an Olympic bobsleigh racer, ride the **Olympia Bob** (p97) in Igls in the Alps of Tyrol.

PARAGLIDING
Drift above the monastery-topped rocks of **Meteora** (p537) in Greece on a tandem or motorised paragliding flight.

GLACIER HIKING
Crunch across glacial ice, passing waterfalls, ice caves and ash from ancient explosions at **Vatnajökull** (p603) in Iceland.

Skiing & Snow Sports

Europe's mountains call as flakes start to fall. Funiculars and cable cars float up to slopes, where you'll find powdery perfection for every taste and ability. The season generally runs from December to Easter, getting longer the higher you go. Ski passes take a hefty chunk out of your budget, but favouring low-key villages over upscale resorts and avoiding school holidays makes it cheaper. Bigger resorts have ski schools offering individual and group lessons. Runs are colour-coded according to difficulty: blue (easy), red (intermediate) and black (expert). Rent gear at sports shops, including **Intersport** *(intersportrent.com)*, which covers 14 countries in Europe.

High Tatras (p997), Slovakia

The terrain is staggeringly varied, from the glitzy World Cup slopes of Kitzbühel (Austria) and St Moritz (Switzerland) in the Alps, to the more offbeat and affordable thrills of the High Tatras in Slovakia and Bulgaria's Mt Vitosha, and aurora-borealis-spangled skiing in the Arctic in Tromsø, Norway.

Water Sports

From Norway's cliff-wrapped fjords down to the clear waters of the Med, Europe is ripe for water adventures. On the coast, sea kayaking raises pulses, whether it's paddling Italy's gorgeous Cinque Terre, exploring Scotland's wild Skye or floating over a sunken city in Kaş, Türkiye.

In summer, divers plunge to reefs, wrecks and grottoes; see **PADI** *(padi.com)* for sites and courses. Winter brings the biggest swells, with waves bashing Atlantic beaches in surf magnets like Nazaré (Portugal) and Newquay (UK); check **Surf Atlas** *(thesurfatlas.com)* for surf resorts, camps and schools. Windsurfing and kitesurfing enthusiasts catch breezes on islands like Naxos in Greece.

Don't forget Europe's rivers and lakes. Highlights include paddling through water lilies in Montenegro's Lake Skadar National Park, kayaking past the limestone cliffs of the Danube's Iron Gates gorge in Serbia and stand-up paddleboarding across mountain-rimmed Hallstätter See in Austria.

VIA FERRATA	BOG WALKING	BLACK-RUN SKIING	DOGSLEDDING
Flirt with mountaineering on a *via ferrata* around Italy's **Lake Como** (p671). These fixed climbing routes deliver knockout views.	Go bogwalking through the prehistoric, bird-rich peatlands of Estonia's **Soomaa National Park** (p351).	Thunder at the speed of light down Europe's longest black run, the 16km-long, near-vertical La Sarenne in **Alpe d'Huez** (p412).	Listen to the howls of huskies, dogsledding through the Swedish Arctic in **Kiruna** (p1108), as the northern lights flash above.

ACTION AREAS

Where to find Europe's best outdoor activities.

Walking/Hiking

1. Jungfrau Region (p1130)
2. West Highland Way (p215)
3. Ruta del Cares (p1060)
4. Tatranská Magistrala (p999)
5. Valbonë Pass (p68)
6. Rota Vicentina (p918)
7. Samaria Gorge (p559)

Skiing/Snowboarding

1. Matterhorn Glacier Paradise (p1129)
2. Kitzbühel (p98)
3. St Moritz (p1131)
4. Tromsø (p862)
5. Chamonix (p407)
6. High Tatras (p997)
7. Bansko (p235)

Extreme Adventures

1. Alpe d'Huez (p412)
2. Vatnajökull (p603)
3. Soomaa National Park (p351)
4. Kiruna (p1108)
5. Igls (p97)
6. Lake Como (p671)
7. Meteora (p537)

Cycling

1. Danube Cycle Path (p977)
2. Verbier (p1128)
3. Bavarian Forest (p495)
4. Camel Trail (p181)
5. Loire Valley (p423)
6. Gap of Dunloe (p631)
7. Ecopista do Dão (p925)

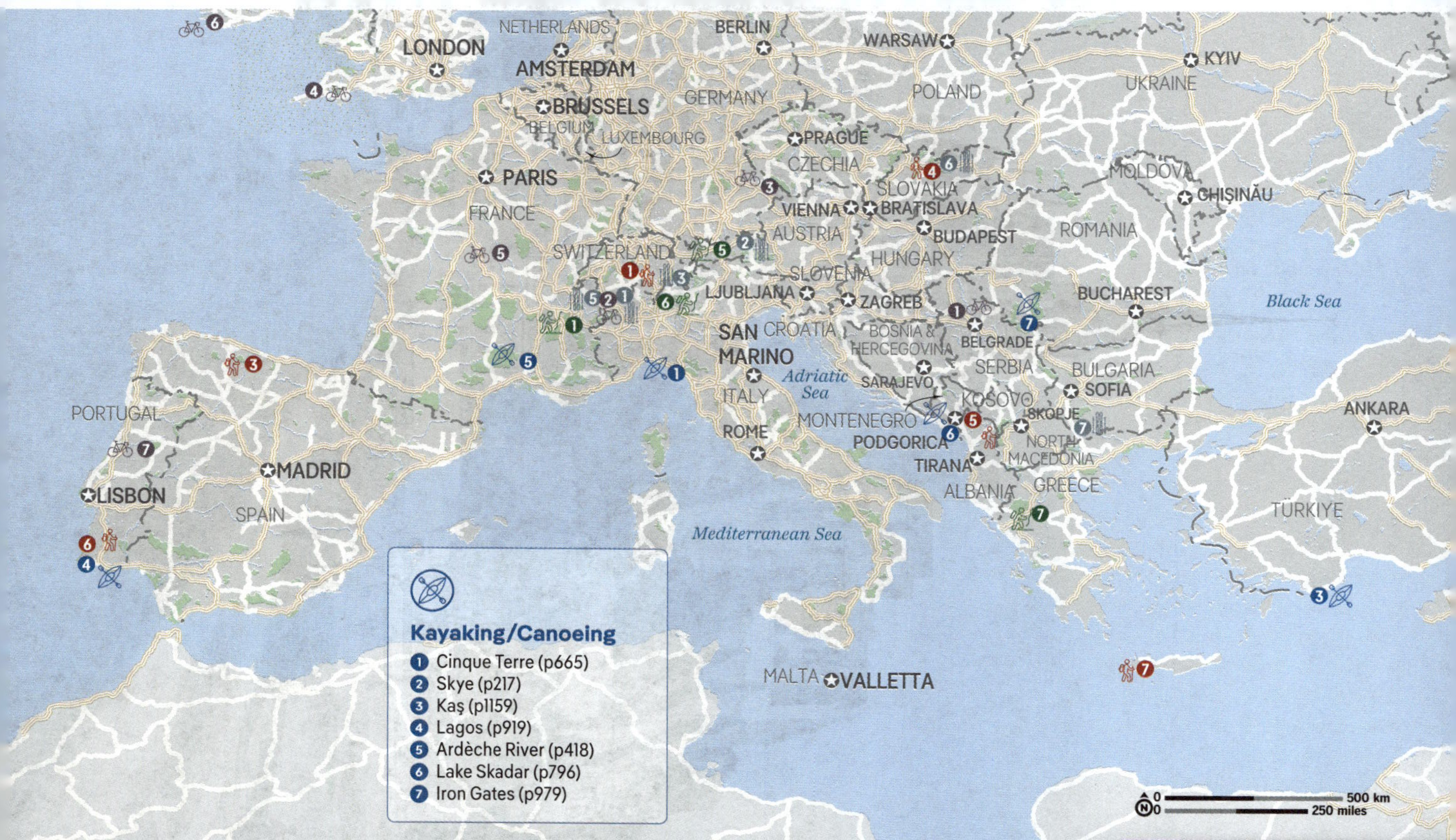
Kayaking/Canoeing
1 Cinque Terre (p665)
2 Skye (p217)
3 Kaş (p1159)
4 Lagos (p919)
5 Ardèche River (p418)
6 Lake Skadar (p796)
7 Iron Gates (p979)
LONDON
NETHERLANDS
AMSTERDAM
BERLIN
WARSAW
KYIV
UKRAINE
BRUSSELS
BELGIUM
LUXEMBOURG
GERMANY
POLAND
PARIS
FRANCE
PRAGUE
CZECHIA
SLOVAKIA
MOLDOVA
CHIŞINĂU
VIENNA
BRATISLAVA
AUSTRIA
BUDAPEST
ROMANIA
SWITZERLAND
HUNGARY
SLOVENIA
LJUBLJANA
ZAGREB
BUCHAREST
Black Sea
SAN MARINO
CROATIA
BOSNIA & HERCEGOVINA
BELGRADE
SERBIA
BULGARIA
SOFIA
Adriatic Sea
SARAJEVO
KOSOVO
ITALY
MONTENEGRO
PODGORICA
SKOPJE
NORTH MACEDONIA
ANKARA
PORTUGAL
MADRID
ROME
TIRANA
ALBANIA
GREECE
LISBON
SPAIN
TÜRKIYE
Mediterranean Sea
MALTA
VALLETTA
0 500 km
0 250 miles

THE GUIDE

Chapters in this section are organised by countries, with each country split into hubs and their surrounding areas. Each hub includes unique experiences, local insights, insider tips and expert recommendations. It's also your gateway to the surrounding area, where you'll see what and how much you can do from there.

Mont St-Michel (p399), France

For places to stay in Albania, see p70

ANDRII MARUSHCHYNETS/SHUTTERSTOCK

Above: Accursed Mountains (p68), Shkodër; Right: Berat (p62)

Curated by
Joel Balsam

Albania

MYSTERIOUS NO LONGER

Cotton-candy-blue waters, spectacular mountain hiking and thousands of years of history etched into crumbling ruins. It's hard to understand why some still skip Albania.

Albania's borders were shut for much of the 20th century due to a brutal strain of communism steered by the iron fist of dictator Enver Hoxha. Even its own residents couldn't get out. But in 1991, communism fell and Albania's doors swung open. What travellers discovered was an enchanting country where the wind whistled through shattered remnants of half-forgotten Roman and Greek ruins and azure water lapped gently at empty beaches. These days, the secret's out, as Instagram reels of dreamy beaches rivalling any in the Mediterranean have put Albania at the top of many a travel list.

Albanians, for the most part, haven't changed. They're still as curious and warm as ever. The prices aren't close to nearby Greece or Croatia. And you can still find quiet beaches and authentic towns. In Tirana, construction cranes and stylish bars are evidence that this European capital is on the upswing, while the Albanian Riviera's cool water is a refreshing respite from the summer heat. Inland, Berat and Gjirokastër's genius Ottoman architecture and alleyways graciously remain intact, and bike-friendly Shkodër is a perfect gateway to breathtaking trails in the Albanian Alps.

Strangely, some still avoid Albania due to the infamous reputation of its overseas mafia, memories of communism and ethnic discrimination. Ignore them and go now before this amazing country gets well and truly swarming.

THE MAIN AREAS

TIRANA & CENTRAL ALBANIA
Up-and-coming capital and UNESCO city. **p60**

THE ALBANIAN RIVIERA
Turquoise water and stone castles. **p64**

THE ALBANIAN ALPS & NORTHERN ALBANIA
Mountain hikes and mysterious history. **p68**

Find Your Way

There are no easy options when it comes to getting around. Public transport is unpredictable and mountain roads are dramatic. Your budget and available time are the main factors.

The Albanian Alps & Northern Albania, p68

Hike to villages in the Accursed Mountains, cruise a high-altitude lake and tour an artsy town.

Tirana & Central Albania, p60

Albania's capital is the place to delve into the country's history, gastronomy and culture. To the south, visit Ottoman-era Berat's wonderful windows.

CAR

Cars provide the most flexibility, especially for exploring lesser-visited destinations. However, roads off the major highways can be dicey. City driving is also a challenge, with narrow streets and drivers who park in the middle of the road.

The Albanian Riviera, p64

Aquamarine water and gorgeous viewpoints along the Ionian coast, plus amazing archaeological sites and a mystical stone city.

FURGON

Albania's main public transport is the *furgon* – a shared van, minibus or car. *Furgons* don't have schedules and make plenty of stops as they go, making arrival times unpredictable.

Himarë (p66)

Plan Your Time

Albania's main cities can be visited in a day or two, but you should leave extra time for delays and infrequent *furgon* if taking public transport.

The Capital & the Coast in a Week

● Start in Tirana to learn about communism at **subterranean bunkers** (p61) and sample *raki* in trendy **Blloku** (p61). Then it's off to the Ottoman town of **Berat** (p62) for winding alleyways. Pick a beach on the Albanian Riviera: there are plenty around **Ksamil** (p65) and **Himarë** (p66). Leave time for ancient **Butrint** (p65).

The Albanian Alps in a Week

● After **Tirana** (p60), head up to cooler climes in **Shkodër** (p68). The city has a young vibe and several excellent museums. Follow up with the multi-day **Valbonë to Theth loop** (p68) over a mountain pass. In Theth, hike to an electric-blue **natural pool** (p69) before returning to Shkodër.

SEASONAL HIGHLIGHTS

SPRING

Albania starts to warm up after Dita e Verës (Summer's Day) on 14 March, though it's often still cloudy and rainy.

SUMMER

Peak season, especially around Sarandë and Ksamil. Make sure to book accommodation ahead of time.

AUTUMN

The best time to travel, with milder temperatures and fewer crowds. September is ideal for hiking in the Alps.

WINTER

Warm up with a *raki* in Tirana then go to the city that makes the masks for Venice during the **Shkodër Carnival** (p69).

Tirana & Central Albania

COMMUNIST HISTORY | CUISINE | NIGHTLIFE

Places

Tirana p60

Berat p62

☑ **TOP TIP**

Albanians are firmly committed to cash payments; few businesses accept credit cards. Both lekë and euros are accepted (except the bus, which only takes lekë), so there's no need to change money. ATMs dispense lekë: Credins and Tirana Bank usually have the lowest fees.

Lively Tirana (Tiranë) has come a long way from its decades of brutal dictatorship, which lasted from 1944 to 1991. The Albanian capital today is bursting with colour, from parks and thoroughfares flourishing with foliage to Soviet-style apartment buildings painted with vibrant murals. Busy traffic rolls past captivating mosque minarets and church domes in this secular though still faithful city, while Tirana's chic locals stroll through clean, safe streets to sprawling patios for an espresso, *raki* (fruit brandy) or fancy cocktail in the dapper Blloku neighbourhood. Look at the modern skyscrapers popping up everywhere, especially around Skanderbeg Sq, for more evidence that this aspiring European Union capital is on the rise.

Then punch the numbers into your time machine and travel back to life under the Ottoman Empire in beautiful Berat. With a story that dates back 2400 years, this UNESCO city is a mountain town with a special kind of magic.

Tirana

Explore the city's heart

Start exploring the Albanian capital at its bustling epicentre: **Skanderbeg Sq**. Walk in a circle to see the epic socialist-realist facade outside the **National History Museum** *(mhk.gov.al; closed for repairs until 2028)*, the **statue** of national

---

 GETTING AROUND

An airport bus (400L) runs every hour from near Skanderbeg Sq and takes 30 minutes. Tirana also has more than 20 municipal bus lines (traditional buses, not *furgon*). Electric taxis like Lux Taxi *(069 844 4487)* are cheaper than official cabs and can pick you up wherever you are. The **Berat Bus**

Terminal is nearly 3km from the historic centre. There are occasional public buses into town, or you can take a taxi. Historic Berat is walkable, although it may be challenging for those with mobility issues.

TIRANA

IS ALBANIA SAFE?

Many who've never been to Albania will warn you not to visit. Ignore them. Albania is as safe as anywhere in Europe, if not safer, with a crime rate lower than Canada's. Pickpocketing isn't common and locals are friendly, curious and welcoming. Stereotypes stem from centuries-old ethnic conflicts between Slavs and Illyrians as well as Christians and Muslims. They also derive from Albania's long communist period and the Albanians' mafia-like crime presence elsewhere in Europe. As the country develops and cracks down on corruption in an effort to join the European Union, this discrimination will inevitably decline. In the meantime, it's travellers' responsibility to share the truth about this friendly country.

hero Skanderbeg and prayer sites for Tirana's large populations of Muslims and Christians: the 19th-century **Et'hem Bey Mosque** *(entry by donation)* and **Resurrection of Christ Orthodox Cathedral**. Around the corner, see where Enver Hoxha (1908–85), a tyrant who ruled Albania during one of Europe's most oppressive dictatorships, coordinated a vast network of spies at **House of Leaves** *(muzeugjethi.gov.al; entry 700L)*.

A short taxi or bus ride will take you further into the paranoid logic of Hoxha and his regime. **Bunk'Art 1** *(bunkart.al; entry 500L)* is a vast network of tunnels spread out over five subterranean floors. It's one of 175,000 bunkers built during the communist period as a backup in case enemies (pretty much everyone except North Korea) attacked. There's also **Bunk'Art 2** *(bunkart.al; entry 500L)* near Skanderbeg Sq, though the lengthy texts are incomprehensible in English.

Capital nightlife

The stylish **Blloku** neighbourhood south of the Lana River is the place to be seen in Tirana. Blocked off for nearly half a century as a heavily guarded home for Communist Party

 EATING IN TIRANA: OUR PICKS

Lakror TeEla: Sample the Korça speciality *lakror* (spinach pie) swigged down with *dhallë* (a salted yoghurt drink). *5am-3pm Mon-Fri, to 2pm Sat & Sun* €

Te Met Kodra: There's just one thing to order here: freshly grilled *qofte* (meatballs) made with meat straight from the farm. *8am-10pm Mon-Sat, to 4.30pm Sun* €

Era: Widely considered Tirana's best restaurant for traditional dishes like *dollma* (stuffed grape leaves), with excellent service and reasonable prices. *11am-midnight* €€

Mullixhiu: Fine dining and bakery in the park from Bledar Kola (a former footballer), who helped kickstart Albania's slow-food movement. *noon-4pm & 6-10pm* €€

GESTUR GISLASON/SHUTTERSTOCK

officials, Blloku's gates were thrown open in 1991 and quickly started filling up with trendy bars and restaurants. Our favourites are **Komiteti** for its many flavours of *raki* (fruit brandy) and **Radio** for creative cocktails with an Albanian twist.

Or attend a wedding performance at **Albanian Night** (*albaniannight.com; entry 3800L*). There's singing, traditional clothing (you'll wear vibrant clothing collected and made by Albanian artisans) and, like any good wedding, plenty of gossip.

Berat

TIME FROM TIRANA: **2HR**

Visit an ancient castle

Imagine life under the Ottoman Empire in beautiful Berat. With a story that dates back 2400 years, this UNESCO World Heritage site and mountain town in central Albania, recognised as a rare example of an architectural character typical of the Ottoman period, has a special kind of magic. Look up and you can't miss **Berat Castle** (*Kalaja e Beratit; 300L*) peeking over the mountain. The castle dates back to the 4th century BCE and was added to by various empires as recently

✕ EATING IN BERAT: OUR PICKS

Eni: Small spot jutting out of the cliffside (the mountain rock is visible) on the Goricë side. An affordable menu, with dishes made from the heart. *11.30am-10.30pm* €

Klea: Castle-top restaurant with a lovely courtyard and fresh Albanian dishes. Breakfast for guests only. *noon-10pm* €

Amalia: Candlelit Goricë alleyway restaurant with an Albanian cuisine tasting menu (€28 for two). Great place to try Berati wine. *11.30am-11.30pm* €€

Lili: Leave with a smile on your face, a full belly and a new friend in English-speaking owner Lili. Reserve ahead. *5.30-10pm Mon-Fri* €€

Berat Castle

WHY I LOVE BERAT

Joel Balsam, Lonely Planet writer
Berat might only occupy a day or two on your trip, and it's clearly not off the beaten track, but it's a guaranteed highlight. There was a chance that multi-faith Berat could have been destroyed under the communists. But it wasn't, which is a huge win for humanity. I love wandering through Berat's stone alleyways, picturing what it might've been like 300 years ago. No matter how many times I visit, I always notice something different. And while I can appreciate a bare stone wall as much as the next world traveller, seeing the Ottoman villas painted in white, with their enchanting wooden windows and roofs, really makes it feel like you've been transported back in time.

as the 19th century. It's a town in and of itself, with more than 100 residential buildings, dozens of towers and church ruins, two mosques and a stone wall that stretches 1.4km. Don't miss the **Onufri Museum** *(Muzeu Kombëtar Ikonografik Onufri; muzeumet-berat.al; 400L)*, a medieval art gallery located inside Cathedral Assumption of Saint Mary (1797).

Ottoman-era neighbourhoods

Below the castle, wander Ottoman-era neighbourhoods for a glimpse at life in Berat from the 16th to 19th centuries. There's **Mangalem**, a neighbourhood of winding stone alleyways, mosques and picturesque windows, earning Berat the nickname 'one above the other windows' or, as it's more commonly known, 'town of a thousand windows'. On the other side of the Osum River is **Goricë**. It has a few stone thoroughfares, a couple of pretty churches and a romantic ambience.

Taste Albanian wine

Say *gëzuar* (cheers) to Albanian wines with grape varieties only found at vineyards located a short 30-minute drive from Berat's historic centre. On the way into Berat, **Çobo Winery** *(cobowine.com; standard/premium €25/45)* does tastings inside its beautiful family-built cottage and in its peaceful garden. Or visit **Alpeta Agrotourism** *(alpeta.al; tastings 2000L)*, located in Roshnik village. It's one of the first agrotourism operations in Albania, with vineyards tumbling down a verdant hillside consisting of 37,000 sq m of land received from the government after the fall of communism. As well as tastings, it does delicious meals and three-hour cooking classes *(per person €50)*.

The Albanian Riviera

SEAFRONT | CASTLE SUNSETS | SEAFOOD

Places

☑ TOP TIP

If beaches are your target, fly to the Greek island of Corfu and take a ferry to Sarandë. Finikas Lines *(finikas-lines.com)* and Ionian Seaways *(ionianseaways.com)* run several daily trips between the two by Flying Dolphin high-speed hydrofoil *(30 minutes, per person €30)* or car ferry *(1¼ hours, per person €20)*.

The Albanian Riviera was a revelation roughly two decades ago, when backpackers discovered the last virgin stretch of coast in Europe and proceeded to flock here in droves, setting up ad-hoc campsites and exploring scores of little-known beaches fronting the out-of-this-world turquoise Ionian Sea. Since then, things have become a lot busier, especially around Sarandë and Ksamil.

But worry not: the water is still a dream to swim in, and if you drive north you'll find plenty of space to throw down a towel and while away the day under a beaming sun, or hire a boat to take you to remote beaches. And all the better if you're looking for fun vibes, as electronic music festivals and beach clubs keep the party popping throughout the summer.

Aside from beach life, the Albanian Riviera has some worthwhile archaeological sites built by various empires, including Hellenistic tribes, the Romans, Venetians and the Albanian-Ottoman despot Ali Pasha.

Sarandë

TIME FROM CORFU: **30MIN** ⛴

Seaside strolls and sunsets

Stroll Sarandë's busy boardwalk, stopping at buzzing rooftop bars, or board a pirate ship for a booze cruise – *yaaarr!* Boat tour operators *(per person 2500L)* can take you to secluded beaches.

⊚ GETTING AROUND

Sarandë is the main hub, where it's easy to walk and catch a bus down the coast to Ksamil (150L) and Butrint (200L), or northbound. Riviera Bus *(rivierabus.com/albania; €50)*, a seven-person air-con minivan, drives from Tirana to Sarandë and back three days a week in summer. The van stops at all major beach towns and also runs from Vlorë to Sarandë for €30 on weekdays in July and August.

Ksamil

At sunset, climb to the ruins of **Lekursi Castle**, an Otto-man castle built in 1537, or the 6th-century **Monastery of the 40 Saints**.

Ksamil

TIME FROM SARANDÉ: **30MIN**

Find your beach bliss

If you've seen photos or videos on social media of the tanta-lisingly turquoise water on the Albanian Riviera, they were probably taken in **Ksamil**. The beach town is lined with breathtaking beaches backed by stark cliffs and stylish bars playing melodic deep house. Bliss out in a beach chair at **Ksamil Beach**, then paddle to the uninhabited islands (**Tre Ishujt**) just offshore. Or go underwater to see WWII and communist-era shipwrecks with **Saranda Diving** (*saranda diving.com; per dive 7000L*).

An ancient 2800-year-old city

The most romantic of Albania's ancient sites, **Butrint** (*butrint.al; entry adult/teen/child 800/500L/free*), has been inhabited for 2800 years. In the 8th century BCE, Hellenist (Greek) tribes built the first *polis* (city) and later Butrint's celebrated site: the

SHIMMERING WATER ON THE ALBANIAN RIVIERA

Pulëbardha Beach: Climb down to this amazing beach at the foot of steep cliffs. It's less busy than the main Ksamil beaches.

Blue Eye: It's not a beach and you can't swim here, but the natural phenomenon that creates electric-blue water 30 minutes from Sarandë is a must-see.

Gjipe Beach: Hike 20 minutes to get here from the parking lot near Himarë; arguably Albania's most stunning beach.

Aquarium Beach: Hike or 4WD drive down to this tiny, hidden beach, where crystal-clear turquoise water splashes under the rocks.

Dhërmi Beach: Electronic music festivals in early June attract those who like to shake it; there's wellness mixed in, too.

EATING IN KSAMIL & SARANDË: OUR PICKS

Ftelea Fish Taverna: Serves only the freshest fish and seafood, grilled, fried or served tucked into pasta or risotto. A Ksamil highlight. *noon-11.30pm* €€

Guvat: On a hill's edge in Ksamil with some of the best views around and often live music at sunset. Service can be slow. *7am-11.30pm* €€€

Taverna Labëria: This family-run restaurant off the Sarandë boardwalk serves terrific portions of steak and seafood at its two busy terraces. *8am-midnight* €€

Manxuranë: Inspired by his mother's cooking, Fatmir's carefully prepared plates are a knockout – as are the Sarandë views. One of Albania's best. *10am-11pm* €€€

ZDENEK MATYAS PHOTOGRAPHY/SHUTTERSTOCK

Gjirokastër Bazaar

Theatre. The Romans followed, building a **Forum**, thermal **Baths** with mosaic wall patterns and more. Then came the Byzantines, who built the well-kept 6th-century **Great Basilica**, and Venetians, responsible for a 16th-century **Tower** and **Triangular Castle**.

Himarë

TIME FROM SARANDË: 1½HR

Budget friendly vibes

Himarë (Himara) is the biggest town on the Riviera and has a less bougie vibe than some other beach resorts along the coast, though the beaches are just as magnificent. Those on a budget will feel especially at home here.

Amazing castles

Taxi up to the ruins of **Himarë Castle** *(entry 300L)*, an enchanting citadel that has existed in some form for 3500 years, with the earliest fortifications dating back to the Hellenistic Chaonians. South of town is the triangular **Porto Palermo Castle** *(entry 300L)*, likely built by the Venetians and expanded upon by Albanian-Ottoman despot Ali Pasha of Tepelenë.

 EATING IN HIMARË: OUR PICKS

Taverna Lefteri: This town has lots of delicious seafood, but Lefteri stands out for its presentation and quality. *noon–4pm & 7pm–midnight* €€

To Steki sti Gonia: Himarë's Hellenistic heritage shines at this Greek restaurant on the seafront. The menu ventures beyond *souvlaki*. *11.30am–midnight* €€

Fig and Olive: With views over Livadhi Beach and twinkly-lit evening meals, this place has a romantic vibe to go along with its seafood dishes. *5.30–10pm* €€

Manolo Beach Bar: Tried-and-true beach bar without the trendiness of some of its competitors. Open year-round. *7.30am–3am* €€

Gjirokastër

Stroll through a stone city

Go for a walk around Gjirokastër to see its fascinating metre-thick stone walls that hold up roofs layered with heavy stone slabs. Start by shopping and eating at the **Bazaar**, found at the top of Gjirokastër's old town at a five-point intersection. Nearby is the 18th-century **Bazaar Mosque**, and beneath it is the atmospheric stone-walled cafe, **Te Kubé**, which doubles as a mini-museum with a communist-bunker tunnel exhibit dedicated to Albanian iso-polyphony music. This chilling vocal art is recognised by UNESCO as a Masterpiece of the Oral and Intangible Heritage of Humanity and celebrates sadness through song. Alternatively, see the 80-room **Cold War Tunnel** *(entry 200L)* on a guided tour led every hour during high season.

Also check out **Gjirokastër Castle** *(entry 400L)*, a medieval fortress dating to the 4th century that later operated as a base for Italian soldiers during the WWII occupation.

Visit historic house museums

Gjirokastër happens to be the birthplace of many of Albania's most important 20th-century figures, and it has museums dedicated to the lot of them. **Kadare House** *(entry 500L)* celebrates the life of Albania's most famous writer, Ismail Kadare (1936–2024), while **Muza Ime Musine Kokalari** *(entry 500L)* is dedicated to Musine Kokalari (1918–83), a feminist writer and social democratic politician. Enver Hoxha was also born here, but his former house has been rebuilt into an interesting **Ethnographic Museum** *(entry 500L)*.

While its former inhabitants aren't as well-known, tour **Zekate House** *(entry 250L)* and **Skenduli House** *(entry 300L)* to see how wealthy families lived during the Ottoman days.

ALBANIAN DISHES TO TRY

Tavë kosi: Lamb baked in a cast-iron pan with yoghurt and rice.

Lakror: Doughy Korçan pie usually stuffed with spinach, and sometimes also cheese, leeks or meat.

Specë/patëllxhan të mbushur: Baked peppers or aubergines stuffed with rice, tomatoes and herbs.

Fërgesë: Dip made with red peppers and ricotta cheese.

Flia (also flija or fli): Layered crepes that can be sweet or sour; from Kosovo and the northern regions.

 ## EATING IN GJIROKASTËR: OUR PICKS

Odaja: Delightful, honest Albanian cooking since 1937 in an upper-floor restaurant. Plenty of vegetarian options. *10am-11pm* €

Kardhashi: A tad pushy, though eminently generous top-of-the-hill restaurant with plenty of outdoor seating. *8.30am-10.30pm* €

Furra: Recently opened spot in the Bazaar with top-quality Albanian casseroles and pizzas. Good vibes, too. *noon-10.30pm* €€

The Barrels: Farm-to-table cuisine beside a vineyard at this wildly popular agritourism destination across the valley. Reserve. *noon-11pm* €€

The Albanian Alps & Northern Albania

MOUNTAIN HIKES | MYSTERIOUS HISTORY | GRILLED CARP

Places

Shkodër p68
Theth p69

☑ **TOP TIP**

Hikes in the Albanian Alps, including the ever-popular Valbonë-to-Theth circuit, take at least two nights – one in Valbonë after taking the Lake Koman Ferry and another in Theth. Allow extra time for a blissful escape from society, and even more if you want to explore Shkodër.

Names don't come much more evocative than the Accursed Mountains (Bjeshkët e Namuna), also known as the Albanian Alps. And the dramatic peaks of northern Albania truly live up to their name. Sure, at under 3000m they might not be as high as the peaks in Switzerland, but the snow-sprinkled mountain pinnacles, deep green valleys and thick forests northeast of the area's only major city, Shkodër, are nothing to scoff at.

Many come here to hike from Valbonë to Theth, a nifty circuit that also includes a three-hour ferry ride. But this popular excursion is far from the only hiking option, and if you ask in-the-know locals, it's not even the best. So find your own favourite mountain trail followed by a plunge into a turquoise blue-eye pool near Theth. And leave time to cycle around Shkodër: it's a lovable, colourful city with historic architecture and a carp-filled lake.

Shkodër

TIME FROM TIRANA: **2HR** 🚌

Hike the Accursed Mountains

Many people come to the Albanian Alps for a single reason: the spectacular three- or four-day circuit from Shkodër, which includes hiking along a section of the multinational **Peaks of the Balkans Trail**. The 14.7km hike over the **Valbonë Pass** (1795m) to Theth takes roughly five to seven hours. The rest of the time will be spent winding over mountain roads in a *furgon*, crossing Lake Koman by ferry and relaxing in mountain tranquillity. Book a self-guided tour that includes transport

---

GETTING AROUND

The most popular way to get around Shkodër is on a bicycle. Most accommodations rent them. Official taxis and public buses (40L), many of which stop at Democracy Sq, can take you to

the lake or the castle. The road to Theth and other roads in the Alps can be rough, windy and covered in snow or black ice as late as June, so take public or private minibuses rather than drive.

and places to stay along the way with any Shkodër accommodation. Alternatively, reserve transport via the **Koman Ferry** website *(komanilakeferry.com)* and pick your own stays.

Understand Albanian culture

See early images of Albanians at the **Marubi National Photography Museum** *(marubi.gov.al; entry 700L)*, which celebrates the work of Pietro Marubi (1832–1903) and his heirs, who documented Albanian life in the late 19th and early 20th centuries. Continue learning about Albanian history at the **Site of Witness & Memory Museum** *(instagram.com/siteofwitnessandmemory; entry 200L)*, which was an interrogation centre and prison for political detainees during the communist era.

Outside the centre, **Rozafa Fortress** *(entry 400L)* was founded in the 4th century BCE during Illyrian times and rebuilt much later by the Venetians and then the Turks. The fortress takes its name from a woman who was allegedly walled into the ramparts as an offering to the gods.

Another key Shkodër spot is the **Venice Art Mask Factory** *(tour €3)*, which is the leading producer of the papier-mâché masks used during Venice's Carnival as well as, of course, **Shkodër's**. Fun fact: the mask worn by Tom Cruise in *Eyes Wide Shut* was made by the artist who founded the Mask Factory.

Theth

TIME FROM SHKODËR: 2HR 🚐

Hike to a waterfall and blue eye

The mountain village of Theth has the most dramatic setting in Albania. Just getting here is quite incredible, whether you cross the mountains on foot from Valbonë or drive from Shkodër. Come to explore **Theth National Park** by hiking to the gushing **Grunas Waterfall**, just 30 minutes from town. Or continue on a six- to seven-hour round-trip to **Blue Eye Kaprre**, an electric-blue natural pool that you can swim in.

See a blood-feud tower

You'll see plenty of stone *kullas* (towers) across Albania, but the one in Theth has a particularly fascinating story. **Reconciliation Tower** *(entry 150L)* dates back 400 years and was used as a 'lock-in tower' during blood feuds – long-standing cycles of violence that were intended to restore honour through vengeance. A tower like this one was meant to protect a family member from an enemy; climb the stairs for an idea of what life was like inside.

KANUN

Northern Albanians traditionally lived according to the Kanun, a legal and moral code from the 1400s (or possibly earlier) that wasn't written down until the early 20th century. This extensive code – 12 books and over 1200 articles – governs everything from what to do when your goat crosses into a neighbour's yard to how to avenge family murders through blood feuds. The Kanun also created the role of 'sworn virgins', women who pledged celibacy in order to benefit from men's social privileges. Despite being declared illegal under Ottoman rule and the Hoxha regime, the Kanun endures to this day: as of 2022, around a dozen sworn virgins remain, and thousands of people escaping blood feuds have sought asylum in Europe over the last two decades.

EATING & DRINKING IN SHKODËR: OUR PICKS

Fisi: Hearty portions and fair prices for mixed grilled meats and friendly service. A Shkodër classic. *11am-10.30pm* €€

Pelikani Kaçurrel: Cycle along Lake Shkodër and have grilled carp at this lovely lakeside restaurant that has its own beach. *8am-11.30pm* €€

Tradita Hotel: Restored 17th-century mansion that once belonged to a local writer; delivers one of the city's finest restaurant experiences. *noon-11.30pm* €€

n'Odë: This bohemian spot gets everyone singing on Saturday nights when a live band takes the stage. It's smack in the centre. *7am-11pm*

Places We Love to Stay

€ Budget €€ Midrange €€€ Top End

Tirana & Central Albania
MAP p61

Tirana

Tirana Backpacker Hostel € Albania's oldest hostel is still going strong, with a vibrant decor reminiscent of the glory days of backpacking. Vegetarian communal breakfast.

Bujtina e Gjelit €€ Tirana's most charming hotel has Ottoman-era vibes with brick archways centred around a pool courtyard. The drawback is that it's far from the centre.

The Plaza €€€ The first of many stylish skyscrapers to open near Skanderbeg Sq was finished in 2016. Modernist design and a great option.

Berat

Berat Backpackers € The best hostel in Berat, and also the oldest, is on the Goricë side. It has dorms, camping, a garden and a fun atmosphere.

Klea Hotel €€ Hilltop hideaway inside the castle, with five compact rooms, pretty patios and a lovely restaurant terrace.

Mangalemi Hotel €€ Built over the pasha's 1764 palace, this is Berat's first post-communist hotel, with beautiful traditional furnishings.

The Albanian Riviera

Sarandë

Central Boutique Hostel € Everything's fresh in this backpacker spot that opened in 2025 – beds with curtains, clean bathrooms and a kitchen that serves a simple breakfast.

Harmony Hotel €€ Minimalist Mediterranean decor away from the loud promenade is a great pick for couples looking for a romantic retreat.

Vila Kalcuni €€€ Watch the boats pass this white mansion on a beachy corner close to Sarandë port.

Ksamil

Ksamil Caravan Camping € Save some cash for the beach by parking your van or pitching a tent at this campground. Open year-round.

Meta Hotel €€ The closest you'll get to the beach at the midrange price point. The stone-shaped headboard cushions might have you feeling like you've woken up in a much comfier Butrint.

Arameras Beach Resort €€€ Go all-out at this beach resort on the far side of Ksamil, with an infinity pool and private beach.

Himarë

Camping Himara € Set up a tent under the olive trees at this camping ground across the main road from Livadhi Beach. Best access to the Aquarium Beach cove.

Vila Kosteli €€ Cliffside apartments run by a friendly couple between Himarë's two beaches. Some rooms have terraces with sun loungers overlooking the sea.

Gjirokastër

Stone City Hostel € Dutch owner Wouter runs Albania's best hostel, with modern-meets-traditional decor and daily activities including fascinating history walks and 4WD tours.

Old Bazaar 1790 €€ Immerse yourself in 18th-century Gjirokastër at this 11-room boutique hotel close to the Bazaar. Rooms have ornate handcrafted bed frames and cute windows with views of the town.

Kerculla Resort €€€ Sleep like a sultan in this palatial hotel overlooking Gjirokastër. Intricate wooden carvings, a relaxing pool area and exquisite views.

The Albanian Alps & Northern Albania

Shkodër

Mi Casa Es Tu Casa € Beautiful mansion that's now a chill, colourful backpackers hostel for all ages. It's not a party vibe.

InTown € Behind the bright orange facade is a lovely B&B with freshly renovated rooms and a tranquil garden steps from the action.

Tradita Hotel €€ Painstakingly restored 17th-century mansion that once belonged to a famous Shkodran writer, now a museum-like boutique hotel with comfortable rooms and locally woven bed linens.

Theth

Molla €€ Have your breakfast in front of a grand mountain amphitheatre and sleep on a comfy bed in a cosy wooden guesthouse. What the Albanian Alps are all about.

Marashi €€€ Recently renovated guesthouse facing the water with an eye-catching standalone tub in the penthouse suite.

Practicalities

LGBTIQ+ Travellers
Albania is often targeted as one of the worst places in Europe for LGBTIQ+ people. The truth is, it isn't great – but it could be worse. Same-sex relationships are legal and discrimination is prohibited. However, LGBTIQ+ people can't get married, adopt or undergo a gender change. Avoid PDA, especially outside of Tirana.

Safe Travel
Stereotypes painting Albania as dangerous date back to historic religious tensions, a brutal dictatorship and the admittedly violent organised crime network. But travelling here is as safe as anywhere in Western Europe, if not more so. Albania has low crime rates and pickpocketing is relatively rare.

Electricity & Connectivity
Albania uses Type F 230V/50Hzv plugs. Local SIM cards and tourist packages are available inside the Tirana airport. Internet connection is spotty in the Alps. Wi-fi is usually decent.

Visas
Citizens of European Schengen Zone countries and nearly 60 other nations can enter Albania without a visa for up to 90 days within a 180-day period. US citizens can stay up to one year.

TRABANTOS/SHUTTERSTOCK

Tirana (p60)

Opening Hours
Most businesses in tourist hubs outside of Tirana shut down from October through May.
Banks 8am–4pm Monday to Friday
Cafes 7am–10pm
Bars noon–midnight
Restaurants 11am–10pm
Shops 9am–8pm
Supermarkets 7am–10pm

Water
Tap water is not drinkable anywhere in Albania, but it's safe enough for brushing your teeth and washing produce.

Public Holidays
New Year's Day 1 January
Dita e Verës (Summer Day) 14 March
Ramadan Bajram/Eid al-Fitr February & March (2026–28)
Sultan Nevruz 22 March
Easter March or April
Labour Day 1 May
Eid al-Adha May (2026–28)
Independence Day 28 November
Liberation Day 29 November
Youth Day 8 December
Christmas 25 December

71

Language

In Albanian – also understood in Kosovo and North Macedonia – *ew* is pronounced as 'ee' with rounded lips, *uh* as the 'a' in 'ago', *dh* as the 'th' in 'that', *dz* as the 'ds' in 'adds', and *zh* as the 's' in 'pleasure'. Also, *ll* and *rr* are pronounced stronger than when they are written as single letters.

Basics

Hello. Tungjatjeta. *toon·dya·tye·ta*
Goodbye. Mirupafshim. *mee·roo·paf·sheem*
Yes. Po. *po*
No. Jo. *yo*
Please. Ju lutem. *yoo loo·tem*
Thank you. Faleminderit. *fa·le·meen·de·reet*
What's your name? Si quheni? *see choo·he·nee*
My name is … Unë quhem … *oo·nuh choo·hem …*
Do you speak English? A flisni anglisht? *a flees·nee ang·leesht*
I don't understand. Unë nuk kuptoj. *oo·nuh nook koop·toy*

Emergencies

Help! Ndihmë! *ndeeh·muh*
Go away! Ik! *eek*
I'm ill. Jam i/e sëmurë. (m/f) *yam ee/e suh·moo·ruh*

Call the doctor/police! Thirrni doktorin/policinë! *theerr·nee dok·to·reen/po·lee·tsee·nuh*

Eating & Drinking

What would you recommend? Çfarë më rekomandoni? *chfa·ruh muh re·ko·man·do·nee*
I'll have… Dua… *doo·a*
Cheers! Gëzuar! *guh·zoo·ar*
I'd like the bill/menu, please. Më sillni faturën/menunë, ju lutem. *muh seell·nee fa·too·ruhn/ me·noo·nuh yoo loo·tem*

Shopping & Services

I'm looking for … Po kërkoj për … *po kuhr·koy puhr …*
How much is it? Sa kushton? *sa koosh·ton*
Cheers! Gëzuar! *guh·zoo·ar*
That's too expensive. Është shumë shtrenjtë. *uhsh·tuh shoo·muh shtreny·tuh*

English & Other Tourist Languages

While most people dealing with tourists on a daily basis speak English extremely well, that's not true of the entire population. English is taught in schools, but the older generations are more likely to know some German, Russian or, along the coast, Italian.

NUMBERS

1
një *nyuh*

2
dy *dew*

3
tre *tre*

4
katër *ka·tuhr*

5
pesë *pe·suh*

6
gjashtë *dyash·tuh*

7
shtatë *shta·tuh*

8
tetë *te·tuh*

9
nëntë *nuhn·tuh*

10
dhjetë *dhye·tuh*

Nënë Tereza International Airport

Arriving & Getting Around

Albania has frequent flights to Tirana. If the beach is your priority, consider taking a ferry from the Greek island of Corfu. Albania also has bus connections to neighbouring Greece, Montenegro, North Macedonia and Kosovo.

By Air
Tirana's **Nënë Tereza International Airport**, 17km from the city centre, is a seamless experience for EU, Canadian and US passport holders. The new **Vlorë International Airport** opened in summer 2025.

By Boat
The best way to get to the Albanian Riviera is via the Flying Dolphin ferry, running from Corfu (Greece) to Sarandë. Ferries also run to Durrës and Vlorë from Bari and Brindisi (Italy).

Furgon
Furgon is the main form of public transport in Albania. Fares are low and you either pay the conductor when you board or before you hop off, which can be anywhere along the route. *Furgon* only leave when full.

Car Hire
Driving in Albania has plenty of issues (aggressive drivers, narrow roads, potholes) but it's the only way to see much of the country and the roads are gorgeous. There are plenty of private car-hire agencies, but few international brands. Speed limits are 40km/h in towns and cities, and 90 to 110km/h on highways. Maps.me is more accurate than Google Maps. Traffic stops are common.

MONEY
Currency: Albanian Lek (L) & Euro (€)

CASH
Cash is still king in Albania. Both Albanian lekë and euros are accepted, and most businesses will give you the actual conversion rate (it's usually 100 lekë to €1). You'll find ATMs dispensing lekë in all major towns and cities; expect a 600L to 850L fee and possibly a conversion percentage in addition to what your home bank charges. Keep smaller bills and change handy, especially if taking the bus.

CARD
Bank and credit cards are almost never accepted in Albania outside of upscale hotels. Even car hire agencies want cash or a bank transfer, and online bookings won't require a credit card if you used one to reserve. If cards are accepted, expect a transaction minimum.

For places to stay
in Austria, see
p101

LIUDMILA KIERMEIER/SHUTTERSTOCK

Above: Stift Melk (p82), Melk; Right: Skiing, Kitzbühel (p98)

Curated by
Kerry Walker

Austria

WHERE CULTURE HITS THE HEIGHTS

No country waltzes so effortlessly between urban and outdoors as Austria. One day you're cresting alpine summits, the next you're swanning around imperial Vienna.

For such a tiny country, Austria is ridiculously big on inspiration. This is the land where Mozart was born, Strauss taught the world to waltz and Julie Andrews grabbed the spotlight with her twirling entrance in *The Sound of Music*. It's where the Habsburgs ruled over their spectacular, sprawling 600-year empire.

These past glories still shine in the resplendent baroque palaces and chandelier-lit coffee houses of Vienna, Innsbruck and Salzburg. Over centuries, the Habsburgs channelled immense wealth into the fine arts and music, collecting palaces the way others do stamps. You'll feel their cultural reverberations today – be it hearing the work of classical masters echo at lavishly gilded concert halls, eyeballing avant-garde art in born-again baroque riding stables, or catching a summer music festival against an uplifting lakeside or mountain backdrop.

Beyond its storybook cities, Austria's trump card is its astonishing natural beauty, which waltzes joyously from the romance of the vine-strewn Wachau to the crystal-clear lakes of Carinthia. Whether you're schussing down the legendary slopes of Kitzbühel, spotting an ibex in the fiery light of sunset as you crest a mountain ridge in Hohe Tauern National Park, or freewheeling along the banks of the mighty Danube, you'll find the kind of landscapes to which no well-orchestrated symphony or singing nun could ever quite do justice.

GEVISION/SHUTTERSTOCK

THE MAIN AREAS

VIENNA
Palaces, coffee houses and galleries galore.
p78

SALZBURG
Mozart, Maria and a resplendent baroque Altstadt. **p85**

GRAZ & THE SOUTH
Cutting-edge art and jewel-coloured lakes.
p92

INNSBRUCK & TYROL
Nonstop alpine backdrops and activities. **p95**

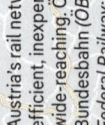
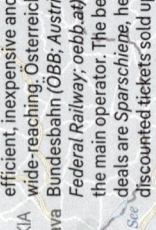

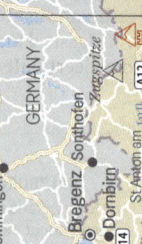

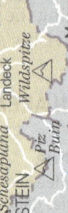

Find Your Way

Austria's public transport network is a dream, with swift, inexpensive trains linking towns and cities, and buses filling the gaps. Car hire gives you greater freedom to explore the country's remotest corners.

CAR

Autobahn (motorways) are well maintained. You can only drive on them with a *Vignette* (motorway tax), available from border crossings and petrol stations. Be prepared for exposed, sharply twisting roads in the Alps.

TRAIN

Austria's rail network is fast, efficient, inexpensive and wide-reaching. Österreiche Bundesbahn (ÖBB; *Austrian Federal Railway; oebb.at*) is the main operator. The best deals are *Sparschiene*, heavily discounted tickets sold up to six months ahead.

Vienna, p78

Baroque streetscapes and imperial palaces set the stage for Vienna's artistic and musical masterpieces alongside its coffee-house culture and vibrant epicurean and design scenes.

Graz & the South, p92

Castle-topped Graz beguiles with medieval looks and edgy art, while beyond rolling hills, vines, orchards and pristine mountain lakes entice.

Salzburg, p85

Legends have been made and born on these grand baroque streets, where you can explore Mozart's 'hood, climb to a medieval castle and catch one of Europe's greatest summer festivals.

Innsbruck & Tyrol, p95

Cultured Innsbruck is the springboard for mountains that make you want to yodel out loud, from summer's patchwork pastures to Christmas-card scenes in winter.

CZECHIA

SLOVAKIA

Laa an der Thaya

Mistelbach

Bratislava

Neusiedl am See

VIENNA

Eisenstadt

Szombathely

HUNGARY

Retz

Hollabrunn

Tulln

St Pölten

Baden bei Wien

Wiener Neustadt

Neunkirchen

Oberpullendorf

Oberwart

Bad Radkersburg

Gmünd

Horn

Krems an der Donau

Melk

Amstetten

Mürzzuschlag

Kapfenberg

Hartberg

Gleisdorf

Feldbach

Leibnitz

SLOVENIA

Maribor

Zwettl

Freistadt

Ems

Steyr

Nationalpark Kalkalpen

Theben

Leoben

Judenburg

Knittelfeld

Wolfsberg

Völkermarkt

České Budějovice

Linz

Wels

Lambach

Gmunden

Ebensee

Bad Ischl

Höher Dachstein

Radstadt

Tamsweg

Murau

St Veit an der Glan

Klagenfurt

Feldkirchen

Villach

Ried

Mattighofen

Salzburg

Bad Gastein

Spittal an der Drau

Drau

Braunau am Inn

Landshut

Rosenheim

Munich

Kufstein

Kitzbühel

Zell am See

Bischofshofen

Hohe Tauern National Park

Lienz

Bressanone

Bolzano

ITALY

Wörgl

Jenbach

Zell am Ziller

Mittersill

Zuckspitze

Innsbruck

Ötztal

GERMANY

Memmingen

Bregenz

Sonthofen

Dornbirn

Feldkirch

Bludenz

Arlberg

St Anton am Arlberg

Imst

Landeck

Silvretta

Piz Buin

Wildspitze

Merano

SWITZERLAND

Chur

Constanz

St Gallen

Konstanz

Vaduz

LIECHTENSTEIN

100 km

50 miles

76

Cycling in the Zillertal (p98)

Plan Your Time

Austria looks deceptively small on a map, but as most of it is vertical there's always a mountain pass, alpine view or hidden hamlet to discover. Avoid peak season for better deals.

Vienna to Salzburg

● Begin with palaces, parks, galleries and world-class concert halls in **Vienna** (p78). An hour west is **Wachau** (p83) on the River Danube, home to twin-spired baroque abbey **Stift Melk** (p83). Next stop is UNESCO-stamped **Hallstatt** (p90). Continue west to **Werfen** (p89) and the **Eisriesenwelt** (p89) ice caves, before rounding out with fortress-topped **Salzburg** (p85).

Into the Tyrolean Alps

● Admire soaring peaks in **Innsbruck** (p95). Roam the Altstadt's medieval lanes, before breezing up to 2334m **Hafelekarspitze** (p97). Skip east to **Swarovski Crystal Worlds** (p97) in Wattens. Detour south to the **Zillertal** (p98) for mountain biking, hiking, whitewater rafting and skiing. From here, head east to **Kitzbühel** (p98) for more action on Olympic slopes.

SEASONAL HIGHLIGHTS

SPRING

Meadows and parks bloom. Snow polishes the highest Alps, but there's cycling and hiking in valleys. Easter markets dazzle.

SUMMER

Light, warm days entice hikers. Cities host open-air festivals, including Vienna's **Donauinselfest** (p81).

AUTUMN

New wine in *Heurigen* (taverns) and highs like **Steirischer Herbst festival** (p93). Cows descend from pastures at the **Almabtrieb** (p100).

WINTER

Alpine slopes buzz, Christmas markets sparkle and Vienna waltzes into ball season. Salzburg gets orchestral at **Mozartwoche** (p87).

Vienna

REGAL HISTORY | HIGH CULTURE | CUTTING-EDGE ARTS

GETTING AROUND

Vienna's historic centre and inner districts are easy to explore on foot, including the Hofburg, museum complexes, modern neighbourhoods with landmarks and low-key nightlife. Schloss Schönbrunn can be easily reached by bus, tram and metro from the centre. Get information at *wienerlinien.at*.

Few cities in the world waltz so effortlessly between past and present, urban and outdoors like Vienna, a capital that has clocked up Mercer's 'most liveable city in the world' for many consecutive years. Its splendid historical face is easily recognised: grand imperial palaces and bombastic baroque interiors, revered opera houses, magnificent squares and art-vault museums curated over the 600-year reign of the Habsburgs.

But Austria's capital isn't bound by its vintage time bubble. Dig deeper, and you'll see a multifaceted Vienna on a spectrum from grandeur to gritty that bridges the classical and the contemporary. You'll need to cover some ground, though – which is easy to do via Vienna's excellent and cheap public transport system.

A stone's throw from Hofburg (the Imperial Palace), the MuseumsQuartier houses provocative and high-profile contemporary art behind a striking basalt facade. In the Innere Stadt (Inner City), up-to-the-minute design stores sidle up to old-world confectioners, and Austro-Asian fusion restaurants stand alongside traditional *Beisln* (small taverns).

Seeking Out Stephansdom

Vienna's symbolic landmark cathedral

Vienna's Gothic masterpiece **Stephansdom** (*stephanskirche. at)* soars above. A mosaic of 230,000 glazed roof tiles crests in between, stamped with the imperial double-headed eagle. It's free to venture into the vaulted, prismatic glass site. You have to pay to enter the central **nave** (*adult/child €7/3, cash only*) for a closer look at the 16th-century sandstone masterwork on the **Pilgramkanzel** (Pilgrim pulpit) and the commanding baroque black marble **High Altar** consecrating the holy space some 100 years later.

Austria's largest bell, the 21-tonne *Pummerin,* is accessible via an elevator journey to the **North Tower** (*adult/child €7/3)*

☑ **TOP TIP**

There's an easy way to know when you've left the circular centre. The grandiose architectural loop of the Ringstrasse surrounding the Innere Stadt, completed on one side of the Danube Canal, is a great orientation point. Beyond this boulevard border, you enter the fringes of the inner districts.

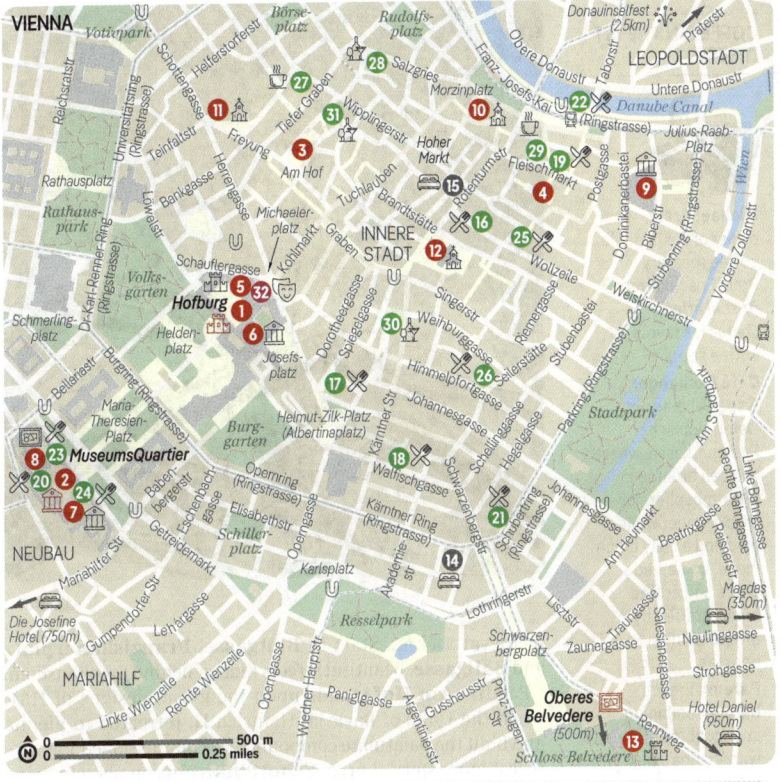

platform overlooking Stephansplatz. Sweeping city views from the **South Tower** (*adult/child €6.50/2.50*) require enough stamina to climb 343 precarious, winding steps to access the peering **Türmerstube** (tower room).

Step into the Middle Ages
Medieval squares and backstreets

Narrow trader alleys, age-old market squares and hidden courtyards – pockets of the Innere Stadt are a window into

COFFEE IN THE 1ST DISTRICT

Michael Prem, owner of sustainable coffee roastery Prem Frischkaffee (*frischkaffee.at*), shares his favourite coffee spots.

Café Exchange: A special place in Österreichische Postsparkasse, where you can breathe in the atmosphere of Otto Wagner while enjoying a daily lunch menu, homemade cakes and coffee brews crafted by award-winning baristas.

Parémi: French bakery combining impeccable coffee with Vienna's best croissant.

Fenster Café: Unique hole-in-the-wall cafe near Schwedenplatz serves its own roast. This is not a space you can enter, but it is the place to get a speciality brew when passing by.

Am Hof

medieval Vienna. Start in **Blutgasse**, **Franziskanerplatz** and **Ballgasse**, beautiful streets hidden behind Stephansdom.

Palatial **Am Hof** stands upon the grand designs of 1154, when the Duke of Bavaria, Heinrich II, retreated to Vienna and built the palatinate compound. He commissioned Vienna's oldest monastery church, **Schottenkirche**, on neighbouring Freyung in 1170.

The courtyard curiosity of **Heiligenkreuzerhof** has its foundations in the 1135-founded Heiligenkreuz Abbey. A time-warp passage between Schönlaterngasse and Grashofgasse, today's courtyard was added in 1771. Neighbouring **Ruprechtskirche**, from 1200, is the oldest in Vienna, overlooking Schwedenplatz and perched on an elevated weave of cobbled alleys that chart the prettiest route down to the Danube Canal.

Habsburg Grandeur at the Hofburg

A palace to out-pomp them all

Nothing epitomises the Habsburgs' extravagant reign more than the humongous 240,000-sq-metre **Hofburg**. Home to

 EATING IN INNERE STADT: WIENER SCHNITZEL

Figlmüller: Proclaimed inventors, where the original *Wiener Schnitzel* (breadcrumbed veal cutlet) has been served since 1905. *11am-10.30pm* €€

Meissl & Schadn: Before feasting, watch the schnitzel beaten and baked through the open salon kitchen in front of the restaurant. *11.30am-11pm* €€€

Gasthaus Reinthaler: It's like time stopped still in this 1977 *Beisl*, one of the historic district's last remaining authentic taverns. *11am-11pm Mon-Fri* €€

Gasthaus zur Oper: Contemporary venue of classic culinary institution Plachutta serves perfectly prepared house recipe *Wiener Schnitzel. 11.30am-midnight* €€

the imperial family for 700 years until 1918, the palace is a tapestry of heritage across its 18 wings and 19 courtyards, showcasing a staggering collection of cultural artefacts and art masterpieces.

Roll back the times in the **Alte Burg** (Old Castle). Enter the **Sisi Museum** and **Kaiserappartements** *(Imperial Apartments; sisimuseum-hofburg.at; adult/child €20/12)* via the marbled Emperor's Staircase – as visitors seeking an audience with Emperor Franz Joseph I once did – and meander through resplendent rooms of court life accompanied by a 75-minute audio guide. Move to the bedazzling belt of living spaces, including bedrooms and bathrooms, studies and saloons, preserved with their chandeliered ceilings, decked walls, regal red silk upholstery and royal gold embellishments.

Burrowed within the wings of the **Schweizerhof** (Swiss Courtyard) are the coveted crown jewels of Austria. The **Kaiserliche Schatzkammer** *(Imperial Treasury; kaiserliche-schatzkammer.at; adult/child €18/free)*. Make a beeline to the bejewelled Crown and Holy Lance of Emperor Rudolf II (Room 2), and the distinguished insignia of the Order of the Golden Fleece (Room 15).

The Hofburg residents today are world-famous white Lipizzaner stallions. Classical skills of horse-riding art and equestrianism have been practised at the UNESCO-listed **Spanische Hofreitschule** *(Spanish Riding School; srs.at; adult/child from €26/reduced)* since 1565. Horses dance gracefully in musical performances in the baroque **Winter Riding School** arena.

Baroque at the Belvedere

Find the world's most famous kiss

Prince Eugene of Savoy's 1723 baroque palace is a masterpiece; the art connoisseur filled it with his collections, which Empress Maria Theresia turned into the Imperial Picture Gallery in 1777, opening Vienna's first public museum. The dual complex is a trove of Austrian art from the Middle Ages to the present day and displays the world's largest collection of Klimt works.

Begin at the **Oberes Belvedere** *(adult/child €21/free; 9am-7pm)*. Top billing goes to Gustav Klimt's most famous work, *Der Kuss* (The Kiss), which, of his 22 paintings here, never leaves the gallery. Stroll the terraced, fountain-splashed, sculpture-strewn gardens down to the **Unteres Belvedere** *(adult/child €18/free, Combi ticket adult/child from €31.50/free; 10am-6pm)* to explore Prince Eugene's illustrious world. He commissioned

BEST FREE MUSIC FESTIVALS

The city of music has events throughout the year, though summer to autumn is when festivities abound.

Film Festival Rathausplatz:
Open-air music films from concert and stage greats, plus pop-up eats at the City Hall square. *Jul-Sep*

Kultursommer Wien:
Music, theatre and dance performances are staged at parks, squares and gardens across the city. *Jun-Aug*

Gürtel Night Walk:
Up-and-coming artists and local bands perform outside the Gürtel (belt) road of bars. *last weekend in August*

Donauinselfest:
Europe's biggest free open-air music festival brings the party to the Donauinsel (Danube Island). *last weekend in June*

 EATING IN THE HISTORIC CENTRE: OUR PICKS

Motto am Fluss: Canal-anchored boat with cafe and restaurant serving contemporary Austrian cuisine. *6-11pm Mon-Sat, to 10.30pm Sun, bar to midnight* €€

Griechenbeisl: Feast on *Wiener Schnitzel* and *Kaiserschmarrn* (sweet pancake) in the city's oldest *Beisl. noon-11pm* €€

Tian: This Michelin-star gourmet vegetarian restaurant is rooted in rare ingredients and experimental cooking. Book well ahead. *6am-11pm Tue-Sat* €€€

Die Cafetière: Revived mid-century modern cafe and purveyors of the tastiest Viennese cheese-and-ham toastie. *7.20am-6pm Mon-Fri, 9am-4pm Sat* €€

mumok

TOP TIPS FOR VISITING MQ

You'll need half a day for just one main museum. Bear in mind that mumok and Kunsthalle Wien are closed on Monday; Leopold Museum on Tuesday. Kunsthalle Wien has free entry 5pm to 9pm Thursday.

Should you wish to dig deeper into the world's largest cultural district, hook onto the one-hour **Secret MQ tour** *(mqw.at/programm/ secret-mq-tour-1-1; English tours 3pm Sat)*. Rest and refuel with organic plates at **MQ Kantine**, takeaway bites and beverages from **MQDaily**, Italian cuisine at **Halle** and Southeast Asian fare at **Café Leopold**.

baroque starchitect Johann Lucas von Hildebrandt to design the opulent summer residence.

A Cultural Dive into the MuseumsQuartier

Tune into Vienna's on-the-pulse arts scene

The former baroque imperial stables have been reborn as **MuseumsQuartier** *(MQ; mqw.at; courtyard open 24/7, museum entry times vary)*, one of the world's largest cultural districts with its arsenal of 11 exhibition spaces.

For modernist art in a brightly lit marble interior, hit the **Leopold Museum** *(leopoldmuseum.org)*, where star exhibits include the world's most comprehensive Egon Schiele collection and Gustav Klimt's *Death and Life* masterwork. Across the way, **mumok** *(mumok.at)* presents a galaxy of contemporary art: from expressionism to the experimental pop of the 1960s and 1970s, and the taboo and tragic in 20th-century Viennese actionism.

Save on individual entry with the MQ Fab 5 ticket *(€39)*; discounted or free entry for children across all museums.

 DRINKING IN THE HISTORIC CENTRE: BARS

Dino's Apothecary Bar: Dark wood-panelled, low-light, classic cocktail bar. Extensive experimental menu. *5pm-2am Tue-Thu, to 3am Fri & Sat*	**Loos American Bar:** Celeb magnet and cult-status bar designed by Viennese modernism architect Adolf Loos. *noon-4am*	**Lamée Rooftop Bar:** The chic and colourful rooftop bar of Hotel Topazz Lamee, with one of the best views of Stephansdom. *11am-1am Sun-Thu, to 2am Fri & Sat*	**Needle Vinyl Bar:** A trendy, retro-styled, record-spinning bar lounge, mixing music and signature cocktails. *5pm-2am*

Beyond Vienna

Waltz beyond the Austrian capital to find some of the country's greatest treasures – from grand abbeys to romantic castle ruins.

Providing popular day-trip material from Vienna, Lower Austria possesses the country's most vibrant cultural landscape: a combination of vineyards and art, monasteries and low wooded hills. Through this enchanting scene flows the mighty Danube, which forms the famous Wachau – one of Europe's most fascinating valleys, watched over by castles and medieval villages.

The stretch of Danube between Krems and Melk is arguably the loveliest along the entire length of this long, long river. Both banks are dotted with ruined castles and medieval towns, and lined with terraced vineyards. You can also indulge in some of Austria's best wines, and local and seasonal dishes at low-key but enormously welcoming *Heurigen* (wine taverns).

Places
Melk p83
Dürnstein p84

Melk
TIME FROM VIENNA: **45MIN**

Benedictine abbey: the Wachau's baroque masterpiece
Perched on a granite outcrop overlooking the Danube, **Stift Melk** (*stiftmelk.at; adult/child €16/8*) is one of Europe's finest ensembles of baroque architecture. Built on the site of a castle, which Leopold II of Babenberg gave to Benedictine monks from Lambach in Upper Austria, it's a huge and imposing place.

The abbey church shines with frescos by baroque master Johann Michael Rottmayr, and Paul Troger, a highly influential painter who ditched the characteristic dark palette of baroque painting in favour of lighter, more vibrant colours. His huge, illusionistic ceiling painting is in the abbey's **Marble Hall**. Around two dozen monks reside in the abbey and surrounding parishes. English-language guided tours of the abbey take place two or three times a day and last around 50 minutes.

The Wachau by boat
Taking a cruise along the Danube is almost part and parcel of spending time in the **Wachau Valley**. It's a nice, lazy way to spend half a day, and the views from the upper deck, enhanced and unobstructed, are very enjoyable – so order yourself a cool spritzer from the onboard bar, sit back and watch the world go by. Tables on the upper deck tend to fill up fast. You can easily combine a boat cruise with a return journey by train or bicycle; don't forget to reserve a place for your bike

GETTING AROUND

Lower Austria is the largest of the country's nine states; however, given Vienna's proximity, transport links are frequent and efficient. There are good rail connections between Vienna and Krems via St Pölten. Along with the famous **Danube Cycle Path**, many areas of Lower Austria are fantastic for cycling, and bikes can easily be rented locally. Bring walking boots, too, as trails above the river lace hills and vines.

ON YOUR BIKE

The **Danube Cycle Path** is one of Europe's greatest long-distance cycle routes – and one of its most beautiful sections is between Krems and Melk, through the UNESCO-listed Wachau Valley. The path follows both banks of the Danube, so you can cycle along one bank and return along the other. Even better, you can take your bike on a boat from Krems to Melk, visiting Dürnstein and Spitz – or on a train from Krems to Emmersdorf (the town opposite Melk), stopping at Dürnstein, Spitz and other places. This makes it nice and easy to combine a river cruise or train ride through the area's legendary vineyards, stopping to soak up some of the Wachau's celebrated cultural sites while sampling its excellent wines.

TRABANTOS/SHUTTERSTOCK

Kuenringerburg castle, Dürnstein

when you book). **DDSG Blue Danube** *(ddsg-blue-danube.at)* offers cruises on the river between Krems and Melk, calling at Dürnstein and Spitz.

Dürnstein

TIME FROM VIENNA: **1HR 10MIN**

Romantic castle ruins

The pretty little town of Dürnstein stands on an impossibly photogenic curve in the Danube, backed by low hills. Rising high above the town, **Kuenringerburg** is the castle where Richard I of England – yes, the Lionheart – was once imprisoned. He ended up here due to a dispute with Leopold V, Duke of Austria, during the Third Crusade. Leopold had Richard incarcerated on his way back from the Holy Land. Leopold was excommunicated for imprisoning a fellow Crusader, and was obliged to have Richard released (following the payment of a sizeable ransom – 35 tonnes of silver).

Only ruins of the castle remain, but they can still be visited, and the view is lovely. It takes 20 minutes to walk up from town following a clearly marked trail.

EATING & DRINKING IN THE WACHAU: OUR PICKS

Gasthof Prankl: Deservedly popular, with delicious food and local wines, in a 500-year-old former ship-owner's house in Spitz. *8am-10pm Fri-Tue* €€

Landgasthaus Essl: Refined dining on Danube's right bank between Spitz and Dürnstein. *11.30am-2.30pm & 6-11pm Wed-Fri, 11.30am-3.30pm & 6-11pm Sat, 11.30am-4pm Sun* €€€

Gasthof Goldenes Schiff: Family-run traditional restaurant and guesthouse, right in the centre of town, with a nice big terrace. *11.30am-8pm Thu-Tue* €€

Klosterhof Spitz: Set in a vineyard on the east side of Spitz, with tables in an atmospheric brick-vaulted interior. *11.30am-7pm Wed-Sun* €€

Salzburg

BAROQUE BRILLIANCE | MOZART'S BIRTHPLACE | ALPINE BACKDROP

The joke 'If it's baroque, don't fix it' could be a perfect maxim for Salzburg: the storybook Altstadt burrowed below steep hills looks much as it did when Mozart lived here 250 years ago. Beside the fast-flowing Salzach River, which divides the city in two, your lifted gaze is raised bit by bit to graceful domes and spires, the formidable clifftop fortress and the mountains beyond. It's a backdrop that did the lordly prince-archbishops and Maria proud.

Beyond Salzburg's two biggest money-spinners – Mozart and *The Sound of Music* – hides a city with a burgeoning arts scene, wonderful food, manicured parks, quiet side streets where classical music wafts from open windows, and concert halls that uphold musical tradition 365 days a year. Everywhere you go, the scenery, the skyline, the music and the history send your spirits soaring higher than Julie Andrews' octave-leaping vocals.

> ### ☑ TOP TIP
>
> During the summer holidays (July and August), Salzburg gets swamped. In December, when the city brims with Christmas markets and festival sparkle, it can get busy and expensive, too. Come in spring or autumn for cheaper flights, lower room rates and fewer crowds.

Salzburg on High

Get a ringside city view

Salzburg is at its most entrancing from above, with domes, spires and rooftops spreading out before you and the turquoise Salzach River unfurling into the mountains. One of the most memorable ways to see the city away from the masses is to get out and stride. Puff up the Nonnbergstiege to Benedictine abbey

GETTING AROUND

Walking is the only way to get a true feel for Salzburg's pedestrianised backstreets. This is one of Austria's most cycle-friendly cities, with a superb network of bike paths along the river, making the transition from city to mountains seamless. Rent touring and e-bikes at **aVelo** at Staatsbrücke.

Getting around by public transport *(salzburg-verkehr.at)* is quick, easy and inexpensive. If you're planning on zipping about town, a *Tageskarte* day pass is better value than single tickets.

Stift Nonnberg (p88), then continue your short but scenic walk along Hoher Weg and Festungsgasse to **Festung Hohensalzburg** *(festung-hohensalzburg.at; adult/child €13.60/5.20)*. The city's crowning-glory fortress has dress-circle views of the baroque Altstadt. Time your walk for midday to hear bells ring out across the city.

You can easily devote an afternoon to wandering the 540m peak of **Mönchsberg**, the cliffs that give Salzburg its dramatic edge. Its sheer, wooded heights are crisscrossed by walking trails. A highly scenic hike leads 3km on from Festung Hohensalzburg, past the **Museum der Moderne** *(museumder moderne.at; adult/child €14/free)* and through woods of beech,

Capuchin abbey

sycamore, linden and oak, to the jovial monastery-founded brewery **Augustiner Bräustübl** *(augustinerbier.at)*. Here you can rest up with a cold foamy one under the chestnut trees in the beer garden.

A leap over the river to the Right Bank brings you to the forested, 640m-high hump of **Kapuzinerberg**, which frames the Altstadt like a postcard. Paths twist past Way of the Cross chapels to the Capuchin abbey at the top. Despite the glorious views, it's rarely busy – hence the reason it is still home to a colony of nimble-footed chamois, which you might spot if you're lucky (and quiet).

The Hills Are Alive

The Sound of Music trail

Ever since Hollywood box-office smash *The Sound of Music* hit big screens in 1965, Salzburg has been inseparable from the world's most famous singing nun. Channel your inner Julie Andrews by devising your own self-guided tour of the movie locations. Start at the very beginning with a cable-car ride to the summit of **Untersberg** *(untersbergbahn.at; return cable car adult/child €34/17)*, where Maria makes her twirling entrance through blooming alpine pastures and the Trapp family flee from the Nazis at the end.

MOZART MAGIC

Mozart's symphonies, sonatas and concertos live on in Salzburg.
Mozarteum: Opened in 1880 and revered for its supreme acoustics, the Mozarteum highlights the life and works of Mozart through chamber music (October to June), concerts and opera. *mozarteum.at*
Mozart Week: In late January, when much-lauded orchestras, conductors and soloists celebrate Mozart's birthday with an 11-day music feast.
Schlosskonzerte: A fantasy of coloured marble, stucco and frescos, the baroque Marmorsaal (Marble Hall) at Schloss Mirabell is the exquisite setting for chamber-music concerts *(adult/child from €42/28)* where internationally renowned soloists and ensembles perform works by Mozart and other well-known composers such as Haydn and Chopin. *schlosskonzerte-salzburg.at*

 EATING IN SALZBURG: BEST ROMANTIC RESTAURANTS

Gasthof Schloss Aigen: This 15th-century country manor does Austrian home cooking with panache. *5.30-10pm Thu, 11.30am-10pm Fri-Sun* €€

Blaue Gans Restaurant: In 650-year-old vaults, this restaurant riffs on regional cuisine in season-spun dishes. *noon-midnight Mon-Sat* €€

Glass Garden: Ingredient-driven sensations at Hotel Schloss Mönchstein's glass-domed, Michelin-starred restaurant. *noon-10pm Thu-Mon* €€€

Esszimmer: Andreas Kaiblinger puts an innovative spin on market-driven French cuisine at this art-slung, Michelin-starred stunner. *noon-10pm Tue-Sat* €€€

ESCAPE THE CROWDS

Hildegard Strohmeyer, an official Salzburg city and hiking guide *(hildastroh. com),* divulges some peaceful spots.

Friedhof St Sebastian: Mozart's father, Leopold, and wife, Constanze, are buried in this cemetery, established in 1600 as an Italian 'campo santo'. Its centrepiece is the mausoleum of Prince-Archbishop Wolf-Dietrich of Raitenau.

Bürgerspitalskirche St Blasius: The civic hospital church near Getreidegasse has an inner courtyard with Renaissance arcades. A Gothic church with 12th-century roots, it impresses with its vault, stained-glass windows and mystical interior.

Waldbad Anif: Rent a bike to pedal south along the Salzach River to this emerald-green lake, perfect in summer.

Schloss Mirabell gardens and Festung Hohensalzburg (p86)

At the foot of Mönchsberg's cliffs, the **Felsenreitschule** is the dramatic backdrop for the **Salzburger Festspiele** (Salzburg Festival) in the movie, where the Trapp Family Singers win the audience over with 'Edelweiss' and give the Nazis the slip with 'So Long, Farewell'. Close by is **Residenzplatz**, where Maria belts out 'I Have Confidence' and playfully splashes the spouting horses of the Residenzbrunnen fountain. Hoof it uphill from here to Benedictine **Stift Nonnberg** *(nonnberg.at; free),* where the nuns waltzed on their way to mass, including the ever-problematic Maria. To see the abbey at its most atmospheric, arrive for the 6.45am Gregorian chant.

Palaces, you say? Romantically rococo **Schloss Leopoldskron** *(schloss-leopoldskron.com),* a 15-minute stroll south of the centre, is where the lake scene was filmed. Its Venetian Room was the blueprint for the Trapps' opulent ballroom, where the von Trapp kids bid their heart-melting farewells. Now you can stay the night in its elegant hotel.

Back in town, the Pegasus fountain, gnomes and steps with fortress views in the **Schloss Mirabell** *(salzburg.info; free)* gardens might inspire a rendition of 'Do-Re-Mi' – especially if there's a drop of golden sun.

 EATING IN SALZBURG: TOP LUNCH SPOTS

Afro Café: Go for fair-trade coffees, lavish brunches and creative day specials at this Afro-chic cafe. *9am-8pm Mon-Sat* €

Green Garden: Tapping into plant power, this vegan cafe rustles up tasty Buddha bowls, brunches and superfood salads. *1-9pm Wed-Fri, 10am-9pm Sat & Sun* €

Heart of Joy: Ayurveda-inspired cafe: all-vegetarian, part-vegan, mostly organic menu of bagels, salads, homemade cakes, juices, daily specials. *8am-7pm* €

Humboldt: Like a blast of nouveau alpine chic, the vibe is cool yet cosy. A good buzz and all-organic, season-driven menu. *10.30am-11pm* €€

Beyond Salzburg

Salzburg is the curtain-raiser to Alps that will make your heart soar and cinematic backdrops that will prompt you to yodel out loud.

You don't need to venture far from Salzburg for high alpine drama. For a memorable day trip, take the quick train ride to Werfen, which thrills with a showstopping medieval castle and the world's biggest ice caves, Eisriesenwelt. Here cliff-skimming trails thread through the rugged peaks of the limestone Tennengebirge, where eagles wheel, winds blow and silence reigns.

Further east, the Salzkammergut wows with alpine and subalpine lakes, deeply carved valleys, high hills and rugged, steep mountains rising to almost 3000m. Rugged paths wind to mountain-top restaurants, caves and salt mines, where the region's 'white gold' once filled the coffers of Habsburg rulers. Swinging south, the unmissable road trip is the Grossglockner High Alpine Road, helter-skeltering below the country's highest peak, 3798m Grossglockner.

Places
Werfen p89
Hallstatt p90

Werfen

TIME FROM SALZBURG: **40MIN** 🚗 OR **1HR** 🚆

Cue the world's biggest ice caves

High above Werfen, the pointed peaks of the Tennengebirge rise like a theatre curtain of solid limestone over the river-woven Salzach Valley. Take the cable car, then hoof it up the steep, scree-strewn trail to **Eisriesenwelt** *(eisriesenwelt.at; adult/ child €42/21),* open from May to October. Stepping through the huge 20m-wide gash in the rock, feeling the frosty blast of 0°C air and seeing the ice twinkle is like pushing through the wardrobe into Narnia.

An old-fashioned carbide lamp illuminates your passage through this pitch-black, glittering underworld of frozen tunnels and passageways, where you will be blown away by the scale and beauty of the ice. But most impressive of all is the echoing, cathedral-like **Eispalast** (Ice Palace), with icicles as big as organ pipes and ice-veined walls.

Big views and birds of prey at Burg Hohenwerfen

Slung high on a wooded clifftop and cowering below the gnarly peaks of the Tennengebirge, **Burg Hohenwerfen** *(burg-hohen werfen.at; adult/child incl lift €17.90/6.10, with guided tour €20.90/7.60)* is visible from afar. For 900 years this turreted beauty of a castle has guarded the Salzach Valley. You'll be mostly captivated by the mountain views from the 16th-century belfry,

GETTING AROUND

Much of the region beyond Salzburg is accessible by public transport (bus and train), removing the need to hire a car unless you crave the independence. There are regional and S-Bahn trains from Salzburg running frequently to Hallein (15 minutes) and Werfen (40 minutes). The two-hour journey to Obertraun often involves a bus-train combo via Bad Ischl.

WATER & WHEELS ON HALLSTÄTTER SEE

Swimming: Hallstätter See reaches about 24°C from June to August. Obertraun and Untersee (near Steeg) have free public beaches with facilities.

Cycling & kayaking: Hire touring bikes, mountain bikes and e-bikes at Dormio Resort Obertraun. For standard city/e-bikes per hour, expect to pay €20/30. There's a charging station at the cable car valley station. Kayak hire for the first hour is €10, and €5 after that.

Lake Connections: Hallstättersee Schifffahrt (hallstattschifffahrt. at) connects the train station on the eastern shore with the town of Hallstatt year-round, timed to trains. From May to September it does southern-end lake circuits and boat rental.

ⒸOKCENTUNC/SHUTTERSTOCK

Saltzwelten Funicular, Hallstatt

but the dingy dungeons (displaying the usual nasties, such as the iron maiden and thumbscrew) are equally worth a look.

Time your visit to catch the stunning **falconry show** (11.15am & 3.15pm daily) in the grounds, where falconers in medieval costume release eagles, owls, falcons and vultures to wheel in front of the ramparts. The brisk walk up from Werfen takes 20 minutes, or you can cheat by catching the lift.

Hallstatt

TIME FROM SALZBURG: **1HR 30MIN** 🚗

Descending into the salt mine

On the western shore of its exquisitely pretty lake, Hallstatt is famous for its salt mine, where mining began over 7000 years ago. Today miners still dig white gold out of the earth. After a short ferry ride across the lake from the train station, you reach a jetty that is a 15-minute walk from the **Saltzwelten Funicular** (salzwelten.at; adult/child €24/12). It's a dramatic ascent into a strange alpine valley with mirrors reflecting the green landscape, a **Skywalk** with stupendous views, and an Iron Age burial ground.

From the top station, it is another 15-minute walk to the mine. After donning protective clothing, you begin the bilingual 90-minute mine tour in **Salzwelten** (salzwelten.at/en/ hallstatt; funicular & tour adult/child €43/21), taking you around 2km through shafts, down miners' slides, and to an illuminated underground lake. Along the way you learn all about the formation of salt, salt mining, and conditions of the miners.

 EATING IN WERFEN: OUR PICKS

Pizzeria im Markt: Pizzas fly out of the oven perfectly thin and crisp at this cosy pick in Werfen's heart. 10am-10pm €

Oedlhaus: At Eisriesenwelt, this 1574m woodsy hut fortifies walkers with grub like Gröstl (pan-fried potatoes, pork and onions) and mountain views. 8am-4pm €€

Stiege No 1: Venison, asparagus, wild garlic – the menu sings of the seasons. In summer, sit in the lantern-lit garden. 11am-10pm Wed-Sun €€

Obauer: Two Michelin-starred restaurant, with alpine, homegrown and locally foraged ingredients. 6-9pm Wed, noon-9pm Thu-Sun €€€

DRIVING THE GROSSGLOCKNER ROAD

Get up close and personal with the Austrian Alps on this sky-high road trip.

START	END	LENGTH
Bruck	Heiligenblut	48km; 5–6hr

Leaving **① Bruck**, enter the mountainous Fuschertal, passing Fusch and **② Wildpark Ferleiten**. Once through the tollgate, the road climbs steeply to **③ Hochmais** (1850m), where glaciated peaks like Grosses Wiesbachhorn (3564m) crowd the horizon. The road zigzags up to **④ Haus Alpine Naturschau** (2260m), which spotlights local flora and fauna. Further on, a 2km side road spirals up to **⑤ Edelweiss Spitze** (2571m), the road's highest viewpoint. Get your camera handy for **⑥ Fuscher Törl** (2428m), with smashing views, and gemstone-coloured lake **⑦ Fuscher Lacke** (2262m) nearby. Here is a small exhibition on the road's construction, built by 3000 men during the Great Depression (1930–35). The road wriggles on through high meadows to **⑧ Hochto**r (2504m), the top of the pass. Next there's a steady descent to **⑨ Schöneck**. Branch off west onto the 9km Gletscherstrasse, passing waterfalls and Achtung Murmeltiere (Beware of Marmots) signs – you may spot one of the burrowing rodents. The Grossglockner massif slides into view on the approach to flag-dotted **⑩ Kaiser-Franz-Josefs-Höhe** (2369m), with memorable views of bell-shaped Grossglockner (3798m) and the rapidly retreating Pasterze Glacier. Allow time for the glacier-themed exhibition at the visitor centre and the Wilhelm-Swarovski observatory. Round out your road trip in **⑪ Heiligenblut**, where a 15th-century pilgrimage church lifts gazes to Grossglockner.

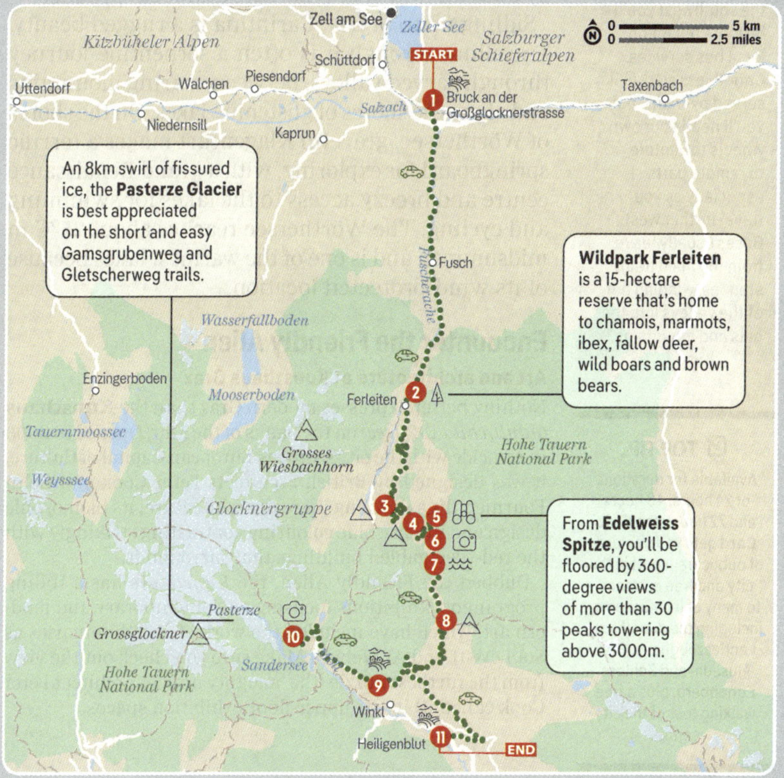

An 8km swirl of fissured ice, the **Pasterze Glacier** is best appreciated on the short and easy Gamsgrubenweg and Gletscherweg trails.

Wildpark Ferleiten is a 15-hectare reserve that's home to chamois, marmots, ibex, fallow deer, wild boars and brown bears.

From **Edelweiss Spitze**, you'll be floored by 360-degree views of more than 30 peaks towering above 3000m.

Zell am See
Zeller See
Salzburger Schieferalpen
START
Kitzbüheler Alpen
Schüttdorf
Uttendorf
Walchen
Piesendorf
Taxenbach
Niedersill
Salzach
Bruck an der
Großglocknerstrasse
Kaprun
①

Fusch

Enzingerboden
Wasserfallboden
Mooserboden
Ferleiten
②
Tauernmoossee
Grosses Wiesbachhorn
Hohe Tauern National Park
Weyssee
Glocknergruppe
③
④ ⑤
⑥
⑦
Pasterze
Grossglockner
⑩
⑧
Hohe Tauern National Park
Sandersee
⑨
Winkl
Heiligenblut
⑪
END

0   5 km
0   2.5 miles

Graz & the South

LAKES | MOUNTAINS | CULTURAL COOL

GETTING AROUND

Styria has a good rail network, with Graz being particularly easy to reach from Vienna, though for the southwest you'll be more reliant on local bus services. Carinthia is also well served by trains, but you'll need your own wheels to venture to remote parts, especially as you travel further west. Buses usually leave from the main train stations, winding out of the valleys into the hills and mountains.

☑ TOP TIP

Available for durations of 24 hours, 48 hours and 72 hours, the **Graz Card** gets you free use of public transport in the city and free entrance to many of its museums, including the *Kunsthaus,* Landeszeughaus, Graz Museum and Schloss Eggenberg, plus a free walking tour of the city centre.

Though Austria's south receives just a trickle of visitors compared to other regions, if you make it this far you'll be richly rewarded. Styria wings you from rolling vineyards, pumpkin fields, wildlife-rich national parks and snow-streaked limestone peaks to the beautiful sweep of the River Mur. UNESCO-listed Graz, Austria's second city, is one of its most vibrant, fizzing with avant-garde arts and a food scene buoyed by abundant farmers markets and local produce.

Sidling up to Styria, Carinthia is a rugged beauty. Travelling through it is often a serpentine journey through carved valleys, between soaring mountains and along the shores of glistening lakes. On the shores of Wörthersee, graceful Klagenfurt makes a terrific springboard for exploring, with a grand Renaissance centre and breezy access to the lakes for swimming and cycling. The Wörthersee reaches about 25°C in midsummer, and is one of the warmest lakes because of its wind-protected location.

Encounter the Friendly Alien

Art and architecture at Kunsthaus Graz

Nothing better expresses modern Graz than the **Kunsthaus** *(adult/child €12/free)* on the banks of the Mur. Opened in 2003 to coincide with the city's stint as European Capital of Culture, it was designed by British architects Peter Cook and Colin Fournier. It's a dazzling piece of architecture, its biomorphic design and intense blue colouring contrasting strikingly with the red-tiled gabled buildings that surround it.

Dubbed the Friendly Alien, the *Kunsthaus* has a rolling program of exhibitions focusing on contemporary and modern art, which have included the work of such luminaries as Sol LeWitt and Ai Weiwei. Make sure you check out the view from the furthest nozzle (the 'naughty nozzle', architect Peter Cook called it) in the upper-floor exhibition space.

GRAZ

Kepler-brücke

Schlossberg

GEIDORF

Zinzendorfgasse

Lendplatz

Josefigasse

LEND

Sauraugasse

Karmeliter-platz

Stadtpark

Elisabethstr

Freiheits-platz

Hofgasse

Leonhardstr

Dom **1**

 Kunsthaus Graz **2**

Südtirolerplatz Hauptbrücke

Hauptplatz

SANKT LEONHARD

Belgiergasse Tegetthoff-brücke

4

INNERE STADT

8 Kaiser-Josef-Platz

GRIES

Kaiserfeldgasse

Joanneumring

Jakomini-platz Reitschul-gasse

Dietrichstein-platz

Brückenkopf-gasse

Radetzky-brücke

10

JAKOMINI

Zweiglgasse Grazbachgasse

0 — 200 m
0 — 0.1 miles

🟠 **HIGHLIGHTS**
1 Dom
2 Kunsthaus Graz
3 Schlossberg

⚫ **SLEEPING**
4 Das Weitzer
5 KAI 36
6 Schlossberg Hotel

🟢 **EATING**
7 Altsteirische Schmankerlstube
8 Geniesserei am Markt
9 Mohrenwirt
10 Scheucher

To the Top of the Schlossberg

Graz' unassailable fortified hill

Schlossberg *(graztourismus.at),* the city's green hill, stands at 473m high above the left bank of the Mur. The old medieval castle underwent a makeover in the mid-16th century courtesy of Italian architect Domenico dell'Allio, who turned it into an impregnable Renaissance fortress. The best way to approach Schlossberg is by skipping up the zigzagging steps from Schlossbergplatz, where it towers above you. Or take the **Schlossbergbahn** *(adult/child €3.20/1.60)* funicular, which was built in 1894 and has a gradient of 61%.

At the top, you'll find the **Bell Tower**, with its 5-tonne bell known as Liesl, the restored casemates and the Schlossberg

---

 EATING IN GRAZ: OUR PICKS

Mohrenwirt: Traditional dishes with a contemporary twist: organic, seasonal local produce. Michelin Bib Gourmand. *11.30am-11pm Wed-Sat* €€

Geniesserei am Markt: Beside the Kaiser-Josef-Platz farmers market. Lunch or the 6pm 10-course surprise menu (book ahead). *9am-10pm Tue-Sat* €€€

Altsteirische Schmankerlstube: Seasonal Styrian and classic Austrian in a homely setting. Vaulted ceiling and wood panelling. *10am-11pm* €€

Scheucher: Michelin-listed restaurant famed for its dry-aged steaks. *11am-2.30pm & 6am-10pm Mon-Fri, 6am-10pm Sat* €€€

BEST FESTIVALS IN GRAZ

This university town has a flurry of festivals, from the International Storytelling Festival (May) to Assembly, the city's Festival of Fashion (September) and Klangnacht, a mesmerising light and sound festival (October).

Elevate: Bills itself as a festival of 'music, arts and political discourse'. *Mar*

Design Month: All of Graz' creative energy condensed into a one-month festival. *May*

Springfestival: Live electronic music and art installations. *Late May/early June*

Aufsteirern: Traditional festival with music, dance, handicrafts and good food. *Sep*

Steirischer Herbst: Edgy, contemporary performing-arts festival, which has been running for over half a century. *Sep/Oct*

branch of the Graz Museum. But the main thing to do up here is enjoy the view over the rooftops of Graz in the beautiful garden on the **Bürgerbastei** – a restored bastion below the clock tower.

Historic Highs in Klagenfurt

Evocative architecture and altar painting

Renaissance romance lives on in Klagenfurt's historic centre. On **Neuer Platz** square is the 16th-century **Dragon Fountain**. This blank-eyed, wriggling statue is modelled on the lindwurm (dragon) of legend, said to have resided in a swamp here long ago, devouring cattle and virgins.

Nearby is the Renaissance **Landhaus** (state parliament), where the highlight is the **Grosser Wappensaal** *(Heraldic Hall; landesmuseum.ktn.gv.at; adult/child €7/free)*, with its magnificent trompe l'oeil gallery painted by Carinthian artist Josef Ferdinand Fromiller (1693–1760). Steps from here, on Pfarrplatz, is the **Stadthauptpfarrkirche St Egid** *(kath-kirche-kaernten.at/pfarren/pfarre/C3080; free)*, where a climb to the 90m-high tower affords a bird's-eye view of town and the surrounding mountains.

Backtracking brings you to the **Dom** *(cathedral; kath-kirche-kaernten.at/pfarren/pfarre/C3074; free)*, with its ornate marble pulpit, sugary pink-and-white stucco and standout altar painting in the chapel by Paul Troger dedicated to St Ignatius.

Swimming & Cycling Wörthersee

Make a splash in Carinthia's biggest lake

Framed by wooded hills and shimmering turquoise-blue, Wörthersee is an instant heart-stealer. In summer all the action is on the lake – open-water swimmers, canoeists, kayakers and stand-up paddleboarders love its placid, tepid waters.

If you prefer to pedal rather than paddle, the 40km **R4 bike route** wraps around the entire shoreline. It's an easy, well-marked ride ticking off swimming spots, beaches and viewpoints. You can hire road and e-bikes at stations in the region, including at the Klagenfurt **tourist office** on Neuer Platz. Boats departing for destinations around the Wörthersee leave from a quay just north of **Strandbad Klagenfurt** (Klagenfurt Bathing Beach). Check times at *woertherseeschifffahrt.at*.

PLAYING YOUR GUEST CARDS RIGHT

Play your guest cards right and you won't need to pay for travelling by regional train around Carinthia. As well as offering various discounts, the free **Wörthersee Plus Card** *(woerthersee.com/card; year-round)* entitles overnight visitors to free train travel throughout Carinthia, including the S1, connecting Friesach in the north with Lienz (in Tyrol, west of Carinthia). It is valid both days of a one-night stay in a participating hotel.

The **Erlebnis Card** *(visitvillach.at/de/erlebnis-card.html)*, Villach's free card, also includes regional travel anywhere in Carinthia and on a few special bus services for the duration of your stay.

The **Kärnten Card** *(kaerntencard.at; adult €60-89, child €31-46)* provides discounts or free admission but not free transport; available in one-, two- and five-week timeframes.

EATING IN KLAGENFURT: OUR PICKS

Princs: Lively kitchen serves pizzas, plates of pasta and 'street food'. Kitchen closes at 9pm. Also with a popular bar. *10am-midnight Mon-Thu, to 2am Fri & Sat* €€	**Dolce Vita:** Local flagship restaurant-*bistretto* with northern Italian cuisine and a local seasonal menu. *11.30am-3pm & 6.30-10pm Mon-Fri* €€	**Ricardo:** Portuguese, tapas, vegetarian (and vegan) dishes, and steaks in a relaxed setting, with outdoor seating. *11.30am-2pm & 6-11.30pm Tue-Sat, 6-11.30pm Mon* €€	**Gasthaus im Landhaushof:** Classic Austrian cuisine, with outdoor seating in the yard and a kitchen open all day. *11am-9pm Mon-Sat, to 3pm Sun* €€

Innsbruck & Tyrol

LIVING HISTORY | HABSBURG CULTURE | HIGH ALPS

Tyrol's capital is a sight to behold. Rising like a theatre curtain above the city, the rock spires of the Nordkette range are so breathtakingly close that when you fly here, it feels as though you're going to smash right into them. It isn't just an illusion: within minutes you can whizz from the late-medieval Altstadt, presided over by a Habsburg palace, to 2000m above sea level and be up among crags where alpine choughs glide and cowbells tinkle.

Beyond Innsbruck, it's all about the outdoors, whether you're pelting down an Olympic bob run, schussing down the legendary slopes of Kitzbühel, cycling the Zillertal or hiking in the Alps with a flawlessly blue sky overhead. Welcome to a place where snowboarders brag under the low beams of a medieval tavern about awesome descents; where *Dirndls* and *Lederhosen* have street cred; and where *Volksmusik* (folk music) features on club playlists.

Palace of Dreams

MAP p96

Discover imperial Innsbruck

Grabbing attention with its pearl-white facade and cupolas, the **Hofburg** *(burghauptmannschaft.at; adult/child €9.50/free)* imperial palace was built for Archduke Sigmund the Rich in the 15th century, expanded by Emperor Maximilian I in the 16th century and given a baroque makeover by Empress Maria Theresia in the 18th century.

Take a romp around the lavish rococo state apartments and you'll be astounded by the 31m-long **Riesensaal** (Giant's Hall), a feast of frescos, weighty chandeliers and Habsburg portraits. Right opposite is the **Hofkirche** *(tiroler-landesmuseen.at; adult/child €14/free),* one of Europe's finest royal court churches. Top billing goes to the crazily ornate black-marble tomb of Emperor Maximilian I (1459–1519), a masterpiece of German Renaissance sculpture. The twin rows of 28 giant bronze figures guarding the sarcophagus include Dürer's legendary King Arthur. Touching the statues is now forbidden,

GETTING AROUND

Innsbruck's compact, pedestrianised, alley-woven Altstadt is a pleasure to explore on foot. Most sights are here, and ultramodern funiculars race you up into the mountains. For outlying sights, such as Bergisel and Schloss Ambras, hop on one of the **IVB** *(ivb.at)* buses; for multiple journeys, invest in a 24-hour ticket. Public transport is free with summer's Welcome Card, the guest card you receive with stays of more than two nights.

☑ **TOP TIP**

Tourist information centres on Burggraben, at the Stadtturm and the Hauptbahnhof are handy first ports of call for maps, tickets, ski passes and information.

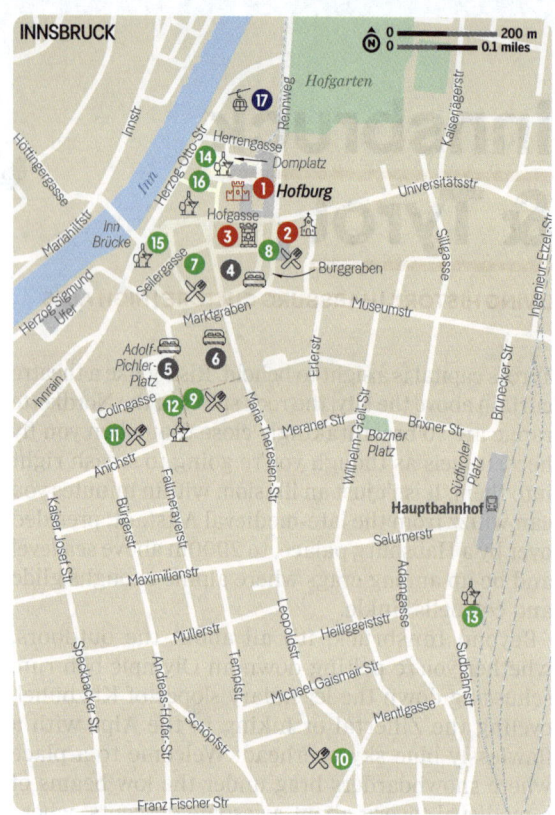

INNSBRUCK

but numerous inquisitive hands have already polished parts of the dull bronze, including Kaiser Rudolf's codpiece!

Innsbruck on High

MAP p96

From city to slopes

You'll be itching to head into the mountains on Innsbruck's doorstep. Zaha Hadid's space-age funicular **Nordketten-bahnen** *(nordkette.com; top of Innsbruck return ticket adult/child €52/31.20)* floats to the slopes in no time, stopping at Hungerburg, where you switch to a cable car to Seegrube and,

 EATING IN INNSBRUCK: OUR PICKS

MAP p96

Olive: Vegetarians and vegans are in their element at this cute bistro with vintage furniture. Book – it gets busy. *5-11pm Mon-Sat* €

Die Wilderin: A modern hunter-gatherer restaurant, where season-spun menus play up farm-fresh and foraged ingredients. *5pm-midnight Tue-Sun* €€

Il Convento: Tucked into the old city walls, this Italian job has dishes like clam linguine and braised veal, and a well-stocked cellar. *11.30am-midnight Mon-Sat* €€

Oniriq: Explosive Austrian flavours are given a foraged twist in ingredient-led tasting menus at this stylishly monochrome pick. *6-11pm Wed-Sat* €€€

finally, 2256m Hafelekar. A 15-minute uphill trudge brings you to 2334m **Hafelekarspitze**, where alpine choughs ride the breeze and gnarly limestone mountains rise in great waves. The views are riveting, reaching all the way to 3798m Grossglockner when it's clear.

Walking trails head off in all directions, including the ridgetop **Goethe Trail**, a 10km, five-hour, out-and-back stomp over meadow and mountain to the **Pfeishütte**. The steep, technically demanding **Nordkette Single Trail** draws hardcore downhill mountain bikers. In winter, the most central place to pound powder is the **Nordpark**. Fearless skiers ride the **Hafelekar Run**, one of Europe's steepest runs, with a 70% gradient.

Life in the Fast Lane

MAP p99

Pick up speed, Olympian-style

For a minute in the life of an Olympic bobsleigh racer, ride the **Olympia Bob** *(knauseder-event.at; bobsleigh ride summer/winter €55/120, skeleton €65)* at the foot of Patscherkofel mountain in **Igls**.

Zipping around 14 curves and picking up speeds of up to 120km/h, the 1.3km bob run, built for the 1976 Winter Olympics, is a single minute of pure hair-raising action. From December to March, you can either join a four-person bobsleigh or throw yourself headfirst down the run on a skeleton. Otherwise, join a pro-bobsled driver from April to October for the summer version. See the website for dates, times and bookings. To reach the bob run, take Bus J from Innsbruck Landesmuseum to Igls Olympiaexpress.

Swarovski Sparkle

MAP p99

Enter a crystal world

The dinky village of **Wattens**, a 30-minute bus ride east of Innsbruck, is the glittering heart of the Swarovski crystal empire. **Swarovski Kristallwelten** *(kristallwelten.swarovski.com; adult/child €26/8)* shines as one of Austria's most-visited attractions.

Against the backdrop of the Alps, the fantasy world begins outdoors with an ivy-swathed giant's head spouting water, a dazzling crystal cloud, bejewelled with 800,000 crystals, floating above a mirrorlike pool, and a stunning modernist, black-and-white carousel glimmering with 15 million crystals by Spanish designer Jaime Hayon. Inside, the Chambers of Wonder zoom in on Alexander McQueen's wintry *Silent Light,*

SKY-HIGH VIEWS

Stadtturm: Onion-domed medieval tower in the heart of the Altstadt. Puff up 133 steps for 360-degree views over Innsbruck's rooftops to the surrounding mountains.

360°: Knockout view of the skyline from the balcony skirting this spherical bar. Nicely chilled spot for a coffee/sundowner.

Lichtblick: Dinner at this slickly minimalist, backlit, glass-walled restaurant takes in the entire sweep of the city and its mountain backdrop.

Buzihütte: This woodsy alpine hut has a peak-gazing terrace for digging into traditional faves like *Käsespätzle* (cheese noodles).

Cloud One: On the 13th floor of Motel One, this glass-fronted bar has tremendous views. Shake your own cocktail or go for a signature pomegranate margarita.

DRINKING IN INNSBRUCK: OUR PICKS

MAP p96

Fuchs & Hase: This vaulted bar is a mellow pick for an expertly mixed cocktail, proper coffee or glass of natural wine. *5pm-1am Tue & Wed, 3pm-1am Fri & Sat*

Stage 12: Backlit, gold-kissed bar with a terrace for summer imbibing, a vintage popcorn machine and talented mixologists. *noon-midnight Sun-Thu, to 1am Fri & Sat*

Moustache: Retro bolthole, with a terrace overlooking Domplatz. Go for cocktails, craft beers and finger food. *10am-2am Tue-Sun, 4pm-2am Mon*

In Vinum: Snug Altstadt wine bar: relaxed choice to sample Austria's finest wines; see website for details of the regular tastings. *11am-midnight Mon-Sat, 4-10pm Sun*

BIKEMP/SHUTTERSTOCK

Hikers, Kreuzjoch

CITY TO SLOPES

The money-saving **Innsbruck Card** *(24/48/72hr €69/79/ 89, child half price)* gets you one visit to Innsbruck's main sights and attractions, a return cable car or funicular journey, a guided city walk and unlimited use of public transport, including the Sightseer and Kristallwelten shuttle bus.

Heading to the slopes? The surrounding region is brilliantly connected by public transport. Distances are generally short and fares inexpensive. Many connections are covered by free guest cards you receive locally, so check this before shelling out on tickets. In winter, Innsbruck's money-saving **Ski Plus City Pass** wraps up 346km of pistes in 12 ski areas around Innsbruck and the glacier-capped Stubaital, and opens the doors at 22 sights and attractions.

South Korean artist Lee Bul's perspective-bending *Into Lattice Sun* and Mexican-Canadian artist Rafael Lozano-Hemmer's *Pulse Voronoi,* a light fantastic walk through 7000 shards of crystal inspired by a Big Bang–style blast.

Outdoor Action in the Zillertal   MAP p99

Hit the slopes

In a stupendously wild pocket of Tyrol, an hour's train ride from Innsbruck, the Zillertal is ripe for outdoor adventure. In summer, hiking trails vein the landscape. Memorable rambles in Zell am See include the 8km round hike to **Zellberg** via the wispy Talbach falls, and the tougher 14km, five-hour stomp up to the 2558m-high, cross-topped summit of **Kreuzjoch**, the highest peak in the Kitzbühel Alps. Mountain bikers are in their element on the 30km **Zillertal Radweg**. For bigger thrills, the **Aktivzentrum** *(aktivzentrum-zillertal.at)* is a one-stop shop for pulse-quickening sports, from paragliding to whitewater rafting and river bugging in raging waters.

When the snow falls, **Mayrhofen**, at the head of the valley, has the downhill edge, with 204km of well-groomed slopes, terrific off-piste and the **PenkenPark** for boarders. One ticket covers the lot: the **Zillertal Superskipass** *(zillertal.at; adult/child €79/35.50).*

Snow Legends in Kitzbühel   MAP p99

World Cup winter wonderland

Winter sparkles brightly in Kitzbühel, right up there among the world's best ski resorts. When flakes blanket the mountains,

TYROL

10 km
5 miles

0
0

Zell am Ziller

200 m
0.1 miles
0
0

★ HIGHLIGHTS
1 Hafelekarspitze
2 Swarovski
  Kristallwelten

SIGHTS
3 Hanglalm
4 Kreuzjoch
5 Zellberg

ACTIVITIES
6 Aktivzentrum
7 Hahnenkamm
8 Kitzbüheler
  Horn
9 Nordpark
10 Olympia Bob

11 PenkenPark

● SLEEPING
12 Pfeishütte

● EATING
13 Buzihütte
14 First Lobster
15 Huberbräu
  Stübert
16 Schulhaus
17 Wirtshaus zum
  Griena

● ENTERTAINMENT
18 Almabtrieb

THE COMING HOME OF THE COWS

In autumn, the Zillertaler celebrate the **Almabtrieb**, or coming home of the cows from their summer pastures to their winter digs in cosy barns. It's a proper taste of the rural Alps to see the cows strut down from the mountains adorned with heavy and elaborate floral headdresses and jangling giant bells.

The centuries-old event is a valley-wide party with feasting, *Volksmusik* with the jaunty melody of accordions and yodelling, locals dressed in *Tracht* (traditional dress), and plenty of schnapps before another harsh, long, snowbound winter of shovelling cow dung. Some of the best celebrations are held in the villages of Fügen, Gattererberg, Hart and Gerlos from mid-September to early October.

ALEXANDER TOLSTYKH/SHUTTERSTOCK

Mayrhofen (p98)

skiers hit the slopes for 233km of downhill. **Hahnenkamm** *(bergwelt-hahnenkamm.at)* is intermediate heaven, **Kitzbüheler Horn** *(kitzski.at)* is much loved by novices, while boarders slide over to Snowpark Kitzbühel at **Hanglalm**, with its rails, kickers, boxes, tubes and obstacles. The **Kitz-Ski Pass** *(2-day pass adult/child €125.50/63)* covers all lifts.

But with so much snow, where to begin? If you're up for a challenge, tackle the tremendously scenic, hut-to-hut, lift-to-lift, 35km **Ski Safari**, linking the Hahnenkamm to Pass Thurn and covering 6000m of vertical. Marked by elephant signs, the full-day alpine tour is a cracking overview to the entire ski area and a free ski bus schleps you back to Kitzbühel at the end.

EATING IN THE ZILLERTAL & KITZBÜHEL: OUR PICKS

Wirtshaus Zum Griena: *Schlutzkrapfen* (cheese-filled pasta) and *Specknödel* (bacon dumplings) at 400-year-old chalet in Mayrhofen.
3-11pm Mon & Thu-Sun €€

Schulhaus: Panoramically perched above Zell am Ziller, this old schoolhouse has sublime views and a Tyrolean seasonal menu.
6-11pm Fri €€

Huberbräu Stüberl: Old-world Kitzbühel haunt with vaults and pine benches, delivering Austrian classics like schnitzel, goulash and dumplings.
9am-11pm €€

First Lobster: Oyster shells mounted on brick walls are a nod to the terrific fish and seafood on the menu at this slick, bistro-style restaurant.
4-11pm Mon-Sat €€

Places We Love to Stay

€ Budget €€ Midrange €€€ Top End

Vienna
MAP p79

Hotel Lamée €€ Glamorous art deco–styled hotel near Stephansplatz, with a city-view rooftop bar.

Die Josefine Hotel €€ Boutique 49-room hotel with *Great Gatsby* vibes; home of stylish Barfly's speakeasy.

Hotel Daniel €€ Smart-luxury, minimalist-style hotel next to Belvedere, with one of the best brunches in town. Vespas and bikes for hire.

Magdas €€ Social business hotel integrating refugees. The sustainable, upcycled design supports NGOs and local artists.

Hotel Imperial €€€ Palatial hotel brimming with decadent features, from the royal staircase to rooms.

Melk & Dürnstein

Hotel Schloss Dürnstein €€€ Opulent rooms in a 17th-century castle – the height of luxury in the Wachau.

Hotel Richard Löwenherz €€€ Beautifully converted from a former medieval convent in Dürnstein, complete with serene monastery garden.

Salzburg
MAP p86

YoHo € Backpacker dream: comfy bunks, cheap beer and *The Sound of Music* screened daily.

Hotel & Villa Auersperg €€ Fuses late-19th-century flair with contemporary. Relax in the vine-swaddled garden or rooftop spa with Kapuzinerberg views.

Hotel am Dom €€ Antique meets boutique at an Altstadt hotel in an 800-year-old building.

Schloss Mönchstein €€€ On a fairy-tale perch atop Mönchsberg and set in hectares of wooded grounds, this 16th-century castle is honeymoon material.

Werfen

Weisses Rössl € Good-value *Pension* (B&B) has great views of the fortress and the Tennengebirge from its rooftop terrace.

Landgasthof Reitsamerhof €€ Rousing views of the Tennengebirge peaks at a sunny yellow, geranium-bedecked chalet just south of Werfen.

Hallstatt

Camping am See € Camping, glamping and upmarket wagons in Obertraun; lake location with beach and sauna-on-wheels.

Hallstatt Hideaway €€€ Modern, beautifully textured suites just back from the lake in Hallstatt. Sauna and private garden on the lake itself.

Graz
MAP p93

Das Weitzer €€ Excellent hotel beside the River Mur and near the Kunsthaus, with a cafe, rooftop sauna and flower-filled lobby.

Schlossberg Hotel €€ Swish art hotel in the former late-16th-century royal carpentry workshops, with an impressive art collection.

Klagenfurt & Wörthersee

Sandwirth €€ Contemporary, comfortable and central, these parquet-floored rooms and apartments are ideal for families.

Seehotel Porcia €€€ In Pörtschach, right on the Wörthersee, with a private beach and elegantly decorated rooms in antique style, some with lake views.

Innsbruck
MAP p96

Hotel Weisses Kreuz €€ This 500-year-old hotel oozes history, with creaking beams, wood-panelled parlours and a twisting staircase.

Stage 12 €€ Design-driven pick lodged in a 16th-century townhouse, with mountain-view rooms, a 6th-floor spa and an upbeat cocktail bar.

Penz Hotel €€€ Behind a sheer wall of glass, this contemporary design hotel has minimalist-chic rooms and a rooftop bar for sunset cocktails.

Zillertal

Schulhaus €€ Charismatic schoolhouse panoramically perched above Zell am Ziller. Rustic rooms, mountain views and a slow-food menu.

Alpenhotel Kramerwirt €€ Big on alpine flair, this rambling 500-year-old chalet in Mayrhofen has warm-hued rooms and a rooftop spa.

Kitzbühel

Snowbunny's Hostel € This friendly, laid-back hostel is a bunny-hop from the slopes.

Villa Licht €€ Pretty gardens, spruce modern apartments with pine trappings, balconies with mountain views – this charming Tyrolean chalet has the lot.

101

Practicalities

HEALTH

The World Health Organization (WHO) recommends all travellers should be covered for diphtheria, tetanus, measles, mumps, rubella, polio and hepatitis B. A UK Global Health Insurance Card (GHIC) or European Health Insurance Card (EHIC) from your healthcare provider covers most emergency medical care in Austria. This is no substitute for good insurance.

ANDRZEJ ROSTEK/SHUTTERSTOCK

LGBTIQ+ TRAVELLERS

Progressive and diverse, Vienna is home to the country's biggest gay community. Positive change is afoot elsewhere, too, though there is still some discrimination, especially in staunchly conservative, Catholic pockets of the country.

MOUNTAIN SAFETY

Every year people die from landslides and avalanches in the Alps. Always check weather conditions before heading out; consider hiring a guide when skiing off-piste. For challenging hikes, ensure you have the proper equipment and fitness. Inform someone at your accommodation where you're going and when you intend to return.

VISAS

Austria is part of the Schengen Agreement. Citizens of the EU, Eastern Europe, Israel, USA, Canada, Central and South America, Japan, Korea, Malaysia, Singapore, Australia and New Zealand don't need visas for stays of up to three months.

OPENING HOURS

Opening hours vary through the year and can differ between cities and small villages.
Banks 9am–3pm Monday to Friday
Cafes 8am–11pm
Post offices 8am–noon and 2–6pm Monday to Friday
Pubs & bars 5.30pm–midnight
Restaurants 11am–2.30pm & 6–11pm
Shops 9am–6.30pm Monday to Friday, to 5pm Saturday
Supermarkets 8am–8pm Monday to Friday, to 5pm Saturday

ACCESSIBLE TRAVEL

Austria scores highly with accessible travel, but a trip still requires careful planning. Ramps into buildings are common but not universal; most U-Bahn stations have wheelchair lifts, but on buses and trams you'll often be negotiating gaps and steps.

PUBLIC HOLIDAYS

New Year's Day 1 January
Epiphany 6 January
Easter Monday March/April
Labour Day 1 May
Whit Monday 6th Monday after Easter
Ascension Day 6th Thursday after Easter
Corpus Christi 2nd Thursday after Whitsunday

Assumption 15 August
National Day 26 October
All Saints' Day 1 November
Immaculate Conception 8 December
Christmas Day 25 December
St Stephen's Day 26 December

Language

The national language of Austria is German. Let's get to grips with the basics here.

Basics

Hello. Servus. *ser*-vus
Hello. Grüss Gott. grewss-got
Good morning. Moagn. *mwah*-gen
Goodbye. Auf Wiedersehen. owf *vee*-der-zay-en
Bye. Tschüss./ Tschau. chüs/chow
Yes. Ja. yah
No. Nein. nain
Please. Bitte. *bi*-te
Thank you. Danke. *dang*-ke
Excuse me. Entschuldigung. ent-*shul*-di-gung
Sorry. Entschuldigung. ent-*shul*-di-gung
What's your name?
Wie ist Ihr Name? (pol) vee ist eer *nah*-me
Wie heißt du? (inf) vee haist doo
My name is …
Mein Name ist … (pol) main *nah*-me ist …
Ich heiße … (inf) ikh *hai*-se …
Do you speak English?
Sprechen Sie Englisch? (pol) *shpre*-khen zee *eng*-lish
Sprichst du Englisch? (inf) *shprikhst* doo *eng*-lish
I don't understand. Ich verstehe nicht. ikh fer-*shtay*-e nikht

Directions

Where's (the station)?
Wo ist (der Bahnhof). vor ist (der *bahn*-hawf)
What's the address?
Wie ist die Adresse? vee ist dee a-*dre*-se
Could you please write it down?
Könnten Sie das bitte aufschreiben? *kern*-ten zee das *bi*-te owf-shrai-ben

Can you show me (on the map)?
Können Sie es mir (auf der Karte) zeige *ker*-nen zee es meer (owf dair *kar*-te) *tsai*-gen

Signs

Ausgang Exit
Eingang Entrance
Damen Women
Herren Men
Heiß Hot
Kalt Cold
Offen Open
Geschlossen Closed
Kein Zutritt No Entry
Rauchen Verboten No Smoking
Verboten Prohibited

Time

What time is it? Wie spät ist es? vee shpayt ist es
It's (10) o'clock. Es ist (zehn) Uhr. es ist (tsayn) oor
morning Morgen *mor*-gen
afternoon Nachmittag *nahkh*-mi-tahk
evening Abend *ah*-bent
yesterday gestern *ges*-tern
today heute *hoy*-te
tomorrow morgen *mor*-gen

Emergencies

Help! Hilfe! *hil*-fe
Go away! Gehen Sie weg! *gay*-en zee vek
I'm ill. Ich bin krank. ikh bin krangk
Call the police! Rufen Sie die Polizei! *roo*-fen zee dee po-li-*tsai*
Call a doctor! Rufen Sie einen Arzt! *roo*-fen zee *ai*-nen artst

NUMBERS
1 eins *ains*
2 zwei *tsvai*
3 drei *drai*
4 vier *feer*
5 fünf *fünf*
6 sechs *zeks*
7 sieben *zee*-ben
8 acht *akht*
9 neun *noyn*
10 zehn *tsayn*

NATALI GLADO/SHUTTERSTOCK

Arriving

Vienna is the main transport hub for Austria, operating services worldwide. The airport is 19km southwest of the city centre. Most low-cost and European carriers operate from Terminal 1, while Terminal 3 is for long-haul flights. Salzburg, Innsbruck and Graz have small, minimal-fuss airports, operating flights to numerous destinations across Europe.

By Rail
Bordering eight countries, Austria's super-central location makes international rail travel a breeze. Vienna is an hour from Bratislava, Innsbruck is 3½ hours from Verona, Linz is four hours from Prague. You get the idea – Europe really is your oyster here.

By Car
There are numerous entry points from Germany, the Czechia, Slovakia, Hungary, Slovenia, Italy and Switzerland. Border crossing points are open 24 hours. Austria is compact – driving from Bregenz in the west to Vienna in the east takes just six hours (traffic permitting).

MONEY

Currency: Euro (€)

CREDIT CARDS

Visa and Mastercard (EuroCard) are more widely accepted than Amex and Diners Club. Upmarket shops, hotels and restaurants will accept cards. Credit cards allow you to get cash advances at ATMs and over-the-counter at most banks. Train tickets can be bought by credit card in main stations.

TAXES & REFUNDS

Mehrwertsteuer (VAT) in Austria is typically 20%. Look for the 'Global Refund Tax Free Shopping' sticker to reclaim about 13% on single purchases over €75 (by non-EU citizens/residents); see *globalrefund.com*. Refund desks are at major department stores, as well as Vienna and Salzburg airports.

TIPPING

Bars About 5% at the bar and 10% at a table.

Hotels One or two euros per suitcase for porters and valet parking in top-end hotels.

Restaurants About 10% (unless service is abominable).

Taxis About 10%.

Getting Around

Austria's public transport network is a dream, with swift, inexpensive trains linking towns and cities, and buses filling the gaps. Car hire gives you greater freedom to explore the country's remotest corners.

Train
Austria's rail system is excellent and inexpensive with a discount card. Österreiche Bundesbahn *(ÖBB; Austrian Federal Railway; oebb.at)* is the main operator. The best deals are *Sparschiene,* heavily discounted tickets sold online up to six months ahead.

JULIA MOUNTAIN PHOTO/SHUTTERSTOCK

Car
You'll find all the major car-hire companies at airports, including Sixt, Hertz and Enterprise. The minimum age for hiring small cars is 19. A valid licence is necessary. Autobahn (motorways) are well maintained. You can only drive on them with a *Vignette* (motorway tax), available from border crossings and petrol stations.

Mountain Railways
When trains stop in the Alps, the only way is up on a *Seilbahn* (funicular) or *Bergbahn* (cable car). Costs quickly mount, meaning it's often cheaper to buy a weekly pass (a ski pass in winter) or use a discount card. Some guest cards get you a free ride.

Bus
Rail routes are often complemented by Postbus *(postbus.at)* services, useful in inaccessible mountainous regions. Buses are fairly reliable, and usually depart from train stations. Aim for weekday travel; services are reduced or nonexistent on weekends.

Bike
Thousands of kilometres of well-signposted bike routes shadow rivers and lakeshores and twist up the Alps. Bike/e-bike rental is ubiquitous and many ÖBB stations rent wheels. Most regional trains transport bikes in the baggage car (you'll need a bicycle ticket). On long-distance trains, reserve online/ use the ÖBB app.

DRIVING ESSENTIALS

Drive on the right.

Winter tyres are obligatory November to mid-April.

50　**100**

Speed limit is 50km/h: built-up areas, 100 km/h: open roads and 130 km/h: motorways.

Curated by
Leonid Ragozin

Belarus

EUROPE'S ODDEST POLITY

One man has defined Belarus for more than 30 years, and he is not going away.

Belarus has been one of Europe's political oddities ever since President Aleksandr Lukashenko came to power in 1994 under the slogans of restoring the Soviet way of life – in which he partly succeeded – as well as the Soviet Union per se, in which he didn't. 'Communism with cappuccino' is how this guidebook series described Belarus in the early 2000s.

Routinely branded as a dictator in the international media, Lukashenko brutally suppressed a peaceful popular uprising against his rule in 2021–22 and allowed Russian troops to launch an attack on Ukraine's capital, Kyiv, in February 2022. However, since Russia withdrew troops from the vicinity of Kyiv the same year, it didn't use Belarusian territory for further attacks on Ukraine and the Belarusian army has never participated in the conflict (though given its unpredictable trajectory, this could change at any time).

Although Lukashenko makes attempts to distance himself from Russia's war in Ukraine and mend relations with the West, Belarus remains under Western sanctions, levied on the country for its role in the war on top of the previous sanctions that punished it for mass human rights violations.

Partly because Belarus began sliding back towards authoritarian rule long before Russia, it has never been on the radar of international travellers. It has few obvious natural or historical attractions, except for Belavezhskaya Pushcha National Park – a piece of primeval forest that's home to a large population of European bison.

Its current geography, demography and urban landscapes were defined by WWII, in which it lost over a quarter of its population – the highest percentage among all European nations. Main Belarusian cities, most notably Minsk, were rebuilt from scratch in the post-war years, giving the country its idiosyncratic hyper-Soviet feel.

ANASTASIA PETROVA/SHUTTERSTOCK

Belarus is currently considered **unsafe to visit**

Left: Obelisk, Belarusian Great Patriotic War Museum; Above: Station Square, Minsk

WHY BELARUS IS A NO-GO ZONE

Warnings against travelling to Belarus issued by major Western governments sound more vague than those pertaining to Russia and Ukraine. Indeed, Belarus has so far avoided turning itself into a battlefield of the Russo-Ukrainian War, even with Russia using its territory in the initial assaults in 2022. Large-scale protests haven't flared up since 2021. But the situation remains fluid: Russian (and Belarusian) war plans are shrouded in secrecy while many anti-Lukashenko Belarusians are only waiting for a sign of weakness from Lukashenko and his patrons in Moscow before taking to the streets again. Belarus remains a very repressive state, more so than Russia. Travelling to Belarus with any politically motivated mission that is deemed undesirable by the regime may result in arrest, deportation or – at worst – a jail sentence. Don't assume any rules exist. Laws are being used arbitrarily or ignored altogether, at least when it comes to political issues.

Belarus Today

Belarus is a country of neat-looking fields, good roads, many lakes and forests, an occasional castle and many sad Jewish memories. Russian language dominates in all spheres of life, despite the efforts to expand the use of Belarusian language (similar to Ukrainian), which is more widespread in the west of the country. There are many vestiges of Polish influence and heritage as well.

The country withdrew into itself following the failure of the anti-Lukashenko uprising and in the wake of the Russian invasion of Ukraine. The uprising, triggered by the jailing of opposition candidates in a presidential election, resulted in 25,000 people being detained between August and November 2020, according to Human Rights Watch. Hundreds of them were subjected to torture. The number of political prisoners peaked at around 1500 in 2023 after which it started slowly diminishing.

The EU stated in 2020 that it doesn't recognise Lukashenko as a legitimate president, which left him as a pariah in Europe. He found himself in even greater isolation when he allowed Russia to use Belarusian territory in its 2022 attack on Ukraine, and Belarus fell under Western sanctions similar to those slapped on Russia.

But things have changed since then. Belarus stayed out of the Ukraine war after 2022, while Lukashenko tried to sell himself as a potential mediator. His efforts paid off when Donald Trump, re-elected in 2024, attempted to stop the war in Ukraine. This led to a frenzy of communication between US officials and Lukashenko, with the latter coaching the former in how to deal with President Putin, according to *Time* magazine.

Ordinary Belarusians have been going about their lives in the meantime. Nobody challenged Lukashenko when he was once again 're-elected' in 2025. Few will be surprised if the same happens in 2030.

History

Belarus means 'White Rus' in Slavic languages, a reference to the fact that its statehood stems from the same root as Russia's and Ukraine's – Kyivan Rus. Its national awakening has been subdued from the outset and remains so today.

Kyivan Rus and Polish-Lithuanian rule

Eastern Slavs from the Krivichi, Dregovichi and Radimichi tribes arrived in what is now Belarus in the 6th to 8th centuries CE. The principalities of Polatsk, Turau, Pinsk and Minsk were formed, all falling under the suzerainty of Prince Vladimir's Kyivan Rus by the late 10th century.

In the 14th century the territory of modern-day Belarus – along with most of today's Ukraine – became part of the Grand Duchy of Lithuania. In the 400 years before Belarus fell under Russian control, Belarusians began separating themselves from Russians and Ukrainians linguistically and culturally.

LATVIA
Rēzekne
RUSSIA
Daugavpils
Panevėžys
Utena
LITHUANIA
Novopolatsk
Polatsk
Vitsebsk
Hlybokoye
Lepel
Smolensk
Kaunas
VILNIUS
Orsha
Marijampolė
Neris (Vilija)
Khatyn
Alytus
Maladzechna
Barysau
Mahileu
(Mogilev)
Krichev
Lida
MINSK
Dudutki
POLAND
Hrodna
Navahrudak
(Novogrudok)
Mir
Babrujsk
Dnipro (Dnieper)
Nyasvizh
Zhlobin
Baranavichy
Slutsk
Białystok
Slonim
Svetlahorsk
Homel
Rechitsa
Kamyanyuki
Zhytkavichy
Bug
Mazyr
Kobryn
Pinsk
Pripyat
Turau
Terespol
Chornobyl
Exclusion Zone
Chernihiv
UKRAINE
Desna
Chornobyl
0 100 km
0 50 miles

After Lithuania united with Poland and became Roman Catholic in 1386, the Belarusian peasantry remained in the Orthodox Church. Lithuania permitted its subjects a fair degree of autonomy, even using their emerging language, yet to be called Belarusian, as the official language.

In 1596 the Polish authorities arranged the Union of Brest, which set up the Uniate Church, bringing much of the Orthodox Church in Belarus under the authority of the Vatican.

Over the next two centuries of Polish rule, Poles and Jews controlled trade and most Belarusians remained peasants. Only after the three Partitions of Poland (in 1772, 1793 and 1795–96) was Belarus absorbed into Russia.

The Russian Empire

Under Russian rule, a policy of Russification was pursued. In 1839 the Uniate Church was abolished, with most Belarusian parishes absorbed by the Russian Church.

During the 19th century Belarus was part of the Pale of Settlement, the area where Jews in the Russian Empire were required to settle. The percentage of Jews in many Belarusian cities and towns before WWII was between 35% and 75%.

The vast majority of Belarusians remained on the land, poor and illiterate. Due to their cultural stagnation, their absence

FAST FACTS

Capital Minsk

Population 9.5 million

Area 207,595 sq km

Official languages Russian & Belarusian

Time zone GMT+3

Currency Belarusian rouble (BYN)

HAY ART OF BELARUS

Driving through Belarus, as we did on multiple occasions prior to 2022, the neatly arranged blandness of its rural landscapes would be occasionally disrupted by a vision that sits somewhere between comical and disconcerting. The country's vast fields are decorated with hay bale sculptures during harvest season and remain throughout winter. Looking like weird agricultural Lego figurines with bales used as the building elements, they might depict a folksy-looking peasant family, with facial features made of paper, Slavic fairy-tale characters or a toy train, with bales arranged as carriages.

This is the kind of aesthetic promoted by and in many ways embodied by Aleksandr Lukashenko, who headed a Soviet collective farm shortly before becoming national leader. A vivid example of political paternalism, he enjoys being called Batka (Daddy) and does so himself – he loves talking about himself in the third person. His political brand might come across as exotic, but in an East European context it is also somewhat typical.

ALENA ZHARAVА/SHUTTERSTOCK

Victory Park, Minsk

from positions of influence and their historical domination by Poles and Russians, any sense among Belarusian speakers that they formed a distinct nationality was very slow to emerge.

The Soviet period

In March 1918, under German occupation during WWI, a short-lived independent Belarusian Democratic Republic was declared, but the land was soon under the control of the Red Army and the Belarusian Soviet Socialist Republic (BSSR) was formed. The 1921 Treaty of Riga allotted roughly the western half of modern Belarus to Poland, which launched a programme of Polonisation. These lands would be annexed by the USSR when Hitler and Stalin divided Poland in 1939.

The eastern half was left to the Bolsheviks and the redeclared BSSR became a founding member of the USSR in 1922. The 1930s also saw industrialisation, agricultural collectivisation and purges in which hundreds of thousands were executed – most in the Kurapaty Forest, outside Minsk.

When Nazi Germany invaded the USSR in 1941, Belarus was at the epicentre of the catastrophe and suffered more than any current European nation. The German occupation was savage and partisan resistance widespread until the Red Army drove the Germans out in 1944, with massive destruction on both sides.

Hundreds of villages were destroyed and much of Minsk was flattened. The Nazis and their auxiliaries locked villagers in their churches and burnt them alive, as happened in Khatyn, now the site of a Soviet-era memorial. At least 25% (over two million people) of the Belarusian population died between 1939 and 1945. At the concentration camp of Maly

Trostenets alone, more than 200,000 people were executed.

In the post-war years, the Soviet authorities reinvented Belarus as the 'assembly shop' of the USSR, transforming it into a major manufacturing and machine-building hub. By the 1980s, Belarus was one of the Soviet Union's most prosperous republics by the 1980s and the wartime population loss was compensated for by the influx of Russian-speaking immigrants.

The 1986 Chornobyl disaster, just over the border in Ukraine, was profoundly felt by the people of Belarus. The radiation cloud released left about a quarter of the country seriously contaminated and it still has effects today.

The Lukashenko decades

Belarus proclaimed itself an independent country after the collapse of the August 1991 coup in Moscow. With no history whatsoever as a politically or economically independent entity, the country of Belarus was one of the oddest outcomes of the disintegration of the USSR.

In July 1994, Aleksandr Lukashenko came to power and has ruled Belarus with an iron grip ever since. His initial promise was reunification with Russia but his relations with Moscow were never ideal and over the years he grew staunchly pro-independence. He has altered the constitution on several occasions to allow himself to remain in office. Resistance to Lukashenko's reign has been muted, though protests have flared up around the time of elections, which all major international observers, including the United Nations Human Rights Council, denounced for failing to meet free and fair standards. These protests occurred when Lukashenko won the presidential vote in 2006 and again in 2010, when he won again with almost 80% of the vote. When the conflict in Ukraine began in 2014, he went on to host peace talks between Russia, Ukraine, France and Germany, which resulted in the Minsk Agreements, which put an end to the initial hot phase of the conflict. Lukashenko's confidence and international clout grew accordingly.

However, his new election bid in 2020 was countered by a united opposition, who made a coordinated attempt at nominating several candidates and launching powerful election campaigns for each of them, despite knowing full well that they would most likely be barred from running. This is exactly what happened, and the candidates and their staffers were arrested. The only opposition personality Lukashenko allowed to run was the last-minute nominee Sviatlana Tsikhanouskaya, the wife of a jailed candidate. Although Lukashenko claimed he won, with 81% voting for him and 10% for Tsikhanouskaya, many believe that she was the real winner. Several EU countries recognise the government in exile she formed after fleeing to Lithuania as the only legitimate body in Belarus. But its influence waned in the years that followed and Lukashenko's confidence grew again. After 'winning' another election in 2025, he released Tsikhanouskaya's husband Siarhei from jail in a prisoner swap organised by the Trump administration.

ZUBR'S COMEBACK

The rescue of the European bison (or *zubr* in Slavic languages) as a species was one of the greatest stories of European cross-border cooperation during the worst periods of the 20th century, in which Belarus played no small part.

The last remaining piece of primeval forest in Central Europe, Belavezhskaya Pushcha was also the last home of European bison before they became extinct in the wild in the 1920s. But 52 bison from Belovezhskaya Pushcha, as well as from the Caucasus, were still living in European zoos. The return of the bison into the wild was championed by pre-war Poland, who controlled the forest in its entirety. The first bison was released in 1929. After WWII, Belavezhskaya Pushcha found itself divided between the USSR and Poland, with no bison on the Soviet side. But almost immediately the Soviet authorities began populating the Belarusian part of the forest with several bison provided by Poland. There were 6244 free-roaming bison in the world by 2020: of these, 2269 were in Poland and 2101 in Belarus.

Curated by
Helena Smith

Belgium & Luxembourg

GABLED BUILDINGS AND OFFBEAT CHARM

Belgium and Luxembourg have all the showy art and architecture you could dream of, as well as little known but appealing towns, cities and verdant landscapes.

Stereotypes of comic books, chips and sublime chocolates are just the start in eccentric little Belgium, which has spent centuries producing some of Europe's finest art and architecture. Bilingual Brussels is the dynamic yet personable EU capital, also sporting what's arguably the world's most beautiful city square. Otherwise, its galleries, cafes and distinctive village-like districts are a delight to explore. Flat, Dutch-speaking Flanders has many other alluring medieval cities, all easily linked by regular train hops: Bruges is the most popular, for its art and exceptional prettiness; but Ghent also features canals, medieval art and beautiful buildings – plus an edgy student scene.

It's a region much beloved by cyclists for its flatness and for its devotion to the Tour of Flanders. Within a Frisbee throw of Bruges, coastal Ostend offers wide sandy beaches, and modern art too. The port city of Antwerp is forever associated with diamonds and the painter Rubens, but it also is known for high fashion. Much of hilly, French-speaking Wallonia is contrastingly rural – its castles and extensive cave systems easier to reach by car – though fascinating Mons is well connected by public transport. Independent Luxembourg, the EU's richest country, is compact and attractive with its own wealth of castle villages, while its capital city is famed both for banking and its fairy-tale UNESCO-listed Old Town.

PECOLD/SHUTTERSTOCK

THE MAIN AREAS

BRUSSELS
Majestic central square
and characterful cafes.
p118

GHENT
Medieval magic and
contemporary life.
p125

BRUGES
Postcard-perfect
canal-side beauty.
p128

For places to stay in Belgium & Luxembourg, see p143

SCSTOCK/SHUTTERSTOCK

Left: *The Adoration of the Mystic Lamb* (p126), Ghent; Above: Grand Place (p118), Brussels

ANTWERP
Rubens, chocolate,
fashion and diamonds.
p134

WALLONIA
Little-visited cities,
wooded Ardennes.
p137

LUXEMBOURG CITY
Fortified bastions,
stunning gorge setting.
p140

Bruges, p128

Bruges grabs the limelight with its fairy-tale confection of pretty canals, soaring towers and step-gabled houses. If the crowds get too much, nip up a quiet side street.

Antwerp, p134

Antwerp is Belgium's second city, biggest port and fizzing hub of cultural cool, known for its glittering diamonds and the baroque canvasses of art superstar Rubens.

Ghent, p125

Ghent has quietly become the country's best-kept secret. Once a European superpower, it is now an unsung treasure with a strong artistic bent and a lively student population.

Brussels, p118

History meets bureaucracy meets bizarre in this multicultural jumble that's fabulous for art, museums, chocolate shops and unforgettable cafe-bars. Brussels' magnificent Grand Place is a global wonder.

Roosendaal

Bergen-op Zoom

Snijder-Rockoxhuis

Onze-Lieve-Vrouwekáthedraal

Museum Plantin-Moretus

Antwerp

North Sea

Knokke-Heist

Zeebrugge

Blankenberge

De Haan *Markt*

Ostend **Bruges**

Nieuwpoort

Veurne A18

Dunkirk

Calais

Terneuzen

Groeninge-museum

Museum Sint-Janshospitaal

The Adoration of the Mystic Lamb

Gravensteen

Belfort **Ghent**

Eeklo A11 St-Niklaas A12

Lokeren A14 Willebroek

Dender-monde

Mechelen

A10 Aalst *Grand Place* A1

BRUSSELS *Musée Horta*

A10

Ninove

Mont des Arts

Halle A7

Waterloo

Diksmuide Torhout

A17 Deinze

Roeselare

Poperinge Zonnebeke

Ypres A19 Menen

Kortrijk

Tourcoing Mouscron

Armentières

Lille

Roubaix

A14 Oudenaarde

Ronse

Leuze A8

Tournai

FLANDERS

Lessines

Enghien

Soignies Nivelles

Mémorial 1815

A16

La Louvière

Lens

Douai Valenciennes

Arras

A7 Mons

Binche

Maubeuge Beaumont

Charleroi

Couvin

Chimay

Amiens

FRANCE

Reims

Find Your Way

The train and bus services are extensive, efficient and affordable (even free in Luxembourg). Wallonia, being less populated, does not have the same coverage as Flanders and Brussels, but cities are well connected.

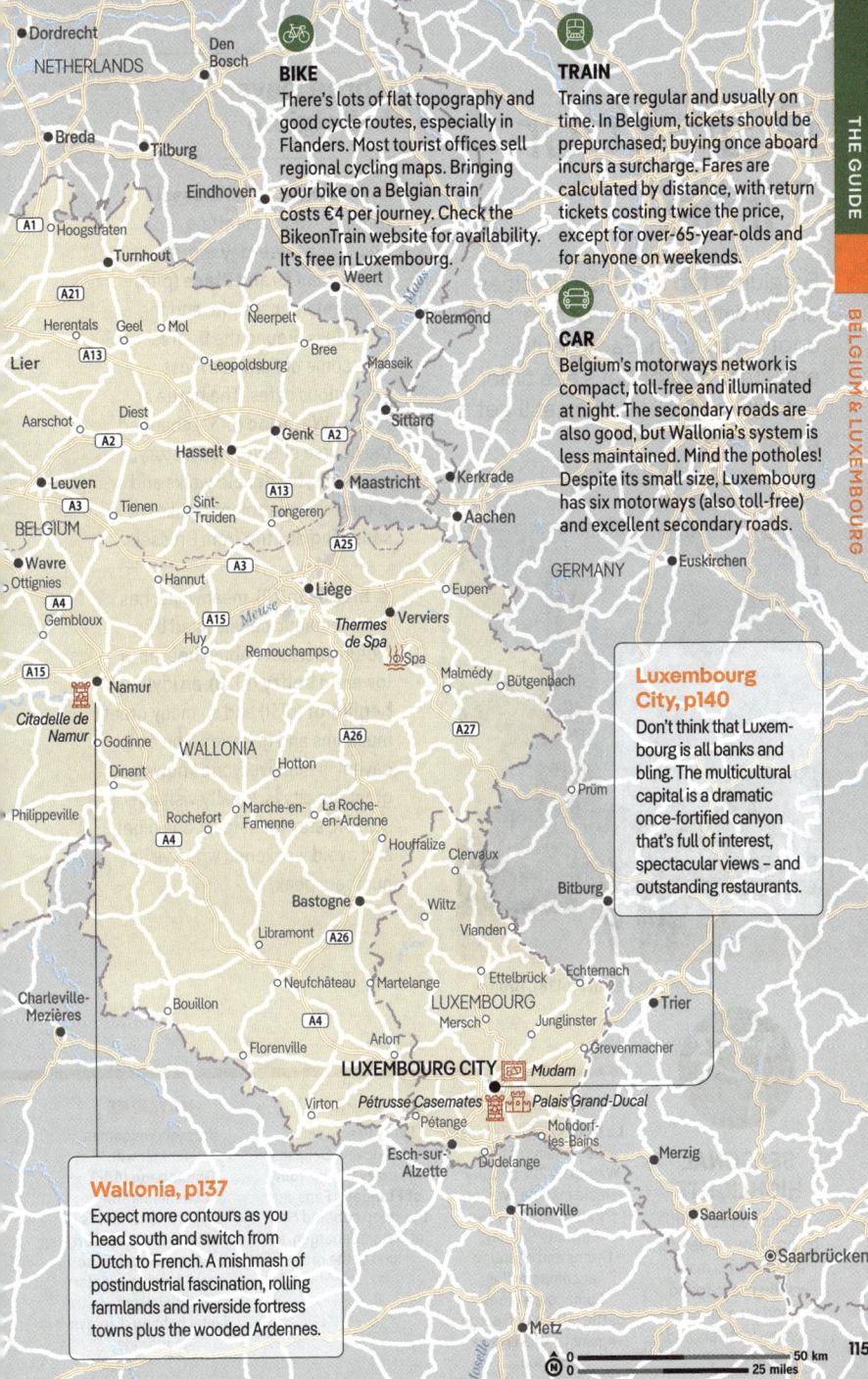

BIKE

There's lots of flat topography and good cycle routes, especially in Flanders. Most tourist offices sell regional cycling maps. Bringing your bike on a Belgian train costs €4 per journey. Check the BikeonTrain website for availability. It's free in Luxembourg.

TRAIN

Trains are regular and usually on time. In Belgium, tickets should be prepurchased; buying once aboard incurs a surcharge. Fares are calculated by distance, with return tickets costing twice the price, except for over-65-year-olds and for anyone on weekends.

CAR

Belgium's motorways network is compact, toll-free and illuminated at night. The secondary roads are also good, but Wallonia's system is less maintained. Mind the potholes! Despite its small size, Luxembourg has six motorways (also toll-free) and excellent secondary roads.

Luxembourg City, p140

Don't think that Luxembourg is all banks and bling. The multicultural capital is a dramatic once-fortified canyon that's full of interest, spectacular views – and outstanding restaurants.

Wallonia, p137

Expect more contours as you head south and switch from Dutch to French. A mishmash of postindustrial fascination, rolling farmlands and riverside fortress towns plus the wooded Ardennes.

Plan Your Time

Belgium's fab four historic cities are all within an hour of one another by train. Each could entertain you for days at a time, but with a week you can still get a good taster.

Belfort (p128), Bruges

OLENA ZNAK/SHUTTERSTOCK

Three Days in Belgium

● Belgium's capital **Brussels** (p118) is a logical starting point for a three-day trip. Its flamboyant **Grand Place** (p118) is a phenomenal sight, and the tiny alleys around the Bourse hide some of Europe's most marvellous cafes. The battle at nearby **Waterloo** (p137) changed the course of European history; museums, battlefield walks and summer reenactments make it a satisfying day trip from Brussels.

● **Bruges** (p128), meanwhile, has it all: romantic canals lined by picture-perfect gabled houses, a towering **belfry** (p128), an idyllic **begijnhof** (p131) and so many great museums and galleries. The one caveat is that everyone knows how great the city is. Ideally visit out of season, stay for at least one night and avoid weekends when visitor numbers peak.

SEASONAL HIGHLIGHTS

Belgium and Luxembourg enjoy moderate, if sometimes rainy, weather year-round – good for a range of events, festivals and gatherings.

FEBRUARY

La Ducasse (p137) sees the remains of Ste-Waudru (a 7th-century female miracle-worker) paraded around town on Trinity Sunday. Drums and chanting accompany the Lumeçon, a mock battle pitting St George against a wickerwork dragon.

APRIL

Every year in spring, cycle-loving Belgians go crazy for the **Tour of Flanders**. Fans line the steep cobbled Muur at Geraardsbergen, an icon of the race.

MAY/JUNE

Brussels welcomes summer with **Ommegang** (p118), commemorating Emperor Charles V's visit in 1549. Up to 1200 costumed locals take part – knights, giants and stilt-walkers – with digital lighting displays on the side.

A Week of Sensational Cities

● Explore Brussels and Bruges as suggested above, then head to gorgeous **Ghent** (p125) with its majestic canal views: this hip and student-filled town feels like a grittier, more lived-in version of Bruges. A day here will leave you wanting more, but it's time enough to climb the tall **belfry** (p125), take a canalboat trip, explore the city-centre medieval castle of **Gravensteen** (p125), check out a cool cafe and adore the fabled *Mystic Lamb* by Flemish Primitive artist **Jan van Eyck** (p126).

● The old core of the city of **Antwerp** (p134) has plenty more, including fabulous museums, an impossibly venerable printworks and Rubens connections at every turn. The city is also a cradle of creativity, where immersive experiences give insights into the diamond industry, chocolate making and brewing.

A Week in Wallonia & Luxembourg

● The old centre of **Namur** (p138) is a fine place to while away a day; the vast bastions of the great fortress make for great explorations and adventures. Afterwards head to **Luxembourg City** (p140) via Dinant and the Meuse Valley. This may be the capital of Europe's richest country, but while much is pricy, there are plenty of free attractions and public transport is gratis. The geography of the city is spectacular, and it is a truly multicultural place.

● The elegant original spa of **Spa** (p139) is a charmer, whether for dining well, 'taking the waters' or otherwise pampering yourself. **Liège** (p139) takes a bit of effort to love, but it's rewarding to stroll around and practise your French with the ebullient, fun-loving locals.

JUNE
Reenactments of the **Battle of Waterloo** (p139) see hundreds of costumed 'soldiers' battle it out on the very field where the conflict took place. Scale and dates vary each year (can be early July).

JULY
The fabulously raucous **Gentse Feesten** (p127) transforms the heart of Ghent into a youthful party, with free music and street theatre, dance workshops and packed streets. Be prepared to party a lot, and sleep little.

AUGUST
A week of raucous celebrations in **Outremeuse** (p139) culminates on 15 August when sermons are read in Walloon dialect, then everyone gets tipsy on *pékèt* (local gin). Expect firecrackers, puppets, dances and a procession of giants.

NOVEMBER
Late November to New Year, embrace the festive holiday spirit as lights illuminate the wonders of Luxembourg City during the winter-lights period.

Brussels

GLOBAL CITY | ARCHITECTURE | NINETEEN VILLAGES

☑ TOP TIP

To see a bunch of top sites, consider the **BrusselsCard** *(brusselscard.be; 24/48/ 72hr €39/51/57)*, which includes free city transport. However, avoid buying one for Mondays when much is closed, or on the first Wednesday afternoon of each month when many major museums are free.

As the capital of a trilingual country with over 180 nationalities, and as the decision-making centre for over 400 million Europeans, Brussels proudly embraces its identity as an open city.

At first glance, Brussels can seem chaotic. Years of uncoordinated urban planning, with little regard for previous heritage, have left the city scattered with mismatched architecture. Grand squares, intricate guildhalls and Gothic churches stand alongside Art Nouveau, Art Deco and sleek glass buildings. This improbable mix has become an integral part of Brussels' landscape, adding to its distinctive character.

It's a city of art, from Flemish masters in the Museum of Fine Arts to avant-garde galleries spread all around town. Comic art has deep roots here: Hergé, creator of Tintin, was born in Brussels. But most of all, the city is all about conviviality and festivities such as Ommegang. With a collection of 19 'villages' and different districts waiting to be discovered, Brussels welcomes you, just as you are.

Brussels' Crown Jewel

Admire the Grand Place

It's impossible not to gawk at the gilded guildhalls of the **Grand Place** (Grote Markt in Dutch). They are a testament to the power and resilience of the guilds and notable figures who rebuilt the Grand Place after the devastating bombing

GETTING AROUND

The heart of Brussels is compact. While the central area, known as the Pentagon, is easily covered by foot, public transport is recommended for visiting other neighbourhoods and attractions, including the distinctive Atomium. The transport network in Brussels consists of metros, trams, buses (operated by STIB/MIVB) and intra-urban trains (SNCB/NMBS). For late-night-goers, Noctis buses (on Friday and Saturday nights) and Collecto, a shared taxi service, are available.

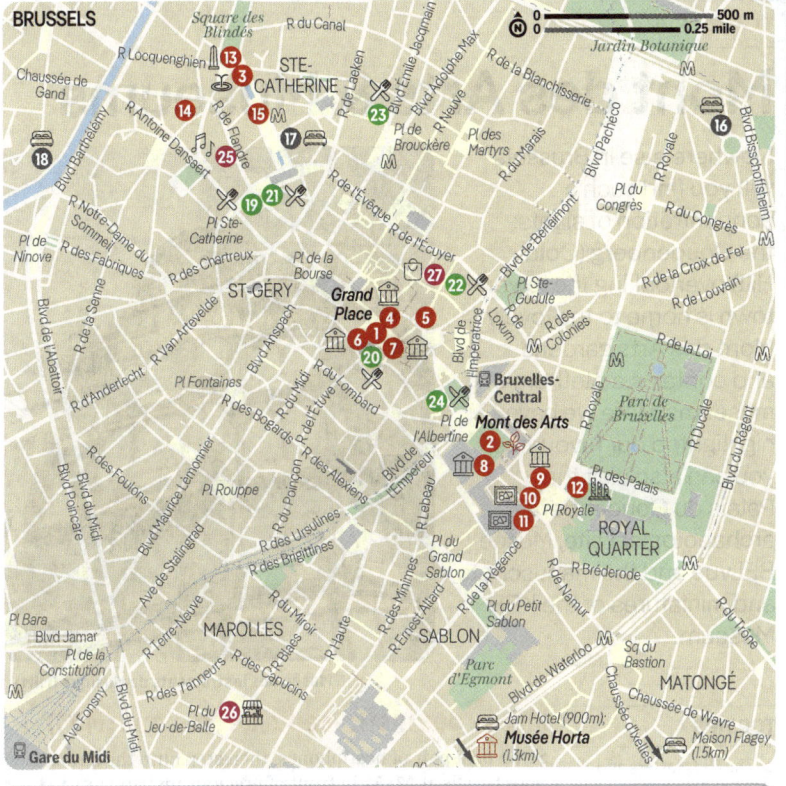

BRUSSELS

⭐ **HIGHLIGHTS**

1 Grand Place
2 Mont des Arts

🔴 **SIGHTS**

3 Anspach Fountain
4 Brussels City Museum
5 Galeries Royales Saint-Hubert
6 Hôtel de Ville
7 Houses of the Dukes of Brabant

8 KBR Museum
9 MIM
see 12 Musée BELvue
10 Musée Magritte
11 Musées Royaux des Beaux-Arts
12 Palais du Coudenberg
13 Pigeon Soldat Memorial
14 Rue de la Cigogne
15 Vismet-Marché aux Poissons

⚫ **SLEEPING**

16 Auberge de Jeunesse Jacques Brel
17 Made in Catherine
18 Meininger Bruxelles City Center

🟢 **EATING**

see 8 albert
19 Chouke
20 Maison Dandoy
21 Mer du Nord

22 Mokafé
23 Super Fourchette
24 Tonton Garby

🔴 **ENTERTAINMENT**

25 La Bellone
see 1 Ommegang

🔴 **SHOPPING**

26 Place du Jeu de Balle Flea Market
27 Tropismes

---

of Brussels by the army of the King of France, Louis XIV, in 1695. The walls of the Gothic city hall remained standing as the sole testimony of the square's medieval past. Its tall and slender tower supports a golden statue of St Michel, one of Brussels' two patron saints. Since 2023, the **Hôtel de Ville** (*City Hall; bruxelles.be/hotel-de-ville; adult €15*) has been open for daily visits. Across from it, the neogothic Maison du Roi now houses the **Brussels City Museum** (*brusselscity museum.brussels; adult/under 18 €10/free*). On the eastern side of the square, the **House of the Dukes of Brabant** is in fact several houses built under the same facade, making it

Mont des Arts & Museums

Nowhere else in Brussels will you find such a concentration of sights: the Coudenberg (Cold Hill) overlooking the lower town is home to the lovely Mont des Arts gardens and contains a plethora of museums. Here we have highlighted our favourites: you can also visit the Palais du Coudenberg archaeological site, Musée BELvue and the manuscripts and miniatures of the KBR Museum.

JOSEFKUBES/SHUTTERSTOCK

Musée des Instruments de Musique (MIM)

TOP TIPS

- The Old Masters and Magritte Museums are free on the first Wednesday of the month from 1pm, and BELVue is on the first Sunday of the month.

- Feeling peckish? **albert**, the National Library's top-floor restaurant, offers splendid views of Brussels and a lovely terrace full of greenery.

PRACTICALITIES

- mim.be, fine-arts-museum.be, coudenberg.brussels, belvue.be, kbr.be/en/museum - Prices vary - Museums close Mondays

Musée des Instruments de Musique (MIM)

Strap on a pair of headphones, then step onto the automated floor panels at **MIM** in front of precious instruments to hear them being played. The museum is housed in the stunning Art Nouveau Old England Building, a former department store built in 1899 by Paul Saintenoy. The rooftop cafe remains closed for renovation.

Musées Royaux des Beaux-Arts

Musées Royaux des Beaux-Arts features 15th-century Flemish Primitives, including Rogier Van der Weyden's *Pietà* with its hallucinatory sky, Hans Memling's refined portraits, and the richly textured *Madonna with Saints* by the anonymous Master of the Legend of St Lucy. Highlights continue with Bruegel the Elder *(The Fall of Icarus)*, Rubens *(Four Studies of a Head)* and Van Dyck *(Portrait of an Elderly Lady)*.

Musée Magritte

With new scenography, **Musée Magritte** holds the world's largest collection of the surrealist pioneer's paintings and drawings. Going from the top floor to the bottom, you can watch his style develop from colourful Braque-style cubism in 1920 through a Dalí-esque phase and a late-1940s period of Kandinsky-like brushwork to his trademark bowler hats of the 1960s.

CAPTUREPB/SHUTTERSTOCK

Place du Jeu de Balle flea market

look like a palace decorated with busts of the several Dukes and Duchesses of Brabant.

A Masterful Design

Visit Horta's own house

At the turn of the 20th century, Victor Horta was already an important architect. He decided to design his own townhouse and workshop, **Musée Horta** *(hortamuseum.be; adult/student/ child €14/6/3.5)* in St-Gilles, and when the two buildings were completed in 1901, it was a true work of total art. Horta meticulously created every aspect, from the letterbox to the mosaics and furniture – today the museum includes some original pieces. The living area's interior is bathed in light, thanks to the windows and a stunning glass roof, showcasing the characteristic Art Nouveau style with its emphasis on glass, metal and curves.

The Spirit of Brussels

Browse and bargain at the Marolles Flea Market

The predominantly working-class and multicultural neighbourhood of **Marolles** (Marollen in Dutch) has always had a rebellious streak and a joke on its lips. The best way to experience it is by visiting the flea market on **Place du Jeu de Balle**. Every morning, starting at 9am, vendors fill up the whole square to sell secondhand clothes, furniture, old cameras, books, paintings... Try your hand at bargaining, or simply enjoy the vibe and have a cup of coffee in one of the many cafes surrounding the square.

THE CONTINENT'S FIRST MALL

Built in 1847, the **Galeries Royales St-Hubert**, just 80m away from Grand Place, is an elegant glass-covered shopping arcade – and was the first of its kind on the continent. With a delightful array of boutiques, chocolatiers, cafes and theatres, intricate architecture and high-end shops, it exudes a timeless charm that attracts both locals and tourists. Do not miss **Tropismes**, Brussels' prettiest bookshop; and have a waffle or *speculoos* biscuit at **Maison Dandoy** or **Mokafé**. Additionally, the Galeries have residential apartments on the upper floors. Fancy living like a resident? We recommend **Hotel des Galeries** or the **Vaudeville B&B**.

EATING IN THE PENTAGON: BUDGET EATS

Mer du Nord/Noordzee: Enjoy your shrimp croquettes at this outdoor venue by a fishmonger's window. *11am-6.30pm Tue-Sun* €

Chouke: Have the best *frites* (chips/fries) in the city centre at this no-frills *fritkot*. Don't miss the homemade burgers. *noon-11pm* €

Tonton Garby: Cheese-loving brothers serve custom sandwiches worth the wait, mixing veggies, fruits and sauces. Friendly, chatty service. *11am-5pm Mon-Fri & Sat* €

Super Fourchette: Vinyl shop meets cafe–*cantine* with homemade, seasonal dishes and a chill vibe. *noon-2pm & 6.30-9.30pm Mon-Fri* €

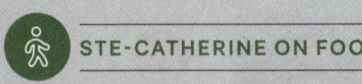 **STE-CATHERINE ON FOOT**

Welcome to Ste-Catherine, one of the oldest Brussels neighbourhoods and former site of the city's inland port.

START	END	LENGTH
Place Ste-Catherine	La Bellone	1km; 45min

Start your walk at ❶ **Place Ste-Catherine**. Until 1854, the square and church area were part of Brussels' port. The city authorities closed it and filled in the basins connected to the Willebroek Canal, which leads to Antwerp. This transformation coincided with the covering of the Senne River and the construction of the Haussmann-inspired Central Boulevards. The current church, designed by Joseph Poelaert, replaced the original one – only the baroque bell tower remains. From here, head to ❷ **Vismet-Marché aux Poissons**, the public space named after the fish market established after the basins were filled in. Though dismantled in the 1950s, the surrounding streets still bear names linked to old merchandise quays. Two artificial basins and several historic fish restaurants recall the area's maritime past. At the end of the second basin, admire the ❸ **Anspach Fountain** with a bas-relief representing an allegory of the Senne River, resting in a tunnel. On the left, notice the Maison du Cheval-Marin, a former inn dating back to the 17th century. Further along, the ❹ **Pigeon Soldat Memorial** pays homage to homing pigeons and their owners during WWI. Next, head to ❺ **Rue de la Cigogne** for Brussels' prettiest street. Rue de Flandre offers an array of good restaurants and independent stores. If open, check out ❻ **La Bellone** for a beautiful surprise.

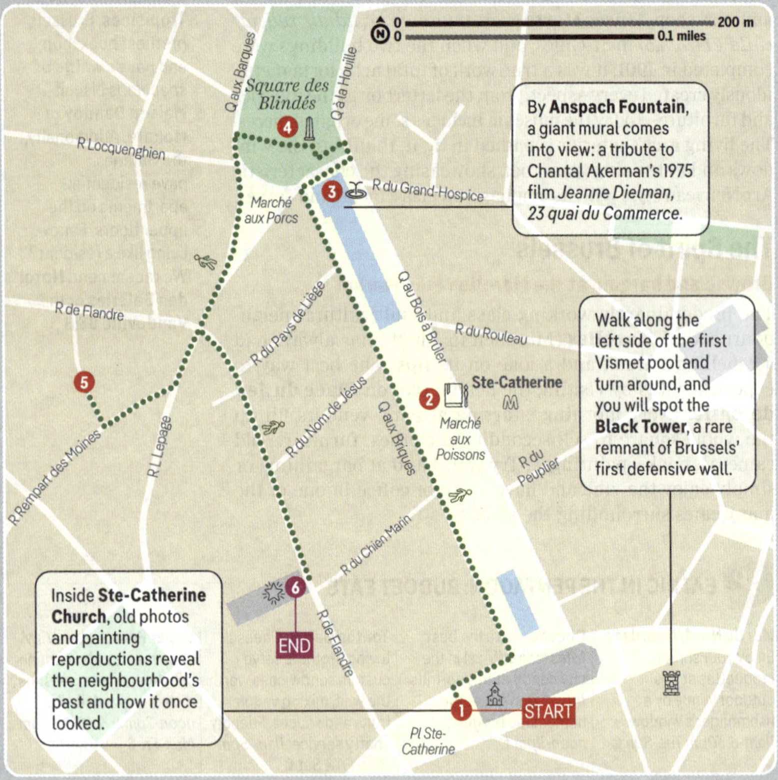

By **Anspach Fountain**, a giant mural comes into view: a tribute to Chantal Akerman's 1975 film *Jeanne Dielman, 23 quai du Commerce*.

Walk along the left side of the first Vismet pool and turn around, and you will spot the **Black Tower**, a rare remnant of Brussels' first defensive wall.

Inside **Ste-Catherine Church**, old photos and painting reproductions reveal the neighbourhood's past and how it once looked.

Map:

N — 0 — 200 m / 0 — 0.1 miles

Q aux Barques
Square des Blindés
Q à la Houille
R Locquenghien
❹
❸ R du Grand-Hospice
Marché aux Porcs
Q au Bois à Brûler
R du Rouleau
R de Flandre
R du Pays de Liège
Ste-Catherine M
❷
Marché aux Poissons
R du Nom de Jésus
Q aux Barques
R du Peuplier
R Rempart des Moines
❺
R L'Escuyer
R du Chien Marin
❻
END
R de Flandre
❶ START
Pl Ste-Catherine

Beyond Brussels

Hop on a train and explore three intriguing cities, rich in history, architecture, and tasty eating and drinking options.

Mechelen (Malines in French) is an unexpected treasure of medieval architecture, with a gorgeous central square, great museums, and an astonishing selection of splendid churches as befits the seat of Belgium's Catholic primate (archbishop equivalent). If possible, time your itinerary so that you over-night here at the weekend which, in complete contrast to Bruges, is when accommodation prices typically fall. Lively Leuven (Louvain in French) elegantly combines history and fun. Today it's home to Flanders' foremost university, and with some 25,000 students in residence between mid-September and June, there's always loads going on.

Places

Mechelen p123
Leuven p124

Mechelen

TIME FROM BRUSSELS: **20MIN** 🚄

Mechelen's Catholic heart

Rising 97m above Mechelen's majestic Grote Markt, the 15th-century tower of **St-Romboutskathedraal** (St-Rombouts Cathedral) is a soaring landmark that you'll find variously framed down gently curved medieval streetscapes. Inside the cathedral there's a 1723 monumental pulpit and a 1630 cruci-fixion scene by Van Dyck.

Beer and history

Mechelen's landmark brewery, **Brouwerij Het Anker**, forms an incongruous addition to the little streets of the city's Grote Begijnhof. But it is heir to a beer-making tradition started here by the *begijns* themselves in 1369. Het Anker beer names are interesting for historico-cultural references relating to Mech-elen's past. There's a well-crafted blonde called Maneblusser meaning 'moon extinguisher' – that's been a self-mocking

---

GETTING AROUND

The main Mechelen train station is around a 20-minute walk south of the Grote Markt. Leuven train and bus stations are a 15-minute walk from the centre straight along Bondgenotenlaan. Dazzling Liège-Guillemins is the main long-distance, high-speed train station, with national and international connections. If you're arriving and want the historic city centre, Liège-St-Lambert station is a more convenient place to alight, though you might need to change at Guillemins.

CHANGE COMES IN WAVES

In 2025, Leuven celebrated the 600th anniversary of its university-city status by installing **Kunst en Wetenschapsroute**, a walking route linking 16 new works of outdoor contemporary art and subtitled in English 'And so, Change comes in Waves'. Many of the artworks are so subtle you need the guide pamphlet to realise that you're actually looking at them. The route starts in the attractive parkland campus around **Arenburg Castle**, where **Dwaaltuin** is the latest monumental artwork by Gijs Van Vaerenbergh. As yet, it's just a monumental steel superstructure, but over coming years the various planted creepers will grow up around the rust-coloured frameworks, creating a circular labyrinth of cascading foliage.

nickname for Mechelen townsfolk since 1687, when cloud-diffused moonlight above the cathedral tower was mistaken for a fire that they tried to put out. The Gouden Carolus range references Holy Roman Emperor 'Golden' Charles V. Ambrio is based on a recipe that was supposedly Charles' favourite ale. Hopsinjoor is a hoppy pun on Op-Sinjoorke, a folklore character.

Leuven

TIME FROM BRUSSELS: **22MIN** 🚆

A Gothic spectacular

Leuven's incredible 15th-century **Stadhuis** is an architectural wedding cake overloaded with terraced turrets, fancy stonework and colourful flags. A phenomenal 235 statues were added in the mid-19th century, each representing a prominent scholar, artist or noble from the city's history.

Flemish Last Supper

If the northwest frontage of the 1425 **St-Pieterskerk** *(free)* looks unfinished, that's because Leuven's unstable subsoil forced builders to abandon plans for a 170m-high tower. However, the interior is lavished with priceless artworks, notably *Het Laatste Avondmaal,* by Leuven-based Flemish Primitive artist Dirk Bouts, who placed Jesus' Last Supper in a typical Flemish dining hall.

Something brewing

Wander into the square called **Oude Markt** any night in the university term time (September to June) and you'll find a surging mass of happy drinkers whose chatter and whoops reverberate around the baroque gables.

Dozens of side-by-side pubs here are collectively nicknamed 'Europe's Longest Bar'. Meanwhile Leuven is home to AB InBev, the world's biggest brewing group. You'll need to pre-book to join a two-hour tour of its vast flagship **Stella Artois Brewery** *(breweryvisits.com; tour €17.50),* usually weekends only. Don't like Stella? Brewery–cafe **Domus** preempted the microbrewery trend decades ago, while **De Blauwe Kater**, open 11am to 2am, has over 100 beers and free blues or jazz gigs on term-time Monday nights.

EATING IN MECHELEN & LEUVEN: OUR PICKS

De Margriet: Courtyard of a historic Mechelen monastery with brasserie-style meals, particularly asparagus or mussels when in season. *11.30am-8.30pm Mon-Sat* €€

Graspoort: Imaginative multicourse 'New World' fusion dinners in atmospheric Mechelen alley, half engulfed by foliage. Close to the Vismarkt. *7-9pm Tue-Sat* €€€

De Werf: Eccentric Leuven student classic, with tables spilling way out into Hogeschoolplein. Popular for back-to-basics fare or just a drink. *9am-9pm Mon-Fri* €

Lukemieke: Serving vegetarian delights for over 50 years in a discreet Leuven townhouse with a rear garden. *noon-2pm & 6-8pm Mon-Fri, closed mid-Jul-mid-Aug* €€

Ghent

MEDIEVAL MASTERPIECES | CANAL-SIDE STROLLS | VIBRANT CULTURE

The seat of the Counts of Flanders, Ghent was a great cloth town that grew to become medieval Europe's largest city after Paris and Constantinople. In the early 19th century, Ghent was the first town in Flanders to harness the Industrial Revolution. Many historical buildings were converted into flax- and cotton-processing mills and the city became known as the 'Manchester of the Continent' after its industrial equivalent in England.

Despite being one of Belgium's most historic cities, Ghent remains small enough to feel cosy but big enough to be a vibrant, relevant centre for trade and culture. There's a wealth of medieval and classical architecture here, contrasted by postindustrial areas undergoing urban renewal that give the city a gritty-but-good industrial feel.

In the centre, tourists remain surprisingly thin on the ground, but Ghent's large student and youth population means there are always people about, enjoying the city's fabulous canal-side architecture, abundance of quirky bars and restaurants, and some of Belgium's best museums.

GETTING AROUND

Ghent's city centre is relatively large, but the different districts are well connected by public transport, including smoothly gliding modern trams. Download the De Lijn app *(delijn.be/en)* to find routes, buy tickets and consult up-to-date information.

Head into Ghent's Past

Medieval monuments

Ghent's UNESCO-listed 14th-century **Belfort** *(historische huizen.stad.gent/en/belfry; adult/child €11/2.20)* or belfry stands 91m high and is topped by a huge and magnificent dragon weather-vane; he's become something of a city mascot. You'll meet two previous dragon incarnations on the 350-stair climb to the top; there are elevators to help some of the way. Enter through the **Lakenhalle**, Ghent's cloth hall that was left half-built in 1445 and only completed in 1903. Hear the carillon at 11.30am Fridays and 11am on summer Sundays.

Flanders' quintessential 12th-century stone castle, the **Gravensteen** *(historischehuizen.stad.gent/en/castle-counts;*

☑ **TOP TIP**

CityCard Gent *(48/72hr €42/48)* gives free entrance to all of Ghent's top museums and monuments and allows unlimited travel on trams and city buses, plus a boat trip and a day's free bike hire. It's excellent value. Buy one at participating museums, major bus offices or the **tourist office**.

★ **HIGHLIGHTS**
1 Belfort
2 Gravensteen
3 The Adoration of the Mystic Lamb

● **SIGHTS**
4 Grasbrug
5 Sint-Baafskathedraal

● **ACTIVITIES**
6 Rederij De Gentenaer

● **SLEEPING**
7 1898 The Post
8 Simon Says
9 Uppelink

● **EATING**
10 't Oud Clooster

● **DRINKING & NIGHTLIFE**
11 Mokabon
12 Rococo

● **ENTERTAINMENT**
13 Handelsbeurs Concert Hall
14 VIERNULVIER

● **INFORMATION**
15 Ghent Tourist Office

adult/child €13/2.70), comes complete with fairy-tale moat, turrets and arrow slits. It's all the more remarkable considering that during the 19th century the site was converted into a cotton mill. Meticulously restored since, the interior sports the odd suit of armour, a guillotine and torture devices. The lack of furnishings is compensated for with a handheld 45-minute movie guide, which sets a tongue-in-cheek historical costumed drama in the rooms, prison pit and battlements. There's a great castle viewpoint on St-Widostraat.

The Mystic Lamb

Flemish Primitive masterpiece

Housed in the towering interior of **Sint-Baafskathedraal** *(sintbaafskathedraal.be; adult/child €16/8),* the Van Eyck brothers' 1432 Flemish Primitive masterpiece **The Adoration of the Mystic Lamb** is one of the earliest-known oil paintings. Completed in 1432, it has 20 luminous panels, which are in the process of a remarkable restoration.

The work represents an allegorical glorification of Christ's death: on the upper tier sits God the Father flanked by the

UHRYN LARYSA/SHUTTERSTOCK

Grasbrug bridge

Virgin and John the Baptist. On the outer panels are the nude Adam and Eve. The lower tier centres on the lamb, symbolising the sacrifice made by Christ, surrounded by religious figures and a landscape dotted with local church towers.

On the Water

Canals, bridges and boat trips

To admire Ghent's towers and gables at their most photogenic, stand just west of the little **Grasbrug** bridge over the Leie river at dusk. The appealing waterfront facades of Graslei aren't as old as they look – they were largely rebuilt to make Ghent look good for the 1913 World Fair.

Join a traditional guided **boat tour** from companies including **Rederij De Gentenaer** (*rederijdegentenaer.be; €10*). These tours take you around the city in 45 minutes to an hour, showing all the highlights with some explanation from a local.

LIVE MUSIC IN GHENT

Liz Aku, Ghent resident, singer and music teacher, reveals her favourite live-music spots. *@lizakumusic*

Bar Bricolage: Urban oasis in Ghent's Old Docks, with sandy boardwalk paths, cultural programming, live DJs and a relaxed campfire atmosphere.

VIERNULVIER: Known for concerts and parties, particularly in the Concert Hall and the new Club Wintercircus.

Handelsbeurs Concert Hall: Beautifully restored venue: intimate setting for jazz, world, soul and acoustic performances.

Gentse Feesten: One of Europe's largest cultural festivals: 10-day celebration; free live music on every corner, from folk to punk to techno. Crowded but amazing experience for all ages.

 DRINKING IN GHENT: BEST BROWN CAFES & COFFEE SHOPS

't Oud Clooster: Atmospheric double-level cafe was once a nunnery. Well-priced meals presented with style. *11.30am–2.30pm & 6-10.15pm Mon-Sat*€€

Mokabon: Ghent's classic old-world coffee shop still serves old-school Belgian coffee with whipped cream. *9am-6pm*€

Rococo: Lit by candles, this classic late-night cafe–bar with carved wooden ceilings is ideal for cosy midnight conversations. *9pm-late Tue-Sun*€€

De Geus van Gent: Congenial cafe with eclectic decor and 20 beers from the barrel. It hosts regular jam nights and live music. *4pm-3am Mon-Fri, 7pm-3am Sat*€

Bruges

GETTING AROUND

The medieval city centre is compact, and walking around it is one of the major pleasures of a visit. The relatively quiet streets also make this a great place to explore by bike. If you're coming from the station, hop on city bus 1 or 2, both of which make loops through the city centre (you can make contactless payments on board), or take a taxi to your hotel.

If you set out to design a fairy-tale medieval town, it would be hard to improve on central Bruges (Brugge in Dutch), one of Europe's best-preserved cities. Picturesque cobbled lanes and dreamy canals link photogenic market squares lined with soaring towers, historical churches and lane after lane of old white-washed almshouses. Medieval Flemish painters were perhaps the first to use oil paint, kicking off a tradition that rivals that of Renaissance Italy. Bruges' galleries and museums are simply outstanding, with many boldly incorporating contemporary works into their historic collections.

For many, though, the Bruges secret is already out; during the busy summer months, you'll be sharing the magic with a constant stream of tourists in the medieval core. To really enjoy Bruges, stay one or two nights – day-trippers miss out on the city's stunning nocturnal floodlighting – and try to visit midweek to avoid weekend crowds.

The Historic Heart of Bruges

Marvellous Markt

The heart of ancient Bruges, **Markt**, the old market square, is lined with pavement cafes beneath step-gabled facades. The buildings aren't always quite as medieval as they look, but together they create a fabulous scene; even the neogothic former post office is architecturally magnificent. The urban panorama is dominated by the 13th-century **Belfort** *(visitbruges.be/nl/belfort; adult/child €15/13)*, towering 83m above the square like a gigantic medieval rocket. There's relatively little to see inside, but it's worth the mildly claustrophobic 366-step climb for the fine views. Look out through wide-gauge chicken wire for panoramas across the spires and red-tiled rooftops towards the wind turbines and giant cranes of Zeebrugge.

The **Historium** *(historium.be; adult/child €26/18)* occupies a neogothic building on the northern side of the Markt. The immersive one-hour audio and video tour aims to take you

☑ TOP TIP

The best times to visit are in spring, when daffodils carpet the tranquil courtyard of the historic *begijnhof* retreat, or outside of Christmas in winter, when you'll have the magnificent, if icy, town almost all to yourself.

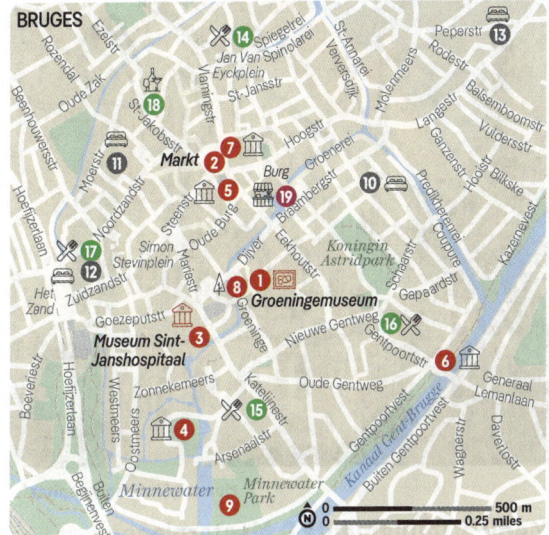

BRUGES

Markt
Burg
Koningin Astridpark
Groeningemuseum
Museum Sint-Janshospitaal
Minnewater
Minnewater Park

0 500 m
0 0.25 miles

⭐ **HIGHLIGHTS**
1 Groeningemuseum
2 Markt
3 Museum Sint-Janshospitaal

🔴 **SIGHTS**
4 Begijnhof
5 Belfort
6 Gentpoort
7 Historium
8 Hof Arents

9 Minnewater

⚫ **SLEEPING**
10 B&B Amaryllis Dieltiens
11 Dukes' Palace
12 Passage Bruges
13 St Christopher's Inn Hostel at The Bauhaus

🟢 **EATING**
14 Blackbird

15 De Bron
16 Patisserie Schaeverbeke
17 That's Toast

🟢 **DRINKING & NIGHTLIFE**
18 De Republiek

🔴 **SHOPPING**
19 Vismarkt

WHY I LOVE BRUGES

Helena Smith, Lonely Planet writer

Bruges is often compared to Venice; both cities are big on canals, Golden Age splendours – and overtourism. But the reason I love both cities is that you can duck down a canal and feel quite alone. Bruges is the kind of place where getting lost is half the fun, and finding your way back is half the fun again. Escape the crowds and venture further afield than Markt or Burg in any direction; you'll have no trouble finding alleys, shops and sights to pique your interest. I enjoy escaping the busy centre on hot summer days and swimming in the Coupure canal, a surreally magical experience in this fairy-tale city.

---

back to medieval Bruges; a fictional love story gives narrative structure, and you can nose around Van Eyck's studio, among other pseudo-historic experiences.

Not So Primitive Art

Artistic highlights in Bruges

The **Groeningemuseum** (*museabrugge.be/en/visit-our-museums/our-museums-and-monuments/groeningemuseum; adult/youth €15/13*) covers a huge sweep of art history, but is best known for its paintings by Flemish Primitives Jan Van Eyck, Rogier Van der Weyden, Hans Memling and Gerard David. These artists depicted the affluence and beauty of Bruges to brilliant effect. Van Eyck's portraits, like those of his counterparts, reflect the abundance of the city, while adding a further dimension of psychological depth. Memling's epic *Moreel Triptych* (1484) is one of the first large-scale group portraits ever painted.

NATALIYA NAZAROVA/SHUTTERSTOCK

Museum Sint-Janshospitaal

Medical Implements & Masterpieces

Preserved hospital building featuring Memling art

In the restored chapel of a 12th-century hospital building, the **Museum Sint-Janshospitaal** *(visitbruges.be/en/sint-janshospitaal-saint-johns-hospital; adult/child €15/7)* shows various torturous medical implements, a hospital sedan chair and a gruesome 1679 painting of an anatomy class. It also incorporates contemporary pieces such as Berlinde De Bruyckere's fallen archangel, a crumple of feathers with fragile legs emerging; and deeply moving video works muse on illness, death and mourning. But most eyes are on seven masterpieces by 15th-century artist Hans Memling, including the enchanting reliquary of St Ursula, which looks like a miniature Gothic cathedral.

 EATING IN BRUGES: VEGAN & VEGGIE-FRIENDLY

Blackbird: All-vegan cafe serving bagels, bountiful happiness bowls, pancakes, fresh juices and cakes. *9am-3pm Wed-Sat, 9.30am-1pm Sun* €

De Bron: By the time this glass-roofed restaurant's doors open, there's a queue of diners keen to get vegetarian fare from *de bron* (the source). *11.45am-2pm Mon-Fri* €

De Republiek: This is a big, buzzing modern bistro with great vegan choices on the menu. *noon-1am Wed-Sun, from 5pm Mon-Tue* €€

That's Toast: Bruges' best breakfast restaurant has gained a following for its all-day brekkies, with several vegan options. *8.30am-4pm Wed-Sun* €€

BRUGES PARKS & CANALS

This walk links some of Bruges' entrancing green spaces, by way of secluded lanes and canals.

START	END	LENGTH
Vismarkt	Vismarkt	3.4km; 2–3hr

The handsome colonnaded 1821 **①** **Vismarkt** (fish market) is still open for business most days. Check out pretty Huidenvettersplein, ringed with archetypal Bruges buildings.

Walk south along Jozef Suvéestraat for a few minutes until you reach local hangout **②** **Koningin Astridpark**, named after the Swedish wife of King Léopold of Belgium; you'll come across her bust when you reach the park. Walking through the park you'll pass a community radio station, bandstand and adventure playground. Beyond the Gothic revival Magdalen Church is scrumptious Patisserie Schaeverbeke. Continue south to **③** **Gentpoort**, one of the town's four medieval gateways. From here, a pleasant footpath leads through the greenery along the water's edge. Follow the

path west until you reach **④** **Minnewater** and its eponymous park, a scenic green space with orderly flowerbeds and secluded paths.

Just north of the park, Wijngaardplein, a touristy but still irresistible square, is ringed by cafes. Over the little arched bridge from the square, the 13th-century **⑤** *begijnhof* is one of the delights of Bruges, its whitewashed buildings encircling a garden with tall trees and swathes of daffodils in spring. It's well worth visiting the church here.

One of the prettiest of this pretty city's hangout spots, **⑥** **Hof Arents** features a humpback bridge, and the clattering hooves of passing carriages that call here. From here, it's a short stroll back to Vismarkt.

Fishmongers have sold North Sea produce at **Vismarkt** for centuries, though now only a few set up on the cold stone slabs.

Look out for the horses' bronze counterparts in the form of Rik Poot's 1987 **Four Horsemen of the Apocalypse** sculptures.

Wijngaardplein
Don't miss the horse fountain – sculpted horses' heads spurt water to fill buckets for the real-life horses.

Beyond
Bruges

Nip up to the coast at Ostend, wander the historic city of Kortrijk or explore WWI history in Ypres.

Places

Ostend p132
Kortrijk p133
Ypres p133

In a region with excellent public transport and short distances between cities and sights, Bruges makes a great jumping-off point to sample the region. Ostend is the focus of the Belgian coast, with wide sand beaches and some fantastic art attractions; take the coastal tram to fascinating Atlantikwall Raversyde to see preserved bunkers and lookouts from both wars. The city of Kortrijk isn't well known on any tourist circuit, but its beautiful historic core and standout textile museum make the place well worth a visit. Entirely rebuilt following WWI, the town of Ypres stands testament to the folly of war; and its major museum, In Flanders Fields, is a sombre but unmissable stop.

GETTING AROUND

Ostend is a quick train trip from Bruges; you can explore Atlantikwall Raversyde and travel to other coastal towns on the Coastal Tram operated by De Lijn *(delijn.be/en)*, a marvellously smooth and frequent service that swooshes you through backstreets and points along the seafront. Kortrijk is a slightly longer train ride away; you'll probably change trains here en route to Ypres, so you could stop for a few hours or overnight on your way to battlefield sites.

Ostend

TIME FROM BRUGES: **14MIN**

Artistic Ostend

Mu.Zee *(muzee.be; adult/child €12/3),* Ostend's foremost gallery, features the work of predominantly local artists. There's a significant collection by symbolist painter Léon Spilliaert (1881–1946), whose most brooding works are reminiscent of Edvard Munch.

But the artistic highlight of Ostend is the house museum dedicated to symbolist artist James Ensor. The **James Ensor House** *(ensorhuis.be; €13/6)* is the place where Ensor worked and lived for the last 32 years of his life. You can visit the artist's painting-lined and object-filled rooms, as well as the bizarrely appealing shop run by his parents.

Bunkers in the dunes

Gripping **Atlantikwall Raversyde** *(raversyde.be/en; adult/child €10/4)* is a remarkably extensive complex of WWI and WWII bunkers, gun emplacements and linking brick tunnels created by occupying German forces. Most bunkers are furnished and 'operated' by waxwork figures, and there's a detailed audio-guide explanation. This is one of Belgium's best and most underrated war sites, but you'll need around two hours and reasonable fitness to make the most of the 2km walking circuit. Take the coastal tram to Domein Raversijde.

Kortrijk

TIME FROM BRUGES: **47MIN**

Serene *begijnhof*

Small but utterly delightful, Kortrijk's enclosed ***begijnhof*** is as charming a cluster of whitewashed old terraced houses as you could hope to find. Designed for single women, the complex was founded by Johanna of Constantinople way back in 1238. The last member of the community died in 2013, and the buildings were restored and now provide affordable housing.

Get in touch with the Texture museum

It's well worth the walk to **Texture** *(texturekortrijk.be; adult/child €8/6),* located in a 1902 flax factory. This museum focuses on the town's flax and linen industry; you'll also see a lovely collection of damasks and laces. The history of flax is told through individual accounts and is surprisingly absorbing; you can touch and smell the fabric itself. The beautifully converted building uses flax chipboard and linen drapes in homage to the museum's content.

Ypres

TIME FROM BRUGES: **1HR 45MIN**

Great War experience

In Flanders Fields Museum *(inflandersfields.be; €12/6)* contains a wealth of letters, household objects, military equipment, maps, newspapers and memorabilia pertaining to WWI. But the real stars of the show are the striking video installations illustrating how families and soldiers on both sides experienced the horrors of the Great War. The audio guide *(per person €2)* includes additional, in-depth listening points. Expect to spend at least two hours here.

THE BATTLE OF THE GOLDEN SPURS

Flanders' French overlords were incensed by the Bruges Matins massacre of May 1302. Philip the Fair, the French king, promptly sent a well-equipped cavalry of aristocratic knights to seek retribution. Outside Kortrijk on 11 July this magnificent force met a ragged, lightly armed force of weavers, peasants and guild members from Bruges, Ypres, Ghent and Kortrijk. But the horseback knights failed to notice a trap: the Flemish townsfolk had disguised a boggy marsh with brushwood. Snared by the mud, the heavily armoured French were immobilised and slaughtered. The event became a symbol of Flemish resistance, and to this day 11 July is celebrated as Flanders' 'national' holiday.

Don't miss the paintings upstairs of Ostend locals.

 EATING IN OSTEND, KORTRIJK & YPRES: OUR PICKS

De Ruyffelaer: Traditional local dishes in a wood-panelled place in Ypres. Chequerboard floors, vintage decor. *11.30am-3.30pm Sun, 5.30-9.30pm Fri-Sun* €€

Frituur Franky: Lovers of the humble fry are spoiled for choice at this excellent Ostend *frituur* (chip shop). *noon-2pm & 5.30-11pm Tue-Sat, 5-10pm Sun* €

't Mouterijtje: Spacious Kortrijk brasserie with bare brickwork: good beers and signature dish *côte-à-l'os* (rib roast). *5pm-midnight Fri-Tue* €€

Bistro Beau-Site: Ostend cafe with jazz on the stereo and art books. Upstairs window seats have beach views. *11am-7pm Mon, Wed & Thu, noon-late Fri-Sun* €€

Antwerp

HIGH FASHION | RUBENS PAINTINGS | LIVE MUSIC

 TOP TIP

Antwerp City Pass
*(antwerpcitypass.be;
24/48/72hr €45/55/65)*
allows entry to over 20
key attractions plus free
public transport. It might
make sense if you're
visiting Chocolate Nation,
De Ruien and De Koninck
Brewery. But almost all
other Antwerp museums
are included in the all-
Belgium **MuseumPass**
*(museumpassmusees.
be; €64.95)*, which lasts a
whole year.

Belgium's second city is also its capital of cool, a
fashion hub and world-leading diamond-trading hub,
yet it still retains an exquisite medieval heart. By the
16th-century Antwerp had taken over from Bruges
as one of Europe's main trading ports, opening the
world's first specially built stock exchange. From the
1560s, iconoclasts, the Dutch Revolt and the inquisition devastated the place, exacerbated later by a
blockade of Antwerp's port. Skilled workers and international trade fled north (hence Amsterdam's rise).
Still, the world's first newspaper was produced here
in 1606, and Rubens hung around to paint baroque
masterpieces. Once the port blockade finally ended
in 1863, wealth quickly returned, and by the 1920s
Antwerp was important enough to host the Olympic
Games and build Europe's first skyscraper. WWII
destroyed much and decimated the significant Jewish
population, but Antwerp rebounded, and today few
cities have a more optimistic 21st-century vision.

Medieval Marvels

Antwerp's antique heart

Other than Europe's first skyscraper (the 1929 Boerentoren), central Antwerp's architecture remains relatively low-rise, such that
the 16th-century belfry of **Onze-Lieve-Vrouwekathedraal**
majestically dominates the cityscape. Ornately magnificent, the

---

GETTING AROUND

Beautiful **Antwerpen-Centraal** is the main
train hub and the nearest station to the
old city centre. Antwerpen-Berchem is a
possible alternative for the Art Nouveau
area of Zurenborg. Antwerpen-Zuid is
marginally nearer Het Zuid. Antwerp has a
well-developed bus and tram system, known

as 'pre-metro' when tunnelling underground.
The easiest way to explore the main sights is
to use the Velo short-hop bicycle-hire system
(velo-antwerpen.be/en). Bike pickup and
drop-off stands are plentiful and the system is
unusually easy to use.

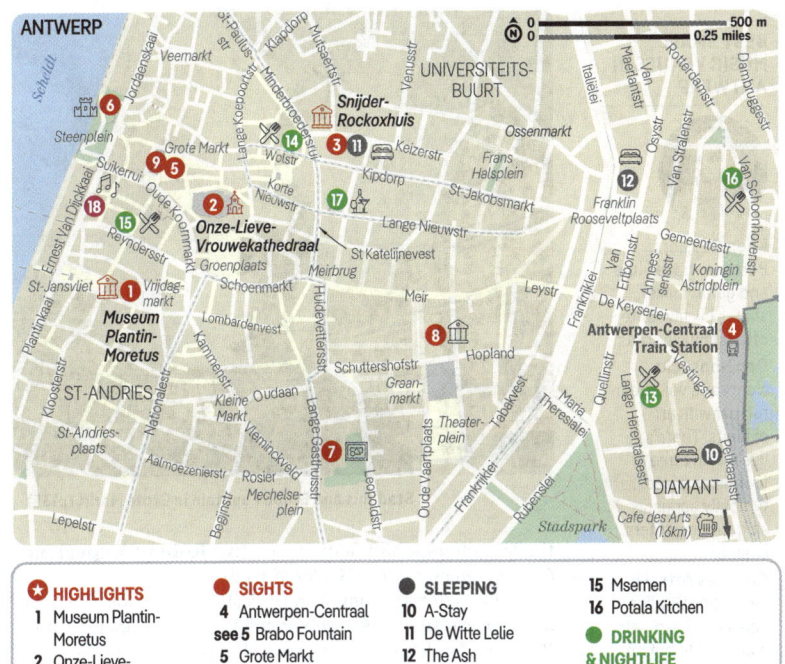

ANTWERP

UNIVERSITEITS-BUURT

HIGHLIGHTS
1 Museum Plantin-Moretus
2 Onze-Lieve-Vrouwekathedraal
3 Snijder-Rockoxhuis

SIGHTS
4 Antwerpen-Centraal
see 5 Brabo Fountain
5 Grote Markt
6 Het Steen
7 Maagdenhuis
8 Rubenshuis
9 Stadhuis

SLEEPING
10 A-Stay
11 De Witte Lelie
12 The Ash

EATING
13 Aahaar
14 Jam

15 Msemen
16 Potala Kitchen

DRINKING & NIGHTLIFE
17 Den Beulebak

ENTERTAINMENT
18 Den Hopsack

123m tower has a habit of popping into view from all kinds of intriguing angles. The cathedral itself is a Gothic masterpiece that took 169 years to finish (1352–1521).

The small streets around the cathedral are abuzz with cafe life, with bars also spilling onto the main market square, **Grote Markt** – a beautiful cobbled space that's lined on three sides by classic step-gabled medieval-style merchant houses. Behind the **Brabo Fountain** is the **Stadhuis**, Antwerp's 1565 city hall with a statue-topped palatial facade that blends Flemish and Italian styles. Inside is a fascinating, map-rich exhibition *(free)* about the city's development, setting out ambitious plans for the future.

Het Steen is Antwerp's dinky but photogenic castle dating from 1200. It contains a tourist office and free-access viewpoint.

Artistic Pedigree

Local artists: Rubens, Van Dyck and Breugel

Peter Paul Rubens (1577–1640) moved to Antwerp in 1609 after lengthy studies in Italy. The house–studio he designed is now the memorable **Rubenshuis** *(rubenshuis.be),* which is undergoing a restoration project until around 2027: meanwhile

BEST SMALL MUSIC VENUES IN ANTWERP

Koen Cassiers, Berchem-based lute and guitar maker, shares his favourite offbeat music spots.

Den Hopsack: Nonprofit, volunteer-run bar with art exhibits. There's live music three or four times a week, typically acoustic singer-songwriters or jazz.

Cafe des Arts: For years, tiny Gitanes cafe on Draakplaats managed to put on little concerts which were essentially rehearsals for the bands. Now the gigs have moved to co-owned Cafe des Arts near Berchem Station, with jazz most Sundays and who knows what on Friday nights.

Den Beulebak: This cute 16th-century building, on a hidden but central courtyard square called St Nikolaasplaats, hosts occasional offbeat folk-music gigs.

Stadhuis and Brabo Fountain in Grote Markt (p135)

the site offers a half-hour interactive **Rubens Experience** *(adult/concession €12/8; closed Wed).*

Antoon (later Anthony) Van Dyck (1599–1641) was the son of an Antwerp silk dealer who honed his art in Rubens' studio. Both Van Dyck and Rubens are well represented at the splendid 17th-century **Snijder-Rockoxhuis** *(snijdersrockoxhuis. be; adult/under-26 €10/6),* gallery–museum.

Dutch-born Pieter Breugel the Elder (c 1525–69) made his home in Antwerp from 1555, and the city still houses several of his masterpieces, notably his brilliantly grotesque 1561 *Dulle Griet* (Mad Meg). See his work at the **Maagdenhuis** *(maagdenhuis.be; adult/under-26 €10/6),* a former 16th-century orphanage/refuge.

The Print Pioneer

The world's oldest surviving presses

In a building that was a print shop from the 1550s, **Museum Plantin-Moretus** *(museumplantinmoretus.be; adult/under-26/under-18 €12/8/free),* retains half a dozen antique presses, including two that are the oldest still in existence anywhere. The medieval building is memorable in itself, with its gilt-leather 'wallpaper', 1622 courtyard garden and 1640 library, not to mention the fabulous collection of paintings.

 EATING IN ANTWERP: BUDGET EATS

Jam: Fresh, imaginative cafe (and terrace) serving flavour-packed snack-lunches inspired by world travels. *11am-6pm Thu-Mon* €

Aahaar: The €12 buffet of authentic Indian vegetarian food is a budget traveller's delight. Good mango lassis. Zero score for decor. *noon-3pm & 5.30-9.30pm* €

Msemen: Moroccan stuffed puff-pastries served with mint tea and tasty harira soup in an invitingly light, bright interior or rear garden. *11am-7.30pm Tue-Sun* €

Potala Kitchen: Simple but great-value Tibetan, Chinese and Pan-Asian meals, mostly costing under €10. On the station area's 'Chinatown' strip. *noon-10pm Thu-Mon* €

Wallonia

INTRIGUING TOWNS | SPORTY OUTDOORS | FORTRESSES

Wallonia is a place of contradictions. It is Belgium's outdoorsy rural underbelly but also the home to cities with heavy industries that brought the country wealth before decaying into an economic malaise during the 1980s. The carnivals are wild (Binche, in particular), the mindset humorous and the language a form of French that amuses visitors from France. Mons is one of Belgium's underrated cultural gems with a crazy dragon-slaying festival to boot – La Ducasse – while Wallonia's capital, Namur, has a lively cultural vibe and an urban cable car that can whisk you to the top of its signature fortress-citadel. Though scarred by 20th-century eyesores, Liège was once an independent prince bishopric and has complex historical layers that reward patient discovery. Spa is the original spa, and there are fortresses galore, from medieval castles to grand châteaux and more recent fortifications.

GETTING AROUND

Train connections are fine for Mons, Liège, Verviers, Namur and Tournai. There's a regular bus to Waterloo from Brussels and river-buses are a pleasure in Namur and Liège. In contrast to much of Flanders, having a car is a great advantage in Wallonia, where many of the attractions are rural and/or awkward to reach by public transport. Free parking is common.

Waterloo

Site of Napoleon's downfall

As you enter the main battlefield site, **Mémorial 1815** *(wat erloo1815.be; adult/under-18/under-10 €24/12/free),* you appear to be descending into the earth. Collect a lanyard to facilitate multimedia quizzes and connect to the internal wi-fi to access *visit.io* on your smartphone for written and spoken extra coverage. Suitably equipped, the museum section then explains the Battle of Waterloo's historical context, from the Enlightenment to the rise of revolutionary France. Then a parade of life-sized soldiers lead you to a 3D film – an intense experience in which you feel really in the thick of the fighting. Then there's a whole lot more about the battle and its repercussions.

Still within Mémorial 1815, continue to the contrastingly old-fashioned **Panorama de la Bataille**, a circular diorama of the battle painted in 1912. It comes complete with sound effects and foreground models of fallen troops and horses. You can

☑ **TOP TIP**

La Roche-en-Ardenne is the mountain-biking capital of the Benelux region. It has some good road-biking routes too, and there are plenty more in the Haute Fagnes area, with riders often basing themselves at Malmédy.

also climb the historical **Lion's Mound**, a memorial erected in the 1820s at the request of the Dutch king, whose son who had been injured while assisting Wellington in the battle here.

Mons

Up at the belfry

Mons hosts four UNESCO-listed features, including one of Europe's most memorable festivals. The medieval city developed around the hilltop site of a Roman camp.

On the highest point of the town, partly ringed by remnant fortifications, the **belfry** (*beffroi.mons.be; adult/senior/under-12 €9/6/free*) is a focal point that marks out Mons from kilometres around. There are great views without climbing it, but paying for entry gets you a lift to the 5th floor, with even finer panoramas and touchscreen view identifiers.

Namur

Bastions and tunnels

The **Citadelle de Namur** covers a whole hillside. To learn more about the city's history – and the fortress, in particular

Its speciality is pork 'berdoulle', ie smothered in thick mustard-onion-tarragon dressing.

 EATING IN WATERLOO, MONS & NAMUR: OUR PICKS

Brasserie de Waterloo: Bistro fare plus beers and spirits created on the premises in this battlefield farmstead. *11am–11pm Wed-Sat, 10.30am-7pm Sun* €€

Chez les Filles: Sweet spot between comfort food and gastronomy. Cosy shop-house on Mons' main dining street. *noon-2.30pm Wed-Sun & 6.30-10pm Wed-Sat* €€

Henri: Mons home-cooking that's been a favourite with local families since 1956. Lunch plates €8.50, cash only. *noon-2pm daily & 6.30-9pm Wed-Sat* €

Le Panorama: High in the Namur citadel, this airy pavilion does a varied menu, ranging from snacks to brasserie-style dishes. *11am-last customer* €€

– it's worth starting a visit at the **Terra Nova visitor centre** *(citadelle.namur.be; adult/student €6/5)*. Audio guides cover the key features, though if you speak French there's a lot more to learn from the swirling information boards.

With a Citadelle Pass *(adult/student €18/16)* you can also visit part of the **souterrains**, a fascinating web of dripping tunnels into which the fortress moved the majority of its key installations in more recent iterations. Guides help bring the past to life using audio-visual displays and 3-D wall projections. Temperatures hover around 13°C (55°F), so dress appropriately.

Liège

Light up the mountain

The sprawling city of Liège is like a living architectural onion, with layer upon layer of history lying beneath a craggily scarred facade; in mid-August look out for the wild **Outremeuse** festival. **Montagne de Bueren** is one of the world's most daunting public stairways, with 374 steps rising vertiginously behind Rue Hors Chateau. On the first Saturday of October, this remarkable sight is transformed into a twinkling beauty during the **Nocturne des Coteaux**, when some 20,000 candles are lit on the steps.

A severed head

In a beautifully adapted cloister-convent, the **Musée de la Vie Wallonne** *(viewallonne.be; adult/concession €7/5)* is thematically chaotic but still the best museum in Liège. In a darkened chamber is the ghoulish showstopper: an original guillotine, and the mummified head of the last man to have felt 'her kiss'.

Spa

The spa at Spa

The **Thermes de Spa** *(thermesdespa.com; 3hr €32)* is the city's contemporary spa centre, located on the hilltop directly above the town centre. It's an indulgent complex of indoor and outdoor baths, hammams and saunas. The centrepiece is a giant, light-filled pool with tall glass windows to contemplate the view. The fun way to arrive from town is by a little funicular *(return €3)* from beside the **Van Der Valk Hotel**.

WATERLOO BATTLE REENACTMENTS

In late June 2025, over 2000 men dressed up in early-19th-century military costumes and replayed scenes from the 1815 battle beside the Lion's Mound. Reenactments on this scale take place every five years, with a grandstand erected for ticketed onlookers *(€42-55)* and a running commentary. Still in character, the 'soldiers' camp overnight at La Cailliou (Napoleonic) and Hougoumont (allies), and a visit to these 'Bivouacs' (also ticketed) is nearly as interesting than the battle show.

In the four years between big reenactments, smaller ones take place, show-fighting around the gates of Hougoumont with around 200 or so participants. The exact weekend (late June/early July) depends on Belgian holidays.

EATING & DRINKING IN LIÈGE & SPA: OUR PICKS

Amon Nanesse/Maison du Pékèt: Rambling antique Liège house with pub fare. Tasters of local gins. *bar 9am-late daily, food noon-2pm & 6-10pm Thu-Mon* €

Brasserie {c}: Medieval buildings that are tasting rooms for Liège's Curtius beer range, but also popular for Belgian food, burgers and *café liégeois*. *noon-11pm Thu-Sun* €€

Little Arthur: Cosy Spa cafe with piled cushions, William Morris wallpaper and a selection of dessert tarts and quiches. *9am-6pm Fri-Tue* €

Rest'O des Amis: Mixing Belgian brasserie and Italian culinary influences to create a locals' dining favourite in the heart of Spa. *11.30am-9pm Wed-Sun* €€

Luxembourg City

☑ TOP TIP

Although the languages you'll most likely encounter are French and German (plus English and Portuguese in some places), Luxembourg's own Germanic language, Luxembourgish (Lëtzebuergesch) is spoken by around 430,000 people. One key word to learn is the general-purpose greeting *'Moien!'*

If you were expecting a city dominated by high-rise banks and anonymous corporate HQ buildings, Luxembourg City will prove a refreshingly charming revelation. The city's old city is in fact a UNESCO-listed layer-cake of bastion walls, footpaths and viewpoints terraced steeply down through parks and fortress remnants to the deep-cut Alzette and Pétrusse river valleys. These scenes are surveyed from many a viewpoint and panoramic walkway, most notably the Chemin de la Corniche, which has been nicknamed the 'most beautiful balcony of Europe'. The atmospheric Grund quarter lies at the riverside below, and it's only when you cross the giant red road bridge (Pont-Grande-Duchesse Charlotte) that you reach the contrastingly brash glass towers of the EU quarter on the Kirchberg Plateau. Add in summer festivals, great art, fine museums and totally free public transport – you don't even pay for the funicular – and you have a gem of a discovery.

Fit for a Grand Duke

The Grand-Ducal palace, inside and out

Luxembourg's hereditary head of state has their office in the **Palais Grand-Ducal**. Built in 1572 as the town hall, an annex was added in 1860 that today houses the Luxembourg Chamber of Deputies (ie parliament). The main building has served as

 GETTING AROUND

Free transport around town includes a useful modern tram linking the main train station and airport via bus hubs and the Kirchberg EU district. Transport systems are completely integrated across the city and the whole Grand Duchy, with real-time best-choice connections given through the *mobiliteit.lu* app.

A funicular and two tall public elevators are handy for dealing with steep cliff ascents. These all run very frequently till 1am.

You do have to pay to use the Velóh *(myveloh.lu)* short-hop shared bicycle-hire scheme: €2/5 for one/three days then free for rides of up to 30 minutes.

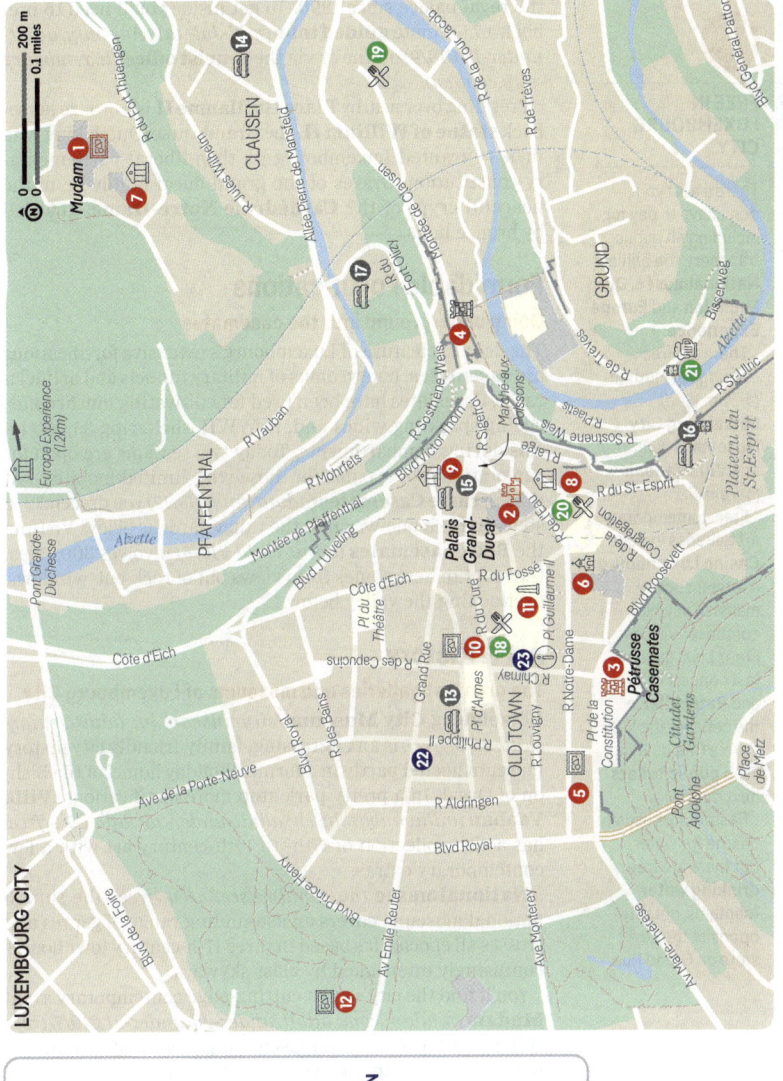

LUXEMBOURG CITY

★ HIGHLIGHTS
1. Mudam
2. Palais Grand-Ducal
3. Pétrusse Casemates

● SIGHTS
4. Bock Casemates
5. Casino Luxembourg
6. Cathédrale Notre-Dame
7. Dräi Eechelen
8. Lëtzebuerg City Museum
9. Nationalmusée
10. Statue of William II
11. Villa Vauban

● SLEEPING
12. Hôtel Les Jardins d'Anaïs
13. Hôtel Français
14. Hôtel Parc Beaux-Arts
15. La Pipistrelle
16. Youth Hostel, Luxembourg City

● EATING
17. Beim Renert
18. Big Beer Company
19. Pizzeria Bacchus

● DRINKING & NIGHTLIFE
20. Scott's

● INFORMATION
21. Drinking water
see 10. Free public toilets
22. Luxembourg City Tourist Office

the royal palace since 1890. To get inside you'll need to pre-book a 75-minute **guided tour** *(mid-Jul–late Aug only, adult/under-13 €18/9)* online or via the **tourist office** *(luxembourg-city.com/en)*.

Presiding over nearby **Place Guillaume II** is a bronze horse-back **statue of William II**, the Grand Duke/Dutch king who in 1841 granted Luxembourg its then-liberal parliamentary constitution. Graves of the grand ducal family lie in the peaceful crypt of the **Cathédrale Notre-Dame**, guarded by bronze lions.

Formidable Fortifications

Going underground into the casemates

The defining feature of Luxembourg's extensive fortifications are **casemates**, honeycombs of military tunnels and artificial caves. Casemates have been used for cultivating mushrooms, ageing sparkling wines and, in WWII, sheltering 35,000 locals during bombardments. Today two sections are open for exploration (not feasible for those with limited mobility). At the **Pétrusse Casemates** *(adult/child €18/12)* you descend 242 steps and exit one-way into the valley gardens below. Visiting the **Bock Casemates** *(adult/child €10/5)* involves 300 steps: the real fun here comes from views out of rock-cut 'windows' overlooking the valley below.

Art & History

The greatest galleries and museums of Luxembourg City

Lëtzebuerg City Museum *(citymuseum.lu; adult/senior/child €5/3/free)*, is an engrossing, family-friendly city history museum hosted partly in a former 'holiday home' of the Bishop of Orval. In a pretty park atop more fortifications, **Villa Vauban** *(villavauban.lu/en; adult/under-26/child €5/3/free)* has a rich collection of 17th- to 19th-century art with a few contemporary extras.

Nationalmusée *(nationalmusee.lu/en; free)*, the superb national museum, covers an astounding range of genres and crosses all epochs. It's based in three 17th-century townhouses confusingly interlinked by glass skyways.

You'll find the city's most cutting-edge contemporary art at **Mudam** *(mudam.com; adult/under-26/under-21 €10/7/free)*. While exhibitions can be fascinating, it's IM Pei's building that makes the experience here so special.

 EATING & DRINKING IN LUXEMBOURG CITY: INFORMAL SPOTS

Pizzeria Bacchus: Cheery, prompt service, decent portions and unusually good value for such a central spot. *noon-9.30pm Tue-Sat* €

Scott's: Casual riverside watering hole with international pub food and grills. *kitchen 6-10pm Mon-Fri, noon-10pm Sat, noon-9pm Sun* €€

Big Beer Company: Microbrewery with Bavarian and Luxembourgish food in the Rives de Clausen nightlife zone. *5am-late Tue-Fri, from noon Sat & Sun* €€

Beim Renert: Fox-themed local cafe–bar with popular terrace and Belgo-Luxembourgish lunches. *10am-12.30am Tue-Sat, kitchen 11.30am-2.30pm* €€

Places We Love to Stay

€ Budget €€ Midrange €€€ Top End

Brussels

MAP p119

Auberge de Jeunesse Jacques Brel € HI-affiliated, no-frills hostel with a great bar, lovely courtyard and free organic breakfast.

Meininger Bruxelles City Center € Set in a restored brewery by the canal, this stylish hostel has spacious rooms (dorms and private), a beautiful bar, kitchen, laundry and bike rentals.

Made in Catherine €€ With just a few rooms, this cosy stay offers a warm welcome and free drinks. Expect exposed beams, vibrant touches, comfy beds and local goodies.

Jam Hotel €€ Jam embraces raw concrete and bold colours, with industrial-chic rooms, a rooftop plunge pool, bar with cosy vibes, and standout gin and tonics.

Maison Flagey €€€ Art Nouveau flair at this characterful B&B near Flagey. Be wowed by the entrance staircase and rooms lovingly decorated with period furniture.

Mechelen

3 Paardekens € Bare-bones rooms and app-activated automated reception, but very central, with a perfect cathedral view from the breakfast terrace.

Hotel Vé €€ Artistic hotel on Mechelen's liveliest nightlife square, retaining elements of the building's former role as a fish smokery.

Leuven

Leuven City Hostel/Hotel Ladeuze € Small, low-key 'grown-ups' hostel with games lounge and quality kitchen. Budget hotel rooms too.

Fourth €€ Super-central in a photo-perfect historic building that's the fourth incarnation of a 1479 guild house.

Ghent

MAP p129

Uppelink € Within a step-gabled canal-side house, the attraction at this super-central hostel is the unbeatable view of Ghent's towers.

Simon Says €€ Get in quick to snap up one of two fashionably styled guest rooms located above its well-patronised, chilled-out coffee shop.

1898 The Post €€€ This boutique offering is housed in Ghent's twin-turreted former post office. Dark and moody in a wonderful way, with great design at every turn.

Bruges

MAP p129

St Christopher's Inn Hostel at The Bauhaus € This backpacker village incorporates a hostel, apartments, a nightclub and a chill-out room.

Passage Bruges € This small hotel has stylish, large and well-priced rooms. Located at the end of a small alleyway, they are also very quiet.

B&B Amaryllis Dieltiens €€ Old and new art fills this lovingly restored classical mansion, which remains an appealing real home run by charming musician hosts.

Dukes' Palace €€€ This large-scale five-star hotel is imposingly tall with a Disneyesque turret. It partly occupies the Prinsenhof building, Bruges' 15th-century royal palace.

Ostend

Hostel De Ploate € This HI hostel is smart, modern and minimal, with no curfew, super-helpful and friendly staff, and a great location.

Thermae Palace Hotel €€€ The beautiful, beachfront Thermae Palace is ageing gracefully and it retains appeal for folks seeking that old-school Euro-beach-resort vibe.

Kortrijk

Hotel Messeyne €€ This grand 1662 townhouse's beamed high ceilings and original fireplaces meld with stylish decor and immaculate rooms.

Center Hotel €€ Attractively modernised rooms at reasonable prices above a subtly fashionable bar with handy 24-hour reception.

Ypres

Yoaké B&B €€ Smart two-room B&B attached to a hip wellness centre. Great breakfasts and a warm welcome.

Main Street Hotel €€€ Jumbling eccentricity with historical twists and luxurious comfort, this is a one-off that oozes character.

Antwerp

MAP p135

A-Stay € The vibe of a great hostel – with common area, sociable bar–cafe, washing-machines etc – but comfortable, hi-tech rooms.

Ash € Big, functional hostel with good kitchen, bar and a handy location for the station. Can overheat in summer.

143

De Witte Lelie €€€ Behind a 16th-century facade, this highly distinctive design hotel has a courtyard garden.

Waterloo

Le 1815 €€ Compact rooms above the Maximus restaurant facing the battlefield, around 300m from the Lion's Mound.

Gîte Ferme d'Hougoumont €€€ Unique rental apartment above the south gateway of the historic Hougoumont farm-museum. Sleeps up to five.

Mons

Mons Dragon House € Guesthouse with stylish decor, very handy location, friendly hosts and communal sitting room/kitchen.

La Maison de la Duchesse de la Vallière €€ Genteel mansion B&B 600m south of the Grand Place set back behind wrought-iron gates. Free private parking.

Namur

Auberge de Jeunesse € It's hard to imagine a better HI hostel, set facing the river with terrace, games room and generous breakfast.

Hôtel Les Tanneurs €€ Contemporary hotel in central Namur, artfully incorporating a series of 17th-century buildings.

Liège

YUST Liège € Hostel accommodation taken to a swanky new level. The rooftop bar surveys Guillemins station. Free coffee in a comfy lounge area.

N° 5 Bed & Breakfast €€ Elegant B&B with sauna, entered through an 18th-century home in the city's most charming historic quarter.

Spa

Manoir de Lébioles €€€ Luxurious 1905 château-style mansion–hotel complex with spa and swimming pools, a 10-minute drive above Spa.

Les Bains de Spa €€€ Choose a 'heritage' room to sleep in the palatial UNESCO-listed 19th-century baths–building, revamped as a five-star hotel in 2025.

Luxembourg City p141

Youth Hostel, Luxembourg City € State-of-the-art HI hostel. Its terrace has great views up towards the Old Town. Bring padlock for lockers.

Hôtel Français €€ Unpretentious but fair-value rooms above a classic brasserie in the city's cafe-life epicentre.

Hôtel Parc Beaux Arts €€€ Exclusive old-town property with original artworks and a 'secret' lounge in the eves.

La Pipistrelle €€€ Four gorgeous B&B suites in an 18th-century property that's carved into the cliff between Grund and the old city.

Hotel Les Jardins d'Anaïs €€€ Oasis of cultured calm with a retro twist, sitting in gardens on a bend of the river, just beyond Claussen.

VIDEO MEDIA STUDIO EUROPE/SHUTTERSTOCK

Manoir de Lébioles, Spa (p139)

Practicalities

ACCESSIBLE TRAVEL

Brussels metro stations have Braille signs and tactile tiles leading up to the platforms. Luxembourg City offers accessible public transport with low-floor buses, trams and an easy-to-use funicular. Cobblestone streets in both countries can be challenging for wheelchairs and those with vision impairments, due to uneven surfaces.

IZI18/SHUTTERSTOCK

LGBTIQ+ TRAVELLERS

Belgium and Luxembourg are among the most welcoming destinations for LGBTIQ+ travellers. Belgium was the second country, after the Netherlands, to legalise same-sex marriage. Both countries offer an inclusive atmosphere; larger cities have thriving queer communities.

ELECTRICITY

The electricity supply is 230V/50Hz. Plugs are type E (Belgium) and type F (Luxembourg).

WEIGHTS & MEASURES

Both countries use the metric system. Also note that the decimal place is indicated by a comma and the thousand by a dot.

LANGUAGES

Belgium is split into Dutch-speaking Flanders (Vlaanderen in Dutch) and French-speaking Wallonia (la Wallonie in French), as well as a small German-speaking region. French, German and Lëtzebuergesch are spoken in Luxembourg. For Dutch see p827, for French see p449 and for German see p519.

CANNABIS POLICY

Contrary to the general perception, possession of cannabis is still illegal in Belgium; it's merely decriminalised. However, carrying a small amount for personal use (3g) is tolerated if you're over 18 years. Luxembourg has passed a similar law. Smoking cannabis in public, even if some people indulge, is still prohibited.

OPENING HOURS

Banks 9am-4pm or 5pm
Bars 6pm-midnight or 1am
Cafes 8am to 8pm
Clubs 10pm-3am (L) or 6am (B)
Restaurants noon-2pm & 6-10pm
Shopping malls 9am or 10am-7pm
Shops 10am-6pm (with a possible midday break)
Supermarkets 8am-8pm

PUBLIC HOLIDAYS

New Year's Day 1 January
Easter Monday March/April
Labour Day 1 May
Europe Day (Luxembourg) 9 May
Ascension Day May
Whit Monday May/June
Luxembourg National Day 23 June

Belgian National Day 21 July
Assumption Day 15 August
All Saints' Day 1 November
Armistice Day (Belgium) 11 November
Christmas Day 25 December
Second Day of Christmas (Luxembourg) 26 December

BJØRN BEHEYDT/SHUTTERSTOCK

Eurostar, Brussels

Arriving

Swift Eurostar trains from London arrive at Brussels Midi station. The major airports are Brussels and Luxembourg; both are about 20 minutes away from their city centres, by train or bus. Low-cost airlines mainly land at Brussels South Charleroi Airport, 45 minutes away from Brussels by shuttle.

By Train
High-speed trains have fast, easy connections between Brussels and London, and between Belgium and the broader French, Dutch and German networks, but such trains require seat reservations and can prove expensive if demand is high.

By Air
Brussels is the country's most globally connected airport and the hub for Belgium's biggest carrier Brussels Airlines *(brusselsairlines. com)*. Charleroi airport, misleadingly described as Brussels-South, attracts budget airlines. Luxembourg Airport is the country's only international airport.

MONEY

Currency: Euro (€)

DIGITAL PAYMENTS
Paying with your phone, smartwatch or contactless bank card has become commonplace since the COVID-19 pandemic. For larger purchases, you will still be asked to enter your PIN. Use contactless payment in Brussels (STIB/ MIVB) and Flanders (De Lijn) public transport.

TAXES & REFUNDS
VAT is always included in both countries. Non-EU residents having bought goods with a minimum invoice of €125.01 (in Belgium) or €74 (in Luxembourg) are entitled to a VAT refund. Request your Tax Free Form, then have it stamped by customs and file it at the airport.

DISCOUNTS
Museums and sights typically offer small discounts to seniors and bigger discounts to those under 26. Accompanied children generally pay even less/go free. Students with an ISIC (International Student Identity Card) might qualify for concession rates.

Getting Around

You can easily move around by public transport in both Belgium and Luxembourg – trains are efficient and services regular. Buses serve areas that the trains don't reach. The scattered towns and villages of Wallonia and Luxembourg are more easily explored by car.

OLRAT/SHUTTERSTOCK

Public Transport
The train and bus services are extensive and affordable (free in Luxembourg), although rush hours often see trains getting delayed. Wallonia, being less populated, does not have the same coverage as Flanders and Brussels, but cities are well connected.

Trains & Trams
A good network of trains makes public transport the best way to visit northern Belgium's cities. The Belgian coast is served by a remarkable tram that runs efficiently back and forth for 70km. Luxembourg's joint railway–bus network is coordinated by CFL (cfl.lu).

Car
In the rustic, less populous south of Belgium, rail-lines are sparse, buses rare and, away from the traffic-jammed motorways, having your own wheels is the easiest way to get around.

Bus
Buses tend to be used in conjunction with train services rather than in competition. Reaching much of rural Wallonia especially, you're likely to need a train–bus combination. Bus frequency is highest on schooldays. Fewer operate on Saturday, while Sunday services can be scant or nonexistent.

Bike
City bikes and electric bikes can easily be hired in many cities in this bicycle-mad region: Flanders is a particularly bike-friendly region. Throughout Belgium you can take your bike on the train for a small fee.

DRIVING ESSENTIALS

Drive on the right.

Seatbelts must be worn by all occupants.

0.5MG

Blood alcohol limit is 0.5mg in Belgium, 0.25mg in Luxembourg.

For places to stay in Bosnia & Hercegovina, see p162

CAYO SEMPERE/SHUTTERSTOCK

Above: Stari Most (p156), Mostar; Right: Sebilj Fountain (p152), Sarajevo

Curated by
Vesna Maric

Bosnia & Hercegovina

RICH HISTORY, WILD NATURE, WARM WELCOME

Bosnia and Hercegovina has stunning natural beauty, charming cities and a fascinating history. Make sure you engage with its friendly people.

Bosnia and Hercegovina's dramatic natural beauty is only matched by its history. Over the centuries, the region has been the meeting point of Byzantine and Roman Christianity, Islam and Judaism, and the Ottoman and Austro-Hungarian Empires – all followed by Yugoslavia's socialism. Most people still associate the country with the heartbreaking war of the 1990s, but while the scars from that time are real, today's visitors will be impressed by the genuine and unassuming human warmth, incredible mountains, wild swimming and rafting, impressive waterfalls and bargain-value skiing.

Major attractions include the historical centres of Sarajevo and Mostar, which counterpoint splendid Ottoman stone architecture with quirky bars, inviting street-terrace cafes, traditional barbecue restaurants and vibrant arts scenes. Nature abounds here, in places like eastern Bosnia's Sutjeska National Park just outside Sarajevo. Hercegovina's incredible Kravica Waterfall and the Ottoman mini-towns of Počitelj and Blagaj are like tiny gems on the horizon, while Jajce in western Bosnia combines cascades, lakes and rivers with fascinating historical sights in its town centre. Rafting and swimming on the gorgeous River Una is an unforgettable experience. According to the *Guardian*, flights from the UK to Bosnia and Hercegovina increased by 284% in 2025, so hurry and visit while the country is still relatively crowd-free and the prices are affordable. This is one of Europe's best-value destinations.

TRABANTOS/SHUTTERSTOCK

THE MAIN AREAS

SARAJEVO	MOSTAR	WESTERN BOSNIA
Bustling Ottoman centre and the nation's best food. **p152**	Celebrity bridge, magnificent Old Town. **p156**	Incredible waterfalls, rivers and verdant towns. **p160**

Find Your Way

Hiring your own car is the best way to explore Bosnia & Hercegovina. For those not wishing to drive, the bus network is reasonably priced and efficient. Trains are limited but pleasant.

BUS & TRAIN

Reasonably priced, with comprehensive coverage and frequent departures. Bus stations pre-sell tickets. Trains are less frequent and with a limited network. ŽFBH (*zfbh.ba*) has an online rail timetable search.

CAR

Hiring a car is the best way to travel at your own pace and to visit regions with minimal public transport. Car rental is easy to organise.

Sarajevo, p152

Stroll around Baščaršija's fascinating Ottoman alleyways, sip Bosnian coffee and savour the nation's best *burek* and *ćevapi*.

Mostar, p156

Gawp at the magnificently rebuilt Mostar bridge, wander the cute Old Town and see one of the most spectacular remnants of Yugoslav architecture.

Western Bosnia, p160

Watch the waterfall tumble photogenically past Jajce's castle-crowned Old Town and raft down one of Bosnia & Hercegovina's fast-flowing rivers.

100 km
50 miles

CROATIA

Novi Grad
Bosanska Dubica
Prijedor
Bosanska Krupa
Bosanski Petrovac
Kulen Vakuf
Bihać

Sremska Mitrovica
Bijeljina
Brčko
Bosanska Gradiška
Banja Luka
Doboj
Tešanj
Kotor Varoš
Ključ
Mrkonjić Grad
Bosansko Grahovo
Glamoč

Prača
Sava
Vrbas
Bosna
Prim

SERBIA

Zvornik
Vlasenica
Srebrenica
Tuzla
Kladanj
Vareš
Žepče
Zenica
Travnik
Bugojno
Tomislav Grad
Livno
Posušje

Drina

SARAJEVO
Sarajevo City Hall
Jahorina
Goražde
Višegrad
Šćepan Polje
Konjic
Jablanica
Stari Most
Mostar
Široki Brijeg
Počitelj
Stolac
Gacko
Trebinje

Neretva
Jezero Rama

GORAŽDE

MONTENEGRO
Nikšić
PODGORICA

Split
BRAČ
HVAR
KORČULA

Adriatic Sea

Dubrovnik

NIGLAYNIK/SHUTTERSTOCK

Buna River (p159), Blagaj

Plan Your Time

Explore Sarajevo and Mostar, but make sure you go into the mountains and river valleys to do some hiking and rafting. This is where the real charm of Bosnia and Hercegovina lies.

If You Only Do One Thing

● In **Sarajevo** (p152), stroll the Ottoman city centre, drink coffee, eat local food and go out with the locals. Alternatively, in **Mostar** (p156), meander around the Old Town and admire the Stari Most and the turquoise Neretva River. Add a visit to nearby **Blagaj** (p159) for beautiful architecture and local trout.

Four Days to Travel Around

● After a day in **Sarajevo** (p152), stop in **Mostar** (p156) on the way to the spectacular **Kravica Waterfall** (p159), where you can spend a few hours and take a dip. Follow this with the hilltop gem of **Počitelj** (p159). The next day, choose between a stop in **Blagaj** (p159) or **Stolac** and the **Radimlja Necropolis** (p159).

SEASONAL HIGHLIGHTS

SPRING
Beat the heat in Hercegovina and see flowers bloom in Bosnia. Rivers are at peak flow. The best time for hiking.

SUMMER
Hot and sweaty, but great for swimming in rivers. The **Sarajevo Film Festival** happens in August.

AUTUMN
The heat is less intense, the nights are cooler and the rains have yet to begin – the ideal time to visit.

WINTER
Skiing gets cheaper after the New Year holidays and the snow usually lasts until mid-March.

Sarajevo

UNIQUE ATMOSPHERE | HISTORY | STREET LIFE

GETTING AROUND

Sarajevo has trams, buses, trolleybuses and minibuses, all operated by GRAS *(gras.ba)*. You can pre-purchase tickets from kiosks or buy them from the driver. They must be stamped once aboard; inspections are common. Tram 3 leaves from Ilidža, passes the National Museum then loops one way (anticlockwise) around Baščaršija. Tram 1 starts at the railway station, then does the same loop as Tram 3.

For reliable on-the-meter fares (2KM plus about 1KM per kilometre) download the Moj Taxi app *(mojtaxi.ba)*. Avoid the taxis waiting outside the airport.

☑ **TOP TIP**

The best way to get a feel for the city is to stroll the Old Town's lanes and avenues, then climb the picturesque slopes of Vratnik for sweeping views..

Ringed by mountains, Sarajevo is a singular city with an atmosphere all its own. Meander around the Ottoman quarter of Baščaršija and enjoy a meal or local coffee at the smoking barbecue restaurants and cafes. Peek into the mosques, churches and synagogues, and marvel at the dilapidating socialist architecture. Then it's time to join the locals in the lively and stylish bars and restaurants. The 20th century thrust Sarajevo into the world's consciousness, from the assassination that precipitated WWI to the successful 1984 Winter Olympics to the brutal almost-four-year siege of the city in the 1990s. Once renowned as the Jerusalem of Europe for its religious diversity, Sarajevo is now a largely divided place, with most of the Serb population living in Istočno Sarajevo (East Sarajevo) on the Republika Srpska side. But the scars are fading with each passing year and Sarajevo has become a wonderful destination to visit. Enjoy its intriguing architectural medley, vibrant street life and irrepressible spirit.

Explore Baščaršija, the Heart of Sarajevo

Atmospheric alleys and architecture

Centred on **Sebilj Fountain**, **Baščaršija** ('barsh-char-shi-ya') is the heart of old Sarajevo. The name for the city's Ottoman-era market is derived from the Turkish for 'main market' and it's still lined with stalls, grand Ottoman mosques and inviting cafes. Splendid 16th-century buildings include the 1531 **Gazi Husrev-beg Mosque** *(vakuf-gazi.ba; 3KM)*, with its 45m minaret, and **Brusa Bezistan**, a former silk-trading bazaar. It now houses a branch of the **Museum of Sarajevo 1878–1918** *(muzejsarajeva.ba; entry 5KM)*.

Religious Harmony Throughout the Centuries

From synagogues to Orthodox cathedrals

Sarajevo has been home to Muslims, Jews and Christians for centuries and it remains so to a lesser degree to this day. The

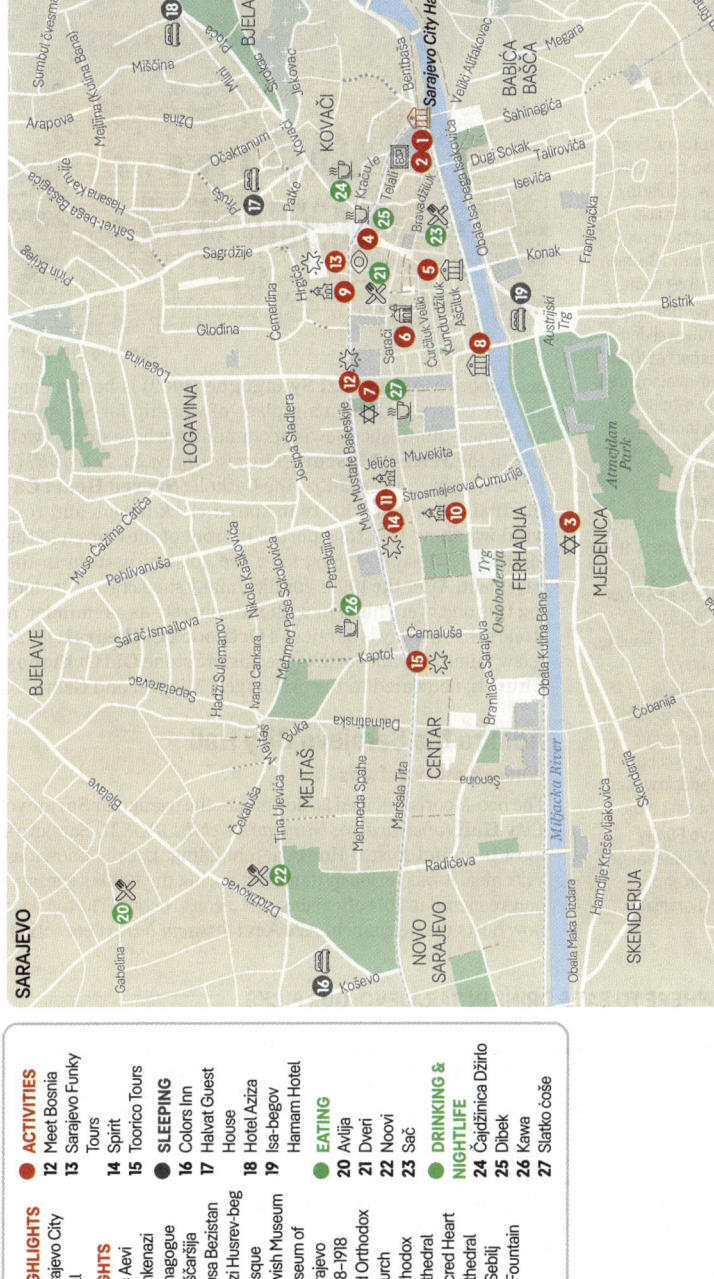

SARAJEVO

● HIGHLIGHTS
1 Sarajevo City Hall

SIGHTS
2 Ars Aevi
3 Ashkenazi Synagogue
4 Baščaršija
5 Brusa Bezistan
6 Gazi Husrev-beg Mosque
7 Jewish Museum
8 Museum of Sarajevo 1878–1918
9 Old Orthodox Church
10 Orthodox Cathedral
11 Sacred Heart Cathedral
see 4 Sebilj Fountain

● ACTIVITIES
12 Meet Bosnia
13 Sarajevo Funky Tours
14 Spirit
15 Toorico Tours

● SLEEPING
16 Colors Inn
17 Halvat Guest House
18 Hotel Aziza
19 Isa-begov Hamam Hotel

● EATING
20 Avlija
21 Dveri
22 Noovi
23 Sač

● DRINKING & NIGHTLIFE
24 Cajdžinica Džirlo
25 Dibek
26 Kawa
27 Slatko ćoše

Sarajevo City Hall

BEST TOURS IN SARAJEVO

Toorico Tours: Ervin leads two-hour walking tours twice daily (by donation). He also offers paid tours and dinners with a Bosnian family in their home.

Spirit: By-donation 90-minute walking tours depart at 10am and 6pm. It also offers a paid two-hour city walking tour and a driving tour to the Tunnel of Hope.

Meet Bosnia: By-donation walking tour that departs at 10.30am and 3pm. Also offers a 3½-hour 'Fall of Yugoslavia' tour and excursions to the country.

Green Visions: Ecotourism specialist has a wide range of hiking, cycling, rafting and, in winter, snowshoeing trips.

Sarajevo Funky Tours: A wide range of tours in and around Sarajevo.

neo-Moorish **Ashkenazi Synagogue** (1902) is both a community centre and the main place of worship for Sarajevo's now much-diminished Jewish community, whose story is well told in the **Jewish Museum** *(muzejsarajeva.ba; entry 5KM)*.

Just nearby, on Ferhadija, the Catholic **Sacred Heart Cathedral** is fronted with twin-spired clock towers and rose windows above the stone portal. In front of the church in the middle of the square, look for a red splatter pattern in the pavement. After the 1990s conflict, many shell craters, including this one, were filled in with red concrete as a reminder. A stone's throw away is Sarajevo's **Orthodox Cathedral** (1872). A few minutes' walk north is the austere stone **Old Orthodox Church**, dedicated to the archangels Michael and Gabriel.

Admire the Sarajevo City Hall

Where history unfolds

The neo-Moorish striped facade makes the triangular **Sarajevo City Hall** *(vijecnica.ba; entry adult/child 10/5KM)* Sarajevo's most beautiful Austro-Hungarian building. Locally known as Vijećnica, it was seriously damaged during the 1990s siege, and only reopened in 2014 after laborious reconstruction. The top floor now hosts the permanent **Ars Aevi** *(arsaevi.ba)* art collection.

 WHERE TO EAT & DRINK IN SARAJEVO: OUR PICKS

Dveri: Sarajevo's best restaurant is this 'country cottage' spot with an enchanting atmosphere. Serves goulash, Bosnian specialities and inky risottos. *8am-11pm* €€	**Avlija**: Locals cosy up here for home cooking in a buzzing covered yard, dangling with trailing pot plants, strings of peppers and the odd birdcage. *8am-11pm* €€	**Noovi**: Gorgeous little courtyard with a small but eclectic menu of steaks, pizzas and vegetarian dishes, plus a good wine list. Local favourite. *noon-11pm Tue-Sun* €€	**Sač**: Bakes everything *ispod sača*-style – under a domed metal lid covered with charcoal. Our pick for Sarajevo's best *burek* and *sirnica*. *8.30am-11pm* €
Kawa: A popular neighbourhood cafe on a hill overlooking the city, yet close to the centre. The views are amazing and the coffee is excellent. *8am-11pm*	**Dibek**: The place to try Bosnian coffee and taste *tucana kahva* (coffee ground in a mortar and pestle) on low stools beneath a central plane tree. *8am-2am*	**Slatko čoše**: Baščaršija's favourite coffee and cake spot, where you can try Bosnian coffee and Turkish tea, and sweeten it up with a Bosnian dessert. *6.30pm-10pm*	**Čajdžinica Džirlo**: Minuscule but brimming with character, Džirlo brews 29 types of tea, many of them made from distinctive Bosnian herbs. *8.30am-11pm*

Beyond Sarajevo

The area around Sarajevo is a patchwork of gorgeous landscapes, interesting towns and good skiing.

Sarajevo is surrounded by some amazing mountains. Make sure you get out and explore them, summer or winter. Aside from the capital, however, eastern Bosnia is largely off the radar for most travellers. The sad legacy of ethnic cleansing has cast a pall over much of the region, although many stop to pay their respects at Srebrenica, the most notorious site of all. The main places of interest include the magnificent Sutjeska National Park and skiing at Jahorina and Bjelašnica. Most sights can be easily reached on a day trip from Sarajevo.

Jahorina
TIME FROM SARAJEVO: **40MIN** 🚗
Ski Olympic slopes
Of Sarajevo's two Olympic skiing resorts, **Jahorina Olympic Centre** *(oc-jahorina.com; entry adult day pass 86KM)*, 26km southeast of the city on the Republika Srpska side, has the widest range of hotels. Stay at the upmarket **Termag Hotel** (p162). **Rajska Vrata** is a charming ski-in alpine chalet off of Jahorina's longest run.

Bjelašnica
TIME FROM SARAJEVO: **1¼HR** 🚗
Winter sports & hiking trails
The modest ski resort of **Bjelašnica** *(ocbjelasnica.com; entry adult day pass 47KM)*, around 25km south of Sarajevo, has eight runs and there's usually enough snow to ski by Christmas. February usually has the best snow. Love competitive mountain walking? Check out the Vučko Trail *(vuckotrail.ba)*.

Sutjeska National Park
TIME FROM SARAJEVO: **2HR** 🚗
Tjentište: A magnificent monument
Tjentište is the site of the **Memorial Complex to the Battle of Sutjeska**. Built in honour of one of the bloodiest WWII battles in Yugoslavia, it was designed by sculptor Miodrag Živković in 1971 and is considered one of the most complex memorials in the former Yugoslav region.

Places
Jahorina p155
Bjelašnica p155
Sutjeska National Park p155

GETTING AROUND
You'll need your own car to get to Sutjeska National Park and the ski slopes.

Mostar

OLD BRIDGE | OLD TOWN | MAGNIFICENT RIVER

GETTING AROUND

Mostar has its own airport, with flights to Belgrade, Zagreb and beyond. However, many use Dubrovnik and Split airports (both in Croatia) to reach Mostar.

The one railway line runs from Ploče (in Croatia) to Mostar and on to Sarajevo through the Neretva Canyon. The main centres are all well connected by bus.

☑ TOP TIP

Many visitors find crossing the Old Bridge a slippery experience – rather than floundering and sliding around on the smooth stone surface, make sure you step firmly on the protruding 'treads' that line the arc of the bridge, like a true Mostarian.

Mostar is the largest city in Hercegovina and the country's biggest tourist attraction. It has a small but thoroughly enchanting Old Town, which is where you'll find the fittingly named Old Bridge, which forms a majestic stone arc between medieval towers and crosses the rushing turquoise waters of the Neretva River below. At dusk the lights of numerous millhouse restaurants twinkle across the gushing streams, while narrow Kujundžiluk bustles with trinket sellers.

After the summer day trippers have departed, savvy travellers who have chosen to base themselves here can enjoy memorable regional attractions as well as ponder the city's darker side. Beyond the cobbled lanes of the attractively restored Ottoman quarter are entire blocks of bombed-out buildings, a poignant legacy of the 1990s conflict. Between November and April most tourist facilities are in hibernation, while summer is scorchingly hot. Spring and autumn are ideal times to visit.

Admire the Splendid Old Bridge

The Balkans' most celebrated span

The world-famous **Stari Most** (meaning 'Old Bridge') is the indisputable heart of Mostar and its pale stone magnificently reflects the golden glow of sunset. The bridge's swooping arch was originally built between 1557 and 1566 on the orders of Suleiman the Magnificent. An engineering marvel in its time, it was pounded into the river during a deliberate Croatian artillery attack in November 1993. The current structure is a faithful 21st-century rebuild.

Don't miss Mostar's best shopping experience, on either sides of the bridge, at the bustling **Kujundžiluk Bazaar**.

MOSTAR

★ **HIGHLIGHTS**
1 Stari Most

● **SIGHTS**
2 Koski Mehmed Pasha Mosque

● **SLEEPING**
3 Kriva Ćuprija 1
4 Muslibegović House
5 Villa Čardak

● **EATING**
6 Hindin Han
see 3 Konoba Taurus
7 Nacionalni Restoran MM
8 Podrum

● **DRINKING & NIGHTLIFE**
9 Club Calamus
10 Duradžik
11 Ima i Može Craft Beer Garden
12 Ljetna Bašta Oscar

● **SHOPPING**
13 Kujundžiluk Bazaar

Watch Divers on the Stari Most

Cold river plunge

Every summer, young men leap from the parapet of Stari Most, plummeting more than 20m into the freezing cold Neretva River. Divers won't leap until 50KM has been collected (in winter it's double). If you want to see professionals compete, watch the **annual diving competition** in late July. In September, the **Red Bull Cliff Diving** *(cliffdiving.redbull.com)* competition attracts international divers and an audience of thousands.

 WHERE TO EAT IN MOSTAR: OUR PICKS

Konoba Taurus: One of Mostar's best, with a terrace next to the Crooked Bridge. Chef Amnerisa cooks traditional food and Dalmatian specialities. *11am-11pm* €€

Podrum: Right at the entrance to the Old Town with a little terrace on the cobbled street, this place is great for *ćevapi* and all kinds of grilled meat. *11am-11pm* €€

Hindin Han: This atmospheric old mill cottage serves a mixture of local dishes. Aim for a table on one of the terraces above the Radobolja River. *11am-midnight* €€

Nacionalni Restoran MM: The perfect place to taste homemade Bosnian food. Try the local favourite, *buredžici – burek* covered in garlicky yoghurt. *8am-6pm* €€

MOSTAR'S HISTORY

Mostar means 'bridge-keeper' and the 16th-century construction of the Stari Most marks an era of prosperity for Mostar during the Ottoman Empire. Under Austro-Hungarian rule in the 19th century, the city's centre of gravity shifted north to Trg Musala, with its lovely neo-Moorish buildings. Before the 1990s conflict, Mostar had one of Yugoslavia's largest proportions of mixed marriages. When the Yugoslav army started bombarding Mostar in April 1992, the city's Bosniaks and Croats banded together, but on 9 May 1993 a conflict erupted between the former allies. A front line emerged north–south along the Bulevar, with Croats to the west and Bosniaks to the east. Every building in the city suffered damage; around 2000 people lost their lives.

GIRAFFE VIDEO STUDIO/SHUTTERSTOCK

Koski Mehmed Pasha Mosque

Climb the Minaret of the Koski Mehmed Pasha Mosque

Classical Ottoman design

First constructed in 1618 and substantially rebuilt after the war, the **Koski Mehmed Pasha Mosque** *(entry without/with minaret 6/12KM)* has a dome painted with botanical motifs and punctuated by coloured-glass windows. Climb the claustrophobic minaret for sweeping town views.

Visit a Fascinating Partisan Memorial

Awe-inspiring architecture

Although sadly neglected and badly vandalised, the **Partisan Memorial Cemetery** is nonetheless a must-visit in Mostar for fans of 20th-century socialist architecture. It was designed by leading Yugoslav-era architect Bogdan Bogdanović and completed in 1965. Paths wind up to the upper section, which contains the gravestones of 810 Mostar partisans who died fighting fascism during WWII.

 WHERE TO DRINK IN MOSTAR: OUR PICKS

Duradžik: This rock-edged bar spills into the central courtyard of the Tabhana (former tannery). There's live music most evenings at midnight. *6pm-3am Mon-Sat*

Club Calamus: Perched on top of an inauspicious-looking office building, this urbane rooftop bar offers cocktails and engrossing city views. It stages live music. *7am-2am*

Ima i Može Craft Beer Garden: Craft-beer lovers will enjoy this open-sided wooden pavilion above the Radobolja River; it has frequent live music and DJ nights. *9am-11pm*

Ljetna Bašta Oscar: Set in a large shady garden, this cafe-bar and chill-out place creates an exotic feel with giant cushions, hammocks and colourful fabrics. *10am-2am*

Beyond Mostar

This is Hercegovina, the sun-scorched south, home to lovely waterfalls and small towns.

Hercegovina's arid Mediterranean landscape encompasses a distinctive beauty punctuated by barren mountain ridges and photogenic river valleys. Famed for its fine wines and sun-kissed fruit, the region is sparsely populated but features historic towns and a toehold on the Adriatic coast. Visit old Ottoman Blagaj and Počitelj, and swim beneath Kravica Waterfall. Hercegovina ('hair-tse-go-vi-na') takes its name from 15th-century Duke Stjepan Vukčić Kosača (*herceg* is 'duke' in the local lingo), under whose rule it became a semi-independent duchy of the Kingdom of Bosnia.

GETTING AROUND

The only railway line runs from Čapljina to Mostar and on to Sarajevo, though the main towns are all well connected by bus. The best way to see the area is to hire a car.

Blagaj

TIME FROM MOSTAR: **20MIN**

Relax by the Buna River

Pretty Blagaj hugs the turquoise Buna River at its source, where it gushes out of a cave to flow past a historical **tekke** *(tekijablagaj.ba/en; entry 10KM)* and Ottoman-era homesteads.

Kravica Waterfall

TIME FROM MOSTAR: **1HR**

Take a dip in emerald pools

In spring, the gorgeous **Kravica Waterfall** *(kravica.ba; entry adult/child 20/10KM)* pounds the water below with a dramatic, steamy fury. In summer it's a more gentle cascade, and the basin offers an idyllic respite from the sweltering heat.

Počitelj

TIME FROM MOSTAR: **40MIN**

An architectural ensemble

This medieval fortified village is one of the most beautiful spots in the country. Cupped in a steep rocky amphitheatre, it's a warren of stairways, stone-roofed houses and pomegranate bushes.

Stolac

TIME FROM MOSTAR: **45MIN**

Admire ancient tombstones

Stolac is one of Hercegovina's prettiest castle towns, with a history going back to Roman times. In the vicinity of Stolac are two sets of classic *stećci* (grave carvings). Beside the Mostar road, 3km west of Stolac, is the famous **Radimlja Necropolis**, a group of around 110 intricately carved white stone tombstones dating back to medieval times.

Western Bosnia

GUSHING RIVERS | GREEN FORESTS | LOVELY TOWNS

GETTING AROUND

Banja Luka is the region's biggest city and transport hub, though Bihać is also well connected.

Bus-hopping from Sarajevo via Visoko, Travnik and Jajce to Banja Luka is relatively straightforward.

Visiting the Una River valley is best done by car. Various Una rafting companies offer client pick-ups from Bihać.

☑ **TOP TIP**

Renting a car is recommended in order to really see the best of this wonderful region.

Travelling through this little-trodden region of green wooded hills, river canyons, lakes and historical towns is a rewarding experience. In the west, the Una River gushes flamboyantly over a series of waterfalls before joining the Sava on its rush to the Danube and, ultimately, the Black Sea. You can hop between the old Ottoman administrative capital Travnik and the gorgeous hilltop settlement of Jajce, with its town-centre cascades and gorgeous lakes for swimming. Make a stop in Visoko to see the weird and wonderful world of the alleged pyramids. Banja Luka is another good pit stop if you're passing through. You'll find yourself passing in and out of Bosniak-Croat Federation territory and the Republika Srpska. You'll know when you're in the latter by the profusion of Serbian flags.

Swim in Jajce's Gorgeous Lakes

Two rivers and a waterfall

Jajce is a historical gem, with a highly evocative walled Old Town clinging to a steep rocky knoll with rivers on two sides. The Pliva River tumbles into the Vrbas River by way of the impressive 21m-high **Jajce Waterfall**, right at the foot of the town walls. Immediately to the west, the Pliva is dammed to form two pretty lakes that are popular with swimmers, strollers, bikers and boaters. Between them lie the Mlinčići, a cute collection of 20 tiny wooden watermills. At the bottom of the lower, smaller lake, boardwalks cross a pretty set of rivulets spilling into a dam basin, which is a popular swimming spot.

Raft, Swim & Admire the Una River

A lush waterway of greens and opals

The adorable Una River has a variety of moods. In the green gorges to the northeast, some sections are as calm as mirrored opal, while others gush over widely fanned rapids. The **Una Aqua rafting centre** *(una-aqua.com; raft trip 100KM per person)* is an attraction in itself, comprising five small islands interlinked with wooden bridges. There's a good swimming

spot, a restaurant, a campsite and a treehouse cabin raised on stilts above a comfy waterside hammock.

The river broadens and gurgles over a series of shallow falls as it passes through the unassuming town of Bihać. Occasionally it leaps over more impressive falls, notably at **Štrbački Buk**, which forms the centrepiece of the 198-sq-km **Una National Park** *(nationalpark-una.ba; entry adult/child 12/8KM)*. A strong contender for the title of the nation's most impressive waterfall, this is a dramatic 40m-wide cascade, pounding 23.5m down three travertine sections, including a superbly photogenic 18m drop-off, overlooked by a network of viewing platforms. The easiest access is 8km along a graded but potholed and unpaved section from Orašac on the Kulen Vakuf road. There are swimming holes to stop at along the way.

Amble Around Pretty Travnik

Castle, cheese and a Nobel laureate

Once the seat of Bosnia's viziers (Ottoman governors), the castle town of **Travnik** is now best known for its sheep's cheese and for being the birthplace of Nobel Prize–winning author Ivo Andrić. Travnik's 15th-century **Old Town Fortress** *(adult/child 3/1.50KM)* surveys the city from a shoulder of hillside. The stone walls gleam so brightly in the sun that they appear to have been scrubbed. The fortress looks over **Plava Voda** (Blue Water), a convivial gaggle of restaurants flanking a gurgling stream, crisscrossed by small bridges. You should definitely have your lunch here.

In the centre of town is the Sulejmanija Mosque, although everyone in Travnik calls it the **Many-Coloured Mosque** *(Šarena Džamija; free)*, a longstanding nickname that references its famous frescoed facade.

TRAVNIK'S LITERARY PRODIGY

Travnik is the hometown of Yugoslav author Ivo Andrić, who won the Nobel Prize in Literature in 1961. The town is the setting of one of his most famous novels, *Bosnian Chronicle*. Although Travnik was under Austo-Hungarian rule when Andrić was born (1892), the author focused mainly on life under the Ottomans, and his lyrical style and perennial theme of the melancholy of passing time earned him the Nobel over authors such as JRR Tolkien, Robert Frost, John Steinbeck and EM Forster, all of whom were in the running that year.

Places We Love to Stay

€ Budget €€ Midrange €€€ Top End

Sarajevo
MAP p153

Halvat Guest House €€ The six rooms at this friendly, family-run guesthouse are clean and spacious, and surprisingly quiet for such a central location. Baščaršija is just down the road.

Colors Inn €€€ Modernist decor is given a dramatic twist with vast, wall-sized black-and-white photos of 20th-century Sarajevo. The 37 comfortable, stylish rooms have a kettle, coffee and chocolates. The breakfast is abundant.

Isa-begov Hamam Hotel €€€ An ornate 19th-century hammam and hotel (originally founded in 1492) has 15 delicious rooms designed to evoke the spirit of the age, with lashings of handcrafted dark-wood furniture. Guests get free use of the hammam.

Hotel Aziza €€€ This comfortable family-run hotel has 17 spacious, light-filled rooms that pay homage to the love story of its owners Mehmed and Aziza Poričanin. A daily sauna is included in the rates.

Jahorina

Termag Hotel €€ Traditional ideas and open fireplaces are given a stylish modern twist, and the rooms have excellent beds and sturdy woodwork. There's an excellent spa centre.

Bjelašnica

Hotel Han €€ Ski-in, ski-out access at the Bjelašnica resort, with stylishly appointed rooms that have been decorated like bleached Mondrian abstracts. In summer, the hotel rents bikes.

Mostar
MAP p157

Muslibegović House €€ An extremely charming boutique hotel, with a variety of room sizes and styles. The excellent modern bathrooms contrast with traditional Bosnian, Turkish and Moroccan design.

Kriva Ćuprija 1 €€ Inhabiting a cluster of stone buildings set around a millhouse restaurant in the heart of old Mostar, this atmospheric place has boutique-style bedrooms and immaculate bathrooms.

Villa Čardak €€ This old stone house on a central lane has been thoroughly modernised and now has seven spacious en-suite rooms; accent walls are emblazoned with forest scenes. There's also a small guest kitchen.

Blagaj

Hotel Blagaj €€ A professional 27-room hotel that has white and lavender walls and a nice terrace. It's just beyond the main car park en route to Blagaj Tekke.

Jajce

Hotel Stari Grad € Heavy beams, wood panelling and a heraldic fireplace give this comfortable place a sense of suavely modernised antiquity. The six standard rooms are somewhat cramped, but nicely decorated and clean.

Una River Valley

Kostelski Buk €€ Set beside a triple set of rapids, this luxurious hotel has stylish rooms with some of the most comfortable mattresses you could hope to sleep on. Some rooms have river views. The restaurant is excellent, too.

Opal Exclusive €€ Hidden away but only 300m north of central Bihać, the Opal's spacious rooms are modern and comfortable. The best have lovely views over the rapids. There's a terrace overlooking the river.

SENAD KOSTIC/SHUTTERSTOCK

Kostelski Buk

Practicalities

LGBTIQ+ Travellers

Homosexuality was decriminalised in 1998, but attitudes remain conservative. Although Bosnia and Hercegovina's gay community still faces many obstacles and prejudice, it is well organised. Pride Festivals have taken place annually since 2019 (with the exception of 2020). Check @bh.povorkaponosa on Instagram. LGBTIQ+ advocacy organisation Sarajevo Open Centre (soc.ba) is active in fighting sexuality-based discrimination.

Dangers & Annoyances

Landmines and unexploded ordnance still affect 2% of Bosnia and Hercegovina's land area. For your safety, stick to paved surfaces or well-worn paths in affected areas, and avoid exploring war-damaged buildings. If you're going hiking, make sure you go with a professional guide.

Accessible Travel

Bosnia's steep townscapes are full of stairways and rough streets that can prove awkward if you have mobility issues. A few places have wheelchair ramps to serve those wounded in the war, but smaller hotels won't have lifts and disabled toilets remain rare.

Smoking

Some consider smoking to be Bosnia's Olympic sport. It is prevalent indoors and out, although new laws mean that there are now designated non-smoking areas in most establishments.

SERGII FIGURNYI/SHUTTERSTOCK

Sacred Heart Cathedral (p154), Sarajevo

Opening Hours

Banks 8am–6pm Monday to Friday, 8.30am–1.30pm Saturday
Bars and Cafes 8am–11pm
Restaurants 7am–10.30pm, or until the last customer
Shops 8am–6pm daily; many stay open later

Etiquette

It's polite to remove footwear before entering a home or guesthouse. If entering a mosque or church, cover legs and shoulders. In mosques, women should cover their hair with a scarf (usually provided).

Public Holidays

New Year's Day 1 and 2 January
Orthodox Christmas 7 January
Republika Day (Srpska) 9 January
Orthodox New Year 14 January
Independence Day 1 March
Easter & Easter Monday (Catholic/Orthodox) March or April
May Day 1 and 2 May
Ramazan Bajram June
Kurban Bajram August or September
All Saints Day 1 November
Statehood Day 25 November
Catholic Christmas 25 December

Language

The official languages are Bosnian, Croatian and Serbian; the guide below is for Bosnian. The official writing system uses both the Roman and Cyrillic alphabets.

Basics

Hello. Zdravo/Здраво. *zdra·vo*
Goodbye. Doviđenja/Довиђења. *do·vee·dje·nya*
Yes. Da/Да. *da*
No. Ne/Не. *ne*
Please. Molim/Молим. *mo·lim*
Thank you. Hvala/Хвала. *hva·la*
Excuse me. Izvinite/Извините. *iz·vee·nee·te*
Sorry. Žao mi je/Жао ми. *zha·o mi ye*

What's your name?
Kako se zovete/zoveš? (pol/inf)
Како се зовете/зовеш?
ka·ko se zo·ve·te/zo·vesh

My name is …
Zovem se … / Зовем се … *zo·vem se*

Do you speak English?
Govorite/Govoriš li engleski? (pol/inf)
Говорите/Говориш ли енглески?
go·vo·ri·te/go·vo·rish li en·gle·ski

I don't understand.
Ne razumijem./Не разумијем.
ne ra·zu·mi·yem

Shopping & Services

I'm looking for…
Tražim … / Тражим…
tra·zhim

How much is it?
Koliko košta …? / Колико кошта …?
ko·li·ko kosh·ta

That's too expensive.
To je preskupo. / То је прескупо.
to ye pre·sku·po

Emergencies

Help! Upomoć!/Упомоћ!
u·po·moch
Go away! Idite!/Идите! *i·di·te*
Call …! Zovite …!/Зовите …!
zo·vi·te

  a doctor ljekara/љекара
  lye·ka·ra

  the police policiju/полицију
  po·li·tsi·yu

I'm lost.
Izgubljen/Izgubljena sam. (m/f)
Изгубљен/Изгубљена сам. (m/f)
iz·gub·lyen/iz·gub·lyena sam

I'm ill.
Ja sam bolestan/bolesna. (m/f)
Ја сам болестан/болесна. (m/f)
ya sam bo·le·stan/bo·le·sna

Eating & Drinking

What would you recommend?
Šta biste preporučili?
Шта бисте препоручили?
shta bi·ste pre·po·ru·chi·li

Do you have vegetarian food?
Da li imate vegetarijanski obrok?
Да ли имате вегетаријански оброк?
da li i·ma·te ve·ge·ta·ri·yan·ski o·brok

Cheers! Živjeli!/Живјели! *zhi·vye·li*

Can I have the bill/menu please?
Mogu li dobiti račun/jelovnik, molim?
Могу ли добити рачун/јеловник, молим?
mo·gu li do·bi·ti ra·chun/ye·lov·nik mo·lim

NUMBERS

1
jedan
један
ye·dan

2
dva/два *dva*

3
tri/три *tri*

4
četiri
четири
che·ti·ri

5
pet/пет *pet*

6
šest/шест
shest

7
sedam/
седам
se·dam

8
osam/осам
o·sam

9
devet/девет
de·vet

10
deset/десет
de·set

FROM LEFT: SMOLLL/SHUTTERSTOCK, TORGONSKAYA TATIANA/SHUTTERSTOCK

Tram (p152), Sarajevo

Arriving & Getting Around

Transport is reasonably priced and generally efficient. Bus services are excellent and inexpensive, while trains are slower, less extensive and cheaper. Driving is the best way to explore the country.

Arriving By Air
Sarajevo International Airport is Bosnia's busiest, with flights connecting to Europe and the Middle East. **Tuzla International Airport** is tiny but a hub for budget airline WizzAir. Mostar also has international flights.

Train
Trains are slower and less frequent than buses, but also slightly cheaper. ŽFBH *(zfbh. ba)* has an online rail timetable. The main routes are Sarajevo–Visoko–Bihać and Sarajevo–Konjic–Mostar–Ploče (in Croatia).

Car
Driving makes sense in more remote areas. There are a few toll roads in the centre of the country; collect your ticket where you enter, then pay at the toll booths when you exit.

Bus
Bus services are excellent and relatively inexpensive. There are often different companies handling each route, so prices can vary substantially. Luggage stowed in the baggage compartment under the bus costs extra (around 2KM a piece). Bus stations pre-sell tickets.

MONEY
Currency: Bosnian Convertible Mark (KM)

ATMS
ATMs accepting Visa and MasterCard are ubiquitous in city centres and towns, but will charge around 10KM for withdrawals. Before withdrawing money, compare the different ATM fees to find the cheapest option.

CREDIT CARDS
Top-end hotels, airline offices and upmarket boutiques generally accept major credit cards. You should be able to pay by card at most restaurants (bar the cheapest ones). Pay by cash in the budget category, whether you are at a hotel, restaurant or bar.

DIGITAL PAYMENTS
You can use digital payments in fancier restaurants, hotels and shops. Outside of major cities, always carry cash.

For places to stay in Britain, see p221

CHRISTIAN MUELLER/SHUTTERSTOCK

Above: London Eye views (p177); Right: Urquhart Castle and Loch Ness (p214)

THE MAIN AREAS

LONDON
Traditional yet boundary-pushing; forever evolving. **p172**

DEVON & CORNWALL
Coast, cliffs and countryside. **p181**

BRISTOL, BATH & THE COTSWOLDS
Innovation, history and English charm. **p185**

THE MIDLANDS
Valleys, villages and soaring hills. **p190**

LIVERPOOL & THE PEAK DISTRICT
Cultural highs and sweeping landscapes. **p194**

Curated by
James March

Britain

AN ANCIENT AND INSPIRING ISLAND

Welcome to Britain, a small island in the North Atlantic with a huge personality. There's much to discover, so dive right in.

From the world-class museums, endless art galleries, renowned attractions, sweeping parks and riverside panoramas of London to the Cotswolds' picturesque villages of golden buildings, thatched roofs and cottage gardens, Britain is immediately enchanting. The remote southwest is a ragged, wind-blasted landscape that's equally dotted with charming coastal villages as with imposing rocks and cliffs. The Midlands is Britain's heartland, where a howling industrial past has given way to dynamic cities, but also where centuries of heritage have been preserved in the quiet, undulating countryside.

Venture out to Britain's western flank and you'll find thunderous rivers, glacial mountain ranges, wave-whipped beaches and ancient forests in Wales, alongside a deep cultural and national pride. The same can be said about Scotland, but its two biggest cities are very different from each other – Edinburgh is ethereal and alluring, while Glasgow is a gregarious delight. Scotland's Highlands bring jagged mountain peaks, brooding castle ruins and stunning drives, before its islands offer Neolithic mystery and wild scenery.

Britain is unlike anywhere else on Earth. Nowhere bombards you with such history, royal heritage, art, culture, food, natural beauty, humour and eccentricity in quite the same way. The country is but a tiny speck on the world map, but it's all right here in Britain. And it's great.

SERGII FIGURNYI/SHUTTERSTOCK

Find Your Way

Transport in Britain can be expensive compared to continental Europe. Bus and rail services are sparse in more remote parts of the country, but between them serve most destinations (expect a more sporadic service at weekends).

TRAIN

The fastest way to reach Britain's main hubs is by train. The ease of travelling between regional towns depends on the train line; if the journey involves several changes, there may be a more direct route by bus.

BUS

For short journeys and for trips outside Britain's main towns, buses are usually the best option if you don't have a car. Buses are often cheaper than trains. Most bus companies accept contactless payment by card.

CAR

Having your own wheels is helpful in most areas because of the flexibility it offers. In others, it's essential, especially in the countryside where public transport can be irregular or nonexistent. Fair warning: parking can be a nightmare in popular spots, particularly during peak seasons.

The Scottish Islands, p217

Wind-blasted shores, ancient monoliths and smoky single malts make Scotland's islands a journey into Britain's wild northern frontier.

Edinburgh, p205

With its mix of meandering medieval alleyways, stately neoclassical terraces and cutting-edge arts festivals, Edinburgh is a cultural capital for the ages.

The Scottish Highlands, p213

Jagged mountain peaks, dune-fringed beaches and brooding castle ruins reveal an untamed side to Scotland.

200 km
100 miles

Shetland

Unst
Yell
Fetlar
Isle of Noss
Mainland
Shetland Islands
Foula
Lerwick

Fair Isle

North Sea

Orkney Islands
Westray
Rousay
Sanday
Skara Brae
Kirkwall
Stromness
Mainland
Hoy
John O'Groats
Wick

Durness
Thurso
Helmsdale

Lochinver
Lairg
Tain
Nairn
Elgin
Banff
Fraserburgh
Peterhead

Ullapool
Dingwall
Inverness
Inverness Castle
Aviemore
Huntly
Aberdeen
Stonehaven

Gairloch
Fort Augustus
SCOTLAND
Montrose

Stornoway
Lewis
The Minch
Kyle of Lochalsh
Portree
Skye
Jacobite Steam Train
Ben Nevis
Pitlochry
Dundee
St Andrews

Harris
Tarbet
Mallaig
Fort William
Loch Lomond & the Trossachs National Park
Perth
Edinburgh
Castle
EDINBURGH
Arthur's Seat
Dunbar
Berwick-upon-Tweed

Outer Hebrides
North Uist
Lochmaddy
Rum
Tobermory
Oban
Stirling
Johnnie Walker Experience
Galashiels
Balivanich
South Uist
Sea of the Hebrides
Coll
Mull
Tarbert
Greenock
Glasgow
M8
M74
Ardrossan

Atlantic Ocean
Tree
Colonsay
Jura
Bute
Arran

Lochboisdale
Barra
Castlebay
Islay
Port Ellen
Brodick
Ayr

St Kilda
Campbeltown

BRITAIN

Liverpool & the Peak District, p194

Stroll Liverpool's famous waterfront before heading inland to a great widescreen playground, combined with fascinating history.

The Midlands, p190

The rolling hills and gentle farmlands of the Midlands are pockmarked by lively cities and the ruins of a pioneering past. Welcome to the heart of England.

London, p172

London's story started nearly 2000 years ago, and it's displayed through instantly recognisable landmarks from the Tower of London and Big Ben to the Shard.

North Wales, p202

Eryri is Britain's most prominent peak, but that's just the start of an adventure through old industry, sublime scenery and villages packed with character.

Cardiff & South Wales, p198

Start in a capital fizzing with creative energy before journeying to a wild coast packed with starry night skies and dense woodlands.

Bristol, Bath & the Cotswolds, p185

Bristol and Bath are a beguiling tandem, while the Cotswolds' dreamy chocolate-box charm is England at its most seductive.

Devon & Cornwall, p181

Welcome to England's wild west, where gorse-clad cliffs, booming surf, white sand and wild coastlines rub shoulders with welcoming towns.

Map labels

NORTHERN IRELAND
Derry
BELFAST
DUBLIN
IRELAND
Newton Stewart
Stranraer
Dumfries
Newcastle-upon-Tyne
Durham
Middlesbrough
Carlisle
Penrith
Keswick
Lake District
Windermere
Barrow-in-Furness
Lancaster
Blackpool
Preston
Blackburn
Skipton
Leeds
York
Thirsk
Scarborough
Middlesbrough
Doncaster
Grimsby
Hull
Sheffield
Lincoln
Skegness
Chatsworth House
Nottingham
Derby
Stoke-on-Trent
Chester
Manchester
Liverpool
ENGLAND
The Beatles Story
Llandudno
Bangor
Holyhead
Isle of Man
Douglas
Irish Sea
Mt Snowdon
Ffestiniog Railway
Eryri National Park (Snowdonia)
Newtown
Aberystwyth
Cardigan Bay
New Quay
WALES
Fishguard
Pembroke
Carmarthen
Swansea
CARDIFF
Cardiff Castle
Cardiff Castle
Brunel's SS Great Britain
Shrewsbury
Birmingham
Shakespeare's Birthplace
Worcester
Hereford
Gloucester
National Museum Cardiff
Coventry
Leicester
Warwick Castle
Stratford-upon-Avon
Oxford
Cheltenham
Bristol
Bath
Roman Baths
Wells
Taunton
Barnstaple
Bude
Exeter
Dartmoor National Park
Plymouth
Torquay
Dorchester
Bournemouth
Southampton
Salisbury
Stonehenge
Swindon
Windsor
Winchester
Isle of Wight
Cowes
Portsmouth
Eastbourne
Brighton
Hastings
Canterbury
Dover
Calais
Strait of Dover
FRANCE
Dieppe
Le Havre
Cherbourg
Rouen
CHANNEL ISLANDS (UK)
Guernsey
English Channel (La Manche)
Truro
Newquay
Penzance
Land's End
Isles of Scilly
St Ives School of Painting
Ely
Cambridge
Peterborough
Northampton
Luton
Grantham
King's Lynn
Boston
Norwich
Sheringham
Great Yarmouth
Ipswich
Colchester
Chelmsford
Southend-on-Sea
LONDON
Tower of London
British Museum
Buckingham Palace
Coventry Cathedral
M1 M6 M62 M5 M4 M11 M20 M25 M3 A1

169

Plan Your Time

Britain is wildly diverse, so planning ahead is key to deciding if you want city strolls, coastal drives, mountain hikes or museum mornings. Then simply choose how long to spend on them.

CRISTIAN M BALATE/SHUTTERSTOCK

Royal Pavilion (p179), Brighton

A Whirlwind Week

● You could spend a month in **London** (p172) and still not feel as though you'd seen enough. It's stuffed to the rafters with museums, bursting at the belt with restaurants to rave about, and with enough nocturnal naughtiness to keep half the world partying – you certainly won't be bored. For starters, visit the **Tower of London** (p175) and **St Paul's Cathedral** (p175).

● If you have the time, take the one-hour train down to **Brighton** (p179), the seaside party city that's England's unofficial LGBTIQ+ capital. From fish and chips along the pier to an astonishing Indian-style pleasure palace, there's nowhere quite like it.

● And for more iconic English sights, the **White Cliffs** (p180) of Dover and **Canterbury Cathedral** (p178) are also just a direct train ride away.

SEASONAL HIGHLIGHTS

Fewer crowds and good weather make the shoulder seasons (March to May, plus September and October) the best time to go.

JANUARY
At a latitude of 60° north, the Scottish island of Shetland is the best place in Britain to catch the colourful **northern lights** (p220) in winter.

MAY
Britain's premier literary festival comes to the borderlands of Hay-on-Wye in May. Catch brilliantly bookish conversations at the **Hay Festival** (p201).

JUNE
Witness the unique sight of the sun rising in line with the Stonehenge's famous stones at its **summer solstice** (p189).

Ten Days to Travel Around

● Start in **Bristol** (p185), the cool capital of the West Country before moving on to nearby **Bath** (p186), home to impeccably preserved Roman baths and remarkable Regency-era architecture.

● This tandem is flanked to the south by **Devon and Cornwall's** (p181) sandy beaches, fishing villages, rolling countryside and stark moorland, while to the north are the chocolate-box villages of the **Cotswolds** (p187).

● In the Midlands, vibrant **Birmingham** (p190) has world-class shopping, Michelin-star restaurants and intriguing industrial history. Just beyond is Shakespeare's hometown of **Stratford-upon-Avon** (p192), where you can see the Bard's birthplace, school and final resting place. Veer north to the wind-whipped scenery and stately homes of the **Peak District** (p194) before finishing in **Liverpool** (p194), home of the Beatles and Liverpool FC.

With More Time

● Kick off a Celtic odyssey exploring Welsh capital **Cardiff** (p198) with its castle, parks and museums, before hitting the remote moors and brooding mountains of **Brecon Beacons National Park** (p201). In North Wales, **Eryri's** (p202) jagged summit is Wales at its most spectacular and **Portmeirion** (p204) its most quirky.

● A Scottish adventure should start in its vibrant capital **Edinburgh** (p205), where highlights include the Royal Mile and medieval Old Town. Then head further north to explore the **Highlands** (p213), from sprawling lochs to mountain trails, lush glens and precious woodland. Don't miss the stunning islands, either. **Skye** (p217) is a misty world of jagged mountain peaks, rich river valleys and plunging cliffs, while **Orkney** (p219) and **Shetland** (p220) are ancient wonderlands illuminated by the northern lights.

AUGUST
The **Edinburgh Festival Fringe** (p205) has an event for anything you care to name – books, art, theatre, music, comedy, marching bands.

OCTOBER
Halloween is an old Celtic festival, so dress up in your spookiest costume, or at least drink in pubs festooned with bats and pumpkins.

NOVEMBER
Guy Fawkes Night (5 November) means the skies across Britain fill with fireworks honouring a failed attempt to blow up parliament back in 1605.

DECEMBER
Colourful **Christmas markets** appear around Britain in December, so get your fix of warming mulled wine amid brightly lit wooden chalets.

London

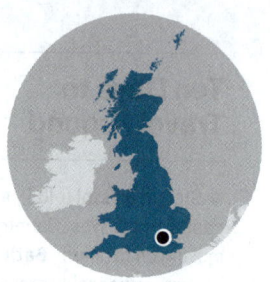

ICONIC SIGHTS | GLOBAL CUISINE | DENSE HISTORY

 TOP TIP

When roaming around the West End, give yourself the freedom to explore. Instead of looking at a map or your phone – simply get lost. Let your intrigue guide you through the little lanes and passages and you may discover a new secret spot. Don't forget to look up: historic details are everywhere.

London's architecture tells a unique and beguiling biography; tireless innovation is built into the city's fabric. The capital's deep-rooted past is accented by modern structures – the Shard, the Gherkin and Tate Modern – that never drown out London's centuries-old narrative. Major projects continue to move London forward, such as the 2022 opening of the Elizabeth line, the 73-mile east–west railway extending across the capital and into neighbouring counties. The regenerated Battersea Power Station, a 1940s power plant turned shopping centre, became accessible to the public for the first time in 2022 with many of its industrial features preserved.

London is a city of concrete plans but also of ideas and imagination – whether it's theatrical innovation, contemporary art, pioneering music, cutting-edge design or global cuisine. It's a place where wide-open vistas and sight-packed streets exist in unison. Add in historic neighbourhoods, leafy suburbs, charming parks and tranquil riverbanks and you have one of the world's great metropolises.

House of Important Pieces

View the world's oldest artefacts

The **British Museum** *(britishmuseum.org; free)* is the country's most popular museum (around 5.8 million visitors

---

GETTING AROUND

London is huge, but the public transport network is generally a well-oiled machine that runs reliably. The Tube, or London Underground – which includes the London Overground, Docklands Light Railway (DLR) and the Elizabeth line – is the fastest and most efficient way of getting around. Some stations are much closer together in reality than they appear on the map. The main sights are clustered around the West End, South Bank and the City of London, and if you plan well, you'll mostly walk.

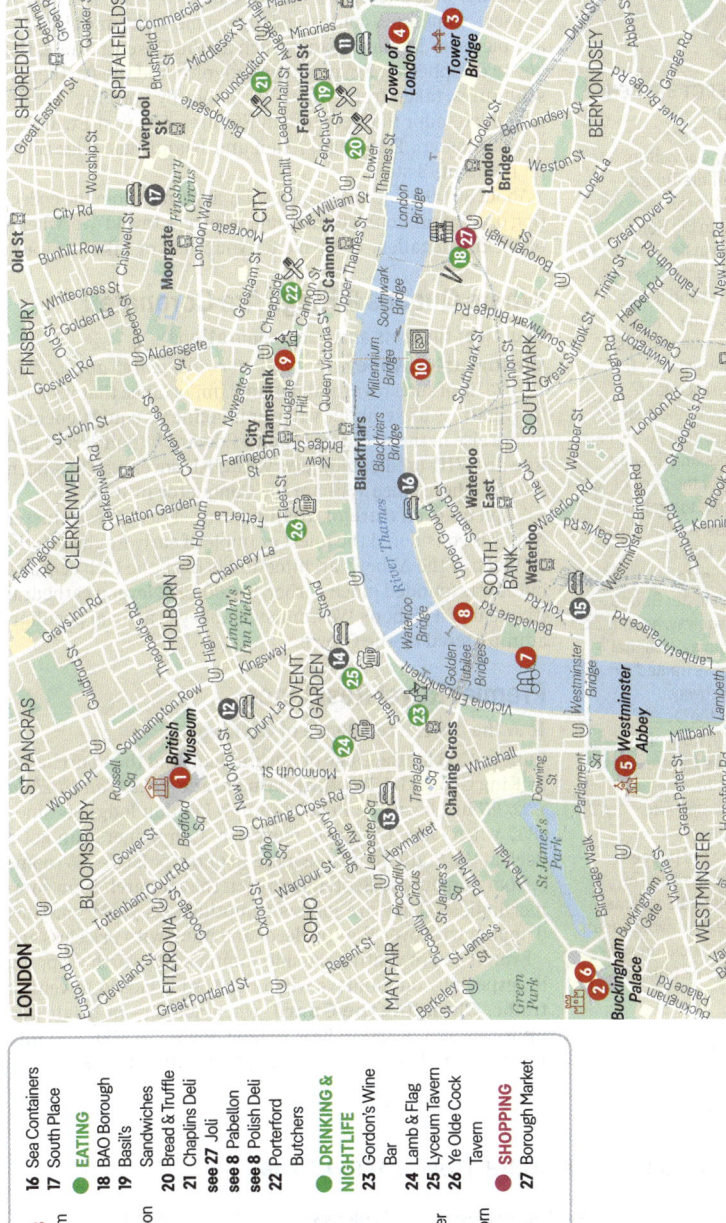

LONDON

★ HIGHLIGHTS
1 British Museum
2 Buckingham Palace
3 Tower Bridge
4 Tower of London
5 Westminster Abbey

● SIGHTS
6 Changing the Guard
7 London Eye
8 Southbank Centre
9 St Paul's Cathedral
10 Tate Modern

● SLEEPING
11 CitizenM Tower of London
12 Hoxton Holborn
13 Londoner
14 One Aldwych
15 Park Plaza

16 Sea Containers
17 South Place

● EATING
18 BAO Borough
19 Basil's Sandwiches
20 Bread & Truffle
21 Chaplins Deli
  see 27 Joli
  see 8 Pabellon
  see 8 Polish Deli
22 Porterford Butchers

● DRINKING & NIGHTLIFE
23 Gordon's Wine Bar
24 Lamb & Flag
25 Lyceum Tavern
26 Ye Olde Cock Tavern

● SHOPPING
27 Borough Market

PERFECT BIG BEN SNAPS

Millions of visitors get off the Tube at Westminster. As home to Big Ben, Westminster Bridge crossing the River Thames and the neo-Gothic Palace of Westminster, it's the perfect spot for an 'I'm in London' selfie. For the best photos, come early in the morning (ideally dusk for the perfect lighting) to avoid the crowds. And try these iconic frames:

● Beneath Westminster Bridge passageway, next to St Thomas' Hospital, for views framed by the archway.

● On the Queen's Walk in front of the Sea Life Centre – best when the clock is illuminated after sunset.

● The red phone box on the edge of Parliament Sq; come off-peak to avoid lines for this social-media-famous picture.

annually) and one of the world's oldest (opened in 1759). It houses – sometimes controversially – some of the most important pieces of human history, such as the Rosetta Stone, the key to deciphering Egyptian hieroglyphs; and the Parthenon sculptures, taken from Athens' Acropolis by Lord Elgin (British ambassador to the Ottoman Empire). The vast Etruscan, Greek, Roman, European, Asian and Islamic galleries carry on humanity's story.

About 80,000 objects are on display at a time (from the collection of eight million). The museum is huge, so avoid overwhelm by picking a gallery or theme for your visit or taking a tour.

Where Queens & Kings Are Coronated
Church of funerals and commemorations

Westminster Abbey *(westminster-abbey.org; adult/child £30/13)* is of such royal and national importance that it's hard to overstress its symbolic value or imagine its equivalent anywhere else in the world. Except for Edward V (murdered) and Edward VIII (abdicated), every English sovereign has been crowned here since William the Conqueror in 1066.

A splendid mixture of architectural styles, Westminster Abbey is considered the finest example of early English Gothic. Much of the Abbey's architecture is from the 13th century, but it was founded much earlier, in 960 CE. Never a cathedral (the seat of a bishop), Westminster Abbey is a 'royal peculiar' administered by the Crown.

Premier Royal Residence
Tour the official residence of the King

Built in 1703 for the Duke of Buckingham and then purchased by King George III, **Buckingham Palace** *(rct.uk; adult/child £32/16)* has been the Royal Family's London lodgings since 1837 when Queen Victoria moved in. Commoners can get a peek at the State Rooms – a mere 19 of the palace's 775 rooms – from mid-July to September when the monarch is on summer holiday. They are just as sumptuous as you'd imagine, dripping with over-the-top decor and hung with priceless art.

Even if you're visiting outside summer, it's worth stopping by, especially on Sundays when the Mall is closed to vehicle traffic. **Changing the Guard**, when soldiers in bright-red uniforms and bearskin hats parade down the Mall and into Buckingham Palace, is madly popular with tourists.

DRINKING IN LONDON: HISTORIC BARS AND PUBS

Lyceum Tavern: On the site of the original Lyceum Theatre; today it's a traditional oak-panelled pub. *noon-11pm Mon-Thu, to midnight Fri & Sat, to 11.30pm Sun*	**Ye Olde Cock Tavern:** London's narrowest pub was frequented by Charles Dickens and Alfred Tennyson. *noon-11pm Mon-Sat, to 7pm Sun*	**Gordon's Wine Bar:** The city's oldest wine bar is a gorgeous candlelit basement and a buzzing terrace. *11am-11pm Mon-Sat, noon-10pm Sun*	**Lamb & Flag:** Tiny and full of old-world charm and history – a pub has been on this West End spot since 1772. *11am-11pm Mon-Sat, noon-10.30pm Sun*

ALEXANDER CHAIKIN/SHUTTERSTOCK

Changing the Guard

A Saintly Symbol of Resilience

Step inside London's mightiest cathedral

A place of Christian worship for more than 1400 years (and pagan before that), **St Paul's Cathedral** *(stpauls.co.uk; adult/child £26/10)* is one of London's most magnificent buildings. For Londoners, the vast dome is a symbol of pride, standing tall since 1710 and surviving an onslaught of Luftwaffe incendiary bombs during the Blitz. The dome, inspired by St Peter's Basilica in the Vatican, rises more than 85m above the floor, supported by eight huge columns.

A Window of Bloody History

London's macabre 1000-year-old royal jail

The unmissable **Tower of London** *(hrp.org.uk/tower-of-london; adult/child £34.80/17.40)* offers a window into 1000 years of gruesome and compelling history. A former royal residence, treasury, mint, armoury and zoo, it's perhaps most remembered as the prison where a king, three queens and many nobles – including Anne Boleyn and Catherine Howard, Henry VIII's second and fifth wives – met their deaths. The immaculately dressed Yeoman Warders (better known as the Beefeaters) live on-site, protecting the spectacular Crown Jewels.

Walk the Thames' Icon

Cross the famous Tower Bridge

With its neo-Gothic towers and sky-blue suspension struts, **Tower Bridge** *(towerbridge.org.uk; adult/child £16/£8)* is one

THE GREAT REBUILD OF LONDON

The Great Fire of London is the reason almost none of medieval London remains and so much of it dates from the late 17th century, yet there's little popular lamentation of this 'wiping out' of the 'old London'. This is because, though London at the time was the third-largest city in the Western world, it wasn't famous for its beauty, architecture or urban design. Writer John Evelyn felt it paled in comparison to the baroque magnificence of Paris and described London as an unplanned, wooden mess. The latter was the main reason the fire spread so quickly and devastatingly, with most properties made of timber and covered in thatched roofing. What was built in their place is the magnificence we still see.

 EATING IN LONDON: BEST STREET FOOD IN THE SOUTH BANK

Pabellon: Indulge in black beans, plantains and Venezuelan arepas at South Bank Food Market. Vegan-friendly. *noon-8pm Fri, noon-11am Sat, noon-6pm Sun* ££

Joli: Singaporean and Malaysian dishes, like tender beef rendang, cooked in a traditional clay pot in Borough Market. *10am-5pm Tue-Fri, 9am-5pm Sat, 10am-4pm Sun* ££

Polish Deli: Barbequed Polish sausages are served with pickles and beer in the South Bank Food Market. *11am-8pm Fri, 10am-6pm Sat, noon-6pm Sun* ££

BAO Borough: Taiwanese joint serving beef short-rib bao buns; wash it down with a fermented pineapple soda. *noon-10pm Mon-Thu, to 10.30pm Fri & Sat, to 9pm Sun* £

A WALK AROUND HAMPSTEAD HEATH

Hampstead Heath's rolling woodlands and wild meadows feel miles away from central London, but you see the city from its hilltops.

START	END	LENGTH
Hampstead Heath station	Holly Bush pub	4 miles; 3–4 hours

Take the London Overground to Hampstead Heath station. Follow the Parliament Hill street into the park to start your climb up to the **1 Parliament Hill Viewpoint** for a panoramic scene of the city.

A web of trails to the north leads to bathing ponds (**2 mixed pond** to the west, **3 men's** and **4 women's** to the east). The men's and women's ponds are open year-round for cold-water swimming and supervised by lifeguards.

Traverse the heath to its northern edge and find the 18th-century **5 Kenwood House**. The free-to-visit gallery has a magnificent collection of art, including paintings by Rembrandt, Constable, Turner, Gainsborough and Vermeer.

Next, head to one of the wonderful pubs nearby for a restorative pint. Exit the heath via the Kenwood House car park and walk southwest along Hampstead Ln. At the heath's edge is the 1585 **6 Spaniards Inn**, where Romantic poets Keats and Byron and artist Sir Joshua Reynolds all paused for a drink.

Stroll to the Jack Straw's Castle bus stop and explore the historic neighbourhood of Hampstead. Loved by artists in the interwar years, it has retained a bohemian feel, with leafy streets, cafes and boutiques. Finish with a gastro-pub dinner at **7 Holly Bush**, a secluded pub with a splendid antique interior.

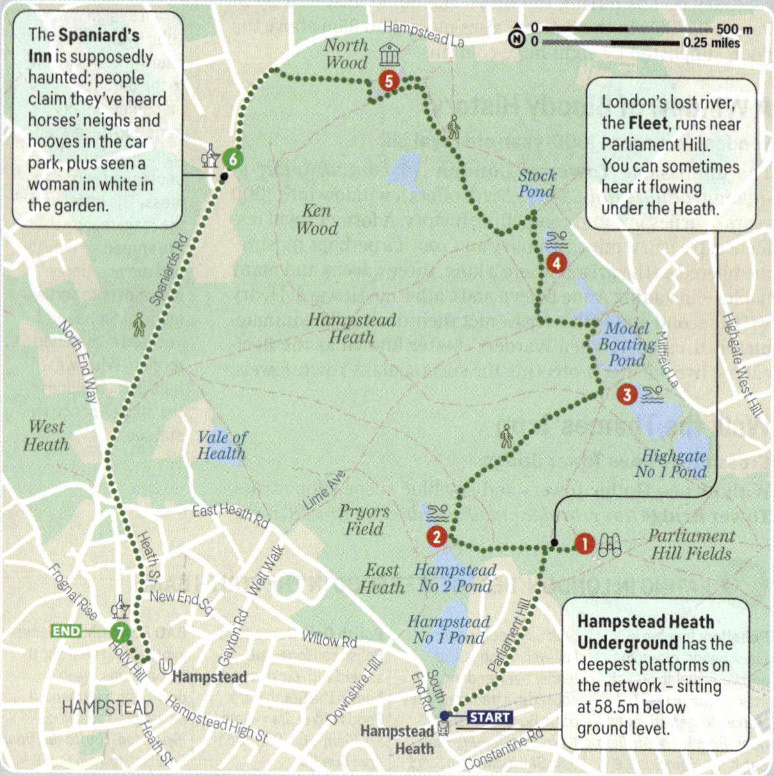

The **Spaniard's Inn** is supposedly haunted; people claim they've heard horses' neighs and hooves in the car park, plus seen a woman in white in the garden.

London's lost river, the **Fleet**, runs near Parliament Hill. You can sometimes hear it flowing under the Heath.

Hampstead Heath Underground has the deepest platforms on the network – sitting at 58.5m below ground level.

North Wood
Ken Wood
Hampstead Heath
Stock Pond
Model Boating Pond
Highgate No 1 Pond
West Heath
Vale of Health
Pryors Field
East Heath
Hampstead No 2 Pond
Hampstead No 1 Pond
Parliament Hill Fields

Hampstead La
Highgate West Hill
Millfield La
Spaniards Rd
North End Way
East Heath Rd
Lime Ave
Heath St
New End Sq
Cayton Rd
Well Walk
Willow Rd
Downshire Hill
South End Rd
Parliament Hill
Constantine Rd
Frognal Rise
Holly Hill
Hampstead High St
Heath St

END 7 Hampstead
HAMPSTEAD
START Hampstead Heath

0 — 500 m
0 — 0.25 miles

of London's most recognisable sights. The city was a thriving port in 1894 when the bridge was built as a much-needed crossing point in the east, equipped with a revolutionary steam-driven bascule (counterbalance) mechanism that could raise the roadway to make way for oncoming ships in just three minutes. The story of building the structure is recounted in the Tower Bridge Exhibition.

Sample Global Flavours

Feast your way through a historic food court

Borough Market *(boroughmarket.org.uk; free)* was initially a wholesale market for greengrocers a millennium ago, but has since transformed into the most renowned food market in London. Today, its hundred-plus high-quality food and drink vendors pull in massive crowds. There are two main areas: Three Crown Square for larger merchants and Green Market for smaller ones. In the third area, Borough Market Kitchen, you'll find street-food traders serving anything from Asian baos to Spanish paella.

Art in a Former Power Station

Dive into Tate Modern's wildest works

The outstanding **Tate Modern** *(tate.org.uk; free)* is a spellbinding synthesis of modern art and industrial brick design. This contemporary-art gallery, housed in the creatively revamped Bankside Power Station, has been extraordinarily successful in bringing challenging work to the masses, both through its free permanent collection and fee-charged temporary exhibitions. The curators have at their disposal more than 60,000 works by Henri Matisse, Andy Warhol, Mark Rothko, Jackson Pollock, Barbara Hepworth, Damien Hirst, Rebecca Horn and more.

Bird's-Eye Views

Take in panoramic scenes from a London landmark

Standing 135m high in a fairly flat city, the **London Eye** *(londoneye.com; adult/child from £29/£26)* is the world's largest cantilevered observation wheel and affords views 25 miles in every direction (as far as Windsor Castle), weather permitting. A ride in one of the 32 glass-enclosed eye-shaped pods takes a gracefully slow 30 minutes.

THE FESTIVAL THAT SHAPED THE SOUTH BANK

The genesis of Europe's largest cultural and artistic hub traces back to the Festival of Britain held between May and September 1951 at a cost of £12 million to showcase great feats in architecture, the arts, science, technology and industrial design. Dubbed a 'tonic for the nation', it was the brainchild of Labour cabinet minister Herbert Morrison to raise spirits and celebrate recovery from WWII, despite austerity, by shining a spotlight on Britain's achievements to millions of visitors. Amid nationwide festivities, South Bank emerged as a thriving focal point, amplifying the festival's resonance. Today, the site of the festival houses the iconic **Southbank Centre**.

 EATING IN LONDON: BEST SANDWICHES IN THE CITY

Porterford Butchers: There are always lunchtime queues out the door for the meat-heavy baguettes at this family-owned shop. *6am-6pm Mon-Fri* £

Basil's Sandwiches: Doorstep-sized club sarnies made with focaccia. The Italian cheese and salami fillings are legendary. *5am-5pm Mon-Fri* £

Chaplins Deli: One for spice o' files, choose from the heaped fillings at the counter of this vintage express joint. *6am-4pm Mon-Fri* £

Bread & Truffle: Freshly baked, gourmet focaccia sandwiches with pesto, mozzarella and basil. *9.30am-5pm Mon-Thu, to 9pm Fri, 10.30am-9pm Sat & Sun* £

Beyond London

South of the capital, where deep and spectacular history meets fun and flair, life is never dull.

Places

England's sunny southeast is where the coastline comes closest to the Continent. Historically, the region has been the frontline of defence against invasion, a past that has left reminders in the form of Norman castles and naval shipyards. This strategic position is brought into focus at Dover Castle and the shore's famous White Cliffs where, from Roman times to the Cold War, the occupiers have prepared for an attack. It's also been the seat of religious life in Britain, with Canterbury Cathedral a beacon of the country's Christianity.

Things are very different a little further west. Ever since the 19th century, when Prince George hosted all-night parties at his opulent Royal Pavilion pleasure palace, Brighton has embraced hedonism. And as home to England's biggest gay scene, it also a place that invites people to be themselves.

GETTING AROUND

It's easy to reach the southeast's main hubs by train from London. The ease of travelling between towns depends on the train line; if the journey involves several changes, there may be a more direct route by bus. Car is generally the easiest way to get around, particularly in rural areas, and driving affords more freedom to explore. However, parking can be expensive in urban centres and traffic can be heavy on the coast.

Canterbury

TIME FROM LONDON: 1HR

The mother church

Rich in historical significance, UNESCO-listed **Canterbury Cathedral** *(canterbury-cathedral.org; adult/child £18/free)* is the spiritual head of the Anglican church and is among Europe's finest cathedrals. Exploring its precincts offers the chance to experience moments of peace and connect with its spirituality, and guided tours illuminate the many treasures and architectural details that tell the story of the cathedral's 1400-year history.

Next to the early Tudor-era Christ Church Gate, head to the visitor centre's upstairs gallery for a superb view of the mostly Gothic cathedral exterior. Before entering the cathedral at the southwest porch, walk further around to its western-most side to see statues of historical figures including Queen Elizabeth II and Prince Philip in the exterior niches.

Inside, the signposted visitor route spotlights the cathedral's most important details. Don't miss the Martyrdom, the spot where Archbishop Thomas Becket was murdered in 1170 by two of Henry II's knights; today it's marked by a flickering candle and modern altar.

AGSAZ/SHUTTERSTOCK

Tomb of Edward, the Black Prince, Canterbury Cathedral

Brighton

TIME FROM LONDON: 1HR

A life of hedonistic excess

Walking down from the train station, the first glimpse of the astonishing 19th-century, Indian-inspired architecture to come is the magnificent **Brighton Dome** *(brightondome. org),* now a concert hall and theatre.

Beyond the dome lies the ostentatious former party palace of King George IV, the **Royal Pavilion** *(brightonmuseums. org.uk; adult/child £19.50/£11.75)* itself. Meticulously planned to wow visitors at every turn, the pavilion's interior is an outlandish fantasy decorated with hand-painted Chinese wallpaper and mirrors to trick the eye.

Retail therapy in the Lanes

The tightly packed **Lanes** form Brighton's popular shopping district. Every twist and turn is packed with jewellers, gift shops, cafes and boutiques, selling everything from upcycled furniture to vegan shoes. Just south of the Brighton train station, the **North Laine** area has a number of partially pedestrianised streets with colourful murals and a more bohemian vibe.

The flea market **Snoopers Paradise** *(snoopersparadise. co.uk)* and nearby **North Laine Bazaar** *(northlainebazaar. com)* are fun places to search for retro collectibles and vintage clothes, records and books, while music lovers could spend hours browsing the vinyl at **Resident Music** *(resident-music.com).*

BEST TOURS IN BRIGHTON

Brighton Regency Routemaster: Afternoon-tea or gin-and-prosecco Regency architecture tours on a converted Routemaster RML 233 double-decker vintage bus.

Piers & Queers: Entertaining 90-minute LGBTIQ+ history tours Friday and Saturday, April to October, visiting famous sights and hidden bars.

Street Art Tour: Two-hour walking tour led by graffiti expert REQ, with insider info on the latest additions to Brighton's street art.

Ghost Walk of the Lanes: Actor and storyteller Rob Marks leads 80-minute Wednesday to Saturday night walks around macabre sights in the Lanes.

Brighton Diver Windfarm Tours: Board a 12m catamaran for a two-hour tour of the offshore New Rampion Windfarm.

 DRINKING IN BRIGHTON: OUR PICKS

Lion & Lobster: Maze of nooks and crannies with three bars, two hidden gardens, a sun-drenched roof terrace and live-music stage. *noon-midnight*

Plotting Parlour: Kemptown speakeasy with ceiling murals and cocktails including seasonal infusions. *4-11pm Sun-Thu, 3pm-midnight Fri & Sat*

Cricketers: Brighton's oldest pub, with flamboyant Victorian interiors. Live music Tuesdays and Fridays. *noon-11pm Sun-Thu, to 2am Fri & Sat*

Joker: Red-brick pub with pressed-tin ceilings and a roof terrace; the cocktail bar has monthly changing cocktails. *4-11pm Mon & Tue, noon-1am Wed-Sun*

STARLING MURMURATIONS ON THE SUSSEX COAST

The sight of thousands of starlings swooping and rising as one is among nature's most mesmerising spectacles. Starling murmurations – in which the glossy black birds react in less than 100 milliseconds to adapt to their neighbours' movements and make near-instant flight-path adjustments – are believed to be a tactic to deter predators and protect the flocks within one confusing, swirling mass.

The best time to see murmurations is during autumn and winter as the late-afternoon light begins to fade. Particularly dramatic displays are often seen near the piers in Eastbourne, Hastings and Brighton, where some 40,000 starlings gather near dusk at the remains of the derelict West Pier.

Join the party at Brighton's seafront

The seafront at Brighton and Hove is an active place, with joggers and dog-walkers zipping along the promenade, past buzzing bars, beachside volleyball games and tarot-card readers. At **Brighton Palace Pier** *(brightonpier.co.uk)*, the screams of thrill-seekers compete with the crashing of waves; take a stroll past doughnut stands and arcade games to the pier-end viewing platform.

For vertical views, hop in the viewing pod to shimmy up the world's tallest moving observation tower, the **i360** *(brighton i360.co.uk; adult/child £17.95/£8.95)*, which tops out at 162m.

Dover

TIME FROM LONDON: 1HR

Visit the famous White Cliffs

Spending a day in Dover offers an introduction to 2000 years of English history and a chance to connect to the emblematic significance and natural beauty of Dover's distinctive cliffs.

Visiting Dover's **castle** *(english-heritage.org.uk; adult/child from £25.90/16.30)* gives a sense of the town's historical role at the frontline of England's defence. From the castle, head 1 mile east to the National Trust–managed **White Cliffs** *(nationaltrust.org.uk)*, standing 106m high and stretching for 8 miles on both sides of Dover; there's parking at the visitor centre on the northern side. Follow the path along the clifftops for a bracing 2-mile walk to the **South Foreland Lighthouse**, where you can eat at the cafe's picnic tables looking out towards France.

Winchester

TIME FROM LONDON: 1HR 10MIN

An awe-inspiring Gothic cathedral

With one of Europe's longest medieval naves, **Winchester Cathedral** *(winchester-cathedral.org.uk; adult/child £13.50/free)* is an imposing Gothic landmark that can be seen from the surrounding hills. Inside, it's a beguiling jumble of architectural styles, with a Norman crypt and ornate Renaissance chantry chapels.

Near the entrance is the **grave of Jane Austen**, marked by a plaque. One of the cathedral's most striking features is the abstract patchwork of the West Window: after the original stained-glass window was destroyed by Parliamentary troops during the English Civil War, the current window was created in 1660 using fragments of shattered glass.

 ### EATING IN CANTERBURY AND WINCHESTER: OUR PICKS

Goods Shed: Canterbury indoor farmers market, food hall and mezzanine restaurant rolled into one. *noon-3pm Sun & Tue, noon-3pm & 5.30-9pm Wed-Sat* ££

Parrot: Dating back to 1370, this snug half-timbered Canterbury pub serves local real ales; has upstairs dining room and a leafy beer garden. *noon-9.30pm* ££

Cart & Horses: Classic pub fare and top Sunday roast are served at this country pub on Winchester's outskirts. *10am-11pm* ££

Wellhouse: All dishes served in this rustic Winchester building are cooked over an open wood-fire. *6.30-9.30pm Mon-Sat, noon-2.30pm & 6.30-9.30pm Sun* ££

Devon & Cornwall

WILD COAST | FRESH SEAFOOD | SPECTACULAR STROLLS

Flung out on Britain's far edge, the southwest is celebrated for its natural charms: craggy cliffs cloaked in gorse, rocky tors on wild moors, golden beaches washed by surf. Every year, millions of visitors flock here to feel the sand between their toes, and with miles of coastline, countryside and clifftops to explore, it's really no wonder.

If you want to experience the region's landscapes at their best, ditch the car and get active. Hiking trails and cycling paths crisscross the countryside, and the South West Coast Path winds around a stunning coastal kaleidoscope. Kayak the rivers, hike the moors, bike the back lanes, surf the waves or coasteer on the cliffs – the adventures never seem to end.

And while the southwest's popularity inevitably means crowds, with the help of a decent map and an adventurous spirit, you'll nearly always be able to find a patch of sand to call your own.

> ### ☑ TOP TIP
>
> The southwest is packed in July and August: it's much more pleasant to visit in spring or autumn, when the big crowds have left and you can appreciate the scenery in (relative) peace and quiet. Book well ahead, too.

Padstow

Cornwall's best-known bike route

Originally a railway line, the **Camel Trail** *(cornwall.gov.uk/cameltrail)* is now Cornwall's most popular bike ride. The trail starts in Padstow and runs east through Wadebridge along the

---

⊘ GETTING AROUND

England's southwestern peninsula is widespread and remote, with just three cities and a handful of major towns. A car brings maximum freedom, but parking can be tricky (and pricey) in popular places, and summer traffic can be a serious headache. The A30 and A38 are the main road routes into the region.

Travelling by bus in the southwest is cheap and usually reliable, but slow. Rural services are less frequent, and in the case of some remote villages, non-existent. Seasonal, hop-on/hop-off buses often run between major attractions in popular areas.

The mainline train between London and Penzance stops at major towns and cities and includes an overnight service six days a week.

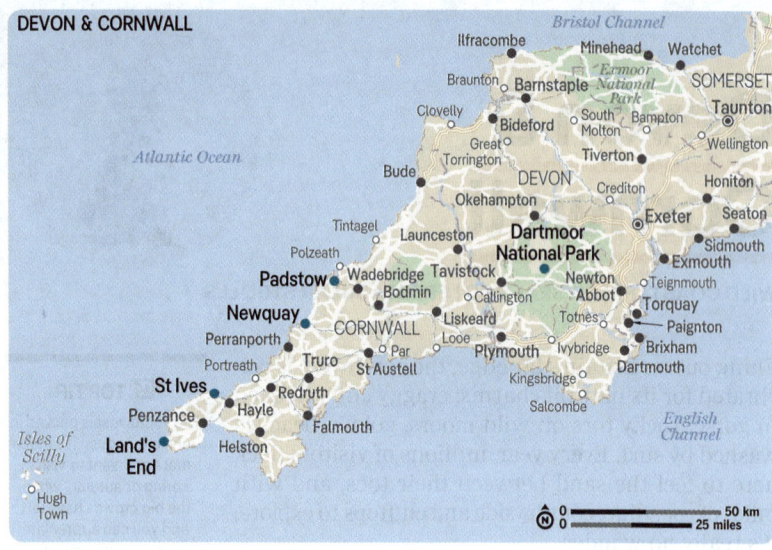

DEVON & CORNWALL

Camel Estuary before continuing through Bodmin (10.8 miles) to Poley's Bridge (18.3 miles) on Bodmin Moor. The Padstow–Wadebridge section makes a lovely half-day excursion, and the scenery is marvellous, but it does get busy in summer.

Bikes can be hired from both ends: in Padstow, try **Padstow Cycle Hire** *(padstowcyclehire.com; adult/child from £17/6)* or **Trail Bike Hire** *(trailbikehire.co.uk; adult/child from £16/8)*. In Wadebridge, try **Bridge Bike Hire** *(bridgebikehire.co.uk; adult/child from £19/10)*.

Fruit of the (Cornish) vines

The sheltered valleys around Padstow are home to several renowned vineyards. **Camel Valley Vineyard** *(camelvalley.com; tours adult £18)* has been producing award-winning still and sparkling English wines since 1989. Visit for one of the guided tours, run at 10.30am Monday to Friday (reduced during harvest and winter), or book a table to sip wines by the glass in the tasting room or on the sun terrace.

Closer to Padstow is **Trevibban Mill** *(trevibbanmill.com; tours £17.50)*. Tours are run seasonally three times a week, or you can book a table for a wine or cider tasting. Alternatively,

 EATING IN PADSTOW: SEAFOOD SPECIALITIES

Seafood Restaurant: The restaurant that started the Stein saga: an elegant, light-filled dining room on the riverside. *noon-9pm* **£££**	**Paul Ainsworth at No 6:** TV chef Ainsworth's Michelin-starred food deserves all the plaudits; it's booked up months in advance. *noon-10pm Tue-Sat* **£££**	**Prawn on the Lawn:** Tiny, ultra-cool seafood bar where the menu changes daily depending on what its fishers have caught. *noon-10pm Tue-Sat* **££**	**Stein's Fish & Chips:** Lines are long and prices above average, but the fresh, battered fish is undeniably good! *noon-8pm* **££**

relax on the viewing balcony (open Tuesday to Saturday) with a sharing platter and a glass of still or sparkling wine or cider.

Newquay

Surf's up

Newquay is Cornwall's surf central. The north coast swells are the most consistent in the UK, and every year they attract thousands of budding boarders looking to catch their first wave or hone their skills. There are scores of schools to choose from; **Escape Surf School** *(escapesurfschool.co.uk; from £30)* and **Fistral Beach Surf School** *(fistralbeachsurfschool.co.uk; £45)* both have good reputations.

Fistral Beach is legendary for its waves, which can reach over 30ft on the infamous Cribbar Reef. Other options within in easy reach of Newquay include **Crantock**, **Holywell Bay** and **Watergate Bay**, where another of the area's best surf schools is based: **Wavehunters** *(wavehunters.co.uk; £45)*.

St Ives

Pick up a brush in Cornwall's art capital

With its fishers' cottages and church towers spread around a brilliant turquoise bay, St Ives is a dazzling sight. If it has inspired you to pick up a brush, book a course at the **St Ives School of Painting** *(schoolofpainting.co.uk; from £12)*, which has been tutoring budding artists since it opened in 1938. Today, the school runs a range of classes and multiday courses focusing on painting in a range of mediums, covering everything from landscapes to life drawing.

Land's End

Take a photo with the Land's End sign

The clue's in the name. The rugged headland of **Land's End** *(landsend-landmark.co.uk; free)* is where Cornwall (and mainland Britain) comes to a screeching halt, and the black granite cliffs fall away into a maelstrom of white surf.

Famous as the last port of call for walkers on the 874-mile slog from John O'Groats in Scotland, the views are epic: the restless Atlantic seems to wrap itself around the horizon, shimmering in the late-afternoon light, and on a clear evening, the sunsets are out of this world. Look out for the **Longships Lighthouse**, 1.25 miles offshore, and the faint outlines of the Isles of Scilly 28 miles out to sea. The photo-op beside

RICK STEIN & PADSTOW

Celebrity chef Rick Stein opened the **Seafood Restaurant** *(rickstein.com)* on the quay in Padstow in 1975 – before he'd even learnt to cook! As his reputation grew, Stein made several TV appearances, rising to fame after his first show, *Taste of the Sea*, in 1995.

The presence of a celebrity chef's flagship restaurant helped boost Padstow's popularity as a holiday destination, turning the town into an upscale foodie hub. Stein now owns four restaurants in Padstow, plus a fishmonger, coffee shop, deli, gift shop and a cookery school – earning the town the nickname 'Padstein'. It's not always affectionately meant: while tourism massively supports the economy, many locals feel Padstow has lost its identity.

 EATING IN ST IVES: OUR PICKS

Porthminster Beach Cafe: Less a beach cafe, more a bistro with a sun-trap terrace and a superb Med-inspired menu. *noon-9pm* ££

Porthminster Kitchen: The beach cafe's in-town sister restaurant, specialising in seafood. *12:30-3pm & 5:30-9pm Mon-Sat, noon-3pm Sun* ££

One Fish Street: The daily seafood-themed tasting menus depend on what's been landed that morning on the quay. *noon-3pm & 7pm-late Mon-Sat* £££

Blas Burgerworks: St Ives' burger joint has choices for carnivores, vegetarians and vegans; also serves breakfasts. *hours vary, closed Mon & Tue* ££

GREAT DARTMOOR WALKS

Lydford Gorge: The southwest's deepest gorge, home to a 30m waterfall and the magical 'Devil's Cauldron' whirlpool.

Wistman's Wood: An easy stroll from the Two Bridges pub to a mossy oak woodland straight from a fairy tale.

Bellever Forest: Several waymarked trails in a dense pine forest: climb Bellever Tor and explore Kraps Ring Bronze Age village.

Princetown Railway Track: Follow the old railway to King's Tor, passing two abandoned quarries, Swell Tor and Foggintor.

Yes Tor & High Willhays: The two highest points on Dartmoor (619m and 621m respectively) afford spectacular views of the moors.

Combestone Tor, Dartmoor National Park

HELEN HOTSON/SHUTTERSTOCK

the famous signpost (New York 3147; John O' Groats 874) is a cliché, but essential nonetheless.

Dartmoor National Park

Hike across Dartmoor's famous tors

Dartmoor's 160 tors are legendary. Though they look like they were dropped upon the landscape by a giant hand, these hilltop outcrops of granite were formed from molten rock some 280 million years ago and left exposed by millennia of erosion. The bizarre shapes of these stacks and monoliths have inspired mankind for centuries. Some were used as places of worship by Dartmoor's ancient inhabitants, others gave rise to folklore and legends that persist to this day.

Some, like the face-shaped **Combestone Tor**, can be seen from the road, while others require a walk. **Haytor** is one of the most popular and easiest to visit: a short walk uphill from the large car park nearby. The moorland trail from here to **Hound Tor** is an ideal introduction to Dartmoor, taking in disused quarries, a clapper bridge and a medieval settlement.

EATING & DRINKING IN DARTMOOR: CLASSIC COUNTRY PUBS

Warren House Inn: Legendary pub halfway along the B3212, near Postbridge, where the fire has remained lit since 1845. *hours vary* ££

Three Crowns: Chagford's lovely, part-thatched inn mixes 13th-century features and a modern atrium dining room. *10am-10pm* ££

Rugglestone Inn: Log fires and home-cooked food in a wisteria-clad stone property in charming Widecombe-in-the-Moor. *hours vary* ££

Dartmoor Inn: Organic open-fire grill cooking and some of the best views of Dartmoor, near Merrivale. *10am-10pm* ££

Bristol, Bath & the Cotswolds

ARCHITECTURE | ANCIENT HISTORY | VILLAGES

Contemporary cities rub shoulders with the ancient past in this region of pastoral landscapes, country pubs and chocolate-box villages.

Bristol is a city that's well and truly on the rise. Disused warehouses have been reimagined as art galleries and museums, old cargo containers now host restaurants serving Modern British dishes with a West Country lilt, and a world-class street-art scene adds colour.

Over in beautiful Bath, its rows of harmonious townhouses and famous crescents still exude the elegance that helped make this the most fashionable city in Georgian Britain. More than 5000 of the city's buildings are now listed by Historic England – part of the reason why Bath is the only city in Britain that's a UNESCO World Heritage site in its entirety.

Just to the north, the Cotswolds burst with charming villages of golden buildings, thatched roofs and picturesque cottage gardens.

> ☑ **TOP TIP**
>
> Bristol Temple Meads train station is beautiful but just on the outskirts of the city centre, so if you have lots of luggage, prepare to order a taxi as the central hotels aren't really walkable.

Bristol

The world's first great ocean liner

Moored in the dockyard in which it was built, **SS Great Britain** *(ssgreatbritain.org; adult/child £19.80/£13.05)* still looks

---

🧭 **GETTING AROUND**

Bristol is well connected to the rest of the UK by rail and bus. Bristol Airport, 8 miles from the city centre, provides links with UK and European cities. With the possible exception of hilly Clifton, it's easy to get around on foot and by bike – Bristol is the UK's first Cycling City, and there's a good network of cycling lanes and routes, plus several bike-rental companies in the city centre. Ferries provide a fun and often quicker way of moving around the harbour.

Bath is a compact and very walkable city, with most of its sights lying in the centre or just to the north, although it's a bit of an uphill climb to reach the Circus and the Royal Crescent.

For the greatest flexibility, and the potential to get off the beaten track in the Cotswolds, having your own car is unbeatable (you just need to find a spot to park).

JANE AUSTEN

Beloved English novelist Jane Austen (1775–1817) topped a 2022 poll as the greatest British author of all time (beating Shakespeare and *Harry Potter's* JK Rowling) but didn't experience fame. Austen published her first novel, *Sense and Sensibility* (1811), anonymously as 'By a Lady', and subsequently *Pride and Prejudice* (1813), *Mansfield Park* (1814) and *Emma* (1816) only as 'By the Author of' her previous works. Austen's other completed novels, *Northanger Abbey* and *Persuasion* (1817), were published posthumously. Social commentary on upper-class, late-18th-century society, especially women's dependence on marriage for status and financial security, were pivotal in her writing, though she wasn't wealthy and didn't marry before her death aged 41.

every bit the groundbreaking steamship it once was. Designed in 1843 by Isambard Kingdom Brunel, this was one of the largest ships ever built, measuring 98m from stern to tip. Brunel used wrought iron instead of wood, allowing for a far bigger hull, and to forego conventional paddle wheels in favour of a propeller. You can see them in the **Dry Dock**, enclosed by the 'glass sea' in which the ship rests. In the **Dockyard Museum**, exhibits chart the ship's chequered history, from a passenger liner to a quarantine ship and coal hulk.

See a grand bridge

Spanning the river below the well-heeled suburb of Clifton is Isambard Kingdom Brunel's awe-inspiring **Clifton Suspension Bridge** *(cliftonbridge.org.uk)*, which took 33 years to build and wasn't finished until 1864, several years after Brunel's death. Cross the bridge to the **Visitor Centre** to discover the story behind this feat of engineering; the free **Weekend Bridge Tours** (year-round) are excellent.

Bath

The world's most famous Roman spa

For over 2000 years, visitors have been drawn to the **Roman Baths** *(romanbaths.co.uk; adult/child £28/£21)* that give the city its name. The Romans established the town of Aquae Sulis around the sight of a sacred spring here in 44 CE and within 100 years had built this ostentatious complex of baths and adjoining temple to the goddess Sulis Minerva. The baths now form one of Europe's best-preserved ancient Roman sites.

The heart of the complex is the atmospheric **Great Bath**, a lead-lined pool filled with steaming jade-coloured water. Though now open-air, the bath was originally covered by a 20m-high barrel-vaulted roof. The Great Bath was fed with water from the **Sacred Spring**, which you can see bubbling away next door.

Taking the waters

While you can't swim at the Roman Baths, you can put the healing powers of thermal waters to the test in Bath.

The cutting-edge **Thermae Bath Spa** *(thermaebathspa.com; from £42.50)* complex is split into the **New Royal Bath** (no children under 16) and, in a separate building across the aptly named Hot Bath St, the more intimate **Cross Bath** (no kids under 12). The highlight is the open-air rooftop pool in the main building, with superb views over the cityscape (especially at dusk).

 EATING IN BRISTOL: OUR PICKS

Pasta Ripiena: Stellar stuffed pasta: handmade, wrapped in front of you, deeply flavoured and delicious. *5.30-11pm Tue, noon-4pm & 5.30-11pm Wed-Sat* ££

Riverstation: Light-filled waterfront restaurant and bar serving modern European cuisine. *11am-9pm Mon-Fri, 10am-9.30pm Sat, 10am-5.30pm Sun* ££

BOX-E: Beautifully cooked seasonal British dishes served in a pair of old shipping containers on Wapping Wharf. *5.30-9.30pm Wed, noon-9.30pm Thu-Sat* ££

Bulrush: Michelin-starred restaurant with British-, French- and Scandinavian-influenced set menus. *6-9.30pm Tue-Thu, noon-1.30pm & 6-9.30pm Fri & Sat* £££

EVANNOVOSTRO/SHUTTERSTOCK

Roman Baths, Bath

The Cotswolds

Get that quintessential England shot

Many of the places for snapping that classic Cotswolds photo have fallen victim to overtourism. Go early in the morning or late in the day to avoid the crowds – it's often when you'll get the best lighting, too.

Starting in **Burford**, Sheep St has vine-covered stone houses set back from the road. In **Bibury**, looking very much like it did when it was built in the 14th century, the cottages of **Arlington Row** are the subject of the occasional visitor controversy; No 9 is available to rent through the National Trust website. While in summer it's hard to get a shot of the bridges over the River Windrush in **Bourton-on-the-Water** without dozens of people, in winter you may snap that elusive snow shot.

Other notable places to visit include the cobblestone **Chipping Steps** in Tetbury; the **Old Mill** at Lower Slaughter; Grade I–heritage listed **Grevel's House** in Chipping Norton; the unfinished, Gothic-revival **Woodchester Mansion**, near Stroud; and the ruins of **Minster Lovell Hall** on the River Windrush near Witney, or **Hailes Abbey** at Winchcombe, both managed by English Heritage.

It goes without saying, respect residents' privacy, and drive on if a coach-load of visitors arrived just before you.

BEST COTSWOLDS OUTDOOR ACTIVITIES OPERATORS

Cotswold Cycles: Rents out all kinds of bikes and has maps and route suggestions from its Moreton-in-Marsh base.

Wild Pig: Hot-air balloon trips over the Cotswolds landscapes from April to October, toasting with bubbles (or tea/coffee).

Cotswold Canoe Hire: Kayaks, open canoes and SUPs for hourly or multiday hire from Lechlade-on-Thames.

Cotswold Mountain Biking: Half- and full-day tours, from flat towpath rides to steep descents and challenging climbs, on electric and traditional mountain bikes.

Cotswold Gliding Club: Sightseeing flights with views of the villages, rivers and rolling hills, plus gliding lessons.

 EATING IN THE COTSWOLDS: BEST COUNTRY DINING

Woolpack Inn: Three-century-old pub near Stroud with dishes like crispy pig's cheek with dandelion. *noon-3pm Mon, noon-3pm & 6-9pm Tue-Sun* ££	**Wheatsheaf Inn:** Seasonal British cuisine served in an elegant dining room and garden in Northleach. *8am-10am & noon-9pm Mon-Sat, noon-8pm Sun* ££	**Bull:** Locally sourced ingredients cooked over a charcoal grill; near Chipping Norton. *5-10pm Mon, noon-3pm & 5-10.30pm Tue-Sat, noon-5pm Sun* ££	**Quince & Clover:** Lovely daytime cafe for dishes like black-pudding sausage rolls in a thatched building near Chipping Norton. *8.30am-4pm Wed-Mon* £

JOAOCIDO/SHUTTERSTOCK

TOP EXPERIENCE

Stonehenge

This mystical ring of monolithic stones is the most famous prehistoric monument in Europe and one of England's most emblematic sights, attracting pilgrims, tourists and New Age travellers for over 5000 years. Despite countless theories about the site's purpose, from a sacrificial centre to an astronomical clock, no one knows exactly why Ancient Britons expended so much time and effort on its construction.

DON'T MISS

Great Trilithon

Heel Stone

Slaughter Stone

Archaeological exhibits

360-degree projection

Neolithic houses

Cursus Barrows

Stone Circle

Walking the visitor path around the circle gets you as close as 5m to the stones to ponder their mysterious origins. Building Stonehenge was a process that lasted over 1000 years. The first phase started around 3000 BCE, when the outer circular bank and ditch were created. Within this were 56 pits – known as Aubrey Holes after John Aubrey, the antiquarian who discovered them in the 1600s – in which cremated remains were buried. These are now marked by concrete plaques.

About 500 years later, Stonehenge's main sarsen stones were hewn from the Marlborough Downs, 20 miles away, and

PRACTICALITIES
● english-heritage.org.uk ● adult/child from £27.20/16.30 ● 9.30am-7pm Jun-Aug, to 5pm Oct-May

dragged to the site. The largest were erected in a horseshoe and crowned by massive lintels to make the trilithons (two vertical stones topped by a horizontal one). The huge slabs of the Great Trilithon were worked to ensure its uprights perfectly framed the setting sun on a midwinter's day.

Surrounding this horseshoe was a ring of 30 sarsens (17 of which are still standing), each one linked to the next by a similar lintel. Four Station Stones were arranged around the edge of the enclosure in a layout that, again, was governed by the movement of the sun. Two additional curving rows of smaller bluestones were hauled here from the Preseli Mountains in South Wales, an incredible 250 miles away, while in 2024 scientists discovered the Altar Stone came from northeast Scotland.

The entrance to the circle is marked by the Heel Stone and, slightly further in, the Slaughter Stone. These stones were aligned to coincide with sunrise at the midsummer solstice.

Crowds flock for **solstice and equinox celebrations**, when free managed access is allowed inside the stone circle.

Stonehenge Landscape

Stonehenge actually forms part of a huge complex of ancient monuments that you can wander around.

North of the circle lie the Cursus Barrows, a humped cemetery of Bronze Age burial mounds. From these, you can make out the ridge of the nearby Cursus itself, an elongated embanked oval built around 1000 years before Stonehenge was raised. More burial mounds, the Old and New King Barrows, sit beside the Avenue, a ceremonial pathway that linked Stonehenge with the River Avon, 1.5 miles away.

The only visible remains of the Neolithic settlement at Durrington Walls, further up the Avon and connected to the river by its own smaller avenue, is the massive henge that was built around it. It's believed Durrington housed the builders of Stonehenge, who also erected nearby Woodhenge.

The National Trust has downloadable walking trails in the Stonehenge Landscape.

Visitor Centre Exhibitions

Engaging displays at the visitor centre, which plot the site's development and show how Stonehenge fits within the landscape and the movement of the sun, give you a good sense of what you're about to see at the stone circle and surrounding landscape. The highlight is a 360-degree projection of Stonehenge, letting you experience the changing seasons (including the midsummer sunrise) from 'inside' the circle. Exhibits include finds unearthed at the site, such as axes, arrowheads and antler picks, and the strikingly lifelike model of the face of a Neolithic man who was buried in a long barrow nearby. Outside, thatch-roofed, white-chalk-walled Neolithic houses replicating those used by Stonehenge's builders were constructed using local materials and ancient methods.

VISITING STONEHENGE

From the visitor centre, frequent shuttle buses make the 1.5-mile trip to the stones. Walking is more atmospheric; ask the driver to drop you at Fargo Woods then follow the trail, past the Cursus and Cursus Barrows. Wear sturdy shoes and bring waterproofs (there's no shelter at the stones). To go inside the circle, book a hosted, out-of-hours **Stone Circle Experience** (maximum 30 people), several months ahead.

TOP TIPS

● The best times to visit are weekdays, before 11am or after 2pm.

● Tickets are by timeslot entry; you can then stay until closing.

● Download English Heritage's free audio tour (bring headphones) for comprehensive guides to the exhibitions, stone circle and surrounding landscape.

● Parking is free if you've prebooked Stonehenge tickets.

● From Salisbury, hop-on/hop-off Stonehenge Tour buses have transport only, or transport and ticket options to Stonehenge and Old Sarum, with combination tickets also available for Salisbury Cathedral. See *thestonehengetour.info*.

The Midlands

CUISINE | INDUSTRIAL HERITAGE | LITERARY LORE

 TOP TIP

Stirchley is Birmingham's neighbourhood *du jour*, particularly if you're a craft-beer fan. But its name doesn't appear on any train map. To visit, take the Cross City Line to Bourneville and exit at Mary Vale Rd.

Though it's comfortably the Midlands' largest metropolis, a combination of Luftwaffe air raids and questionable town planning gave Birmingham a somewhat dismal image during the late 20th century, but fresh new architecture, gleaming trams and the arrival of some fabulous restaurants have helped make it the Midlands' renaissance city. World-class shopping and unique museums bring the smart centre plenty of buzz, but make time for neighbourhoods like Harborne and Moseley, where creative locals put their hearts into some fine artisan shops, bars and cafes.

The leafy countryside outside the Second City reveals some serious history, from imposing castles to the home of a certain 16th-century playwright. There are also grand adventures found in Shropshire, while over in Nottingham, there's far more to the city than its famous tights-wearing outlaw, Robin Hood. These days, the crowds come to Nottingham for its bumping music scene, creative restaurants and an infectious youthful dynamism.

Birmingham

Stroll Birmingham's historic waterways

'More canals than Venice' is the tongue-in-cheek phrase often used by locals when discussing Birmingham's famous

GETTING AROUND

The Midlands is a large landlocked region in the centre of England. It features hubs of various sizes, though Birmingham is the best place to start, as it offers public transport links in every direction. Hubs can be reached quickly and easily by train, with regular departures from Birmingham New Street station. Different train companies running various routes may feel confusing at first, but the countryside rides are smooth and relaxing.

Driving is the most practical way of exploring rural areas like Shropshire. Having your own wheels is especially handy for accessing viewing points, country houses and villages.

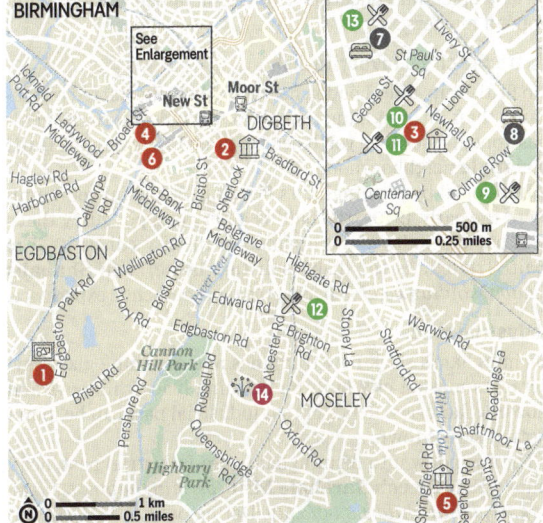

BIRMINGHAM

SIGHTS
1 Barber Institute of Fine Arts
2 Birmingham Back to Backs
3 Coffin Works
4 Gas Street Basin
5 Sarehole Mill
6 Worcester & Birmingham Canal

SLEEPING
7 Bloc
8 Grand Hotel Birmingham

EATING
9 Adam's

10 Albatross Death Cult
11 Opheem
12 Shababs
13 Wilderness

ENTERTAINMENT
14 Moseley Folk & Arts Festival

BIRMINGHAM'S BEST FESTIVALS

Moseley Folk & Arts Festival: Laid-back three-day music festival in Moseley Park at the end of August. Bring a blanket and a fold-up chair.

Brum Brew Fest: Weekend beer trail by the Brum Beer Babs group. Visit the city's best pubs, tick them off and receive a unique badge.

Birmingham Pride: One of the UK's biggest queer celebrations. Join the colourful street party on Hurst St and watch shows in Smithfield Sq.

Birmingham Cocktail Weekend: A weekend-long showcase of Birmingham's finest mixologists at different locations, with wallet-friendly prices.

Birmingham Mela: The UK's biggest South Asian music festival in Smethwick's sprawling Victoria Park. Very family-friendly, too.

waterways. Once used as fume-ridden trade routes in the 18th and 19th centuries, the city's canals are clean, pleasant and pass by some of Birmingham's prettiest scenery.

With its jaunty waterside pubs, bars and bistros, **Gas Street Basin** is the lively epicentre of Birmingham's canals. Enjoy the atmosphere here before walking the 45-minute stretch of the **Worcester and Birmingham Canal** south to the Birmingham University grounds. This tranquil trail finishes amid some fine Edwardian architecture and it's just a short walk to the **Barber Institute of Fine Arts** (*barber.org.uk;*

Opheem's sensational Aloo Tuk is Birmingham's best dish.

EATING IN BIRMINGHAM: BEST FINE DINING

Albatross Death Cult: Sublime seafood-heavy 12-course tasting, with unbeatable sake pairings. *7-10pm Wed-Sat, 1.30-3.30pm Fri & Sat* £££

Adam's: Superb seven-course tour de force of creative modern British cuisine from chef Adam Stokes. *noon-5pm & 6.30pm-midnight Wed-Sat* £££

Wilderness: Ten-course tasting experience amid charcoal-black interior and pounding rock soundtrack. *6-9pm Wed-Sat, 12.30-2pm Fri & Sat* £££

Opheem: Aktar Islam's seasonal 10-course Indian fine dining is a revelation; two Michelin stars *5.30-9.30pm Wed-Sat, noon-1pm Fri & Sat* £££

SHAKESPEARE & STRATFORD

While most of William Shakespeare's greatest works were written in London, he was born in Stratford and spent his formative years here, as well as his final years.

Born on 23 April 1564, he was the third of eight children and the eldest surviving son of John Shakespeare and Mary Arden. He was likely educated at Kings New School which, amazingly, still exists. At 18, he married 26-year-old Anne Hathaway with whom he had three children.

At some point in the mid-1580s, he left for London where he became the playwright we know today. At the age of 49, he retired home to Stratford where he died three years later, in 1616.

free), a splendid collection of lesser-heralded works by European masters.

Taste the city's favourite dish

No British city after London has more Michelin-starred restaurants than Birmingham, though for a window into the city's gastronomic heritage you'll need to jump in a taxi to the **Balti Triangle** neighbourhood.

Developed by Birmingham's fledgling Pakistani community in the early 1970s, the balti is a fiery one-pot curry that's still popular today and is a symbol of the city's diversity. The Balti Triangle is the dish's spiritual home, with **Shababs** *(shababsindian.co.uk)* offering the most authentic experience.

Industrial relics

Birmingham's sleek new tramlines and gleaming glass skyscrapers mask a city built on belching black chimneys and howling factories. Relics of that industrial past can be found dotted across town.

For a window into Birmingham's pre-industrial past, head out to Hall Green's **Sarehole Mill** *(birminghammuseums. org.uk; adult/child £8.80/5.50).* Dating back to 1771, the old watermill next to the River Cole was originally used to grind wheat but years later fascinated a young JRR Tolkien, who used the bucolic surroundings in his writings.

Back in the city centre, the **Birmingham Back to Backs** *(nationaltrust.org.uk; adult/child £11/5.50)* are the last surviving 19th-century back-to-back houses, and show how working people lived as the industrial age took over British society. On a more macabre note, the quirky **Coffin Works** *(coffinworks. org; guided tour £10)* is a beautifully preserved factory where accoutrements to coffins were once made – funerals were big business in Victorian Birmingham.

Stratford-upon-Avon

Stroll through Shakespeare's hometown

While a walk through Stratford-upon-Avon starts and ends with major Shakespeare sites, the town is also a fascinating journey through medieval, Elizabethan, Georgian and Victorian architecture.

Start at **Shakespeare's Birthplace** *(shakespeare.org.uk; adult/child £25/12.50),* where the world's most famous playwright was born. Further in town lies the black-and-white timber frame of **Harvard House**, dating back to 1596 and built

DRINKING IN STRATFORD: BEST PUBS

Ya Bard: Friendly and compact five-tap craft-beer bar that feels like you're in someone's living room. *3-8pm Tue-Thu, noon-8pm Fri & Sat, noon-4pm Sun*

Dirty Duck: Classic actors' post-show haunt opposite the Royal Shakespeare Company. *noon-11.30pm Mon-Thu, to midnight Fri & Sat, to 10pm Sun*

Stratford Alehouse: The finest spot for real ale and cider, with walls covered in colourful beer mats. *3-10pm Mon-Thu, 1-10pm Fri & Sat, 1-7pm Sun*

Garrick Inn: Timber-framed and supposedly haunted, this 15th-century pub is the town's oldest. *9am-11.30pm Mon-Thu, to midnight Fri & Sat, to 11pm Sun*

by Thomas Rogers, grandfather to the benefactor of Harvard University, John Harvard. Next door is the similar-looking **Garrick Inn**, Stratford's oldest public house named after the influential 18th-century actor David Garrick. Make sure to drop by **Holy Trinity Church** *(stratford-upon-avon.org; free)*, the scene of the Bard's baptism, marriage and burial.

Warwick

A mighty fortress

With its rising turrets, formidable walls and regular reenactment events, **Warwick Castle** *(warwick-castle.com; adult/child £26/21)* resembles the sort of monolithic fortress typically seen in movies or adventure books. Its oldest parts date back to the 11th century and the entire structure is still in remarkably good condition.

Coventry

Marvel at two very different cathedrals

The fragmented walls and soaring spire of **Coventry Cathedral** *(coventrycathedral.org.uk; free)* are what provokes a reaction more than anywhere else here. Devastated by a ferocious German bombing blitz during WWII, its nave suffered a direct hit and was left a smoking ruined shell. But its survival was inspiring, and the stained-glass windows in the modernist **New Cathedral** next door reflect a gaudy kaleidoscope of colours.

Nottingham

Taste history in Nottingham inns

Residing beneath the cliff of Nottingham Castle's lofty hilltop site, **Ye Olde Trip to Jerusalem** *(greeneking.co.uk/pubs)* claims to be the oldest of Nottingham's historic watering holes. Dating back to (allegedly) 1189, its low-sloping sandstone ceilings, silver suit of armour and spectacular Rock Lounge are an alluring combination. **Ye Olde Salutation Inn** *(salutation-inn.com)* has parts dating back to 1240, yet has somehow found a new life as a lively rock-and-metal pub, whereas the **Bell Inn** *(greeneking.co.uk/pubs)* has been looking onto Old Market Sq for almost 600 years.

THE WORLD'S OLDEST FOOTBALL CLUB

Notts County aren't the most popular team in Nottingham (that distinction goes to local rivals Nottingham Forest), but one thing that can never be taken away is their status as the oldest professional football club in the world. Formed in November 1862 as Nottingham Football Club, the team predates the Football Association itself, which wouldn't be founded until 1863. But despite their pioneering history, County haven't been particularly successful on the pitch, with an FA Cup their only top-flight honour (and that was way back in 1894). Football (soccer) is the world's most popular team sport, but the basis for every club began here in Nottingham.

 EATING IN NOTTINGHAM: OUR PICKS

Bar Iberico: Spanish tapas in the heart of Hockley, with cosmopolitan outdoor seating underneath red awnings. *11.30am-10pm Mon-Sat* ££

Restaurant Sat Bains: Two-Michelin-star restaurant on the edge of town with a sublime 10-course tasting menu. *5-7.30pm Wed-Fri, 1-7.45pm Sat* £££

Annie's Burger Shack: Retro American diner serving thick burgers and craft beers. *1-9pm Mon-Thu, 10am-10pm Fri & Sat, 10am-9pm Sun* ££

Cod's Scallops: A new standard for fish and chips, especially alongside oysters, cockles and whelks. *11.30am-9pm Mon-Thu, to 9.30pm Fri & Sat* ££

Liverpool & the Peak District

Preston
Blackburn
Southport   Huddersfield
Wigan   Manchester
Liverpool
Warrington   Sheffield
Macclesfield   Hope
Chester   Valley
Nantwich   Bakewell
Wrexham   Stoke-on-Trent

BEATLES LORE | HUGE HILLS | OPULENT HOMES

☑ TOP TIP

The Peak District is lovely all year round, but autumn is arguably the finest time to visit. Its quaint villages and countryside are a beautiful canvas of red, orange and gold, while its walking trails are a little quieter after the summer's rush of visitors.

A romantic collection of yawning valleys, stone villages, soaring hills and historic homes, the Peak District is is a widescreen outdoor playground where the Midlands meets the north. From the wind-sculpted hills of the Hope Valley to charming chocolate-box towns such as Eyam and Buxton, this is England at its most alluring. At its heart is Bakewell, a small town best known for its sweet indulgent puddings but also considered a gateway into the Peak District. From here, you can wander pretty riversides or hop on a bike into rolling hills and valleys.

Once you've had enough of the elements, the lively cities of the north await and few are more captivating than Liverpool. Arguably northern England's most distinct city, with its rejuvenated waterfront and a soundtrack provided by the greatest band of all time, Liverpool has a friendly character that adds warmth to its wealth of unique attractions.

Liverpool

Liverpool from above

A trio of iconic Edwardian buildings known together as the Three Graces – the **Cunard Building**, the **Port of Liverpool Building** and the **Royal Liver Building** – make up the recognisable skyline of Liverpool's Pier Head waterfront.

GETTING AROUND

Small-town Bakewell is comfortably walkable, but bear in mind there's no train station. Hiring a car is a good idea if you're planning to stay a few days in Bakewell, as some villages and heritage sites can be time-consuming to reach by bus and expensive by taxi. The hiking area around Edale is well served by the Hope Valley Line trains running between Sheffield and Manchester.

Liverpool is a very walkable city, albeit slightly hilly in parts. Buses or taxis are best for heading out to the football stadiums or Beatles hot spots like Penny Lane, while the train is best for Crosby Beach and heading in from Liverpool John Lennon Airport.

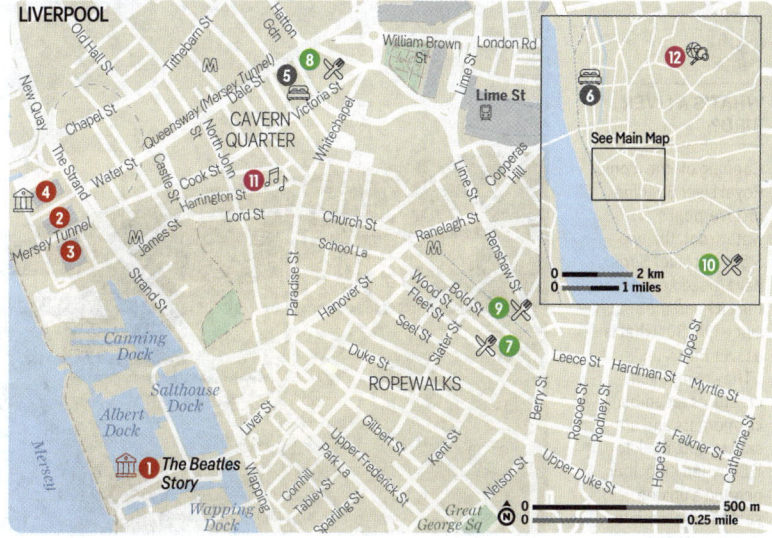

Map Legend

HIGHLIGHTS
1 The Beatles Story

SIGHTS
2 Cunard Building
3 Port of Liverpool Building
4 Royal Liver Building

ACTIVITIES
see 12 Anfield Stadium Tour

SLEEPING
5 Municipal Hotel & Spa
6 Titanic Liverpool

EATING
7 Bamboo
8 Dale Street Kitchen
9 LEAF
10 Pippins Corner

ENTERTAINMENT
11 Cavern Club
12 Liverpool Football Club

Topped by the mythical Liver Birds, the Royal Liver Building (pronounced 'lie-ver') soars to a height of 98m; it's now possible to enjoy beautiful panoramic views of the city from its wind-whipped summit by taking the **Royal Liver Building 360 Tour** *(liverbuildingtour.com; adult/child £17.50/12.50)*.

The Fab Four

Learn about Liverpool's most famous export at **The Beatles Story** *(beatlesstory.com; adult/child £20/11)* at the Albert Dock. Stroll north along Pier Head and grab a selfie with the excellent **statue of the band** in front of the Cunard Building. And of course, a night singing and dancing at the legendary **Cavern Club** *(cavernclub.com)* is a rite of passage (though not the original club, its atmosphere is cracking).

Make it a party with their Bottomless Brunch.

 EATING IN LIVERPOOL: BEST BRUNCH SPOTS

LEAF: Chic spot with high ceilings and a vast brunch menu, including shakshuka, and steak and eggs. *9am-10pm* ££

Dale Street Kitchen: Elegant corner spot serving award-winning breakfasts, including pancakes and a full English. *8am-5pm* ££

Bam Boo: Stylish Bold St brunch joint with floral decor and a strong French-toast game. *9am-5pm Sun-Fri, to 6pm Sat* ££

Pippins Corner: Hearty brunches with plenty of veggie options, too. Check the specials board. *9am-6pm* ££

WHAT'S A LIVER BIRD?

Capping off the iconic Royal Liver Building on Liverpool's waterfront, the two 5.5m-tall Liver Birds have looked out over the city and the sea since 1911. But what is a Liver Bird?

They're mythical creatures resembling cormorants and are said to date back to 1207, when King John needed a unique seal to differentiate documents and sterling from his territory when registering Liverpool as a borough. Centuries later, in 1797, they also appeared on the city's coat of arms.

Their cultural identity with Liverpool waned afterward, but their appearance at the summit of the city's lavish new skyscraper in 1911 shot the bird back into public consciousness – which is where it's stayed ever since.

Meet the Reds

A 15-minute bus ride from the city centre, the iconic **Anfield** stadium is the flag-waving, scarf-raising church where **Liverpool Football Club** plays, and attending a game – while not easy to get a ticket – should be a bucket-list item for any football fan. Failing that, the **stadium tour** *(bookings.liverpoolfc.com/stadiumtours; adult/child £25/16)* will get you up close to the famous Kop End and into the team dressing rooms.

Bakewell

Enter a grandiose world

The handsome landscape surrounding Bakewell is the backdrop for some of England's most opulent historic estates. **Chatsworth House** *(chatsworth.org; adult/child £35/10)* is a lavish 16th-century mansion recognisible for its appearances in various adaptations of Jane Austen's *Pride & Prejudice*. The grand estate contains the famous Devonshire art collection and a majestic 105-acre garden. Nearby **Haddon Hall** *(haddonhall.co.uk; adult/child £28/free)* has a medieval chapel on-site and a marvellous 16th-century Long Gallery, while **Hardwick Hall** *(nationaltrust.org.uk; adult/child £21/10.50)*

 EATING & DRINKING IN BAKEWELL: BEST PUBS

Red Lion: This 17th-century coaching inn with oak beams and stained-glass windows has excellent Sunday roasts. *noon-10pm* £	**Manners:** Slightly away from Bakewell's busy centre, with quality cask ale and pub classics. *noon-11pm Mon-Sat, to 10pm Sun* £	**Rutland Arms:** At this Georgian landmark hotel there's a fine front terrace to watch the world go by. *11am-11pm*	**Joiners Arms:** Specialist micropub with a revolving selection of cask and keg beer on tap. *noon-11pm Sun-Thu, to midnight Fri & Sat*

TIM M/SHUTTERSTOCK

Chatsworth House, Bakewell

is an Elizabethan architectural masterpiece, decked out with magnificent tapestries and oil paintings.

Taking back a trail

The trend for repurposing Britain's discontinued train lines has been a wonderful boon for those who love the outdoors. Free for walking, cycling and jogging, the **Monsal Trail** is a meandering 8-mile delight on the old Manchester, Buxton, Matlock and Midland Junction Railway, which was built by the Midland Railway in 1863 to link Manchester with London and closed in 1968. Opened in 1981, the trail takes in dense forest, historic lime kilns and cinematic Victorian viaducts between Bakewell and the Topley Pike junction. Start in Bakewell and soak in the views from the spectacular **Headstone Viaduct** near Monsal Head.

Hope Valley

Adventures on the biggest scale

With its snaking mountain trails, ragged limestone edges and tranquil lakes, the Hope Valley provides a glorious windswept canvas for enjoying the great outdoors. The Peak District's hiking epicentre is the village of **Edale**, where several great walks begin. The panoramic views from the summit of **Mam Tor** are remarkable, and the 4.3-mile hike is moderately challenging, while the difficult **Kinder Scout Loop** climbs the Peak District's highest point. An evocative cycling trail flanks the edges of **Ladybower Reservoir** and **Derwent Reservoir** – the site where the Dambusters practised their famous Operation Chastise (a legendary WWII attack on German dams using 'bouncing bombs').

THE BEST VIEWPOINTS IN THE PEAK DISTRICT

Mam Tor: Gorgeous 360-panorama of the Hope Valley and Derbyshire from its 517m summit. It can get very blustery.

Monsal Head: A sigh-drawing English landscape – rolling hills, broccoli-like oak forests and a tall arching railway viaduct complete the scene.

The Roaches: Gritstone edges and craggy rocks looking over a sprawling pastoral scene. Including them makes for great photographs.

Bamford Edge: Rocky overhang that's a nerve-shredder to stand on. One of the Peak District's finest sunset spots.

Winnats Pass: Limestone gorge just south of Mam Tor. Rising ridges on either side are the region's most stunning drive.

Cardiff & South Wales

Bannau
Brycheiniog
(Brecon
Beacons)
National Park
Llandrindod
Wells
Hay-on-Wye
Hereford
Brecon
Abergavenny
Carmarthen
Llanelli
Swansea
Merthyr
Tydfil
Bridgend
Newport
CARDIFF
Porthcawl
Barry

GRAND CASTLES | MISTY MOORS | GOLDEN COAST

South Wales wings you from a capital fizzing with creative energy to mountains of myth and a wild coast of cliffs, coves and islands.

Buzzing with urban renewal, capital city Cardiff mixes a lively gastronomy scene with sweeping green spaces and grand historic sites. On the English border, the river-woven Wye Valley is a beer and literary haven. To the west, the Brecon Beacons hoist great sails above chequered fields, heather-misted moors and sheep-bobbled valleys, with single-track lanes forcing you to curse and reverse, trails cresting glacier-scoured summits, and country pubs filled with low beams, real ales and singsong voices.

And the coast just keeps getting better the further west you go. From the sweeping golden sands of Gower and Carmarthenshire to the cliff-flanked coves, coast path and puffin islands of Pembrokeshire, the call of the sea here is irresistible.

GETTING AROUND

South Wales takes up around a quarter of the country. While it looks small on a map, it's a journey of around 140 miles (three hours) from Chepstow in the east to St Davids in the west. The best way to explore is by car, especially in the remotest reaches of the mountains and coast. The region's main transport hubs (Cardiff, Swansea, Abergavenny, Haverfordwest) have decent train connections, but the smaller lines are slow (if scenic).

Cardiff

A headfirst plunge into history

Defiant and hulking, **Cardiff Castle** *(cardiffcastle.com; adult/child £16/10.50)* has presided over the capital for two millennia. These walls have seen it all: Romans (who built the first fort), Normans (the mighty motte-and-bailey keep), medieval lords (the Black Tower) and the Bute family (from 1766 to 1947), who gave it a mock-Gothic makeover in Victorian times.

Download the free Cardiff Castle app to access a self-guided audio walking tour. The keep is one of the best places to get your bearings. Climb 50 stone steps up the side of the motte, then continue to the viewing platform for panoramic views over the castle grounds and the city centre.

TOP TIP

Wales attracts rain like moths to a flame, so always prepare for wet weather. Always pack a waterproof coat and shoes, especially if you're out in the sticks.

An engrossing romp through time

Cardiff's largest museum is the all-encompassing **National Museum Cardiff** *(museum.wales; free)*. The building oozes classical style, with hefty granite steps leading to bronze front

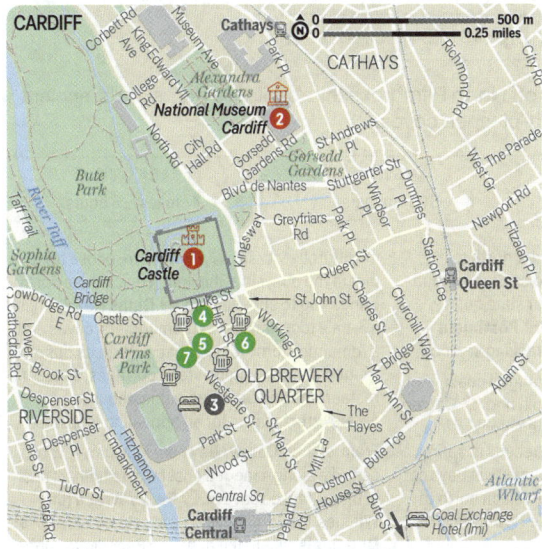

★ **HIGHLIGHTS**	● **SLEEPING**	5 City Arms
1 Cardiff Castle	3 Parkgate Hotel	6 Old Arcade
2 National Museum	● **DRINKING &**	7 Tiny Rebel
Cardiff	**NIGHTLIFE**	
	4 Blue Bell	

doors, opening to the polished marble entrance hall capped with a 30m-high dome.

Most of the ground floor is dedicated to the **Evolution of Wales** exhibition. This fascinating walk through 4600 million years has interactive displays, space specimens, artefacts and images to illustrate how Wales came to be. The **natural history** exhibit is a snapshot of Wales' flora and fauna, from butterflies and seascapes to a 7.5m basking shark. Upstairs is all about art. The **permanent galleries** showcase over 500 years of paintings, illustrations, sculptures, ceramics and more from Wales and the world.

Hay-on-Wye

Wales' literary wonderland

Hidden in the Welsh hills, the Georgian market town of Hay-on-Wye has extraordinary cultural cachet as the host of Britain's

BEST ART IN THE NATIONAL MUSEUM

San Giorgio Maggiore at Dusk: This technicolour sunset, painted by Monet, is from a series of studies of an island in Venice.

Landscape at Auvers in the Rain: Finished three days before his suicide, this moving Van Gogh oil painting shows slashes of rain distorting a colourful landscape.

La Parisienne: Referred to as 'The Blue Lady', this striking Renoir oil painting is one of the museum's centrepieces.

Dorelia McNeill in a Feathered Hat: Welsh artist Augustus John painted Dorelia, his common-law wife, repeatedly for over 60 years.

The Empty Mask: A Magritte painting embodying the surrealist fascination with the subconscious.

The house bitter is worth trying.

 DRINKING IN CARDIFF: OUR PICKS

Old Arcade: Ever-popular pub with an outdoor area. Hearty food and plenty of choice on the bar. *11am–11pm Sun & Mon, to midnight Fri & Sat*

Tiny Rebel: Pub/bar from local brewery Tiny Rebel, with a great range of drinks and occasional live music. *noon–1am Sun–Wed, to 2am Thu–Sat*

Blue Bell: One of Cardiff's oldest pubs has a traditional, cosy atmosphere with locally sourced Welsh food. *11am–midnight*

City Arms: Traditional pub opposite the Principality Stadium, with a vast array of Welsh and British beers. *noon–11pm Sun–Thu, to midnight Fri & Sat*

BEST OF THE PENINSULA ROAD TRIP

This 38-mile drive shows off North Pembrokeshire's wildlife-rich islands, ancient hillforts and gorgeous cliff-clasped coves.

START	END	LENGTH
St Davids	St Dogmaels	47 miles; 2½ hours

Starting in ❶ **St Davids**, meander north to ❷ **Abereiddi**, where the turquoise Blue Lagoon glimmers in a sheer-sided former slate quarry. In the hook-shaped harbour of ❸ **Porthgain** nearby, the Shed entices with cracking seafood.

Breeze 4 miles north along the ragged coast, and just past the village of Trefin you'll find ❹ **Carreg Samson**, a 5000-year-old dolmen plonked in a farmer's field. Carpeted with bluebells in spring, a wooded valley dips to the sublime twin bays of ❺ **Abermawr and Aberbach**. Push on north to lighthouse-topped ❻ **Strumble Head**, which bears the brunt of the Irish Sea.

In culturally vibrant ❼ **Fishguard**, pause for a pint in the quayside Ship Inn. A quick drive north brings you to cliff-rimmed ❽ **Dinas Head**, where a 3-mile loop walk reveals smugglers' coves and a romantic storm-ruined chapel. With its dune-fringed beach, sagging stone cottages, excellent restaurants and boutique-y guesthouses, ❾ **Newport** makes for an appealing rest stop.

From wild ❿ **Ceibwr Bay** near Moylgrove, you can hike along a ragged coast where fulmars nest in the collapsed cave of ⓫ **Pwll y Wrach** (the Witches' Cauldron). Wind up in estuary-side ⓬ **St Dogmaels**, where the ruins of a Benedictine abbey nod to its origins as a Celtic monastic community.

Carreg Samson takes its name from the local legend that 6th-century bishop and missionary St Samson of Dol lifted the 12-ton capstone into place with just his little finger.

Gorse-clad **Strumble Head** has an edge-of-the-world quality on bleak, windy days. Grab binoculars to spot Arctic skuas, storm petrels, seals and porpoises.

At **Abermawr and Aberbach**, the stumps of a drowned, 8000-year-old forest emerge at very low tide.

Irish Sea

Cemaes Head

Cardigan

Strumble Head

Garn Fawr
Goodwick

Fishguard

Nevern

Mynydd CarnIngli

Pembrokeshire Coast National Park

Cwmcerwyn

PEMBROKESHIRE

St Davids Head

Pembrokeshire Coast National Park

St Davids
Solva
Newgale

START

Ramsey Island

St Brides Bay

Haverfordwest

A487 · A40 · B4330 · A487 · A40

0 ——— 10 km
0 ——— 5 miles

Addyman Books, Hay-on-Wye

THE LADY OF THE LAKE

The glacial lake of **Llyn-y-Fan Fach** appears in Welsh epic *The Mabinogion*. Legend tells that a young farmer peered into the lake and saw a beautiful maiden. He coaxed her ashore and begged for her hand in marriage. They lived happily and raised three sons, but when the farmer struck his wife three times, she returned to the fairy world forever.

Here myth merges with fact, as the sons were the first in a long line of royal healers. The village of Myddfai was a medieval centre for herbalist activity. Today, Pant-y-Meddygon (Physicians' Valley) on Mynydd Myddfai is still rich in the plants used to make the remedies described in the late-14th-century *Red Book of Hergest*.

most feted literature and arts festival. Held over 11 days from late May, **Hay Festival** *(hayfestival.com)* attracts both major and emerging talent. Politics, poetry workshops, book signings, concerts, comedy performances and kids' activities aim to generate ideas and ponder life's biggest questions.

If you can't snag festival tickets, come for a romp around the town's 20-plus independent bookshops, from the vast, immaculately catalogued shelves of **Richard Booth's Bookshop** *(boothbooks.co.uk)* to rare, out-of-print tomes at **Addyman Books** *(hay-on-wyebooks.com)*.

Bannau Brycheiniog (Brecon Beacons) National Park

Climb South Wales' highest mountain

Rain, bog and fog be damned: puffing up to the highest peak in the Brecon Beacons, **Pen-y-Fan** (886m), is irresistible. On cloud-free days, views stretch all the way over bald, glacier-scoured peaks and deep valleys to the Black Mountains, Bristol Channel and Eryri (Snowdonia) beyond.

The quickest stomp to the top begins at **Pont ar Daf** car park on the A470, 10 miles southwest of Brecon. It's a steep but straightforward ascent (4.5 miles return; allow three hours). Dodge the biggest crowds by choosing one of the longer routes on the north side of the mountain, starting at **Cwm Gwdi** car park, for instance (a 7-mile, four-hour round trip).

EATING AROUND THE BRECON BEACONS: MEALS TO REMEMBER

Felin Fach Griffin: Beamed, fire-warmed bar and stunning menus raiding the kitchen garden for ingredients. *noon-2.30pm & 6-9pm* ££

Newbridge on Usk: Exquisite regional food beside a stone bridge on the River Usk. *6-9pm Mon & Tue, noon-3.30pm & 6-9pm Wed-Sat, noon-8.30pm Sun* ££

1861: Fresh farmed and foraged produce shines in the tasting menus at this Cross Ash restaurant. *noon-3pm & 6.30-11pm Wed-Sat, noon-3pm Sun* £££

Bell at Skenfrith: Dreamy pub on the River Monnow's banks, with garden-grown produce on the creative menu. *noon-2.30pm & 6.30-8.30pm Wed-Sat* £££

201

North Wales

SCENERY | HERITAGE TRAINS | SEASIDE TOWNS

Imagine thunderous rivers, glacial mountain ranges, dune-fringed, wave-whipped beaches and ancient forests folded into 823 glorious sq miles of national park. This is Eryri (Snowdonia), the country's mountainous, Welsh-speaking, richly cultured heart. Welcome to Wales at its wildest: chockablock with trails, swim spots and scrambles over rocky terrain.

Sharp peaks pierce the heavens, with Yr Wyddfa (Snowdon) – Wales' highest mountain (1085m) – dominating the skyline. Seven trails lead to the top of Cymru's cap, with snaking queues in peak season. Beyond, adventure mounts at former quarries and historic slate mines reimagined into thrilling zipwire zones, underground trampolines, and accessible cycling routes.

Further south, rolling hills tumble into Victorian resort towns, sandy beaches and one bizarre Italianate village, while heritage rail lines showcase one of the most unique ways to see one of Britain's most cinematic landscapes.

Eryri National Park (Snowdonia)

Hike to the summit of Yr Wyddfa (Mt Snowdon)

Thousands of pro hikers and outdoor newbies flock to **Yr Wyddfa** (Mt Snowdon), Eryri's most popular and incredibly

 GETTING AROUND

Covering some 5175 sq miles, this region may seem small, but the roads wrap around several mountain ranges, meander through a national park and wiggle along the coast. Take your time to enjoy it fully.

A car is helpful in most areas and essential in the countryside, where public transport can be irregular or nonexistent, though parking can be a nightmare in popular spots, particularly during peak seasons.

Trains link many major destinations, particularly along the north and west coast (as far south as Aberystwyth). However, services are slow, and same-day travel is expensive. To get between North and Mid-Wales, you'll need to change in Shrewsbury, England.

GYVAFOTO/SHUTTERSTOCK

Llanberis Path, Eryri National Park (Snowdonia)

photogenic peak, year-round. In peak summer season, you'll see snaking queues of selfie-seekers leading to the 1085m summit.

The **Llanberis Path** is the go-to summit route for most hikers. Starting from Llanberis village, it's a more gradual ascent that follows the **Snowdon Mountain Railway** *(snowdonrailway.co.uk; prices vary)*, making it a top choice for first-timers and less confident walkers. It's a steady climb, usually taking three to four hours. On a clear day, the astonishing views from the summit stretch as far as Ireland and the Isle of Man.

Blaenau Ffestiniog

Jump on a winding heritage train

Chugging away since 1832, the **Ffestiniog Railway** *(fest rail.co.uk; prices vary)* is the world's oldest narrow-gauge railway. **Mountain Spirit** is the flagship Ffestiniog Railway experience, with carriages typically pulled by 150-year-old Double Fairlie locomotives. Your epic 13.5-mile journey starts in Porthmadog and crosses the Cob Estuary, climbing steadily through lush fields, dense forests and lakes towards

STARGAZING SPOTS IN ERYRI

Eryri is designated an International Dark Sky Reserve. Here are some of the best places for stargazing.

Bwlch y Groes: As one of the highest-tarmacked passes in Wales, this site has expansive views of the Dyfi Valley, Cader Idris and the Berwyn Mountains, and unparalleled stargazing.

Llyn y Dywarchen: Situated above Drws-y-Coed in Dyffryn Nantlle, this fishing lake is a scenic dark location for stargazing, free from urban light pollution.

Llyn Geirionnydd: Located in Gwydir Forest near Betws-y-Coed, this accessible star-spotting site has parking and toilets.

Llynnau Cregennen: At the foothills of Cader Idris, these twin lakes provide an atmospheric setting for stargazing and astrophotography.

 EATING & DRINKING IN BLAENAU FFESTINIOG: OUR PICKS

De Niro: Family-friendly cafe known for hearty soups, proper good toasties and veggie offerings. *10am-3pm Mon-Sat* £	**Trish & Chips:** Classic fish and chips; it also serves pies, sausages and scampi. *4-8pm* £	**Y Manod:** Classic, community-led boozer with local ales, live music and lively quiz nights. *hours vary* £	**Y Pengwern:** Community-owned pub in Llan Ffestiniog, with lovely wood-burning fire and classic pub grub. *hours vary* ££

WALES' OLDEST PIER

Aberystwyth's **Royal Pier** *(royalpier.co.uk)* holds the accolade of being the oldest pier in Wales. This retro, Grade II–listed structure opened in 1865. It was Eugenius Birch's brainchild and initially extended 244m into the sea. Sadly, a fierce storm in 1866 took out a 30m section, but it was soon extended and refurbished, adding a tearoom and bandstand. In 1896, the Prince of Wales inaugurated a grand iron-and-glass pavilion holding 3000 people. Miraculously, the weathered pier has survived despite numerous challenges, including the Great Storm of 1938 and going into administration in 2016. Today, there's ongoing debate and plans on how best to regenerate the Victorian-era pier and restore it to its former glory.

Blaenau. Upgrade to gold service and book 'Observation Bay' seats for the best view.

Zipline over a former quarry

Situated among the former slate mines of Blaenau Ffestiniog, **Zip World Llechwedd** *(zipworld.co.uk; from £10)* is a high-adrenaline historical adventure. Strapped in on a four-person parallel zip line, you'll soar high above slate mountains dotted with patches of green and glittering lakes at speeds of over 50mph. Below you, the old slate quarry is a reminder of the area's industrious past. But it's not just about the zip-line thrills. As part of the **Titan 2** experience, a former army truck will take you to a height of 430m overlooking the human-made mountains while a guide explains the history of the mining community.

Portmeirion

A most unusual Welsh village

Resembling a technicolour fever dream, pastel-coloured **Portmeirion** *(portmeirion.wales; adult/child £20/13)* is no ordinary Welsh village. Designed by visionary architect Clough Williams-Ellis between 1925 and 1973, the Italian Riviera–style buildings hugging the Dwyryd Estuary are set amid lush woodlands and groomed gardens. Alongside its colourful architecture, the ticketed site features two historic hotels, a spa, self-catering cottages, gift shops, a swanky restaurant and an Italian-style *gelateria*.

Aberystwyth

Find beaches for all occasions

If you were to play British Seaside Holiday Bingo, Aberystwyth's three beaches would be a full house. Backed by a faded Victorian promenade, the sweeping stones of Blue Flag **North Beach** have everything you'd need for a nostalgic dip: donkey rides, chilly waters, penny arcades and a pier. On the other side of the castle is **Aberystwyth South Beach**, a quiet curl of slate-grey sand and shingle, and beyond the harbour wall is pebbly **Tanybwlch Beach**. This is where you'll find the locals.

 EATING IN ABERYSTWYTH: OUR PICKS

Medina: Indie Middle Eastern cafe and food shop; come here for Neapolitan-style pizzas. *9.30am-8.30pm Mon-Fri, to 9.30pm Sat* ££

Ultracomida: Trendy Spanish deli and tapas bar. Excellent selection of continental wines, cheeses and Iberian ham. *10am-4pm Mon-Sat* ££

Mama Fay's: Caribbean-inspired dishes including spicy jerk chicken, curried goat or Jamaican potato curry. *5-10pm Tue-Sat* ££

Dragonfly Bistro: Great for vegan and vegetarian eaters; expect creative dishes that are both fresh and colourful. *hours vary* ££

Edinburgh

MAJESTIC ARCHITECTURE | TWISTING STREETS | COSY CAFES

It all began with fire and rock. The rugged landscape of modern-day Edinburgh was formed by three volcanoes, which rose 350 million years ago. The first of these (Castle Rock) is the most recognisable, with its long-extinct volcanic plug now home to moody Edinburgh Castle. The second (Calton Hill) sits to the east of the New Town, topped with mighty monuments and panorama-loving picnickers. And the third (Arthur's Seat) has become the go-to place for hikers, bikers, dog-walkers and kite-fliers, who ascend its crag-fringed slopes for views across Holyrood Park.

Most visitors to Edinburgh stick around the city's ancient, volcanic heart, with its mishmash of narrow streets, winding alleys and underground vaults. But hike up any of Edinburgh's extinct volcanoes and it becomes clear just how much lies beyond. The New Town's leafy squares, the West End's splendid architecture, Leith's fancy restaurants and Holyrood's hipster bars – varied and vibrant, Edinburgh begs to be explored.

Festival City

Edinburgh's crazy August days

August is festival season in Edinburgh, and it's the greatest show on Earth. The main attraction, of course, is the **Edinburgh Festival Fringe** *(edfringe.com)*. Over the course of three weeks, tens of thousands of performances of comedy, theatre, dance, circus, cabaret and kids' shows fill venues throughout the Old Town and beyond.

Yet the Fringe is just one of several major festivals taking place here in August. There's the **Edinburgh International Festival** *(eif.co.uk),* with its packed program of classical music, theatre and opera. The **Edinburgh International Book Festival** *(edbookfest.co.uk)* stages talks from big-name authors from around the world. And don't miss the **Edinburgh Art Festival** *(edinburghartfestival.com),* which sees specially commissioned artworks scattered around the city.

GETTING AROUND

With the narrow medieval alleyways of the Old Town, the grandly proportioned streets of the New Town and the well-marked footpaths snaking up Arthur's Seat, Edinburgh is a very walkable city. The tram provides hassle-free access from the airport to the city centre (a 30-minute journey), and continues to Newhaven, making it a great way to hop between the West End, New Town and Leith. Services run daily from around 4.30am to midnight.

☑ TOP TIP

For a taste of the cramped conditions of years gone by, dive off from the Royal Mile into the narrow closes on either side. Just a short walk down an alley will reveal a whole other world of quaint little courtyards, pretty whitewashed houses and surprising city views.

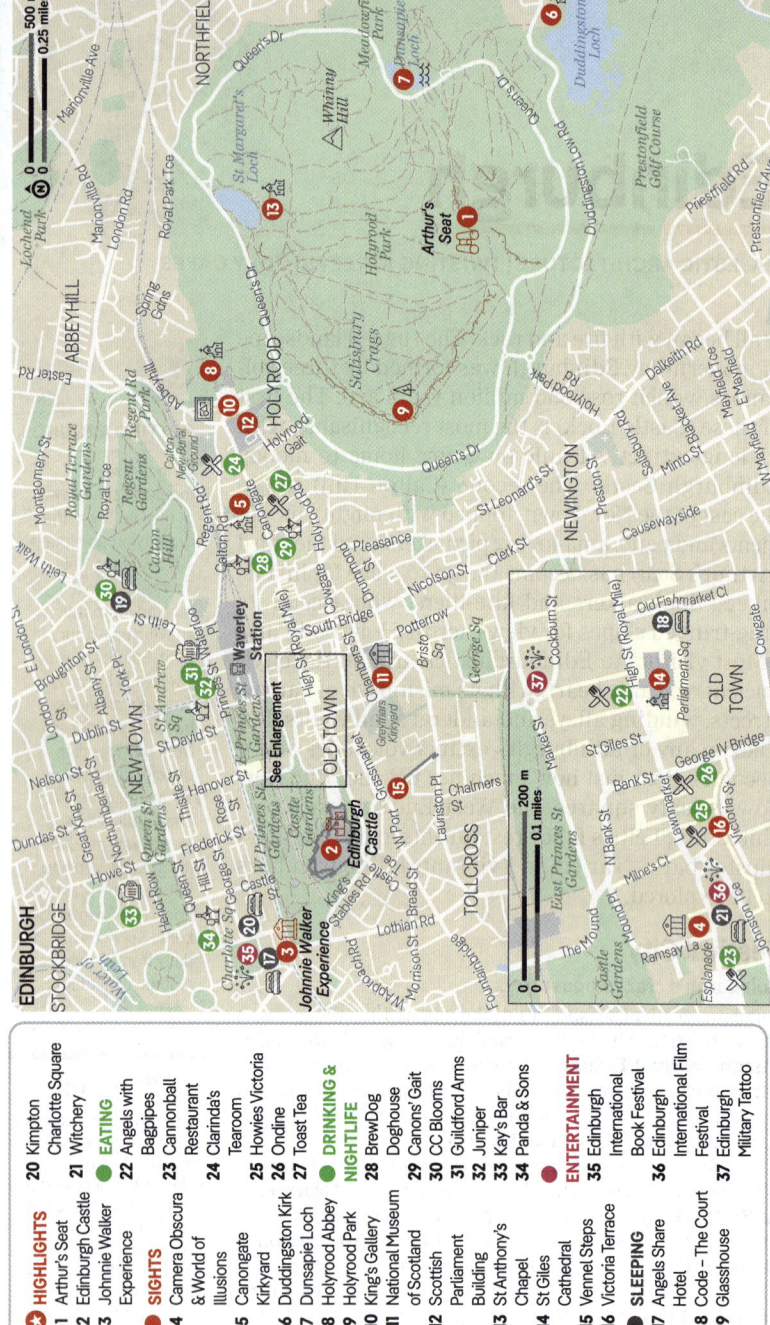

EDINBURGH

STOCKBRIDGE

NEW TOWN

OLD TOWN

Johnnie Walker
Experience

Edinburgh
Castle

TOLLCROSS

ABBEYHILL

NORTHFIELD

HOLYROOD

Holyrood
Park

Arthur's
Seat

NEWINGTON

OLD TOWN

See Enlargement

HIGHLIGHTS
1 Arthur's Seat
2 Edinburgh Castle
3 Johnnie Walker
Experience

SIGHTS
4 Camera Obscura
& World of
Illusions
5 Canongate
Kirkyard
6 Duddingston Kirk
7 Dunsapie Loch
8 Holyrood Abbey
9 Holyrood Park
10 King's Gallery
11 National Museum
of Scotland
12 Scottish
Parliament
Building
13 St Anthony's
Chapel
14 St Giles
Cathedral
15 Vennel Steps
16 Victoria Terrace

SLEEPING
17 Angels Share
Hotel
18 Code – The Court
19 Glasshouse

20 Kimpton
Charlotte Square
21 Witchery

EATING
22 Angels with
Bagpipes
23 Cannonball
Restaurant
24 Clarinda's
Tearoom
25 Howies Victoria
26 Ondine
27 Toast Tea

DRINKING &
NIGHTLIFE
28 BrewDog
Doghouse
29 Canons' Gait
30 CC Blooms
31 Guildford Arms
32 Juniper
33 Kay's Bar
34 Panda & Sons

ENTERTAINMENT
35 Edinburgh
International
Book Festival
36 Edinburgh
International Film
Festival
37 Edinburgh
Military Tattoo

Edinburgh Castle from Princes St Gardens

There's also the **Edinburgh International Film Festival** *(edfilmfest.org),* the world's oldest film festival with regular premieres and red-carpet stars. And the **Royal Edinburgh Military Tattoo** *(edintattoo.co.uk)* brings eye-popping displays of military marching bands.

Scotland's Chief Royal Castle

Visit the fortress on the hill

The most potent symbol of the Scottish capital, **Edinburgh Castle** *(edinburghcastle.scot; adult/child £21.50/13)* has stood on the brooding crags high above the city for the best part of a millennium. As well as being one of the city's most visible and recognisable sights, it's also one of its most interesting, with attractions ranging from ancient stone chapels to sparkling crown jewels.

Between April and September each year, knowledgeable guides offer 30-minute tours from just inside the Main Gate – a perfect introduction to the castle before you go and explore it for yourself.

Identity Meets Politics

Where unique architecture houses Scotland's decision-makers

The **Scottish Parliament Building** *(parliament.scot; tours free),* conceived by Catalan architect Enric Miralles and

BEST VIEWS IN THE OLD TOWN

National Museum of Scotland: The rooftop terrace here offers far-reaching vistas of Edinburgh Castle and the city below.

Castle Esplanade: On a clear day, you can see out to Leith and beyond from this viewpoint beside the castle.

St Giles Cathedral: Accessible by guided tour, the church's roof offers great views along the Royal Mile.

Vennel Steps: Climb halfway up this staircase from Grassmarket for a remarkable view of Edinburgh Castle.

Victoria Terrace: Head down tiny Fisher's Close to emerge on this terrace with views of colourful Victoria St.

EATING IN THE OLD TOWN: BEST RESTAURANTS

Angels with Bagpipes: Popular Royal Mile restaurant, named for the statue in St Giles Cathedral, serving Scottish cuisine with inventive twists. *noon-9pm* **££**	**Howies Victoria:** Opt for the bargain lunch menu of seasonal Scottish fare, from salmon to venison, or treat yourself to a seafood dinner. *noon-10.30pm* **££**	**Cannonball Restaurant:** Italian-influenced Scottish cuisine served in a chic but informal restaurant by the castle. *noon-10pm Mon-Thu, to 10.30pm Fri & Sat* **£££**	**Ondine:** Sample the best oysters in Edinburgh, along with other seafood specialities and seared steaks, at this fine-dining restaurant. *noon-10pm Tue-Sat* **£££**

SERGII FIGURNYI/SHUTTERSTOCK

Arthur's Seat

BEST CHURCHES IN HOLYROOD & ARTHUR'S SEAT

Holyrood Abbey:
In the Palace of Holyroodhouse grounds, these ruins were once one of Europe's grandest abbeys.

Canongate Kirkyard:
This unusual-looking church (and cemetery full of famous locals) was a favourite of the late Queen Elizabeth II.

St Anthony's Chapel:
A popular stop on the way up Arthur's Seat, this ruined chapel provides great views across the city to Leith.

Duddingston Kirk:
This eye-catching Anglo-Saxon church is one of Edinburgh's oldest, built around 1124 and expanded in the 1630s.

King's Gallery:
Formerly the Queen's Gallery, this art collection is housed in the shell of the 19th-century Holyrood Free Church.

completed by his widow, Benedetta Tagliabue, is a brazenly modern construction of polished concrete, granite and steel, without a neo-Gothic clock tower in sight. Few passers-by are immediately convinced by its starkly out-of-place exterior, but venture inside and you may just change your mind. The lobby is a playful space of concrete pillars, oak panels, glass walls and eye-catching works of art. Join a guided tour to walk the sloping corridors, see the debating chamber and learn more about the architect's intentions of creating a building to represent a national identity.

The Roof of the City

Hike to Edinburgh's highest point

An unmistakable feature of the Edinburgh skyline, the craggy, gorse-covered **Arthur's Seat** rises up behind the towers of the Palace of Holyroodhouse. Earn your porridge with a 45-minute climb to its 251m summit.

The trail starts across from the car park on Queen's Dr, and gently climbs up and away from the road. Take a short diversion to see the medieval ruins of **St Anthony's Chapel**, including fine views towards North Edinburgh, before doubling back and continuing your way into the heart of **Holyrood Park**. Divert left off the main trail onto a narrower path,

 EATING & DRINKING IN HOLYROOD & ARTHUR'S SEAT: BEST CAFES & PUBS

Clarinda's Tearoom: A Canongate institution, this quaint tearoom has been serving homemade scones for half a century. *9.30am-4.30pm Tue-Sun* £

Toast Tea: As the name suggests, this Asian cafe serves breakfast toasts alongside good coffee, tea and homemade soft drinks. *10am-6pm Mon-Sat* £

Canons' Gait: This ever-popular Royal Mile pub has a good selection of ales and unfalteringly friendly service. *noon-11pm Sun-Wed, to midnight Thu-Sat*

BrewDog Doghouse: There's craft beer galore coming out of the 30 taps here. If you find you've overindulged, simply check into the on-site hotel. *7am-1am*

which becomes increasingly steep and rocky as it approaches a plateau – a chance to catch your breath while looking over pretty **Dunsapie Loch**. From here, a final 10-minute push along the mountain ridge brings you to the top of the hill. Drink in the marvellous city panorama before heading back the way you came.

Family Fun with Victorian Roots
Escape into a world of optical illusions

It may be 170 years old, but Edinburgh's bewitching **Camera Obscura** *(camera-obscura.co.uk; adult/child £24.95/17.95)* continues to baffle and delight visitors to this day. Enter from Castlehill, near the top of the Royal Mile, and climb up to the Outlook Tower for a taste of true Victorian ingenuity. Here, live images from the streets below are projected onto a canvas table. Think CCTV, 19th-century style. The rest of the building is given over to the **World of Illusions**, a collection of hands-on exhibits showcasing a variety of optical illusions, light puzzles, mirror mazes, 3D holograms and vortex tunnels; enough to keep the kids entertained for an hour or two, but not quite matching the magic of the camera obscura above.

Bringing Whisky to Life
A spiritual experience like no other

Part animated history lesson, part interactive theatre show, part theme-park extravaganza, the no-holds-barred £150 million **Johnnie Walker Experience** *(johnniewalker.com; tours & tastings from £30)* is an all-singing, all-dancing introduction to the life and times of Mr Johnnie Walker. It starts slowly with a questionnaire (designed to work out your flavour preferences) but then the real fun begins, with the immersive, full-sensory Journey of Flavour tour. The highlight is a storytelling segment in which actors recount the brand's long journey from a humble grocer's shop to the world's best-selling Scotch, but the entire thing is an all-consuming experience of energetic live performances, top-drawer visual effects and eardrum-splitting soundscapes. After an hour or so, you emerge blinking into a tasting room, where a choice of whiskies and cocktails awaits.

LGBTIQ+ EDINBURGH

Edinburgh has a small but long-established LGBTIQ+ scene. Most of the city's gay-friendly bars and clubs are centred around the New Town's Broughton St and top of Leith Walk (also known as 'the Pink Triangle'). For two of the most popular, head to Greenside Place. Here, you'll find **CC Blooms** *(ccblooms. co.uk),* a mainstay of Edinburgh's gay scene since the early 1990s, with its two floors playing a mix of dance and disco music – as well as hosting the odd cabaret night. Just a few doors down from here is **Planet Bar & Kitchen**, a lively gay bar known for its nightly entertainment, ranging from karaoke and bingo to Showtime Fridays drag queen shows.

 DRINKING IN THE NEW TOWN: BEST PUBS & BARS

Guildford Arms: Pretty pub, all wood panels and elegant plasterwork, with good beer and whisky. *11am-11pm Sun-Thu, to midnight Fri & Sat*

Juniper: Sip imaginative cocktails (like peaty whisky with peach iced tea) in a colourful, plant-filled interior. The steaks are tasty, too. *noon-11pm*

Panda & Sons: Easily missed, Prohibition-style speakeasy tucked away behind a fake barbershop exterior and down a staircase. *hours vary Tue-Sun*

Kay's Bar: Tiny, cosy and friendly, this coach house turned local pub has an extensive whisky selection. *11am-11pm Sun-Thu, to midnight Fri & Sat*

Beyond
Edinburgh

Where Scotland's biggest and most
gregarious city sidles up alongside a
majestic national park.

Places

Glasgow p210

**Loch Lomond & the
Trossachs National Park**
p212

Stepping out of Central Station reveals the flutter and swirl
of a metropolis. Crowds throng the sidewalks, queuing buses
and honking taxis fill the streets, and an eclectic mix of modern and Victorian architecture looms overhead. Welcome to
the heart of Scotland's biggest city.

Yet Glasgow's lively city centre is just the start of the story.
Explore the East End for the city's oldest surviving buildings,
Merchant City for some of the best restaurants, shopping and
nightlife, and the West End for bohemian bars and cafes.

Just to the north of Glasgow, the stunning Loch Lomond
and the Trossachs National Park are a majestic escape. Here
you'll find an all-you-can-explore banquet of sprawling lochs,
mountain trails, lush glens and precious woodland.

Glasgow

TIME FROM EDINBURGH: **1HR**

Classical architecture meets provocative art

Glasgow's **Gallery of Modern Art** (*glasgowlife.org.uk; free*)
features works from local and international artists, housed
in a neoclassical building on elegant Royal Exchange Sq. The
original interior is an ornate contrast to the inventive art on
display; all exhibitions are temporary and free to visit. There
are also valiant efforts made to keep the kids entertained,
from museum trails to art clubs.

Outside the museum stands the horseback **statue of the Duke
of Wellington**, which is invariably crowned with a traffic cone
– an iconic symbol of Glaswegian humour and defiance. Street
artist Banksy claims it's his favourite work of art in the UK.

GETTING AROUND

Glasgow's grid layout makes walking easy,
albeit with steep hills. The Subway has
15 stops and travels in a loop – the most
convenient way of getting between the centre
and the West End. City bus services, mostly
run by First Glasgow, are also frequent; buy
tickets when boarding.

Loch Lomond and the Trossachs National Park
is a road-trip dream come true, with incredible
drives and 'Scenic Route Viewpoints' along
the way. Loch Lomond is easily accessed from
the Central Belt on public transport. ScotRail
services run from Glasgow to Balloch, Arrochar,
Tarbet and Ardlui.

Barrowland Ballroom, Glasgow

Marvel at medieval majesty

Glasgow Cathedral *(glasgowcathedral.org; free)* has a rare timelessness. It's a shining example of Gothic architecture and, unlike nearly all of Scotland's cathedrals, it survived the Reformation mobs almost intact.

The wooden roof has been restored many times since its original construction, but some of the timber dates from the 14th century. Many of the cathedral's stunning stained-glass windows are modern – Francis Spear's 1958 work *The Creation* fills the west window. The cathedral is divided by a 15th-century pulpitum (choir screen), decorated with carved figures that may represent Jesus' disciples. Beyond this, note the impressive shields on the roof, which create a path leading to the four stained-glass panels of the east window, also by Francis Spear and depicting the Apostles. At the northeastern corner is the entrance to the 15th-century upper chapter house, now used as a sacristy.

Take a trip to the Barras

Visiting the **Barras Market** is an essential Glasgow weekend experience. The Barras preserves a democratic old-time feel with its no-nonsense stalls, traditional cafes and the sense that some of the wares might have fallen off the back of a truck. Check out the down-at-heel secondhand market under the **Barrowland Ballroom** *(barrowland.co.uk),* a brilliant old dancehall and music venue.

GLASGOW SCHOOL OF ART

In 1896, aged 27, Charles Rennie Mackintosh won a competition to design a new building to house the Glasgow School of Art, where he had studied. Completed in phases between 1896 and 1909, the British art nouveau-style 'Mackintosh Building' (as it came to be known) was arguably his supreme architectural achievement – and became an instant city landmark. Tragically, just as it was close to reopening after a devastating 2014 fire, another (even larger) blaze in 2018 destroyed the painstakingly reconstructed interiors and severely damaged the building. The city has committed to reconstructing it in Mackintosh's distinctive style; it is scheduled to reopen in 2030.

 EATING IN GLASGOW: OUR PICKS

Finnieston: Gastropub with a below-decks atmosphere and a menu focusing on Scottish seafood. *noon-midnight Sun-Thu, to 1am Fri & Sat* **££**

Mother India: A stalwart among Glasgow curry houses – the quality and innovation at this Indian restaurant are second to none. *hours vary* **££**

Stravaigin: Constantly pushing the boundaries of originality without breaking the bank, this is a popular choice for a Sunday roast. *noon-midnight* **££**

Hanoi Bike Shop: This upbeat Ruthven La spot has creative takes on Vietnamese food, using fresh ingredients and homemade tofu. *noon-9pm* **££**

ROB ROY

The wilds of the Trossachs and the historic network of cattle-droving roads were once stomping ground for Clan MacGregor – most famously, the notorious outlaw and folk hero Rob Roy MacGregor. Born in the village of Glengyle in 1671, Rob Roy was a skilled cattle thief and an exceptional swordsman. He was an illustrious character, described as Scotland's answer to Robin Hood; his exploits are romanticised in the writings of Sir Walter Scott and played out on the big screen in the 1995 film *Rob Roy* starring Liam Neeson. Follow in his footsteps with a drink at the **Drover's Inn** *(thedroversinn. co.uk)*, a reputedly haunted 300-year-old pub, and visit his **final resting place** in the graveyard at Balquhidder Old Kirk.

Disguised by an unremarkable facade, **Randall's Antique & Vintage Centre** has some two-dozen vendors peddling an excellent range of vintage objects. And look out for **Barras Art & Design** *(baadglasgow.com)*, with its pop-up stalls, regular weekend events, busy courtyard bar and menu of fusion food. It's quite a contrast to the rest of the market but it works well.

Loch Lomond & the Trossachs National Park
TIME FROM EDINBURGH: **2HR** 🚗

Forests, gardens and glens

The **Great Trossachs Forest National Nature Reserve** *(lochlomond-trossachs.org)* is undergoing a major regeneration project, with two million trees already planted as part of a 200-year plan. Experience this precious medley of scenery on the 30-mile **Great Trossachs Path** from Callander to Inversnaid or choose from one of nine waymarked walking trails in Glen Finglas.

Take a leisurely, low-level walk through the woods at **Loch Ard** near Aberfoyle. Six miles away, following part of the iconic Duke's Pass, is the **Three Lochs Forest Drive**. This 7-mile driving route takes in Lochan Reòidhte, Loch Drunkie and Loch Achray.

The national park extends across to the remote Cowal Peninsula and the ever-enchanting Puck's Glen. Nearby, **Benmore Botanic Garden** *(rbge.org.uk; adult/child £9/7.80)* has 49 hectares of rare plants, vibrant rhododendrons and giant trees.

Lochs, islands and boat trips

Swarms of visitors gravitate towards Loch Lomond and its bonnie banks, especially when the sun makes an appearance. A range of water-sports activities are available with **Loch Lomond Leisure** *(lochlomond-scotland.com; rental £20-25)* at Luss and Rowardennan.

Cruise the loch for a closer look at its islands and islets: **Sweeney's Cruises** *(sweeneyscruiseco.com; adult/child from £16/10.50)* departs from Balloch, while **Cruise Loch Lomond** *(cruiselochlomond.co.uk; from £16)* offers trips and water-bus services from various locations. From Luss, take the water bus to **Inchcailloch**, a national nature reserve. Ascend the short summit path for incredible views, visit the ancient burial ground and picnic on the golden-sand beach.

EATING IN LOCH LOMOND & THE TROSSACHS NATIONAL PARK: OUR PICKS

Broch: Family-run establishment in Strathyre offering homemade soda bread, Italian coffee and full Scottish breakfasts. *10am-4pm Thu-Tue* £

Boatshed: A picture-perfect cafe with outdoor decking overlooking Loch Goil: soup, toasties, coffee and cake with a view. *10am-4pm* ££

Oak Tree Inn: Post-hike pub classics, burgers and pizzas in Balmaha; tables outside plus adjoining ice-cream parlour and coffee shop. *8am-11pm* ££

Clachan Inn: Hearty meals in Scotland's oldest licensed pub; try the haggis bonbons. Located in Drymen. *11am-11pm Mon-Thu, 12.30-11pm Sun* ££

The Scottish Highlands

EPIC DRIVES | VIEWS | DRAMATIC HISTORY

The Highland landscapes may seem timeless, but they haven't always been this empty. In the blink of an eye, following the Clearances of the late 18th century, the Highlands became some of Europe's least populated places. Centres such as Inverness, Fort William and Aviemore have bounced back, but there remain many wild and empty spaces just waiting to be explored. All you need to do is decide where to go first.

The smart city of Inverness, with its hilltop castle, is a fine starting point before escaping into the rugged hills, rock and heather of Cairngorms National Park or searching for monsters on shimmering Loch Ness. You can ascend the snow-hazed summits of the Nevis Range, or join scarf-wearing *Harry Potter* fans on the steam train to Glenfinnan.

Wherever your journey takes you, you can end each day with a warming whisky in front of a crackling pub fire.

Inverness

Discover the transformed Inverness Castle

Inverness city centre is dominated by the baronial turrets of hilltop **Inverness Castle** *(invernesscastle.scot; adult/child £20/14)*. Dating from the 1840s, it replaced a medieval castle blown up by the Jacobites in 1746. The castle served as courthouse and prison until 2020, and reopened in 2025 after a regeneration project.

Gorgeous gardens and terraces surround the castle, with panoramic views south towards the Great Glen and north to the looming Ben Wyvis. Look out for the statue depicting Flora MacDonald with her collie dog, Flossie, gazing west towards Skye where she helped Bonnie Prince Charlie escape to France in the aftermath of the Battle of Culloden.

Inside the castle, colourful installations and interactive displays regale you with stories of Highland history and Gaelic culture, guided by the spirit of a *seanchaidh* (Gaelic for a traditional storyteller) and culminating in an immersive flythrough of Highland landscapes.

GETTING AROUND

The Highlands cover a huge swathe of northern Scotland, from the Cairngorms to John O'Groats. By far the best way to explore the region, having your own wheels allows you to stop whenever you like to soak up the scenery. Buses (mainly run by Scottish Citylink) and trains (run by ScotRail) connect the region's bigger towns, such as Inverness, Fort William, Aviemore, Ullapool and Wick.

☑ **TOP TIP**

Be careful when driving in this part of Scotland. Some roads can get very narrow, not to mention how remote they are, too. Prepare for all kinds of weather and watch out for sheep and deer on the roads.

THE JACOBITE REBELLIONS

The Jacobite rebellions of the 18th century were not about Scotland vs England. This was a civil war between the armed forces of the Hanoverian monarchy that had ruled Britain since 1688, and supporters of the exiled King James (hence the name 'Jacobites' – from Jacob, Latin for James) who wanted to restore a Catholic Stuart king to the British throne. From the Battle of Killiecrankie in 1689 to the final showdown at Culloden in 1746, there was no simple divide – Scots, English and Irish, Catholics and Protestants, Highlanders and Lowlanders, fought on both sides of the conflict.

QUINNY74/SHUTTERSTOCK

Culloden Visitor Centre

Comprehending Culloden

The last pitched battle ever fought on British soil took place on the eastern edge of Inverness in 1746. The Battle of Culloden saw the crushing of Bonnie Prince Charlie's dream of a restored Stuart monarchy. The Jacobite defeat sounded the death knell for the traditional Highland way of life; the horrors of the Clearances, when thousands were forcibly evicted from their homes, soon followed.

The sombre moor where the conflict took place has scarcely changed in almost three centuries. The National Trust for Scotland's **Culloden Visitor Centre** (*nts.org.uk; adult/child £16.50/12*) explains the battle, including the lead-up and the aftermath, with perspectives from both sides. An innovative 360-degree movie puts you in the middle of the mayhem. After a look around the museum, join a 45-minute guided tour of the battlefield where 1500 Jacobites were slaughtered by government forces in less than an hour.

The Nessie phenomenon

The ideal way to fathom the mystery of the Loch Ness Monster takes half a day and comes in two parts, both beginning at **Drumnadrochit** – a village seized by monster madness, its

 EATING IN INVERNESS: OUR PICKS

MacGregor's: Gastropub serving Scottish food and beer by day, and traditional Scottish music by night. *11am-midnight Mon-Sat, from noon Sun* ££

Bad Girl Bakery & Cafe: Breakfast and lunch spot in the Victorian Market, with fresh pastries and top-notch coffee. *9am-6pm Mon-Sat, 10am-5pm Sun* £

Mustard Seed: Bustling riverside restaurant with a Mediterranean vibe serving seafood, steak and vegetarian dishes. *noon-2.30pm & 5-9.15pm* ££

Rocpool: Stylish bistro with a Med-influenced menu focusing on quality Scottish produce, especially seafood. *noon-2pm & 5.30-9pm Tue-Sat* £££

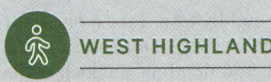

WEST HIGHLAND WAY IN A DAY

If you don't have time to hike the whole trail, you can walk (or mountain bike) this scenic stretch in a day.

START	END	LENGTH
Bridge of Orchy	Glencoe Mountain Resort	12 miles; 6 hours

From the train station, cross the main road to the **1 Bridge of Orchy** that gives the village its name, built in 1752 by General Caulfield as part of a military road-building project to pacify the Highlands.

Cross the bridge and take the footpath on the left. The trail climbs steeply over a ridge, following the route of Caulfield's road; pause at **2 Mam Carraigh** viewpoint for a grand panorama over Loch Tulla before descending to the Inveroran Hotel.

Continue on the tarmac to its end at **3 Forest Lodge**, where a gate marks the continuation of the trail along the route of the old road built by

Thomas Telford in 1811 (the main road to Glen Coe until the 1930s).

The stony trail crosses wild moorland with the hills of the Black Mount to your left, crossing Telford's **4 Ba Bridge** at the halfway point and passing the gloriously isolated ruin of **5 Ba Cottage**, a 19th-century shepherd's house.

As you round the shoulder of the hill, you'll get a **6 view of Buachaille Etive Mor** guarding the entrance to Glen Coe before the trail descends to **7 Glencoe Mountain Resort**. An hourly Citylink bus service stops at the junction with the main road and will take you back to your starting point or on to Fort William.

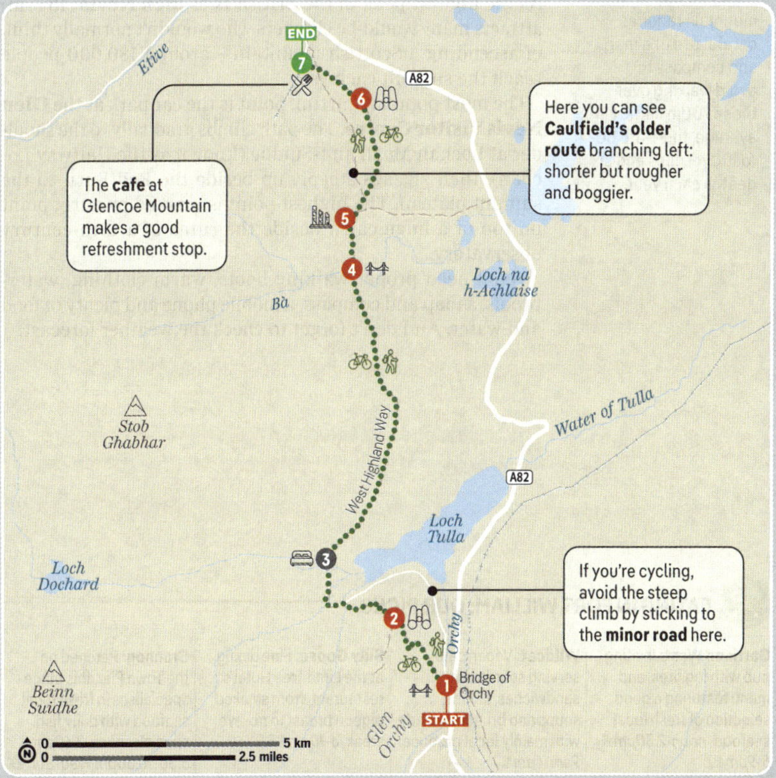

The **cafe** at Glencoe Mountain makes a good refreshment stop.

Here you can see **Caulfield's older route** branching left: shorter but rougher and boggier.

If you're cycling, avoid the steep climb by sticking to the **minor road** here.

215

BEN NEVIS FACTS

Here are a few hard facts to mull over before you try racing up the tourist track to the top of Ben Nevis.

The summit plateau is bound by 700m-high cliffs and has a sub-Arctic climate. At the summit, it can snow on any day of the year. The summit is wrapped in cloud nine days out of 10. In thick clouds, visibility at the summit can be 10m or less, and in such conditions, the only safe way off the mountain requires careful use of a map and compass to avoid walking over those 700m cliffs. On average, there are 80 to 100 rescues and six deaths each year.

gift shops bulging with Nessie cuddly toys. Take a one-hour **Deepscan Cruise** *(lochness.com/cruises; adult/child £21/18),* and get a feel for the huge size and depth of the loch while keeping a close eye on the boat's echo sounder. Then join a guided tour of the **Loch Ness Centre** *(lochness.com;adult/child £13.95/12.55),* an entertaining introduction to the history of the monster and a clear-sighted look at the evidence for and against its existence.

Fort William

All aboard the Harry Potter Express

The **Jacobite Steam Train** *(westcoastrailways.co.uk; adult/child £65/36)* travels the scenic two-hour run between Fort William and Mallaig. One of the great railway journeys of the world, the route crosses the historic Glenfinnan Viaduct, made famous in the *Harry Potter* films.

Trains depart from Fort William train station at 10.15am and (in peak season only) 2.40pm, and return from Mallaig at 2.10pm and 6.40pm. There's a brief stop at Glenfinnan station, and you get 1½ hours in Mallaig (two hours on the afternoon service).

Climbing Ben Nevis

As the highest peak in the British Isles, **Ben Nevis** (1344m) attracts many would-be climbers who wouldn't normally think of ascending a Scottish mountain – around 130,000 people reach the summit each year.

The most popular starting point is the car park at the **Glen Nevis Visitor Centre**. The path climbs gradually to the shoulder at Lochan Meall an t-Suidhe (known as the Halfway Lochan), then zigzags steeply up beside the Red Burn to the summit plateau. The highest point is marked by a trig point on top of a huge cairn beside the ruins of a 19th-century observatory.

You'll need proper walking boots, warm clothing, waterproofs, a map and compass, a mobile phone and plenty of food and water. And don't forget to check the weather forecast.

 EATING IN FORT WILLIAM: OUR PICKS

Garrison West: Inviting pub with log fires, and menu featuring a good selection of fresh local seafood. *noon-2.30pm & 5-9pm* ££

Wildcat: Vegan cafe serving sourdough sandwiches, salads, soups and brunches made with mainly local produce. *9am-4pm* £

Silly Goose: Fine dining at the Lime Tree Hotel's restaurant, from smoked pigeon breast to rib-eye steak. *6-10pm* £££

Crannog: Perched on the Town Pier, this place specialises in fresh local seafood with daily fish specials. *noon-2.30pm & 5.30-10.30pm Wed-Sun* ££

The Scottish Islands

MOUNTAINS | NEOLITHIC SITES | ISLANDS

Scotland's islands are wild, windswept and epic. These untamed corners of Britain aren't easy to travel, but the reward is some of the country's most remarkable scenery.

The main draw is Skye, an island of big landscapes: sharp-toothed mountain peaks, emerald-green river valleys and crashing cliff-edge waterfalls. Visitors flock here in their thousands to see the jagged peaks of the Quiraing or to skirt along the ridge of the Black Cuillin mountains. But there's Portree, too, a pretty harbourside settlement with colourful houses overlooking a sheltered bay, as well as top-notch whisky distilleries.

Or you can venture further afield to Scotland's far-flung northern islands like Orkney and Shetland. These starkly beautiful islands, their coastlines chiselled by North Sea storms and Atlantic gales, are a haven for wildlife and a hotbed of history. Prehistoric stone circles, Caribbean-like beaches, seabird-studded cliffs and Viking-inspired festivals await.

GETTING AROUND

Getting to the islands is easiest by ferry, either as a foot passenger or with your car. The main operators are CalMac and Orkney Ferries. Loganair flights are available between many of the islands. Once on the islands, travelling by car is by far the most efficient way of getting around.

Skye

Take to the water

The staggering landscapes of Skye can make it tempting to stay on terra firma, but those who head out to sea get to experience the island from a whole new perspective. Sign up for Rona boat trips from Portree with **Seaflower Skye** *(seaflowerskye.com; incl lunch £145),* or get closer to the water (and the wildlife) on a sea kayak with **Sea to Skye Xperience** *(seatoskyexperience.co.uk; half-/full day £45/95),* departing from Broadford. Prefer to be in the water rather than on it? Join a multiday diving expedition with **Dive & Sea the Hebrides** *(dive-and-sea-the-hebrides.co.uk; 3 days from £355)* to explore some of the incredible marine life, reefs and wrecks around the island. However you choose to take to the water, remember to look back at the Skye shoreline for stunning views of the Old Man of Storr and the Cuillin Hills.

☑ **TOP TIP**

These sparsely populated islands have limited accommodation, so it's important to book well in advance to secure a hotel or B&B for your time here. Also, not everything (restaurants, museums, etc) is open year-round, so plan ahead.

The drive of your life

Turning out of **Broadford** (30 minutes' drive south of Portree) and onto the B8083, it doesn't feel like you're about to embark on one of Scotland's most dazzling drives. But as the road narrows to a single-track lane, you'll notice the round-topped Beinn na Caillich mountain and know your adventure has begun.

The next 30 minutes of driving is a blur of unbelievable vistas: the picturesque valley of Strath Suardal, the roofless ruin of a church overlooking Loch Cill Chriosd, and the views of the solemn Bla Bheinn mountain across Loch Slapin. As you approach **Elgol**, traditional crofts lead the way down to the town's pier, which has perhaps the best vista of all: the Cuillin Hills jutting skywards across the water.

A duo of drams

Founded in 1830, Talisker was Skye's only legal whisky distillery for the better part of two centuries and a globally popular single malt. But today, following the 2021 release of the first whiskies by new local producers, whisky lovers can visit multiple distilleries on a day tour.

Start where it all began at **Talisker Distillery** *(malts.com; tours from £15)*, around 30 minutes' drive southwest of Portree. The distillery tour and tasting allow you to sample a mix of smoky, salty classic whiskies and rare, sweet expressions matured in sherry and port casks. After a brief walk along the sands of Talisker Bay (for some sobering sea air), travel south to the Sleat peninsula to visit **Torabhaig Distillery** *(torabhaig.com; tours from £15)*. Sit in the courtyard, flanked by old stone farmhouses, to savour its lightly peated, vanilla-sweetened single malt.

Ring of Brodgar, Orkney

Orkney

A wild Neolithic heart

At the centre of Orkney, and spanning much of the West Mainland, lies the **Heart of Neolithic Orkney** *(historicenviron ment.scot)*, a UNESCO World Heritage site. This is a good starting point for the islands' wider archaeological heritage. Made up of **Skara Brae** *(adult/child £10/6)*, the **Ring of Brodgar** *(free)*, the **Standing Stones of Stenness** *(free)* and **Maeshowe** *(adult/child £10/6)*, these fascinating sites are all within a stone's throw from one another. They have forced archaeologists to rethink settlement patterns throughout Neolithic Britain and offer a tantalising glimpse into life 5000 years ago.

Entry to Skara Brae and Maeshowe should be booked online as far in advance as possible. The best plan for visiting the sites in summer is to book Skara Brae for 4pm and Maeshowe for 7pm.

BEST SIGHTS ON SKYE'S TROTTERNISH PENINSULA

Lealt Falls: Gaze upon the 90m cascade and look out for ruins of the old diatomine factory and salmon smokehouses below.

Old Man of Storr: This eye-catching, 50m-high shard of rock is a 45-minute hike from the main road car park.

Kilt Rock: Admire this high cliff face of vertical basalt columns (which look like pleats on a kilt).

Skye Museum of Island Life: Learn about traditional island crofting life at this preserved village of thatched cottages.

Fairy Glen: Explore a Hobbiton-esque landscape of impossibly green hillocks, placid pools and castle-like rock formations.

An Corran Beach: Go in search of 165-million-year-old dinosaur footprints at low tide.

EATING IN PORTREE (SKYE): OUR PICKS

| **Café Arriba:** Climb the steep stairs to this laid-back cafe for a hearty Scottish breakfast or seafood-filled lunch. *8am-4pm Thu-Tue £* | **Pizza in the Skye:** Street-food truck serving thin-crust wood-fired pizza and garlic bread. Order online in advance. *noon-8pm Tue-Sat £* | **Sea Breezes:** This place is all about seafood: opt for the platter with salmon, mussels and langoustines. *noon-2pm & 5.30-9pm Tue-Sat ££* | **Dulse & Brose:** Try modern Scottish cuisine with an Asian twist, featuring fresh Skye seafood, venison and cheese. *5-10pm £££* |

THE NORTHERN LIGHTS

Shetland lies 60 degrees north of the equator, putting it at a similar latitude to Anchorage, Alaska and the southern tip of Greenland. This makes it the best place in Britain to see the northern lights (aurora borealis), known in the local dialect as the 'mirrie dancers'. Midwinter is the best time for viewing; **AuroraWatchUK** (*aurorawatch.lancs. ac.uk*) predicts when the aurora is likely to be visible.

Shetland's high latitude also results in the phenomenon known locally as the 'simmer dim'. A few weeks on either side of midsummer (21 June), the sun doesn't set until 10.30pm and rises again five hours later. Between sunset and sunrise there is no proper darkness, just a modest twilight. Not quite the midnight sun, but close.

THE TRIGGERHAPPYDOC/SHUTTERSTOCK

Puffins, Isle of Noss, Shetland

Shetland

Seabirds and seals

The little **Isle of Noss** (*nature.scot*) lies just 3 miles east of Lerwick, on the far side of Bressay. Awe-inspiring sea cliffs on its east coast rise to 180m, providing nesting sites for more than 100,000 pairs of breeding seabirds, including gannets, guillemots, kittiwakes, shags and puffins – one of the great seabird spectaculars of Shetland.

Book a two-hour boat tour with **Seabirds & Seals** (*seabirds-and-seals.com; adult/child £60/30*) to get up close and personal with the birds; trips depart from **Victoria Pier** in Lerwick up to six times daily.

 EATING IN LERWICK (SHETLAND): OUR PICKS

Peerie Shop Cafe: An absolute gem of a place, serving the best coffee, soups, scones and sandwiches in town. *8am-4pm Tue-Sat* £	**Fjarå:** Scandi-style cafe-bar with superb sea views and great breakfast, lunch and dinner menus. *8am-10pm Tue-Sat, 9am-5pm Sun* ££	**No 88 Kitchen & Bar:** Hip and relaxed, with seasonal dishes championing Shetland seafood and lamb. *10am-10pm Wed-Sat, noon-4pm Sun* ££	**Mareel Cafe:** Waterside arts-centre cafe serving locally made sandwiches, soups, wraps and salads. *10am-9pm Tue-Thu & Sun, to midnight Fri & Sat* £

Places We Love to Stay

£ Budget ££ Midrange £££ Top end

London
MAP p173

Hoxton Holborn ££ Ultra-chic yet affordable, with hip rooms full of design details and leather, velvets and mid-century furniture. Its social spaces are always happening.

CitizenM Tower of London ££ If you don't get the room with windows framing Tower Bridge, there's always the roof terrace.

Londoner £££ The sexy Leicester Sq newcomer has multiple trendy eateries and a wellness retreat with a big pool.

One Aldwych £££ An independent hotel in a historic building, One has been renovated with relaxing plush, neutral decor, and has fabulous theatre views.

South Place £££ A hip, design-led five-star hotel with all the trimmings of luxury, including a Michelin-starred seafood restaurant.

Sea Containers £££ Luxury hotel with the best views of the skyline as well as a spa, a cinema and an award-winning cocktail bar.

Park Plaza £££ Four-star hotel in a central location with views to die for. You can see the London Eye right from your window.

Padstow

Trewornan Manor £££ Posh B&B in a 17th-century, Grade II–listed manor house surrounded by 25 glorious acres.

Harbour Hotel Padstow £££ Formerly the Metropole, this period beauty commands a panoramic view over the estuary.

Land's End

Old Success Inn ££ Sennen Cove's beloved seaside pub has plush, colourful rooms and glorious coastal views.

Land's End Hotel £££ Perched on the very edge of Britain, this hotel has luxurious rooms and hard-to-beat sea views.

Bristol

Artists Residence ££ Georgian townhouse with a range of industrial-chic rooms, a cafe, kitchen and lounge bar.

Number 38 £££ Upmarket B&B with sweeping city views from contemporary rooms on the edge of the Downs.

Bath

Brooks ££ A scattering of antiques meet plush modern furnishings at this comfy, fairly central bolthole with an honesty bar.

Queensberry £££ Stylish Queensberry is Bath's luxury choice. Heritage roots meet snazzy furnishings in these Georgian townhouses.

Birmingham
MAP p191

Bloc £ Smart Japanese pod-style rooms alongside golden design touches nodding to the historic Jewellery Quarter's past.

Grand Hotel Birmingham £££ Plush art deco hotel where Winston Churchill once stayed. Don't miss the indulgent afternoon tea at Parisian-style cocktail bar Madeleine.

Stratford-upon-Avon

Arden Hotel ££ Rustic rooms and a magnificent brasserie, perfectly located across the street for attending performances by the Royal Shakespeare Company.

Hotel du Vin ££ Smart Georgian boutique hotel with a French bistro, a wine cellar and 46 cosy rooms. Short walk to the train station.

Nottingham

St James Hotel ££ Stylish hotel with contemporary rooms, an art gallery and a fine location near Nottingham Castle.

Lace Market Hotel ££ Georgian townhouse in Lace Market area with 51 individual bedrooms, suites and feature rooms.

Liverpool
MAP p195

Titanic Liverpool ££ Former dockside warehouse packed with character and huge amounts of space. Don't miss the Rum bar pouring sweet spirits from Guyana, Barbados and Cuba.

Municipal Hotel & Spa £££ Lavish Victorian building topped by a soaring clock tower. Hosts a glittering palm court alongside a spa and fitness centre.

Bakewell

Rutland Arms Hotel ££ Nineteenth-century coaching inn offering 32 refurbished bedrooms, an excellent restaurant and an extensive wine menu.

H Boutique Hotel ££ Luxury boutique hotel with 10 stylish suites, each telling a local story beginning with 'H'.

Cardiff
MAP p199

Coal Exchange Hotel ££ Former hub of global coal trading transformed into a

221

55-room hotel with restaurant. Historic features, Jacuzzi baths and great location.

Parkgate Hotel £££ Luxury city-centre hotel next to Principality Stadium. Lovely on-site spa, bar and restaurant. Rooms are spacious and comfortable.

Bannau Brycheiniog (Brecon Beacons) National Park

Lodge ££ Blissfully poised on Llanfrynach's fringes, this B&B has country flair and lovingly tended gardens overlooking the hills.

Peterstone Court £££ On the banks of the Usk, this Georgian manor brims with period charm and Beacons views. The spa and heated outdoor pool are huge draws.

Portmeirion & Blaenau Ffestiniog

Treks Bunkhouse £ This family-run bunkhouse high in the Moelwyn mountains makes a terrific base for cycling, hiking and canoeing. There's a barbecue area with mountain views.

Hotel Portmeirion £££ Historic hotel in Portmeirion, with Dwyryd Estuary views. Gourmet dining, a heated outdoor pool and substantial breakfasts.

Edinburgh   MAP p206

Code – The Court £ Colourful, charming and cheap, this old courthouse prison turned luxury hostel has extremely comfy pod beds and tasty waffle-heavy breakfasts.

Angels Share Hotel ££ Connected to the longstanding bar of the same name, this hotel offers compact, individually designed rooms adorned with tartan and portraits of famous Scots.

Witchery £££ One of Edinburgh's most uniquely decadent stays, this historic hotel is all about plush antique furniture, indulgent themed suites and candlelit fine dining.

Kimpton Charlotte Square £££ Seven Georgian townhouses were combined to make this charming hotel, with elegant rooms and suites, a small spa and two exceptional restaurants.

Glasshouse £££ Chic, modern and luxurious, this magnificent stone- and glass-fronted hotel at the top of Leith Walk is renowned for its elegant rooftop garden.

Glasgow

Citizen M ££ Modern, business-focused hotel offering minimalist rooms with king-sized beds, decent showers and an app controlling the lighting, thermostat, blinds and more.

Glasgow Grosvenor Hotel ££ Historic hotel opposite the Botanic Gardens offering classically stylish rooms, plus a fine restaurant and gin bar.

Alamo Guest House £££ Antique furnishings and modern comforts combine in this elegant, family-run guesthouse, located on the edge of Kelvingrove Park.

Inverness

Rocpool Reserve £££ The swishest place in town is a Georgian manor with River Ness panoramas, sunken baths, hot tubs and private balconies.

Culloden House £££ A converted mid-18th-century Palladian manor house where Bonnie Prince Charlie once stayed.

Skye

Carters Rest ££ This Neist Point–adjacent B&B has large bedrooms, great food and wonderful coastal views.

Skeabost House Hotel £££ Once a hunting lodge, this luxury lochside hotel has one of Skye's best restaurants.

Shetland

Rockvilla Guest House ££ A relaxing, welcoming retreat in a stone-built villa with a pretty garden in central Lerwick.

Belmont House £££ This 18th-century Georgian country house close to the Unst ferry pier provides luxurious B&B accommodation.

Hotel Portmeirion

Practicalities

HEALTHCARE
When Britain left the EU, it lost the reciprocal healthcare agreement provided by the European Health Insurance Card. Travellers from the EU and other nations must now have private travel insurance to cover any medical care. Choose your policy carefully and make sure you get one that includes emergency flights home.

DAVE SMITH 1965/SHUTTERSTOCK

VISAS
Citizens of Australia, Canada, EEA (European Economic Area) nations, Israel, Japan, New Zealand, Switzerland and the USA can visit Britain without a visa. Check the latest visa rules before you travel (gov.uk/check-uk-visa).

LGBTIQ+ TRAVELLERS
Britain is regarded as one of the most LGBTIQ+-friendly travel destinations in the world. London, Brighton, Manchester, Birmingham, Bristol, Edinburgh and Cardiff all have flourishing gay scenes, while other cities and small towns have active communities, too. However, LGBTIQ+ hate crime, particularly transphobia, is on the rise. Some areas still harbour pockets of homophobic hostility as well.

ELECTRICITY
Unlike most of the world, Britain uses the plug type G, which is the plug with three rectangular pins in a triangular pattern (on a 230V supply voltage and 50Hz) - so it's wise to bring an adaptor.

OPENING HOURS
Banks 9.30am–4pm or 5pm Monday to Friday (some to 1pm Saturday)
Pubs and bars Noon–11pm Monday to Thursday, to midnight or 1am Friday and Saturday, 12.30pm–11pm Sunday
Restaurants Lunch noon–3pm, dinner 6–9pm or 10pm (later in cities)
Shops 9am–5.30pm (6pm in cities) Monday to Saturday, 11am–5pm Sunday

LANGUAGES
The number of Welsh, Scots, Scottish Gaelic and Cornish speakers in Britain is on the rise. Meanwhile, both Polish and Romanian are spoken by over 500,000 people in the UK, with Punjabi and Urdu not far behind.

PUBLIC HOLIDAYS
New Year's Day 1 January (plus 2 January in Scotland)
Easter March/April (Good Friday to Easter Monday inclusive)
May Day First Monday in May

Spring Bank Holiday Last Monday in May
Summer Bank Holiday Last Monday in August
Christmas Day 25 December
Boxing Day 26 December

WORLDOFDOMINIC/SHUTTERSTOCK

Liverpool Street tube station

Arriving

Most visitors reach Britain by air and generally arrive at one of London's two largest airports: Heathrow (often chaotic and crowded; 15 miles west of central London) and Gatwick (busy; 30 miles south of central London). The capital has three other airports: Stansted, Luton and London City. Other options for arriving in Britain are by boat and by train.

By Air
European travellers can, for the most part, fly to all corners of Britain. Long-haul travellers will almost always fly into Heathrow. London's new Elizabeth Line is the most cost-efficient way to head into the capital once through immigration and baggage.

By Boat & Train
Britain has several passenger ports, with the most significant being Southampton, Dover and Liverpool, which handle a mix of ferries and cruise ships. Eurostar trains from Paris, Amsterdam and Brussels arrive at London St Pancras station.

MONEY

Currency: Pound sterling (£)

WAYS TO PAY
An increasing number of shops, bars and restaurants only accept card payments. While contactless is king, keep some change handy for local markets, toilets and seasonal car parking (especially on the coast).

TIPPING
Not obligatory, but tipping around 10% in restaurants and cafes is the norm. Tips may be added to your bill as a 'service charge' (12.5% in London). Unless you're eating and receiving table service, there's no need to tip bar staff.

HOW TO SAVE MONEY
Between Edinburgh's £7.50 pints and £163.40 train tickets for London to Manchester, Britain can make your credit card cry. Booking ahead saves money. Reserve B&Bs and private rooms in hostels at least two months in advance (book direct for the best deals). Swap trains for coaches (or book off-peak train travel 12 weeks in advance). Build itineraries around free museums such as the Scottish National Gallery and the British Museum.

Getting Around

Transport in Britain can be expensive compared to continental Europe. Bus and rail services are sparse in more remote parts of the country, but between them serve most destinations (expect a more sporadic service at weekends). In coastal regions, some bus services only run during the summer season.

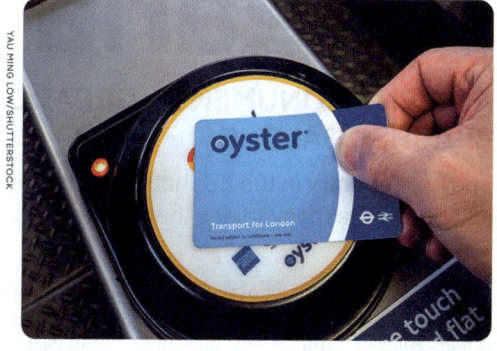

YAU MING LOW/SHUTTERSTOCK

Best Ways to Get Around
A car is useful for visiting remote regions in the countryside, mountains and on the coast. You're unlikely to need one in major cities. Trains are a good alternative, with frequent and extensive countrywide coverage. Coaches offer cheap city-to-city travel.

Local Networks
Traveline *(traveline.info)* covers bus, coach, train and taxi services nationwide. It offers online timetables, a journey planner and limited fare information. **National Rail Enquiries** *(nationalrail. co.uk)* has downloadable maps of the rail network. **National Express** *(nationalexpress.com)* has interactive route maps for its coaches.

Coaches
Long-distance buses (called coaches in Britain) are nearly always the cheapest way to get around. **National Express** *(nationalexpress.com)*, **Scottish Citylink** *(citylink. co.uk)* and **Megabus** *(uk. megabus.com)* are the major operators. Book early or off-peak for the cheapest fares.

Tickets & PlusBus
Ticketing in Britain is interconnected. If the train doesn't get you all the way to your destination, add a **PlusBus** *(plusbus.info)* supplement when reserving to validate your train ticket for onward travel by bus.

Driving
Having a car or motorbike means you can be independent and reach remote places. Most roads are in good or very good condition, but downsides include traffic jams, the high cost of fuel, pricey city parking and, in London, the Congestion Charge.

DRIVING ESSENTIALS

Drive on the left side

17

Driving age is 17

Speed limit is 70mph on motorways, 60mph on single-carriageway roads and generally 30mph in urban areas

Curated by
Leonid Ragozin

Bulgaria

ANCIENT MONUMENTS, GREAT OUTDOORS, BEACHES GALORE

The only country in the EU that uses the Cyrillic alphabet is just one of the many things that makes Bulgaria special.

Occupying a large chunk of the Balkans, Bulgaria is a land of sombre mountains ranges, some of Europe's most ancient cities, lovely countryside, the beautiful (if overdeveloped) Black Sea coast and rose shrubs on every corner. It was at the centre of action in Europe through much of antiquity and into the Middle Ages, with succeeding empires and kingdoms each leaving an architectural and cultural footprint, starting with Rome. The supranational structure it now finds itself a part of is the EU: Bulgaria joined the Schengen Area in 2025 and replaced its currency with the euro in 2026.

The capital, Sofia, is a city that has some of the best features of southeastern Europe: an easygoing atmosphere, a lively and increasingly sophisticated restaurant and cafe scene, and plenty of historical monuments, from Roman to communist. Two other major historical hubs, Plovdiv and Veliko Târnovo, are also filled with millennia-old stories and monuments. The mountains south of Sofia are the country's outdoor nexus, with multiple opportunities for skiing and hiking. The Black Sea coast is also steeped in ancient history, with settlements like Nesebâr tracing its roots back to ancient Greece. Although it's endowed with beautiful sandy beaches, this region does suffer from overtourism.

ROSSHELEN/SHUTTERSTOCK

THE MAIN AREAS

SOFIA
Bulgaria's historic but youthful capital. **p230**

BLACK SEA COAST
Sandy beaches, ancient Greek legacy. **p237**

CENTRAL BULGARIA
Roman ruins and Bulgarian heritage. **p241**

For places to stay
in Bulgaria, see
p245

JOVAN M/SHUTTERSTOCK

Left: Stadium of Philippopolis (p242), Plovdiv; Above: Aleksander Nevski Cathedral (p231), Sofia

Find Your Way

International airports at Sofia, Burgas and Varna serve as the main entry points for travellers. An extensive network of bus routes and ramshackle trains connect most places around the country.

BUSES & TRAINS

Travelling around Bulgaria means combining buses and trains. Buses (book tickets on *oblet.com*) are often faster and the network is more extensive. Trains (book tickets on *bileti.bdz.bg*) provide more leg space, but little else.

CAR

Renting a car is a fun and rewarding way to explore Bulgaria. The main rental hubs around the country are Sofia, Varna and Burgas. To avoid unexpected charges, it's best to book directly from local operators, such as *toprentacar.bg*.

Sofia, p230

Bulgaria's capital is full of life and youthful energy, and peppered with architectural monuments from different epochs.

Central Bulgaria, p241

Plovdiv and Veliko Tărnovo are quintessentially Bulgaria and have heaps of cultural heritage.

Black Sea Coast, p237

Bulgaria's beaches are wide, sandy and filled to the brim during a rather short season. But there are also ancient treasures to explore.

ROMANIA • Ruse • Dobrich • Varna • Shumen • Razgrad • Targovishteo • Veliko Tărnovo *Archaeological Museum* Nesebŭr *Black Sea* Burgas Sozopol Sredets Yambol Sliven Kazanlăk Stara Zagora *Centralen Balkan* Pleven • Lovech Troyan • Panagyurishte Plovdiv Pazardzhik *Ferros (Maritsa)* Haskovo Kărdzhali Komotini Cherven Bryag Shiroka Lŭka Gotse Delchev Velingrad Vratsa Montana *Aleksander Nevski Cathedral* *Sveta Sofia Church* *Rilski Rila manastir* Bansko *Pirin National Park* Sandanski **SOFIA** Pernik Dupnitsa Blagoevgrad *Strumica* Petrich Kyustendil Kalotina SERBIA NORTH MACEDONIA GREECE

100 km / 50 miles

SERGII FIGURNYI/SHUTTERSTOCK

Veliko Târnovo (p244)

Plan Your Time

Distances are large and trains are slow, so factor in extra time to get around. It's best to plan your trip in advance.

Three Days

● Spend two days in **Sofia** (p230) and explore its numerous monuments and museums; enjoy the city's easygoing ambience. Take a hike up **Mt Vitosha** (p233) and make sure you visit the ancient **Boyana Church** (p233). On day three, take a tour to the **Rila Monastery** (p234) and try to fit a visit to the **Seven Rila Lakes** (p234) into your itinerary.

With More Time

● Follow the three-day itinerary, then head to **Veliko Târnovo** (p244) and immerse yourself in the essence of Bulgaria. Make your way to **Varna** (p237) and begin exploring the **Black Sea coast** (p237), moving south to **Burgas** (p238) via **Nesebãr** (p238). Return to Sofia via **Plovdiv** (p241), where you can visit the Roman ruins and the wonderful Old Town.

SEASONAL HIGHLIGHTS

SPRING
The Black Sea is too cold for swimming, but everything is in bloom. An ideal time for hiking and exploring culture.

SUMMER
As the temperatures climb, locals seek refuge in the mountains and by the sea. Beaches fill up with sunseekers.

AUTUMN
September is prime festival season in seaside cities, but the mercury drops soon after, most in the mountains.

WINTER
Snow blankets the mountain peaks: time to get out the skis and enjoy a white Christmas.

Sofia

ROMAN RUINS | MEDIEVAL CHURCHES | MOUNTAIN AIR

GETTING AROUND

Sofia has a convenient public transit system: the three metro lines are supplemented by multiple bus and tram routes going in all directions from the metro stations. Electronic tickets are available at metro stations, and the metro also conveniently connects the city to the airport.

While you don't need a car in the city, it is a good place to pick one up for further travels. Rental agencies, like *greenrentacar.bg*, are located at the airport and in shopping malls. A bike-share network exists, but leaves much to be desired.

☑ TOP TIP

Sofia has its own nature park on Mt Vitosha, with dozens of hiking trails in summer and ski slopes in winter.

The chef who prepared this spicy cultural stew chose to throw a bit of everything into the mix. Tramlines and fin-de-siècle buildings give Sofia a measure of Central European charm with more than a whiff of imperial grandeur. Mosques and Turkish baths provide a strong Levantine flavour. Communist-era neoclassicism and Cyrillic script add an air of political intrigue. Sun-drenched streets, Roman ruins, cafe tables scattered in squares and mountains in the distance remind travellers that they are within the Mediterranean cultural universe. And the best time to visit Sofia is now: it's fairly well organised, easy to get around and increasingly cosmopolitan, but thankfully still devoid of the slick sterility of richer European capitals. Its captivating ambience feels organic, deriving from the natural charm of its friendly and energetic inhabitants.

Central Sofia

Roman foundations

The heart of Sofia is a peculiar organism that lives above and below ground: the **Ancient Serdica Complex** *(entry free),* plus two medieval churches, all wrapped up in a subway transfer hub and topped with a massive Soviet-style government compound known as the **Largo**.

The Serdi, the Celtic tribe that lived here in antiquity, gave its name to Ulpia Serdica, a Roman settlement and the precursor of today's Sofia. The two connected metro stations, **Serdika** and **Serdika II**, envelope two large Roman ruins from this era. You'll see fragments of eight streets, an early Christian basilica, and baths and houses dating from the 4th to 6th centuries.

Surrounded on all sides by the Serdica site, the quaint **Sveta Petka Samardzhiiska Church** hails from another era. It was built during the early years of Ottoman rule (late 14th century), hence its subterranean position and inconspicuous exterior. Inside are some 16th-century murals.

★ HIGHLIGHTS
1 Aleksander Nevski Cathedral
2 Sveta Sofia Church

● SIGHTS
3 Ancient Serdica Complex
see 3 Largo
4 National Museum of Archaeology
5 Red Flat
6 Sveta Nedelya Cathedral
7 Sveta Petka Samardzhiiska Church
8 Sveti Georgi Rotunda

● SLEEPING
9 Agora Boutique Hotel
10 Art Hotel 158
11 Hostel Mostel
12 Hotel Les Fleurs
13 Hotel Niky

● EATING
14 Dark Sister
15 Fake French
16 Izbata Tavern
17 Krâchme Divaka
18 Made in Blue
19 Manastirska Magernitsa
20 MoMa Bulgarian Food & Wine
21 Yum

● SHOPPING
22 Ladies' Market

The vast courtyard formed by the Largo complex conceals an ancient gem: the **Sveti Georgi Rotunda**. This red-brick church was built in the 4th century CE, which makes it Sofia's oldest preserved building. It was initially designed as a Roman bath house but was repurposed as a church in the Roman or early Byzantine times. The murals inside were painted between the 10th and 14th centuries.

Dig into Bulgarian history

If you only get to visit one museum in Sofia, make it the **National Museum of Archaeology** (*Национален археологически музей; naim.bg; entry adult/concession €6/1.50*). Housed in a former mosque built in 1496, it displays a wealth of Thracian, Roman and medieval artefacts. Highlights include a mosaic floor from the Church of Sveta Sofia, a Thracian gold burial mask (4th century BCE) and a magnificent bronze head, thought to represent a Thracian king. Also look out for the heart-warmingly cute zoomorphic figurines from the prehistoric Chalcolithic period.

The original Sofia

Believed to be a contemporary of the Hagia Sophia in Istanbul, the **Sveta Sofia Church** (*Света София*) was built on the foundations of four earlier churches – as well as a Roman amphitheatre. The church dates back to the 4th century, during the reign of Roman emperor Constantine. In the 14th century, it gave the city its current name. A **subterranean museum** (*sofiahistory museum.bg; entry adult/concession €4/1.50*) houses an ancient necropolis, with 56 tombs and the remains of four other churches.

Church of fallen soldiers

One of the symbols not just of Sofia but of Bulgaria itself, the awe-inspiring **Aleksander Nevski Cathedral** (*Свети*

RED DECADES

Bulgaria was ruled by the Communist Party for 43 years. Memories of this period range from total resentment to deep nostalgia. Vestiges of the communist past are scattered around Sofia, with the **Largo complex** presiding over the centre and monuments on display at the **Museum of Socialist Art**. The main legacy is the sea of apartment blocks. Check out the **Red Flat** museum if you're curious about life during the communist era.

ANCIENT SERDICA

In addition to the main Largo ruins, remnants of ancient Serdica pop up throughout the centre. Excavated sites include the following:

Western Gate: Remains of two towers, by the St Joseph Catholic Cathedral at Tsar Boris I.

Amphitheatre: Incorporated into the Arena di Serdica hotel at Budapeshta 2.

Roman Thermal Baths: Remnants of a Roman spa and temples by the Turkish Mineral Baths.

Konstantinov Quarter: Sophisticated Roman residential complexes in the courtyard of the President's Office.

Remains of Northern Wall: Stones from a 6th-century wall, built during the reign of Emperor Justinian.

BORYANA MANZUROVA/SHUTTERSTOCK

Mt Vitosha

Александър Невски; cathedral.bg) was built between 1882 and 1912 in memory of the 200,000 Russian soldiers who died fighting for Bulgaria's independence during the Russo-Turkish War (1877–78). It was named in honour of a 13th-century Russian warrior-prince. The crypt houses the **Museum of Christian Art** *(nationalgallery.bg; entry adult/concession €4/1.50),* Bulgaria's biggest and best collection of icons, stretching back to the 5th century.

Cafe culture and mountain views

The attraction of Sofia's main pedestrian strip, **Vitosha Boulevard**, reveals itself immediately. The magnificent view of Mt Vitosha, which the street seems to abut (but doesn't), is always there – no matter if you're strolling around or sipping on a latte. The Byzantine silhouette of **Sveta Nedelya Cathedral** at the Serdika end of the boulevard is also quite imposing.

Built in the 20th-century interwar period, Vitosha Boulevard's arcades have a predictable array of high-end fashion brands and tourist-oriented cafes. If you'd like to enjoy a glass of wine or a meal, bear in mind that the best options are located in the smaller streets that run parallel to the main drag.

 WHERE TO EAT IN CENTRAL SOFIA: OUR PICKS

Dark Sister: A bohemian haunt disguised as a sidewalk cafe. Food encompasses the Balkans and the Middle East, from hummus to schnitzel. *noon-10.30pm* €€

Izbata Tavern: One of the best places in town to sample Bulgarian food. The menu comes with an intriguing vegetarian section, plus lots of meat. *11am-11pm* €€

Moma Bulgarian Food & Wine: An update on a traditional *mehana* (tavern). Try the *gozba* pork stew cooked in a bread loaf and Bulgarian wine. *12.30-11.30pm* €€

Fake French: Not at all fake, but instead a creative take on French standards (eg onion soup), with a merry brasserie ambience. *6.30-11pm* €€

Fruit of the land

The city's oldest open-air market is known as the **Ladies' Market** *(Женски пазар)*; it stretches for several blocks along bul Stefan Stambolov, ending at the **Lions' Bridge**, a prominent landmark. The name derives from the Ottoman policy that forbids women from shopping anywhere else but this area. The section of the market closer to Serdika metro has lately acquired a more gentrified look, but further on, the place morphs into a much livelier traditional East European market, where mountains of fruit and vegetables adorn simple metal stalls and sellers chat amicably with customers.

Mt Vitosha Area

A breath of fresh mountain air

Not only does **Mt Vitosha** serve as a decorative element in Sofia's cityscape, but it also happens to be the capital's favoured hiking and skiing destination. There are dozens of clearly marked trails, a handful of hotels, cafes and restaurants, and numerous huts and chalets. The sightseeing highlight is **Zlatnite Mostove** *(Златните мостове)* – a spray of large boulders (a 'stone river') that tumbles down a slope from 1700m to 1350m.

Neither of the two cable-car services that once served Mt Vitosha were operational at the time of writing. It's best to either take a taxi or bus 63, which runs from the Krasno Selo metro station to the mountaintop, terminating near Zlatnite Mostove. This is the best place to start exploring the mountain.

Medieval frescoes

A visit to Mt Vitosha can be easily combined with a serious dive into history and art. One way to access the park is to take bus 64 to the final stop, which drops you off at the UNESCO-protected **Boyana Church** *(Боянска Църква; boyanachurch.info; entry adult/concession €6/1.50)*, one the most enchanting religious structures in the country and one of the rare examples of medieval Bulgarian religious art. Inside is a hall of 90 frescoes, the most important of which was painted in 1259 and depicts biblical scenes as well as portraits of the local overlord Kaloyan and his wife Desislava, who had commissioned them.

From the church, it's an arduous 3.1km climb to the **Boyana Waterfall**, followed by a 3.2km hike to Zlatnite Mostove. Or you can take bus 63 instead; hop on at the Kv Boyana bus stop.

BEST HIKES ON MT VITOSHA

Boyana Church–Zlatnite Mostove: Ask for directions to Boyana Waterfall. From there, obvious paths lead to Zlatnite Mostove (three hours).

Zlatnite Mostove–Mt Cherni Vrâh: A challenging hike, via Kumata Hut and Mt Sedloto (2018m; three hours).

Aleko–Mt Cherni Vrâh: Popular but steep trail (90 minutes on foot).

Aleko–Zlatnite Mostove: Follow the trail to Goli Vrâh, skirt around Mt Sredets (1969m) and pass Hotel Bor (three hours).

Dragalevtsi–Boyana: An easy 5km low-altitude route connecting two main entry points into Vitosha Nature Park.

WHERE TO EAT IN CENTRAL SOFIA: OUR PICKS

Yum: Feast on Chinese dumplings, noodles and delicious salads in this tiny and intimate establishment with impeccable service. *noon-10pm €€*	**Krâchme Divaka:** In an appealing old house, this is a good choice for traditional Bulgarian food. Try the signature chicken soup cooked in a bread loaf. *noon-11pm €€*	**Manastirska Magernitsa:** Enormous and entertainingly idiosyncratic menu featuring recipes collected from monasteries across the country. *noon-11pm €€*	**Made in Blue:** A blue-coloured house with art on the wall and an outdoor patio. Middle Eastern flavours and seafood stand out on the eclectic menu. *noon-11pm €€*

Beyond Sofia

South of Sofia, Bulgaria's tallest mountains rise above the country's most important monastery, top ski resort and beautiful lakes.

Places

Rila Monastery p234
Seven Rila Lakes p234
Bansko p235

Two mountain ranges east of the road that connects Sofia to Greece are home to some of Bulgaria's most popular destinations. The Rila Mountains are the first chain you'll encounter when travelling south from the capital. This is where the heart of Bulgarian cultural identity was preserved at Rila Monastery, the holiest of the country's Orthodox sites. Also here are seven gorgeous mountain lakes that are strung together at the centre of prime hiking territory. Further south are the Pirin Mountains, Bulgaria's highest range and the home of Bansko, a once traditional mountain town that's become a favourite with skiers and digital nomads.

GETTING AROUND

It's best to explore these areas by car, especially if you're pressed for time. Buses from Sofia's central bus station are convenient for Bansko. The tour company Traventuria (*rilamonasterybus. com*) runs shuttle buses from Sofia to Rila Monastery and Seven Rila Lakes.

Rila Monastery

DISTANCE FROM SOFIA: 1¾HR 🚗

The holiest ground

Ensconced within a remote wooded enclave along the Rilska River, the **Rila Monastery** (*rilskimanastir.org; entry free*) is a living testament to centuries of faith, resilience and architectural artistry. This is Bulgaria's largest and most famous Orthodox monastery, and it's hard not to be awed by its spiritual significance, imposing scale and sheer grandeur of the fortress-like sanctuary: arcaded balconies are set around a cobblestone courtyard and the surrounding residential wings can house over 300 pilgrims. Plan on spending a couple of hours here. The monastery is in the Rila Mountains at an elevation of 1147m.

Seven Rila Lakes

DISTANCE FROM SOFIA: 1¾HR 🚗

Hike Bulgaria's lake country

Alpine vistas, glistening lakes and craggy mountain peaks – hiking the **Seven Rila Lakes** is arguably the most attractive

WHERE TO EAT: RILA MONASTERY & SEVEN RILA LAKES

Bakery: Just outside the monastery walls, this bakery sells freshly baked bread and *mekitsi* (Bulgarian donuts) accompanied by buffalo milk. *9.30am-4.30pm* €

Gorski Kut Hotel & Restaurant (p245): Right on the river with gorgeous forest views, five minutes from the monastery. The fresh trout is excellent. *10am-10pm* €€

Restaurant Gayzera: Traditional Bulgarian dishes, plenty of outdoor seating and a fireplace in colder weather. Located in Sapareva Banya. *noon-11.30 pm* €€

Lovna Hut: Serves traditional Bulgarian cuisine in a forested setting and also has accommodation. Walking distance from the Panichishte Chairlift. *10am-8pm* €€

Rila Monastery

open-air adventure in Bulgaria, and delivers some of Eastern Europe's most dramatic highland scenery for comparatively little effort. Cradled in the Rila Mountains, the area is defined by its seven glacial lakes, each named after its shape and connected via a complex system of streams.

To begin, take the **Panichishte Chairlift** *(€9 return)* to the start of the trailhead just outside **Rila Lakes Hut**. From here, follow a steep and rocky path up to a moderately challenging trail that traces a high ridge on a well-marked circular route. You'll tick off each member of the crystal-clear septet as you go, from Kidney Lake (2100m) to Tear Lake (2500m), which remains frozen for nine months of the year.

Bansko

DISTANCE FROM SOFIA: **2½HR**

From skiing to mountain biking

Sitting 925m above sea level in the foothills of the **Pirin Mountains**, Bansko has transformed itself from a quiet revival-era town of cobbled streets, *mehana* (traditional taverns) and timber-framed houses into the country's busiest year-round resort. In winter, its slopes buzz with high-octane energy as skiers and snowboarders race down its groomed pistes, lured by the Alpine-style terrain at Balkan prices. In summer, the slopes become the playground of hikers and mountain bikers who fan out across the UNESCO-listed wilderness, tackling the park's craggy ridges and 118 glacial lakes.

AN ALPINE BASE

Over the past decade, Bansko has reinvented itself as one of Europe's digital nomad hubs. What began with a single coworking space has since blossomed into an international community of remote workers, drawn by the town's affordability, scenery and nomad scene. Each summer, the Bansko Nomad Fest attracts hundreds of laptop-toting wanderers, with a full schedule of talks, workshops and activities – it's the largest digital nomad gathering in the world. Outside of the week-long celebration, Bansko retains its cosmopolitan flair with coworking spaces like Altspace *(altspacecoworking. com)* providing reliable infrastructure and an instant network of new connections for the constant stream of temporary residents looking for a slice of mountain paradise.

 WHERE TO EAT IN BANSKO: OUR PICKS

Mehana Vodenitsata: Next to main square, this timber-and-stone *mehana* serves grilled Bulgarian classics in generous portions, with a warm welcome. *noon-late* €€

Baryakova: Cosy mountain tavern known for grilled meats, seasonal dishes, wine and slow-cooked pork knuckle. *5pm-late Mon-Fri, from 11am Sat & Sun* €€

Dedo Yonkata: Family-run, 100-year-old house near the gondola, serving Pirin specialties in clay pots over wooden embers; spacious garden for dining. *10am-late* €€

Dedo Tase: This Old Town favourite has large portions of traditional fare: smoked meats, hearty soups, local cheeses and lamb skewers. *5-11pm Fri-Wed* €€

A SANCTUARY OF SPIRIT & IDENTITY

The hermit St John of Rila founded the Rila Monastery in the first half of the 10th century and it has been an active centre of worship and devotion ever since. Beyond its spiritual significance, it also played an important role in preserving Bulgaria's national identity, especially during Ottoman rule from the 15th to 19th centuries. During this time, the monastery not only protected monks from religious persecution but also safeguarded the Bulgarian language by preserving ancient manuscripts and books. Many of these are now displayed in the Church History Museum. The current buildings, including the main church, largely date from 1834–37, and were rebuilt after earlier structures were destroyed by fire.

Vihren Peak

Hit the trail in Pirin National Park

There are over a dozen different trails in **Pirin National Park**, from short 30-minute treks – such as the trail from **Vihren Hut** to **Okoto Lake**, which promises stunning views with minimal physical exertion – to longer and more strenuous multi-day treks. Most hikes begin at **Vihren Hut**, which you can reach in about 30 minutes by car or taxi, or via a local shuttle (€6, one hour) from town. From the trailhead parking lot, it's a 20-minute walk past the 1300-year-old **Baykusheva Mura**, Bulgaria's oldest coniferous tree. Alternatively, you can hike up from Bansko via the ski slopes in three to four hours – less if you take the gondola to its midway station.

For a more challenging hike, summit **Vihren Peak** (2914m), Bulgaria's second-highest mountain. The trail from the Vihren Hut takes five to six hours return and involves steep, mostly continuous climbing. However, there are plenty of scenic stops to rest and admire the views and glacial lakes along the way. It's also possible to reach the summit from **Banderitsa Hut** via a wooded trail that cuts through alpine meadows and granite-filled valleys, and passes the **Snezhnika Glacieret**, the southernmost glacial mass in Europe, en route. The final section involves some scrambling; a chain helps you up some of the steepest sections. From the summit, you can continue down to Vihren Hut for lunch before heading back to Bansko.

For more experienced mountaineers seeking an even greater thrill, **Koncheto Ridge**'s famous knife-edge traverse (about 400m long and half a meter at its narrowest) awaits. Connecting Kutelo Banski and Suhodol Peaks, it has nearly vertical drops on both sides. A metal safety cable aids passage, but only those comfortable with heights should attempt it.

Black Sea Coast

ANTIQUITY | VIBRANT CITIES | BEACHES

Blessed with golden sands, ancient ruins and a near-subtropical climate, the Black Sea coast is Bulgaria's greatest asset. Unfortunately, mass tourism in its most oppressive form is now the single dominating feature of the region. But this is not a reason to pass it by, but rather to adjust your plans. Paradoxically, its two coastal cities, Burgas and Varna, now provide a more rewarding beach experience for independent travellers. Varna in particular has the perfect combination of laid-back atmosphere, ancient monuments, interesting restaurants and a nice beach (although the one in Burgas is better). The rest of the coast is best savoured outside the July and August holiday mayhem. This is particularly true when it comes to the two main destinations, Nesebâr and Sozopol, both former Greek towns with illustrious histories.

Varna

Ancient stones, precious metals

Elegant and eclectic, ancient and modern, partially spruced-up and simultaneously run-down, Varna is charmingly authentic. Despite its seaside resort feel, with a long sandy beach and vast maritime gardens, it provides a welcome respite from the holidaying crowds that occupy the rest of the Bulgarian coast.

Varna was a major hub of civilisation in prehistoric times. Archaeologists have unearthed metal objects here, including what is reputed to be the world's oldest piece of golden jewellery. These finds are the pride of the excellent **Archaeological Museum** *(Археологически музей; museumvarna.com; entry adult/student €5/1.50)* and there is more here, too: dark-coloured Thracian pottery and Roman marble, as well as touching Hellenistic items like a Greek marble plaque listing the names of the city's school graduates in 221 CE.

Other remnants of antiquity are still a part of Varna's landscape. Deep inside the historic quarter, the well-preserved

Places

Varna p237
Nesebâr p238
Burgas p238
Sozopol p240

GETTING AROUND

Varna and Burgas both have international airports, with flights to Sofia and a number of European and Turkish destinations. Trains from Varna run to Veliko Târnovo and Sofia. From Burgas, Sofia trains pass through Plovdiv. Frequent buses connect all major destinations along the coast.

☑ TOP TIP

There are a lot of seafood restaurants on the coast and many of them serve creatures that don't live in the Black Sea, like squid and octopus. Take a look at the boxed text on p239 to learn more about which fish are local.

ruins of Varna's 2nd-century **Roman Thermae** (*Римски терми; museumvarna.com; entry adult/student €5/1.50*) are the largest in Bulgaria and the fourth largest of their kind in Europe (after two in Rome and one in Trier, Germany).

Nesebâr

Town of medieval crosses

On a small rocky outcrop 37km northeast of Burgas and connected to the mainland by a narrow, artificial isthmus, pretty-as-a-postcard **Nesebâr** is famous for its numerous, albeit mostly ruined, medieval churches. Bulgaria's main package-tourism hub, Sunny Beach (Slânchev Bryag), is just across the bay; hence every conceivable water sport is on hand.

Greeting visitors at the town's medieval gates, the fine **Archaeological Museum** (*Археологически музей; ancient-nesebar.com; entry adult/concession €4.60/2.30*) tells the story of Mesembria, as the place was known to the ancients. Greek and Roman pottery, statues, tombstones, Thracian gold jewellery and ancient anchors are all on display. Europe's Dark Ages were not that dark here, as suggested by the partly excavated remains of 6th-century **Byzantine baths** (*Ранновизантийски терми*), which was one of the region's biggest and best spas, renowned for its curative waters.

Burgas

Beach and gardens

A gateway to the Bulgaria seacoast for many visitors, Burgas is a beach destination in itself, with arguably better access to the sea and nature than some of the drab coastal resort towns nearby.

The pride of Burgas is its subtropical **Maritime Gardens**, which stretch along the Black Sea coast and are filled with manicured flower beds, fountains, busts of Bulgarian worthies, abstract sculptures and cafes. There are spectacular views over the sea from the terraces, and steps lead down to the 3km-long beach, which is surprisingly pretty given its urban location.

History lessons

The compact Old Town, with low-rise houses from the 19th and early 20th centuries, is enveloped in an extensive pedestrian area filled with street cafes and idle strollers. There are a couple of interesting museums to peek into. The small **Archaeological Museum** (*Археологически музей; burgasmuseums.bg;*

TOURS OF VARNA

Just arrived in Varna? Sign up for a free two-hour walking tour through the **Tourist Information Centre** (*visit.varna.bg*) from June to September. Tours leave at 10.30am and cover major sights, especially churches. Tours run almost daily in July and August, and less frequently in June and September. Contact the office for dates and to book a spot. Alternatively, try a half- or full-day cycling tour of Varna run by **Plateau Cycling** (*plateucycling.com*), which also offers trips around the Black Sea coast and eastern Bulgaria. Tours include hybrid bikes and gear, as well as pick-ups, drop-offs, luggage transfers and cold drinks.

 WHERE TO EAT & DRINK IN VARNA AND NESEBÂR

Stariya Chinar: Upmarket Balkan soul food at its best. Try the baked lamb, made to an old Bulgarian recipe, or the divine BBQ pork ribs. In Varna. *8am–midnight* €€	**Bacaro:** A stylish fusion restaurant in Varna that leans towards Asian cuisine and has a garden across the road. *5–11pm Tue-Sat* €€	**Arnautova Kâshta:** Find refuge from Nesebâr's tourist crowds in this sweet rustic courtyard. The menu is standard, but the cooking is soulful. *11am-10pm* €€	**Pri Maykla:** An idiosyncratic little bar in Nesebâr designed as a cave with fake stalagmites, turtles and waterfalls. Long list of cocktails. *noon-midnight*

Aquae Calidae

KNOW YOUR FISH

Pretty much every restaurant on the coast serves seafood, but many, if not most, offer fish and molluscs that don't even live in the Black Sea, due to its low salinity. Black Sea classics are smaller fish, especially bluefish *(chernokop)*, gobies *(popcheta)*, red mullet *(barbun)* and the needle-headed garfish *(zargan)*, famous for its phosphorescent bones. Larger fish include sea bream *(tsipura)*, sea brill *(kalkan)* and sea bass *(lavrak)*. Another famous Black Sea speciality is mussels, but which mussels wind up on your plate in the EU single-market zone is anyone's guess – unless you're eating at a mussel farm.

entry adult/concession €3/1.50) houses a diverting collection of local finds, including Neolithic flint tools, a wooden canoe from the 5th century BCE, Greek statuary and the remarkably well-preserved wooden coffin of a Thracian chieftain. It's all well laid out and signposted in English. The lively **Ethnographic Museum** *(Етнографически музей; burgasmuseums.bg; entry adult/concession €3/1.50)* displays a rich collection of folk costumes, jewellery and furniture. You may notice that the people dressed in traditional garments in large photos at the entrance are museum staffers who sell tickets and provide guide services.

Bathe like a sultan

How about combining a plunge into ancient history with some 'me time' in a modern spa? Hot springs in what is now **Vetren**, off the Sofia motorway 14km from Burgas, have been known since Thracian times and associated with a cult of river nymphs. The baths were famous across the ancient world under the name of Thermopolis. In Ottoman times, Suleiman the Magnificent converted it into an opulently decorated hammam. Today, the ruins of Thermopolis are enveloped by the modern spa complex **Aquae Calidae** *(aquae-calidae.com; entry adult/child €13/7.70)*. Visitors get to see the **ruins of the anicient spa** *(adult/student €8/7)* and an informative animation video inside the restored hammam. Afterwards,

WHERE TO EAT & DRINK IN BURGAS AND SOZOPOL

8 Mammas: You'll feel mothered by the kind women making and serving home-style Bulgarian-Turkish specialities at this tiny patio in Burgas. *11.30am-11pm €*

Ethno: An old-time Burgas favourite in a new location. The menu departs from the tourist-trap routine towards more unusual Bulgarian flavours. *11am-11pm €€*

Palikari (Doctor's House): This upmarket place in Sozopol has a perfect cliffside setting in Sozopol with postcard sea views. *11am-midnight €€*

Metalhead Brewery: Combine your spa visit to Aquae Calidae with some popular local craft produce in the immediate vicinity. *2-10pm Wed-Sun*

THERE I WAS ON A JULY MORNING

It might hark back to the solar cults of the ancient Thracians, but this tradition was nonetheless born in the communist period and it's even framed today as a subtle protest against the regime. Crowds of hippies would meet in the area of Yaylata, north of Varna, to greet the sunrise on the morning of 1 July. Why this particular date? Because of Uriah Heep – the ritual was based on listening to the British band's most famous hit, 'July Morning', while watching the sun rise from the sea. The tradition persists today, with big municipalities – like Burgas – placing it on the city calendar. In 2007, Uriah Heep's John Lawton finally made it to Bulgaria and performed the song live.

RNDMS/SHUTTERSTOCK

Church of Sveta Bogoroditsa

enjoy the modern spa and end the day with a glass of ale at the nearby Metalhead Brewery.

Sozopol

History unwrapped

Sitting atop an island-like peninsula, Sozopol was designed to provide plenty of shade and allow its residents to marvel at the surrounding beauty, sweeping views of the sea and a fishing harbour. To get an idea of what it was like to live in one of the revival period houses here, drop into the local **Ethnographic Museum** *(Етнографски музей; sozopol-museums.bg; entry adult/concession €1.5/0.50)* located in the former dwelling of a wealthy Greek merchant, who resided here until the early 20th century. Even when it's scorching hot outside, the wooden structure continues to breathe, taking in the cooling sea breeze and keeping the heat out.

Another unmissable heritage building is the 15th-century **Church of Sveta Bogoroditsa** *(Църква 'Света Богородица'),* its quaintness being the product of the Ottoman policy that limited the height of Christian temples – architects bypassed the rule by building churches below street level. Set in a courtyard with a giant fig tree, it's one of the most picturesque places in town, with an exquisite wooden iconostasis and a pulpit carved with bunches of grapes.

Having emerged as the ancient Greek polity of Apollonia, Sozopol has a long and illustrious history. Though the building itself is drab, the **Archaeological Museum** *(Археологически музей; sozopol-museums.bg; entry adult/concession €3.50/1.50)* has a small but fascinating collection of local finds from its Apollonian glory days. In addition to a wealth of Hellenic treasures, the museum occasionally exhibits the skeleton of a local 'vampire', found with a stake driven through its chest. Enter from the building's north side.

Central Bulgaria

ROMAN RUINS | BULGARIAN HERITAGE | URBAN DELIGHTS

Central Bulgaria is where you can trace the footprints of civilisations past and savour the best of Bulgaria's own civilisation, with its unique blend of ancient Slavic and Orthodox heritage, enriched with Byzantine, Ottoman, West European and Russian influences. One of Europe's oldest settlements, Plovdiv also happens to be one of contemporary Bulgaria's liveliest cities where Roman ruins and Ottoman-era quarters mix with a vibrant modern cafe and restaurant scene. Further north, Veliko Târnovo is the cradle of Bulgarian statehood and identity. It elicits the perfect blend of quintessentially Balkan elements when it comes to architecture, ambience, food and lifestyle. Venture into the heartland to walk the winding lanes of hilly Old Towns, savour the best of the country's cuisine at *mehana* taverns, and immerse yourself in a culture and history that's extremely idiosyncratic but also essential to understanding Europe as a whole.

Places

Plovdiv p241
Stara Zagora p242
Veliko Târnovo p244

☑ TOP TIP

The Free Plovdiv Tour (freeplovdivtour.com) begins at 11am outside the City Hall. Running 365 days a year and led by friendly local guides, it's a great way to get a quick overview of the city. Tips are expected: pay what you can.

Plovdiv

More ancient than most

A seductive fusion of Roman, Hellenistic and Thracian foundations with a pinch of Ottoman spice, Plovdiv is Bulgaria's cultural heart and its second-largest metropolis. First settled over 8000 years ago, it ranks among Europe's oldest cities and its rich historical legacy lies just beneath the central pedestrianised

---

 GETTING AROUND

Plovdiv is on the main railway line between Sofia and Burgas. There are also train services to Stara Zagora, from where you can embark on a spectacular rail journey to Veliko Târnovo. The latter is located 7km from Gorna Oryahovitsa on the Sofia–Varna line. Buses

run between Sofia and all the cities mentioned here. Plovdiv is best explored on foot. If you need to go further, hop on a city bus, an easy and affordable way to get around. A single ride costs just €0.50, payable in cash on board. Veliko Târnovo is also walkable.

A FORGOTTEN ARENA

It boggles the mind to think that until the 1970s, people had absolutely no idea that a vast Roman stadium lay beneath Plovdiv's main commercial street. Such collective amnesia is less a mark against the people who have come and gone in the centuries since, though, and more a testament to the metropolis' continuing evolution over 6000 years, such that even the imperial triumphs of a monumental 250m-long gladiatorial arena fell into irrelevance as ever greater chapters of its historical story unfolded. As each new construction project presents a potential new twist to its legacy, Plovdiv is a city that reminds us that history is a living thing, forever in dialogue with the present.

spaces. One of the most fascinating landmarks is the ancient **Stadium of Philippopolis** *(ancient-stadium-plovdiv.eu; entry adult/child €3.50/1.50)*. It was only discovered around 50 years ago, when reconstruction work revealed its curved rows, marble seating and subterranean passages. Built in the 2nd century CE under Emperor Hadrian when Plovdiv was known by its Roman name, Philippopolis, the historic stadium staged everything from chariot races to gladiatorial duels.

Regional archaeological museum

If the stadium whetted your appetite for mortal combat, continue your journey into the past at the **Archaeological Museum** *(archaeologicalmuseumplovdiv.org; entry adult/child €4/1)*. One of Bulgaria's oldest cultural institutions, it opened in 1882 and houses a collection of gladiatorial artefacts that illuminate the lives of those who once battled for fame, such as funerary stelae of fallen gladiators. Beyond the arena, the museum documents the city's 8000-year-long heritage – from Neolithic settlements and Thracian rituals to Hellenistic artistry and Roman grandeur – via a rich 100,000-strong collection of artefacts.

Ottoman aromas

Though Bulgaria eventually won its freedom from nearly 500 years of Ottoman rule in the late 19th century, traces of that era still infuse Plovdiv. Not just in its architecture, culture and cuisine, but also in the lingering aroma of Turkish coffee from the cafe beside the **Dzhumaya Mosque** in the city centre. Begin your morning with a cup here, best enjoyed from the upholstered, street-facing seats that offer both shade and prime people-watching. Coffee is served with rose water, a fragrant flourish born from the country's long-standing love affair with the flower, which was first cultivated during Ottoman times. Afterwards, step inside the adjoining 14th-century mosque. Shoes come off at the door, a small but humbling act of respect. If you're here on a Friday, prayers led by the local Muslim community – today less than 5% of the population, down from 80% in the 15th century – offer a glimpse into living faith.

Stara Zagora

Return to the dawn of history

Stara Zagora is an appealing mid-sized city that also happens to be one of Europe's oldest continually inhabited settlements – and it has the archaeological pedigree to prove it. One of

 WHERE TO EAT IN PLOVDIV: OUR PICKS

Rahat Tepe: Traditional cuisine paired with stunning panoramic views. Known for its sizzling hot-plate dishes, generous portions and fresh salads. *10am-late* €€	**Oleander Garden Restaurant:** Charming restaurant serving fresh, locally inspired dishes in a relaxed setting. *noon-4.30pm & 6.30-10pm Tue-Sat, noon-5pm Sun* €€	**Restaurant Philippopolis:** A must for meat lovers, featuring a spacious hidden garden and interiors adorned with Bulgarian artwork. *11am-late* €€€	**Hebros Restaurant:** Elegant fine-dining in a historic house and hotel. Freshly prepared, homemade-style regional dishes are on the menu. *noon-10.30pm* €€€

Roman Theatre, Stara Zagora

the most stunning finds in Europe, the **Neolithic Dwellings** *(Neolitni Zhilishta; rimstz.eu; entry adult/child €3.50/2)* were discovered in 1969 on the fringes of the city hospital. Now covered by a protective shell, the museum displays a family farmstead destroyed by fire some time around 5800 BCE. At first it may look like a pile of rubble, but it gradually becomes a source of wonder once your eyes become accustomed to what's there: walls, pots and hearths are all discernible, while a millstone and storage vessels reveal its importance as a grain store. A basement room houses a compelling collection of Neolithic pots and cult figures, and an intimate museum takes you right back to the source of European civilisation. Back in the city centre, the remarkably well-kept open-air remains of a **Roman Theatre** *(entry free)* recall the town's 2nd-century CE heyday during the reign of Emperor Marcus Aurelius. Learn more about this heritage at the nearby **History Museum** *(rimstz.eu; entry adult/child €2/1)*, which preserves a stretch of Roman street lined with statues of citizens, togas neatly draped over shoulders.

Enjoy a cross-mountain rail journey

Few Bulgarian journeys are as dramatic as the train ride from **Stara Zagora to Veliko Târnovo**, which wends its way over the Stara Planina mountains before arriving at the medieval capital. The route passes through the corn and sunflowers of the Valley of the Roses before climbing into the highlands, the thickly forested hills passing by in a kaleidoscopic flash of green. Nearing the summit, the line corkscrews its way through curving tunnels to gain height. The train then descends towards Tryavna and passes through the limestone gorge of the Dryanovo River before gliding into Veliko Târnovo station. Around five trains make the trip at roughly two-hour intervals throughout the day; fare prices start at around €4.50 and the journey takes about three hours.

HISTORY OF TSAREVETS FORTRESS

Tsarevets Fortress (p244), atop strategic Tsarevets Hill, has been settled since time immemorial. Thracians and Romans used the hill as a defensive position, but the Byzantines built the first significant citadel here between the 5th and 7th centuries. The fortress was rebuilt and fortified by the Slavs and Bulgars between the 8th and 10th centuries, and again by the Byzantines in the early 12th century. When Târnovgrad became the Second Bulgarian Kingdom's capital, the fortress was truly magnificent, but it was sacked and destroyed during the Ottoman invasion in 1393. Tourists can thank the communists for returning it to a semblance of its former glory, although some archaeologists grumble about the faithfulness of the restoration.

VALENTIN VALKOV/SHUTTERSTOCK

Tsarevets Fortress

Veliko Târnovo

Cradle of the nation

When people mention the heartland of Bulgarian history and culture, it's Veliko Târnovo and the Central Mountains that they're talking about. This region is where the roving Bulgar khans first settled down and formed a state, the country's medieval tsars built their capitals, and the mountain-cradled monasteries and prosperous highland villages nurtured the country's 19th-century revival. If you want to come to grips with how Bulgaria became Bulgaria, this is the place you should start.

Set aside a few hours to scramble around **Tsarevets Fortress** *(museumvt.com; entry adult/child €7.50/3),* the sprawling hilltop citadel that once served as the seat of Bulgaria's tsars during the glory days of the Second Kingdom. The fortress's walls and towers have been partially reconstructed to provide an idea of what it once looked like. Although the historical accuracy of what you see is debatable, it's a hugely evocative site. Rising up from the summit of **Tsarevets Hill** is the reconstructed former patriarchate, centred on the **Cathedral of the Holy Ascension**. Heartstopping views of the city and its surroundings from the church steps are more impressive than the church itself, which contains kitschy modern murals of Bulgarian medieval leaders.

 WHERE TO EAT IN VELIKO TÂRNOVO: OUR PICKS

Bey House: Upscale hotel restaurant offers a gourmet take on Bulgarian cuisine, with great wines and delicious sweets in a walled garden. *9am-11pm* €€€

Han Hadzhi Nikoli: Courtyard dining in a beautifully restored inn, with an exciting blend of Bulgarian-European cuisine. *10am-11pm* €€

Hotel-Mehana Gurko: Traditional-style tavern with great views and tasty Bulgarian specialities, washed down with local wine. *noon-9pm* €€

Bakery for Kadaif: Syrupy *kadaif,* a traditional Bulgarian sweet with Turkish roots, as well as baklava made on the premises. *10am-6pm* €

 # Places We Love to Stay

€ Budget €€ Midrange €€€ Top End

Central Sofia   MAP p231

Hostel Mostel € A popular hostel in a renovated 19th-century house. The dorms come in all sizes; there are a couple of singles and doubles, too.

Art Hotel 158 €€ An artsy boutique hotel with a homey feel in the heart of the city. Spacious rooms and laudable breakfasts.

Pop Bogomil €€ This small hotel has 15 small but comfortable rooms, individually decorated and priced. In the Lion's Bridge area, to the north of the city.

Agora Boutique Hotel €€ In the middle of action just off Vitosha Boulevard, this mansion has comfortable rooms.

Hotel Niky €€ Funky common areas, comfortable rooms and gleaming bathrooms. The smart suites come with kitchenettes.

Hotel Les Fleurs €€€ Features gigantic blooms on the facade, a surreal interior design and a floral motif in the more stylish rooms.

Oborishte 63 Boutique Hotel €€€ In the nicest part of central Sofia, this luxurious salmon-pink 1930s home has a view over the Aleksander Nevski Cathedral.

Rila

Gorski Kut €€ Riverside hotel with mountain views, seven minutes from Rila Monastery, midway to Bansko and Seven Lakes.

RILA 6ATO Hotel & Restaurant €€ The chairlift to the Seven Lakes is 5km away. Good value with detached wooden cabins.

Bansko

Hotel Orphey € Big rooms at this family-friendly hotel opposite City Park. Free parking and shuttle to the gondola.

Velinov Boutique Hotel €€ Super cosy with mountain views and typical Bulgarian touches right next to St Trinity Church.

Amira Boutique Hotel €€€ Premium mountain hotel 400m from the lifts with an excellent restaurant, terrace views and free shuttle.

Varna

Yo Ho Hostel € This pirate-themed place has four- and 11-bed dorm rooms and private options.

Hotel Hi €€ Well-appointed rooms designed in a classical style. Location is spot on.

Graffit Gallery Hotel €€ With its own gallery and themed rooms, this is one of Varna's more colourful options.

Black Sea Coast

Boutique Hotel St Stefan €€ Art-filled rooms with views over the harbour and the Black Sea from old Nesebâr.

Guest House Tony €€ A popular oldie in an excellent location overlooking the sea in Nesebâr; it fills up quickly. No-frills but homey, with a great host.

Hotel St Nikola €€ Bland but comfortable rooms in a traditional-looking house in a superb location in Nesebâr.

Burgas & Beyond

Boutique Guest House Ruvan €€ A neat family hotel in heart of Old Town. Spacious rooms come with balconies.

Hotel Chiplakoff €€ This attractively restored art nouveau mansion features original spiral staircases.

Hotel Briz €€ Spacious rooms with sea views in a quiet location at the far end of Sarafovo. The perfect place to land before flying in or out of Burgas.

Plovdiv

Hostel Ginger House € Walking distance to attractions. Velin, the super friendly owner, makes this a highly recommended stay.

Boutique Guest House Yes For You €€ Stylish accommodation with character and a welcoming vibe. Close to sights, cafes, bars and restaurants.

Villa Flavia Boutique Hotel €€€ Steps from the Roman Theatre. Chic rooms, superb breakfast and a recently discovered ancient bath beneath the hotel.

Veliko Târnovo

Hotel-Mehana Gurko €€ On the city's oldest street, with blooms spilling over the balconies and great views. Book in advance.

Hotel Kiev €€ Much better inside than it appears at first glance. Excellent value, great central location and spotlessly clean.

Bey House Royal Hotel €€€ Fancy property in the residence of the area's last Ottoman governor.

Bridges Residence €€€ Spacious boutique hotel suites in the city's historic core; contemporary conveniences and grand views.

Practicalities

Weather
Summer heat in Bulgaria can be oppressive, and the number of days with temperatures over 33°C has been consistently rising year on year. In winter, expect cold, icy conditions, especially in the mountains.

LGBTIQ+ Travellers
Same-sex partnerships are permitted in Bulgaria, though these unions do not enjoy the full legal protections granted to hetero partnerships. Sofia and Varna are home to large LGBTIQ+ communities, though gay culture tends to stay on the down low. GLAS (glasfoundation.bg/en) is a leading NGO that protects and promotes the rights of lesbian, gay, bisexual and transgender people.

Accessible Travel
Bulgaria is a signatory to the UN Convention on Rights of Persons with Disabilities, which mandates that all new construction meet minimum standards of accessibility. The country is far behind, however, in retrofitting existing facilities. Sofia Airport is fully modernised and meets accessibility requirements.

Smoking
Smoking is banned in all indoor public spaces, including restaurants, bars, hotels, cinemas and offices, but the rule is sometimes loosely enforced. In reality, most restaurant tables are located outdoors where smoking is permitted, so brace for tobacco-scented meals on occasion.

NATALIA SILYANOV/SHUTTERSTOCK

Vitosha Boulevard (p232), Sofia

Opening Hours
Banks 9am–5pm Monday to Friday
Museums 10am–5pm
Post Offices 8am–7pm Monday to Friday
Restaurants 9am–11pm
Shops 10am–7pm Monday to Friday, 11am–5pm Sat and Su

Language
Bulgarian is a southern Slavic language. The Cyrillic alphabet was first developed here in the 9th century and later adopted by other Slavic languages.
Hello *Здравейте* zdra·vey·te
Goodbye *Довиждане* do·veezh·da·ne
Do you speak English? *Говорите ли английски?* go·vo·ree·te lee ang·lees·kee
Thank you *Благодаря* bla·go·dar·ya
Yes *Да* da
No *He* ne

Public Holidays
New Year's Day 1 January
Liberation Day 3 March
Orthodox Easter April/May
May Day 1 May
St George's Day/Bulgarian Army Day 6 May
Cyrillic Alphabet/Culture and Literacy Day 24 May
Unification Day 6 September
Bulgarian Independence Day 22 September
Christmas 25 & 26 December

FROM LEFT: SIMON RICHMOND/LONELY PLANET, JOHNER IMAGES/GETTY IMAGES

Station, Varna (p237)

Arriving & Getting Around

Bulgaria has three main international airports: Sofia, Varna and Burgas. Plovdiv airport gets some EU flights. All airports are modern and have regular flights between one another.

Bus
The most reliable transport between cities is by bus. Local buses reach most villages, though these services are infrequent, or seasonal in ski or beach destinations. Comfort levels vary wildly.

Train
Slower than buses, trains are a scenic way to cover ground in Bulgaria. Sometimes they serve some out-of-the-way places. Comfort inside the carriages is truly substandard, so pay extra for first class.

Car
The most convenient way to get around, especially if heading to small Bulgarian villages. Car hire can be arranged in the main airports. Book with local providers, such as *toprentacar.bg*.

Road Conditions
Road conditions are patchy, but generally satisfactory. There are several motorways, some of which are only partly finished. The longest connects Sofia to Burgas and serves as the main transport axis between western Bulgaria and the Black Sea coast. The north–south axis is not particularly fast, with serpentine roads crossing mountain ranges.

MONEY
Currency: Euro (€)

CARDS
You cannot rely exclusively on credit or debit cards in Bulgaria. Cards are commonly accepted in hotels, restaurants and shops in big cities, towns and tourist resorts; less so in more rural areas.

ATMS
ATMs that accept major credit cards (Visa and MasterCard) are common in all sizable towns and cities. Choose ATMs affiliated with major banks instead of private ATMs, where the conversion rates may be much higher.

CHANGING MONEY
Foreign-exchange offices can be found in all large towns, and rates are displayed prominently. They are no longer allowed to charge commission, but that doesn't stop them trying. Always check the final amount before handing over your cash.

For places to stay
in Croatia, see
p271

TRAVELLINGIN/SHUTTERSTOCK

Above: City walls (p266), Dubrovnik; Right: Krk (p261)

Curated by
Anja Mutić

Croatia

LIVING UP TO THE HYPE

A must-visit destination ever since *Game of Thrones* showcased the country's magnificent architecture and coastline, Croatia is still having its moment in the sun.

Despite the bucket-list fame of recent years, Croatia's pleasures are still more timeless than trendy. Crystalline water laps gently at a 1778km-long coast and some 1185 islands. Away from the coast, eight national parks protect pristine forests, karstic mountains, rivers, lakes and waterfalls in a landscape of primeval beauty. The culture is as varied as the scenery, with a parade of Roman, Venetian, Austro-Hungarian and Italian occupiers leaving Croatia with a unique identity. Marvel at ancient treasures and medieval towns preserved over thousands of years.

Tourism to the country is nothing new. The Habsburg Empire set up shop on the coast more than 140 years ago and opened swank health resorts, many of which are still open. Later came President Josip Broz Tito's push for international guests in the 1970s, which poured funding into impressively modern hotel architecture along the coast and created Croatia's burgeoning tourism industry. This all came to a halt during the Homeland War from 1991 to 1995, when the nation was engaged in battles with its fellow ex-Yugoslavia neighbours. While the country bounced back, it took a couple of decades for travellers to return in significant numbers. But today, they're certainly back. With an exciting gastronomy scene, an array of islands and beaches, fascinating history and culture, and spectacular nature, Croatia is a trove of delights.

ILIJA ASCIC/SHUTTERSTOCK

THE MAIN AREAS

ZAGREB
Croatia's cosy, pocket-sized capital. **p254**

ISTRIA & KVARNER
Forward-thinking port city, delightful islands and foodie delights. **p258**

SPLIT & DALMATIAN ISLANDS
Iconic Roman-palace quarter and gorgeous beaches. **p262**

DUBROVNIK
Medieval walls, scenic streetscapes and beaches. **p266**

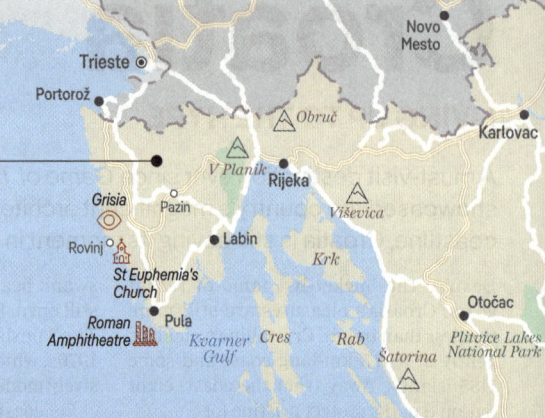

Find Your Way

Smooth, winding seaside roads with incredible views link the mainland villages, towns and cities of this long, thin and predominantly coastal country, but the rural inland areas are just as scenic and peaceful to explore.

Istria & Kvarner, p258

A h;eart-shaped peninsula on the northern Adriatic with seaside gems, foodie enclaves and the most underrated stretch of Croatia's coast, with a forward-thinking port city.

BUS

Croatia has a vast bus network, operated by local companies such as Arriva and international fleets like FlixBus, which often travel the length of the country and are the quickest intercity option.

CAR

Driving a car is the easiest way to explore Croatia, particularly if you plan to visit some rural, off-the-beaten-path gems. The best rental prices are found in Zagreb, Split and Rijeka.

FERRY

Ferry links in Croatia are cheap and efficient, so reaching the islands is entirely doable DIY, no matter your transport situation. National ferry company Jadrolinija connects the mainland to all inhabited islands throughout the year.

0   100 km
0   50 miles

HUNGARY

Čakovec

Varaždin

Koprivnica

Zagreb, p254

A laid-back little capital city, big on coffee culture and vivacious street life, with a clutch of offbeat museums, green spaces and a mountain on its doorstep.

Subotica

SERBIA

Museum of Broken Relationships

Bjelovar

Virovitica

Našice

Osijek

ZAGREB

Kupa

Kutina

Vukovar

Bačka Palanka

Petrinja

Sisak

Slavonska Požega

Sava

Nova Gradiška

Đakovo

Vinkovci

Slavonski Brod

Brčko

Bihać

Una

BOSNIA & HERCEGOVINA

Banja Luka

Bosansko Petrovac

Split & Dalmatian Islands, p262

The heart of Dalmatia, this buzzing city showcases the monumental Diocletian's Palace, while the islands sport gorgeous beaches and sweet coastal towns.

Gračac

Knin

Krka National Park

SARAJEVO

Šibenik

Sinj

Diocletian's Palace

Dubrovnik, p266

With the mesmerising beauty of its walled old town featuring marbled lanes and architectural showpieces, this Adriatic city is a stunner lined with dazzling beaches.

Split

Riva

Mostar

Brač

Zlatni Rat

Bol

Hvar

Vis

Metković

Korčula

Neum

Mljet

Nikšić

City Walls

MONTENEGRO

Dubrovnik

Herceg Novi

Plan Your Time

Timing is crucial in Croatia, a country with 48 inhabited islands and seasonal ferry and flight schedules. Outside of summer, many places along the coast shut down and transport options are limited, so plan in advance.

PILLIP/SHUTTERSTOCK

Trg Bana Jelačića (p257), Zagreb

A Quick City Break

● Top of everyone's city-break list is enchanting **Dubrovnik** (p266), which deserves all the accolades. The walled old town's wide, marble-paved streets lined with monumental baroque churches and Gothic palaces dazzle visitors, while glorious beaches make for the perfect place to rest after a few days of sightseeing.

● Off-the-radar Kvarner is a gorgeous coastal region and an up-and-coming playground for foodies. Explore the dynamic port city of **Rijeka** (p260), with its edgy arts and culture scene.

● And there's **Zagreb** (p254), Croatia's stellar capital which is fun to visit year-round, even in winter (Advent is particularly great with its happening Christmas markets). The city is packed with lively cafes, museums and galleries, and music venues to dive into.

SEASONAL HIGHLIGHTS

Croatia gets busy in the summer. If possible, visit during spring or autumn for the same scenery but fewer travellers. The country has lots of traditional events.

FEBRUARY

The bombastic **Rijeka Carnival** (p261) is usually in early to mid-February, or head to Dubrovnik for the mighty Feast of St Blaise.

MARCH/APRIL

Good Friday processions are particularly elaborate in Dubrovnik, where the walls are lit with flame.

MAY

The last Sunday in May is Wine Day, when winemakers open their cellars and offer tastings of their vintages.

A Week to Spare

● The winning first-timers' trip to Croatia begins with a couple of nights in buzzy **Split** (p262), where you can take in the ancient Roman city centre inside **Diocletian's Palace** (p262) followed by local beach bars and cool restaurants.

● Next, hop on a ferry to one or two of the Dalmatian islands. After a couple of nights in **Hvar** (p265; for nightlife) or **Brač** (p264; for beaches), ferry onwards to spend a final few days in **Dubrovnik** (p266), the mesmerising showpiece of Croatia's coast, with its awesome architecture within the storied old town, gorgeous beaches and all-around elegance making up for the crowds.

Slow-Travel Sojourn

● If you're location-independent or travelling long term, renting a place for a month as a base from which to explore can save you a lot of euros and ease the pace of travel. **Split** (p262) is the most popular place for digital nomads on the coast of Croatia, but **Dubrovnik** (p266) also has expat scenes worth discovering.

● If you're looking for an extended break to switch off and relax, a month on an island such as **Hvar** (p265) or at a mainland spot such as rural **Istria** (p258) rewards with quaint, less-frequented villages steeped in local culture, food and tradition, as well as incredible wineries.

JULY

Film lovers flock to Pula in July for the **Pula Film Festival** (p258) and its nighttime screenings under the stars.

AUGUST

Okolo/Around (p257) brings public art installations and urban interventions to Zagreb's streets – many in the Upper Town – for about 10 days each August.

SEPTEMBER

September is when truffle hunters in Istria go into the forest in search of the elusive Magnatum Pico.

DECEMBER

Advent festivities in Zagreb have been drawing increasing numbers of visitors, who come to explore the fun and colourful Christmas markets.

Zagreb

ANCIENT TOWN | QUIRKY MUSEUMS | VIBRANT STREET LIFE

GETTING AROUND

Zagreb is a small and compact city made for strolling. Taking one of the iconic blue trams is part of the fun and a good way to reach the highlights beyond the city centre. Buy your ticket from the driver, at a kiosk or through an app, and make sure to validate it at a yellow machine on board.

☑ TOP TIP

Noon comes with a bang in Zagreb, and locals set their watches by it, so brace yourself for a loud blast. You'll likely get startled, but fear not; it's not an explosion, but the sound of the Grič cannon from the **Lotrščak Tower**; it's been marking midday for the last 100 years.

No more a mere stopover en route to the coast, Croatia's capital is firmly on the map of small European capitals on the rise. The wintertime Advent festivities have done much to extend the season, bringing droves of visitors to Zagreb for its Christmas markets. Beyond the big events that dot the calendar, Zagreb has an understated charm: it's the type of city that grows on you in a slow-burn kind of way. Among its chief appeals? It's a laid-back micro-metropolis made for strolling. Wander through the Upper Town's red-roof and cobblestone splendour, peppered with church spires. See the domes and ornate upper-floor frippery of the Lower Town's mash-up of Secessionist, neo-baroque and art deco buildings. Check out its collection of quirky museums and dive into its small but burgeoning art scene, its vibrant street life and its many nature parks and forests.

Upper Town

As the oldest part of Zagreb, the Upper Town (Gornji Grad) is a storybook maze of cobblestone streets and squares that make for some wonderful roaming. Spread across two small hills – Gradec and Kaptol – connected by a string of steps and passageways, this is where the city originally began in medieval times. When the two settlements merged in 1850, Zagreb was born. Today, its streets are speckled with baroque palaces, neoclassical mansions, medieval towers and neo-Gothic churches. This cobblestone feast of historic architecture has dashes of vibrant life – from perennially full cafe-bars that line the buzzy Tkalčićeva to quirky museums.

Browse Dolac Market

Indulge your senses at this central farmers market dotted with iconic red parasols and countless stalls overflowing with fresh fruit and veg. With its pops of colour, the 'belly of Zagreb' offers a field day for photo ops. **Dolac Market** has been

HIGHLIGHTS

1 Museum of Broken Relationships

SIGHTS

2 Cathedral of the Assumption of the Blessed Virgin Mary

3 Galerija Klovićevi Dvori
4 Lotrščak Tower
5 Museum of Illusions
6 Trg Bana Jelačića
7 Zrinjevac

SLEEPING

8 Esplanade Zagreb Hotel
9 Hotel Jägerhorn

10 Stay Swanky
11 Stellar Boutique Modules

EATING

12 BioMania Bistro
13 Broom44
14 Gostionica Ficlek
15 Heritage

16 Otto & Frank
see 14 Pod Zidom
17 Salo
18 Vinodol

SHOPPING

19 Dolac Market

trader-central since the 1930s, when the city authorities set up a market space on the 'border' between the Upper and Lower Towns. Today, vendors from all over Croatia descend daily to hawk their garden-fresh produce and assorted edible goods.

Cathedral glory and city icon

The twin spires of Zagreb's **Cathedral of the Assumption of the Blessed Virgin Mary**, Croatia's largest sacral building, have soared over the city for eight centuries. The original structure has been transformed and rebuilt many times due to fires and earthquakes, but its signature neo-Gothic look came about at the turn of the 20th century. The cathedral has unfortunately been closed and under lace-like scaffolding since the 2020 earthquake.

ZAGREB ADVENT

In the last 10 years, Zagreb's Christmas market has grown from a small happening to the peak of the city's calendar, drawing in crowds from across the country and the world. Hotels and restaurants book up quickly, so it's best to plan a visit way ahead. Advent put wintertime Zagreb on the map; before that, it was a sleepy city where families celebrated Christmas by getting together at home. Now, everyone heads out to the decked-out streets, squares and parks, which come alive with buzzy food stalls, craft pop-ups, live music, mulled wine, dance parties and art happenings. Held at various locations around the city centre and beyond, Advent typically runs from late November into January.

IVAN KLINDIC/SHUTTERSTOCK

Bandstand, Zrinjevac

The pastel-coloured charm of Tkalča

Strolling up and down **Tkalča**, a charming pedestrian street that winds uphill from Trg Bana Jelačića, is a favourite pastime for locals. Centuries ago, a stream lined with watermills ran in its place, separating the medieval settlements of Kaptol and Gradec. Today, Tkalča, as Tkalčićeva is called by locals, is lined with pastel-coloured townhouses and cafe terraces bustling with life day and night. Pick your pavement table for great people-watching and city-vibe-soaking, drink in hand.

See the Museum of Broken Relationships

From romances that withered to broken family connections, the wonderfully weird **Museum of Broken Relationships** *(brokenships.com; entry adult/child €7/5.50)* explores the mementos left behind after a relationship ends. On display in the string of all-white rooms are donations from around the globe that range from the hilarious to the heartbreaking; each comes with a story attached. Check out the adjacent shop – the 'bad memories eraser' is a bestseller.

EATING IN THE UPPER TOWN: BEST BRUNCH SPOTS

Salo: This bright bistro-bakery on Opatovina doles out artisan breads, small creative plates and speciality coffee. *8am-4pm Wed-Sat, 9am-2pm Sun* €

Broom44: Right on Dolac, with tables spilling into the market, Broom44 serves world-cuisine-inspired dishes, mostly plant-based. *6.30am-3pm Mon-Sat, 8am-2pm Sun* €€

Otto & Frank: Hearty breakfasts of eggs, French toast and the like till noon; yummy burgers and bar vibes after. *8am-11pm Mon-Sat, 9am-5pm Sun* €

BioMania Bistro: Plant-based, seasonal dishes that span the usual international favourites (think burgers and pasta). Great desserts, too. *11am-11pm Tue-Sun* €€

Lower Town

The Lower Town (Donji Grad) pretty much consists of the entire city centre of Zagreb below the Upper Town – basically anything below the historic hills stretching towards the north. It has a distinct old-world flair and central European flavour, plus some of the city's most offbeat museums and contemporary art galleries, as well as fine examples of grand Habsburg-era architecture. With its leafy U-shaped series of seven parks and squares known as Lenuci's Horseshoe, it's perfect for strolling and exploring Zagreb's vibrant cafe culture. The Lower Town is also the site of many festivals and street happenings that span almost the entire year.

The buzz of Trg Bana Jelačića

Zagreb's geographic heart and the separation line between the Upper and Lower Towns is **Trg Bana Jelačića**. If you enjoy people-watching, sit in one of the cafes and watch the tramloads of people getting out, greeting each other and dispersing among the newspaper kiosks and flower stalls lining the strip towards Dolac Market. The equestrian statue of Jelačić and the nearby clock tower are the main rendezvous points.

Zrinjevac's tree-lined beauty

Officially called Trg Nikole Šubića Zrinskog, but known as **Zrinjevac**, this verdant square is a major hangout during sunny weekends and hosts pop-up stalls during spring, summer and Advent. It acts as a venue for many festivals and events, often centred on the ornate music pavilion that dates from 1891.

Amazing Museum of Illusions

Visitors of all ages are treated to heaps of fun at the **Museum of Illusions** *(muzejiluzija.com; entry adult/child €12/9)*, a fantastic little sensory adventure that started in Zagreb in 2015 and has since spread to franchises across the world, including New York, Dubai and Athens. The Tilted Room and the Mirror of Truth are among 70-plus intriguing exhibits, hologram pictures, puzzles and educational games that offer a fun mental workout.

UPPER TOWN'S BEST SUMMER FESTS

Grič Evenings: A series of concerts held every July in the atrium of the **Galerija Klovićevi Dvori**, with everything from chamber music to world tunes. *(facebook.com/VeceriNaGricu)*

Okolo/Around: This annual event brings public art installations and urban interventions to Zagreb's streets for 10 days in August. *(@okoloaround)*

Zagreb International Folklore Festival: A celebration of traditional culture every July, this festival takes place around the city centre and the Upper Town. *(msf.hr/en)*

Le Grič: For four Saturdays in August, sip wine and champagne and mingle at this seasonal event on the walkway behind the Zagreb City Museum. *(facebook.com/legric)*

 EATING IN THE LOWER TOWN: BEST CROATIAN CUISINE

Vinodol: Upscale Central European fare with a modern twist. Go for succulent lamb or veal and potatoes under a *peka* (domed baking lid). *noon-midnight* €€	**Heritage:** Petit snack bar and delicatessen churning out traditional Croatian finger food. Tricky to get a table. *noon-8pm* €	**Gostionica Ficlek:** Real-deal Zagreb mainstays served in a cosy bistro space, grandma-style. Right by Dolac Market, so as fresh as it gets. *11am-11pm* €	**Pod Zidom:** Upmarket bistro next to Dolac Market, with a focus on modern cuisine with market-fresh ingredients. *noon-11pm Tue-Sun* €€

Istria & Kvarner

SEASIDE TOWNS | ANCIENT HISTORY | GASTRONOMIC DELIGHTS

Places

GETTING AROUND

The main cities, towns and islands of Kvarner and Istria are well served by public transport. Arriva *(arriva.com.hr)* is the main bus carrier. The freedom of your own wheels makes exploration easiest. The highways and artillery roads here are well maintained, smooth, scenic and easy to drive.

☑ TOP TIP

Wine lovers, don't miss the last Sunday in May (Wine Day), when cellar doors swing open and you can sample Istria's local vintages.

The Kvarner region (formerly known as Liburnia) may be less famous than coastal counterparts in the south, but therein lies its appeal. Framed by Adriatic waters and separated from Dalmatia by the mountains that form its borderlands, Kvarner showcases the dynamic port city of Rijeka and a string of forest-strewn islands. The adjoining sun-drenched peninsula of Istria is tucked into the North Adriatic Sea with its heart-like shape. Its shorelines are lined with hotel complexes and pretty beach-resort towns welcoming sunseekers in summer, while the verdant interior features hilltop towns and neat rows of vineyards and olive groves, providing the excellent wine and olive oil Istria is known for, as well as black-and-white truffles growing in dense forests.

Pula

TIME FROM ZAGREB: **3HR** 🚙

Seaside Pula is Istria's largest city, occupying the southwestern tip of the peninsula. Its well-preserved 1st-century Roman amphitheatre is the main drawcard. Other remnants of its past live on in the old town's Roman street plan, from ancient arches and mosaics to temples and theatres. During Austro-Hungarian times, Pula was an important naval base, as well as a centre for shipbuilding for over 150 years. The bilingual street signs are a reminder that Pula is one of the Istrian cities where Italian is an official second language.

On the Roman trail

Any visit to Pula starts at its harbour-facing **Roman Amphitheatre** *(arenapula.hr; entry adult/child €10/5)*, known locally as the Arena. Built in the 1st century, this limestone-built landmark is one of only six remaining Roman amphitheatres in the world. Gladiators once entertained 20,000 spectators here; today it seats 5000 for open-air concerts and the annual **Pula Film Festival**.

Rovinj

Near the amphitheatre lies the 1st-century **Small Roman Theatre**, revived in 2023 when the stage and semicircular seating area of ancient stones got a much-needed upgrade. Today it's an atmospheric venue for concerts and cultural events, seating up to 1700.

Rovinj

TIME FROM PULA: **40MIN**

Seaside Rovinj is one of Croatia's most iconic destinations and an absolute must-visit. Set on a hilly peninsula, it seems to rise out of the sea with the Church of St Euphemia soaring above the city's rooftops. Standing cheek by jowl along the waterline are pretty buildings with their lime-plaster facades painted in pleasing pastel shades. The egg-shaped peninsula that Rovinj stands on was once an island –it was connected to the mainland in 1763. Rovinj had a strong maritime industry in the 17th century, and its fishing tradition continues today.

Tracing Rovinj's landmarks

The **Grisia** is a lane of slippery cobbles lined with artists' galleries and studios that slopes upwards to Rovinj's highest point

THE WORLD'S BIGGEST TRUFFLE

The truffle is a tuber that grows underground in dense forests and can only be sniffed out by specially trained dogs. While the black truffle is available year-round, the pungent white truffle can only be found for a few months of the year – generally September to January – hence its status as a luxury delicacy.

It was in Istria's Motovun forest that the world's biggest truffle was dug up in 1999, fetching a price tag of US$5000. Giancarlo Zigante and his dog Diana unearthed the 1.31kg white truffle and earned themselves a Guinness World Record. Today, Giancarlo runs **Restaurant Zigante** in nearby Livade and has a line of truffle products under the brand name Zigante (*zigantetartufi.com*).

DINING IN ROVINJ: TOP SPOTS

Snack Bar Rio: Much more than a snack bar, this cheerful sea-facing restaurant cooks up elevated seafood, pastas and salads. *8am-10pm Tue-Sun* €€

Brasserie Adriatic: Smack on the main square with Mediterranean cuisine and Istrian specialities, including vegan options. *7am-10pm* €€

Maestral: Enjoy an alfresco meal with superb views of the old town. Fish dominates the menu, but there are plenty of other tasty options. *10am-11pm* €€

Puntulina: Feast on plates of seafood at this stunning spot on the edge of the water. Bookings are a must. *noon-10pm Thu-Tue* €€€

259

and most important landmark: the 18th-century **St Euphemia's Church**. Its 60m-high bell tower is topped with a bronze statue of its patron saint. For superb views over the terracotta rooftops and nearby islands, brave the 200 steps to the top.

Grisia has had its own festival since 1967: on the second Sunday of August, the **Grisia Art Fair** celebrates the city's artistic tradition with the creations of local artists covering every available nook and cranny.

Rijeka

TIME FROM ZAGREB: **2HR**

Rijeka (meaning 'river' in Croatian) is often overlooked in favour of its Dalmatian counterparts, but this underrated cultural metropolis has nothing to prove. Its left-leaning residents enjoy their coastal city without the crowds of mass tourism, making it one of the most affordable places to live like a local and enjoy the thriving music and food scenes – and it's a five-minute drive from a beach. As well as being a punk-rock hub, Croatia's third-largest city is forward-thinking, open-minded and a lot of fun to visit.

Rijeka's gritty grandeur

The Rijeka we know today is a product of town planning by the Austrian Habsburgs, who rebuilt their biggest seaport following a devastating earthquake in the 1750s. Most of the grand, ornate architecture in the town centre dates to the late 1800s, when the city was home to the Habsburg navy and cultural institutions. Look for the baroque **City Clock Tower** above the arched city gate, renovated by Filbert Bazarig in 1876, and the **Ivan Zajc Croatian National Theatre** (*hnk-zajc.hr*), which was rebuilt in 1885.

Baška Beach

Palace Modello, designed by Buro Fellner & Helmer and built in 1885, is another impressive remnant of the era, and the colossal **Palača Adria** (Adria Palace), a neo-Renaissance layer cake completed in 1897, started out as an administrative centre for the Austro-Hungarian government.

Krk Island

TIME FROM RIJEKA: 1HR

Croatia's largest island is known for its gorgeous seaside towns, sprawling beaches and rich cultural heritage. From the ancient Liburnians and industrious Romans to dynastic Frankopan lords and Slavic priests, Krk is steeped in history. It's a hugely popular destination for both international tourists (around 100,000 visit every summer) and Croatian visitors alike. The mainland-connecting highway bridge makes for seamless travel, the island has abundant outdoor opportunities and the enchanting old towns round out Krk's intoxicating arsenal.

Baška in the sun

There's no getting around it – Krk is touristy. In July and August, sunseekers are spread towel-to-towel across many of the island's best beaches, including the fine crescent beach set below barren hills in Baška. One of the island's prettiest stretches, **Baška Beach** sits directly across from the peaks of the mainland, evoking a sense that the sea is an alpine lake enveloped by soaring highlands. The drive to the southern end of Krk is dramatic, too, passing through a fertile valley bordered by eroded mountains, before petering out in the Baška. Outside of the highest season, it's an immensely pleasant town, with a small 16th-century core of Venetian townhouses and nice hiking trails into the surrounding mountains.

RIJEKA'S WILD FIFTH SEASON: CARNIVAL

Every year on the last Sunday before Christian Lent commences, Rijeka holds the gargantuan **Rijeka Carnival** (*rijecki-karneval.hr*). A parade of 10,000 costumed people dance, march and party down the length of the Korzo, led by the city's mayor, the Carnival queen and the honorary mayor of the day, Meštar Toni, who is handed keys to the city for the duration. Not quite winter, not yet spring, it's dubbed Rijeka's 'fifth season'.

The highlight of the parade is saved for last. A group of 100 men, the *zvončari* bell ringers, wear striped shirts and are masked as imaginary but ferocious animals. The noise of their bells is said to scare away bad spirits, the winter and – as legend would have it – the Ottoman army.

Split & Dalmatian Islands

GORGEOUS BEACHES | ICONIC PALACE | HEAPS OF HISTORY

Places

Split p262
Brač Island p264
Hvar Island p265

GETTING AROUND

Split's compact old town is easy to explore on foot. To explore further, try **Promet** (promet-split. hr), the excellent public bus system. Local taxis tend to be overpriced – try Uber or Bolt instead. Ferry services connect Split to nearby islands, such as Hvar and Brač, but there are also private boat taxis, charters and private tours that can whisk you to any town with a port.

☑ **TOP TIP**

If you'd like to cycle around Split, look out for the Nextbike (nextbike.hr) bike-share stations. A handy app lets you rent bicycles and e-bikes at a budget-friendly hourly rate.

A couple of decades ago, Split was little more than a transit town to pause in before catching a ferry to the islands. Despite the magnificence of its star attraction, the World Heritage–listed Diocletian's Palace, the city stood forlorn and overlooked, with parts of it even described as a ghetto. Meanwhile the Riva, the city's now beloved seaside promenade, was a thoroughfare for car traffic.

Today, Split is one of Croatia's most visited cities, drawing crowds of tourists even during the shoulder seasons. It's a popular halt for cruise ships and a coveted destination for Croatia's growing tribe of digital nomads. The fact that many scenes from *Game of Thrones* were filmed here may also have something to do with its popularity.

No longer a mere launchpad to the islands, Split has finally attracted the attention it deserves, though the Splićani (the people of Split) are still learning to adjust to their city's new star status.

Split

Roam ancient Roman quarters

Diocletian's Palace is one of the world's largest and most complete Roman edifices. The fortress-like palace was built in the 4th century as Emperor Diocletian's swanky retirement home. The sprawling 38,700-sq-metre complex consists of roughly 200 buildings and has been inhabited for 2000 years, but only a few hundred tenants remain today.

Don't miss the handsome **Peristyle** (courtyard), the **Cathedral of St Domnius** – originally built as Emperor Diocletian's mausoleum and today's the world's oldest working Catholic cathedral that still has its original structure – the Temple of Jupiter (now the Baptistery), and the **Vestibule**, a domed rotunda that once opened onto the imperial corridor and the emperor's apartments.

Stone-slabbed Decumanus is the palace's thoroughfare. It's bookended by the **Silver Gate** at its eastern limit and the

CENTRAL SPLIT

⭐ **HIGHLIGHTS**
1 Cathedral of St Domnius
2 Diocletian's Palace

🔴 **SIGHTS**
3 Iron Gate
4 Model of Diocletian's Palace
5 Model of Old Town
6 Peristyle
7 Republic Square
8 Riva
9 Silver Gate
10 Vestibule

⚫ **SLEEPING**
11 Divota Apartment Hotel
12 Heritage Hotel 19
13 Hotel Vestibul Palace

🟢 **EATING**
14 Konoba Fetivi

Iron Gate to the west. It separated the emperor's residence from the military quarters, and intersects with north–south Cardo at the Peristyle. Interconnecting these arteries is a labyrinth of passageways lined with ancient buildings occupied by shops, cafes and restaurants.

City life by the sea

A favourite pastime for Split residents is a relaxed stroll on the seaside promenade. The Quay of the Croatian National Revival is the official name of this 250m-long stretch of waterfront, but for the Splićani, it's the **Riva**. Come early evening, chattering swallows swoop between the Riva's neat rows of palms while families amble up and down the footpath.

At the eastern end, look for the bronze 3D **Model of Old Town** and, a few steps away, a similar **Model of Diocletian's Palace**. Ramble along the white stone walkway while browsing for wooden souvenirs, handmade jewellery, locally produced wine and honey, and a range of other goodies, including dried figs, herbal teas and natural soaps. Then do like the Splićani and sit down for a cup of coffee. On Saturday mornings, people go to town in their Sunday best, and

---

🍽 **EATING IN SPLIT: OUR PICKS**

Up Cafe: Fuel up on tofu burritos, veggie burgers, falafel wraps and plant-based cakes at this casual cafe. *7am-8pm Mon-Fri, 8am-5pm Sat* €€

Dvor: Overlooking Firule beach, this upscale restaurant delights with its shady garden and imaginative fish dishes. *noon-midnight Sun-Thu, to 1am Fri & Sat* €€

Mokosh: At this art nouveau villa set in an elegant garden, you'll find fresh fish and meat dishes, plus several vegetarian options. *8am-midnight* €€

Konoba Fetivi: A longstanding favourite for its laid-back vibe and traditional Dalmatian cuisine. Try the black risotto or octopus salad. *noon-8pm Mon-Sat* €€

THE GUIDE

CROATIA SPLIT & DALMATIAN ISLANDS

SPLIT'S BEST BEACHES

Bačvice: This sandy beach with buzzing bars is also a favoured spot for players of *picigin* (a local ball game).

Firule: Popular horse-shoe-shaped sandy beach with cliffside cafes and a scene that continues way past sundown.

Žnjan: One of the bigger beaches in Split, with several bays of white pebbles and views of the mountainous coastline stretching southeast.

Kašjuni: A narrow pebble beach and sunset party spot that curves around the bay on the south side of Marjan Forest Park.

Bene: On the northern side of the Marjan Peninsula, this rocky beach has plenty of shade thanks to the many pine trees.

the long row of cafes buzzes with chitchat and the clinking of cups on saucers.

At the Riva's western end, you may catch the distinctive whiff of sulphur from the healing waters that have sprung up in this spot since Diocletian's time. Some believe these therapeutic springs are the reason he built his palatial retirement home here.

From here, venture to the handsome Venetian-inspired **Republic Square** to admire the vibrant red facades and elegant arches of its three-sided colonnade.

Brač Island

TIME FROM SPLIT: **50MIN** 🚢

Brač, Croatia's third-biggest island, is all about perfect beaches, dramatic mountain landscapes, delightful fishing villages and rustic stone hamlets locked in time. The island is also home to Vidova Gora, the highest mountain in the Adriatic archipelago, and the country's best-known beach, Zlatni Rat. The island's history has been shaped by its exceptional natural resources. The olive tree is a symbol of Brač: the rocky landscape is blanketed with groves of more than a million

EATING IN HVAR TOWN: OUR PICKS

Mediterraneo Dine & Wine: Book ahead to eat at this family-run Hvar institution. An extensive wine list complements the large menu. *noon-midnight* €€

Giaxa: Traditional Dalmatian cuisine prepared with high-quality produce. Ask about the catch of the day. *noon-11pm* €€

Štajun: A rustic restaurant offering a fine-dining menu of raw, warm and cold appetisers, with meat or fish as the main. *noon-midnight* €€€

Dalmatino: Smack in the heart of Hvar Town, this bustling dining spot serves up dishes of fish and steak. *noon-11pm Mon-Sat* €€€

Zlatni Rat

trees and neat rows of vineyards. Brač is also famous for its high-quality limestone, quarried here since Roman times and used to build many of Croatia's most notable architectural treasures.

White pebbles and turquoise water

Zlatni Rat is Croatia's best-known and most-photographed beach, and it doesn't disappoint. In the delightful town of Bol on the island's southern side, its long V shape magically shifts and changes with the waves and tides. The fine white pebbles are soft on the soles of the feet and don't stick to your skin. Then there's the astonishingly aquamarine water, as clear as a bath, making swimming a true delight. The beach can be reached from Bol along a 2km shady promenade lined with umbrella pines. A tourist train and taxi boat also make the trip from Bol's port.

Hvar Island

TIME FROM SPLIT: 1HR

Hvar has become synonymous with swank, thanks to Hvar Town's image as a posh destination for the jet set who sail in on their luxury yachts and its buzzy nightlife. But if you're not a fan of the glitterati or all-night parties, fear not, there's the rest of the island to explore. **Stari Grad**, one of the oldest Croatian towns, is charming, easier on the wallet and close to the lush Stari Grad Plain – a UNESCO World Heritage Site. Other highlights include scenic bays ribboned by gorgeous beaches, fields of fragrant lavender and superb local wines.

HVAR'S BEST BEACHES

Mekićevica: Follow the path eastwards from Pokonji Dol to reach this small, sublime and secluded cove of white pebbles.

Malo Zaraće: This pocket-sized beach, embraced by limestone rocks lapped by cobalt-blue waters, is the perfect sunset spot.

Dubovica: After a steep, zigzagging descent, your reward is a strand of white pebbles and two-tone waters of impossible blue.

Lučišća: A magical cove carved out of a rocky cliff face with clear green-blue waters. Best reached by boat.

Jagodna: A series of tiny pebbly coves opens to shallow aquamarine waters. Arrive early.

Brusje: On the less-frequented northern coastline lies this beautiful bay with a lovely stretch of beach.

Dubrovnik

MEDIEVAL WALLS | HISTORIC STREETS | BEACHES

☑ **TOP TIP**

Dubrovnik suffers terribly from overtourism. June, July and August are the busiest months. If you don't need to swim, come in March, April or November. Otherwise, aim for May, September or October. Beat the busiest crowds by exploring the old town early in the morning or after dark.

Dubrovnik's extraordinary old town never fails to dazzle. Its magnificent walls enclose a romantic vision of honey-coloured stone and terracotta roofs, virtually unchanged since the 17th century. The vivid colours of the Adriatic lapping at its edges add an extra level of irreality to a scene that already appears to come straight from a fairy tale.

Dubrovnik is busier now than it has ever been, and like Venice – its one-time overlord – it's in danger of being loved to death. *Game of Thrones* is partly responsible for the upsurge in visitors, as the HBO series brought a new generation of admirers to its streets.

But there's so much more to Dubrovnik than just the old town. It's also a regional hub for education, employment and cultural events, so take your time and get to know the city outside the walls, as well as within.

Walk the City Walls

Heaps of history and dazzling views

Croatia's number-one tourist attraction, Dubrovnik's majestic **city walls** *(citywallsdubrovnik.hr; entry adult/child €40/15; 8am-7pm, reduced hours Nov-Mar)* are its defining feature. Stretching a monumental total of 1940m in length, the ramparts are among the largest and most well-preserved in Europe. Circling the old town in one unbroken loop, they're as

 GETTING AROUND

The entire old town is a pedestrian zone, and **Libertas** *(libertasdubrovnik.hr)* buses will get you everywhere else you need to go. Timetables are available on the Libertas app or online. Tickets (€2.50) can be purchased on the bus, but they're slightly cheaper if bought at a *tisak* (newsstand) and free if you've

purchased a Dubrovnik Pass (p269). **Mynt** *(rentmynt.com)* is a handy pay-as-you-go app for moped (scooter) hire. Uber operates here and is considerably cheaper than regular taxis. Parking is expensive, so you're better off not hiring a car until you're ready to leave the city.

DUBROVNIK

★ HIGHLIGHTS
City Walls

SIGHTS
1 City Walls
2 Fort Lovrjenac
3 Fort St John
4 Pile Gate
5 Ploče Gate
6 Rector's Palace
7 Sponza Palace

● ACTIVITIES
8 Buža
9 Du Kayak Tour
10 Porporela
11 Šulić Beach
12 X-Adventure

● SLEEPING
13 Karmen Apartments

● EATING
14 Gradska kavana Arsenal
15 Lady Pi-Pi
16 Nautika
17 Nishta
18 Peppino's
19 Republic
20 Restaurant 360
21 Restaurant Dubrovnik

● DRINKING & NIGHTLIFE
22 Beach Bar Dodo
23 Buža
24 D'vino

Belvedere Beach
Sveti Jakov Beach (2km)
Petra Krešimira IV

Banje Beach (300m);
Hotel Excelsior (500m)

Old Harbour

Fort Revelin

Trg Oružja

City Walls

Braće Andrijića

Put Iza Grada

Restićeva

Luža Sq

Pred Dvorom

Žudioska

Peline

Prijeko

Lučarica

Gundulićeva Poljana

Držićeva Poljana

M Kaboge

C Zuzorić

Buničićeva Poljana

Androvićeva

Zagrebačka

Fort Minčeta

Kunićeva

Od Sigurate

Izmedu Polača

Mihe Pracata

Siroka

Od Puča

Poljana Rudera Boškovića

Strossmayerova

Gučetića

Restaurant 360

Od Kaštela

Plača (Stradun)

Zlatarićeva

Dubrovačkva

Poljana Paska Miličevića

Za Rokom

Od Rupa

Na Andiji

Brsalje

Brsalje

Izmedu Vrta

Bisalje

Sv. Đurđa

Od Tabakarije

Guest House Bilišić (530m)

Hotel Bellevue (1km)

Branitelja Dubrovnika

Danče Beach (2km)

PILE

Adriatic Sea

Od Pustijerne

Ispod Mira

Stulina

Od Kaštela

0   200 m
0   0.1 miles

267

THE REPUBLIC OF RAGUSA

Before the Slavic name stuck, Dubrovnik was known as Ragusa. By the end of the 12th century, Ragusa had become a significant trading centre. Venice took the city in 1205, but Ragusa was able to break free in 1538 and declare itself a republic.

By the 15th century, Ragusa had extended its borders to include the entire coast from Ston to Cavtat, as well as the islands of Lastovo and Mljet. Centuries of peace and prosperity allowed art, science and literature to flourish.

The beginning of the republic's economic decline came with a major earthquake in 1667, which killed as many as 5000 people and left the city in ruins. The final coup de grâce was dealt by Napoleon, whose troops entered the city in 1808.

beautiful as they are imposing. From the sea, the juxtaposition of pinkish grey stone and azure waters is mesmerising. For those walking them, the walls provide views over the tight maze of church steeples and terracotta roofs enclosed within.

If you keep a consistent pace and don't stop for photos or refreshments at the cafes, walking the full loop of the walls will take around an hour. There are three entrance points: near the **Pile Gate**, the **Ploče Gate** and **Fort St John**. You can buy a ticket at the gate, but you're better off purchasing a Dubrovnik Pass, which grants free entry.

To avoid accidents, congestion and general confusion, the path leads in an anticlockwise loop only. Along the way are various forts and towers to explore, the highlight being **Fort Minčeta** at the highest point on the landward side. While you're walking, keep an eye out for the two basketball courts tucked away in different corners of the city.

Dubrovnik's patron and protector, St Blaise, adorns the walls of **Fort Lovrjenac**, which was constructed atop a 37m-high promontory adjacent to the old town. Built in 1301 to stand guard over the city's western approach, its walls range from 4m to 12m in thickness. It's fairly empty inside, but it's worth popping in for the incredible views of the old town over the bay. Entry is included with the city walls ticket, or you can pay €15 for just the fort.

Experience the Glory of Ragusa

Majestic palaces and history galore

Apart from its many churches, the most resplendent buildings in the old town are a pair of remarkable palaces that largely survived the earthquake of 1667. If you want to get a feel for the glory days of the Republic of Ragusa, the **Rector's Palace** *(dumus.hr; entry adult/student €15/8)* is the place to start. For nearly 400 years, the palace served as the official residence of the elected official who governed Ragusa. The palace contains his office, private chambers, public halls, administrative offices and a dungeon. It was initially built in the 1430s in Gothic style, with the Renaissance porch added later. During the rector's one-month term, he was unable to leave the building without the permission of the senate. Today, the palace has been turned into a fascinating cultural-history museum; you'll need at least an hour to do it justice. Admission for the palace is included if you've bought the Dubrovnik Pass; it's closed Mondays from November to March.

 EATING IN THE OLD TOWN: BEST CONTEMPORARY CUISINE

Nishta: Imaginative and beautifully presented vegan food incorporating Greek, Middle Eastern, Indian and Mexican flavours. *11.30am-10pm Mon-Sat* €€

Nautika: Contemporary Croatian cuisine in a romantic clifftop location just outside the city walls. The service is faultless. *6pm-midnight* €€€

Restaurant 360: Michelin-starred spot within the city walls delivering fine dining at its best, with prices to match. *6.30-10.30pm Tue-Sun* €€€

Restaurant Dubrovnik: Upmarket restaurant serving modern Mediterranean cuisine on a covered rooftop terrace. *6-11pm Easter-December* €€€

Rector's Palace

The nearby **Sponza Palace** has the old town's most beautiful facade. It was completed in 1522 as a customs house and now houses the state archives. Architecturally, it's a mixture of influences. It's usually possible to pop your head in to admire the sweeping, column-lined cloister. Just inside the door is the Memorial Room of the Defenders of Dubrovnik, a moving exhibition honouring those who died during the Homeland War (1991–95).

Find a Beach for You

Swimming, suntans and glam

If the summer heat saps your enthusiasm for sightseeing, a trip to the beach is the best remedy. The main resorts are on the Lapad Peninsula, west of Gruž Harbour, but there are excellent swimming spots to be found all around Dubrovnik, including right in the shadow of the famous city walls. If you tire of the mainland options, catch a ferry to one of the nearby islands, such as Lokrum, Koločep, Lopud or Šipan.

For family fun, head to Lapad Bay, where the main beach has safe and inviting shallow waters. Close to the old town,

DUBROVNIK PASS

If you're planning to walk the **city walls** (p266), buying a Dubrovnik Pass (*dubrovnikpass.com; 1/3/7 days €40/50/60*) is a no-brainer, as the admission for the walls alone is the same price as the day pass.

All passes include free buses, along with admission to the city walls, **Rector's Palace**, Franciscan Monastery, Maritime Museum, Museum of Modern Art, archaeological exhibitions and five other small sights. On top of that, there are discounts to other attractions throughout the county, including **Ston Walls**.

You can buy your pass online or at various shops, sights and hotels, and at any of the official tourist offices.

DRINKING IN DUBROVNIK: BEST BARS

D'vino: If you're interested in sampling top-notch local wine, this convivial and atmospheric bar in the old town is the place to go. *11am-11pm Mon-Sat*

Buža: This ramshackle cliff-edge bar by the city walls feels like a discovery, but it's often packed, especially around sunset. Cliff divers provide free entertainment. *9am-1am*

Beach Bar Dodo: Local favourite, open all day for beers, burgers and chilled vibes under the watchful eye of Fort Lovrjenac. *10am-8pm*

Cave Bar More: Choose between a seat by the water on Lapad Bay or in an actual cave with stalactites and a flooded cavern. *8am-midnight*

BBA PHOTOGRAPHY/SHUTTERSTOCK

TOP TIPS FOR VISITING THE CITY WALLS

It makes no sense to purchase the city walls ticket separately. The one-day **Dubrovnik Pass** (p269).) is the same price and includes public transport and many other sights.

The entrance near the Pile Gate is usually the busiest. Skip the queues by entering from the Ploče side, which has the added advantage of getting the steepest climbs out of the way first.

There's little shade, so wear a hat and time your visit for the beginning or end of the day. You'll avoid the worst of the crowds, too.

Take water with you, as the stalls along the route are expensive.

Dubrovnik city walls (p266) and Lokrum

check out **Banje Beach**, Dubrovnik's busiest and most famous, just beyond the Ploče Gate, and also **Porporela**, **Buža**, **Šulić** and **Dance** beaches. For local vibes, go to **Sveti Jakov** or **Belvedere**, while the best of beach glam can be found at **Copacabana**.

Kayaking & Snorkel Tours

See the city walls from the sea

If you're an active traveller, there's lots to do on the shores of Dubrovnik. Sea kayaking is big business in the city, with tours departing from Banje Beach, Sveti Jakov Beach and little Šulić Beach under Fort Lovrjenac. **X-Adventure** (*kayak-dubrovnik.com; tours €30-40*) and **Du Kayak Tour** (*dukayaktour.com*) depart from directly beneath the walls, near Pile Gate. The views of the city walls are incredible from the sea, and most tours will take you to **Lokrum** and Betina Cave, a snorkelling spot that can only be reached from the water. Sunset tours are popular.

Outdoor Croatia (*outdoorcroatia.com; from €88*) offers a kayak and snorkel tour of the Elaphiti Islands and includes the ferry from Gruž Harbour to Lopud.

 EATING IN THE OLD TOWN: BEST BREAKFASTS & SNACKS

Gradska kavana Arsenal: A top breakfast perch, with a terrace overlooking Dubrovnik's finest buildings and a Viennese-style interior. *8am-midnight* €€

Lady Pi-Pi: Start your day overlooking the old town's terracotta roofs from this little rooftop by the upper walls. *9am-9pm* €€

Republic: Gourmet burger bar on a side lane, also serving pizza, pasta and *ćevapi*. Veggie and vegan burgers available. *11am-11pm* €€

Peppino's: Dubrovnik's best and creamiest gelato, with an array of interesting, artisanal flavours and fair prices. *11am-8pm* €

Places We Love to Stay

€ Budget €€ Midrange €€€ Top End

Zagreb

MAP p255

Stay Swanky € Happening backpacker joint, with a garden bar, seasonal pool, dorms, private rooms inspired by artisans, apartments and Soi, an Asian-fusion restaurant.

Hotel Jägerhorn €€ Zagreb's oldest hotel dates back to 1827 and is a peaceful oasis in a passageway just off Ilica, with subdued, classic elegance and a terrace cafe.

Stellar Boutique Modules €€ Designer hotel along tram-lined Vlaška, with smallish all-white rooms inspired by space, artwork on the ceilings, an all-day cafe-bar serving food and a rooftop bar.

Esplanade Zagreb Hotel €€€ The grande dame of Zagreb hotels is this 100-year-old belle époque beauty with plush rooms and two restaurants, steps from the main train station.

Istria & Kvarner

Old Town Inn €€ Bang in the old town, surrounded by some of Rijeka's coolest addresses and Roman ruins, with modern rooms and historic touches.

Boutique Hotel Valsabbion €€€ Small beachside hotel in quiet Pješčana Uvala, close to Pula, with plush rooms. Perks include its own beach area, heated pool and medical spa.

Hotel Adriatic €€€ A chic design hotel on Rovinj's seafront with art-filled rooms and an elegant bar and brasserie.

Split & Dalmatian Islands

Divota Apartment Hotel €€€ A diffused hotel of apartments and rooms in multiple restored stone houses in charming Veli Varoš.

Heritage Hotel 19 €€€ An elegant boutique hotel in a heritage property with a courtyard garden and romantic vibe.

Hotel Vestibul Palace €€€ Seven rooms make up this elegant hotel with a bar and restaurant tucked just behind the palace's vestibule.

Villa Giardino Heritage Boutique Hotel €€€ A charming villa with elegant rooms in a leafy garden in the heart of Bol on Brač Island.

Maslina Resort €€€ A slice of luxury amid olive groves on a quiet bay near Stari Grad. Ingredients for the restaurant are sourced from the organic garden.

Dubrovnik

MAP p267

Karmen Apartments €€ These four character-filled apartments enjoy a great location near the harbour in Dubrovnik's old town. Book well ahead.

Guest House Biličić €€ This long-standing guesthouse is surrounded by a gorgeous subtropical garden. Bedrooms are simple and clean, with private bathrooms across the corridor.

Hotel Bellevue €€€ On a cliff at the beginning of the Lapad Peninsula, this classy hotel has modern decor, excellent facilities and a beach beneath.

Hotel Excelsior €€€ A Yugoslav-era mash-up of a 1913 hotel with a modern annex, this luxurious hotel has renovated rooms, plus indoor and outdoor pools.

IVO ANTONIE DE ROOIJ/SHUTTERSTOCK

Esplanade Zagreb Hotel

Practicalities

LGBTIQ+ Travellers

Croatia ranked #48 on the 2025 Spartacus Gay Travel Index, which is quite low compared to other European countries. In short, Croatia is still a conservative society dominated by traditional Catholic values. Though attitudes are slowly changing, the LGBTIQ+ community prefers to stay under the radar, fearing harassment if they reveal their sexual orientation.

Digital Nomads

Croatia introduced a temporary stay permit for digital nomads in 2021. Valid for up to 18 months, any non-EU/EEA national who works remotely as an employee or is self-employed can apply for the permit as long as they do not provide services to Croatian companies.

Electricity & Connectivity

Type F plug
220V/50Hz
Free wi-fi is available at the airport and most hotels and cafes, while major cities and tourist centres have a free public wi-fi service.

Drinking Water

Croatia is known for its high-quality, abundant water resources. Tap water is perfectly safe to drink.

JULIA LAV/SHUTTERSTOCK

Rijeka (p260)

Opening Hours

Many shops close on Sundays outside of summer.
Banks 8am–6pm Monday to Friday
Bars 10am–2am
Cafes 7am–11pm
Restaurants 10am–11pm
Shopping malls 9am–10pm
Supermarkets 7am–9pm

Public Holidays

New Year's Day 1 January
Epiphany 6 January
Easter Monday March/April
Labour Day 1 May
Statehood Day 30 May
Corpus Christi 60 days after Easter
Day of Antifascist Resistance 22 June
Homeland Thanksgiving Day 5 August
Feast of the Assumption 15 August
All Saints' Day 1 November
Remembrance Day for Victims of the Homeland War 18 November
Christmas 25 & 26 December

Language

In Croatian, every letter is pronounced and its sound does not vary from word to word.

Basics

Hello. Dobar dan. *do·bar dan*
Goodbye. Zbogom. *zbo·gom*
Yes. Da. *da*
No. Ne. *ne*
Please. Molim. *mo·lim*
Thank you. Hvala vam/ti (pol/inf). *hva·la vam/ti*
Excuse me. Oprostite. *o·pro·sti·te*
Sorry. Žao mi je. *zha·o mi ye*
What's your name? Kako se zovete/zoveš? (pol/inf) *ka·ko se zo·ve·te/zo·vesh*
My name is ... Zovem se ... *zo·vem se*
Do you speak English? Govorite/Govoriš li engleski? (pol/inf) *go·vo·ri·te/go·vo·rish li en·gle·ski*
I don't understand. Ne razumijem. *ne ra·zu·mi·yem*

Directions

Where's (the station)? Gdje je (stanica)? *gdye ye (sta·ni·tsa)*

10 Phrases to Sound Like a Local

Šta ima? – What's up?
Kužim/Ne kužim – I understand/I don't understand.
To je fora! – That's cool!
To je mrak! – That's awesome!
Idemo na cugu – Let's go for a drink.
To je puno love – That's a lot of money.
Nema šanse! – No way!
Nema veze – Never mind.
Idemo na klopu – Let's go for some food.
Nema frke – No problem.

What's the address? Koja je adresa? *koy·a ye a·dre·sa*
Could you please write it down? Možete li to napisati?/Možeš li to napisati? (pol/inf) *mo·zhe·te li to na·pi·sa·ti/mo·zhesh li to na·pi·sa·ti*
Can you show me (on the map)? Možete li mi to pokazati (na karti)? *mo·zhe·te li mi to po·ka·za·ti (na kar·ti)*

Time

What time is it? Koliko je sati? *ko·li·ko ye sa·ti*
It's (10) o'clock. (Deset) je sati. *(de·set) ye sa·ti*
Half past (10). (Deset) i po. *(de·set) i po*
morning jutro. *yu·tro*
afternoon popodne. *po·pod·ne*
evening večer. *ve·cher*
yesterday jučer. *yu·cher*
today danas. *da·nas*
tomorrow sutra. *su·tra*

Emergencies

Help! Upomoć! *u·po·moch*
Go away! Maknite se! *mak·ni·te se*
Call ...! Zovite ...! *zo·vi·te*
   a doctor liječnika *li·yech·ni·ka*
   the police policiju. *po·li·tsi·yu*

Eating & Drinking

What would you recommend? Što biste nam preporučili? *shto bi·ste nam pre·po·ru·chi·li*
Cheers! Živjeli! *zhi·vye·li*
I'd like the bill please. Mogu li dobiti račun, molim. *mo·gu li do·bi·ti ra·chun mo·lim*

DONATIONS TO ENGLISH

Did you know that the words Dalmatian and cravat come from Croatian?

NUMBERS

1	**jedan** *ye·dan*
2	**dva** *dva*
3	**tri** *tri*
4	**četiri** *che·ti·ri*
5	**pet** *pet*
6	**šest** *shest*
7	**sedam** *se·dam*
8	**osam** *o·sam*
9	**devet** *de·vet*
10	**deset** *de·set*

Zagreb International Airport

Arriving

It's always thrilling to arrive in Croatia, whether landing at one of the nine airports, coming by sea or arriving overland as the verdant landscapes and island-dotted coastline sweep by. It's busiest during the high summer season (July and August), but with vistas this stunning, a trip any time of the year is a delight.

By Air
Zagreb International Airport (Franjo Tuđman Airport) is Croatia's main hub. During summer, additional low-cost connections from European destinations fly to Brač, Dubrovnik, Osijek, Pula, Rijeka, Split and Zadar.

By Land
With limited train services in the Balkans, many travellers find the affordable, long-haul buses run by companies such as FlixBus and Arriva to be the best way of getting to Croatia. There are regular international services to Zagreb and Rijeka.

MONEY

Currency: Euro (€)

CASH

Cash is still king in Croatia, especially in villages and smaller towns on the islands, where cafes and restaurants are likely to take cash only. Check with your accommodation in advance, particularly if staying in rural or remote spots or in a hostel.

TIPPING

Croatia doesn't have a tipping culture, but gratuities are always appreciated. Round up the bill in bars and cafes, and leave a 5% to 10% tip in restaurants. If you pay by card, leave the tip in cash.

CARDS & ATMS

You can pay by card or phone in all large chain stores in Zagreb, Zadar, Split, Dubrovnik and other urban areas. Have small change ready for small purchases, bus tickets and the like. ATMs operated by banks are widespread and reliable. Avoid Euronet ATMs – these charge high fees and offer terrible exchange rates.

Getting Around

Croatia is relatively small – it takes just seven hours to drive from one end to the other via the highways. That said, if you plan to visit the islands, a lot of your journeys will likely involve ferries, so don't rush and allow for slow travel days.

PAUL PRESCOTT/SHUTTERSTOCK

Bus
Arriva, Autotrans and FlixBus all serve Zagreb, Pula, Rijeka, Zadar, Split and Dubrovnik, where you can change to cheap, mostly punctual, local buses (Arriva and Autotrans) that journey onwards to the major islands and more rural destinations.

Ferry
Ferries connect the mainland with the islands; Jadrolinija is the biggest company. Its schedule ramps up come peak season, and other companies like Krilo serve useful routes such as Split–Dubrovnik during summer.

Car
Hiring a car is undoubtedly the best way to explore Croatia. The best prices are found in Zagreb or Rijeka; expect to pay double in Split or Dubrovnik. Highways have tolls in many parts; get a ticket at the entrance and pay at the exit.

DRIVING ESSENTIALS

Drive on the right

50

Speed limit is 50km/h on urban roads, 90km/h on main roads and 130km/h on highways

While Croatians are courteous drivers, don't expect locals to stick to the speed limits

Train
Croatia is not well served by train. Arriving from Slovenia, Hungary, Austria and other neighbours into Zagreb Glavni Kolodvor station (pictured above), the only onward route you're likely to use is the Zagreb–Split train, which is best booked in advance.

Bicycle
Long-distance cycling is popular with visitors. Nextbike is a public bike-sharing system (e-bikes too), and you can rent a bike from terminals without needing a phone. Look for docking stations in 30 locations across Croatia.

Curated by
Mark Baker

THE GUIDE

CZECHIA

Czechia

BREATHTAKING CASTLES AND EVEN BETTER BEER

Find dramatic historical architecture, charming towns,
quirky sights and a vibrant, youthful culture.

Since the fall of communism in 1989 and the opening up of Central and Eastern Europe, Prague has evolved into one of Europe's most popular travel destinations. And for very good reason. Czechia's capital city offers an intact medieval core that transports you back – especially when strolling the hidden streets of the Old Town – some 600 years. The 14th-century Charles Bridge, linking two historic neighbourhoods across a slow-moving river – with Prague Castle pitched dramatically in the backdrop – is one of the continent's most beautiful sights. But Prague is not just about history. It's a vital urban centre with a rich array of cultural offerings, including fantastic museums, concert halls, restaurants and clubs.

Outside the capital, in the provinces of Bohemia and Moravia, castles and palaces abound – including the audacious hilltop chateau at Český Krumlov – which illuminate the stories of powerful dynasties whose influence was felt throughout Europe. Bohemia was famous in the 19th century for its regal spas, and Karlovy Vary still shows off this old-school splendour. Beer afficionados will make a beeline for Plzeň (Pilsen), where modern-day lager was first invented. Moravia lies a bit further off the beaten path. The provincial capital of Brno abounds in student-fiilled bars and cafes and ghoulish underground sights. The city of Olomouc has much of the architectural beauty of Prague, with just a fraction of the crowds.

FOTOKON/SHUTTERSTOCK

THE MAIN AREAS

PRAGUE
Czechia's breathtaking and energetic capital. **p280**

BOHEMIA
Castles, historic spa resorts, beers and bones. **p289**

MORAVIA
Underground adventure and baroque beauty. **p295**

DALIU/SHUTTERSTOCK

For places to stay in Czechia, see p300

Left: Beer, Plzeň (p290); Above: Charles Bridge (p285), Prague

Find Your Way

A sampling of the best of Czechia. We've picked out some of the must-see sights in Prague, plus highlights for excursions further afield into the provinces of Bohemia and Moravia.

Moravia, p295

Experience Czechia without the tourists, including visiting a vibrant provincial capital and an underappreciated baroque beauty.

Prague, p280

Immerse yourself in centuries-old historic architecture, followed up with a pint at a pub or a classical concert.

Bohemia, p289

Discover castle-topped hills and charming historic towns, and then treat yourself to possibly the world's best beer tour.

TRAINS & BUSES

You won't need a car to get around. The extensive train and bus network can take you to all the places covered here. We've noted where either the train or bus might be faster or cheaper.

CAR

Don't use your own vehicle to get around Prague. The city's metro and trams are much more practical. Outside the capital, a car gives you flexibility to explore the country at your own pace.

GERMANY

POLAND

SLOVAKIA

AUSTRIA

Katowice

Ostrava

Opava

Frýdek-Místek

Rožnov pod Radhoštěm

Nový Jičín

Olomouc

Přerov

Kroměříž

Blansko

Šumperk

Svitavy

MORAVIA

Moravia River

Brno

Labyrinth under the Vegetable Market

Villa Tugendhat

Třebíč

Jihlava

Litomyšl

Havlíčkův Brod

Chrudim

Hradec Králové

Ústí nad Orlicí

Sedlec Ossuary

Kutná Hora

Mladá Boleslav

Elbe River

Labe River

Děčín

Bohemian Switzerland National Park

Dresden

Chemnitz

Ústí nad Labem

Louny

Kladno

Žatec

Most

Chomutov

Karlovy Vary

Mariánské Lázně

Domažlice

Plzeň (Pilsen)

Klatovy

Beroun

Příbram

Písek

Tábor

Benešov

PRAGUE

Prague Castle

Old Town Square

Vltava River

Český Krumlov State Castle

Šumava National Park

České Budějovice

Český Krumlov

Třeboň

Jindřichův Hradec

BOHEMIA

Munich

GERMANY

Danube

Odra

Odra

0   50 miles

0   100 km

N

Prague (p280)

Plan Your Time

Three days is sufficient for Prague, and you can then pick and choose what you'd like to see in Bohemia or Moravia. With a car you can cover the highlights in a week.

Three Days in Prague

● Experience the exciting combination of a glorious past and energetic present in Prague. Take in the grandeur of **Prague Castle** (p281), cross **Charles Bridge** (p285) and wander Prague's Old Town. Take in the spectacle of **Old Town Square** (p286) and the **Astronomical Clock** (p286) and then explore the **Prague Jewish Museum** (p286). Spend a third day on the train going to see spectacular **Karlštejn Castle** (p288).

A Week in Czechia

● Begin in **Prague** (p280) before heading west for the spa scene at **Karlovy Vary** (p289). Balance the virtue and vice ledger with a few brews in **Plzeň** (p290), before heading south to **Český Krumlov** (p292). Take in the 'Bone Church' in **Kutná Hora** (p293) and then head east to enjoy the underground sights of **Brno** (p295). From Moravia's largest city, it's just a skip to stately **Olomouc** (p298).

SEASONAL HIGHLIGHTS

SPRING

Trees and flowers start budding in April and the country comes alive after the long winter. May and June days are often warm and sunny.

SUMMER

Hot, sunny days are perfect for escaping the city. That said, it's high season. Thousands of visitors stream through Prague daily.

AUTUMN

September and October tend to be quieter but still offer reliably good weather. Locals decamp to the forests to pick mushrooms.

WINTER

The Christmas and New Year's holidays enliven the long, cold winter. Hotel rates drop, but some attractions, including gardens, close.

Prague

RIVETING HISTORY | STIRRING VIEWS | REGAL ARCHITECTURE

☑ TOP TIP

Prague can get very crowded, particularly in midsummer and over major holidays. To avoid disappointment, book things like meals at popular restaurants as well as theatre and concert tickets as far in advance as possible.

The ups and downs of centuries past, of empires, wars, plagues and prosperity, are etched into Prague's soul like the lines carved onto the facades of its Gothic towers and Renaissance palaces. Some 35 years ago, Prague re-emerged on the European stage after languishing for years under communism, and the world was agog. Those years trapped behind the Iron Curtain left the city looking neglected and rundown, but it was obvious Prague's rich history and intrinsic beauty – the hypnotic, visual tension between Charles Bridge and Prague Castle – had survived intact.

Indeed, that's the real pleasure of a trip to Prague now that the scaffolding is down and the appeal is obvious to everyone: to take in the beauty as you wander slowly from Prague Castle down through the historic Malá Strana quarter, across Charles Bridge, over the Vltava River and into the arms of the Old Town.

Prague Castle & Hradčany

The hilltop neighbourhood of Hradčany, home to Prague Castle, retains a whiff of exclusivity centuries after the emperors and kings who once lived here have gone. The main attractions include the Prague Castle complex and stately St Vitus Cathedral, which stands within the castle walls. Strahov Monastery has been here since at least 1140; the

---

◎ GETTING AROUND

Prague has an excellent public transport system of metros, trams, buses and night trams, but when it comes to moving around the relatively compact historic neighbourhoods of Staré Město (Old Town), Malá Strana and Prague Castle, it's more convenient – and more scenic – to travel by foot. Use the metro to cover longer distances or to convenient stations located near Staré Město, Malá Strana and central Wenceslas Square. Use the tram for shorter stretches. Tram 22 runs to near Prague Castle and can spare you the climb up to the castle district.

Old Royal Palace

monks' adjoining library is one of the most beautiful in Europe. Scattered among the incredible palaces are pubs, restaurants and breathtaking views out over Malá Strana and the Old Town.

Take in sprawling Prague Castle

Looming high above the Vltava River, **Prague Castle** *(hrad.cz; tours from adult/child 300/200Kč),* with its serried ranks of spires and palaces, dominates the city. Within its walls lies a fascinating collection of historic buildings, museums and galleries, home to some of Czechia's greatest artistic and cultural treasures. The grounds of the castle complex are free to enter, though to see the interiors (including adjoining St Vitus Cathedral) requires a combined admission ticket. Buy tickets online at **Ticketportal** *(ticketportal.cz)* or at the **castle information centre**.

The high point for most visitors is the **Old Royal Palace**, situated in the castle's third courtyard. This is one of the oldest surviving parts of the castle, dating from 1135. Don't miss the **Vladislav Hall** (Vladislavský sál), which is famous for its beautiful, late-Gothic vaulted ceiling. Beyond the Old Royal Palace, the **Basilica of St George** is Czechia's best-preserved Romanesque basilica. You can also stroll **Golden Lane**, where writer Franz Kafka stayed at No 22 (from 1916 to 1917).

EARLY STORY OF HRADČANY

Hradčany got its first royal residents in the 9th century. A ducal palace was built here to accommodate the early ruling Přemyslid dynasty. The 12th century saw significant expansion. A grander ducal palace was completed. In 1140, the Premonstratensian Monastery was founded in Strahov. In the 14th century, Emperor Charles IV rebuilt the castle to more properly represent Prague's status as seat of the Holy Roman Empire. He also embarked on construction of St Vitus Cathedral.

In 1541, a tragic fire engulfed the district and damaged many buildings, including the castle and cathedral. Yet the fire created large, empty lots that eventually gave way to today's mega-palaces, including the **Schwarzenberg Palace** and the **Archbishop's Palace**.

EATING & DRINKING NEAR PRAGUE CASTLE: OUR PICKS

Klášterní Pivovar Strahov: Convivial pub near Strahov Monastery serves its own St Norbert beers – and very good Czech food. *10am-10pm* €€

Vinobona Wine & Bistro: Tiny, romantic spot; perfect for breakfast/ lunch. Dress smartly for pricier dinner tasting menu. *9am-3pm, 6-10pm Thu-Mon* €€€

Kuchyň: Book well in advance to secure one of the popular terrace tables. Excellent Czech standards. *11.30am-11pm* €€

Lobkowicz Palace Café: The best pit stop for drinks and light meals within the Prague Castle complex. Superb views from the back balcony. *10am-6pm* €€

PRAGUE

38 St Nicholas Church
39 St Vitus Cathedral
40 Strahov Library
41 Strahov Monastery
42 Velvet Revolution
Memorial
43 Wenceslas Statue

● **SLEEPING**
44 Ahoy! Hostel
45 Design Hotel Josef
46 Dominican
47 Dům U Velké Boty
48 Golden Well Hotel

49 Icon Hotel
50 Little Quarter Hostel
51 Mosaic House
52 Sophie's Hostel

● **EATING**
53 420 Restaurant
54 Café Savoy
55 Čestr
56 Garden's
57 Ichnusa Botega Bistro
58 Kantýna
59 Kuchyň

60 Lobkowicz Palace Café
61 Mincovna
62 Naše Maso
63 Terasa U Zlaté Studně
64 U Modré Kachničky
65 V Kolkovně
66 Vinobona Wine & Bistro

● **DRINKING**
& NIGHTLIFE
67 Duplex
68 Klášterní Pivovar
Strahov

● **ENTERTAINMENT**
see 33 Dvořák Hall
69 Lucerna Music Bar
70 National Theatre
71 Prague State Opera
72 Reduta Jazz Club
see 22 Smetana Hall

● **INFORMATION**
73 Castle Information
Centre

● **TRANSPORT**
74 Praha Hlavní Nádraží

BEST VENUES FOR CLASSICAL MUSIC

Rudolfinum: Gorgeous neo-Renaissance building with **Dvořák Hall**, home of the Czech Philharmonic Orchestra. The season runs September–June. (*rudolfinum.cz; standing tickets from 200Kč*)

Smetana Hall: Centrepiece stage of the Municipal House and home of the Prague Symphony Orchestra. (*fok.cz; tickets from 400Kč*)

Church of St James: Features a splendid pipe organ. Pop in on Sunday mornings at 10am for a free organ recital. (*praha.minorite.cz; free*)

Church of St Nicholas: Chamber concerts here are visually splendid (though acoustically average). (*svmikulas.cz; tickets from 300Kč*)

Estates Theatre: Branch of the National Theatre hosting occasional baroque music concerts. (*narodni-divadlo.cz; tickets from 400Kč*)

St Vitus Cathedral

Admire towering St Vitus Cathedral

Built over almost 600 years, **St Vitus Cathedral** (*katedrala svatehovita.cz*) is one of Central Europe's most richly endowed cathedrals. It is pivotal to the country's cultural life, housing treasures that range from the tombs of St Wenceslas and Charles IV to the baroque silver tomb of St John of Nepomuk and the ornate Chapel of St Wenceslas. Step inside to see the massive nave flooded with colour from stained-glass windows created by eminent Czech artists of the early 20th century – note the one by Alfons Mucha in the third chapel on the northern side. The high points include the **tomb of St Vitus** and spectacular silver **tomb of St John of Nepomuk**. The **Wallenstein Chapel** contains the graves of cathedral architects Matthias of Arras and Peter Parler. The most beautiful of the side chapels is the **Chapel of St Wenceslas**. Its walls are adorned with gilded panels containing polished slabs of semiprecious stones.

The world's prettiest library?

Tucked away in a quiet corner of Hradčany, the **Strahov Monastery** (*strahovskyklaster.cz; library tours adult/child 150/80Kč*) has stood here since 1140, when it was founded by Duke Vladislav II. The biggest attraction is the magnificent **library**. Guided tours allow you to peer into the two baroque halls. The stunning interior of the two-storey 'Philosophy Hall' features floor-to-ceiling walnut shelving. The older 'Theology Hall' is even more breathtaking.

Malá Strana (Lesser Town)

Visitors are often surprised to discover that Malá Strana (Lesser Town) is in some ways more beautiful than Staré Město (Old Town). In the 17th and 18th centuries, noble families built their sumptuous palaces and plotted out spacious gardens here. The neighbourhood is home to many top sights, including the impressive baroque of St Nicholass Church and the elegant Wallenstein Garden. The best way to explore is to amble along the cobblestoned backstreets, or through **Kampa Park** along the river, and admire the handsome buildings and tiny squares.

Walk across Charles Bridge

Who knew a bridge could ever be this beautiful or that mounting 30 baroque statues along its edges might elevate a handsome Gothic structure into a public work of art? **Charles Bridge** *(Karlův most, free)* is a world-class attraction. The bridge began life in 1357 when Emperor Charles IV commissioned Peter Parler (architect of St Vitus Cathedral) to replace an older, 12th-century bridge that had been washed away by floods. The new bridge was completed in 1390. The statues came three centuries later, when the bridge's first monument, the Crucifix near the eastern end, was mounted in 1657. The most famous figure is the monument to **St John of Nepomuk**. Tradition says if you rub the bronze plaque, you'll one day return to Prague.

Take in grand St Nicholas Church

Praguers generally have a love-hate affair with baroque architecture. Everyone, though, loves **St Nicholas Church** *(Kostel svatého Mikuláše; stnicholas.cz; adult/child 140/80Kč)*; its big green dome can be seen from just about anywhere in the centre. The building was begun by famed baroque architect Christoph Dientzenhofer; his son Kilian continued the work and Anselmo Lurago finished the job in 1755. Mozart himself tickled the ivories on the 2500-pipe organ in 1787. Take the stairs up to the gallery to see Karel Škréta's emotive, 17th-century *Passion Cycle* paintings. On the ceiling, Johann Kracker's 1770 *Apotheosis of St Nicholas* is Europe's largest fresco.

Climb Petřín Hill

This 318m-high **Petřín** is one of Prague's largest green spaces. It's great for quiet, tree-shaded walks and fine views over the 'city of a hundred spires'. Climb up or take the **Petřín Funicular** to find the views and a handful of kid-friendly attractions. The **Petřín Lookout Tower** *(adult/child 220/150Kč)*, a 60m-high Eiffel Tower lookalike (though smaller at a ratio of 1:5), offers dramatic vistas. Just near the lookout tower is a **Mirror Maze** *(adult/child 120/80Kč)*. Younger children will get a kick out of the distorting funhouse mirrors and labyrinth.

Staré Město (Old Town)

Staré Město, Prague's Old Town, has been the city's beating heart for more than 1000 years. The grand buildings, churches

HOUSE SIGNS OF NERUDOVA

Steep Nerudova street leads from Malá Strana to Prague Castle. It has a long, rich history – much of it written on the playful symbols that adorn the fronts of the houses. The **House at the Three Fiddles** (Nerudova 12) once belonged, fittingly, to a family of violinmakers. **St John of Nepomuk House** (No 18) is adorned with an image of the patron saint himself. **Bretfeld Palace** (No 33) was a social hot spot, entertaining the likes of Mozart and Casanova. The **House of the Golden Horseshoe** (No 34) is named after St Wenceslas' horse, allegedly shod with gold. Czech writer and journalist Jan Neruda, after whom the street is named, lived at the **House of the Two Suns** (No 47) from 1845 to 1857.

 EATING IN MALÁ STRANA: OUR PICKS

| **U Modré Kachničky:** This feels like an old-fashioned hunting lodge, with quiet, candlelit nooks. The traditional roast duck is very good. *noon-11pm* €€€ | **Terasa U Zlaté Studně:** Perched atop a Renaissance mansion close to the castle, the 'Golden Well' has truly fine dining. *noon-4pm & 6-11pm* €€€ | **Ichnusa Botega Bistro:** Superb Italian food and wines ferried to Prague directly from the owner's homeland of Sardinia. *11am-10pm* €€ | **Café Savoy:** Elegant Viennese-style coffeehouse, with terrific Czech specialties and homemade desserts. *8am-10pm Mon-Fri, from 9am Sat & Sun* €€ |

IN THE FOOTSTEPS OF KINGS

The **Royal Way** (Královská cesta) was the former processional route followed by the Bohemian kings on their way to St Vitus Cathedral for coronation. The first king to ride the route was the Habsburg ruler Albert II, in 1438; the last was Emperor Ferdinand I of Austria, in 1836.

The coronation route ran right through the heart of Staré Město. It began at the Powder Gate. From here, the route followed Celetná to Old Town Square and the adjacent Little Square (Malé náměstí). From the squares, the route traced Karlova street to Charles Bridge and then across to Malá Strana. On the Malá Strana side, the coronation route proceeded along Mostecká street to Malostranské náměstí (Lesser Town Square) before climbing up Nerudova to Prague Castle.

and squares, the Old Town Hall and Astronomical Clock stand as testimony to the growing wealth and influence over the centuries of Prague's merchants and artisans. This splendour came to rival that of the kings and noble families on the other side of the river. The best way to take in Staré Město's sights is to wander at will. The street plan appears to have little logic at all; perfect for getting lost in.

Explore Old Town Square

One of Europe's most beautiful and busiest urban spaces, **Old Town Square** has been Prague's principal public square since the 10th century and was its main marketplace until the beginning of the 20th century.

The most important building, the **Old Town Hall** *(staromestskaradnicepraha.cz; tower adult/child 300/200Kč)*, was founded in 1338 to serve as Staré Město's independent seat of government. These days it no longer has a formal governing function. The main admission ticket includes entry to the tower, which affords dramatic views of the square below. The Town Hall's best-known attraction is the **Astronomical Clock** *(free)* on its south-facing exterior. On the hour, from 9am to 9pm, spectators are treated to a 45-second mechanised marionette display straight out of the Middle Ages.

Beyond the Old Town Hall, the most dramatic structure on the square is the twin-spired **Church of Our Lady Before Týn**, across the way, which stands incongruously behind a row of baroque facades. The 14th-century **House at the Stone Bell** is considered the square's oldest building. Find another important church, the baroque **Church of St Nicholas**, wedged into the northwestern corner.

Two pieces of statuary in the middle of the square are integral to this public space. Praguers love the dramatic art nouveau depiction of Czech religious reformer **Jan Hus** by Ladislav Šaloun. The newer **Marian Column** was only installed in 2020, and it's fair to say locals haven't quite warmed up to it yet.

Tour Prague's Jewish Museum

The **Prague Jewish Museum** *(jewishmuseum.cz; from adult/child 600/400Kč)* isn't simply one museum but a grouping of historic synagogues and an ancient burial ground. The holdings constitute possibly the world's biggest collection of sacred Jewish artefacts, many rescued from synagogues destroyed by Nazi Germany during WWII. The crumbling **Old Jewish Cemetery** is a must. The weatherworn headstones mark just

EATING IN STARÉ MĚSTO: OUR PICKS

420 Restaurant: Opulent dining room with baroque statues. Traditional Czech dishes given fusion upgrade. Book ahead. *11.30am-10.30pm* €€€

Mincovna: Best of an average bunch of restaurants on Old Town Square. Decent pork knee, schnitzels and duck. *11.30am-11pm* €€

Naše Maso: Tiny butcher with stand-up tables at the forefront of Prague's rush to embrace the foodie philosophy of locally sourced meat. *11am-10pm* €€

V Kolkovně: Operated by Pilsner Urquell Brewery. Stylish, modern take on traditional Prague pub; fancy-ish versions of classic Czech dishes. *11am-midnight* €€

CAVAN-IMAGES/SHUTTERSTOCK

Old Town Square

a fraction of the thousands buried here. Other important sites include the **Old-New Synagogue**, **Pinkas Synagogue**, **Maisel Synagogue**, **Spanish Synagogue**, **Klaus Synagogue** and **Ceremonial Hall**. One basic admission ticket allows entry to all of the main monuments, including the Old-New Synagogue. Buy tickets via the museum website or at the Museum Reservation Centre (Maiselova 15).

Admire art nouveau elegance

The **Municipal House** *(obecnidum.cz; guided tours adult/ child 320/270Kč)* is Prague's most exuberantly art nouveau building. The building, constructed between 1906 and 1912, was a lavish joint effort by around 30 leading Czech artists, including Alfons Mucha. Every detail of its design and decoration was carefully considered. Guided tours in English can be booked via the website or at the venue box office. The tour's highlight is the octagonal Lord Mayor's Hall, the windows of which overlook the main entrance.

Nové Město (New Town)

The busy streets of Prague's main commercial area are where Prague starts to feel like a real city (and less like a living museum). Nové Město translates as 'New Town', but there's little 'new' about it. It was laid out by Emperor Charles IV in the mid-14th century to alleviate overcrowding in Staré Město.

EPIC HISTORY OF WENCESLAS SQUARE

Wenceslas Square has witnessed a great deal of Czech history. In 1848, during the revolutionary anti-Habsburg upheavals of that year, a giant mass was held here. In 1918, at the end of WWI, thousands gathered to celebrate the creation of the newly independent Czechoslovakia from the ruins of the old Austro-Hungarian Empire.

For many Czechs (and Slovaks), Wenceslas Square will forever be linked to the 1989 Velvet Revolution. Not far from the square, on Národní street, find a **memorial** to the spot where demonstrators and riot police first clashed on 17 November. In the days afterwards, angry citizens gathered on the square night after night to protest and cheer on the efforts of dissident leader Václav Havel.

 EATING IN NOVÉ MĚSTO: OUR PICKS

Kantýna: Choose your own piece of meat at the counter for the chefs to prepare, and enjoy it in an opulent former bank building. *11.30am-11pm* €€

Čestr: Splurge-worthy steakhouse behind the 'New Building' of the National Museum. Pair a meal with a trip to the museum or State Opera. *noon-11pm* €€€

Garden's: A passage opposite the entrance to the Lucerna Palace leads to a secret garden. Book ahead. *11am-10pm Mon-Sat, to 8pm Sun* €€

Hostinec na Výtoni: Duck is a beloved staple of Czech cuisine and at this picturesque inn by the river they do it better than anyone else in town. *11.30am-11pm* €€

BEST FOR A
FUN NIGHT OUT

**State Opera
(narodni-divado.cz):**
Prague's pre-eminent
venue for opera is
heavy on traditional
Italian opera at a very
high standard.

**National Theatre
(narodni-divadlo.
cz):** Performs virtually
anything from Czech
opera to avant-garde
dance.

**Reduta Jazz Club
(redutajazzclub.
cz):** Smartly dressed
patrons squeeze
into tiered seats and
lounges to soak up
the big-band, swing
and Dixieland.

**Lucerna Music Bar
(musicbar.cz):** Host
all kinds of live rock
bands – from Czech
superstars to visiting
indie rockers from
around the world.

**Duplex (duplex.
cz):** Visiting live
DJs, several rooms,
rooftop chillout zone.
Often considered the
best dance club
in town.

Nové Město is home to the city's most important public gathering area, Wenceslas Square, as well as many excellent museums, restaurants, hotels and concert venues. Many of the great moments of Czech history took place here.

Tour the National Museum

Nové Město's most important building looms high above Wenceslas Square. The neo-Renaissance bulk of the **National Museum** *(nm.cz; adult/child 300/200Kč)*, designed in the 1880s as an architectural symbol of the Czech National Revival, highlights not only the history of the Czech lands from the 8th to 20th centuries, but presents thorough exhibitions on natural history, the 'miracles of evolution' and much more. The holdings are divided into two buildings. In addition to the main historical building, the **annex** is home to two more attractions: the interactive Children's Museum and the Museum of the 20th Century, narrating last century's gripping events.

See Kafka's head on a swivel

Nové Město is home to two of Czech artist David Černý's *(davidcerny.cz)* most-popular installations. Don't leave Prague without checking out **K**, a giant rotating bust of Franz Kafka. The bust gives a mesmerising show, as Kafka's face rhythmically dissolves and re-emerges.

The Lucerna Palace shopping arcade holds Černý's oddest installation: **Kůň** (Horse). A giant dead horse – with St Wenceslas sitting astride – hangs from the marbled atrium. It's a wryly amusing counterpart to the more imposing equestrian statue of the Bohemian patron **St Wenceslas** on Wenceslas Square.

Outside of Prague

TIME FROM PRAGUE: **45MIN**

Tour majestic Karlštejn Castle

Once you've had your fill of Prague, one fun, easy day trip is to catch the train out to Karlštejn, 35km southwest of the capital, to see magnificent **Karlštejn Castle** *(hrad-karlstejn.cz; basic tour adult/child from 300/240Kč)*. This glorious pile was conceived by Emperor Charles IV in the 14th century and wouldn't look at all out of place on Disney World's Main Street. After seeing the interior, stroll through the charming town that surrounds the structure.

Two main guided tours of the castle are available, but most visitors opt for the shorter, hourlong 'basic' tour. This option provides a good introduction. You'll get glimpses into the Knight's Hall – still daubed with the coats of arms and names of the knight-vassals – as well as views of Emperor Charles IV's bedchamber, the Audience Hall and the Jewel House.

Bohemia

HISTORIC SPA | BREATHTAKING ARCHITECTURE | BIRTHPLACE OF BEER

Czechia's western province of Bohemia, with its forests and rolling hills, surrounds Prague on all sides. The region is peppered with unique sights and UNESCO World Heritage listings. To the west, the lustrous spa region – centred on Karlovy Vary – attracted the rich and famous from all around Europe in the 19th and early 20th centuries and still has the impressive architecture to match. To the south, the medieval resplendence of Český Krumlov and its glorious Renaissance castle rival Prague in terms of wow factor. Just south of Prague, the sweet aroma of hops drifts in the air in the city of Plzeň (Pilsen), where lager was invented in the 19th century and brewing traditions are still based on Bohemia's crystal-clear water and award-winning Saaz hops. Other highlights in this incredibly varied wedge of Central Europe include the magnificent former silver-mining town of Kutná Hora. People come here not just to tour the old mines but to visit the shocking, must-be-seen-to-be-believed 'Bone Church'.

☑ TOP TIP

If you've only got time for one destination in Bohemia, make it Český Krumlov, one of Europe's prettiest small towns. Plan to stay overnight, as the three-hour travel time from Prague each way can be too long for a comfortable day trip.

Karlovy Vary

TIME FROM PRAGUE: 1½HR 🚌

Karlovy Vary, or simply 'Vary' to Czechs, perhaps more than any other town in Central Europe best captures the lost glamour and elegance of 19th-century spa culture. The

---

 GETTING AROUND

Bohemia is well covered by buses and trains, though if you don't have your own wheels, the destinations listed here are probably best approached as a return trip from Prague. Whether the train or bus is best depends on the destination. For Karlovy Vary and Český Krumlov, opt for the bus, while Plzeň and Kutná Hora both lie an easy train journey away. For drivers, roads are good but get crowded on weekends. The D5 motorway whisks you from Prague to Plzeň in under an hour.

289

SOUVENIRS FROM KARLOVY VARY

Becherovka: This strong-tasting herbal liquor, made to a secret recipe, is available at every bar and grocery store.

Moser Glass: Visit the **Moser Glasswork Shop** at the Grandhotel Pupp for an eternal reminder of your trip.

Spa cups: Among the most popular Bohemian souvenirs are these curiously shaped sipping cups, available from spa kiosks.

Porcelain: Head to **Porcelain Pokorný** (*nábřeží J Palacha 924/6*) for a wide choice of locally produced wares.

Spa wafers: Typical Czech-spa tooth-rotters available at stalls in the spa zone.

Petrified roses: Roses left in the spring water accumulate mineral residue, essentially turning to stone; buy one from kiosks in the Vřídelní Colonnade.

promenades, colonnades and grand neoclassical buildings dazzle the eye. In the resort's heyday, royals like Russia's Peter the Great and members of the Habsburg monarchy hobnobbed here with the greatest thinkers, writers and composers of their time. These days, visitors come to admire the architecture and stroll the impressive colonnades, sipping on the health-restoring sulphurous waters from spouted ceramic drinking cups.

Stroll the colonnades

The best way to experience Karlovy Vary is to get out walking and see the magnificent colonnades up close. Start your stroll at the northern end of the spa area, whose entry is marked by the landmark communist-era **Hotel Thermal** (1976), built in the modern 'brutalist' style.

Inside, you'll find **Saunia** (*saunia.cz*), with access to the hotel's famous rooftop pool and views across the town. Walk south into the spa zone to find the cast-iron **Park Colonnade**. Then continue for 300m along the Teplá River to the biggest and most impressive colonnade, the neo-Renaissance **Mill Colonnade**, with five different springs.

Keep walking along Lázeňská street to the impressive **Market Colonnade**; one of its two springs, the pramen Karla IV (Charles IV Spring), is the spa's oldest. The street Stará Louka continues south for more splendour. At the end of the stroll stands the magnificent **Grandhotel Pupp**, the resort's choicest hotel.

Hit Vary's high points

For the best high-level views of pretty Karlovy Vary, make your way up to the **Diana lookout tower**, reached by **funicular railway** from behind the Grandhotel Pupp. The tower is free to climb and affords memorable views across the spa and the surrounding forested hills. There's a restaurant and cafe here and other attractions, including a worthwhile **Butterfly House** (*papilonia.cz*).

Plzeň (Pilsen)

TIME FROM PRAGUE: 1HR 🚆

Bohemia's second-biggest city of Plzeň (Pilsen) is a grainy, industrial place with a couple of stellar attractions that make it worth the trip from Prague. Beer drinkers will head straight for the Pilsner Urquell Brewery and Brewery Museum to pay homage to the place where modern lager was first produced (and still made to the original recipe). Parents with kids in

 EATING IN KARLOVY VARY: BEST FOR A SPECIAL MEAL

La Hospoda: Upscale take on a traditional Czech pub, serving staples as well delicacies like baked goose and roast boar. *11am-10pm* €€

Ukrajina: Serves the huge, local Ukrainian refugee community, offering filling fare from their war-torn home country. *11am-10pm* €€

Tusculum: The best lunch or dinner option in town, Tusculum features organic, locally sourced ingredients. Lots of vegetarian options. *noon-10pm* €€

Embassy Restaurant: The restaurant of the Embassy Hotel plates up top-notch Czech standards for Munich prices. *noon-10pm* €€€

MICHAELA JILKOVA/SHUTTERSTOCK

Pilsner Urquell Brewery

tow may bypass the brewery in favour of Techmania, a giant, hands-on science museum and arguably the best children's attraction in the country.

Learn how lager is made

The number one reason people come to Plzeň is to visit the famous **Pilsner Urquell Brewery** *(prazdroj.cz; entry 380Kč),* where Pilsner lager was first cooked up in 1842. Arguably Czechia's best known and most copied beer, it was 'invented' when a Bavarian brewer named Groll, whose task it was to upgrade the slurry the locals were forced to drink, came up with a new way of brewing. The drink – pils lager – quickly spread to Prague's pubs and the world beyond. Entry to the brewery is by guided tour. Highlights include the old cellars (dress warmly) and a glass of unpasteurised nectar (tasting far better than the Urquell you get in pubs). Get beer merch at the brewery shop.

Across the Radbuza River, close to the town's big main square, is the **Brewery Museum** *(prazdrojvisit.cz; entry 150Kč),* which offers an insight into how beer was made (and drunk) in the days before Pilsner Urquell. Highlights include a mock-up of a 19th-century pub, a huge, wooden beer tankard from Siberia and a collection of beer mats.

THANKS, AMERICA!

At the end of WWII, the area around Plzeň was liberated from Nazi Germany by the US army (not the Soviet Red army), and the people here have never forgotten. Throughout the communist era this was a problematic event – the communists even went so far as to claim Soviet troops in US uniforms freed Plzeň.

After the Velvet Revolution it became possible to talk more openly about how WWII ended in this part of Europe. Plzeň goes further than that, organising its May **Slavnosti Svobody** (Liberation Festival) with a dwindling number of US soldiers who were here in '45 as guests of honour. The 'General Patton' and 'Díky, Ameriko!' ('Thanks America!') monuments are permanent reminders of the US Army's greatest moment in Bohemia.

 EATING IN PLZEŇ: OUR PICKS

Lokál pod Divadlem: The Plzeň branch of a popular pub-restaurant serving Czech standards and good beer. *11am-11.30pm* €

Na Spilce: The pub-restaurant at the Urquell Brewery is a great place to end the day in Plzeň. *11am-10pm* €€

U Salzmannů: Plzeň's oldest tavern, with a proud tradition of serving well-chilled Urquell and belly-filling Bohemian cuisine. *11am-11pm* €€

Šenk na Parkánu: At the Brewery Museum, the beer at this typically Czech pub-restaurant is tops, but so is the traditional food. *11am-late* €€

EGON SCHIELE IN ČESKÝ KRUMLOV

Art fans may be interested in knowing the celebrated Austrian expressionist painter Egon Schiele (1890–1918) loved Český Krumlov and had a deep connection to the town through his mother, Marie Soukupová, who was born here. Schiele himself lived in Krumlov in 1911, spending most of his time painting his *Dead Towns* pictures, a far cry from the explicit nudes for which he is famous. However, things did not go well when he returned to those naked female forms. He raised the ire of the townsfolk by hiring underage girls as nude models and was eventually chased out of town.

Get 'technical'

The interactive **Techmania Science Centre** *(techmania.cz; adult/child/family 280/280/1040Kč)* is one of the best ways to entertain kids that Czechia has to offer. If you arrive in the morning, you can almost guarantee you'll be dragging your reluctant-to-leave offspring out of the door at closing time eight hours later.

It's based in a huge, former heavy-engineering workshop, and kids are free to roam all day, trying out myriad experiments as they go. Sit back and relax as your little ones mess about with magnets, splash around in the water world, become TV news presenters in front of a green screen, see if they can out-run a cheetah and build towers out of thousands of wooden blocks. There are also excellent science demonstrations, a 3D planetarium and full-sized historic trains manufactured at the Škoda engineering works.

Český Krumlov

TIME FROM PRAGUE: **3HR**

Wrapped around a tight bend in the Vltava River, deep in Bohemia's south, the must-see town of Český Krumlov is a gem in every sense of the word. It's a Prague in miniature – a UNESCO World Heritage Site, with a huge castle complex, an old town, Renaissance and baroque architecture and hordes of tourists milling through the streets – but all on a smaller scale. You can walk from one end of town to the other in 20 minutes.

Lose yourself among cobbled lanes

The best way to see the town is simply to wander the Inner Town. Pass through the narrow streets packed with tiny shops and cafes to reach **Svornosti Square**, a small, painfully pretty piazza where there's always something going on – this is the focus of the Five-Petalled Rose Celebrations and the venue for the town's Christmas market. The town hall rests on six Gothic arches on the square's northeast flank, one of them providing shelter for the tourist office. There are also a few hotels and restaurants occupying prime spots. Radiating out from Svornosti are cobbled lanes, alleyways and streets that are sheer joy to explore.

Explore Krumlov's XL castle

Wherever you wander, you can't miss Český Krumlov's dramatic **Renaissance castle** *(zamek-ceskykrumlov.cz; tours adult/child from 300/90Kč)*, which stands atop a promontory high above town. The castle began life in the 13th century and acquired

EATING IN ČESKÝ KRUMLOV: OUR PICKS

Krumlovský Mlýn: This huge, heavy-beamed tavern right on the tourist trail serves Bohemian staples and has seating next to the Vltava. *11am-10pm* €€

Krčma v Šatlavské: Slightly upmarket medieval cellar with a meat-heavy menu. Reservations essential. *11am-midnight* €€

U Dwau Maryí: Old Bohemian recipes washed down with mead and ale at this tavern where time has stood still. *11am-10pm* €€

Cikánská Jizba: Raucous, tightly-packed pub-restaurant that's been around forever. Nightly gypsy music. *5pm-midnight Mon-Sat* €€

Český Krumlov

its present appearance in the 16th to 18th centuries under the stewardship of the noble Rožmberk and Schwarzenberg families. The interiors are accessible by guided tour only, though you can stroll the grounds unsupervised. Note there are over 360 rooms in the castle, though the tours examine only a small fraction.

Three tour routes are available: Tour 1, the standard tour, takes in the opulent Renaissance and baroque interiors; Tour 2 visits the Schwarzenberg portrait galleries and their 19th-century apartments. Tour 3 explores the chateau's nearly perfectly preserved baroque theatre.

Even if you don't take the tour, part of the fun here is getting lost in the passages, arcading and gangways on the south side, which lead to the **Cloak Bridge** – an amazing Renaissance structure rising incredibly high above the gorge.

Kutná Hora

TIME FROM PRAGUE: 1HR 🚆

Enriched by silver ore, the medieval city of Kutná Hora became the seat of Wenceslas II's royal mint in 1308 and once rivalled Prague in importance. By the 16th century, the mines began to run dry, and the town's demise was hastened by the Thirty Years' War. Kutná Hora became a UNESCO World Heritage Site in 1996, luring visitors with a smorgasbord of historic sights. One of those sights is the Sedlec Ossuary, aka the 'Bone Church', a chapel decorated with thousands of stacked human bones.

FIVE-PETALLED ROSE CELEBRATIONS

Bohemia's biggest medieval bash is the **Five-Petalled Rose Celebrations** (slavnostipetilister-uze.cz), a three-day Renaissance party that takes place each June. The entire historical centre is roped off (you need a ticket to get in even if you are just sightseeing) and countless events take place in every street, park and courtyard.

The biggest day is the Saturday, which sees a huge procession featuring many a silly costume somehow squeeze its way through the crooked medieval streets. In the evening, the focus is on Svornosti Square, where there are sword fights, puppeteers, medieval music and tons of food and drink. In other places there are demonstrations of horsemanship, archery, folk music, street theatre and more food.

 EATING IN KUTNÁ HORA: OUR PICKS

Restaurace V Ruthardce: Old Bohemian tavern with heavy Czech favourites and views of the St Barbara Cathedral. *11am-11pm* €€

Dačický: An old Bohemian, wood-panelled beerhall with lager and dumplings galore. *11am-8pm* €€

U Šneka Pohodáře: Enjoy a pizza and a Bernard beer at the 'Easy-going Snail'. *11am-10pm* €

Kavárna na Kozím plácku: Cute cafe with big timber beams and mismatched 1950s furniture. *9am-7pm* €

FIVE CENTURIES IN THE MAKING

It took over 500 years to complete Kutná Hora's Cathedral of St Barbara. Construction began in 1380 under Jan Parléř, son of Petr Parléř, Charles IV's favoured architect.

The Hussite Wars soon intervened and work was interrupted, but between 1489 until his death in 1506 another star architect Matěj Rejsek (of Prague's Prašná brána fame) added the cathedral's impressive vaulting, and another architectural superstar Benedikt Ried (of Old Royal Palace at Prague Castle fame) finished off the naves after that. But when the silver ran out, construction work was abandoned completely in 1558, and for over three centuries nothing much happened. It was only in the late 19th century that the cathedral was completed in neo-Gothic style.

MIKHAIL MARKOVSKIY/SHUTTERSTOCK

Sedlec Ossuary

Gasp at a ghoulish spectacle

When the Schwarzenberg royal family purchased the Sedlec Monastery (about 2.5km northeast of the town centre) in 1870 they allowed local woodcarver František Rint to get creative with the bones in the crypt (the remains of an estimated 40,000 people), resulting in the spooky **Sedlec Ossuary** *(Kostnice; sedlec.info; adult/child 220/150Kč)*, a remarkable 'bone church'. The skeletons found their way into the church when the surrounding cemetery was reduced in size. The human remains here are mostly plague victims and those who perished in the Hussite Wars of the 15th century. Garlands of skulls and femurs are strung from the vaulted ceiling, while in the centre dangles a vast chandelier containing one of each bone in the human body.

Tour the old silver mines

Originally part of the town's fortifications, the Hrádek (Little Castle) was rebuilt in the 15th century as the residence of Jan Smíšek, administrator of the royal mines, who grew rich from silver mined illegally under the building. It now houses the **Czech Silver Museum** *(cms-kh.cz; adult/concession 90/60Kč)*. There are two guided tours; the second includes a visit down an ancient silver mine.

Gaze up at the miners' cathedral

Kutná Hora's greatest monument is the Gothic **Cathedral of St Barbara** *(chramsvatebarbory.cz)*. It rivals Prague's St Vitus in size and magnificence, its soaring nave culminating in elegant, six-petalled ribbed vaulting, and the ambulatory chapels preserve original 15th-century frescoes, some of them showing miners at work. Take a walk around the outside of the church; the terrace at the eastern end enjoys the finest view in town.

Moravia

URBAN FUN | BEAUTIFUL BAROQUE | SPOOKY UNDERGROUND

Venture into Czechia's easternmost province, Moravia, for a rurally resplendent flip on its western counterpart, Bohemia. Here, instead of industry as in the west of the country, tradition and folklore take centre stage. A dedication to vineyards and wine surpasses breweries, and big-hitter sites fill tiny towns, chronicling the former dynasties of medieval Moravia to the Habsburg Empire.

At Moravia's core is its provincial capital of Brno. The province's gateway and trendsetting student city carves a somewhat rebellious, artistic path in creating a new identity above ground, while showing off its historic cache beneath. Come here to experience the pleasures of urban Czechia – with its sights, restaurants and bars – but without the crowds of Prague.

Olomouc, to the northeast, was Moravia's first capital and a former Habsburg stronghold. This relatively sleepy city conceals its baroque beauty in a bubble – the prettiest city in the region is surprisingly overlooked. This is the place for peaceful walks through resplendent public squares while surrounded by grand churches and statues. An active student scene keeps the bar and cafe scene fresh.

Brno

TIME FROM PRAGUE: **2HR** 🚆

Prague may garner more attention, but Brno isn't trying to compete. Sure, the city isn't as pretty as Prague, but it feels somehow more authentic. Brno's vibrancy comes from its university students and start-ups that fill the city with youthful energy and creative enterprise. While Brno boasts a grand town hall and hilltop castle, many of the biggest attractions lie below ground, where history is burrowed in medieval labyrinths and subterranean cellars and crypts. Architecture buffs won't want to miss touring the early-20th-century functionalist icon, the Villa Tugendhat.

Places

Brno p295
Olomouc p298

GETTING AROUND

Both Brno and Olomouc are easily reachable by train or bus from Prague. Brno is accessible by bus or train from Vienna, Budapest and Bratislava. Long-distance and international bus companies like Flix and RegioJet use a small bus station opposite the Grandhotel Brno in the centre of the city. By car, Czechia's main D1 motorway links Prague with both Brno and Olomouc, though parking is limited. Within Moravia, fast trains run between Brno and Olomouc.

☑ TOP TIP

Guided tours of Brno's UNESCO-listed **Villa Tugendhat** (p296) are very popular and often oversubscribed. Buy tickets in advance of travelling.

Poke around Brno's underground

The fun of a visit to Brno is the chance to explore the many underground passages etched into the earth here over the centuries. Make your way first to the central **Vegetable Market** (Zelný trh), a fixture since the 13th century. Just next to the market find the entrance to a kilometre-long maze of chambers and passageways in a multilevel den from the Middle Ages. Tour the cellars of old city merchants and alchemists on a one-hour walk through the **Labyrinth under the Vegetable Market** (*podzemibrno.cz; adult/child 180/90Kč*). The nearby **Ossuary at the Church of St James** (*podzemibrno.cz; adult/child 160/80Kč*) is a more sombre walk through history: find a floor-to-ceiling, bone-stacked burial shaft of some 50,000 people who perished in the Thirty Years' War of the 17th century and the plagues. For something even more ghoulish, the **Capuchin Crypt** (*hrobka.kapucini.cz; adult/child 120/70Kč*), below the Church of the Discovery of the Holy Cross on Capuchin Square, holds a truly macabre encounter. For over 100 years, until 1784, the Friars of the Christian Capuchin Order were given a simple – respectful – burial here as mummified remains.

Climb up for Old Town vistas

Brno's medieval **Old Town Hall** (Stará radnice) features a 13th-century vaulted treasury and 16th-century judicial-themed, fresco-daubed hall, but be sure to climb the 173 wooden stairs through the clocktower centriole to the 63m-high panoramic **Renaissance pavilion** (*gotobrno.cz; adult/child 90/50Kč*), and take in the city spires and pastel veneers.

Wander the halls of spooky Špilberk Castle

The mid-13th-century fortification of **Špilberk Castle** (*spilberk.cz; adult/child 160/95Kč*) turned 18th-century notorious Habsburg lockup is today a museum complex. Top exhibitions include the **Prison of Nations** with dungeon and torture exhibits; the eight-part, artefact-packed **Brno on Špilberk** timeline from medieval stronghold to the Capital of Moravia; and a preserved 18th-century **Baroque Pharmacy** set-up. Other rooms are chock-full of artworks from Austrian Moravia to the modern day.

Tour the UNESCO-listed Villa Tugendhat

Brno was no exception to the 1920s interwar boom in modern architecture, with **Villa Tugendhat** being its greatest example of functionalist architecture. This simple, purist-style living

---

MORE ON MENDEL

It's fascinating to think that the foundations of modern genetics were laid not in a high-tech lab but on a simple lawn. Between 1856 and 1863, Gregor Mendel cross-bred pea plants in a monastery garden, studying how combinations and traits like colour and size were inherited. Being a humble monk with a green-thumbed hobby, his work was largely overlooked by the scientific community at the time.

It wasn't until the mid-20th century when genetics was studied in the context of DNA and chromosomes that Mendel's pioneering research gained the recognition it deserved. His initial observations revealed the patterns of generational inheritance and predictable ratios – discoveries now known as 'Mendel's Laws'.

 EATING IN BRNO: OUR PICKS

Bucheck: Teeming food truck tucked off the side of the Vegetable Market (Zelný trh) serving banging pulled-pork burgers. *11.30am until sold out Tue-Sun* €

Lokál U Caipla: Traditional Czech eats from goulash soup to grilled meats served with a perfectly poured beer. *11am-midnight Mon-Thu, to 1am Fri & Sat, to 1pm Sun* €€

Eggo Truck Brno: Punk rock tunes with your mimosa or coffee-fuelled breakfast or brunch at this uber-cool bistro. *9am-1pm Mon, 8am-2pm Tue-Sat, 9am-1pm Sun* €

Cà Phê Cô: Of all the Vietnamese restaurants in Brno, this trendy joint has the tastiest street-food style pho, rolls, rice and banh mi. *11am-10pm* €€

Venus of Dolní Věstonice

space, designed by German-born architect Ludwig Mies van der Rohe, was completed in 1930 for the Jewish industrialist family of Greta and Fritz Tugendhat, though they had to flee eight years later. Entry is by a 60- or 90-minute **guided tour** *(tugendhat.eu; adult/child 400/250Kč)*, ideally booked at least a month in advance. However, free garden access is without reservation, linking to the art nouveau **Villa Löw-Beer** that belonged to Greta's parents.

Admire the world's oldest ceramic figurine

The **Moravian Museum** *(mzm.cz; adult/child 170/110Kč)* has a repository of six million natural history, archaeology and ethnography artefacts housed in the reconstructed 1616 Dietrichstein Palace. Collections span the Palaeolithic era to the Middle Ages, and despite the lack of English text, come here for the museum's prized exhibit: the 30,000-year-old **Venus of Dolní Věstonice** – considered to be oldest ceramic figurine in the world, found during an excavation in the South Moravian village in 1925.

Discover the origins of genetic science

In the mid-19th century, Augustinian monk Gregor Mendel began experimenting with pea plant breeding in a monastic

BRNO'S BEST COFFEE

Adam Neubauer, three-time Barista of the Year from Brno's top coffee shop, MONOGRAM Espresso Bar, shares his favourite spots. *monogramespresso-bar.cz*

Take 5 If you want to feel like a local, head to this place in the eastern Židenice neighbourhood. There's great coffee, excellent pastries, and friendly owners behind the bar. **Kafe Fridrich** Head north of the centre to this cosy cafe. They serve tasty coffee and incredible vegan sweet treats – the banana bread is possibly the best in the city. **Typika** Brno's recently opened hangout has a coffee garden in the courtyard of the Moravian Gallery. Spacious and comfortable; you might end up staying a few hours. **Kimono** This small and hip espresso bar has a stylish wood-panelled interior and serves top brew classics and speciality coffees.

DRINKING IN BRNO: OUR PICKS

Super Panda Circus: Find the door behind the circus curtain, ring the buzzer and indulge in this unique, hidden cocktail world. *7pm-2am Mon & Tue, 6pm-2am Wed-Sat*

Bar, Který Neexistuje: The 'bar that doesn't exist' is the city's trendy-decked cocktail bar behemoth. *5pm-2am Sun-Tue, to 2.30am Wed & Thu, to 3.30am Fri & Sat*

4pokoje: This neon-lit, exposed-brick hipster hangout turns buzzing early-hours bar after its daytime bistro persona. *5pm-1am Mon & Tue, to 3am Wed, to 4am Thu-Sat*

Schrott: Brewery and bar with courtyard garden in an old industrial building with unique upcycled scrap decor. *3pm-1am Mon-Sat, 3pm-midnight Sun*

WHY I LOVE OLOMOUC

Becki Enright, Lonely Planet writer

There's Prague's showy magnificence and Brno's alternativeness, but what is it about Olomouc that makes it unmatched by any other Czech city? Its cobblestone core is a cultural evolution – you can walk through the riverside gardens below the old walls, have coffee in an old Jesuit commune, step inside baroque, Renaissance and art nouveau houses, dine in part of the old fortress and admire modern murals. I love Olomouc because it has nothing to prove; it's grand without being flashy. Like its Holy Trinity Column construction, the city's admiration comes from its own people; for us visitors, its modesty is its majesty.

Hercules' Fountain, Olomouc

garden in a suburb of Brno; humble observations that unknowingly founded genetic science. Only after his death was Mendel revered as the 'Father of Genetics' for his discovery. The **Mendel Museum** (*mendelmuseum.muni.cz; adult/child 130/100Kč*), an institution of the Masaryk University, is in the precinct of the abbey where Mendel lived and details his life's work and the story of his revolutionary findings through audiovisual exhibits and personal objects.

Olomouc

TIME FROM BRNO: **1HR**

Somehow, Olomouc has evaded discovery; Czechia's prettiest city outside Prague flies entirely under the radar. Once the seat of the Czech monarchy and Moravia's first capital before it moved to Brno, the town is plump with grandeur. Its well-preserved urban core is a municipal conservation area, protecting its main squares ringed with baroque buildings, fountains and the centrepiece UNESCO World Heritage monument the Holy Trinity Column. Olomouc was a barricaded city and Habsburg military centre until the end of the 19th century, and is now fringed by remnants of the medieval and crown fortresses.

Admire squares, fountains & UNESCO monuments

The star of Olomouc's main **Upper Square** (Horní náměstí) is the 32m-high **Holy Trinity Column** (Sloup Nejsvětější

 EATING & DRINKING IN OLOMOUC: OUR PICKS

Hanácká hospoda: Modern-twist beer hall in an old Renaissance palace, with contemporary-traditional Czech classics and share platters. *hours vary* €€

Long Story Short: From fortress bastion and military bakery to contemporary cuisine eatery, with small bites, grill plates and veggie dishes. *8am-10pm Mon-Sun* €€

Konvikt Bistro & Bar: Trendy hangout in a former 17th-century Jesuit house with ecclesiastical trims. Come here for the veggie-laden lunch menu. *8.30am-10pm Mon-Fri* €

Café na cucky: Have breakfast and brunch in this arty lounge cafe that's also a gallery and theatre space. *1-9pm Mon, 8am-9pm Tue-Sat, 9am-7pm Sun* €

Trojice), an 18th-century devotional masterpiece carved by local artists with depictions of 18 saints, 12 light bearers, 12 apostles, and the Assumption of Mary and the Holy Trinity. It took 37 years to build. The largest and tallest baroque sculpture in Europe, it was inscribed on the UNESCO World Heritage list in 2000.

The Gothic-towered, 15th-century **Town Hall** (Radnice) is known for its **Astronomical Clock,** renovated in the 1950s communist era in the style of socialist realism. The mosaic is topped by the folk tradition *Ride of the Kings* and worker murals at its base. Its moving procession of proletariat workers can be seen at noon. South of the action, **Lower Square** (Dolní náměstí) is an alfresco square of cafes punctuated with the 1715 Marian Plague Column.

Around these landmarks are six mythological baroque fountains built between 1683 and 1735. On Upper Square: the **Hercules' Fountain** (Herkulova kašna) and **Caesar's Fountain** (Caesarova kašna), and **Mercury's Fountain** (Merkurova kašna) north of it. On Lower Square: **Neptune's Fountain** (Neptunova kašna) and **Jupiter's Fountain** (Jupiterova kašna). The Rome-inspired **Tritons' Fountain** (Kašna Tritonů) is on the road to the cathedral.

Visit palaces, cathedrals & churches

The city's origins trace back to **Ostrava Castle** on **Wenceslas Square** (Václavské náměstí). Little remains of the medieval site where the Přemyslid dynasty ended with the assassination of King Wenceslas III in 1306. Some ruins are visible in the **Archdiocesan Museum**, packing 1000 years of Olomouc Archdiocese culture into art collections and the Romanesque **Bishop's Palace** *(muo.cz; adult/child from 250/150Kč)*.

The bastion is the 100m-high **St Wenceslas Cathedral** *(Katedrála sv Václava; katedralaolomouc.cz)*, a 12th-century Romanesque basilica rebuilt in Gothic style, with a crypt entombing Olomouc bishops. The adjacent **Archbishop's Palace** *(arcibiskupskypalac.cz; tours 180/120Kč)* has been the headquarters for Olomouc archbishops since 1685 and was where Franz Joseph I was declared Emperor of Austria in 1848.

The Olomouc Archdiocese's significance is reflected in its mass of Roman Catholic churches. The 15th-century Gothic **St Maurice** (Chrám sv Mořice) houses Central Europe's largest organ with 10,000 booming pipes. The tri-domed 17th-century **Church of St Michael** (Kostel sv Michala) glimmers with neo-baroque interiors, while the 18th-century **Church of the Virgin Mary of the Snow** (Kostel Panny Marie Sněžné) pops with colourful stucco. The tiny **Chapel of St Jan Sarkander** (Kaple sv Jana Sarkandra) was built in 1909 upon the prison site where priest John Sarkander was tortured to death in 1620 for refusing to divulge confessions. His canonisation as Moravia's patron saint occurred in 1995 in Olomouc with Pope John Paul II.

OLOMOUC'S PRESTIGIOUS PUNGENT CHEESE

Love it or hate it, you haven't been to Olomouc until you've tasted its culinary speciality. *Olomoucké tvarůžky* is a distinctive Czech delicacy, a matured cheese with a pungent aroma and piquant flavour. This tiny yellow dairy disk is a Haná region tradition dating back to the 15th century; it is considered Czechia's oldest cheese and an integral part of Moravian heritage. You'll find it on menus around the city, served fresh, fried, spread and garnished. The cheese is so important that it is celebrated annually at the Olomouc Cheese Festival in April: a mix of folk pageantry, chef presentations and musical revelry, with cheese and its best accompaniment, beer.

Places We Love to Stay

€ Budget €€ Midrange €€€ Top End

Prague

MAP p282

Malá Strana (Lesser Town)

Little Quarter Hostel €
Gleamingly clean and perched halfway between Charles Bridge and Prague Castle. Book early.

Dům U Velké Boty €€ The quaint 'House at the Big Boot' is set on a quiet square, five minutes' walk from the castle and Charles Bridge.

Golden Well Hotel €€€ A secluded, elegant Renaissance house that is a popular choice for honeymooners in Prague.

Staré Město (Old Town)

Ahoy! Hostel € A pleasant, welcoming and peaceful hostel (definitely not for the pub-crawl crowd).

Design Hotel Josef €€ The work of London-based Czech architect Eva Jiřičná; the minimalist theme is evident in the stark white lobby with glass staircase.

Dominican €€€ Housed in the former monastery of St Giles, this luxury hotel is bursting with character and is full of delightful period details.

Nové Město (New Town)

Sophie's Hostel € Chic step up from a typical hostel; contemporary style, with oak-veneer floors and stark, minimalist decor. Book way in advance.

Icon Hotel €€ Pretty much everything in this gorgeous boutique hotel on a hidden street behind Wenceslas Square has a designer stamp on it.

Mosaic House €€ Modern, clean and eye-catching, fully in keeping with the hotel's 1930s functionalist design ethos.

Bohemia

Karlovy Vary

Villa Basileia €€ Long-established guesthouse by the Teplá River, with very cosy rooms and a restaurant within walking distance of the city's sights.

Hotel Romance Puškin €€ Superb spa-area location, with very comfortable rooms and a cooked breakfast.

Pension Villa Rosa €€ Perched high above the river, the family-run Villa Rosa combines traditionally furnished rooms with a spectacular location.

Plzeň (Pilsen)

Hotel Astory € The most convenient hotel for the main train station and the Prazdroj Brewery, with clean and well-kept 21st-century rooms.

Hotel Rango €€ Plzeň's most character-packed boutique hotel, with sumptuous rooms, a great restaurant and a convenient location.

Český Krumlov

Hotel Myší Díra €€ This hotel has a superb location overlooking the river, and bright, spacious rooms with lots of blonde wood and quirky handmade furniture.

Hotel Konvice €€ An attractive, old-fashioned hotel with romantic rooms and period furnishings. Many rooms have impressive old wood-beamed ceilings.

Moravia

Brno

10-Z Bunker € An extraordinary stay in a former nuclear fallout shelter, foregoing comforts for a more authentic experience, even if just for one night.

Hotel Avion €€ Reconstructed functionalist-style hotel designed by Czech architect Bohuslav Fuchs. A National Cultural Monument with colour block rooms and a design museum.

Barceló Brno Palace €€€ Prestigious heritage building from the 1850s turned luxury hotel with 199 rooms, a courtyard lobby bar and fine-dining restaurant.

Olomouc

Miss Sophie's Olomouc €€ Restored 14th-century listed monument building with eight boutique-antique rooms. The in-house cafe serves a local coffee roast and homemade food.

Long Story Short €€ Sophisticated hostel with dorms and private rooms. The on-site cafe, bistro and bakery nods to the site's former use as a military bakery.

Practicalities

LGBTIQ+ Travellers
Czechs are generally tolerant of same-sex couples. Prague is the most open-minded city; the industrial areas of north Bohemia and north Moravia have the most conservative views. Rarely will openly gay couples experience any kind of negative reaction. Same-sex registered partnerships have been possible since 2006.

Health
Tap water is safe to drink and there are no serious threats to health. Watch for ticks, though, when hiking or camping in forests and grasslands. Ticks can carry two serious diseases: tick-borne encephalitis and Lyme disease. Use repellents, cover exposed legs and periodically check your skin for bites.

Insurance
Insurance is not compulsory to travel to Czechia but it's good to have. Consider a policy that covers flight cancellation and medical care. Alternatively, or additionally, EU travellers can apply for the European Health Insurance Card (EHIC) that covers emergency medical treatment free of charge.

Public Toilets
Public toilets are more plentiful in Prague than elsewhere in the country. Nearly all Prague metro stations have a public toilet. Most public toilets charge either 10Kč or 20Kč. Have small change ready.

EGOTRIPONE/SHUTTERSTOCK

Charles Bridge (p285), Prague

Opening Hours
Banks 8am–5pm Monday to Friday
Bars noon–2am
Clubs 11pm–4am Thursday to Saturday
Restaurants 11am–10pm
Supermarkets 7am–10pm
Shops 9am–5pm Monday to Friday, 9am–1pm Saturday

Accessible Travel
Authorities have made steady progress in making Czechia accessible to all, though challenges remain. Prague's airport is mainly barrier-free and has 20 contact points from which passengers with disabilities can call for assistance. As for getting around Prague, many (but not all) metro stations have lifts. Choose accommodation carefully, as only the most modern hotels have fully accessible facilities.

Public Holidays
New Year's Day 1 January
Easter Monday March/April
Labour Day 1 May
Liberation Day 8 May
Sts Cyril & Methodius Day 5 July
Jan Hus Day 6 July
Czech Statehood Day 28 September
Republic Day 28 October
Struggle for Freedom & Democracy Day 17 November
Christmas Eve/Day 24/25 December
St Stephen's Day 26 December

Language

An accent mark over a vowel in written Czech indicates it's pronounced as a long sound. Note that air is pronounced as in 'hair', aw as in 'law', oh as the 'o' in 'note', ow as in 'how', uh as the 'a' in 'ago', kh as the 'ch' in the Scottish loch, and zh as the 's' in 'pleasure'. Also, r is rolled in Czech and the apostrophe (') indicates a slight y sound.

Basics

Hello. Ahoj. *uh·hoy*
Goodbye. Na shledanou. *nuh·skhle·duh·noh*
Excuse me. Promiňte. *pro·min'·te*
Sorry. Promiňte. *pro·min'·te*
Please. Prosím. *pro·seem*
Thank you. Děkuji. *dye·ku·yi*
Yes. Ano .*uh·no*
No. Ne. *ne*
What's your name? Jak se jmenujete *yuhk se yme·nu·ye·te*
My name is ... Jmenuji se ... *yme·nu·yi se ...*
Do you speak English? Mluvíte anglicky? *mlu·vee·te uhn·glits·ki*
I don't understand. Nerozumím. *ne·ro·zu·meem*

Transport

bus	autobus	*ow·to·bus*
plane	letadlo	*le·tuhd·lo*
train	vlak	*vluhk*

One ... ticket jízdenku ... *yeez·den·ku*
to (Telč), do (Telče), *do (tel·che)*
please. prosim. *pro·seem*
one-way. jedno-směrnou. *yed·no·smyer·noh*
return. zpátečni. *zpa·tech·nyee*

Emergencies

Help! Pomoc! *po·mots*
Go away! Běžte pryč! *byezh·te prich*

Call the doctor/police! Zavolejte lékaře/policii! *zuh·vo·ley·te lair·kuh·rzhe/po·li·tsi·yi*
I'm lost. Zabloudil. *zuh·bloh·dyil*
I'm ill. Jsem nemocný. *ysem ne·mots·nee*
Where are the toilets? Kde jsou toalety? *gde ysoh to·uh·le·ti*

Eating & Drinking

What would you recommend? Co byste doporučil/doporučila? (m/f) *tso bis·te do·po·ru·chil/ do·po·ru·chi·luh*
Do you have vegetarian food? Máte vegetariánskájídla? *ma·te ve·ge·tuh·ri·ans·ka yeed·luh*
I'd like the bill/menu, please. Chtěl/Chtěla bych účet/jídelníček prosím. (m/f) *khtyel/khtye·luh bikh oo·chet/ yee·del·nyee·chek ... pro·seem*
I'll have ... Dám si ... *dam si ...*
Cheers! Na zdraví! *nuh zdruh·vee*

Shopping & Services

I'm looking for ... Hledám ... *hle·dam ...*
How much is it? Kolik to stojí? *ko·lik to sto·yee*
That's too expensive. To je moc drahé. *to ye mots druh·hair*
bank. banka. *buhn·kuh*
post office. pošta. *posh·tuh*
tourist office. turistická informační kancelář. *tu·ris·tits·ka in·for·muhch·nyee kuhn·tse·larzh*

NUMBERS	
1	**jedan** *ye·dan*
2	**dva** *dva*
3	**tři** *trzhi*
4	**čtyři** *chti·rzhi*
5	**pět** *pyet*
6	**šest** *shest*
7	**sedam** *se·dam*
8	**osm** *o·sm*
9	**devět** *de·vyet*
10	**deset** *de·set*

Tram, Prague (p280)

Arriving & Getting Around

Václav Havel Airport Prague is the main air gateway. From the airport, taxis and public transport quickly bring you to the centre. Prague's main train and bus stations are connected to major European cities and the gateways for onward travel within Czechia.

Public Transport in Prague
The public transport network of metros, trams and buses is comprehensive and relatively cheap. Buy tickets at ticketing machines in metro stations or on tram cars, and validate tickets in special yellow stamping machines.

Prague Ticket Costs
Tickets for Prague's buses, trams, metro and trolleybuses are timed with 30-minute (30Kč) and 90-minute (40Kč) validity. One-day (120Kč) and three-day (330Kč) passes are also available and can make for good value.

Driving Essentials
Hire cars at Prague airport or points around the country, and drive on the right. The speed limit is 50km/h in urban areas, 90km/h on secondary roads and 130km/h on motorways. The blood alcohol limit is 0g/L.

Long-Haul Train & Bus Travel
Train and bus routes cover the entire country and are practical for moving around. Trains are best for covering large distances, such as from Prague to Brno or Olomouc. Buses are more practical for shorter distances and select routes, as from Prague to Karlovy Vary or Český Krumlov. Most trains depart from **Praha Hlavní Nádraží** (main station). Most buses use Prague's **Florenc Bus Station**.

MONEY
Currency: Czech crown (Koruna česká; Kč)

CHANGING MONEY
Avoid private exchange booths at Prague airport or around heavily touristed areas, as these places invariably charge high commissions. Instead, withdraw cash from bank ATMs using your own debit or credit card. Czech ATMs require a four-digit PIN.

CARD PAYMENTS
Paying with credit or debit cards is common around the country and often preferable to cash. The only exceptions might be smaller shops in outlying areas. Ticket machines at Prague metro stations and on trams also allow for card payments.

TIPPING
Tipping is not widespread in Czechia but very much appreciated in restaurants and cafes. Tip 10% to reward good service or round up to the nearest 10Kč or 100Kč increment (depending on the amount).

Curated by
Anthony Ham

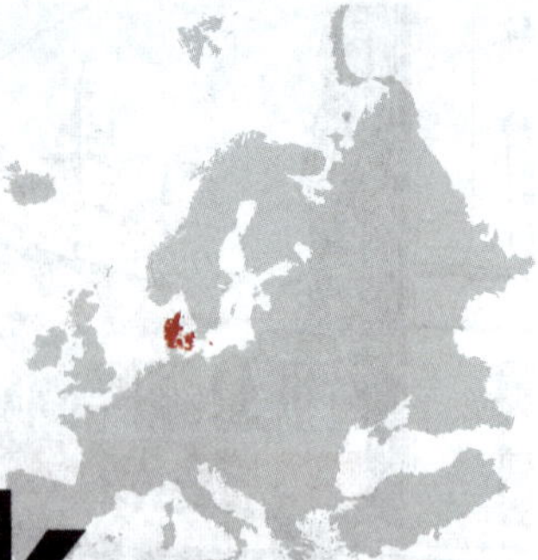

Denmark

VIKINGS, HYGGE, CASTLES AND CULTURE

Spiritual home of the fairy tale, the gentle land of Hans Christian Andersen is a whirl of whimsical castles, picture-book villages and cutting-edge creativity.

The Danes first made their mark more than a millennium ago when seafaring Vikings set out from the archipelago on conquests to Northern Europe and beyond. Much smaller than Norway and Sweden, Denmark continues to resonate far beyond its shores through design, literature, gastronomy, sustainability and, of course, hygge (cosiness, comfort and togetherness) – a cornerstone of Danish culture.

The Danes are a contented bunch, at home in one of the happiest and most liveable nations on earth. Cutting-edge yet functional design, urban planning that puts people (and bikes) before cars, and all-important work-life balance are Danish hallmarks.

Nowhere is this more palpable than in the coolest Scandinavian capital of them all: cycle-friendly and ever-so-hip Copenhagen, where travellers can find world-class museums, trendy shopping, cool nightlife and vibey neighbourhoods. It's also a foodie paradise, home of perfect pastries, artful smørrebrød and a New Nordic cuisine movement that puts Denmark top of the table.

ELENARTS/SHUTTERSTOCK

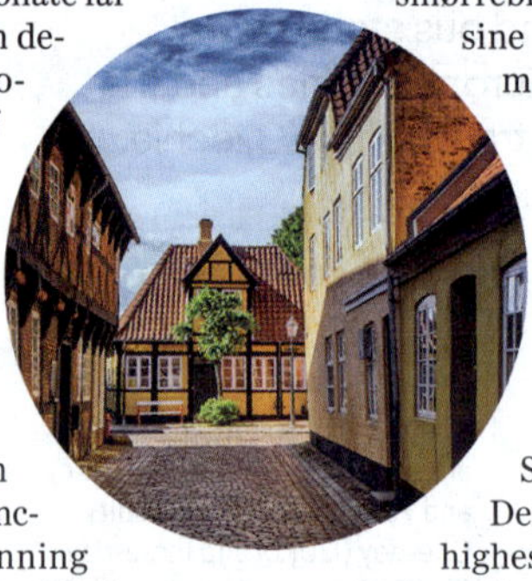

Denmark has so much more to offer visitors. Right on the doorstep are history havens Helsingør and Roskilde; further afield, there's Odense and Aarhus, packed with cultural treasures. Unlike its Scandinavian neighbours, Denmark is pancake-flat (the highest point is a mere 171m), yet its bucolic countryside, white-sand coast and island escapes mean that the great outdoors is a large part of its appeal.

THE MAIN AREAS

COPENHAGEN
Effortlessly cool, culture-rich capital. p308

ROSKILDE
Royal tombs and rock stars. p317

BORNHOLM
'Sunshine island' far away in the Baltic. p320

AARHUS
Denmark's creative second city. p324

RIBE
Medieval history and a wild tidal coastline. p327

For places to stay in Denmark, see p330

THE GUIDE

DENMARK

GREG V KING/SHUTTERSTOCK

Left: Ribe (p327); Above: Viking ship reproduction, Viking Ship Museum (p318), Roskilde

Find Your Way

Denmark is a small country, with cultural and historical sights aplenty, as well as dramatic coastline and cosy countryside. We've picked the places that help you experience the very best of this *hyggelig* nation.

CAR

Having your own wheels gives you freedom and convenience. For more remote destinations, such as northern Jutland, it's the best option. Electric charging stations are becoming commonplace, making it possible to go green.

PUBLIC TRANSPORT

The extensive national train network connects most cities and towns; however, it's wise to reserve a seat. Smaller places are served by regular buses, while the islands have car-ferry links.

Copenhagen, p308

Elegant, eclectic, designed-for-life Copenhagen is a foodie-focused, cycle-friendly joy. Denmark's crown jewel.

Roskilde, p317

Fjord-side former capital and royal resting place, home to a spectacular cathedral, a Viking ship museum and northern Europe's biggest music festival.

Bornholm, p320

Adrift in the Baltic, Denmark's 'sunshine island' is a Danish holiday hot spot and blissful escape for craftspeople and creative types.

Aarhus, p324

Denmark's youthful second city charms at every turn, from the iconic rainbow atop its art museum to the cobbles and cafes of the Latin Quarter.

Ribe, p327

Ribe's 12th-century cathedral stands proud over Denmark's oldest town. A slice of living history and gateway to the birdlife-rich Wadden Sea National Park.

Map labels

SWEDEN

GERMANY

NORTH SEA

Kattegat

Skagerrak

COPENHAGEN
KBH
Torvehallerne
Amalienborg

Roskilde
Roskilde Domkirke
Viking Ship Museum

Bornholm
Bornholms Kunstmuseum
Hammershus Slot
Østerlars Kirke
Rønne

Aarhus
Aarhus Domkirke
AROS Aarhus Kunstmuseum

Ribe
Ribe Domkirke
Ribe Kunstmuseum

ZEALAND (SJÆLLAND)
FUNEN (FYN)
JUTLAND (JYLLAND)
Lolland
Falster
Bornholm

Limfjord
Nissum Fjord
Ringkøbing Fjord
Wadden Sea
Lille Bælt
Store Bælt
Sejrø Bugt
Isefjord
Køge Bugt
Fakse Bugt
Smålandsfarvandet

Skagen, Ålbæk, Hirtshals, Hjørring, Løkken, Sæby, Brønderslev, Aalborg, Aabybro, Åsaa, Hals, Hadsund, Skørping, Hobro, Aars, Farsø, Skive, Viborg, Karup, Silkeborg, Ikast, Herning, Holstebro, Struer, Lemvig, Agger, Hurup, Nykøbing, Thisted, Fjerritslev, Mors, Randers, Auning, Bjerringbro, Ebeltoft, Rønde, Grenå, Hadsten, Horsens, Juelsminde, Vejle, Give, Billund, Varde, Esbjerg, Ribe, Tønder, Skærbæk, Bramming, Vejen, Kolding, Haderslev, Christiansfeld, Aabenraa, Tinglev, Padborg, Sønderborg, Nordborg, Fåborg, Svendborg, Assens, Middelfart, Odense, Nyborg, Korsør, Slagelse, Kalundborg, Holbæk, Roskilde, Køge, Næstved, Vordingborg, Præstø, Stege, Nakskov, Maribo, Sakskøbing, Nykøbing, Nordby, Ærøskøbing, Rudkøbing, Fredericia, Helsingør, Hillerød, Frederiksværk, Gilleleje

Læsø, Vesterø Havn, Østerby Havn

Samsø

Rømø, *Fanø*

Nyhavn (p308), Copenhagen

Plan Your Time

Bridging Scandinavia and continental Europe, Denmark is part mainland and part island chain. Discover your own Denmark through an activity-packed city break or countryside escape.

If You Only Do One Thing

● Walk through Copenhagen's **Nyhavn** (p308) dockyard and hop on a **boat tour** (p308), then visit the **Amalienborg Slot** (p314) palaces and the **Designmuseum Danmark** (p315). Refuel with smørrebrød at **Torvehallerne** (p313) then tour the opulent **Christiansborg Slot** (p313) palace and swot up on Viking history at the **Nationalmuseet** (p316).

One Week to Travel

● Feast your eyes on the astonishing cathedral and **Viking Ship Museum** (p319) in Denmark's former capital **Roskilde** (p317). At once holiday town, artistic centre and filled with historical interest, **Bornholm** (p320) is delightful. Round out your trip with time in **Aarhus** (p324) and **Ribe** (p327).

SEASONAL HIGHLIGHTS

SPRING
Spring brings **wildflowers** and **blossoms** as Copenhagen's world-famous **Tivoli Gardens** (p309) reopens after its winter break.

SUMMER
Warm, long days are punctuated by the occasional rain shower and plenty of festivals (including legendary **Roskilde Festival** (p319).

AUTUMN
Summer attractions have mostly shut, autumnal **harvests** are in full swing, **craft weeks** take over Bornholm, and **birders** flock to Ribe.

WINTER
Nights draw in, countered by twinkling lights, warming *gløgg* (mulled wine) and *æbleskiver* (spherical pancakes) at Christmas markets.

Copenhagen

VIBRANT NEIGHBOURHOODS | CULINARY JOY | HISTORIC ARCHITECTURE

GETTING AROUND

Copenhagen Airport is 8km from the city centre, with frequent train and metro connections. Metro tickets start at 24kr for a single journey. Copenhagen is very walkable, with small distances: Tivoli to Nyhavn is just 1.5km through the old centre. There's nothing more Copenhagen than jumping on a bike. Use an orange **Donkey Republic** (donkey.bike) bike by downloading the app.

☑️ **TOP TIP**

A **Copenhagen Card** (copenhagencard. com) is valid 24 hours to five days, and includes entrance to almost 90 attractions (including Tivoli, Christiansborg and Nationalmuseet) as well as public transport. Buy it in advance and activate on arrival to cover public transport from airport into town.

Encompassing candy-coloured houses, historic ports, palaces and extraordinary cuisine, Copenhagen is one of Europe's most enticing capitals. This charismatic harbour town is likely to tempt you to start dreaming of a Scandi life, whirring along on your bicycle, dressed in tastefully muted colours, with a bunch of sunflowers in your basket. There are the classic attractions such as Tivoli Gardens, the Little Mermaid statue, the royal palaces and canals, but it's the people-centred focus and visionary design that is the allure: all those well-thought-out museums, free harbour baths where you can swim in clean canal water, the nightlife of Nørrebro and Vesterbro, the bohemian flavour of Christiania. With nine centuries of royal history, some enlightened city planning and a seemingly ever-growing wave of grassroots creativity, this elegant and egalitarian city, UNESCO World Capital of Architecture 2023–2026, seems set to continue reinventing itself.

Postcard-Perfect Nyhavn

Stroll around Copenhagen's iconic dockyard

If there's one defining image of Copenhagen – or even Denmark – it's probably **Nyhavn**, a lineup of perfectly pastel townhouses along a canal. King Christian V had this 'New Harbour' dug by Swedish prisoners of war in 1673 to connect more easily to his newly cobbled plaza Kongens Nytorv (King's New Sq). Nyhavn's oldest surviving building, No 9, dates to shortly afterwards in 1681.

Copenhagen by Boat

Explore the city's waterways

Copenhagen is a city on water, so naturally one of the best ways to explore is by boat. Straightforward one-hour **Canal Tours** (stromma.com) depart from either Nyhavn or

Tivoli Gardens

TRIALS OF THE LITTLE MERMAID

Sitting on a rock in the harbour, the **Little Mermaid** (Den Lille Havfrue in Danish) has become synonymous with Copenhagen. Beer baron Carl Jacobsen commissioned her after seeing a Royal Danish Theatre ballet of the Hans Christian Andersen tale. Unveiled in 1913, the mermaid has had a torrid time over the decades: beheaded in 1964, an arm severed (then returned) in 1984, another attempted beheading in 1990 followed by a successful one in 1998. In 2003 explosives blew her off her perch, but thankfully she was discovered in the harbour and returned to her rightful spot. In 2025 there was talk of removing her because her nudity offended some... So if you find the 1.25m statue underwhelming, you can at least admire her resilience.

Gammel Strand and take in the Inner Harbour, Christianshavn, Slotsholmen Canal and the **Little Mermaid**. Localled **Hey Captain** *(heycaptain.dk)* runs boat tours for up to 12 people.

Kayak Republic *(kayakrepublic.dk)* rents out kayaks and stand-up paddleboards on Slotsholmen, and runs a 'green kayak' scheme (free rental as you collect trash while paddling; grabby-arm provided). Hire an electric-powered boat via **GoBoat** *(goboat.dk)* or **FriendShips** *(friendships.dk)*.

Another option is the **Harbour Bus** (Havnebus), a small ferry that's part of the public transport system (routes 991/992), making 10 stops between Teglholmen in the south and Orientkaj in the north.

Fairy-Tale Fun in the City

Enchanting Tivoli Gardens

One of the world's oldest operating amusement parks, **Tivoli Gardens** *(tivoli.dk; adult/child 349/174kr)* first opened in 1843. It's whimsically pretty, with vintage rides, wandering peacocks and a boating lake. Refuel at hot-dog stalls or at **Tivoli Food Hall**, which serves different world cuisines. Tivoli's landmark Japanese pagoda features a roster of Michelin-starred chefs.

Tivoli is only open during set seasons: Easter, summer, Halloween and winter, each with its own decorative theme. 'Fredagsrock' concerts take place on the outdoor Plænen stage on Friday evenings in summer.

CENTRAL COPENHAGEN & THE OLD CITY

⭐ HIGHLIGHTS
1 Amalienborg Slot
2 Nationalmuseet
3 Torvehallerne KBH

🔴 SIGHTS
4 Børsen
5 Christiansborg Slot Tower
6 Designmuseum Danmark
7 Freetown Christiania

8 Marmorkirken
9 Ny Carlsberg Glyptotek
10 Nyhavn
11 Rådhuspladsen
12 Rundetårn
13 Thorvaldsens Museum

🔴 ACTIVITIES
14 FriendShips
15 GoBoat

16 Hey Captain
17 Kayak Republic

⚫ SLEEPING
18 71 Nyhavn Hotel
19 Andersen Hotel
20 Bedwood Hostel
21 Coco Hotel
22 Danhostel Copenhagen City
23 Hotel Alexandra

24	Hotel Danmark
25	Hotel Nimb
26	Hotel Skt Petri
27	Kanalhuset
28	Steel House Copenhagen
29	Urban House Copenhagen by MEININGER
30	Villa Copenhagen

● **EATING**

31	Aamanns 1921
32	Hallernes Smørrebrød
33	Lillian's Smørrebrød
34	Restaurant Kronborg
35	Tivoli Food Hall

● **ENTERTAINMENT**

| 36 | Tivoli Gardens |

● **SHOPPING**

37	AC Perch's Thehandel
38	Hay House
39	Illums Bolighus
40	Magasin du Nord
41	Reseller
42	Time's Up Vintage

Art under the Dome

Inside Ny Carlsberg Glyptotek

Just south of Tivoli, the **Glyptotek** (*glyptoteket.dk; adult/ under 18yr 125kr/free*) houses superb sculptures by Rodin, plus paintings by Gauguin, Cézanne, Van Gogh, Pissarro, Monet and Renoir. There are also Egyptian mummies and Roman death-mask paintings, and a glorious colonnaded atrium. Many of the works on display are from early Carlsberg brewing magnate Carl Jacobsen's private art collection. The gallery is closed Mondays.

 EATING IN CENTRAL COPENHAGEN: TYPICAL DANISH

| **Lillian's Smørrebrød:** Tuck into a classic at this good-value sandwich bar, open weekdays only. *9am-2pm Mon-Fri* € | **Restaurant Kronborg:** Wood-beamed Kronborg serves classic smørrebrød on Royal Copenhagen china. *11am-5pm Sun-Wed, to 10pm Thu-Sat* €€ | **Hallernes Smørrebrød:** Inside Torvehallerne, this spot has beautifully prepared, seasonal smørrebrød. *10am-7pm Mon-Fri, to 6pm Sat & Sun* €€ | **Aamanns 1921:** Creative smørrebrød by Chef Adam Aamann at this elegant old-town restaurant. *11.30am-10pm Mon-Sat, to 5.30pm Sun* €€€ |

Christiansborg Slot

COPENHAGEN'S BEST SHOPPING

Reseller: Designer clothes are curated and resold. Great place to hunt for bargains.

Hay House: Founded by Mette and Rolf Hay, it stocks stylish, practical homewares and furniture.

Illums Bolighus: Multi-storey emporium of Danish design, selling everything from iconic Danish lighting to sheepskin mittens.

Time's Up Vintage: High-scale vintage boutique all about Euro flamboyance and glamour.

AC Perch's Thehandel: Beautifully packaged teas in a historic shop with attached tearoom.

Magasin du Nord: The city's largest and oldest department store, with lots of local labels and design, plus the excellent Hallernes Smørrebrød up top.

Gourmet Grazing at Torvehallerne

A superb covered food market

The web of streets spreading east and northeast of Tivoli is the oldest part of Copenhagen. This 800-year-old settlement is overflowing with world-class museums, compelling buildings and culinary delights. On the site that was Copenhagen's vegetable market until the 1950s, **Torvehallerne KBH** *(Market Halls; torvehallernekbh.dk)* is a delicious ode to the fresh, tasty and artisanal. Find upwards of 80 meat, fish and vegetable vendors, including high-end street-food places with anything from Korean *hotteok* pancakes to traditional Danish pickled herring and smørrebrød.

A Palace of Power

Government grandeur at Christiansborg Slot

Christiansborg Slot *(christiansborgslot.dk; adult/under 18yr 195kr/free)* has been the seat of Danish political power since the 1400s, and today is home to Folketinget (Danish parliament), prime minister's office and supreme court. Visitors can check out the king's chandelier-and-stucco-decorated chambers, the vast royal kitchen, royal stables and palace chapel. It's also possible to go underground to explore the 11th-century ruins of the former castle.

Kødbyen

Just to the north of the palace complex is the Greco-Roman-style **Thorvaldsens Museum** *(thorvaldsensmuseum. dk; adult/under 18yr 100kr/free)*, designed to house the work of superstar Danish sculptor Bertel Thorvaldsen (1770–1844).

Copenhagen from Above
Climb the Rådhus tower

Soaring above **Rådhuspladsen** (Town Hall Sq) and the Latin Quarter, the romantic Rådhus (town hall) was built in 1905. Inside, the eccentrically elaborate World Clock was designed by astro-mechanic Jens Olsen (1872–1945). The vintage interior is magnificent, but the main reason to visit is a guided tour that runs up its 105m-tall **tower** *(admission 40kr)* two or three times daily. City views at the top – count 300 steps – are fabulous.

An easier ascent can be had at the nearby 35m-tall **Rundetårn** *(Round Tower; rundetaarn.dk; adult/child 40/10kr)*, built as an observatory for astronomer Tycho Brahe in 1642. You reach the top by a gently spiralling ramp.

Royal Life at Amalienborg Slot
Visit the royal residences

Facing each other across a cobbled square, the **Amalienborg Slot** *(kongernessamling.dk/amalienborg; adult/under 18yr 125kr/free)* palaces are the main residences of the Danish royal family. Former Queen Margrethe II has lived in Christian IX's palace since 1967, while her successor, King Fred and his wife Queen Mary, live at Frederik VIII's palace. Don't miss the Royal Life Guards in tall bearskin caps, marching to the palace of Christian VIII from Rosenborg Slot for the changing of the guard at noon.

A short walk northwest is **Marmorkirken** *(Marble Church; marmorkirken.dk; dome tour adult/child 50kr/free),* also known as Frederik's Church. At 1pm on weekends, you can climb inside its enormous green-and-gold dome as part of a tour.

Design Danish-Style

Explore Denmark's design museum

The **Designmuseum Danmark** *(designmuseum.dk; adult/ under 18yr 130kr/free),* closed Mondays, is a must for fans of applied arts and industrial design. Its stupendous collections explore the evolution of Danish design, from the homespun practicalities of mid-century design stars Arne Jacobsen, Poul Henningsen, Nanna Ditzel and Finn Juhl, to exhibitions on contemporary sustainable design.

Hippy Vibes at Freetown Christiania

Denmark's alternative commune district

Set on a former military barracks and parts of Christian V's 17th-century Fortification Ring, **Freetown Christiania** *(christiania.org)* is an autonomous community established by squatters in 1971. Once notorious for 'Pusher Street', where weed and hash were sold openly, today the area feels more like a traveller hangout.

With its DIY homes, cosy garden plots, eateries, beer gardens, music venues and waterfront trails, countercultural Christiania is a fascinating foil to perfectly coiffed Copenhagen. On weekends year-round and daily in July and August, resident-led **tours** *(60kr)* depart from the Prinsessegade entrance at 3pm. Many places (including tour guides) don't accept cards, so bring cash.

Nighttime Fun in the Meatpacking District

Copenhagen's coolest corner

Once a massive abattoir complex, Copenhagen's **Kødbyen** *(kodbyen.kk.dk)* – literally 'meat town', aka the Meatpacking District – is today one of the city's biggest nightlife and creative clusters, and sits at the heart of confident, dynamic Vesterbro. It's worth a visit here by day or by night to take in the variety of extraordinary restaurants, energetic galleries and ample choice of bars, breweries and nightclubs, open late into the night.

THE STOCK EXCHANGE

In April 2024 a huge fire destroyed parts of **Børsen**, Copenhagen's historic stock exchange. The shock to the city was comparable to that of Paris' Notre Dame cathedral going up in flames. The exchange is currently undergoing restoration, but you can still see the stark, fire-blackened remains on Slotsholmen, close to Christiansborg Slot. The 400-year-old building was gutted by the fire, which also caused the collapse of its famous 52m-high spire. The spire featured four dragons with tails twisted into a spear, symbolising close ties with neighbours Norway and Sweden. According to legend, the spire preserved the building from enemy attacks and fire, so it must have taken its eye off the ball.

Nationalmuseet

Denmark's **National Museum** is the repository for all manner of Stone Age tools, Viking weaponry, rune stones and medieval jewellery. Major cutting-edge exhibitions change every couple of years and include themes such as Viking raids. It's great for kids, and there's a wonderful children's wing.

DIEGO GRANDI/SHUTTERSTOCK

Artefacts

TOP TIPS

- Allow at least three hours to do the museum justice.
- There are various free tours during the day, or you can download a free audio tour.
- The restaurant is great, serving tasty Danish cuisine.

PRACTICALITIES

- nationalmuseet.dk
- 10am-5pm ● adult/ under 18yr 140kr/free

Ground Floor

Exhibitions start with the Stone Age, and show extraordinary artefacts from the Iron Age and beyond. This is where the most splendid Viking artefacts are: huge rune stones, the 3500-year-old Trundholm sun chariot, the extraordinary Gundestrup Cauldron and a well-preserved Viking warship. There are also hefty gold hoards and Viking shields.

Also on the ground floor, the fabulous **children's wing** is designed for under 12s and offers kids the chance to play at being Vikings, shopkeepers and even pupils in a 19th-century schoolroom.

Upper Floors

The excellent **Voices from the Colonies** exhibition concentrates on personal stories to examine Denmark's colonial history in the West Indies, India, West Africa and Greenland. Look out also for Egyptian mummies, Assyrian reliefs, splendid dollhouses and a 1970s Danish sitting room.

Viking Sorceress

Don a headset and take in several rooms of audio-visual thrills narrated by a Viking sorceress at this temporary exhibition (until 2027). This conceptual section is followed by a fascinating collection of artefacts evoking the 10th century, the time when she lived.

Roskilde

EPIC HISTORY | VIKING STORIES | FAB FESTIVAL

The fjordside former capital of Roskilde has rip-roaring Viking heritage and one of Europe's largest music festivals. The unparalleled Viking Boat Museum, set against the picturesque fjord, showcases five remarkably preserved Viking boats that date back over a thousand years. Roskilde came to prominence in the Viking Age, when King Harald Bluetooth built Zealand's first wooden-stave Christian church here in 980 CE. On the same spot in the centre of town now stands UNESCO-listed Roskilde Cathedral, spanning 850 years of Danish history. As the royal mausoleum, it's also the final resting place for Danish royalty, akin to a lavish indoor cemetery.

Roskilde is famous for its namesake music festival, but the music doesn't stop when the festival packs up. The Musicon, a reimagined post-industrial neighbourhood, is home to Ragnarock, an innovative and experiential museum of modern music, where you can dive into Danish and international pop culture from the 1950s to today.

Walk among Royal Tombs

Cathedral crypts of Roskilde

The Gothic spires of **Roskilde Domkirke** *(roskildedomkirke. dk; adult/under 18yr 70kr/free)* soar majestically over the city centre. Dating back to 1170, and much changed over the centuries, the magnificent cathedral is a living testament to 850 years of Danish history, architecture and leadership. It's a regal cemetery, with 21 kings and 18 queens buried here – a sarcophagus has already been prepared in one of the 11 chapels for Margrethe II, who abdicated in 2024 after 52 years on the throne. Every hour, a mechanical clock dating to 1500 sees St George slay the dragon, prompting it to let out a death wail.

GETTING AROUND

If you're driving to Roskilde, there's unlimited free parking in front of Museumsøen and the Viking Ship Museum. Trains between Copenhagen and Roskilde (25 minutes) run up to six times an hour. Central Roskilde is compact enough to visit the main sights on foot or by bike. Bike lanes run most of the way between Roskilde and Copenhagen; it's about 30km on Roskildevej/Route 156 or about 40km on the Danish National Cycle Route 4.

☑ TOP TIP

Accommodation is relatively limited in Roskilde because it's so straightforward to get here from Copenhagen by rail. Consider staying in the capital and visiting Roskilde for an extended day trip; trains run 24/7.

THE GUIDE

ROSKILDE **DENMARK**

SHAKESPEAREAN IMAGINATION

Despite setting one of his most famous plays at **Kronborg Slot**, calling it Elsinore (the anglicised word for Helsingør, 70km northeast of Roskilde), Shakespeare had never been to Denmark. It's thought that the setting for *Hamlet* (1602) was inspired by tales of the newly expanded castle spread by both travelling players and Danish nobles, Frederik Rosenkrantz and Knud Gyldenstierne, who met the Bard in England in the 1590s. Their surnames might sound familiar – the two were written into the play as Hamlet's childhood friends. *Hamlet* was first staged at Helsingør's castle in 1816, and you can still see a performance for yourself at Kronborg Slot every August during the open-air **Shakespeare Festival** *(hamlet scenen.dk)*.

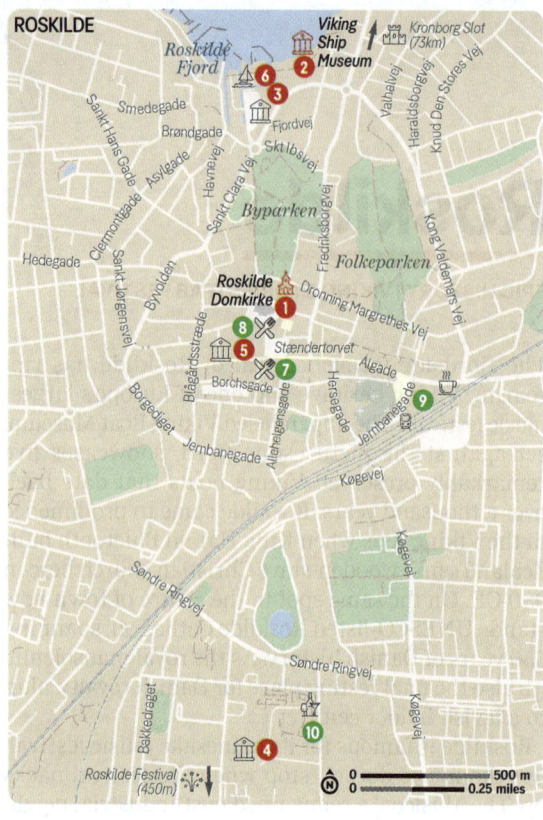

HIGHLIGHTS
1 Roskilde Domkirke
2 Viking Ship Museum

SIGHTS
3 Museumsø
4 Ragnarock
5 Sankt Laurentius

ACTIVITIES
6 Nordic Longboat Trips

EATING
7 PROP Vin og Tapasbar
8 Raadhuskælderen

DRINKING & NIGHTLIFE
9 Kaffekilden
10 Musicon Mikrobryggeri

Just 200m south of the cathedral, overlooking Roskilde's main square, is **Sankt Laurentius** *(sanktlaurentius.dk; adult/child 50kr/free)*. Summit the bell tower – spared demolition after the Reformation – then descend into the basement, where the skeletal remains of medieval graves await.

Recreate the Viking Past

Vikings and their ships

Set against a fjord-facing glass wall in the **Viking Ship Museum** *(vikingeskibsmuseet.dk; adult/under 18yr 160kr/free)* are five original Viking vessels that seem almost ready to float. Discovered at the bottom of a channel in the adjacent fjord system, they'd been weighed down with stones more than 1000 years ago. Excavated in 1962, the five 'Skuldelev ships' (named after the place they were discovered) are 25% to 75% preserved and reassembled on frames.

At the adjoining **Museumsø** boatyard, replicas of Viking ships are moored alongside traditional Scandinavian wooden vessels. From May to September, you can take to the water daily on amusing **Nordic Longboat Trips**, during which you propel a craft through the water using a mixture of sailing, rowing and ducking overhead ropes. Boat trips are included in the museum admission.

MORE ANCIENT SHIPS

Head to the **Vasamuseet** (p1095) in Stockholm to see an impeccably preserved 17th-century ship at what is Scandinavia's most visited museum.

The World of Music

Roskilde Festival and a music museum

Founded in 1971, the legendary **Roskilde Festival** *(roskilde-festival.dk; entire fest 2400kr)* is northern Europe's largest music festival. Past headliners have included Blur, Charlie XCX, Bob Dylan and Bob Marley. The event spans four days in late June/early July, plus a four-day 'warm-up' period. Plan ahead to score tickets and camping spot.

Anchored by the neon-and-gold facade of music museum **Ragnarock** *(museumragnarock.dk; adult/under 18yr 110kr/free),* the factory-turned-neighbourhood of Musicon sits between the festival grounds and Roskilde's centre. The museum delivers a multi-sensory journey through rock and youth culture from the 1950s to the present.

EATING & DRINKING IN ROSKILDE: OUR PICKS

Raadhuskælderen: Danish dishes in a modernised ancient cellar or pretty garden with cathedral view. *11am-9pm Tue-Sat* €€

PROP Vin og Tapasbar: In a lane off car-free Skomagergade, this is a low-key tapas place with wine. *noon-10pm Mon-Thu, to midnight Fri & Sat* €€

Kaffekilden: Cosy up with coffee and cake at this unpretentious cafe near the train station. *8am-8pm Mon-Fri, 9am-7pm Sat, 10am-7pm Sun*

Musicon Mikrobryggeri: Paninis and pints at this itty-bitty container-built brewery in Musicon. *2pm-midnight Mon-Thu, noon-2am Fri & Sat, to 10pm Sun*

Bornholm

ISLAND VIEWS | ARTISAN CRAFTS | VACATION VIBES

GETTING AROUND

DAT flights to Bornholm depart from Copenhagen year-round, and from Aarhus June to August. A car ferry sails to Rønne from Ystad (Sweden). An overnight car ferry sails to Rønne from Køge, south of Copenhagen, with free bunk beds.

Once on the island, the BAT bus system is comprehensive. Car hire is available at the airport.

☑ **TOP TIP**

Valid for one week, Bornholm's **Museum Pass** is a bargain. The 170kr version includes entry to the Bornholms Kunstmuseum, Bornholms Museum, Hjorths Fabrik, and Erichsens Gård in Rønne; Melstedgård (aka the farming museum) just outisde Gudhjem, and the highly-rated NaturBornholm.

A distant dot way out in the Baltic Sea, sunny Bornholm is a geopolitical enigma, an artistic retreat and a summer holiday hot spot for Danes. The boulder-strewn island surprises cyclists with precipitous slopes swooping down to the northern coastal fringes, offering taxing gradients and glorious vistas. Ferries and flights arrive in patchily attractive Rønne, Bornholm's biggest town. Cosy Gudhjem, quaint Allinge-Sandvig and arty Svaneke all have more charm and historical pedigree, and make nicer bases for touring the island. Bornholm is small enough to visit anywhere from anywhere else, but large enough to offer days of discoveries, from mysterious standing stones to cutting-edge museums. In food terms, it punches well above its weight, with old-world smokehouses and a Michelin-starred outpost of Copenhagen's Kadeau.

In 1658, Denmark lost Bornholm and most of what's now southern Sweden to its Scandinavian neighbour. Bornholm alone was returned, however, hence its isolation from the rest of modern Denmark.

Culture on the Coast

The many charms of Gudhjem

Thronged with visitors in summer, picturesque Gudhjem snakes steeply down from a prominent windmill to a pretty little port. The coastal strip features cafes, ice-cream parlours and Bornholm's oldest glass studio **Gudhjem Glasrøgeri** *(gudhjem-glasroegeri.dk; free),* occupying a former smokehouse. On the town's upper heights, the **Gudhjem Museum** *(gudhjemmuseum.dk; adult/under 18yr 50kr/free)* has set up shop in a former train station, and focuses on local art and handicrafts; it's closed Monday to Wednesday.

BORNHOLM

Inset: Gudhjem

BALTIC SEA

Nørresand
Løkkegade
Gudhjem Harbour

18
5
12
11

Ertholmene Islands

0 ——— 200 m
0 ——— 0.1 miles

Sandvig
7 15
13
8
10 17 Allinge
2
Hammershus Slot

Vang
Olsker
Tejn
14

1
Bornholms Kunstmuseum
See Gudhjem
6 Melsted

BALTIC SEA

Hasle
4
Klemensker
Rø Plantage
3 *Østerlars Kirke*
Østerlars

Nyker
Østermarie
9 Østermarievej Svaneke

Almindingen
Hallegaard
Årsdale

Rønne
Rytterknægten
Ssøndre Ringvej
Nylars
Åkirkeby
Rønnevej
Nexø

Arnager
Søndre Landevej
Pedersker
Poulskervej
Balka
Snogebæk

16
Strandmarksvej
Dueodde

N
0 ——— 10 km
0 ——— 5 miles

⭐ **HIGHLIGHTS**
1 Bornholms Kunstmuseum
2 Hammershus Slot
3 Østerlars Kirke

🔴 **SIGHTS**
4 Grønbechs Gård

5 Gudhjem Glasrøgeri
6 Gudhjem Museum
7 Hammeren
8 Hammeren Fyr
see 1 Helligdomsklipperne
9 Louisenlund
10 Madsebakke

🔴 **ACTIVITIES**
11 M/S Thor

⚫ **SLEEPING**
12 Gudhjem Vandrerhjem
13 Nordlandet
14 Stammershalle Badehotel

15 Strandhotellet

🟢 **EATING**
see 4 Hasle Røgeri
16 Kadeau
17 Nordbornholms Røgeri
18 Norresan

THE BORNHOLM UPRISING

In 1658, after Denmark lost a series of wars, it was forced to cede large swathes of territory – including Bornholm – to Sweden. The island's residents, fiercely loyal to Denmark and unhappy with Swedish rule, soon rebelled. Led by local leader Jens Pedersen Kofoed, they launched a coordinated uprising on 8 December 1658, assassinating Swedish commander Johan Printzensköld and overwhelming the small garrison. Recognising the headache of holding Bornholm and its limited strategic value, Sweden chose not to reconquer the island. By 1660, under the Treaty of Copenhagen, Bornholm alone was officially returned to Denmark to become an isolated outpost just off the coast of what is now southern Sweden.

Gudhjem Glasrøgeri (p320)

Several times a day in summer, the wooden cutter **M/S Thor** *(ms-thor.dk; round trip adult/child 140/90kr)* departs from Gudhjem's dainty harbour for a 30-minute cruise along a coastline etched with towering granite pillars and deep caves. The boat stops at a jetty beside **Helligdomsklipperne** ('sanctuary cliffs'), once a place of pilgrimage. Disembark and climb rocky steps to the island's top art gallery, **Bornholms Kunstmuseum** *(bornholms-kunstmuseum.dk; adult/under 18yr 100kr/free),* closed Monday. Instead of returning to Gudhjem by boat, you can take the popular clifftop walk (6km, 1½ hours); it's especially pretty at sunset.

Spiritual Bornholm

Round churches and sacred stones

Around 5km south of Gudhjem, **Østerlars Kirke** *(oesterlars kirke.dk; adult/child 25/10kr)* is the biggest and most memorable of Bornholm's four highly distinctive round churches from the 12th and 13th centuries. With heavy buttresses, conical spires and 2m-thick walls, they are different from any other churches in Denmark. At Østerlars, visitors can squeeze through a claustrophobic staircase to the upper levels, where slot-like shooting holes support the theory that these churches were originally used as defence towers to guard against raiders.

Far older than the round churches are Bornholm's various standing stones. Some are natural 'erratics' known as *rokke-stenen* – rocking boulders that pivot miraculously. Other stones were erected at Iron Age and Viking-era gravesites, most impressively at **Louisenlund**, hidden in woodlands 4km east of Østermarie. On **Madsebakke**, a hill behind Allinge, bronze-age petroglyphs etched on to boulders depict curvaceous boats, footprints and sun wheels, evidence of a ritualistic culture on Bornholm some 3500 years ago.

Hammer of History

Medieval fortress and majestic views

At Bornholm's northern tip, the gargantuan ruins of **Hammershus Slot** *(free)* loom ominously over the windblown coast like a set from *Game of Thrones*. A beautifully designed visitor centre explains the history of the 'hated castle' that symbolised the imposition of power on Bornholm by tyrannical outsiders.

To reach the ruins, you could hike in from Sandvig, a fairly easy 3km on a path passing Hammersø, Bornholm's largest lake with zip-lining in the adjacent quarry pond. Longer and taxing but more interesting alternatives loop around, or over, the windswept craggy headland called **Hammeren**. With a car, you could drive right to Hammeren's highest point, **Ørnebjerget** (Eagle's Hill), for panoramic vistas towards Sweden from atop **Hammeren Fyr** lighthouse.

Back along the coast, the northern twin towns of **Allinge-Sandvig** delight with chocolate-box cottages, classy seaside hotels, a wealth of summer dining options and two working smokehouses.

Island of Creativity

Meet Europe's first 'World Craft Region'

What draws so many artisan craftspeople, chefs, artists and nature lovers to Bornholm? The island's clay certainly inspires ceramicists, and glass-making is a particularly well-established art form – so much so that Denmark's Royal Academy runs its glass and ceramics programme on the island. The World Crafts Council bestowed the title of 'World Craft Region' on Bornholm, the planet's first island community to receive it. For a comprehensive introduction to the craft scene, start by visiting **Grønbechs Gård** *(groenbechsgaard.dk; adult/under 18yr 75kr/free),* a one-stop crafts showcase housed in a restored 19th-century warehouse in Hasle. Its craft shop is probably the best on the island.

If you want to explore a single village on a relaxed craft-based day out, a good choice is the loveable harbour town of **Svaneke**. A central cluster of venues includes artist studios, shops selling glassware and jewellery, and hands-on workshops. On Wednesday and Saturday mornings, the **Svaneke Torvedage** market fills the central square. At the top of town, the bizarre three-legged concrete pyramid is in fact a surrealist water tower from 1952 by Danish architect Jørn Utzon (who went on to design the Sydney Opera House).

BORNHOLM'S SMOKEHOUSES

Buildings in Bornholm with distinctive, upturned Y-shaped chimneys were originally smokehouses *(røgerier)* for curing herring, using alder-wood smoke. Locals insist that 19th-century Scottish visitors to Christiansø introduced this method, which later became an economic mainstay. Gudhjem became known as the '100-chimney town' for its many smokehouses, and across Denmark it's still associated with a classic *smørrebrød* (open-faced sandwich) of smoked herring on rye bread with chives and raw egg yolk called *Sol over Gudhjem* ('sun above Gudhjem'). Despite the West Baltic fishing ban, Bornholm has a dozen working *røgerier* smoking herring imported from Jutland. Hasle's *røgeri* still uses century-old equipment.

 EATING IN BORNHOLM: OUR PICKS

Norresan: Lavish smørrebrød, cakes and rhubarb gin in a whitewashed Gudhjem smokehouse by the water. *noon-9pm* €	**Nordbornholms Røgeri:** This highly regarded Allinge smokehouse serves locally smoked fish, salads and soup. *11am-10pm* €€	**Hasle Røgeri:** Great value, all-you-can-eat buffet heavy on the herring. Sit inside a handsome Rønne building or on a lawn with sea views. *10am-9pm* €€	**Kadeau:** Bornholm's Michelin-starred wunderkind, with impeccable sustainability credentials, is improbably remote. *6-11.30pm Thu-Sun, lunch Fri & Sun Jul* €€€

Aarhus

ART & CULTURE | MUSEUMS | LOCAL GASTRONOMY

GETTING AROUND

Aarhus Airport is 45km northeast of the city. Airport buses are timed to sync with international departures and arrivals. Trains to Copenhagen (three to 3½ hours) leave Aarhus roughly half-hourly. If you don't plan on cycling to sights beyond the centre, make use of Aarhus' local bus network. Bus 18 runs to Moesgaard Museum; buy tickets on board or using the Midttrafik app. The Aarhus light rail (Letbane) has a handy stop at Dokk1.

☑ **TOP TIP**

Most of the city is walkable. To speed things up or roam further, grab a bicycle. Download Donkey Republic's smartphone app to rent an orange bike from locations around the city, or try **Refurbish Bike** *(179kr per month),* a start-up which salvages abandoned bikes and gets them roadworthy again.

Buzzing with students, vibrant and creative, Denmark's youthful second city is like a mini Copenhagen, with world-class museums and galleries, waterside fun and fabulous dining. Aarhus (pronounced 'oar-hus') also goes by the nickname 'Smilets By' (City of Smiles), a slogan adopted in the 1930s that's stuck around – nothing to do with those happiness indexes, even if Aarhus does tend to come out on top.

The city's earliest origins were in the Viking settlement of Aros ('mouth of the river'), roughly where the cathedral is today. In the 1930s, the city filled in its river and some questionable planning saw a multilane road and fenced-in rail track block access to the waterfront. Thankfully, the river was reclaimed in 1958, the road narrowed and new attractions appear to be added every year. As elsewhere in Denmark, you can swim close to the city, and eating, drinking and leisure activities bejewel the waterfront.

Rainbow Over Aarhus

Art adventure at ARoS museum

ARoS Aarhus Kunstmuseum *(aros.dk; adult/under 18yr 180kr/free)* is a fantastic art museum, not even considering its roof-mounted rainbow crown. The work of Danish-Icelandic artist Olafur Eliasson, Your Rainbow Panorama is a 150m-long looping skywalk of multicoloured glass from which you can soak up dreamy, Kodak-filtered panoramas of the city.

Highlights inside the red-brick building include *Boy,* an astonishingly lifelike sculpture of a crouching child by Australian artist Ron Mueck. At 5m tall, the child's vulnerability is incredibly vivid. In 2026 a new extension to the museum opens, featuring a vast and ambitious architectural artwork entitled *The Dome, a Skyspace* by American artist James Turrell.

Allow at least half a day here, or make an evening of it: ARoS is open until 9pm on weekdays, except Monday when it's closed.

Bohemian Aarhus

Stroll through the colourful Latin Quarter

Aarhus's **Latin Quarter** (Latinerkvarteret) is a kernel of cobbled streets lined with mustard-yellow and ochre tiled-roof buildings. It's the city's prettiest district, with independent boutiques, cute cafes and creative bistros competing for your attention. Comprising part of the city's old Viking core, this central area extends north and west from Aarhus Domkirke.

History-hunters can dig up some handsome half-timbered merchant houses, especially along narrow **Mejlgade**. If headed westwards, make for idyllic **Møllestien**, a picture-book cobblestone street of pastel-hued cottages and rambling roses.

Sacred Spire of Aarhus

Denmark's tallest church

The pointed tower of **Aarhus Domkirke** *(aarhusdomkirke. dk; free),* Denmark's tallest and longest church, is a local landmark. Inside, its whitewashed interior safeguards pre-Reformation frescoes, including a 1497 depiction of St George in which an almost cartoonish dragon lies on its back, vanquished by the saint. A stunning gilt altarpiece (1479) by late-Gothic

PARTY IN AARHUS

Youthful Aarhus – home to up to 44,500 university students during term time – loves to make a night of it. Drinkers gravitate to the Latin Quarter for wine bars and hip hangouts; **Frederiksgade** for boisterous pubs and live jam sessions; and **Frederiksbjerg**, south of the station, for craft cocktails and brewpubs. To drink like a local, order an 'Aarhus Set': a Ceres Top beer with a chaser of liquorice-like Arnbitter; both were originally created in Aarhus. With arguably Denmark's best music scene, Aarhus features eclectic offerings, from **Musikhuset Aarhus** (*musikhusetaarhus. dk*) concert hall to live-music events at **Train** (*train.dk*), as well as the excellent arthouse cinema **Øst for Paradis** (*paradisbio.dk*).

Aarhus Rådhus

German sculptor Bernt Notke is folded in five different ways to display different narratives at different times of year. Climb the cathedral **tower** *(adult/child 20/5kr),* inaccessible during services, for a view over the city rooftops.

Mid-Century Design Icon

Arne Jacobsen's town hall

The grey-marble-clad **Aarhus Rådhus**, co-designed by pioneer of Danish modernism Arne Jacobsen, was completed in 1942. It almost didn't have a clock tower until citizens looked at the plans and found them lacking. Pop inside to admire the clean lines, parquet floors and vintage elevators, or sign up for a guided tour with **Aarhus Guiderne** *(aarhusguiderne. dk; adult/child 125/50kr).*

 EATING IN AARHUS: OUR PICKS

Aarhus Street Food: Sprawling hive of global food-truck fare and bars, in an old bus garage. Many dishes are under 100kr. *11.30am-9pm* €

OliNico: Laid-back vibes, huge portions of mussels and a three-course dinner menu for 175kr. *noon-2pm & 5.30-9pm Mon-Sat, 5.30-9pm Sun* €

Restaurant Hærværk: New Nordic cuisine breaks the mould with sustainable menus that change daily. *5-11pm Tue-Sat* €€€

Substans: This 11th-floor, Michelin-starred spot spins work-of-art dishes from local produce; fabulous port views. *6pm-midnight Tue-Thu, from noon Fri & Sat* €€€

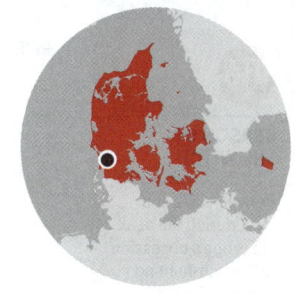

Ribe

OLD TOWN | MEDIEVAL CATHEDRAL | NIGHT TOURS

The jewel in the crown of southern Jutland is Ribe. The country's oldest town and historic Denmark at its most photogenic, this is where a night watchman still plods through antique streets, spinning yarns as he goes. A host of half-timbered chocolate-box houses huddle around the nation's first cathedral, with its 52m-high tower looking out over marshes to the shimmering wetlands of the Wadden Sea.

Such is the sense of living history in Ribe that the entire old town is a designated preservation zone. You can sup a beer in one of Denmark's oldest inns, patrol cobblestones after dark on a free nightly guided tour, then bed down in antique lodgings with wonky floors and low ceilings. Throw in a fine-art gallery showcasing Denmark's Golden Age masters, museums about Vikings and witches, and you've got the history part of any southern Jutland tour wrapped up.

Jewel of the Marshes

Ramble through historic Ribe

Designed in the Romanesque style of the early Middle Ages, **Ribe Domkirke** *(ribe-domkirke.dk; free)* dates from around 1225. Later Gothic additions include the 52m-tall **Commoners' Tower** *(adult/child 25/15kr)*, which you can climb for inspiring views out to the Wadden Sea. A museum partway up the climb details the cathedral's construction history, explaining how an earlier tower collapsed on Christmas morning 1283, killing several townspeople.

After exploring the cathedral, cross the south side of the square to **Kannikegården** *(free)*, a contemporary red-brick building sheltering the excavations of Denmark's oldest Christian cemetery. On nearby Puggårdsgade is a 16th-century manor house, the charmingly crooked **Taarnborg**, where a succession of Ribe bishops lived. Take Grønnegade to duck into narrow alleys that lead down and across pretty Fiskergade to

---

GETTING AROUND

Ribe is easy to explore on foot. Most sights and the train station are within a 10-minute walk of Torvet, the central square. Hire bicycles from **Danhostel Ribe** (p330) or electric bikes from **Ribe Cykellager** *(ribecykellager.dk)*. Danhostel Ribe has free four-hour parking for motorists, or drive a bit further on Saltgade for free 48-hour parking.

Ribe is connected by rail to Esbjerg, where you can change trains for Aarhus.

☑ TOP TIP

The **Night Watchmen** tour isn't the only themed walk on offer in Ribe. In summer, weekly ghost walks depart from Museet Ribes Vikinger on Wednesday evenings, recounting spooky tales like that of Maren Spliid, Ribe's most famous witch. Tours are in Danish and English.

SEASON OF THE WITCH

Between 1572 and 1652, during the peak of Europe's obsession with witch-hunting, Ribe conducted 22 witch trials. The most famous by far was against Maren Spliid, the wife of a tailor and a wealthy, respected citizen. After the case was roundly dismissed at trial, her accuser – another tailor, albeit less successful than Maren's husband – appealed to the Danish king, who was more than a bit obsessed with magic and devilry. Spliid was tried a second time, but again acquitted. The case then went to the Supreme Court where, unfortunately for Maren Spliid, the king himself was the judge. She was tortured and burned at the stake near Ribe in 1641.

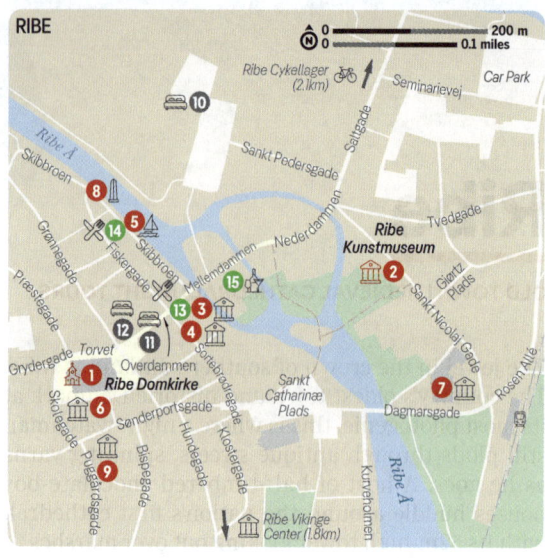

RIBE

⭐ **HIGHLIGHTS**
1 Ribe Domkirke
2 Ribe Kunstmuseum

🔴 **SIGHTS**
3 Hex! Museum of Witch Hunt
4 Jacob A Riis Museum
5 Johanne Dan
6 Kannikegården
7 Museet Ribes Vikinger
8 Stormflodssøjlen
9 Taarnborg

⚫ **SLEEPING**
10 Danhostel Ribe
11 Hotel Dagmar
12 Weis Stue

🟢 **EATING**
13 Quedens Gaard
14 Sælhunden
see 12 Weis Stue

🟢 **DRINKING & NIGHTLIFE**
15 Terpager & Co

Skibbroen and the riverfront. Here you'll find the **Johanne Dan**, an old sailing boat with a flat bottom. Close by, **Stormflodssøjlen** shows the high-water mark of a flood in 1634 that claimed hundreds of lives.

On the lookout for floods, fires and ne'er-do-wells were the night watchmen, a job abolished in 1902 then reinstated in the 1930s as a tourist attraction. The free **Night Watchmen Tour** (in Danish and English) takes place nightly from May to October. Meet outside the **Weis Stue** (p330) inn at 8pm; no booking required.

 EATING & DRINKING IN RIBE: OUR PICKS

Quedens Gaard: Have breakfast Danish-style in a cobbled courtyard or snack on sandwiches, burgers and salads. *10am-6pm €*

Weis Stue: Meat-heavy mains, fish platters and lunchtime smørrebrød beneath beams in one of Denmark's oldest inns. *11.30am-3pm & 5-9pm €€*

Terpager & Co: Historic spot for nibbles and wine, a passion of the family owners. Fine food shop and deli, too. *11am-5.30pm Mon-Fri, 10am-4pm Sat €€*

Sælhunden: Black-and-white riverfront spot serving fish-centric Danish fare and smørrebrød on starched white tablecloths. *11.30am-10pm €€€*

Vikings, Witches & Watercolours

Ribe's wonderful museums

In a grand mansion from 1864, **Ribe Kunstmuseum** *(ribekunstmuseum.dk; adult/under 18yr 90kr/free)* has been around long enough to acquire some of Denmark's best artworks. Ribe is one of Scandinavia's oldest towns, and **Museet Ribes Vikinger** *(ribesvikinger.dk; adult/under 18yr 110kr/free)* does a fine job of unwrapping its history from its origins as a Viking trading post in the 700s through the thriving Middle Ages and beyond.

The compelling **Jacob A Riis Museum** *(jacobariis museum.dk; adult/under 18yr 95kr/free)* tells the tale of a boy from Ribe who emigrated to the US in 1870 and went on to become a noted social reformer. Sharing the same space, **Hex! Museum of Witch Hunt** *(hexmuseum.dk; adult/under 18yr 110kr/free)* ramps up the fear factor with displays that put light and sound to ingenious use.

Kids can embrace their inner Viking at **Ribe VikingeCenter** *(ribevikingecenter.dk; adult/ child 145/75kr),* a hands-on experience featuring costumed performers, traditional workshops and even 'warrior training'. It's 3km south of town.

VIKING DENMARK
See five original Viking vessels in Roskilde's excellent **Viking Ship Museum** (p319).

Places We Love to Stay

€ Budget €€ Midrange €€€ Top end

Copenhagen MAP p310

Urban House Copenhagen by MEININGER € Cheery, central hostel with rooms – all en-suite – sleeping from three to 10 people.

Steel House Copenhagen € Excellent hostel close to the central Lakes area. Pods provide a sense of privacy, while facilities include a pool and a gym.

Danhostel Copenhagen City € Fantastic views from a tower block overlooking the harbour, just south of Tivoli. Dorms and private rooms are bright, light and modern.

Bedwood Hostel € Cosy hostel with six- to 12-bed dorms, in a historic wood-beamed warehouse from 1756 on Nyhavn waterfront. Privacy curtains and bedside power sockets.

Hotel Danmark €€ Cosy boutique hideaway with muted colours inspired by the nearby Thorvaldsen Museum. Heavenly beds, tactile fabrics and restrained, elegant Danish furniture.

Andersen Hotel €€ White-on-white gives way to bold, playful design; Molten Brown bathroom amenities and complimentary evening wine (5pm to 6pm).

Hotel Alexandra €€ The furniture of Danish design deities such as Arne Jacobsen and Verner Panton graces the interiors of refined yet homey Alexandra.

Hotel Skt Petri €€ Former department store, designed with a charcoal palette softened by blonde-timber flooring and rich splashes of colour. Best views are from the 4th floor and above.

Kanalhuset €€ Beautiful rooms and apartments with softly glowing colours, set in a historic canal-side building. Book well ahead.

Rye 115 €€ Lovely location close to the Lakes and bars, boutiques and restaurants of Nørrebro. Simple *hyggelig* rooms have lots of charm.

Coco Hotel €€ Chic hotel with a Parisian vibe, and fresh greens and blues in the rooms; some have views over the rooftops.

Hotel Nimb €€€ Part of historic Tivoli Gardens, this boutique belle has antiques, contemporary comfort (especially in the new wing), a rooftop bar and a pool. Some suites have a terrace with view.

Villa Copenhagen €€€ Between Tivoli and Copenhagen Central, this stylish hotel is a handsome conversion of the palatial former Post and Telegraph Head Office. Rooftop pool.

71 Nyhavn Hotel €€€ Character, comfort and great views in two striking, 200-year-old canal-side warehouses.

Bornholm MAP p321

Gudhjem Vandrerhjem € Half-timbered hostel with fabulously central coast-facing location. Dorms are only available in low season.

Strandhotellet €€ Historic sea-facing hotel in Sandvig, given a loving makeover by its recent husband-and-wife owners. Great quality meals too.

Nordlandet €€€ Splurge at this classy seafront getaway, raised above rock pools south of Sandvig. By the folks behind Michelin-starred restaurant Kadeau.

Stammershalle Badehotel €€€ One of Bornholm's top choices is this imposing, early-20th-century bathing hotel overlooking a rocky stretch of coast between Gudhjem and Tejn. Excellent restaurant. Book well ahead.

Aarhus MAP p325

Hotel Guldsmeden €€ A top pick for its excellent location, warm staff, rooms with Persian rugs, pretty garden oasis and relaxed, stylish ambience.

Hotel Oasia Aarhus €€ Great city-centre choice with Hästens beds (some of the most comfortable in the world) and light-filled, minimalist rooms.

Villa Provence €€€ Provençal country style dominates Aarhus' most charming boutique hotel. Superior rooms are larger but standard have the same attention to detail.

Ribe MAP p327

Danhostel Ribe € Skyline views, quiet location and a short walk into the old centre. Bike hire available. Occasional rambunctious school groups.

Hotel Dagmar €€ Billed as Denmark's oldest hotel, Dagmar comes with sloping floors and cathedral views, charming old-world tiling, artworks and antiques.

Weis Stue €€ Eight small, wonky rooms above Ribe's oldest inn, all with creaking floorboards and bags of character. Bathrooms are shared.

Practicalities

Tourist Information

Denmark is generally well served by helpful tourist offices and multilingual staff. Each town and region publishes an annual brochure covering the things travellers need to know, and has a website covering accommodation options and practical info.

Visas

Schengen country citizens can enter freely for any length of stay. From late 2026, visitors from the UK, US, Canada, Australia and New Zealand will need an ETIAS travel authorisation. Nationals from other countries should check *nyidanmark.dk*.

Time

Time in Denmark is one hour ahead of GMT/UTC. Clocks are moved forward one hour for daylight saving time from the last Sunday in March to the last Sunday in October. Denmark uses the 24-hour clock system.

Smoking

Danes are surprisingly heavy smokers – around 16% of the adult population smokes. Smoking is banned in restaurants, bars and clubs, but allowed in some small pubs.

PHOTOKARI.COM/ALAMY

Public Holidays

New Year's Day 1 January
Maundy Thursday Thursday before Easter
Good Friday Friday before Easter
Easter Sunday in March/April
Easter Monday Monday after Easter
Great Prayer Day Fourth Friday after Easter
Ascension Day Sixth Thursday after Easter
Whitsunday Seventh Sunday after Easter
Whitmonday Seventh Monday after Easter
Constitution Day 5 June
Christmas Eve 24 December
Christmas Day 25 December
Boxing Day 26 December
New Year's Eve 31 December

Opening Hours

Banks 10am–4pm Monday to Friday
Bars and clubs 4pm–midnight, to 2am or 5am Friday and Saturday
Cafes 8am–6pm
Restaurants noon–10pm (earlier on weekends)
Shops 10am–6pm Monday to Friday, to 2pm or 4pm Saturday, often closed Sunday (except supermarkets)

Etiquette

• Trains and tours run on time and aren't a minute late. Danes operate similarly in social situations.
• When you go to just about any place there can be a queue, there's invariably a machine dispensing numbered tickets. Grab a ticket as you enter.
• As you raise your glass to make a toast, say *'Skål!'* (Cheers!) and make eye contact with everyone.

Language

Many visitors to Denmark get around without speaking a word of Danish, but just a few phrases go a long way in making friends, inviting service with a smile, and ensuring a rich and rewarding travel experience – you could be invited in for some hygge, experience a sublime meal or grab that great shopping bargain.

Basics

Hello. Goddag. *go·da*
Goodbye. Farvel. *faar·vel*
Yes. Ja. *ya*
No. Nej. *nai*
Please. Vær så venlig. *ver saw ven·lee*
Thank you. Tak. *taak*
Excuse me. Undskyld mig. *awn·skewl mai*
Sorry. Undskyld. *awn·skewl*
What's your name? Hvad hedder De/du? *va hey·dha dee/doo*
My name is … Mit navn er … *mit nown ir …*
Do you speak English? Taler De/du engelsk? *ta·la dee/doo eng·elsk*
I don't understand. Jeg forstår ikke. *yai for·stawr i·ke*

Directions

Where's …? Hvor er …? *vor ir …*
What's the address? Hvad er adressen? *va ir a·draa·sen*
Could you please write it down? Kunne De/du skrive det ned? *koo·ne dee/doo skree·ve dey nidh*
Can you show me (on the map)? Kan De/du vise mig det (på kortet)? *kan dee/doo vee·se mai dey (paw kor·tet)*

Signs

Indgang/Udgang Entrance/Exit
Åben/Lukket Open/Closed
Ledige værelser Rooms available
Varm/Kold Hot/Cold

Time

What time is it? Hvad er klokken? *va ir klo·ken*
It's (two) o'clock. Klokken er (to). *klo·ken ir (toh)*
Half past (one). Halv (to) (lit: half two). *hal (toh)*
morning morgenen *mor·nen*
afternoon eftermiddagen *ef·taa·mi·da·en*
evening aftenen *aaft·nen*
yesterday i går *ee gawr*
today i dag *ee da*
tomorrow i morgen *ee morn*

Emergencies

Help! Hjælp! *yelp*
Stop! Stop! *stop*
Go away! Gå væk! *gaw vek*
I'm ill. Jeg er syg. *yai ir sew*
Could you help me, please? Kan De/du hjælpe mig? *kan dee/doo yel·pe mai*
Call …! Ring efter …! *ring ef·ta …*
 a doctor en læge. *in le·ye*
 the police politiet. *poh·lee·tee·et*

Eating & Drinking

What would you recommend? Hvad kan De/du anbefale? *va kan dee/doo an·bey·fa·le*
What's the local speciality? Hvad er den lokale specialitet? *va ir den loh·ka·le spey·sha·lee·teyt*
Cheers! Skål! *skawl*

NUMBERS

1
en *in*

2
to *toh*

3
tre *trey*

4
fire *feer*

5
fem *fem*

6
seks *seks*

7
syv *sew*

8
otte *awte*

9
ni *nee*

10
ti *tee*

Copenhagen

Arriving & Getting Around

Most travellers will enter at Copenhagen airport. It's only 8km to the city centre and takes less than 15 minutes by train or metro; taxis take longer.

Booking Trains
Buy train tickets from station machines, ticket offices or via the DSB website or app. Reservations are not free, but for longer distances it can be worthwhile.

Rejsekort
Fares are cheaper with a *rejsekort,* an electronic ticket system for travelling by bus, train, metro and water taxi. Download the Rejsekort app and touch in and out on public transport.

Hiring a Car
The best rental deals are found on foreign booking sites. Several apps offer hourly rentals – Share Now has electric and petrol cars, and GreenMobility operates EV fleets.

Bicycle
Copenhagen is widely considered the world's best bike city. In Copenhagen, Helsingør, Roskilde and Aarhus, Donkey Republic rents orange bicycles by the minute via the app.

MONEY
Currency: Danish krone (kr or DKK)

CREDIT CARDS
Visa and MasterCard are widely accepted, American Express and Diners Club less so. Hotels, petrol stations, restaurants and shops may charge a fee for foreign cards.

CASH & ATMS
Some cash machines exchange foreign currency. You don't need to carry much cash in Denmark as shops and services are increasingly cashless.

TIPPING
Hotels Usually 10kr to 20kr is sufficient for carrying bags to your room. **Taxis** It's not really expected, as service is included in the quoted price. **Restaurants** It's not expected, but tipping is becoming more common. Round up or add 10% when service is especially good.

For places to stay in Estonia, see p352

MATT MUNRO/LONELY PLANET

Above: Tallinn (p338); Right: Festival, Setomaa (p347)

Curated by
Angelo Zinna

Estonia

A CULTURAL CROSSROADS

Ruled and influenced by different empires throughout its history, Estonia has developed a distinct character all its own.

Estonia has long been defined by its strategic position at the crossroads of Northern Europe's sea routes. It was part of the Hanseatic League trading bloc during the Middle Ages and later absorbed into the Swedish kingdom, and its identity grew increasingly tangled as the Russian Empire conquered its territory in the early 18th century. Independence followed the Russian Empire's collapse in 1917, but Estonia's larger neighbours never ceased to view this tiny nation as an essential pawn on their geopolitical chessboard. Estonians would have their nationhood removed by both Nazi and Soviet forces during WWII, a conflict followed by nearly five decades of USSR rule. Today, most Estonians tend to resent the 'post-Soviet' label, although a large portion of the population – over 20% – is composed of ethnic Russians who either moved in Soviet times or are descended from migrants. Despite its convoluted past, Estonia is a nation looking forward. In cities, folk music festivals go hand in hand with a thriving contemporary art scene, and former industrial districts live a second life as design-centric creative hubs filled with galleries and international restaurants. Outside urban areas, nature maintains a central role in the local way of life. Half the country is covered by forests and 2000 islands spill from the coastline. Whether you're visiting to escape the crowds or to decipher its layered culture, Estonia awaits discovery.

ALEXANDER GAFARRO/SHUTTERSTOCK

THE MAIN AREAS

TALLINN
Modern capital with a medieval heart. p338

TARTU & THE SOUTH
Cradle of culture. p344

PÄRNU & THE WEST
The summer capital. p348

Find Your Way

Over half of Estonia is covered by forests and a third of the population is concentrated in the capital, leaving the majority of the country dotted with small settlements surrounded by nature.

BUS & TRAIN

With patience, all of Estonia can be visited using public transport. Cheap, reliable buses run regularly. The northern train line links Tallinn to Narva and Paldiski, while two lines travel south to Pärnu and Tartu (book via elron.ee).

CAR

Your own vehicle is the fastest way to move around the country, which can be crossed from north to south in three hours. Major rental companies operate in Tallinn and Tartu.

Tartu & the South, p344

Home of Estonia's first university, Tartu is a friendly place, kept vibrant by its seasonally changing student population.

Tallinn, p338

Dynamic, tech-driven capital with a UNESCO-listed Old Town. Discover medieval roots, some of the Baltics' best museums and art-filled parks.

Pärnu & the West, p348

Estonia's summer capital is the country's prime beach destination, a wellness-centred, family-friendly town with resorts and 19th-century villas.

Gulf of Finland

Loksa

TALLINN
Tallinn Great Town Guild Hall
Maardu
Keila
Paldiski
Kehra
Jõhvi
Iisaku
Rakvere
Tamsalu
Mustvee
Lake Peipsi
Kallaste
Estonian National Museum
Tartu
University of Tartu Museum
Vastse-Kuuste
Võru
Rõuge
Alüksne
Põltsamaa
Paide
Türi
Võhma
Suure-Jaani
Lake Võrtsjärv
Viljandi
Viljandi Teutonic Order Castle
Karksi-Nuia
Elva
Otepää
Tõrva
Valga
Strenci
Valka
Smiltene
Valmiera
LATVIA
Rūjiena
Põltsamaa
Vändra
Sindi
Pärnu
Pärnu River
Soomaa National Park
Lihula
Virtsu
Haapsalu
Vormsi
Muhu
Onissaare
Saaremaa
Kuressaare
Kuressaare Episcopal Castle
Kärdla
Käina
Hiiumaa
Kolka
Sääre

Lake Pihkva
Pskov
RUSSIA

40 km
20 miles

N

336

MO WU/SHUTTERSTOCK

Town Hall Square (p338), Tallinn

Plan Your Time

Tallinn tends to grab all the attention with its cultural attractions, but save some time to explore the islands and rural towns of the south.

A Day in the Capital

● Spend your morning exploring Tallinn's Old Town, from **Town Hall Square** (p338) to elevated **Toompea** (p340). Seek traces left behind by the Hanseatic League in the **Great Guild Hall** (p339), then enter the stunning **Alexander Nevsky Cathedral** (p340), before lunch in **Telliskivi** (p340).

● In the afternoon, stroll Kadriorg Park and visit the art museum **Kumu** (p342). Conclude at the **Estonian Maritime Museum** (p343) and its extension at **Seaplane Harbour** (p343).

Three Days to Explore

● Dedicate a few days to discovering southern Estonia's fascinating culture. Walk through Tartu's Old Town and climb up Toomemägi to the remains of **Tartu Cathedral** (p345). Head to **Aparaaditehas** (p346) for a tour of this refurbished industrial area's galleries.

● Spend day two touring the **Setomaa** (p347), home of the musical Seto minority, starting in the village of Värska and continuing to Obinitsa. On day three head to charming **Viljandi** (p347).

SEASONAL HIGHLIGHTS

SPRING
Soomaa National Park experiences a 'fifth season' as floods transform it into a kayaking playground.

SUMMER
Estonia celebrates Jaanipäev (Midsummer's Day) on 24 June with huge bonfires and folk music festivals.

AUTUMN
The weather is typically moody in autumn. Prices tend to decrease together with tourism numbers.

WINTER
Winters are famously harsh in Estonia, but Christmas markets light up the squares of Tallinn and Tartu.

Tallinn

MEDIEVAL CAPITAL | MUSEUMS | HARBOUR CITY

GETTING AROUND

Tallinn's Old Town is best explored on foot, but to reach many of the sights in the suburbs you'll need to get on a bus or rely on the electric scooters that seem to have taken over the city. Bus tickets can be purchased with contactless cards directly on the bus (cash is not accepted) or online at tallinn. pilet.ee. Timetables are available at *transport.tallinn.ee.*

☑ TOP TIP

Tallinn's train station sits northwest of Old Town. Buses depart from the station 2km southeast of the centre. The compact inner city is walkable, while trams and intercity buses link the suburbs. You can purchase one-hour public transport tickets by tapping your contactless card on the vehicle, or via tallinn.pilet.ee.

Soon after Tallinn entered the Hanseatic League mercantile alliance in the late 13th century, it became the most important port of the Gulf of Finland and a crucial junction on the Baltic Sea's trade routes. The resulting wealth led to the construction of the best-preserved medieval city of Nordic Europe, still contained within its original walls and guarded by 26 red-roofed watchtowers. Old Town (Vanalinn) is divided into two equally attractive sections – Toompea, on the hill, and the Lower Town – but the historic heart of the city once known as Reval is only part of the allure.

When the centre starts feeling a bit too much like a medieval theme park, exit the walls to find neighbourhoods of traditional wooden houses, modernist structures built for the 1980 Moscow Olympics and glass office towers housing an ever-growing tech sector. From the creative district of Telliskivi to the imperial art park of Kadriorg, getting to know Tallinn rewards a few days of any visitor's time.

The Heart of Old Town

Under the eye of Old Thomas

The oldest cobbled alleys of Tallinn's historic core all seem to converge in **Town Hall Square** (Raekoja Plats), the epicentre of the Lower Town expanding under the shadow of the Town Hall's spire. Functioning as a marketplace until the end of the 19th century, Raekoja Plats is now the ideal starting point to explore the UNESCO-listed Old Town, the open-air museum tributing the Hanseatic roots of Estonia's capital.

Tallinn's Gothic **Town Hall** *(raekoda.tallinn.ee; entry adult/child €7/5),* rising tall on the square's southern side, is one of the oldest municipal buildings in Northern Europe. Originally erected in the 15th century, it continues to dominate Old Town's skyline with its 64m spire, topped by a statue of Old Thomas (Vana Toomas), Tallinn's most notable icon and guardian of the city since 1530. You can visit the building's

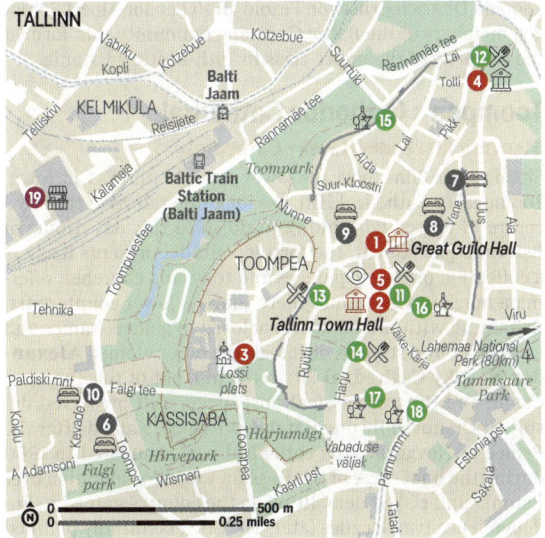

TALLINN

HIGHLIGHTS
1 Great Guild Hall
2 Tallinn Town Hall

SIGHTS
3 Alexander Nevsky Cathedral
4 Estonian Maritime Museum
5 Town Hall Square

SLEEPING
6 ibis Styles Tallinn
7 Imaginary Hostel
8 Schlössle Hotel
9 St Olav Hotel
10 von Stackelberg Hotel

EATING
11 Ill Draakon
12 Katusekohvik Maru
13 Peet Ruut
14 Pegasus

DRINKING & NIGHTLIFE
15 Botaanik
16 Sessel
17 Valli Bar
18 Whisper Sister

SHOPPING
19 Telliskivi Flea Market

interior between 25 June and 31 August, or on a private visit with a certified guide during the rest of the year (book ahead).

Hanseatic Wall St

Inside the Great Guild Hall

The **Great Guild Hall** *(ajaloomuuseum.ee/great-guild-hall; entry adult/child €14/9)* stands as one of Pikk St's most prominent buildings, its imposing size reflecting the wealth and power of the merchant guilds that once met here. Completed in 1410, its design reflects the real-estate tax system of 15th-century Northern Europe – the wider the facade, the higher the tax bill. Behind its entry doors, adorned with two lion head knockers, a vaulted hall was designed for public celebrations and meetings of major international traders. The Guild Hall served as Tallinn's main business centre until the 19th century, with stock-market negotiations eventually moving into the palace. Much of what is known about the Hanseatic League today comes from documents such as the ancient ledgers on display in the museum, used for record-keeping by merchants. While the main hall is devoid of decorations, the small guild hall features lunette paintings from 1869 by

 EATING IN TALLINN'S OLD TOWN: OUR PICKS

Peet Ruut: Organic cuisine at its best, Peet Ruut cares as much about flavours as the origins of each ingredient. *6-10pm Mon-Sat €€*

Pegasus: This restaurant has been serving fine food for half a century, but you can't tell from its modern cuisine. *noon-11pm Mon-Thu, noon-midnight Fri & Sat, 1-10pm Sun €€*

Ill Draakon: Eel soup and sausages in a playful, medieval-inspired Town Hall Square tourist restaurant. *11am-10pm €€*

Katusekohvik Maru: Access the 'Fat Margaret' rooftop by booking a table in Maru's outdoor terrace overlooking the city walls. *10am-10pm €€*

Leopold Dietrich Ernst von Pezold and Theodor Albert Sprengel, members of the Baltic German community that formed the majority of the upper class in 19th-century Estonia.

Toompea's Orthodox Cathedral

Step into Alexander Nevsky Cathedral

Sitting some 30m above the lower part of Tallinn's Old Town, Toompea, or Cathedral Hill, has long functioned as the city's centre of power, continuing to do so to this day. Home of Estonia's parliament, the fortified citadel presents itself as a collection of stately palaces and towering churches, offering a much quieter atmosphere than its lower counterpart. Brimming with sacred icons enclosed in golden frames and candles lit by Orthodox devotees, the onion-domed **Alexander Nevsky Cathedral** sits right in front of the Toompea Castle and the neoclassical post office, well preserved despite its historically unpalatable presence. Named after the Prince of Novgorod, the cathedral was completed in 1900 during the final stage of the Russian Empire's dominion over Estonia and risked demolition as the country gained its independence two decades later. The Soviets initially planned to convert the church into a planetarium – it didn't happen, and the Alexander Nevsky Cathedral was shut for 50 years, reopening to the public in 1991.

Telliskivi Creative City

Eat, drink and thrift in Tallinn's former industrial district

'Craft', 'artisanal', 'organic' and other trendy buzzwords recur often in graffiti-decorated Telliskivi, the area that resulted from the 2009 regeneration project of this industrial corner of Tallinn north of the railway station. Rundown warehouses and former factories located in the once-dodgy Kalamaja district are now home to an eclectic mix of cafes, bars, shops and galleries – plus a **weekly flea market**. It's lively both day and night.

Kadriorg's Art, Classical & Contemporary

Imperial gardens turned museum hub

Removed from the bustle of Tallinn's Old Town, Kadriorg Park is the unchallenged art centre of Estonia's capital, housing museums brimming with classical and contemporary

A BRIEF HISTORY OF THE HANSEATIC LEAGUE

Much of what you see today in Tallinn's Old Town is the result of the city's role as a commercial hub on the Baltic coast. While the Hanseatic League had a major impact on the development of Baltic cities, its history remains largely obscure. Emerging in the 12th century and flourishing from the 13th to the 17th centuries, its primary purpose was to protect the economic interests and trading privileges of an emerging merchant class, ensuring safe passage for goods across the Baltic and North Seas. Tallinn, then known as Reval, became a crucial member of the Hanseatic League in 1285. Its strategic location brought immense prosperity to Reval, resulting in the construction of Tallinn's fortified walls, merchant houses and grand churches.

DRINKING IN TALLINN: OUR PICKS

Whisper Sister: A tiny plaque on Pärnu St (no 12) marks this speakeasy-style cocktail bar – blink and you'll miss it. *6pm-12.30am Sun-Thu, to 2.30am Fri & Sat*

Valli Bar: Historic bar in front of the Sõprus cinema, attracting a local crowd with its cheap beer. *noon-1am Mon-Fri, to 2am Fri & Sat, to midnight Sun*

Sessel: Walk through a souvenir shop to get to Sessel, a cocktail bar overlooking Viru St that also offers sushi. *noon-1am Sun-Thu, to 3am Fri & Sat*

Botaanik: An intimate, welcoming corner cocktail bar serving some of the best cocktails in town. Book ahead to secure a table. *6pm-midnight Thu, to 1am Fri & Sat*

Lahemaa National Park

Covering 725 sq km, Lahemaa National Park is Estonia's largest national park. Hiking, cycling, camping, kayaking and other activities are all great ways to explore the bogs, bays, lakes and forests of this rural landscape, easily reached from Tallinn. A number of villages and glamping facilities dot the area, allowing you to stay close to the action and away from the crowds.

Viru Bog Trail

Bog Walking on the Viru Trail

The **Viru Bog Trail** extends above the bogs formed in prehistoric times, considered the oldest landscapes in Estonia. The boardwalk runs between the lakes before connecting to a hiking path that runs through the pine forest. The full loop is 5.5km.

Manors & Palaces

The Baltic German nobility built opulent villas in Lahemaa, some of which still stand today. **Palmse Manor**, first built in 1720 and later reconstructed, is Lahemaa's prime historic building, housing the park's visitor centre, a museum with period furniture and clothing, and a restaurant. South of the beach town of Võsu is **Sagadi Manor**, a late baroque complex built by the von Fock family in the mid-18th century. Besides a hotel, the complex is also home to a Forest Museum run by Estonia's State Forest Management Centre.

Village Hopping

In Viinistu, a fish processing plant has been converted into the **Viinistu Art Museum**, housing the private artwork collection of Jaan Manitski, the Viinistu-born businessman and former Minister of Foreign Affairs of Estonia. In charming Käsmu, the **Käsmu Sea Museum**, housed inside a Russian-era border-guard station, displays hundreds of sea-related objects that offer a glimpse into the settlement's long-standing relationship with the Gulf of Finland.

TOP TIPS

● The Lahemaa Visitor Centre is found at Palmse Manor, in one of the former stables of the complex.

● Loksa is the main town within the park's borders, followed by Võsu. Both are small, but are connected to Tallinn via public transport.

PRACTICALITIES

● Hiking-trail info is available at rmk.ee or via the RMK app.

● For bus schedules see transport.tallinn.ee.

ESTONIA'S SONG FESTIVAL

The UNESCO-inscribed Estonian Song Festival is the country's most important music event, held in the Song Festival Grounds near Kadriorg Park every five years. The event, first held in Tartu in 1869, is more than just a concert. Gathering up to 70,000 spectators, it's a powerful expression of Estonian identity.

During Soviet rule it served as a covert form of protest and a way to preserve national culture – the event's immense scale and its role in keeping the Estonian language and traditions alive make it the single most important gathering in the country. A parade running through Tallin's central streets, where choirs wear the traditional clothing of their regions, inaugurates the start of the event.

works on the lush grounds first commissioned by Russian Tsar Peter the Great in the early 18th century. Manicured gardens, mirror-like ponds and oak-shaded paths blend in this 70-hectare park on the outskirts of the city centre. The architectural centrepiece of Kadriorg Park is its homonymous palace, a baroque construction backed by a symmetrical French garden Peter the Great had built as a gift to his wife, Empress Catherine I, between 1718 and 1725.

Today, the palace is home to a branch of the Art Museum of Estonia. The main hall of **Kadriorg Art Museum** is one of Northern Europe's most impressive pieces of baroque architecture, with intricate stucco decorations symbolising the tsar's power and the initials of Peter and Catherine nestled above the opposing fireplaces. The Estonian Art Museum, or **Kumu**, is contained inside a futuristic, semicircular building designed by Finnish architect Pekka Vapaavuori and showcases the evolution of Estonian art from the 18th century to the present day. Begin with the heritage Baltic German painters such as Oskar Georg Adolf Hoffmann and Carl Timoleon von Neff, moving forward to the early-20th-century constructivist movement known as the Group of Estonian Artists, which depicts society's entrance into tech-driven modernity.

Estonian Maritime Museum

Tallinn & the Baltic Sea

Visit the Estonian Maritime Museum and Seaplane Harbour

Much of Tallinn's history took place on the water. Two kid-friendly museums retrace the evolution of seafaring from the Middle Ages to modern times – from epic battles to marine archaeology and Cold War spy games. Set inside an artillery tower known as 'Fat Margaret' is the **Estonian Maritime Museum**. Here a collection of over 700 exhibits, including the 20m *Koge* shipwreck dating to the 14th century, traces the history of navigation in the Baltic Sea. Of the 17 model ships exhibited around the archaeological remains, eight come to life thanks to augmented reality.

Under the three concrete domes of the 1917 hangar known as **Seaplane Harbour**, you'll find one of Europe's most intriguing maritime museums, opened in 2012 after a long restoration process and updated in 2024. Occupying a large section of the hangar is the 59.5m *Lembit* submarine, built in the UK between 1935 and 1937 for the Estonian navy. You can enter its claustrophobia-inducing interiors to get a feel of life underwater and walk through the vessel's eight sections, from the engine rooms to the sleeping quarters.

FESTIVALS IN TALLINN

Besides the Song Festival, Tallinn hosts many events, especially during the summer months.

Old Town Days: Old Town's largest cultural festival celebrates ancient traditions in early June.

Tallinn Street Food Festival: In early June, the Song Festival Grounds turn into a huge, open-air restaurant filled with food trucks.

PÖFF Black Nights Film Festival: One of the Baltics' most important film festivals takes place in November.

Tallinn Craft Beer Weekend: Tallinn's Craft Beer Weekend celebrates the local beer scene by gathering breweries small and large in the city's Creative Hub in May.

Tallinn Music Week: International acts are hosted all around the city during the capital's loudest week, in April.

Tartu & the South

Places

Tartu p344
Viljandi p347
Setomaa p347

☑ TOP TIP

The Tartu Smart Bike Share has made 750 regular and e-bikes available to the public at 69 stations around the city. You can rent a bike *(starting at €2 per hour)* via the Tartu Smart Bike mobile app and drop it off at any station in town.

Fresh off a year as European Capital of Culture, Estonia's second city has long been defined by its role as a cradle of ideas. The Livonian Brothers of the Sword made Dorpat, as the city was then known, their regional power centre in the 1220s and within decades the city joined the Hanseatic League and became the third-most-important Livonian city, after Riga and Tallinn. Since 1632, when the Kingdom of Sweden founded the Academia Gustaviana, the city has attracted bright minds and innovators in the arts and the sciences. A calm city of less than 100,000, Tartu remains vibrant thanks to its population of international students. Around Tartu, religious and linguistic minorities keep ancient traditions alive in the picturesque countryside. On the shores of Lake Peipsi, Europe's largest transboundary lake, Russian-speaking descendants of Old Believers keep ancient rituals alive in their onion-domed churches. Further south, the musically gifted Setos perform hypnotic chants.

Tartu

Musical Town Hall Square

The *Kissing Students* statue – a city symbol recently renovated as part of the 2024 Capital of Culture programme – stands in

---

GETTING AROUND

Although Tartu is Estonia's second-largest city, its centre is small and best visited on foot. Public transport runs frequently to sights outside of Old Town – take bus 7 to get to the Estonian National Museum and Raadi Park, and bus 1 or 2 to reach Aparaaditehas. Both sides of the Emajõgi River are lined with cycling paths, allowing you to easily explore the city on two wheels. Exiting the city is best done by car, but many places are reachable by public transport. **Go Bus** *(gobus.ee)* runs services from Tartu's bus station to most towns in the region. Buses are efficient and on time, but not frequent – check the schedule on peatus.ee, as some areas are only covered once or twice a day.

Tartu Cathedral

Tartu's **Town Hall Square**. This open space is framed by restaurant terraces that converge towards the 18th-century **Town Hall** (Raekoja plats), built by German architect Johann Heinrich Bartholomäus Walter following a fire that destroyed much of the city in 1775. The Town Hall still serves as the local government's seat – only the Tartu Visitor Centre and the historic pharmacy found on the ground floor can be accessed. The baroque tower topping the Town Hall houses Estonia's biggest carillon, a system of 34 bells that play five times a day at 9am, noon, 3pm, 6pm and 9pm.

Ruins of the cathedral

The Gothic skeleton of **Tartu Cathedral**, the largest in the country, has stood on top of Toomemägi since the 13th century, when the knights of the Livonian Order conquered the city. The cathedral took two centuries to complete before being largely destroyed during the Livonian War (1558–83) and ceasing to function as a place of worship, leaving Toomemägi with just its ruins ever since. In the early 19th century, the University of Tartu rebuilt parts of the cathedral and turned its main hall into a library. Today, the cathedral houses the **University of Tartu Museum** (*muuseum.ut.ee; entry adult/child €9/6*). You can visit the elegant White Hall; on its balcony are all the gifts given to

INTELLECTUAL PRIDE

Since the 17th century, the University of Tartu has functioned as the city's cultural pillar. Named Academia Gustaviana after Swedish King Gustavus Adolphus, the university operated from 1632 to 1699, when it was moved to Pärnu, only to be shut down a decade later. It was reopened in Tartu by Tsar Alexander I of Russia in 1802, growing to become Estonia's prime research centre at the turn of the 20th century. When the Soviet and German armies clashed in the 1944 Battle of Tartu, the university lost 15 of its buildings. But it survived, and continues to operate as one of Estonia's most important educational institutions, drawing many international students each year.

 EATING & DRINKING IN TARTU: OUR PICKS

Gunpowder Cellar: Former military storehouse serving heartwarming dishes and a long list of local beers and ciders. *noon-10pm Sun-Tue, to 1am Wed-Sat* €€

Kampus: With a show kitchen facing pedestrian Rüütli, Kampus offers a Spanish-influenced menu of light lunch meals and hearty mains. *noon-9pm Tue-Thu, to 1am Fri-Sun* €€

Ihamaru Pizza & Käbliku Brewery Taproom: Pair excellent wood-fired pizza with one of the craft beers from the Käbliku. *4-11pm Mon-Thu, noon-11pm Fri-Sun* €

Kolm Tilli: Serving international cuisine from brunch to dinner, with a street-food menu if you're just looking for something light. *9am-11pm Mon-Fri, to 1am Sat, 10am-10pm Sun* €

SETO LEELO

The ancient polyphonic singing tradition known as *leelo* has long been one of the defining features of the Seto people, and continues to be performed during festivals, and events such as funerals and weddings. It's typically performed by a group of women led by a 'song mother'. While many songs are passed down through generations, 'song mothers' are praised for their ability to improvise, creating verses on the spot to form a hypnotic rhythm, somewhere between a lament and a lullaby. Recently, the Estonian Literature Museum has created a digital platform to collect historic recordings of Seto music – on the website of **Seto Singing Heritage** *(laul.setomaa.ee)* you can now listen to original songs dating as far back as the 1920s and learn about the structure of melodies.

TRABANTOS/SHUTTERSTOCK

the university by prominent guests. The core of the exhibition is found in the Morgenstern Hall, spanning the 5th and 6th floors, where besides the historic library you'll find some of the oldest models of the cathedral and the university's founding act.

Estonia's cutting-edge national museum

The **Estonian National Museum** *(erm.ee; entry adult/child €15/10)* was designed to reflect Raadi Park's history as a military airport – the impressive glass-clad building was created as an extension of the asphalt airstrip – and has over 140,000 objects covering the history of Estonian customs and traditions. While this may seem like an unusual location for such an important institution – Raadi Park is 2.7km from Tartu's city centre – it is worth the trip. Most of the space is used for the 'Encounters' permanent exhibition, a massive showcase of everyday objects tracing the transformation of everyday life in Estonia, from the Stone Age to independence.

From 'everything factory' to creative hub

Bombed in 1941, the Aparaaditehas quarter was reborn in the Soviet era as a multifunctional industrial site where boots, refrigerators, umbrellas and car parts were produced to be shipped all over the USSR. In the 1970s, during Aparaaditehas' peak, more than 1500 people were employed here. Today, **Aparaaditehas** follows in the footsteps of Tallinn's Telliskivi (p340) and other European 'creative districts', with its buildings repurposed as a culture hub. A large abstract mural is the focal point of the courtyard, where art galleries and artisanal bakeries share the industrial architecture with coworking spaces, record stores and tattoo studios.

Viljandi Teutonic Order Castle

Viljandi
TIME FROM TARTU: 1¼HR

Viljandi's medieval fortress

Charming Viljandi is celebrated for its cultural scene, which comes to life during summer through major open-air events such as the Viljandi Folk Music Festival. Set on a hill overlooking **Lake Viljandi**, the crumbling remains of the **Viljandi Teutonic Order Castle** stand as the region's most treasured landmark. German Knights of the Catholic Teutonic Order settled in Viljandi in the early 13th century, erecting the fortress in 1224. The Polish-Swedish wars of the 1600s brought the castle to its ruinous state. Reach the leafy hill where the archaeological site is found via the 1879 suspension bridge running for 50m across the ditch on the southern side of the park.

Setomaa
TIME FROM TARTU: 1¼HR

Home of the Setos

Setomaa is home to the Seto minority, a group of Orthodox Christians whose Finno-Ugric language finds its best expression in the *leelo* polyphonic singing tradition. To get a glimpse of rural life in Setomaa visit Värska's **Seto Farm Museum**, a complex of wooden houses and stables depicting the living and working conditions of families in the pre-industrial era. The **Obinitsa Seto Museum** offers a window into the region's history, with an emphasis on the role of women in Seto society. Women have been historically leading the preservation of the *leelo* singing tradition and 'song mothers' continue to be respected figures in the community. An important piece of living culture is the **Obinitsa Kunstisaal** (Obinitsa Art Gallery), run by writer Kauksi Ülle and her husband, painter and silversmith Evar Riitsaar.

347

Pärnu & the West

18TH-CENTURY GRANDEUR | THE BEACH | SPA LIFE

Places

✅ TOP TIP

During summer months many concerts are held in Pärnu, both in old-school venues such as the Kuursaal, a former casino turned restaurant, and in parks such as Vallikäär and Munamäe.

As spring ends and the weather warms up, Pärnu comes to life with Estonians, Finns and Latvians heading to the Baltic Sea. Doubling as a relaxing, wellness-oriented resort and party town, Pärnu attempts to cater to both families and hedonists. Its historic core boasts a collection of colourful palatial residences dating back centuries as well as a vibrant restaurant scene, while the shallow water lapping its sandy beach favours slow strolls over long swims. With so much to detain visitors in Pärnu itself, the resort's hinterland is often neglected, despite offering plenty of its own charm. Haapsalu provides for visitors in search of coastal relaxation, while boggy Soomaa National Park offers canoeing, kayaking, bog walking, or simply observing the scenery from a hammock. The wild, windswept West Estonian Archipelago is worth a detour, starting from Saaremaa, the largest island in the region.

Pärnu

Mapping the Old Town's magnificence

The 15th-century **Red Tower**, once part of Pärnu's medieval fortress, is the only piece of architecture from the Hanseatic era to survive (reconstructed) and houses a small **museum** *(parnumuuseum.ee/tower; entry adult/child €7/5)* tracing the

---

 GETTING AROUND

Pärnu centre's pedestrian streets make for pleasant walks, but, with cycle paths crisscrossing the city and its surroundings, greater Pärnu is best explored by bicycle. The Baltreisen Bicycle Rental shop rents bikes for €11 per day from under the giant mural on Pühavaimu St. For a relaxing cruise with **Pärnu**

Cruises *(parnucruises.ee)*, hop on the 1963 MS *Kuha*, departing four times a day from Tallinn Gate. The coast and countryside is best explored with your own vehicle. Organised tours to Soomaa National Park usually include transport, and a bicycle can get you far, given the low traffic on the flat roads of western Estonia.

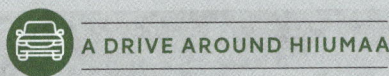

A DRIVE AROUND HIIUMAA

This road trip around the West Estonian Archipelago's second island can be done in one (long) day, or broken into two with a night's stop in Kärdla.

START	END	LENGTH
Sõru Harbour	Heltermaa	160km; 7hr+

From the tiny **❶ Sõru Harbour** make your way north to the Kõpu Peninsula along the island's western flank. Near the imposing **❷ Kõpu Lighthouse**, originally built by Hanseatic League merchants in the 16th century, find the red **❸ Ristna Lighthouse** and the surfing beach at **❹ Surf Paradiis**. A 31m **❺ wooden copy of the Eiffel Tower** awaits in a small amusement park of quirky structures built by local craftsman Jaan Alliksoo in Reigi, followed by the **❻ Hiiumaa Military Museum** and the **❼ Tahkuna Lighthouse** on the Tahkuna Peninsula. Following the 80 road, you'll reach the **❽ Hill of Crosses**, a collection of hundreds of wooden crucifixes built by 18th-century Swedes, then Kärdla, Hiiumaa's

capital. Stop for lunch at the **❾ Hiiumaa Pruulikoja Resto** and after a stroll through the town, drive south toward Kassari. Make a brief stop at the **❿ Lavendlitalu** (lavender field). Continue south to Käina, Hiiumaa's second town, where the modern **⓫ Windtower Experience** (Elamuskeskus Tuuletorn) houses a five-floor, family-friendly museum dedicated to nature's role in shaping Hiiumaa's identity, plus a 20m climbing wall, the highest in all the Baltics. South of Käina is the Kassari Reserve, extending to the promontory **⓬ Sääre Tirp**, a wild, hikable strip of land emerging from the sea. **⓭ Heltermaa** is Hiiumaa's port town, connecting the island with the outside world.

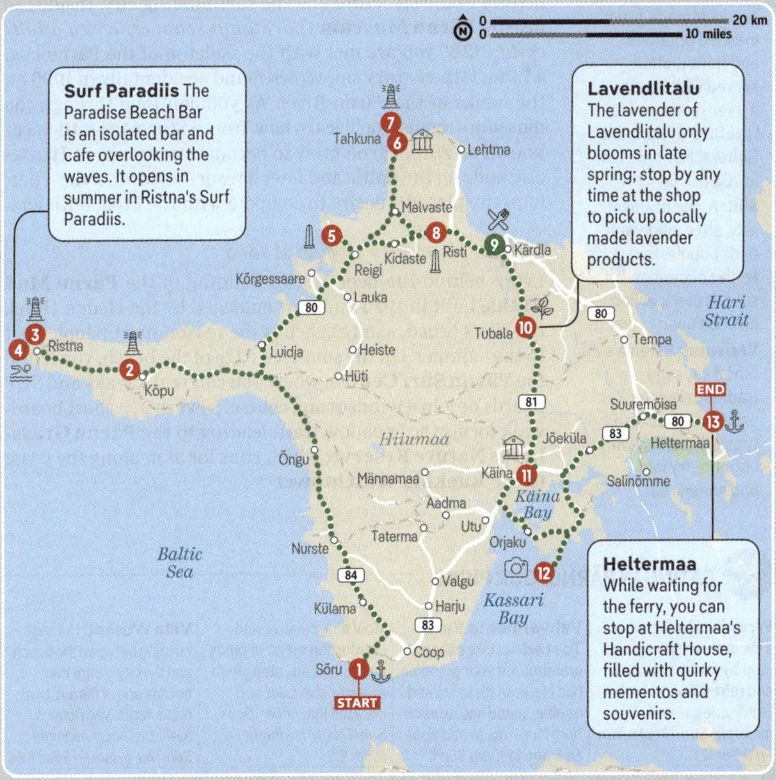

Surf Paradiis The Paradise Beach Bar is an isolated bar and cafe overlooking the waves. It opens in summer in Ristna's Surf Paradiis.

Lavendlitalu The lavender of Lavendlitalu only blooms in late spring; stop by any time at the shop to pick up locally made lavender products.

Heltermaa While waiting for the ferry, you can stop at Heltermaa's Handicraft House, filled with quirky mementos and souvenirs.

0 ——— 20 km
0 ——— 10 miles

Hari Strait

Baltic Sea

Kassari Bay

Käina Bay

Hiiumaa

Tahkuna · Lehtma · Malvaste · Kõrgessaare · Reigi · Kidaste · Risti · Kärdla · Lauka · Tubala · Tempa · Luidja · Heiste · Hüti · Õngu · Männamaa · Aadma · Utu · Käina · Jõeküla · Suuremõisa · Salinõmme · Heltermaa · Nurste · Taterma · Orjaku · Valgu · Harju · Külama · Sõru · Coop · Ristna · Kõpu

80 · 81 · 83 · 84 · 83

START

END

FLAVOURS OF ESTONIA

Simple and hearty, Estonian cuisine reflects the country's climate and connection to nature. Here are some key dishes to look for:

Baltic herring *(räim)* **and sprats** *(kilu):* A recurring presence in Estonian cuisine – try a *kiluvõileib* (sprat sandwich; sprat served on dark rye bread with butter and a hard-boiled egg).

Mulgipuder: Some consider it the national dish – a filling porridge made from mashed potatoes and barley, often served with bacon. It even made it onto UNESCO's Intangible Cultural Heritage list in 2024.

Sült: A savoury meat jelly, often made with pork, popular for festive occasions. If it sounds unappealing, just wait until you see it.

Verivorst: Estonia's blood sausage is a traditional winter and Christmas dish, typically served with lingonberry jam and sauerkraut.

ALEXANDRE.ROSA/SHUTTERSTOCK

history of the structure and the surrounding city. Inside the nearby **Pärnu Museum** *(parnumuuseum.ee; entry adult/child €12/9)* you are met with the skeleton of the Pärnu cog, a 7.9m, 14th-century shipwreck found accidentally in 1990 on the banks of the Pärnu River. As you continue through the museum's rooms, you'll learn how, from a Stone Age settlement known as Pulli, Pärnu grew to become an important Hanseatic node on the Baltic and later a resort town with the – perhaps misplaced – desire to compete with the French Riviera.

Estonia's favourite stretch of sand

Lying behind the neoclassical building of the **Pärnu Mud Baths**, built in 1926 and now managed by the Hedon Hotel, the city's broad, sandy beach is the reason most people visit in the summer. On the southern edge of the beach, you'll find the **Pärnu Surf Centre**, where you can rent kayaks and SUP boards or join a windsurfing course. Next to it, a short boardwalk forms the 'meadow trail', leading to the **Pärnu Grasslands Nature Reserve**, which runs for 3km along the coast to the **Raeküla Watchtower**.

 EATING IN PÄRNU: OUR PICKS

Wrapimaja: Between a swim and a spa session stop by for tasty wraps and refreshing rhubarb lemonades. *noon-midnight Sun-Thu, to 2am Fri & Sat* €

Vehverments Bar & Tostadas: Like eating at grandma's, if your grandma had Mexican tostadas and a selfie-suited house. *noon-11pm Mon-Thu, to midnight Fri & Sat, to 10pm Sun* €

VoVa: A creative and comforting menu of tapas and full meals, along with an extensive beer and cocktail list. *noon-10pm Sun-Thu, to midnight Fri & Sat* €€

Villa Wesset: Heritage building between the beach and the city centre that houses one of Pärnu's best restaurants. Veg options available. *noon-midnight Sun-Thu, to 1am Fri & Sat* €€€

ESTONIA PÄRNU & THE WEST

Pärnu Mud Baths

Soomaa National Park

TIME FROM PÄRNU: **40MIN**

Experience the 'fifth season'

Covering an area of some 360 sq km, **Soomaa National Park** is well known for turning hikers into kayakers during the 'fifth season' in spring, when the rain and snow melt causing the rivers to overflow. The park's **visitor centre** is in the middle of the park, 12km from Jõesuu. The easy Riisa study trail is a popular walking path, running for 4.8km on a boardwalk.

Haapsalu

TIME FROM PÄRNU: **2HR**

Spa-town heritage

Stretching around the crumbling remains of **Haapsalu Episcopal Castle**, the city's **Promenade** is ideally positioned for summer evenings strolls along the bay. Haapsalu has been welcoming wellness tourists to its spas for over a century and the relaxed atmosphere is still part of the allure. From the onion-domed **Church of Mary Magdalene**, reach the dreamy **Haapsalu Kuursaal**, a green and white wooden villa on the seaside promenade that used to be a favourite holidaying destination for the 19th-century Russian aristocracy.

Kuressaare

TIME FROM PÄRNU: **3HR**

Inside Kuressaare's Episcopal Castle

With a population of just over 13,000 people, Kuressaare, the capital of Saaremaa, is the obvious starting point to explore the West Estonian Archipelago. At its core sits the **Kuressaare Episcopal Castle**, one of the best-preserved fortifications in Estonia. Inside, the **Saaremaa Museum** (*samu.ee; entry adult/ child €12/9*) covers the country's history from medieval times.

Places We Love to Stay

€ Budget €€ Midrange €€€ Top End

Tallinn

MAP p339

Imaginary Hostel € One of Old Town's long-standing hostels (and often the cheapest), with mixed dorms only and beehive-like beds that offer a little more privacy than usual.

St Olav Hotel €€ Excellent location and price, but to get to your room you'll need to find your way through a labyrinth at this historic hotel. Rooms are more spacious than other basic Old Town hotels and a buffet breakfast is included.

ibis Styles Tallinn €€ A safe bet right outside Old Town's walls by Lindamägi. Modern, bright clean rooms, 24-hour reception and comfy beds at a budget friendly price, close to the railway station and Kalamaja.

von Stackelberg Hotel €€ Access this elegant property from the courtyard surrounding a fountain and stay in tastefully furnished rooms away from the crowds but near all the sights.

Schlössle Hotel €€€ The colourful exterior of this Old Town palatial hotel contrasts with the elegant stonework and plush decor of the interior.

Lahemaa National Park

Viinistu Art Hotel €€ A former fish-processing plant in front of the local art museum has been converted into a simple waterfront hotel filled with paintings. Great breakfast and restaurant.

Palmse Distillery Guesthouse €€ Nestled behind the manor house and the greenhouse, this converted 19th-century distillery makes you feel at home on the historic Palmse property.

Vihula Manor €€€ The most luxurious of the Baltic German manor houses converted into hotels, with sophisticated rooms designed for relaxation and on-site spa treatments available.

Tartu

Hektor Design Hostel € Matching the vibe of the surrounding Aparaaditehas, this 'smart' hostel comes with a sauna and a gym, plus many modern touches and a laundry room.

Villa Margaretha €€ An elegant art nouveau villa in the picturesque Karlova district, with an excellent restaurant.

Hotel Tartu €€ A midrange choice in an updated 1960s building that offers straightforward rooms near the bus station, the river and Old Town.

Antonius Hotel €€€ An Old Town boutique hotel with elegant, antique furniture and top-notch service.

Pärnu

Tiia Guesthouse € The cheapest rooms in town are in this basic but clean wooden

home, close to the action. Shared bathrooms.

Tervise Paradiis €€ A large family-oriented hotel, with an adjoining waterpark and beach views from the balconies.

Villa Andropoff €€ In the secluded beachside forest of Valgeranna, this modernist hotel once used by the Soviet political elite is now an architectural monument.

Villa Ammende €€€ This art nouveau villa has been successfully restored to become one of Pärnu's most refined boutique hotels.

Haapsalu

Päeva Villa €€ Pastel rooms, each with their own theme, in a family-run guesthouse with a peaceful atmosphere.

Hestia Hotel & Spa €€€ This contemporary hotel is all about relaxation. Spa treatments are the main draw, but the views aren't bad either.

Kuressaare

Hotel NOSPA €€ Modern (although a little anonymous) rooms by St Nicholas Church, with balconies, powerful showers and a shared kitchen. Automated check-in and little to no staff around.

Ekesparre €€€ A refined 10-room historic boutique hotel right in front of the Episcopal Castle. Originally built in 1908, it's now Kuressaare's top hotel.

Practicalities

LGBTIQ+ Travellers
Estonia is generally considered a safe and welcoming destination for LGBTIQ+ travellers. While attitudes can be more conservative in rural areas, major cities like Tallinn have a visible LGBTIQ+ scene. In 2024, Estonia legalised same-sex marriage.

Health
Apart from tick-borne diseases, which can be a danger in grassy and forested areas, and slippery streets during icy winters, there are no major health concerns specific to Estonia. The main thing to keep in mind is that you may find yourself far from a doctor or a hospital when visiting remote areas.

Russian Travellers
Following Russia's invasion of Ukraine in 2022, Estonia closed its border to most Russian citizens. Russian citizens with a short-term Schengen visa are not allowed to enter Estonia for tourism, regardless of the visa-issuing country. Also, as of 2025, Estonia no longer recognises non-biometric passports issued by Russia.

Ice Roads
In winter, Estonia has official ice roads linking the islands to the mainland. These seasonal routes form across the frozen Baltic Sea in the coldest months and are regulated by special rules, including recommended speeds and distances between vehicles.

MNSTUDIO/SHUTTERSTOCK

Tallinn (p338)

The RMK App
The 'RMK Loodusega koos' app, developed by the State Forest Management Centre (RMK) provides information and tools for hiking and camping in Estonia's forests and natural areas. Find hundreds of trails and maps, with details on where you can stop for the night if you're going to be out for consecutive multiple days.

Tap Water
Tap water is generally considered good to drink in Estonia; you can always fill up your water bottle in public restrooms without any concerns.

Public Holidays
New Year's Day 1 January
Independence Day (Iseseisvuspäev) 24 February
Easter March/April
Spring Day (Kevadpüha) 1 May
Whit Sunday May/June
Victory Day (Võidupüha) 23 June
St John's Day/Midsummer's Day (Jaanipäev) 24 June
Independence Restoration Day (Taasiseseisvumispäev) 20 August
Christmas Eve 24 December
Christmas Day 25 December
Second Day of Christmas 26 December

Language

Double vowels in written Estonian indicate they are pronounced as long sounds. Note that air is pronounced as in 'hair', aw as in 'law', ea as in 'ear', eu as the 'u' in 'nurse', ew as 'ee' with rounded lips, oh as the 'o' in 'note', ow as in 'how', uh as the 'a' in 'ago', kh as in the Scottish loch, and zh as the 's' in 'pleasure'.

Basics

Hello. Tere. *te·re*
Goodbye. Nägemist. *nair·ge·mist*
Excuse me. Vabandage/Vabanda. (pol/inf) *va·ban·da·ge/va·ban·da*
Sorry. Vabandust. *va·ban·dust*
Please. Palun. *pa·lun*
Thank you. Tänan. *tair·nan*
Yes. Jaa. *yaa*
No. Ei. *ay*
What's your name? Mis on teie nimi? *mis on tay·e ni·mi*
My name is … Minu nimi on … *mi·nu ni·mi on …*
Do you speak English? Kas te räägite inglise keelt? *kas te rair·git·te ing·kli·se keylt*
I don't understand. Ma ei saa aru. *ma ay saa a·ru*

Transport

boat laev *laiv*
bus buss *bus*
plane lennuk *len·nuk*
train rong *rongk*
One … ticket (to Pärnu), Üks … pilet (Pärnusse), *ewks … pi·let (pair·nus·se)*
please. palun. *pa·lun*
one-way ühe otsa *ew·he o·tsa*
return edasi-tagasi *e·da·si·ta·ga·si*

Emergencies

Help! Appi! *ap·pi*

Go away! Minge ära! *ming·ke air·ra*
Call the doctor/police! Kutsuge arst/politsei! *ku·tsu·ge arst/o·li·tsay*
I'm lost. Ma olen ära eksinud. *ma o·len air·ra ek·si·nud*
Where are the toilets? Kus on WC? *kus on ve·se*

Eating & Drinking

What would you recommend? Mida te soovitate? *i·da te saw·vit·tat·te*
Do you have vegetarian food? Kas teil on taimetoitu? *kas tayl on tai·met·toyt·tu*
I'd like the bill/menu, please. Ma sooviksin arvet/menüüd, palun. *ma saw·vik·sin ar·vet/me·newt pa·lun*
I'll have a … Ma tahaksin … *ma ta·hak·sin …*
Cheers! Terviseks! *tair·vi·seks*

Shopping & Services

I'm looking for … Ma otsin … *ma o·tsin*
How much is it? Kui palju see maksab? *ku·i pal·yu sey mak·sab*
That's too expensive. See on liiga kallis. *sey on lee·ga kal·lis*
bank pank *pank*
market turg *turg*
post office postkontor *post·kont·tor*

NUMBERS

1
üks *ewks*

2
kaks *kaks*

3
kolm *kolm*

4
neli *ne·li*

5
viis *vees*

6
kuus *koos*

7
seitse *say·tse*

8
kaheksa *ka·hek·sa*

9
üheksa *ew·hek·sa*

10
kümme *kewm·me*

Tallinn Baltic Station

Arriving & Getting Around

Tallinn is the main point of entry for those who reach Estonia by sea or air. Overland travellers can easily reach Estonia from Latvia – Riga is just a couple of hours away from the border.

By Ferry from Helsinki
A dozen ships a day arrive from Helsinki, on the opposite side of the Gulf of Finland, docking at the Estonian capital's harbour. From Tallinn's port, Old Town can be reached on foot in under 20 minutes.

Arriving by Air
Tallinn Airport is the main gateway, offering frequent connections to major European cities. Frequent buses provide easy access to the city centre. Tartu has Estonia's second international airport.

Driving Essentials
Car-rental prices start at around €40 per day. Given the short distances between cities, a small car is usually enough. The speed limit is 50km/h in urban areas, 90km/h outside of cities. The blood alcohol limit is 0.2g/L.

Public Transport
Buses serve rural areas only once or twice per day, so make sure to check schedules if you're planning a day trip. Intercity buses such as those with Lux Express or Flixbus are generally comfortable. Train tickets are slightly cheaper when bought online at elron.ee. The railway system is small and very efficient. As of 2025, the three Baltic capitals can be reached within a single day by train.

MONEY
Currency: Euro (€)

CASH
Cash seems to be disappearing from Estonian cities, although it's still commonly used for smaller transactions in markets. It's a good idea to keep some euros in your pocket, but it's likely that you won't end up using them. Currency exchange points are easy to find in cities, but ATMs generally offer better rates.

CREDIT & DEBIT CARDS
Credit and debit cards are accepted almost everywhere in Estonia, especially Visa and MasterCard. You won't have trouble using them in hotels, restaurants, larger shops and for online bookings. Occasionally, smaller establishments or shops in remote areas might only accept cash.

DIGITAL PAYMENTS
Digital payments, including mobile payment apps and contactless payments, are popular in Estonia, a country known for its advanced digital infrastructure.

For places to stay in Finland, see p374

ARTBBNV/SHUTTERSTOCK

Above: Saimaa (p368); Right: Helsinki (p360)

Curated by
Anthony Ham

Finland

SCENERY, DESIGN AND FASCINATING CULTURE

Regionally, Finland is a curious melting pot blending
Arctic climes, charming, history-heavy coastal towns
and beguiling modern cities.

Is Finland a Scandinavian country? The debate is long-running; to weigh in you need to go. Finland is, in many ways, the black sheep of the Nordics – a middle child shaped culturally by East and West, as well as northern indigenous heritages. A history of devastating wars and invasion, from north to south, over centuries sets it apart – and sure makes being titled the 'world's happiest country' even more impressive.

Finland has rebuilt itself from the ashes (literally and figuratively) again and again to become a prime example of abundant living, from its summer cottage lifestyle to world-renowned contemporary design and architecture, and vibrant music and gastronomy scenes. Sisu (an untranslatable word for being determined and resilient), the nation's most

valued trait, can be traced across Finnish culture, whether it be sauna stamina, tenacious Olympians or all its plucky wilderness – even Finland's seal population is successfully fighting back against extinction. The natural beauty has character: the capricious aurora borealis (northern lights) and those endless coasts, lending the mighty nickname 'Land of a Thousand Lakes', are prime examples. Human-made marvels across city blocks and showrooms are sure to keep eyeballs busy, too. Savour all this stimuli, and most importantly, the infectious, fun-loving Finnish spirit – Finns are warm-hearted beyond the top-layer reserve. Whether it be festivals, outdoor thrills or ancient ruins, Finland and its unique mystique make for incredible explorations.

FIIPHOTO/SHUTTERSTOCK

THE MAIN AREAS

HELSINKI
Northern coolness with a neighbourly twist. **p360**

TURKU
Scandinavia's seaside rendition of southern charm. **p364**

SAIMAA LAKELAND
Lakes, seals and scenic roads. **p368**

ROVANIEMI & THE NORTH
Lapland hub, Arctic landscapes and Sámi culture. **p371**

Find Your Way

Finland is one of Europe's largest countries –
Helsinki is some 1000km from the Arctic Circle.
Lapland, easily the country's biggest
region, alone stretches 500km
south to north. Most adventures
start in Helsinki.

CAR

Having your own vehicle is by far
the easiest way to go. Watch out for
wildlife on the roads, know where
the next petrol station is, and in
winter use snow tyres and check
the weather.

PUBLIC TRANSPORT

You can set your watch by Finnish
transport. Trains (vr.fi) are most
comfortable; buses (matkahuolto.
fi) are slower but more frequent.
Busy train routes are best booked
in advance. Ferries connect
islands and mainland.

Saimaa Lakeland, p368

Find out why Finland is the
'Land of a Thousand Lakes'.
Savour breathtaking coasts
during cycling tours, hikes,
watersports and cottage
living.

Rovaniemi & the North, p371

Meet northern locals
including Santa Claus in an
Arctic Circle hub, discover
the Sámi's ancestral home,
and spend days sleighing,
sledding, snowmobiling and
reindeer-spotting.

Turku, p364

Fascinating medie-
val architecture in
Finland's oldest city
and former capital.
From here, little port
towns strung along
the southern coast
and archipelago are
prime for exploring.

Helsinki, p360

Impressive art and engineering,
nearby lake life and exciting tastes
from farm to forest. In the capital
of the 'world's happiest country',
there's something for everyone.

Nuorgam
Lakselv
Utsjoki
Karasjok
Sevettijärvi
Karigasniemi
Kaamanen
Kilpisjärvi
Inarijärvi
Siida
Inari
Nellim
Ivalo
Raja-Jooseppi
Enontekiö
Saariselkä
Lokan
tekojärvi
Kittilä
Tulppio
Kolari
Savukoski
Sodankylä
Pelkosenniemi
Pello
Kemijärvi
Salla
Sinettä
Rovaniemi
Arktikum
Tornio
Ranua
Kuusam
Kemi
Pudasjärvi
Gulf of
Bothnia
Oulu
Puolanka
Raahe
Liminka
Suomussalmi
Kalajoki
Oulujärvi
Ontojärvi
Kokkola
Ylivieska
Pyhäntä
Kajaani
Kuhmo
Jakobstad
Haapajärvi
Sonkajärvi
Nurmes
Björköby
Kaustinen
Lestijärvi
Pihtipudas
Lieksa
Vaasa
Pielinen
Seinäjoki
Viitasaari
Alavus
Saarijärvi
Kuopio
Virrat
Suonenjoki
Joensuu
Parkano
Jyväskylä
Pieksämäki
Varkaus
Jämsä
Saimaa Lakeland
Pori
Puulavesi
Savonlinna
Orivesi
Mikkeli
Olavinlinna
Rauma
Tampere
Saimaa
Huittinen
Heinola
Imatra
Hämeenlinna
Lahti
Lappeenranta
Forssa
Riihimäki
Kouvola
Åland
Turun Linna
Turku
Vanha
Kauppahalli
Kotka
Mariehamn
Turun
Tuomiokirkko
HELSINKI
Aboa Vetus
Ars Nova
Architecture
& Design
Museum
Suomenlinna
Hanko
Åland Sea

SWEDEN

RUSSIA

ESTONIA

0   100 km
0   60 miles

Suomenlinna (p362)

Plan Your Time

Finland is great for road trips, or combining public transport with car hire. More than three-quarters of Finland is forested and there's 4600km of coastline – spending time in nature is essential.

A Long Weekend

● **Helsinki** (p360) is a great place to start, with its impressive architecture, great gastronomy and historic digs. Wander through the inner city, gaping at buildings or the Design District's backstreet windows, then take the ferry to the UNESCO-listed **Suomenlinna** (p362) sea fortress, where historic fortifications and barracks dot an 18th-century military stronghold.

A Finland Week

● For a true northern adventure, take the night train from **Helsinki** (p360) to **Rovaniemi** (p371), Lapland's capital and the 'official hometown of Santa Claus'. In two days you can visit its excellent museums and soak up some nature, before heading north to discover Sámi cultural landmarks at **Siida** (p373) and cruise **Lake Inari** (p372), Lapland's largest lake.

SEASONAL HIGHLIGHTS

SPRING
Winter activities are sometimes possible into March. As spring unfolds, days lengthen and temperatures warm.

SUMMER
Summer has festivals and ***mökki*** (cottage) getaways. Head north for extreme climes, including no-night summers.

AUTUMN
While Finns go back to work, it's a great time to travel though outside cities. Some attractions close until late May.

WINTER
Short, bitterly cold days, but the northern lights are possible. December brings Christmas markets and ***glögi*** (hot punch).

Helsinki

NORTHERN COOLNESS | CUTTING-EDGE ARCHITECTURE | SEASIDE CAPITAL

GETTING AROUND

Helsinki has Finland's only metro system, plus an efficient public tram and bus network and the City Bikes bike-share scheme, with some 1500 bikes at 150 stations citywide, April to September. The compact city centre is easily covered on foot.

Inexpensive local buses zip out to nearby villages, and local ferries serve island destinations including Suomenlinna. Check schedules and buy tickets online at *hsl.fi* or via the app.

When Prussian architect Carl Ludwig Engel set foot in Helsinki in 1816, the city held a mere 4000 inhabitants. Seven years earlier, Finland had been annexed by Russia after more than 600 years of Swedish rule. Russia's Alexander I happily transferred the capital from Turku closer to home – and tasked Engel with transforming an impoverished, war-torn city into a worthy capital for the new Grand Duchy of Finland.

For Engel, who reluctantly rebuilt Helsinki until his dying breath, today's city would be mind-boggling. Diverse, interesting architecture abounds, as Engel's neoclassical builds mingle with Jugendstil (art nouveau) and early-20th-century creations. Fine-dining restaurants, hip bars and design studios smack of cool, modern creativity. Yet such vibrancy is just the backdrop to everyday life in this laid-back harbour city. Parks, beaches and other natural escapes provide a great quality of life for the 600,000 inhabitants. If only Engel could see Helsinki today!

A Tsar's Tribute

Spot grand architecture

Looming above the pastel-coloured buildings of Helsinki's shoreline, **Helsinki Cathedral** *(Tuomiokirkko; helsingin tuomiokirkko.fi; adult/child €8/free)* dominates the city's skyline. The cathedral was built between 1830 and 1852 in honour of Tsar Nicholas I of Russia, the Grand Duke of Finland. It was designed by Engel, but after his death it was noticed that the church's proportions were not in perfect symmetry and the 12 rooftop statues of the Apostles were added.

☑ **TOP TIP**

One of the best ways to feel the sea breeze is to rent a city bike. The yellow bikes are dotted around the capital and work with the HSL app *(hsl.fi)*.

HELSINKI

Töölönlahti

TÖÖLÖ

Kaisaniemenpuisto

University Botanical Gardens

KRUUNUNHAKA

KLUUVI

Lastenlehdon puisto

Hietalahti Flea Market

Sinebrychoffin puisto

Architecture & Design Museum

Vanha Kauppahalli

EIRA

Kaivopuisto

Tähtitorninvuoren puisto

Korkeasaari

Hylkysaari

Kruununvuorenselkä

Katajanokka

Eteläsatama

Valkosaari

Luoto (Klippan)

Ryssänsaari

Pikkuluoto

Katajanokanluoto

Puolimatkansaari

Pohjoinen Uunisaari

Sirpalesaari

Liuskasaari

Harakka

Gulf of Finland

Suomenlinna

Suomenlinna

Lonna (1.2km)

0 — 500 m
0 — 0.25 miles

THE GUIDE

FINLAND HELSINKI

★ HIGHLIGHTS
1 Architecture & Design Museum
2 Suomenlinna
3 Vanha Kauppahalli

● SIGHTS
4 Helsinki Cathedral
5 Kampin Kappeli

6 Market Square
7 National Museum of Finland
8 Suomenlinna-Museo
9 Uspenski Cathedral

● ACTIVITIES
10 Allas Sea Pool

● SLEEPING
11 Hobo Hotel Helsinki
12 Home Hotel Jugend
13 Hostel Suomenlinna
14 Hotel Haven
15 Hotel Mestari
16 Scandic Grand Central

● EATING
see 13 Cafe Silo
17 El Fant
18 Erikssonin Osteribaari
19 Kolme Kruunua
20 Magu
21 Palace
see 18 Story

ELIEL SAARINEN'S HELSINKI

Not as well known as Alvar Aalto, architect Eliel Saarinen (1873–1950) helped shape modern Helsinki in the early 20th century. His style is noticeable as soon as you arrive – the four huge male figures holding spherical lamps at the central railway station are an unmissable feature of the art nouveau structure designed by Saarinen in 1919. Nearby is the towering, church-like **National Museum of Finland** (under renovation until 2027), tracing Finland's history from the Stone Age. Saarinen completed this in 1910, inspired by the medieval architecture of rural Finland. This building is one of the most important examples of the National Romantic style that appeared in Nordic countries at the turn of the century.

A Garrison Getaway

Explore a UNESCO-listed sea fortress

Helsinki has more than 300 islands, and the main sight among them is **Suomenlinna** (*suomenlinna.fi*) sea fortress, dating from the 1740s and Helsinki's only UNESCO World Heritage site. On the island, be prepared to walk as Suomenlinna's fortifications and barracks host multiple little museums, from toy and military collections to **Suomenlinna-Museo** (*adult/child €9/4*), which showcases the fortress' history. If you fancy a tasty cinnamon bun, try **Cafe Silo** (*silo.fi*) near the main entrance.

HSL ferries (*hsl.fi*) leave from **Market Sq** (Kauppatori). Buy zone AB tickets (*single adult/child €2.95/1.50*) at the platform, online or via the app.

Steamy Views

Helsinki's favourite sauna

In summer from Tuesdays to Saturdays, make time to visit **Lonna** (*lonna.fi*), an island just offshore from Suomenlinna; booking is advised. Tiny Lonna makes a cute excursion from Helsinki, and its public loft saunas have calming sea views. The sauna can be combined with dips in the sea – note that it's a mixed sauna for all genders. Bring your own swimsuit, if you wish, as well as slippers to walk into the sea. The ferry (10 minutes) leaves from Kauppatori (Market Sq) and is operated by **FRS Finland** (*frs-finland.fi/suomenlinna; adult/child/under 6yr €6.80/3.40/free*).

A Pool with a View

Take a swim and a sauna

Open year-round, **Allas Sea Pool** (*allasseapool.fi; adult/child/under 2yr from €18/10/free*) is an urban spa oasis right beside Market Sq. The spa has fresh and saltwater pools, as well as sauna and wellness facilities. The pools are open till 9pm or 10pm, which, especially in autumn and winter, offers possibilities for moonlight swims. Take in Helsinki's city lights from the upper-floor bar after you've had a relaxing steam in the sauna.

 EATING IN CENTRAL HELSINKI: OUR PICKS

Magu: Vegan fine dining. Try the eight-course option and the small producers' eco-wines. *4-10pm Wed-Sat* €€€

Kolme Kruunua: Homey Finnish dishes – meatballs, fried vendace, salmon soup. *4pm-1am Mon-Thu, to 1.30am Fri, noon-1.30am Sat, to 1am Sun* €€

Palace: Finland's only two-Michelin-starred restaurant has 1950s modernist decor, seasonal Nordic cuisine and balcony views. *6-11.30pm Wed-Sat* €€€

El Fant: Natural wine, light lunches from sourdough toasties to pasta, and ice tea on a cobbled street near Senate Sq. *11am-varies Tue-Sun* €

Russian Influence

An Eastern Orthodox Church

Uspenski Cathedral *(hos.fi),* perched on a Katajanokka hill overlooking the city, is one of the most visible symbols of Helsinki's Russian influence. Built in 1868, it's the largest Eastern Orthodox church in Western Europe, distinguished by its red-brick facade, golden domes and intricate Byzantine-Russian architecture. Inside, visitors are greeted by icons, chandeliers and richly decorated altars. The cathedral's position offers panoramic views of Helsinki, adding to its allure.

Fine Finnish Foods

Taste the traditions

Adjoining the bustling Kauppatori (Market Sq), **Vanha Kauppahalli** *(Old Market Hall; vanhakauppahalli.fi)* features stall after stall selling traditional Finnish foods and international flavours. Built in 1889, the market hall retains its revered knowledge of modern food trends – in fact, it has been featured in listings of the world's best foodie spots. Try the traditional creamy salmon soup at **Story** *(story-restaurants.fi),* or sit down at **Erikssonin Osteribaari** *(kalatukkueriksson.fi)* for oysters hailed as Helsinki's best. The market also has a selection of Finnish meats, such as moose, bear, reindeer, Karelian pies and fried vendace.

Dashing Designs

Enjoy the art of living

On the border of design-central Punavuori and neighbouring Kaartinkaupunki, the **Architecture & Design Museum** *(designmuseum.fi; adult/child €20/free)* is for anyone intrigued by the Finns' take on creating bold everyday objects. The exhibits vary from Ilmari Tapiovaara's woodwork and Eero Aarnio's chairs and lamps, to Lotta Nieminen's contemporary take on design. The museum is closed Mondays from September to end of May.

For glasswork aficionados, a trip to the design museum's satellite space in Arabianranta's **Iittala & Arabia Design Centre** *(iittala.com; free)* is a must. Take tram 6 from the central railway station.

Silence in the City

Escape the clamour of the city centre

Beside the busy Kamppi shopping centre, the conical wooden structure of **Kampin Kappeli** *(Kamppi Chapel; kampin kappeli.fi)* is an ecumenical place to promote a very Finnish virtue: silence. Everyone is welcome to enter and sit in silence, surrounded by some of the busiest parts of the city. Eye-catching from the outside, the chapel is particularly beautiful inside with its curving wooden walls. Visit in winter (September to May) for free; other times adults pay €5.

OLYMPIC DRINK

In 1952, Helsinki was set to host the long-awaited Olympic Games. However, there was a problem: the city, emerging from WWII, lacked bars and experienced bartenders to cater to the thirsty visitors' needs. A ready-made cocktail was needed. Enter Lonkero, a combination of gin and grapefruit soda – a uniquely sour and lightly carbonated cocktail manufactured by Hartwall brewery. Lonkero quickly gained popularity, becoming a staple in Finnish culture and social settings. Over the years, various flavours emerged – from cranberry and lemon to mango – but the classic gin and grapefruit combination remains. Today, Lonkero is a symbol of Finnish summer. Sip one in most bars or buy it at any supermarket.

Turku

MEDIEVAL ARCHITECTURE | ARCHIPELAGO GATEWAY | CULTURE HUB

GETTING AROUND

Downtown Turku is easily explored on foot. Bikes and ride-sharing scooters are popular in summer. Airport service is limited; usually it's cheaper to reach Turku from Helsinki by car or train, or Stockholm by ferry. If you fly into Turku, take bus 1 from the airport to get to the city centre in approximately 20 minutes (tickets €3). Multiple ferries depart daily from the city's harbour to Åland, taking around six hours to reach Mariehamn.

☑ **TOP TIP**

All day, the free mini ferry **Föri** shuttles walkers and bikers across the Aura in two minutes flat. Chugging since 1904, the orange commuter is Finland's oldest daily transport. Find it a few blocks southwest of the Martinsilta (St Martin's Bridge).

Turku (Åbo in Swedish) is Finland's second city – or first, by some accounts, as it was the capital until 1812. Dating from the 13th century, when Turku was founded, the majestic Turun Linna (Turku Castle) and Gothic wonder Turun Tuomiokirkko (Turku Cathedral) are testaments to the city's storied past. Contemporary Turku is even more enticing, challenging Helsinki's cultural preeminence with cutting-edge art galleries, summer music festivals and innovative restaurants. The University of Turku is Finland's oldest, established in 1640 by the Swedish king as the Royal Academy of Turku, and it still draws young minds to the city. Students keep cafes and clubs buzzing, while designer boutiques and second-hand shops offer limitless scope for browsing beauty and buried treasure. Through the ancient network of atmospheric streets and squares, the Aurajoki (Aura River) meanders picturesquely out to sea. For nature lovers, the city is the gateway to the glorious Turku archipelago.

Feudal Fortress

Finland's largest castle

Founded in 1280 as a Swedish military outpost at the mouth of the Aurajoki, the gargantuan **Turun Linna** *(turunlinna.fi)* is easily Finland's biggest castle. It's free for visitors to roam the outdoor courtyard's annexes; admission to the **museum** *(adult/child €14/6)* is worthwhile, too. The labyrinthine layout features dungeons, banquet halls and the castle's impressive Old Bailey, exhibiting objects and artefacts once belonging to the ruling elite. The castle was seriously damaged by Soviet bombing in 1941 and brought back to its former glory after the war.

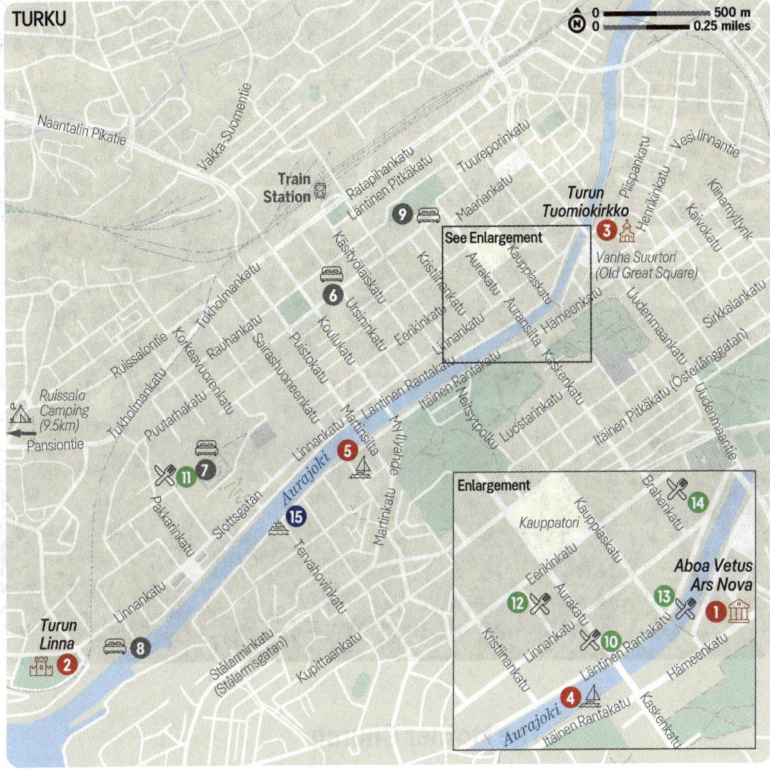

HIGHLIGHTS
1 Aboa Vetus Ars Nova
2 Turun Linna
3 Turun Tuomiokirkko

ACTIVITIES
4 MS Aurella
5 MS Rudolfina

SLEEPING
6 Bridgettine Sisters' Guesthouse
7 Hotel Kakola
8 Laivahostel Borea
9 Park Hotel

EATING
10 Blanko

11 Kakolanruusu
12 Kauppahalli
13 Smör
14 Tiirikkala

TRANSPORT
15 Föri Ferry

Masterpieces Old & New

Avant-garde art meets archaeology

The riverside **Aboa Vetus Ars Nova** *(Museum of Archaeology & Contemporary Art; avan.fi; adult/child €16/11)* draws visitors underground to Turku's medieval streets with imposing stone ruins. Some 37,000 artefacts, from ceramics to buried gold, have been unearthed from the site below (digs still continue) and are now exhibited between 14th- and 15th-century cellars, church foundations, and building walls buried following the great fire of 1827.

The Mother Church

Finland's most important religious building

Consecrated in 1300, **Turun Tuomiokirkko** *(Turku Cathedral; turuntuomiokirkko.fi)* was rebuilt many times after damaging fires, but still looks majestic. Besides the impressive Gothic interior and the 1836 altarpiece depicting the Transfiguration of Jesus, a small **museum** *(adult/child €2/1)* is filled with religious artefacts and ritualistic tools from the 15th and 16th centuries. In summer, try to catch a Turku International Organ Concert – the cathedral hosts free concerts performed by musicians from around the globe (8pm Tuesdays in June, July and August).

 EATING IN TURKU: OUR PICKS

Smör: Enjoy organic, locally sourced dishes by flickering candles in a vaulted cellar. *5-11pm Wed-Thu, to midnight Fri, 4pm-midnight Sat* €€€

Tiirikkala: Cool brunch and cocktails in a wooden house; live jazz and blues on weekends. *9.30am-9pm Tue-Thu, to 11pm Fri & Sat, 11am-4pm Sun* €€

Blanko: Hip venue with great lunch specials and the best Sunday brunch in town. *11am-11pm Mon-Thu, to 3am Fri, noon-3am Sat, 1-9pm Sun* €€

Kakolanruusu: Modern fare, open-fire cooking in a former prison warehouse. *4-11pm Tue-Thu, noon-2.30pm & 4pm-midnight Fri, from 1pm Sat* €€€

Turun Tuomiokirkko

Finnish Food Tour

Eat your heart out in Turku

Turku's fabulous **Kauppahalli** *(Market Hall; kauppahalli. fi)* is easily its most atmospheric lunch spot. The historic covered market, built in 1896, is where locals of all ages gather for bites and coffee-break chatter across rich wood counters and tables. Vendors sell local delicacies, including artisan cheeses, meats, seafood and baked goods; there's also multicultural cuisine and a vegan kitchen. It's closed on Sundays.

Cool Cruises

Head out into the archipelago

Archipelago and river cruises are popular in summer, with most boats departing from the Martinsilta quay. **MS Rudolfina** *(rudolfina.fi; from €37))* provides lunch and dinner harbour cruises overlooking Turku Castle, Pikisaar Island and Ruissalo Island, while evening cruises show off Naantali Harbour and the Kultaranta (president's summer residence). If you're short on time, the **MS Aurella** *(river-cruises.fi; from €9)* takes you along the Aurajoki on 1½-hour guided tours.

ONCE UPON A CAPITAL

Åbo (Turku's original Swedish name), once Sweden's second-largest town, comes from a settlement *(bo)* on a river *(å)*. When the Russians took over, the city – still deeply connected to Sweden – lost its capital status to Helsinki and became a commerce hub. The name Turku is an archaic Russian word for 'marketplace'.

Today, the Aurajoki, lined with terrace restaurants and cultural sights, is Turku's hub for local life. These riverbanks, though, have been inhabited over millennia. Archaeological finds date back to the Stone Age, but Turku was founded with a Catholic settlement in 1229. In the 14th century, a new church and the Turku Castle saw the city consecrated as an administrative and spiritual base.

Saimaa Lakeland

MEDIEVAL CASTLE | WATER ACTIVITIES | LOCAL FOOD

Places

Savonlinna p368

Kolovesi & Linnansaari National Parks p369

Saimaa's reputation in Finland is almost mythical. It seems like the labyrinth of lakes and islands has been here forever – in fact, it was created 11,000 years ago when the glaciers of the last Ice Age withdrew across Finland, carving landmasses and leaving thousands of lakes behind. Around this time, a population of ringed seals separated from their pack in the Arctic Ocean and were left stranded in freshwater. These ringed seals are now endemic to Saimaa, and while they remain endangered, their numbers have risen from dozens to more than 400 in recent decades. The seals are a lovely attraction, but Finns also flock to Saimaa to bask in the summer sun, staying in lake-shore cottages as the region's villages come to life with outdoor terraces and small festivals. In winter, the lakes are covered with ice and snow – as well as locals ice-hole fishing, skating and skiing.

GETTING AROUND

Saimaa's 14,500km lake coastline is the world's longest, and the region's small towns and villages are few and far between. The area is best explored by car or from the water – trains and buses won't reach many of the best spots. City-hop between bigger hubs like Savonlinna and Lappeenranta by public transport. The bus from Lappeenranta to Savonlinna (3¾ hours) changes in Mikkeli; the train (just over two hours) curves near the Russian border, with a change in Parikkala.

Savonlinna

Saimaa's king of the castle

Savonlinna, with its medieval castle and busy summer harbour, is the jewel of Saimaa. On its own island, **Olavinlinna** *(St Olaf's Castle; kansallismuseo.fi/fi/olavinlinna; adult/child €14/7)* dates from the 15th century when Sweden wanted to protect its eastern regions against the Novgorodians. In July, Olavinlinna hosts an annual **Opera Festival** *(operafestival.fi)*, started by Finnish opera singer Aino Ackté in 1912. The dimly lit castle's slightly claustrophobic corridors and staircases are fun to explore. Guided tours in English run hourly, June to August.

Neighbouring **Riihisaari**, wich used to harbour Olavinlinna's war boats until Finland's border shifted further east in 1617, holds **Savonlinna Museum** *(savonlinna.fi/riihisaari; adult/child €10/free)* with a History of Saimaa exhibit, featuring life-sized Saimaa ringed seals and intriguing sailing and sea-life paraphernalia.

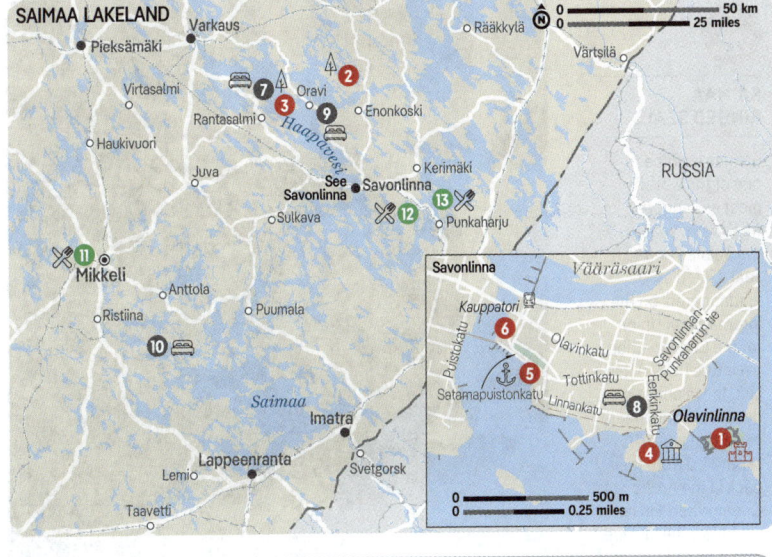

⭐ **HIGHLIGHTS**
1 Olavinlinna

🔴 **SIGHTS**
2 Kolovesi National Park
3 Linnansaari National Park

4 Riihisaari
5 Savonlinna Harbour
6 Savonlinna Market Square

⚫ **SLEEPING**
7 Hotel & Spa Resort Järvisydän
8 Hotel Saima

9 Oravi Village
10 Uhkua

🟢 **EATING**
11 Kirjalan Paahtimo
12 Museoravintola Lusto
13 Wanha Koulu

Linnankatu is a cobblestoned street leading from the castle to the harbour. Savonlinna's **Market Sq** (Kauppatori) and **Savonlinna Harbour** (Satama) sit side-by-side and are best experienced in summer when local delicacies such as fried vendace and *lörtsy* (turnover) are sold at stalls.

Kolovesi & Linnansaari National Parks

Aquatic excursions and seal-spotting

Kolovesi and **Linnansaari National Parks** (*nationalparks. fi*) are located on islands on Lake Saimaa. In summer, **Järvisydän Resort** (p374) provides kayak and boat excursions to Linnansaari. An excellent starting point for exploring both parks is **Oravi Village** (p374), offering diverse accommodation from cosy cabins and tree tents on Linnansaari island to modern apartments and lakeside glass houses in the village.

From Oravi, you can take a boat taxi to Linnansaari. When the lake is frozen, Linnansaari can be reached from Oravi and Järvisydän on marked trails, but don't stray from the path – it's important to provide a peaceful breeding period for the Saimaa ringed seals. If you're looking for seals, it's best to go

☑️ **TOP TIP**

Ask a tourist office about summer cycling trips around the lakeland. Two popular circular routes are the 154km Saimaa archipelago and 60km Puumala archipelago routes. Both include ferry rides and ridges winding across the lakes, and have hotels, restaurants, cafes and swimming.

SAIMAA RINGED SEALS

Saimaa is home to one of the world's most endangered freshwater seals, the Saimaa ringed seal. Listed as 'Endangered' on the International Union for the Conservation of Nature (IUCN) Red List, these animals descend from ringed seals that were separated from their pack in the Arctic Ocean when the land rose after the last Ice Age, some 9500 years ago. Now, due to a tenacious protection campaign, there are about 400 seals living in Saimaa. The seals are typically under 1.5m and weigh 50kg to 90kg. The best time to spot the elusive creatures is between May and mid-June when the seals climb on top of rocks to moult, but you can make sightings till September.

SEPPO ULMANEN/500PX

Saimaa ringed seal

on a guided tour, not least because the Saimaa ringed seal is a protected species. One of the best ways to take in the beauty of Saimaa and spot the seals is on an eco-boat ride – try **LakelandGTE** *(lakelandgte.fi; adult/child €65/50)* – silently gliding between Saimaa's many islands for an intimate feel of the landscape. A 75-minute eco-boat trip from Puumala includes informative narration by the skipper. Binoculars, coffee and cinnamon buns are available.

Trails of various lengths crisscross Linnansaari, the highlight being a climb to **Linnanvuori**, a rocky cliff with views of Saimaa's blue horizon.

EATING AROUND SAIMAA: OUR PICKS

Wanha Koulu: Summer restaurant-cafe in an old school (hence the name Old School) in Savonlinna. *10am-6pm Mon-Sat, from noon Sun* €€

Museoravintola Lusto: Museum restaurant with local organic meat, lake fish and mushrooms from nearby forests. *11am-7pm* €€

Kirjalan Paahtimo: Small cafe-roastery with Mikkeli's best breakfast, the Taste Saimaa Breku. *7.30am-5pm Mon-Fri, 9.30am-3pm Sat* €

Uhkua: Order dinner baskets of local delicacies at this floating cottage. Foodie events like foraged dinners. Booking required. *hours vary* €€

Rovaniemi & the North

SANTA'S HOME | ARCTIC ACTIVITIES | SÁMI CULTURE

Rovaniemi (Roavvenjárga in Northern Sámi) is known as the capital of Lapland, the country's largest and northernmost region. Lapland stretches for over a quarter of Finland's surface, though many people think it begins some 150km further up. Rovaniemi's calling card is – you guessed it – Santa Claus, who resides year-round in the village northeast of town and magically multiplies in winter to greet the tens of thousands of peak-season visitors. Further north, deeper into the Arctic, the small, spread-out village of Inari occupies a big and important place in the Lapland picture as the seat of the Sámi Parliament in Finland and effectively the Sámi people's cultural capital in Finland. Today, Inari is a hub of tourism in northern Lapland, a good base for local walks and lake trips, winter husky sledding and aurora borealis viewing. For all its many attractions, it remains agreeably low-key, far from overwhelmed by its visitors.

Rovaniemi

Learn about the Arctic

Arktikum (*arktikum.fi; adult/child/family €20/5/45*) is the best place to start your Lapland journey. Inside one of Rovaniemi's most iconic buildings, the two-storey gallery is covered by a glass ceiling resembling a frozen finger pointing to the North Pole. Rovaniemi's main cultural institution takes you on a journey through the region's history, from the Iron Age to the contemporary era. Learn how Rovaniemi evolved from an agricultural settlement first mentioned in 1453 to an official town in 1960.

Pay a visit to Santa

About 8km northeast of the city centre is the official residence of **Santa Claus Village** (*santaclausvillage.info; free*), open 365 days a year for visitors from all corners of the globe. Christmas is serious business in Finland – surrounded by

Places

Rovaniemi p371

Inari p372

GETTING AROUND

Rovaniemi airport is 8km northeast of the city centre. City bus 11 runs to/from the centre (Ruokasenkatu) every 40 minutes, December to February. **Airport Express** (*airportbus. fi*) minibuses run to the centre (reduced service outside winter). The city is walkable. It's a four-hour, 326km drive north to Inari, although you can fly to **Ivalo Airport**, 49km south of Inari and take a bus or rent a car from there. For more information, see *visitinari.fi*.

WHERE IS THE ARCTIC?

Running through Santa Claus Village is the line that marks the border of the Arctic Circle, the southernmost latitude at which the sun will not rise all day during the winter solstice. While the boundary makes for a great photo opportunity, you may not be standing in the right spot when visiting Rovaniemi.

This is because the Arctic Circle is not fixed – rather, it's moving slightly season after season. Because of variations in the Earth's axial tilt caused by gravitational interactions with the moon and other celestial bodies, the actual Arctic Circle shifts north or south by several metres each year.

☑ TOP TIP

There's usually snow from mid-November to late April. In December and early January the sun is up less than four hours a day. Despite that, and temperatures well below zero, peak season is December and January. Book ahead at that time.

---

forests, the red village is part shopping centre, part theme park, with restaurants serving slow-cooked reindeer stews, souvenir shops brimming with all things Arctic and design stores of Finnish brands such as Marimekko and Pentik. Enter Santa's Office (under the 'Meet Santa' sign) for a three-minute chat with Santa himself. The encounter will be photographed and filmed by elves; download the results for €50 (or €35 for an A4 print). Also in the village centre is the **Santa Claus Post Office**. Any mail sent from here is stamped with a special Arctic Circle/Santa/Reindeer postmark. To get to **Santa Claus Village**, catch local bus 8, the seasonal **Santa Claus Bus** (*santaclausbus.fi*) or the bus to the airport.

Inari

Sail to a sacred island

A great way to experience Inarijärvi, Finland's third-largest lake, is to take a summer cruise from the dock at the Siida car park in the 120-seat catamaran operated by **Visit Inari** (*visitinari.fi*). The boat sails to – but doesn't land on – **Ukonsaari** (Ukko Island), an old Sámi sacred site. Departures are at 1pm from mid-June to mid-September, and 5pm in July. On request, the 1pm cruise will drop you at Pielpavuono, from where you can walk back to Inari via **Pielpajärven Erämaakirkko**, an *erämaakirkko* (wilderness church) that dates back to 1760.

Visit Inari, with an office next to **Hotel Inari** (p374), offers a range of other activities, such as reindeer- and husky-farm visits, snowmobiling and aurora borealis outings, with transport from Inari included.

Immerse yourself in Sámi culture

Designed by Oulu-based architectural firm Halo in 2012, the curved wooden structure housing the **Sámi Cultural Centre Sajos** (*sajos.fi*) is an impressive landmark in the heart of Inari. The Sámi Parliament in Finland operates from the oval meeting hall, while a Sámi library, **Café Čaiju** and a crafts store are in other rooms. To learn about the functioning of the Sámi Parliament, you can book a 45-minute guided tour (*€300 per group*), although the building is publicly accessible free of charge. The **Sámi Duodji** shop here is the official shop of the Sámi handicrafts association; its trademark guarantees that an item is an authentic Sámi handicraft.

TOP EXPERIENCE

Siida

Siida, a Sámi term referring to a traditional community, offers an introduction to Sámi culture through superb presentations of Sámi artefacts and northern Lapland nature. Learn about Sámi history and the holistic connection between livelihoods, nature and language of Europe's only recognised indigenous peoples.

ALEXANDERSTOCK23/SHUTTERSTOCK

Siida Open-Air Museum

Nature & Nurture

The permanent exhibition combines huge photo panels that illustrate the region's ecosystems and the cycle of the seasons, with artefacts showing how the relationship to Arctic nature continues to influence Sámi culture. From clothing to hunting and cooking tools, geography has shaped the Sámi way of life – how climate change will affect future generations is a question the museum leaves open.

The Return of Sámi Artefacts

In 2021, the National Museum of Finland returned thousands of objects from its Sámi collection to Siida, in a government-backed repatriation project that aimed to return heritage artefacts to their homeland and reconnect communities. A glass case displays part of the collection – many are still being studied as their origin is unknown – providing a new context for artefacts that have been tied to Finland's colonial history for the past century.

Open-Air Museum

The Siida Open-Air Museum offers a glimpse into the architectural heritage of the Sámi people. Explore nearly 50 structures, including traditional Sámi pole tents, storage buildings and traps, along an 800m trail. The museum also showcases Sámi livelihoods and lifestyles, dating back 10,000 years, through artefacts, dwellings and archaeological findings.

TOP TIPS

● Guided tours are available on request, for both the permanent exhibition and the open-air museum.

● The 2023 documentary *Mácchan – Homecoming* tells the story of the Sámi collection's repatriation.

PRACTICALITIES

● siida.fi ● 9am-6pm daily Jun-Sep, 10am-5pm Mon-Sat Oct-May ● adult/ child/under 6yr €18/7/free

Places We Love to Stay

€ Budget   €€ Midrange   €€€ Top End

Helsinki
MAP p361

Hostel Suomenlinna € Mixed and female dorms, as well as double and family rooms, on the UNESCO World Heritage–listed fortress island of Suomenlinna.

Hobo Hotel Helsinki €€ Great value for money; Hobo's restaurant and urban retro vibes keep you happy, bang in the city centre.

Home Hotel Jugend €€ Located in a castle-like 1908 stone building, with modern and stylish rooms and beautiful original features elsewhere.

Hotel Haven €€€ Five-star hotel with one of the city's best breakfast views over Old Market Hall and Market Sq.

Scandic Grand Central €€€ Find 1930s railway romance in the Eliel Saarinen–designed building, which also hosts Helsinki's central railway station.

Hotel Mestari €€€ Excellent-value hotel located close to Kamppi shopping centre, but with a feeling of calm thanks to dim lighting and dark-panelled rooms.

Turku
MAP p365

Bridgettine Sisters' Guesthouse € Run by nuns, this Catholic convent's guest wing is a haven with austere, spotless rooms.

Laivahostel Borea € The SS *Bore*, a passenger ship turned hostel, docks outside the Forum Marinum museum.

Ruissalo Camping € On Ruissalo island, this campground has grassy sites, great cabins, saunas and Turku's closest beaches.

Park Hotel €€ In an art nouveau building overlooking a hilly park, this hotel has characterful rooms, classical music and a lobby parrot.

Hotel Kakola €€€ Former prison transformed with plush, warm Scandinavian design – including a 'jailhouse chic' cell room.

Saimaa Lakeland
MAP p369

Oravi Village €€ Located between Linnansaari and Kolovesi National Parks, Oravi has an eco-hostel and tree tents on Linnansaari island as well as budget-friendly apartments on the mainland.

Hotel Saima €€ A lovely wooden villa in central Savonlinna with six rooms equipped with vintage furniture – the suite is particularly spacious, and there's a room offering castle views.

Uhkua (p370) **€€€** The essence of Saimaa shines in Uhkua's floating cottage and sauna, as well as its nature-driven activities, from kayaking to foraging tours.

Hotel & Spa Resort Järvisydän €€€ The lakeside spa and the glass-walled suites are the draws here; organised activities in the surrounding area are a bonus.

Rovaniemi & the North

Hostel Cafe Koti € Centrally located, popular hostel with 24 rooms and two dorms in neat, clean Nordic style.

Arctic City Hotel €€ Rooms are compact but plush fabrics give them an intimate feel; the location is super central.

Hotel Inari €€ Well-run, comfortable, medium-sized lakeside hotel in the middle of Inari with great views from the restaurant.

Arctic Light Hotel €€€ Inspired conversion of the former city hall with individually designed, Arctic-themed rooms and a superb breakfast.

Glass Resort €€€ Luxurious two-floor 'glass apartments': glass bedroom ceilings and full-wall glass windows for comfortable aurora borealis viewing.

Lomakylä Inari €€€ Comfy and modern two-to-four-person cabins 1km from the village centre. Some are right by the lakeshore with a glass ceiling for aurora spotting; others have a private sauna.

Wilderness Hotel Inari €€€ Inari's classiest rooms, at the lakeside Wilderness Hotel Inari and the riverside Wilderness Hotel Juutua.

Practicalities

Tourist Information
The main website of the Finnish Tourist Board is *visitfinland.com*. Cities, large towns and major tourist destinations also have tourist offices.

IGOR EFREMYCHEV/SHUTTERSTOCK

Visas
Schengen country citizens can enter freely for any length of stay. Travellers from the UK, Canada, New Zealand, the US and Australia can stay for up to 90 days in any six-month period, but, from late 2026, they will need an ETIAS travel authorisation.

Time
Finland is on Eastern European Time (EET), an hour ahead of Sweden and Norway. In winter it's two hours ahead of UTC/GMT.

Smoking
Smoking is not allowed inside public buildings. Most restaurants and cafes don't have smoking sections. Cigarette packets are sold by cashiers in shops.

Public Holidays
New Year's Day 1 January
Epiphany 6 January
Good Friday Friday before Easter
Easter March/April
Easter Monday Monday after Easter Sunday
Labour Day 1 May
Feast of the Ascension 40th day after Easter
Pentecost Seventh Sunday after Easter
Midsummer Saturday between 20 and 26 June
All Saints' Day Saturday between 31 October and 6 November
Independence Day 6 December
Christmas Day 25 December
St Stephen's Day 26 December

Opening Hours
Banks 10am–4.30pm weekdays
Bars 3pm–2am weekdays
Cafes 8am–7pm weekdays
Clubs 8pm–5am Friday and Saturday
Restaurants 11am–9.30pm
Shopping malls 10am–8pm
Shops 10am–6pm Monday to Friday, 11am–5pm weekends

Etiquette
• Greet men, women and children with a brief but firm handshake and make eye contact.
• Finns value conversation but don't engage in small talk; silence is considered preferable.
• Shower before entering a sauna (pictured). Nudity is the norm (a towel is required in mixed saunas), but check first.
• Finns are very punctual and expect the same in return.

375

Language

Finnish is not closely related to any language other than Estonian and Karelian and a handful of other rare languages. There is a Swedish-speaking minority in Finland and all Finns learn Swedish in school.

Basics

Hello. Hei/Terve (pol) Moi (inf). *hay/tehrr-veh/moy*

Goodbye. Näkemiin (pol)/Moi (inf). *na-keh-meen/moy*

Yes. Kyllä (pol)/Joo (inf). *kül-lah/yoo*

No. Ei. *ay*

Please. There's no frequently used word for 'please' in Finnish. Often kiitos (thank you) is used.

Thank you. Kiitos/Kiitti (inf). *kee-toss/keet-ti*

Excuse me. Anteeksi. *uhn-teehk-si*

Sorry. Olen pahoillani/Sori (inf). *o-lehn puh-hoyl-luh-ni/so-rri*

What's your name? Mikä teidän nimenne on?/Mikä sun nimi on? (inf) *mi-ka tay-dan ni-mehn-neh on/mi-ka sun ni-mi on*

My name is ... Minun nimeni on .../Mun nimi on ... (inf). *mi-nun ni-mehn-ni on .../mun ni-mi on...*

Do you speak English? Puhutko englantia? *pu-hut-ko ehng-luhn-ti-uh*

I don't understand. En ymmärrä. *ehn üm-marr-rra*

Directions

Where's ... (train station)? Missä on ... (juna-asema (inf)/rautatie-asema)? *mis-sa on ... (yu-nuh-uh-se-muh/row-tuh-ti-eh-uh-se-muh)*

I'm looking for...? Etsin....? *et sin...*

Can you show me (on the map)? Voitko näyttää minulle (kartasta)? *voyt-ko na-üt-taa mi-nul-leh (kuhrr-tuhs-tuh)*

Time

What time is it? Paljonko kello on? *puhl-yon-ko kehl-lo on*

It's (one) o'clock. Kello on (yksi). *kehl-lo on (ük-si)*

morning aamu *ah-mu*

afternoon iltapäivä *il-tuh-pa-i-va*

evening/night ilta *il-tuh*

today tänään *ta-naan*

Emergencies

Help! Apua! *uh-pu-uh*

Go away! Mene pois!/Häivy! (inf). *meh-neh poys/ha-i-vü*

I'm ill. Minä olen sairas. *mi-na o-lehn sai-rruhs*

Call the police Soittakaa poliisi! *soyt-tuh-kah po-lee-si*

Eating & Drinking

What would you recommend? Mitä suosittelisit? *mi-ta su-o-sit-teh-li-sit*

Can I see the menu please? Saisinko ruokalistan? *sai-sin-ko-ru-o-kuh-lis-tuhn*

NUMBERS

1
yksi *ük-si*

2
kaksi *kuhk-si*

3
kolme *kol-meh*

4
neljä *nehl-ya*

5
viisi *vee-si*

6
kuusi *koo-si*

7
seitsemän *sayt-seh-man*

8
kahdeksan *kuhkh-dehk-suhn*

9
yhdeksän *ükh-dehk-san*

10
kymmenen *küm-meh-nehn*

Helsinki (p360)

Arriving & Getting Around

Helsinki-Vantaa Airport is the primary point of entry for most visitors arriving in Finland. The airport has a railway station underneath.

Bus & Train
Bigger cities are well connected by trains and buses. In Lapland, Tornio, Rovaniemi, Kemijärvi and Kolari can be reached by train. Buses and trains are reliable and comfortable; in winter snow might cause delays.

Train Tickets
Finland's train provider is **VR** *(vr.fi)*. Tickets are cheaper if purchased online at least a month in advance. Long-distance tickets must be bought before boarding the train. Stations have ticket machines and some have service desks.

Hiring a Car
Cars are best rented in bigger cities or airports; prices tend to be higher in Åland. Both manual and automatic options are available. You can also rent hybrid or electric cars.

Road Conditions
Bigger highways are in good shape, but the remoter the road, the bumpier it gets. Take notice when you see warning signs for moose/deer. Rental cars will have studded or friction tyres in winter.

MONEY
Currency: Euro (€)

CREDIT CARDS
Hotels, cafes, restaurants and shops accept credit cards, as do most stalls in the market squares, especially in bigger cities. In more remote spots it is convenient to have some cash at hand in case credit-card machines are down. In Helsinki, a few establishments have started endorsing a no-cash policy.

DIGITAL PAYMENTS
Digital payments are growing in popularity. MobilePay is the most popular app for mobile payments in Finland but other apps, such as ApplePay, work as well.

TIPPING
Tipping is not customary, although some restaurants have started providing the option for tipping, especially when paying by card. Cafes might have a tip jar by the till.

Curated by
Anna Richards

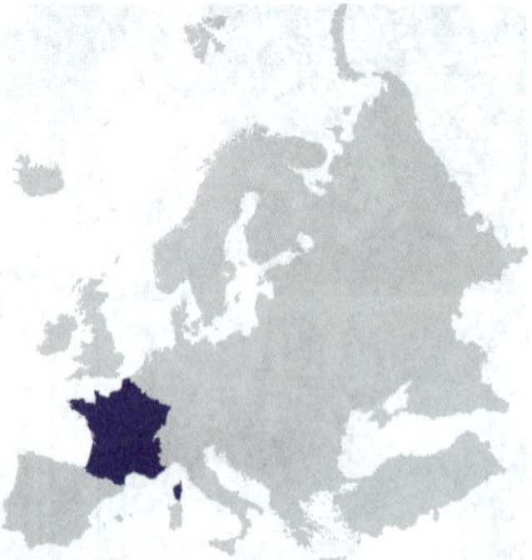

France

WINE, CHEESE AND WILDLY VARIED SCENERY

Endless coastline; mountains that provide thrills, be it summer or winter; and a gastronomy so good it invented Michelin stars.

Who doesn't dream of France? Ever since rich Europeans flocked to the Riviera in the 18th century and English alpinists conquered mountain peaks to unveil tourism in the Alps, it has been a highly desirable place to go.

A little bit of everything got sprinkled into the mix in France. Beaches along the Côte d'Azur that range from sugar-soft spun gold to rocky limestone inlets, mountain giants (including the highest peak in the Alps, Mont Blanc) that soften to hills peppered with lavender fields and olive groves in Provence, châteaux that span rivers and pierce the sky with a hundred turrets. Wherever you are in the country, you're never far from a wine region, and you can bet there'll be plenty of local, AOP cheeses too.

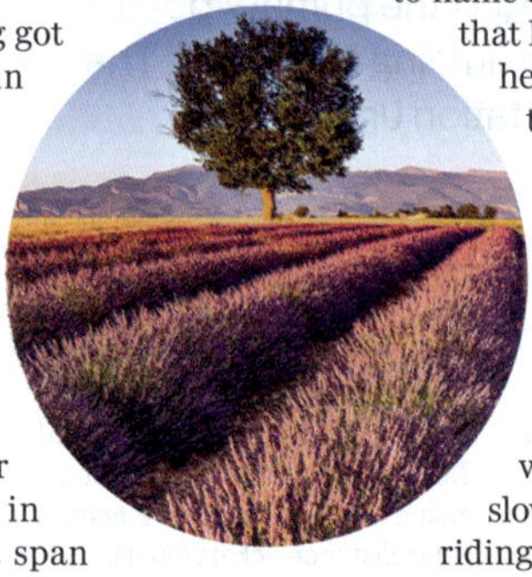

Throw in some of the most instantly recognisable monuments in the world – the Eiffel Tower, Notre-Dame and the Louvre to name a few – and it's no surprise that France consistently hits the headlines as 'the world's top tourist destination', notching up 100 million annual visitors in 2024. Making it even easier to get around responsibly, greening public transport and encouraging longer sojourns are top priorities for a country whose new 'dream big, live slow' road map has one overriding goal: becoming the global benchmark for sustainable tourism by 2030. Travel slowly, and if you can, avoid July and August.

EMPERORCOSAR/SHUTTERSTOCK

THE MAIN AREAS

PARIS
Herculean culture, history and joie de vivre. **p384**

MONT ST-MICHEL
Island abbey on a tidal throne. **p399**

FRENCH ALPS
One of Europe's true mountain epics. **p406**

LYON
Unmatched cuisine in a city with soul. **p413**

For places to stay in France, see p446

MISTERVLAD/SHUTTERSTOCK

Left: Plateau de Valensole (p433), Gorges du Verdon; Above: Notre Dame (p389), Paris

LOIRE VALLEY
Châteaux, vineyards
and cyclepaths.
p420

PROVENCE
Sun, sea and rosé
p424

BORDEAUX
Historic, wine-infused
port city.
p436

Mont St-Michel, p399
When the tide rises, this monastery is completely cut off from the mainland, guarded by bobbing seals and wheeling seabirds.

Loire Valley, p420
Hundreds of châteaux framed by vineyards and waterways characterise this postcard-perfect region, which was once home to the French royal family.

Bordeaux, p436
Synonymous with wine, Bordeaux is well watered by its viticultural neighbours. Not all its history is edifying, though, and much of Bordeaux's wealth was ill-obtained.

ENGLAND

The Channel (La Manche)

CHANNEL ISLANDS (UK)

Guernsey

Jersey

North Sea

Strait of Dover

Dover
Hastings
Dunk
Calais
Boulogne-sur-Mer
A2
A16
Abbeville
Dieppe
Amiens
A29
Beauvais
Rouen
Cherbourg
Le Havre
Bayeux
Caen
Lisieux
Musée Louvre
A13
Eiffel Tower
Évreux
PARIS
St-Lô
Flers
Dreux
Cathédra Notre Dan de Par
Alençon
Chartres
A10
A1
Abbaye du Mont St-Michel
A84
St-Malo
Mont St-Michel
Morlaix
St-Brieuc
Brest
Carhaix-Plouguer
Quimper
Rennes
Laval
Châteaudun
A11
A81
Le Mans
Orléa
A28
Loire Valley
Lorient
Vannes
Atlantic Ocean

Loire
Angers
Tours
Blois
Château Chambor
A11
A87
A85
Château d'Azay-le-Rideau
Château de Chenonceau
Bourg
A71
Nantes
Cholet
Châteauro
La Roche-sur-Yon
A83
Poitiers
A10
Les Sables-d'Olonne
Montluç
A20
Niort
La Rochelle
A10
Saintes
Angoulême
Limoges
La Cité du Vin
Périgueux
Brive-la-Gaillarde
Bordeaux
A89
Musée d'Aquitaine
Sarlat-la-Canéda
Arcachon
Dordogn
Aurilla
Bay of Biscay
A20
Cahors
Rode
A62
Garonne
Agen
A63
A65
Montauban
Mont-de-Marsan
Auch
Toulouse
Castre
Bilbao
Biarritz Bayonne
A64
Pau
Tarbes
A64
Carcassonne
A61
Donostia-San Sebastián
Lourdes
Vignemale
The Pyrénées
Pamplona
ANDORRA
ANDORRA LA VELLA
Lleida
Barcelon
SPAIN
Tarragona

CAR

Driving is the best way to see much of the French countryside, but it can be expensive, and *péages* (tolls) on highways quickly cost as much as, or more than, fuel. Cut costs by using a ridesharing platform like BlaBlaCar (*blablacar.fr*).

TRAIN

One of the best ways to get around. High-speed TGV train services link many of France's major cities, including Paris–Lyon (two hours), Paris–Bordeaux (two hours) and Paris–Marseille (3½ hours). Slower, TER services also run between cities, as well as to more rural areas.

BUS

Long-distance buses, including BlaBlaCar Bus and FlixBus, are often the cheapest way of travelling long distances (particularly into neighbouring countries like Spain, Switzerland and Italy), although they tend to take longer than the train.

Find Your Way

Once the laughing stock of Western Europe for frequent strikes and delays, France's public transport is now one of the best out there. The strikes still happen, but they're generally scheduled in advance – check *cestlagreve.fr* for information.

Paris, p384
City of light and love, the place that inspired everyone from Hemingway to Fitzgerald, Paris' reputation precedes it.

French Alps, p406
Legendary for skiing, but increasingly a summer destination, as locals and tourists escape ever-common heatwaves to hike and mountain-bike through Europe's most dramatic scenery.

Lyon, p413
Hungry travellers arrive here guided by their stomachs, and find a city that's older than Paris, with architecture spanning Roman to Renaissance to avant-garde.

Provence, p424
A region that veers from wildly enthralling city life to tranquil village idyll – complete with fine wine, lavender fields and coastal castaway coves.

381

Plan Your Time

You could spend years in France and not see it all. If pushed for time, pick a region or two to savour.

Château de Chenonceau (p422), Chenonceaux

Paris in a Day

● Montmartre's slinking streets and steep staircases are enchanting, especially in the early morning when tourists are few. Head to the hilltop **Sacré-Cœur** (p393) basilica to soak up views over Paris. Wander down to Pigalle for lunch, to rub shoulders with fellow diners at the long tables at **Bouillon Pigalle** (p392).

● In the afternoon, potter through the Île de la Cité, site of **Notre Dame** (p389), painstakingly restored after the 2019 fire, and climb the 422 steps up the South Tower. Then put your feet up with a good book at **Shakespeare and Company** (p393).

● In the evening, ascend the **Eiffel Tower** (p384) to experience glittering *la ville lumière* (City of Light) by night, before changing perspective over dinner and drinks at floating restaurant **Francette** (p385), looking up at the tower.

SEASONAL HIGHLIGHTS

France is strictly seasonal. Visit the Alps in May, for example, and you'll find very little open. Shoulder season often has the best of both worlds.

FEBRUARY

It's the height of **ski season** in the Alps, but the school holidays mean sky-high prices and packed pistes in ski resorts. In Provence, Nice celebrates an epic **carnival** (p428) for a fortnight in late February and early March.

APRIL

The arrival of spring means **Lyon's rivers** come to life, with *péniche* (narrowboat) beer gardens spilling onto the banks. Water levels are high for **kayaking** the Ardèche River, although it's chilly for swimming.

MAY

In a month splattered with public holidays, many choose to *faire le pont* and take long weekends. **Cannes Film Festival** (p428) turns the city into a celebrity-spotting frenzy.

ANDRE QUINOU/SHUTTERSTOCK

A Few Days Château-Hopping in the Loire

● Start at the **Château Royal de Blois** (p421), a compelling introduction to château architecture and the bloody history of the Loire, then stroll along the riverfront and up to Blois' medieval quarter. At dinner, sample a local dry white wine.

● Spend the next day exploring **Château de Chambord** (p421), its dazzling rooftop and the formal French gardens, and take a picnic lunch. Rent a bike/boat to enjoy in the sprawling grounds in the afternoon.

● On day three, explore the yew-tree maze and architecture at castle-turned-bridge, **Château de Chenonceau** (p422), much of which was designed by women. In the afternoon, drive to **Château de Villandry** (p423), famed for its unparalleled Renaissance gardens.

A Week in Provence

● Begin in **Marseille** (p430), France's second city. Marseille develops in dog years; however often you visit, there's always new hip restaurants and bars to discover, with grab-and-go street food on every corner. Take a day to escape the city to the **Îles du Frioul** (p430), only 20 minutes away.

● Once you've had your fill of edgy bars and street art, head to the splendid coastal **Calanques** (p431) on a build-your-own adventure: kayaking, hiking or even climbing. Next, head inland for an adventure fix at the **Gorges du Verdon** (p433), France's answer to the Grand Canyon. If you're touring in June or July, tack on a detour to the purple-hued **Plateau de Valensole's lavender fields** (p433). Finish up in Avignon to visit the **Palais des Papes** (p435).

JUNE	JULY	SEPTEMBER	DECEMBER
Lavender is everywhere in Provence; for a dreamy photoshoot, visit the **Plateau de Valensole** (p433) – responsibly. **Nuits de Fourvière** (p414) brings Lyon's Roman amphitheatre back to life with almost two months of concerts.	Thousands take to the streets to embrace the wild parties and living lesson in Basque culture during Bayonne's exuberant **Fêtes de Bayonne** (p441). The French summer holidays start in early July: expect crowds in the south.	The vendange, or **grape harvest**, begins in wine regions around the country. On the **Journées du Patrimoine** (usually the third weekend in September), many monuments usually closed to the public open their doors.	Strasbourg's **Christmas markets** light up the city. Expect fairy-light-covered craft stalls, mulled wine and treats. In the Loire, Christmas spirit takes hold at châteaux, including Azay-le-Rideau, Chenonceau and Villandry.

383

Paris

HERCULEAN CULTURE | HISTORY | JOIE DE VIVRE

GETTING AROUND

Most international airlines fly to Aéroport de Charles de Gaulle (28km northeast) or Aéroport d'Orly (19km south). Paris also has five major train stations with international service, and trains are the easiest public transport into the city. The metro is the fastest way to get around, and RER express trains save time crossing the city and serve the suburbs and airports. With no stairs, buses are good for parents with prams/strollers and people with limited mobility.

☑ **TOP TIP**

Craving green spaces? Join joggers, families and art lovers in the former royal hunting grounds, the **Bois de Boulogne** in western Paris, or **Bois de Vincennes** in the east.

A visit to the seductive French capital is a timeless experience. Be it sipping Champagne atop the Eiffel Tower, lunching cheek by jowl in a neighbourhood bistro, or people-watching on a buzzing cafe pavement terrace, the *art de vivre* (art of living) in the City of Light is utterly contagious.

Paris' cityscapes are instantly recognisable – Notre Dame cathedral, the iron Eiffel Tower, the Arc de Triomphe guarding the glamorous Champs-Élysées, lamplit bridges spanning the Seine, cafes spilling onto wicker-chair-lined streets. A short stay or first-time visit can entice you to linger in the historic centre – the Louvre, the islands, St-Germain and the Latin Quarter – with its myriad monuments and 'must-sees'.

Dining is a quintessential part of any Parisian experience, whether at intimate restaurants, Michelin-starred temples of gastronomy, *boulangeries* (bakeries) or lively street markets.

One of the world's great art repositories, Paris' priceless treasures are showcased in palatial museums, contemporary galleries and innovative multimedia spaces.

Exploring an Icon

Metal asparagus or iron lady?

Named after its designer, Gustave Eiffel, the **Eiffel Tower** *(toureiffel.paris, 2nd floor access using the stairs adult/youth/child from €14.50/7.30/3.70)* was built for the 1889 Exposition Universelle (World's Fair). It took 300 workers, 2.5 million rivets and two years of nonstop labour to assemble. Upon completion, the tower became the tallest human-made structure in the world (324m) – a record held until the 1930 completion of New York's Chrysler Building. A symbol of the modern age, it faced opposition from Paris' artistic and literary elite, and the 'metal asparagus', as some snidely called it, was originally

The Eiffel Tower and the Seine

slated to be torn down in 1909. It was spared only because it proved an ideal platform for the transmitting antennas needed for the newfangled science of radiotelegraphy. Now a local nickname for the tower is *La dame de fer* (Iron Lady). Of the tower's three floors, the 1st (57m) has the most space, with a broad wooden deck for lounging, but the least impressive views. The glass-enclosed Pavillon Ferrié houses an immersion film along with a small cafe, pizza bar and souvenir shop. This level also hosts the restaurant **Madame Brasserie**. Views from the 2nd floor (115m) are grand – impressively high but still close enough to see the details of the city below. Also up here are toilets, souvenir shops, a macaron bar and Michelin-starred restaurant **Le Jules Verne** (accessible by a dedicated lift in the south pillar). Views from the wind-buffeted top floor (276m) stretch up to 60km on a clear day. At this height the sweeping panoramas are more thrilling than detailed. You'll exit the lift onto a glass-enclosed level with directional panels orienting many of the world's cities. Then take one of the two small sets of metal stairs to the highest tier, which is open-air. Celebrate your ascent with a glass of bubbly from the Champagne bar at this topmost level – or

continued on p388

SPARKLES & A PAINT JOB

Every hour on the hour, the entire tower sparkles for five minutes with 20,000 6-watt lights. They were first installed for Paris' millennium celebration in 2000 – it took 25 mountain climbers five months to install the current bulbs and 40km of electrical cords. For the best view of the light show, head across the Seine to the Jardins du Trocadéro. By day, admire the paintwork. Every seven years, a 50-person crew works at night to strip the old paint and then repaint the entire structure. The tower has sported six different colours throughout its lifetime. The most recent golden hue, unveiled for the 2024 Olympics, was the yellow-brown shade originally conceived by Gustave Eiffel.

 EATING NEAR THE EIFFEL TOWER: OUR PICKS

Les Deux Abeilles: Homemade delights await at this old-fashioned tearoom that's adored by regulars. *9am-7pm Tue-Sat* €

Bistrot des Fables: A zinc bar contributes to the old-world charm, along with traditional classics like herring potato salad, devilled eggs and beef stew. *hours vary* €€

Francette: Toast the tower from the deck of this floating restaurant moored right on the quay. For the best views, reserve an outside table. *noon-1am* €€

Arnaud Nicolas: The charcuterie maestro stocks a boutique and runs this restaurant with a lunch menu changing every two weeks. *noon-2.30pm & 7-10pm Tue-Sat* €€

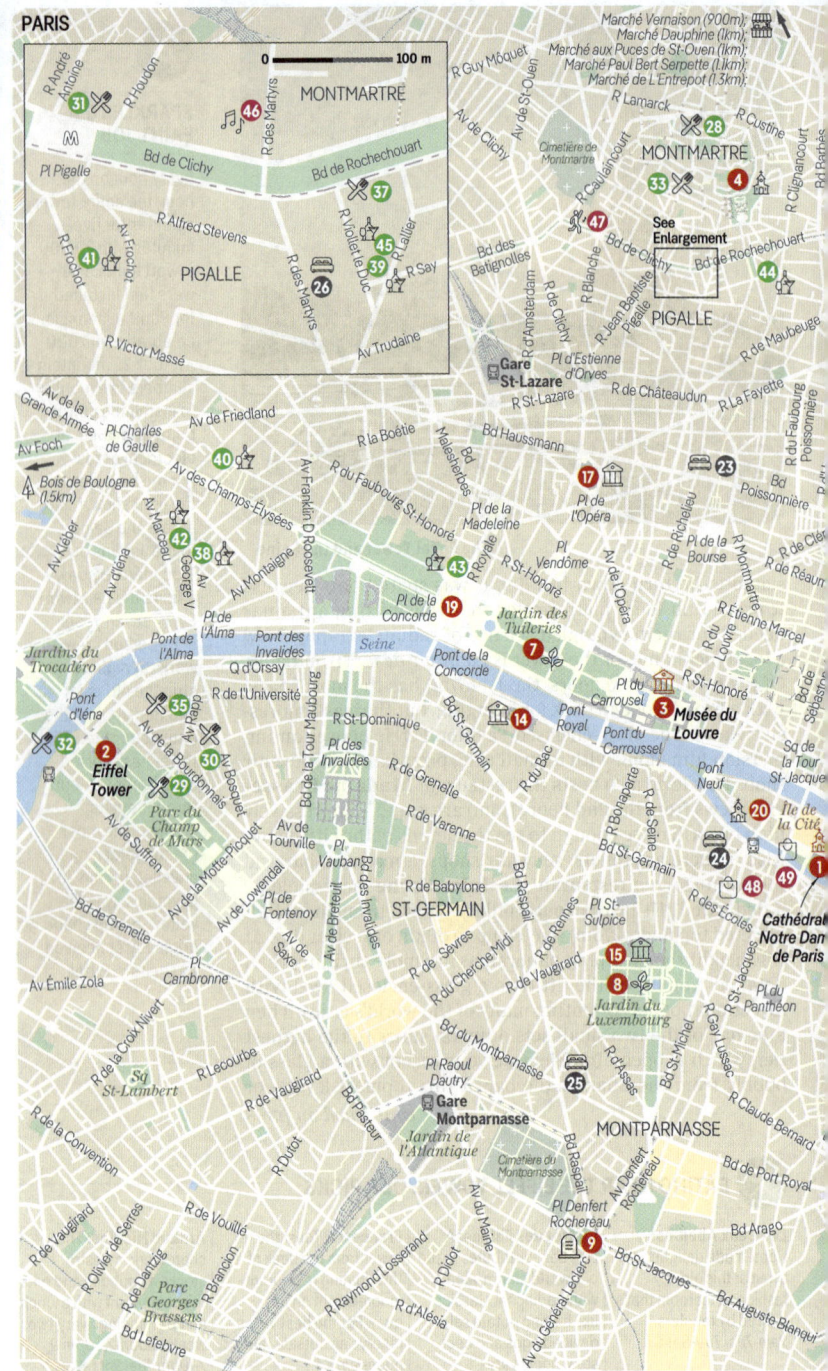

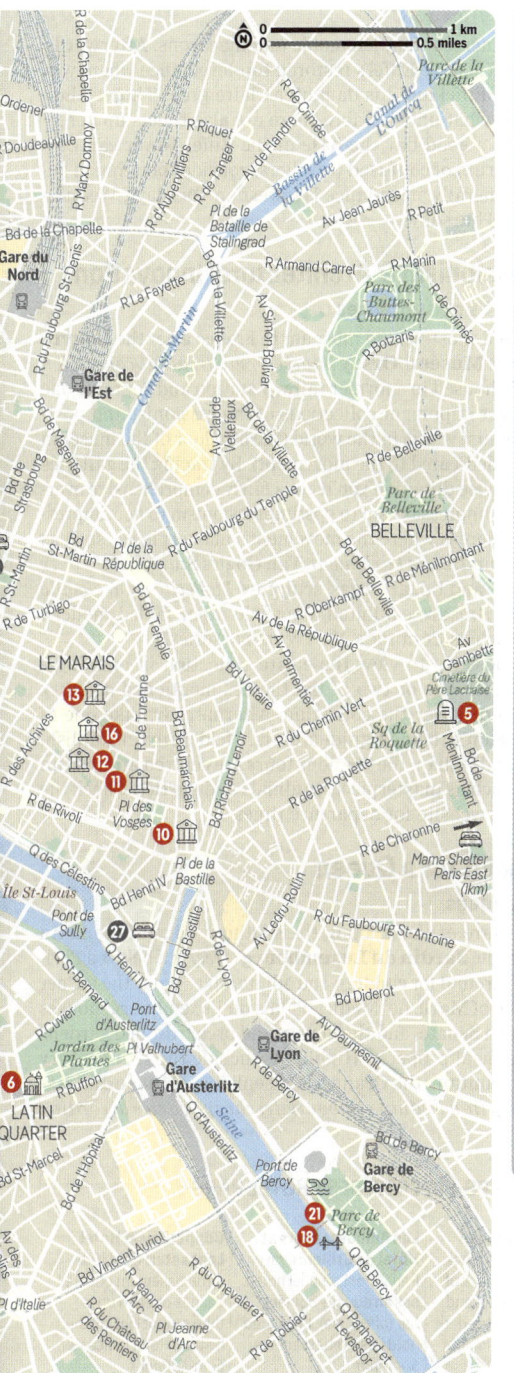

FRANCE PARIS

0 ___ 1 km
0 ___ 0.5 miles

★ HIGHLIGHTS
1 Cathédrale Notre Dame de Paris
2 Eiffel Tower
3 Musée du Louvre

● SIGHTS
4 Basilique du Sacré-Cœur
5 Cimetière du Père Lachaise
6 Grande Mosquée de Paris
7 Jardin des Tuileries
8 Jardin du Luxembourg
9 Les Catacombes
10 Maison de Victor Hugo
11 Musée Carnavalet
12 Musée Cognacq-Jay
13 Musée de la Chasse et de la Nature
14 Musée d'Orsay
15 Musée du Luxembourg
16 Musée National Picasso-Paris
17 Palais Garnier
18 Passerelle Simone de Beauvoir
19 Place de la Concorde
20 Sainte-Chapelle

● ACTIVITIES
21 Bercy Swimming Area

● SLEEPING
22 123 Sebastopol
23 Hôtel Chopin
24 Hotel Dame des Arts
25 Hôtel des Académies et des Arts
26 Hôtel HoY
27 People Marais

● EATING
28 Aléa
29 Arnaud Nicolas
30 Bistrot des Fables
31 Bouillon Pigalle
32 Francette
33 La Part des Anges
see 2 Le Jules Verne
35 Les Deux Abeilles
see 2 Madame Brasserie
37 Maggie

● DRINKING & NIGHTLIFE
38 Bulgari Bar at Bulgari Hotel Paris
39 Classique
40 CopperBay at Hotel Lancaster
41 Dirty Dick
42 Le Bar at Four Seasons Hotel George V
43 Les Ambassadeurs at Hôtel de Crillon
44 Minore
45 Sister Midnight

**●
ENTERTAINMENT**
46 Madame Arthur
47 Moulin Rouge

● SHOPPING
48 Abbey Bookshop
49 Shakespeare and Company

continued from p385

opt for mineral water, lemonade and macarons. Afterwards, peep into Gustave Eiffel's restored top-level office where wax models of Eiffel and his daughter Claire greet Thomas Edison. Somewhat unbelievably, there are also toilets up here.

Even on a good day the base of the Eiffel Tower can be a chaotic scrum of confused travellers; consider booking in advance. Generally attendance is lowest on Tuesdays, Wednesdays and Thursdays.

Impressionism & Architectural Innovation

See Monet's masterpieces

The second-most-visited museum in France after the **Louvre** (p390), the **Musée d'Orsay** *(musee-orsay.fr; adult/concession €16/13)* is housed in a former railway station and contains one of the most important collections of impressionist and post-impressionist works in the world (the 5th floor of the museum is largely dedicated to the movement). By tracing the galleries in a clockwise direction you'll get a fairly comprehensive overview from impressionism to postimpressionism to neo-impressionism. Here is where the movement's masterpieces, such as Monet's *Londres, le Parlement,* Van Gogh's *Starry Night over the Rhône*, and Edgar Degas' sculpture *La Petite Danseuse de Quatorze Ans* are exhibited alongside other fabled modern works, such as Cézanne's *Nature morte* series.

It's impossible to view the entire collection in one day – instead, pick one or two of the themes mentioned as entry points to discover the collection. Alternatively, take one of the museum's themed guided tours. Held daily in English, French and Italian, the 1½-hour tours are centred around fun themes such as masterpieces, animals and parties. Check the museum's website for departure times.

A Park Fit for a Queen

Royal gardens

A 22-hectare expanse along the southern edge of the Latin Quarter, the **Jardin du Luxembourg** *(free)* is a beloved Parisian playground for children and adults alike. Today the former residence of Marie de' Medici, Palais du Luxembourg, houses the French Senate, and the flower- and orchard-filled gardens are its official property. Highlights include the 17th-century Medici Fountain, the Orangerie greenhouse, **Musée du Luxembourg** *(museeduluxembourg.fr; charge varies according*

OFF WITH THEIR HEADS!

Created in 1772, **place de la Concorde** sits on what was once a dry moat and fields surrounding the **Jardin des Tuileries** and the former royal palace. It's famously where Louis XVI and Marie-Antoinette were guillotined in 1793 during the French Revolution, along with many others, gaining the square the name place de la Révolution. Renamed place de la Concorde in 1795, it was redesigned between 1836 and 1846 to add the two fountains, Fontaine des Mers and Fontaine des Fleuves, and the statues representing various French cities that sit around the edge of the square. But its most famous monument is the 3300-year-old Egyptian Luxor Obelisk, erected in 1836 after France received it as a gift from Egypt's ruler.

 DRINKING NEAR THE CHAMPS-ÉLYSÉES: BEST HOTEL BARS

Le Bar at Four Seasons Hotel George V: Cocktails crafted with the latest techniques at elegant and cosy gentlemen's-club-style bar. *5pm-1am*	**Bulgari Bar at Bulgari Hotel Paris:** Sleek black bar hidden at the back of Bulgari Hotel: a cool and sexy setting for after-dark cocktails. *10am-midnight*	**Les Ambassadeurs at Hôtel de Crillon:** One of Paris' most palatial hotels has an equally opulent bar (of course): the gilded gold Les Ambassadeurs. *5pm-1am*	**CopperBay at Hotel Lancaster:** Cool 10th arrondissement cocktail bar has opened up a third outpost inside the historic Hotel Lancaster. *5pm-1.30am*

NEIRFY/SHUTTERSTOCK

Palais du Luxembourg and Jardin du Luxembourg

to exhibition) and lovely statues scattered among treelined paths. In the spring and summer months, the pond springs to life, as toy sailing boats (available to rent) race across its waters. Tennis and pétanque courts, chess tables...there's a bevy of recreational activities, not to mention the delights for young children, including a playground and Paris' oldest merry-go-round, designed by Charles Garnier (the architect of the **Palais Garnier**), and topped with an ancient ring-tilting game that's a rite of passage for Parisian kids.

Gargantuan Gargoyles

The most famous cathedral in the world

Majestic and monumental, Paris' iconic French Gothic cathedral **Notre Dame** *(notredamedeparis.fr; treasury adult/ child €12/6)* reopened in December 2024 after the 2019 fire. Long considered the city's geographic and spiritual heart, it went through a massive restoration and, amazingly, because everything – including undamaged elements – was cleaned, the cathedral looks brand-new.

This is an actively working church, and also the capital's most visited free sight – more than 29,000 people come daily. The masterpiece we see today was begun in 1163 and largely completed by the early 14th century. It was badly damaged during the Revolution, prompting architect Eugène-Emmanuel Viollet-le-Duc to oversee extensive renovations between 1845 and 1864. That's when many of the magnificent forest of ornate flying buttresses that encircle the cathedral chancel and support its walls and roof were added. A constant queue marks the entrance to the Tours de Notre Dame *(tours-notre-dame-de-paris.fr)*, the cathedral's bell towers. Climb the 422 spiralling steps to the 69m top of the South Tower (the one on the right as you face the church). On your way up, you'll pass through a *continued on p392*

REBUILDING NOTRE DAME

On the evening of 15 April 2019, a blaze broke out under the roof of Cathédrale Notre Dame de Paris. Firefighters were able to control the fire and ultimately save the church, but the damage was catastrophic. The restoration involved over 1000 artists and not only repaired fire-damaged elements, but cleaned and restored everything to the untarnished condition of the era of Viollet-le-Duc. It cost about €900 million (via donations).

SAIKO3P/SHUTTERSTOCK

TOP EXPERIENCE

Musée du Louvre

The Louvre is undeniably Paris' pièce de résistance, with 35,000 works of art on display, including iconic masterpieces, spread across four floors. Glancing at each piece for one minute would take 24 days without sleeping, not to mention the time needed to appreciate the museum's grand surroundings. Therefore, careful planning is essential to fully experience the world's largest art museum.

DON'T MISS

Mona Lisa

Winged Victory of Samothrace

Venus de Milo

The Sphinx's Crypt

Le Salon Carré

Cour Marly and Cour Puget

First Time at the Louvre?

Entering the museum for the first time can be intimidating. The key to approaching the vast collections of the Louvre is to consider them from two significant perspectives: Western Art spanning from the Middle Ages to the mid-19th century, and the art and crafts of five ancient civilisations that preceded and influenced it. Simultaneously, immerse yourself in the museum's captivating architecture shaped by multiple sovereigns. To navigate the museum, just remember that it is made of three wings: the parallel Richelieu (North), Denon (South) and Sully (East).

PRACTICALITIES
● louvre.fr/en ● adult/child €22/free ● 9am-6pm Thu & Sat-Mon, to 9pm Wed & Fri

The Louvre can be both awe-inspiring and overwhelming. Possibly the best way to visit it is to allow yourself to choose, explore and be pleasantly surprised. Don't worry about seeing every masterpiece – enjoy the journey itself!

Guided by Ancient Civilisations

The antiquities department showcases pieces dating from the Neolithic period to the decline of the Roman Empire. Exploring chronologically, the treasures of ancient civilisations will primarily lead you through the ground floor, with an additional area dedicated to Egyptian antiquities on level 1. Begin your journey in the Richelieu wing, exploring the Mesopotamian art (considered the earliest human civilisation). Continue to the Sully wing to descend into the Sphinx's Crypt and uncover Egyptian art. Proceed to the Denon wing to see Greek, Etruscan and Roman art.

Gardens of Sculptures

Sculpture enthusiasts should not miss the atmospheric Cour Marly and Cour Puget, on level 1 of the Richelieu wing. These indoor courtyards bathed in natural light house French masterpieces created under Louis XIV. The Cour Marly provides an atmospheric setting reminiscent of its original location in one of the king's residences. Interestingly, in an arrangement that may seem counterintuitive, ascending to the upper level will transport you back in time to medieval French sculpture. Moving through the Richelieu wing on the ground floor, you'll then encounter more sculptures from the 17th to 19th centuries.

A European Tour of Masterpieces

The top floors showcase European paintings and decorative arts from the Middle Ages to the mid-19th century. Many visitors explore these floors towards the end of their visit, following the sequential order of the rooms. If you're a painting enthusiast, you should prioritise these floors during your visit. They are must-visit areas for iconic artworks like the *Mona Lisa*, as well as monumental paintings such as the *Wedding at Cana* and the *Raft of the Medusa*. In addition, don't miss the impressive Great Gallery, the historic Salon Carré (the precursor to exhibition salons), and the opulent Galerie d'Apollon adorned with stunning murals and golden embellishments.

Around the Louvre, Around the World

As no ordinary museum, the Louvre takes you on a journey to different eras and continents. Don't miss the apartments of Napoléon III, almost untouched for nearly 150 years, at the end of the Richelieu wing on the first level. For a broader cultural experience, explore the small section dedicated to American, African, Asian and Oceanic arts, situated in a remote part of the Denon wing (access through level 1).

ANTIQUE MYSTERY

The oldest displayed piece is the statue of *Aïn Ghazal* (Room 303, Sully Wing), unearthed in the 1980s in Jordan. Its subject is still a mystery: was it a man, a child, a god? In comparison, the *Winged Victory of Samothrace* and the *Venus de Milo*, both date back to the 3rd and 1st century BCE, which means more than 8000 years separates them from the enigmatic statue!

TOP TIPS

● Make sure to book your ticket online in advance, as you won't need to line up at the museum desk and there may be special offers available.

● The website is a valuable resource for finding inspiration and planning your visit, with thematic itinerary ideas.

● Arriving early will give you the opportunity to explore the galleries with fewer crowds.

● Wear comfortable shoes – you'll be walking through 403 halls and nearly 15km of corridors!

● If you're visiting with children, take a break at the Studio (Richelieu wing, level 1), which provides creative materials for them to enjoy.

FÊTE DE LA MUSIQUE

If you are in Paris on 21 June, the longest day of the year, get ready for the Fête de la Musique (Festival of Music). During this jovial annual celebration, which was launched in 1982 by the French government to encourage and support amateur music, the city's streets are filled all day and night with every kind of music genre imaginable. Concerts include big-hitter names, and are even held in unique venues, including the Louvre, but one of the best ways to experience the festival is to just stroll around by foot in neighbourhoods like Bastille, encountering concerts by chance. Check the full schedule at *fetede lamusique-paris.fr*, concerts generally run from 6pm to midnight.

PATRICK KERWIN/SHUTTERSTOCK

Sainte-Chapelle

continued from p389

room with displays on the cathedral's history before you reach the Galerie des Chimères (Gargoyles Gallery). These grotesque statues divert rainwater from the roof to prevent masonry damage, with the water exiting through their elongated, open mouths. Although they appear medieval, they were installed by Viollet-le-Duc in the 19th century. There's a 1000-visitor maximum per day, so book your timed-entry ticket in advance.

It is absolutely worth the fee to enter the *trésor* (treasury), which houses Notre Dame's dazzling sacred jewels and relics in the cathedral's southeastern transept. Check out the wonderful Les Camées des Papes (Papal cameos), sculpted with incredible finesse in shell and framed in silver. The 268 pieces depict every pope in miniature, from St Pierre to Benoît XVI.

Shimmering Stained Glass of Sainte-Chapelle

Glorious Gothic chapel bedazzlement

No sight in Paris is as dazzling as the radiant Holy Chapel called **Sainte-Chapelle** *(sainte-chapelle.fr; adult Jun-Sep €18, Oct-May €13, incl Conciergerie Jun-Sep/Oct-May €25/20, child free)*, hidden away like a precious gem within the city's

EATING IN MONTMARTRE & PIGALLE: OUR PICKS

Aléa: Simple market-led cuisine. Local favourite. *noon-1.30pm & 7.30-9.30pm Wed & Thu, noon-1.30pm & 7.30-10pm Fri, noon-2pm & 7.30-10pm Sat, 12.30-2pm Sun* €€

La Part des Anges: Laid-back local spot with great traditional food like *magret de canard. 7pm-10.30pm Tue-Thu, 7pm-10.45pm Fri, noon-2.30pm & 7-11pm Sat* €€

Bouillon Pigalle: Terrific value, this *bouillon* is one of several not to miss for escargot and steak-frites. *noon-midnight Sun-Thu, from 11.30am Fri & Sat* €

Maggie: Vintage-style dining space (with vestiges of its days as a 1920s dancing hall) serves traditional French food. Rooftop bar with city views. *7-10pm Tue-Sat* €€

original, 13th-century Palais de Justice (Law Courts) and Palais de la Cité, the former royal residence. Paris' oldest, finest stained glass laces its sublime Gothic interior – best viewed on sunny days when light floods in, creating an entrancing rainbow of bold colours. Built in just six years and consecrated in 1248, it was conceived by French king Louis IX to house his collection of holy relics, including the famous Ste-Couronne (Holy Crown, Jesus' wreath of thorns), which he acquired in 1239 from the Emperor of Constantinople for a sum easily exceeding the amount it cost to build the chapel. There are discounts on entry on Wednesdays from April to September.

Beautiful Bookshops

English-language spots with Parisian soul

French literary giants and expatriate authors found creative refuge in both the city's cafes and bookshops, like the whimsical **Shakespeare and Company** *(shakespeareandcompany.com)*, a hub for expats since 1919. There's also the cosy, Canadian-run **Abbey Bookshop** *(abbeybookshop.org)*, where towering stacks of books and regular readings invite lingering. Along the Seine, the *bouquinistes* continue to sell vintage books, posters and magazines from green wooden stalls.

Where Cabaret Meets Cocktails

Glamour and after-dark revelry

Since the Belle Époque, Pigalle has been Paris' playground of after-dark pleasures. Its reputation truly took shape after WWII, when it became a hub for neon-lit sex shops, cabarets and smoky bars. While many of its infamous establishments are fading, Pigalle's spirit endures in legendary venues like the **Moulin Rouge** *(moulinrouge.fr; adult €103)*, where since 1889, high-kicking dancers and extravagant sets bring the cancan to life in nightly shows at 9pm and 11pm. Cabaret **Madame Arthur** *(madamearthur.fr)* is a fun evening out of live music and gender-bending performances, keeping Pigalle's legacy of spectacle and seduction alive. Beyond the show lights, Pigalle's warren of small spaces has always been central to its illicit charm, once home to shadowy dens, opium-fuelled escapades and whispered rendezvous. Today, these tight quarters have found a new life as cocktail bars, where locals and visitors mingle over expertly crafted drinks. Spots like **Sister Midnight**, **Dirty Dick**, **Minore** and **Classique** shake up inventive cocktails, blending Pigalle's hedonistic past with a squeakier-clean present.

A Basilica With a View

Paris' sacred heart

Rising above Montmartre (the hill of martyrs), the **Basilique du Sacré-Cœur** *(sacre-coeur-montmartre.com; adult/child/groups €8/5/6, tickets available on-site only, email for guided visits)*, dedicated to the Sacred Heart of Jesus, is a vantage point, a sanctuary, a Parisian rite of passage, and one of the

GHOSTS OF ARTISTS PAST

Pigalle has long been a stage for Paris' most electrifying performers and artists. In the late 19th century, Toulouse-Lautrec immortalised its cabarets, painting La Goulue and Jane Avril, the high-kicking stars of the Moulin Rouge. The district pulsed with bohemian energy, drawing poets and painters. By the 1920s, Josephine Baker mesmerised crowds at the Folies Bergère, while Édith Piaf sang in Pigalle's streets before becoming the soul of French *chanson*. Jazz musician and writer Boris Vian added his avant-garde flair to the area's clubs. After WWII, Pigalle's neon glow lit up a world of jazz, burlesque and underground culture. Today, its music halls, cabarets and cocktail bars keep the spirit of its legendary artists alive.

city's most visited landmarks. From its gleaming domes to one of the world's largest mosaics, its grandeur stuns. Designed in a striking Roman-Byzantine style, the basilica took five architects over four decades to complete (1875–1919). Visitors can climb the 300 steps to the dome for breathtaking panoramic views of Paris, while inside, chapels, stained-glass windows, and a crypt bathed in natural light create a contemplative atmosphere. The basilica's perpetual adoration prayer cycle, which began in 1885, continues uninterrupted, and on Sundays, the grand organ resonates through the sacred space during Mass and vespers. You can spend the night at the Basilica from 11pm to 7am if you pray for at least an hour, as part of the continuous prayer cycle, unbroken since 1885 (sign up on the Basilica website, dorms from €15).

Grab a Bargain

France's most famous flea market

Founded in 1885, the **Marché aux Puces de St-Ouen** *(puces deparissaintouen.com)* is the world's largest antiques market, located just beyond Paris' northern edge. It spans 12 distinct markets spread across 7 hectares, with antiques, vintage furniture, rare collectibles, fashion and curiosities. For serious collectors or intrigued wanderers, the mazelike alleys have endless inspiration and irresistible old-world charm.

The allure of Les Puces lies in the diversity and distinct rhythm and charm of each market. **Marché Vernaison**, the oldest, is a warren of open-air lanes lined with vintage postcards, embroidered linens and costume jewellery. **Marché Paul Bert Serpette**, the crown jewel, draws a discerning crowd of interior designers and collectors who come for 20th-century design icons, museum-worthy antiques and impeccably curated vignettes. Inside the vaulted glass pavilion of **Marché Dauphine**, the atmosphere is more freewheeling: vinyl records, retro cameras, tribal artefacts and the occasional taxidermied bird. **L'Entrepot** is one of the smallest markets but it's mighty and has a bunch of old zinc-top brasserie bars and spiral staircases from houses all over the country.

Haggling is part of the charm at Les Puces. Approach vendors with a smile, and you might knock 10% to 20% off the price. While some accept cards, cash is often preferred for smaller items or better deals.

Urban Swimming

Go for a dip in the Seine

In 1900, during the first edition of the Olympic Games in Paris, swimming races took place in the River Seine. Decades of industrialisation polluted the waters until a nadir was reached in the 1970s. After a mass clean-up operation, including the construction of water-treatment plants and rainwater-storage basins, swimming was possible once again for the 2024 Games. Since the summer of 2025, the public has also been able to bathe in the famous river,

MORE CITY DIPS

Urban 'wild' swimming is on the rise, and there are plenty of other European cities where you can take a plunge, including Barcelona, Amsterdam and Berlin.

PETR KOVALENKOV/SHUTTERSTOCK

Grande Mosquée de Paris

MARCHE DES FIERTÉS

Running in Paris since 1981, the **Marche des Fiertés** *(marchedes fiertes.org)* has its origins in the Gay Pride marches that began in New York. In Paris the annual parade is attended by over 500,000 people and includes support from more than 200 volunteers. Organisation of the event is led by the group Inter-LGBT, who brings together around 90 organisations. Their shared mission is to 'combat discrimination based on sexual orientation or gender identity, as part of the promotion of human rights and fundamental freedoms'. Open to all, whether you identify as an ally or part of the community, the event is a celebratory and political day filled with music, costumes, placards, floats, a final concert and dance-filled afterparties.

including at the **Bercy swimming area** by the **Simone de Beauvoir footbridge**. The area is supervised, marked with buoys and equipped with showers and lockers.

Calm at the Paris Mosque

A North African oasis for food and relaxation

One of the biggest mosques in France, and Paris' central mosque, the **Grande Mosquée de Paris** *(grandemosqueede paris.fr)* has a striking Moorish-style minaret, which peeks out from behind smooth white walls as you approach along the street. Visit the interior to see the intricate tile work and calligraphy. There is also a North African hammam (steam bathhouse) with timings for women and men, a pretty courtyard **restaurant** *(la-mosquee.com)* that serves delicious couscous, tagines and meat skewers, as well as a tearoom with sweet, fragrant mint tea and traditional cakes. There is also the possibility of smoking shisha in the front garden.

Pay Respects to Wilde & Morrison

The resting place of artists

When commissioned to design the new Parisian cemetery, **Père Lachaise**, in the early 19th century, architect Alexandre-Théodore Brongniart envisioned a space that would embody nobility without grandiosity, and simplicity without neglect, and invoke religious sentiments without fear. Inspired by English gardens, the cemetery was meticulously planned, with winding paths and a significant portion dedicated to nature. Today, as you enter, the cacophony of the city fades away and the graves seamlessly blend into the undulating landscape, creating a feeling of beautiful strangeness, as if you were suspended between two worlds.

continued on p398

TAKASHI IMAGES/SHUTTERSTOCK

Hall of Mirrors

Versailles

Sprawling over 900 hectares, the monumental, 400-year-old Château de Versailles is France's most famous and grand palace. It's situated in the leafy, bourgeois suburb of Versailles, 22km southwest of central Paris. The estate is divided into three main sections: the 580m-long palace; the gardens, canals and pools to the west of the palace; and the Trianon Estate to the northwest.

DON'T MISS

The Palace

Hall of Mirrors

King's and Queen's State Apartments

Formal gardens and fountains

Lunch near the Grand Canal

History

The estate began in 1623 as a hunting lodge for Louis XIII. Subsequently, Louis XIV transformed it into a vast, baroque château. Some 30,000 workers and soldiers toiled on the property, the bills for which all but emptied the kingdom's coffers.

The Château de Versailles was the kingdom's political capital and the seat of the royal court from 1682 up until the fateful events of 1789 when revolutionaries massacred the palace guard. Louis XVI and Marie Antoinette were ultimately dragged back to Paris, where they were ingloriously

PRACTICALITIES

● en.chateauversailles.fr ● adult/child from €21/ free ● 9am-5.30pm Tue-Sun

guillotined. In the 19th century, Napoléon and Josephine lived on the estate, as did Charles de Gaulle in the 1940s.

The Palace

Work on the palace began in 1661 under the guidance of architect Louis Le Vau (Jules Hardouin-Mansart took over from Le Vau in the mid-1670s); painter and interior designer Charles Le Brun; and landscape artist André Le Nôtre, whose workers flattened hills, drained marshes and relocated forests as they laid out the seemingly endless gardens, ponds and fountains.

Le Brun and his hundreds of artisans decorated every moulding, cornice, ceiling and door of the interior with the most luxurious and ostentatious of appointments: frescoes, marble, gilt and woodcarvings, many with themes and symbols drawn from Greek and Roman mythology.

Few alterations have been made to the château since its construction, apart from most of the interior furnishings disappearing during the Revolution and many of the rooms being redecorated by Louis-Philippe (r 1830–48), who opened part of the château to the public in 1837. The château is in the final stages of a lavish €400 million restoration.

Hall of Mirrors

The palace's opulence peaks in its shimmering Galerie des Glaces (Hall of Mirrors). This 75m-long ballroom shines with 17 sparkling mirrored features comprising 357 individual mirrors on one side and an equal number of windows overlooking the gardens and the setting sun on the other.

King's & Queen's State Apartments

Luxurious, ostentatious appointments adorn every feature of the palace's Grands Appartements du Roi et de la Reine (the King's and Queen's State Apartments). Rooms are dedicated to Hercules, Venus, Diana, Mars and Mercury.

Other Notable Rooms

The **Galerie des Batailles** (Battle Gallery) is longer than the Hall of Mirrors and features 33 huge paintings that recall mostly forgotten French military victories. Savour the thematic decor in the **Salon de la Guerre** (War Room) and the **Salon de la Paix** (Peace Room), which bookend the Hall of Mirrors.

Gardens, Estate & Equestrian Academy

A walk through the sprawling and artful formal gardens, natural areas, huge Grand Canal and the Trianon palaces is a highlight. Or take in a horse show at the **National Equestrian Academy of Versailles**.

HISTORIC VERSAILLES

Don't miss the historic centre of Versailles town. Build a superb picnic at the market stalls of **Les Halles de Versailles** on the **place du Marché**. In the old St-Louis quarter, next to the **Cathédrale St-Louis**, the **Potager du Roi** (King's Kitchen Garden) dates from the time of gourmand Louis XIV.

TOP TIPS

● Prepurchase tickets on the château's website for a dedicated time slot.

● Consider getting tickets for a concert in the Royal Chapel or Royal Opera for a unique palace experience.

● Download the official Château de Versailles app – loaded with audio tours and info for the entire estate.

● The four-person rental electric carts are limited to a set route covering a fraction of the estate. Rental bikes and e-bikes allow the most freedom. Explore the Grand Canal with a rowboat. The shuttle train is very slow.

● Versailles is best reached by the RER C line, which ends at Versailles Château Rive Gauche (some trains continue elsewhere). Other stations with Versailles in their names are a much longer walk from the château and town centre.

BASTILLE'S ANCIENT FORTRESS

Nothing remains of Bastille's fortress, originally constructed in the 14th century to defend the eastern flank of Paris against the English during the Hundred Years' War. By 1417 the royal castle took on an unusual new aspect: it formally became a state prison, housing inmates for centuries until it was destroyed during the 1789 revolution. On 14 July 1789, the inhabitants of the Faubourg St-Antoine, sick of prolonged food shortages due to an ongoing siege of Paris, stormed Bastille prison. When the guards refused to surrender, rebels seized 250 barrels of gunpowder, freed prisoners and put the military governor's head on a pike. This was the first episode of the French Revolution.

MIKHAIL GNATKOVSKIY/SHUTTERSTOCK

Les Catacombes

continued from p395

Overlooked at the time of its inauguration, the cemetery faced challenges in gaining popularity due to its location far from the city. However, to enhance its appeal, the city of Paris relocated the graves of famous figures like Molière and La Fontaine. Over time, politicians, scientists, artists and writers followed, solidifying Père Lachaise's reputation as the eternal resting place of the renowned. Oscar Wilde's tomb has long been the object of passionate kisses believed to bring luck in love, and the ritual offerings left on Jim Morrison's grave perpetuate a cult (mainly based on alcohol). Download the cemetery map from a QR code at the entrance; this will help you locate specific graves and landmarks, and choose the right entrance. There are five different ones, but only three of them are near metro stations.

An Underground Ossuary

The ghosts of Paris past

In 1785, subterranean tunnels of an abandoned quarry were upcycled as storage rooms for the exhumed bones of corpses that could no longer fit in the city's overcrowded cemeteries. By 1810 the skull- and bone-lined catacombs – resting place of millions of anonymous Parisians – had been officially born.

The route through **Les Catacombes** (*catacombes.paris.fr; adult/child €31/12*) begins at its spacious entrance on av du Colonel Henri Rol-Tanguy. Walk down 131 spiral steps to reach the ossuary itself, with a mind-boggling number of bones and skulls of millions of Parisians neatly packed along the walls. Visits cover about 1.5km of tunnels in all, at a cool 14°C. People with claustrophobia may experience some anxiety in the confined environment. It's closed Mondays.

Mont St-Michel

BIODIVERSE BAY | TIDE-WALKING | WONDROUS ABBEY

For a millennium, Mont St-Michel has entranced visitors with majestic views that metamorphose with the tides. When the seas rise, a 1000-year-old Gothic abbey crowns the top of an island of craggy rock. Conceptualised from a dream in which an archangel bids a bishop to build a place of devotion in an impossible place, Mont St-Michel captures the imagination of anyone who crosses its sandy paths. The sometimes-island itself changes as quickly as the sea; only a handful of inhabitants live there in comparison to the millions of annual tourists who crowd the winding streets that ascend to the pointed top.

Once you've snapped your photo of the extraordinary sight and have heard the bells ring in the abbey, the next best step is to immerse yourself in the incredible biodiversity of the bay. With slow and careful observation and turning off the tourist paths, you can find yourself in a vivid, waking dream full of flora, fauna and culinary delights.

Nocturnal Visits & High Tide

A night visit to the bay

The traditional approach to the **Abbaye du Mont St-Michel** (*abbaye-mont-saint-michel.fr; adult/child €16/free*) is an established, elevated wood-plank path with guardrails, next to the road where shuttles ferry visitors back and forth all day. But in the spirit of Robert Frost: the road less travelled makes all the difference. If you're pressed for time, try to go as early as possible to avoid the crowds, and plan on eating and sleeping off the almost-island to avoid handing over a lot of cash for mediocre tourist traps.

Take the unconventional route and sink your toes in the sometimes-moving quicksand with local guide **Romain Pilon** (*labaiecderomain.fr; tours per person from €15*), native of the bay and a guide for over two decades. Fishing enthusiasts can go shrimping with Romain during select windows throughout the year, usually mid-September through October and a short

GETTING AROUND

The nearest train stop is Pontorson (just short of five hours from Paris), where buses will take you 350m from the entrance of Mont St-Michel. But a car is your best bet to get around the bay and surrounding villages, though parking near Mont-St-Michel is pricey. Getting to the island of Mont St-Michel itself is fairly straightforward: walk or queue up for an all-day shuttle bus (free). To walk across the bay, it's best to hire a guide and check tide changes: *ot-montsaintmichel .com/marees*.

☑ TOP TIP

Avoid the summer months (July and August) for the best views and fewer crowds. If you find yourself here during high season, try to go at dusk or dawn to beat the rush.

BEST ANNUAL FÊTES/FESTIVALS IN NORMANDY

Dîner sur la Digue:
Join thousands of guests at this dinner party alongside the boardwalk in Cabourg. Reserve, pack your picnic or grab a meal from vendors.

Cabourg Mon Amour Festival: Annual three-day, open-air music festival, with styles from electro to rap. *cabourgmon amour.fr*

Fête des Marins:
Every Pentecost weekend (the seventh Sunday after Easter), get suited in sailor stripes in Honfleur for parades, concerts, photos and more.

Offcourts Festival:
September festival celebrating French and Québécois short films. Free screenings, concerts and festivities.

American Film Festival: Each September, stars gather in Deauville to celebrate American cinema. *festival-deau ville.com*

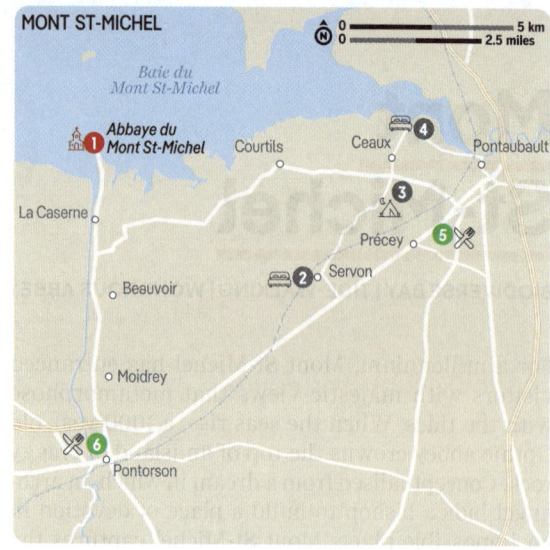

MONT ST-MICHEL

Baie du Mont St-Michel

HIGHLIGHTS
1 Abbaye du Mont St-Michel

SLEEPING
2 Auberge Sauvage

3 Camping La Baie du Mont St-Michel
4 Chambres d'Hôte Les Bruyères du Mont

EATING
see 2 Auberge Sauvage
5 La Brocante
6 Le Grillon
see 1 Le Logis Sainte Catherine

window in April. But year-round, the best way to see Mont St-Michel is with his 'Sortie Nocturnes'.

Night owls will meet at 7.30pm and then skulk around the bay as evening falls. Enter a hidden world over the next few hours, bathed in the light of the spectacular sunset and surrounded by the cries of geese and migratory birds – identified by your guide – and the moving waters and sound of the shifting shores. The visit ends at 11.30pm, cloaked in the mystical magic of night, where you'll emerge with uncovered secrets and views of the bay.

EATING NEAR MONT-ST-MICHEL: OUR PICKS

Auberge Sauvage:
Michelin-starred haven set in a 16th-century presbytery. Local produce and foraged delicacies dominate. *7.30pm-midnight Thu-Mon* €€€

La Brocante: Enjoy simple snacks, sandwiches, crêpes, coffees and wines in this retrofitted old auto shop. *10am-6pm Mon, Thu & Fri, 11am-6pm Sat & Sun* €

Le Grillon: Unpretentious and unfussy spot to taste lamb chops made from the sheep that graze the salty fields. *12.30-1.30pm Sat-Wed, 7-8.30pm Fri-Tue* €€

Le Logis Sainte Catherine: Rotating menu with innovative plates like *moussette* rillettes. Dazzling terrace, elegant decor. Book online. *hours vary* €€€

Abbaye du Mont St-Michel (p399)

Go Birding or Become a Bird

Bird-watching and paragliding

If you're travelling with a group, flock together and book the **Birding Bus** (*birding-msm.com; from €10*), run by ornithologist and biologist-by-training Sébastian Provost, who showcases bird-watching as a fascinating artform that brings to life hidden worlds. At various points along the bay, you'll encounter birds, seals and even dolphins.

For those who like to fly solo, jump for a bird's-eye view of Mont St-Michel and its surroundings – literally. With experienced and competition-winning paraglider **Léo Hamard** (*parapenteenbaie.fr; flights from €80*), you can float above the abbey and the bay like a bird. Watch your feet dangle and be dazzled by the singular feeling of lightness and freedom flying on the winds. Adrenaline junkies and first-timers alike can spring for the 'acrobatic' flight option (weather contingent) for a truly head-spinning flight. Reserve a date in advance online, but the jumping-off point is dictated by the winds.

MAD FOR MOUSSETTES IN MAY

Crab lovers, take note of *moussettes*, the nickname of a variety of young spider crab (under two years old) found all over fish markets in La Manche from April to June, and especially bountiful during the month of May. They're known for their sweet, subtle and abundant flesh; enjoy them without any condiments needed, although if you're partial to one, homemade mayonnaise is the most traditional (our advice: wear a bib and gloves to avoid the mess). You can buy them cooked or boil in water for 20 minutes. As a bonus, eating *moussettes* also helps out the local ecosystem, since the spider crabs have infiltrated the Normandy region and pose a threat to mussel producers.

Beyond Mont St-Michel

Explore the bucolic Norman countryside and wild Breton coast, toasting your adventures with crisp apple cider.

Places

Giverny p402

Étretat p403

D-Day Landing Beaches p404

St-Malo p405

GETTING AROUND

Various towns and cities like Le Havre, Étretat and St-Malo are easily accessible by direct trains from Paris. More isolated areas, including the D-Day beaches, require more planning, with sparse bus services. A car is most convenient to explore the less touristy areas (Breton highways are toll-free, Norman highways are not!). In both Normandy and Brittany, hiking and cycling are some of the best ways to take in coastal scenery.

To the east of Mont St-Michel, Normandy's breathtaking landscapes singlehandedly inspired the impressionist art movement; painter Claude Monet obsessively painted sunrise at Le Havre and his backyard water lilies in Giverny. From the world-famous and epically surreal Mont St-Michel abbey, all the way to the cliffs of Étretat, the Normandy coast is replete with famed destinations. History buffs can immerse themselves in D-Day reenactments, and even breakfast on tables made from reassembled German planes. Westwards, Brittany has some of nature's most wonderful sights with unspoiled rawness. Over 2000km of coastline, the ocean's mystical draw and mesmerising landscapes never fail to enchant visitors. That's got to be worth braving the rain.

Giverny

TIME FROM MONT ST-MICHEL: **3HR**

Skip the crowds at Monet's secret island

Monet's residence of over four decades, **Maison et Jardins de Claude Monet** (*claudemonetgiverny.fr; adult/child/under 7yr €12/6.50/free*) is a powerful testament to the lasting legacy of a visionary artist: his world-famous water lilies and his eccentric, brightly coloured home dotted with his collection of Japanese block prints are flocked to by thousands of tourists each year. The queue for the water lilies, which tears through the house at a frenetic pace, can be intimidating – but if you pause and gaze out of the window and focus on a flower, you'll surely be left with an impression of the painter's life. Reservations are strongly recommended (weekdays are slightly less crowded than the weekend) and beware of big holiday weekend crowds.

To contemplate his life with more breathing room, walk up to his humble grave and contrast it with the greatness of his legacy. Better yet, picnic at the lesser-known **Île aux Orties**, a patch of land Monet owned at the confluence of where the Epte River meets the Seine, that once turned into an island during heavy rain periods. To get there, walk past the windmill near the car parks the along the small rue des Batards

MB_PHOTOGRAPHER/SHUTTERSTOCK

Maison et Jardins de Claude Monet, Giverny

until you reach the river for a more isolated experience of one of his rarer, inspired landscapes.

Étretat

TIME FROM MONT ST-MICHEL: 2½HR 🚗

Coast along the renowned alabaster cliffs

France's famous and trafficked cliffs, Étretat's staggering arches have been sculpted over millennia by winds and the whims of the sea, and immortalised by Monet over 80 times. More recently, the cliffs have also unfortunately been the cause of deaths due to reckless photos – skip the selfies at the top and don't stray off established paths.

Falaise d'Aval and the adjacent Aiguille are the most iconic, featuring a needle shooting from the water alongside an arch; and the **Falaise d'Amont** has a bird's-eye view of Étretat. Hikes here are choose-your-own-adventure: opt for the steep steps to the neo-Gothic stone church, **Chapelle Notre-Dame-de-la-Garde**, for a peaceful (yet windy) picnic – the view from the church is better than a visit inside. Hardcore hikers, head to the intensive and rewarding five-hour Roc Vaudieu Loop. If you're short on time, take the Porte d'Amont Loop that starts at Chemin de Criquetot. To wade deeper into the waters, head to **Voiles et Galets** *(voilesetgalets.com; rentals from €15)* in Étretat for an unforgettable kayak or paddleboard ride

✖ EATING IN GIVERNY: OUR PICKS

Au Coin du Pain'tre: Simple plates like quiches and baguette sandwiches. The highlight: relaxing over breakfast or lunch with a garden view. *9am-7pm* €

Cocorico: Pop-up food truck with fresh sandwiches, burgers and desserts at reasonable prices for a takeaway picnic, when the sun's out. *hours vary Apr-Oct* €

Les Nymphéas: Family-friendly garden restaurant: crêpes, fondue, raclette, burgers and salads. *9am-6pm Apr-Oct* €€

Oscar: Gourmet bistro in a stylish setting with refined plates by acclaimed chef David Gallienne. *10am-6pm Mon-Thu, to 9pm Fri & Sat* €€€

**Memorial Museum
of Omaha Beach:**
Memorial of steel
shooting out of
the sand stops
the breath, while
well-curated museum
pays tribute to fallen
soldiers.

**Utah Beach
Landing Museum:**
Westernmost beach
hosts one of biggest
museums built on
German fortifications.
Glimpse an original
B-26 bomber.

La Pointe du Hoc:
View ravages of
a battlefield and
old bunkers at this
powerfully sobering
memorial point. Many
stairs.

Overlord Museum:
Collectors' paradise:
restored trucks,
vehicles, dioramas
and veteran tributes.

Airborne Museum:
Near historic church
Ste-Mère-Église, this
museum focuses on
the airborne troops
and hosts an original
glider and a C-47
plane.

under some epic scenery; no reservations, as rentals depend on weather conditions. Don't miss a paddle out to the **Plage du Fourquet** to enjoy a secluded beach.

D-Day Landing Beaches

TIME FROM MONT ST-MICHEL: 1½HR 🚗

A night at a WWII museum

When US soldiers landed on Normandy's Omaha Beach on the morning of 6 June 1944, the ensuing crescendo to WWII left indelible scars on the French countryside. From west to east, the 80km stretch of sand comprises the American landing beaches of Utah and Omaha; Gold Beach, where the British landed; **Juno Beach** for the Canadians; and then another American landing destination, Sword Beach. Decades later, D-Day remains a monolithic legend that has left countless memorial and military sites, cemeteries, museums and remains of what was once the largest harbour in the world.

Bringing history to life are the wife-and-husband team behind guesthouse **D-Day Aviators Le Manoir** *(ddayaviatorslemanoir.fr)*. Anne Florence and Paul Hontang are both pilots with passions. Paul is a history expert, constantly on the hunt to add to their impressive collection of war detritus: a plane cockpit adorns the living room, and guests breakfast on a table made from a German plane engine. Anne has a personal collection of over 500 dentelles, traditional lace bonnets and hats worn to signify the different life stages of a woman. Ask her for a peek in the garage next door. Situated in Arromanches-les-Bains, where the world's largest artificial harbour was assembled by the Allied Forces, the manor house is centrally placed for visiting all along the D-Day Landing Beaches and right next to the renovated **Musée du Debarquement** *(musee-arromanches.fr; adult/child €12.90/8.30)*, a stunningly detailed presentation of why and how the critical events of 6 June 1944 took place.

For a wilder ride, head to the family-friendly **La Batterie du Holdy Guesthouse** *(batterie-du-holdy.com)*, just south of Utah Beach. Be transported back to the events of 6 June 1944, with cinematic and immersive reenactments in the very buildings where WWII action took place. Booking a night here is well worth it – an impassioned Jeep tour is included without steep prices. The real goldmine is the anecdotes Jean generously shares with his guests, and the delight of breakfast served in a 1940s-era grocery store.

Go behind enemy lines

On the coast along the English Channel, known as La Manche, near Utah Beach, there are a few German artillery batteries to visit. The **Batterie de Crisbecq** *(batteriedecrisbecq.fr; adult/child €12.50/8.50)*, also known as the Battery of St Marcouf, is the largest and most spectacular. Built in 1941 by the German military engineering group Todt, the bunker today lets you walk in German soldiers' footsteps – the former trenches have been excavated and now serve as walking paths between the 22 blockhouses. View up-close battle scars, grenade traps and visible damage. The **Batterie d'Azeville** *(batterie-azeville.manche.fr; adult/child €8/4)* is smaller in scale, but stands intact today due to a one-in-a-million chance: on D-Day, an American destroyer successfully shot a shell through the opening of the blockhouses. The shell miraculously didn't explode but crossed through the blockhouse and ended up a dud behind the fields.

If you want to go underground in WWII sites, head to the under-the-radar **Radar Museum 1944** *(musee-radar.fr; adult/under 10yr €7.50/free)*, a former German listening station that has preserved its original state. Run by friendly and impassioned volunteers, the guided visits at this lesser-known museum are well worth reserving in advance.

St-Malo

TIME FROM MONT ST-MICHEL: **50MIN**

Pirates and privateers

'Not French, not Breton, I am Malouin.' St-Malo's slogan sets the tone. Circled and protected by its commanding ramparts yet resolutely open to the sea, it takes great pride in its very distinctive identity. One of the most prosperous ports in France from the 15th century onwards, it became home to great seafarers such as Jacques Cartier, the first European to make his way to Canada in the 16th century. But St-Malo is most famous for the high number of privateers who enriched the city in the 17th and 18th centuries. Commissioned by the King of France to pillage enemy boats during war times, privateers owned hundreds of armed ships in the port of St-Malo towards the end of the 18th century. The city walls, which originally date back to the 12th century, were expanded and fortified to better defend these accumulated treasures, and quickly became emblematic of the city.

Standing imperiously on a rocky island facing the sea, St-Malo's **Fort National** *(fortnational.com; adult/child €5/3)* was built in 1689 and was originally intended to protect the city's port. Throughout the centuries, it has been the stage of legendary attacks and epic battles – and has also known darker days during WWII, when it was used as a prison by the Germans. The site is now open to visits every day in the summer, and during some school holidays and bank holidays. Opening hours depend on the time of the day: you'll need to wait for the tide to be low to walk across **Plage de l'Eventail** to reach the fort. You can book a 35-minute guided tour in English by email, with written translations also available in a number of other languages.

THE PRICE OF LIBERATION

The old town of St-Malo as we know it today came very close to not surviving at all. In August 1944, after four years of German occupation, St-Malo and its surroundings were relentlessly bombed by the Allies. When the city was liberated on 17 August 1944, 80% of the old town was destroyed. The ramparts, miraculously, were still standing. However, instead of razing the remains to the ground and rebuilding afresh, everything was reconstructed just as it was: a colossal, complex project that took years, including 18 months just to clear out the 500,000 cu metres of ruins. In 1972, when Cathédrale St-Vincent was inaugurated, St-Malo was officially completely restored.

 EATING IN ST-MALO: OUR PICKS

Doma: A cosy room and a short, tasty menu based on seasonal produce that is reasonably priced. *noon-1.30pm Wed-Sat, 7.30-9.30pm Tue-Sat* €€

La Touline: Classic crêperie with high-quality ingredients at the heart of the *intra muros. hours vary* €

Les Flibustiers: A warm spot with a terrace in the centre offering no-fuss *planches* (platters), salads, tartines, quiches and soups. *hours vary* €

Bouliche: Away from the crowds, near to Cité d'Alet, a local gem with creative plates. *noon-2pm Tue, 7-10pm Wed, noon-2pm & 7-10pm Thu-Sat* €€

French Alps

MOUNTAIN SCENERY | ADRENALINE | CHEESE

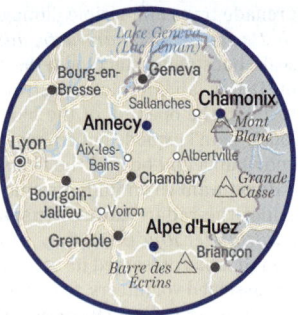

 TOP TIP

Travelling without kids? Take your skiing holiday in late January or late March: you'll miss all the school holidays (French and European) and rates are much lower. Low season in the Alps is from late April to early June and late September to late November, and many mountain towns all but shut up shop.

Heart-thumping adventure and pastoral tradition share the same starting gate in this high-octane playground, dedicated to safeguarding ancestral savoir-faire. The French Alps is where beauty of the most breathtaking nature and action collide. Glacier-carved national parks and shark-toothed mountain summits, ice-blue lakes and sky-high cols: the call of the wild is fierce in this eastern swathe of France, even more so for outdoor adventurers in town to bag the highest, longest feat – on skis, bike or simply your own two feet.

Rumbling across seven European countries, the Alps climax with western Europe's highest peak, Mont Blanc (4805m). The hypnotic snow-white crown of this storied mountain spirographs a kaleidoscope of magical shadows over the renowned ski and mountaineering town of Chamonix in Savoie (Savoy). Inhabited since prehistoric times, the French Alps have been fiercely contested since time immemorial. The desire to conquer that they arouse burns brighter

---

⊙ GETTING AROUND

Embracing the *départements* (departments) of Savoie, Haute-Savoie and Isère, the French Alps cover a vast area – not easy to navigate swiftly, thanks to valleys and mountains blocking direct routes. Roads to many ski stations are steep and serpentine. Snow clearing is frequent, but winter tyres or chains stowed in your trunk are obligatory from November to March. Many cols (mountain passes) are snowbound and closed in winter; in early/late summer, check road conditions before setting out. Buses link Moûtiers train station with Les Trois

Vallées and Bourg-St-Maurice station with Val d'Isère/Tignes. Modane is the rail stop for the Vanoise, linked by bus to Bonneval-sur-Arc. For Chamonix, hop on the Mont Blanc Express train at TGV station St-Gervais-Le Fayet. The long-distance GR5 or Grande Traversée des Alpes walking trail crosses the entire French Alps en route from Lake Geneva to the Med (674km). Shorter trails tackle the entire region, and are the loveliest way of slow-hopping between remote hamlets, farms and mountain *refuges* (shelters).

FRANCOIS ROUX/SHUTTERSTOCK

Mer de Glace (p408), Chamonix

than ever regardless of the season, be it the Vallée Blanche ski descent or Europe's longest black run in winter, or epic hiking trails in summer (the Tour du Mont Blanc spans three countries). Lakeside towns like Annecy offer a choice between the slow pace of life – glacial dips and languid paddleboarding in the crystalline waters of Lake Annecy – or yet more adrenaline, and it's one of the most popular spots in the country for paragliding.

All that effort tends to work up an appetite, and culinary specialities in the French Alps are of the 'roll-me-down-the-mountain' type: belt-busting troughs of fondue, gooey tartiflette and heady raclette.

Chamonix

MAP p408

Off-piste ride of a lifetime

Free-rider king of the French Alps and springboard to some of Europe's most fêted mountain adventures, Chamonix has always been one ski spin ahead of the curve. Just walking down Chamonix's pedestrian main street, loomed over by Mont Blanc's snow-white dome, it's impossible not to feel a sassy new spring in your step: the palpable buzz and anticipation of the next outdoor thrill around the corner.

Tales of skiers cruising along and suddenly disappearing from sight are rife in La Vallée Blanche annals. Then again, skiing across a snow bridge and tumbling metres like a rag doll into a dark ice-blue crevasse as the ruptured bridge collapses happens with surprising frequency.

This is just one reason why Europe's most legendary off-piste ski route – an astounding 2800m descent through a landscape of eerie, unearthly beauty – must be tackled with a certified guide. Starting at a dizzying 3842m, at the top

MOUNTAIN TOOLKIT

Lift passes: Find details of all passes at *montblancnatural resort.com*.

Mountain guides: Compagnie des Guides de Chamonix (*chamonix-guides. com*), inside the Maison de la Montagne, has guides for snowshoeing, ice-climbing, off-piste skiing, summer mountaineering, climbing and canyoning.

Trail access and conditions: The Office de Haute Montagne (*chamoniarde.com*), also in Maison de la Montagne, has information on hiking, climbing and ski-touring trails – including trail conditions.

Chamonix mobile app: Tourist office app (*en.chamonix.com*): weather forecasts, webcams, maps; purchase and top-up lift passes, too.

407

BEST ALTERNATIVE MOUNTAIN THRILLS IN THE FRENCH ALPS

Moon-biking: Ride snowy trails in Courchevel astride a silent, electric snow bike with front sled blade and rear caterpillar track.

Fat biking: Speed down on snow bicycles with ultra-fat tires in La Plagne.

Acro-speleology: Go with a guide to Grottes de St-Christophe caves for mixed climbing-canyoning in Massif des Chartreuse.

Electric mountain biking: Along the Via 3 Vallées, a 34km cycling itinerary links Courchevel, Méribel, Les Menuires and Val Thorens.

Mushing: Sled (up to 50km/h) with American Eskimo, Greenland or Alaskan dogs through sugar-dusted firs in several ski resorts

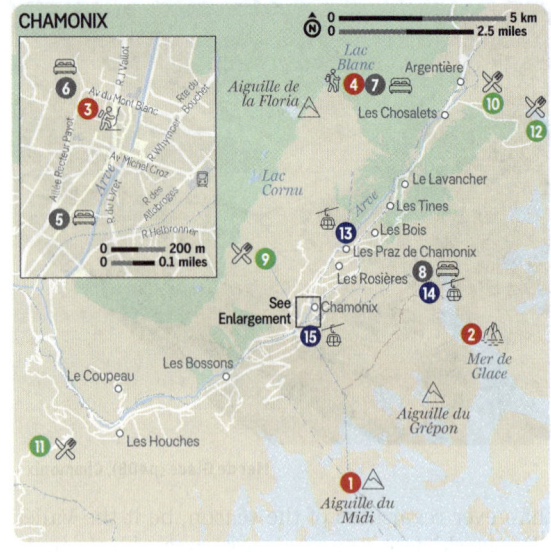

● **SIGHTS**
1 Aiguille du Midi
2 Mer de Glace

● **ACTIVITIES**
3 Compagnie des Guides de Chamonix
4 Lac Blanc

● **SLEEPING**
5 Hôtel Richemond
6 La Folie Douce
7 Refuge du Lac Blanc
8 Refuge du Montenvers

● **EATING**
9 La Bergerie de Planpraz
10 La Crèmerie du Glacier
11 Les Vieilles Luges
12 Refuge de Lognan

● **TRANSPORT**
13 Télécabine de la Flégère
14 Télécabine de la Mer de Glace
15 Téléphérique de l'Aiguille du Midi

cable-car station of the **Téléphérique de l'Aiguille du Midi** (*aiguilledumidi.montblancnaturalresort.com/en; adult/child return €78/66.30*), the challenging 20km ski route follows three serpentine glaciers down to the lower, moraine-scarred reaches of France's longest glacier, the **Mer de Glace** (Sea of Ice).

Here, at around 1700m, the glass-sided **Télécabine de la Mer de Glace** (*montenversmerdeglace.montblancnatural resort.com; adult/child return incl train, cable car & ice cave €39.50/33.60*) – a state-of-the-art cable car directly above an ice cave – whisks Vallée Blanche skiers back up to Gare du Montenvers at 1913m. From here Montenvers' cherry-red cogwheel train trundles down to Chamonix town in 20 minutes. This leg of the trip is also an exhilarating day trip for nonskiers year-round.

Late March to early April is the best time to tackle the Vallée Blanche, only suitable for confident skiers comfortable on black pistes and ungroomed terrain. Hook up with a guide from **Compagnie des Guides de Chamonix** (*chamonix-guides. com*) on a **small-group expedition** (*per person €155, plus lift passes €90*), with an overnight at 3613m at the **Refuge des Cosmiques** (*incl lift pass €425*) on the Col du Midi glacier or – most magically of all – on a **moonlight descent** (*2 people €430*).

Get up high on Chamonix's most popular hiking trail

Don trainers or sturdy walking shoes for the short but steep, rocky hike up to **Lac Blanc** (2352m). Despite horrific summertime crowds (avoid in July and August), marvelling at razor-sharp reflections of Europe's highest peak in the picture-postcard alpine lake is mind-blowing. Wild dipping in the crystalline water is prohibited.

Beat the crowds by hitting the trail at 8.30am when cable cars open; count three to four hours to cover the 8.5km return hike from the top of **Téléphérique de la Flégère** *(adult/child return €24/20.40)* at 1877m. Alternatively, overnight in Lac Blanc's lakeside mountain hut **Refuge du Lac Blanc** *(refuge-lac-blanc.fr; per person incl full board €85)* to gorge on sunrise views in splendid isolation. The WWII-era, 40-bed hut with basic cafe is open June to September.

Summiting the Aiguille du Midi

This rocky tooth of an alpine peak – **Aiguille du Midi** (3842m) in the Massif du Mont Blanc, easy to spot for miles around – ensnares France's highest cable-car station at 3777m, promising spine-tingling adventure for mountain enthusiasts and privileged access to a spectacular fairy-tale ice world for first-timers to high altitudes. Since it's weather dependent, check the website for variable hours *(aiguilledumidi.montblanc naturalresort.com; adult/child €88/68.90)*.

The giddy anticipation of new heights to be conquered is electric as you glide from Chamonix's bottom Téléphérique de l'Aiguille du Midi cable-car station to its top station at 3842m. The change of cabin at mid-station Plan d'Aiguille du Midi (2317m) is a prime opportunity to grab a coffee or *vin chaud* (warm mulled wine) at mountain hut Bar Plan d'Aiguille and acquaint yourself with the numerous aiguilles sculpting Chamonix's distinctive skyline.

At the futuristic top station, dimly lit tunnels spaghetti from the cable car, past wintertime skiers donning crampons to tackle the Vallée Blanche off-piste descent, to a succession of outdoor panoramic terraces. Information panels identify what's what in the surrounding breathtaking sea of snowy peaks.

Follow signs to Le Tube – a 34m-long metal pipe wrapped around part of the rocky spur. Take your time to traverse the cylindrical walkway, perforated with five slit windows overlooking ant-sized rock climbers in summer dangling on Pointe Rébuffat. Information boards impress with mind-blowing facts such as the 300 cu metres of concrete, 80 tons of steel and 500-plus helicopter trips it took to construct this wild, gravity-defying gallery.

CHEESY SAVOYARD SPECIALITIES

Savoyard fondue: In Savoie equal parts of grated Comté, gruyere and Beaufort cheese are melted with white wine in a garlic-smeared pot.

Tartiflette: Reblochon sliced and layered between potatoes, diced bacon, cream and nuts in this classic oven-baked dish.

Raclette: Melted raclette – occasionally smoked/peppered – is scraped from a standing grill onto boiled potatoes.

Burgdorf: Slices of Abondance cheese are oven-baked with Savoie white wine, sweet Madeira wine, nutmeg and pepper until bubbling, crisp and golden.

Crozet gratin: Savoyard 'pasta' squares are oven baked with Beaufort or Reblochon to create a gooey, crisp-crust gratin.

 EATING IN CHAMONIX: BEST MOUNTAIN LUNCHES — MAP p408

| **Refuge de Lognan:** The blueberry tart is a rite of passage at this mountain shelter on Argentière's Intégrale run. Cash only. *noon-2pm Jun-Sep & Dec-Apr* € | **La Crèmerie du Glacier:** A 1920s forest cabin famed for gratins, fondues and *croûtes* (wine-soaked bread, oven-baked with toppings). *11:30am-3pm* €€ | **Les Vieilles Luges:** A roaring fire welcomes skis at the Old Sledges, an 18th-century farmhouse on the slopes in Les Houches. *12.30-3pm Tue-Sun Dec-Apr* €€ | **La Bergerie de Planpraz:** The cozy Sheepfold gazes at Mont Blanc from its sunny terrace perched at 2000m. Order fire-grilled meat. *noon-3pm Dec-Apr* €€€ |

BEST SWIMMING BEACHES

Imperial Beach: Picnic-friendly lawns, sandy beach volleyball court, pétanque, children's playground, concreted shallows to paddle in and seasonal beach bar – by Annecy's pre-WWI casino-turned-luxury hotel.

Marquisats Beach: Grass-fringed pebble beach, a 15-minute stroll from Annecy's Jardins de l'Europe on the western lakeshore.

St-Jorioz Beach: Lake Annecy's only natural sand beach is in St-Jorioz. Vintage diving tower (lifeguards July and August), changing cabins, showers and snack bar.

Angon Beach: Beach volleyball and pétanque, 2km south of Talloires.

Choseaux Beach– Clos Berthet: Untamed grass and pebbles in Sévrier, a 10-minute walk south from busy municipal beach.

Ride the lift up to Pas dans le Vide, a glass-walled and -floored cabin overhanging a 1000m drop which, at 3830m, sits just 12m short of the summit. This is the highest point of the Aiguille du Midi tourist site, and views down are predictably exhilarating or terrifying, depending on your head for heights.

Annecy

Timeless romance in a handsome old town

Colourful facades and flower-fringed canals characterise Annecy's Vielle Ville (old town), nicknamed 'Venice of the Alps'. Commanding views across ochre rooftops and flower-festooned canals to the lake and burly Massif des Bauges beyond, **Château d'Annecy** *(musees.annecy.fr; adult/under 12yr €7/free)* is the crowning glory. Residence to the Counts of Geneva in the 13th and 14th centuries, it was abandoned three centuries on.

From the château, drop steeply down along stone-paved Rampe du Château to prison-turned-history museum **Palais de l'Isle** *(adult/child €5/2.50)*. The best views of this eye-catching stone building, squatting on a triangular islet in the Canal du Thiou since 1325, are from Pont Perrière, the old town's distinctive canal bridge safeguarded by baroque **Église St-François de Salès**. The Venetian atmosphere here is undeniable.

Fly with the birds above Col de la Forclaz

It requires no skill – just guts or the dream to fly with birds – to paraglide over Lake Annecy. April to November, tandem flights take off from the **Site de Montmin** (1276m) up high near the **Col de la Forclaz** (1150m) at the lake's southern tip. They land 10 to 20 minutes later at official landing zones in Doussard (next to the D281) or in Perroix (2km south of Talloires).

Dozens of *parapente* (paragliding) schools offer tandem flights. Several operate from wooden huts at the Doussard landing field, from where minibuses shuttle clients up to the pass. In Annecy's old town, adventure-sports specialists **Takamaka** *(annecy.takamaka.fr; from €95)* has an office at 23 rue du Faubourg Ste-Claire where you can pick up info, check weather/flying conditions and reserve flights.

Paddling and surfing Lake Annecy

Don't let the garish rubber rings outside the *épicerie* (grocery) at the entrance to Doussard Plage on the lake's southern tip put you off. Once afloat a stand-up paddleboard (SUP), you'll find the serenity of less-tamed shores here is intoxicating.

 EATING IN ANNECY: OUR PICKS

Marché de la Vieille Ville: Open-air street market in the old town, stalls with Savoyard cheeses, charcuterie and food to go. *7am-1pm Tue, Fri & Sun €*

Les Baigneurs Café: Breakfast, brunch, specialist coffee and lunchtime tartines on a sun-soaked terrace. *8.30am-5.30pm Wed-Fri, from 9am Sat & Sun €*

Bon Pain Bon Vin: Local produce fuels this old-school buvette with 1960s interior, traditional cuisine and specials chalked on the board. *10am-1am €€*

Saba: Feast on creative French-Japanese fusion with local foodies at this sassy old-town bistro. *noon-1.30pm & 7-9pm Mon, Tue, Thu & Fri, 7-9pm Wed €€€*

🚲 CYCLING LAKE ANNECY

Lap up big mountain views and bijou villages on this 42km lake-loop ride.

START	END	LENGTH
Annecy Town	Annecy Town	42km; 3–4 hours

Hire a bicycle/e-bike from ❶ **Cyclable** (annecy-bonlieu.cyclable.com) and set off clockwise (300m elevation). Pick up the two-way cycling path in front of Veyrier-du-Lac, and cruise 6km alongside the D909, past Mont Veyrier (1291m) on your left. Climb up to place de l'Église in Menthon-St-Bernard, 3km south; its fairy-tale ❷ **Château de Menthon-St-Bernard** is a 2km detour uphill. At ❸ **Café de la Place**, refuel on coffee and a *tarte écureuil* (caramelised walnut tart) from the bakery.

Stay alert on the steep downhill swoop to Talloires. It was in this pretty lakefront village

cradling 17th-century ❹ **Abbaye de Talloires** that Cézanne painted in 1896. This is the lake's narrowest point where the built-up 'grand lac' (north) spills into the wilder 'petit lac' (south). Thirty minutes (8.7km) on a dedicated cycling path takes you to the lake's southern tip. Doussard is the springboard for walks in the ❺ **Réserve Naturelle du Bout du Lac d'Annecy**. A greenway now takes you to Duingt: pedalling through a defunct railway tunnel heralds your arrival. Park and follow the footpath 10 minutes to hillside ❻ **Grotte de Notre Dame du Lac** for breathtaking lake views. It's 13km back to Annecy.

Lakeside **Château de Duingt** hosts seasonal exhibitions.

Climb the **Tour de Brauvivier** to watch paragliders dropping over rocky Dents de Lanfon (1824m) and Lanfonnet (1793m).

Along the reserve's circular boardwalk, keep your eyes peeled for beavers.

SKIING LES TROIS VALLÉES

The world's largest ski area connects three valleys with 600km of pistes and 200 lifts. Key resorts:

Méribel (1450m): Best for intermediate skiers: 150km of blue and red runs, two snow parks and a wild après-ski scene. Linked by gondola to budget Brides-les-Bains (600m). *(meribel.net)*

Courchevel (1850m): Tree-fringed playground for the super-rich; La Tania (1400m) lower down is less flash. *(courchevel.com)*

Val Thorens (2300m): Europe's highest ski resort, meaning the longest snow-sure season (usually late November to mid-May. *(valthorens. com)*

St-Martin de Belleville (1450m): Traditional village option: chic accommodation and dining ranging from gourmet mountain hut to Michelin-starred. *(st-martin-belleville. com)*

THOMAS DEKIERE/SHUTTERSTOCK

Paragliding over Lake Annecy (p410), Annecy

Help yourself to an inflatable board, paddle and life vest – via the Equip Sport app – from the ingenious SUP vending machine on the lawn section of Doussard Beach. April to October, head to beach cafe **Le Cadre** *(lecadre74.com),* at the beach's opposite end by the pleasure port, where water-sports school **SkiWake74** *(skiwake74.com; rental per hr €17)* rents kayaks and SUPs. You can also water-ski, wakeboard or surf the waves of the latest speedboat here.

Alpe d'Huez

Fly down Europe's longest black run

Winter or summer, in the ski town of Alpe d'Huez, riding the two legs of the **Télépherique du Pic Blanc** *(skipass. alpedhuez.com)* up to Lac Blanc (2700m) and beyond to Pic Blanc (3330m) is dizzying. Prepare for bitter cold on the wind-whipped glacier – frequently -20°C in winter and -10°C on a sun-scorched spring day. A spectacular ski-swoosh down to Alpe d'Huez beckons – on Europe's longest black run, 16km-long **La Sarenne** with a 2km vertical drop. Except for a handful of steep, ungroomed segments polka-dotted with moguls, the snowy descent is more like a wide, roller-coaster red with a maddeningly long green at the end. Skip the final 'flat' by cutting off at Pont du Gua to take the Chalvet chairlift up, then ski the red Campanules down. To admire Pic Blanc and its glacier in an alternative, magical light, ski La Sarenne at sunrise with a *pisteur* (ski patroller) or after sunset by head-torch with a guide; book at the tourist office *(alpedhuez.com)* on place Joseph Paganon.

Nonskiers zoom down Europe's longest black run on two wheels during April's Sarenne Snowbike *(skipass.alpedhuez .com/hiver/sarenne-snowbike)* and in July when thousands of intrepid bikers rip down ice, slush and rocks at speeds of up to 100km/h during Megavalanche, the world's longest downhill mountain-bike event.

Lyon

FINE WINE | UNPARALLELED DINING | VARIED HISTORY

First the Roman capital of the Gauls in the 1st century BCE, then European capital of the silk trade in the 16th century, Lyon's past has been multifaceted. As it industrialised and motorists began to pass through, it rose to prominence in the Michelin road guide, leading to the discovery of the city's unusual cuisine and *bouchon* restaurants.

Lyon today is wonderfully liveable, and still deservedly wears the crown as France's gastronomic capital. It has a sprinkling of everything: great food and wine, proximity to the mountains, immense parks, a buzzing nightlife (watered by fine wines from Beaujolais to the north and the Rhône Valley to the south), and architecture that yo-yos between Roman, Renaissance, Baroque and art deco. In recent years, the city council has invested in all things green, meaning that bike paths are often as wide as car lanes, and footpaths and parks run along much of the riverbanks.

Before Lyon Came Lugdunum
Think about the Roman Empire

Until 43 BCE, Lyon was little more than a Gaulish village. Lucius Munatius Plancus, governor of Gaul, was sent to found a Roman colony by the Senate, and Lugdunum was born. Under Emperor Augustus (27 BCE to 14 CE) the city mushroomed, and many vestiges of its Roman origins are still standing today. The 1st-century-CE amphitheatre is home to summer

☑ **TOP TIP**

Some of the best art installations are under your feet. Incognito street artist Ememem is Lyon's answer to Banksy, only they're solving the city's pothole problem by filling them in with mosaics.

 **GETTING AROUND**

Lyon's metro is comprehensive and reliable *(€2.10/journey)*. A **Lyon City Card** *(24hr/48hr/72hr/96hr €32/€44/€56/€68)* from **Only Lyon Tourist Office** includes entry into multiple museums, public transport, guided visits and certain boat trips. Download the

Vélo'v app (electric and regular bikes) for easy, pay-per-use rental in the city. To get to the city centre from the airport, take the **Rhône Express** *(rhoneexpress.fr; one way €15.20)*, or the C200 bus *(€2.10)* to **Vaulx-en-Velin La Soie** metro.

WHAT'S A BOUCHON?

In other parts of the country, a *bouchon* is either a wine cork or a traffic jam. In Lyon, they're meat-heavy traditional restaurants formerly run by *Mères Lyonnaises* (Lyonnaise mothers), who'd feed workers cheap, cheerful and filling plates of offal, washed down with red wine. Restaurants sticking to tradition dish up *andouillette* (sausages made from pig intestines), kidney and tripe, and many of the upmarket *bouchons* manage to make it quite palatable (though beware tourist traps in Vieux Lyon). The truly traditional even serve *mâchon*: bottomless brunch with a Lyonnais twist. Instead of eggs and avocado, the menu includes *rognons de veau* (calf kidneys) and *tête de veau* (calf's head) all washed down with large quantities of wine...at 9am.

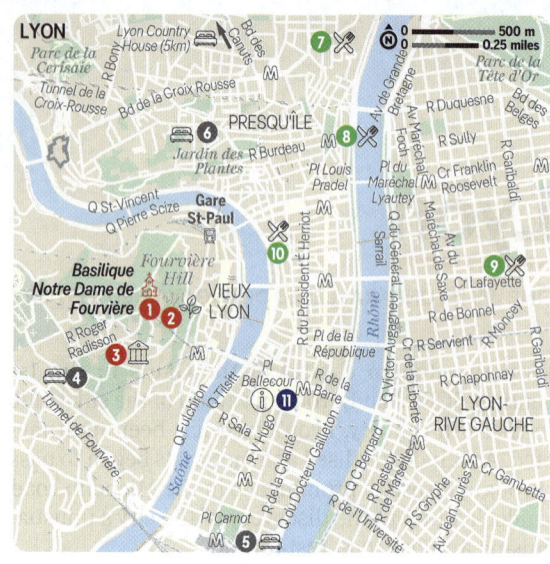

⭐ **HIGHLIGHTS**	⬤ **SLEEPING**	9 Ayla
1 Basilique Notre Dame de Fourvière	4 Fourvière Hôtel	10 Circle
	5 Hotel de Verdun 1882	⬤ **INFORMATION**
🔴 **SIGHTS**	6 Pilo	11 Only Lyon Tourist Office
2 Jardin du Rosaire	🟢 **EATING**	
3 Musée Gallo-Romain de Fourvière	7 Alebrije	
	8 Astral	

concerts; **Nuits de Fourvière**, in June and July, is the largest. There's a great museum, the **Musée Gallo-Romain de Fourvière** *(lugdunum.grandlyon.com; adult/child €7/3)*, that thoroughly explores Lyon's origins and has plenty of interactive displays for kids, including one section where they can dress up as gladiators.

Discover Secret Passageways

Traboules crisscross the city

Over 400 *traboules*, covered passageways originally used for transporting silk, wind their way through Lyon. Many are in private buildings, making them difficult to explore independently. Lyon's free **walking tour** *(freetourlyon.com)* – give what you like – in English and run by a Dutch expat, shows places many locals don't even know exist. Choose from a tour of Vieux Lyon (the Old Town), or Vieux Lyon and Croix-Rousse, and expect to return with a mine of fun facts. Who knew that the predecessor to computers was Lyon's silk-weaving Jacquard loom?

Virgin Mary statue, Basilica Notre-Dame de Fourvière

High on the Basilica Domes

A hill with history

It's difficult to imagine Lyon without **Basilica Notre-Dame de Fourvière** *(fourviere.org; free),* which dominates the skyline, but was only built at the end of the 19th century. The golden statue of the Virgin Mary predates the basilica: it was built by a local sculptor in 1852 and erected on the spires of the basilica to commemorate Lyon's liberation from the plague epidemic in 1643 (rumour has it that the disease never crossed the Rhône and stayed confined to the other side of Pont de la Guillotière).

Views from the top of Fourvière Hill are already impressive: they take in Lyon's twin rivers, the Saône and the Rhône, and (when you stand next to the basilica) the Alps. However, the highest point is from the basilica's domes. Inside the cathedral, stained-glass windows and ceilings adorned with golden stars and chandeliers of epic proportions create scenes straight out of a fairy tale. **Tours** *(booking.fourviere.org; adult/child €14/7)* run daily from April to September. To get here, take the funicular from Vieux Lyon, or walk up through **Jardin du Rosaire**.

WHY I LOVE LYON

Anna Richards, Lonely Planet writer

Lyon bewitched me when I first visited as a backpacker over a decade ago. From our hilltop hostel we looked over the towers of Cathédrale St-Jean, cylindrical l'Opéra and silhouettes of the distant Alps. The scent of praline brioche wafted up from chimneys, and *péniches* sank lower into the Rhône under the weight of stomping feet dancing the night away in floating clubs. I've now lived here for years, but I'll never grow tired of discovering the latest fusion restaurant to open, or picnicking beside immense botanical greenhouses in urban parks. In winter I can go skiing all day and be back drinking Beaujolais on a boat bar at night – how many cities can you say that about?

EATING IN LYON: PROPER GOOD GRUB

Circle: Six- or eight-course tasting menus where the quality of the simplest ingredients, like olive oil, shines through. *noon-1.15pm & 8-9.15pm Tue-Sat* €€€

Ayla: Franco-Lebanese sharing plates, as much of a feast for eyes as bellies. The tempura vine leaves stand out. *noon-2pm & 7.30-9.30pm Tue-Sat* €€

Astral: Classic French cuisine done well, managed by a young team. It also runs wine tastings in the cellar. *noon-2pm & 7-9.30pm Thu-Mon* €€

Alebrije: Franco-Mexican fusion from one of Lyon's top chefs, Carla Kirsch Lopez, who draws on inspiration from her two cultures. *7.30-9pm Tue-Sat* €€€

Beyond Lyon

Towering limestone gorges, prehistoric caves and the seat of the European Parliament are easily reachable from Lyon.

Places

Strasbourg p416
Gorges de l'Ardèche p417
Gorges du Tarn p419

Limestone pillars higher than skyscrapers mask warrens of prehistoric caves, and forests teem with wildlife. The many twists and turns of the Ardèche River and Tarn River cut through their prospective limestone plateaus and snake through the middle to form the Gorges de l'Ardèche and the Gorges du Tarn. To the northeast, the impossibly photogenic city of Strasbourg is a flurry of twisting backstreets lined with crooked half-timbered houses, scenic canals, flower-filled courts and opulent shops. Inviting *winstubs* (traditional Alsatian taverns) cower beneath the soaring magnificence of the cathedral, a medieval marvel in pink sandstone. It may look like something out of a fairy tale, but Strasbourg has got its finger on the pulse, and this city is the seat of the European Parliament.

GETTING AROUND

Strasbourg is a major transport hub, and has high-speed (TGV) connections to Paris (from one hour 50 minutes). There's also an airport serving several European destinations.

Strasbourg city centre is relatively small, so easy to walk.

Both the Gorges de l'Ardèche and the Gorges du Tarn are difficult to reach using public transport: take a car to avoid wasting hours waiting for virtually nonexistent buses. The scenic roads with sweeping bends are popular with motorcyclists.

Strasbourg

TIME FROM LYON: **4HR**

Awe-inspiring architecture

Strasbourg walks a fine tightrope between France and Germany, and between a medieval past and a progressive future.

Completed in all its Gothic grandeur in 1439, **Cathédrale Notre-Dame** (*cathedrale-strasbourg.fr; astronomical clock adult/child €4/2, platform €8/5*) is the unchallenged Strasbourg icon in the heart of the city. The lace-fine facade lifts the gaze little by little to flying buttresses, leering gargoyles and a 142m spire. The interior is exquisitely lit by 12th- to 14th-century stained-glass windows. We love the quirky Gothic-meets-Renaissance astronomical clock that strikes solar noon at 12.30pm with a parade of figures portraying the lives of the Apostles. A spiral staircase twists up to the 66m-high viewing platform. To appreciate the cathedral in peace, visit in the early evening, when the crowds have thinned.

Visit the European Quarter

About 2km northeast of central Strasbourg, the European Quarter is a city within the city, with its own architecture and unique energy. Overlooking the River Ill, the oval-shaped building of the **Parlement Européen** (*europarl.europa.eu*) is striking. You can take an audioguide tour or sit in on debates ranging from lively to yawn-a-minute.

Cathédrale Notre-Dame's astronomical clock, Strasbourg

DINING AT A WINSTUB

For a memorable culinary experience in Strasbourg, dine at a *winstub*: a traditional Alsatian restaurant renowned for its warm, homely atmosphere. Most dishes are based on pork and veal; specialities include *baeckeoffe* (meat stew), *wädele* or *jambonneau braisé* (braised pork knuckles), *fleischschnäcke* (minced meat rolls) and *choucroute garnie* (sauerkraut garnished with meat or fish). Vegetarians can usually order *bibelaskäs* (soft white cheese mixed with fresh cream) and *pommes sautées* (sautéed potatoes). Also look for restaurants serving *tarte flambée* (a thin-crust pizza dough topped with crème fraiche, onions and lardons). Alsatian specialities are best accompanied with Alsatian white wines.

A futuristic glass crescent, the Council of Europe's **Palais de l'Europe** *(coe.int)* across the River Ill can be visited on free one-hour weekday tours (ask to join a group); see the website for reservations. You can also take a virtual tour at *70.coe.int/virtual-tour-en.html*.

It's just a hop across the Canal de la Marne to the swirly silver **Palais des Droits de l'Homme** *(European Court of Human Rights; echr.coe.int),* the most eye-catching of all the EU institutions. It ensures that 46 European states abide by the European Convention on Human Rights.

Gorges de l'Ardèche

TIME FROM LYON: **3HR**

Prehistoric cave paintings

Grotte Chauvet 2 *(grottechauvet2ardeche.com; adult/child 10-17/under 10yr €18/9/free)* may be a replica of the original cave, which is closed to the public to avoid damaging the cave paintings, but it's a good one. The original, discovered in 1994, is a UNESCO World Heritage Site, and features cave paintings thought to be over 30,000 years old, composed of handprints and sketches of cave bears, cave lions and mammoths. From the paintings it's possible to deduce incredible amounts of information, including the rough age and the gender of the artists. The replica includes exceptionally informative guided

 EATING IN STRASBOURG: OUR WINSTUB PICKS

Chez Yvonne: Near the cathedral, Chez Yvonne is an institution. Traditional decor and excellent Alsatian dishes. *11.45am-2pm & 6.30-10pm Tue-Sat* €

Le Tire-Bouchon: Arguably the best *choucroute* of Strasbourg is served at this snug, amiable *winstub. 11.30am-9.30pm* €

Au Pont Corbeau: The essence of Alsace quaintness: dark timber, checked tablecloths and hearty grub. *noon-2pm & 7-9.30pm Mon-Fri, noon-2pm Sun* €

Le Clou: The menu is packed with classics – *wädele, bibelaskäs* – all of which marry nicely with a glass of local pinot noir. *11.45am-2.30pm & 6-10pm* €

KAYAKING THE ARDÈCHE RIVER

A roller-coaster adventure by water through France's prehistoric playground. Shorter 7km and 13km routes are also possible.

START	END	LENGTH
Vallon Pont d'Arc	Sauze	32km; 7 hours/2 days

Kayaking the Ardèche River reaches motorway levels of busy in high season; a website is in place to predict how busy the river will be. Canoë Malin can be consulted via the tourist office website (gorges-ardeche-pontdarc.fr).

Start at ❶ **Vallon Pont d'Arc**:it's a sprawling mass of rental shops without a clearly defined centre. There's plenty of choice and, so long as your kayak is seaworthy, rentals are much of a muchness, supplying laminated maps and a watertight tub for your belongings, and organising your return transfer at the end of whichever distance you choose to tackle. Aïgue Vive (aigue-vive.com) is helpful and efficient.

It doesn't take long to reach the showstopper, the ❷ **Pont d'Arc** (4km), but what those who've taken the land route don't see are the caves inside the rock arch itself. By kayak, you can dip in and out of the caves and crane your neck to take in the 54m-high rock arch from the water.

Keep moving with the current, over rapids (Grade II/Grade III) and between limestone cliffs, to reach two wild campsites: ❸ **Bivouac de Gaud** and ❹ **Bivouac de Gournier**. If splitting the trip over two days, you'll need to camp at one of these. For the final few kilometres to ❺ **Sauze**, the limestone cliffs shrink, and you can often see vultures wheeling overhead.

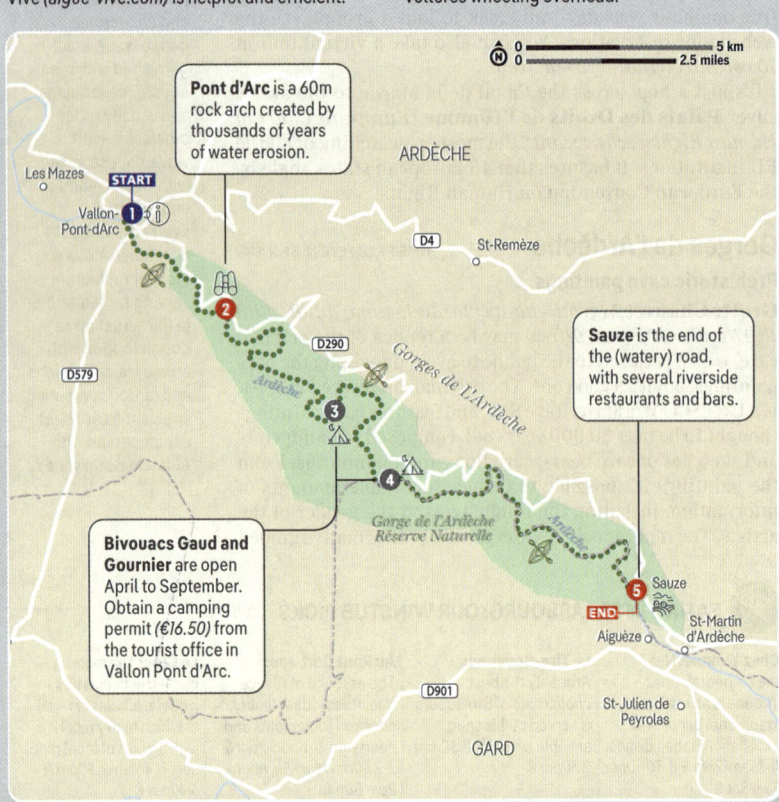

Pont d'Arc is a 60m rock arch created by thousands of years of water erosion.

Sauze is the end of the (watery) road, with several riverside restaurants and bars.

Bivouacs Gaud and Gournier are open April to September. Obtain a camping permit (€16.50) from the tourist office in Vallon Pont d'Arc.

Gorges du Tarn

BEST LONG-DISTANCE HIKES NEAR THE GORGES DU TARN

For more information, see *gr-infos.com*.

GR67: Considered the ultimate guide to the Cévennes on foot, the 130km GR67 is a loop hike that begins and ends in Anduze, summiting Mt Aigoual.

GR68: The GR68, aka the Mont Lozère loop, never actually climbs the mountain, rather using it as the axle around which the 115km hike revolves.

GR736: From Albi to Villefort, this 317km route encompasses the entire Causses et Cévennes.

GR4: Passes through the Causses et Cévennes on its way from the Atlantic to the Mediterranean.

GR70: The Stevenson Trail, famously trekked by Robert Louis Stevenson and his donkey Modestine, running from Le Puy-en-Velay to Alès.

visits and immersive sound-and-light shows. The visit lasts approximately one hour; factor in extra time for the sound-and-light show. Audioguides in English available.

Gorges du Tarn

TIME FROM LYON: 3½HR 🚗

Road trips and watery adventures

One of France's most spectacular natural wonders, the Gorges du Tarn, is found in the zone where the Cévennes becomes the Causses: a biodiverse region of shifting mountain-scapes. If you have a car, prepare for one of the country's truly spectacular, and slightly unnerving, drives. The gorge runs for around 50km, but a good entry point is the pretty village of Ste-Énimie. From here, the D907 balcony road scrapes its way past vertiginous cliffs, which occasionally hang right over the road.

Midway along is the stunning La Malène village, the best point to go boating. **Les Bateliers des Gorges du Tarn** (*gorgesdutarn.com; €26*), the revered local boaters, steer you down the river in a green wooden boat. Kayaking and canoeing are popular alternatives, and the river is safer for beginners here than Ste-Énimie. **Canoë 2000** (*canoe-kayak-gorgesdu tarn.com*) and **Canoe au Moulin de la Malène** (*canoeblanc. com*) rent all the necessary equipment and drive you back to the village at the end. In **Ste-Énimie**, try **Canoë Méjean** (*canoe-mejean.com*). Back on the road, at **Le Rozier** you can turn east into **Gorges de la Jonte**, which has another stunning gorge drive on wider, less crowded roads.

 EATING IN GORGES DU TARN: BEST RESTAURANTS

L'Alicanta: Seasonal ingredients (often linked to beef, pork or lamb) with good-value set menus in Le Rozier. *7-8.30pm* €€

Le Petit Paris: Try regional dishes, such as *aligot* (cheesy mashed potato served with sausage) in Ste-Énimie. *hours vary Fri-Tue* €€

Capluc Kfé: Charcuterie and cheeseboards, river trout and *aligot* with pork sausages in onion gravy are hearty at this Le Rozier favourite. *hours vary* €€

Auberge du Moulin: Terrace dining in Ste-Énimie, overlooking the gorge, with French cuisine staples such as roast leg of lamb with vegetables. *Thu-Tue Apr-Oct* €€

Loire Valley

RIVERSIDE CASTLES | VINEYARDS | SERENE CYCLING

☑ TOP TIP

Thirsty? Head to one of the Loire's many *guinguettes*. A kind of pop-up riverbank restaurant with a beer-garden vibe, *guinguettes* originated in Paris during the Belle Époque. Open from spring to early autumn, they bring together wooden furniture, deckchairs, hanging fairy lights, local wine, tasty food and, often, live music.

If you're looking for French splendour, style and gastronomy, the Loire Valley will exceed your expectations, no matter how great. Poised on the crucial frontier between northern and southern France – and just a short train or *autoroute* (tolled motorway) ride from Paris – the region was once of immense strategic importance. Kings, queens, dukes and nobles came here to build feudal castles and, later on, sumptuous Renaissance pleasure palaces – that's why this fertile river valley is sprinkled with hundreds of France's most opulent aristocratic estates, many sporting crenellated towers, soaring cupolas and twinkling banquet halls.

The Loire, much of it a UNESCO World Heritage Site, is also known for its outstanding wines – reds, whites, rosés and sparkling – and vineyards stretch along both banks of the Loire from the Blésois, westward through Touraine and Anjou, to the Atlantic. A network of walking trails, bike paths and tertiary roads makes it easy to visit both glittering châteaux and vine-encircled *domaines* (wine-growing estates) in a single afternoon.

Fans of French urban life will find medium-sized cities that are renowned for their *douceur de vivre* (the gentle pleasures of life), with verve and energy added by tens of thousands of students. Tours, Angers and Nantes are graced with handsome avenues, historic

---

 GETTING AROUND

Having your own wheels is the easiest and quickest way to visit châteaux and vineyards, but if you stay in the city centre in Tours, Angers and Nantes, a car can be a liability, as parking is in short supply and is time-limited and/or pricey. Tours-Centre, the Loire Valley's

main rail hub, has direct services to over a dozen Loire destinations.

Direct TGV trains link Paris Montparnasse with St-Pierre-des-Corps (3km from Tours), Angers-St-Laud and Nantes. Zipping along backroads on a *vélo* is a fantastic way to tour the Loire.

quarters traversed by narrow medieval streets and excellent (and moderately priced) dining, as well as an abundance of lovely gardens and romantic riverside promenades.

Blois

Royal château with a bloody history

Seven French kings lived in the **Château Royal de Blois** *(chateaudeblois.fr; adult/child €14.50/7.50)*. Its four grand wings were built during four distinct periods in French architecture: Gothic (13th century), Flamboyant Gothic (1498–1501), early Renaissance (1515–20) and classical (1630s). You can easily spend a half-day immersing yourself in the château's dramatic and bloody history and its extraordinary architecture. An informative audioguide costs €3; a HistoPad, offering augmented-reality views, is free at the *consigne* (checked-luggage facility). The most sumptuous part of the Gothic wing is the richly painted Estates General Room, from the 13th century. The King's Chamber was the setting for one of the bloodiest episodes in the château's history, the assassination of Duke Henri I de Guise in 1588.

Every night from early April to late September, a 45-minute **Son et Lumière** *(adult/child €12/7.50)*, held in the interior courtyard, brings the château's history and architecture to life with dramatic lighting and narration.

Chambord

The Loire's most magnificent château

One of the crowning achievements of French Renaissance architecture, the **Château de Chambord** *(chambord.org; adult/child €19/free)* – with 426 rooms, 282 fireplaces and 77 staircases – is the largest, grandest and most visited château in the Loire Valley. Rising through the centre of the structure, the world-famous double-helix staircase ascends to the great lantern tower and the rooftop, where you can gaze out across the vast grounds and marvel at a mind-blowing skyline of cupolas, domes, turrets, chimneys and lightning rods. To add virtual-reality furnishings to some of the rooms, pick up – at the entrance to the château itself – a HistoPad tablet computer *(€6.50, 1½ hours)*. In July and August, hour-long guided **tours** *(adult/child €7/4)* in English begin daily at 11.15am; reserve online or at the ticket counter.

THE GUIDE

FRANCE LOIRE VALLEY

WINE TOURING IN THE LOIRE

It's easy to put together a web of wonderful wine-tasting itineraries in the Loire, drawing on 350 wine cellars producing reds, rosés, whites, dessert wines and crémants (sparkling wines). A tourist office or *maison des vins* (wine visitor centre) can supply you with local options and – assuming it's reissued – *À la Découverte des Vins de Loire* (Discovering Loire Wines): a free map with an excellent, colour-coded presentation of the winegrowing areas that stretch from Blois to the Atlantic. It is produced by the region's winegrowers' association, Vins de Loire *(vinsdeloire.fr)*; its website has plenty of information in English and downloadable brochures under 'Tourist circuits'.

EATING IN BLOIS: OUR FRENCH PICKS

Poivre et Sel: Traditional French cuisine served on rustic tables, with old-style wood beams overhead. *noon-1.45pm & 7-9.30pm Mon-Sat* €€

L'Arboré Sens: A city-centre brasserie with a pretty terrace, a good selection of salads, reasonable prices and, on some evenings, live music. *11am-midnight Mon-Sat* €

Côté Loire-Auberge Ligérienne: On the riverfront, French cuisine in a rustic dining room and, when it's warm, on a lovely terrace. *noon-1.30pm & 7.30-9pm Tue-Sat* €€

Au Rendez-Vous des Pêcheurs: Elegant bistro specialising in fish (salmon, cod, zander), served on gorgeous ceramic plates. *12.15-1.15pm & 7.15-8.30pm Tue-Sat* €€€

VINEYARD-HOPPING & FLOATING ABOVE THE VINEYARDS

Private companies offer well-organised minibus tours that take in various combinations of châteaux, sometimes coupled with vineyard visits, as well as specialised tours featuring cycling or wine-tasting. Tourist offices and their websites have details. Floating peacefully in a *montgolfière* (hot-air-balloon) is a gorgeously romantic way to see the Loire countryside. Operated by about a dozen companies, flights are generally possible from April to October, weather permitting, with departures early in the morning or in the evening. Tourist offices (eg Tours and Amboise) and their websites can provide contact information and help with reservations.

VICTOR TORRES/SHUTTERSTOCK

Château de Chenonceau, Chenonceau

The château is surrounded by Louis XIV-style formal gardens (château tickets required) and extensive grounds (open 24 hours). At the Embarcadère (boat dock), rent bicycles, quadricycles, electric golf carts and electric boats from early April to October. Outdoor spectacles held in the warm season include a 45-minute **equestrian show** *(adult/child €18/14.30, adult incl château €32)* in which horses and colourfully clad riders take you through five centuries of Chambord's history. Shows are held from early April to September and begin at 11.45am and/or 4pm from Tuesday to Sunday.

Chenonceaux

Elegant arches and delightful gardens

Spanning the languid Cher River atop a graceful arched bridge, the **Château de Chenonceau** *(chenonceau.com; adult/child €18/15)* is one of France's most elegant castles. It's hard not to be moved and exhilarated by the glorious setting, the formal gardens, the magic of the architecture and the château's fascinating history. Chenonceau is largely the work of several remarkable women – hence its nickname, the Château des Dames. The distinctive arches and the eastern formal garden were added by Diane de Poitiers, mistress of Henri II. Catherine de Médici completed the château's construction and added the yew-tree maze and the western rose garden. The most singular contribution of Louise of Lorraine's was her black-walled mourning room on the top floor, to which she retreated when her husband, Henri III, was assassinated in 1589.

The château's pièce de résistance is the 60m-long, checkerboard-floored Grande Galerie over the Cher River, scene of many an elegant party hosted by Catherine de Médici and Madame Dupin. Used as a military hospital during WWI, it served from 1940 to 1942 as an escape route for *résistants*, Jews and other refugees fleeing from the German-occupied zone (north of the Cher) to the Vichy-controlled zone (south of the river). There's an excellent 1¼-hour audioguide *(€5)* in 12 languages. Chenonceau's elegant restaurant, L'Orangerie, serves brunch-style French meals from noon to 3pm and becomes a *salon de thé* (tearoom) from 3pm to 4.30pm You can taste Touraine wines in the château's historic wine cellar, the Cave des Dômes (closed November to January). Chenonceaux (the name of the village has an X at the end) is an easy train ride from Tours.

Villandry
Exquisite gardens à la Française

The gardens of the **Château de Villandry** *(chateauvillandry. com; adult/child €14/8, gardens only €8.50/5.50, winter €2)* are among France's most beautiful, with more than 6 hectares of cascading flowers, ornamental vines, manicured lime trees, razor-sharp box-hedges and tinkling fountains. Try to visit when the gardens – all of them organic – are blooming (ie between April and October). Tickets are valid all day (get your hand stamped if you leave). An audioguide costs €4. For many, the highlight is the 16th-century-style *Potager Décoratif* (Decorative Kitchen Garden), where cabbages, leeks and carrots create nine geometrical, colour-coordinated squares.

Azay-le-Rideau
Renaissance castle par excellence

Romantic, moat-ringed **Château d'Azay-le-Rideau** *(azay-le-rideau.fr; adult/child €16/free)*, built almost exactly 500 years ago on a natural island in the middle of the Indre River, is wonderfully adorned with elegant turrets, exquisitely proportioned windows, delicate stonework and steep slate roofs. The famous, Italian-style loggia staircase overlooking the central courtyard is decorated with the salamanders and ermines of François I and Queen Claude. Audioguides *(€3; 1½ hours)* are available in five languages. From mid-July to late August, you can take a *flânerie nocturne* (nighttime stroll; adult/child €8/4) around the illuminated gardens, accompanied by ancient music, from nightfall until 11.15pm.

CYCLING THE LOIRE

The Loire Valley is fabulous cycling country – pedal through villages, vineyards and forests on your way from one château to the next. **La Loire à Vélo** *(Loire by Bike; loirebybike.co.uk)* maintains 900km of signposted routes from Nevers to the Atlantic; pick up a free guide from a tourist office or access information (details on route options and bike hire) from the website. Individual *départements*, including Indre-et-Loire (Touraine), Loir-et-Cher (Blésois) and Maine-et-Loire (Anjou), have their own cycling networks and brochures. Les Châteaux à Vélo *(chateauxavelo.co.uk)* maintains over 500km of marked bike routes in the Blésois. The Geovelo smartphone app recommends routes that follow bike paths and avoid heavy traffic.

Provence

SEDUCTIVE BEACHES | LAVENDER FIELDS | COLOURFUL CITIES

TOP TIP

Don't dismiss Provence in winter. The crowds have left and prices are much lower, but the temperature remains balmy. Some of the best parties happen in winter, including Nice's carnival, which lasts for two weeks each February.

When you find yourself awash in Provence's famous light, it becomes clear why so many artists have been magnetically drawn here for centuries, seeking to unlock something bigger than themselves. This land epitomises springtime, having inspired great post-impressionist painters Cézanne and Van Gogh to create their seminal works. As the mistral wind howls down the Rhône Valley towards the sea, slamming the wooden shutters of homes throughout the night and clearing the skies for what feels like endless sunshine, it creates a climate that is not only inviting for travellers but also ideal for farming. Sampling the fresh produce nurtured here is an essential part of the journey, especially in the busy markets and endless stretches of vineyards. For a month or two every year, from June to early July, the region glows purple as Provençal lavender comes into bloom.

The region's palpitating heart is Marseille, France's second-largest city, with its vibrant cultural energy, street art, eclectic nightlife and world-class dining scene. It's constantly evolving, and increasingly attracts partygoers looking to discover 'France's Berlin'. To the east, the Côte d'Azur, France's glittering

GETTING AROUND

Away from the coast, driving in this region can be a joy. To spontaneously stop in tiny villages or wind your way to far-flung vineyards is a luxury. Provence is one of the best cycling areas in France, thanks to its endless backroad options. In the cities, ditch the car as fast as you can. Marseille has two metro lines and an extensive bus network, while Nice is best explored by bus or tram. Both cities also have pay-per-use bike-rental schemes.

The comprehensive ZOU! bus service runs lines all around the region. Great for connecting villages and sights, but, with infrequent services, it's not so great if you want to dine at a restaurant outside of town or have booked accommodation in the countryside. However, it is a good way of avoiding extortionate parking charges and summer traffic jams along the coast.

blue coast, maintains its glorious longtime allure with its intoxicating mix of sun, sea, culture, food and wine. The sun shines down 300 days a year on Nice's Renaissance old town, movie capital Cannes and the glitzy beach clubs of St-Tropez.

Whether you're stretched out by the sea, driving quiet countryside roads or lost in nature, Provence is a sensuous Mediterranean experience waiting to be discovered.

Nice

MAP p426

Soak up the history

Nice's UNESCO heritage can be seen in around 800 buildings across the city, and their art deco detailing and Belle Époque flourishes can be admired from the street. The excellent Explore Nice Côte d'Azur app *(explorenicecotedazur.com/en/discover-the-unesco-heritage-routes)* organises some of the most noteworthy sites into a series of self-guided neighbourhood walks, complete with a pop-up historical outline of each building listed. You can also deep dive into this protected heritage at the **Musée Massena** *(massena-nice.org; adult/child €10/free)* on the **Promenade des Anglais**. Much of the permanent collection is dedicated to the history of Nice.

Cycling the Prom

The combo of Nice's public e-bike fleet and the dedicated, flat bike lane that extends the entire 6km length of the Promenade des Anglais (and then some) is one of the city's best pairings. The Prom is scattered with bike pickup and drop-off points.

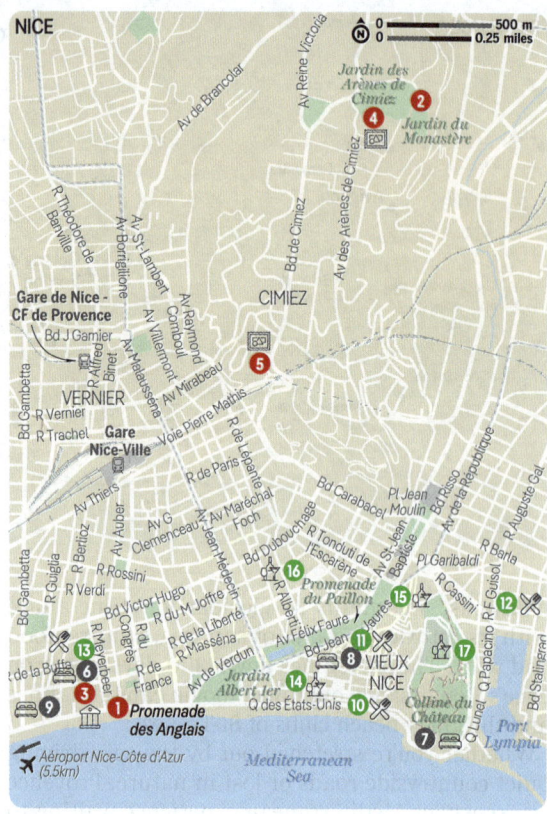

⭐ **HIGHLIGHTS**
1 Promenade des Anglais

🔴 **SIGHTS**
2 Monastère Notre Dame de Cimiez
3 Musée Masséna
4 Musée Matisse
5 Musée National Marc Chagall

⚫ **SLEEPING**
6 Hostel Meyerbeer Beach
7 Hôtel La Pérouse
8 Hôtel Rossetti
9 Le Negresco

🟢 **EATING**
10 Babel Babel
11 Lavomatique
12 Le Bistrot de Jan
13 Le Canon

🟢 **DRINKING & NIGHTLIFE**
14 Cave Bianchi
15 Cave de la Tour
16 La Part des Anges
17 Rouge

Propelled by the battery and the fresh sea air, you'll reach **Aéroport Nice-Côte d'Azur** in less than 20 minutes (if starting out at the eastern end opposite the arcades of **Vieux Nice**).

Two masters and their museums

It is a truth universally acknowledged that the light on the Côte d'Azur has an allure unlike anywhere else in the world. Countless artists have been drawn to the region in search of it: two in particular have left their mark (or, perhaps it's the other way around?): Marc Chagall and Henri Matisse. Dedicated museums to both artists occupy sprawling grounds in

 EATING IN NICE: OUR PICKS ──────────────── MAP p426

Lavomatique: Trendy bistro with natural wines in Vieux Nice. Shared plates cooked in an open kitchen. *noon-1.45pm & 7-10pm Tue-Fri, 7-10pm Mon* €€

Babel Babel: Med cuisine, served across from the Med. Don't miss the panisse with homemade za'atar. *10am-midnight Mon, Thu & Sun, to 2am Fri & Sat* €€

Le Bistrot de Jan: More casual sibling to the Michelin-starred Jan next door. The decor is straight from a design magazine. *noon-3pm & 7pm-12.30am Tue-Sat, 11am-3pm Sun* €€

Le Canon: Neighbourhood fave with a hyperlocal focus: each farmer is named on the menu. *noon-2pm Mon, Tue, Thu & Fri, 7.30-11.30pm Mon-Fri* €€

Musée Massena (p425), Nice

Cimiez, the leafy residential neighbourhood in the north of Nice, and can be visited on the same day. Start at the **Musée National Marc Chagall** *(musees-nationaux-alpesmaritimes .fr/chagall; adult/child €10/free)*, where the most extensive public collection of the Belarusian artist's work hangs. The 12 monumental canvases depicting scenes from the Old Testament are spellbinding in colour and detail, and will linger in your memory long after you've left. A further 20 minutes' walk (or Ligne d'Azur bus 5) and you'll arrive at the **Musée Matisse** *(musee-matisse-nice.org; adult/child €10/free)*. The setting, in a coral-red Genoese villa dating from the 17th century, is magic, with olive groves and ancient ruins. Matisse is buried in the **Monastère Notre Dame de Cimiez** at the eastern end of the parkland. Both museums are closed Tuesdays.

The coolest street in town

The strip and the surrounding streets of **rue Bonaparte** are Nice's hip LGBTIQ+ district, having earned the nickname le petit Marais, a nod to Paris' famous bohemian gay quarter. A part of the road is painted rainbow, à la San Francisco's Castro District, and the stretch between place Garibaldi and place du Pin is now fully pedestrianised. This is where you should head if you are looking for a guaranteed evening buzz,

WHAT IS NIÇOISE CUISINE?

Nice's street-food culture, including chickpea-based *socca* and *panisse*, *pan bagnat (salade niçoise* in a bread roll) and *pissaladière* (onion-topped dough), is based on the colourful vegetables and legumes that thrive in the poor, water-deprived soils of the Mediterranean coastline. It feels closer to Italy in nature and flavour than the heavier, sauce-based cuisine of northern France. The city brims with cheap and cheerful street-food stops, as well as more classic local bistros. If you see the Cuisine Nissarde sticker displayed at a restaurant's entrance, you know their dishes respect local culinary traditions. Beyond the traditional places, a new wave of chefs is putting a fine-dining twist on local dishes, elevating them to a semi-gastronomic standing.

🍸 DRINKING IN NICE: BEST WINE BARS ────────────── MAP p426

Rouge: Sleek spot just back from Port Lympia serving up stylish, modern tapas plates, washed down with organic wines. *noon-10.30pm*

Cave de la Tour: Enjoy 1940s jazz, an interior that has hardly changed, and Nice wine by the glass. *8am-2.30pm & 6-8.30pm Tue-Sat, 8am-12.30pm Sun*

La Part des Anges: A treasure of natural and organic wines in the city centre; voted best wine bar in France in 2020. *10am-8.30pm Mon-Sat*

Cave Bianchi: History seeps out of every nook of this atmospheric Vieux Nice wine shop and bar across from the Opera. *9.30am-7.30pm, to 10.30pm Fri & Sat*

VV SHOTS/SHUTTERSTOCK

BEST EVENTS IN NICE

Carnaval de Nice:
For two weeks in late February and early March, floats and flower battles take over the streets. One of Europe's brightest carnivals, running since the Middle Ages.

Lou Queernaval:
France's first queer carnival runs adjacent to the Carnaval de Nice; expect glitter, dazzling floats and drag queens.

Nice Jazz Festival:
Jampacked four-night calendar of performances in Jardin Albert Ier, and fringe concerts popping up all around town.

Pink Parade (Pride):
Crowds swarm Nice's main streets for July's Pink Parade (Pride); the afterparty lasts all night.

Noël à Nice: Sip bubbles with fresh oysters and ride on a giant Ferris wheel; festive Nice lights up during December.

Jardin Exotique d'Èze, Èze

as new bars or restaurants are always opening – just remember that you're still in the provinces, and even the most lively bars shutter by 1am, particularly out of season.

Èze

Exotic flowers and panoramic sea views

Although you'll increasingly need to swerve around selfie-stick-wielding visitors as you meander through it, the **Jardin Exotique d'Èze** (*jardinexotique-eze.fr; adult/child €5/free*) is still one of the region's most delightful experiences. Around the ruined 12th-century château above the terracotta rooftops of the village, a peaceful cactus garden grows: it's more than worth the entry fee for the sweeping sea views that extend beyond Cannes alone.

Cannes

Festival fever

For two weeks every May, Cannes rolls out the red carpet for a galaxy of stars during the annual **Festival de Cannes** (the Cannes Film Festival). The harbourfront **Palais des Festivals et des Congrès** is the epicentre. For the remainder of the year, the gloss barely fades. Follow the trail of over 400

EATING & DRINKING IN CANNES: OUR PICKS

Poissonnerie Forville:
Fish counter outside Marché Forville serving fresh treats such as oysters and sea urchins (in season). *7am-2.30pm Tue-Sun* €€

Le Pompon: A menu of creative small plates that changes daily with the season. Colourful ingredients and beautiful presentation. *12.15-1.30pm & 7.15-9.30pm Tue-Sat* €€

Bar Fouquet's: Hôtel Barrière Le Majestic's bar serves artful cocktails, where homemade bitters, jellies, even edible perfumes, are standard. *10am-midnight*

Maison Grenache:
Atmospheric wine bar next to the Marché Forville with ultra-knowledgeable owners. *9am-5pm, to 10.30pm Fri & Sat*

stars who have cast their handprints in stainless steel along the **Chemin des Étoiles** (path of stars) outside the Palais. Dates for **tours** *(adult/child €6/3)* inside the Palais are only scheduled six weeks in advance by the tourist office (conveniently housed in the building), depending on the upcoming event calendar, and are only in French. When visits do run, you're given a 1½-hour behind-the-scenes insight into one of cinema's most legendary venues.

St-Tropez

Life's a beach

Sexy St-Tropez might be the most desired destination on the Côte d'Azur and a byword for lithe, tanned bodies dancing on tables at trendy beach bars along buttercream Plage de Pampelonne, but it hasn't always been the jet-set magnet it is today. The sleepy fishing village was thrust into the global spotlight in the 1950s, when a young Brigitte Bardot filmed *And God Created Woman* here. If bling isn't your thing, that doesn't mean you should bypass St-Tropez. Meander cobbled lanes in the old fishing quarter of La Ponche, watch games of pétanque beneath plane trees on place des Lices, fill your picnic basket at its produce market (don't forget a bottle of local rosé), or hike along the coast from beach to beach on the Presqu'île de Saint-Tropez peninsula. Just be aware: in summer, every inch of space is jampacked.

The seaside scene revolves around sandy clubs and restaurants, all with their own style. Most are open May to September, and advance bookings are highly recommended. Beaches also have public areas where you can lay down your towel. The 5km-long, celebrity-studded **Plage de Pampelonne** is the most famous of the beaches and has the largest selection of exclusive clubs and restaurants. It's the place to see and be seen – you'll want to reserve a lounger and lunch. Atmosphere? Indulgence, glitz and relaxation. **Le Club 55** *(leclub55.fr)* is the longest-running Pampelonne club, originally the crew canteen during *And God Created Woman* and still catering to incognito celebs. **Nikki Beach** *(nikkibeach.com/sttropez)* is favoured by dance-on-the-bar glitterati, and those who just want to be seen. For a more chill vibe, try **Le 1051** *(le1051.com)*.

Looking for a quieter beach experience without sacrificing luxury? Book ahead for **La Cabane Méditerranée** *(laca banemediterranee.com; loungers from €30)*, on the edge of **Plage d'Héraclée**. About 10km further south from St-Tropez, the beach is wilder than Pampelonne, and the club is tucked into the edge of a rock.

Hit the open seas

Get out on the water to take in the gorgeous coast. It can be as easy as taking a ride on **Les Bateaux Verts**, with boat excursions throughout the region. Or opt for a water-skimming catamaran on Golfe de St-Tropez at sunset with **Sport Decouverte** *(sport-decouverte.com; €40)*, where you can sip an *apéro* suspended in the nets of the catamaran, sandwiched between the blues of the sea and the sparkling sky.

BEST ARTS EXPERIENCES & EVENTS IN CANNES

Festival d'Art Pyrotechnique: Global competition to win best fireworks show crown. Six nights in summer.

Les Plages Électroniques: Epic three-day dance festival on the beach: eight stages and over 50,000 festivalgoers. In August.

Musée Bonnard: Neoimpressionist painter Pierre Bonnard (1867–1947) was known as the Painter of Happiness, and Le Cannet, at Cannes' northern fringes, was his happy place.

La Malmaison: Showcase of contemporary art in a historic, renovated building.

Le Suquet des Artistes: Small but avant-garde exhibition space in the former city morgue that brings local artists to the fore.

STEFANO BOLOGNINI/SHUTTERSTOCK

CLEANLINESS IS CLOSE TO GODLINESS

Following the cholera outbreaks of the early 1830s, which claimed thousands of lives, a plan was devised to improve public health by channelling water from the Durance River in the Alps. By 1869, Marseille's **Palais Longchamp** was opened to the public as a 'hymn to water', celebrating this remarkable engineering achievement.

Marseille's famous soap (Savon de Marseille) also played a significant role in reducing infant mortality and the spread of contagious diseases during the 19th century. Originally made with olive oil and free of colouring and perfume, it now comes in various shapes and smells. The **Savonnerie Marseillaise de la Licorne** has free daily tours of its factory.

Chateau d'If, Marseille

Marseille

MAP p430

Mix with the locals in lively squares

Marseille has an edge. France's second-largest city puts its arms around you as a drunken friend would – passionately and deliriously. It is a city that revels in its status as France's underdog. Sooner or later, you'll end up on the **cours Julien** (known locally as 'le cours Ju') for a drink, and for good reason. As a pedestrian area slathered with street art and bohemian yearnings, this is the home of some great bars and restaurants, which remain open day and night. Wander the narrow side streets, packed with bookshops, galleries and tattoo parlours, until you reach the noisy and elongated main square, a destination for a solid night out, and a microcosm of the city itself. You are likely to hear boomboxes blasting, guitars strumming and African drums pounding as soon as the sun comes out.

Place Jean-Jaurès, also known as La Plaine, is another vast square surrounded by bars and restaurants. For years it has been the battleground for left-wing militants and artists. Buzzing day and night in the spring and summer months, it remains a beating heart for locals escaping the tourist traps, whether in the bars or in the public seating areas beneath the trees. La Plaine is only a 10-minute walk east from cours Julien.

Escape to the Château d'If

For a quick and easy trip out to sea, hop on the Frioul-If ferry to Marseille's closest islands: the Île d'If (for historians) and the **Îles du Frioul** (for nature lovers). Commanding access to Marseille's Vieux Port, the **Chateau d'If** (*chateau-if.fr; adult/child €7/free*) was immortalised by Alexandre Dumas in his classic 1844 novel, *The Count of Monte Cristo*. At the 16th-century island prison with three towers, one giving a great view across the bay, you can wander unaccompanied or visit with an audio or guided tour; the contrast between the cells for the wealthy and the dungeon pit strikes a tone. This is the ferry's first stop; it's 20 minutes from the Vieux Port.

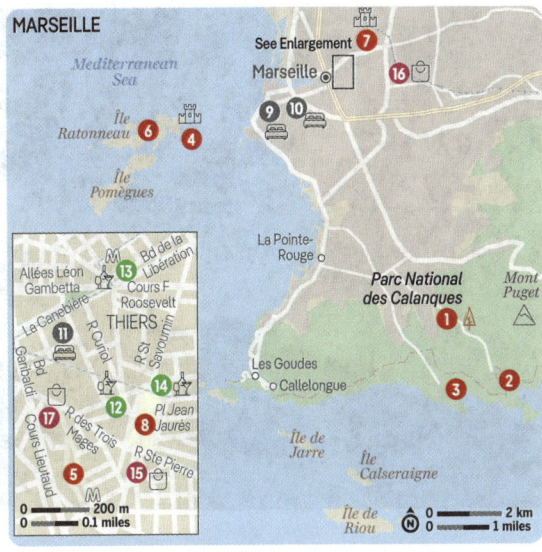

MARSEILLE

Mediterranean Sea

See Enlargement

Marseille

Île Ratonneau

Île Pomègues

La Pointe-Rouge

Parc National des Calanques

Mont Puget

Les Goudes
Callelongue

Île de Jarre

Île Calseraigne

Île de Riou

Allées Léon Gambetta

Bd de la Libération

Cours F Roosevelt

THIERS

La Canebière

R Curiol

R St-Savournin

Bd Garibaldi

Pl Jean Jaurès

Cours Lieutaud

R des Trois Mages

R Ste Pierre

0   200 m
0   0.1 miles

0   2 km
0   1 miles

⭐ HIGHLIGHTS
1 Parc National des Calanques

● SIGHTS
2 Calanque de Morgiou
3 Calanque de Sormiou
4 Château d'If
5 Cours Julien
6 Îles du Frioul

7 Palais Longchamp
8 Place Jean-Jaurès

● SLEEPING
9 Hotel Peron
10 La Relève
11 Le Ryad

● DRINKING & NIGHTLIFE
12 Bar des Maraîchers

13 Grand Bar du Chapitre
see 10 La Relève
14 PMU le blabla

● SHOPPING
15 Bière de la Plaine
16 Cristal Limiñana
17 Savonnerie Marseillaise de la Licorne

THE GUIDE

FRANCE PROVENCE

DISCOVER THE HISTORY OF PASTIS

The apéritif pastis is easy to spot: a milky-looking concoction served in a tall glass that adorns outdoor tables across Provence. In 1932 in Marseille, Paul Ricard developed his aniseed-and-liquorice-based liqueur (*pastis* means 'mix' in Occitan) after absinthe was banned in France for fear it caused hallucinations and madness. Since then, it has become a drink that is synonymous with the city. Ricard may now be part of a multinational conglomerate based in Lille, but there are still independent producers in Marseille where you can arrange a visit, including **Cristal Limiñana** (*cristal-liminana.com*) and the independent brewery **Bière de la Plaine** (*Distillerie de la Plaine; @distillerie_de_la_plaine*).

It's another 15 minutes to the next stop, the Port du Frioul, your entry point to two of the Îles du Frioul, Pomègues and Ratonneau, which are connected by a dam. Attacking the unspoiled jagged rock of Pomègues is liberating. Following the seawall after you dock will lead to the Fort de Cavaux, leaving you lost at sea on an uninhabited island, revisiting ghosts in the bunkers of WWII. The island of Ratonneau has a few small shops and restaurants and is popular for its beaches and tiny village. There's a chapel that resembles a Greek temple and the ruins of the Hôpital Caroline, which once housed quarantined travellers, but the highlight is the St-Estève beach, where you can swim safely, protected from the wind.

The ticket pier for **lebateau ferries** (*lebateau-frioul-if.fr; 1/2 islands return €11.10/16.70*) is at the Vieux Port. When facing the port, get in line at its large booth on the left. The Château d'If is closed on Mondays.

Outdoor adventures in the Parc National des Calanques

It feels like a miracle to find a refuge like the **Parc National des Calanques** only a short distance from Marseille. In parts

WHAT IS A CALANQUE?

Calanques are coastal geological features typical of the Mediterranean region. These picturesque coves, formed in limestone and located between Marseille and Cassis, are characterised by steep cliffs rising above vibrant turquoise waters. When the sun shines, the small beaches within these narrow bays, comprising either pebbles or fine sand, attract crowds. Escaping to them has become a way of life for city dwellers, leading to various regulations protecting the natural sites. Access by car can be challenging, and most routes are closed between June and October as the arid conditions during this period place the parks at a high chance of wildfires. The strong mistral winds that can sweep through the area further intensify the risks.

MARAAO85/SHUTTERSTOCK

of this diminutive 85-sq-km patch of scrubby promontories, it's easy to believe you're miles from civilisation. Then a twist in a pine-clad gully reveals the entirety of France's second metropolis spread out within apparent touching distance; the *calanques* (inlets) appear almost as its uninhabited suburbs. But with their light-shifting geometry, rich plant and animal life and idyllic hidden coves, Les Calanques are so much more than that. They are beloved of the Marseillais, who come for the sun and to hike over pine-strewn promontories, mess about in boats and generally refresh their souls.

Of the many *calanques* along the coastline, the most easily accessible are **Calanque de Sormiou** and **Calanque de Morgiou**. Remote inlets such as **Calanque d'En-Vau** and **Calanque de Port-Miou** take dedication and time to reach, either on foot or by kayak. Note that overland access is often limited from June to September, due to fire danger; always check first on the app: *calanques-parcnational.fr/fr/application-mobile-officielle-mes-calanques*. The app is also excellent for up-to-date info on the park and activities. There is also a reservation system in place for two of the most popular *calanques* in summer: **Calanque de Sugiton** and **Calanque des Pierres Tombées**. See *calanques-parcnational.fr*.

DRINKING IN MARSEILLE: BEST PASTIS BARS

MAP p430

Bar des Maraîchers: Listen to '80s radio hits with owner, Serge, who features in his own hilarious fresco of the *Last Supper. 3pm-2am*

Grand Bar du Chapitre: A young crowd in a leafy square at the top of the main thoroughfare, La Canebière. *10am-12.30am*

PMU le blabla: Super cheap and one of the best suntraps protected from the wind in the city. *6.30am-9pm*

La Relève: In the Endoume neighbourhood. Pastis can still be fancy and here it's served with great food and music. *8am-10pm Mon-Sat, 9am-5pm Sun*

Calanque d'En-Vau

There's no shortage of outdoor activities here: hiking, kayaking, stand-up paddleboarding, swimming, diving and rock climbing are all incredible. You'll find guides and gear rental in both Marseille and Cassis. From October to June, hiking trails lead through the maquis (scrub). Marseille's tourist office leads guided walks and has an excellent hiking map of the various *calanques,* as does Cassis' tourist office. For access by public transport take bus 19 from Marseille's Castellane bus station down the coast to its terminus at La Madrague, then switch to bus 20 to Callelongue. Note that the road to Callelongue is only open to cars on weekdays from mid-April to May and closed entirely from June to September.

Gorges du Verdon

Sustainable lavender visits

Dive into the new face of ecologically responsible lavender production by visiting an organic lavender farm on the **Plateau de Valensole**. To start with, look for the lavender fields that have let golden grass grow up between the rows of purple – these farms are doing their part to preserve the soil for the next generation. Many farms are open year-round to guests, but run special tours during the harvest season. And no visit would be complete without trying some lavender-based products straight from the source, such as essential oils, soaps and perfumes produced on-site using sustainable methods.

The lavender fields of Valensole are usually the highlight of a photography tour of Provence. Visit in late June or early July, but no later. During this time, the fields are alive with colour and fragrance, providing a stunning backdrop for your photos. To get the perfect shot, you'll have to get up early – sunrise has the longest 'soft-light' period, which reduces shadows and harsh glare. Don't go tramping in the fields,

LOOK UP

The Gorges du Verdon is home to one of France's most impressive bird populations, including griffon, cinereous and Egyptian vultures. These massive birds ride the thermals above the cliffs, often visible from Route des Crêtes or trail lookouts. Bring binoculars and look for their broad wingspans and slow, soaring flight – especially active on warm afternoons with rising air currents. The two-hour **Treguier Botanical Trail** (start/finish Moustiers-Ste-Marie) is a relatively easy circular walk; great for spotting birdlife. Spring is the best time for twitchers, although the wallcreeper bird tends to only make an appearance in winter.

LAVENDER FARMS ON THE PLATEAU DE VALENSOLE

La Ferme du Riou: This organic farm runs distillery visits during the harvest season and farm visits year-round.

Lavande Bio Berenger: Organic producer with a cabin in the fields during harvest season. Otherwise, stop into the shop in Valensole.

Lavandes Angelvin: Runs distillery visits during high season and guided visits on Tuesdays at 3pm.

Terraroma: Very photogenic lavender and almond farm, with a few sunflower fields to complete the mosaic.

Les Lavandes d'Isabelle et Sébastien: Technically off the plateau and closer to Manosque, this little family lavender farm is less crowded and has a small boutique to find your favourite products.

ZORAN PAJIC/SHUTTERSTOCK

Tablet in use, Palais des Papes, Avignon

but tread carefully between rows – these are precious crops for local farmers. What to wear? Consider colours that will complement the lavender fields. Soft pastels, earthy tones and neutral colours work well in this setting. Avoid wearing bright colours that may clash with the lavender or draw too much attention away from the landscape's natural beauty.

Hike the Sentier Blanc-Martel

This 16km one-way trek from **Chalet de la Maline** to **Point Sublime** is one of France's most legendary hikes. Named after the first geologists to explore the canyon, the trail hugs the cliffs and drops down to the riverbed, with ladders, tunnels and dizzying views along the way. It's demanding but not extreme – suitable for fit beginners with proper footwear. Book the Navette Blanc-Martel *(navette.parcduverdon.fr)* in advance for transport to the trailhead and pickup at the end. Hikers should carry plenty of water, snacks and a torch for the tunnel. Get an early start to avoid the heat and crowds.

Cycle the Route des Crêtes

This 24km balcony road loops out from La Palud-sur-Verdon, rising over 650m in elevation and offering heart-stopping views straight into the canyon. Originally designed for motorised day-trippers, parts of the Route des Crêtes are now restricted or closed to vehicles on select days, giving cyclists a stretch of silence and space. The ride is challenging but manageable with an e-bike – rentals are available in La Palud. Spring and autumn are the best times to ride, with cool weather and lighter traffic. Stop at *belvédères* (lookouts) along the way, where vultures and climbers share the same dizzying vertical playground. A helmet, water and good brakes are essential.

Raft the Verdon River

From April to June, when the river is flowing strong, rafting the Verdon is a wild, splashy ride through limestone corridors and rolling rapids. Most trips depart from Castellane, on the gorge's eastern end. Rapids range from easygoing to intense (Class I to IV), making this a good fit for both beginners and adrenaline junkies. Book ahead with a certified company such as **Yeti Rafting** *(verdon-rafting.net; per person from €40)* – gear and guides are included. Minimum age varies by route (usually seven to 16), and all participants must be able to swim. It's a half-day adventure that takes you deep into the canyon, with moments of calm water to catch your breath between the thrills.

Avignon

The home of seven popes

The vast rooms and shady arcades of 14th-century **Palais des Papes** *(palais-des-papes.com; adult/child €12/€6.50)* give a glimpse into medieval life, when Avignon was the centre of the Catholic world. A visit is supported by tablets (available in multiple languages) that digitally restore lost frescoes and furniture. It's a surprising example of tech that genuinely deepens the experience, bringing rooms to life with audio-visual storytelling and changing art installations. The **Great Chapel** represents the largest covered space in the palace. Construction began in 1348 but was slowed by the Black Death pandemic. In the 14th century, the windows were of stained glass with a carpeted floor and walls covered with drapery dominated by green tones.

Buy tickets online to save time at the entrance, especially during the busy summer season and July theatre festival, and don't miss the Jardins du Palais, designed in the English style and accessible from the former apartments of the Pope – his place for wandering reflection.

THE GREAT SCHISM

Avignon first gained its ramparts – and reputation for arts and culture – during the 14th century, when Pope Clement V fled political turmoil in Rome. From 1309 to 1377, seven French-born popes invested huge sums in the papal palace and offered asylum to Jews and political dissidents. Pope Gregory XI left Avignon in 1376, but his death two years later led to the Great Schism (1378–1417), during which rival popes (up to three at once) resided at Rome and Avignon, denouncing and excommunicating one another. Even after the matter was settled and an impartial pope, Martin V, established himself in Rome, Avignon remained under papal rule. Avignon and Comtat Venaissin (now the Vaucluse *département*) were ruled by papal legates until 1791.

 EATING IN AVIGNON: BEST RESTAURANTS

Numéro 75: Chic restaurant in a *hôtel particulier* with a private courtyard, excellent Med menu and stellar wine list. *noon-2.30pm & 7-10pm Mon-Fri* €€€

Graines de Piment: Good-value, tasty bistro on place de la Principale that gives disadvantaged youth a chance to gain work experience. *12.15-1.30pm Mon-Fri* €

Fou de Fafa: Four-course dinners at this Avignon staple, drawing on Mediterranean and Provençal cuisines. Reserve. *7-11pm Thu-Mon* €€

L'Épicerie: Classic French bistro with rustic decor in the heart of old Avignon. Plenty of hearty meat-based dishes; vegan options too. *noon-2.15pm & 7-10pm Thu-Mon* €€

Bordeaux

WINE | GASTRONOMY | ART AND ARCHITECTURE

Bordeaux's mood board hasn't changed since French novelist Victor Hugo (1802–85) visited in 1839, waxing lyrical in letters to his wife back in Paris about the city's elegant squares and quaysides, fountains and monumental theatre that reminded him of Versailles. He wrote 'and you will love Bordeaux, even if you only drink water'.

Bordeaux's heady cocktail of old and new – not to mention its legendary wine cellars, bistros, *bars à vin* and restaurants bursting with prestigious vintages – is as intoxicating as ever. From this Gallo-Roman city's golden past as medieval wine trader and key port in Europe during the Age of Enlightenment, to famous vineyards, a spirited student population and a buoyant undercurrent of creativity, France's sixth-largest city brims with surprising and enthralling stories at every turn. Paired with an exceptional dining scene and captivating river life, there is no tastier marriage.

The Epic Story of Bordeaux Wine

Learn and taste in city museums

Bordeaux's intoxicating wine story begins in the ancient trading district of riverside Chartrons. The city's life-blood wine trade originates here. Discover the role of *négociants* (merchant traders) in the 18th and 19th centuries at the **Musée du Vin et du Négoce** *(museeduvinbordeaux.com; adult/child*

 GETTING AROUND

Tram line A is the cheapest, quickest way to get into town: 45 minutes from **Aéroport de Bordeaux** *(bordeaux.aeroport.fr)* in Merignac, 10km west. The same tickets *(single/10-ticket card €1.90/15)* are valid on Bat3 riverboats, likewise run by public-transport company

TBM *(infotbm.com)*. TBM's public bike-sharing scheme **Le Vélo** has stations with classic and electric wheels all over town. Free-floating electric scooters by **Pony** *(getapony.com)* and **Dott** *(ridedott.com)* fill the gaps.

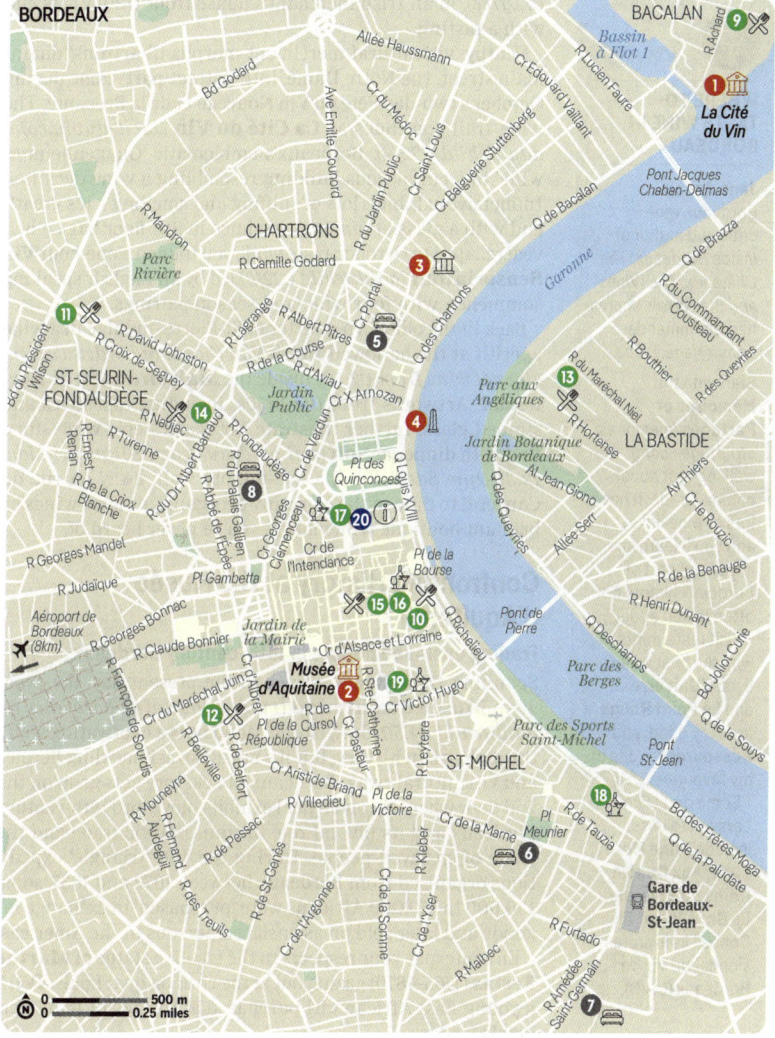

HIGHLIGHTS
1 La Cité du Vin
2 Musée d'Aquitaine

SIGHTS
3 Musée du Vin et du Négoce
4 Statue of Marthe Testas

SLEEPING
5 Chez Dupont
6 Hôtel La Zoologie
7 Jost
8 La Maison du Lierre

EATING
9 Bar de la Marine
10 Chiocchio

11 Le Pavilion des Boulevards
12 L'Univerre
13 Magasin Général
14 Ressources
15 Soif

DRINKING & NIGHTLIFE
16 Aux Quatre Coins du Vins
17 Bar à Vin
18 Le Point Rouge
19 Wine More Time

INFORMATION
20 Bordeaux Tourist Office

WHERE TO TASTE WINE IN BORDEAUX

Jane Anson, Bordeaux wine critic and author of *Inside Bordeaux: The Châteaux, The Wines and the Terroir,* shares her recommendations. @jane.anson

Start with the **Mémoires et Partages** *(memoires etpartages.com)* walking tour about colonial trade. It has lots of wine links and you'll learn an important part of Bordeaux history not often talked about.

Visit restaurants with the best wine lists: **L'Univerre** and **Le Point Rouge** are very good, and **Ressources** is one of my favourites.

Some great wine bars not to miss include **Wine More Time, Aux Quatre Coins du Vins** and **Le Bar à Vin** at the Conseil Interprofessionnel du Vin de Bordeaux (CIVB).

€12/free), in an Irish merchant's house from 1720. Visits end with a tasting.

Nearby, viticultural merriment morphs Chartrons' quaint main street, rue Notre Dame, into a street-party zone during October's two-day Fête du Vin Nouveau et de la Brocante. The wine trail continues at **La Cité du Vin** *(laciteduvin.com; adult/child €22/9)*, Bordeaux's emblematic 'Guggenheim of wine' in a curvaceous building resembling a wine decanter. Immersive exhibits (lots of sniffing and smelling – it's great!) end with a glass of *vin* or grape juice in 8th-floor bar Le Belvédère. April to October, taste while you tour on a one-hour **Via Sensoria tour** *(adult/child €22/9)* led by an English-speaking sommelier, with four wine-and-season pairings.

Back in the old-town quarter of St-Pierre, indulge in a wine apéritif at the hallowed **Bar à Vin** *(baravin.bordeaux.com; glass of wine from €2.50)* inside the **Maison du Vin de Bordeaux**. Artworks from the 1950s, including tapestries and stained glass, further illustrate Bordeaux's epic wine story. End with dinner at **Soif** *(soif-bordeaux.com; 7-11pm Fri-Mon, 12.30-2pm Sat & Sun)*, a five-minute walk away on rue du Cancera, to dine in the company of organic, natural wines by brilliant boutique winemakers you've never heard of.

Confronting History at the Musée d'Aquitaine

Trading enslaved people in 18th-century Bordeaux

Spanning Gallo-Roman times to the present day, the evocative **Musée d'Aquitaine** *(musee-aquitaine-bordeaux.fr; adult/child €4.50/free)*, closed Monday, is a captivating waltz through urban history. But it's not all swashbuckling heroics and viticultural swag. Bordeaux's backstory gets grim on the 2nd floor where chronological exhibits move into 18th-century Bordeaux and its pivotal role in transatlantic trade and the trade of enslaved people. During the 480 'triangle' expeditions organised from Bordeaux between 1672 and 1837, some 130,000 to 150,000 Africans were 'purchased' in exchange for goods and later sold on as enslaved persons in the Americas.

En route, pay your respects to the emotive statue of **Marthe Testas** (1765–1870) gazing out at the river on quai Louis XVIII, a young East African girl purchased at the age of 16 by Bordelais traders.

 EATING IN BORDEAUX: FAVOURITE TERRACES

Magasin Général: France's largest organic restaurant, with vintage sofas. *8am-7.30pm Mon-Fri, from 9am Sun, to 11.30pm Fri, 9am-11.30pm Sat €*

Bar de la Marine: Nothing beats the €20 three-course lunch served in a summer flower garden in Bacalan. Cool 1950s memorabilia too. *9am-5pm Mon-Fri €*

Chiocchio: Tasty Franco-Tuscan fare on an urban terrace, foxy street art and prime people-watching on cafe-beaded place du Palais. *noon-3pm & 7-11.30pm Mon-Sat €€*

Le Pavillon des Boulevards: Seasonal gastronomy on terracotta-paved patio perfumed with magnolia. *noon-2pm Wed, noon-2pm & 8-10pm Tue & Thu-Sat €€€*

Beyond Bordeaux

An unmatched sensory feast, trips beyond Bordeaux deliver pink-hued cities, go-slow sea adventure and France's finest wine.

Bordeaux is a gateway to vine-ribboned countryside and Atlantic Coast sand dunes. North, where the Dordogne and Garonne Rivers meet, spills the Gironde Estuary and the prestigious vineyards of the Médoc. South of the city, the Côte d'Argent (Silver Coast) takes centre stage with endless shimmering-gold beaches backed by dark-green pine forests. Surfers catch waves and enjoy incredible sunsets in celebrity Biarritz, while Basque culture reigns supreme in Bayonne. To the southeast, the pink city of Toulouse feels lived in and laid-back, thanks to its large student population, yet still has lofty dreams of aiming for the stars: it's a hub for the manufacture of airplanes and rockets.

Places

St-Émilion p439
Arcachon p440
Bayonne p440
Biarritz p441
Toulouse p442

St-Émilion

TIME FROM BORDEAUX: 1HR 🚗

Visit an eco-winery and lunch between vines

The first vines were planted on the picturesque Troplong Mondot estate carpeting the highest point of St-Émilion in the 1700s, and by 1745 the winemaker was rich enough to have a handsome château built from the local creamy limestone on his land. Today, guided tours of **Château Troplong-Mondot** (*troplong-mondot.com; 90min guided tour with tasting €50*) walk you around one of the region's most innovative, green-thinking wineries. Vineyards are ploughed exclusively by a dozen hefty working horses; a pig and several hens recycle organic waste; and the estate's swanky barrel cellar with 12m-high cathedral ceiling is underground to avoid spoiling the centuries-old bucolic landscape.

Tours end with tastings of two vintages and there's a swish boutique where you can buy the premier *grand cru* wines. Alternatively, reserve a table at the château's Michelin-starred

 GETTING AROUND

A car isn't vital along the southwest coast, but needed in rural areas and those with poor public transport (northern part of the Médoc and the Basque hinterland). High-speed TGVs service Bordeaux, Biarritz and Bayonne (four hours direct from Paris Montparnasse).

Toulouse also has TGVs to Paris Montparnasse (just under five hours), and regular trains to Spain. Walking or cycling the city centre is easiest. Toulouse also has a well-served international airport.

restaurant, Les Belles Perdrix *(weekday lunch/dinner menus from €50/85)*, overlooking vines, to indulge in outstanding modern French cuisine and perfect pairings. It's 20 minutes (2km) on foot from St-Émilion village to Troplong-Mondot.

Arcachon

TIME FROM BORDEAUX: 1HR

Climb Europe's largest sand dune

Breathtakingly cold in winter and as hot as burning coals in the height of summer it might be, but barefoot is the most thrilling way to romp around the golden sands of Europe's largest dune. Local lore claims the shifting **Dune du Pilat**, 10km south from Arcachon, has swallowed trees, a road junction, even a hotel. What is certain is the spectacular panorama from the top. Looking west, see sandy shoals at the mouth of the Bassin d'Arcachon, Cap Ferret and bird-rich Banc d'Arguin. Facing east, dead black trees killed by forest fires polka-dot rich green forest.

April to November, a staircase – around 150 steps – is built on the dune's eastern slope to help tourists stagger breathlessly to the top. Otherwise, use the locals' 'secret' shortcut to arrive midway up the dune: uphill past fashionista lunch hangout **La Co(o)rniche** on av Louis Gaume, then right onto the unmarked footpath between the bike stand and No 31 on av des Dunes. To understand the fragility and diversity of Pilat's vulnerable sand scape, join a guided nature walk, sunrise or sunset hike, telescope workshop or storytelling sessions organised by the **Espace Accueil** *(ladunedupilat.com)* at the dune entrance. Snack bars and eco-boutiques here only sell local artisan fare.

Bayonne

TIME FROM BORDEAUX: 2HR

Learn about traditional Basque culture in Bayonne

Funerary rites, fishing, folklore, pastoral life and *pelota*: Petit Bayonne's riverfront **Musée Basque et de l'Histoire de Bayonne** *(musee-basque.com; adult/under 26yr €8/free; closed Mon & Thu)* has brought Basque history, culture and crafts vividly to life since 1924. Its 20 rooms fill a 17th-century warehouse, built on the wharf by a merchant to store his goods once offloaded from the ship. Get orientated with a scale model of Bayonne port in 1805, showing Grand Bayonne, which the Romans founded on a hill between the town's two rivers, and Petit Bayonne on the Nive's opposite riverbank, which flourished as a trading and shipbuilding hub from the 12th century. Spot the Gothic twin spires – one now clean-cream, the other

---

LA VÉLODYSSÉE

As its evocative name suggests, **La Vélodyssée** *(cycling-lavelodyssee. com)* is a coastal odyssey by *vélo* (bike) along France's Atlantic Coast, linking Roscoff in Brittany with Hendaye on the French–Spanish border, 1270km away in Pays Basque.

The scenic Gironde stretch is 81km (four hours) from the tip of the Médoc south to Lacanau, just north of the Bassin d'Arcachon. Flat and reasonably unchallenging, the well-marked cycling itinerary kicks off with ethereal sea and Cordouan lighthouse views from Pointe de Grave (it's 108 steps up the cape's own, 28m-tall Phare de Grave lighthouse) before plunging through pine forests and past sand dunes, beaches, lake and lagoon on its route 7.5km south to Soulac-sur-Mer and beyond.

EATING & DRINKING IN ARCACHON: OUR PICKS

La Pâtisserie de Ma Fille: Gourmet breakfasts, brunch, crêpes and cakes on market square place des Marquises. *8am-7pm Mon-Thu, to 10pm Fri-Sun* €€

Café de la Plage – Chez Pierre: A Mira craft beer brewed next door in La Teste-de-Buch or lavish shellfish platter: this timeless seafront duo delivers. *8am-2am* €€

Coquille: All-day ceviche, burgers, bowls, salads and meat/fish mains in a cosy, sea-inspired bistro near the market. *9am-midnight Tue-Sat, to 4pm Sun* €€

Club Plage Pereire: Enjoy oysters, seafood, cocktails and a great gin made from Cognac vine blossoms at this pop-up on Plage Pereire. *10am-midnight Apr-Sep* €€

Dune du Pilat, Arcachon

dirty dark-grey – of 13th-century **Cathédrale Ste-Marie** *(free)* and its peaceful cloister on place Louis Pasteur, and the 17th-century ramparts encircling the city.

Don't miss the rooms dedicated to *pelote Basque (pelota)* – the catchall name for more than a dozen traditional Basque ballgames, including *main nue* (played barehanded) and *jaï alaï* (the most high-octane variant). Art, short films and players' kit shine light on the rules, the *fronton (pelota* court), how to use the scoop-like basket called a *chistera*, etc. Post-museum, pass by **Trinquet St-André**, a 17th-century covered *jeu de paume* court on rue du Jeu de Paume, later adapted for *pelota*. Enjoy a drink in its bar-brasserie from 1943 and catch a game in action.

Biarritz

TIME FROM BORDEAUX: 2HR

Lunch cheap on oysters and white wine

Fashionable surf villages and fishing ports bead the seashore south of Biarritz. Ruins of medieval ovens once used to melt whale blubber rub shoulders with trendy beach bars, bodegas and eco-boutiques. *Pintxos, poissons* and paella at Biarritz' renowned bistro-bodega **Bar Jean** *(barjean-biarritz.fr)* has been a Biarrot rite of passage since 1930. The round-the-clock festive vibe on the street terrace alone is memorable (unusually, food is served nonstop from 10.30am to 1am).

FÊTES DE BAYONNE

Thousands of revellers fill Bayonne for five days during July's Fêtes de Bayonne *(fetes. bayonne.fr)*. White with a red sash and neck-scarf is the non-negotiable dress code. The street revelry starts on the last Wednesday in July or first in August with the traditional throwing of the city keys from the balcony of Bayonne's town hall. Fireworks and a *bal* (dance) follow. Brass bands, DJs and choirs perform all over town and there's folk dancing, *pelota*, omelette championships, espadrille throwing, tugs-of-war and stone lifting in *festivals de force basque* (strength competitions). Thursday's Journéee des Enfants has kids' activities. Less savoury are the Basque *courses des vaches* ('running of the bulls' but with horned cows) and *corridas* (bullfights).

 EATING IN BAYONNE: GOOD-VALUE DINING

Bistrot Pépite:	**Cantine du Musée:**	**Cidrerie Ttipia:**	**Basa:**
Modern bistro fare: duck hearts with port, curried mussels, veggie beignets. *7.30-9.30pm Tue-Fri, noon-1.30pm & 7.30-9.30pm Sat* €	Excellent-value bistro serves seasonal Basque fare with lashings of 'bonne humeur'. *12.15-1.30pm Tue, 12.15-1.30pm & 7.30-9.30pm Wed-Sat* €€	A juicy *txuleta* (beef steak) for two, fries, salad and a cider is the thing at this rustic, noisy cider hall. *noon-2pm & 7-11pm Tue-Sat, noon-2pm Sun* €€	Good-value lunches in a brasserie with peaceful garden patio. Try smoked octopus with beetroot and caramelised dill. *noon-10pm Mon-Sat, to 2pm Sun* €€

BEST BIARROT BEACHES FOR SURFING & SUNBATHING

Grande Plage: Biarritz' main golden-sand beach, much-loved since the days of Napoléon II and Eugénie.

Plage de la Côte des Basques: Long golden sand beach with trendy bars. A surfers' and sunset lovers' favourite.

Plage d'Ilbarritz: Another strip of powder-soft sand, enlivened with the summer terrace of beach bar Blue Cargo, a dance floor after dark.

Plage de l'Océan: Fringed by protected sand dunes and a golf green, this is the wildest of Anglet's back-to-back swathe of sand beaches. Sunset drinks at beach bar Ozeanoa are a must.

Plage des Sables d'Or: Cafes, surf shops and several sandy beach-volley courts in Anglet.

ANIBAL TREJO/SHUTTERSTOCK

Capitole, Toulouse

To keep things cheap, dive into **Les Halles** *(halles-biarritz. fr; 6/12 oysters with glass of wine €8/14)* opposite. Swimming with the day's catch from 7.30am to 2pm daily, the fish hall buzzes with vendors flogging crab claws, whelks, seasonal sea urchins and an ocean of fish. Oyster farmers shuck various sized *huîtres* for seafood lovers to devour standing up or slurp around shared tables on a no-frills mezzanine upstairs.

Toulouse

TIME FROM BORDEAUX: 2½HR

It's a Capitole idea to visit Toulouse

Toulouse's city hall, the **Capitole** *(free)*, demonstrates many facets of the city's cultural character. With its rose terracotta and white brick neoclassical facade, complete with eight pink and cream marble Corinthian columns, it is one of Toulouse's signature buildings. The exterior's architectural display is balanced by the interior's impressive frescoes and paintings, which decorate the chambers and halls. Enter from the **Place du Capitole**, the city's social focal point; its perimeter arcades are packed with patrons of its Belle Époque bistros and brasseries. Inside, follow the entry signs through security. Once through, climb the elegant main staircase, overlooked by Renaissance-style murals. At the top, local artist Henri Martin's huge postimpressionist canvases fill Salle Henri-Martin, while painted scenes from Toulouse's history

EATING IN BIARRITZ: HIP PICKS IN BIBI BEAURIVAGE

Bleach: Lunch with sassy locals over homemade food in a retro, 1950s-styled cafe in Biarritz' coolest no-tourists 'hood. *9am-3pm Mon-Fri* €

Club Sandwich: Chicken burgers, truffle clubs, falafel salad by day. Vinyl nights, DJ sets, club nights come dark. *noon-3pm & 7pm-midnight Tue-Sat, noon-3pm Sun* €

Restaurant Hernani: Spend an evening in Spanish Basque country at this lively bodega. The sangria flows. *7.30-11pm Tue-Sat* €€

Chéri Bibi: Off-grid modern neighbourhood bistro: expertly curated local produce with natural wines on a wooden people-watching deck. *7pm-midnight Thu-Sun* €€

decorate the **Salle des Illustres** (Hall of the Illustrious). The southern end of the building hosts the **Théâtre du Capitole** (*opera.toulouse.fr*), where the city's ballet and opera companies perform regularly. Try to catch one of the occasional €5 lunchtime recitals (book in advance).

Towpath adventures

The Canal de Garonne runs east from the Atlantic; the Canal du Midi runs west from the Mediterranean. They meet in Toulouse, forming one continuous, navigable coast-to-coast waterway. Exploring the towpaths, which are shaded by regimented parades of plane trees, can be as simple as a leisurely stroll or a daylong cycling trip. For the latter, rentals are available from the city's 400 bike stations using the vélôToulouse (*velotoulouse.tisseo.fr*) bike-sharing app.

A more substantial waterway, the Garonne River cleaves its way through the heart of the city. Get onto the water with **Les Bateaux Toulousains** (*bateaux-toulousains.com; from €8*), with 30-minute cruises from July to October. The same boats are used for canal cruises from March to June.

Conquering the skies

Toulouse has long been seen as the world capital of aeronautics. And aviation, space and technology enthusiasts have not one, but four major landmarks in store. Of them, the most impressive is **Aeroscopia** (*aeroscopia.fr; adult/child €15/12*), which brings together scores of planes, among them some of the world's largest. You can walk through a Concorde (its 1970s style seats and complex control panels preserved in place behind perspex) and an Airbus A380 on the tarmac outside, where parts of the fuselage and flooring are stripped back to expose the complicated wiring. Nearby, **Ailes Anciennes Toulouse** (*Old Wings Toulouse; aatlse.org; €7*), open only a few days a week, holds a fine collection of 47 heritage planes, including a French Dassault Mirage, British De Havilland Vampire T11, and a US Lockheed T-33 Shooting Star. **Let's Visit Airbus** (*manatour.fr; adult/child €16/13*) runs tours of the Airbus Factory.

Nothing martials humanity's scientific advances like the exploration of space. Toulouse's contribution to our airborne feats beyond the stratosphere are celebrated at the vast **Cité de l'Espace** (*cite-espace.com; adult/child €29/22.50*) space museum. Highlights include boarding a Mir space station, riding the Apollo mission simulator and seeing real pieces of moonrock.

CITY OF VIOLETS

It is dubbed the Rose City but Toulouse is also a city of violets. Specifically, the flowers that are cultivated locally in winter and used to make *liqueur de violette* (a popular ace up the sleeve with local mixologists); *violettes de Toulouse* candies; and Paris-Toulouse pastries, consisting of hazelnut praline and violet-infused Chantilly cream. If used well, violet flowers create a subtle fragrant note, rather than the soapy flavour you might expect. To buy violet products, check out **La Maison de la Violette**, a shop in a canal barge. In a nod to this violet heritage, the local football team, Ligue 1's Toulouse FC, play in purple and even released a third kit in the 2024–25 season emblazoned with violet flowers.

 EATING IN TOULOUSE: OUR PICKS

Chez Tran: Playful neon lighting and paper lanterns. Try its signature bo buns. On rue Pargaminières, known as the 'street-food half-mile'. *hours vary* €

Au Bon Graillou: Try the excellent-value seasonal three-course menu for lunch, using ingredients from Marché Victor Hugo downstairs. *noon-3pm Tue-Sun* €€

L'Oncle Pom: Sagely takes a potato-forward approach: first, select your preparation (gratin, French fries etc) before choosing a meat or fish to accompany. *hours vary* €€

Restaurant Emile: Michelin Guide–level *cassoulet* served in clay bowls. Book ahead for terrace seating. *noon-1.30pm & 7.30-9.30pm* €€€

HELP ME PICK:

Where to Taste Wine

The French thirst for wine dates to Roman times when oenophiles identified fertile pockets of Gaul to plant *vignobles* (vineyards) to spawn France's most celebrated wine regions: Burgundy, Bordeaux, Champagne, Alsace, the Loire and Rhône valleys, Provence and Languedoc. Quality wines in France are Appellation d'Origine Contrôlée (AOC) or Appellation d'Origine Protégée (AOP): the wine has met stringent regulations governing where, how and under what conditions it was grown and bottled. Some regions have a single AOC (like Alsace); others dozens. Bordeaux has 65!

Where to go if you love...

Full-Bodied Reds

Monks in Burgundy began making wine in the 8th century, believing divine spirits in the soil spoke to them through wine. Burgundy vineyards remain small and are divided into *climats* – a viticultural patrimony UNESCO-listed since 2015. Winegrowers in **Côte d'Or**, **Chablis**, **Châtillon** and **Mâcon** produce small quantities of excellent reds from pinot noir grapes. The best Bourgogne vintages demand 10 to 20 years to age. Despite Burgundy's global fame (and the sky-high prices its wines now fetch), many winemakers remain modest – owner-operators who prune their own vines and consider themselves caretakers rather than creators.

Bubbles

Champagne's beloved bubbles were once thought to be a fault in the region's still wine. It wasn't until Dom Pierre Pérignon, a Benedictine monk at Hautvillers Abbey, started to master the art of winemaking that the sparkling wine began to be appreciated. 'Come quickly, I am tasting the stars!' is what he reportedly exclaimed upon tasting Champagne in 1693. For centuries, Champagne was the celebratory drink for French coronations, giving it the reputation as 'the wine of Kings and the King of wines'. Today, the famous Champagne houses welcome visitors to underground caverns, perfectly manicured vineyards and exquisite tasting rooms.

BARMALINI/SHUTTERSTOCK ©

Crisp Whites

The Loire Valley produces France's greatest variety of wines, some in troglodyte caves. Light delicate whites from **Pouilly-Fumé**, **Vouvray**, **Sancerre**, **Bourgueil** and **Chinon** are excellent. Muscadet, cabernet franc and chenin blanc grapes contrast with chardonnay grapes that go into Burgundy's great whites. There are also plenty of reds, particularly in Chinon, most made from cabernet franc grapes, aged in caves carved out of *tuffeau*, the soft local limestone, which offers the ideal temperature and humidity.

Pale Rosé

Chilled, fresh pink rosé wines are synonymous with the hot south, and 80% of the wine produced in Provence is rosé. **Côtes de Provence**, with 20 hectares of vineyards between Nice and Aix-en-Provence, is France's sixth-largest appellation. Look for rosés from **Bandol**, **Coteaux d'Aix-en-Provence**, **Palette** and **Coteaux Varois**.

Burgundy Wineries are almost impossible to visit; buy from *négociants* (wine merchants) in specialist wine shops instead.

Champagne Most Champagne houses are in Reims, Épernay or in between the two. Tastings often require reservation and include a tour, and are much more expensive than in other wine regions, starting from €27 per person.

Loire Valley Hundreds of vineyards welcome visitors, although advance reservations are preferred. Visit *vinsdeloire.fr/caves -touristiques* for information and an interactive map.

Provence Many vignerons (growers) open their doors to visitors; taste two or three vintages before buying. In Provence fill your own container with cheap *vin de table* (table wine) at the local wine cooperatives.

Oeno-tourism

E-bike tours are common in areas like Beaujolais, Jura and the Loire; or in the Dordogne and Ardèche, wake up to sunrise yoga sessions among the vines. In the Alps, try heady combinations like snowshoe walks to taste wine in forest tipis, or take blind tasting up a level by combining speleology and wine tasting in the Ardèche's caves. Wine-infused runs are increasingly popular, too. The Marathon du Médoc is now almost 40 years old, and obtaining a place is reminiscent of getting tickets for Glastonbury or Coachella. Bigger and more popular year-on-year, the riotous Marathon du Beaujolais is a popular alternative, but even that sells out well in advance. Look out for smaller wine runs, and prepare to don full fancy dress.

When buying wine from a shop, visit a caviste rather than a supermarket. Often the price difference is nominal, and they'll have a greater selection of wines from small producers.

445

Places We Love to Stay

€ Budget €€ Midrange €€€ Top end

Paris   MAP p386

Hôtel Chopin € A rare budget hotel in Paris, and in the unique location of one of the city's historical *passages couverts*. This historic hotel originally opened in 1846 and features classic, period-inspired rooms overlooking the Paris rooftops.

People Marais € This modern hostel is built for community, with well-equipped dorms, communal kitchens, and a light-filled sociable cafe and restaurant.

123 Sebastopol €€ A cinema-themed hotel, where each floor is dedicated to a film director or film-music composer, with an entertaining atmosphere. It is family-friendly and conveniently located between Sentier and Le Marais.

Hôtel des Académies et des Arts €€ An effortlessly cool design hotel housed in the building where Modigliani once had his studio (book room 52 if you want to sleep in it). The hotel also has its own art atelier downstairs.

Hotel Dame des Arts €€ This hip hotel is one of St-Germain-des-Prés coolest addresses, with design-led rooms and a rooftop terrace with fantastic views that pulls in locals as well as guests.

Hôtel HoY €€ One of the most restful places to stay; there's a yoga studio and in-room mats. The highlight is the ground-floor flower shop and the excellent MESA, serving up creative plant-based dishes steeped in Latin American flavours.

Mama Shelter Paris East €€ This cool Philippe Starck–designed, 170-room hotel draws a younger, creative crowd to its off-grid location, thanks to its bold industrial decor, rooftop bar and playful touches such as cartoon-mask lampshades.

Mont St-Michel   MAP p400

Chambres d'Hôte Les Bruyères du Mont € Find an enchanted garden and gracious host Nadine in this guesthouse near Mont St-Michel.

Camping La Baie du Mont St-Michel €€ A well-maintained, no-frills campsite with friendly hosts and plenty of hot water for showers.

Auberge Sauvage €€€ Farmhouse chic aesthetic with a garden and tennis courtyards – and a Michelin-starred restaurant.

Annecy

Hôtel du Château €€ Family-run hotel in Annecy with panoramic breakfast terrace and free parking, on a hill across from the château's imposing gatehouse.

Chamonix   MAP p408

Le Chamoniard Volant € Veteran favourite of climbers and ski bums on a budget, with bunk dorms and communal kitchen in a self-catering chalet.

Hôtel Richemond € Third-generation family hotel, with old-school rooms in a grand old building from 1914; exceptional value.

La Folie Douce €€ The famous après-ski brand's only hotel parties hard inside a monumental Belle Époque palace.

Refuge du Montenvers €€ Mourn France's longest but fast-melting glacier at this elegant grand dame, an 1880 vintage with chic retro-styled rooms, restaurant and summer terrace above Mer de Glace.

Lyon   MAP p414

Pilo € Almost too stylish to be a hostel, with oodles of plants, Friday-night DJ sets alfresco, boules pitches and frequent visiting tattoo artists.

Hotel de Verdun 1882 €€ Beautiful rooms in a historic building formerly belonging to the founders of Lyonnais institution Brasserie Georges.

Lyon Country House €€ A breath of fresh air just 15 minutes from the city centre, with lodges, treehouses and suites.

Fourvière Hôtel €€€ Chic, upmarket hotel in a former convent. The old altar and confessional booths spill over with house plants.

Loire Valley

Hôtel de Biencourt € Just 150m from the entrance to Azay-le-Rideau, 17 charming rooms in a one-time school from the 17th and 18th centuries.

Côté Loire-Auberge Ligérienne € Facing the river in Blois, this establishment – an inn since 1675 – has eight spotless rooms, some with 350-year-old beams and/or great Loire views.

Le Bois des Chambres €€ A very classy 39-room hotel, 300m from Chaumont-sur-Loire, that occupies a 19th-century barn and ecofriendly, modern pavilions surrounded by gardens.

Hôtel Le Grand Monarque €€
An 18th-century coaching inn transformed into a charming hotel just five minutes on foot from the château. Rooms are spacious, with a mix of 21st-century mod cons and antique touches.

Relais de Chambord €€€
Chambord's former kennels are now a luxury hotel with an unbeatable château-adjacent location, country-chic rooms, a sensational bar, a spa and a *bistronomique* restaurant.

Nice MAP p426

Hostel Meyerbeer Beach €
Friendly hostel with a cracking city-centre location, just three minutes from the beach. Dorms are mixed.

Hôtel Rossetti €€ Charming three-star boutique hotel with seven rooms in the shadow of Cathédrale Ste-Réparate in Vieux Nice. The hidden terrace is lovely.

Hôtel La Pérouse €€€ Clinging to the Colline du Château with a hidden pool and sea views, this delightful four-star hotel is one of Nice's finest.

Le Negresco €€€ The grande dame of Nice's hotels, set across from the beach. Each room is unique and styled to a theme. The art collection is priceless.

Marseille MAP p431

Hotel Peron €€ Wes Anderson–style hotel with views of the corniche and beyond. Art deco from every angle and a friendly reception.

Le Ryad €€ North African–inspired hotel that has a sanctuary of a garden to drink fresh mint tea in after a long day.

La Relève €€ There are only four rooms, so book in advance for this 1950s-inspired guesthouse that is attached to a very cool bar in the 7e.

St-Tropez

Hôtel Ermitage €€ Self-consciously retro, with sweeping views over town.

Hôtel Lou Cagnard €€€ Lovely jasmine-scented garden patios and welcoming feel. Open year-round.

Bordeaux MAP p437

Jost € A new-gen lifestyle hostel with a Spritz-fuelled bar around a rooftop pool (guests only). Tip-top Italian tapas too.

Chez Dupont €€ B&B-style rooms decorated with vintage furniture and curiosities, on Chartrons' old-world main street.

La Maison du Lierre €€ As serene as its name, the House of Ivy has quaint boutique rooms and serves breakfast in a vine-draped garden.

Hôtel La Zoologie €€€
Four-star luxury in Bordeaux's historic Institute of Zoology, a glorious 1903 mashup of brick, stone and glass.

Hotel Peron, Marseille

Practicalities

MONEY & CURRENCY

The currency in France is the euro (€). Payment by card is widespread and can be contactless up to €50; smaller shops can impose a minimum payment (€10 or €15). In rural France, many B&Bs, *fermes auberges,* produce markets and taxi drivers don't accept cards. You cannot hire a car without a credit card.

BILLION PHOTOS/SHUTTERSTOCK

SMOKING

Smoking in France is illegal in indoor public spaces, summer forests and – since July 2025 – in public parks and gardens, beaches, bus shelters, sports facilities and outdoor spaces around schools.

HEALTHCARE

Pharmacies – an illuminated green cross indicates they're open – sell a wide range of medicines without *ordonnance* (prescription). Details of the closest *pharmacie de garde* open at night and on Sundays are displayed in pharmacy windows. Call 118 or Europe-wide 112 for an ambulance.

LGBTIQ+ TRAVELLERS

The rainbow flag flies high in France. 'Laissez-faire' perfectly sums up France's liberal attitude towards homosexuality and people's private lives in general, in part because of a long tradition of public tolerance towards unconventional lifestyles.

OPENING HOURS

In many French towns and villages, shops close on Monday.
Banks 9am–noon and 2pm–5pm Monday to Friday or Tuesday to Saturday
Bars 7pm–1am
Cafes 7am–11pm
Clubs 10pm–3am, 4am or 5am Thursday to Saturday
Restaurants Noon–2.30pm and 7pm–9pm or later six days a week
Shops 10am–noon and 2pm–7pm Monday to Saturday

ACCESSIBLE TRAVEL

France presents constant challenges for *visiteurs à mobilité réduite* (visitors with reduced mobility) and *visiteurs handicapés* (visitors with disabilities), but inroads are being made into helping them get around more easily. Paris metro is not good for accessibility, but Paris buses are 100% accessible.

PUBLIC HOLIDAYS

New Year's Day 1 January
Easter Sunday & Monday Late March/April
May Day 1 May
WWII Victory Day 8 May
Ascension Thursday May; 40th day after Easter
Pentecost & Whit Monday Mid-May to mid-June; seventh Sunday after Easter
Bastille Day (Fête Nationale) 14 July
Assumption Day 15 August
All Saints' Day 1 November
Remembrance Day 11 November
Christmas Day 25 December

Language

Standard French is taught and spoken throughout France. This said, regional accents and dialects are an important part of identity in certain regions, but you'll have no trouble being understood anywhere if you stick to standard French.

Basics

Hello. Bonjour. *bon-zhoor*

Goodbye. Au revoir. *o-rer-vwa*

Yes. Oui. *wee*

No. Non. *non*

Please. S'il vous plaît. *seel voo play*

Thank you. Merci. *mair-see*

Excuse me. Excusez-moi. *ek-skew-zay-mwa*

Sorry. Pardon. *par-don*

What's your name? Comment vous appelez-vous? *ko-mon voo-za-play voo*

My name is ... Je m'appelle ... *zher ma-pel ...*

Do you speak English? Parlez-vous anglais? *par-lay-voo ong-glay*

I don't understand. Je ne comprends pas. *zher ner kom-pron pa*

Directions

Where's ...? Où est ...? *oo ay ...*

What's the address? Quelle est l'adresse? *kel ay la-dres*

Could you write the address, please? Est-ce que vous pourriez écrire l'adresse, s'il vous plaît? *es-ker voo poo-ryay ay-kreer la-dres seel voo play*

Can you show me (on the map)? Pouvez-vous m'indiquer (sur la carte)? *poo-vay-voo mun-dee-kay (sewr la kart)*

Signs

Entrée Entrance

Fermé Closed

Ouvert Open

Sortie Exit

Toilettes/WC Toilets

Time

What time is it? Quelle heure est-il? *kel er ay til*

It's (8) o'clock. Il est (huit) heures. *il ay (weet) er*

Half past (10). Il est (dix) heures et demie. *il ay (deez) er ay day-mee*

Morning Matin. *ma-tun*

Afternoon Après-midi. *a-pray-mee-dee*

Evening Soir. *swar*

Yesterday Hier. *yair*

Today Aujourd'hui. *o-zhoor-dwee*

Tomorrow Demain. *der-mun*

Emergencies

Help! Au secours! *o skoor*

Leave me alone! Fichez-moi la paix! *fee-shay-mwa la pay*

I'm ill. Je suis malade. *zher swee ma-lad*

Call ... Appelez... *a-play*

    a doctor un médecin. *un mayd-sun*

    the police la police. *la po-lees*

Eating & Drinking

What would you recommend? Qu'est-ce que vous conseillez? *kes-ker voo kon-say-yay*

Cheers! Santé! *son-tay*

That was delicious. C'était délicieux! *say-tay day-lee-syer*

NUMBERS

1 un *un*

2 deux *der*

3 trois *trwa*

4 quatre *ka-trer*

5 cinq *sungk*

6 six *sees*

7 sept *set*

8 huit *weet*

9 neuf *nerf*

10 dix *dees*

TRAVELVIEW/SHUTTERSTOCK

Charles de Gaulle airport

Arriving

For many, touchdown in Paris, at Charles de Gaulle or Orly airports, is their first taste of France, although there are international airports across the country. Trains link much of continental Europe and the UK with France, with many ferry connections joining the UK to northern France, too. Cruises dock on much of the French coast, particularly along the Mediterranean.

By Air
Charles de Gaulle, Paris, is the largest international airport in France, and most flights linking non-European countries arrive here. There are international airports in Lyon-St-Exupéry, Marseille-Provence, Nice-Côte d'Azur, Bordeaux-Mérignac and Toulouse-Blagnac, among others.

By Train
Eurostar *(eurostar.com)* is currently the only trans-Channel service to the UK; book tickets to/from London St Pancras in advance for best rates. Renfe *(renfe. com)* runs France–Spain connections, and Trenitalia *(trenitalia.com)* serves the France–Italy route.

Getting Around

There's excellent public transport but you'll also want your own wheels to explore deeper. EU nationals don't need a visa to visit France, but by the end of 2026, it is anticipated that arrivals from the UK, US, Canada and New Zealand, among others, will have to fill in a pre-arrival, online form to meet the EU's new electronic vetting system *(etiasvisa.com)*.

Train & Bus
France's SNCF rail network has frequent services (both high-speed TGVs and regional TER trains). Principal rail lines radiate out from Paris, making services between towns on different spokes slow or nonexistent. Bus services are reduced weekends and school holidays.

GREGORY_DUBUS/GETTY IMAGES

Bicycle & E-Bike
Dedicated cycling paths are widespread; many skirt canal towpaths or retired railway lines (*voies verts* or greenways). Long-distance itineraries like La Vélodyssée (p440) favour roads with light traffic and are ideal for bike-packing. Bike rental – road and mountain bikes, regular and electric-assisted – is omnipresent.

Hiring a Car
Driving is a delight in backstage France, but a car is a liability in traffic-plagued city centres. Find rental agencies at airports and by train stations; many offer electric cars. Some cities have a public car-sharing scheme, ideal for an out-of-town day flit. Consider car-sharing platforms *ouicar.fr* and *fr.getaround.com*.

Using Motorways
Autoroutes (motorways) command *péages* (tolls). Take a ticket on entering, pay when exiting. Cash payers: drive into a tollbooth displaying a green arrow – booths showing a white card symbol only accept cards. Check traffic conditions, motorway services etc on *bison-fute.gouv.fr*.

Ridesharing
Covoiturage (ridesharing) in France is a national institution. BlaBlaCar *(blablacar.fr)* is the most popular app, connecting passengers with drivers. In towns and cities, hitchhikers can stand in front of an *'Arrêt sur le pouce'* sign to be picked up by a vetted driver in the Rézo Pouce network *(rezopouce.fr)*.

DRIVING ESSENTIALS

Any car entering an intersection (including a T-junction) from a road on your right has the right of way unless street signs indicate otherwise.

There's generally a tollbridge, but some motorways have phased this out; pay within 72 hours online at *sanef.com*.

Approx. €1.72/L

For places to stay in Germany, see p516

CANADASTOCK/SHUTTERSTOCK

Brandenburger Tor (p458), Berlin

Curated by
Barbara Woolsey

Germany

TRANQUIL LANDSCAPES AND FESTIVE TRADITIONS

Travel in Germany is just like its culture: direct and efficient. In a world of options, Germany is serious about the joy of simple pleasures.

Germany's take on fun and adventure is just like how it brews its beer: an age-old recipe that never wavers from tradition and values good taste. If you're on a roller-coaster, multicountry Eurotrip, what Germany offers is a breath of fresh air (literally) in forests, beer gardens and laid-back cities where parks and nature are a must.

Getting from A to B is efficient on the autobahn, the world's fourth-longest highway system, and a train network where high-speed and wide-spanning regional services tick like clockwork. There's something undeniably artistic in the way scenery unfolds here; the corrugated, dune-fringed coasts of the north; the moody forests, romantic river valleys and vast vineyards of the centre; and the off-the-charts splendour of the Alps, carved into rugged glory by glaciers and the elements. All of these are integral parts of a magical natural matrix that's bound to give your legs a good workout.

Experiencing Germany is all about your belly, too. Local food is so much more than sausages and pretzels. Beyond the clichés awaits a cornucopia of seasonal palate-teasers and ingredients varying greatly from region to region. Dishes are a formidable means of consuming Germany's culture and history, and understanding its regional differences. In many ways, the country is akin to its hodgepodge dinner staples like *Eintopf* (one-pot stew) and *Auflauf* (casserole) – a vibrant mix of flavours and influences offering new surprises in every bite.

THE MAIN AREAS

BERLIN
Germany's nonconformist capital. **p458**

POTSDAM
Palaces and gardens galore. **p470**

COLOGNE
Energetic yet ancient Roman city. **p471**

DÜSSELDORF
Germany's fashion capital. **p476**

HAMBURG
Northern charms – medieval and maritime. **p479**

LÜBECK
Sweets and picture-book streets. **p484**

MUNICH
World-class beer and museums. **p485**

BAVARIA
Modern fairy-tale landscapes. **p490**

STUTTGART & THE BLACK FOREST
Fast cars and enchanting greenery. **p496**

BREMEN & LOWER SAXONY
Dramatic scenery and architecture. **p500**

DRESDEN & LEIPZIG
Historical elegance, countercultural stride. **p504**

CENTRAL GERMANY
Intellect and innovation on the heartland. **p507**

FRANKFURT AM MAIN
Manhattan vibes on the Maine. **p509**

Find Your Way

Wherever you go in Germany's north, water is a loyal travel buddy. Hop on a car or train for a couple of hours, and landscapes shift from wild nature to quaint countryside and lively small-city life.

Hamburg, p479

Germany's largest port boasts cosmopolitan vibes and urban dwellers with cash to spend. Urban renewal, counterculture and a vibrant nightlife create excitement.

Berlin, p458

Berlin's alternative spirit, eclectic food scene, layered history and anything-goes nightlife enthral. Cavernous museums and industrial nightclubs outnumber rainy days.

CAR

Useful for travelling at your own pace or visiting nature-heavy regions and national parks where public transport is meagre. Frequent rest stops make for comfortable journeys, and the experience of blasting down speed-limit-free autobahn.

TRAIN

An extensive network of long-distance and regional trains have frequent departures. The national operator Deutsche Bahn has a monopoly on tracks and can be fairly expensive; private operators offer some deals. Carriage chaos ensues on weekends and public holidays.

AIR

Only useful for longer distances, such as Hamburg to Munich or Berlin to Munich. It's sometimes cheaper than trains but not necessarily faster when you factor in check-in, security and getting into the city centre; trains drop you right into the downtown action.

Central Germany, p507

Germany's heartland of nature and history. Ancient beech forests, rococo castles atop vine-clad hills, historic redoubts of German culture and lively university towns all await.

Bavaria, p490

Traditional Germany bottled into one region. Intoxicating landscapes – rolling vineyards, storybook forests and alpine peaks – spiked with castles, palaces and breweries along the way.

Munich, p485

Its reputation as the 'City of Art and Beer' is well earned. Attack the art quarter's museums and galleries; drink up beer-garden vibes and brewhouse traditions.

Stuttgart & the Black Forest, p496

Exciting thrills from fast Swabian cars to the outdoor action of Black Forest firs. Hike, swim and ski, then sink into healing thermal waters.

Cologne, p471

Feel your spirits soar in the cathedral's luminous beauty, then come back to earth with a Kölsch beer, fantastic shopping and museums.

Frankfurt am Main, p509

Europe's de facto financial hub offers fine dining and art museums against an iconic skyline; further out, regional discoveries span mystical villages, castles and forests.

0 km 100
0 miles 50

PRAGUE

VIENNA

CZECHIA

AUSTRIA

SWITZERLAND

FRANCE

BELGIUM

LUXEMBOURG

LUXEMBOURG CITY

455

Plan Your Time

Seeing Germany's different landscapes makes for a special journey. Beyond capitals like Berlin and Munich, countryside and small-city life are worth exploring – especially where scenic rivers run through.

MAJONIT/SHUTTERSTOCK

Kölner Dom (p471), Cologne

Weekend in the Capital

● A few days in **Berlin** (p458) is all it takes for key cultural highlights and a high-level perspective on German history. In Historic Mitte, trace the past against evocative landmarks: sobering WWII commemoration at the **Holocaust Memorial** (p460), Cold War divide at **Checkpoint Charlie** (p460), and finally, celebrating today's reunified Republic of Germany at the **Reichstag** (p460) and **Brandenburger Tor** (p458).

● On the UNESCO-listed **Museumsinsel** (p463), former Prussian palaces are prime for discovering ancient Egyptian history as well as globetrotting ethnology and Asian art at the **Neues Museum** (p463) and **Humboldt Forum** (p464) respectively. On an easy day trip to Potsdam, **Sanssouci Palace** (p470) and **sumptuous gardens** (p470) drive home Prussian glory days.

SEASONAL HIGHLIGHTS

Germany embraces all seasons, with events spread across the year. Weather and even public holidays range wildly across states.

MARCH
Longer-lingering daylight puts a spring in even the most gruff Germans' steps. Fresh **herring** hits coastal menus, and dishes prepared with **Bärlauch** (wild garlic) are all the rage.

APRIL
The Easter Bunny? Pfff. Germany's springtime mascot is the village Asparagus Queen, ushering in the nation's favourite cream-coloured crop. From markets to menus, **white asparagus** is everywhere.

MAY
Surprisingly warm and sunny, May is perfect for clinking in **beer gardens**. It's also packed with public holidays; trains and highways become awfully busy.

A Week's Southerly Quest

● Exploring southern Germany is an odyssey meandering high and low. Over two weeks, make your first impression in **Munich** (p485), Bavaria's cosmopolitan capital, visiting world-class museums of **Kunstareal** (p488) and tipping beer in **Englischer Garten** (p489). Wander from the famous piazza, **Marienplatz** (p485), to the truly urban **Viktualienmarkt** (p487) farmers market.

● Next, chase the superlative and fantastical within the Bavarian Alps: Germany's highest point, the **Zugspitze** (p492), and the Disney-inspiring **Schloss Neuschwanstein** (p492). Along the southern border, continue following fairy tales into the **Black Forest** (p498) and along the **Romantic Road** (p494). Backtrack to **Stuttgart** (p496) to discover further German legends – the **Porsche** (p496) and **Mercedes-Benz** (p497) museums.

A Few Days in the East

● Challenge historical assumptions about eastern Germany, chasing cultural highlights that reveal royal elegance and artsy modern gumption. Spin through **Berlin** (p458), Germany's wild-child capital with its eclectic neighbourhoods, iconic nightlife and GDR history. Hop over to **Dresden** (p504), exploring its baroque elegance and treasure troves of art.

● From there, it's just a zip over to **Leipzig** (p506), dubbed the City of Heroes for its role in razing the Berlin Wall. Immerse yourself in a cultural heritage to a soundtrack by Bach, Mendelssohn and Wagner, as well as today's modern rhythms of industrial nightlife and contemporary art. Some say 'Hypezig' is the better Berlin; go ahead and judge for yourself.

JUNE

it's **festival season** and there's fresh, local produce in supermarkets. Life moves fully outdoors upon summer solstice's blessed 9.30pm sundown.

JULY

School's out, and peak season begins. Pre-book accommodation – mountain or coast. Dip into lakes, rivers and Baltic or North Sea waters.

SEPTEMBER

It's sunny, but not hot. Summer is over but **wine** and autumn festivals (also, **Oktoberfest**) ease the season out. Changing leaves excite.

DECEMBER

Cold, sun-deprived days are brightened by **Advent** festivities, **Christmas markets** and twinkle-light canopies across streets, beer halls and restaurants.

Berlin

WORLD-FAMOUS MUSEUMS | MONUMENTAL HISTORY | GASTRONOMY

☑ TOP TIPS

Today, the site of the **Führerbunker** lies beneath an unremarkable car park, revealing its grim history only by a modest information panel. A diagram outlines the vast bunker network alongside construction data and the site's post-WWII fate. The Soviets blew up the interior in 1947, sealing off one of the darkest chapters of the 20th century.

Berlin is a city built on sand, water and the refusal to sit still. From its orderly Prussian foundations to its roaring industrial boom, through wartime destruction, Cold War division and the euphoric tearing down of the Wall, it's reinvented itself more times than most capitals can fathom. Former French culture minister Jack Lang said it well when he quipped that Paris will always be Paris, but Berlin will never be Berlin. True, although that's the city's magic. It's always becoming.

What keeps Berlin magnetic is sheer variety. Swoon over Nefertiti on Museum Island in the morning, raise your pinkie at afternoon tea at posh Hotel Adlon and sip natural wine in a trendy bar by evening. Street art decorates Berlin's facades like a second skin; weekend flea markets are a citywide ritual. Even club culture still exudes global pull, from marathon Berghain techno sessions to summer raves and sex-positive parties.

Historic Mitte

MAP p459

Symbol of division and unity

Brandenburger Tor (Brandenburg Gate) is Berlin's most famous – and most photographed – landmark. Trapped right behind the Berlin Wall during the Cold War, it symbolised division for decades before becoming an emblem of German reunification when the hated barrier fell in 1989. Today, it's a photogenic backdrop for New Year's Eve parties, concerts, festivals and mega-events, including FIFA World Cup finals.

 GETTING AROUND

Berlin is a sprawling city, but key areas are compact. Most blockbuster sights are found between Alexanderplatz and Zoo Station. Walking around Berlin's *Kieze* (neighbourhoods) is a joy, but to travel between them you'll need the excellent public transport – or a bicycle. Bike lanes, rental stations and app-based bike- and e-scooter-sharing services abound. Bicycles may be taken aboard specially marked U-Bahn, S-Bahn and tram carriages but require a separate *Fahrradkarte* (bike ticket).

HISTORIC MITTE, MUSEUMSINSEL & ALEXANDERPLATZ

Crowned by the Quadriga (Johann Gottfried Schadow's sculpture of the Roman goddess of victory), the Brandenburg Gate looks over **Pariser Platz**, which was completely flattened in WWII. Look around now: the US, French and British embassies and the venerable **Hotel Adlon** once again frame the square.

Beacon of German democracy

It's been burned, bombed, rebuilt, buttressed by the Berlin Wall, wrapped in fabric and finally reimagined by Norman Foster

BEST SHOPPING IN HISTORIC MITTE

Frau Tonis Parfum: This made-in-Berlin perfume boutique offers scent tests to help you choose a matching fragrance plus bespoke blends.

Ritter Sport Bunte Schokowelt: Colourful flagship store with classic, limited-edition, vegan, organic and personalised chocolate bars, and a bean-to-bar exhibit.

Dussmann – Das Kulturkaufhaus: Eldorado for bookworms, with a huge music selection, free concerts and high-profile book readings and signings.

Rausch Schokoladenhaus: Emporium of truffles and pralines with replicas of Berlin landmarks and a cafe with a view of Gendarmenmarkt.

KPM Berlin: Store and outlet for handmade porcelain from the royal KPM manufactory, established by Frederick the Great in 1763.

Holocaust Memorial

as the modern seat of Germany's parliament, the Bundestag. Topped with a glistening glass dome, the iconic **Reichstag** (*bundestag.de; free*) now stands as the symbolic and architectural heart of the surrounding Federal Government District, built in the 1990s after German reunification.

Reserve a time slot online for the lift to the rooftop terrace for fabulous views and access to the glass dome. Resembling a giant glass beehive, the glistening cupola is open at the top and bottom, and hovers directly above the plenary chamber, serving as a visual metaphor for political transparency.

Confronting Holocaust history

The **Holocaust Memorial** (*stiftung-denkmal.de; free*) was dedicated in 2005 to commemorate the six million Jewish victims of the Holocaust. Designed by New York architect Peter Eisenman, the football-field-size area is filled with 2711 concrete stelae, rising in sombre silence from undulating ground and inviting quiet reflection on loss, absence and memory.

You're free to access this massive concrete maze at any point and make your individual journey through it. Lose yourself in the narrow passageways and connect with its metaphorical sense of disorientation, claustrophobia and oppression. Remember that this is a space for respectful reflection.

Alfa, Bravo...Checkpoint Charlie

Checkpoint Charlie was the principal Cold War–era border crossing for foreigners and diplomats between the American

EATING IN HISTORIC MITTE: OUR PICKS

MAP p459

India Club: Curries are culinary poetry at this elegant North Indian outpost led by top toque Manish Bahukhandi. *5-11.30pm Wed-Mon* €€€

Crackers: Cosmopolitan gastro-cathedral where the lofty ceiling matches the dishes made with sustainably sourced provisions. *6pm-1am* €€€

Ganymed Brasserie: Paris meets Berlin at this charming and historic all-day riverside spot for French classics and seafood. *9am-midnight* €€€

Zollpackhof: Hearty German fare and Bavarian beer in a riverside beer garden or historic dining room with a crackling fireplace. *noon-11pm* €€

A LEISURELY TIERGARTEN STROLL

Clear your head with a spin around Tiergarten, one of the world's largest inner-city parks.

START	END	LENGTH
Potsdamer Platz	Tiergarten S-Bahn station	6km; 2 hours

From **1 Potsdamer Platz**, make your way to **2 Luiseninsel**, an enchanting enclosed garden adorned with statues and flowerbeds. Follow the waterway west to **3 Rousseau-Insel**, a teensy island and memorial to 18th-century French philosopher Jean-Jacques Rousseau.

Continue to the **4 Siegessäule** (Victory Column) to climb up to the skirt hems of its gilded Victoria statue for fabulous city views. Following Spreeweg north takes you past snowy-white **5 Schloss Bellevue**, a palace originally built for Frederick the Great's brother and now the residence of the German president.

Meander along the Spree River, then check out the latest art exhibit at the **6 Akademie der Künste**.

Walk south through the park to reach the Neuer See, a romantic lake fronted by the charming **7 Café am Neuen See** restaurant and beer garden.

Stroll north on Tiergartenufer along the Landwehrkanal until you reach Schleuseninsel to strike see the wacky **8 Rosa Röhre**, a massive piglet-pink pipe snaking around a university research facility painted cornflower-blue.

Then arrive at the magnificent **9 Charlottenburger Tor**, a counterpart to the Brandenburg Gate. If you're hungry, drop by **10 Capt'n Schillow**, a quirky fish-focused restaurant boat moored below the gate. Otherwise follow Strasse des 17 Juni east to wrap up your tour at **11 Tiergarten S-Bahn station**.

On Sundays you can browse **Berliner Trödelmarkt**, Berlin's oldest flea market, which sets up along Strasse des 17 Juni.

The **Hansaviertel quarter** is a showcase of modernist 1950s buildings designed by Gropius, Niemeyer and other big mid-century architects.

A **memorial** below Lichtenstein Bridge marks where the body of revolutionary Rosa Luxemburg was thrown into the Landwehr Canal after her 1919 murder.

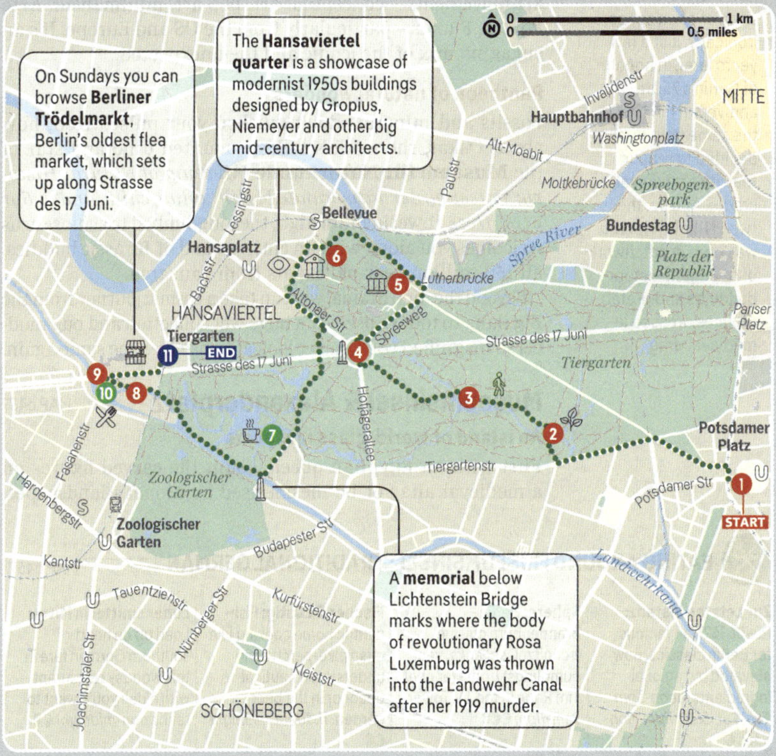

MEDIEVAL REBOOT

The area west and south of the TV Tower was once the bustling heart of medieval Berlin. Back in the 13th century, traders set up shop along the Spree, giving rise to the twin towns of Berlin and Cölln. Many of the old buildings and crooked lanes survived until WWII, but in the aftermath, East German city planners bulldozed most of what remained, sparing only a few token landmarks like the Marienkirche that now stands forlorn in a sea of open space. Ironically, just a few years later, in honour of Berlin's 750th anniversary in 1987, the same government decided to rebuild the city's medieval cradle. And so, the twee **Nikolaiviertel** was born, a patchwork of relocated historic buildings and prefab replicas dressed in medieval drag.

sector in West Berlin and Soviet-controlled East Berlin. It got the name 'Charlie' because it was the third Allied checkpoint to open – hence the third letter in the NATO phonetic alphabet.

These days, the recreated checkpoint, complete with young men in uniform posing for tips, may scream 'tourist trap', but there are a few genuinely worthwhile exhibits that help you connect with this historic site.

For a crash course in Cold War milestones, check out the photos and documents of the free outdoor **Checkpoint Gallery**. Stories of daring escapes across the Wall are at the heart of the **Mauermuseum** *(mauermuseum.de; adult/child €18.50/12.50)*.

Edgy art in a Nazi bunker

Pick up on the vibes of war, vegetables and whips still clinging to the labyrinthine warren now housing the **Sammlung Boros** *(Boros Collection; sammlung-boros.de; adult/student €18/10)*, one of Berlin's most exciting private art spaces. A fresh exhibition rolls out every four years. Tours (also in English) run for 90 minutes and tend to sell out fast, so book early.

All aboard the art train

Housed in a grand old train station, **Hamburger Bahnhof – Nationalgalerie der Gegenwart** *(hamburgerbahnhof.de; adult/child €16/free)* is one of Germany's top spots for contemporary art. Its collection spans the full arc of post-1960s art movements – conceptual art, pop art, minimalism, Arte Povera, Fluxus – particularly from the US and Europe. It's an engaging mix of the iconic and the unexpected.

Pantheon of natural wonders

Fossils and minerals don't quicken your pulse? Well, how about Oskar, the world's tallest mounted dino and star of the **Museum für Naturkunde** *(Museum of Natural History; museumfuernaturkunde.berlin; adult/child/under 6yr €11/5/free)*. Towering 13m high, the long-limbed brachiosaurus welcomes you along with an entire squad of Jurassic buddies, all 150-million-year-old expats from Tanzania.

Beyond the dino drama, you can take a cosmic journey from the Big Bang to today, discover a huge wet collection and bug models so magnified you'll never look at house flies the same again.

Museumsinsel & Alexanderplatz   MAP p459

An island of world-class museums

Flirt with an Egyptian queen, count the carved figures on a medieval altar or be mesmerised by Monet's landscapes.

EATING AROUND MUSEUMSINSEL: TRADITIONAL GERMAN ——— MAP p459

Zur Letzten Instanz:	Sphere: Berlin–	Fischer & Lustig: Fish-	Lebensmittel in Mitte:
Rustic 1621 lair famous for Berlin classics, now elevated by regional ingredients. *noon-3pm Tue-Sat, 5.30-11pm Mon-Sat* €€	Brandenburg cuisine (schnitzel, *soljanka*, veal dumplings) from star chef Tim Raue in the TV Tower. *9am-11pm* €€€	centric home cooking like crisp pike-perch amid understated nautical decor or in the beer garden. *11.30am-midnight* €€	Load up on hearty southern German fare in this woodsy restaurant with a deli you'll want to raid. *noon-midnight* €€

SEANPAVONEPHOTO/GETTY IMAGES

Fernsehturm (p464)

DOWN INTO THE UNDERBELLY

Berliner Unterwelten *(berliner-unterwelten. de; adult/child from €17/13)*, a nonprofit committed to preserving the city's hidden depths, is your gateway to exploring Berlin's mysterious underbelly on a guided tour. The most popular is 'Dark Worlds', a 90-minute descent into a civilian air-raid shelter beneath Gesundbrunnen U-Bahn station. Inside, you'll pick your way through claustrophobic rooms, narrow corridors and heavy steel doors, and past haunting wartime relics like hospital beds, gas masks and guns. The guides bring alive the chilling reality of ordinary Berliners cooped up here, crammed and scared, as the bombs rained down on the city. The minimum age is seven; children under 14 must be accompanied by an adult. Tickets are only available online.

Welcome to **Museumsinsel** *(Museum Island; smb.museum; day pass adult/child €24/free)*. Berlin's renowned repository of 6000 years of art, artefacts and sculpture from Europe and beyond is spread across five grand buildings.

The grand neoclassical **Old Museum** holds historical antiquities and the **New Museum** has a show-stopping Egyptian collection. The Greek-temple-style **Old National Gallery** is a tribute to 19th-century European art while the palatial **Bode-Museum** brings together several period-spanning collections under one grand roof. Note that the **Pergamonmuseum**, Museum Island's crown jewel, will remain closed for renovation until at least 2027.

Iconic Egyptian collection

For over 60 years, the **Neues Museum** *(New Museum; smb. museum; day pass adult/child €24/free)* sat in ruins. But today it's one of the city's most celebrated attractions and a standout on Museumsinsel.

With her elegant neck and eternal good looks, Egyptian queen Nefertiti is definitely the head-turner of the **Egyptian Museum and Papyrus Collection**. Berlin's world-renowned Egyptian collection shares a roof with the **Museum of Pre- and Early History**, a rather clunky name for a trove of fascinating finds from the Stone Age to the Middle Ages.

The entire museum building was a wartime ruin resurrected by David Chipperfield, who ingeniously incorporated salvaged remnants.

Pantheon-inspired antiquities

The Neues Museum shares top billing on Museumsinsel with the **Altes Museum** *(Old Museum; smb.museum; day pass adult/child €24/free)*. The first museum to open on Museumsinsel

BERLIN'S BEST FLEA MARKETS

Our picks beyond the Mauerpark (all are held on Sunday).

Trödelmarkt Arkonaplatz, Mitte: Ride the retro frenzy with upmarket furniture, accessories, clothing, vinyl and books at this weekly market.

Flohmarkt Boxhagener Platz: Fun finds and bargains abound at this year-round Friedrichshain charmer.

Nowkoelln Flowmarkt, Neukölln: Canal-side hipster market with handmade treasures and impromptu concerts every other Sunday from April to December.

NK Kranoldplatz Flohmarkt, Neukölln: Idyllic vintage, art and bric-a-brac market held every other Sunday from mid-March to mid-November.

Flohmarkt am Rathaus Schöneberg: Hunt for deals and collectables next to where JFK gave his 'Ich bin ein Berliner' speech.

in 1830, its Pantheon-inspired rotunda is the centrepiece. The ground level is home to sculptures, vases, tomb reliefs and jewellery that delve into Greek mythology, daily life in cities and the royal courts, and the importance of theatre. Two sculptures are standouts: the *Praying Boy* behind the rotunda and the *Berlin Goddess* off to the right. Upstairs, the busts of Caesar and Cleopatra are especially striking.

Atop Germany's tallest structure

No matter where you are in Berlin, chances are you'll spot the **Fernsehturm** *(tv-turm.de; adult/child from €29.50/19.50)*. The TV Tower – Germany's tallest structure – is as iconic to the city as the Eiffel Tower is to Paris. It has stretched its slim frame to a dizzying 368m (including the antenna) since its 1969 debut.

Up top, pinpoint city landmarks from the glass-fronted **observation deck** at 203m, complete with a bar and a slow spin (twice an hour). The TV Tower's newest attraction is the rotating restaurant **Sphere** (p462); it's now helmed by Tim Raue, whose two-starred eponymous restaurant, **Restaurant Tim Raue** *(tim-raue.com)*, has long made foodies swoon.

Explore Berlin's royal cathedral

Spirituality meets spectacle at the **Berliner Dom** *(berliner dom.de; adult/student €10/7.50)*, which pulls quadruple duty as church, museum, concert hall and royal crypt. Inside, the former royal court church is gilt to the hilt, featuring an altar of marble and onyx, a 7269-pipe Sauer organ and lavish chapels, including one housing the sculpted sarcophagi of Friedrich I and Sophie Charlotte. For more dead royals, albeit in less extravagant coffins, head down to the crypt. There's an optional leg workout: a 270-step climb to the dome for glorious 360-degree views.

Berlin's newest cultural hub

After 20 years of debate, planning, construction and delays, Berlin's newest culture hub finally fully opened in 2022. Housed in a replica of the baroque Prussian city palace, the **Humboldt Forum** *(humboldtforum.org; prices vary, many exhibits free)* was named after Enlightenment-era brothers Wilhelm and Alexander von Humboldt. At its heart lie the dazzling collections of the **Ethnologisches Museum** and the **Museum für Asiatische Kunst** – your ticket to tapping into centuries of culture and creativity from across Africa, Asia, the Americas and Australia. It's open Wednesday to Monday.

Prenzlauer Berg

MAP p465

From death strip to urban living room

No other park in Berlin has pulled quite as radical a transformation as the **Mauerpark** *(mauerpark.info)*. Once part of the Berlin Wall death strip, it now pulses with a free-spirited vibe, especially on Sundays during the outdoor season. That's when thousands of locals, expats, tourists and bleary-eyed clubbers flood in to forage for treasure at the **Flohmarkt**

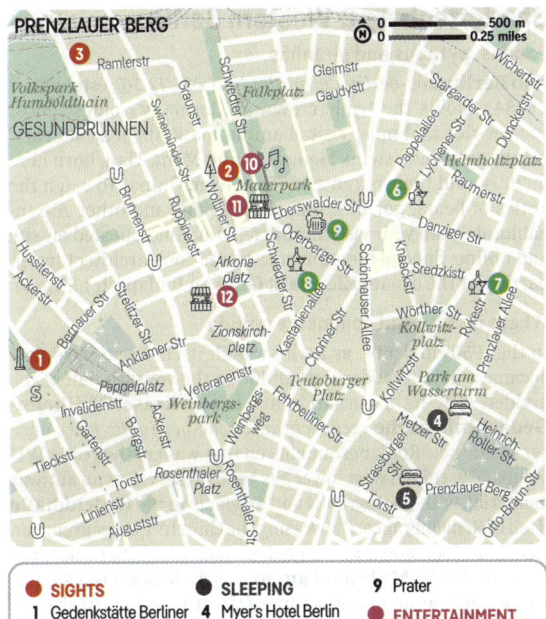

PRENZLAUER BERG

0   500 m
0   0.25 miles

● SIGHTS		● SLEEPING		9 Prater
1	Gedenkstätte Berliner Mauer	4	Myer's Hotel Berlin	● ENTERTAINMENT
2	Mauerpark	5	Soho House Berlin	10 Bearpit Karaoke
● ACTIVITIES		● DRINKING & NIGHTLIFE		● SHOPPING
3	Berliner Unterwelten	6	August Fengler	11 Flohmarkt im Mauerpark
		7	Bryk Bar	12 Trödelmarkt Arkonaplatz
		8	Pluto	

im Mauerpark, snack at street-food stalls, chill in the beer gardens or stake out **Bearpit Karaoke** in the amphitheatre

Legend of a divided city

Though dismantled over 30 years ago, the Berlin Wall continues to capture our collective imagination. You'll find answers to just about any Wall-related question at the **Gedenkstätte Berliner Mauer** (*Berlin Wall Memorial; stiftung-berliner-mauer.de; free*). Along with the superb 1.4km-long outdoor exhibition, visit the **Documentation Centre**'s exhibition – called '1961/1989. The Berlin Wall' – for a concise, engaging history (it's closed on Mondays).

BUDGET-FRIENDLY SIGHTSEEING

One of Berlin's best bargains is a DIY city tour aboard buses 100, 200 and 300, whose routes pass by many of the capital's greatest hits, all for the price of a standard public transport ticket (tariff AB). You have two hours to ride, hop off or switch lines. Better yet, get the 24-hour ticket to explore without the rush.

Bus 100 travels between Berlin-Zoo station and Alexanderplatz, and provides glimpses of landmarks such as the Gedächtniskirche, the Siegessäule, the Reichstag and the Brandenburg Gate.

Bus 200 also links Berlin-Zoo station and Alexanderplatz through a more southerly route via Potsdamer Platz.

Bus 300 connects the Philharmonie and U-Bahn/S-Bahn station Warschauer Strasse via Alexanderplatz and the East Side Gallery.

DRINKING IN PRENZLAUER BERG: OUR PICKS

MAP p465

Prater: Berlin's oldest beer garden (1837) offers custom pilsner and snacks; also has a woodsy beer hall with a full menu. *noon-11.30pm*

Bryk Bar: Sophisticated neighbourly cocktail lab, with classic and next-gen drinks, some starring the house-made Bryk gin. *7pm-1am Tue-Sat*

Pluto: Unpretentious wine bar with burgundy walls, serving biodynamic European wines and seasonal small plates. *5pm-late Thu-Mon*

August Fengler: The flirty party vibe, wallet-friendly prices and mix of locals and visitors make this 1936-born spot a Berlin classic. *6pm-4am*

BEST MURALS IN KREUZBERG

Astronaut/ Kosmonaut Mural: Victor Ash's monumental stencil-style piece was inspired by the US–Soviet space race.

Pink Man Mural: A lone terrified figure crouches on the finger of Blu's scary creature built from writhing pink bodies.

Rounded Heads Mural: Berlin artist Nomad's faceless figure hugs a hooded character in his signature pictogram style, inspired by punk and hip-hop culture.

Yellow Man Mural: Brazilian twins Os Gemeos painted a yellow-skinned, gender-neutral figure in eccentric attire, blending folklore with social messaging.

Nature Morte: Belgian artist ROA's depiction of animal carcasses reflects on the life-and-death cycle of native species within the urban environment.

Charlottenburg & Western Berlin MAP p467

Pandas, pythons and piranhas

Zoo Berlin *(zoo-berlin.de; adult/child €25/12.50)*, established in 1844, holds the triple crown as Germany's oldest, most species-rich and most visited animal park. Its biggest heart-throbs are panda twins Meng Hao and Meng Tian, born here in 2024, and their parents, on loan from China. To catch the antics of bears, gorillas, hippos, sea lions and other zoo inhabitants, plan your visit around feeding times, posted on-site and online. Special mention goes to the zoo's architecture, in particular the ornate **Elephant Gate** on Budapester Strasse.

Where history and commerce collide

In the 1950s and '60s, as Berlin rebuilt itself, Breitscheidplatz became a hub of modern urban life in the western half of the divided city. Its main landmark is the **Kaiser-Wilhelm-Gedächtniskirche** *(gedaechtniskirche-berlin.de; free),* once a majestic neo-Romanesque church that was crushed by WWII bombs. The ruined west tower has been preserved as an antiwar memorial, with photographs and artefacts in the **Gedenkhalle** (Hall of Remembrance) showcasing the church's former grandeur.

Outside, look down at the golden crack in the steps north of the church: the **Mahnmal am Breitscheidplatz** is a simple, striking memorial to the victims of the 2016 terror attack here.

From Hitler to Hertha BSC

Berlin's monumental **Olympiastadion** *(olympiastadion.ber lin; adult/student/under 14yr €11/8/6, tours €17-25),* built by the Nazis for the 1936 Olympic Games, is one of the city's few surviving Third Reich architectural relics. Revamped for the 2006 FIFA World Cup, the coliseum-like venue is now a state-of-the-art space for concerts, sports and major events. It's also the home turf of Berlin soccer team, Hertha BSC.

On non-event days (check the website first), explore the stadium with an optional multimedia guide *(€4).* To see the locker rooms and stadium roof, join a guided tour (some are offered in English).

In the footsteps of Prussian royalty

Schloss Charlottenburg *(spsg.de; day pass to all open buildings adult/student/under 7yr €19/14/free)* is an exquisite palace ensemble and the best place in Berlin to soak up the grandeur of the Hohenzollern clan, who ruled Brandenburg and later Prussia from 1415 to 1918. A visit is especially pleasant in summertime when you can fold a picnic in the palace park into a day of peeking at art, treasures and period rooms. It's closed on Mondays.

 DRINKING IN CHARLOTTENBURG: CLASSIC PUBS MAP p467

Zwiebelfisch: Cosy pub popular with artsy barflies, exemplifying Charlottenburg at its boho best since the 1960s. *noon-2am*

Schleusenkrug: Next to a canal lock, Schleusenkrug has a charming 1950s interior but truly rocks the beer-garden season. *11am-10pm*

Diener Tattersall: Signed stills of celeb patrons decorate this artist pub founded by a heavyweight boxer. *6pm-2am Mon-Sat*

Dicke Wirtin: Stuffed with knick-knacks, this long-standing pub doles out homemade schnapps and hearty local fare. *11am-midnight Wed-Mon*

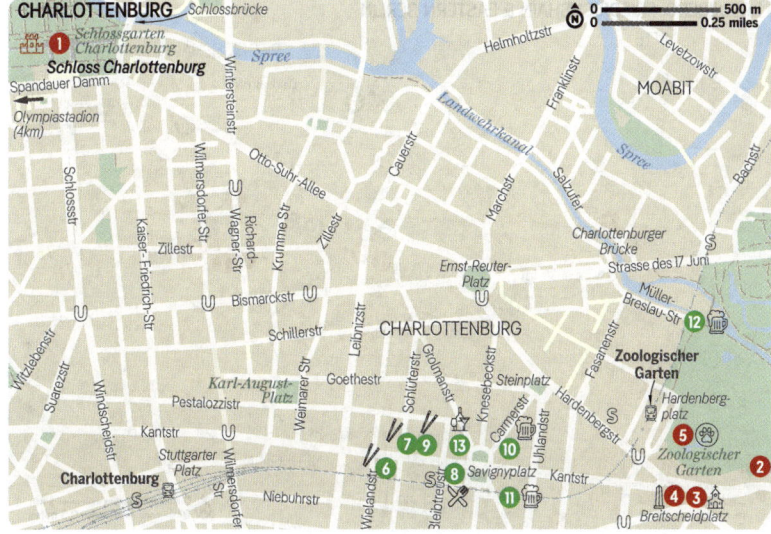

CHARLOTTENBURG — Schlossbrücke

⊕ HIGHLIGHTS
1 Schloss Charlottenburg

● SIGHTS
2 Elephant Gate – Zoo Berlin Entrance

3 Kaiser-Wilhelm-Gedächtniskirche
4 Mahnmal am Breitscheidplatz
5 Zoo Berlin

● EATING
6 893 Ryōtei
7 Good Friends
8 Lo Fūfu
9 Madame Ngo

● DRINKING & NIGHTLIFE
10 Dicke Wirtin
11 Diener Tattersall
12 Schleusenkrug
13 Zwiebelfisch

Kreuzberg

MAP p468

Beacon of enlightenment

The **Jüdisches Museum** *(jmberlin.de; free),* Europe's largest Jewish museum, is an eye-opening destination for anyone curious about Jewish history and culture, regardless of background or belief. The building alone is a showstopper: the zigzagging, zinc-clad masterpiece by American-Polish architect Daniel Libeskind stands as a powerful metaphor for the fractured yet enduring journey of the Jewish people in Germany over the past 1700 years.

Street-food pioneers

Berlin has embraced the global street-food frenzy with the fervour of a newfound convert. It all started back in 2013 with

EATING ON KANTSTRASSE (CHINATOWN): ASIAN RESTAURANTS MAP p467

Lo Fūfu: Bold Italian pairs happily with Japanese precision in this sleek open kitchen. *6-10pm Mon, Thu & Fri, from 1pm Sat & Sun €€*

893 Ryōtei: Glam Japanese den behind a graffiti facade, serving aroma-rich bites with Nikkei influences. Bookings a must. *6-11pm Tue-Sat €€€*

Madame Ngo: This Hanoi-style brasserie makes pho-nomenal soups but also plays with French colonial influences. *noon-10pm €€*

Good Friends: Old-school Chinese-community darling has a long Cantonese menu and great weekday lunch specials. *noon-10.45pm Fri-Wed €€*

467

KREUZBERG, FRIEDRICHSHAIN & EASTERN BERLIN

⭐ **SIGHTS**	**7** Rounded Heads Mural	**12** Katerschmaus	**17** Galander Kreuzberg
1 Astronaut Mural	**8** Tempelhofer Feld	**13** Markthalle Neun	**18** Limonadier
2 East Side Gallery	**9** Yellow Man Mural	**14** Michelberger	
3 Jüdisches Museum	● **SLEEPING**	● **DRINKING**	🔴 **SHOPPING**
4 Karl-Marx-Allee	**10** Kiez Hostel	**& NIGHTLIFE**	**19** Flohmarkt Boxhagener
5 Nature Morte	● **EATING**	**15** Apotheken Bar	Platz
6 Pink Man Mural	**11** Aleppo Supper Club	**16** Bar Franzotti	**20** Nowkoelln Flowmarkt

the launch of **Street Food Thursday** at **Markthalle Neun** (*markthalleneun.de)*, a historic market hall that also hosts a popular farmers market on Friday and Saturday. The weekly Thursday snack-athon, which runs from 5pm to 10pm, remains a solid fixture on Berlin's culinary lineup and has also propelled numerous aspiring chefs to prominence.

Neukölln

MAP p468

Field of freedom

The airfield of **Tempelhofer Feld** (*tempelhoferfeld.de; free)* that so gloriously handled the Berlin Airlift of 1948–49 has been repurposed as one of the world's largest urban parks. In this steadily evolving open-sky adventure playground, cyclists

 DRINKING IN KREUZBERG: COCKTAIL BARS ──────── MAP p468

Apothekenbar: Get your hands on a potent Penicillin at this charming cocktail bar in a retired 150-year-old pharmacy. *6pm-1am or later*

Limonadier: Top-shelf spirits make for a night of sophisticated drinking at this cocktail cavern with a sensuous 1920s vibe. *7pm-2am Tue-Sat*

Bar Franzotti: Overwhelmed by the 1000+ spirits at this vintage-style bar? Let the bartender whip up a cocktail tailored for you. *7pm-2am Mon-Sat*

Galander Kreuzberg: Leather armchairs and flattering lighting create an intimate ambience for the expert drinks at great prices. *6pm-1am Wed-Sun*

and bladers zip down old runways, while fun zones include barbecue areas, community gardens and basketball courts. In spring, Skudde sheep roll in to serve as natural lawnmowers.

Friedrichshain & Eastern Berlin

MAP p468

Political oppression in East Germany

Thousands of offices across 40 buildings served as the nerve centre of East Germany's most feared institution, the Ministry of State Security, better known as Stasi, until 1989. House 1 is now home to the **Stasimuseum** (stasimuseum.de; adult/student/under 12yr €12/6/free, tours additional €5), where exhibits unpack the organisation's origins, working methods and far-reaching grip on East German society and beyond.

Secrets, cells and fear

Victims of Stasi persecution often ended up at the infamous **Stasi Prison** (stiftung-hsh.de; adult/concession €9/5), now a memorial site called Gedenkstätte Berlin-Hohenschönhausen. Between 1951 and 1989, over 11,000 suspected regime opponents were held in this vast remand facility, about 30 minutes' ride on tram M5 from Alexanderplatz.

Book a time slot online for a punch-in-the-gut tour through this claustrophobic warren, including peeks inside cells and interrogation rooms. Don't be shy to ask questions. For a deeper understanding of prison life and the Stasi surveillance machine, budget some time for the two on-site exhibitions.

Grim history, glorious art

Along Mühlenstrasse, a 1.3km stretch was saved from the Berlin Wall to become the **East Side Gallery** (eastsidegalleryberlin.de; free). Featuring more than 100 paintings by international artists, the world's largest open-air gallery stands as a testament to the peaceful revolution unfurling German reunification.

The East Side Gallery runs between Ostbahnhof and the Oberbaumbrücke; kick off your stroll at either end. Each mural has a QR code you can scan to learn about the artwork and its creator. Also watch out for the shiny information stelae with historical bites. On many weekends, multilingual guides stand by to answer any burning Wall-related questions.

EAST BERLIN'S MONUMENTAL BOULEVARD

Friedrichshain brims with monumental architecture, but nothing quite matches the pomp and scale of **Karl-Marx-Allee**, a 2.3km stretch of socialist showmanship between Frankfurter Tor and Alexanderplatz. Stroll down this 90m-wide boulevard, known until 1961 as 'Stalinallee'. Bilingual information panels unpack the architecture and history. Restaurants, galleries and shops inject contemporary vibrancy.

Living in these monumental 'workers' palaces' was considered a privilege reserved for party loyalists. The apartments featured central heating, lifts, tiled baths and built-in kitchens – serious luxury for the time. The most impressive buildings, riffing on Moscow's wedding-cake style, were constructed from 1952 to 1960 between Strausberger Platz and Frankfurter Tor.

 EATING IN FRIEDRICHSHAIN: OUR PICKS MAP p468

Michelberger: Locally adored all-day spot with upscale bistro fare made with ingredients from small producers and its own farm. *7am-11pm* €€	**Katerschmaus:** Light lunches and a meat-focused dinner menu, plus Spree views, at this spot below Holzmarkt. *noon-3pm & 6-10pm Mon-Sat* €€	**Aleppo Supper Club:** At his pint-sized cafe, Samer Hafez dishes up Syrian soul food enriched with 'secret' spices and made for sharing. *11.30am-11pm* €€	**Hafenküche:** Marina spot with self-service lunches, modern German dinners and Spreedeck beer-garden snacks. *noon-3pm Sat & Sun, 6-9.30pm Wed-Sun* €€

Potsdam

FAIRY-TALE PALACE | COLD WAR HISTORY | LAKESIDE DELIGHTS

GETTING AROUND

Potsdam is about 35km southwest of Berlin. It can be reached in under an hour from central Berlin, on the S-Bahn (S1 or S7). The city lies within Berlin's C fare zone, so you'll need an ABC ticket.

Walking or cycling are the best ways to explore Potsdam; rent a bike from Pedales outside the Hauptbahnhof. Schloss Sanssouci is 3km from the train station and is served by buses 614 and 695.

☑ TOP TIP

The Potsdam tourist office maintains a branch at the Mobiagentur Potsdam in the Hauptbahnhof and another on Alter Markt in the historic centre near Museum Barberini. Sanssouci Park sits west of the Altstadt, while the Neuer Garten with Schloss Cecilienhof is north. Babelsberg is about 4km east of central Potsdam.

Potsdam, the state capital of Brandenburg, is home to magnificent palaces and gardens embraced by lakes and the Havel River. It's an essential stop if you're spending any time in the region at all. Leading the roll call of royal pads is Schloss Sanssouci, a charming mini-Versailles and summer refuge of Frederick the Great with a splendid park. No wonder UNESCO gave World Heritage Status to large parts of the city in 1990.

Most people visit on a day trip from Berlin, but you'll need more time if you don't want to miss out on its many other attractions. Find out why there's a Dutch Quarter, visit the palace that hosted the Potsdam Conference, peer behind the walls of a sinister KGB prison and soak up splendid vistas on a cruise along the tranquil lakes embracing this enticing city.

Stepping into Potsdam's Past

Restored historic centre

Potsdam's biggest stunner is **Schloss Sanssouci** (*Sanssouci Palace; spsg.de; adult/student/under 7yr €22/17/free*). The rococo palace sits daintily above vine-draped terraces with Frederick the Great's grave nearby. Sanssouci's resplendent **park** (*free*), Potsdam's oldest, is dotted with palaces reflecting the Italian obsession of successor Friedrich Wilhelm IV (1795–1861).

Although much of Potsdam's historic town centre fell victim to WWII bombing and socialist town planning, it's been nicely restored for exploring on foot. Potsdam's own **Brandenburger Tor** (*free*), modelled after Rome's Arch of Constantine, is a gateway to the main shopping street, Brandenburger Strasse. The pedestrian drag links with the scenic **Holländisches Viertel** (Dutch Quarter).

Alter Markt, the old market square, is anchored by an obelisk and lorded over by the domed **St Nikolai-Kirche** (*nikolai-potsdam.de*); clamber up 216 steps to the church's viewing **platform** (*€5*). Finally, in **Altstadt**, don't miss exploring Impressionist masterpieces at the **Museum Barberini** (*museum-barberini.de; adult/child €18/free*).

Cologne

GRAND CATHEDRAL | RHENISH JOIE DE VIVRE | ART MUSEUMS

Founded by the Romans, Cologne (Köln) offers a mother lode of attractions, led by its famous cathedral with filigree twin spires dominating the skyline. The museum scene is outstanding when it comes to art, but the city will also inspire fans of chocolate, sports and history.

Cologne's spirited locals are known for their liberal outlook and zest for life. Join them in the Pride celebration (one of Germany's biggest) in July, and in the beer halls of the Altstadt or bars in the student-centric Zülpicher Viertel, trendy Belgisches Viertel or gritty Ehrenfeld. Cologne also has an excellent electronic-music club scene.

Shopping is a popular pastime, with a fun mix of eclectic boutiques, and designer and vintage stores scattered throughout the neighbourhoods. For mainstream shopping, stroll along Hohe Strasse in the city centre, one of Germany's oldest pedestrianised shopping strips. Souvenir hunters should seek out the classic outlets selling the famous eau de cologne.

GETTING AROUND

Cologne is eminently walkable, and places further afield can easily be reached by public transport, bicycle or e-scooter. Radstation behind the Hauptbahnhof rents bikes.

Cologne's Pride & Joy

Uncover endless cathedral treasure

Cologne's geographical and spiritual heart is the magnificent, UNESCO-listed **Kölner Dom** *(koelner-dom.de; tower adult/ child €8/4)*. It's a treasure-packed, centuries-long pilgrimage site, home to a powerful diocese centre.

Top billing inside belongs to the jewel-encrusted, gilded **Shrine of the Magi** (main altar). The basilica-shaped sarcophagus allegedly contains the remains of the three kings who followed the celestial star to Bethlehem. The bones were spirited out of Milan in 1164 by Emperor Barbarossa.

The Dom's newest stained-glass window, unveiled in 2007, is the **Richter Fenster** (south transept). The work of Germany's most important living artist, Cologne-based Gerhard Richter, it weaves together 11,500 square glass panes in 72 vibrant hues (a twist on Richter's 1974 work, *4096 Colors*).

☑ **TOP TIP**

The city's excellent website *(museenkoeln.de)* has information on most of Cologne's museums. The **MuseumsCard** *(individual/ family €18/30)* is good for one-time admission to all municipal museums on two consecutive days and free public transport on the first day. Buy it online, at the tourist office opposite the cathedral or at participating museums.

Take the 533 steps up the Dom's **south tower** that dwarfed all European buildings before the Eiffel Tower. En route to the 95m-high viewing platform, admire the 24-tonne **St Peter's Bell**, the world's largest free-swinging working bell.

From the Dom's heights, saunter into the vaulted medieval cellars of the **Domschatzkammer** (treasury), which practically spills over with precious reliquaries, robes, sculptures and liturgical objects.

A Romp Around Western Art

Visit a dazzling art museum

Museum Ludwig (*museum-ludwig.de; adult/child €12/free*), in a shed-roof building near the Dom, owes its reputation to a sublime collection of global modern art. In light-filled galleries you can binge on Picasso, pop art, Pollock and photography, or linger over German expressionists and the Russian avant-garde. Works rotate regularly because there's only room to show off one-third of the collection at a time, with the rest of the space reserved for temporary exhibitions. These dig into everything from post-colonial critique and identity politics to rising voices in global contemporary art and less well-known chapters of modernism.

Kölner Dom (p471)

Hail to the Ancient Romans

Tracking down Cologne's origins

Some 2000 years ago, Cologne was a thriving Roman city with temples, paved roads, an aqueduct and stone houses. Nobody knows how much of its ancient history still lurks beneath the modern city, but plenty of what's been dug up already can be admired in the **Römisch-Germanisches Museum** (*roemisch-germanisches-museum.de; adult/child €6/free*).

While its original 1970s home by the Dom is getting a serious facelift until at least 2030, highlights from its vast collection are on view in the Belgisches Haus near Neumarkt (closed Tuesdays). Standouts include a sculpture of Hercules mid-battle with a lion and a delicate marble torso dubbed the 'Kölsche Venus'. There's also remarkably well-preserved glassware and items from daily life like toys, tweezers, lamps and jewellery, the designs of which have changed little over time.

Ancient Roman ruins are scattered all over town. When checking out the dome, stop by the **Roman Arch** on the cathedral plaza, once part of the northern gateway to the Roman colony. Over at Zeughausstrasse 13 is the **Römerturm**

EXPLORING DOM DEEPER

Construction of Cologne's landmark cathedral began in 1248 in the French Gothic style but was suspended in 1560 for lack of money. The half-built church lingered for nearly three centuries and even served as a horse stable and prison during the Napoleonic occupation. A sizeable cash infusion from Prussian king Friedrich Wilhelm IV finally led to its completion in 1880. Miraculously, the cathedral got through WWII bombing raids with nary a shrapnel wound.

Kölner Dom has plenty of delights that must be experienced on guided tours (in English, upon request). Dive into the building's Roman-era roots on an archaeological tour, or climb to lofty heights to study its industrial-era filigree-iron roof truss or to get close-ups of its famous bells. Book on *domfuehrungen-koeln.de*.

EATING IN COLOGNE: OUR PICKS

Neobiota: Michelin-starred lair with breakfast until 3pm and innovative multicourse dinners in a casual setting. *10am-3pm & 7-11pm Tue-Sat* €€€

Bei Oma Kleinmann: Old-school, family-owned restaurant that has fed generations with schnitzel and other German fare. *5pm-midnight Mon-Sat* €€

Chum Chay: First-class plant-based Vietnamese at economy prices in Belgian Quarter; try the curry with rambutan and lychee. *noon-10pm Mon-Sat* €

Bad Ape: Cheerful lunch spot that doles out gourmet salads, low-gluten sandwiches and excellent coffee; lots of vegan options. *10am-6pm Tue-Sat* €

KÖLSCH PRIMER

Cologne has its own style of beer, Kölsch, which is light, hoppy, slightly sweet and served cool in *Stangen* – skinny, straight glasses that only hold 0.2L. In traditional Cologne beer halls and pubs you don't order beer so much as subscribe; the constantly prowling servers, called *Köbes*, will ply you with another round until you indicate you've had enough by placing a beermat on top of your glass.

A ceaseless flow of *Stangen* filled with Kölsch, along with earthy humour and platters of meaty local foods, are the hallmarks of Cologne's famed beer halls. A local speciality served on select days is *Reibekuchen* (or *Rievkooche* in the local dialect), traditional potato pancakes.

PAI VEGA/SHUTTERSTOCK

Schokoladenmuseum

(Roman Tower) that formed the northwest corner of the 4km-long Roman city wall.

Chocolate Paradise

Sweet museum treat

Cologne's **Schokoladenmuseum** (*schokoladenmuseum.de; adult/student/under 6yr Mon-Fri €15.50/9/free, Sat & Sun €17/10.50/free*) is a sleek, boat-shaped temple to the 'elixir of the gods' (as the Aztecs referred to chocolate), anchored at the tip of the old city port just south of the Altstadt. Its centrepiece is a walk-through **chocolate factory** that lifts the lid on the bean-to-bar process. Watch chocolatiers handcraft truffles and pralines, and find out how hollow bunnies are born. The interactive 'Cocoa's Journey Through Time' exhibition traces 5000 years of the cultural history of chocolate, from its pre-Columbian origins to its rise as a royal indulgence and the dawn of the chocolate vending machine. For an extra €3, you can cap your tour with a 30-minute **tasting session** (also offered in English). Or head straight to the glorious finale: dipping a wafer into the museum's famous 3m-high **fountain** flowing with 200kg of warm melted Lindt chocolate.

Dodge the crowds by visiting on a weekday, and save time by buying your time-slot ticket online.

Cologne's Creative Underbelly

Ehrenfeld street-art exploration

While Cologne is celebrated for its fine-arts scene, the city's streets are just as expressive. Murals, stencils, stickers, graffiti

– it's all out there, especially in Ehrenfeld, a former working-class *Veedel* (Cologne slang for 'neighbourhood') that's evolved into an eclectic cross-cultural cauldron of creativity.

Urban art royalty like Herakut, El Bocho, Stohead and M-City have splashed colour across once drab walls, often as part of the **CityLeaks Urban Art Festival** *(cityleaks-festival.de)*. The festival's been on hiatus since 2021 (a revival is planned) but the CityLeaks crew still runs street-art tours of Ehrenfeld and the Südstadt. Tours are also offered by **Alternative Cologne Tours** *(alternativecolognetours.com)*.

One of the most powerful pieces is right at Ehrenfeld train station: a tribute to local Nazi resistance group Edelweiss-piraten by hometown spraymeisters Captain Borderline. It's on Schönsteinstrasse, right under the railway arch where the SS publicly hanged 13 of the group's members in late 1944.

Christian Art Progressively Staged

Religious museum for the 21st century

Art, history, architecture and spirituality collide brilliantly at **Kolumba** *(kolumba.de; adult/child €8/free)*, the quietly striking art museum of the Archdiocese of Cologne. Designed by renowned Swiss architect Peter Zumthor, the minimalist structure encases the ruins of the late-Gothic church of St Kolumba, destroyed during WWII.

Start in the airy foyer, where an oversized steel door swings open into a cavernous, almost meditative space. A wooden walkway zigzags over exposed archaeological layers going back to Roman times, while soft daylight dancing through the perforated facade creates a sense of calm and mystery.

The actual galleries are up a steep staircase and are changed every September. However, the concept stays the same: modern art juxtaposed with sacral objects, creating a surprising dialogue between old and new. A wood-panelled library with leather chairs invites quiet reading or simply zoning out. Don't skip the **Madonna in the Ruins** chapel, an octagonal structure built from war debris in 1950; its separate entrance is on Brückenstrasse.

CARNIVAL: FOOLS, FLOATS & REVELRY

Called the 'fifth season', **Karneval** *(koelnerkarneval.de)* is one of Cologne's wildest parties, when the city collectively loses the plot over street parades, packed pubs and way too much Kölsch. Festivities peak in the week before Lent, kicking off on **Weiberfastnacht** (Thursday), when women playfully chop off ties and take charge. Over the weekend, parades featuring wacky homemade floats criss-cross the local neighbourhoods. By the time it all comes to a head with the big parade on **Rosenmontag** (Rose Monday), the entire city has come unglued. Swaying and drinking while crammed in a pub, or following other costumed fools behind a huge bass drum leading to who-knows-where, you'll be swept up in one of the world's most unhinged celebrations.

 EATING IN COLOGNE: FAST FOOD

Kebapland: Cologne's top kebab: marinated meat, charcoal-grilled and served with local flavour in Ehrenfeld. *11.30am-1am Sun-Thu, to 3am Fri & Sat* €

Freddy Schilling: Burgers in the Zülpicher Viertel student quarter: meaty or plant-based organic patties, home-made sauces, hand-cut fries. *noon-10pm* €

Rievkoochebud: Made-to-order local-style potato pancakes, a perfect preparation for an Altstadt drink-a-thon. *noon-8pm Wed-Sat, to 6pm Sun* €

Curry B: Join the queue for Cologne's *Currywurst* – fried bratwurst, slivered and slathered with house-made spicy curry ketchup. *11am-8pm Mon-Sat* €

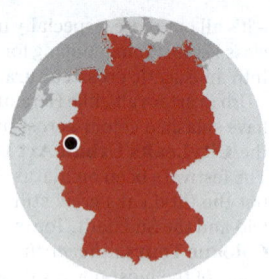

Düsseldorf

ALTBIER BARS | AVANT-GARDE ART | BOLD ARCHITECTURE

GETTING AROUND

Rheinbahn *(rheinbahn. de)* operates an extensive network of U-Bahn trains, trams and buses throughout Düsseldorf. Tickets are available from bus drivers and vending machines at U-Bahn and tram stops, and must be validated upon boarding. Tickets bought inside vehicles are pre-validated.

Düsseldorf impresses with edgy architecture, nightlife that doesn't quit and an art scene to rival many flashier cities. At first, the capital of North Rhine–Westphalia may seem all buttoned-up business: banking, advertising, fashion and telecoms have helped make it one of Germany's wealthiest cities. Yet all it takes is a bar-hop around the Altstadt to realise that locals have no problem letting their hair down once they shed those Boss jackets. Nicknamed the 'longest bar in the world', this historic riverside quarter is packed with enough energy to keep things going well into the night. Down by the redeveloped harbour, Medienhafen is a parade of bold avant-garde architecture by international design-meisters. Urban explorers should check out creative and style-savvy neighbourhoods like Flingern and Unterbilk that offer fun shopping, laid-back cafes and good people-watching. For prime ramen and sushi, venture to Little Tokyo, the hub of Düsseldorf's huge Japanese community.

The Altstadt Beyond Beer

Hidden wonders, history, culinary delights

Düsseldorf's Altstadt is (in)famous for its 300-plus bars. Beyond partying, museums and historical gems make a case for visiting during daytime.

The **K20** *(kunstsammlung.de; adult/student/chld €9/5/ free)* is a powerhouse of modern art, from Klee, Picasso and Mondrian to seminal non-European heavyweights like Etel Adnan, Lygia Pape and Rasheed Araneen. Veer off Rheinufer-promenade to the **Hetjens Museum** *(duesseldorf.de/hetjens; adult/child €5/free),* covering 8000 years of world ceramic art.

On Burgplatz, the **Schlossturm** *(schifffahrtmuseum.de; adult/child €3/free)* is all that remains of Düsseldorf's old palace; it houses a small Rhine-focussed **museum**. The **Markt am Carlsplatz** *(carlsplatz-markt.de)* is a prime foodie playground.

☑ **TOP TIP**

The **Düsseldorf tourist office** *(duesseldorf-tourismus.de)* in the Altstadt has a wealth of printed information and staff eager to help with lodging, events tickets and the Düsseldorf Card. It also organises well-done city tours, including an Urban Art Walk, an Altstadt Beer Safari and a Sound of Düsseldorf music expedition.

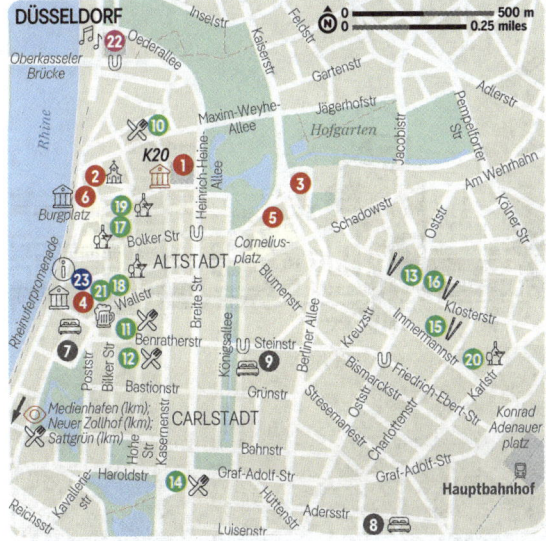

DÜSSELDORF

Inselstr *Oederallee* *Oberkasseler Brücke* *Feldstr* *Gartenstr* *Adlerstr* *Kaiserstr* *Maxim-Weyhe-Allee* *Jägerhofstr* *Jacobistr* *Pempelforter Str* *Heinrich-Heine-Allee* *Hofgarten* *Am Wehrhahn* *Bölker Str* *Cornelius-platz* *Schadowstr* *Oststr* *Kölner Str* *Blumenstr* *ALTSTADT* *Breite Str* *Königsallee* *Berliner Allee* *Kreuzstr* *Klosterstr* *Immermannstr* *Karlstr* *Wallstr* *Benratherstr* *Steinstr* *Bismarckstr* *Friedrich-Ebert-Str* *Konrad Adenauer platz* *Bastionstr* *Grünstr* *Stresemannstr* *Charlottenstr* *Bilker Str* *Kasernenstr* *Hohe Str* *CARLSTADT* *Bahnstr* *Graf-Adolf-Str* *Graf-Adolf-Str* *Haroldstr* *Hüttenstr* *Adlerstr* *Hauptbahnhof* *Reichsstr* *Kavallerie str* *Luisenstr*

Rhine • Rheinuferpromenade • Burgplatz • K20

Medienhafen (1km); Neuer Zollhof (1km); Sattgrün (1km)

0 — 500 m
0 — 0.25 miles

● **HIGHLIGHTS**
1 K20

● **SIGHTS**
2 Basilika St Lambertus
3 Dreischeibenhaus
4 Hetjens Museum
5 Kö-Bogen I & II
6 Schlossturm & SchifffahrtMuseum

● **SLEEPING**
7 Hotel Orangerie

8 Max Hotel Garni
9 Ruby Coco Hotel

● **EATING**
10 Brauerei im Füchschen
11 Markt am Carlsplatz
12 Münstermann Kontor
13 Naniwa
14 Pelican Fly
15 Takumi
16 Yabase

● **DRINKING & NIGHTLIFE**
17 Elephant Bar
18 Et Kabüffke
19 Melody
20 Sakura Bar
21 Uerige

● **ENTERTAINMENT**
22 Tonhalle

● **INFORMATION**
23 Tourist Office – Altstadt

DÜSSELDORF'S ARCHITECTURAL MARVELS

Kö-Bogen I & II: Daniel Libeskind's Kö-Bogen I caps the Königsallee with angular glass and limestone. Kö-Bogen II is practically a vertical park.

Basilika St Lambertus: The twisted spire of this Gothic church is not a design quirk – warped by a storm, it was deliberately left that way.

Tonhalle: An expressionist 1920s jewel, Düsseldorf's premier concert hall has a ribbed blue dome and started out as a planetarium.

Dreischeibenhaus: This 94m-high tower gets its name from the three offset slim slabs *(Scheiben);* it was a symbol of Germany's postwar economic recovery.

Neuer Zollhof: Stainless steel meets playful asymmetry in a trio of shimmering buildings that turned Medienhafen into a contemporary art piece.

Industrial Harbour Reimagined

Architectural port of call

Where dockworkers once hauled cargo, creative minds now forge ad campaigns and brainstorm headlines. The **Medienhafen** *(Media Harbour; medienhafen.de)* is Düsseldorf's boldest urban revitalisation project. The old commercial harbour is now a striking lineup of avant-garde buildings by top architects. Frank Gehry's **Neuer Zollhof** draws the most

---

🍸 **DRINKING IN DÜSSELDORF: ALTSTADT FAVES**

Uerige: Traditional Altbier brewpub with hearty snacks, local colour aplenty and a merry crowd that often spills into the street. *10am-midnight*

Et Kabüffke: Chase your Altbier with a shot of Killepitsch (local liqueur blending 90 fruits, herbs and spices) served through the window. *11am-midnight*

Melody: Island of sophistication among the boisterous Altstadt bars, with quality cocktails and eggnog made by the owner. *10pm-late Wed-Sat*

Elephant Bar: Good drinks and good times at this James Bond–style '60s bar with complexion-friendly lighting and mellow sounds. *6pm-late Wed-Sat*

SAIKO3P/SHUTTERSTOCK

Medienhafen (p477)

camera clicks – a trio of warped towers sheathed in stainless steel, red brick and white plaster, respectively.

For a different selfie angle, head to the promontory below the Hyatt Regency Hotel, anchored by a silver-clad, egg-shaped bar that buzzes in summer. From this spot, the full sweep of Medienhafen with the Rheinturm TV tower is Insta-gold. There's also a two-hour **Media Harbour Tour** *(€20)* run by Düsseldorf Tourism.

Japanese Flavours & Culture

Tokyo on the Rhine

Düsseldorf's **Little Tokyo** is the commercial heart of the city's sizeable Japanese expat community. Centred on Immermannstrasse, just outside the Hauptbahnhof, this buzzing strip is chock-a-block with ramen joints, sushi bars, manga shops and Japanese supermarkets. Local faves for slurping ramen include **Takumi** and **Naniwa**, while **Yabase** is tops for sushi and **Sakura Bar** for cocktails.

 EATING IN DÜSSELDORF: OUR PICKS

Münstermann Kontor: Buzzy bistro with seasonal pan-European dishes that are both creative and down-to-earth. *noon-8pm Tue-Fri, from 11am Sat* €€€

Brauerei Im Füchschen: Boisterous and full of local colour – the 'Little Fox' is a true Rhenish beer hall. *11am-midnight Wed-Sun, from 3pm Mon & Tue* €€

Pelican Fly: 'Berlin-style *Imbiss*' (snack bar) reborn as a fries-and-wine bar in a retro-styled pavilion. *noon-3pm & 5pm-midnight Mon-Thu, noon-midnight Fri & Sat* €

Sattgrün: Cheerful vegan self-service buffet with international dishes in three sizes and two branches in the Medienhafen and Flingern. *noon-10pm* €

Hamburg

MARITIME HISTORY | INNOVATIVE ARCHITECTURE | NIGHTLIFE

Hamburg is one of Europe's coolest, most affluent cities, but most people don't know that – the vibe is just that unpretentious. Germany's largest port and second-largest city merits its historic label 'the gateway to the world'. It's been hustling since medieval times, especially in the late 19th and early 20th centuries, cultivating quiet wealth via global trade. Innovative architecture and sustainability shape a stylish, media-savvy modern city, yet Hamburg stays true to its maritime soul – embodied in endless, glimmering blues and squawking gulls. Today's zeniths include vibrant subcultures, lively neighbourhoods, and a performance scene defined by rising stars (which once included the Beatles). No, hamburgers weren't invented here (though patties are inspired by local cooks). And yes, the nightlife extends far beyond the notorious Reeperbahn red-light district. Rest assured, no matter where you drop anchor in Hamburg, it's a safe haven for letting the good times roll.

☑ **TOP TIP**

Undeterred by the infamous *Schmuddelwetter* (drizzly weather), Hamburgers have come up with inventive ways to enjoy the Elbe. No matter the weather, **StrandPauli** *(strandpauli. de)*, a sandy beach bar, is a lively favourite. If it's chilly, board the moored party boat **Frau Hedi** *(frauhedi. de)* where disco evenings get sweaty.

From Chambers to Courtyard
Uncover City Hall's hidden features

Hamburg's 1897 **Rathaus** *(hamburg-travel.com; tours adult/ child €5/free)* is a 647-room beehive full of fascinating, beautiful details. Currently the seat of Senate and Parliament, it's

GETTING AROUND

Hamburg's excellent public-transport system (trains, buses, trams) will take you all around the city and into suburban neighbourhoods.

Bikes are free on public trains outside peak hours (6am to 9am and 4pm to 6pm). Download the **StadtRAD** *(stadtrad.hamburg. de)* app for cross-city bike-sharing. Driving is easy, but parking is a pain. Uber vehicles are limited and not worth long pickup waits; rely on taxis instead.

For an authentically local experience, board a **Hadag commuter ferry**. The **St Pauli Piers** is the key hub for seven Elbe lines used primarily by locals. The most important for sightseers is 62 – a seven-minute commute to the **Elbphilharmonie** (p481) pier.

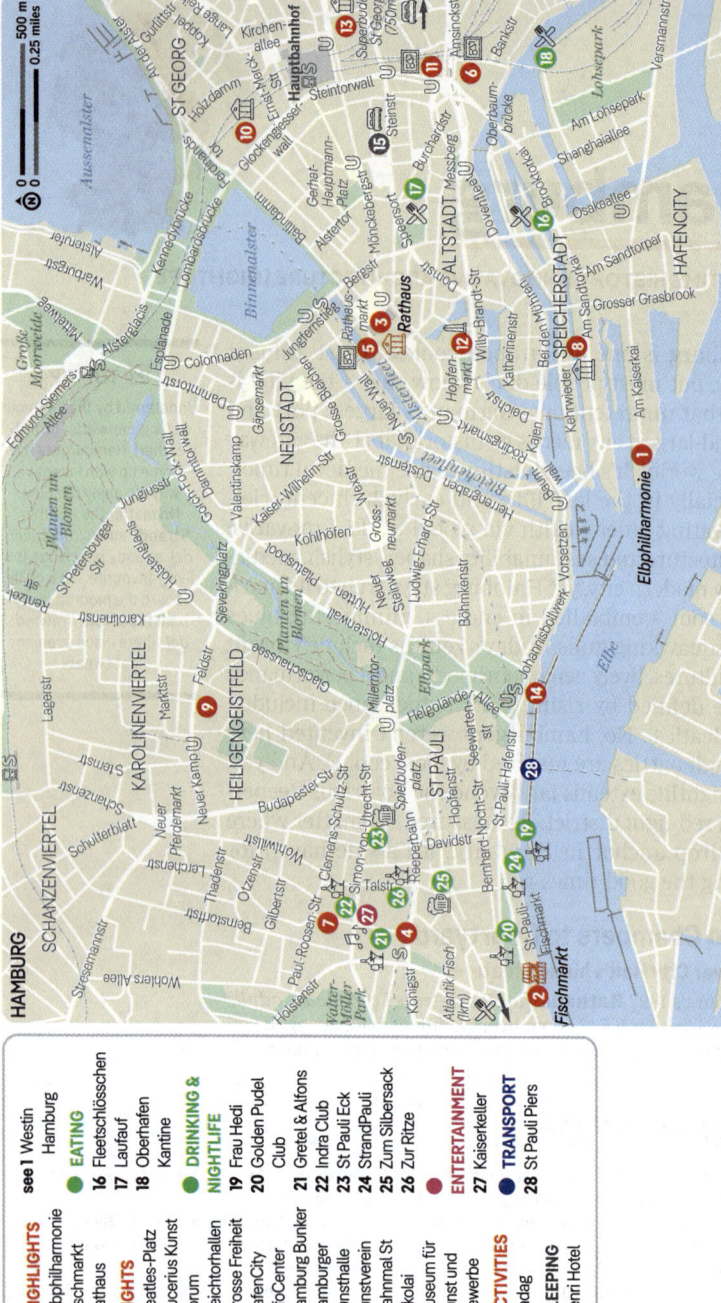

HAMBURG

one of Europe's most opulent, still-functioning government buildings.

On a guided tour (see the website for booking information), you'll wind through a fraction of the building's maze of chambers. The most renowned are the **Kaisersaal** (Emperor's Hall), a lavish, neobaroque vision once designed to host Emperor Wilhelm II during visits, and the **Grosser Festsaal** (Great Hall) ceremonial room.

Tours aside, march through the Grand Entrance Hall during opening hours and take in its 'hidden' courtyard. Take breaks on comfy chairs with tables overlooking the eternally gorgeous Hygieia Fountain. The female bronze figure, the Greek goddess of health, commemorates Germany's last major cholera epidemic in 1892.

Historic Fish Sammies

Wake up early for the Fischmarkt

Wake up early on Sunday (or stay up Saturday night) to hit Hamburg's legendary **Fischmarkt** (*fischauktionshalle.com; free*), a port tradition since 1703. Over 70,000 people attend the weekly market, which is open from 5am to 9.30am April to October and from 7am November to March. Whether you're a morning person or not, the Fischmarkt is a truly energising, one-of-a-kind sunrise experience. Get caught up in its signature tidal wave of high-sensory shenanigans, from noisy vendors to smoky fish grilling.

The iconic specialities are the *fischbrötchen* (fish sandwiches) topped with decadent North Sea and Elber River delights. The assortment is incredible: pickled herring, smoked salmon, fried or grilled fish fillets, regional shrimp or crab, you name it.

Breakfast in hand, head to the historic **Fish Auction Hall**, inaugurated in 1896 and a testament to Hamburg's long-standing maritime heritage. While the building once hosted fish auctions, today it's a live-entertainment venue. Consider German *Schlager* (cheesy pop) and rock cover bands your 6am wake-up call.

Musical Heights & Iconic Architecture

Discover the Elbphilharmonie

Perched majestically over the Elbe River, the **Elbphilharmonie** (*elbphilharmonie.de; tickets €20-150*) is one of Europe's most exciting and recent architectural feats.

The landmark 2017-unveiled building harmonises old and new. Striking glass rises high above Hamburg's skyline, framing a

WELCOME TO THE WATERFRONT

The **Speicherstadt** is the largest warehouse district in the world, where the buildings stand on timber-pile foundations – oak logs, in this particular case. The seven-storey red-brick warehouses lining the Speicherstadt archipelago are a famous Hamburg symbol and they're increasingly filled with fine museums.

Meanwhile, the neighbouring **HafenCity** quarter, part of the port area where Speicherstadt is located, is a world seemingly being created before your eyes. Wander around and check out the Kesselhaus (Old Boiler House) where the **HafenCity InfoCenter** (*hafencity. com/infocenter*) is located; the information office is closed on Mondays. A room-sized scale model of Hamburg shows the full vision of HafenCity's expected completion in 2030 (it's only about 50% there).

 EATING IN HAMBURG: NORTHERN GERMAN SPECIALITIES

Fleetschlösschen: Overlook a Speicherstadt canal while eating Northern-style fish dishes with cucumber salad and remoulade. *11am-10pm* €€

Laufauf: North German dishes like *Bratheringe* (fried herring) in Altstadt. Well-priced lunch specials. *11.30am-10pm Mon-Fri, from 1pm Sat* €€

Oberhafen Kantine: Traditional Hamburg fare beneath a HafenCity train bridge. *5-9.30pm Tue, noon-9.30pm Wed-Sat, noon-5.30pm Sun* €€

Atlantik Fisch: Altona-based cafe run by a seafood vendor; offering 20 different *Fischbrötchen* (fish sandwiches). *6am-4pm Mon-Fri, from 7am Sat* €€

HAMBURG'S ART MILE

Enjoy Hamburg's five-pack of renowned art institutions, aka the Kunstmeile, with a three-day **Art Mile Pass** (kunstmeile-hamburg.de; €35).

Hamburger Kunsthalle: World-renowned museum with a treasure trove of period-spanning masterpieces.

Bucerius Kunst Forum: Private art museum with four annual exhibitions; multimedia links contemporary society and antiquity.

Museum für Kunst und Gewerbe: Europe's foremost, oldest applied arts institution: sculptures, jewellery, ceramics and more.

Deichtorhallen: Two industrial halls – one for modern/documentary photography, another for large-scale contemporary art.

Kunstverein: Long-established local art association for emerging contemporary and conceptual art.

Hamburg Bunker

restored historic brick warehouse. Inside, a one-of-a-kind concert hall has exceptional acoustics and a stunning auditorium orchestrating immersive symphony and musical experiences.

Architects allegedly drew inspiration from the Ancient Greek theatre at Delphi, sport stadiums and tents. The building's glass structure with its wave-like roof is meant to mimic the ethereal, floating quality of a hoisted sail, water wave, iceberg or quartz crystal. It provides contrast to the 1963-built heavy brick warehouse it sits atop.

Catching a concert in the state-of-the-art surrounds here is an unforgettable experience. Don't miss taking Europe's longest escalator up to the viewing platform, a 360-degree wrap-around balcony providing dizzying city and harbour perspectives.

Concrete Rooftop Garden

Scale the Hamburg Bunker

An anomaly on Hamburg's skyline, the brooding WWII concrete structure **Hamburg Bunker** (hamburgbunker.com;

 DRINKING IN ST PAULI: PUB CRAWL

Zur Ritze: Pass between the painted legs of this Reeperbahn pub's entrance. Inside, it's a serious drinking den. *hours vary*

Golden Pudel Club: Tiny bar-club in a 19th-century bootleggers' jail. Programming prize underground bands and vinyl DJs. *10pm-6am*

Zum Silbersack: Diverse crowd and cheap drinks make for weird and wild evenings. Down an infamous caraway shot. *5pm-2am Mon-Thu, to 3am Fri & Sat, to 1am Sun*

St Pauli Eck: A quintessential German pub: jukebox, stiff pours and gruff staff behind a cluttered bar. *5pm-late Mon-Sat*

free) – a former air-raid shelter – was transformed in 2024 into a panoramic cultural attraction. Climb the cement-poured 'mountain path' up to a rooftop urban garden for unparalleled, 360-degree views across the city.

Though it's a gargantuan, painful reminder of the Nazi era, demolition was never realistic here. The amount of explosives required for demolition would likely raze the surrounding residential area. Today, it endures as a multi-purpose building holding everything from a hotel to a nightclub and cafe.

The highlight, however, is a 10,000-sq-metre rooftop garden with over 20,000 trees and more flora. Follow a spiralling staircase to get here; the ascent's 300-plus steps provide historical info along the way.

Finding the Fab Four
German Beatlemania

Long before forging rock-and-roll history, the Beatles paid their dues performing in Reeperbahn pubs. On the famous **Grosse Freiheit** party mile, the band set the stage for its meteoric rise. Stand atop the vinyl-record-shaped **Beatles-Platz** next to abstract steel sculptures of the Fab Four (including a hybrid of Ringo Starr and the band's original drummer during Hamburg days, Pete Best).

Down Grosse Freiheit, the band's name is featured outside the **Kaiserkeller** *(docksfreiheit36.de/kaiserkeller)*. Meanwhile, a small outside plaque commemorates the Beatles' inaugural German gig at the **Indra** *(indramusikclub.de)*. Another plaque at **Gretel & Alfons** claims this particular pub to be the boys' favourite haunt. Legend has it Paul McCartney ran up (and forgot) a considerable tab here. He eventually returned to pay up decades later.

Sacred War Memorial
Take in the views from Mahnmal St Nikolai

Mahnmal St Nikolai *(mahnmal-st-nikolai.de; observation deck & museum adult/child €5/3)* was the world's tallest building from 1874 to 1876, and it remains Hamburg's second-tallest structure (after the TV Tower). Today, the bombed-out remains of St Nikolai Church encompass a war memorial and **crypt history museum**. Take the elevator up to the church's 76.3m-high **observation tower** inside the surviving spire for awesome views. Down below, walk among church remnants in an open-air courtyard.

PATCHWORK CITYSCAPE

Harmonising surviving prewar structures, functionalist feats and seafaring motifs, Hamburg's architecture is a fascinating mishmash. During WWII, Hamburg's city centre – mostly Gothic and neo-Gothic architecture – was destroyed. The Rathaus remains as enduring style icon, while 19th-century Speicherstadt highlights the city's neo-Gothic-influenced era. Mid-20th-century functionalism saw classic architecture razed for unappealing, utilitarian structures. The period's 'high point' is the Fernsehturm (TV Tower), still Hamburg's tallest building. The exception to this architectural 'reset' was the indestructible WWII Hamburg Bunker. Now, city architects are incorporating maritime motifs along the harbour – the Elbphilharmonie and HafenCity are examples.

Lübeck

MEDIEVAL ARCHITECTURE | HANSEATIC HISTORY | MARZIPAN CAPITAL

GETTING AROUND

Lübeck's Altstadt is on an island encircled by the canalised Trave River. The Hauptbahnhof and central bus station are 500m west of the Holstentor. Walking around is easy; many streets are pedestrianised and off limits to all but the vehicles of hotel guests. Lübeck is an hour's drive from Hamburg or about 40 minutes by train.

☑ TOP TIP

The **Lübeck Day Pass** *(1/2 days €12/16)* is excellent value. It offers access to all of Lübeck's museums; the **Day Pass Plus** *(1/2 days €18/22)* also includes the St Petri observation deck and St Marien churches.

Lübeck's global claim to fame is certainly its Christmas confections – but this Hanseatic city proves to be much sweeter than its marzipan. A 12th-century gem in Germany's northernmost state of Schleswig-Holstein, Lübeck has more than 1000 historic buildings. Picture-book streets are an enduring reminder of its role as the mighty Hanseatic League capital, a status that earned it the nickname 'the Queen of the Hanse'.

Designated a UNESCO World Heritage site in 1987, Lübeck's well-preserved Altstadt (old town) is abundant with delightful ornate facades and narrow cobblestone streets. It offers an alluring silhouette from its waterfront position on the Trave River, which leads towards the Baltic Sea and from there to Scandinavia. Beyond the medieval spires and red-brick buildings, Lübeck is a lively provincial city blending old-world character with urban impulses.

Hanseatic History & Medieval Gems

Tour Lübeck's museums

Lübeck's most impressive treasure, **Holstentor** (Holsten Gate) is among the best-known surviving medieval city gates in Germany. The **Museum Holstentor** *(museum-holstentor.de; adult/child €8/free)* sheds light on the city's mercantile glory days.

Essentially an open-air historical exhibit on Brick Gothic architecture, the cobblestoned **Museumsquartier St Annen** *(museumsquartier-st-annen.de; free)* comprises an old synagogue, church and several medieval buildings. The namesake **St Annen Museum** *(adult/child €8/free)* details the area's history tracing 700 years of art and culture; the adjoining **St Annen Kunstalle** has ecclesiastical and contemporary art.

The **Europäisches Hansemuseum** *(European Hanseatic Museum; hansemuseum.eu; adult/child €16/free, incl guided tour €21)* offers fascinating accounts of Hanse's far-reaching network via high-tech audiovisuals and artefacts. The ticketing system 'personalises' tours according to your interests, bringing interactive experiences to another level. 'Choose your own adventure' across four thematic fields and one of 50 trading sites.

Munich

WORLD-CLASS ART | BREWING TRADITIONS | METROPOLITAN VIBES

Munich isn't called Germany's secret capital for nothing. Nowhere else in the Bundesrepublik will you find such a lively blend of past and present, in a city that manages to combine Mediterranean flair with alpine flavours, traditional oompah culture with the freakishly modern, and horrible history with eco-tech.

And Munich's nickname isn't 'the City of Art and Beer' for nothing, either. Prepare for an art attack at the world-class museums in the Kunstareal, an entire quarter of the city centre given over to galleries and museums. There are also plenty more throughout the city. Then there's the beer, celebrated nightly in countless beer gardens and beer halls including the world's most famous, the Hofbräuhaus. It's so good that the annual Oktoberfest attracts over six million drinkers – and there are other beer festivals, such as the Starkbierzeit, that draw many an elbow-bender to the Bavarian metropolis.

The Altstadt & Residenz

Meet Munich on Marienplatz

The Altstadt's heart and soul, **Marienplatz** heaves from dawn till dusk and beyond with throngs of tourists, revellers and locals. Save for the 1638 **Mariensäule** (St Mary's Column) and the 1950s **Fischbrunnen** (Fish Fountain), the inventory of the square is limited. Completely dominating its northern side, the neo-Gothic **Neues Rathaus** *(New Town Hall; muenchen. travel; tower adult/child €7/3)* features gargoyles and other statuary. Pinpoint Munich's landmarks while catching the lift up the 85m-tall tower. Upcoming renovations here could last years. Arrive in front of the Neues Rathaus at 11am, noon or at 5pm (March to October) and see the famous Glockenspiel.

How Bavarian royalty lived

Munich's most visited sight, the **Residenz** *(residenz-muenchen. de; adult/child €20/free)* was the family home of the ruling Wittelsbach dynasty for over five centuries, from 1508 until WWI. Generations of big-egoed Bavarian royals shunned their

GETTING AROUND

The airport is around 30km northeast of the city centre. To reach the centre, take the S1 or S8 S-Bahn (around 40 minutes) to the Hauptbahnhof. An Uber costs €60 to €70.

Trams are good for getting around the centre and to the suburbs. The underground railway, the U-Bahn, serves the centre and the inner suburbs. There are eight lines; the main interchanges are at the Hauptbahnhof and the Sendlinger Tor. The S-Bahn lines go outside the city.

☑ **TOP TIP**

The Hauptbahnhof area has one of the highest concentrations of accommodation options in Munich. This location puts you within walking distance of many sights. However, during Oktoberfest bagging a room anywhere in Munich is almost impossible unless you book a year ahead.

485

MUNICH

Massmann-park

Olympiapark (3.2km); Olympiatum (3.2km)

Gästehaus Englischer Garten (1.2km); Kleinhesseloher See (1.2km); Hirschau (1.9km)

MAXVORSTADT

Kunstareal

Englischer Garten

Englischer Garten

Hauptbahnhof

Alter Botanischer Garten

Hofgarten

Munich Residenz

LEHEL

Maximilians-brücke

Augustiner Bräustuben (800m)

Frauenplatz

Hofbräuhaus

ALTSTADT

Theresienwiese (300m)

Kaiser-Ludwig-Platz

Nussbaum-park

GLOCKENBACHVIERTEL

Cornelius-brücke

0   500 m
0   0.25 miles

predecessors' living quarters, preferring to commission their own, hence the sheer size and scale. Among several resplendent rococo and gilded rooms, the climax is Ludwig I's **Royal Palace**. The **Schatzkammer**, containing the Wittelsbachs' collections of jewel-encrusted priceless bling, is also not to be missed.

Mother of all Munich churches

Munich's top temple is the **Frauenkirche** (*muenchner-dom. de; south tower adult/child €7.50/5.50*), instantly recognisable on the city's skyline – no building in the Altstadt can stand taller than its 99m. Built in the 15th century but severely damaged during WWII and rebuilt, it has some interesting

LET GO MEDIA/SHUTTERSTOCK

Hofbräuhaus

SIGHTSEEING MADE EASY

Don't get your Pinakotheken in a twist while sightseeing in Munich. The city centre's bus route, the 100, aka **Museenlinie**, links over 20 museums and other interesting localities en route. The Königsplatz, Lenbachhaus, the Kunstareal and the English Garden are all linked by this ordinary *Stadtbus* (city bus). Leaving every 10 minutes in both directions (every 20 minutes on weekends), the 100 also serves as a kind of budget hop-on/hop-off route, especially with a day pass. The whole route takes around 25 minutes to complete, connecting to U-Bahn, S-Bahn and trams at both ends.

For the Kunstreal, the official website has an interactive stroll which eases some of the overwhelm here.

features including the tomb of Ludwig the Bavarian in the **crypt**. The highlight (though a rather pricey one) for most visitors is climbing the 98m **south tower** to peer out the small windows across all of Munich.

Check out the Hofbräuhaus

Even committed teetotallers should at least poke their heads around the door of the **Hofbräuhaus** *(hofbraeuhaus.de)*, Munich institution and the world's most celebrated beer hall. For those into Central European lager, a night on the Hofbräu is like the culmination of a hop-scented pilgrimage. It's a beer hall and tourist attraction rolled into one: take a seat in the main hall or in the horse-chestnut-shaded garden, order a *Mass* (1L tankard) and some Bavarian food and sway with the other tourists to the oompah band. The place is open every day of the year, even Christmas Day.

Feast at Munich's city-centre market

Bio *Weisswurst,* alpine cheese or pickled anything – **Viktualienmarkt** *(viktualienmarkt-muenchen.de)* has it all. Just steps from the Marienplatz, this 200-year-old, open-air market occupies 22,000 sq metres.

This is no ordinary farmers market. Over the past two decades it has become a dining hot spot, with countless stalls

 EATING IN THE ALTSTADT: FINE DINING

Alois – Dallmayr Fine Dining: Enjoy the double-Michelin-starred menu at this top-drawer Munich stalwart. *12.30-3pm Thu-Sat, 7pm-midnight Wed-Sat* €€€

Les Deux: The modern French cuisine at this restaurant near the Frauenkirche has earned it a Michelin twinkler. *noon-midnight Mon-Sat* €€€

Tohru: Minimalist Michelin Japanese cuisine in a retro dining room prepared by German-Japanese chef, Tohru Nakamura. *7pm-midnight Tue-Sat* €€€

Le Stollberg: Intimate little restaurant serving Bavarian food with Mediterranean touches. *11.30am-2.30pm & 6pm-midnight Wed-Fri, 4.30-11pm Sat* €€€

TOP EXPERIENCE

Kunstareal

The Kunstareal, Munich's cultural quarter, is made up of two areas. The heart and soul of Maxvorstadt is the Königsplatz, commissioned by Ludwig I as part of his 'German Athens' vision for Munich and resembling a city in the ancient world. The addition of the various Pinakotheken, the area's second focus, over the decades expanded the Kunstareal into today's starring attraction.

Lenbachhaus

TOP TIPS

● On Sundays, try the €1 challenge (expect to be exhausted). Many institutions close Mondays.

● Main works from the closed Neue Pinakothek can be seen at the Sammlung Schack and the Alte Pinakothek.

● The lawns around the Alte Pinakothek are popular for picnics.

PRACTICALITIES

● kunstareal.de
● admission varies ● each institution has one late opening day

On Königsplatz

The **Lenbachhaus** *(lenbachhaus.de; adult/child €10/free)* specialises in members of the Munich-born modernist group *Der Blaue Reiter* (The Blue Rider) including Wassily Kandinsky and Paul Klee.

Meanwhile, the **State Museum of Egyptian Art** *(smaek. de; adult/child €7/free)* traces 5000 years of Egyptian and Sudanese history in one of Europe's finest collections.

Kunstareal Museums

With its vast collection of art from the 14th to the 18th centuries, the **Alte Pinakothek** *(pinakothek.de; adult/child €9/free)* is a world-class art museum. if you're going to choose just one gallery to visit in the Kunstareal, many would say this should be it. Da Vinci, Cranach the Elder, Dürer, Memling, Bruegel the Elder, Rubens, Botticelli, Rafael, Titian, Velázquez, Raphael...the list of big names and priceless masterpieces goes on room after room.

Germany's largest modern-art museum, the cavernous **Pinakothek der Moderne** *(pinakothek.de; adult/child €10/free)*, comprises four museums in one – engaging (and often confusing), but there's something for everyone. The abstract, multi-hued **Museum Brandhorst** *(museum-brandhorst.de; adult/child €9/free)* showcases art from the 1960s onwards – Warhol, Hirst and co. Temporary exhibitions challenge the art world.

offering tasty gourmet (and not so gourmet) snacks. Put together a (very pricey) picnic or grab lunch. The market has its very own chestnut-shaded beer garden, the Altstadt's best and a Munich institution since 1807. All of Munich's main breweries take turns serving here, but in summer you'll have a long wait for a table.

Schwabing

Endlessly stroll an English Garden

Strolling through the vast meadows of the sprawling city park is how the good folk of Munich escape the stresses of the 21st century. The **Englischer Garten** *(English Garden; free)* is one of the world's largest urban parks. Dodge the joggers and high-speed cyclists to discover a tranquil world of woodland, birdsong and students swotting up in the sun.

In the park's middle, the **Monopteros** (1838) is a Greek temple with city-centre views. A short walk north lies the **Chinesischer Turm** *(Chinese Tower; chinaturm.de),* the unlikely setting for a classic beer garden.

Further north, the English Garden becomes wilder, despite two 'tamed' spots: **Kleinhesseloher See**, a lovely lake for boating around three little islands, and **Hirschau** *(hirschau-muenchen.de)* beer garden, one of Munich's best.

Theresienwiese & Olympiapark

Munich's best beer hall?

The vast, ear-shaped **Theresienwiese**, aka the *Wies'n* (meadow), is the home of Oktoberfest but it's a big, vacant, gravelly space the rest of the year. Just north, another lager-related attraction, the **Augustiner Bräustuben** *(braeustuben.de),* is a smarter stop. The oldest, second-largest of the 'big six', Augustiner is the last Munich brewery storing lager in oak barrels. The atmosphere in the evenings is slightly more authentic than its city-centre cousins.

Exploring Olympian levels

The **Olympiapark** *(olympiapark.de; free)* was the site of Munich's 1972 Summer Olympics – a chance to break with the past and the Nazi-era Berlin Olympics. It became better known for tragedy. Today, you can go up to the 190m-high viewing platform of the **Olympiaturm** *(adult/child €13/10).* The fast lift is nausea-inducing but these are Munich's best views bar none. Sometimes, the Alps are visible.

BEST MUNICH TOURS

Olympiapark Tour: Fascinating stadium experiences include a vertigo-inducing Stadium Roof Tour and zip-lining 35m above the pitch.

Radius Tours: Themed tours of Munich and beyond (Neuschwanstein, Salzburg). Its Third Reich tour is a classic.

Dark History Tours: Themed walks led by local-expert guides specialising in the Third Reich, WWII and medieval gore.

Munich Walk Tours: All kinds of walking tours in English including beer tours, the English Garden and cycling trips.

OzTour Munich: Award-winning city tours, Dachau trips and days out at Schloss Neuschwanstein.

Heart of Munich: Family-run agency offering city walking tours plus interesting Third Reich and Munich Suburbs tours.

 EATING IN THE ALTSTADT: TRADITIONAL BAVARIAN PLACES

| **Augustiner Stammhaus:** Monster beer hall with different rooms and a tranquil, old-world courtyard. *10am-midnight* €€ | **Fraunhofer:** Wonderfully characterful, 19th-century Bavarian inn with a tiny theatre at the back. *5pm-1am* €€ | **Schneider Brauhaus:** One of Munich's classic beer halls, with a rabble-rousing oompah band. *9am-10pm* €€ | **Bratwurstherzl:** Sausages are the focus at this old Munich tavern with a Franconian twist. *10am-11pm Mon-Sat* €€ |

Bavaria

ALPS | STORYBOOK CASTLES | ROMANTIC FOREST

 TOP TIP

Nuremberg's **Christkindlesmarkt** *(christkindlesmarkt.de)* in December is often touted as Germany's best. Fairy-lit stalls proffer Yuletide baubles, roasted chestnuts, toffee and mead bottles against medieval splendour. Famous local bratwurst and *Glühwein* (mulled wine) scent the air. Weekends get busy with locals and Czech tourists – visit on a weekday for a less shuffling experience.

Bavaria packs a lot into its 70,000 sq km, from the glorious Alps and fertile Danube plain to the moody Bavarian Forest and the toytown-medieval Romantic Road. Devouring a vast chunk of Germany's south, Bavaria is like a country unto itself (many locals nostalgically dream it still is), with multilayered diversity and sophistication to match. If you came to Germany to see storybook castles and half-timbered towns, the Free State keeps its promises.

But incredibly varied Bavaria offers much more than the chocolate-box, felt-hat idyll. Descend from the Alps to learn about the rise and fall of the Nazis in Nuremberg, to follow the Wagner trail in Bayreuth or to sample a different local wine in every tavern in Würzburg. Destinations are often described as possessing 'something for everyone', but in Bavaria's case it just happens to be true. The Free State is no bargain, but it's worth every cent to see.

Ettal

Marvel at Ludwig II's alpine escape

A 45-minute drive from Garmisch-Partenkirchen, in a wide valley hemmed by peaks rising over 1700m in places, UNESCO-listed **Schloss Linderhof** *(schlosslinderhof.de; adult/child €10/free)* is the most remote and smallest of all Ludwig II's

---

🧭 GETTING AROUND

Getting around Bavaria is simple, if slightly more expensive than it once was. With its smooth, fast and toll-free autobahn, Bavaria is best explored by car, though in big cities parking can be costly.

The vast majority of medium to large centres are linked by rail. The Bayern Ticket (aka Bayern Regional Day Pass) gives 24-hour access to all of Bavaria's rail system (except high-speed services).

There are no domestic flights within Bavaria.

castles and the only one he lived to see fully built. It's a bizarre yet unforgettable castle experience.

Explore a Benedictine monastery

The definite highlight of the famous, alpine-topped Benedictine monastery **Kloster Ettal** *(kloster-ettal.de; entry free, tour adult/child €5/free)* is a rococo basilica housing the monks' prized possession, a marble Madonna. On guided tours (German only), explore the monastery's architecture, beer brewery and liqueur factory.

Oberammergau

Admire Oberammergau's painted buildings

Any visit to this small town should begin with a wander around the centre to admire the numerous examples of *Lüftlmalerei*. These huge, decorative murals on house facades can be found throughout the Alps, but the style was invented here. Common motifs include biblical stories, and fairy tales are also popular. The **Little Red Riding Hood House** and **Hansel & Gretel House** depicts scenes from the Brothers Grimm's best-known tales.

CLIMBING THE NEUSCHWANSTEIN HILL

There are a number of ways to get up to Neuschwanstein. The cheapest is to walk – it costs nothing, but it's a long and relentless climb. If you want to visit Marienbrücke first, as we suggest you do, follow the signs as you near the top – there's a steep cut-through to the bridge. The other options are to take a horse-drawn carriage, but it takes you directly to the castle, which means you need to climb past Neuschwanstein and then back again. Unless you like the walk up, we recommend taking the shuttle bus up (it drops you at the start of the short trail to Marienbrücke), then walking down to the castle before following the road down on foot.

PHOTOGRAPHY IS ON/SHUTTERSTOCK

Zugspitze cable car station, Garmisch-Partenkirchen

Garmisch-Partenkirchen

Ascend Germany's tallest mountain

At 2962m, the **Zugspitze** (*zugspitze.de; adult/child €75/37.50*) is Germany's tallest mountain with the country's only (and shrinking) glacier. Going up is the most magical anywhere in the German Alps; dedicate at least half a day to the experience.

A cogwheel train called the **Zugspitzbahn** chugs up in a 75-minute, valley-viewing journey. At the **Zugspitzplatt**, a plateau below the summit, you can rent skis and snowboards (*skiverleih-garmisch.com*). A 10-minute cable car takes you up the final vertical metres to the top.

Füssen

A fairy-tale German castle

Rising amid the forested peaks like a fantasy vision, **Schloss Neuschwanstein** (*neuschwanstein.de; adult/child €23.50/2.50*) was the model for Disney's Sleeping Beauty castle. King Ludwig II's fairy-tale Schloss Neuschwanstein is Bavaria's most visited attraction, and as it comes into view from **Marienbrücke**, it's instantly obvious why.

You'll enjoy your visit more if you plan ahead. It can only be visited on guided tours (in German or English, about 35 minutes). Outside the peak summer season, tickets are available on-site, but reserving online is recommended – especially in summer.

EATING IN FÜSSEN: OUR PICKS

Vinzenzmurr Metzgerai: Sample hearty food like *Leberkäse* (meatloaf) in a bun, goulash soup, bratwurst or schnitzel. *9am-6pm Mon-Fri, 8am-1pm Sat* €

Beim Olivenbauer: Tyrol meets the local Allgäu region at this fun eatery. Try the *Maultaschen* (pork and spinach ravioli) and a mug of local beer. *noon-11pm* €€

Zum Franziskaner: Specialises in *Schweinshaxe* (pork knuckle) and schnitzel as well as other meaty Bavarian and Allgäu staples. *11.30am-10pm Thu-Tue* €€

Zum Hechten: Füssen's best hotel restaurant keeps things regional with Allgäu favourites like schnitzel, noodles and venison goulash. *11am-10pm* €€

Ludwig's childhood palace

You get two for your money visiting Neuschwanstein. The 'other' castle, where King Ludwig II grew up, **Schloss Hohenschwangau** (*hohenschwangau.de; adult/child €26/14.50, incl Neuschwanstein €48.50/17*), is just as interesting, if not as dreamily storybook-ish.

Climb high into the Alps

In summer, the cable car **Tegelbergbahn** (*tegelbergbahn.de; adult one-way/return €20.50/31, child €8.50/13*) ascends Tegelberg (1881m) to a mountain chalet. From the summit, and despite the relatively low altitude, the views seem to extend forever.

Augsburg

Pop into a Renaissance city

Ranking among Germany's oldest towns – its story dates back around 2000 years – Augsburg is worth as much time as you can give it. The city centre's offering is varied, from the fascinating **Fuggerei** (*fugger.de; adult/child €8/4*) settlement's social and architectural history, to memorable churches and great food. Its puppet or marionette theatre, **Augsburger Puppenkiste** (*puppenkiste.de; tickets from €10, museum adult/child €5/3.30*), is one of southern Germany's most underrated museums.

Rothenburg ob der Tauber

Magical medieval streets

Few large villages or small towns in Germany are so impressively medieval as Rothenburg. Painstakingly preserved architecture makes the city centre a period piece of gables, turrets and half-timbered facades encircled by tower-dotted stone walls. A visit here is all about wandering around; the small square of **Plönlein** is a magical evocation of Rothenburg's charm. Arguably the best views are from the **Rathausturm** (*adult/child €4/2*), the tower of the town hall.

Würzburg

Big, baroque and beautiful

The vast UNESCO World Heritage–listed **Residenz** (*residenzwuerzburg.de; adult/child €10/free*), once the home of local prince-bishops, is one of Germany's most beautiful baroque palaces. Commissioned in 1720 by prince-bishop Johann Philipp Franz von Schönborn, it took almost 60 years to complete. Today the 360 rooms are home to government institutions,

BAVARIA'S MEDIEVAL CITY WALLS

Rothenburg ob der Tauber: Extending over 2.5km, Rothenburg's ancient walls encircle the town – walk their length and admire them from afar.

Dinkelsbühl: Also 2.5km long, the walls at Dinkelsbühl are much quieter than Rothenburg's but just as beautiful.

Nördlingen: Dating back to the 14th century, Nördlingen's walls are almost perfectly circular.

Landsberg am Lech: One of Bavaria's least-known walled cities, Landsberg has fine, 15th-century fortified gates and imposing stone ramparts.

Nuremberg: Beginning opposite the Hauptbahnhof and extending around the Altstadt, Nuremberg's walls are a constant presence in the city.

 EATING IN ROTHENBURG OB DER TAUBER: OUR PICKS

Zur Höll: Medieval wine tavern in Rothenburg's oldest building, offering regional specialities and Franconian wines. *5-11pm Mon-Sat* €€

Gasthof Butz: Family-run inn in a former brewery serving no-nonsense southern German dishes. *11.30am-2pm & 6-9pm Tue, Wed & Fri-Sun* €€

Mittermeier: Savour a finely crafted menu at one of Rothenburg's oldest fine-dining establishments. *6-9pm Tue-Sat* €€€

Weinstube zum Pulverer: Ancient spot serving classic German cooking in a tranquil ambience. *5-11pm Wed-Fri, noon-11pm Sat & Sun* €€€

The Romantic Road

From the vineyards of Würzburg to the foot of the Alps, the almost 400km-long Romantic Road (Romantische Strasse) is by far Germany's most popular tourist route. It passes through more than two dozen cities, towns and villages in a ribbon of half-timbered quaintness. This is the Germany many expect to see, with perfectly conserved towns delivering on all the promises seen pre-trip on Instagram.

KONSTANTIN YOLSHIN/SHUTTERSTOCK

Schloss Weikersheim, Weikersheim

VITAL STATS

Length 460km

Visitors Around 30 million annually

Year created 1950

Number of official stops 29

Number of castles and palaces 22

Number of UNESCO sites 4

Largest city Augsburg (population 301,000)

Smallest stop Röttingen (population 1681)

Number of autobahns 0

Most visited town Rothenburg ob der Tauber

PRACTICALITIES

● romantischestrasse.de

North to South

The Road is designed to be driven north to south. Leaving from Würzburg, the scenery becomes more magnificent. Getting to Würzburg is straightforward via regular trains from Munich (two hours), Bamberg, Frankfurt and Nuremberg (one hour from each). Spend a few days in Würzburg, including an afternoon at **Festung Marienberg** (schloesser.bayern.de; adult/child €4/free) with its 800-year-old bastions. The Romantic Road ends in Füssen, where **Schloss Neuschwanstein** (p492) is unmissable. From Füssen, Austria's Alps are nearby.

Romantic Road Coach

For those who aren't driving or cycling the Romantic Road, the **Romantic Road Coach** (romanticroadcoach.de) is a seasonal bus service (May to September) connecting towns not serviced by regular rail. The most popular routes are day trips (sometimes with wine tastings) from Würzburg or Frankfurt am Main to Rothenburg ob der Tauber. After Rothenburg, **Deutsche Bahn** (bahn.de) trains service 15 stations, including Dinkelsbühl, Harburg, Nördlingen, Donauwörth, Augsburg, Landsberg am Lech, Füssen and Munich. The coach route's midway stop is effectively in Weikersheim, a pretty small town straddling the Tauber River with the finest palace along the entire Road, **Schloss Weikersheim** (schloss-weikersheim.de; adult 60/80min tour €9/11).

university faculties and a museum, but the grandest 40 have been restored for visitors to admire.

Nuremberg

Revisit the Nuremberg trials

You can visit the courtroom where the Nazi leaders were tried for crimes against peace and humanity, now the **Memorium Nuremberg Trials** *(memorium-nuremberg.de; adult/child €7.50/2.50)*. Courtroom No 600 has been left pretty much as it was back then, and there's a multimedia exhibition telling the story of one of the world's most famous legal processes.

Regensburg

Explore religious Regensburg

The austere **Dom St Peter** *(bistum-regensburg.de; free),* dominating Regensburg's skyline, is a masterpiece of Gothic grandeur in Bavaria. Beyond incredible architectural features, the **Domspatzen** is a boys' choir that has been around for over 1000 years; they accompany the 10am Sunday service during the school year. Attached to the church, the **Domschatzmuseum** (Cathedral Treasury) overflows (and overwhelms) with lavish monstrances, tapestries and other treasures.

Bavarian Forest

Hiking and biking in the Bavarian Forest

Apart from the obvious attractions of the Bavarian Alps, there's no better place in the Free State to pull on hiking boots than the **Bavarian Forest National Park** *(nationalpark-bayerischer-wald.de)* and surrounding areas. The park extends for around 24,250 hectares along the Czech border, from Bayerisch Eisenstein in the north to Finsterau in the south. You'll encounter far fewer people on the trails here than in the Alps and there's also more wildlife to spot.

The European long-distance E6 hiking route cuts through the Bavarian Forest, but with over 350km of trails amid thick mountain spruce in the park, there are countless other routes to follow. Popular hikes include those to the summit of **Mt Lusen** (1373m), to the top of **Mt Grosser Arber** (1456m), the park's highest, and along the ridge that divides Bavaria from West Bohemia. Some paths in the national park are out of bounds from November to July.

Other activities include mountain biking, trail running, skiing and snowshoeing. The maps produced by Kompass – sheets 195, 196, 197 and 198 – are invaluable companions. They are available from tourist offices, some bookshops, the park visitor centre and online.

BASES FOR THE BAVARIAN FOREST

The German part of the Bavarian Forest is fringed by villages and small towns, all of which work as bases for exploring the national park. The more accessible ones can be reached via the Waldbahn railway line.

Zwiesel is the largest town just outside the park, with plenty of accommodation, places for eating and provisioning, a well-stocked, helpful **tourist office** *(zwiesel.de),* and a museum about local traditions. Another option for the south of the national park, **Grafenau** has shops, accommodation, a spa and a **tourist office** *(grafenau.de).* And if you're looking to combine the region's glass-making traditions with time spent exploring the park, **Frauenau**, very near the park's boundary, has the **Glasmuseum** *(glasmuseum-frauenau.de; adult/child €5/free, Sun €1).*

Stuttgart & the Black Forest

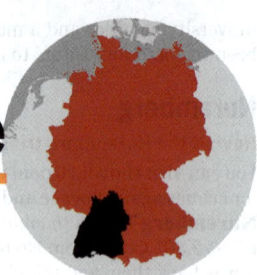

ENCHANTING WOODLAND | SPAS | INNOVATION

☑ **TOP TIP**

The money-saving **SchwarzwaldCard** *(schwarzwaldcard.shop; adult/child from €51/35)* is good for three days of free or reduced entry to over 200 attractions, including cable cars, museums, adventure parks and swimming pools. Popular inclusions are the Triberger Wasserfälle and Europa-Park.

Welcome to the southwest, known as the sunniest region in Germany. You're in the state of Baden-Württemberg, where locals are renowned for their inventiveness, prosperity and work-hard, play-hard mentality. Stuttgart, the region's capital, has a proud history of engineering that has given the world the automobile, spark plugs and the pretzel. Freiburg, one of the world's greenest cities, is also a gateway to exploring the depths of the Schwarzwald.

The Black Forest (Schwarzwald), a sprawling mass of spruce trees, tight-knit villages and pocket-sized lakes, is a place that both adventure seekers and slow travellers will be captivated by. The name itself casts a mysterious spell over the region, and you wouldn't be blamed for expecting to see a wicked witch straight out of a Brothers Grimm fairy tale cackling in the sky. But with one step into the undergrowth, you'll soon discover the only mystery here is how they make such a delicious cake.

Stuttgart

Rev your engines

There's nothing more synonymous with Stuttgart than fast cars. At the **Porsche Museum** *(porsche.com; adult/child €12/6),* almost 100 Porsche vehicles are on display. There are kids' exhibits, a racing simulator and a comprehensive audio

 GETTING AROUND

Covering Germany's southwest corner, the state of Baden-Württemberg is well connected by train, bus and autobahn. Trains run regularly and are your best option for getting around, though driving allows you to see and do more. Towns are best explored on foot.

Even the smallest of towns have dedicated bike paths. However, navigating long distances on two wheels may see you riding in the slip lane a fair bit. Bike routes such as the **Bodensee Radweg** *(bodensee-radweg.com)* are good options.

STUTTGART & THE BLACK FOREST

0 ——— **50 km**
0 ——— **25 miles**

Homburg
Zweibrücken
Neustadt
Speyer
Landau
Heidelberg
Sinsheim
Rothenburg ob
der Tauber
Wissembourg
Bruchsal
Karlsruhe
Heilbronn
Schwäbisch
Hall
Haguenau
Pforzheim
Ludwigsburg
Schwäbisch
Gmünd
Aalen
FRANCE
Rastatt
Baden-
Baden
Bühl
Stuttgart
Sindelfingen
Esslingen
Göppingen
Heidenheim
an der Brenz
Strasbourg
Kehl
Ruhestein
**Black Forest
National Park**
Tübingen
Kirchheim
unter Teck
Günzburg
Offenburg
Freudenstadt
Reutlingen
Nordschwarzwald
Neckar
Ulm
Hechingen
Rust
Balingen
Europa-Park
*Mittlerer
Schwarzwald*
Triberg
Rottweil
Colmar
Waldkirch
Villingen
Tuttlingen
Bad
Sulgau
Biberach
Freiburg
Titisee
Messkirch
Memmingen
Feldberg
Donaueschingen
Bad
Waldsee
Todtnau
Südschwarzwald
Singen
Ravensburg
Leutkirch
Lörrach
Koblenz
Schaffhausen
Konstanz
Friedrichshafen
Wangen
Kempten
Basel
Rhine
SWITZERLAND
Winterthur
*Lake
Constance*
Lindau
Bregenz AUSTRIA
Sonthofen

tour. You can even splash out and rent a Porsche for the day from the ticket desk.

Across town lies the 'competition'. The **Mercedes-Benz Museum** (*mercedes-benz.com; adult/child €16/8*) celebrates the evolution of the car over 135 years, contextualised through world history. From the first internal combustion engine to a history-making road trip in 1888 and the Silver Arrows sports-car hall of fame and the Popemobile, the collection is impressive and vast. The museum itself is an architectural marvel earning an entry in the Guinness World Records for the world's biggest artificial tornado – an atrium feature designed to extract smoke in case of fire.

EATING IN FREIBURG: LOCAL CUISINE

Grosser Meyerhof: Altstadt tavern specialising in local Badish dishes such as *Maultaschen* (pork and spinach ravioli). *11.30am-11pm €€*

Heiliggeist Stüble: Dine on local specialities with the sound of church bells at this stylish tavern under the Münster. *11.30am-11pm €€*

Martin's Bräu: Home-brewed ales and meaty snacks like ox-tongue salad, bratwurst or pork knuckle. *11am-11pm Sun-Thu, to midnight Fri & Sat €€*

Schmidt: This is the best place to enjoy a fluffy, rich Black Forest cake and coffee. Big breakfast menu, too. *9am-6pm Mon-Sat €*

BLACK FOREST HAM

The tradition of smoking meat dates to the Middle Ages, and *Schwarzwälder Schinken* (Black Forest ham) still uses traditional methods today. This dry-cured, cold-smoked ham is known for its smoky aroma, dark outer crust and tender, salty-sweet interior. The process begins with pork leg, which is seasoned with salt, garlic, coriander, juniper and pepper, then cured for several weeks. It's smoked over fir and spruce wood before being air-dried at high altitudes, giving it its distinct character. Only ham made in the Black Forest region can carry this name, in efforts to ensure it's made using traditional methods and authentic regional ingredients. It's often enjoyed with thick slices of bread or added to *Flammkuchen* (Alsatian pizza).

Freiburg

Strolling the Altstadt

Spend a day walking the Altstadt, starting at the bustling farmers market (Monday to Saturday) on **Marktplatz**, where delicious produce and snacks abound. Work that off by climbing the 333 spiral steps up the spire of the 800-year-old **Freiburger Münster** (*freiburgermuenster.info; tower adult/child/under 7yr 5/3/free*) to be rewarded with Freiburg's best vistas. The cathedral is in constant need of maintenance, so expect to see some scaffolding (the only removal was for the Pope's 2011 visit). While wandering, look down at 19th-century, coloured stone mosaics (the stone came from the Rhine); they depict business emblems or cultural motifs – even pretzels.

Running along the Altstadt, the **Bächle water canals** (once medieval firefighting trenches) are as Freiburg-iconic as the Münster spire. Today, you'll likely find kids tugging sailboats along them, dogs taking a refreshing drink or locals dipping in. Local legend has it that if you set foot in a canal, you'll marry a local.

Europa-Park

Get your pulse racing

Europa-Park (*europapark.de; adult/child from €52/44*) is one of Europe's biggest and best theme parks. You can easily spend a whole day here and not see it all. Of 13 high-adrenaline roller-coasters, the standout Icelandic-themed **Blue Fire Megacoaster** blasts to 100km/h in just 2.5 seconds.

Black Forest National Park

A wild adventure

The **Nationalpark Schwarzwald** (*nationalpark-schwarzwald.de*) is a 10,000-hectare area best explored on foot. Magnificent flora and fauna abound. For a real adventure, you can even stay a night in the wilderness at a secret nature camp only accessible on foot. The visitors centre at Ruhestein offers maps and an exhibition on the project.

Triberg

Going cuckoo for a waterfall

The busy tourist town's claims to fame are cuckoo clocks and Germany's highest waterfall. **Triberger Wasserfälle** (*triberg.de; adult/child €8/7.50*) is impressive – winding boardwalks

DRINKING IN THE BLACK FOREST: LOCAL TIPPLES

Rothaus: Visit the Black Forest brewery in Grafenhausen to taste what makes its cult beer, the Tannenzapfle, so special. *11am-6pm*	**Alpirsbacher Klosterbrau:** Tour the family-owned brewery in Alpirsbach that has been crafting award-winning brews since 1880. *hours vary*	**Black Forest Distillers:** Pre-book a distillery tour in Lossburg to try Monkey 47, an award-winning dry gin made using 47 botanicals. *noon & 2pm Sat*	**Emil Scheibel Schwarzwald-Brennerei:** Learn to make great fruit schnapps at this distillery in Kappelrodeck. *9am-5pm Mon-Fri, 10am-1pm Sat*

and scenery-heavy trails abound – and cuckoo clocks less so, with many cheap imports. **Oli's Schnitzstube** *(olisschnitzstube.de)* still produces handcrafted clocks while **Rombach und Haas** *(black-forest-clock.de)* does ultra-modern ones.

Titisee

Make a splash

Titisee's scenic alpine lake is alive in summer with a quaint tourist village and plentiful water activites. The 7km shoreline has plenty of quieter swimming spots; in the town, there are good restaurants and souvenir boutiques. If weather isn't co-operating, the **Badeparadies Schwarzwald** *(badeparadiesschwarzwald.de; adult/child from €23/19)* indoor pool complex is a forest-hidden oasis.

Feldberg

'Tis the ski-son

Ski through the Black Forest mountains on **Feldberg**, the Black Forest's highest peak at 1493m. It's family-friendly and offers ski hire. Cross-country skiing is also popular, with 120km of marked trails winding through snowy enchantment – there's also snowshoeing and toboggan runs. Afterwards, hit the après-ski bars in small resort towns such as Todtnau and Feldberg.

Todtnau

Swing through the trees

From the **Blackforest Line suspension bridge** *(blackforestline.de; adult/child €12/9)*, get a bird's-eye view of the multi-tiered **Todtnauer Wasserfall** *(todtnauer-wasserfaelle.de; adult/child/under 6yr €2.50/1.50/free)*, one of the highest natural waterfalls in Germany. A combined ticket gets you entry to both the bridge and the waterfall, with a 2.4km circular walk connecting the two.

BEST SHORT HIKES IN THE BLACK FOREST

Uhrwaldpfad Rohrhardsberg: This 8km circular hike through dense forest features over 30 cuckoo clocks along the path from April to October.

Mummelsee to Hornisgrinde: From picturesque Mummelsee, this 4km loop ascends to Hornisgrinde, the highest peak in the northern Black Forest.

Allerheiligen Wasserfälle: This trail near Oppenau leads hikers 4.2km through a series of stunning waterfalls in a lush forest.

Gauchach Gorge Gourmet Trail: Challenging 5.6km trail through the wild Gauchach Gorge with its many waterfalls.

Muggenbrunn Barefoot Path: Feel spruce cones, bark mulch and fresh mountain water underfoot on this 600m-long trail. Great for kids.

WINTER FUN
Check out the ski resorts of **Garmisch-Partenkirchen** (p492) in Bavaria if you're keen on more winter adventures.

Bremen & Lower Saxony

Hamburg
Bremerhaven
Oldenburg
Bremen
Lüneburg
Uelzen
Cloppenburg
Verden
Nienburg
Celle
Bergen-Belsen
Wolfsburg
Osnabrück
Minden
Hanover
Herford
Hamelin
Braun-schweig
Bielefeld
Hildesheim

ART MUSEUMS | WWII HISTORY | RICH GREENERY

GETTING AROUND

Rail connections are excellent and often integrated with bus services. ICE fast trains service main hubs like Bremen and Hanover, and there's an extensive regional network.

To reach Bergen-Belsen Memorial Site, take an ICE or regional train to Celle. Take bus 900 from Schlossplatz and change to bus 110 at 'Küsterdamm, Winsen' stop. It's best to avoid Sunday, as only a *Rufbus* (call bus) completes the journey from Winsen and needs to be booked ahead.

☑ TOP TIP

During trade fairs, hotels and private accommodation in Hanover and nearby towns are booked out, so it's important to always run a quick check online *(visit-hannover.com/ Messen-Kongresse)* before coming. As an alternative, visit Bremen first.

Lower Saxony, spilling northwards to the North Sea and in most parts flat as a pancake, is the largest German state after Bavaria. For the traveller, it's a low-key place with an understated character to its the landscape: wide-open spaces and heath, occasional hilly country-side, and tidal mudflats that submerge and reappear in daily cycles. Hanover, its capital, has several excellent museums, as well as large swathes of green space that invite a stroll. An hour's drive from Hanover, the Bergen-Belsen Memorial Site, a former concentration camp, reveals Lower Saxony's stark contrasts.

Meanwhile, Bremen is a city-state unto itself with its own port, Bremerhaven. Bremen brings together culture, particularly the fine arts, and plenty of nightlife in one small bundle. Within a short space of time, you can wind down medieval streets, duck into another gallery featuring unusual expressionism, stroll along the 'museum mile' and rest up in some great cafes and student places.

Bremen

MAP p501

All about expressionism

Bremen's longstanding ties with expressionism are best reflected in the architecture along **Böttcherstrasse**. Red-brick houses sport unique facades; some are now artisan shops and art museums. The **Paula Modersohn-Becker Museum** *(museen-boettcherstrasse.de; adult/child €12/free)* showcases the early expressionist and member of movement-founding Worpswede artist colony. The adjoining **Roselius-Haus Museum** *(museen-boettcherstrasse.de; adult/child €12/free)*, in a 16th-century patrician house, primarily displays 16th- and 17th-century art. The standout is a section dedicated to Lucas Cranach the Elder.

Works of Gerhard Marcks

Next to Gerhard Marcks' **Town Musicians of Bremen Statue** on the Marktplatz, the same Brothers Grimm fairy tale it's

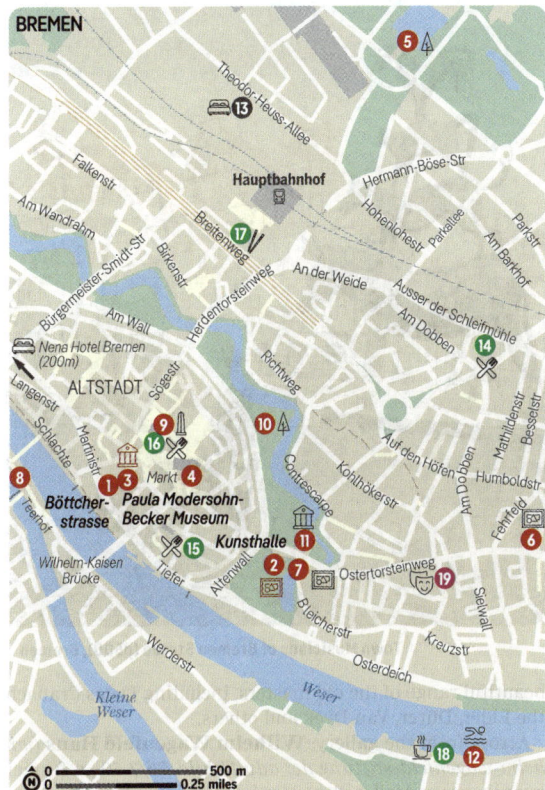

BREMEN

inspired by is charmingly re-enacted at noon from May to September. It's a beautiful, lighthearted performance honouring an artist condemned as 'degenerate' during Nazi times. The excellent **Gerhard Marcks Haus** *(marcks.de; adult/child €5/ free)* exhibits the artist's own donated works.

Bremen's cultural mile

The **Kunsthalle** *(kunsthalle-bremen.de; adult/child €15/ free)* is Bremen's premier art exhibition space with a large, permanent collection of paintings, sculpture and copperplate engravings, spanning medieval to present times. There's a

---

✂ **EATING IN BREMEN: OUR PICKS** ─────────────── MAP p501

Hanoi Deli: Sushi, Vietnamese dishes and some pan-Asian classics; large servings. *11.30am-10pm Mon & Wed-Fri, from noon Sat & Sun* €€

Bremer Ratskeller: Hearty traditional German cuisine beneath the Rathaus. Gorgeous vaulted ceilings. *noon-9.30pm Sun-Thu, to 10pm Fri & Sat* €€

Argana: Moroccan cooking in the Schnoor quarter. Lots of meat-based tajines, and veg offerings. *noon-3pm & 5.30-10pm Tue-Fri, 2.30-11pm Sat, 5.30-10pm Mon* €€

Al Pappagallo: Delicious Italian dishes prepared in an open kitchen and elegantly presented. *noon-2pm & 6-11pm Mon-Fri, 6-11pm Sat* €€€

ROSSHELEN/SHUTTERSTOCK

Town Musicians of Bremen Statue (p500), Bremen

BEST BREMEN PARKS & QUIET SPOTS

Wallanlagen: Bremen's town fortifications were converted into parkland in the 19th century, with ponds and meadows.

Teerhof: This quarter on the spit of land in the Weser River has a slightly abandoned feel, despite its gentrified housing. On the same peninsula but reached by ferry from Sielwall, the **Weser Strand** (Weser Beach) is a summer bathing spot, and **Café Sand** a popular retreat.

Bürgerpark Bremen: Northeast of the centre, an enormous stretch of parkland with lakes, trails, forests and meadows. It also has a small animal park, popular with kids.

Bibelgarten: The Bibel Garden is a tranquil yard at the entrance to the Bleikeller crypt.

beautiful range of the old masters, including Lucas Cranach the Elder, Dürer, Van Dyck and others.

Across from the gallery, **Wilhelm Wagenfeld Haus** *(wilhelm-wagenfeld-stiftung.de; adult/child €6/3.50)*, a former guardhouse and jail, now houses contemporary design from industrial to photography. It's named after a Bauhaus luminary.

Bremen's cultural mile gives way to great cultural venues in **Das Viertel**, such as the **Mensch, Puppe** *(menschpuppe.de; matinee adult/child €10/8, evening incl drink €25/15)* puppet theatre and a handful of galleries including the outstanding **Galerie Kramer** *(galeriekramer.de; free)*.

Hanover

Relax in royal parkland

Hanover's highlight is **Herrenhäuser Gärten** *(hannover.de/herrenhausen)*, a sprawling constellation of gardens. Start in the **Grosser Garten** *(incl museum & Berggarten adult/child €10/free)*, known for baroque golden sculptures, a maze and the beloved Niki de Saint Phalle Grotto. A path leads down to the Grosse Fontäne, one of Europe's tallest fountains jetting to 80m high. In summer, dancing fountain shows, **garden illuminations** *(adult/child €6/free)*, concerts and fireworks competitions delight.

The **Museum Schloss Herrenhausen** *(incl Grosser Garten & Berggarten adult/child €10/free)* recounts the grounds' history from the 17th century to their Hanoverian royal creators.

Exploring the old town

Despite severe WWII damage, Hanover's small old town retains much historic character. The most interesting buildings on Am Markte, the central square, are the medieval **Altes Rathaus** *(Old Town Hall; altes-rathaus-events.de)* and the Gothic **Marktkirche** *(Market Church; marktkirche-hannover. de; free)*. **Leibnizhaus** on Holzmarkt was once the home of the renowned mathematician and philosopher Gottfried Wilhelm Leibniz (1646–1716) and has an attractive, reconstructed Renaissance facade. The nearby **Aegidienkirche** soberly recollects wartime horrors; the medieval church remains in bombed-out condition since 1943.

Not to be missed along the river are the voluptuous and fluorescent-coloured **Die Nanas** sculptures. These Venus figures are Hanover's beloved landmarks.

Into the sky, onto a lake

The **Neues Rathaus** *(adult/child €4/3.50)* has an unusually curved lift leading up to its green dome. A glass ceiling and floor make for an ascent that's nerve-tingling and claustrophobic (six-person capacity and busy in summer). Afterwards, stroll through parkland to **Maschsee** for endless splashy fun including rental pedalling and rowing boats. Ferries – some solar-powered – ply the lake from Easter to October (weather depending).

Bergen-Belsen

Visit a Holocaust memorial

Visiting the **Bergen-Belsen Memorial Site** *(bergen-belsen. stiftung-ng.de; free)*, a former concentration camp, takes you to where Anne Frank died in 1945. The modern **Documentation Centre** chronicles the fates of the people who passed through and the grounds' evolution from a forestry workers' barracks to a POW camp.

HANOVER PLANNING PRACTICALITIES

The **Hanover Tourist Office** *(hannover. de/tourismus)* is located opposite the Hauptbahnhof and has an excellent website. Its **HannoverCard** *(1/2/3 days €13/20/26)* gives you free or discount admission to sights and free public transport. There's an accommodation booking service on the website, as well as a telephone booking service that's especially useful for rooms with private hosts during peak trade-fair periods. Also consult the website for information on accessibility and barrier-free offerings.

The Museum Schloss Herrenhausen is closed Mondays. The Herrenhäuser Gärten themselves have reduced winter hours but are open all year, though illuminations are only in summer.

DRINKING IN HANOVER: OUR PICKS

Waterloo: This beer garden is on the way to football club Hanover 96's home ground, with *Wurst* and more on the menu. *hours vary*

Brauhaus Ernst August: Sprawling brewpub with food, parties and live music, serving its own beers. *11am-11pm Mon-Thu, to late Fri & Sat*

Holländische Kakao-Stube: Historic (1895) Dutch coffeehouse with a great selection of pastries and a maritime ambience. *10am-6.30pm Mon-Sat*

Cafe Mezzo: Cafe and bar alongside the Pavillon cultural venue; the latter has live music and lots of events. *9am-midnight Mon-Sat, to 11pm Sun*

Dresden & Leipzig

BAROQUE | ROYAL TREASURES | ART

GETTING AROUND

Both cities are best explored on foot. In Dresden, trams connect the Altstadt and Neustadt and serve every corner of the centre. In Leipzig (1½ hours from Dresden by car or train), the distance between most attractions is walkable. For Plagwitz, KarLi and Connewitz, you'll need to catch a tram from the Hauptbahnhof or Augustusplatz. Install the Nextbike app on your phone to book municipal bicycles available in both cities.

☑ TOP TIP

Sold at tourist information centres, the Leipzig Card allows unlimited travel within one or three days and entitles you to discounts at most of the important museums.

With a colourful history as an independent entity, a quasi-empire at times, Saxony is the most distinctive East German region. It takes pride in speaking a dialect that other Germans – according to regular national opinion surveys – appear to dislike. This might be a secret strategy to keep others away from a land that is truly blessed.

Dresden's 18th-century cultural heyday is evident in the Altstadt's baroque wonders and their precious art collections. Across the river, Dresden's Neustadt has dozens of restaurants and shops and one of the liveliest nightlife scenes in Germany's east. In the north, Leipzig is an energetic and progressive metropolis that rivals Berlin as the country's hippest destination. Leipzig has nurtured some famous composers and scientists as well as important German painters, and has a plethora of fascinating museums and a world-class picture gallery. It's an all-round liveable city, half of which is covered by lakes and wood-like parks.

Dresden

A cityscape to die for

Before anything else, take in marvellous views from **Brühl's Terrace** (aka the Balcony Europe). Dark-green, untamed Neustadt banks juxtaposed against the blackened stones and baroque curves of Altstadt provide an intense visual experience.

Another marvel is the **Frauenkirche** *(frauenkirche-dresden.de),* a magnificent cathedral resurrected after being reduced to WWII rubble. Next, take in **Residenzschloss** *(skd.museum; adult/child €16/free),* a Renaissance palace home to Saxony's rulers for around 400 years. Its collections include the unmissable **Historisches Grünes Gewölbe** *(€16, incl other collections €28),* a real-life Aladdin's cave of precious ivory, silver, diamonds and jewels. Reconstruction on the bombed-out palace began in the 1960s and was finally completed in 2013.

Nearby, the **Albertinum** *(skd.museum; adult/child €14/free),* a former Renaissance-era arsenal, is the stunning home

Brühl's Terrace and Frauenkirche, Dresden

of the **Galerie Neue Meister** (New Masters Gallery), which has paintings by the likes of Caspar David Friedrich, Claude Monet and Marc Chagall.

Private Eden

At **Zwinger** *(der-dresdner-zwinger.de; adult/child €16/free)* palace, discover an Earthly version of paradise for the chosen – Saxon royals and their guests.

Inside, the **Gemäldegalerie Alte Meister** (Old Masters Gallery) is an astounding collection of 16th- to 18th-century European art including Raphael's famous *Sistine Madonna* (1513), and works by Titian and Cranach.

The extraordinary **Porzellansammlung** brings together 17th- and 18th-century porcelain from China and Meissen. The **Tiersaal** (Animal Hall) is the ultimate highlight with hundreds of porcelain animals. Lastly, the **Mathematisch-Physikalischer Salon**, a collection of scientific implements, will delight anyone interested in the Enlightenment.

Sounds of Dresden

Dresden's opera house, the **Semperoper** *(semperoper.de)*, is another architectural jewel in the Altstadt. Destroyed by Allied air raids, it was resurrected in 1945. Counting premieres of famous works by Strauss and Wagner, it still hosts world-class concerts today (buy tickets well ahead).

Dresden's other top venue for classical music is a strikingly different piece of GDR-era brutalism. The **Dresdner Philharmonie** *(dresdnerphilharmonie.de)* is home to one of Germany's best orchestras.

BEST DRESDEN FESTIVALS

Dixieland Fest: A May parade of Dixieland bands riding retro and steampunk vehicles; concerts are also held aboard steamships.

Filmfest Dresden: Held in April, the international short-film festival takes place in various city locations, including on giant screens in Altstadt.

Flottenparade: The full might of the Saxon navy is displayed in the I May parade, with Dresden's famous steamships floating past the Altstadt.

Louisenfest: 'Party, music, food' is the motto of this late-June festival celebrating the city's happening street. Visual arts are also on the menu.

Elbhangfest: A late-June festival organised by people living on the high bank of the Elbe between Pillnitz and Loschwitz.

 EATING IN LEIPZIG & DRESDEN: OUR PICKS

Bayerische Bahnhof: Gose beer and stylish food in the intriguing setting of a defunct Leipzig railway station's waiting room. *noon-I0pm* €€

Café Puschkin: KarLi's flagship hangout is well past its heyday, but it still draws a merry Leipzig crowd and has an eclectic menu. *9am-2am* €€

Lila Sosse: Intriguing vegan and meaty concoctions served in glass preserve jars inside Dresden's Kunsthof-passage courtyard complex. *4-IIpm* €€

PlanWirtschaft: A quiet courtyard setting in the heart of Dresden's Neustadt and a menu alluding to GDR-era culinary standards. *5-IIpm Tue-Sun* €€

Leipzig

You want a revolution?

Leipzig's **Nikolaikirche** *(nikolaikirche.de)* is famous for the 'peace prayers' held here every Monday at 5pm since 1982. Starting in September 1989, the prayers kicked off a chain reaction of events leading to East Germany's collapse and Germany's reunification.

The **Zeitgeschichtliches Forum** *(hdg.de; free)* further covers East German political history with an enormous exhibition, while the darker side of Communist times is chillingly documented by the **Stasi Museum** *(runde-ecke-leipzig.de; adult/student €5/4),* located in the former secret police headquarters. English-language audio guides accompany displays (in German) on propaganda, surveillance devices, recruitment and other machinations.

Singing city

The 800-year-old boys' choir **Thomanerchor** still performs at its original base in the Gothic **Thomaskirche** *(thomaskirche. org).* Bach repertoire honours the composer who led it for 27 years until his death. Bach's remains lie buried beneath a bronze plate afront the altar. The church hosts other musical events – some are free – including **Bachfest** *(bachfestleipzig.de)* in June.

Notes and notables

Walk the footsteps of Leipzig's famous composers along the 5km **Leipziger Notenspur** *(Leipzig Music Trail; notenspur-leipzig. de).* Each of the 23 stops has information panels and phone numbers to call and listen for music or additional commentary. There are six museums along the route, most doubling as concert venues, including **Mendelssohn-Haus** *(mendelssohn-stiftung. de; adult/child €10/free),* the house where Schumann composed the *Spring Symphony,* Wagner's former school, and apartments Edvard Grieg stayed in. At the interactive **Bach-Museum Leipzig** *(bachmuseumleipzig.de; adult/child €10/free),* learn how to date a Bach manuscript, listen to baroque instruments or treat your ears to any of his compositions.

Treasures of knowledge

Leipzig University is one of the world's oldest, founded in 1409 by scholars fleeing the Hussite uprising in Prague. The list of alumni is stellar – from Goethe and Nietzsche to former German Chancellor Angela Merkel. Located in Augustusplatz, its contemporary home known as **Paulinum** looks like an airport terminal devouring a Gothic cathedral. It's a boldly postmodern tribute to the 13th-century university church, which stood here until East German authorities blew it up in 1968.

Thankfully, the university's treasure trove of scientific collections was left unscathed. The **Museen im Grassi** *(grassi-leipzig.de)* includes the **Musikinstrumenten-Museum** *(adult/child €6/free)* where you can discover five centuries' worth of music in an interactive sound laboratory. There's also the **Museum für Völkerkunde** *(free)* exploring global cultures and the **Museum für Angewandte Kunst** *(free)* flaunting Art Nouveau and Art Deco furniture, porcelain, glass and ceramics.

Central Germany

HISTORY | ANCIENT BEECHWOOD | BROTHERS GRIMM

Central Germany is truly the heart of the country. Plenty of sites in Thuringia, Lower Saxony, Saxony-Anhalt and Hesse have a special historical resonance or even a mythic significance. And so much of the national story has unfolded here – key sites in intellectual, religious and political developments that have shaped modern Germany, Europe and beyond. Look no further for the seedbed of Germany's most revered artists, writers and thinkers from Goethe to Nietzsche and Bach.

Here, beyond the time-worn churches, half-timbered, 16th-century merchants' houses and grim fortresses of tourist brochures, you'll find glowing examples of the German rural ideal. Ancient swaths of beech and conifer forest, the low mountains and farmsteads of Brothers Grimm stories, and broad fields of corn and sunflowers are abundant. There's room to stretch your legs, to cycle, to swim and to get back to basics in some of the largest nature reserves in Central Europe.

Weimar

Discover Goethe's Weimar

Johann Wolfgang von Goethe (1749–1832), the colossus of German letters, spent much of his life in Weimar. He lived in the 18th-century *Wohnhaus* (residence) on Frauenplan square for more than 50 years. The house now houses the **Goethe-Nationalmuseum** *(klassik-stiftung.de; adult/student €10/4)*, the world's largest collection of Goethe manuscripts and artefacts.

Allow several hours to explore the residence and the superbly curated permanent exhibition, **Lebensfluten – Tatensturm** ('Floods of Life – Storm of Action') including where he wrote *Faust*. Meanwhile, the **Goethe Gartenhaus** *(klassik-stiftung. de; adult/student €7/3)* is where he lived prior to the *Wohnhaus*. The lovely cottage, surrounded by the garden that Goethe himself laid out, is within the 58-acre, UNESCO-listed **Park an der Ilm** *(free)*.

GETTING AROUND

This region is most easily explored by car. In the towns, you can mostly get around on foot.

Deutsche Bahn *(bahn.de)* runs most services in Central Germany. The major rail hubs are Kassel and Halle, though there are regular connections throughout. Private operator **FlixTrain** *(flixtrain.com)* runs between Halle and Berlin but comfort is lacking. The region's bus network is efficient and much cheaper than rail.

☑ TOP TIP

In Weimar, head for the tourist office and get a Weimar Card. It's seriously good value – for €32.50 you'll get 48-hour access to the many museums and historic sites of the Klassik Stiftung Weimar ensemble, plus a guided walking tour and free 'iguide'.

507

MUSEUMS FOR EXPLORING GREAT MINDS

Schiller Museum: Friedrich Schiller's *Wohnhaus* includes a permanent exhibition on the 18th-century author.

Liszt-Haus: Where composer Franz Liszt lived from 1869 until his death in 1886.

Museum Neues: The former Grand Ducal Museum hosts a permanent exhibition on early modernist art spanning the Weimar School to Henry van de Velde.

Haus Hohe Pappeln: An unusual house designed by the Belgian Art Nouveau architect-designer himself.

Nietzsche Archiv: Where the troubled philosopher and nihilist lived out his final years.

House of the Weimar Republic: Exhibit on the story of Germany's short-lived first democracy.

Bauhaus beginnings

The **Bauhaus Museum Weimar** *(klassik-stiftung.de; adult/ student €10/4)* commemorates the Bauhaus (literally 'building house') school founded in Weimar in 1919. The collection here focuses on the early days. To actually see Bauhaus architecture, **Haus Am Horn** *(adult/student €5/2)* is Weimar's only truly Bauhaus building.

The dark history of Buchenwald

Buchenwald concentration camp has been preserved almost untouched as a memorial, the **Gedenkstätte Buchenwald** *(buchenwald.de; tour adult/student €7/3, multimedia guide €5)*. Visitors are encouraged to wander quietly and freely around its numerous structures, including the crematorium.

Kassel

Deep dive into fairy tales

Kassel is an ideal launching pad for exploring the **Märchenstrasse** (Fairy Tale Road), one of Germany's most beguiling tourist routes. The 600km route stretches from Hanau, the birthplace of the Brothers Grimm, to Bremen. Of the 50-odd fairy-tale-associated stops, five are 'life stations' of the brothers: Hanau, Steinau, Marburg, Kassel and Göttingen. All make for excellent day trips or overnight destinations. Before heading off, discover the Brothers' legacy in Kassel at **Grimmwelt** *(grimmwelt.de; adult/student/under 3yr €10/7/ free)*, the world's leading museum and archive on their work.

Dessau

The wonderful world of Bauhaus

Bauhaus, considered the most influential school of design and architecture of the 20th century, reached its creative peak in Dessau. The purpose-built **Bauhaus-Dessau Museum** *(bauhaus-dessau.de; adult/child €10/free)*, home to wonderful exhibitions curated from 49,000 pieces, is the world's second largest after Berlin. Also obligatory is the **Bauhausgebäude** *(adult/child €10/free)*. The iconic modernist building, designed by Gropius himself, is a teaching institution but permits audio guided tours inside.

Wittenberg

Lutheran churches and sights

The Lutherstadt-Wittenberg is UNESCO-recognised for its wealth of Reformation-related sites. Most important is the **Schlosskirche** *(schlosskirche-wittenberg.de; tower €3)* where Martin Luther nailed his *Ninety-Five Theses* to the door. There's also **Stadtkirche Wittenberg** *(stadtkirchengemei nde-wittenberg.de)*, where Luther conducted the world's first Protestant worship services in 1521.

Frankfurt am Main

SKYLINE VIEWS | APPLE WINE | ART MUSEUMS

Glinting with glass, steel and concrete skyscrapers, Frankfurt am Main (pronounced 'mine') is unlike any other German city. 'Mainhattan' is a high-powered finance and business hub, home to one of the world's largest stock exchanges and the gleaming headquarters of the European Central Bank, and it famously hosts some of the world's most important trade fairs, attracting thousands of business travellers. Yet, at its heart, Frankfurt is an unexpectedly traditional and charming city, with half-timbered buildings huddled in its quaint medieval Altstadt (old town), cosy apple-wine taverns serving hearty regional food, village-like neighbourhoods filled with outdoor cafes, boutiques and street art, and beautiful parks, gardens and riverside paths. The city's cache of museums is second in Germany only to Berlin's, and its nightlife and entertainment scenes are bolstered by a spirited student population. The area around the Hauptbahnhof is the red-light and drug district, and while it offers the cheapest accommodation, you should avoid it.

Frankfurt's Historic Heart

Roman market square

The **Römerberg** is Frankfurt's old central square, buzzing with tourists and street performers. Ornately gabled half-timbered buildings, reconstructed in the 1980s after WWII bombings, give an idea of how beautiful the city's medieval core once was. The photogenic **Rathaus** building, with its three step-gabled 15th-century houses, is one such example. In the time of the Holy Roman Empire, it was the site of celebrations during the election and coronation of emperors. Today, it houses the office of Frankfurt's mayor.

GETTING AROUND

Frankfurt is a surprisingly compact, small and navigable city. It is very walkable and the River Main acts as a primary landmark to guide your journey. To get a real feel for the city, try to take it in on foot as much as you can. Public transport is also robust and easy to use, with commuter trains, buses, trams and a subway system. If renting a car, parking can be a bit expensive, so prepare to pay €1 for every 20 minutes in most cases.

☑ **TOP TIP**

The **Moselle Valley** is especially scenic walking country. Variants of the Mosel Erlebnis Route follow the entire Moselle Valley along both banks of the river. Expect some steep climbs if you venture away from the river, such as on the 185km-long Moselhöhenweg, which sticks to high ground but offers spectacular vistas.

BEST FESTIVALS IN FRANKFURT

Christopher Street Day: A colourful Pride parade in mid-July, as well as a *Strassenfest* (street festival) at Konstablerwache.

Rheingauer Weinmarkt: At this 10-day late-summer festival, enjoy a taste of over 600 wine varieties from the surrounding Rheingau region.

Apfelweinfestival: Frankfurt's famous *Apfelwein* is celebrated in August with tastings, music and storytelling in dialect.

Frankfurt Book Fair: The largest annual global book fair, Frankfurter Buchmesse, takes place at Frankfurt Messe in mid-October. Book early to get a hotel room.

Christmas Market: Every December, Frankfurt's Christmas market in the Altstadt brings cheer with choirs, *Glühwein*, stalls and traditional foods.

HIGHLIGHTS
1 Kaiserdom
2 Römerberg
3 Städel Museum

SIGHTS
4 Deutsches Filmmuseum
5 Deutsches Romantik-Museum
6 Historisches Museum Frankfurt
7 Museum für Kommunikation

ACTIVITIES
8 Primus Linie

SLEEPING
9 Ruby Louise Hotel
10 Steigenberger Frankfurter Hof

EATING
11 Im Herzen Afrikas
12 Kleinmarkthalle
13 Occhio D'Oro
14 Pizzeria Montana
15 Ramen Muku
16 Zu den 12 Aposteln

Regal History
Climb the Kaiserdom

The red-sandstone Imperial Cathedral of St Bartholomew, aka **Kaiserdom** (*dom-frankfurt.de; tower adult/child €3/1.50*) or Frankfurt Cathedral, is located in the heart of the Altstadt. An unmatched view of the city is your reward if you climb the 328 steps up the cathedral's Gothic tower to the viewing platform at an impressive 66m. The cathedral itself, the construction of which began in the 13th century, houses many regal memories as the German emperors and kings of the Holy Roman Empire were either crowned or elected here. The original chapel where the elections took place is now used only for silent prayer. The cathedral was rebuilt after an 1867 fire and again after the bombings of 1944, which left it a burnt-out shell.

A Soaring Romantic Journey
Learn about German Romanticism

The **Deutsches Romantik-Museum** (*German Romanticism Museum; deutsches-romantik-museum.de; adult/child €12/3*)

Kaiserdom

is the very first of its kind in the world, deep-diving into the art and ethos of the German Romantic movement.

The first-level Goethe gallery contains over 5000 paintings from 1750 to 1850. The 2nd-floor gallery broadens the scope to explore Romanticism as a whole, focusing heavily on the literary works from the era. Weave through a maze of mirrors and standing panes with varying definitions of Romanticism imprinted on them; you can even type out your very own ode to love. The 3rd-floor gallery brings the intense feelings of the German Romantics to life. Learn how philosophers, poets, novelists, painters and fine artists throughout Europe began to gain inspiration from the German Romantics.

Down the Main

Relax on a river cruise

The Main River divides the city, with Frankfurt proper on the northern bank, and Sachsenhausen on the southern. You can appreciate the city's many charms while bobbing down the river on a boat. Hour-long sightseeing cruises with **Primus Linie**

 EATING IN FRANKFURT: CHEAP EATS

Kleinmarkthalle: Traditional market hall with stalls selling artisan smoked sausages, cheese and pastries, plus espresso bar. *8am-6pm Mon-Fri, to 4pm Sat* €

Pizzeria Montana: Thin-crust pizzas with premium ingredients prepared fresh and cooked in a wood-fired oven. *11.30am-10pm Mon-Fri, from noon Sat & Sun* €

Ramen Muku: One of Frankfurt's excellent Japanese restaurants serves homemade ramen noodles and sashimi. *noon-1.30pm & 6-9.30pm Wed-Sun* €

Startorante: Social enterprise offering hospitality training and apprenticeships to young women; it serves three-course lunches. *11.30am-2pm Tue-Fri* €

(primus-linie.de) leave hourly from Eiserner Steg, or catch an evening cruise to see the city's glittering skyline as dusk falls.

Longer full-day and multi-day cruises often begin in Frankfurt and float onwards to Mainz where the river meets the Rhine. At the Rhine–Main junction, you can continue on through the spectacular Rhine Valley.

Get Your Culture Fix

Explore Museum Embankment

On the southern bank of the Main River, nine world-class museums line up like dominoes. A further three jostle for position on the opposite side under the name **Museumufer** (Museum Embankment). You'd need weeks to visit them all, so focus on the heavy hitters.

Founded in 1815, **Städel Museum** *(staedelmuseum.de; adult/child €16/free)* is a world-renowned art gallery with an outstanding collection of European art from masters like Rembrandt, Rubens and Cézanne. It also features temporary photography exhibits, included in the ticket price.

Next door is the **Museum für Kommunikation** *(mfk-frankfurt.de; adult/child/under 5yr €8/2/free)*, which promises to revive some nostalgia as you trace the history of communication from Mesopotamian writing stones through to today's ultra-connected tech, with engaging, hands-on exhibitions.

Movie buffs will love the **Deutsches Filmmuseum** *(German Film Museum; dff.film; adult/child/under 6yr €8/4/free)*, where you can try your hand at editing, play around with green screens and explore iconic props, costumes and film posters.

Jump back across the river to visit the **Historisches Museum Frankfurt** *(historisches-museum-frankfurt.de; adult/child €8/free)*. This museum focuses specifically on the long and storied history of Frankfurt. Don't miss the giant snow globe on the bottom floor.

 EATING IN FRANKFURT: OUR PICKS

Zu den 12 Aposteln: German food such as Frankfurter schnitzel with *Grüne Sosse* and *Käsespätzle* under dim lamplight. *noon-11pm* €€

Druckwasserwerk: German cuisine in a beautiful building from 1899. Outside, there's an umbrella-shaded terrace. *5pm-midnight Mon-Sat* €€€

Occhio D'Oro: On the rooftop of the Flemings Hotel, this Italian restaurant with stunning city views serves regional cuisine. *6pm-midnight Mon-Sat* €€

Im Herzen Afrikas: Eritrean cuisine at a rustic tavern with a sandy floor and colourful murals transporting you to Africa. *4-11pm Mon-Fri, from 1pm Sat* €€

Beyond Frankfurt

Leave behind Frankfurt's towering cityscape to discover quiet charm, Gutenberg's legacy, medieval castles...and, of course, Riesling after Riesling.

Straddling the Rhine, Mainz offers a chance to explore the region's quieter side. The hometown of Johannes Gutenberg, the inventor of the printing press, Mainz has a sizeable university and a rich wine culture. Strolling along the Rhine and sampling local wines in a half-timbered tavern is as much a part of any Mainz visit as its fabulous sightseeing.

Between Rüdesheim and Koblenz, the Rhine cuts deeply through the Rhenish Slate Mountains, meandering between hillside castles and steep fields of wine-producing grapes. This is Germany's landscape at its most dramatic – forested hillsides alternate with craggy cliffs and near-vertical terraced vineyards. Idyllic villages appear around each bend, their half-timbered houses and Gothic church steeples seemingly plucked from the world of fairy tales.

Places
Mainz p513
Heidelberg p515
Rüdesheim am Rhein p515
Koblenz p515

Mainz

TIME FROM FRANKFURT: **50MIN**

Birthplace of the printing press

The **Gutenberg-Museum Mainz** *(mainz.de; adult/child €10/4)* is a proud homage to the history of the printed word and the 15th-century Mainz native who invented it – Johannes Gutenberg. The museum's most incredible exhibits, kept under dim light, are the two copies of the 42-line **Gutenberg Bible**,

---

⊘ GETTING AROUND

ICE trains run frequently from Frankfurt's Hauptbahnhof via the airport and are the easiest and quickest way to reach Mainz. All main attractions are within walking distance from the train station. The public bus and tram systems are easy to use.

Navigate the Romantic Rhine Valley by renting a car. Only two train lines run along this section of the Rhine. The Linke Rheinstrecke (Left Rhine Line) runs along the west bank from Cologne to Mainz, passing through

Boppard, St Goar, Oberwesel and Bacharach. The Rechte Rheinstrecke (Right Rhine Line) runs along the east bank and passes through Braubach, Kaub, Assmannshausen and Rüdesheim.

KD runs cruises and scheduled services up and down the river between Cologne and Mainz. Travelling end to end takes over 11 hours, or you can opt for shorter sections such as St Goar to Bingen.

SADMAN/SHUTTERSTOCK

Drosselgasse, Rüdesheim am Rhein

printed in 1455 and hand-decorated. Don't miss the 20-minute demonstrations of Gutenberg's printing press to understand the ingenuity of his invention.

Chagall's blue-hued church

Around 200,000 pilgrims make their way to the **St-Stephan-Kirche** *(bistummainz.de/pfarrei/mainz-st-stephan)* every year. This would be just another Gothic church rebuilt after WWII were it not for the nine brilliant-blue stained-glass windows created by the Jewish artist Marc Chagall in the final years of his life, which serve as a symbol of Jewish–Christian reconciliation. Pick up an audio guide inside the church to learn more about each individual artwork.

Marvel at the Mainz markets

Three times a week year-round, open-air markets fill the pretty squares around **Mainzer Dom** *(bistummainz.de/mainzer-dom),* the city's immense 12th-century cathedral built from deep-red sandstone blocks. Many of the stall-holders have been selling local produce, smoked meats and more at these markets for generations. On Saturdays from March to November, you can enjoy the **Market Breakfast** with Mainz winegrowers. In front of the cathedral, treat yourself to a *Worscht un Woi,* a sausage served with a roll and wine. In December, these markets become even more festive, with Christmas shopping, holiday-themed stalls and carol music.

Heidelberg

TIME FROM FRANKFURT: 1HR

A majestic hilltop castle

Hit the Romantic Road for Heidelberg's Altstadt and the ruined Renaissance **Schloss Heidelberg** (*schloss-heidelberg.de; adult/child €11/5.50*). The castle gardens are worth strolling for views of the Neckar River and the Altstadt rooftop. The castle cellar is also home to the **Heidelberg Tun (Großes Fass)**, the world's biggest wine barrel. The Schlossticket combines entrance to the castle and a ride on the **Bergbahn** funicular railway (a steep walk up is also an option).

Rüdesheim am Rhein

TIME FROM FRANKFURT: 1HR

It's wine o'clock

Although Rüdesheim is an unofficial starting point on a journey up the Rhine (day-tripping coach tourists abound), it stays surprisingly small and maintains its old medieval charms. Explore the kitschy, colourful town centre and, especially, the famously narrow medieval alley **Drosselgasse**.

Rüdesheim is primarily a winemaking town and its vineyards are UNESCO-listed. The town has its own delicious white variety, called the Rheingauer Riesling, which you can sample at **RheinWeinWelt** (*rheinweinwelt.de*).

Koblenz

TIME FROM FRANKFURT: 1½HR

Fall in love with Festung Ehrenbreitstein

Perched 118m above the Rhine, the **Festung Ehrenbreitstein** (*Ehrenbreitstein Fortress; tor-zum-welterbe.de/festung-ehrenbreitstein; adult/child €10/5.50*) was indestructible for decades until Napoleonic troops arrived. To prove a point, the Prussians rebuilt it as one of Europe's mightiest fortifications. Inside, there are several museums and fabulous views from its ramparts and viewing platform, from where you can see the confluence of the Rhine and Moselle rivers. The most fun way to travel up is the **Seilbahn** (*seilbahn-koblenz.de; one-way adult/child €12/6*) cable car.

Where the rivers meet

At the point of confluence of the Moselle and the Rhine, the **Deutsches Eck** (German Corner) is a testament to German unity lost and found. The stone pedestal links up to a grassy promenade for the most perfect riverside stroll.

TASTE THE WINE ROUTE

One of Germany's oldest tour routes, the **Deutsche Weinstrasse** (German Wine Route) traverses the heart of the Palatinate (Pfalz) – a region of vine-covered hillsides, rambling forests, ruined castles, 35 picturesque hamlets and thriving fruit orchards. The drive is especially pretty during spring (March to mid-May) and harvest (September to October). Starting in Schweigen-Rechtenbach, on the French border, the route winds north for 85km to Bockenheim an der Weinstrasse, although it can be driven in either direction. Key stops along the way include the postcard-perfect medieval Riesling villages of **Bacharach** and **Oberwesel**, as well as fairy-tale landmarks in **St Goar**.

Places We Love to Stay

€ Budget €€ Midrange €€€ Top End

Berlin   MAP p459, p465 & p468

Generator Berlin Alexanderplatz € Huge and high-energy, this modern designer hostel has cheerfully painted private rooms and dorms, plus industrial-chic public areas.

Kiez Hostel € Central, squeaky-clean base with a welcoming homey vibe and imaginatively designed dorms, but limited check-in hours.

Cosmo Hotel €€ The lobby's extravagant lamps and armchairs set the tone for crisply angular rooms with silvery design accents and floor-to-ceiling windows.

Park Inn by Radisson Berlin Alexanderplatz €€ This sleek tower is honeycombed with 1029 generic but comfy rooms featuring panoramic windows, wooden floors and noiseless air-con.

Myer's Hotel Berlin €€ Feeling like your rich uncle's manor, this 56-room boutique hotel has antique-style rooms, a clubby bar and a cosy cellar spa.

Sly Berlin €€ Modern luxury meets local flair across four revamped factory-era buildings, anchored by a lush atrium and crowned with a rooftop sauna.

Hotel Château Royal €€€ Hip and haute boutique hotel in two listed buildings and a Chipperfield-designed annex features elegant rooms and site-specific art throughout.

Soho House Berlin €€€ This celeb-fave offers vintage-styled rooms in multiple sizes and access to members-only areas like the spa and rooftop pool.

Cologne   MAP p472

Hostel die Wohngemeinschaft € This next-gen hostel turned creative space has smartly designed rooms with themes from spaceship to Bollywood.

Hotel Chelsea €€ Originals created by international artists, in exchange for lodging, grace the public areas and 39 rooms, including the eye-catching deconstructivist top floor.

Wasserturm Hotel Cologne €€€ A-list sanctuary in a landmark water tower with quirky-luxe design, top gym and rooftop bar.

Düsseldorf   MAP p477

Max Hotel Garni € Modern self-check-in hotel near the Hauptbahnhof is a solid bargain base, with 11 snug but comfortable and quiet rooms.

Ruby Coco Hotel €€ 'Lean luxury' hotel with rooftop terrace, channeling Coco Chanel in rooms with glass-fronted shower cubicles.

Hotel Orangerie €€€ Stylish refuge in a neoclassical mansion in a quiet corner of the Altstadt within staggering distance of pubs, the river and museums.

Hamburg   MAP p480

Superbude St Georg € Design hotel-hostel combo with comfy beds, sleek private bathrooms and a 'rock star suite' – another location in St Georg near Central Station.

Henri Hotel €€ Kidney-shaped tables, plush armchairs, vintage typewriters – 1950s chic à la Don Draper. Rooms and studios for urban lifestyle junkies.

Westin Hamburg €€€ Hamburg's premier address, inside the lower half of the Elbphilharmonie. Rooms are stylish and minimalist. Splurge on an upper-floor room with city or harbour views.

Munich   MAP p486

Flushing Meadows €€ Up-to-the-minute minimalist design on the top two floors of an industrial building in the hip Glockenbachviertel. There are views, designer styling and a restaurant to enjoy.

Gästehaus Englischer Garten €€ Occupying a 200-year-old ivy-clad mill, this small guesthouse on the edge of the English Garden offers an intimate, pre-millennium experience in individually done-out, antique-speckled rooms.

Das Kleine Hotel in München €€ There's a dearth of accommodation in Maxvorstadt, so this 'little hotel in Munich' with its parquet floors, slightly dated fabrics and art sprinkled throughout is a well-used but welcome place to unpack.

Bayerischer Hof €€€ In a super-central location since 1841, this is one of the grandes dames of the Munich hotel world. Elegant rooms, impeccably regimented staff, antique-dotted public spaces and five fabulous restaurants.

Garmisch-Partenkirchen

Reindl's Partenkirchner Hof €€ Five-star everything here includes wine bar, gourmet restaurant and folk-themed rooms.

Gasthof zum Rassen €€
Behind a 14th-century frescoed facade, this guesthouse has modern rooms, antique public areas and Bavaria's oldest folk theatre.

Rothenburg ob der Tauber

Hotel Herrnschlösschen €€€
Occupying a 900-year-old Rothenburg mansion, this top-class hotel is a blend of ancient and new, Gothic and faux-retro.

Altfränkische Weinstube €€€
This 650-year-old Rothenburg inn has heaps of medieval character and an excellent restaurant.

Würzburg

Hotel Zum Winzermännle €€
Family-run converted winery in the heart of Würzburg with old-fashioned rooms, some with balconies.

Hotel Rebstock €€€
Würzburg's best hotel inhabits a renovated rococo town house, with great facilities, service and Altstadt location.

Bremen

MAP p501

Prizeotel Bremen City €
Good-value hotel, with large rooms in fluorescent colours and soundproofed windows close to the station. Prices vary, but it's great value during quiet times.

Nena Hotel Bremen €€€
Design hotel on the river in the centre, with indoor pool and wellness area.

Dresden

Hostel Mondpalast € Each playful room is designed to reflect a sign of the zodiac in this out-of-this-world hostel-bar-cafe in Neustadt.

Hotel am Terrassenufer €€
This brutalist GDR-era block looming over Altstadt features large rooms with panoramic views of the river.

Gewandhaus Hotel €€€ In Altstadt, the 18th-century trading house has sleek public areas plus beautiful and bright rooms.

Leipzig

Hostel Five Elements € Super-central and well-equipped hostel featuring dorms, cheap

private rooms, comfy common spaces and cooking facilities.

Gwuni Mopera €€ No-nonsense rooms and an on-site restaurant-bar in a quiet courtyard across the ring road from Altstadt.

Townhouse €€€ Boutique gem with sound-sculpture lamps, Bach manuscript wallpaper and views of the Thomaskirche.

Weimar

Labyrinth Hostel € Artist-designed rooms in an extremely friendly and well-run hostel, close to the Weimarhallen Park.

Hotel Alt Weimar €€ Good-value rooms in the former home of 19th-century occultist, archivist and architect Rudolf Steiner.

Frankfurt am Main

MAP p510

25hours Goldman € Artfully decorated rooms in the east end, a 10-minute tram ride from Römer. Score the best deals and early check-in by booking directly. Paid parking.

Ruby Louise Hotel €€ Find a super-trendy vibe at this designer hotel featuring a rooftop terrace and reception on level 6.

Steigenberger Frankfurter Hof €€€ Luxurious rooms, full spa, bar and restaurant with outdoor dining. Perfect location-wise for exploring the city.

HELGA KING/SHUTTERSTOCK

Bayerischer Hof, Munich

Practicalities

HEALTH

Health care in Germany is of a high standard. German *Drogerien* (chemists) do not sell any kind of medication, not even aspirin. Even *rezeptfrei* (over-the-counter) medications for minor health concerns are only available at an *Apotheke* (pharmacy), so bring what you need along with you. Tap water is drinkable.

BALKANSCAT/SHUTTERSTOCK

ELECTRICITY

Germany's electricity supply is 230V, and plugs are of the European two-round-pin type (Type C and Type F). Most sockets accept both. Three-pin sockets are not used, so you'll only need standard European adapters.

DAYS OF CLOSURE

On Sundays, Germany observes *Ruhetag* (day of rest) when supermarkets, malls and individual retailers are closed. Don't expect to get any shopping done on these days. Some supermarkets are open in major train stations – these are helpful in a pinch, though expect long queues. Museums and restaurants stay open on Sundays but they might close on a Monday and/or Tuesday (check ahead).

PRIVACY

Photographing individuals in public places is not allowed in Germany unless you check with the person first. This is taken very seriously. Do not take photos of children. Many nightlife establishments ban photography completely.

OPENING HOURS

Opening hours vary seasonally and between cities and villages.
Banks 9am–4pm weekdays
Bars 8pm–2am
Cafes 10am–6pm
Restaurants 11am–10pm (food until 9pm)
Shops 10am–6pm Monday to Saturday
Supermarkets 8am–8pm Monday to Saturday (earlier in rural areas)

SMOKING

Smoking is legislated differently in every state. Some bars, pubs and cafes allow smoking. Bavaria bans it practically everywhere, while in Berlin and Hamburg smoker-friendly bars abound. Look for a sign out front reading *Raucherkneipe* (smoking bar) to indicate such establishments.

PUBLIC HOLIDAYS

Germany observes 11 national public holidays. Additional holidays vary between states.
New Year's Day 1 January
Easter March/April; Good Friday, Easter Sunday and Easter Monday
Ascension Day 40 days after Easter

Labour Day 1 May
Whit/Pentecost Sunday and Monday 50 days after Easter
Veteran's Day 15 June
German Unity Day 3 October
Christmas Day 25 December
Boxing Day 26 December

Language

German belongs to the West Germanic language family, with English and Dutch as close relatives.

Basics

Hello. Servus. *ser*-vus
Hello. Grüss Gott. grewss-got
Good morning. Guten Morgen. goo-ten *mor*-gen
Goodbye. Auf Wiedersehen. owf vee-der-zay-en
Bye. Tschüss./ Tschau. chüs/chow
Yes. Ja. yah
No. Nein. nain
Please. Bitte. *bi*-te
Thank you. Danke. *dang*-ke
Excuse me. Entschuldigung. ent-*shul*-di-gung
Sorry. Entschuldigung. ent-*shul*-di-gung
What's your name?
Wie ist Ihr Name? (pol) vee ist eer *nah*-me
Wie heißt du? (inf) vee haist doo
My name is ...
Mein Name ist ... (pol) main *nah*-me ist ...
Ich heiße ... (inf) ikh *hai*-se ...
Do you speak English?
Sprechen Sie Englisch? (pol) *shpre*-khen zee *eng*-lish
Sprichst du Englisch? (inf) shprikhst doo *eng*-lish
I don't understand. Ich verstehe nicht. ikh fer-*shtay*-e nikht

Directions

Where's (the station)?
Wo ist (der Bahnhof). vor ist (der *bahn*-hawf)
What's the address?
Wie ist die Adresse? vee ist dee a-*dre*-se
Could you please write it down?
Könnten Sie das bitte aufschreiben? *kern*-ten zee das *bi*-te owf-shrai-ben

Can you show me (on the map)?
Können Sie es mir (auf der Karte) zeige *ker*-nen zee es meer (owf dair *kar*-te) *tsai*-gen

Signs

Ausgang Exit
Eingang Entrance
Damen Women
Herren Men
Heiß Hot
Kalt Cold
Offen Open
Geschlossen Closed
Kein Zutritt No Entry
Rauchen Verboten No Smoking
Verboten Prohibited

Time

What time is it? Wie spät ist es? vee shpayt ist es
It's (10) o'clock. Es ist (zehn) Uhr. es ist (tsayn) oor
morning Morgen *mor*-gen
afternoon Nachmittag *nahkh*-mi-tahk
evening Abend *ah*-bent
yesterday Gestern *ges*-tern
today Heute *hoy*-te
tomorrow Morgen *mor*-gen

Emergencies

Help! Hilfe! *hil*-fe
Go away! Gehen Sie weg! *gay*-en zee vek
I'm ill. Ich bin krank. ikh bin krangk
Call the police! Rufen Sie die Polizei! *roo*-fen zee dee po-li-*tsai*
Call a doctor! Rufen Sie einen Arzt! *roo*-fen zee *ai*-nen artst

NUMBERS	
1	
eins *ains*	
2	
zwei *tsvai*	
3	
drei *drai*	
4	
vier *feer*	
5	
fünf *fünf*	
6	
sechs *zeks*	
7	
sieben *zee-ben*	
8	
acht *akht*	
9	
neun *noyn*	
10	
zehn *tsayn*	

NIKADA/GETTY IMAGES

Frankfurt International Airport

Arriving

Most travellers arrive in Germany by air or by rail and road from neighbouring countries. Frankfurt International is Germany's busiest airport (and one of Europe's largest), servicing some 300 destinations; it's the headquarters for Germany's flag carrier, Lufthansa. Non-EU visitors will probably enter into Europe and go through customs here, even if their final stop is elsewhere.

By Air
Most large and many smaller German cities have their own airports, and numerous carriers operate domestic flights within Germany. However, unless you're flying from one end of the country to the other, planes are only marginally quicker than trains.

By Rail
Rail services link Germany with virtually every country in Europe. **Deutsche Bahn** (*bahn.de*) handles ticketing. In the EU's Schengen (free-movement zone) crossing borders is visa-less; there are no passport controls entering from the Netherlands, Belgium, Austria and Switzerland, among others.

MONEY
Currency: Euro (€)

CASH
Cash is king in Germany. Always carry some and plan to pay cash at places like cafes and pubs. Since the pandemic, e-payments are catching on, but setting aside smaller bills for tips and emergencies is always a good idea. Barkeepers and kiosks may gripe about big notes.

CREDIT CARDS
Plastic is essential for booking hotels and sometimes for reserving tables at high-end restaurants. In Berlin, a small yet rising number of coffee and nightlife joints only take electronic payments, too. Usually Visa and Mastercard are accepted (not American Express or Diners Club). Kiosks usually require a minimum purchase of €10.

TIPPING
Quality of service and setting dictate how Germans tip. Say either the amount you want to pay, or *'Stimmt so'* for no change.

Hotels €1 to €2 per bag/cleaning day.

Restaurants Most Germans will tip 5% to 10%.

Cafes and bars Simply round up to the nearest euro.

Getting Around

For speedsters on tight schedules, driving a car on the autobahn's limitless stretches will be deeply satisfying, but parking in cities is a pain. Germany's excellent train system makes for efficient travel too – it's stress-free, you can stretch your legs and mind your carbon footprint. Last-minute bookings can be expensive during busy periods (weekends and holidays).

WERNER SPREMBERG/SHUTTERSTOCK

Public Transport
Germany's cities and larger towns have efficient public transport systems. Bigger cities such as Berlin and Munich integrate buses, trams, U-Bahn (underground) trains and S-Bahn (suburban) trains in one network. Fares are determined by zones or time travelled (sometimes both).

Car
German roads are excellent and no tolls are charged on any public roads. The country's pride and joy is its 13,000km network of autobahns (motorways). Every 40km to 60km, you'll find elaborate service areas with 24-hour petrol stations, toilets and restaurants.

Ridesharing
In cities, car-share apps like **Miles Mobility** (miles-mobility. com) offer renting cars by short duration or distance. Check out long-distance carpooling (travel in someone's private car in exchange for some petrol money) via **BlaBlaCar** (blablacar.com) and **Mitfahrzentrale** (mifaz.de).

Train
Intercity Express (ICE) trains are high-speed sprinters, and Regional Express (RE) are slower but more affordable public trains. Some private operators offer significantly cheaper fares, though on slower, older (and less comfortable) trains. Reserving seats is always smart.

Ferry
Ferries connect Germany's two seas, and provide convenient transport in its lake- and river-filled interior. Frequent ferries connect popular North and Baltic Sea islands; short-distance ferries shuttle passengers and vehicles along the Rhine and Elbe River.

DRIVING ESSENTIALS

Drive on the right

No general speed limits – usually 50km/h in urban areas, 80km/h on secondary roads, 130km/h recommended on motorways

0.05%

Blood alcohol limit is 0.05%

Curated by
Kate Armstrong

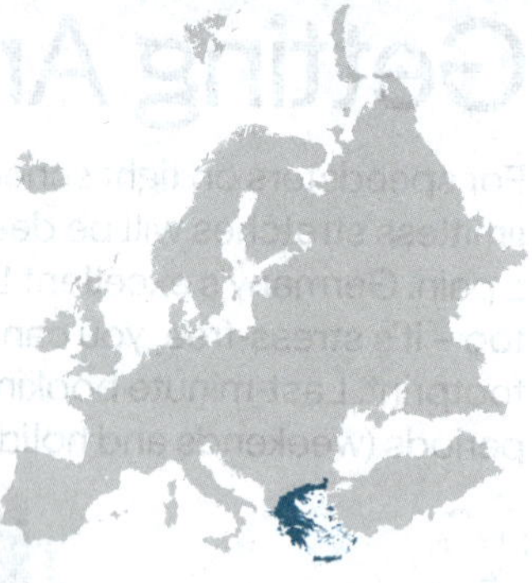

Greece

THE PLACE FOR EPIC ADVENTURES

Greece's legendary status is defined by its astonishing ancient civilisations, stunning azure seas, fresh culinary delights and mind-blowing museums.

Greece is a legendary destination in every sense. Literally speaking, it's where many myths of gods and giants originated, and it's not hard to see why. With wide skies, an island-speckled ocean and a varied and stunning terrain, it's made for adventure, relaxation and imagination.

You can evoke the essence of Ancient Greek civilisation at the Acropolis in Athens, consult the oracle at Delphi and reach lofty heights in the monasteries of Meteora in central Greece. Then wander under clear blue skies and white domes of the Cyclades, or even live out your inner knight in Rhodes' medieval Old Town. Eat your way through the local dishes in Crete and wander through fortresses and the ancient Palace of Knossos.

IMARZI/SHUTTERSTOCK

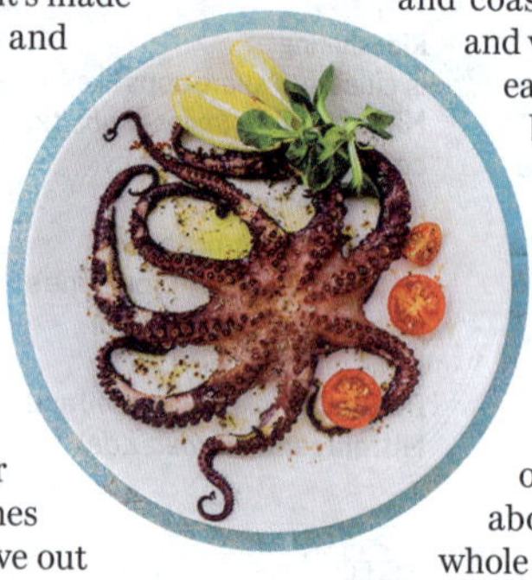

As for Greek cuisine? *Nostimo!* (Delicious!) Greek food is renowned across the globe for its wholesome, hearty dishes and philosophy of simple but superior-quality local ingredients, from mountain meats and coastal seafood to wild herbs and vegetables. And Greeks love eating out, sharing impossibly big meals with family and friends in a drawn-out, convivial way. Whether you're eating octopus at a seaside table or sampling a contemporary lamb recipe under the floodlit Acropolis, dining out in Greece is never just about what you eat but the whole sensory experience.

Finally, whether you're after beaches, ancient sites, mountain walks or city life, Greece has you covered.

THE MAIN AREAS

ATHENS
Greece's riveting, ancient capital.
p528

CENTRAL & NORTHERN GREECE
Full of history, with Greece's coolest city.
p534

PELOPONNESE
Filled with amazing archaeological sites.
p540

CYCLADES
Blue, white, gorgeous and ever popular.
p544

For places to stay in Greece, see p560

MIKHAIL MARKOVSKIY/SHUTTERSTOCK

Left: Grilled octopus; Above: Ancient Delphi (p535)

DODECANESE
A stunning array of history and beauty.
p547

CORFU
A pearl of the Ionian Islands.
p552

CRETE
Cretan cuisine, Minoan civilisation and fun.
p556

N

0 — 100 km
0 — 50 miles

Central & Northern Greece, p534

The focus is Meteora, famous for its Byzantine monasteries; Delphi, the centre of the ancient world; and Thessaloniki, Greece's creative city-by-the-sea.

Corfu, p552

Stroll atmospheric alleys between two fortresses, and explore world-class museums and gilded churches, all set against Venetian, French and British architecture.

Peloponnese, p540

Home to Nafplio, Greece's first capital, amazing archaeological sites of Mycenae and Epidavros, and Ancient Olympia, the spiritual home of the modern Olympics.

BULGARIA

NORTH MACEDONIA

Prilep · Gevgelija · Paleokastro · Doirani · Sidirokastro · Dra

Ohrid · Bitola · Kajmakčalan · Kilkis · Serres · Kava

Lake Ohrid · Lake Prespa · Florina · Edessa · Kerkini Reservoir · Strymnas

Korça · Kastoria · Naoussa · Giannitsa · Thessaloniki · A2

Veria · Alexandria

Vlorë · ALBANIA · Mt Grammos · Ptolemaida · A2 · Katerini · A24

Mt Smolikas · Kozani · Thermaic Gulf

Lecce · Grevena · Mt Olympus

Otranto · Saranda · Konitsa · Metsovo · Moni Megalou Meteorou · A1 · Elassona

ITALY · Corfu · Ioannina · Kalambaka · Trikala · Larissa

Palaio Frourio · Corfu Town · Mon Repos · A2 · Igoumenitsa · Karditsa · Farsala · Volos

Achilleion Palace · Parga · Arta · A3 · A1 · Skiathos · Skiathos Town

Ionian Sea · Paxi · Preveza · Karpenisi · Lamia · Isteia · Skopelos

Lefkada Town · Agios Konstantinos · Kym

Lefkada · Agrinio · Ancient Delphi · Mt Parnassos · A1 · Halkida · Evia

Fiskardo · Messolongi · Nafpaktos · Itea · Livadia · National Archaeolog Museum

Ithaki · Gulf of Corinth · Thiva · Karys

Argostoli · Sami · Patras · A8 · Loutraki · ATHENS · Rafina

Kefallonia · A5 · Xyiokastro · Acropolis · A8 · Piraeus · Acropolis Museum · Lav

Agios Nikolaos · Kyllini · Amaliada · Corinth · A7 · Aegina Town · Aegina · Kea

Zakynthos · Pirgos · PELOPONNESE · Argos · Poros Town · Kythne

Zakynthos Town · Olympia Archaeological Museum · Tripoli · Nafplio · Theatre of Epidavros · Hydra Town · Hydra

Megalopoli · Astros · Spetses Town

Kyparissia · Sparta · Mia

Kalamata · Mt Profitis Ilias

Mediterranean Sea · Pylos · Kardamyli · Gythio

Areopoli · Neapoli

Kythira

Antikythira · Venetia Harbou

Kissamos · Hania

Paleohora · Hora Sfakio

Gavdos

Find Your Way

Given its complex geography, Greece has an extensive network of domestic flights. Ferries link all the islands. Buses run on the larger islands, and a car or motorbike is the best way to explore most islands.

CAR

Given the vastness of mainland Greece, a car is useful as it allows you to get off the beaten track. Your own wheels can be useful on islands, too, where bus services may be limited.

BOAT

Greece's extensive ferry network includes fast modern ferries and overnight boats with cabins. Departures are subject to delay during poor weather. Schedules change annually, and services are greatly reduced between mid-October and Easter. In high season, book ahead. For schedules and tickets, *ferryhopper.com* is reliable.

BUS

The bus network on larger islands and in Athens is comprehensive and fares are cheap; buy tickets at the office (sometimes on board). Corfu (and some other Ionian islands) can be reached from Athens by bus – the fare includes ferry ticket price. Village services can be more limited.

Athens, p528

Ogle world-renowned treasures in one of the cradles of civilisation, from the Acropolis to the historic backstreets.

Cyclades, p544

Be mesmerised by white-and-blue architecture, dramatic cliffs and epic sunsets. The largest island, Naxos, has ancient ruins, mountain hamlets and white-sand beaches.

Dodecanese, p547

The historic centre of the Dodecanese, Rhodes Town is a medieval time capsule, while Kos Town is a charmer, with fabulous ancient ruins and more.

Crete, p556

Explore Minoan culture at the Palace of Knossos, enjoy the best of fresh and local Cretan cuisine, and hike through gorges to open sea.

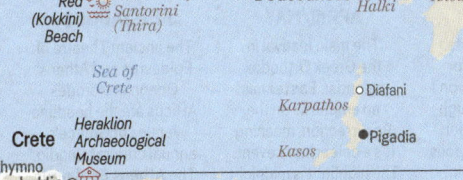

525

Plan Your Time

You can choose to spend more time in Athens and visit just one (or two) islands, or go crazy and do a ferry-heavy (or flight-focused) whirlwind trip to get a taste beyond the mainland.

YASEMIN OZDEMIR/SHUTTERSTOCK

Erechtheion, Acropolis (p529)

Mainland Greece in a Week

● Spend two days in the Greek capital, meandering around **central Athens** (p528) and visiting the **Acropolis** (p529), the **Acropolis Museum** (p530) and the Plaka district.

● Then catch the bus to **Delphi** (p534) and enjoy the sacred ruins. Alternatively, head to **Meteora** (p536) to visit the monasteries before hiking through the surreal landscape (connections are difficult and time-consuming between Delphi and Meteora).

● Afterwards, catch another bus to **Thessaloniki** (p537) and indulge in the city's restaurants, museums and artistic spaces, before returning to Athens. Another mainland itinerary option is to take the bus from Athens to **Nafplio** (p538). Explore the historic town and surrounding archaeological sites before heading west to **Ancient Olympia** (p543).

SEASONAL HIGHLIGHTS

Greece is a year-round destination. Many islands are 'closed' during winter. What you're looking for should dictate when you go.

FEBRUARY

With fewer tourists, it's a great time for sightseeing – you won't have to push through crowds at the major sights like the Acropolis or Roman Agora in Athens.

APRIL/MAY

The main festival in the Greek Orthodox calendar, **Easter** has an emphasis on the Resurrection, meaning it's a celebratory event. The highlight is midnight on Easter Saturday, when fireworks and a procession hit the streets.

JUNE/AUGUST

The ancient Theatre of Epidavros and Athens' Odeon of Herodes Atticus are the headline venues of Greece's annual cultural shindig. The **Athens Epidaurus Festival** (p543) features music, dance, theatre and much more.

Two Weeks to Explore

● Follow the **Athens** (p528) itinerary, then on day three catch the bus to **Delphi** (p534) for a night to experience the sacred ruins, and return to Athens.

● Next, fly to **Corfu** (p552) and spend several days exploring the Old Town and the **Achilleion Palace** (p555) before enjoying a beach day. Take a one-hour ferry to **Paxi** (p555) where you can relax for a day or two amid the olive groves, seaside villages and beach coves.

● Return to Corfu and take the ferry to Igoumenitsa, where you can catch a bus to Kalambaka (via Ioannina) for **Meteora** (p536). Fill two days with visits to the rock monasteries and outdoor pursuits before heading back to Athens.

Ten Days to Travel Around

● Start on Crete by flying in to **Hania** (p557). Spend a day strolling the Venetian fortifications or people-watching from a cafe by its charming harbour. Enjoy a day trekking the **Samaria Gorge** (p559) and another day at the Minoan ruins of **Knossos** (p559) and the state-of-the-art **Heraklion Archaeological Museum** (p558) in Iraklio.

● From Iraklio, either fly to **Rhodes** (p548) or get the twice-weekly, 11-hour ferry (less time from Sitia). On historic Rhodes, explore its atmospheric medieval **Old Town** (p549).

● To end your journey, take a three- to five-hour ferry ride to the island of **Kos** (p550). Here, experience its own ancient Old Town, before venturing out to beaches and archaeological sites.

SEPTEMBER

In early September, sample widely at the **wine festival** (p542) that celebrates the Nemea region's *agiorgitiko* red grape with tastings, concerts and more.

OCTOBER

A simple 'no' (ohi in Greek) was the famous response when Mussolini demanded passage for his troops on 28 October 1940. Now, **Ohi Day** is a national holiday with remembrance services and parades.

NOVEMBER

Around 150 films are crammed into 11 days of screenings, alongside concerts, exhibitions, talks and theatrical performances at the **Thessaloniki Film Festival** (p539).

DECEMBER/ JANUARY

This season brings joyful, light-festooned harbours, honey cookies and good cheer. New Year's Day brings the **Feast of Agios Vasilios** (St Basil), a church ceremony. This is time for the *vasilopita* (cake with a lucky coin).

Athens

ANCIENT LANDMARKS | ARCHITECTURE | CONTEMPORARY CULTURE

☑ **TOP TIP**

You could skip all the sights in Athens and still feel you have the city's pulse just by strolling along the pedestrian Dionysiou Areopagitou street around sundown. Lights glow on the Acropolis above, and the road is filled with tourists, snack vendors, musicians and local couples out for a promenade.

Cradle of European civilisation and democracy, Athens is a master of reinvention, serving a thrilling mashup of architectural gravitas, bodacious street life and inspiring creativity. With both grace and grunge, Athens creates a heady mix of ancient history and contemporary cool. The cultural and social life of the city plays out amid and within ancient landmarks, and the magnificent Acropolis remains the hub around which Athens' neighbourhoods revolve. This citadel crowns a rocky outcrop with ancient temples (including the jewel, the Parthenon) and serves as a daily reminder of Greece's heritage and the city's many transformations.

With a past rooted in mythology, drama, philosophy, Byzantine churches and, more recently, the 2004 Olympic Games, the city continues to pulse with art, community spirit and political debates. It's a must for most visitors to Greece. Athens can be chaotic, but take the pressure off by people-watching at a cafe or retreating to a wooded hilltop.

 GETTING AROUND

The transit system uses the **Ath.ena Ticket**, a reloadable card available from metro ticket offices and machines. Load it with credit, rides (€1.20 each, discount for 5 or 10) or travel pass (24 hours/5 days €4.10/8.20). These exclude airport transfer. Three-day tourist tickets (€20) include airport transfer. Swipe at metro turnstiles or, on buses/trams, validate in the machine. One swipe gives you 90 minutes, including transfers.

The Piraeus port is massive – 12 quays from which ferries and cruises depart to most Greek island groups and the Peloponnese. The metro line 1 (green) and suburban rail line 3 (blue) from Athens terminate at gate E7. A free shuttle bus runs regularly along the northern quays inside the port from gate E7 to E1.

Direct bus X96 to Eleftherios Venizelos International Airport stops outside the metro and along the road outside the port. The T7 tram departs from outside E8. Bus 040 goes to Athens, as does express X80 (May to October).

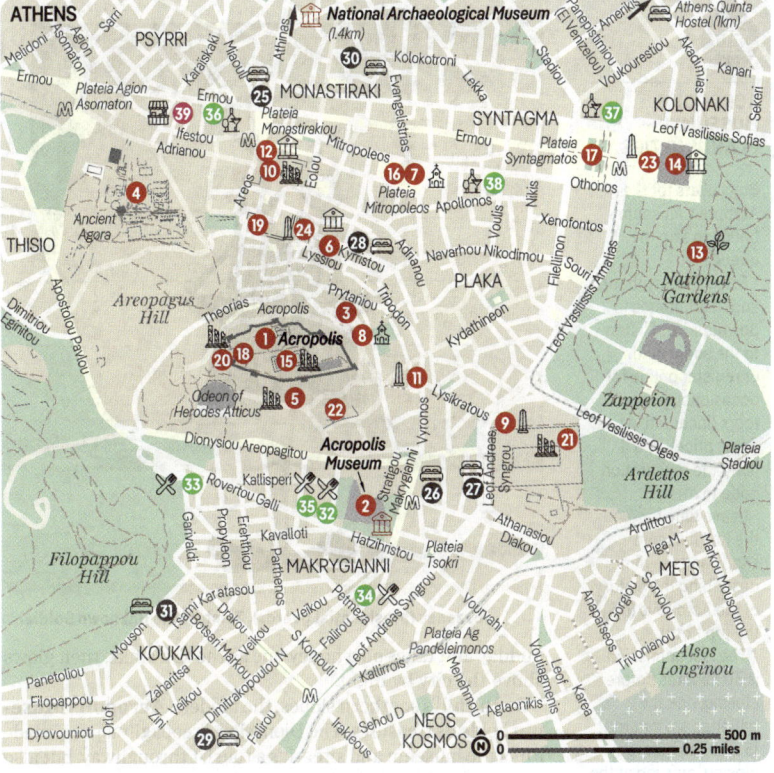

Map labels

ATHENS

PSYRRI

MONASTIRAKI

SYNTAGMA

KOLONAKI

National Archaeological Museum (1.4km)

Athens Quinta Hostel (1km)

THISIO

PLAKA

National Gardens

Areopagus Hill

Acropolis

Odeon of Herodes Atticus

Acropolis Museum

Zappeion

Ardettos Hill

METS

Filopappou Hill

MAKRYGIANNI

KOUKAKI

NEOS KOSMOS

Alsos Longinou

500 m
0.25 miles

⭐ **HIGHLIGHTS**
1 Acropolis
2 Acropolis Museum

🔴 **SIGHTS**
3 Anafiotika
4 Ancient Agora
5 Asclepieion & Stoa of Eumenes
6 Bath House of the Winds
7 Church of Agios Eleftherios
8 Church of St George of the Rock

9 Hadrian's Arch
10 Hadrian's Library
11 Lysikrates Monument
12 Mosque of Tzistarakis
13 National Gardens
14 Parliament
15 Parthenon
16 Plateia Mitropoleos
17 Plateia Syntagmatos
18 Propylaia
19 Roman Agora
20 Temple of Athena Nike
21 Temple of Olympian Zeus

22 Theatre of Dionysos
23 Tomb of the Unknown Soldier
24 Tower of the Winds

⚫ **SLEEPING**
25 A for Athens
26 Athens Backpackers
27 Athens Gate
28 Athens Muses Suites
29 Marble House Pension
30 Mosaikon
31 Neoma

🟢 **EATING**
32 Ellevoro
33 GH Attikos
34 Mani Mani
35 Point A

🟢 **DRINKING & NIGHTLIFE**
36 Couleur Locale
37 GB Roof Garden
38 Metropolis Roof Garden

🔴 **SHOPPING**
39 Monastiraki Flea Market

Athens' Crown Jewel

Epic monuments and vistas at the Acropolis

The **Acropolis** (*odysseus.culture.gr; adult/child €30/free*) is the most important ancient site in the Western world, and a glimpse of this magnificent monument cannot fail to exalt your spirit. Crowned by the Parthenon, it's visible from almost everywhere in Athens. Its marble gleams white in the

ACROPOLIS MUSEUM PLANNING TIPS

Buy tickets for the Acropolis Museum online to skip the queue.

Bring a smartphone and headphones to download and listen to the audio guide, or register online for occasional guided tours (included in the ticket price). You'll need the registration code to attend.

Leave time for the fine museum shops and the film describing the history of the Acropolis (on the top floor).

The last admission is 30 minutes before closing, and the galleries are cleared 15 minutes before closing, starting at the top floor.

The ground-floor shop and cafe are accessible without a ticket.

Every Friday and Saturday the 2nd-floor restaurant is open until midnight.

THANASIS F/SHUTTERSTOCK

Evzones (presidential guards), Tomb of the Unknown Soldier

midday and takes on a honey hue as the sun sinks, then glows above the city by night.

On the hill's southern slopes, the modern **Acropolis Museum** holds its treasures. The Dionysiou Areopagitou promenade links the museum and site – it's a tourist throughway, but also a favourite spot for locals to stroll at sundown. Entering from the southeastern entrance (near the museum), you come to the ancient **Theatre of Dionysos** before ascending the stairs towards the **Asclepieion** temple ruins. Continue on the trail and, as you climb the final steps, look up to see the **Temple of Athena Nike**. Then, like so many pilgrims before you, pass through the **Propylaia**, the monumental entrance to the Acropolis. The **Parthenon**, one of the largest Doric temples ever completed in Greece, looms before you.

Ancient Masterpieces

Admire the treasures of the Acropolis Museum

The state-of-the-art **Acropolis Museum** (*theacropolismuseum.gr; adult/child €20/free*) displays the surviving treasures

 EATING AROUND THE ACROPOLIS: STYLISH SPOTS

Mani Mani: i Dig into herb-filled cuisine from the Mani peninsula region in the Peloponnese, like seafood orzo with wild fennel. *2-11pm* €€

GH Attikos: Greek classics in a casual, airy setting with Acropolis views and an open terrace. *noon-4pm & 6-9pm Mon-Sat* €€

Ellevoro: Family-run, decorated with candles and mini-chandeliers and serving trad Greek dishes. *7pm-midnight Wed-Mon, from noon Sun* €€

Point A: Rooftop restaurant of the Herodion Hotel, with stunning Acropolis and Acropolis Museum views. *7pm-midnight* €€€

from the temple hill, with emphasis on the Acropolis as it was in the 5th century BCE, the apotheosis of Greece's artistic achievement. Layers of history are revealed and interpreted: glass floors expose subterranean ruins, and the Acropolis itself is visible through the floor-to-ceiling windows, so the masterpieces are always in context.

As you enter the museum, look down through the glass floor to view the ruins of an ancient Athenian neighbourhood that were uncovered during the museum's construction and had to be preserved and integrated into a new building plan.

The Finest Collection of Greek Antiquities

A pilgrimage to the National Archaeological Museum

Housed in an enormous 19th-century neoclassical building, the 11,000 treasures of the **National Archaeological Museum** *(namuseum.gr; adult/child €12/free)* date from prehistoric to Classical periods – a comprehensive overview of historic Greek art. It's impossible to appreciate all the exquisite sculptures, pottery, jewellery and frescoes in one go, and whatever you see will be a treat. You'll need time here to do it justice or make a beeline for the big-ticket items: the Mask of Agamemnon, Vaphio gold cups, the colossal Sounion Kouros and the Antikythera Mechanism.

Watch the Changing of the Guard

A photo op at the Tomb of the Unknown Soldier

Located on Athens' principal plaza, Plateia Syntagmatos, an essential photo op is of the traditionally costumed *evzones* (presidential guards) flanking the **Tomb of the Unknown Soldier**, a cenotaph dedicated to Greek soldiers killed in war, which stands just below the neoclassical **Parliament** building. Every hour, on the hour, the guard changes. On Sunday at 10.30am, a whole platoon, accompanied by a band, sets off from the Presidential Guard complex on Irodou Attikou, and marches down Vasilissis Sofias to the tomb for the 11am ceremony. The *evzones*' uniform of the fustanella (skirt) and pompom shoes reflects the attire worn by the klephts, the mountain fighters of the War of Independence.

GUIDED TOURS

On Foot: Athens Walking Tours *(athenswalkingtours. gr)* and **Alternative Athens** *(alternative athens.com)* have expert guides. **This is Athens** *(thisisathens. org)* has a free program to team up visitors with locals for themed walks.

By Bike: E-bike tours by **We Bike Athens** *(webikeathens.gr)* in Thisio, **Solebike** *(solebike.eu)* near the Acropolis and **Roll in Athens** *(facebook. com/rollinathens)* near Syntagma take the strain out of pedalling uphill. **Coco-Mat.Bike Tours** *(coco-mat. bike)* in Gazi gains cool points for unique ash-wood-frame bikes (regular and e-bikes). Or rent your own bike at **Funky Ride** *(funkyride.gr)*.

On the Bus: Hop-on, hop-off with **City Sightseeing Athens** *(city-sightseeing.com)* or **Athens Happy Train** *(athenshappy train.com)*.

 DRINKING IN MONASTIRAKI & SYNTAGMA: ROOFTOP BARS

A for Athens: The rooftop cafe-bar at this Monastiraki hotel is grand, with sweeping 360-degree views. *4pm-midnight*	**Couleur Locale:** In a Monastiraki arcade, this all-day bar-restaurant has Acropolis views. *10am-2am Sun-Thu, to 3am Fri & Sat*	**Metropolis Roof Garden:** Head to the top of luxe Electra Metropolis Athens Hotel for creative cocktails and inventive cuisine. *1-6pm & 7-11pm*	**GB Roof Garden:** Glam it up on the top of the Grande Bretagne Hotel on Plateia Syntagmatos, with radiant Acropolis views. *1pm-2am*

Central Athens Meander

Boisterous, monument-packed central Athens is best explored on foot. The historic centre and the main archaeological sites, major landmarks, museums and attractions, are quite close to one another. The main civic hub of Athens, Plateia Syntagmatos, merges into the historic Plaka and Monastiraki neighbourhoods, which mesh one into the next and make for a super stroll (3km, three hours) for soaking up the city-centre history and life.

❶ Plateia Syntagmatos

Plateia Syntagmatos, considered the centre of Athens, has been a favourite place for protests since the rally that led to the granting of a constitution on 3 September 1843. Time your visit with the hourly changing of the guard at the **Tomb of the Unknown Soldier** (p531) in front of Parliament.

❷ Temple of Olympian Zeus

Stroll through the lush **National Gardens**, exiting south to the striking **Temple of Olympian Zeus** or what remains of the largest temple ever built. Teetering on the edge of the traffic alongside the temple, **Hadrian's Arch** is the ornate gateway marking the boundary of Hadrian's Athens.

❸ Lysikrates Monument

Cross Leoforos Vasilissis Amalias and walk up Lysikratous into Plaka. Built in 334 BCE, the **Lysikrates Monument** is the only remaining example of monuments that once lined this street to the **Theatre of Dionysos** (p530), site of dramatic contests.

PIC MEDIA AUS/SHUTTERSTOCK

Temple of Olympian Zeus

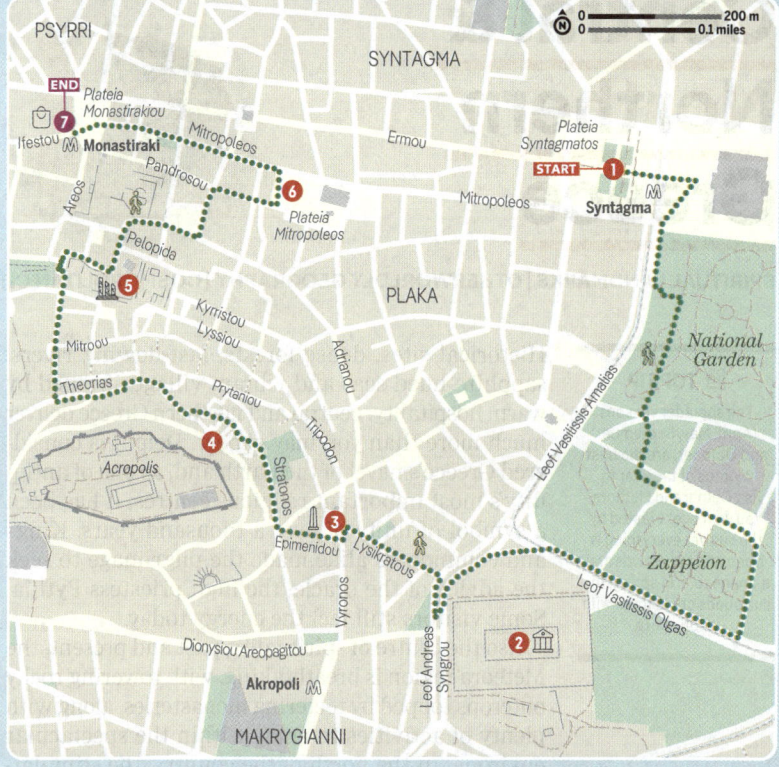

The monument commemorates one chorus' victory.

④ Anafiotika

Ascend the Epimenidou steps, turn right into Stratonos, and **Church of St George of the Rock** marks the entry to **Anafiotika**, a picturesque maze of whitewashed houses. Explore a bit, then emerge at Theorias road, above the old Athens University (1837–41). Descend on pedestrianised Diaskouron for views of the **Ancient Agora**.

⑤ Roman Agora

Descend as far as the ruins of the **Roman Agora** where you can see its **Tower of the Winds**, a classical time-and-weather station. Across the road, duck into **Bath House of the Winds**, a historical Turkish

hammam. Northeast of the Roman Agora, the ruins of **Hadrian's Library** sit next to 1759 **Mosque of Tzistarakis**.

⑥ Plateia Mitropoleos

Jaunt north to **Plateia Mitropoleos**, where you'll find Athens Cathedral and its smaller, more historically significant neighbour, 12th-century **Church of Agios Eleftherios**, which was built from pieces of ancient temples and earlier Christian monuments.

⑦ Monastiraki Flea Market

Cruise up Mitropoleos and you'll reach colourful, chaotic Plateia Monastirakiou. To the left, down Ifestou, is **Monastiraki Flea Market**, a gateway to shopping throughout the district.

Central & Northern Greece

SPIRITUAL LANDMARKS | OTHERWORLDLY GEOGRAPHY | COSMOPOLITAN CITY

 ☑ TOP TIP

The shoulder seasons (April, May, September and October) are the best months of the year to visit Delphi and Meteora. You won't get blasted by the sun yet everything is open and the crowds are manageable. In spring, the surrounds are abloom with wildflowers.

Historical sites, dense forests, fast-flowing rivers, sapphire-hued seas and vibrant villages framed by warm hospitality: central and northern Greece deliver much more than you may expect. Delphi is considered Greece's navel of the Earth and, as one of antiquity's most important religious centres, it has been a symbol of unity of over a thousand years. Kings and commoners alike made the pilgrimage to seek the advice of the oracle, the high priestess Pythia. Some visitors still feel the energy today.

Also the centre of spirituality, past and present, the Meteora region is breathtaking, with towering rocky outcrops topped by teetering monasteries, along with plenty of activities to enjoy within the spectacular environs. In the north of the country, the stimulating and stylish city of Thessaloniki always surprises and is considered Greece's most cosmopolitan city (shhh, don't tell the Athenians). Expect excellent cuisine, bars and shopping here, too.

Delphi

Legend has it that Zeus released two eagles from opposing ends of the Earth to locate its centre. They crossed paths above Delphi. In the 8th century BCE, the cult of Apollo was established here. Leaders and commoners alike from the Mediterranean and Asia Minor made the pilgrimage to the oracle of sacred Delphi to consult a mysterious high priestess, Pythia,

---

⊘ GETTING AROUND

Central Greece is the country's largest region. Meteora (Kalambaka) is easily reached by train from Athens; for Delphi, catch a direct KTEL bus from Athens' Liosion bus terminal. Connections between Delphi and Meteora are surprisingly tricky. There are limited bus services, though these are long and you must change at Trikala, 22km east of Kalambaka. For exploring central Greece, having a car is best as it allows you to reach historical sites, remote mountain villages and far-flung beaches.

APOLLO'S VOICE: THE ORACLE

Perched in the Temple of Apollo, the Delphic oracle ranked high among the sacred sites of Ancient Greece. Devotees flocked here asking for Apollo's guidance in making decisions. Wars were fought, colonies created, marriages sealed, leaders chosen and journeys begun on the strength of the oracle's advice.

Apollo's instrument of communication, the Pythia (priestess), was usually an older woman who sat on a tripod in the temple. Although there's no evidence for the theory that she inhaled vapours of ethylene from cracks in the rocks below the sanctuary, evidence shows she made her prophesies in a trancelike state.

The Pythia's pronouncements were notorious for their ambiguity, which left the interpretation up to the recipients.

who prophesied on everything from matters of the heart to a city-state's decision to go to war. The joy of staying right in the town of Delphi is that you can easily walk to all the ancient sites and museums.

One of Greece's top sights

As you ascend the archaeological site of **Ancient Delphi** *(ody sseus.culture.gr; incl museum adult/child €20/free)*, look out across the olive-grove-carpeted valley and Gulf of Corinth below, close your eyes and tap into Delphi's divine energy. Get here early to avoid the crowds, take snacks and water. And time!

Like the original pilgrims, start your visit at the **Sanctuary of Athena Pronaia**, a 20-minute walk east past the region's highlights while taking in the sweeping views down to the Gulf of Corinth. The fenced site is always open. You'll pass the **Castalian Spring**, a sacred source for Delphi.

You can scamper about the hilly site in a sweat-soaked, manic hour, but why? It's better to take it slow, ponder the many individual features and tease out the surviving nuances. Gaze out over the views and find quiet, shady spots to contemplate the deep meaning it has held over the millennia. Just thinking of the countless feet that have trod the **Sacred Way** and who they've belonged to, will give all but the dullest minds pause.

Taking a tour with a local guide is a wonderful way to evoke the sense of place. Try English-speaking **Penny Kolomvotsou** *(kpagona@hotmail.com)*.

Treasures and masterpieces

Save the unmissable **Delphi Archaeological Museum** *(ody sseus.culture.gr; incl site adult/child €20/free)* for the afternoon, when the outdoor sites swelter in the midday sun. Entry is by time slot, so reserve ahead. You'll gain a clearer

METEORA'S HISTORY

The name Meteora is derived from the Greek adjective *meteoros*, meaning 'suspended in the air' (the word 'meteor' comes from the same root).

Hermit monks began inhabiting the scattered natural caverns of Meteora during the 11th century. By the 14th century, the power of the Byzantine Empire was waning, and with Turkish incursions into Greece on the rise, monks fled the bloodshed for a safe haven here.

Ruins of abandoned communites in sites that now seem utterly inaccessible dot the area. Removable ladders were used at first. Later, windlasses hauled the monks up in nets. When curious visitors asked how frequently the ropes were replaced, the monks' straight-faced reply was 'when the Lord lets them break'.

JOAQUIN OSSORIO CASTILLO/SHUTTERSTOCK

Sphinx of the Naxians, Delphi Archaeological Museum

understanding of the context of where the treasures were found. You can have a deeply rewarding visit in under two hours and you'll come away with a clearer picture of how lavish Ancient Delphi must have been and the wealth it attracted. Get more info on selected exhibits in 3D via the Digital Delphi phone app or the comprehensive *Delphi Monuments and Museum* by Photios M Petsas.

The collection starts with some impressive bronze works: a bronze figurine believed to depict Apollo, the forerunner of stone-carved *kouros* statues; the **Sphinx of the Naxians** (560 BCE), with the face of a woman, the body of a lion and the wings of a bird; and the crown jewel, the life-size **Bronze Charioteer** (478–474 BCE).

Meteora

Meteora's otherworldly stone pillars rise up vertically from the vast Thessaly plain. This geological marvel came about some 11 million years ago: earthquakes, wind and rain gradually sculpted a mass of rocks, sand and sediment. It's hard to comprehend how monasteries were built atop these precipitous cliffs and into rockfaces.

Has a fabulous beer menu of regional brews!

 EATING IN DELPHI: OUR PICKS

Taverna Gargadoyas: Welcoming, no-frills traditional taverna at the west end of town, serving great grilled meats. *1-11pm* €

Dion Tavern: Classic Greek dishes, like rice-stuffed tomatoes and souvlaki, are well executed. Tables inside and out; stark decor. *noon-11pm* €

Taverna Vakhos: Well-crafted Greek fare, including vegan dishes; seasonal artichokes and mountain herbs from the garden. *noon-10.30pm* €

To Patriko Mas: Elevated views to go with the elevated Mediterranean fare. Game casseroles are a speciality. *noon-3pm & 6-10pm* €€

Free-climbing, cave-dwelling ascetics were the first to make Meteora home in the 11th century. Deemed a holy place, Meteora was where the first Orthodox monastic communities formed in the 12th century. At its peak, 24 monasteries were hosted here; today, six remain active and open to visitors in this UNESCO-listed destination.

Moseying about monasteries

There's enough variation between the opening hours of Meteora's monasteries that crafting an itinerary is a bit like a jigsaw puzzle. As always, try to hit top sights such as Moni Megalou Meteorou as early as possible.

All six of Meteora's monasteries – **Moni Megalou Meteorou**, **Moni Varlaam**, **Moni Agiou Stefanou**, **Moni Agias Varvaras Rousanou**, **Moni Agias Triadas** and **Moni Agiou Nikolaou Anapafsa** – are impressive in their own way. With precision planning, you might see four in one day, but this would be a stunt. To enter the monasteries, visitors are required to cover their shoulders and legs; shawls are available to buy or borrow at most monasteries. Be prepared to scale between 140 and 300 steps at all but the accessible Moni Agiou Stefanou.

Each monastery charges the same admission *(adult/child €5/free)*. Good sources of information include **Visit Meteora** *(visitmeteora.travel)* and the **Kalambaka Tourist Office** *(infotouristmeteora.gr)*.

Thessaloniki

Map p538

It's easy to fall in love with Thessaloniki. Greece's second-largest (and arguably coolest) city is built along the water, and the view over the Aegean Sea to snowcapped Mt Olympus is superb. Old and new coexist in architectural anarchy: here, the ruins of Byzantine churches give way to 1960s apartment blocks, and Ottoman-era *hammams* and historic buildings have been repurposed into art spaces, cafes, bars and shops.

Boardwalk empire and people-watching

Walking along the waterfront promenade is a way of life in Thessaloniki. It even has its own word in Greek: *volta*. Start walking the Nea Paralia from the port, where a crop of new cafes and restaurants have opened up in this once seedy area. Head towards the 15th-century **White Tower** *(lpth.gr; adult/child €6/free)*, Thessaloniki's most iconic image, and continue to the strikingly contemporary **Thessaloniki Concert Hall**. The total distance is 3.5km.

BEST ACTIVITIES IN METEORA

To arrange these, see visitmeteora.travel.

Hike to hermit caves: Trace the routes of the earliest monks on a trek to cave hermitages and chapels. Guides offer more options.

Mountain biking: Fly along oak-forest trails, across rockfaces and through a verdant valley, all while glimpsing stellar views.

Rock climbing: Navigate adventurous climbing routes with local experts. Residents hit the rocks in April on the feast day of St George.

Paragliding: Soar above Meteora's towering columns of rock on a tandem or motorised paragliding flight.

Meteora Photo Tour: Venture to out-of-the-way spots that capture the colossal rock columns and monasteries in their best light.

 EATING & DRINKING IN KASTRAKI & KALAMBAKA: OUR PICKS

| **Taverna Gardenia:** Kastraki taverna with a huge front patio and snug old-fashioned interior. Open-air grill/spit-roast mains. *12.30-11pm* € | **Qastiro:** Stylish wine bar in Kastraki serving Med-accented meals from a short menu. Enjoy quality coffee on the stone terrace. *10am-midnight* €€ | **Fortounis Tsipouradiko:** Long-standing Kalambaka *ouzerie* (place serving ouzo and food) that gets a lively, late crowd. *11am-midnight* € | **Ambrosia Taverna:** Modern Greek place in Kalambaka that does creative fresh fare served with aplomb. Fine wine list. *noon-11pm* €€ |

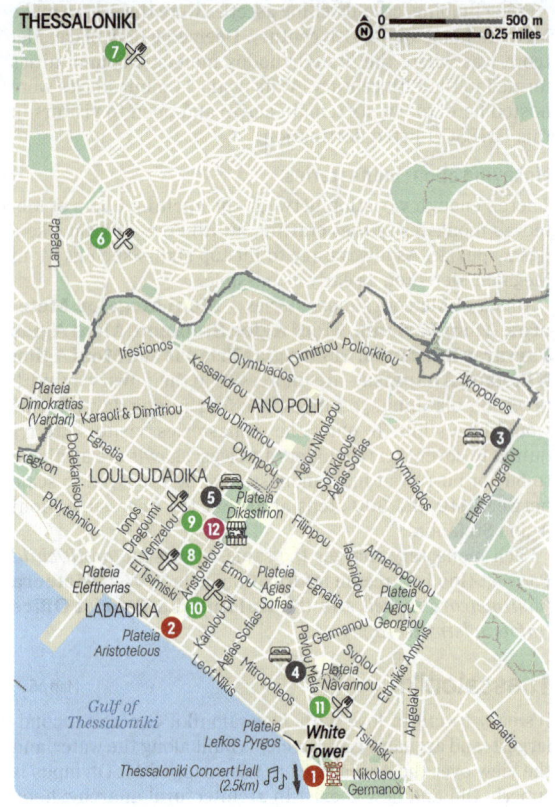

THESSALONIKI

★ **HIGHLIGHTS**
1 White Tower

● **SIGHTS**
2 Plateia Aristotelous

● **SLEEPING**
3 Little Big House
4 Trilogy House
5 Zeus is Loose

● **EATING**
6 Bougatsa Bantis
7 Milano Bakery
8 Modiano Market
9 Stou Mitsou
10 Terkenlis
11 Trigona Elenidis

● **SHOPPING**
12 Kapani Markete

Afterwards, relax in **Plateia Aristotelous**, Thessaloniki's heartbeat. It's a cross between a Parisian boulevard, Bologna's covered arcades and Venice's Piazza San Marco, with an unmistakably Greek flair. Elsewhere, the port of Thessaloniki is the city's hotbed for contemporary art. Just up from the port is the **Ladadika** neighbourhood, where former brick warehouses have been converted into tavernas, cafes and bars.

Thessaloniki's markets

Rich in both history and culinary delights, Thessaloniki is a city that can be best appreciated through its markets.

 EATING IN THESSALONIKI: BEST PASTRY SHOPS ──────── MAP p538

Milano: Hands down the city's best *tiropita* (cheese pie) can be found at this bakery in the Neapoli neighbourhood. *8am-7pm* €

Trigona Elenidis: A flaky triangle stuffed with custard and dripping in sweet syrup, the *trigona* found here is a hallmark Thessaloniki dessert. *9am-11pm* €

Bougatsa Bantis: Salty cheese or sweet custard is layered in filo, cut in squares and served warm. It's the ideal breakfast. *6.30am-2.30pm* €

Terkenlis: *Tsoureki* is a slightly sweet, yeasted loaf with a mastic flavour; try it covered in chocolate and stuffed with chestnut puree. *7am-11pm* €

White Tower (p537), Thessaloniki

The **Modiano Market** *(agoramodiano.com)* was originally built in 1930 by renowned local Jewish architect Eli Modiano, and quickly became the centre of daily life for Thessalonikians. Today, the revamped, cavernous, glass-and-brick structure is home to dozens of stalls, divided into 'neighborhoods' by food type. From fruits and veg to syrupy pastries to third-wave coffee, you can find almost anything here. The space is now also used for events and concerts.

Food lovers should make a beeline for the **Kapani Market** *(kapani.gr)*. Located in the city centre, this is the place to stock up on Greek products like mountain tea, mastic from Chios and pine-tree honey. In addition to non-perishables, you can stroll through the fresh fish and meat sections. Grab lunch at **Stou Mitsou**, a *tsipouradiko* selling delicious grilled and fried dishes between the market stalls.

LIGHTS, CAMERA, ACTION

Each year, Thessaloniki hosts its **international film festival**, the most important silver-screen event in the country. First launched in 1960 as a national film festival, it has adapted to the times: in its earliest years, it focused on New Greek Cinema, and then, following the end of Greece's military dictatorship, the festival promoted much more political cinema. These days, the focus is still on arthouse cinema, with an emphasis on voices from the Balkans. For 11 days each November, the city is awash in screenings, premieres, lively talks and discussions. It's an event cinephiles shouldn't miss. See *filmfestival.gr* for more info.

Peloponnese

ARCHAEOLOGICAL WONDERS | ANCIENT OLYMPIA | MYTHICAL MOMENTS

☑ **TOP TIP**

Nafplio is a good base from which to explore the sites of Mycenae and Epidavros; for Ancient Olympia, it's best to spend a night or two in Olympia.

With secluded beach coves, bucolic cypress forests, lofty peaks and concealed villages, mainland Peloponnese has the charm of a seasonal island all year round. The region is legendary – fables are central to its culture and landscape. It's where many a Greek god and human hero performed their deeds in historical sites, classical temples, Mycenaean palaces, Byzantine cities and Venetian fortresses. You can commune with the ghost of Agamemnon at Mycenae, a once-great civilisation, or test your sprinting skills at Ancient Olympia, spiritual home of the Olympics. Or recite the lines of Oedipus at the Theatre of Epidavros and be captivated by Mystras where the Byzantine civilisation ended in the 14th century. If 'ancient' isn't your thing, explore the natural surroundings instead. The region's cuisine is among the best in Greece thanks to its fresh seafood, mountain meats and wild greens. The Peloponnese has the best of everything.

Nafplio

Explore the Old Town Nafplio

Nafplio is one of Greece's prettiest towns and admirers revel in its knockout waterside location. The town is a sum of its

 GETTING AROUND

The Peloponnese is one of Greece's largests region with distinct sub-areas and varied topography. Various KTEL bus networks link main towns and remote villages throughout the region. Buses run from Athens to both Nafplio and Ancient Olympia. For the former, you can take a direct bus or, if you're in or near the Peloponnese, you can change at the interchange known as KTEL Isthmus, located near the Corinth Canal and gateway to the

region. Similarly, to get to Ancient Olympia from Nafplio, you'll need to head first to KTEL Isthmus and change buses at Pyrgos, from where you can get a small train or bus to Olympia. Apart from this train, the main train network no longer operates in the region, except for the *proastiako*, a handy suburban network that runs between Athens Airport and Kiato, on the outskirts of Corinth (town). For remote regions, having your own wheels allows you more access.

Panagiotis Zotos
is a history lover
and co-owner of
Pension Marianna
(hotelmarianna.gr).

**What is
Acronafplia?** An
'acro-polis' was the
upper fortified part
of town where, when
attacked, the locals
went for protection.
Acronafplia is
Nafplio's oldest
castle; it dates to
Mycenaean times
(1750 BCE). Over time,
different conquerors
changed its
fortifications. Finally,
when it was no longer
considered secure,
it moved to Palamidi
(16th century).

Why visit? It's a
beautiful and quiet
place, especially at
sunrise. When you
walk inside, you feel
like you're in the
pages of history; you
can see the different
architectural styles
and construction
stages over the
different periods.

**Another interesting
fact?** The name
Nafplio means 'ship'.
When you're up here,
you understand why:
it feels like you're
sailing through the
ocean waters.

parts: enchanting narrow streets, elegant Venetian houses
and neoclassical mansions.

All alleys seem to lead to the bustling **Plateia Syntagma**,
the heart of the Old Town. Here, the cafes afford views of the
Trianon, a former mosque, the handsome former **National
Bank building** (1932) and the **Archaeological Museum**
(odysseus.culture.gr; adult/child €10/free), a former Venetian warehouse. The outstanding collection includes bronze
armour from near Mycenae.

The **Peloponnesian Folklore Foundation Museum** *(bpf.
gr; adult/child €5/free)* displays Greek cultural items. Further
on is **Plateia Kapodistrias**, named after Ioannis Kapodistrias, the first governor of the modern Greek state, who was
murdered outside the church of Aghios Spiridonas. A block
south of here is the **Land Gate**, identifiable by the lion carving. In the first Venetian occupation it was the only entrance
to the city by land.

Power to the fortresses

Nafplio's imposing landmark, the citadel known as **Palamidi** *(odysseus.culture.gr; adult/child €20/free),* stands on a
216m-high outcrop of rock. An hour or so within its walls
will give you time to wander the grounds and enjoy bird's-eye
views over the sea and landscape. Built by the Venetians between 1711 and 1714, the fortress is regarded as a masterpiece
of military architecture. To get there, you can go by road via
taxi or tackle the 911 steps that begin southeast of the bus
station. Climb early or towards sunset.

Back on the waterfront, boats run the five-minute journey
(half-hourly) between the waterfront and the **Bourtzi** *(incl
boat ride €12),* an islet fortress about 500m off the port. A

THE WINE ROUTES OF NEMEA

The rolling hills 37km northwest of Nafplio are part of the Nemea region, one of Greece's premier wine-producing areas that's particularly famous for its *agioritiko* grape and full-bodied reds. Look out also for wine made from *roditis,* a local variety of white grape. Nemea has been known for its fine wines since Mycenaean times, when nearby Phlius supplied the wine for the royal court at Mycenae.

There are dozens of wineries in the region. Many of these are open to the public; for tastings, most – but not all – require bookings. Visits usually include a winery tour and a tasting, sometimes with accompanying nibbles. To hop between vineyards, you'll need your own transport.

A **wine festival** in early September marks the beginning of the vintage.

MATYAS REHAK/SHUTTERSTOCK

Lion Gate, Ancient Mycenae

half-hour or so allows time to 'recreate' the events of the fortress 'of the rock'. Constructed between 1471 and 1472 by the Venetians, it helped defend the city for 350 years under different conquerors. Explanatory signs are in English.

Ancient Mycenae

Where myth and history are linked

The region's must-see historical attraction is **Ancient Mycenae** *(odysseus.culture.gr; adult/child €20/free),* 24km northwest of Nafplio, in the barren foothills of Mt Agios Ilia and Mt Zara. Ancient Mycenae was the home of the legendary King Agamemnon, ruler of the Greeks during the Trojan War. It was, for four centuries in the second millennium, the most powerful kingdom in Greece. One of Greece's most impressive ancient sites, it provides context to understanding Mycenaean influence over Ancient Greece.

KTEL buses from Athens and Nafplio drop you at Fichti village; it's an uphill slog for 3.5km to the site. It's easiest to have your own wheels.

 EATING IN NAFPLIO: OUR PICKS

Pidalio: A 10-minute walk west of the Od Town, Pidalio prepares some of the best mezedhes around. Just ask locals. *1.45-11.15pm Wed-Mon* €€

I Gonia Tou Kavalari: Some of the best contemporary Greek mezedhes around, from *spetsofaï* (sausage) to *apaki* (fried pork). *noon-late* €€

To Omorfo Tavernaki: Modern twist to traditional cuisine: creative salads and excellent meats, plus tasty starters. Always busy. *11.30am-late Fri-Wed* €€

Antica Gelateria di Roma: Nafplio's original gelateria, run by Italians – as genuine as they come. Handmade on premises, any flavour is good. *9am-1am* €

Epidavros

The stage of ancient dramas

Built of limestone, yet one of the best-preserved Ancient Greek structures in existence, the late-4th-century-BCE **Theatre of Epidavros** (*argolisculture.gr; incl Sanctuary of Asclepius adult/child €20/free*) will have you singing. Part of the Sanctuary of Asclepius (an ancient health sanctuary), and considered to have played an important role in the cultural life of ancient times, it's renowned for its symmetry and amazing acoustics; a coin dropped in the theatre's centre can be heard from the highest seat. The theatre is now used for performances during the annual **Athens Epidaurus Festival** (*aefestival.gr*).

In high season, buses head here from Nafplio. If visiting by car, follow the signs to Ancient Theatre (not to P Epidavros or A Epidavros).

Ancient Olympia

In the footsteps of glory

It's worth the energy to reach Olympia, if only for one impressive site. This is **Ancient Olympia** (*odysseus.culture.gr; adult/child €20/free*), birthplace of the modern Olympic Games, where states come together for the sake of friendly competition just as they did here some 2800 years ago. This atmospheric site is also fun: sprint the 192.27m in the stadium and the ghosts of cheering crowds are guaranteed to make your skin prickle. At the ruins of the gymnasium, conjure up an aroma of sweat and oil (athletes smeared their bodies with this).

There's no right way to approach the site; the QR code at the entrance helps recreate the buildings in 3D, thereby revealing the sanctuary's former glory, and there are good information panels in Greek, English and German. But you'll need at least half a day for the site and Archaeological Museum. Archaeological or sports buffs might like one to two days to visit all museums. A guide will bring the site alive.

One ticket includes access for one day to the **Archaeological Site of Olympia**, **Olympia Archaeological Museum**, the **Museum of the History of the Olympic Games in Antiquity**, and the **Museum of the History of the Excavations in Olympia**. These are located within walking distance of the site, on the way to Olympia village.

ANCIENT OLYMPIA TIPS

Niki Vlachou is a guide and owner of **Niki Olympic Tours** (*olympictours.gr*).

What's the 'must visit' at the site?
The stadium. Close your eyes and feel the energy as you imagine the young men who were trying to fulfil their dreams to become Olympic champions. You can almost 'hear' the roar of the crowds.

And the 'must see' at the museum?
The East and West pediments of the temple of Zeus, like an ancient movie theatre where the statues are like actors conveying the tales.

Something people might not know about the site? When the Roman Emperor Nero competed in the games (around 67 CE), he made his own rules. In a chariot race, he fell off the chariot, yet declared himself the winner!

 DRINKING IN NAFPLIO: OUR PICKS

Allotino: The place to be seen for daytime coffee and evening cocktails. Also serves salads and club sandwiches. *8am-3am*	**Mavros Gatos:** Nafplio's popular hangout, especially the young and trendy, with music and good drinks. *8am-3am*	**A!Ladokampos Gold:** Olive oil and wine tastings (think organic wine) in this store-cum-bar run by a Greek-American. *10am-12.30am Wed-Mon*	**3Sixty:** A posh wine bar in a hotel of the same name, it has a more international feel, a snob factor and high-end cocktails. *9am-midnight*

Cyclades

INCREDIBLE VISTAS | BEACHES | BLUE-AND-WHITE DOMES

 TOP TIP

If flying, give yourself extra time when leaving from Santorini Airport as the small terminal can be mayhem. Fira can become crammed with people, especially when the cruise ships are in port.

What do you think of when you think of the perfect Greek island? Why, one of the Cyclades, of course. This circular archipelago is Greece from central casting: rugged, sun-drenched outcrops of rock anchored in turquoise waters and strewn with gleaming white hamlets and blue-domed churches. Add to that a fabulous set of culinary flavours, fantastic hiking, plentiful beaches and a good dose of sophistication, and you really get the best of Greece's ample charms.

Of all of the Cyclades, one island seems to be the principal actor. Santorini (Thira) exudes in-your-face charm, including sheer cliffs and a snowdrift of white Cycladic houses. But beauty brings admirers and the island is slammed by them in peak season (so much so that the strain on the infrastructure is a huge concern). The more relaxed alternative, Naxos, has an entrancing variety of attractions including grand beaches, mountains and a lovely historic town.

GETTING AROUND

Conventional and fast ferries connect both Santorini and Naxos with Athens' Piraeus and Rafina ports. Ferries also link the two islands (two to three hours). In Santorini, Athinios port sits at the cliff base; buses and taxis meet ferries and cart passengers up to Fira. Consult **KTEL Santorini Buses** *(ktel-santorini.gr)* for schedules and prices. May to September buses are overcrowded. Having a car is the best way to explore the island, but traffic in high season is a menace. Fira's taxi stand is on Dekigala, near the bus station.

Naxos' small airport has several daily flights to/from Athens. Buses leave from the end of the ferry quay in Hora; timetables are posted outside the bus information office. While there are frequent buses to the villages, they can take a long time to get there and back. Buy tickets from the office or the machine outside (not from the bus driver). For larger exploration, get your own wheels; taxis are useful only for short hops.

CYCLADES

Santorini (Thira)

Booming caldera town and more

Santorini's main town, **Fira**, is a busy place, its caldera edge layered with swish cave hotels, infinity pools and restaurants. It's backed by narrow streets packed with shops, and more bars and restaurants. Sitting 220m below Fira – three minutes by cable car, or 587 steps on foot – the **Old Port** (Fira Skala) is mainly used by cruise-ship passengers visiting for a day. **Santorini Cable Car** (scc.gr; adult/child €10/5) is swamped with those same passengers, especially in the morning and afternoon. Views over the multicoloured cliffs are breath-taking, and come sunset, crowds gather at the caldera edge.

Fira merges into two more villages: **Firostefani** (about a 15-minute walk north) and posher **Imerovigli** (about a half-hour walk from Fira). All are loaded with stores – browse for original art, ceramics, woodwork, local foodstuffs, high-end fashion and junk. Fira is also the island's nightlife hot spot. Nine kilometres further on, with white dwellings hewn into the volcanic rock, **Oia** is a gleaming gem and a famous place to watch a sunset. It, too, gets packed – your only hope is to

 EATING IN SANTORINI: OUR PICKS

Aroma Avlis: Part of the Artemis Karamolegos winery, this terrific restaurant does brilliant things with local ingredients. 1-11pm €€

Fistikies: Head to this restaurant in an elegant courtyard in Kamari for seafood, pasta and Greek fare. 2-11pm €€

Pelican Kipos: Gorgeous garden and good food in central Fira, plus a good selection of wines. 8am-11.30pm €€

To Krinaki: Superb, all-fresh, all-local ingredients are paired with local beer and Santorini-grape wine; just east of Oia. noon-11pm €€€

545

BEST
ANCIENT SI

BEST BEACHES ON NAXOS

Agios Prokopios: Sandy and shallow beach set in a sheltered bay south of Cape Mougkri.

Agia Anna: Merging with Agios Prokopios, this is a stretch of crowded white sand, with development along its length.

Glyfada and Plaka: Sandy beaches and turquoise waters, with accommodation and restaurants, perfect for a chilled-out stay.

Mikri Vigla: Golden granite boulders divide the beach into two; it's big on the kitesurfing scene, with reliable wind conditions.

Pyrgaki: Windsurfing and kitesurfing spot reachable via an unpaved road past the Aliko promontory.

Hawaii Beach: Shines with calm, limpid blue waters just north of the promontory.

venture out in the very early morning. Walking here takes three hours (9.1km); bring water, sunscreen and a hat.

For swimming, the famous **Red (Kokkini) Beach**, near Ancient Akrotiri in the south, has particularly impressive red cliffs, loungers and restaurants. You can walk from a parking lot over the eastern point to reach it. Or, catamaran cruises from all over the island plus caïques from pretty **Akrotiri Beach** go there and on to the sheltered cove of **White (Aspri) Beach** before visiting **Black (Mesa Pigadia) Beach**, with a beachside taverna.

Naxos

The largest of the Cyclades – and a centre of Classical Greece and Byzantium, with Venetian and Frankish influences – Naxos impresses. Its main town of Hora backs a lively waterfront with a web of steep cobbled alleys climbing to its dramatic hilltop *kastro,* a testament to three centuries of Venetian rule. Within easy reach are excellent beaches, fascinating mountain villages, inspiring ancient sites and bizarre-looking marble quarries.

Labyrinthine old town and ancient icons

Hora (Naxos Town) is enchanting, especially with the remnants of the fortified Venetian **kastro** looming above the waterfront. This was the seat of power for Marco Sanudo, the 13th-century Venetian who founded the town and made Naxos the heart of the Duchy of the Aegean. The tangle of steep footpaths is divided into two historic Venetian neighbourhoods: Bourgos, where the Greeks lived, and the hilltop Kastro, where the Roman Catholics lived.

Hora is easily managed on foot, though it's almost impossible not to get lost in the old town, but it's just as easy to find your way again. And that's half the fun. Within the *kastro,* the remnants of Sanudo's castle, the **Tower of Sanoudos**, is surrounded by gorgeous Venetian mansions.

Reach the two marble columns with a crowning lintel of the **Temple of Apollo** via a causeway to Palatia islet.

EATING IN HORA: OUR PICKS

Avaton 1739: Atop Hora's *kastro,* don't miss the exalted panorama – a favourite for sunset cocktails and creative cuisine. *8.30am-2am* €€

O Apostolis: Occupying a tiny plaza right at the heart of labyrinthine Bourgos, with good traditional dishes in a pretty courtyard. *7pm-midnight* €€

Doukato: Magical setting in a former monastery, with top Naxian specialities like *kalogeras* (beef, eggplant and cheese). *6pm-midnight* €€

Kamaraki: Excellent taverna frequented by locals, with traditional dishes such as *horta* and fried fish, and tables in a pretty alley. *noon-11.30pm* €

Dodecanese

STUNNING COVES | VARIED LANDSCAPES | ANCIENT CULTURES

Timeless charm and natural beauty, historic ruins and tranquil beaches – welcome to the Dodecanese, which has all that epitomises old Greece. Meaning '12 islands' (these are the main ones, though there are more), the archipelago curves through the southeastern Aegean parallel to the ever-visible shoreline of Türkiye. The footprints of everyone from Greeks and Romans to crusading medieval knights and Byzantine and Ottoman potentates to 20th-century Italian bureaucrats are found here.

Admittedly, Rhodes and Kos are magnets for package tourism and cruise-ship crowds, but you can find your own corners on each of these islands. They offer two very different experiences, so you can commune with the ghosts of the knights over one or two nights in Rhodes, and the ghost of Hippocrates in the Asklepieion, an ancient healing centre in Kos, the next. Both islands also have beautiful beaches that are perfect for swimming.

☑ **TOP TIP**

If you're only visiting Rhodes for a short time, perhaps as part of an island-hopping itinerary, there's plenty to see in Rhodes' Old Town without venturing further afield. Beware that in high season, the Old Town gets terribly crowded with tourists.

 GETTING AROUND

Direct ferries connect Rhodes with Kos (between two and four hours, depending on the service).

Rhodes has an excellent bus network. Buses leave from the urban bus stop on Mandraki Harbour; buy tickets on board. If you're based in Rhodes Old Town, you can't drive into that district, so it makes sense to rent a car only for the actual day(s) you'll use it. Rhodes Town's main taxi rank is on the northern edge of the Old Town, just east of

Plateia Rimini; a board displays set fares for specific destinations.

In Kos, cycling is very popular, with plenty of bicycles for hire, and it's a great way to get around. Cycle lanes thread all through Kos Town, with the busiest route running along the waterfront to connect the town with Lambi to the north and Psalidi to the south. Taxis congregate on the south side of the port. The line of boats moored in Kos Town offer excursions around Kos and to nearby islands.

RHODES' HISTORY

The Minoans and Mycenaeans established early outposts on Rhodes, around the 16th century BCE, followed by the Dorians. Over the next centuries, Rhodes switched allegiances like a pendulum between Athens, Persia, Sparta and Alexander the Great; the island was assimilated into the Roman Empire in 70 CE, then the Byzantine province of the Dodecanese. When the Crusaders seized Constantinople, it was granted independence. Later, the Genoese gained control followed by the Knights of St John, who ruled Rhodes for 213 years from 1309. They were ousted after two sieges by the Ottomans, who were kicked out by the Italians nearly four centuries later. In 1947, after 35 years of Italian occupation, Rhodes, along with the Dodecanese Islands, became part of Greece.

Rhodes Town

Rhodes Town sits at the island's northern peak and is made up of the Old and New Towns, each its own entity. Sealed like a medieval time capsule behind a double ring of high walls and a deep moat, the Old Town is a magical labyrinth. The New Town is a modern Mediterranean resort, with busy beaches, nightlife and waterfront bars.

Trace the history of the knights

An easy walk down the somewhat forbidding **Street of the Knights** is the quintessential Rhodes Town experience, not least because its architecture speaks of the various historical

 EATING IN RHODES TOWN: BEST RESTAURANTS

Paradosiako Kafeneio I Symi: Rhodes' cutest terrace and some of the best seafood and fish you're likely to taste. *1-11pm Mon-Sat* €€

Romios Restaurant: Traditional, elegantly presented Rhodian dishes in a tree-canopied Old Town courtyard. *noon-midnight* €€

Kelari Pantieras: Taste the meze and listen to live bouzouki music in this gorgeous neighbourhood taverna. *5pm-midnight Mon-Sat* €

4 Rodies: Eat perfectly prepared Rhodian dishes in the leafy garden of this locally loved, family-run restaurant. *1.30-11pm Wed-Mon* €€

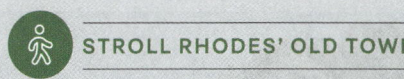

STROLL RHODES' OLD TOWN

A walk around the historical capsule of Rhodes' Old Town will take you through millennia of history.

START	END	LENGTH
D'Amboise Gate	Jewish Museum of Rhodes	2.5km; 2–3 hours

Start from the 16th-century **① D'Amboise Gate**, one of the most impressive of the nine approaches to the Old Town; it's protected by two massive concentric towers. Go down Orfeos and turn into the Street of the Knights. The austere mansions (known as inns) that line the arrow-straight streets of the **② Knights' Quarter** were home to the medieval occupying army of the Knights of St John.

From the outside, the 14th-century castle-like **③ Palace of the Grand Master** looks much as it did when erected by the Knights Hospitaller, though it has fascist-style interiors. Walk to Apellou street and the **④ Archaeological Museum**, located inside the magnificent 15th-century Knights' Hospital.

Carry on south down Apellou, and you'll reach Sokratous street and **⑤ Hora**, the so-called Turkish Quarter that occupies the central bulk of the Old Town. Look out for the **⑥ Mosque of Suleyman**, built in 1522 to commemorate the Ottoman defeat of the knights, and renovated in 1808 (not open to visitors). The peaceful **⑦ Muslim Library**, founded in 1793, sits in an inviting little garden courtyard opposite the mosque.

Head back down Sokratous to the Old Town's southeast corner and the **⑧ Jewish Quarter**, once home to a population of 5500 Jewish people. End the walk at the **⑨ Jewish Museum of Rhodes**, entered via the 1577 Kahal Shalom Synagogue.

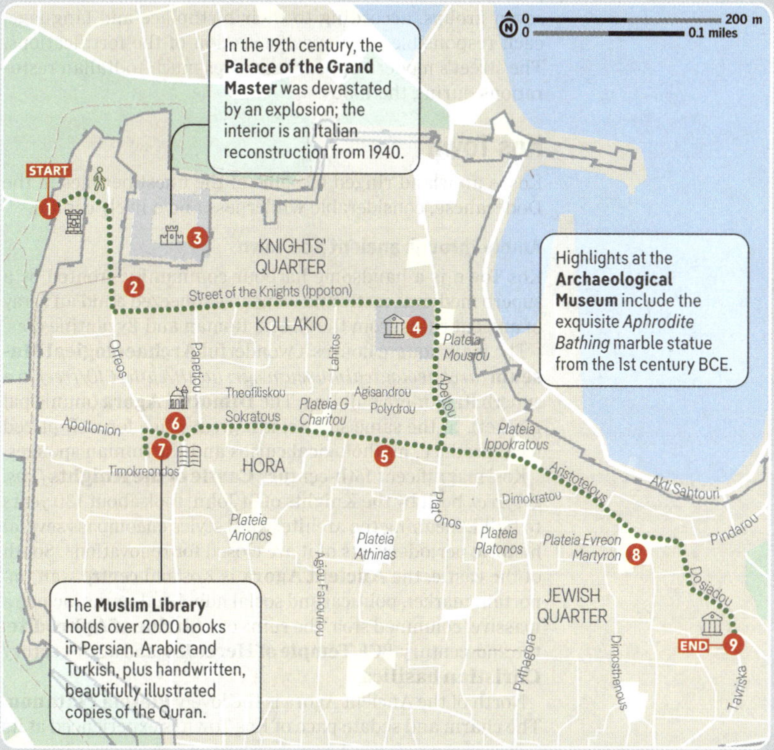

In the 19th century, the **Palace of the Grand Master** was devastated by an explosion; the interior is an Italian reconstruction from 1940.

Highlights at the **Archaeological Museum** include the exquisite *Aphrodite Bathing* marble statue from the 1st century BCE.

The **Muslim Library** holds over 2000 books in Persian, Arabic and Turkish, plus handwritten, beautifully illustrated copies of the Quran.

START

KNIGHTS' QUARTER

Street of the Knights (Ippoton)

KOLLAKIO

Orfeos

Panetiou

Theofiliskou

Sokratous

Plateia G Charitou

Agisandrou Polydrou

Lahitos

Plateia Mousiou

Apellou

Plateia Ippokratous

Apollonion

Timokreondos

HORA

Aristotelous

Akti Sahtouri

Dimokratou

Platonos

Plateia Arionos

Agiou Fanouriou

Plateia Athinas

Plateia Platonos

Plateia Evreon Martyron

Pindarou

JEWISH QUARTER

Pythagora

Dimotheandous

Dosiadou

Tavriska

END

0 ——— 200 m
0 ——— 0.1 miles

rulers of this Mediterranean island. It should take you no more than 20 minutes.

From the 14th century, this was home to the Knights Hospitaller who ruled Rhodes. The knights were divided into seven groups, according to their birthplace and language, each responsible for a specific section of the fortifications. The street's modern appearance owes much to Italian restorations during the 1930s.

Kos Town

Kos is an island ringed by some of the finest beaches in the Dodecanese, considerable wilderness and a lively capital.

Amble through ancient Kos Town

Kos Town is a handsome harbour community, fronted by a superb medieval castle and somehow squeezed amid an array of ancient ruins from the Greek, Roman and Byzantine eras.

The main square houses a wonderful **Archaeological Museum** *(archaeologicalmuseums.gr; adult/child €10/free)* in a superb Italian-era building. The **Dimotiki Agora** (municipal market), in the same square, is a great place for well-priced local produce, mythological curios and Kalymnian sponges.

Kos' magnificent 15th-century **Castle of the Knights** *(kos. gr; free),* built by the Knights of St John, took about 130 years to build, meaning the architectural styles encompass several historic periods. Parts of it are closed for renovations. South of the castle, the **Ancient Agora** is Kos' old centre – an important market, political and social hub. Landmarks include a massive, columned stoa, the ruins of a **Shrine of Aphrodite**, the 2nd-century-BCE **Temple of Hercules**, and a 5th-century **Christian basilica**.

North of the Ancient Agora is the lovely **Plateia Platanou**. The charm and sedate pace of Kos Town is experienced at its

TRABANTOS/SHUTTERSTOCK

Asklepieion, Kos

best in this lovely cobblestone square. Sitting in a cafe here, you can pay your respects to **Hippocrates' plane tree**. Hippocrates himself is said to have taught his pupils in its shade – though this is legend, since plane trees don't usually live for more than 200 years.

Discover the ancient site of healing

The island's most important ancient site, **Asklepieion** *(kos. gr; adult/child €15/free)* stands on a pine-covered hill 3km southwest of Kos Town, commanding lovely views towards Türkiye. A religious sanctuary devoted to Asclepius, the god of healing, it was also a healing centre and a school of medicine. It was founded in the 3rd century BCE, according to legend by Hippocrates himself, the Kos-born 'father' of modern medicine. He was already dead by then, though, and the training here simply followed his teachings. Bus 3 runs hourly from Kos Town to the site. It's also a pleasant, if uphill, bike ride.

BEST BEACHES ON KOS

Magic Beach: Great spot for a nature-based experience with few(er) resources, in the island's southwest.

Exotic Beach: If you like to get into your birthday suit, this spot near Magic Beach is the nudist option.

Lagada Beach: Lovely and simple, also referred to as Banana Beach.

Agios Stefanos Beach: Sadly, this beach has been ruined by a massive resort behind it. Nevertheless, the small beachfront promontory has the photogenic islet of Kastri, topped with a tiny church, within swimming distance offshore.

Agios Theologos Beach: On the west coast, backed by meadow bluffs carpeted in olive groves, it feels far removed from the resort bustle.

 EATING ON KOS: OUR PICKS

Haihoutes: In a ghost village, this tastefully restored cafe serves history, traditional food and good coffee. *3pm-midnight €*

O Makis: In Mastihari, this is a genuine Greek experience with friendly Makis, serving seafood and grills at incredible prices. *10am-midnight €*

Oria Taverna: Walk up for 15 minutes to this idyllic taverna, near old Pyli Castle, for the best views on Kos and traditional food. *9am-9pm €*

Restaurant Agios Theologos: Set above Agios Theologos Beach, this much-loved seafood taverna enjoys the best sunsets in Kos. *10am-9pm €€*

Corfu

COSMOPOLITAN VIBE | MIGHTY FORTRESSES | REGAL REFUGE

 TOP TIP

Parking and car congestion can be a nightmare in Corfu Town. It's best to find a space where you can leave your car; the centre is largely pedestrianised and you won't need it while you're in town.

Still recognisable as the idyllic refuge where the ship-wrecked Odysseus was soothed and sent on his way home, Corfu – one of the seven main Ionian Islands – continues to attract travellers with its lush scenery, bountiful produce and pristine beaches. While certain parts of the island have succumbed to overdevelopment, it's possible to escape the crowds.

Imbued with Venetian elegance, historic Corfu Town (Kerkyra) stands halfway down the island's east coast. Located between two strongholds (each topped by a fortress built to withstand Ottoman sieges), the UNESCO-listed Old Town unfolds as a tight-packed car-free warren of cobbled lanes. Some are lined with fine restaurants, lively bars and intriguing shops; others exude a timeless charm, with flowery side alleys and weathered facades. The Old Town's majestic architecture includes the splendid Liston arcade, high-class museums, and many churches.

By day, streets buzz with cruise-ship passengers and day-trippers; come evening, the atmosphere thrives around teeming bars.

GETTING AROUND

Corfu's Old Town is compact and mostly pedestrianised, so getting around is best done on foot.

Corfu City Bus *(astikoktelkerkyras.gr)* serves points around Corfu Town and the nearby communities in central Corfu; most lines depart from the main local bus station near San Rocco Sq (aka Plateia Theotoki). Line 15 goes to the airport and the port, New Limani. Buy tickets at vending machines or kiosks; tickets bought from bus drivers are more expensive.

Buses to destinations in northern and southern Corfu leave from the **Green Buses** *(ktelkerkyras.gr)* terminal in the New Town, a 15-minute walk south of the centre. Green Buses has frequent services to major beaches and island communities, the port and airport. Services are reduced on weekends and outside peak season.

To thoroughly explore the island, you'll need your own transport. Car and motorbike rentals are widely available at the airport, in Corfu Town and at the resorts. Prebook in summer.

CORFU

0 ___ 200 m
0 ___ 0.1 miles

BEST ORGANISED TOURS

Corfu Walking & Food Tours: Guided tours of Corfu's Old Town, plus island coach tours, including a Durrell-themed one. *(corfuwalkingtours. com)*

Corfu Perspectives Guided Tours: Insightful tours focus on Corfu's lesser-known sides, personalities and locations. *(corfu guidedtours.com)*

Aperghi Travel: Island hikes, from guided one-day treks up Mt Pantokrator to two-week self-guided Corfu Trail expeditions. *(aperghitravel.gr)*

S-Bikes & Cycle: Acharavi-based company leads guided mountain-bike tours around northern Corfu and e-bike tours of Corfu Town. *(cyclecorfu.com)*

Ionian Cruises: Day cruises to Paxi and Antipaxi, to Parga and Syvota islands and across to Albania. *(ionian-cruises.com)*

⭐ **HIGHLIGHTS**	7 Liston	13 Marina's Taverna
1 Palaio Frourio	8 Neo Frourio	14 Papagiorgis
	see 6 Palace of St	15 Tsipouradiko
🔴 **SIGHTS**	Michael & St	16 Venetian Well
2 Archaeological	George	
Museum	9 Spianada	🟢 **DRINKING &**
3 Byzantine Museum of		**NIGHTLIFE**
Antivouniotissa	⚫ **SLEEPING**	17 Imabari Seaside
4 Casa Parlante	10 Bella Venezia	Lounge
5 Church of Agios	11 Locandiera	
Spyridon		🔵 **INFORMATION**
6 Corfu Museum of	🟢 **EATING**	18 Aperghi Travel
Asian Art	12 Chrisomalis	

A Stroll Through History

Explore Corfu's Old Town

A Corfu Town landmark, the elegant **Liston** is an arcaded building dating back to Corfu's Napoleonic occupation (1807–14). These days, it houses see-and-be-seen cafes. Across the grassy expanse known as the **Spianada**, the imposing **Palaio Frourio** *(odysseus.culture.gr; adult/child €10/free)* fortress was built in the 14th century by the Venetians to

Neo Frourio

defend against Ottoman attacks. Previously, it enclosed the entire Byzantine city within massive stone walls; spend half an hour clambering up to the viewpoints.

After a sightseeing respite at **Imabari Seaside Lounge** on Faliraki Beach, follow the waterfront to reach a pale-yellow 15th-century church that houses the **Byzantine Museum of Antivouniotissa** *(odysseus.culture.gr; adult/child €5/3)*. Then wander through a web of lanes and alleyways, where bougain-villea plants blaze in pink and red across pastel-painted walls.

The **Church of Agios Spyridon** shelters the remains of Corfu's patron saint. Cross the pretty Plateia Agios Spyridon for an ice cream at **Papagiorgis** *(papagiorgis.gr)*, an old-school patisserie from 1924, before popping into **Casa Parlante** *(casaparlante.gr; adult/child €10/6)* to gain the sense of the lifestyle of a 19th-century merchant family.

On the other side of town looms the **Neo Frourio** *(odysseus. culture.gr; adult/child €5/free)*, or New Fort, another Venetian masterpiece of military engineering built in the 16th century. The bastion can be accessed via the stairway at the western end of Solomou. It's open from April to October.

Eastern Masterpieces

Greece's only collection of Asian art

Looming over the northern end of the Spianada is the neo-classical **Palace of St Michael and St George**. Built by the British as a residence for the high commissioner, it also served as the seat of the Ionian Parliament and summer palace of the Greek royal family. Today, it's home to the prestigious **Corfu Museum of Asian Art** *(matk.gr; adult/child €10/free)*, which features 15,000 artefacts, mostly from Japan and China, donated by private collectors.

Archaeological Treasure Chest
Catch a glimpse of Corfu's distant past

South of the city centre, the **Archaeological Museum of Corfu** *(adult/child €10/free)* should be on the to-do list of anyone interested in Ancient Greek history and art. Its fine collection of pieces unearthed around the island provides an insightful survey of Corfu's rich archaeological heritage, from prehistoric to Roman times.

Forest, Royals & Ruins
Discover Corfu's regal connections at Mon Repos

The rambling wooded estate of **Mon Repos** sits partly on top of Palaeopolis, an ancient settlement dating back to the 8th century BCE. The park's centrepiece is a neoclassical mansion, showcased as the **Museum of Palaeopolis** *(odysseus. culture.gr; adult/child €10/free)*. It was built in 1830 as the summer retreat of Corfu's British governors and used as a residence by Greek royals from 1864 until 1967. Perhaps its biggest claim to fame is as the place where Prince Philip of Greece, later Duke of Edinburgh and husband of Queen Elizabeth II, was born in 1921.

Mon Repos is about 2km south of the Old Town and served by bus 2a from the Spianada or San Rocco Sq. Pack a picnic and water, as there are no cafes or shops on the grounds or nearby.

Royal fans, garden lovers and mythology buffs should make the 10km trip south to **Achilleion Palace** *(achillion-corfu. gr; adult/child €7/5)*, the splendid summer retreat of Empress Elisabeth of Austria, aka Sissi. It was completed in 1892, and Sissi only got to enjoy a few years here before her tragic assassination in 1898. To get here, hop on Blue Bus 10 at San Rocco Sq.

PAXI & ANTIPAXI

A mere 10km off the south of Corfu island, and measuring 13km from tip to toe, Paxi packs a lot of punch in its pint-sized frame. Its sublime beaches are bound to bring a smile to your face. Facilities are concentrated in three peaceful harbour villages on its easeetern shores – Lakka, Loggos and the ferry port of Gaios. The vibe is laid-back but sophisticated. From Gaios, it's a short hop to sister island Antipaxi, a wonderful day-trip destination for its beach coves.

Paxi does not have an airport. Passenger-only ferries operated by Joy Cruises, Lefkada Palace and Kerkyra Lines serve Paxi from Corfu Town, while Kamelia Lines leaves from Lefkimmi in southern Corfu (free bus shuttle from Corfu Town). Kerkyra Lines and Kerkyra Seaways link Paxi with Igoumenitsa.

 EATING IN CORFU TOWN: OUR PICKS

Tsipouradiko: Pick from plenty of mezedhes at this rustic old mansion with tables under a tree and occasional live music. *6.30pm-midnight* €€

Chrisomalis: Going strong since 1904, this little taverna was a Durrell family fave. Warm service and good people-watching. *12.30pm-midnight* €€

Marina's Taverna: Tables strewn around a cobbled square, and home-cooked dishes made from tried-and-true family recipes. *noon-midnight* €€

Venetian Well: Local recipes elevated with contemporary techniques and cosmopolitan flair. It's tucked on a romantic square. *7-11.30pm* €€€

Crete

STUNNING COASTS | VIBRANT CULTURE | HISTORIC WONDERS

☑ **TOP TIP**

Hania is known for having some of the best food on the island, from prized meats to seasonal vegetables. Be sure to try cheeses, preserves and olive oil.

Crete is a treasure chest of splendid beaches, ancient marvels and striking landscapes, weaving in entrancing cities and throwback villages where residents share uniquely Cretan traditions. There's something undeniably artistic in the way Crete's landscape unfolds, from the sun-drenched beaches in the north to the rugged canyons spilling out at the cliff- and cove-lined southern coast. In between, valleys cradle moody villages, and round-shouldered hills are the overture to often snow-dabbed mountains.

Crete's natural wonders are equalled only by the richness of its history. The Palace of Knossos is but one of many vestiges of the mysterious ancient Minoan civilisation (as seen in the unmissable Archaeological Museum in Iraklio). Then there are Venetian fortresses, Turkish mosques and Byzantine churches – Hania and Rethymno showcase these spectacularly. The island's beauty is rivalled by its food, with rural tavernas often producing their own ingredients and catching their own seafood.

 GETTING AROUND

KTEL buses serve the island and link Iraklio, Hania and Rethymno. Local buses head from Iraklio to the Palace of Knossos.

If you're driving to Hania, park on the periphery (there are car parks to the south) and walk to the Old Town. From the airport, insist to your driver that they stick to the posted fixed price before setting off.

The historic quarter of Rethymno is mostly car-free and best enjoyed on foot. Parking is always a problem; try the huge car park east of the Municipal Park or the paid parking on Kriari. The bus station is at the western edge of the commercial centre.

Most places of interest in Iraklio are within the city centre, which is largely pedestrianised. Leave the car in your hotel garage, a 24/7 car park or use the free parking at the Cultural Centre on Giannikou. The airport is 4km east of the centre; access is a breeze. The ferry port is even closer.

CRETE

Sea of
Crete

Kolymbari   Stavros
Kissamos   ● Hania
                Panormo   Bali   Dia
Samaria Gorge Georgioupolis Rethymno   Iraklio Palace of
    Sougia   Perama Anogia Knossos Malia
Paleohora   Agia Plakias Spili Zaros Agia Varvara Kastelli Neapoli Agios Sitia Palekastro
       Roumeli Hora   Arhanes   Nikolaos
            Sfakion Agia Galini Arkalohorion Mt Istron Mohlos
              Tymbaki   Mires   Dikti   Makrygialos Zakros
                        Pyrgos   Myrtos   Xerokampos
                          Arvi Ierapetra
Gavdos   Gaïdouronisi Koufonisi
                                       (Hrysi)
                    Libyan
                     Sea

Mt Pahnes   Mt Psiloritis   Mt Dikti

0 ——— 50 km
0 ——— 25 miles

Hania

Hania (also spelt Chania) is Crete's most evocative city. Wandering its tangle of alleys and lanes is one of the island's pleasures. It was historically the seat of Venetian, Turkish and then Cretan rule, and remnants of Venetian and Turkish architecture abound, with ancient synagogues, plus old townhouses now transformed into atmospheric restaurants and boutique hotels.

Explore the Venetian Harbour

There are few places where Hania's historic charm and grandeur are more palpable than in the **Venetian Harbour**. Lined by pastel-coloured buildings that punctuate a maze of narrow lanes lined with shops and tavernas, its oldest parts date to the 15th century. The eastern side is dominated by the domed **Mosque of Kioutsouk Hasan**, now an exhibition hall. On the west side, short and steep streets lead up to the remains of the Venetian fortifications. (It's worth ascending the steps for the somewhat hidden high Venetian-era terrace, to enjoy views across the city and harbour.)

Heading east around the harbour, the restored **Grand Arsenal** houses the **KAM Centre of Mediterranean Architecture**. Continuing on, the somewhat dilapidated, 15th-century **Neoria**, or **Venetian shipyards**, are a historic treasure hiding in plain sight.

Following the waterfront out onto the 14th-century **breakwater**, you can clamber over the huge blocks of stone as you take in captivating views back to the Old Town. Imagine the port filled with Venetian sailing ships laden with valuable cargo. Parts of the magnificent 21m-high **lighthouse** date to 1595. It was rebuilt by the Egyptians in the 1820s in the shape of a minaret.

Heraklion Archaeological Museum, Iraklio

HANIA TOURS & INFO

Boats of every shape and size tour Hania's harbour and coast, especially at sunset. Touts offer a choice of glass-bottom, vintage or sailing boats and more. Some tours are all-day affairs and visit the remote beaches on the Rodopou Peninsula and **Balos Beach** on the Gramvousa Peninsula, which are difficult to reach via land.

Tours on land cover much of Western Crete. Check durations carefully – for instance, the trip for the hike in the **Samaria Gorge** lasts from dawn until after dusk.

Hania's **municipal tourist office** (*explorechania.gr*) has limited hours but is an excellent resource for special events and getting around the region without a rental car. Check its official website and phone app.

Treasures in the Archaeological Museum of Chania

For greater historical insight, don't miss the **Archaeological Museum of Chania** (*amch.gr; adult/child €15/free*) where artefacts from across the island are displayed in two light-filled galleries, with plenty of signage offering details and context. For time out, relax in the breezy cafe with views from the deck to the Aegean. The museum is 1.5km east of the Old Town. Come in the afternoon, and after the visit walk back along the shoreline for pre-sunset views plus glimpses of hidden beaches below a tiny park and the remains of waterfront tanneries that were a major Hania industry 100 years ago.

Iraklio

Minoan culture at the Heraklion Archaeological Museum

Snake goddesses, bull leapers and the Prince of the Lilies are among the intriguing characters you'll encounter in the unmissable **Heraklion Archaeological Museum** (*heraklionmuseum.gr; adult/child €12/free*). This is the world's premier museum of the Minoan culture, widely considered the first civilisation in Europe. Reaching a peak of development beginning in 2000 BCE, their art, architecture and culture are celebrated in the 27 rooms of this visitor-friendly museum.

A two-hour spin around here will greatly enhance your understanding of Cretan history, help put any archaeological site on Crete in context, and shine a spotlight on aspects of daily life and the development of Cretan societies. It's best to visit after 3pm in summer when it's less busy. The simple

 EATING IN HANIA: BEST TAVERNAS

Pinaleon Fine Kitchen: A menu of the greatest hits of Greek classics is served in this spiffy yet unpretentious corner taverna. *1-10pm €€*

Kouzina Epe: Stylish cafe on a relaxed square serving an appealing mix of modern Greek fare and daily specials. *noon-7.30pm €€*

Christostomos: Behind the harbour, popular for its classic Cretan cuisine cooked over wood or in a pot with homegrown ingredients. *1-11pm €€*

Kalderimi: A traditional, busy taverna in Topanas. Cretan standards cooked with creative flair, plus dishes from around the Med. *8.30am-11pm €€*

cafe is good for refreshments and has shady outdoor seating overlooking architectural digs.

Palace of Knossos

The grand capital of Minoan Crete

Crete's must-see attraction is the **Palace of Knossos** (*knossos-palace.gr; adult/child €26/free*), just 5km south of Iraklio. Combining a visit here with Iraklio's excellent Archaeological Museum is highly recommended and will give unparalleled insight into Crete's Minoan civilisation. The setting is awe-inspiring and the ruins and recreations impressive, incorporating an immense palace, courtyards, private apartments, baths, lively frescoes and more. To beat the crowds and avoid the heat, get to Knossos either at 8am or after 3pm. Skip ticket-booth queues by buying timed-admission tickets online. Plan on spending at least two hours to do the place justice.

Samaria Gorge

Crete's world-class hiking

Samaria Gorge (*samaria-gorge.gr; adult/child €10/free*) is one of Europe's top geological wonders. The best way to experience the gorge is by hiking its 18km length from the starting point in the hillside village of **Xyloskalo** near Omalos. You begin at an elevation of 1230m and end at sea level. The national park ends at the 13km mark just north of the almost abandoned village of **Palea Agia Roumeli**, from where it's a further 3km to the sea. All along the route stay alert for *kri-kri*, a mountain goat that's native to Crete, and enjoy the wildflowers blooming in profusion.

Day trips to the gorge are heavily marketed to tourists across Crete and it gets crowded in summer. Start as early as you can manage to get ahead of the crowds. The park's north entrance is open from 7am to 1pm May to October. After closing, visitors are not permitted to walk on the entire trail, as everyone needs to be out of the park by 4pm. Sturdy shoes are a must. Day trips to Samaria Gorge start at the park entrance and include a pick-up from either Sougia or Hora Sfakion, after a ferry ride from Agia Roumeli. The Samaria Gorge website has excellent details on the hike and how to get there.

BEST WINERIES BEYOND IRAKLIO

Boutari Winery: One of Greece's largest wine producers has a vast, airy tasting room in Skalani.

Stilianou Winery: Rustic and down-to-earth, it specialises in organic wines made with local varietals only; in Kounavi.

Titakis Wines: Huge facility and garden in Kounavi, with sample plots of 11 Cretan varieties.

Digenakis Winery: In Peza, with an artful tasting room and unusual vintages.

Agelakis Winery: In a bare-bones facility around a Peza courtyard. Vines cover just 4.5 hectares.

Domain Paterianakis: This organic specialist has views as big as its tasting room off the main road in Alagni.

 EATING IN IRAKLIO: OUR PICKS

Peskesi: Culinary magic forged from family-farm ingredients and served amid unpretentious sophistication in a Venetian mansion. *1pm-1am €€*	**Thigaterra:** This rustic-elegant slow-food champion at Ammoudara Beach gives traditional Greek dishes the next-gen workout. *4pm-midnight €€*	**Vourvouladiko:** Turkish-infused Cretan cuisine in an enchanted Lakkos garden with historic photographs. A genteel retreat. *7pm-1am €€*	**Apiri:** Stylish but relaxed corner bistro with a tightly curated menu of modern Greek cuisine, cocktails and craft beer. *noon-midnight €€*

Places We Love to Stay

€ Budget €€ Midrange €€€ Top end

Athens
MAP p529

Athens Backpackers € Aussie-run backpackers near the Acropolis, with spotless dorms, a courtyard, well-stocked kitchen and busy social scene. Also has Athens Studios.

Athens Quinta Hostel € Friendly hostel in an old Exarhia mansion, furnished with velvet sofas and patterned tile floors.

Marble House Pension € In a quiet cul-de-sac in Koukaki, this pension offers well-maintained rooms and one apartment; some have small balconies. Air-con is extra.

Athens Gate €€ Stunning views over the Temple of Olympian Zeus from the spacious front rooms, and a central (if busy) location.

Athens Muses Suites €€ Renovated townhouse up on the slopes of Plaka with small, well-kept rooms.

Mosaikon €€ One in a cluster of high-end, reasonably priced suite hotels in the heart of Monastiraki.

Neoma €€€ Light and airy, with sensational Acropolis views from the rooftop bar and pool, on the edge of Filopappou Hill.

Delphi

Fedriades Hotel € Attractive, value-for-money three-star hotel with comfortable, family-friendly rooms and terrific mountain views. Breakfast features homemade food. Free bikes.

Hotel Tholos € Minimalist (not to say humdrum), central and great value. Has sea-view balconies and caring owners.

Meteora

Meteora Central Hostel € Well-managed spot in Kalambaka and one of Greece's best hostels. Dorm rooms are spotless, with good lockers; also private doubles.

Doupiani House €€ Breakfast in a carefully tended garden with uninterrupted Meteora views at this warmly welcoming family-run Kastraki hotel.

Thessaloniki
MAP p538

Zeus is Loose € Hostel (or rather, poshtel) with a muted colour scheme, big windows, sleek furniture and a rooftop bar.

Little Big House € Choose from private doubles or small dorms in this cute and eclectic hostel in charming Ano Poli.

Olganos VL €€ Lovely, family-run boutique hotel in the old Jewish quarter of Veria, close to all the archaelogical sites.

Trilogy House €€ Design buffs will feel at home in this restored 1920s building, where modern fixtures mix with neoclassical lines.

Nafplio

Pension Marianna €€ Vibrant place with convivial owners, Greek *filoxenia* (hospitality) and wide-vista setting – you can't get better for value. Organic breakfasts.

Aetoma €€€ Intimate yet comfortable, the five rooms in a classic mansion have dark, heavy and stylish furnishings. Generous traditional breakfast.

Grand Sarai €€€ This renovated pink mansion is sleek and modern on the inside, with stylish rooms. Most have marvellous views; some have balconies.

Olympia

Hotel Pelops €€ Our pick for Olympia's most welcoming lodgings, with comfortable rooms and a delightful, sunny lounge. Greek-Australian Suzanne is a fount of knowledge.

Pension-Tavern Bacchus €€ Located only a few kilometres from the ancient site in the village of Ancient Pissa, this pleasant spot has wonderful valley views, a swimming pool and a decent tavern.

Santorini (Thira)

Spiros & Hiroko Hotel €€ Behind a huge bloom of geraniums on Perissa's main street, Japanese-Greek couple Hiroko and Spiros run an immaculate 10-room hotel. No kids.

Aroma Suites €€ Overlooking the caldera at the quieter southern end of Fira, this boutique hotel has charming service and six cave-house rooms and suites.

Chelidonia Traditional Villas €€€ Traditional Oia cliffside dwellings that have been in the owner's family for generations. It has beds in cosy alcoves, and private patios with caldera views.

Villa Blanca €€€ A superb option away from the crowds amid Megalohori's vineyards, this luxury villa is built in traditional Cycladic style with a hot tub and ocean view.

Naxos

Hotel Grotta €€ Located on high ground overlooking the *kastro* and Hora, this excellent family-run hotel has immaculate rooms, great sea views, and a cool indoor hot tub.

Hotel Glaros €€ A well-run and immaculate 13-room boutique hotel with an indoor hot tub. The beach is only a few steps away. Adults only.

Rhodes Town

S Nikolis Hotel €€ Set across several restored buildings and a flowery courtyard, the stylish, split-level rooms feature four-poster beds, marble floors and stone walls. Breakfast is superb.

Marco Polo Mansion €€ This 15th-century pasha's house lovingly recreates an Ottoman ambience. Some rooms are in the mansion itself; the rest open onto the stunning garden.

Spirit of the Knights €€€ With their thick rugs, dark woods, stained-glass windows and sense of tranquillity, the six opulent suites in this gorgeous boutique hotel ooze medieval atmosphere.

Kos Town

Hotel Afendoulis € There may be plusher hotels in Kos, but none with such spirit. Clean rooms with small balconies, a homely lounge area and delicious breakfasts.

Kos Aktis Art Hotel €€€ Bedrooms are minimalist affairs of glass, light and wood. The view of the Aegean and, by night, Bodrum glittering like a giant chandelier is romantic.

Corfu   MAP p553

Locandiera €€ This stylish guesthouse in a historic building in Corfu Town is a standout for its superb breakfasts and rooms with a subtly artsy vibe.

Manessis Apartments €€ Lovely two-bedroom apartments with balconies facing Kassiopi's harbour, framed by flower-filled gardens and managed by a caring owner who ensures everything goes smoothly.

Rolling Stone €€ Indie travellers' favourite on Kontogialos (Pelekas) Beach, with a shared outdoor kitchen and hosts who organise

barbecue evenings and boat rides to hidden caves.

Bella Venezia €€€ This city hotel in a neoclassical villa on a peaceful street features compact but well-equipped rooms and a flowery breakfast terrace.

Hania

Kumba Hostel € Restored, hip hostel east of the centre. Bright cafe–bar, spacious and modern dorms, and rooms that are quiet and comfortable.

Ionas Boutique Hotel €€ Historic building with nine contemporary rooms and a rooftop terrace, located in the labyrinth old Splantzia quarter.

Malmo Historic Hotel €€ Beautifully restored hotel arching over the pedestrianised street in Splantzia. Rooftop deck; nightlife is right outside the door.

Iraklio

Intra Muros Boutique Hostel € Family-run and central, with a fully equipped communal kitchen and a veranda for socialising.

Olive Green Hotel €€ Contemporary hotel with minimalist white and olive-green decor. It gets eco-cred from solar panels and sustainable building materials.

Lato Boutique Hotel €€ Iraklio goes Hollywood – with all the sass but sans the attitude – at this mod boutique hotel overlooking the old harbour.

JAYSKYLAND IMAGES/ALAMY

Hotel Grotta, Naxos

Practicalities

FAMILY TRAVEL

Greeks love children, and yours will be fussed over wherever you go. While there may not be specific tourist infrastructure for families, the country is crammed with fascinating history, thrilling ferry rides and sandy beaches. Children receive discounted admission at nearly all museums and sights.

SVEN HANSCHE/SHUTTERSTOCK

SMOKING

Be aware: while smoking is prohibited in all enclosed public spaces, including restaurants and bars, enforcement can be lax. And outdoors (including restaurant/bar terraces) is another matter – it's permitted (and enjoyed) by many.

HEALTH & SAFE TRAVEL

Probably the biggest danger travelling in Greece is heatstroke; much of Greece experiences seaside breezes, so it's easy to become overexposed to the sun without realising it. Be careful, too, at isolated swimming spots that may have powerful currents. Mosquito repellent can be hard to find; bring some with you. Cannabis is illegal and brings heavy fines and/or imprisonment.

VISAS

Visitors from the UK, Canada, New Zealand, the US and Australia are among nationalities that can stay for up to 90 days in any six-month period without a visa.

OPENING HOURS

Opening hours vary throughout the year, the following are high-season hours.
Banks 8.30am–2.30pm Monday to Thursday, 8am–2pm Friday
Restaurants 11am–11pm
Cafes 9am–midnight
Bars 8pm–late
Shops 8am–3pm Monday, Wednesday and Saturday; 9am–2pm and 5.30pm–9pm Tuesday, Thursday and Friday

LGBTIQ+ TRAVELLERS

Same-sex marriage was legalised in Greece in 2024; attitudes to the LGBTIQ+ community have grown more liberal across Greece. However, the Orthodox Church plays a prominent role in shaping society's views, so attitudes outside major cities and gay-friendly islands are more conservative.

PUBLIC HOLIDAYS

New Year's Day 1 January
Epiphany 6 January
Lent First Sunday in February
Greek Independence Day 25 March
Good Friday April/May
Orthodox Easter Sunday April/May
May Day (Protomagia) 1 May

Whit Monday (Agiou Pnevmatos) 50 days after Easter Sunday
Feast of the Dormition 15 August
Ohi Day 28 October
Christmas Day 25 December
St Stephen's Day 26 December

Language

With just a little Modern Greek under your belt, you'll have a richer understanding of this language's impact on contemporary Western culture; and even if you learn only the very basics, your travel experience will be the better for it.

Basics

Hello. Γειά σας. *ya*·sas (polite/plural)
Γειά σου. *ya*·su (informal/singular)
Good morning. Καλημέρα. ka·li·*me*·ra
Good evening. Καλησπέρα. ka·li·*spe*·ra
Goodbye. Αντίο. an·*di*·o
Yes./No. Ναι./Όχι. ne/*o*·hi
Please. Παρακαλώ. pa·ra·ka·*lo*
Thank you. Ευχαριστώ. ef·ha·ri·*sto*
Sorry. Συγγνώμη. sig·*no*·mi
My name is … Με λένε … me *le*·ne …
Do you speak English?
Μιλάτε αγγλικά mi·*la*·te an·gli·*ka*
I (don't) understand.
(Δεν) καταλαβαίνω.
(dhen) ka·ta·la·*ve*·no

Directions

Where is …? Πού είναι …; pu *i*·ne …
What's the address?
Ποια είναι η διεύθυνση
pia *i*·ne i dhi·*ef*·thin·si
Can you show me (on the map)?
Μπορείς να μου δείξεις
(στον χάρτη)
bo·*ris* na mu *dhik*·sis (ston *har*·ti)

Signs

ΕΙΣΟΔΟΣ Entry
ΕΞΟΔΟΣ Exit
ΠΛΗΡΟΦΟΡΙΕΣ Information
ΑΝΟΙΧΤΟ Open
ΚΛΕΙΣΤΟ Closed
ΓΥΝΑΙΚΩΝ Toilets (Women)
ΑΝΔΡΩΝ Toilets (Men)

Time

What time is it? Τι ώρα είναι; ti *o*·ra *i*·ne
It's (2 o'clock).
Είναι (δύο η ώρα). *i*·ne (*dhi*·o i *o*·ra)
It's half past (10).
Είναι (δέκα) και μισή. (*dhe*·ka) ke mi·*si*
today σήμερα *si*·me·ra
tomorrow αύριο *av*·ri·o
yesterday χθες hthes
morning πρωί pro·*i*
(this) afternoon
(αυτό το) απόγευμα
(af·*to* to) a·*po*·yev·ma
evening βράδυ *vra*·dhi

Emergencies

Help! Βοήθεια! vo·*i*·thya
Go away! Φύγε! *fi*·ye
I'm lost. Εχω χαθεί. *e*·kho kha·*thi*
There's been an accident.
Έγινε ατύχημα. *e*·yi·ne a·*ti*·hi·ma
I'm ill.
Είμαι άρρωστος. *i*·me a·ro·stos (m)
Είμαι άρρωστη. *i*·me a·ro·st (f)
I'm allergic to (antibiotics).
Είμαι αλλεργικός/αλλεργική
(στα αντιβιωτικά).
i·me a·ler·yi·*kos*/a·ler·yi·*ki* (m/f)
(sta an·di·vi·o·ti·*ka*)

Eating & Drinking

What would you recommend?
Τι θα συνιστούσες;
ti tha si·ni·*stu*·ses
That was delicious.
Ηταν νοστιμότατο!
i·tan no·sti·*mo*·ta·to
Cheers! Εις υγείαν! is i·*yi*·an

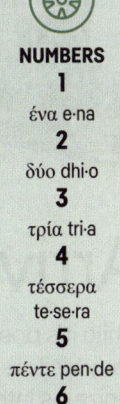

NUMBERS
1
ένα e·na
2
δύο dhi·o
3
τρία tri·a
4
τέσσερα te·se·ra
5
πέντε pen·de
6
έξι e·xi
7
επτά ep·ta
8
οκτώ ok·to
9
εννέα e·ne·a
10
δέκα dhe·ka

MARKUS MAINKA/SHUTTERSTOCK

Eleftherios Venizelos International Airport

Arriving

While it's possible to drive south via the Balkans, many visitors arrive by air into Eleftherios Venizelos International Airport (Athens) or one of the four other international airports. Visitors from the UK, Canada, New Zealand, the US and Australia are among nationalities that can stay for up to 90 days in any six-month period without a visa.

By Air

Greece is easy to reach by air, particularly in summer. There are five main international airports: Athens and Thessaloniki, as well as two on Crete and one on Rhodes. Kos and Corfu receive year-round flights and these increase in high season.

By Boat

Ferries reach Greece from ports in Italy (Ancona, Bari, Brindisi). Services to Patras are useful for the Peloponnese (specifically Ancient Olympia), while those that head to Igoumenitsa are handy for ongoing journeys to Kalambaka (Meteora) or Delphi. See *ferryhopper.com*.

MONEY

Currency: Euro (€)

CREDIT & DEBIT CARDS

Big resorts and hotels accept payments by credit and debit card, but family-owned properties often don't. MasterCard and Visa are the most widely accepted.

CASH

Cash is accepted everywhere and helps businesses avoid extra fees from banks (and in some cases, the tax office). ATMs are found at banks in cities and towns.

TIPPING

Hotels Tip porters €1 per bag and housekeepers €1 per night.

Restaurants Even if a service charge is included, a small tip is customary for good service. Round up the bill or tip around 10%.

Taxis Not expected but rounding up to nearest euro is a welcome gesture.

Getting Around

Given its complex geography, Greece has an extensive network of domestic flights and ferries. Intercity buses (KTEL network) are frequent, cheap and air-conditioned; services to remote villages are limited though not impossible. A car remains the best way to explore off-the-beaten track locations, but roads can be narrow and winding, especially in mountainous terrain and mountain villages.

LYDIAREI/SHUTTERSTOCK

Boat
Greece's network of ferries includes fast modern ferries and overnight boats with cabins. For safety, departures are subject to delay during poor weather. Schedules change annually, and services are greatly reduced between mid-October and Easter. In high season, book ahead.

Bus
The bus network is comprehensive and fares are cheap. It's mostly run by public companies under the **KTEL** (ktelbus.com) umbrella. Towns on the mainland have frequent connections to Athens. The island of Corfu can also be reached from Athens by bus (ferry ticket may be included).

Taxi
Taxis are widely available in Greece. They are reasonably priced by European standards, making them a viable alternative to hiring a car if you aren't exploring much. Beware of meter scams. In Athens, useful apps to avoid rip-offs include Beat and Uber.

Car Hire
Hire cars are available on all but the smallest of islands; local firms often have the best rates. Some islands are becoming jammed with hire vehicles, and parking can be challenging in summer. You'll need a good dose of road smarts.

Driving Conditions
Main highways in Greece are in good condition. However, some island roads aren't paved. Road surfaces are also prone to weathering and subsidence, and roads passing through mountainous areas can be littered with rocks (or, in winter, ice and snow).

DRIVING ESSENTIALS

Drive on the right

 50   **120**

Speed limit is 50km/h in urban areas, 90km/h on secondary roads and 120km/h on highways

0.05

Blood alcohol limit is 0.05%

Curated by
Kata Fári

Hungary

STUNNING ARCHITECTURE AND THERMAL SPAS

Hungary is home to one of Europe's most stunning capitals, thermal waters galore and people whose language you'll probably never speak, but who you'll definitely want to meet.

Hungary might be small, but it packs quite a punch. The country is steeped in history and tradition, its bounty of Art Nouveau architecture is astonishing, its thermal waters are restorative and its cuisine is as delicious as it is hearty. Budapest lays claim to the crown of most stunning capital in Europe, but it's so much more than a pretty face. With parks brimming with activity, museums filled with treasures, pleasure boats on the Danube and Turkish-era thermal baths belching steam, the Hungarian capital is a delight both by day and night.

In a country as flat as a *palacsinta* (pancake), Northern Hungary is as hilly as it gets, with towns rich in culture, vineyards renowned the world over and villages that cherish their traditions. Northwest of Budapest, the Danube Bend is a region of low peaks and attractive river towns steeped in history and the cultures of those who settled here. Southwest is Central Europe's largest lake, Lake Balaton (aka the Hungarian Sea), the favourite summer destination of locals, where sailing, soaking and stand-up paddleboarding is a way of life.

To the south and east is Hungary's heartland, the Great Plain, an intoxicating cocktail of countryside imbued with moody romance, splendid architecture and national parks.

BUDAPEST SPAS

THE MAIN AREAS

BUDAPEST
Scenic beauty, high culture, hot nightlife. **p570**

DANUBE BEND
Historical river towns vie for visitors' attention. **p582**

LAKE BALATON
Warm days at Central Europe's largest lake. **p585**

THE GREAT PLAIN
Horse shows and charming countryside. **p585**

NORTHERN HUNGARY
Wine, baroque architecture, folklore and forests. **p586**

For places to stay in Hungary, see p588

MARAKO85/SHUTTERSTOCK

Left: Lukács Baths (p570), Budapest; Above: Széchenyi Chain Bridge (p575), Budapest

568

Find Your Way

Hungary has no domestic flights as the country is small enough to get around by train, bus or boat. The public transport system is reliable and the roads are good. A car is only needed for rural Hungary.

TRAINS & BUSES

MÁV (*mavcsoport.hu*) operates reliable services to Hungary's major towns. Volánbusz runs an extensive bus network. The **Hungary Pass** (*18,900Ft*) provides unlimited travel throughout Hungary (available via the BudapestGO and MÁV apps or BKK, MÁV and Volánbusz ticket offices).

BOAT

Mahart PassNave (*mahartpassnave. hu*) runs excursion boats and hydrofoils on the Danube River from Budapest to places like Szentendre, Visegrád and Esztergom from April to September. **Balaton Shipping Company** (*bahart.hu*) passenger ferries serve about 20 ports on Lake Balaton.

0   50 miles
0   100 km

Danube Bend, p582
Flanked by attractive towns, the Danube makes its bend 50km north of Budapest, flowing west towards Western Transdanubia.

Northern Hungary, p586
Comparatively hilly, with main attractions that can be found around Eger and, 130km to the east, Tokaj.

Budapest, p570
The Queen of the Danube awaits with astonishing architecture, healing thermal baths and an unforgettable nightlife scene.

Lake Balaton, p585
Hungary's largest body of water. The 235km shoreline is dotted with villages a few minutes' drive from one another.

AUSTRIA
SLOVAKIA
BRATISLAVA
Eisenstadt Mosonmagyaróvár
Fertö-Hanság National Park
Jánosháza
Szombathely
Sopron
Győr Tatabánya
Kisbér
Székesfehérvár
Veszprém
Balaton Uplands National Park
Tihany
Balatonfüred
Hévíz
Nagykanizsa
Lake Balaton
Kaposvár
Zselic Region
Ormánság Region
CROATIA
Dráva River
Osijek
Pécs
Szekszárd
Tamási
Duna-Dráva National Park
Baja
Dunaföldvár
Dunaújváros
Kiskunság National Park
Kecskemét
Bugac
Kiskunfélegyháza
Szeged
SERBIA
Sárköz Region
Békéscsaba
Körös-Maros National Park
Szolnok
Great Plain
Kunszentmárton
Hortobágy National Park
Oradea
ROMANIA
Berettyóújfalu
Püspökladány
Debrecen
Polgár
Nyíregyháza
Satu Mare
Kisvárda
Rakamaz
Tokaj
Szerencs
Miskolc
Bükk National Park
Valley of the Beautiful Women
Eger
Füzesabony
Lake Tisza
Salgótarján
Mátra National Park
Mád-Dely National Park
Pászto
Gödöllő
Gyömrő
Open-Air Ethnographical Museum
Esztergom
Danube River
Visegrád
Szentendre
BUDAPEST
Parliament
Liberty Monument

CLARI MASSIMILIANO/SHUTTERSTOCK

Royal Palace (p574), Budapest

Plan Your Time

Hungary holds so much to see and do that you could easily fill a fortnight, but if you have less time, follow your interests to create your own curated trip.

Pressed for Time

● If you only have a day or two, focus on beautiful Budapest and explore both sides. Head up to the historic Castle District on the **funicular** (p574) and take in the views from the **Royal Palace** (p574) and **Fisherman's Bastion** (p574). Spend the afternoon soaking at **Széchenyi** (p570) or **Gellért Baths** (p570); in the evening take a river cruise offered byone of the various boat companies downtown.

A Week-Long Stay

● A week is enough to balance culture, nature and relaxation. After exploring **Budapest** (p570), you can day-trip to the **Danube Bend** (p582) to see charming local towns. In summer, **Lake Balaton** (p585), Central Europe's largest lake, is a must for sailing, stand-up paddleboarding and soaking. In autumn, **Northern Hungary** (p586) is best for hikes and discovering Hungary's world-renowned wine culture.

SEASONAL HIGHLIGHTS

SPRING

From March to June, Hungary is in full bloom, and Easter traditions are in full swing in historic Hollókő.

SUMMER

Scorching summer begins with Tihany's **Lavender Festival** (p585) in late June. The perfect time to relax at scenic Lake Balaton.

AUTUMN

Hungary's forests turn a riot of red and brown; it's a great time for hiking and touring the wine regions, particularly Tokaj-Hegyalja.

WINTER

Winter may be mighty cold, but it's the perfect time to relax in thermal baths and enjoy marvellous Christmas markets.

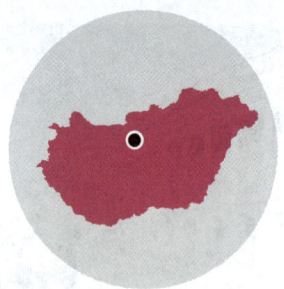

Budapest

SCENIC BEAUTY | HISTORIC SPAS | NIGHTLIFE

GETTING AROUND

Budapest is easy to navigate. The Danube clearly defines west and east: Buda and Pest. The public transport system is safe, efficient and inexpensive, and taxis are reasonably priced. You can also get around by bicycle, electric scooter or on foot. The BudapestGO app for public transport in the city offers several key features, including ticket and pass purchases, real-time route planning, a map, timetables and service updates. The city's official bike-sharing scheme is with the green MOL Bubi bikes.

☑ **TOP TIP**

Public transport tickets not only have to be purchased but also validated. Digital tickets come with a QR code scanner that you can use on machines at stations or the side of buses and trams before boarding, and passes have a QR code for inspection.

Budapest is a dazzling gem of a city, but its beauty is not all God-given: humankind has also played a role in shaping its pretty face. The city is an architectural treasure trove, with enough baroque, neoclassical, eclectic and Art Nouveau buildings to satisfy everyone. Overall, Budapest has a fin-de-siècle feel, for it was in the late 19th century, during the capital's golden age, that much of what you see today was built.

With parks brimming with activity, museums filled with treasures, pleasure boats on the Danube and Turkish-era thermal baths belching steam, the Hungarian capital is a delight both by day and night. Stroll along the Duna korzó, Pest's riverside embankment walkway, or cross any of the Danube bridges, and you'll pass young couples embracing passionately. It's then that you'll feel the romance of a place that, despite all the attempts from both within and without to destroy it, has never died.

Soak Away Your Worries

Take the plunge in a thermal bath

Hardly anything feels more relaxing in Budapest than plunging into a thermal pool and soaking away your stress in muscle-melting mineral-rich waters. Taking the waters is a way of life here, and the country – especially its capital – is a paradise for those seeking relaxation, healing and a bit of quirky local culture. Budapest lies on a geological fault line separating the Buda Hills from the Great Plain, and some 40,000 cubic metres of warm, mineral-rich water spurt forth each day. Hence the sobriquet, the 'City of Spas' – find the perfect combination of relaxation and restoration at one of several bathhouses in town. The most notable are Gellért Baths (unfortunately closed for renovations until 2028), the most beautiful bathhouse of all; **Széchenyi Baths** (*szechenyibath.hu; 10,000-17,000Ft*), Europe's largest spa complex in a wedding-cake-like building; **Lukács Baths** (*lukacsfurdo.hu; 3600-8300Ft*), a more local, health-oriented

Széchenyi Baths

WINE WITH A VIEW

Every September, the Royal Palace becomes a magnificent backdrop for the **Budapest Wine Festival**, when wooden kiosks are set up side-by-side at this historic venue to serve the country's finest red, white and sparkling wines from various regions, as well as a plethora of foreign bottles. A wide range of gastronomic delights is also available – many are prepared especially for the occasion and pair perfectly with the wines on offer. Various events, wine-focused workshops and concerts also take place in the gorgeous setting. This is one of the most elegant wine festivals in the country, and a perfect place to get familiar with lesser known but highly praised wines from all over the country. Tasting is by the glass, but bottles are also available.

destination; **Rudas Baths** *(rudasfurdo.hu; 9800-15,800Ft),* an original Turkish baths with a contemporary touch and a rooftop hot tub; and **Veli Bej Baths** *(irgalmasrend.hu/site/velibej/home; 4500-6000Ft),* a traditional Turkish bath with a modern twist.

Walk Down Memory Lane

Explore the Castle District on foot

The World Heritage–listed Castle District is home to historic sights, charming cobblestone streets, fascinating museums and stunning viewpoints that set the stage for a journey back in time. With a majestic monument on practically every corner, it's unparalleled when it comes to sightseeing. There's hardly another neighbourhood in the city with so many heavyweight sights crammed into such a compact space: the Royal Palace (p574), Fisherman's Bastion (p574) and neo-Gothic Matthias Church (p574) are all steps away from one another. Wear comfortable shoes for the cobblestone streets.

 EATING & DRINKING IN THE CASTLE DISTRICT: OUR PICKS

White Raven Skybar & Lounge: Atop the Hilton Budapest, the city's highest sky bar offers jaw-dropping views and delicious drinks and finger food. *noon-10pm* €€€

Royal Guard Restaurant & Cafe: With a facade adorned with intriguing statues and weaponry, the Royal Guard houses a lovely cafe-restaurant. *11.30am-9.30pm* €€

Savoyai Terasz: Delicious coffee and dazzling views right at the foot of the Royal Palace. Plenty of musical events in the warmer months. *10.30am-8pm* €€

4 perc és kávé: This bite-sized cafe is fully vegan, making java mostly from oat milk. *8.30am-6pm Mon-Fri, from 9am Sat & Sun* €

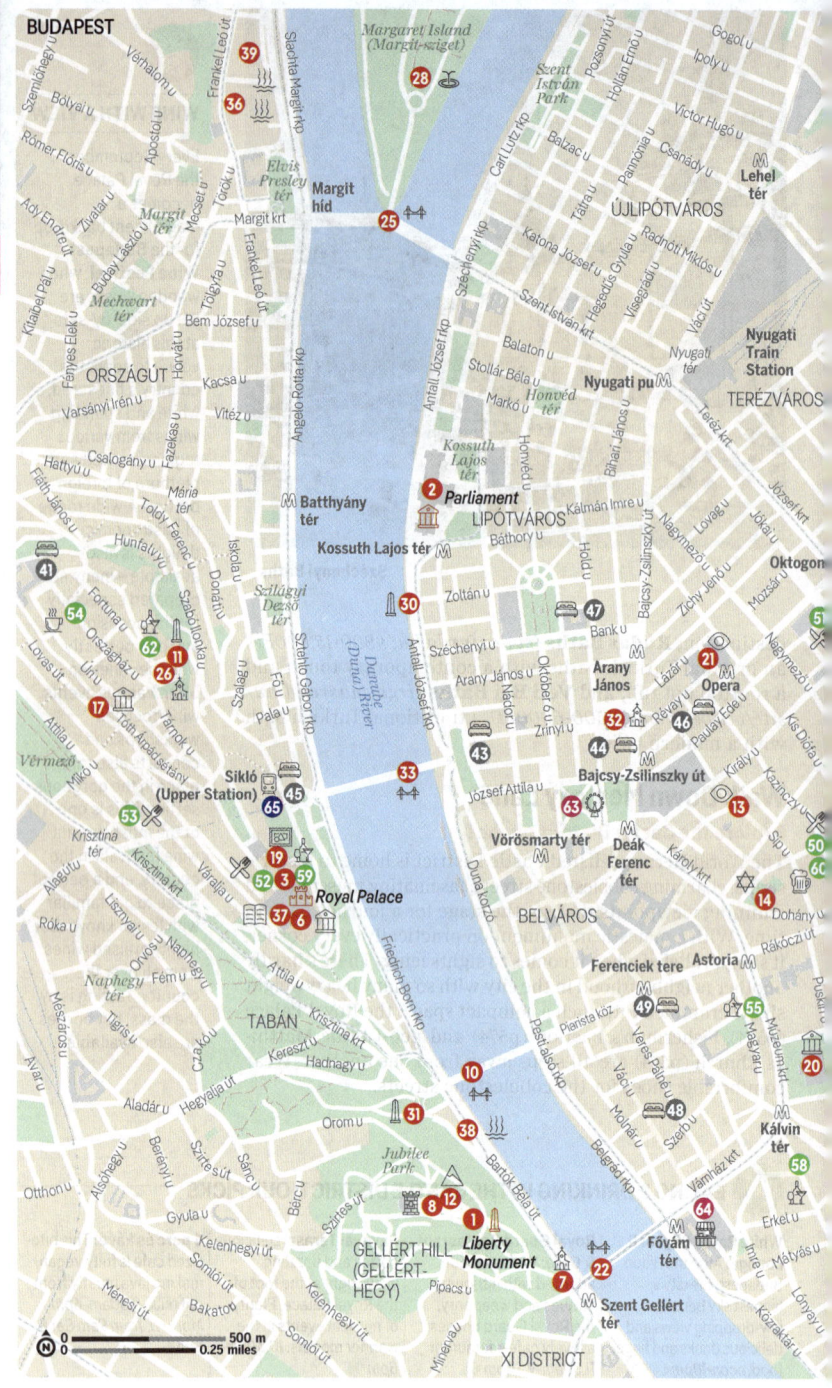

BUDAPEST

*Margaret Island
(Margit-sziget)*

*Szent
István
Park*

*Elvis
Presley
tér*

**Margit
híd**

Margit krt

*Margit
tér*

ÚJLIPÓTVÁROS

**Lehel
tér**

*Mechwart
tér*

ORSZÁGÚT

*Mária
tér*

**Nyugati
Train
Station**

Nyugati pu

TERÉZVÁROS

*Kossuth
Lajos
tér*

Oktogon

**Batthyány
tér**

Parliament

LIPÓTVÁROS

Kossuth Lajos tér

*Szilágyi
Dezső
tér*

*Danube
(Duna) River*

Bank u

**Arany
János**

Opera

Vérmező

**Siklò
(Upper Station)**

Royal Palace

Bajcsy-Zsilinszky út

Vörösmarty tér

**Deák
Ferenc
tér**

*Krisztina
tér*

BELVÁROS

TABÁN

Ferenciek tere

Astoria

**Kálvin
tér**

*Napheg
tér*

**Gellért Hill
(GELLÉRT-
HEGY)**

*Jubilee
Park*

*Liberty
Monument*

**Fővám
tér**

**Szent Gellért
tér**

0   500 m
0   0.25 miles

XI DISTRICT

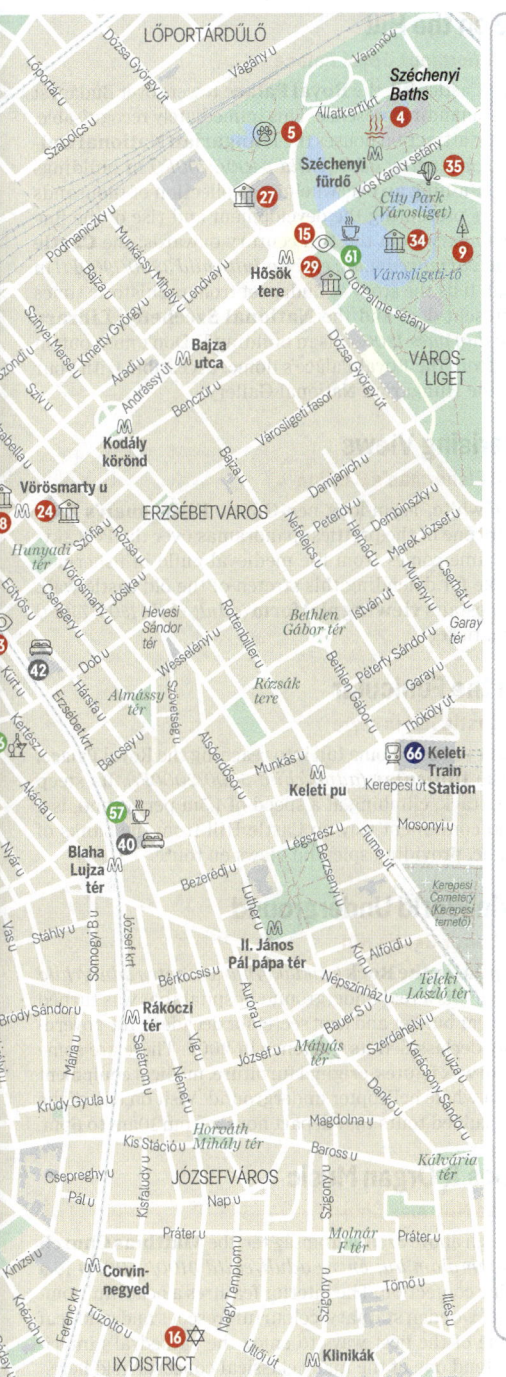

TIVADAR KOSZTKA CSONTVÁRY

Though he never sold a painting in his life, many critics consider Csontváry Hungary's greatest painter. A pharmacist by profession, he produced most of his artworks in just a few years, starting when he was about 41. In 1949 he had an exhibition in Paris, where Picasso spent an hour after closing time admiring Csontváry's paintings and praised the Hungarian artist. Acknowledged abroad but criticised at home, Csontváry died penniless just after WWI. Don't miss his paintings, including *Ruins of the Greek Theatre at Taormina* (1905) and *Pilgrimage to the Cedars of Lebanon* (1907), on the 2nd floor of the Hungarian National Gallery's Building C.

Castle on the Hill

Visit the enormous Royal Palace

Crowning Castle Hill, the **Royal Palace** towers over Budapest with a commanding presence. This immediately recognisable, emblematic attraction houses the **Hungarian National Gallery** *(mng.hu; entry adult/child 5400/2700Ft)* in buildings A to D, containing an overwhelming collection of thousands of artefacts presenting the development and rise of the fine arts in Hungary from the 11th century onwards; the **Castle Museum** *(varmuzeum.hu; entry adult/child 3800/1900Ft)* in building E tells the story of Budapest from prehistoric times to the present day; and the **National Széchenyi Library** *(oszk.hu; day pass 1200Ft)* is in building F. Don't miss out on the view from the Royal Palace's dome, accessible with your ticket to the Hungarian National Gallery.

Mesmerising Views

Marvel at Fisherman's Bastion

The bone-white, 140m-long neo-Gothic **Fisherman's Bastion** offers one of the prettiest panoramas over the Pest skyline. Its name comes from the medieval guild of fishermen responsible for defending this stretch of the old castle wall. Only the upstairs **viewing platform** *(adult/child 1500/750Ft)* requires a ticket.

Fun on the Funicular

Ascend Castle Hill in style

If you want to sneak some fun into reaching the Royal Palace, hop on the **funicular** *(adult/child 5000/2000Ft)*. Its steep 95m-long track, climbing at a speed of 1.5m per second, is a quick and convenient way up Castle Hill from the banks of the Danube, providing splendid views en route.

An Eerie World Underground

Venture below Castle Hill

The **Hospital in the Rock** *(sziklakorhaz.eu; entry adult/child 9500/4800Ft)* is a real underground hospital that was turned into a nuclear bunker and kept secret for decades – the government only declassified its existence in 2002. There are some 200 lifelike wax figures, original furniture, medical equipment and even a whole helicopter underground. Visit on one of the one-hour guided tours that depart hourly from 10am to 6pm.

Frescoes & Organ Music

Admire the Matthias Church

Perched high above Szentháromság tér, the **Matthias Church** *(matyas-templom.hu; entry adult/child 3100/2500Ft)* is a neo-Gothic confection. The interior features a beautiful combination of wooden statuary, colourful frescoes and gold-leaf detail. One of the best ways to enjoy the cathedral's interior is to attend one of the many classical concerts held here.

Fisherman's Bastion

All Aboard the Cutest Ride
Take a trip on the Children's Railway

One of the best ways to explore the Buda Hills, a favourite hiking spot of locals, is by riding the **Children's Railway** *(gyermekvasut.hu; entry adult/ child 1000/500Ft)*, which is operated almost entirely by kids. The staff, aged 10 to 14 and dressed in smart uniforms, hold all the positions on the railway, from conductors to signallers, while a little adult supervision keeps things on track (the engineers, thankfully, are grown-ups). The Children's Railway operates year-round, giving you a different view of the Buda Hills each season.

An Island in the Middle of the City?
Walk around Margaret Island

Neither Buda nor Pest, Margaret Island (Margit-sziget) sits in the middle of the Danube. Just 2.5km long, it's not graced with many significant sights, but you can easily spend half a day exploring its swimming complexes, thermal spa, gardens and centuries-old ruins; on a hot summer afternoon, it makes for a lovely escape. The main attraction is the **Musical Fountain** that puts on a dramatic display five times a day, with jets 'dancing' to music and shooting up to 10m in the air. Catch the last show at 9pm, when the fountain is illuminated by hundreds of coloured lights.

Strenuous Climb for Splendid Views
Climb Gellért Hill

You can climb one of Budapest's most iconic landmarks, the 235m-high, tree-dotted **Gellért Hill**, surmounted by the **Citadel** and the **Liberty Monument**, a proud lady watching over Budapest with the symbol of peace, a palm branch, in her hands.

KNOW YOUR BRIDGES

While there are over a dozen bridges in Budapest, you'll spend most of your time photographing or crossing only a handful of them. One of the most striking and the star of many a photograph is the **Széchenyi Chain Bridge**, which was the first permanent bridge connecting Buda and Pest when it was inaugurated in 1849. The second was **Margaret Bridge**, which doglegs in the middle allowing it to stand at right angles to the Danube where it converges at the southern tip of Margaret Island. Sage-green **Liberty Bridge** is the locals' favourite, while slender and elegant gleaming-white **Elizabeth Bridge** connects the city centre with Gellért Hill. In WWII all of Budapest's bridges were blown up, though later rebuilt.

RAZAK.R/SHUTTERSTOCK

FRANK WAGNER/SHUTTERSTOCK

Parliament

From the top, the views of Buda, the Pest skyline and the gently curving Danube River are unbeatable. On the way, expect peaceful rest stops, a playground and slide park, and even the **Cave Church** *(sziklatemplom.hu; entry adult/child 1200/1000Ft)*, a functioning church set inside a cave – a real sight to behold.

Ghosts of Communism Past

Explore this huge open-air park

Memento Park *(mementopark.hu; entry adult/child 3000/1200Ft)* provides a sneak peek behind the Iron Curtain, guarding the gigantic statues of Lenin, Marx, Engels, homegrown heroes and other types of communist propaganda that were removed from the streets of Budapest after the fall of the Berlin Wall in 1989. You can opt for a guided tour or wander around on your own, but don't miss the park's top attraction, a pair of gigantic boots. It's a replica of the original 8m-high bronze statue of Stalin that was pulled down from its plinth on Dózsa György út in City Park during the 1956 Uprising and sawed apart until only the boots remained.

 EATING IN BUDAPEST: HUNGARIAN FOOD

Városliget Café: A long-standing restaurant serving tasty local fare, from traditional bean soup to schnitzel, along with lake views. *noon-10pm* €€

Menza: Retro-chic place with a modern take on Hungarian cuisine plus international favourites; try the red-wine beef stew. *11am-11pm* €€

Gettó Gulyás: The best place to try *pörkölt* (traditional beef stew) and *gulyás*, Hungary's favourite soup. *noon-11pm* €€

Stand25: Hungarian classics like goulash and *somlói* cake by Bocuse d'Or Europe winner Tamás Széll. *noon-4pm & 6pm-midnight Mon-Sat* €€

Hungary's Largest Building
Tour the Parliament

The **Parliament** (*parlament.hu; entry adult/child from 4500Ft*) stretches for 268m along the left bank of the Danube in Pest. It's a vast, stately building and repository of national treasures, a symbolic counterweight to the Royal Palace on Castle Hill across the river. The building is a blend of many architectural styles (neo-Romanesque, neo-baroque). You can take a 45-minute tour by audio guide of the North Wing; be sure to see one of the country's most important national symbols, the Holy Crown of Hungary.

History's Dark Side
A moving Holocaust memorial

On the Danube embankment south of the Parliament is a monument to Hungarian Jews shot and thrown into the river by members of the fascist Arrow Cross Party in 1944. Called **Shoes on the Danube**, it's a simple but poignant display of 60 pairs of old-style boots and shoes in cast iron along the riverbank.

The Country's Most Sacred Catholic Church
Visit the Basilica of St Stephen

The neoclassical cathedral, the largest in Budapest, is in the form of a Greek cross and can accommodate 8000 worshippers. The interior of **St Stephen's Basilica** glimmers in low-lit splendour, with Károly Lotz' golden mosaics on the inside of the dome seeming to produce a light all of their own. Its major drawcard is the Holy Dexter (or Holy Right), the mummified right hand of St Stephen, first king of Hungary, who was credited with establishing the Kingdom of Hungary and introducing Christianity as the state religion. The top of the dome, which offers fantastic views, can be reached on foot or via lifts. There are three ticket types: for the basilica, the treasury and the dome.

A Quick Spin
Short but sweet Ferris wheel flight

Dominating Erzsébet tér, the **Ferris Wheel of Budapest** (*oriaskerek.com; entry adult/child from 4300/2300Ft*) offers stunning panoramic views of Pest and across the Danube to Buda, and it's an easy way to get a view of the capital. Board after dark; the flight is particularly impressive at night.

A Night at the Opera
Music, laughter and a beautiful building

The neo-Renaissance **Hungarian State Opera House** (*opera.hu*) was completed in 1884 and is among the most beautiful buildings in Budapest. It's worth a visit as much to admire the incredibly rich decoration inside as to view a performance and hear the perfect acoustics. Tickets range from affordable to astronomical, but standing room costs next to nothing – or join one of the three one-hour daily **tours** (*9000Ft*) in English, which include a 10-minute performance at the end.

WHO WAS ST GELLÉRT?

A hill, a bath, a hotel, a city square and a metro station are all named after one man: St Gellért. But who was this guy? St Gellért was an Italian missionary who ended up in Hungary around 1020, after a storm disrupted his pilgrimage. King Stephen convinced him to stay, tutor his son and convert the masses to Christianity. After being named a bishop, he went on to live the life of a hermit. Unfortunately, legend has it that after the king died in 1038, the pagan Magyars hurled the bishop to his death in a spiked barrel. His **statue** now stands on the spot of his martyrdom, gazing peacefully down over the city.

THE SUPERSTAR PIANIST

Screaming young fans at concerts of their musical idols is nothing new under the sun. But would you have thought that this phenomenon started in the classical concert halls of 19th-century Europe? 'Lisztomania' was a term first coined by German poet and Franz Liszt's contemporary, Heinrich Heine. Biographer Oliver Hilmes wrote in his work *Franz Liszt: Musician, Celebrity, Superstar* that 'women tore at each other's hair in trying to lay hands on a glass or handkerchief that Liszt had used'. One of the greatest pianists that has ever lived was a true performer – he would toss his hair and sway over the keyboard, completely captivating his often hysterical audiences.

In the Footsteps of Franz Liszt
Music academy and museum

Opened in 1875, the **Liszt Ferenc Academy of Music** (*zeneakademia.hu*) is today housed in a newer Art Nouveau building built in 1907 and is both a university and Budapest's top classical-music venue. The renovated interior is worth visiting on a **guided tour** (*5300Ft*) if you're not attending a performance. The wonderful little **Liszt Ferenc Memorial Museum** (*lisztmuseum.hu; entry adult/child 3000/1500Ft*), housed in the Old Music Academy, is where the great composer lived in a 1st-floor apartment for five years until his death in 1886. The rooms are filled with his instruments, furniture, books, portraits and personal effects.

The Continent's First Metro
Take a ride on the historic underground

One of Budapest's four metro lines, the **Millennium Underground Railway** is by far the oldest. Indeed, it was the first underground railway to open in continental Europe, preceding the Paris metro by 14 years. Today it runs for 4.4km below Andrássy út, serving 11 stations; to change direction, you must exit and cross the street.

Descend into Darkness
See the House of Terror

The **House of Terror** (*terrorhaza.hu; entry adult/child 4000-2000Ft*) is a moving museum focusing on the atrocities of Hungary's fascist and Stalinist regimes and commemorates their victims. It's set up in the former headquarters of both the Arrow Cross Party (Hungarian Nazis), and, later, the Communist Secret Police, used for interrogating and torturing 'enemies of the state'. The walls were allegedly extra thick to muffle the screams.

A Trip Back to the Belle Époque
The most beautiful cafe in the world

An ever-present queue outside the **New York Café** (*newyorkcafe. hu*), once voted the most beautiful coffee house in the world, will certainly catch your eye in Erzsébetváros. Inside, you can immerse yourself in authentic 19th-century coffee-house culture amid gilded and marble surfaces, etched glass and frescoes, and live Hungarian music. During Hungary's belle époque, renowned writers were often seen putting pen to paper here.

Europe's Largest Synagogue
Explore the Great Synagogue

With its crenellated red-and-yellow glazed-brick facade and two enormous Moorish-style towers, Budapest's stunning **Great Synagogue** (*jewishtourhungary.com; entry adult/child 13,000/10,500Ft*), also called the 'Dohány utca Synagogue', is the largest Jewish house of worship in Europe, seating 3000 people. Visit for its majestic architecture, the Hungarian Jewish Museum and Archives, and the Holocaust Tree of

Gozsdu udvar

Hungary's two most famous spirits are *pálinka* and Unicum. *Pálinka* is distilled from a variety of fruits and is akin to a strong brandy or eau de vie. It kicks like a mule and is served in most bars, some of which carry an enormous range – and almost all Hungarian households have suspicious mineral water bottles filled with homemade *pálinka*. Unicum's medicinal-looking bottle is instantly recognisable. The bitter aperitif has been around since 1790 – prepared according to a secret formula and aged in oak casks, it's available in four different tastes. The liqueur was apparently baptised by Austro-Hungarian Emperor Joseph II; when tasting it for the first time, he exclaimed, *'Das ist ein Unikum!'* (This is unique!).

Life Memorial. Admission includes an informative 45-minute tour in eight languages – tours start every 30 to 60 minutes.

Let the Party Begin

One long courtyard, lots of fun

Erzsébetváros has Budapest's most exciting nightlife, and **Gozsdu udvar** is its heart. It's a continuous 'courtyard' running a few hundred metres between Király utca 13 and Dob utca 16. A residential complex of seven blocks and six interconnecting courtyards when it was built in 1901, and part of the Jewish Ghetto during WWII, it's now lined with bars, clubs, cafes and restaurants, and pulses with music from dusk to dawn.

Harrowing History

Reminisce at the Holocaust Memorial Centre

The **Holocaust Memorial Centre** *(hdke.hu; entry adult/child 3600/1600Ft)* is the only public collection in the country that deals exclusively with the history of the Holocaust. Housed in a striking modern building that opened in 2002, the thematic permanent exhibition traces the rise of anti-Semitism in Hungary and follows the path to the genocide of the country's Jewish and Roma communities. A sublimely restored synagogue in the central courtyard, designed by Leopold Baumhorn and completed in 1924, hosts temporary exhibitions on the mezzanine level.

Romkocsma Is Where It's At

Boozing at ruin bars

Throwing back drinks at a ruin bar *(romkocsma)* filled with the most random knick-knacks is a real Budapest experience. The granddaddy of them all is **Szimpla Kert** *(szimpla.hu)*

HUNGARIKUMS

The culinary heritage of Károly Gundel (founder of City Park's famed Gundel Restaurant) is a Hungaricum, alongside many other wonderful things such as *lángos* (deep-fried dough with toppings), *pálinka* (fruit brandy), Herend porcelain, *teqball* and PICK salami. But what is a Hungarikum? The term refers to a collection of unique, culturally significant and nationally recognised products, practices or values from Hungary that embody the essence of the country's heritage. These can include food and beverages, agricultural practices, folk art, traditions, inventions and even natural phenomena. Being recognised as a Hungarikum is a mark of prestige and a point of national pride, signifying the importance of these products or practices to Hungarian identity and heritage.

Nagycsarnok

in Erzsébetváros, and some say it's still the best. **Instant-Fogas** *(instant-fogas.com)* is where two ruin bars merged to form the biggest in town. The quirkiest one is **Csendes Létterem** *(facebook.com/csendesvintagebar)* in Belváros and a slightly more upscale one is **Púder Bárszínház** *(puderbar.hu)* in Southern Pest.

The History of Hungary

Visit the Hungarian National Museum

The **Hungarian National Museum** *(mnm.hu; entry adult/child 3500/1750Ft)* houses the nation's most important collection of historical relics. It traces the history of the Carpathian Basin from the Stone Age and that of the Magyar people and Hungary from the 9th-century conquest to the fall of communism. If you visit just one museum in Budapest, make it this treasure trove.

The Biggest Deal in Town

Shop and eat at Nagycsarnok

Nagycsarnok *(piaconline.hu)* or the 'Great Market Hall', opened in 1897 and is the city's biggest market. Gourmets will appreciate the variety of treats available here for less than you'd pay in the shops on nearby Váci utca. Head up to the 1st floor for Hungarian folk costumes, dolls, painted eggs, embroidered tablecloths, leather goods, carved hunting knives and other souvenirs, as well as cooked foods like *kolbász* (sausage), *pörkölt* (stew) and *lángos* (deep-fried dough with toppings).

Diamonds & Rust on Sale

Flea-market finds

One of the biggest flea markets in Central Europe, **Ecseri Piac** *(piaconline.hu)* sells everything from antique jewellery and Soviet army watches to top hats (and a fair amount of stolen antique goods too, it's said). Early Saturday is the best time to go for treasures. To get here, take bus 54 from Pest's Boráros tér, or for a quicker journey, express bus 84E, 89E or 94E from the Határ út stop on the M3 metro line.

A Park with Pizzazz
Spend an afternoon in City Park

Serene **City Park** (Városliget) is the Pest side's green lung and Budapest's favourite recreational space. But don't just think plentiful picnic spots and groomed gardens; City Park is home to major landmarks such as the world-renowned Széchenyi Baths (p570); the city's most famous plaza, Heroes' Square; the faux-historic but fairy-tale **Vajdahunyad Castle**; the enormous **Budapest Zoo and Botanical Garden**; a lovely lake (and ice-skating rink in winter), and a handful of outstanding museums. And all of this within just 15 minutes of the city centre.

Meet Hungary's Heroes
Awe at Heroes' Square

This picture-perfect plaza concluding tree-lined Andrássy út is Budapest's largest and most symbolic square, serving as an elegant gateway to City Park. Framed by monumental statues narrating the tale of Hungary's formation and resilience and flanked by two major museums, the **Museum of Fine Arts** and the **Palace of Art** (Kunsthalle), **Heroes' Square** offers a blend of culture, striking architecture and history. It's especially majestic at night.

Take Flight in a Hot-Air Balloon
Have a go at BalloonFly

If you observe Budapest's cityscape, you'll likely spot a hot-air balloon adding a dash of red and white to the Pest skyline. This is **BalloonFly** *(balloonfly.hu; entry adult/child 10,000/5000Ft),* which takes visitors for a flight up to 150m above City Park, providing a stunning bird's-eye view, with landmarks like Széchenyi Baths, Vajdahunyad Castle and Heroes' Square en route.

WHY I LOVE BUDAPEST

Kata Fári, Lonely Planet writer
You know that sudden gush of love you get when you look at somebody you've known forever but for a split second realise again just how beautiful they are? For me, this happens every time I cross a bridge in Budapest. My love story with the city has seen splashes at stunning spas, nights lost at random ruin bars, hikes through the Buda Hills, laps around Margaret Island, books read at century-old coffee houses, romantic boat trips on the Danube, and daily dog walks in a park centred by a castle. I love Budapest because it's elegant, historic, romantic, bohemian and random all at once, and even though I know it like the back of my hand, it still manages to surprise me time and again.

Beyond Budapest

WINE | LAKES | THE DANUBE

Places

☑ **TOP TIP**

The best time to visit Hungary is during the shoulder seasons of spring (March–May) and autumn (September–November), which have pleasant weather and generally fewer crowds. Lake Balaton is at its best but busiest in summer, while the country is a winter wonderland during the Christmas holidays.

Though Budapest is a superstar city and the main reason why most travellers visit Hungary, the country has much more to offer, from vineyards to tranquil countryside. Central Europe's largest lake, Lake Balaton, is the favourite summer destination of locals, where beaching and boating is a way of life. The wine regions in Northern Hungary grow grape varieties you may have never heard of but will end up gushing about. The Danube Bend's romantic towns are perfect for a quick spring getaway, while in the colder months, the hiking trails and the Great Plain's rural romance are ready to steal your heart.

Danube Bend

TIME FROM BUDAPEST: **1HR**

The Danube Bend is lined with romantic riverside towns that vie for visitors' attention. Travelling upriver from Budapest, the Danube draws you deeper into its spell as you leave the day-trippers behind in the arts-focused town of Szentendre (St Andrew), round the eponymous bend and pass the impressive citadel of Visegrád. Beyond that, the Danube swirls past Esztergom, which, like Visegrád, was once a royal seat of sorts but in contrast, Esztergom is a religious centre dominated by a vast hilltop basilica, which is Hungary's largest church. Due to its close proximity and easy accessibility, the Danube Bend makes a perfect getaway from Budapest.

Szentendre's open-air ethnographical museum

Situated 5km from **Szentendre** (take bus 878), this **ethnographical museum** *(skanzen.hu; entry adult/child 4000/2000Ft)* is an unusual plunge into a fascinating 'alternative village reality'. As you wander or ride on a hire bike through the grounds, you'll find yourself transported into a picturesque setting of immaculately reconstructed Hungarian rural architecture and

GETTING AROUND

Travelling around the country is easy and affordable, and Hungary is also a manageable size, with most inland journeys from Budapest only taking a couple of hours. Trains take you most places, while buses take care of the rest.

Sailing up the Danube Bend or cycling are fun alternatives. Driving is only necessary if you're planning to see the country's remote corners. For those travelling extensively, the Hungary Pass provides unlimited public transport.

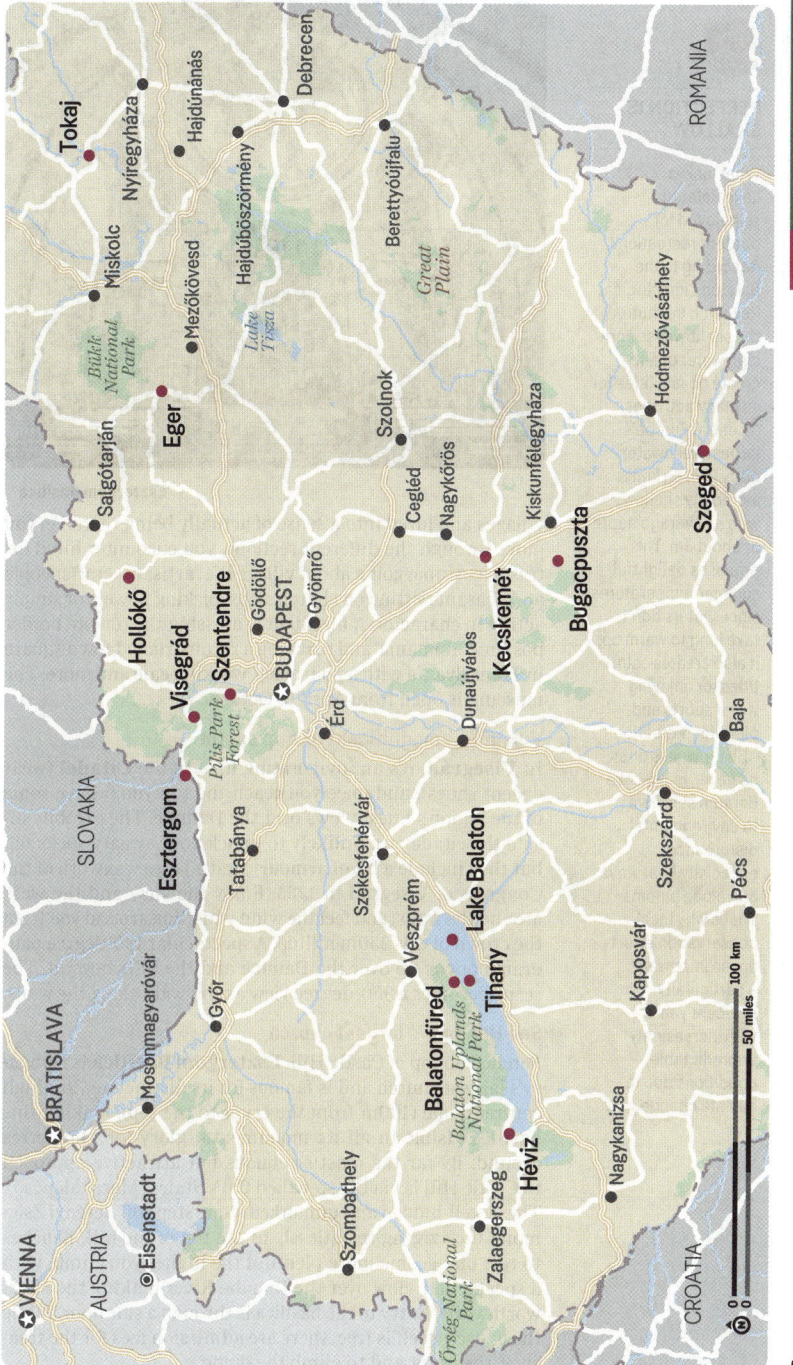

ROMANIA

Tokaj

Nyiregyháza

Hajdúnánás

Debrecen

Miskolc

Hajdúböszörmény

Berettyóújfalu

Mezőkövesd

Bükk
National
Park

Lake
Tisza

Great
Plain

Hódmezővásárhely

Szolnok

Eger

Salgótarján

Cegléd

Nagykőrös

Kiskunfélegyháza

Szeged

Hollókő

Szentendre

Gödöllő

Gyömrő

BUDAPEST

Kecskemét

Bugacpuszta

Visegrád

Pilis Park
Forest

Érd

Dunaújváros

Baja

Esztergom

Tatabánya

Székesfehérvár

SLOVAKIA

Veszprém

Lake Balaton

Szekszárd

Pécs

Győr

Tihany

Kaposvár

Balatonfüred

Balaton Uplands
National Park

BRATISLAVA

Mosonmagyaróvár

Nagykanizsa

Hévíz

Zalaegerszeg

VIENNA

Eisenstadt

AUSTRIA

Szombathely

Őrség National
Park

CROATIA

100 km

50 miles

0

0

MIKHAIL MARKOVSKIY/SHUTTERSTOCK

Esztergom Basilica

villages and lured into a sense of actually being there. As you move through the different sections, you encounter hired extras in costume going about village life: artisans, craftspeople and peasants sitting on church steps, picking flowers or simply acting in character. A highlight is crossing the remote border post into 'Romania' and reaching a reconstructed town square in Transylvania with a pharmacy, working cafe and more. The museum is open from April to October.

Visegrád's magnificent hilltop castle

In **Visegrád**, it's an invigorating hike to the **Citadel** (wear decent shoes), and once you reach the top you'll have some of the region's finest views over the Danube. The exhibits inside the citadel are unlikely to knock your sweaty socks off, but they include a bit of armoury and a large waxwork of the Congress of Visegrád in 1335. Enjoy the view and the walk around the walls, and feel the wind whistling around you from the crown of this 330m hilltop. A spectacular 180-degree panorama opens up over the Danube and the hills beyond. The scene becomes a 360-degree view as you walk along the walls.

See Hungary's largest church

Perched on top of Castle Hill, **Esztergom Basilica** is Hungary's largest church and is famous for its distinctive 72m-high central dome (100m from the crypt to the top), making this basilica visible in all its monumental glory for kilometres around. By far the most strenuous but attractive approach to Castle Hill is via the so-called Cat's Stairs (Macskalépcső). These well-hidden and unmarked stone steps off Berényi Zsigmond utca zigzag relentlessly to the top of the hill. Benches to rest on become more plentiful the higher you climb, with a spectacular view over the Danube River making the effort worthwhile. Entry to the basilica is through a side door. While the church itself is free, there are admission fees for the treasury, the crypt and to climb the dome.

Lake Balaton

Historical wonders, impressive food and wine, and an unparalleled spa scene: Lake Balaton is where Hungarians relish the good life. During the dog days, resorts and guesthouses are packed with holidaymakers beaching and boating in opaque, turquoise-hued waters. Beyond the postcard-perfect marinas and famously shallow swimming waters, Central Europe's biggest lake has a wealth of attractions that may be surprising – Balaton is equal parts quaint and chic. Thermal spas, wellness centres and campsites reel visitors in, but it's Balaton's hearty 'everything stew' of outdoorsy experiences that makes the destination highly memorable: sipping wines overlooking handsome vineyards, cycling adventures passing dreamy coasts and lavender fields, and tiny towns packed with historical treasures.

Catch lavender fever in Tihany

No visit to Lake Balaton is complete without seeing **Tihany**. The town's famous lavender fields traditionally blossom from mid-June to early July. During this time, aromatic purple fields explode around the peninsula and coincide with activities and events for the annual **Lavender Festival**. Lavender picking is only allowed in public areas, for example on the so-called **Lavender Trail**.

Swimming and shoreside fun in Balatonfüred

There's no better spot to wade into Lake Balaton's famously comfortable waters than from the two main beaches at **Balatonfüred**, **Esterházy Strand** (*balatonfuredistrandok.hu*) and **Kisfaludy Strand**. Unfolding along the row of bars and restaurants of the **Tagore Sétány** (the lake-hugging promenade), both beaches (walking from the marina, Esterházy comes first, followed by Kisfaludy) are known for their lively atmosphere. Lots of water activities are on offer at both, from paddleboating to SUP rentals, as well as shady spots for relaxing between dips and good toilet and changing facilities.

Soak in miracle waters in Hévíz

Just under 9km from Keszthely at the western tip of Lake Balaton, the village of **Hévíz** lays claim to the world's largest swimmable thermal lake, which is fed by 80 million L of thermal water daily. **Hévízi-tó** (*heviz.hu/en/lake-heviz*) is an incredible sight. The temperature averages 33°C and never drops below 22°C, even in winter, allowing you to bathe when the surrounding fir trees have turned icy.

The Great Plain

TIME FROM BUDAPEST: 2HR

What the Outback is for Australians or the Wild West for Americans, the Great Plain is for Hungarians. The Hortobágy region is the home of Hungarian cowboys and amazing horse shows, while Kecskemét and Szeged are cities to explore for culture, architecture and that charming countryside feel.

VISEGRÁD GROUP

The centrepiece of the citadel is a waxwork that graphically depicts how the Visegrád Group began. The year was 1335 and the kings of Bohemia, Hungary and Poland came together in Visegrád to make deals, form an anti-Habsburg alliance, resolve disputes and eat well, judging by this waxy portrayal. This was the first diplomatic cooperation between the so-called 'Visegrád countries'. In 1991, the Visegrád Group was formed between Hungary, Czechoslovakia and Poland to promote cooperation and mutual interests. It later became the Visegrád 4 when Slovakia became an independent country. Friction over approaches to the war in Ukraine have tested the glue holding the group together, but so far their shared interests have prevailed over their differences.

ASZÚ, THE KING OF WINES

Volcanic soil, a sunny climate, two rivers and mountains have helped make Tokaj-Hegyalja Hungary's most renowned wine region. It is most famous for Tokaji Aszú, a sweet golden nectar made with ripe grapes infected with 'noble rot': *Botrytis cinerea* mould that almost turns them into raisins on the vine, but grows only in years with the right climatic conditions (not too rainy, not too dry). Aszú can be blended from any of the six grape varieties grown in the Tokaj region but the most important is the indigenous Furmint. Aszú wines are rated according to the number (five or six) of *puttony* (25L carriers of individually picked grapes) of Aszú paste added to each barrel of base wine to increase sweetness.

Paintings, peacocks and majolica in Kecskemét

Lying halfway between the Danube and Tisza Rivers in the southern Great Plain, **Kecskemét** boasts some of the finest architecture of any small city in Hungary. Along with colourful Art Nouveau and Secessionist buildings, its museums and the region's excellent *barackpálinka* (apricot brandy) are major draws as well. An Art Nouveau masterpiece, **Cifrapalota** *(kkjm.hu; entry adult/child 1800/900Ft)* was built in 1902–03 by Géza Márkus. The grand townhouse is a visual feast with a whimsical majolica facade, a grand hall flaunting peacock motifs and a courtyard with fairy-tale flair. Exhibits inside include 19th- and early-20th-century Hungarian art as well as artefacts from Avar graves – mystical remnants from 6th-century Central Asian warriors.

Horse tricks and sand steppes

About 35km south of Kecskemét, **Bugacpuszta** *(bugacpuszta.hu)* is the easiest gateway to the rambling and disjointed Kiskunság National Park. Steer straight to the **Karikás Csárda**, a traditional inn, to buy tickets to the park and the popular Horse Show offered on Wednesdays, Fridays, Saturdays and Sundays between May and September. During this tightly choreographed 40-minute spectacle, horse herders crack their bullwhips and ride five horses at full tilt while standing on the rear two.

Flowers, leaves and waves in Szeged

The cultural capital of the Great Plain and Hungary's third-largest city, **Szeged** is an embracing town that's easy to love. A romantic symphony of lily-and-ivy motifs dancing across an undulating facade that juts out like a ship's bow, **Reök Palace** (1907) is an architectural showstopper and the crown jewel of Szeged's rich Art Nouveau scene. Step inside and you'll be just as wowed by the interior, especially the frilly wrought-iron staircase. Afterwards, pop into the street-level cafe **Reök Kézműves Cukrászda** for artisanal French pastries crafted by a two-time national cake champion.

Northern Hungary

TIME FROM BUDAPEST: 3HR

Northern Hungary is as hilly as the country gets. Hike on forested trails amid lovely rolling hills and scout castle ruins. Towns rich in culture, world-famous vineyards and villages that cherish their traditions make Northern Hungary an excellent place to connect with the country's spirit and history.

Eger's valley of the wine cellars

Cradled by vineyards and brimming with ornate baroque buildings, **Eger** (pronounced 'egg-air') is a jewellery box of a town with loads to see and do. A wine lover's fantasy come true, the famed **Valley of the Beautiful Women** *(Szépasszony-völgy; szepasszonyvolgy.info),* about 2km southeast of Eger's city centre, is home to several dozen wine cellars that welcome visitors who'd like to sample local vintages. Most open from 10am or noon to 6pm, until 8pm or later June to September,

ZEDSPIDER/SHUTTERSTOCK

Hollókő Castle

and some close on Mondays. Carved into volcanic rock, they're arrayed along a horseshoe-shaped road with a park in the middle, with a row of restaurants on the side.

Quick trip to centuries past

Long the home of the minority Palóc people, **Hollókő** *(holloko.hu)* is famous for the folk architecture of its **Old Village** (Ófalu), a UNESCO World Heritage Site since 1987. Unchanged for well over a century, its whitewashed wattle-and-daub houses – with carved balconies and overhanging porch roofs, bedecked with flowers in summer – are arrayed along a single main street, Kossuth utca. Although geared towards tourists (almost all domestic), Hollókő still manages to feel like a living, breathing village. The Old Village can be visited year-round but not much is open from November to March. Many visitors begin by walking from the tourist office through the woods to the hilltop **Hollókő Castle** *(Hollókői Vár; 3000Ft)*, a distance of 1km. Built in the 13th century, the imposing stone structure looks like the setting for a fairy tale.

Taste Tokaj's liquid gold

At the confluence of the Bodrog and Tisza Rivers, the town of **Tokaj** is the commercial and touristic hub of the 27-village Tokaj-Hegyalja wine region. To sample the Tokaj region's extraordinary wines, head to a wine cellar *(pince)*, cafe or restaurant that offers wine by the glass – they're dotted around the town centre.

THE BETYÁRS: BANDITS OF THE PUSZTA

The Great Plain highwaymen were infamous outlaws who ruled the vast, wild spaces of the *puszta* (Great Plain) in the 19th century. Many were landless farmers, seasonal workers, former soldiers or unemployed herders who turned to ambushing travellers and horse carriages to make ends meet. Operating in small, tight-knit gangs, these bandits struck fear into the hearts of travellers and traders passing through the unpatrolled, remote areas. Their daring heists and narrow escapes became the stuff of legend, with tales spreading far and wide. While they were definitely criminals, some saw them as Robin Hood–like folk heroes rebelling against social injustice. Eventually the law caught up with them, leading to their decline by the late 1800s.

Places We Love to Stay

€ Budget €€ Midrange €€€ Top End

Budget MAP p572

Shantee House € Share a yurt with your friends or that special someone in the Zen-like garden of Budapest's first hostel.

Loft Hostel € Friendly backpacker magnet with great kitchen, TV room with skylight, funny artwork and super-helpful staff.

Hotel President Budapest €€ Welcoming 150-room hotel on a beautiful street, with a stunning rooftop bar and a huge jadeite *turul* (falcon-like totem of the ancient Magyars and now a national symbol) in the lobby.

Baltazár €€ Family-owned boutique hotel offering individually decorated rooms with vintage furniture.

Hotel Central Basilica €€ The name says it all at this very central hotel opposite the basilica with 47 rooms, 10 of which face it.

Four Seasons Gresham Palace Hotel €€€ This one-of-a-kind luxury 179-room hotel was created out of the stunning Art Nouveau Gresham Palace (1906).

Párisi Udvar Hotel €€€ This stunner of a 110-room hotel is in the heart of one of the most beautiful buildings in Pest.

Anantara New York Palace Hotel €€€ Blends grandeur and comfort with luxurious rooms, an excellent spa and the historic New York Café next door.

Hotel Clark Budapest €€€ Stay at adults-only Hotel Clark for relaxation by the foot of the Chain Bridge and head up to the rooftop bar for lovely views.

Hotel Moments Budapest €€€ Stunning Art Deco hotel with 99 large rooms, an impressive lobby and an enviable location on UNESCO-listed Andrássy út.

Corinthia Hotel Budapest €€€ The hotel's lobby – a double atrium with a massive marble staircase – is among the most impressive in the city.

Szentendre

Bükkös Hotel & Spa €€€ Adults-only hotel pitching especially to couples on romantic breaks, with spa and massages. Central location, contemporary atmosphere and good breakfasts.

Visegrád

Hotel Silvanus €€€ On a forested hillside near the citadel, this large hotel has great views, an outdoor pool and spa. It was given a makeover in 2024.

Esztergom

Alabárdos Panzió és Apartmanház €€ Immaculate, quiet and very professionally run pension at the foot of the basilica and close to the museums. It also has apartments.

Tihany

Houses of History €€€ Charming B&B rooms set in 19th-century thatched-roof buildings formerly belonging to an abbey. Boasts a pool and also public beach access.

Balatonfüred

Füred Camping € Bungalows and caravans, plus a pool and direct lake access, offer relaxation on a budget. One of the largest camping grounds on the lake.

Anna Grand Hotel €€€ Once a sanatorium, today it's Balatonfüred's most historic grand hotel. Period antiques alongside modern furnishings abound; views of the hotel's courtyard and Gyógy tér square.

Kecskemét

Boutique Hotel Center €€ Slicked up in 2020, this pet-friendly outpost in the heart of town sports modern designer rooms accented with abstract art. Rates include a breakfast buffet.

Szeged

Noir Hotel €€ Superb, central pad marries high style with affordability and has spacious studios with sleek black-surface kitchens, ultra-comfy beds and terraces or balconies.

Eger

Hotel Estella €€ Half a block south of the Old Town, on the upper floors of a late-communist-era university building. Rooms are modern and well kept. Excellent value.

Hollókő

Tugári Vendégház €€ Old cottage in Hollókő with four charmingly furnished rooms and a communal kitchen for making food and friends.

Tokaj

Toldi Fogadó €€ Eclectic art adds a contemporary touch to this town-centre inn with good-sized rooms, a 15m pool, Jacuzzi and sauna.

Practicalities

LGBTIQ+ Travellers

While Budapest has a solid gay scene and gay visitors generally have a good time in Hungary, the country's stance on LGBTIQ+ issues is out of step with many other parts of Europe. The Hungarian government strongly promotes a conservative Christian agenda and still imposes laws against the local LGBTIQ+ community. While travellers aren't generally affected, be aware that PDA may attract unwanted attention.

Health

Hungary doesn't have any serious health risks, but it's still wise to make predeparture preparations. The European Health Insurance Card (EHIC) allows EU citizens to receive emergency state-provided healthcare.

Scams to Avoid

Dodgy restaurants and clubs in Budapest's party district (inner District VII) may overcharge foreigners, so check prices before you order. Don't hail taxis off the street and avoid the seemingly friendly touts waiting outside popular places – call a reputable company instead.

Bottled Drinks

When buying bottled or canned drinks in Hungary, you'll pay an additional 50Ft deposit per bottle, refundable when you return your empty bottles to any of the designated redemption machines inside bigger supermarkets.

ALLA SIMACHEVA/SHUTTERSTOCK

Funicular (p574), Budapest

Solo Travel

Hungary is a popular and generally safe destination for solo travellers. Budapest has a massive array of budget-friendly and social accommodation options, including hostels that organise pub crawls and other outings. Women travelling alone should not encounter any particular problems besides some mild local machismo.

Public Holidays

New Year's Day 1 January
Memorial Day of the 1848 Revolution 15 March
Easter March/April
Labour Day 1 May
Whit Monday May/June
Foundation of the State 20 August
Memorial Day of the 1956 Revolution 23 October
All Saints' Day 1 November
Christmas Day 25 December

589

Language

A symbol over a vowel in written Hungarian indicates it's pronounced as a long sound. Double consonants should be drawn out a little longer than in English. Note also that **aw** is pronounced as in 'law', **eu** as the 'u' in 'nurse', **ew** as 'ee' with rounded lips, and **zh** as the 's' in 'pleasure'. Finally, keep in mind that **r** is rolled in Hungarian and that the apostrophe (') indicates a slight **y** sound.

Basics

Hello. Szervusz/Szervusztok. (sg/pl) *ser·vus/ser·vus·tawk*
Goodbye. Viszlát. *vis·lat*
Excuse me. Elnézést kérek. *el·ney·zeysht key·rek*
Sorry. Sajnálom. *shoy·na·lawm*
Please. Kérem/Kérlek (inf/pol) *key·rem/keyr·lek*
Thank you. Köszönöm. *keu·seu·neum*
Yes. Igen. *i·gen*
No. Nem. *nem*
What's your name? Mi a neve/neved? (pol/inf) *mi o ne·ve/ne·ved*
My name is ... A nevem ... *o ne·vem ...*
Do you speak English? Beszél/Beszélsz angolul? (pol/inf) *be·seyl/be·seyls on·gaw·lul*
I don't understand. Nem értem. *nem eyr·tem*

Transport

bus busz *bus*
plane repülőgép *re·pew·leū·geyp*
train vonat *vaw·not*
One ... ticket to (Eger), Egy ... jegy (Eger)be. *ej ... yej (e·ger)·be*
 one-way csak oda *chok aw·do*
 return oda-vissza *aw·do·vis·so*

Emergencies

Help! Segítség! *she·geet·sheyg*
Go away! Menjen innen! *men·yen in·nen*

Call the doctor! Hívjon orvost! *heev·yawn awr·vawsht*
Call the police! Hívja a rendőrséget! *heev·yo o rend·ēūr·shey·get*
I'm lost. Eltévedtem. *el·tey·ved·tem*
I'm ill. Rosszul vagyok. *raws·sul vo·dyawk*
Where are the toilets? Hol a vécé? *hawl o vey·tsey*

Eating & Drinking

What would you recommend? Mit ajánlana? *mit o·yan·lo·no*
Do you have vegetarian food? Vannak Önöknél vegetáriánus ételek? *von·nok eu·neuk·neyl ve·ge·ta·ri·a·nush ey·te·lek*
I'll have ... ... kérek. *... key·rek*
Cheers! Egészségetekre! *e·geys·shey·ge·tek·re*
I'd like the ... ... szeretném. *... se·ret·neym*
 bill A számlát *o sam·lat*
 menu Az étlapot *oz eyt·lo·pawt*

Shopping & Services

I'm looking for ... Keresem a ... *ke·re·shem o ...*
How much is it? Mennyibe kerül? *men'·nyi·be ke·rewl*
That's too expensive. Ez túl drága. *ez tūl dra·go*
market piac *pi·ots*
post office postahivatal *paw·sh·to·hi·vo·tol*

NUMBERS	
1	**egy** *ej*
2	**kettő** *ket·tēū*
3	**három** *ha·rawm*
4	**négy** *neyj*
5	**öt** *eut*
6	**hat** *hot*
7	**hét** *heyt*
8	**nyolc** *nyawlts*
9	**kilenc** *ki·lents*
10	**tíz** *teeze*

Tram, Budapest (p570)

Arriving & Getting Around

For most travellers visiting Hungary, Budapest is the main point of entry. Ferenc Liszt International Airport is about 16km southeast of the city centre. The main international train station in Budapest is Keleti railway station.

From the Airport

Shuttle bus 100E to/from central Pest (stop: Deák Ferenc tér) runs daily round the clock. A combination bus (200E) and metro is a bit cheaper but slower. Taxis are the fastest way to get to/from the airport.

Hungary Pass

If you're planning on travelling around the country, consider buying a Hungary Pass, good for unlimited travel throughout Hungary. It's valid for almost all services with **Budapest Public Transport** *(BKK; bkk.hu)*, suburban and regional buses, HÉV suburban railways and regional trains.

Validating Tickets

Budapest public transport tickets have to be validated after purchase. Digital tickets have a QR-code scanner (codes are on the sides of buses, trams and on ticket machines) and passes have their own QR codes that controllers check.

BudapestGO

The BudapestGO mobile app for public transport has several key features. You can buy and store digital tickets and passes directly on the app (don't forget to validate tickets with QR codes and show passes to inspectors). It also provides route planning and a map, timetables, and information on routes, connections and travel times, as well as updates on potential delays and other relevant information.

MONEY
Currency: Hungarian Forint (Ft)

CASHLESS PAYMENTS

Most restaurants, hotels, shops, car-hire companies and petrol stations across Hungary accept credit cards, especially Visa and MasterCard. American Express isn't always accepted.

CASH

When travelling outside Budapest, it's wise to carry cash in case it's not possible to pay by card. Smaller shops and ice-cream parlours appreciate coins and might struggle to break larger banknotes.

TIPPING

Add at least 10% for table service at restaurants. Instead of leaving money on the table, tell the server how much you want to pay in total, including the tip. Many restaurants already add a service fee of about 12% to 15% – check the receipt or ask before paying.

For places to stay
in Iceland, see
p608

Above: Northern lights, Reykjavík (p596); Right: Whale near Húsavík (p607)

Curated by
Anthony Ham

Iceland

THE WILD POWER OF NATURE

Adventure awaits in Iceland, with one of Europe's largest wilderness areas – changing shape with every volcanic eruption – and with its fascinating capital and small towns.

Iceland is a magical place, where it's as if the world is being created before your very eyes. In this vast volcanic laboratory, the earth itself is restless and alive. Admire thundering waterfalls, glittering glaciers carving their way to black-sand beaches, explosive geysers, rumbling volcanoes and contorted lava fields.

In summer, permanent daylight energises the already zippy inhabitants of Iceland's lively capital, Reykjavík, with its wonderful cafe and bar scene. Fashion, design and music are woven into the city's fabric, and the museums are tops.

In winter, with luck, you may see the aurora borealis shimmering across the sky. Year-round, though, adventure tours abound, getting you up close and personal with sights and sounds that will stay with you for life.

The warmth of Icelanders is disarming, as is their industriousness. They've worked hard to recover from financial upheaval, and to transform Iceland into a destination that, thanks to its popularity with visitors, can host more than six times its population each year. Pause and consider a medium-sized city in your country – then give it far-flung universities, airports and hospitals to administer, 30-odd active volcanoes to monitor, and hundreds of hotels to run. How might they cope? Could they manage as well as the Icelanders, and still have time left over to create spine-tingling music and natty knitwear?

TATONKA/SHUTTERSTOCK

THE MAIN AREAS

REYKJAVÍK
Nightlife and culture.
p596

THE GOLDEN CIRCLE
Hot springs and
history. **p600**

SOUTHEAST ICELAND
Ring Road highlights
and mountain treks.
p602

**AKUREYRI &
THE NORTH**
Northern whale-
watching heartland.
p605

Find Your Way

Iceland is a fantastic road-trip destination. You can head out from Reykjavik on the famous Ring Road, but make time to deviate along the way to find less visited corners and wonders.

BUS & TOUR

Buses (*straeto.is*) are a reasonable option during summer, with daily departures between towns and villages along the Ring Road. When in doubt, join a tour for added convenience and further reach.

CAR & CAMPER

Hire a car or camper, preferably a 4WD, to have the most freedom. Gravel roads are common in rural locations. Outside summer, especially, drivers should check *weather.is*, *umferdin.is* and *safetravel.is*.

Akureyri & the North, p605

Look for northern lights over the snow-capped mountains of Iceland's northern capital, in a region known for outstanding whale-watching.

Southeast Iceland, p602

The country's southeast is best known for black beaches, dramatic waterfalls and subglacial volcanoes.

The Golden Circle, p600

One of the most memorable driving routes on the planet, including mega-attractions Þingvellir, Gullfoss and Geysir.

Reykjavik, p596

Iceland's human heart: a big city in a tiny package next to powerful nature, with volcanoes bubbling on the Reykjanes Peninsula.

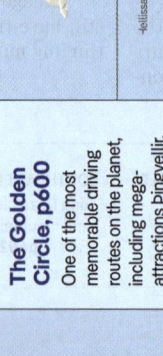

Skaftafellsjökull (p603)

Plan Your Time

Iceland's biggest draw is that natural wonders are literally everywhere. We've picked the places that best capture its landscape and culture, but each is a springboard for you to uncover your very own Iceland.

A Long Weekend

● Two days is a minimum for getting to know **Reykjavík** (p596). For the third day, rent a car or join an organised tour and head for the **Golden Circle** (p600), the approximately 300km loop extending from Reykjavík to **Þingvellir National Park** (p600), and to the grand **Gullfoss** (p601) waterfall and **Geysir** (p601), the original hot-water spout after which geysers are named.

Ten Days in Iceland

● Complete the classic Ring Road loop around the country. Start in **Reykjavík** (p596), explore the **Golden Circle** (p600), then head along the south coast, stopping around **Vík** (p602), **Skaftafell** (p603) and **Jökulsárlón** (p604). Loop around the east, then head north to go whale-watching in **Húsavík** (p607) and spend time in **Akureyri** (p605).

SEASONAL HIGHLIGHTS

SPRING

Temperatures rise slowly, but it's only May when you might feel some warmth. The northern lights season fades out.

SUMMER

Mid-June marks the start of the **festival season**. Mountain roads and **hiking trails** are open. Attractions are very busy.

AUTUMN

The **northern lights** and cooler weather. By November, it's safe to access ice caves. The last of puffins and whales leave Iceland.

WINTER

Icy weather, short days and many side roads are closed. **Ice caves** are a highlight. Reykjavík hosts a handful of **festivals**.

595

Reykjavík

ICELANDIC ARCHITECTURE | LOCAL CULTURE | FINE FOOD

GETTING AROUND

Old Reykjavík is compact and walkable. **Strætó** *(bus.is)* local buses connect the suburbs and run to Akranes, Borgarnes, Hveragerði and Selfoss. Buy tickets *(per ride adult/teen/child 650kr/325kr/free)* at the bus terminal, on board (no change given) or with the Strætó Klappið app or Klapp card. Parking in central Reykjavík is limited and governed by meters/payment apps. It's easiest to park on the edge and walk in. Book taxis online or via the Hreyfill app.

☑ **TOP TIP**

Nightclubs in the Old Reykjavík quarter have some of the city's best late-night DJ sets and intense dance scenes, but they start late – after midnight. To get deals on drinks, pop in early for happy hour, circling back to dance in the wee hours.

Reykjavík is Iceland's human heart. Nearly two-thirds of all Icelanders live in the capital region: 240,000 inhabitants of colourful corrugated houses, grey suburbs and an ever-growing number of apartment complexes. The most common bird, the joke goes, is the building crane. Construction projects are everywhere, transforming the world's most northerly capital from an oversized fishing village into an international city.

To first-time visitors, the capital tends to be warmer than expected and spread over a wider area, though the city centre – from Old Harbour to the Hlemmur bus terminal – is less than 3km long, making it easy to explore on foot. When you slip behind the shiny tourist-centric veneer, you'll find a place and a populace that mixes aesthetically minded ingenuity with an almost quaint, know-your-neighbours sense of community.

Add a backdrop of snow-topped mountains, churning seas and clean, clear air, and the chances are you'll fall helplessly in love, heading home already saving to return.

Swans, Scenery & Sculptures

Explore Old Reykjavík

Historic Miðborg, or the area dubbed Old Reykjavík, is the jaunty heart of the capital and its cultural centre. Anchored by a placid lake, the neighbourhood is tops for a wander.

When the weather is fine, take a stroll around idyllic lake **Tjörnin** and you'll find lots of surprises. It echoes with the honks and squawks of more than 40 species of visiting birds, including swans, geese and Arctic terns. Pretty, sculpture-dotted parks like **Hljómskálagarð2ur** line the southern shores, and their paths are much used by cyclists and joggers.

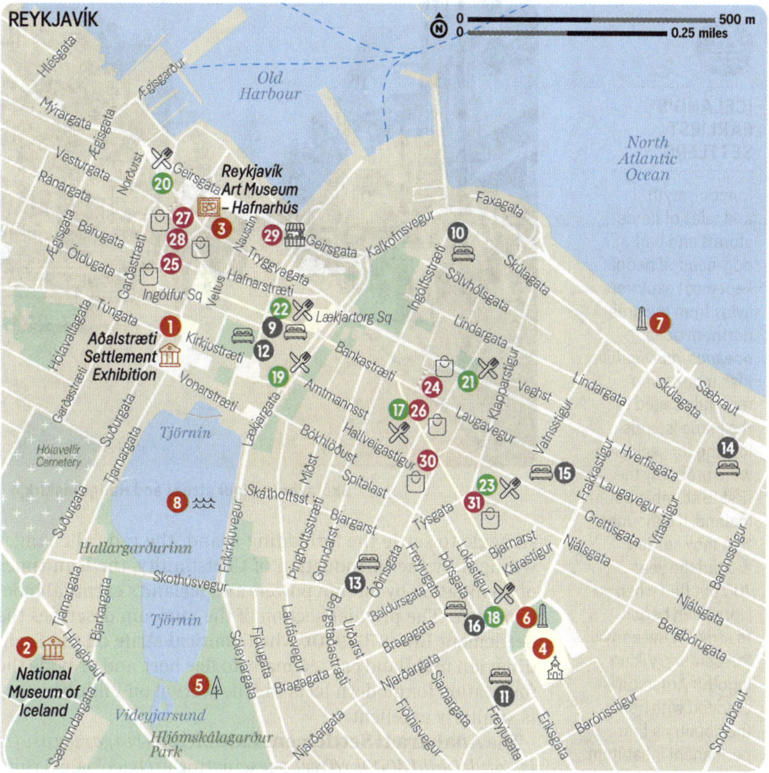

REYKJAVÍK

0 500 m
0 0.25 miles

Old Harbour

North Atlantic Ocean

Reykjavík Art Museum – Hafnarhús

Aðalstræti Settlement Exhibition

Tjörnin

Hólavöllur Cemetery

Hallargarðurinn

Tjörnin

National Museum of Iceland

Viðeyjarsund

Hljómskálagarður Park

⭐ **HIGHLIGHTS**

1 Aðalstræti Settlement Exhibition
2 National Museum of Iceland
3 Reykjavík Art Museum – Hafnarhús

🔴 **SIGHTS**

4 Hallgrímskirkja
5 Hljómskálagarður Park

6 Leifur Eiríksson Statue
7 Sun Voyager
8 Tjörnin

⚫ **SLEEPING**

9 Apotek
10 CenterHótel Arnarhvoll
11 Freyja Guesthouse
12 Hótel Borg
13 Hótel Holt
14 KEX Hostel
15 Sand Hotel

16 Sunna Guesthouse

🟢 **EATING**

17 101 Reykjavik Street Food
see 9 Apotek Kitchen + Bar
18 Café Loki
19 Icelandic Street Food
20 Le Kock
21 Mat Bar
22 Pósthús Mathöll
23 Skál

🔴 **SHOPPING**

24 Epal
25 Fischersund
26 Kaolin
27 Kirsuberjatréð
28 Kogga
29 Kolaportið
30 Rammagerðin
31 Skúmaskot

Reykjavík Art Museum (*artmuseum.is; adult/child 2430kr/free*) is Iceland's largest institution dedicated to the visual arts. It's split across three locations. The **Hafnarhús**, near the waterfront in Old Reykjavík, is a marvellously restored warehouse converted into a soaring steel-and-concrete exhibition space for cutting-edge contemporary Icelandic art.

The superb **National Museum of Iceland** (*thjodminjasafn. is; adult/child 3000kr/free*) provides a meaningful overview of Iceland's history and culture. You'll see how this wild volcanic island over 600km from its closest neighbour became a country. Brilliantly curated exhibits lead you through the

Skólavörðustígur street and Hallgrímskirkja

ICELAND'S EARLIEST SETTLERS

Rumour, myth and tales of fierce storms and barbaric dog-headed people kept most explorers away from the great northern ocean, *oceanus innavigabilis*. Irish monks who regularly sailed to the Faroe Islands looking for seclusion were probably the first to stumble upon Iceland. It's thought that they settled around the year 700 but fled when Norsemen began to arrive in the early 9th century. Viking Ingólfur Arnarson is credited with being the country's first permanent inhabitant. The Norwegian fugitive landed in Southeast Iceland, before continuing around the coast. He made his home in this promising-looking bay that he named Reykjavík (Smoky Bay), after the steam from its thermal springs.

struggle to settle the forbidding island, the radical changes wrought by the introduction of Christianity, the lean times of domination by foreign powers and Iceland's eventual independence. The premier section of the museum describes the Settlement Era (870–930), when political strife on the Scandinavian mainland caused many to flee here and provide the foundation for modern Iceland. The section on Viking history is similarly excellent.

The **Aðalstræti Settlement Exhibition** (*borgarsogusafn. is; adult/child 3000kr/free),* a fascinating archaeological ruin-museum spanning Aðalstræti 10 and 16, is based around a 10th-century Viking longhouse and other Settlement Era finds from central Reykjavík, and reconstructs how the city came to be, with fascinating multimedia displays.

The huge industrial building near the harbour hosts **Kolaportið flea market** (*kolaportid.is),* a Reykjavík institution, on weekends from 11am to 5pm. It's a vast tumble of second-hand clothes (including wool sweaters), old toys, antiques, food and cheap imports. Bring cash in case that must-have-item's seller doesn't take cards or digital payments.

 ## EATING IN OLD REYKJAVÍK: OUR PICKS

Pósthús Mathöll: Lively, central food hall with loads of options including popular Funky Bhangra (burger meets Indian). *11.30am-10pm* €€

Le Kock: Some of Reykjavík's best burgers paired with drinks at Tail and donuts at its bakery Deig (which has earlier hours). *11.30am-11pm* €€

Icelandic Street Food: Showcases home-cooked food, from fish stew and lamb soup to sugar-dusted waffles. *11am-10pm* €€

Apotek Kitchen + Bar: Delicious small plates and top-flight cocktails inside a historic pharmacy. *11.30am-10pm Sun-Thu, to 11pm Fri & Sat* €€€

Reykjavík's Beating Heart

Discover Laugavegur

Reykjavík's main street for shopping and people-watching is bustling, often-pedestrianised Laugavegur. The narrow, one-way lane and its side streets blossom with the capital's most interesting shops, cafes and bars. At its western end, its name changes to Bankastræti, then Austurstræti. Running uphill off Bankastræti, artists' street **Skólavörðustígur** ends at a spectacular modernist church. The waterfront offers excellent views of Faxaflói bay and majestic Mt Esja, from the iconic **Sun Voyager** sculpture. This is prime Reykjavík, where colourful houses hide boutiques, galleries and cafes. On weekend nights, it becomes the centre of the city's *djammið* (party scene).

Reykjavík's soaring church defines the city skyline and is one of the tallest structures in Iceland, visible from 20km away. **Hallgrímskirkja** *(hallgrimskirkja.is; tower adult/child 1400/200kr)* is also one of the best places to get a bird's-eye view of the city.

Head to the top of the 74.5m-high tower to look out on Reykjavík's colourful houses, the Atlantic Ocean and Mt Esja. On a clear day, it's possible to see as far as the Snæfellsjökull glacier. A lift carries visitors part of the way up the tower, but you have to climb a few flights of stairs to reach the very top. On the church's front plaza, gazing proudly into the distance, is a **statue** of the Viking Leifur Eiríksson, the first European to reach America.

BEST DESIGN SHOPPING

Skúmaskot: Handmade porcelain, women's and kids' clothing, paintings and cards.

Kirsuberjatréð: Handmade clothes, fish-skin-leather purses and bowls made from radish slices. *(kirs.is)*

Rammagerðin: Souvenir shop loaded with woollens, crafts and collectables. *(icelandgiftstore.com)*

Fischersund: Concept store by Sigur Rós frontman Jónsi and his sisters: perfumes, herbs and art. *(fischersund.com)*

Epal: Large Icelandic home-goods store. *(epal.is)*

Kaolin: Interesting array of ceramic arts and crafts. *(kaolin.is)*

Kogga: Tiny ceramic studio in the lower level of an old Reykjavík house. *(kogga.is)*

 EATING IN LAUGAVEGUR: ICELANDIC PICKS

Skál: Unusual flavours (fermented garlic, birch sugar, Arctic thyme salt) and Icelandic ingredients. *5-11pm or midnight daily, plus noon-3pm Wed-Sun* €€€	**Mat Bar:** Fuses Mediterranean and Nordic cuisine in tapas-sized shared plates, along with cocktails. *5-10pm Mon-Thu, to 11pm Fri & Sat* €€€	**Café Loki:** Convenient cafe for classic home-style Icelandic dishes and *skyr* (yoghurt-like dessert), across from Hallgrímskirkja. *8am-10pm* €€	**101 Reykjavik Street Food:** Casual spot perfect for a quick bowl of soup, *plokkfiskur* (fish stew) or fish and chips. *11am-10pm* €€

The Golden Circle

**NATIONAL PARK | ERUPTING GEYSIR |
BEAUTIFUL WATERFALLS**

GETTING AROUND

The Golden Circle is easy to drive on your own, allowing you to overnight in the area and explore further afield.

There's paid parking at Almannagjá, Þingvellir, and Kerið volcano crater. There are numerous bus/van/Jeep tours, which take about eight hours. Many operators offer activities like ATV rides, horse riding, glacial adventures and Blue Lagoon or Sky Lagoon visits. No regular buses serve the main sights of the Golden Circle, but Strætó buses 72 and 73 loop south of it.

Diving in glacial waters, absorbing the grandeur of the first-ever parliamentary site and watching the earth belch boiling water 30m high – the Golden Circle has it all. The 300km route features three knockout sights: Þingvellir, where tectonic plates meet; Geysir, where water erupts more than 100 times a day; and the roaring and voluminous waterfall Gullfoss.

The Golden Circle straddles two continental plates. The first stop on the itinerary is Þingvellir National Park, which marks the tectonic plate boundaries for Europe and North America, pulling apart the landscape with canyons and cracks. But there's an added layer of history that makes this UNESCO World Heritage site all the more unique: Iceland's Alþingi or parliament was founded at Þingvellir in the year 930 CE.

In summer, if you can, plan your visits for early morning or late in the day to avoid the bulk of the tours plying this route throughout the day.

Þingvellir National Park

Walk through history

UNESCO World Heritage site **Þingvellir National Park** *(thingvellir.is; admission free, parking from 1000kr)* is Iceland's most important historical spot. Viking settlers established the world's first democratic parliament, the Alþingi (pronounced 'al-thingk-ee'), here in 930 CE. Come see where, until 1798, meetings were conducted outdoors in an immense, fissured rift valley, with rivers and waterfalls all around. This is the kind of place that will make even hardcore urbanites grab a pair of hiking boots.

Þingvellir (pronounced 'thing-vet-lir') sits on the tectonic-plate boundary where North America and Europe are tearing away from each other at 1–18mm per year. The plain is scarred by dramatic fissures, ponds and rivers, including the great rift

Almannagjá. A path descends into the fault between the clifftop **Hakið Visitor Centre** and the **Alþingi Site**. There's also a viewing platform, and trails are 1.5km to 10.5km long, so it's easy to find a hike to suit. South is **Þingvallavatn**, Iceland's largest lake, where you can descend into Silfra gorge between the tectonic plates.

Geysir

See the steaming earth

Geysir (pronounced 'gay-zeer', literally 'gusher') is the original hot-water spout after which all other geysers are named. Set in the beautiful Haukadalur geothermal region, about a 90-minute drive from Reykjavík, the Great Geysir has been active for around 800 years.

You'll see smoke rising on the horizon as you approach Haukadalur. Vibrant shades of yellow (sulphur), green (copper) and red (iron) colour the ground. You'll also find mud pools, hot springs and fumaroles – vents in the earth that emit volcanic gas.

The best-known geyser, **Geysir** *(parking 1000kr),* used to gush water up to 80m. Earthquakes can stimulate activity, though nowadays eruptions are rare. Luckily for visitors, trusty **Strokkur**, the valley's most active geyser, sits alongside, shooting an impressive 15m to 30m plume before the water vanishes down its enormous hole. Strokkur may not shoot water as high as Geysir, but it's far more reliable, going off about every 15 minutes.

Gullfoss

Iceland's most famous waterfall

Gullfoss *(Golden Falls; gullfoss.is; free)* is a spectacular double cascade dropping a dramatic 32m. As it descends, it kicks up magnificent walls of spray before thundering down a rocky ravine. On sunny days the mist creates shimmering rainbows, while in winter the falls glitter with ice. Although it's popular, its remote location on the edge of the highlands still makes you feel the awesome forces of nature.

Dropping into the rugged canyon of the Hvítá river, Gullfoss has two cascades: the first drop is 11m and the second is 21m. In summer, Gullfoss is at its fullest, and around 38 million tonnes of water charge through daily.

A tarmac path leads from the main car park and visitor centre to a grand lookout over the falls. Stairs continue down to the level of the falls. A path (don't stray off) continues down the valley towards the falls for the most captivating video shots. There's also a lesser-known viewing spot on the eastern riverbank.

TOWNS OF THE SOUTH

The Haukadalur and Hvítá valleys are dotted with farms and geothermal greenhouses – a sustainable-produce paradise.

Reykholt: This rural township – one of several Reykholts around the country – is centred on the Reykjahver hot spring and is traditionally a greenhouse village. The main attraction is the deep Hvítá river, South Iceland's centre for whitewater rafting.

Flúðir: This little agrarian community is connected to Reykholt via a bridge on Rte 359.

Laugarás: Hamlet with new lagoon and kid-favourite **Slakki Petting Zoo**.

Selfoss: The largest gateway town, on the river Ölfusá. It has an impressive array of grocery stores and eating and accommodation options.

☑ TOP TIP

A little planning will pay off for travellers seeking a more subdued experience; check the live traffic monitor operated by **Visit Iceland** *(visiticeland.com)* to analyse peak hours at main destinations. During summer, for instance, constant daylight hours allow for a lot of flexibility.

Southeast Iceland

GLACIAL LAGOONS | DEEP CANYONS | YEAR-ROUND ACTIVITIES

Places

The mighty Vatnajökull – Europe's most massive ice cap – dominates Southeast Iceland, with its huge rivers of frozen ice cracking steep-sided valleys. Blow your mind as you traverse the 200km stretch of Ring Road from Kirkjubæjarklaustur to Höfn, transporting yourself across vast deltas of grey glacial sand, past marooned-looking farms, around the toes of craggy mountains, through surreal lava fields and by groaning glacier tongues and ice-filled lagoons.

The giant Vatnajökull's twisting tongues of frozen ice carve valleys opening at the sea. One of several glacial lagoons, Jökulsárlón is a photographer's paradise where wind and water sculpt calving icebergs into fantastical shapes and sweep them out to Fellsfjara where they sparkle in the sun like diamonds. With so much natural upheaval on display, it's not surprising that Skaftafell (the southern branch of the enormous Vatnajökull National Park) is such a popular oasis for sightseers and hikers.

GETTING AROUND

The Ring Road from Hella to Vík gets busy over summer. Traffic eases up the further east you go. Most sights are roadside or within 10km from the Ring Road. Gravel roads are rare. Vík is a major stop for all Reykjavík–Höfn bus routes; buses stop at the N1 petrol station in the centre of town. Kirkjubæjarklaustur is another stop (at the N1). Buses travelling east call at Skaftafell and Jökulsárlón. Almost all Reykjavík-based tour companies head south. Many southern operators also pick up in Reykjavík.

Vík

Walk along a black-sand beach

On the western side of Reynisfjall, the high ridge above Vík, Rte 215 leads 5km down to the famed black-sand beach **Reynisfjara** *(parking 1000kr)*. Braving weather and crowds, you'll be rewarded with a broad sweep of beach backed by an incredible stack of basalt columns that look like a magical church organ, and outstanding views west to Dyrhólaey.

Immediately offshore, you'll see the towering **Reynisdrangur sea stacks**. A bracing walk up from Vík's western end takes you to the top of **Reynisfjall** (340m), which provides superb views.

At all times watch for rogue waves: people are regularly swept away, including a nine-year-old child in August 2025.

Skaftafell

Glaciers and waterfalls

Vatnajökull is the world's largest ice cap outside the poles, and huge outlet glaciers, pleated with crevasses, flow down from the heights to the lowlands along Iceland's south coast. At Skaftafell, a popular trail offers an easy one-hour walk from **Skaftafellsstofa Visitor Centre** (path S1; 3.7km return) to the glacier tongue of **Skaftafellsjökull**.

Another trail (path S2; 5.3km return) leads to **Svartifoss** (Black Falls), a stunning, moody-looking waterfall flanked by geometric black basalt columns. On the return, head back via the big views of Sjónarsker and traditional turf-roofed farmhouse **Sel**. This two-hour return walk, including Svartifoss, is classified as easy.

Go on a glacier hike

One highlight of any visit to the southern reaches of Vatnajökull is a glacier hike, where you get to strap on crampons and crunch your way around (atop) a glacier. You can see waterfalls, ice caves, glacial mice (moss balls, not actual mice!) and different-coloured ash from ancient explosions. Never venture out onto one without both a guide and the right equipment. **Icelandic Mountain Guides** (*mountainguides.is*) and **Arctic Adventures** (*glacierguides.is*) have information and booking huts beside Skaftafellsstofa Visitor Centre.

Go beneath the ice

The glorious dimpled caverns (ice caves) of exquisite blue light beneath the glacier are truly things of wonder. The caves can be viewed only from November to March, not least because they become unstable and unsafe in warmer weather. They must be visited with guides, who will ensure safety and correct equipment. We recommend you go with a local company. **From Coast to Mountains** (*fromcoasttomountains.com; 3hr tour per person 27,500kr*) and sister company **Local Guide** (*localguide.is; 3hr tour per person 23,900kr*) are the regional experts on ice caves in Southeast Iceland.

Fjaðrárgljúfur

Look into a storied canyon

The verdantly twisting, picturesque **Fjaðrárgljúfur canyon**, topped by waterfalls and carved out by the river Fjaðrá, has been well and truly discovered, thanks to Instagrammers and one Justin Bieber (who filmed a video clip here). Park at the main (lower) car park and walk the 2km up to the viewing platform. Along the way there are plenty of places to gaze into the gorge's rocky, writhing depths and emerald-green surrounds. The canyon is just west of Kirkjubæjarklaustur, 3km north of the Ring Road via Rte 206.

JÖKULHLAUP

The section of Ring Road that passes across Skeiðarársandur was the last bit of the national highway to be constructed, in 1974 (until then, folks from Höfn had to drive to Reykjavík via Akureyri). Long gravel dykes have been strategically positioned to channel floodwaters away from this highly susceptible artery. They did little good, however, when within a few hours in late 1996 the Grímsvötn (or Gjálp) eruption created a massive *jökulhlaup* (glacial flood) releasing up to 3000 billion litres of water and dragging icebergs the size of three-storey buildings – three Ring Road bridges were washed away like matchsticks. There's a memorial of twisted bridge girders and an information board along the Ring Road just west of Skaftafell.

☑ TOP TIP

Budget for plenty of stops on the route beyond Vík and run at the sound of 'Katla is erupting'. The region is home to Iceland's most notorious volcanoes, including Eyjafjallajökull, Katla, Hekla and Öræfajökull. Reserve accommodation well ahead – the area gets booked out every summer.

BEST LOCAL TOUR OPERATORS

From Coast to Mountains: Owner Einar, Iceland's first ice-cave guide, offers climbing, cave and puffin tours. *(fromcoasttomountains.com)*

Local Guide: Family-owned and in the area for generations; first-rate local knowledge, year-round glacier hikes and ice climbs. *(localguide.is)*

Heading North: Small groups with a maximum of six people make for outstanding glacier and ice-cave tours. *(headingnorth.is)*

Vivid Iceland: Excellent private and small-group glacier tours by a park ranger and qualified glacier guide. *(vividiceland.is)*

Fellsfjara

Jökulsárlón

Glacier, lagoon and a 'diamond' beach

Spectacular, luminous-blue icebergs drift through Jökulsárlón (pronounced 'yokul-sar-lon') glacier lagoon, right beside the Ring Road. The icebergs calve from Breiðamerkurjökull and can spend five years floating in the 25-sq-km, 250m-deep lagoon, melting, refreezing and occasionally toppling over with a mighty splash, startling the birds and the seals that like to frolic in the shallows here.

There are many ways to explore this miraculous place. From June to September, park rangers lead a free guided walk (one hour) at 11am around the lagoon. To get up close to the glacier by water, take a Zodiac tour with **Ice Lagoon Adventure Tours** *(icelagoon.com; per person 15,900kr)*. Another fine option is to kayak the lagoon. **IceGuide** *(iceguide.is; per person 16,900kr)* leads hour-long paddles from May to early October. And there's the novelty of amphibious boat tours operated by **Glacier Lagoon** *(icelagoon.is; adult/child 6900/3500kr)*; trips run from from May to October.

Cross from the lagoon car parks underneath the Ring Road bridge out to the mouth of the Jökulsá river. The 'Diamond Beach' or **Fellsfjara**, is where icebergs glitter on the black-sand beach on their final journey into the ocean.

 EATING AROUND JÖKULSÁRLÓN: OUR PICKS

Heimahumar: This food truck by the main car park does a warming lobster bisque, lobster roll, hot dogs and hot drinks. *11.30am-5pm mid-May–mid-Sep €*

Northern Light Bite: Another of the Jökulsárlón food trucks, this one keeps it simple with fish (local cod) and chips. *11.30am-4pm mid-May–mid-Sep €*

Fancy Sheep: Next to the other food trucks, Fancy Sheep holds its own with lamb or beef burgers, pumpkin soup or fries. *11.30am-5pm mid-May–mid-Sep €*

Jón Ríki: Stylish farmhouse restaurant at Hólmur with a small brewery; try the grilled langoustine and the jalapeno-and-pumpkin ale. *6-8.30pm Mon-Fri €€*

Akureyri & the North

NORTHERN CAPITAL | WHALE-WATCHING | CULTURAL LIFE

Akureyri stands strong as Iceland's second city, albeit with only around 20,000 residents. Despite its diminutive size, expect cool cafes, quality restaurants and something of a late-night scene on the Hafnarstræti pedestrian street – a far cry from other towns in rural Iceland.

Akureyri sits at the head of Eyjafjörður, Iceland's longest (60km) fjord, at the base of snow-capped peaks. In the early days, Danish merchants shaped its character by promoting the planting of trees in well-tended gardens, laying the foundation for the Scandi-style public parks at Kjarnaskógur and Lystigarður. The harbour is the second-busiest port of call for cruise ships, just a stone's throw from the Arctic Circle. Akureyri also serves as a gateway town for Húsavik, an hour's drive away and one of the best places in the world to see whales.

With its relaxed attitude and extensive accommodation choices, Akureyri is the natural base for exploring North Iceland.

Akureyri

Sea monsters and storybooks

For an overview of Akureyri's history, don't miss the **Akureyri Museum** *(minjasafnid.is; adult/child 2600kr/free)*, about a 30-minute walk from the centre in the old town. Its highlight is the Schulte Collection – the world's largest collection of historical maps of Iceland and elsewhere in Scandinavia. Some date back to the early 16th century, complete with sea monsters and other denizens of the deep.

Just below the **Akureyrarkirkja** *(akureyrarkirkja.is)*, Akureyri's landmark church, is the **Gilið** or 'ravine' – Akureyri's art street, lined with several small galleries and craft shops, sporting a rainbow-hued sidewalk and crowned by the **Akureyri Art Museum** *(listak.is; adult/child 2200kr/free)*. This ambitious museum is by far the best art museum outside of Reykjavík, with frequently changing exhibitions.

Places

GETTING AROUND

Akureyri city buses *(straeto.is)* are free but don't service the airport. Call 461 1010 for a taxi. During summer, buses go twice daily between Akureyri and Reykjavík via Skagafjörður. Buses serve Húsavík, although it's easier to drive (one hour). To pay for parking in Akureyri, download EasyPark or Parka apps; free parking is widely available. Rent a scooter via the Hopp app. Runners and cyclists enjoy the smooth 14km path between Hof Culture House (home to tourism information) and Hrafnagil.

WHALE-WATCHING TOURS

North Sailing (*northsailing.is*) and **Gentle Giants** (*gentlegiants.is*) are the two largest operators, both with 70- to 90-passenger boats and offices high on the foreshore overlooking the harbour. **Friends of Moby Dick** (*friends ofmobydick.is*) is a smaller operator with personalised tours led by a marine biologist and a boat that takes about 40 passengers. Warm overalls (which you pull on over your own warm clothing) are provided by all companies. North Sailing, Gentle Giants and **Húsavík Adventures** (*husavikadventures. is*) also offer tours on Rigid Inflatable Boats (RIBs) or Zodiacs. A three-hour tour costs around 13,000/7000kr per adult/child, but many hotels in the region have their own promotion code for online bookings.

ALESSANDRO FAVARO/ALAMY

Hot springs of Akureyri

Akureyri is famously sunny, but this is still North Iceland. What better way to beat the chill than with a warm soak? Some years ago, during the building of the Vaðlaheiðar Tunnel on Akureyri's outskirts, the construction crew was struck by a stream of hot water midway into the 7km mountain dig. Fast forward several years and the result of that discovery is the **Forest Lagoon** (*forestlagoon.is; adult/child 6900/3450kr*), open since 2022 and the winner of our vote for Iceland's best luxury hot springs. Enjoy the plunge pools, Finnish sauna, city views and soothing forest surroundings.

 EATING IN AKUREYRI & THE NORTH: OUR PICKS

Eyja: Akureyri wine bar and bistro with three-course options and a fish-of-the-day main. *4-10pm Sun-Thu, to midnight Fri & Sat* €€

Gamli Baukur: Among shiny nautical relics in Húsavík, timber-framed Gamli serves spaghetti with shellfish and cod with green pesto. *11.30am-9pm* €€

Strikið: Akureyri restaurant known for Icelandic brunches and local focus (super-fresh sushi, lamb shoulder, shellfish soup). *11.30am-2pm & 5-9pm* €€€

North Restaurant: Chef Gunnar Gíslasson elevates Nordic cuisine with Icelandic ingredients and creative menus. At Hotel Akureyri. *6-9.30pm Wed-Sat* €€€

Puffins, Lundey

Húsavík

Look for humpbacks off Húsavík

Although it's possible to see whales closer to Akureyri, Húsavík is world-class. Three-hour boat tours head out in a variety of forms into Skjálfandi, a bay rich in krill, plankton and fish that draw whales, white-beaked dolphins and seabirds, especially in summer.

Most tours take place in converted wooden former fishing vessels or Zodiacs. We're surprised it's taken this long, but a handful of operators (North Sailing is one) now offer a tour in a 'silent' electric-powered boat. The main whale-watching season runs from June to September, with mostly humpbacks. Blue whales are elusive, but your best chance is April and May, or October to December.

Some companies offer an add-on to the usual three-hour whale-watching trip to **Lundey** (aka Puffin Island), a summer nesting ground of these engaging, much-loved little birds. The island is close in to the shore, north of Húsavík.

Back in port, don't miss the **Húsavík Whale Museum** *(whalemuseum.is; adult/child 2200kr/free)*, which displays one of only four complete blue-whale skeletons in existence.

☑ **TOP TIP**

There's a choice to be made as you travel between Akuryeri and Húsavík: take the 7km-long **Vaðlaheiðar Tunnel** *(tunnel.is; 2150kr)* or Rte 84; the latter is free and very scenic, but it does add 16km to your trip. If you take the Akureyri tunnel, pay online within 24 hours.

Places We Love to Stay

€ Budget €€ Midrange €€€ Top End

Reykjavík

MAP p597

Sunna Guesthouse € Rooms and apartments are simple and sunny, with honey-coloured parquet floors. Several have Hallgrímskirkja views. Limited free parking.

KEX Hostel € Megahostel with heaps of style (think vaudeville meets rodeo). Unofficial headquarters of backpackerdom and popular local gathering place.

Freyja Guesthouse €€ Beautiful, welcoming rooms with shared bathrooms in the residential streets near Hallgrímskirkja. Also has a family suite with private bathroom.

CenterHótel Arnarhvoll €€ Glossy waterfront hotel with unimpeded views of the bay and Mt Esja. Small, Scandi-design rooms with large windows.

Hótel Borg €€€ Art-deco luxury hotel on Reykjavík's main square with a glamorous restaurant and a fab spa.

Apotek €€€ Iconic 1917 building designed by Guðjón Samúelsson, with contemporary rooms in muted tones and a popular restaurant-bar.

Sand Hotel €€€ Art-deco echoes meet Nordic design and 21st-century luxury: in-room espresso machines, bluetooth speakers, fine linens and soft towels.

Hótel Holt €€€ Cool blast to the luxurious past. Built in the 1960s as one of Reykjavík's first hotels, Holt is decked out with original art.

The Golden Circle

Geysir Campground € Simple campground, a short walk from the geysers, with mountain views, laundry and a playground.

Hótel Geysir €€ Stylish hotel with 77 rooms, a five-minute walk from its namesake geyser.

Lake Thingvellir Cottages €€ Four pine cottages with kitchenettes and views of the lake sit near the national-park entrance along Rte 36.

Náttúra Yurtel €€€ Mongolian yurts with electricity, private toilets, underfloor heating.

Hótel Gullfoss €€€ Clean rooms and comfortable beds as close to the waterfall as you can get. Ask for a room facing the valley. Hot-pots and a restaurant.

Ion Adventure Hotel €€€ Chic, with sustainable practices, Ion has a geothermal pool, a spa and a restaurant.

Southeast Iceland

Skaftafell Campsite € Large, year-round site with laundry facilities and paid hot showers. No cooking; wi-fi in visitor centre.

Potato Storage €€ Brand-new apartments on a peaceful Svínafell farm offer welcome respite after a day's hiking.

Hótel Skaftafell €€€ One of very few hotels in the area (so in hot demand despite being merely functional), with a restaurant.

Fosshotel Glacier Lagoon €€€ Superb four-star hotel out on the plains with sleek Nordic design and all-encompassing views.

Akureyri & the North

Hamrar Campsite € Family favourite just south of town on the edge of Kjarnaskógur forest, with a playground operated by the local scout group.

Akureyri Backpackers € A chilled vibe, popular bar, central location and rooms of varying size sharing bathrooms. Showers are in the basement; no kitchen.

Hótel Akureyri €€ Boutique-style hotel on the edge of town with well-equipped rooms (the front ones have fjord views).

Gamli Skólinn €€ A perfect Húsavík base, with three beautifully decorated four- and six-person apartments on a quiet side street near the Húsavík Museum.

Árból €€ This 1903 heritage house has a leafy setting and spacious rooms spread over three levels. There's no kitchen.

Húsavík Cape Hotel €€€ A boutique option overlooking the harbour with fresh, modern rooms – ask for a corner room with views – and a breakfast buffet.

Practicalities

Tourist Information
Visit Iceland (visiticeland.com)
Reykjavík (visitreykjavik.is)
Southwest Iceland
(visitreykjanes.is; south.is)
Southeast Iceland (south.is; visitvatnajokull.is; vatnajokulsthjodgardur.is)
North Iceland (northiceland.is; visitakureyri.is)

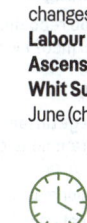

ENRIQUE REMBIS/SHUTTERSTOCK

Visas
Schengen country citizens don't need a visa for visits under 90 days. From late 2026, citizens or residents of the US, Australia, Canada, the UK, Japan and New Zealand will need an ETIAS travel authorisation.

Time
Iceland's time zone is the same as GMT/UTC (London). There is no daylight saving time. Iceland uses the 24-hour system, and all transport timetables and business hours are posted accordingly.

Smoking
Smoking is illegal in enclosed public spaces, including in cafes, bars, clubs, restaurants and on public transport. Most accommodation is nonsmoking.

Public Holidays
New Year's Day 1 January
Easter March or April (changes annually)
Labour Day 1 May
Ascension Day 18 May
Whit Sunday Monday May or June (changes annually)

Independence Day 17 June
Commerce Day First Monday in August
Christmas Eve 24 December
Christmas Day 25 December
Boxing Day 26 December

Opening Hours
Supermarkets 7am–midnight; some 10am–8pm
Government-owned liquor stores (Vínbúðin) 11am–6pm Monday to Saturday; some remote stores only 4–6pm
Shops 9am–6pm; weekend hours may vary
Bars 10am–1am Sunday to Thursday, until as late as 5.30am Friday and Saturday

Etiquette
● Remove your shoes when entering someone's home.
● Leave your pram and baby outside when visiting boutiques and cafes (yes, you read that correctly).
● Strip and shower thoroughly before entering a hot-pot or pool.
● Don't use drones in national parks.
● Don't drive off-road and don't ignore signs advising that roads or sites are closed – this is due to safety reasons.

Language

Most Icelanders speak English, so you'll have no problems if you don't know any Icelandic. However, any attempts to speak the local language will be much appreciated.

Basics

Hello. Halló. *ha·loh*
Goodbye. Bless. *bles*
Yes. Já. *yow*
No. Nei. *nay*
How are you? Hvað segir þú gott?
kvadh say·yir thoo got
Fine. And you? Allt fínt. En þú? *alt feent en thoo*
Thank you. Takk/Takk fyrir.
tak/tak fi·rir
Excuse me. Afsakið. *af·sa·kidh*
Sorry. Fyrirgefðu. *fi·rir·gev·dhu*
My name is … Ég heiti …
yekh hay·ti …
Do you speak English?
Talarðu ensku? *a·lar dhoo ens·ku*
I don't understand. Ég skil ekki.
yekh skil e·ki

Directions

Where's the (hotel)? Hvar er
(hótelið)? *kvar er (hoh·te·lidh)*
What's your address? Hvert
er heimilisfangið þitt? *kvert er
hay·mi·lis·fown·gidh thit*
Can you show me (on the map)?
Geturðu sýnt mér (á kortinu)?
ge·tur·dhu seent myer (ow kor·ti·nu)

Signs

Inngangur Entrance
Útgangur Exit
Opið Open
Lokað Closed
Bannað Prohibited
Snyrting/Salerni Toilets

Emergencies

Help! Hjálp! *hyowlp*
Go away! Farðu! *far·dhu*
I'm lost. Ég er villtur/villt. (m/f)
yekh er vil·tur/vilt
Call …! Hringdu á …! *hring·du ow …*
   a doctor lækni *laik·ni*
   the police lögregluna
   leukh·rekh·lu·na
Where are the toilets? Hvar er
snyrtingin? *kvar er snir·tin·gin*

Eating & Drinking

What would you recommend?
Hverju mælir þú með? *kver·yu
mai·lir thoo medh*
Cheers! Skál! *skowl*
Do you have vegetarian food?
Eruð þið með grænmetisrétti?
er·udh thidh medh grain·me·tis·rye·ti
breakfast morgunmat *mor·gun·mat*
lunch hádegismat *how·day·yis·mat*
dinner kvöldmat *kveuld·mat*

Shopping & Services

I'm looking for … Ég er að leita að …
yekh er adh lay·ta adh …
How much is it? Hvað kostar
þetta? *kvadh kos·tar the·ta*
It's faulty. Það er gallað. *thadh er
gat·ladh*
Where's the …? Hvar er …? *kvar er …*
   bank bankinn *bown·kin*
   market markaðurinn
   mar·ka·dhu·rin

NUMBERS

1
einn *aydn*

2
tveir *tvayr*

3
þrír *threer*

4
fjórir *fyoh·rir*

5
fimm *fim*

6
sex *seks*

7
sjö *syeu*

8
átta *ow·ta*

9
níu *nee·u*

10
tíu *tee·u*

FROM LEFT: WIRESTOCK CREATORS/SHUTTERSTOCK, ESPRESSO77/SHUTTERSTOCK

Ring Road (p595)

Arriving & Getting Around

International travellers flying to Iceland arrive at Keflavík International Airport, 49km southwest of Reykjavík. A weekly ferry service runs between northern Denmark and Seyðisfjörður.

Airport Bus
Flybus *(re.is)* connects Keflavík Airport with Reykjavík in under an hour. Bus and flight schedules are coordinated. For some hotels, you can pay for an additional transfer (on a smaller bus) from the main bus station.

Buses
Reykjavík has an extensive bus system, but it's harder to bus beyond Selfoss on the southern coast and Borgarnes to the north. Download the Strætó Klappið app to purchase individual bus tickets. Activate your ticket before you ride.

Road Conditions
Major roads in Iceland are paved and well maintained. Secondary roads may be gravel. F-roads are challenging summer-only mountain roads. Check road conditions at *road.is*.

Ridesharing
Because ridesharing services like Lyft and Uber aren't allowed, carpooling is a popular option for getting between cities. People submit routes they're driving on *samferda.net* and passengers can request rides and offer to split costs.

MONEY
Currency: Icelandic króna (kr or ISK)

CASH OR CARD?
Most places in Iceland accept credit cards and digital payments, even for small purchases. Some public restrooms require payment, so keep some coins on hand if you're taking a long-distance road trip.

TAXES & REFUNDS
Iceland's standard VAT is 24%. Books, food and accommodation are taxed at a lower 11%. Visitors from outside Iceland can claim a tax refund on transactions of 6000kr or more – ask for a form to fill in and a receipt from the shop, and drop these off at the airport.

TIPPING
Taxes and service charges are always included in Iceland. However, rounding up restaurant bills or leaving an additional tip for exceptional service is always appreciated.

PATRYK KOSMIDER/SHUTTERSTOCK

For places to stay in Ireland, see p640

Above: Cliffs of Moher (p635); Right: General Post Office (p619), Dublin

THE MAIN AREAS

DUBLIN
Ireland's characterful capital. **p616**

KILKENNY
Medieval heritage, arts, crafts and design. **p621**

CORK
Urban buzz, artisan producers, wild coastline. **p624**

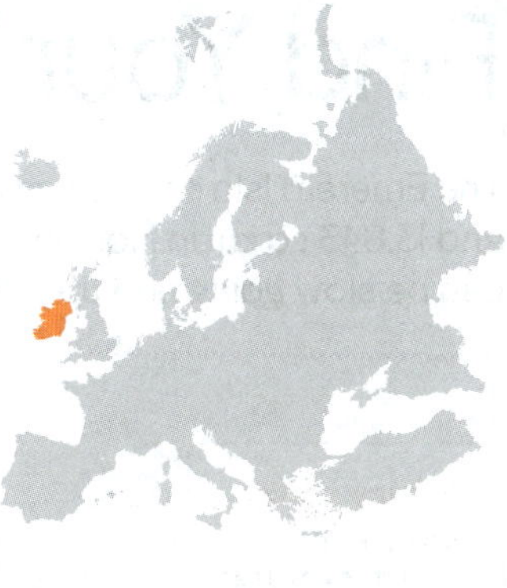

Ireland

ANCIENT HISTORY, SPELLBINDING SCENERY AND SPIRITED CULTURE

The wild Atlantic coastline, misty mountains, monastic ruins, medieval castles, colourfully painted villages and cities teeming with culture enchant visitors to Ireland.

For a small island at Europe's western edge, Ireland's history is immense. Forged by glacial events during the last ice age that formed its mountains, valleys and drumlins, and laid the foundations for its waterways and bogs, it has had a human presence stretching back to the pre-Celts, Celts and early Christians. Following St Patrick's arrival in 433 CE, some of Europe's most significant – often mystical – ancient and monastic sites are scattered across the Irish landscape. Marauding Vikings plundered Irish monasteries from 795 to 841, establishing settlements throughout the country, including economic powerhouse Dublin.

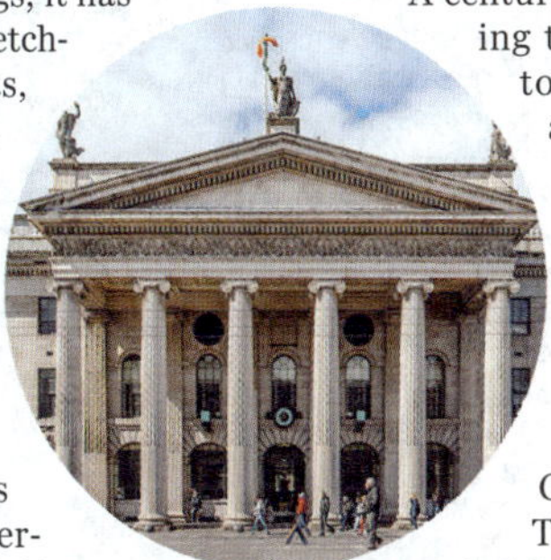

The battle between the forces of the high king, Brian Ború, and king of Leinster, Máelmorda mac Murchada, in 1014 set in motion events that have reverberated ever since. Helped by MacMurrough, in 1169 Welsh and Norman barons captured areas in Ireland's southeast, beginning an 800-year occupation by Britain.

A centuries-long struggle – including the Great Famine that led to a worldwide diaspora, and revolutionary period in the early 20th century – resulted in the 1922 formation of the Irish Free State, with six Northern Ireland counties gaining legislative and executive authority under 1998's Good Friday Agreement.

These events have shaped this thriving contemporary country today, but haven't altered the cultural expression spanning storytelling to trad-music sessions and the revival of ancient festivities such as Samhain (Halloween), and warmth and spirit at Ireland's heart.

KERRY
The jewel in Ireland's scenic crown.
p628

GALWAY
Vibrant festivals, trad music, rugged landscapes.
p632

BELFAST
Revitalised port city filled with history.
p637

Find Your Way

The Emerald Isle covers just 84,421 sq km in the Republic of Ireland and 13,843 sq km in Northern Ireland, but plan ahead as backroads can be slow going and there's a lot to see.

Belfast, p637

Belfast's enduring links to the *Titanic* and its recent history are explored throughout this engaging and revitalised city.

Galway, p632

Home to evocative landscapes including Connemara National Park, as well as a creative city with a fabulous trad-music scene.

Dublin, p616

Georgian architecture, distilleries and breweries, sights celebrating a rich literary heritage and legendary nightlife infuse Ireland's absorbing capital.

Kerry, p628

Spectacular scenery spans Ireland's highest mountains, two national parks, charming peninsulas and remote islands including the remarkable Skellig Michael.

THE GUIDE

IRELAND

Portrush
Coleraine
Letterkenny
Dungloe
Derry A26
Ballymena Larne
A6
Strabane Bangor
A5
Donegal BELFAST
N15
Omagh NORTHERN
Bundoran IRELAND Lough Neagh
Dungannon
Enniskillen A3 A1
Sligo A4 Armagh
Belmullet Newry
N2
Ballina N4 Dundalk
Carrick-on- Cavan Carrickmacross
Castlebar N5 Shannon N3
Westport M1
Ballyhaunis Navan Drogheda
N17 Longford
Clifden Roscommon
Lough Corrib Tuam Mullingar M3
Athlone M4 DUBLIN
Galway M6
IRELAND Tullamore
Aran Islands M7 Naas
M18 Roscrea Portlaoise Wicklow
Lahinch Nenagh M9
Ennis M7 Carlow M11
Kilkee Limerick M8 KILKENNY Gorey
Shannon Cashel Enniscorthy
Listowel New Ross Wexford
Tralee N20 Clonmel M8
Dingle Killarney Mallow Waterford
Carrantuohil Tramore
Waterville Macroom Dungarvan St George's Channel
Kerry Kenmare CORK
Kinsale Cobh
Bantry Clonakilty
Skibbereen

North Channel
SCOTLAND
Dumfries
Isle of Man
Douglas
Irish Sea
Atlantic Ocean
Fishguard WALES
Carmarthen
Swansea

N
0   100 km
0   50 miles

CAR
A car gives you the most freedom and is essential in out-of-the-way areas. Get off the main roads when you can: narrow, winding secondary or tertiary roads lead to some of Ireland's most magical scenery.

BUS & TRAIN
Ireland's extensive network of public and private buses is the most cost-effective way to get around, with services to and from most inhabited areas. A limited rail network links Dublin to all major urban centres.

Guinness Storehouse (p620), Dublin

Plan Your Time

Quality, not quantity, should be your goal: instead of a hair-raising race to see everything, narrow down destinations and give yourself time to linger for the most memorable Irish experiences.

If Time Is Tight

● Start in Ireland's dynamic capital, **Dublin** (p616), visiting its collection of Georgian showpieces, history museums, literary sites, **Guinness Storehouse** (p620) and whiskey distilleries, and legendary music venues and pubs. Then explore **Kilkenny city** (p621) along its medieval mile, linking its landmark cathedral and castle. Browse Irish crafts and design in the castle stables, or stroll the riverbanks into the green countryside.

Two Weeks to Explore

● After Dublin and Kilkenny, make your way to the Republic's buzzing second city, **Cork** (p624). Detour to picturesque harbours **Cobh** (p627) and **Kinsale** (p627), then see majestic scenery in **Killarney National Park** (p628), the **Cliffs of Moher** (p635) and Galway's **Connemara** (p635). Save a night for **Galway city** (p632) for live music at its rollicking pubs, before finishing with *Titanic* history in **Belfast** (p637).

SEASONAL HIGHLIGHTS

SPRING

St Patrick's Day festivities liven up often-chilly March. April and May can be glorious times to visit before the crowds descend.

SUMMER

From June to August, days are at their longest, everything is open and **beaches** get busy. Activities take place both indoors and out.

AUTUMN

Outdoor adventures are prime amid September/ October's blazing colours. Parades celebrate ancient Celtic **Samhain** (Halloween).

WINTER

Christmas brightens up December. In January and February, pubs with roaring turf fires, trad sessions and craic are cosy refuges.

EVAN HAMMONDS/500PX

Dublin

HISTORY | FOOD & DRINK | LITERATURE

A small city with a huge reputation, Dublin exudes an irresistible mix of heritage and hedonism. Dublin has been making noise since around 500 BCE, when Celtic settlers set up camp at a crossing on the River Liffey. They called it Áth Cliath – the 'Ford of the Hurdles' – and the name lives on today as the Irish for Dublin, Baile Átha Cliath. It's still Ireland's busiest hub, with over a quarter of the country's population living in or around the capital. While the city centre is fairly small, Dublin spreads wide: it's a city of neighbourhoods, each with its own personality. It's not the prettiest capital, and Dubliners won't pretend otherwise. But they'll also tell you that charm beats beauty, and they'll point you towards show-stopping Georgian squares or Victorian shopfronts and remind you that it's easy to love a city that's lovely, but real affection is rooted in character.

Academic Grandeur

Roam the hallowed Trinity College

All elegant courtyards and ivy-clad buildings, Ireland's most prestigious university, **Trinity College Dublin** *(visittrinity. ie; €16-33.50)* is home to the twin treasures of the **Old Library's** vaulted, oak-scented Long Room and the *Book of Kells;* created around 800 CE by monks on the island of Iona,

---

 GETTING AROUND

Dublin is compact and flat, with most major sights within walking distance. The city has a rent-and-ride Dublinbikes scheme, a two-line light-rail system called the Luas, a suburban DART train that runs along the coast, and an extensive bus network for getting beyond the centre. The easiest way to pay for public transport is with a Leap Visitor Card (p643).

Daily **Mary Gibbons' Tours** *(newgrange tours.com; per person €75)* from Dublin visit Newgrange and the Hill of Tara. **St Kevins Bus Service** *(glendaloughbus.com; adult/ child return €23/14)* departs from St Stephen's Green North (stop 181) for Glendalough. Otherwise, both are easily reached by car.

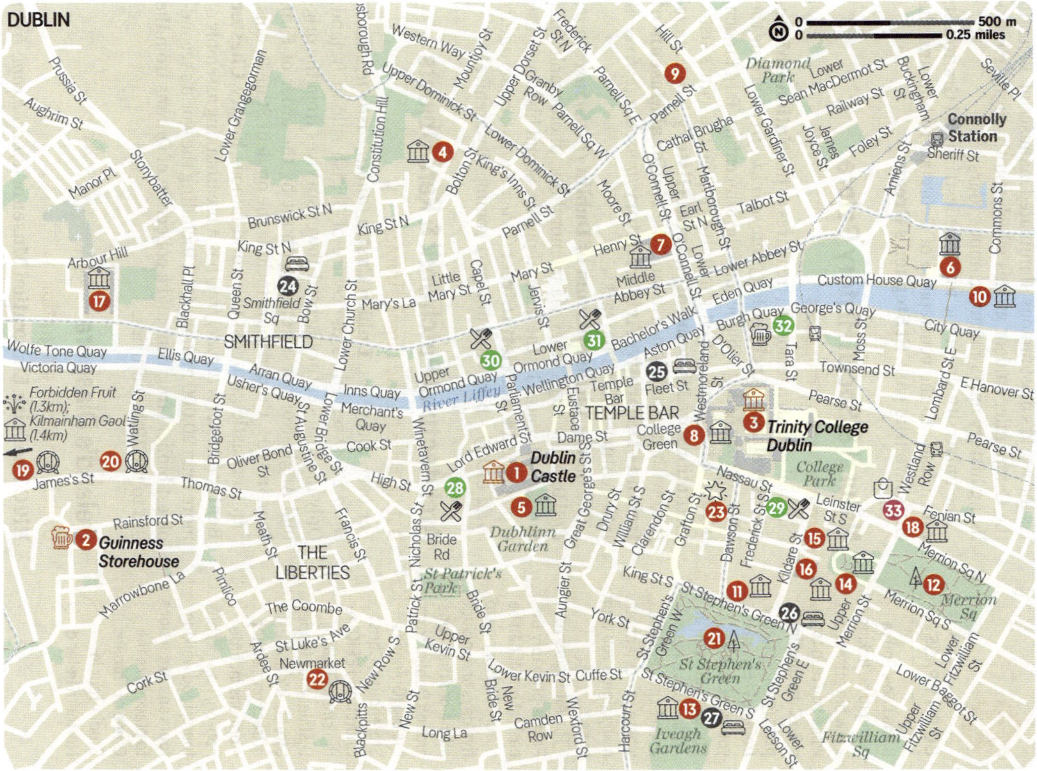

DUBLIN

★ HIGHLIGHTS
1 Dublin Castle
2 Guinness Storehouse
3 Trinity College Dublin

● SIGHTS
4 14 Henrietta Street
5 Chester Beatty
6 EPIC The Irish Emigration Museum
7 General Post Office
see 7 GPO Museum
8 Irish Whiskey Museum
9 James Joyce Centre
10 Jeanie Johnston
11 Little Museum of Dublin
12 Merrion Square
13 Museum of Literature Ireland
14 Museum of Natural History
15 National Library of Ireland
16 National Museum of Ireland – Archaeology
17 National Museum of Ireland – Decorative Arts & History
18 Oscar Wilde House
19 Pearse Lyons Distillery
20 Roe & Co Distillery
21 St Stephen's Green
22 Teeling Distillery

● ACTIVITIES
23 Dublin Literary Pub Crawl

● SLEEPING
24 Generator Hostel
25 Morgan Hotel
26 Shelbourne
27 Staunton's on the Green

● EATING
28 Leo Burdock's
29 Library Street
30 Soup Dragon
31 Winding Stair

● DRINKING & NIGHTLIFE
32 John Mulligan's

● SHOPPING
33 Sweny's Pharmacy

GO CITY PASS

If you know you're going to be ticking off a few big attractions while you're in town, a **Go City Dublin pass** *(gocity.com; from €69)* can save you some cash. Choose between an All-Inclusive Pass or an Explorer Pass, where you select how many sights you want to see.

The All-Inclusive Pass is probably the easiest bet. It can be purchased for one to five days and includes all major attractions around Dublin, from the big (Guinness Storehouse, Christ Church and EPIC) to the small (Teeling Distillery, 14 Henrietta Street). It's not just attractions, either – options include hop-on/hop-off bus tours, food walking tours and excursions to places like the Game of Thrones Studio Tour in Northern Ireland.

it's the world's most famous illuminated manuscript. Beneath the Campanile, student guides whisk you through Trinity's living history on 45-minute campus tours.

The university sits at the top of pedestrianised Grafton St, which leads to the centrepiece of Georgian Dublin and the city's favourite park, **St Stephen's Green**.

Natural & Social History Galore

Explore Dublin's museums

Cultural and archaeological treasures at the **National Museum of Ireland – Archaeology** *(museum.ie; free)* include the 12th-century Ardagh Chalice and the 8th-century Tara Brooch, both masterpieces of Celtic metalwork. The museum's sister institutions are **Museum of Natural History** *(museum.ie; free)* with its stuffed beasts and the **National Museum of Ireland – Decorative Arts & History** *(museum.ie; free)*, at 18th-century Collins Barracks.

The quirky **Little Museum of Dublin** *(littlemuseum.ie; €18)* tells the city's story via memorabilia, photographs and artefacts donated by the general public. Social history is also explored at **14 Henrietta Street** *(14henriettastreet.ie; adult/child €10/6)* – part museum, part community archive.

Architectural Patchwork & Rare Objects

Dublin's castle and famous library

For over 700 years, **Dublin Castle** *(dublincastle.ie; adult/child €8/4)* served as the centre of British rule in Ireland. Only the 13th-century Record Tower survives from the original Anglo-Norman stronghold built by the order of King John in 1204. Guided tours include the opulent State Rooms.

In the castle grounds, the world-famous library **Chester Beatty** *(chesterbeatty.ie; free)* has a breathtaking assembly of more than 20,000 manuscripts, including the world's second-oldest biblical fragment and a collection of Qurans from the 9th to the 19th centuries.

Ireland's Diaspora

Understand Irish emigration

EPIC The Irish Emigration Museum *(epicchq.com; from €28)* charts Ireland's global story in interactive galleries spread through vaulted stone tunnels, where you discover why millions left, where they landed and how 70 million people now claim Irish roots.

 EATING IN DUBLIN: OUR PICKS

Leo Burdock's:
Dublin's most famous fish-and-chip shop is a rite of passage for many. *11.30am-midnight Sun-Thu, to 1am Fri & Sat* €

Soup Dragon: This cafe has been a budget favourite for years. The daily soup, bread and fruit deal is a bargain. *8am-5pm Mon-Fri* €

Winding Stair: Contemporary Irish cuisine in an elegant 1st-floor dining room. *noon-3.30pm & 5.30-10.30pm* €€

Library Street: Sophisticated, superb sharing plates from Michelin-trained Kevin Burke. *5-11.30pm Tue-Thu, from 2.30pm Fri & Sat* €€

EPIC The Irish Emigration Museum

Combination tickets are available with the **Jeanie Johnston** *(jeaniejohnston.ie; adult/child €15/10),* a replica 19th-century 'coffin ship' that carried starving Irish emigrants across the Atlantic during the 1845–52 Great Famine.

The Struggle for Nationhood

Learn about Irish independence

A quintessential Dublin landmark, the **General Post Office** served as command HQ for the rebels during the 1916 Easter Rising; you can still see the pockmarks of the struggle in the Doric columns outside. Its interactive visitor centre, **GPO Museum** *(gpomuseum.ie; adult/child €15/7.50),* serves as a fitting tribute to its role in the creation of the Irish state, exploring the Rising's origins to its aftermath.

Grim prison **Kilmainham Gaol** *(kilmainhamgaolmuseum. ie; adult/child €8/4),* built in 1796 and closed in 1924, played a pivotal role in nearly every chapter of the country's long resistance to British rule.

City of Literature

Leaf through literary Dublin

A UNESCO City of Literature, Dublin is the vanguard for Irish writing, superbly covered at the **Museum of Literature Ireland** *(moli.ie; adult/child €14.50/12).* The **James Joyce Centre** *(jamesjoyce.ie; adult/child €7/5)* has evocative exhibits and also leads walking tours of his novels' settings. Overlooking elegant **Merrion Square**, the childhood home of Oscar Wilde is now the **Oscar Wilde House** *(oscarwildehouse.com; tour €25)* with guided tours. And on a two-hour **Dublin Literary Pub Crawl** *(dublinpubcrawl.com; adult/ student €20/18),* actors lead you on a jaunt between pubs associated with famous Dublin writers.

JOYCEAN PILGRIMAGE

Every year on 16 June, fans of James Joyce roam the streets of Dublin in boater hats, round spectacles and petticoats to celebrate Bloomsday, the day on which *Ulysses* is set. When Bloomsday rolls around, there are several performances in tiny **Sweny's Pharmacy**, which is featured in the book and looks exactly as it did in the 1850s. Otherwise, the shop is open year-round, with readings held on Thursday evenings.

The reading room of the **National Library of Ireland** is where Stephen Dedalus mused on Shakespeare in *Ulysses.*

James Joyce was a regular and set a scene from *Dubliners* in the back room of **John Mulligan's** on Poolbeg St, which began life as a spirit grocer's back in 1782 and was licensed as a pub in 1852.

Sláinte! (Cheers)

Dublin's brewing and distilling history

Dublin's most popular attraction is the **Guinness Storehouse** (*guinness-storehouse.com; experiences €26-350*). Seven floors of foam, folklore and flawless pours, it's part brewery, part immersive brand shrine. Toast your visit at the rooftop Gravity Bar, pint in hand, city skyline laid out before you.

Distilling has been revived in the surrounding Liberties neighbourhood in recent years, with **Teeling Distillery** (*teelingwhiskey.com; tours €20-35*), **Pearse Lyons Distillery** (*pearselyonsdistillery.com; tours €22-32*) and **Roe & Co** (*roeandcowhiskey.com; from €25*) in the art deco Guinness Power Station all offering tours and tastings.

If you want to taste a few different spirits and not just one brand, head to the **Irish Whiskey Museum** (*irishwhiskey museum.ie; tours €23-35*) near Trinity College.

Testament to Prehistoric Humankind

Day trip to Newgrange

Located 54km north of central Dublin in County Meath, the vast Neolithic necropolis known as **Brú na Bóinne** (*heritage ireland.ie; tour & Newgrange chamber adult/child €18/12*) is one of the most extraordinary sites in Europe. A thousand years older than Stonehenge and a UNESCO World Heritage site, the complex's tombs were the largest artificial structures in Ireland until the construction of the Anglo-Norman castles 4000 years later. The area consists of many different sites; a startling 80m in diameter and 13m high, **Newgrange's** circular stone ramparts, topped by a grassy dome and fronted by a wall of blazing white quartz, look eerily futuristic. Underneath lies the finest Stone Age passage tomb in Ireland.

Magical Mountain Monastery Ruins

Day trip to Glendalough

Tucked into a narrow valley in the Wicklow Mountains 51km south of central Dublin, **Glendalough** (*glendalough.ie; car park €4*) is one of Ireland's most important early Christian sites. With its stone ruins scattered amid forest and misty lakes, it's not difficult to see why monks came seeking solitude and pine-scented silence. In the late 5th century, St Kevin, a bishop, established a monastery here. The most fascinating ancient structures lie in the lower part of the valley east of the Lower Lake; the Upper Lake has the best scenery. Bring walking boots for its trails.

Kilkenny

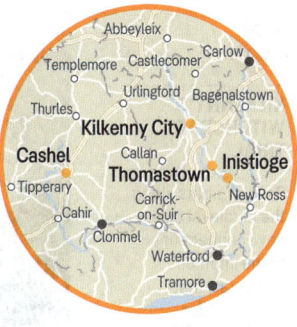

HISTORY | ARCHITECTURE | FESTIVALS

County Kilkenny's centrepiece is its namesake city. Known as the Marble City for its dark, fossil-speckled limestone, it bewitches visitors with medieval alleys winding between a historic cathedral and an imposing castle that fulfils every storybook fantasy of what one should look like, along with craft studios, traditional pubs and glorious riverside walks and cycle trails. Surrounding it, the county too is a delight, a place of rolling hills where tiny roads navigate the valleys alongside trout-filled rivers, moss-covered stone walls, idyllic towns and villages, and relics of centuries of Irish religious history.

Across the border in County Tipperary, Cashel was once the seat of the high kings of the province of Munster. Among the country's most majestic religious sites, the extraordinary Rock of Cashel emerges out of the craggy landscape on a limestone bluff above the Golden Vale. This is one of the most enchanting corners of Ireland's Ancient East.

> ### ☑ TOP TIP
>
> Guided tours give a great insight into Kilkenny city. Options span historian-led **Pat Tynan Kilkenny Walking Tours** *(kilkennywalkingtours.ie)*, craic-filled **Shenanigans** *(shenaniganswalks.com)*, 'Spooktacular' tours of haunted sights with **Kilkenny Ghost Tours** *(kilkennyghosttours. com)*, sunset tours with **Kilkenny Cycling Tours** *(kilkennycyclingtours. com)* and castle-view river cruises with **Boat Trips Kilkenny** *(boattrips.ie)*.

Kilkenny City

Sightseeing along the medieval mile

Kilkenny city's medieval mile connects its major historic sites. Marking its southern end beside the River Nore is **Kilkenny Castle** *(kilkennycastle.ie; self-guided tours adult/child €8/4,*

> ### ⊘ GETTING AROUND
>
> Kilkenny city's centre is easily walkable, though its narrow streets can get crowded. Cycling is an enjoyable option; **Bolt** *(bolt.eu)* has app-based e-bikes, or rent bikes from **Kilkenny Cycling Tours** *(kilkennycyclingtours.com)*.
>
> Located 1.2km northeast of Kilkenny Castle (around a 15-minute walk) across the River
>
> Nore, **MacDonagh Train Station** is on the line from Dublin Heuston south via Thomastown to Waterford city. Cashel is just 60km southwest of Kilkenny city, but there's no direct public transport; you'll need a car, or catch a bus from Cork city (1¾ hours).

St Canice's Cathedral, Kilkenny City

KILKENNY'S WITCHCRAFT TRIAL

Several sights along the medieval mile have connections to the infamous witchcraft trial of Dame Alice Kyteler. In medieval Kilkenny, Dame Alice established **Kytelers Inn** (kytelersinn. com) on St Kieran's St in the early 14th century (it's still full of atmospheric spaces for a pint). After Dame Alice's four wealthy husbands died in mysterious circumstances, she fled Ireland to avoid conviction for witchcraft; in her absence, her maid, Petronella de Meath, was burned at the stake in 1324 just north of St Mary's Church, where Kilkenny's Tholsel (City Hall) was built in 1761. The central tower of St Canice's Cathedral collapsed in 1332 after Dame Alice's son, William, was made to carry out roof repairs as penance.

guided tours €12/6); book tickets up to a week ahead. Dating back to the Anglo-Norman conquest, it was built in stone in 1192 and over the centuries it has undergone successive adaptations; three of its four round towers survive. Strolling its richly decorated rooms, gardens and 21 hectares of public parkland evokes its past. The castle's former stables and coach houses, Castle Yard, is now the **National Design & Craft Gallery** (dcci.ie; free).

Early-13th-century St Mary's Church houses the **Medieval Mile Museum** (medievalmilemuseum.ie; audio tour adult/child €7/3, guided tour €10/5), putting 800 years of city history into context. Artefacts include maces, sceptres, keys, coins, civic records and skeletons. Works are underway to combine it with the adjacent **Tholsel** (City Hall) to create the Museum of Medieval Kilkenny.

Accessed via an arched entry and stone steps, **Butter Slip** is a dark, narrow walkway built in 1616 and once lined with the stalls of butter vendors. To the north, **Rothe House & Garden** (rothehouse.com; self-guided tours adult/child €8.50/4, guided tours €10/6), a Tudor merchant's house, dates from 1594.

St Canice's Cathedral (stcanicescathedral.ie; adult/child €7.50/5, incl guided tour & tower climb €16/9) was built between 1202 and 1285. Rising 30m outside, the remarkably preserved round tower dates from the 9th century. Heading southwest on Abbey St through the **Black Freren Gate** (the medieval

EATING IN KILKENNY CITY: OUR PICKS

Arán Deli & Bakery: This deli/bakery uses great sourdoughs in its gourmet sandwiches, plus savoury and sweet pastries. 7am-3pm Wed-Mon €

Foodworks: In a restored bank, with all-day brunch dishes that incorporate the owners' vegetables, herbs and reared pigs. 8.30am-4pm Wed-Sun €€

Petronella: Modern Irish cuisine in a stone-walled, oak-beamed building on the medieval Butter Slip. noon-2.30pm & 4-9.30pm Tue-Sat, noon-5pm Sun €€€

Campagne: Michelin-starred chef Garrett Byrne creates regional French cuisine from seasonal Irish produce. 5.30-9pm Wed-Sat, 12.30-2.30pm Sun €€€

city walls' only surviving arch), you'll reach the **Black Abbey** *(dominicans.ie; by donation)*, a Dominican priory built in 1225.

Thomastown

Unearth architectural treasures

Thomastown (Baile Mhic Andáin; historically known as Grennan), 17km southeast of Kilkenny city, centres on a quadrant of streets lined by colourfully painted buildings and enticing galleries and cafes. One of the most complete Cistercian abbey ruins in Ireland, the 12th-century **Jerpoint Abbey** *(heritageireland.ie; adult/child €5/3)* lies 2.5km southwest.

Sprawling across a hectare of pastoral landscapes 9km northwest of Jerpoint Abbey, **Kells Priory** *(heritageireland.ie; free)* was founded in 1193. Extensive ruins of this fortified Augustinian monastery remain, including a nave, chancel, chapel, bread oven and mill.

Inistioge

Fall for Inistioge's charms

With its 18th-century, 10-arch stone bridge and central green ringed by churches, cafes and pubs, Inistioge (Inis Tíog), 26km southeast of Kilkenny, is one of Ireland's prettiest villages. Just outside, 1.5km south at **Woodstock Gardens & Arboretum** *(woodstock.ie; per car €5),* 20 hectares of formal and informal gardens have been restored to the Victorian era of 1840 to 1890, with long avenues lined with noble fir and monkey puzzle trees. Foxgloves, lavender and cornflowers on the terraced flower garden are linked to the rose garden by the yew walk.

Cashel

Explore ecclesiastical history

Bristling with medieval towers on a limestone outcrop above green fields, the **Rock of Cashel** *(heritageireland.ie; adult/ child €8/6)* is one of Ireland's most spectacular sights. Sturdy 15th-century walls surround an enclosure containing a 13th-century Gothic cathedral, early-12th-century 28m-tall round tower, and 15th-century choristers' kitchen and dining hall. The highlight is **Cormac's Chapel**, with its beautifully carved doorways and Ireland's only surviving Romanesque frescoes. The best photo opportunities are from the hauntingly beautiful ruins of **Hore Abbey**, 1km west.

KILKENNY FESTIVALS

St Patrick's Festival Kilkenny: Celebrations over four days in March include marching bands, a funfair, fireworks and parade.

Kilkenny Tradfest: This four-day mid-March event has gigs, sessions, workshops and a trad-music trail.

Kilkenny Roots Festival: Bluegrass, swing, folk and Cajun music play during May's four-day fest.

Cat Laughs Comedy Festival: Uproariously funny Irish and international comedians perform over four days in June.

Kilkenny Arts Festival: Over 250 artists perform in more than 150 events at historic venues during August.

Savour Kilkenny: Harvest celebrations in October include cookery demonstrations, market stalls and a craft brewery and distillery marquee.

Yulefest: Winter cheer warms the city from late November to late December.

 DRINKING IN KILKENNY CITY: OUR PICKS

Sullivan's Taproom: Reviving local brewing with its Black Marble Stout, Maltings Red Ale and Irish Gold. Huge beer garden. *noon-11pm Sun-Thu, to 12.30am Fri & Sat*

Tynans Bridge House Bar: Charming former grocery/pub with original timber cabinetry opposite St John's Bridge. *10.30am-11.30pm Sun-Thu, to 12.30am Fri & Sat*

Dylan Whisky Bar: Cosy snugs, old advert-etched mirrors, open turf fire and tasting flights from its 200-strong whiskey collection. *5pm-midnight Mon-Fri, from 3pm Sat & Sun*

Left Bank: In an 1870s Bank of Ireland building, with nine bars, regular live music, a heated courtyard and 1st-floor nightclub. *noon-11pm Sun-Thu, to 2am Fri & Sat*

Cork

FOOD & DRINK | HISTORY | WILD COASTLINE

Ireland's second city, Cork – a thriving metropolis made glorious by location and its almost Rabelaisian devotion to the finer things in life – has an understated confidence grounded in its plethora of food markets and an ever-evolving cast of creative eateries, and in its selection of pubs, entertainment and cultural pursuits including copious festivals.

Surrounding it is an undulating landscape dotted with charming villages. The country's largest county, Cork can fairly lay claim to being the nation's food and drink capital, with lush pastures and coastal fishing fleets, as well as 60% of the country's artisan producers located here – traditional cheesemakers, craft bakers, boutique coffee roasters... Seafood-famed Kinsale is the gateway to the 2500km-long Wild Atlantic Way; heading west, narrow roads wind around rugged, rock-girt coastlines and pass through a dozen or more old fishing villages where boats bob at their moorings and harbourside bars entice you in for a pint.

Cork City

Enter a Victorian prison

Behind towering walls dating from 1818, the imposing **Cork City Gaol** (*corkcitygaol.com; adult/child €11/7, audio guide or guided tour extra €2*) received its first inmates in 1824. Poverty was the most common crime, especially during the desperate

---

GETTING AROUND

Cork city's centre can be explored on foot; there's also a network of buses. **Kent Train Station** has frequent services via Midleton and Fota to Cobh, useful for day trips in either direction. No trains serve the west of the county; you have to go by car or bus. Regular buses run from Cork city to destinations including Kinsale.

A car is pretty much essential for exploring away from the main towns. Major car rental companies are located at **Cork Airport**, 8km south of the city. Avoid city-centre parking problems by using **Black Ash Park & Ride** on the South City Link Rd.

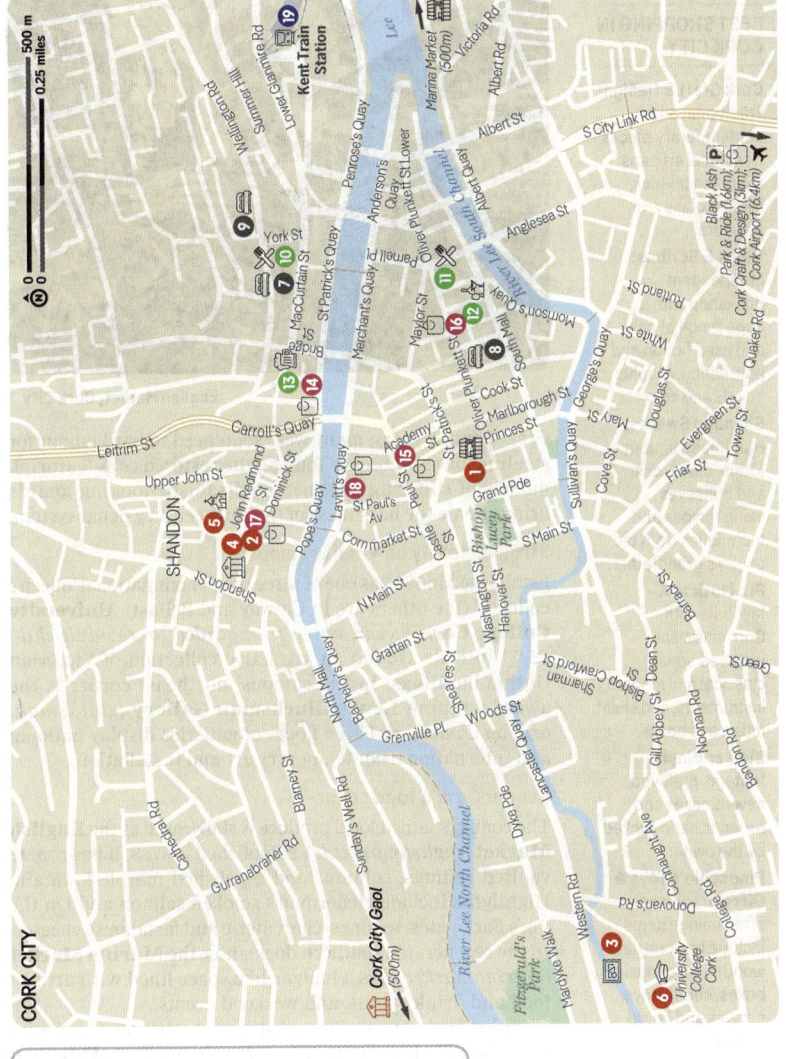

CORK CITY

SIGHTS
see 4 Cork Butter Museum
1 English Market
2 Firkin Crane
3 Lewis Glucksman Gallery
4 Old Butter Market
5 St Anne's Church
6 University College Cork

SLEEPING
7 Hotel Isaacs
8 Imperial Hotel
9 Sheila's Hostel

EATING
10 Glass Curtain
11 Market Lane

DRINKING & NIGHTLIFE
12 Crane Lane Theatre
13 Sin É

SHOPPING
14 Bunker Vinyl
15 Pinocchio's Toys & Gifts
16 Pro Musica
17 Shandon Sweets
18 Vibes & Scribes

TRANSPORT
19 Kent Train Station

BEST SHOPPING IN CORK CITY

Cork Craft & Design: Traditional and contemporary pieces from local artisans including textiles, framed glass and furniture.

Vibes & Scribes: Independent bookshop with a huge range of new and used fiction and non-fiction, graphic novels and comics.

Shandon Sweets: Handmade liquorice, fudge, clove rocks and bullseyes using recipes and techniques from the owner's grandfather.

Pro Musica: A favourite with Cork musicians, with traditional, classical and modern instruments, and sheet music and books.

Bunker Vinyl: Vintage, preloved, new releases and reissues hand-picked by the owner.

Pinocchio's Toys & Gifts: Traditional, often unique items include baby rattles, wooden toys, music boxes, cuddly toys, puzzles and board games.

English Market, Cork City

Great Famine years; many were sentenced to hard labour for stealing loaves of bread. Touring the restored cells featuring models of suffering prisoners and sadistic-looking guards brings home the harshness of the 19th-century penal system.

Stroll a stately university campus

Established in 1845 as one of three nondenominational 'queen's colleges' (the others are in Galway and Belfast), **University College Cork** *(ucc.ie; entry free; guided tours adult/child €5/3)* spreads around an attractive collection of Victorian Gothic buildings. In the campus' northeast corner is the award-winning **Lewis Glucksman Gallery** *(glucksman. org; by donation)*. Three floors of galleries display national and international contemporary art and installation.

Savour Cork's food scene

The county's famed local produce is showcased at the **English Market** *(englishmarket.ie)*. Established in 1788, it has ornate vaulted ceilings, columns and a polished marble fountain. Highlights include Hederman's smoked salmon and On the Pig's Back patés, terrines, charcuterie and farmhouse cheeses. In the regenerated southern docklands, the **Marina Market** *(marinamarket.ie)* is a hangar-like space lined with artisan food and drink stands, and weekend events.

Guided food tours visiting producers throughout the city include Cork Tasting Trails (2½ to three hours) from **Fab Food Trails** *(fabfoodtrails.ie; €80)* and the Cork Culinary Tour (three hours) from **Bonner Travel** *(bonner-travel.com; €130)*.

 EATING & DRINKING IN CORK CITY: OUR PICKS

Market Lane: Bright bistro with a hearty menu reflecting what's fresh at the English Market. *noon-9.30pm Sun-Wed, to 10pm Thu & Fri, to 10.30pm Sat* €€

Glass Curtain: Contemporary Irish cuisine like lamb belly with black garlic and whey, in a 19th-century bakery. *5.30-10.30pm Tue-Thu, from 5pm Fri & Sat* €€€

Crane Lane Theatre: Three bars, a covered laneway beer garden, roaring 1920s decor, live bands from jazz and bluegrass to rock plus DJ sets. *4pm-2.30am*

Sin É: A true craic-filled pub, long on atmosphere and short on pretension, with live music almost every night. *12.30-11.30pm Sun-Thu, to 12.30am Fri & Sat*

In Cork pubs, locally brewed Murphy's and Beamish stouts, not Guinness, are the preferred pints.

Ring the Shandon bells

Overlooking the city centre, hillside Shandon (from the Irish Sean Dún, meaning 'old fort') is an atmospheric spot to wander. Built in 1855, the large, circular **Firkin Crane** *(firkincrane. ie)* is where Cork's butter was weighed and packed for export; it now houses a dance centre. Neoclassical columns adorn the facade of the **Old Butter Market**; the trade's history is told at the adjacent **Cork Butter Museum** *(thebuttermuseum. com; adult/child €5/1.50)*.

Shandon is dominated by the 1722 **St Anne's Church** *(stan neshandon.ie; church €3, incl tower climb adult/child €9/5)*; on the tower's 1st floor, aspiring campanologists can ring the **Shandon Bells** then continue up the 132 steps to the top for 360-degree views of the city.

Kinsale

Tour Kinsale's picturesque harbour

Kinsale (Cionn tSáile), 25km south of Cork city, is one of many colourful gems strung along County Cork's coastline. Guarded by a huge 17th-century fortress, the star-shaped artillery **Charles Fort** *(heritageireland.ie; adult/child €5/3)*, its narrow, winding streets are lined with galleries, lively bars and superb seafood eateries.

Discover the history of the town by joining Dermot Ryan of **Kinsale Heritage Town Walks** *(kinsaleheritage.com; adult/child €5/free)* for a one-hour walking tour. To get out on the water, take a one-hour boat trip of the harbour with **Kinsale Harbour Cruises** *(kinsaleharbourcruises.com; adult/child €15/7)* or a two-hour open-topped adventure boat trip with **Kinsale Sea Safari** *(kinsaleseasafari.ie; €53)*.

Cobh

Contemplate Cobh's Titanic heritage

Cobh (pronounced 'cove'), 23km east of Cork city, is dotted with brightly coloured houses and overlooked by the single-spire, Gothic Revival–style **St Colman's Cathedral** *(cobhcathed ralparish.ie; by donation)*.

This was the final port of call for RMS *Titanic* in 1912. The original White Star Line offices on Cobh's waterfront, where passengers embarked, now house the poignant **Titanic Experience Cobh** *(titanicexperiencecobh.ie; adult/child €13/9)*; guided tours provide an insight into the ill-fated liner's first and final voyage.

Sail to a prison island

Clearly visible offshore, **Spike Island** *(spikeislandcork.ie; adult/child incl ferry & guided tour €27.95/14.95)* lies low and green in Cork Harbour, topped by a huge 18th-century artillery fort that commanded the harbour entrance. During the Irish War of Independence and from 1984 to 2004, it served as a prison, gaining the nickname 'Ireland's Alcatraz'.

THE GREAT FAMINE

The Great Famine of 1845–52 remains Ireland's greatest national tragedy. With farmers already crippled by repressive Penal Laws, when a blight hit potato crops, prices soared. Most tenants fell into arrears and were evicted or sent to the dire conditions of the workhouses. Yet Ireland was forced to export its food to Britain. Lord Dufferin and GF Boyle, who journeyed from Oxford to Skibbereen in 1847 to see if reports of the Famine were true, reported: 'The accounts are not exaggerated – they cannot be exaggerated – nothing more frightful can be conceived'. The Poor Law deemed landlords responsible for the maintenance of their poor and encouraged many to 'remove' tenants from their estates by paying their way to America aboard the scourged 'coffin ships'.

Kerry

SCENERY | OUTDOOR ACTIVITIES | HISTORY

☑ **TOP TIP**

Kerry's standout sight, Skellig Michael, needs to be booked well in advance but sea crossings can be cancelled at short notice due to bad weather, so have a plan B just in case.

County Kerry (Irish: Chiarraí) contains some of Ireland's most iconic scenery: surf-pounded sea cliffs, soft golden strands, emerald-green farmland stitched by stone walls, mist-shrouded bogs and mountain peaks. Offshore, the jagged, improbable outpost of Skellig Michael is one of the Republic's two UNESCO World Heritage sites.

With one of the country's finest national parks as its backyard, the lively tourism hub of Killarney spills over with colourful shops, restaurants and pubs with spirited trad music. The town is the jumping-off point for the famed Ring of Kerry driving route, which skirts the Iveragh Peninsula, with photo-worthy views at every twist and turn.

To Killarney's north, the Dingle Peninsula is like a condensed version of its southern neighbour, with the Slea Head Drive linking ancient prehistoric ring forts, beehive huts, Christian sites and sandy beaches looping from the charming fishing port of Dingle, renowned for its seafood, traditional culture and music-filled pubs.

Killarney National Park

Clip-clop in a jaunting car

Traditional horse-drawn jaunting cars provide tours from Killarney town to Ross Castle and Muckross Estate, complete

---

 GETTING AROUND

County Kerry covers a large area, much of it mountainous and remote, with narrow winding roads. Rail is more useful for getting to Kerry from Dublin or Cork than getting around. Regular bus services run from Killarney to Kerry Airport, and from Killarney to Dingle town.

Local minibuses serve the Ring of Kerry and Dingle Peninsula though services can be infrequent, so a car is preferable. Find car rental outlets in Killarney and at Kerry Airport. Bicycles are ideal for exploring the Killarney region; try your accommodation or **Killarney Rent A Bike** (killarneyrentabike.com).

Gap of Dunloe (p631), Killarney National Park

with amusing commentary from the 'jarvey' (driver). Cars typically fit up to four people; expect to pay around €20 per person for a one-hour tour. Pick them up at Kenmare Pl or book tours online with companies such as fifth-generation-run **Killarney Jaunting Cars** *(killarneyjauntingcars.com)*.

Explore Muckross Estate

The impressive Victorian mansion of **Muckross House** *(muck ross-house.ie; adult/child house & farms €16/10, house or farms only €9/6)* was built as a hunting and fishing lodge for the Herbert family in 1843. Sloping down to the Middle Lake, beautiful **Muckross Gardens** are free to explore. Also here are three recreations of 1930s **Muckross Traditional Farms** (closed November to February).

Visit Ross Castle

A lovely 2.6km walk or bike ride southwest of Killarney town's St Mary's Cathedral pedestrian entrance through the park (you might spot deer along the way), **Ross Castle** *(heritageireland. ie; adult/child €5/3)* is a traditional tower house and keep from the 15th century, when it's thought to have been built by Irish chieftain O'Donoghue Mór. Entertaining 45-minute guided tours provide an easily digested medieval history lesson.

KILLARNEY TOWN'S TOURISM EVOLUTION

Set amid lakes, waterfalls and woodland beneath heather-clad peaks, Killarney town is the natural base camp for excursions into the neighbouring national park. In the business of welcoming visitors since 1747, when Thomas Browne (fourth Viscount Kenmare) tapped into its tourism potential, followed by the railway's arrival in 1853 and the 2014 launch of the Wild Atlantic Way, the town is a well-oiled tourism machine, with competition keeping standards high. Green initiatives, such as the 2023 ban on single-use coffee cups (BYO or pay a €2 deposit for a reusable 2GoCup), and the Killarney Hotels Sustainability Charter (eliminating single-use items, reducing properties' carbon footprints, minimising food waste and using local suppliers) are paving the way for its sustainable future.

 EATING IN KILLARNEY TOWN: OUR PICKS

Lir Café: Brews some of Killarney's best coffee; the food spans toasties, pastries, cakes and handmade chocolates. *7am-7pm* €

Mad Monk: Fresh seafood from its own fishing fleet with hand-cut chips in a bright, bare-brick space. *12.30-8.30pm Sun-Thu, to 9pm Fri & Sat* €€

Cronin's Restaurant: Kerry produce includes Skellig prawns, Kenmare salmon and MacGillycuddy Reeks venison. *4-9.30pm Mon-Fri, from 3pm Sat & Sun* €€

Brícín: Charmer with antique lamps, stained glass and vintage art; try the house-speciality boxty (potato pancake). *6-9.30pm Tue-Sat* €€

RING OF KERRY ROAD TRIP

This circuit of the Iveragh Peninsula winds past pretty villages, pristine beaches, craggy mountains and sparkling loughs, with views of the island-dotted Atlantic.

START	END	LENGTH
Killarney	Killarney	170km; 1 day

South of Killarney, the summit of the narrow pass known as **①** **Moll's Gap** is worth a stop for the great views towards the Gap of Dunloe and breakfast at Avoca Cafe. The N71 road descends via swooping bends to **②** **Kenmare**, with a neat triangle of streets lined with craft shops, art galleries and cafes. West on the N70, the pretty village of **③** **Sneem** is split by a river, with a picturesque waterfall tumbling below the old stone bridge.

The coastal scenery ramps into overdrive as the road winds over the hill to tiny **④** **Caherdaniel**, hidden among the trees at Derrynane Bay. A short detour leads to beautiful Derrynane Beach.

The N70 now climbs high above the sea, passing Beenarourke viewpoint, with grandstand views over scattered islands, before descending to the old-fashioned seaside (and golf) resort of **⑤** **Waterville**. Stay on the N70 (or detour via the Skellig Ring before continuing north) to **⑥** **Cahersiveen**, the main town on the Ring and home to the excellent Old Barracks heritage centre.

Follow the N70 to the family-favourite, recreated 19th-century **⑦** **Kerry Bog Village** museum, with the thatched homes of the turfcutter, blacksmith, thatcher and labourer, and a dairy, and meet Kerry bog ponies. Continue on the N70 to Killorglin, then the N72 back to Killarney.

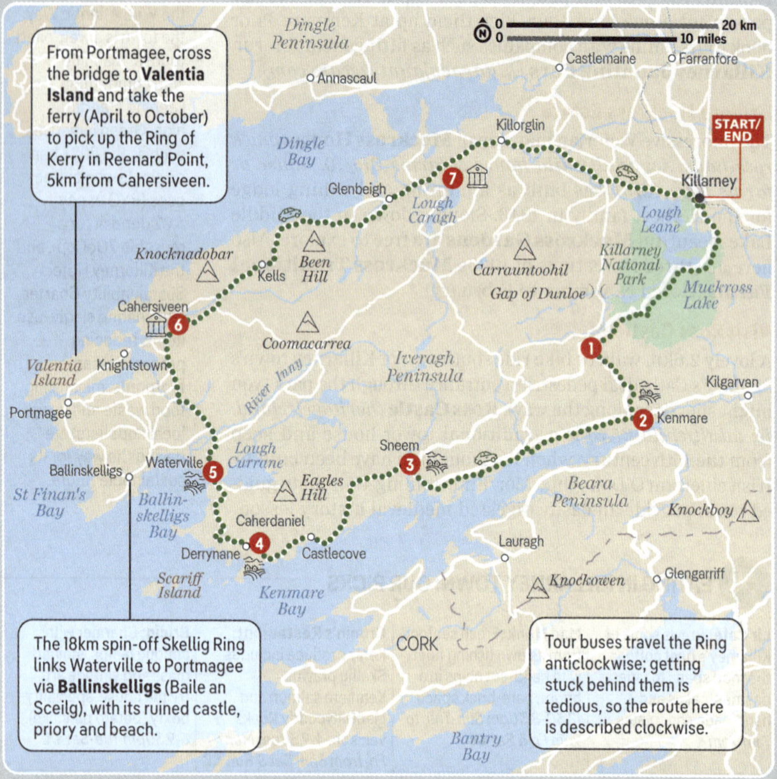

From Portmagee, cross the bridge to **Valentia Island** and take the ferry (April to October) to pick up the Ring of Kerry in Reenard Point, 5km from Cahersiveen.

The 18km spin-off Skellig Ring links Waterville to Portmagee via **Ballinskelligs** (Baile an Sceilg), with its ruined castle, priory and beach.

Tour buses travel the Ring anticlockwise; getting stuck behind them is tedious, so the route here is described clockwise.

Killarney Lake Tours *(killarneylaketours.ie; waterbus adult/child €15/10)* departs out front, and traditional **open boats** *(€15/10)* nearby at **Reen Pier**.

The Gap of Dunloe by boat and bike

A boat trip across the lakes followed by a bike ride through the mountain scenery of the **Gap of Dunloe** is the classic Killarney experience; organise it with your accommodation or book online at **Gap of Dunloe Tours** *(gapofdunloetours.com)*. Boats depart from Reen Pier at 11am, with bikes propped in the bow for the 1½-hour cruise. Disembarking at 19th-century hunting lodge **Lord Brandon's Cottage**, the cycling section begins with a 4.5km climb to the head of the Gap; at the summit, you're rewarded with stunning views back to the Upper Lake and forward into the narrow pass of the Gap itself, a wild and scenic glaciated valley. The total distance cycled is 23km. Allowing for stops, you should be back in Killarney by 3.30pm.

Skellig Islands

Voyage to a remote island monastery

The jagged, 217m-high rock of **Skellig Michael** *(Sceilg Mhichíl; heritageireland.ie; landing tour/non-landing ecotour per person from €130/50)* rises dramatically out of the sea 11.5km off the coast, topped with the remains of an early Christian monastery that famously featured in two *Star Wars* movies. Reached by 618 steps cut into the steep rockface (no handrails), the 6th-century monastery is a miracle of masonry, set on platforms built on the vertiginous slope using nothing more than drystone walls and earth. Birdlife includes puffins from around April to early August.

Landing tours (around five hours) usually run from mid-May to September, weather permitting; dates and tour-boat permits are announced each year. Most boats depart from Portmagee. Numbers are limited, so book well ahead (landings are still subject to conditions on the day). Children must be over 12.

Dingle

Discover the Slea Head Drive

Beyond Dingle town, the peninsula's scenery goes into overdrive. The 42km **Slea Head Drive** passes through the villages of Ventry, Dunquin and Ballyferriter, taking in a host of superbly preserved structures from the ancient past including beehive huts, ring forts, inscribed stones and early Christian sites. Allow at least half a day.

PÁIRC NÁISIÚNTA NA MARA, CIARRAÍ

Known by its Irish name **Páirc Náisiúnta na Mara, Ciarraí** *(nationalparks.ie/mara-ciarrai)*, the **Kerry Seas National Park** became Ireland's first marine national park when it was officially designated in April 2024. Centred around the Dingle Peninsula, its 290 sq km take in islands off the Kerry coast (including Skellig Michael), offshore marine reefs (notably the deep limestone Kerry Head Shoal), and coastal mainland sites such as the fore dunes and fixed dunes at **Inch** (both a Special Area of Conservation and a Special Protection Area), **Mt Brandon** uplands and the peninsula's spectacular **Connor Pass**. The park's coast is home to seabird colonies including puffins, storm petrels and Manx shearwaters, with other bird species including gannets, fulmars, kittiwakes, guillemots and razorbills.

 DRINKING IN DINGLE TOWN: OUR PICKS

Foxy John's: This classic Dingle shop-pub stocks stout and whiskey. *10.30am-11.30pm Mon-Thu, to 12.30am Fri & Sat, noon-11.30pm Sun*

Dick Mack's: Snugs inside, tables in the courtyard, plus the pub's own craft beers from its restored 19th-century brewhouse. *noon-11pm*

Curran's: Shop-pub with original stained-glass snugs; regular spontaneous trad sessions. *noon-11.30pm Sun-Thu, to 12.30am Fri & Sat*

John Benny's: Local musos pour in most nights for trad sessions at this stone-floored pub. *11.30am-11.30pm Tue-Thu & Sun, to 12.30am Fri & Sat*

Galway

MUSIC | FOOD & DRINK | SCENERY

 TOP TIP

Numerous companies offer day trips from Galway city to highlights of Galway's Connemara region like Kylemore Abbey, Clare's Cliffs of Moher and Burren National Park in Clare, and the ancient, starkly beautiful Aran Islands (a geological extension of the Burren), off the coast of both counties. Try **Lally Tours** (lallytours.com).

The halfway point of the weaving 2500km Wild Atlantic Way, County Galway's exuberant namesake city is a swirl of colourful shop-lined streets filled with buskers and performance artists and enticing old pubs that hum with trad-music sessions, hosting some 120 festivals held throughout the year.

Some of Ireland's most spellbinding scenery fans out from Galway's city limits, particularly in the breathtaking Connemara region, where tiny roads wander along a coastline studded with islands, dazzling white-sand beaches and intriguing villages; the interior shelters heath-strewn boglands, glassy lakes, looming mountains and isolated valleys. Stone walls and sheep are always on the horizon.

To Galway's south are the windswept landscapes of County Clare, including the ocean-pounded coast, eroding rock into fantastic formations, sea stacks and sheer precipices including those at the Cliffs of Moher and the moonscape-like bare limestone Burren, together forming a UNESCO Global Geopark.

Galway City

Take a traditional music pub crawl

For the best of Galway's toe-tapping tunes, head to the **Latin Quarter**, named for the city's historic trading links with Spain and Portugal.

GETTING AROUND

Galway city is well connected with other major towns by both bus and train. Bus Éireann has limited services in most of Connemara. Driving is the best way to explore, getting you to remote spots. Fuel up in larger towns when you can. If you're driving from County Kerry, stop off in Clare en route to Galway.

Galway's city centre is easily explored on foot. Buy a Visitor Leap Card to save up to 30% on fares. Use the Coca-Cola bike-share scheme to get around the city. A bus connects Shannon Airport to Galway city.

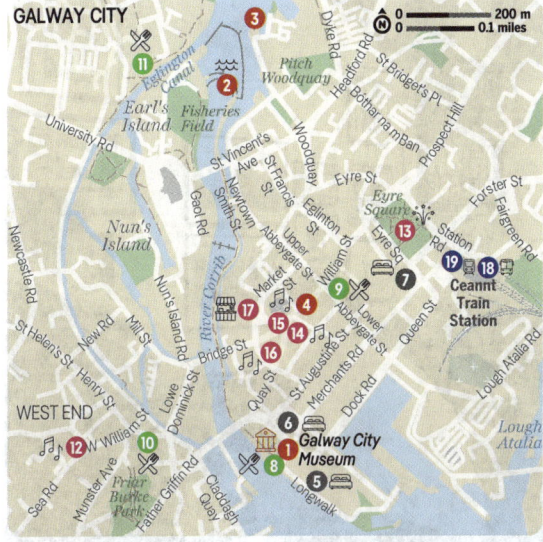

GALWAY CITY

HIGHLIGHTS
1 Galway City Museum

SIGHTS
2 Salmon Weir

ACTIVITIES
3 Corrib Princess
4 Galway Food Tours

SLEEPING
5 Heron's Rest

6 House Hotel
7 Kinlay Hostel

EATING
8 Ard Bia at Nimmo's
9 Food for Thought
10 Oscars Seafood Bistro
11 Sult

ENTERTAINMENT
12 Crane Bar

13 Galway Christmas Market
14 Taaffes Bar
15 Tig Cóilí
16 Tigh Neachtain

SHOPPING
17 Galway Market

TRANSPORT
18 Bus Éireann
19 Train Station

The fire-engine-red **Tig Cóilí** (*tigchoiligalway.com*) is a favourite among local musicians. This atmospheric gem hosts two evening trad sessions, usually around 6pm and 9.30pm. **Taaffe's** (*taaffesbar.ie*) is across the road, popular with locals and GAA sports fans. Heading down to Quay St, you'll find family-run **Tigh Neachtain** (*tighneachtain.com*), founded in 1894, the heart of the Galway music scene.

Cross the Wolfe Tone Bridge to the West End, where the **Crane Bar** (*thecranebar.com*) holds nightly Irish music sessions.

Board a boat for Lough Corrib

Join a 90-minute cruise aboard the open-top **Corrib Princess** (*corribprincess.ie; adult/child €20/10*) passing ruined castles along the River Corrib en route to the Republic's largest lake – Lough Corrib, the haunt of herons, swans and, if you're lucky, leaping salmon. From May to September, there are two or three departures daily from Woodquay, just north of the **Salmon Weir**.

GALWAY CITY'S BEST FESTIVALS

Cúirt International Festival of Literature: April sees one of Ireland's premier literary festivals, featuring a week of talks, interviews, poetry sessions and readings.

Blas na Bealtaine: 'A Taste of May' is a month-long celebration of Galway's culinary scene including farm tours, foraging, cookery demos and more.

Galway International Arts Festival: The biggest event on the calendar is held in late July, a two-week fiesta of theatre, comedy, music and art.

Galway Races: A week of horse racing begins on the last Monday in July, drawing tens of thousands of punters.

Galway International Oyster & Seafood Festival: Going strong since 1954, the world's oldest oyster festival takes place over the last weekend in September.

ROBERT ORMEROD/LONELY PLANET

Crane Bar (p633), Galway City

Dip into Galway's colourful past

Exhibits at the modern **Galway City Museum** *(galwaycity museum.ie; free),* by the Spanish Arch, engagingly convey the city's archaeological, political, cultural and social history. Look out for the Galway hooker fishing boat suspended from the ceiling, and gold Claddagh ring dating from around 1700.

Catch the weekend markets

Galway's bohemian spirit comes alive at its **markets**. Saturdays and Sundays from 8am to 6pm are the standout for food, when farmers and fisherfolk sell fresh produce alongside stalls selling flowers, arts, crafts and street food; buskers add to the festive atmosphere. Additional markets take place from noon to 6pm daily in July and August, and there's an atmospheric **Christmas Market** from 14 to 24 December.

Galway's gastronomic delights

From Michelin-star dining to the freshest fish and chips, Galway's food scene runs the gamut. Book an outing with

 EATING IN GALWAY CITY: OUR PICKS

Ard Bia at Nimmo's: Long-established cafe-restaurant beside the Spanish Arch, working with local producers. *10am-3pm daily, 6-9pm Tue-Sun* €€

Food for Thought: Good-value organic, vegetarian and vegan sandwiches and wholesome lunch dishes. *8am-5pm Mon-Sat, noon-3.30pm Sun* €

Oscars Seafood Bistro: Outstanding West End restaurant helmed by cookbook author Michael O'Meara. *6-9pm Tue-Thu, to 9.30pm Fri & Sat* €€€

Sult: Riverside cafe-bar-restaurant on Galway University campus, with prices half of those in city centre. *8.30am-8pm Mon-Fri* €

Galway Food Tours *(galwayfoodtours.com; per person €90)* to sample everything from local oysters and craft beers to artisan cheese and chocolate.

Connemara

Ramble in Connemara National Park

Connemara National Park, once part of the privately owned Kylemore Estate, opened to the public in 1980. Set in the northern part of County Galway, near the village of Letterfrack, it encompasses 20 sq km of mountain, bog, heath and woodland, showing off the region's wild, rugged landscape at its best, and is home to rare plant species, wild red deer and Connemara ponies. Park rangers lead free guided walks from the **Connemara National Park Visitor Centre** *(nationalparks.ie; free)*. Pick up free trail maps here and check out the exhibits describing the peatland landscape and conservation projects.

Tour postcard-perfect Kylemore Abbey

Perched photogenically on the shores of Pollacapall Lough, 4km east of Letterfrack, the crenelated neo-Gothic **Kylemore Abbey** *(kylemoreabbey.com; adult/child €18/free)* looks like a scene from a fairy tale. Mitchell Henry, the son of a wealthy cotton merchant, originally built this 19th-century structure as a country house, then called Kylemore Castle. In 1920, the castle was purchased by a community of Benedictine nuns, becoming the first Benedictine abbey in Ireland. A pleasant 20-minute walk or a free shuttle-bus ride west, past little Maladrolaun Lake, is an extravagant Victorian walled garden.

Cruise Killary Harbour

Slicing 16km inland and more than 45m deep in the centre, Killary Harbour is strikingly scenic and often referred to as Ireland's only fjord. The small village of Leenane sits on its southern shore, nestled among the Mweelrea, Devilsmother and Maamturk Mountains. Hop aboard the catamaran operated by **Killary Fjord Boat Tours** *(killaryfjord.ie; adult/child €27/free)* for a 90-minute cruise along the harbour to Barna island and back; keep your eyes peeled for dolphins.

Set out on Clifden's Sky Road

A definitive stop on any tour of Connemara, Clifden (An Clochán, meaning 'stepping stone') is an appealingly picturesque Victorian-era market town presiding over the head of the narrow bay where the River Owenglin tumbles into the sea. Its triangle of central streets is home to a colourful collection of craft shops, galleries, designer boutiques and lively pubs. The 20km scenic **Sky Road** loop drive starts and ends here.

Cliffs of Moher

Feel the sea spray from Ireland's famous cliffs

Rising to a height of 203m in a series of receding headlands, the Cliffs of Moher are the most popular sight outside Dublin (with crowds to match). One of Ireland's most important

BURREN & CLIFFS OF MOHER GEOPARK

The geology that underlies the rugged scenery of the Burren and the Cliffs of Moher is protected as a UNESCO **Global Geopark** *(burrengeopark. ie)*. During the Carboniferous period 350 million years ago, this whole area lay at the bottom of a warm, shallow sea. The remains of coral and shells fell to the sea bed, then coastal river deltas dumped sand, silt and mud on top. Time and pressure turned the sediments to stone, with fossil-rich limestone below and stratified shale and sandstone above, while continental collisions tilted and folded the rock layers. As you travel south, you move from the limestone landscapes of the Burren into the overlying shale and siltstones exposed in the Cliffs of Moher.

CLADDAGH RINGS

Proudly adorning fingers around the world, the Claddagh ring is traditionally a symbol of love. The two open hands represent friendship and hold a heart that signifies love. They're topped by a crown of loyalty. Traditionally, how you wore the ring would indicate your relationship status.

Single: On your right hand, with the point of the heart facing your fingers and away from your heart.

In a relationship: On your right hand, with the point of the heart pointing at your wrist and heart.

Engaged: On your left hand, with the point of the heart facing your fingers.

Married: On your left hand, with the point of the heart facing your wrist.

Burren National Park

seabird-nesting sites, the vertical, west-facing cliffs are home to more than 35 species including the mainland's largest colony of puffins on the grass-topped promontory below O'Brien's Tower viewpoint. Sunsets are spectacular.

Cut into the hillside, the state-of-the-art **Cliffs of Moher Visitor Centre** *(cliffsofmoher.ie; parking at gate/booked online €15/8, cyclists & pedestrians free)* has engaging exhibitions on the cliffs' fauna, flora, geology and climate.

Burren National Park

Hike in the Burren National Park

The Burren National Park protects 15 sq km of limestone landscapes centred on the small hills of Mullaghmore (191m) and Slieve Roe, whose dramatic scenery and rare flora are emblematic of the greater Burren region that covers some 360 sq km. Hiking details and a free shuttle bus to the trailhead are available from the **National Park Information Point** *(nationalparks.ie)* in Corofin.

No matter when you visit the Burren, wildflowers are in bloom. The region supports an incredibly diverse range of flora, with more than 70% of Ireland's 900 native species and many of the country's native orchids.

THE GUIDE

IRELAND BELFAST

Belfast

HISTORY | CULTURE | LANDSCAPES

The capital of Northern Ireland and gateway to its spectacular landscapes, beaches and dramatic natural features, Belfast has transformed into a modern city with a thriving cultural life and arts scene. Belfast today is a different city from the Belfast of the Troubles (from the late 1960s until the signing of the Good Friday Agreement of 1998). Though political tensions remain, the years of paramilitary campaigns and sectarian violence have been left in the past. Over recent years, Belfast has also emerged as a major film and TV production destination, beginning with blockbuster series *Game of Thrones*. Since then, the filming of further productions has helped rebrand Belfast as a 21st-century city. But history is rarely far from mind here. The murals of West Belfast reflect issues of national identity at the root of the conflict. Meanwhile, no visitor to Belfast leaves without learning about the Belfast-built liner *Titanic*.

☑ TOP TIP

For a scenic walk or bike ride from Belfast's leafy Queen's Quarter, stroll or cycle through the Botanic Gardens to Stranmillis Embankment, then follow the path north for 3km along the west bank of the Lagan to reach Queen's Bridge, just east of the city centre.

Historic Landmarks

Public buildings, public house and markets

Opposite the 1895-built **Grand Opera House** *(goh.co.uk),* the **Crown Liquor Saloon** *(nicholsonspubs.co.uk)* is a historical monument decorated with ornate tiles and a crown mosaic at the entrance.

Belfast's architectural centrepiece is the council's domed, Renaissance-style **City Hall** *(belfastcity.gov.uk; tours adult/*

GETTING AROUND

Belfast is small and easy to navigate. The city centre, Cathedral Quarter and Titanic Quarter are best tackled on foot, while buses and trains link the centre with neighbourhoods further afield. The city's cycling network includes a number of traffic-free stretches;

bikes can be rented through the Belfast Bikes bike-share scheme.

From the Laganside Bus Centre, Goldliner bus 221 runs via the world's oldest whiskey distillery at **Bushmills** to the Giant's Causeway (1½ hours).

CAVE HILL HISTORY

Evidence suggests that people lived on **Cave Hill** as far back as the Stone Age: a stone cairn on the summit dates from the Neolithic period (4500–2500 BCE). Flint arrowheads from the period have also been discovered nearby; they can be seen in **Belfast Castle**.

There are several *ráths* (defensive earthen ring forts) dating from early Christian times (400–1200 CE), including **McArt's Fort**, on a high rocky outcrop. It was here that members of the United Irishmen looked down over the city in 1795 and pledged to fight for Irish independence.

Between 1840 and 1896, limestone was extracted from Cave Hill for use in the shipping industry. You can see the remains of a limestone quarry on the hills southern slopes.

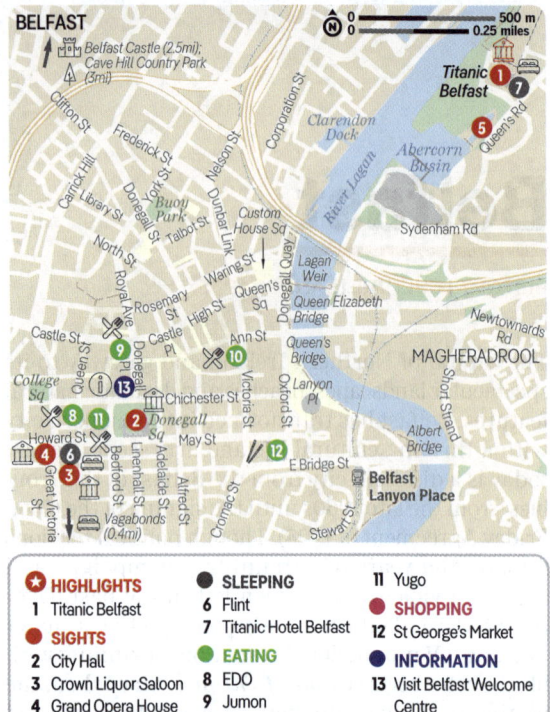

⭐ **HIGHLIGHTS**	⚫ **SLEEPING**	11 Yugo
1 Titanic Belfast	6 Flint	🔴 **SHOPPING**
🔴 **SIGHTS**	7 Titanic Hotel Belfast	12 St George's Market
2 City Hall	🟢 **EATING**	🔵 **INFORMATION**
3 Crown Liquor Saloon	8 EDO	13 Visit Belfast Welcome
4 Grand Opera House	9 Jumon	Centre
5 SS Nomadic	10 Pocket	

child £6/free), with stained-glass windows, Greek columns and Italian marble, visitable on 45-minute tours.

Housed in a Victorian-era building with sandstone porticos and a glazed roof, **St George's Market** *(belfastcity.gov.uk)* has live music and food, drink, antiques and craft stalls on market days (Friday to Sunday).

Titanic Quarter Icon

Learn about the Titanic

The shipyards where the *Titanic* was built are now part of the redeveloped Titanic Quarter. At the head of the slipway is **Titanic Belfast** *(titanicbelfast.com; incl SS Nomadic adult/child £26.95/13),* a state-of-the-art multimedia exhibition that charts the liner's history from its construction to its launch, fit-out and ill-fated maiden voyage. Highlights include a high-tech ride through a noisy, smells-and-all recreation of the city's shipyard, and the Belfast-built **SS Nomadic** *(nomadicbelfast.com),* the last remaining vessel of the White Star Line.

Belfast Backstories

Political murals and a Victorian prison

West Belfast developed with the linen mills that propelled the city into late-19th-century prosperity. It was an area of

Titanic Belfast

low-cost, working-class housing where sectarian divisions became yet more entrenched from the early 1970s, as paramilitary groups ramped up their campaigns. These days the area is safe and visitors are welcome.

Black taxi tours of West Belfast's murals stop to see the Solidarity Wall, the Bobby Sands mural and the murals of the Shankill. The **Visit Belfast** *(visitbelfast.com)* tourist information office on Donegall Sq can arrange a one- to two-hour **black taxi tour** *(for 2 people around £70)* with local cabbies.

In the Footsteps of Giants

Explore a geological phenomenon

Equally exhilarating when cloaked in mist or bathed in sunshine, the **Giant's Causeway** *(nationaltrust.org.uk; causeway free, visitor centre incl parking adult/child £15/7.50)* is a UNESCO World Heritage wonder. Uneven stacks of over 40,000 hexagonal basalt columns along the water's edge form a causeway that inspired the legend that the stones were put in place by a giant. From the **visitor centre**, it's a gentle 10- to 15-minute walk (or £1 shuttle-bus ride) downhill to the Causeway itself, where you can walk out onto the stones.

 EATING IN BELFAST: BRUNCH & SMALL PLATES

Yugo: Asian fusion dishes in an industrial-style dining room. Sit at the counter to watch the chefs at work. *5-9pm Tue, noon-2.45pm & 5-9.30pm Wed-Sat* ££

Pocket: Creative brunch dishes (like the excellent Ulster Fry), speciality coffee and booze. *8am-3pm Mon-Thu, to 4pm Fri & Sat, 8.30am-4pm Sun* ££

Jumon: Vegan/vegetarian Southeast Asian fusion; has an upbeat atmosphere and wall murals. *5-10pm Mon-Thu, noon-3pm & 5-10pm Fri & Sat* ££

EDO: Modern European tapas, perfect for sharing. Dishes are cooked over apple and pear wood in a Bertha oven. *noon-9.30pm Tue-Sat* ££

Places We Love to Stay

€ Budget €€ Midrange €€€ Top End

Dublin
MAP p617

Generator Hostel € Bright hostel on Smithfield Sq with a fun design, comfy dorms and a lively social scene.

Staunton's on the Green €€ This handsome Georgian house has charming bedrooms and a beautiful garden.

Morgan Hotel €€ Temple Bar hotel right in the middle of the action; some rooms have balconies.

Shelbourne €€€ Dublin's most famous hotel was founded in 1824 and is the height of old-school luxury.

Kilkenny City

Langton's Hotel Kilkenny €€ Kilkenny empire with historic and modern rooms, gardens, multiple restaurants and bars, and nightly live music.

Hibernian Hotel €€ Central 18th-century Georgian bank now housing 46 contemporary guest rooms, a brasserie restaurant and bar.

Butler House €€€ In private gardens with an entrance to Castle Yard, this 1786 mansion has 17 sumptuous period-furnished rooms.

Cork City
MAP p625

Sheila's Hostel € Popular backpacker's hostel in a handy location for exploring the city, with great facilities including a cinema room and sauna.

Hotel Isaacs €€ Housed in a Victorian furniture warehouse in a buzzing central location, with spacious, well-decorated rooms.

Imperial Hotel €€€ History-filled, two-century-old landmark in the heart of Cork with lavish rooms and contemporary amenities and spa.

Kinsale

Giles Norman Townhouse €€ Stylish guest rooms with elegant bathrooms, espresso machines and a discount at the downstairs gallery.

Old Presbytery €€€ Luxury self-catering apartments set in a gorgeously refurbished 18th-century Georgian property.

Killarney

Black Sheep Hostel € Eco-focused, traveller-designed hostel with custom-made bunks and built-in lockers, free breakfast and attached coffee shack.

Fleming's White Bridge Caravan & Camping Park € Lovely, sheltered family-run campsite on the banks of the River Flesk 2.5km southeast of town.

Crystal Springs €€ Wonderfully relaxing B&B just outside the centre, with a glass-enclosed breakfast room overlooking the river. Two-night minimum.

Cahernane House Hotel €€€ Grand manor dating from 1877, with antique-furnished rooms (some with a claw-foot bath or Jacuzzi).

Killarney Plaza Hotel €€€ Central 198-room modern hotel channelling art-deco-era style, with a lavishly tiled pool, sauna, steam room and spa.

Dingle Town

Rainbow Hostel & Camping € Set in large gardens 1.5km northwest of town, this bright, fresh bungalow is also the nearest place to town you can pitch a tent.

Base Dingle €€ Contemporary lodgings in Dingle's heart, offering 30 sleek rooms that can sleep two to five people (no breakfast).

Castlewood House €€€ A haven of country-house quiet and sophistication 10 minutes' stroll from town.

Galway City
MAP p633

Kinlay Hostel € Centrally located hostel just off Eyre Sq, a stroll away from the traditional pubs of Shop St.

House Hotel €€ Boutique hotel in a converted warehouse with an amazing location in the Latin Quarter.

Heron's Rest €€€ Boutique B&B in a lovely row of houses on the banks of the Corrib; sit outside and enjoy the views. Breakfast hampers include organic local produce.

Belfast
MAP p638

Vagabonds £ Within walking distance of the city centre, this popular, well-run hostel has dorms, private rooms and common areas for socialising.

Flint ££ Suites here have a small kitchen and a table for eating or working. Located right by City Hall.

Titanic Hotel Belfast £££ Located in the Harland & Wolff shipping company's old headquarters; the hotel's interior design references the city's shipbuilding past.

Practicalities

INSURANCE

Travel insurance is not required to enter Ireland, but comprehensive insurance is highly recommended to cover theft and loss as well as any medical problems. EU citizens carrying a free European Health Insurance Card (EHIC) are covered for most emergency medical care but not for emergency repatriation.

LANGUAGE

Irish (Gaeilge) is the country's official language. In 2003, the government introduced the Official Languages Act, whereby all official documents, street signs and official titles must be either in Irish or in both Irish and English.

REPUBLIC OF IRELAND ENTRY REQUIREMENTS

Ireland and Britain are part of the Common Travel Area (CTA). No UK ETA is required for the Republic. The Republic is in the EU but isn't a member of Schengen, and isn't planning to implement ETIAS (European Travel Information and Authorisation System) launching in late 2026.

BEACH SAFETY

Rip currents are the leading hazard for beachgoers. If lifeguards aren't present, ask locals whether the water is suitable to enter. For more advice on keeping safe in and around the water, see *watersafety.ie*.

NORTHERN IRELAND ENTRY REQUIREMENTS

Northern Ireland, as part of the UK (and no longer the EU post-Brexit), requires visa-exempt visitors to obtain a UK ETA (Electronic Travel Authorisation; *gov.uk/eta*), whether arriving directly or from the Republic. While the 'soft' border between the Republic and Northern Ireland means there are no passport controls, visitors still require a UK ETA for Northern Ireland.

OPENING HOURS

Pubs 10.30am–11.30pm Monday to Thursday, 10.30am–12.30am Friday and Saturday, noon–11pm Sunday
Restaurants noon–10.30pm
Shops 9.30am–6pm Monday to Saturday (to 8pm Thursday in cities), noon–6pm Sunday

PUBLIC HOLIDAYS

New Year's Day 1 January
St Brigid's Day 1st Monday in February (Republic of Ireland)
St Patrick's Day 17 March
Easter Monday March/April
Easter Tuesday March/April (Northern Ireland)
May Holiday 1st Monday in May
Spring Bank Holiday Last Monday in May (Northern Ireland)
June Holiday 1st Monday in June

The Twelfth 12 July (Northern Ireland)
August Holiday 1st Monday in August (Republic of Ireland)
Summer Bank Holiday Last Monday in August (Northern Ireland)
October Holiday Last Monday in October (Republic of Ireland)
Christmas Day 25 December
St Stephen's Day (Boxing Day) 26 December

TUPUNGATO/SHUTTERSTOCK

Ryanair planes, Dublin Airport

Arriving

Dublin is the main point of entry for most travellers to Ireland. Flights arrive at Dublin Airport, 10km north of the city centre, which has two interconnected terminals with ATMs, restaurants and convenience stores. Buses connect Dublin Airport with towns and cities across Ireland. You can also fly to Belfast, Shannon and Cork, and smaller airports including Kerry (near Killarney).

US Preclearance
When travelling from Dublin or Shannon airports to the US, passport and immigration formalities are handled before boarding at US Preclearance; allow extra time. When you arrive in the US, the flight is treated as a domestic arrival.

Ferry
Car ferries from Liverpool in England, Holyhead in Wales and Cherbourg in France arrive at Dublin ferry port, 5km east of the city centre. Belfast has ferry links with Scotland and England. Ferries sail between Rosslare in County Wexford and Britain, France and Spain.

MONEY
Currency: Euro (€) – Republic of Ireland; Pound sterling (£) – Northern Ireland

TIPPING

Accommodation
Hotel porters €1–2/£1–2 per bag; cleaning staff at your discretion. Not expected in small B&Bs.

Pubs Not expected unless table service is provided, then €1–2/£1–2 for a round of drinks.

Restaurants Check whether your bill includes a service charge. For decent service 10%; up to 15% in more expensive places.

Cafes Not expected; many have an optional tip jar on the counter.

Taxis Round up to an even amount.

Toilet attendants Loose change; no more than 50c/50p.

MONEY-SAVING TIPS

Many attractions offer discounted rates if you buy tickets online in advance. You can also buy visitor passes that include entry to a number of attractions, such as the Dublin Pass. The Heritage Card includes free entry to all Office of Public Works–managed sites; it can be a good deal depending on how many spots you plan to visit.

Getting Around

Transport in Ireland by bus and train is efficient and reasonably priced to and from major urban centres; smaller towns and villages along those routes are well served. Service to destinations not on major routes is less frequent and often impractical. Exploring Ireland's wildest and most beautiful corners is easiest by car.

Leap Visitor Card
In Dublin, the Leap Visitor Card includes all Dublin Bus, Luas tram, DART and commuter train travel (though not Aircoach and Dublin Express airport bus services) for one, three or seven days. It's easiest to buy it in Dublin (online purchases require postage); points of sale include Dublin Airport.

4KCLIPS/SHUTTERSTOCK

Irish Explorer Rail Pass
If you're travelling around Ireland by train, the Irish Explorer rail pass includes five days of unlimited rail travel in the Republic within 15 consecutive days. It's sold at larger train stations (not from ticket machines or online).

TFI Live App
Download Transport for Ireland's TFI Live app (*transportforireland.ie/available-apps/tfi-live*) to plan bus, train and tram trips using real-time departure information.

Toll Roads
Ireland currently has 11 toll roads; 10 have barrier toll plazas where you pay at the cashier's booth. Dublin's M50 toll plaza is barrier-free; pay online (*eflow.ie*) before 8pm the following day. Peak rates are charged on weekday mornings and evenings at the Dublin Tunnel.

Rural Road Hazards
Ireland's rural roads can be steep, narrow and winding. Single-track roads with blind bends can be challenging; if you see an oncoming vehicle, the etiquette is for the car nearest to a passing place to reverse; thank the driver with a wave.

DRIVING ESSENTIALS

Drive on the left-hand side

Speed limits are in kilometres per hour in the Republic and miles per hour in Northern Ireland

0.05

Blood alcohol limit is 0.05%

Curated by
Cristian Bonetto

Italy

EUROPE'S CULTURAL AND CULINARY PARADISE

World-famous art, architecture, food and passion, wrapped up in some of Europe's most magnificent natural landscapes.

A favourite destination since the days of the 18th-century Grand Tour, Italy may appear to hold few surprises. Its iconic monuments and masterpieces are known the world over, while cities like Rome, Florence and Venice need no introduction.

Yet Italy is far more than the sum of its sights. Its fiercely proud regions maintain centuries-old customs and culinary traditions, making the country feel more like a collection of mini nations – each with its distinct identity, specialities, architecture and festivals. After all, Milan and Turin are closer to Paris and Munich than they are to Palermo, while the latter's souk-like markets and Arabesque flourishes serve as a constant reminder that Tunis is much closer than Rome.

The extraordinary contrasts extend beyond the lively streets and piazzas, spilling into the very landscapes that frame them. Italy offers an amazing suite of natural backdrops: icy northern Alps and glacial lakes, gentle Tuscan hills, vertiginous Campanian coastlines and spitting Sicilian volcanoes. Few countries can claim such breadth and beauty in such a compact area.

Then, Italy has always had a knack for superlatives – from ancient glories and Renaissance masterpieces to fashion, design, food and wine. No other country matches its number of UNESCO World Heritage Sites, and few others seduce with such effortless style and heart-on-sleeve charm. *Benvenuti* to Europe's most intoxicating, theatrical stage.

RAUL JICHICI/SHUTTERSTOCK

THE MAIN AREAS

ROME	NORTHERN ITALY	FLORENCE & TUSCANY	NAPLES & THE AMALFI COAST	SICILY
Italy's ancient, eternal capital. **p650**	High fashion, lakeside villas, gondolas. **p662**	Renaissance masterpieces and a lopsided icon. **p683**	Hyperactive street life, coastal beauty. **p694**	A Greek, Arab and Norman melting pot. **p705**

For places to stay in Italy, see p714

SERGEY NOVIKOV/SHUTTERSTOCK

Left: Tuscany (p683); Above: Cattedrale di Santa Maria del Fiore (p687), Florence

TRAIN & BUS

Fast, efficient and well connected, Italy's train network is best for travelling between major cities and along the coast. It works in conjunction with an efficient regionalised bus network, which can be useful for reaching smaller towns.

CAR

Cars aren't needed for getting around Italian cities and major towns, where historic centres are walkable and public transport is generally reliable. Beyond urban areas, a car offers flexibility to explore rural, off-the-beaten-track locations at your own pace.

FERRY

Ferry and hydrofoil services connect the Italian mainland to various islands, including regular overnight services between Naples and Sicily. Regular high-speed hydrofoils run year-round between Naples, Capri and other islands in the Bay of Naples, with seasonal services connecting Amalfi Coast towns.

Northern Italy, p662

Operatic encores in Milan, glittering mosaics in Venice, stunning hikes along the plunging Cinque Terre: Italy's well-heeled north isn't short of blockbuster moments.

Florence & Tuscany, p683

Birthplace of the Renaissance, Florence is Italy's preeminent city of art. Hop between masterpieces, then detour to a Tuscan town or an infamously crooked tower.

GERMANY

AUSTRIA

SWITZERLAND

LIECHTENSTEIN

SLOVENIA

CROATIA

FRANCE

MONACO

CORSICA

SAN MARINO

Adriatic Sea

Ligurian Sea

Salzburg
Innsbruck
Bregenz
VADUZ
Zürich
Lucerne
Bellinzona
Lugano
Como
Varese
Novara
Biella
Vercelli
Turin
Asti
Alba
Bra
Pinerolo
Susa
Courmayeur
Aosta
Ivrea
Chamonix
Mont Blanc (Monte Bianco)
Monte Rosa
Amécy
Chambéry
Gap
Grenoble
Cuneo
Sanremo
Imperia
Albenga
Savona
Genoa
Rapallo
La Spezia
Alessandria
Pavia
Milan
Lecco
Bergamo
Brescia
Cremona
Piacenza
Parma
Reggio Emilia
Modena
Bologna
Imola
Forlì
Cesena
Ravenna
Porto Garibaldi
Ferrara
Legnago
Mantua
Verona
Vicenza
Padua
Venice
Chioggia
Treviso
Pordenone
Belluno
Cortina d'Ampezzo
Bolzano
Trento
Rovereto
Riva del Garda
Sondrio
Domodossola
Verbania
Bobbio
Massa
Lucca
Pisa
Livorno
Cecina
Pistoia
Florence
Siena
San Gimignano
Arezzo
Grosseto
Orvieto
Piombino
Portoferraio
Bastia
Porto Santo Stefano
Viterbo
Terni
Rieti
L'Aquila
Spoleto
Foligno
Perugia
Gubbio
Urbino
Pesaro
Rimini
Ancona
Ascoli Piceno
Civitanova Marche
Giulianova
Pescara
Ortona
Zadar
Pula
Rovinj
Trieste
Monfalcone
Udine
Portogruaro
LJUBLJANA
Klagenfurt
Villach
Maribor
Graz
Lienz
Marmolada
Monte Disgrazia
Monte Ortles
Gran Paradiso
Monviso
Monte Argentario
Elba
Capraia
Giglio
Corno Grande
Basilica di San Marco
Gallerie dell'Accademia
Piazza del Duomo
Piazza del Campo
Leaning Tower
Duomo
Cannes
Nice
Adige
Po
Arno
A22
A23
A4
A13
A14
A1
A15
A21
A4
A7
A26
A5
A10
A6
A12
A11
A12
A1

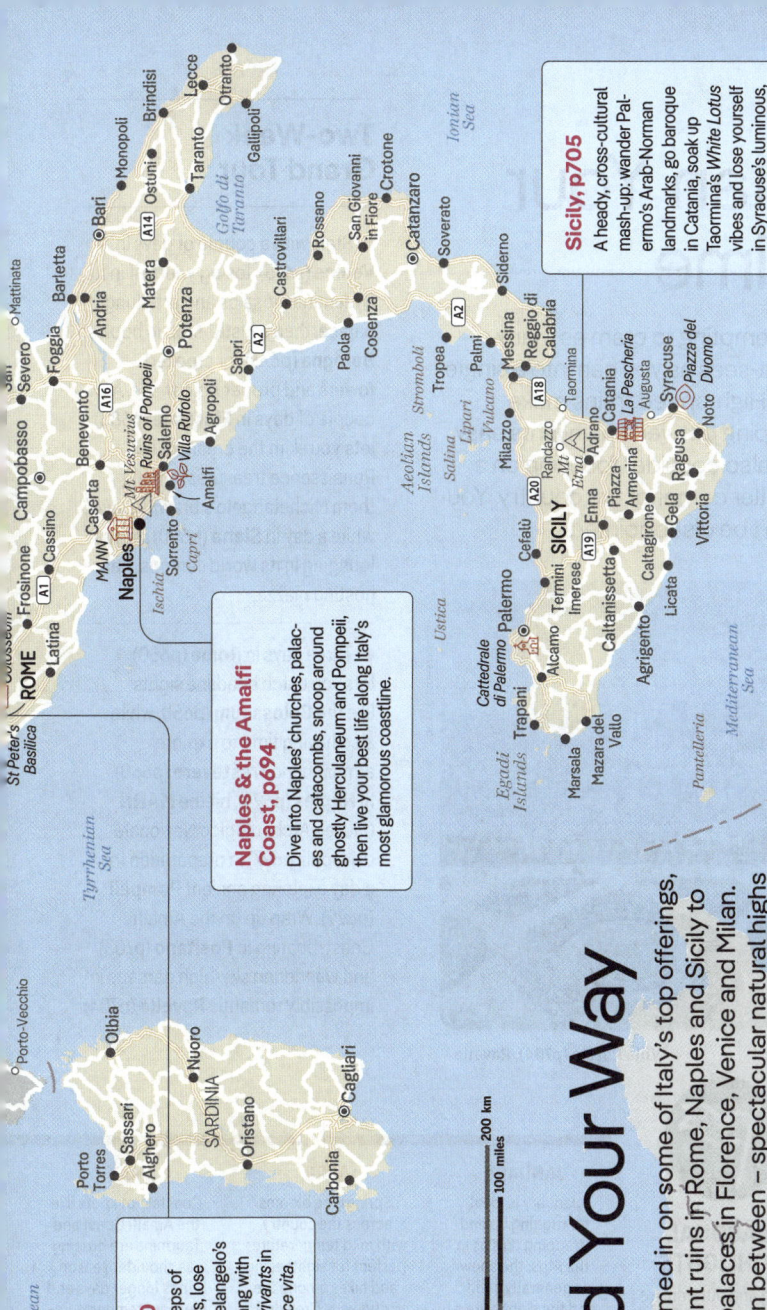

Sicily, p705

A heady, cross-cultural mash-up: wander Palermo's Arab-Norman landmarks, go baroque in Catania, soak up Taormina's *White Lotus* vibes and lose yourself in Syracuse's luminous, labyrinthine streets.

Naples & the Amalfi Coast, p694

Dive into Naples' churches, palaces and catacombs, snoop around ghostly Herculaneum and Pompeii, then live your best life along Italy's most glamorous coastline.

Rome, p650

Trace the footsteps of Roman emperors, lose yourself in Michelangelo's frescoes, and hang with Trastevere *bon vivants* in the city of *la dolce vita*.

Find Your Way

We've zoomed in on some of Italy's top offerings, from ancient ruins in Rome, Naples and Sicily to art-slung palaces in Florence, Venice and Milan. Speckled in between – spectacular natural highs and some lesser-known treasures.

0 — 200 km
0 — 100 miles

Plan Your Time

It's tempting to cram as many must-sees as you can into a single trip. High-speed trains make hopping between highlights easy, but also consider focusing on a smaller corner of the country. You won't be disappointed.

ARCADY/SHUTTERSTOCK

Villa Rufolo (p704), Ravello

Two-Week Grand Tour

● Start with a couple of days in **Venice** (p675), losing yourself in its Byzantine mosaics and art-slung palace, then whistle-stop in bookish **Bologna** (p673) for crooked towers and proper *bolognese*. A couple of days in **Florence** (p683) lets you skim the cream of its Renaissance treasures, among them Michelangelo's brawny *David*, while a day in **Siena** (p690) means lounging in its world-famous, Palio-hosting piazza.

● Three days in **Rome** (p650) lets you catch headline sights like the **Colosseum** (p651), while also having time to explore atmospheric **Trastevere** (p660). In **Naples** (p694), hit the **MANN** (Museo Archeologico Nazionale di Napoli; p697) in preparation for a day exploring ancient **Pompeii** (p699). Wrap up on the Amalfi Coast, boating in **Positano** (p703) and wandering sky-high gardens in impossibly romantic **Ravello** (p704).

SEASONAL HIGHLIGHTS

Spring and autumn are ideal for sightseeing. Summer heat packs the coasts, while winter snows fuel alpine skiing.

JANUARY

January is ideal for rugging up and strapping on skis in the Alps: the snow is generally solid, and the slopes are a little calmer after the Christmas and New Year's holiday rush.

APRIL

Springtime blooms across the country, with mild temperatures perfect for sightseeing and hikes among the wildflowers. Crowds are generally lighter than summer, though Easter brings busy streets and higher prices.

MAY

Coastal hot spots like the Amalfi Coast and Taormina are buzzing as shoulder season brings longer days and pleasant temperatures without the sweltering summer crush. Epicureans hit local markets for prime-time asparagus.

Six Northern Days

● Strut straight into Italy's fashion-and-finance capital, **Milan** (p667), for a couple of days. Scale its spindly **Duomo** (p669), take in Leonardo da Vinci's **The Last Supper** (p670) and dive into the Navigli's canal-side **aperitivo scene** (p670). Book ahead to catch a show at the world-famous opera house **La Scala** (p667).

● Head west for a few days in Italy's former capital, **Turin** (p665) – elegant, faintly French and home to royal palaces, grand cafes and the **Museo Egizio** (p667), Europe's greatest repository of Egyptian antiquities. Then, trade the city's stately arcades for the dramatic coast of the **Cinque Terre** (p662). Spend another two days or so hiking between its pastel villages, take a dip in turquoise coves and linger over Liguria's famous seafood, pesto and focaccia.

Sicily in Short

● Time-poor? Sicily's Ionian Coast delivers easy-to-reach thrills, from ancient Graeco-Roman ruins and jaw-dropping coastal towns to baroque splendour and vibrant street life. Start with two days in **Syracuse** (p711), indulging in Ortigia's island charm and roaming the vast **Parco Archeologico della Neapolis** (p713).

● Then continue up the coast to **Catania** (p708), Sicily's second-largest city, where UNESCO-listed piazzas, stuccoed churches and a raucous fish market make light work of a couple of days. The dining is sensational and its youthful, student energy invigorating. Then slow down with a day or so in polished **Taormina** (p710). Stroll old-world alleys, savour clifftop views of moody Mt Etna, and catch a moonlit show at the resort town's spectacular, millennia-old **Teatro Greco** (p711).

JUNE

School is out and the summer holidays begin, with tourist numbers increasing significantly across the country. Warm days and evenings herald outdoor festivals, from opera and theatre to Pride parades.

JULY

Hot days, packed beaches, and wild blueberries in full bloom. Outdoor festivals continue and Siena's Piazza del Campo hosts the thrilling horse race **Palio** (p692) on 2 July (a second edition is held on 16 August).

OCTOBER

While central and southern Italy still enjoy mild days, northern regions may see the season's first snow. Leaves are ablaze and autumn produce shines, from pumpkin-filled tortellini to roasted chestnuts.

NOVEMBER

Truffle season hits its peak in northern Italy, especially for the prized white Alba truffle. Gourmands flock to truffle festivals and waiters shave it fresh over steaks, pastas and warming risottos.

Rome

ROMAN ARCHITECTURE | BAROQUE LANDMARKS | LA DOLCE VITA

☑ **TOP TIP**

Trastevere's riverfront is the place to be in summer as the Lungo il Tevere street carnival revs into action. Stalls, pop-up bars, restaurants and even dance floors set up on the waterfront between Ponte Sisto and Ponte Sublicio between June and September.

Ever since its golden age as the ancient *caput mundi* (world capital), Rome has been seducing visitors. Its thrilling cityscape, piled high with martial ruins and monuments, is achingly beautiful, and its museums and churches harbour some of Europe's finest masterpieces.

Managing the twin demands of tourism and modern civic life has increasingly become a reality of governing Rome, a city whose population of 2.7 million is dwarfed by the annual influx of Italian and foreign visitors. The result of all this is a city that can sometimes appear to be living on the edge of perpetual chaos. And while Rome is undeniably busy, and is often scruffy and noisy, it's not the giant free-for-all it's occasionally portrayed as. Look closer and you'll see most drivers are wearing their seatbelts, and that few people are smoking in banned public places. In Rome, first impressions can be gloriously misleading.

Ancient Rome

Just to the south of the city centre, Ancient Rome is a thrilling mix of ancient treasures, iconic monuments and mesmerising views. This is where you'll find Rome's most celebrated ruins and showstopping landmarks: the Colosseum, Palatino (where

continued on p654

 GETTING AROUND

Rome is best explored on foot: the main sights are clustered in and around the *centro storico* (historic centre), the centre is relatively flat, and traffic is restricted in many areas. Driving is stressful, parking scarce and scooters better left to locals. Public transport fills the gaps: the metro (lines A and B) links Termini to the Colosseum and the Vatican. There are no metro stations in the *centro storico*, but you can walk from Barberini, Spagna and Flaminio stations. Spagna is also useful for Villa Borghese. Buses cover much of the *centro storico* and trams run to Trastevere. Tickets are easy to buy at stations and kiosks.

TOP EXPERIENCE

Colosseum

The Colosseum is the most thrilling of Rome's ancient monuments, an electrifying, spine-tingling sight commissioned by Vespasian in 72 CE and inaugurated by Titus in 80 CE. This is where gladiators met in mortal combat and prisoners fought off wild beasts in front of baying, bloodthirsty crowds. Two thousand years on and it remains the city's most popular attraction.

VIACHESLAV LOPATIN/SHUTTERSTOCK

Making the Most of Your Visit

Even without a ticket, the outer walls – originally covered in travertine and with statues in the niches – impress. The upper level, punctuated by square window openings and slender Corinthian pilasters, had supports for 240 masts, which held a giant awning over the arena.

Once you make it inside, steep steps lead to the first and second tiers. From here you can look over the partially rebuilt arena floor and down into the underground areas. On the 2nd floor you'll also find the small **Museo del Colosseo** illustrating the Colosseum's history. You'll need a Full Experience ticket (€24) to gain access to the upper floors, where women spectators would have sat. The Full Experience ticket also allows you to walk on the arena floor and explore the subterranean sections, which once served as the stadium's backstage.

Demand for all tickets is high, so book well in advance, even a month ahead for peak periods; check the website for details. You can buy same-day tickets (subject to availability) at ticket offices on Piazza del Colosseo (credit/debit cards only) and Largo della Salara Vecchia.

TOP TIPS

● Tickets include the holder's name, so bring photo ID to enter.

● Reckon on about an hour inside the Colosseum. Try to visit first thing or late afternoon, when it's cooler, less crowded and there's better lighting.

● Free interactive audio guides are available on the official MyColosseum app.

PRACTICALITIES

● colosseo.it ● adult/reduced €18/2 ● 8.30am-1hr before sunset, last entry 1hr before closing

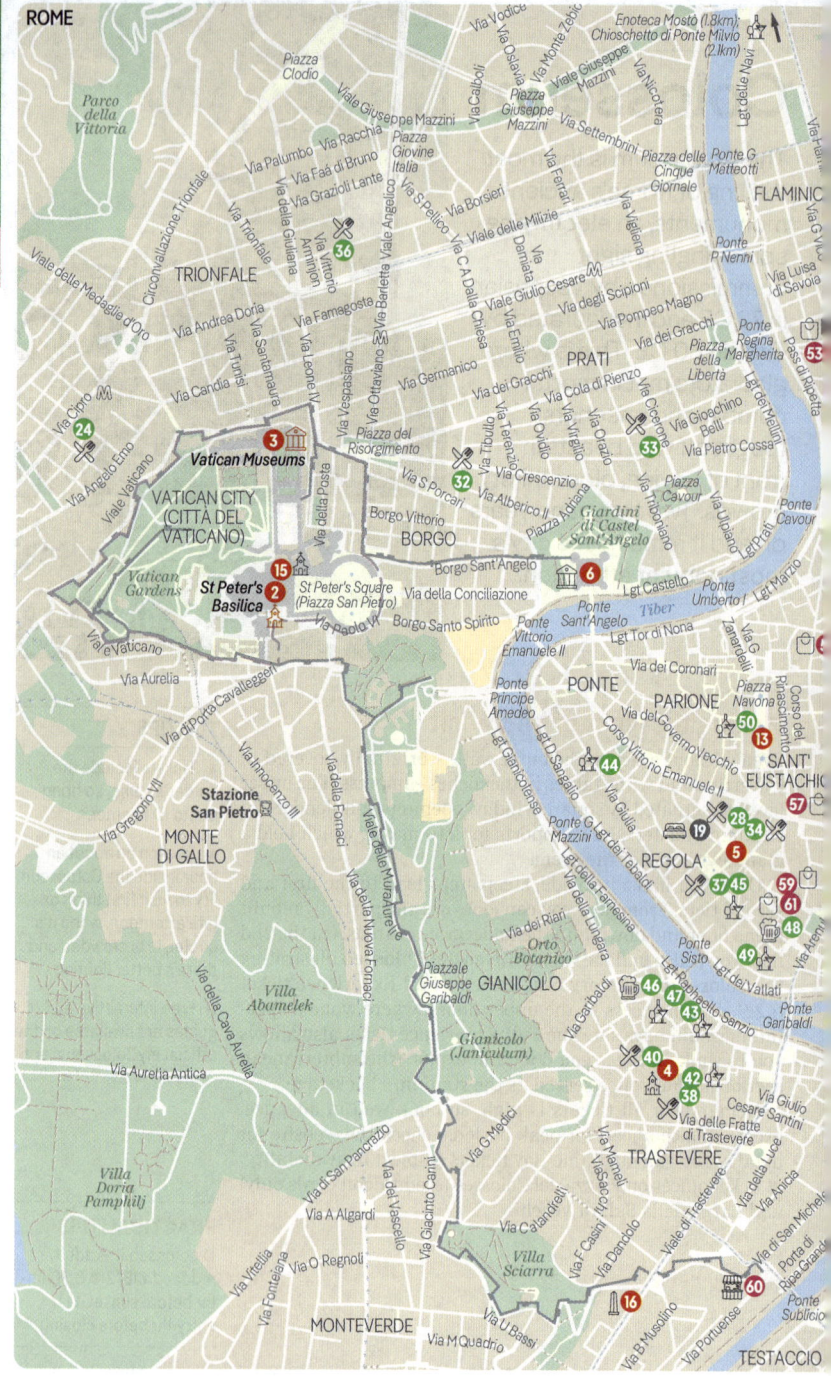

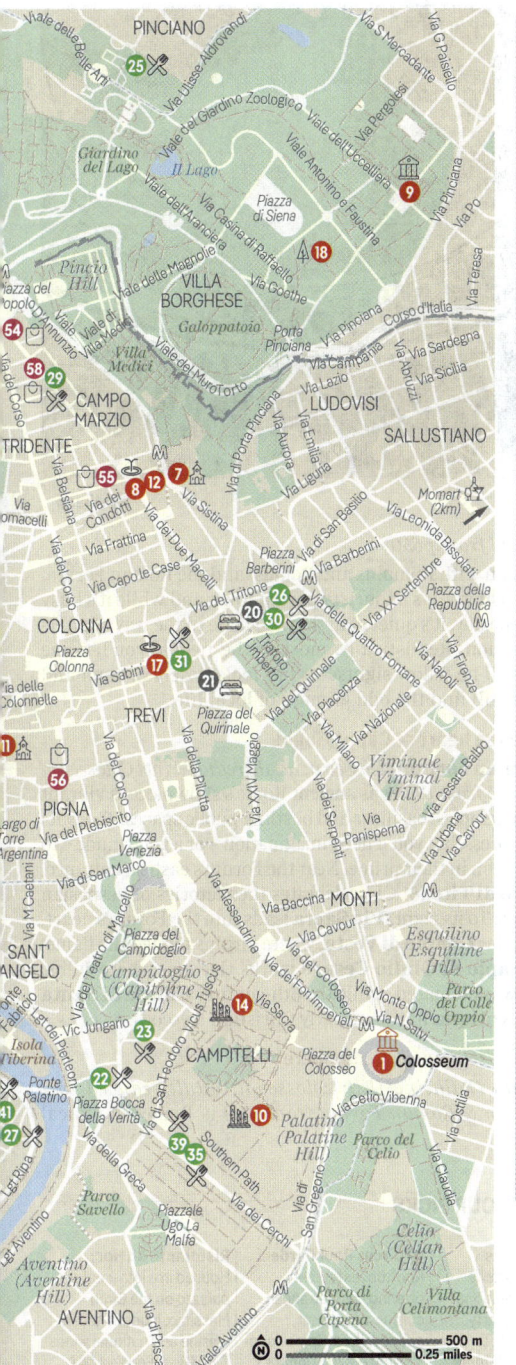

ANCIENT HIGHLIGHTS

Darius Arya, a Rome-based archaeologist, highlights some must-sees. *@dariusaryadigs; ancientromelive.org*

The Forum and Palatino are the real heart of Rome's history. You'll want to get the Super pass to have access to the 'secret' sites and monuments like Santa Maria Antiqua and the Curia Iulia. Due to new openings, everyone should walk up Domitian's ramp (which once connected to the palace on top) and through the substructures of the Domus Tiberiana.

For the Colosseum, try to take the elevator ride to the top or the hypogeum (underground chambers). They are both wonderful experiences that bring you closer to the Colosseum's history.

RESUL MUSLU/SHUTTERSTOCK

Pantheon

continued from p650

it all began with Romulus and Remus) and the Roman Forum. Unsurprisingly, it's a touristy part of town and while it's busy during the day, it's quiet at night with little in the way of after-hours action. Realistically, most of the people you'll come across will be fellow sightseers but look closely enough and you can still find the odd glimpse of local life.

Explore the heart of Caput Mundi

The **Roman Forum** *(colosseo.it; adult/reduced incl Colosseum & Palatino from €18)* was ancient Rome's showpiece, a vibrant centre of temples, basilicas and bustling public spaces. Today its ruins impress, but you'll need imagination – or a good guide – to picture them in their prime. Near the Forum's eastern entrance, the **Arco di Tito** (81 CE) celebrates the victories of Vespasian and Titus. To its right, **Via Sacra** leads into the Forum's heart, passing the **Tempio di Vesta**, where virgins tended the flame. The **Tempio di Giulio Cesare** marks the spot where Julius Caesar was cremated, while the 6th-century **Chiesa di Santa Maria Antiqua** harbours early Christian frescoes.

Roam where emperors slumbered

Palatino *(Palatine Hill; colosseo.it; adult/reduced incl Colosseum & Roman Forum from €18)* is Rome's mythical

EATING IN ANCIENT ROME: OUR PICKS

Alimentari Pannella Carmela: A workaday food store ideal for sandwiches. *8.30am-2.30pm Mon-Sat, 5-8pm Mon-Fri* €

Osteria Circo: This Circo Massimo *osteria* specialises in traditional Italian fare and hearty Roman pastas. *12.30-3.30pm & 7.30-11.30pm* €€

47 Circus Roof Garden: Rooftop restaurant offering Mediterranean cuisine and sunset *aperitivi* (from 4pm). *noon-3.30pm & 7-10.30pm* €€€

Ristorante Ad Hoc: Housed in a 16th-century *palazzo* on the Circo Massimo. Modern Italian cuisine and national wines. *7-10.30pm Fri-Wed* €€€

birthplace, where Romulus supposedly founded the city in 753 BCE. Archaeology reveals Iron Age huts from the 9th century BCE. Later, emperors lived in palatial luxury, most notably in Domitian's 1st-century palace, divided into the public **Domus Flavia**, private **Domus Augustana**, and sunken **stadio**. Highlights include Augustus' frescoed **Casa di Augusto**, the **Orti Farnesiani** gardens with stunning Forum views, and the towering **Domus Tiberiana**, the Palatino's first palace. The **Museo Palatino** chronicles the hill's development, though you'll need a Forum Pass Super *(€18)* or Full Experience *(€24)* ticket to access the museum, as well as the Aula Isiaca and Loggia Mattei, Casa di Augusto and Domus Tiberiana. Allow about three hours to explore the Palatino and adjoining Forum.

Centro Storico

A tangled knot of cobbled alleyways, Renaissance palaces and baroque piazzas, Rome's *centro storico* (historic centre) is the city many visitors come to find. The Pantheon and Piazza Navona are the star turns, but walk around and without even trying you'll come across a whole host of monuments, museums and churches, many containing masterpieces. But it's not all high culture. There's plenty of fun to be had just strolling the area's theatrical streets, taking in its romantic nooks and enjoying the many boutiques, cafes, *trattorias* and bars. Just make sure to bring some comfortable shoes for the uneven cobbles.

Admire an engineering marvel

Built by Hadrian around 125 CE on the site of Marcus Agrippa's earlier temple, the 2000-year-old **Pantheon** *(pantheon roma.com)* is the best-preserved of Rome's ancient monuments. Step through its immense bronze doors and you're met with the largest unreinforced concrete dome ever built – a feat so breathtaking it inspired Michelangelo before he designed the dome of St Peter's Basilica. The temple-turned-church, whose tombs include that of Raphael, is best visited early to avoid the biggest crowds, and it's wise to book **tickets** *(portale.mu seiitaliani.it; adult/reduced €5/2)* online in advance to skip long queues. Return at night to see it illuminated.

Pose on a perfect piazza

A cinematic sweep of fountains and baroque *palazzi* (mansions), **Piazza Navona** has long been a hub of city life. For close on 300

WATER FOUNTAINS

Sightseeing can be thirsty work in Rome. Fortunately, you can get free drinking water throughout the city, courtesy of 2500 or so fountains known as *nasoni* (or 'big noses'). First introduced in the 1870s, these cast-iron fountains supply a constant flow of safe, refreshingly cool, *acqua potabile* (drinking water), which you can use to fill up your bottles or drink directly. To do so, block the main spout and cup the water as it spurts through the hole in the top of the nozzle. You'll find *nasoni* in Piazza della Rotonda and Piazza Navona, among other places. To locate the nearest one to you, check out the free app Acea Waidy Wow.

A hip trattoria with piazza seating.

EATING & DRINKING IN THE CENTRO STORICO: OUR PICKS

Osteria La Quercia: On a charming square near Piazza Farnese eat Lazio regional classics. *noon-3.30pm & 7-11.30pm* €€

Ditirambo: Central location, informal vibe and seasonal, organic cuisine. Roman pastas to thoughtful vegetarian offerings. *12.30-3pm & 6.30-11pm* €€

Rimessa Roscioli: Gourmets adore this place, with its wine-pairing dinners, tastings, tours and classes. Book ahead. *5-11pm Mon-Sun* €€

Luciano Cucina Italiana: Near Campo de' Fiori, this spot serves renowned carbonara and inventive mains. *12.15-3pm & 7.15-11pm* €€€

years it hosted Rome's main market, and still today it attracts a daily circus of street artists, hawkers and tourists. It stands on the 1st-century **Stadio di Domiziano**, whose underground remains can be visited from Via di Tor Sanguigna. The piazza's centrepiece is Bernini's 1651 **Fontana dei Quattro Fiumi**, featuring four river gods. Dominating the square's western flank, the domed **Chiesa di Sant'Agnese** in Agone was designed by the revered baroque architect Francesco Borromini. To catch the piazza at its most alluring, come first thing in the morning before the crowds or after dark when the fountains are illuminated.

Browse on the Campo

Hanging out on a busy piazza is a quintessential Roman experience. And nowhere does piazza life quite like **Campo de' Fiori**. Colourful, noisy and always busy, the square hosts a well-known market during the day and teems with life at night as visitors and young locals pack its restaurants and brash bars.

Amid the piazza's hurly-burly, you'll see a statue of a hooded monk. This is the philosopher Giordano Bruno, who was burned here for heresy in 1600.

Tridente & Trevi

Tridente, named after the three streets that form a trident as they lance off Piazza del Popolo, is a glamorous district, full of old money, fashionable bars and swish hotels. It's also Rome's premier shopping district, home to luxury designer boutiques and flagship stores. But once the shops close, the area quietens, leaving few after-hours distractions.

To the south, the Trevi Fountain stands out in a knot of dark, narrow streets, which teem throughout the day as crowds stop off to toss their coins into the *Dolce Vita* fountain.

Climb some famous steps

Few spots in Rome are as iconic (or romantic) as **Piazza di Spagna**, especially in April or May, when its famous Steps are adorned with azaleas. Once dubbed *'il salotto di Roma'* (Rome's parlour), the square takes its name from the 17th-century Spanish embassy still standing here. At its heart is Pietro and Gian Lorenzo Bernini's **Fontana della Barcaccia**, which depicts a seemingly sinking boat. Rising above, the 1725 Scalinata della Trinità dei Monti – better known as the **Spanish Steps** – links the piazza to the 16th-century **Chiesa della Trinità dei Monti** and its striking frescoes. Make sure not to sit on the Steps as hefty fines apply.

DRINKING IN THE CENTRO STORICO: OUR PICKS

L'Angolo Divino: Near Campo de' Fiori, this snug wine bar serves interesting Italian wines and tasty dishes. *11am-3pm Tue-Sat & 5pm-1am Mon-Fri*

Open Baladin: Modern pub near Campo de' Fiori with 40 craft beers on tap and up to 100 bottled brews. *noon-1am, to 2am Fri & Sat*

Il Goccetto: An old-school *vino e olio* (wine and oil) shop with a bottle-lined interior and a fabulous wine list. *noon-midnight Tue-Sat, from 5pm Mon*

Terrazza Borromini: Bask in sunset views over Piazza Navona from this rooftop bar atop a 17th-century *palazzo*. Reservations recommended. *noon-midnight*

Spanish Steps, Piazza di Spagna

Relive a Fellini scene

The **Trevi Fountain** is Rome's most famous, and most flamboyant, baroque masterpiece. Designed by Nicola Salvi in 1732, it fills an entire piazza, with Oceanus riding a shell chariot, tritons and seahorses symbolising the sea's moods. Fed by the Aqua Virgo aqueduct, it will be forever tied to Fellini's *La Dolce Vita,* in which a glamorous Anita Ekberg wades through its waters (don't try it – bathing is banned). Spot the odd stone urn on the right, rumoured to have been placed there by Salvo to block the view of a rude, meddling barber during construction. And don't skip the ritual: back turned, eyes closed, coin tossed with your right hand over your left shoulder.

Vatican City & Borgo

The Vatican City sits across the river to the northwest of the historic centre. Officially it's an independent sovereign state – the world's smallest, with an area of 44 hectares – but in practice it's more like a city neighbourhood. It's also one of Rome's most visited areas, home to priceless treasures and revered masterpieces, many housed in St Peter's Basilica, the Vatican Museums and Sistine Chapel.

A short walk from St Peter's Square, Castel Sant'Angelo looms over the quaint Borgo district. Originally, this was a much larger medieval quarter, but much of it was destroyed in 1936 to make way for Via della Conciliazione.

TRIDENTE'S BEST SHOPS

Bomba: Designer Cristina Bomba's atelier creates gorgeous pieces that hit the wallet hard but are oh so worth it.

Artisanal Cornucopia: Jewellery, handbags and homeware are for sale at this stylish independent boutique on Via dell'Oca.

Borsalino: On Piazza del Popolo, Borsalino showcases headwear for both men and women, selling classic and newer models.

Fabriano: Fabriano stocks stylish stationery, including delightful leather-bound journals and notebooks, at its store in Via del Babuino.

c.u.c.i.n.a.: If you've always dreamed of owning a *caffettiera* and other Italian kitchen essentials, then this is the place for you.

EATING AROUND TRIDENTE & TREVI: OUR PICKS

Colline Emiliane: Regional delicacies of Emilia-Romagna, according to what's in season. *12.45-2.45pm & 7.30-10.45pm Tue-Sat* €€

Hostaria Romana: A textbook Italian *trattoria* serving up delicious Roman classics. *12.30-3pm & 7.15-11pm, closed Sun & Mon lunch* €€

Il Chianti: Enjoy Tuscan classics, from soups to steaks, or select pizzas at this ivy-clad location. *noon-1am* €€

Da Edy: A chic restaurant, with high-ceilinged interiors and painting-covered walls. *noon-3pm & 6.30-11pm Mon-Sat* €€

TOP EXPERIENCE

Vatican Museums

The Vatican Museums claim more masterpieces than some countries, and with 7km of exhibition halls, they are rightly considered one of the world's greatest art museums. While exploring the entire complex would take several days, even a single visit is sure to leave you star-struck as you take in its never-ending collection of world-famous artworks, culminating in Michelangelo's frescoes in the Sistine Chapel.

Galleria delle Carte Geografiche

TOP TIPS

● Save time by booking tickets online (for a small surcharge) or joining a guided tour.

● Rainy days are busiest and afternoons tend to be quieter than mornings.

● The museums are free (and very busy) on the last Sunday of the month.

PRACTICALITIES

● museivaticani.va
● adult/reduced €20/8, free last Sun of the month
● 8am-8pm Mon-Sat, 9am-2pm last Sun of month

Must-See Treasures

Start your explorations by heading to the **Pinacoteca**, often overlooked but full of treasures, among them a trio of works by Raphael, Leonardo da Vinci's *San Gerolamo* and Caravaggio's moving *Deposizione*.

The ground-floor **Museo Pio-Clementino** houses classical sculptures, and many top pieces are found in the Cortile Ottagono, including the *Laocoön* and *Apollo Belvedere*. Elsewhere, the Sala delle Muse houses the famous *Torso Belvedere,* while the Sala Rotonda displays the towering bronze *Hercules.*

The Simonetti staircase leads up to the popular **Galleria delle Carte Geografiche**, a 120m-long corridor adorned with Renaissance topographic maps. The so-called **Stanze di Raffaello**, once part of Pope Julius II's private apartments, astounds, with its frescoes by Raphael and his pupils, including *La Scuola di Atene* and scenes of Constantine.

They're a fitting prelude to the grand finale – the inimitable **Sistine Chapel**. Start by gazing at Michelangelo's ceiling from the east wall, then take in the *Last Judgement* on the western wall and the side frescoes of Moses and Christ. Just remember photography is strictly forbidden in the Sistine Chapel. Time wise, allow at least three hours to cover the Vatican Museum's highlights.

Vatican City (p657)

Make a pilgrimage to St Peter's

St Peter's Basilica *(basilicasanpietro.va)* is the pinnacle of Rome's artistic and architectural brilliance. Built over St Peter's supposed burial site, Constantine's 4th-century church gave way to the current basilica, consecrated in 1626. Inside lies Michelangelo's hauntingly beautiful *Pietà*, a red floor disc marking Charlemagne's coronation spot, and Bernini's towering baldachin, soaring beneath Michelangelo's 133m-tall dome. Don't miss the bronze statue of St Peter, its foot worn smooth by centuries of pilgrims' caresses. Dress modestly (cover shoulders and knees), and plan to visit at lunch or late afternoon to avoid the longest lines. To the right of the main portico is entry to the dome, which offers magnificent views of the city.

Scale a mighty fortress

With its distinctive round keep, **Castel Sant'Angelo** *(castel santangelo.beniculturali.it; adult/reduced €16/2)* is an immediately recognisable landmark. Built as a mausoleum for Emperor Hadrian, it was converted into a papal fortress in the 6th century. Nowadays it houses a fascinating collection of paintings, sculpture, military memorabilia and medieval firearms. Many of these weapons were used by soldiers fighting to protect the castle, which is linked to the Vatican by a 13th-century passageway, the Passetto di Borgo.

VATICAN CURIOSITIES

The Vatican is quite the curious place, besides being a repository for some of the world's greatest artworks. It might be a tiny pocket of Rome, but officially it's an independent state, the world's smallest, complete with its own flag, army (the Swiss Guards), postage stamps, licence plates and, of course, head of state (the pope). And another thing – while Italian is widely spoken throughout the Vatican, Latin is technically the official state language. That means that if you want to withdraw some money at a Vatican ATM, you will find Latin among the possible language options.

 EATING IN VATICAN CITY, BORGO & AROUND: OUR PICKS

Bonci Pizzarium: Some of Rome's best sliced pizza, served with tonnes of creative toppings. *11am-11pm Tue-Sat, 11am-3pm & 5-11pm Sun* €

Il Sorpasso: A popular spot in Prati, serving everything from salads to pizza to *trapizzini* (pizza pockets). *9am-1am Mon-Fri, 9.30am-1am Sat* €€

Osteria dell'Angelo: Authentic neighbourhood *trattoria* offering fixed-price menus. *12.30-2.30pm & 7.30-11pm Mon-Fri, 7.30-11pm Sat* €€

L'Arcangelo: Treading the line between informal and chic, this restaurant enjoys a stellar local reputation. *7.15-10.45pm Mon-Sat* €€€

COBBLESTONES & PIETRE D'INCIAMPO

It pays to look down as you're walking your way through Trastevere, and not just because its oh-so-picturesque cobblestones can be notoriously treacherous and slippery, especially when wet. But among the regular cobblestones, you will sometimes find gilded *pietre d'inciampo* (stumbling stones). Every single one of these bronze squares is engraved with the name of a Jewish Roman citizen and marks the spot where he or she was rounded up by Nazi troops during WWII and deported to one of the Reich's concentration camps. More than 1000 Jewish residents were forcibly removed from their homes, and many of the stones appear in a group with several others – marking where entire families were taken.

LACHRIS77/GETTY IMAGES

Pincio Hill, Villa Borghese

Museum highlights include the papal apartments on level five and the terrace, immortalised by Puccini in his opera *Tosca,* from where you can enjoy a truly spectacular view over Rome.

Trastevere

On the left bank of the Tiber – hence the name *trans Tevere,* 'across the Tiber' – Trastevere is one of Rome's most attractive areas, an endlessly photogenic pocket of cobbled lanes, medieval piazzas and ochre, ivy-clad *palazzi*. It's beautiful any time of day but really comes into its own at night when street sellers set up camp on its picturesque alleyways and crowds swarm to its many restaurants, bars and cafes.

This beauty and carnival-like atmosphere has made it popular with visiting students and foreign home buyers. But while gentrification has undeniably changed the area, it hasn't eradicated its unique character.

Ponder medieval mosaics

The **Basilica di Santa Maria in Trastevere** is one of Rome's oldest churches dedicated to the Virgin Mary. Tradition places its founding in the 3rd century, though the current building

Located right in the heart of Trastevere.

 EATING IN TRASTEVERE: OUR PICKS

Tonnarello: Always packed but rightfully so, since it serves up all the delicious staples of Roman cuisine. *11am-11pm* €€

Da Enzo: Tiny *trattoria* with a menu made from locally sourced Lazio ingredients. *12.15-3pm & 7-11pm Mon-Sat* €€

Osteria Nannarella: A great place to sit down and enjoy everything from carbonara to fried artichokes. *11.30am-11.30pm* €€

Trattoria da Teo: A textbook *trattoria* that's perfect for digging into platefuls of Roman standards. *12.30-3pm & 7.30-11.30pm Mon-Sat* €€

– featuring 24 Roman columns from the Baths of Caracalla and stunning medieval mosaics – is a 12th-century rebuild. The portico was added at the beginning of the 18th century, with various pieces of Roman marble forming another informal mosaic to echo those found inside. Legend holds the basilica stands atop a miraculous oil fountain, marked inside near the altar, though scholars suggest it may have been a polluted water source. To catch the mosaics in the best light, visit early morning or late afternoon.

Treasure-hunt at a flea market

Every city needs its own giant flea market, and the **Mercato di Porta Portese** fills that role for Rome. With more than 500 stalls selling everything from secondhand clothes and everyday home stuff to antiques, paintings, books and picture frames, the sprawling open-air market takes over the area around Porta Portese every Sunday morning. While undoubtedly chaotic, it's the perfect way to truly immerse yourself in the local atmosphere of Trastevere.

Villa Borghese

For a leisurely stroll, a family bike ride or an outdoor yoga class, **Villa Borghese** is the place. The gateway to Rome's affluent northern suburbs, it's the city's central park – an 80-hectare oasis of shadowy glades, gardens and grassy banks. Among its attractions are a small boating lake, the Giardino del Lago; a panoramic viewing terrace on the Pincio Hill; and several excellent museums, including the superlative Museo e Galleria Borghese.

Schmooze with the masters

Set in a lavishly decorated villa, the **Museo e Galleria Borghese** *(galleriaborghese.beniculturali.it; adult/reduced €17/4)* boasts some of the city's greatest Renaissance and baroque masterpieces. Among them are Bernini's *Apollo e Dafne* and *Ratto di Proserpina,* not to mention Canova's daring depiction of Napoleon's sister, Paolina Bonaparte Borghese, as *Venere vincitrice.* Caravaggio dominates Sala VIII with six intense canvases, including his much-loved *Giovane col Canestro di Frutta.* Upstairs, Titian's early masterpiece *Amor Sacro e Amor Profano* is one of the museum's most prized works. Tickets must be booked in advance, with timed-entry ensuring you can savour the highlights sans the hordes. Bring photo ID.

GOFFREDO MAMELI

The Palazzo Corsini was the theatre of one of the most violent battles of the Siege of Rome of 1849 – and among the many soldiers who were fatally wounded was a poet and patriot named Goffredo Mameli, barely in his early 20s. His compositions included the 1847 'Canto degli Italiani', literally 'Song of the Italians'. His fellow patriot Michele Novaro arranged it into music, and that song is now known as the 'Inno di Mameli', or 'Hymn of Mameli' – Italy's national anthem, recognised as provisional in 1946 and made official in 2017. While Mameli's original text includes six verses and a refrain, the anthem is performed by repeating the first verse twice and adding the refrain at the end of the second repetition.

 DRINKING IN TRASTEVERE: OUR PICKS

Ma Che Siete Venuti a Fà: A paradise for beer lovers, with a wide selection of beers on tap and by the bottle. *11am-2am*

Meccanismo: Cool, hip and good at any time of day, from morning coffee to afternoon tea or late-evening cocktails. *8am-2am*

Freni e Frizioni: Cool, lively and with a young crowd. Ideal for an afternoon *aperitivo* or post-dinner cocktail. *6.30pm-2am*

Bar San Calisto: Packed with locals at every hour of the day and night. Come here for a taste of authentic Trastevere. *6am-2am*

Northern Italy

ICONIC CHURCHES | OPULENT PALACES | STUNNING HIKES

 TOP TIP

If you plan on buying Murano glass, beware of foreign-made imposters. As a rule of thumb, if it's not expensive, it's probably not made locally (expect to pay upwards of €35 for a single handblown tumbler). Certified artisans are listed on *muranoglass.com* and display 'Vetro Artistico Murano' labels.

Italy's well-heeled north is the country at its most powerful and creatively charged. Home to names like Missoni, Maserati and Kartell, it's here that Italian style, creativity and flair reach their enviable zenith, shaping trends across the world. Its biggest city, Milan, is the country at its sharpest and chicest – a place where past and future collide with spectacular effect. Celebs and mere mortals sigh collectively over villa-flanked Lago di Como, while others fall madly for Liguria's wilder, equally stunning Cinque Terre. Do you feast in mouthwatering Bologna, museum hop in orderly Turin, or catch a summer opera in Verona's ancient Roman arena? Then, of course, there's the fairest of them all: Venice. The world's most improbable masterpiece, no city quite blurs the line between reality and fantasy like this one. Tread lightly and respectfully, and it promises to reward you with its own extraordinary treasures.

Cinque Terre

Clinging like timeworn citadels to Liguria's precipitous coast, Cinque Terre – namely Riomaggiore, Manarola, Corniglia, Vernazza and Monterosso al Mare – are five diminutive fishing villages linked by a network of ancient cliff-side footpaths that are

GETTING AROUND

Spanning several regions – including Lombardy, Piedmont, Liguria and the Veneto – northern Italy is well served by trains, buses and tolled *autostrade* (freeways). Frequent high-speed services link Turin and Milan with Verona, Venice, Bologna and cities further south, while *regionale* (regional) trains and buses connect smaller towns.

Milan and Venice are major international gateways, with airports offering domestic and global connections. Outside urban areas, driving can be rewarding, but Liguria's cliffside roads are not for the faint-hearted, especially in summer.

Within cities, public transport – including buses, metro lines, trams, and in Venice, *vaporetti* (passenger ferries) – makes getting around easy. For short distances, walking remains the most convenient option.

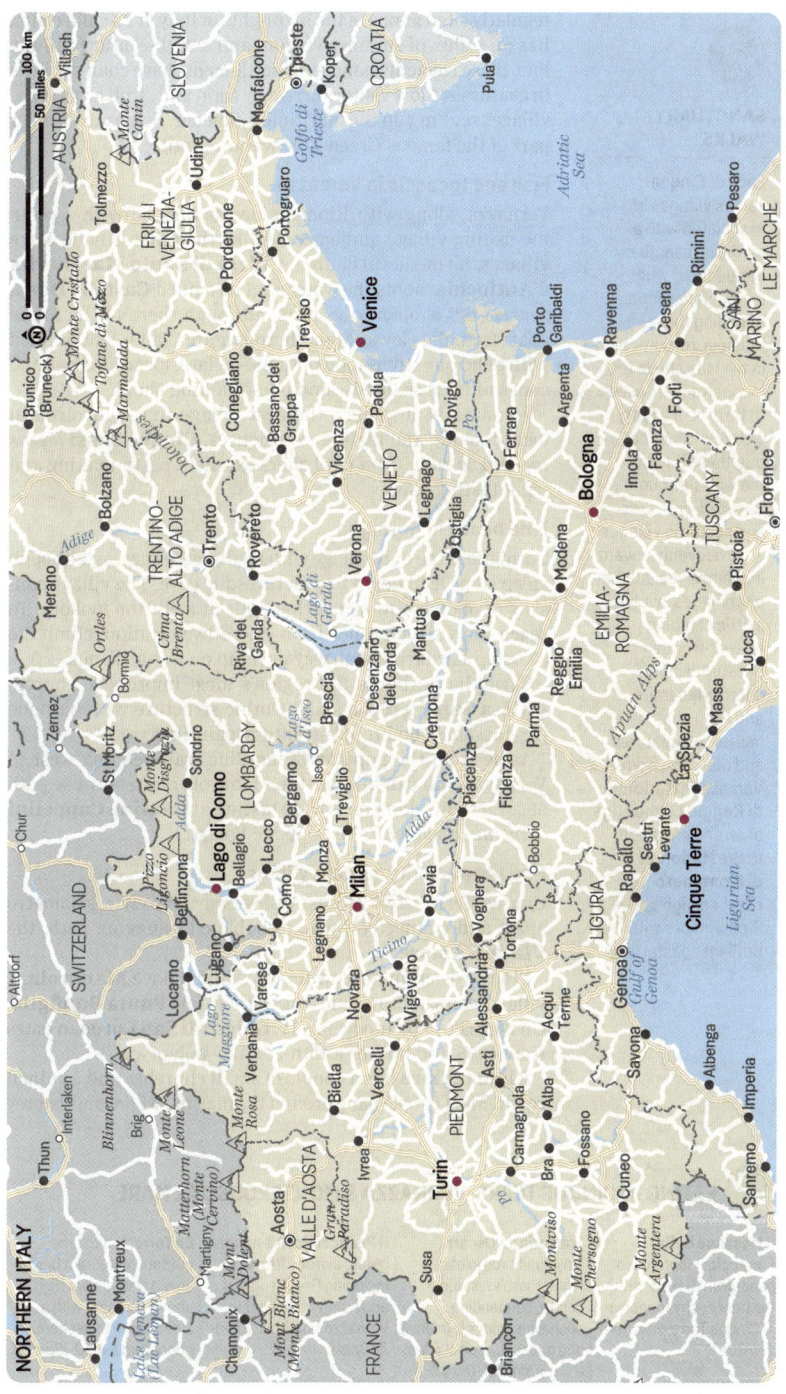

NORTHERN ITALY

SANCTUARY WALKS

Each of Cinque Terre's villages is associated with a medieval sanctuary bequeathed with a holy Marian icon. Reaching these religious retreats, high in the hills above the Mediterranean, used to be part of a hefty Catholic penance but, these days, the walks through terraced vineyards and soporific villages are a heavenly reward in themselves. All the pilgrimages involve a little climbing on well-trodden but surprisingly uncrowded trails and each church has its own features and nuances, from Vernazza's **Madonna di Reggio** on the edge of an ancient wood, to the **Madonna di Montenero** perched high above Riomaggiore with brilliant coastal views.

regularly cited as one of the highlights of Italy. It's a valid claim. Bar an influx of summer visitors and a 19th-century railway line, these ruggedly handsome settlements have changed little in centuries. Most visitors arrive by train and stroll around the villages soaking up the maritime ambience. Some tackle all or part of the famous Green-Blue walking trail.

Fish and focaccia in Vernazza

Vernazza, along with Riomaggiore, is imbued with a genuine fishing village ambience. Unlike the other Cinque Terre villages, its medieval church, **Chiesa di Santa Margherita d'Antiochia**, abuts the water, and its ruined **Castello Doria** *(tickets €2)* is open to visitors (although there's little to see apart from the views). Main thoroughfare Via Visconti is lined with delicious street-food options – gelato, focaccia slices and cones of fried seafood – and one-of-a-kind shops.

Vernazza is, arguably, the best village to get involved in local cooking and tasting experiences. **Cinque Sensi** *(5sens ivernazza.com; from €50)* offers excellent pesto-making and wine-tasting classes.

Find peace in Corniglia

Corniglia is the only village with no direct sea access, although steep steps lead down to a picturesque cove. The village consists of one narrow street that ends at a clifftop lookout. To reach the village proper from the railway station, climb the 377-step Lardarina stairway or jump on a shuttle bus.

Corniglia harbours the region's most impressive church, **Chiesa San Pietro**, a small Gothic structure with baroque frescoes and sombre 18th-century paintings.

Aside from the popular Green-Blue trail heading west to Vernazza, you can hike east to Manarola on free-to-use path 583. En route, don't miss wine tasting at **Cantina Cappellini** *(cantinacapellini.it)* just outside Volastra.

Hop between the eastern villages

Cinque Terre's two closest villages are barely a kilometre apart and connected by a strollable cliff-hugging path, the **Via dell'Amore**.

Vineyards cram narrow terraces high above **Manorola**, a village known for its cafes and panoramic **Punta Bonfiglio**. On Piazzale Papa Innocenzo IV, **Chiesa di San Lorenzo** dates from 1338 and houses a 15th-century polyptych.

Riomaggiore has a couple of small churches and a ruined castle. Most people hang around the marina, where multistorey

EATING IN CINQUE TERRE: VERNAZZA & MONTEROSSO AL MARE

| **Il Massimo della Focaccia:** Monterosso beachfront bakery with the best crispy focaccia in Cinque Terre. *9am-7pm Thu-Tue* € | **Trattoria da Oscar:** Tiny family-run joint in Monterosso's historic centre; outstanding anchovies, *vongole* (clams) and gnocchi. *noon-2.30pm & 7-9.30pm Sat-Thu* €€ | **Il Porticciolo:** All-natural gelato in fruity flavours, including Greek yoghurt and honey, right next to Vernazza's harbour. *10am-7.30pm* € | **La Torre:** Handsome outdoor restaurant beside an old watchtower high above Vernazza with a steep climb to get here. *noon-4pm & 6.30-10pm* €€ |

Chiesa di Santa Margherita d'Antiochia, Vernazza

pastel houses glow romantically at sunset. This is the best place in Cinque Terre to rent a kayak or organise a diving or snorkelling excursion. A short walk to the east brings you to pebbly, wave-battered **Spiaggia di Fossola**.

Kayak the coast

Laced with caves and beaches, some of them only accessible by boat, Cinque Terre lends itself to the pulse-raising pursuit of sea-kayaking. When the weather is cooperating, it's possible to paddle into the harbours of all five towns in one day. Riomaggiore is the best launch point and has a reliable rental point, **Cinque Terre Adventure** (*cinqueterreadventure.com; kayak rental 1/2hr €10/20),* in the marina. For extra safety and insider knowledge, join a guided trip.

Turin

Turin has abundant history moving through its streets and sailing down its river, the mighty Po. What was once a small settlement of the Taurini people in the 3rd century BCE became a Roman colony first and a Renaissance duchy after. But most of Turin's current look comes from the 19th and 20th centuries: grand royal palaces in the city centre, which speak to its former status as a capital of the Kingdom of Italy and seat of the country's royal family, and industrial suburbs

PARCO NAZIONALE DELLE CINQUE TERRE INFO

The whole Cinque Terre area is part of the **Parco Nazionale delle Cinque Terre** *(parconazionale 5terre.it).* Park authorities maintain the various hiking trails that surround the five villages and preserve the surrounding seas, which are included in a protected marine area. The park's useful website is worth visiting when you are planning your trip, and there are also information points at each Cinque Terre train station and in La Spezia. Check out the two options for the Cinque Terre Card ahead of your visit. Opt for the Trekking Card if you just want to hike on the SVA between the villages, and the Treno MS Card if you want to also include unlimited train travel.

 EATING IN CINQUE TERRE: CORNIGLIA

Ristorante Cecio: Large portions of risotto, pasta and fish served by charismatic staff who treat you like family. *noon-3pm & 6.30-10pm* €€

Alberto Gelateria: Often touted as offering the best ice cream in the five villages, using local herbs to augment its fruity flavours. *9am-10pm* €

Pan e Vin: Friendly staff serve hearty breakfasts, focaccia sandwiches, wine and the best Nutella cake on the Riviera. *7am-8pm Fri-Wed* €

Enoteca Il Pirun: Spread across two floors of an old village house, this trad *trattoria* offers earthy Cinque Terre classics. *noon-3pm & 7-10pm* €€

TARA VAN DER LINDEN PHOTO/SHUTTERSTOCK

Palazzo Reale, Turin

THE HOLY SHROUD

Don't expect to see the Holy Shroud when you visit the **Cattedrale di San Giovanni Battista** – it's usually kept locked inside a very specific case to prevent any damage, and pilgrims can only stop in front of the chapel that houses it. The Shroud is, however, exhibited to the public at irregular intervals – with years potentially separating them, considering the last ones were in 2013, 2015, 2020 and 2021, with some of the viewings only being via TV. These are always announced beforehand on its official website *(sindone.org)*. If you happen to visit around the time of an *ostensione* (showing) and want to take advantage, prepare for some considerable queues.

dating back to when Turin was one of the engines behind Italy's modernisation process.

Tap into the city of kings

The **Palazzo Reale** *(museireali.beniculturali.it; full/reduced €15/2)* was once the official residence of the House of Savoy. Close by is **Palazzo Madama**, also used by members of the royal family as a residence. Both palaces are museums in their own right, but also host exhibitions. Passing through the Palazzo Reale's courtyards will lead you to the relaxing **Giardini Reali**.

Just off the side of the Palazzo Reale, the **Cattedrale di San Giovanni Battista** contains the **Chapel of the Holy Shroud**, which houses the famous Shroud of Turin, believed to be the cloth used to wrap the body of Jesus Christ after his crucifixion.

Piazza-hop *alla torinese*

The quickest way to gain a sense of Turin's atmosphere is to get lost in the perfectly parallel, grid-like streets of its city centre. Linger in its piazzas, like **Piazza Statuto** – not too far from the Porta Susa railway station – or the sprawling

 EATING IN TURIN: OUR PICKS

Barbagusto: Tiny, cosy and featuring a menu bursting with all the delicacies the Piedmontese culinary tradition has to offer. *12.30-3.30pm & 7.30-10pm Wed-Sat, 7.30-10pm Sun* €

Osteria Antiche Sere: Your textbook Turin restaurant in both looks and food, on a quiet street away from the most beaten tourist tracks. *7.30-10.30pm Mon-Sat* €€

Pasticceria Ghigo: This incredibly *torinese* cafe is perfect for sitting under the Via Po porticoes. Try their *nuvola*, a little *pandoro* (sweet bread) that's renowned throughout the city. *7.30am-8pm* €€

Vintage 1997: Enjoy a Michelin-starred meal at this elegant place. Tasting menus include local dishes and quirkier creations. *12.30-2.30pm & 8-11pm Mon-Thu, 12.30-2.30pm & 7.30-11pm Fri, 7.30-11pm Sat* €€€

Piazza Vittorio Veneto, or the tiny **Piazza Carlo Emanuele II**, which locals know as 'Piazza Carlina'.

Getting from one to the other is simple, thanks to Turin's porticoes. When put together, the city's monumental porticoes are almost 20km long, lining the major avenues of its centre and allowing people to be outside even when the weather isn't the nicest.

Enjoy a museum day

Rainy days are the perfect occasion to explore one of Turin's many museums. History buffs can head to the **Museo Nazionale del Risorgimento Italiano** *(museorisorgimento torino.it; full/reduced €10/8)*, housed inside the magnificent **Palazzo Carignano**, or the nearby **Museo Egizio** *(museo egizio.it; full/reduced €18/3)*, which hosts the second-largest collection of Egyptian antiquities after the one in Cairo. If you prefer cinema, then head to the **Museo Nazionale del Cinema** *(museocinema.it; full/reduced €16/14)*, located inside the skyline-defining **Mole Antonelliana**.

For something a little different, car lovers should try the **Museo Nazionale dell'Automobile** *(museoauto.com; full/reduced €15/12)* a few kilometres outside the city centre.

Milan

MAP p668

Milan is an industrial powerhouse, a fashion capital and global trendsetter in architecture and design. The birthplace of Prada and Alfa Romeo, Italy's wealthiest city continues to nurture innovation, but for many residents its finest attributes have nothing at all to do with financial clout or iconic labels. This is a place of countless, only-in-Milan experiences. It's sinking into a red velvet chair and waiting for the curtain to rise at La Scala. Or enjoying a balmy summer evening at a canal-side cafe while watching the world stroll past, wandering through a provocative art installation or happening upon a glowing Duomo at sunset.

Watch the curtain rise at La Scala

Onc of the most famous opera stages in the world, **La Scala** *(teatroallascala.org)* is where Maria Callas made her debut, Verdi triumphed and Toscanini established his legacy as a virtuoso conductor. Sitting in the crimson and gilt boxes of Teatro alla Scala among the Milanese dressed to impress is one of those moments you won't forget. The opera season kicks off on 7 December, the day of Sant'Ambrose – Milan's patron saint – and it typically runs until mid-July. If you're not a fan

LOCAL DRINKS

If you want to truly take a sip of Turin, then you can't leave the city without having tried two of its most typical drinks. First up is the *bicerin* (quite literally 'small glass' in the local dialect), a shot of espresso carefully layered with chocolate and milk. Try it at **Caffè al Bicerin**, where it was supposedly invented at the beginning of the 18th century. Then there's vermouth, an aromatised and fortified wine whose modern version was first produced right here in Turin around the same time the *bicerin* was invented. It's usually drunk as an *aperitivo*, even though you'll find that a good number of the city's cafes serve it around the clock.

EATING NEAR MILAN'S DUOMO: OUR PICKS

MAP p668

Trattoria Milanese: Generous goblets of wine, hearty servings of traditional Milanese (try pan-fried risotto). *noon-2.30pm & 7-10.30pm Mon-Fri* €€

Peck: Restaurant and deli; Milanese specialities like *osso buco* (veal and vegetables in broth) and *mondeghili* (meatballs) with chicory. *9am-7.30pm Tue-Sat, from 3pm Mon* €€

Rinascente Food Hall: On the 7th floor of Rinascente department store; excellent options include Il Bar, with Duomo views. *10am-midnight* €€

Il Marchese: A beautiful courtyard and photogenic bar, with decadent dining on Roman specialities like pasta carbonara. *12.30pm-2am* €€€

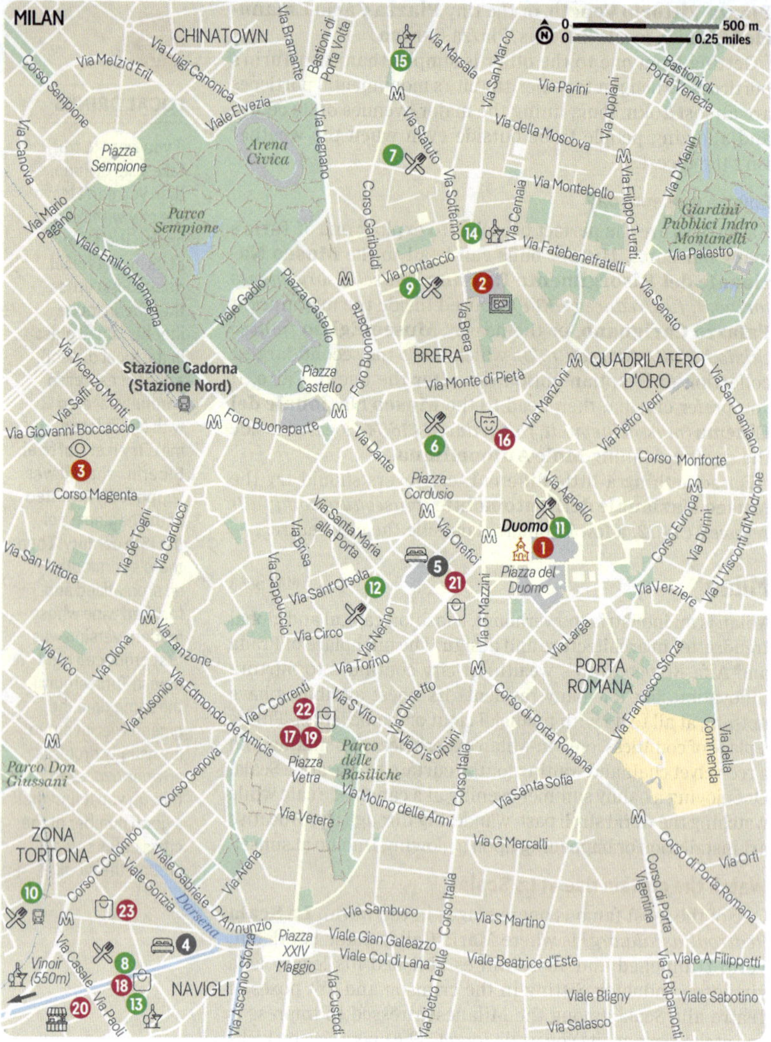

MILAN

CHINATOWN

500 m
0.25 miles

Piazza Sempione

Arena Civica

Parco Sempione

Giardini Pubblici Indro Montanelli

Stazione Cadorna (Stazione Nord)

BRERA

Piazza Castello

QUADRILATERO D'ORO

Foro Buonaparte

Piazza Cordusio

Duomo

Piazza del Duomo

PORTA ROMANA

Piazza Vetra

Parco delle Basiliche

ZONA TORTONA

Piazza XXIV Maggio

NAVIGLI

Vinoir (550m)

● HIGHLIGHTS
1 Duomo

● SIGHTS
2 Pinacoteca di Brera
3 The Last Supper

● SLEEPING
4 Maison Borella
5 Spadari al Duomo

● EATING
6 Il Marchese
7 Le Tre Regioni
8 Luca & Andrea
9 Osteria da Fortunata
10 Osteria del Binari
11 Rinascente Food Hall
12 Trattoria Milanese

● DRINKING & NIGHTLIFE
13 Mag Cafè
14 N'Ombra de Vin
15 Radetzky Cafe

● ENTERTAINMENT
16 Teatro alla Scala

● SHOPPING
17 Cavalli e Nastri Uomo
18 Dischivolanti
19 Frip
20 Mercatone dell'Antiquariato
21 Peck
22 Scout
23 Tenoha

Duomo, Milan

of operatic glory, you can also see theatre, ballet and classical-music concerts here year-round (except during August).

Swoon over the Duomo

Milan's pink-marble **Duomo** *(duomomilano.it)* was begun by Giangaleazzo Visconti in 1387. Canals were dug to transport the vast quantities of marble, and new technologies invented to cater for the never-before-attempted scale. During his stint as king of Italy, Napoleon offered to fund its completion in 1805. Neo-Gothic details were piled on – the petrified pinnacles, cusps, buttresses, arches and more than 3000 statues are almost all 19th-century additions.

Inside, stare up, and up, to the enormous stained-glass windows, with 144 panes illuminating stories from the Bible. Climbing to the roof terraces, you'll be within touching distance of the elaborate 135 spires and their forest of flying buttresses. The good-value €22 combination ticket covers the cathedral, roof terraces and more.

Trawl the Pinacoteca

Upstairs from Brera Academy, the **Pinacoteca di Brera** *(pinacotecabrera.org)* houses Milan's impressive collection of old masters, much of it 'lifted' by Napoleon during his Italian campaigns.

LA SCALA TICKETS

Tickets with a full view of the stage typically cost from €65 to €320. Buy tickets online or from the box office up to four months before the performance. The box office also sells discounted same-day tickets, available online two hours before the performance or from the box office one hour before opening.

Keep in mind that the cheapest seats (which can start at €10) may be partial or no view. Located in the highest galleries, you'll either be forced to stand or crane your neck just to put a face to those angelic voices. But you'll still get to revel in the butterflies-inducing energy of a performance at La Scala – at an unbeatable price.

 EATING & DRINKING IN BRERA: OUR PICKS ———————— MAP p668

Le Tre Regioni: Tiny family-run deli – compile a delicious sandwich from quality cold cuts and Lombard cheeses. *7.30am-8pm Mon-Sat* €

Radetzky Cafe: Fabulous banquette and window seating on a stylish, pedestrianised strip make it popular for an *aperitivo*. *8am-2am* €€

N'Ombra de Vin: Atmospheric former Augustine refectory with top wines, meat boards and tapas-style dishes. *10am-midnight Mon-Wed, to 1am Thu-Sat, 6pm-midnight Sun* €€

Osteria da Fortunata: Go early to beat the long lines at this perennially popular spot, famed for its homemade pasta. *noon-12.30am* €€

Running directly south of the Duomo, the Via Torino chain shops gradually morph into the city's hippest streetwear strip, Corso di Porta Ticinese.

Frip: The small boutique is a showcase for avant-garde fashion, from cutting-edge to more subtle designs.

Cavalli e Nastri Uomo: A beautifully curated collection of vintage menswear. The women's store is across the street.

Dischivolanti: This canal-side shop is a must for vinyl lovers, with a great selection of classic and hard-to-find LPs.

Tenoha: Direct from Tokyo, this Japanese concept store features beautiful objects for home and wardrobe, plus a stylish restaurant and bar.

Scout: Affordable, attractive and well-made basics by the well-known Italian retailer.

Rembrandt, Goya and van Dyck are included, but you're here to see the Italians: Titian, Tintoretto, Veronese and the Bellini brothers. Much of the work has tremendous emotional clout, notably Mantegna's brutal *Lamentation over the Dead Christ*. Allow several hours to cover 38 rooms at a reasonable pace. Among the highlights is Room IX, a showcase of Venetian Renaissance masters. Don't miss Caravaggio's *Cena in Emmaus* (Supper at Emmaus) in Room XXVIII, or the Rubens, Van Dyck and Jan Fyt paintings in Rooms XXXI and XXXIII.

Attend the Last Supper

Milan's most famous painting, Leonardo da Vinci's **The Last Supper** *(cenacolovinciano.org/en)*, is hidden away on a wall of the refectory adjoining the Basilica di Santa Maria delle Grazie. Depicting the moment when Jesus drops the bomb of his impending betrayal, the mixed reactions of his disciples rendered through their gestures and expressions – what da Vinci described as 'motions of the soul' – are utterly enthralling. The illusion of a 3D space created by various tricks of perspective only adds to the image's realism. Online reservations are released quarterly (mid-March for June, July or August visits); tickets go quickly. If sold out, book a **Viator city tour** *(from €80)*, which guarantees a visit.

Hang out by the canals

Milan was once laced with waterways that da Vinci himself had a hand in developing. Sadly, in the 1930s the fascist regime closed them for supposed hygiene reasons and to accommodate the increasing number of cars. Now you can have a drink on the photogenic **Naviglio Grande** and **Naviglio Pavese**, and imagine what might have been. Naviglio Grande is *the* place for *aperitivo* and on Saturday nights it feels like the whole city is here. On the last Sunday of the month, it hosts the **Mercatone dell'Antiquariato** *(navigliogrande.mi.it)*, a sprawling antiques market.

Lago di Como

Set in the shadow of the snow-covered Rhaetian Alps and hemmed in on both sides by steep, verdant hillsides, Lago di Como (aka Lake Lario) is spectacular. Shaped like an upside-down Y, the lake is littered with villages, including exquisite Bellagio. Where the southern and western shores converge is the lake's main town, Como, an elegant, prosperous city that was once a powerful rival of Milan. Among the area's siren

EATING & DRINKING IN NAVIGLI: OUR PICKS ⎯⎯⎯⎯⎯⎯ MAP p668

Luca & Andrea: Tiny place overlooking the canal. Chalkboard menu of classic fare with standouts like *osso buco* and summer pastas. *8am-2am* €€

Osteria del Binari: Bedrock of quality Milanese fare with a Liberty Style design interior and garden terrace. *7am-3pm & 7.30pm-1am* €€

MAG Cafe: Canal-side cocktails crafted with curious herbs and syrups, served in vintage glassware by knowledgeable barkeeps. *9am-2am*

Vinoir: Small, spare bar at Navigli Grande's quieter end, harbouring unusual natural wines and delicious small plates. *noon-3pm & 5pm-midnight*

Bellagio and Lago di Como

calls are extraordinarily sumptuous villas, often graced with gardens bursting with plant and animal life. The mountainous terrain provides numerous opportunities for bird's-eye views of the lake. Prepare to swoon.

Ride the cable car to Brunate

The 1894 **Funicolare Como–Brunate** *(funicolarecomo.it; one way €3.60)* takes seven minutes to trundle up to the quiet hilltop village of **Brunate** (720m), revealing a memorable perspective of mountains and lakes. Once at the Brunate funicular stop, continue to nearby baroque **Chiesa di San Andrea**. With its faded pink exterior and giant bell peeking out of the tower, it's hard to miss. If you want to keep going, allow another 30 minutes or so for the steep walk (1.3km) up to **San Maurizio**. There you can scale 143 steps to the base of **Faro di Volta**, a lighthouse built in 1927 to mark the centenary of the physicist Alessandro Volta's death.

Fall in love with Bellagio

Flanked by blue waters and lined with villas, cypress groves, oleanders and lime trees, **Bellagio** lives up to its moniker as the 'pearl' of Lago di Como. From the port, wander up the stony stairs of Salita Serbelloni, stopping to peruse the wine and silk shops. At Via Garibaldi, if you turn left and walk for

 EATING & DRINKING IN BELLAGIO: OUR PICKS

Enoteca Cava Turacciolo: Bellagio's most charming wine bar is in a candlelit, stonewalled space down a lane near the waterfront. *noon-11pm Thu-Tue* €

Trattoria San Giacomo: Cosy spot in the heart of town, with reasonably priced homemade pasta and lake fish. *noon-2.30pm & 7-9.30pm Wed-Mon* €€

La Grotta: Satisfying pizzas, pastas and seafood in an understated dining room with vaulted ceilings. *noon-2.30pm & 7-9.30pm Tue-Sun* €€

Dispensa 63: Small, creative, seasonally inspired menu with hits like risotto with scallops and roe. *noon-2pm Thu-Sat & 7-9pm Tue-Sat* €€€

VERONA VERITÀ

Alice Ronconi, former craft-beer publican, is a barista at Amaro. @alice_beerland

When she isn't pursuing hops, her perfect Verona day goes something like this:

I recommend starting your morning with a *risino* (shortcrust pastry filled with rice and custard) at **Pasticceria Scapini** and a nice walk to Castel San Pietro for the best view of the city; nearby there's the archaeological museum of Teatro Romano. Weather permitting, you can continue walking to one of the greenest places in the centre of Verona, **Parco delle Mura**, where you can have a picnic or simply relax. The perfect day in Verona ends with an Americano *aperitivo* at **Archivio** and a tasty plate of *bigoli* with donkey *ragù* at **Osteria al Duca**.

10 minutes you'll hit **Punta Spartivento**, the northernmost tip of the town where there's a swath of green and pretty views. You'll pass the town's brick Romanesque church en route, worth ducking into for its stark simplicity. But the real stars of Bellagio are its **villa gardens**.

Hike Menaggio's ancient pathways

A narrow cobblestone lane that was once part of a Roman road along the western side of Lago di Como has been preserved in sections. The **Antica Strada Regina** traverses wooded greenery, passes through age-old villages and offers fine views over the shoreline – at times from 150m heights. One of the best sections to walk is the 7km stretch (about a three-hour walk) between Menaggio and Rezzonico. If you don't want to walk back, return on the C10 bus (22 minutes).

Verona

Best known for its Shakespeare associations, Verona attracts a multinational gaggle of tourists to its pretty piazzas and knot of lanes, most in search of Romeo and Juliet. But beyond the heart-shaped kitsch and Renaissance romance, it's a bustling city whose centre is dominated by a mammoth, remarkably well-preserved 1st-century amphitheatre, the venue for an annual summer opera festival. Add to that countless churches, a couple of architecturally fascinating bridges, regional wine and food from the Veneto hinterland and some impressive art, and Verona shapes up as one of northern Italy's most attractive cities.

Beyond Romeo and Juliet

Avoid the crowds leaving lovelorn graffiti at **Casa di Giulietta** *(adult/reduced €22/13)* – which some might say is…ahem… much ado about nothing.

Verona's actual teen lovers climb up to the hilltop terraces of **Castel San Pietro** for spectacular views. Art lovers shouldn't miss the **Galleria d'Arte Moderna Achille Forti** *(gam.comune.verona.it; adult/reduced €6/4)*, nor the extraordinary **Palazzo Maffei** *(palazzomaffeiverona.com; adult/reduced €15/13)*, overlooking wonderful **Piazza delle Erbe**.

Veronetta, on the right bank of the Adige, is the authentic part of the city. It's home to the beautiful Renaissance garden **Giardino Giusti** *(giardinogiusti.com; adult/reduced €13/9)* and the striking **Teatro Romano e Museo Archeologico**

 EATING IN VERONA: OUR PICKS

Café Carducci: Storied 1920s-style bistro in classic surrounds (mirror-lined interior, linen-topped tables with candles). Exquisite for charcuterie and local cheeses. *8am-3pm & 6-10pm Tue-Sat* €

Hostaria la Vecchia Fontanina: The tables at this historic eatery fill mostly with Italians – a good sign. Excellent food at easy-to-digest prices. *noon-2.30pm & 7-10.30pm Mon-Sat* €

Osteria da Ugo: Back-alley *osteria* with a wonderful courtyard; Veronese specialities are executed with creative flair and smart service. *noon-2.30pm & 7.30-10.30pm Mon & Wed-Sat, noon-2.30pm Sun* €€

Casa Perbellini: World-class, three-star Michelin dining, such as warm spaghetti, lemon, anchovy, chicken and spring-onion emulsion (tasting menus from €220). *12.30-2pm & 7.30-9pm Tue-Fri, 12.30-2pm Sat* €€€

(museoarcheologico.comune.verona.it; adult/reduced €9/6), both worthwhile pit stops.

An arena of arias

The eighth-biggest amphitheatre in the Roman Empire and predating the Colosseum in Rome, the 1st-century **Arena di Verona** *(arena.it; adult/reduced €12/9)* is an engineering marvel. Book tickets online to avoid long queues, then pass through its ancient corridors to re-emerge into the massive, sunlit stone arena (head to the top!).

The arena is at its best during the **Arena di Verona Opera Festival** *(arena.it; tickets €30-365)*, which runs from June to September and draws international stars. There's no need to spring for top-end tickets – the numbered stone steps are fine. Rent a cushion and prepare for an unforgettable evening.

Bologna

Bologna is a city of two intriguing halves. One side is a high-tech city located in the super-rich Po valley, where opera-goers waltz out of regal theatres and into some of Italy's finest restaurants. The other is a bolshie, politically edgy city that hosts the world's oldest university and is famous for its graffiti-embellished piazzas filled with tipsy students.

No wonder Bologna has earned so many historical monikers: *La Grassa* (The Fat One) for its rich food legacy, *La Dotta* (The Learned One) for its university, and *La Rossa* (The Red One), a nod to its medieval terracotta and long-standing penchant for left-wing politics.

A medieval marvel

The foundations of Bologna's forward-thinking ethos were laid in the Middle Ages. Home to the world's oldest continually operating university, founded in 1088, the city welcomed everyone from Dante to Petrarch.

On this day-long sojourn, all roads lead to 13th-century **Piazza Maggiore**, dominated by **Basilica di San Petronio** *(basilicadisanpetronio.org)*. On the western flank is **Palazzo Comunale** (**Palazzo d'Accursio**), home to the Bologna city council since 1336 and the **Collezioni Comunali d'Arte** *(museibologna.it; adult/reduced €6/4)*, a collection of 13th- to 19th-century paintings, sculptures and furniture. Head up the attached 13th-century **Torre dell'Orologio** *(Clock Tower; bolognawelcome.com)* for panoramic views, including of the

A DAY OFF IN BOLOGNA

Daniele Bendanti, chef at **Oltre**, one of the city's top modern *trattorias*, shares some insights from his days off in the city. *@d.bendanti*

You can't miss a great breakfast at **Gino Fabbri Pasticcere** *(ginofabbri.com)* in La Caramella, a bit outside Bologna but worth it. Take a nice walk at **Giardini Margherita**, the city park that raised me. Eat something from Alessandro, my meat supplier at **Macelleria Con Cucina Agnoletto Bignami** *(facebook .com/Macelleria .Agnoletto.Bignami)*, and stop for a glass of wine or two at the **Osteria del Sole**. Towards evening, cuddle up with a nice plate of *tagliatelle* at **All'Osteria Bottega** *(osteriabottega.com)*, where I worked as a chef for five years and to which I'm very attached.

 EATING IN BOLOGNA: OUR PICKS

I Panini di Mirò: Friendly Mirò holds court at this glorified food stall with over 50 versions of great-value gourmet *panino* (roast pork, caramelised onions, pecorino). *noon-11pm* €

Delizie Bolognesi: Forging incredible, seasonally driven gelato, often with surprising local ingredients. Try Nettuno (Cervia salt, Bourbon vanilla, Sorrento lemon, orange-scented pistachio brittle). *11am-midnight Tue-Sun* €

Al Sangiovese: A convivial husband-and-wife team as generous with their portions as they are with their hospitality runs this somewhat off-the-beaten-path *trattoria*. *12.15-2.30pm & 7-10.30pm Mon-Sat* €€

Oltre: Trendy Oltre bucks tradition with creative nightly specials, without foregoing outstanding modern takes on classics. *12.30-2.30pm & 7.30-11pm Mon, Sat & Sun, 7.30-11pm Thu & Fri* €€€

SAN MARCO'S BEST SHOPPING

Piedàterre: Stylish, colourful *furlane* (Venetian slippers), hand-stitched by Italian artisans.

Merchant of Venice: Locally inspired perfumes, toiletries and home fragrances sold in a neo-Gothic pharmacy.

Giuliana Longo: A milliner and living institution, crafting everything from fascinators to classic Panamas.

Rubelli: Silk foulards and lavish handbags from a world-renowned textile house.

Chiarastella Cattana: Elegant, understated tablecloths, napkins, tea towels, cushions, robes and more from Venetian textile designer Chiarastella Cattana.

Libreria Linea d'Acqua: A high-end treasure trove of antiquarian books, first editions, maps, sculptures and engravings driven by a genuine love of Venice.

COLLECTION MAYKOVA/SHUTTERSTOCK

Torre degli Asinelli and Torre Garisenda, Bologna

leaning 97.2m-high **Torre degli Asinelli** and its neighbour, **Torre Garisenda**. Finally, there's **Basilica di Santo Stefano** (*santostefanobologna.it*), a labyrinth of interlocking ecclesiastical structures dating to the 11th century.

Taste-test the city

A misnomer, spaghetti *bolognese* is about as Bolognese as Yorkshire pudding, and Bologna's fiercely traditional *trattorias* don't serve it. Instead, the city prides itself on a vastly superior meat-based sauce called *ragù*, which sees slow-cooked minced beef and pork added to a *soffritto* (sautéed onions, celery and carrots), enlivened with a liberal dash of red wine and simmered for hours.

Ragù is one of a long list of renowned specialities birthed in the kitchens of what is arguably Italy's culinary capital, Emilia-Romagna. Lasagne, tortellini, *mortadella* and *passatelli* (pasta made with breadcrumbs, eggs and Parmesan) all hail from here.

It's generally difficult to eat badly in Bologna (though you'll need reservations at the best places, at least a week in advance). At **Trattoria Bertozzi** (*trattoriabertozzibologna.it*; *meals €30-45*), locals in the know indulge in authentic local

DRINKING IN BOLOGNA: OUR PICKS

Enoteca Storica Faccioli: This storied – if somewhat touristy – *enoteca* features Italy's best natural, organic and biodynamic juice. *4-10pm Mon-Wed, from noon Thu-Sat*

Ruggine: Locally driven craft mixology down a serene alleyway near Piazza Maggiore: house-made shrubs, Venetian aperitifs, Romagnan brandies. *6pm-1am*

Le Serre dei Giardini Margherita: Bologna's unique alfresco bar; a part co-working/event space and vegetarian restaurant immersed in greenery. *8am-midnight Mon-Fri, from 9am Sat & Sun*

Il Punto: Bologna's best and most Italian-focused craft-beer bar, with eight taps and 150 choices by the bottle. *6pm-12.30am Tue & Sun, to 1am Wed-Thu, to 2.30am Fri & Sat*

specialities. And at richly traditional **Al Cambio** *(ristoranteal cambio.it; meals €42-55)* the incredible lasagne is the pinnacle by which all others are judged. Make these your can't-miss meals in Bologna (reservations mandatory).

Walk it all off around the city's old food market, a squared grid of narrow lanes just off the southeast corner of Piazza Maggiore known as the **Quadrilatero**. For a deeper dive into local kitchens, get cooking with **Cesarine** *(cesarine. com; per person €65-214)*.

Venice

MAP p676

The French novelist Marcel Proust famously declared: 'When I went to Venice, I discovered that my dream had become – incredibly but quite simply – my address'. In this city of masks, storybook palaces and ghostly winter fogs, the line between reality and fantasy can be very thin indeed.

For over 1000 years, Venice was the capital of the Republic of Venice, a sovereign state which, at its peak, ruled lands as far away as the Peloponnese, Crete and Cyprus. Trading with Asia Minor, Persia and the Mongol Empire, La Serenissima was also one of the world's most cosmopolitan commercial hubs, its *calli* (streets) graced with the silks, spices and languages of distant lands. This melting pot would leave an indelible mark on the city's architecture, cuisine and culture. To this day, these worldly influences are palpable, whether it be in the Islamic flourishes of its Palazzo Ducale or the sweet-and-sour flavour of the city's signature *sarde in saor* (deep-fried sardines).

Eye-up Venice's keepsakes

Taking up most of the Procuratie Nuove and Procuratie Nuovissime (Ala Napoleonica) wings of Piazza San Marco, **Museo Correr** *(correr.visitmuve.it; adult/reduced €14/11)* offers a crash course in Venetian history, with an inventory that includes Doge Francesco Morosini's buff coat and sword.

Part of the 1st floor houses the **Museo Archeologico Nazionale** and its Graeco-Roman relics. If you're pressed for time, skim it and focus instead on Museo Correr's old globes and maps, its extraordinary cache of weapons and trophies from Venetian battles, and the magnificent reading room of the 16th-century **Biblioteca Nazionale Marciana**. Upstairs, the **Pinacoteca** explodes with four centuries of masterpieces, including works by Paolo Veronese.

continued on p679

THE CAPPELLA MARCIANA CHOIR

Marco Bellussi, director and composer. *@bellussiteatro*

Attend Sunday morning mass at the **Basilica di San Marco** (p678) to hear the magnificent Cappella Marciana choir, which has performed at the church for more than 700 years. Occasionally the choir performs works in the Venetian polychoral style, a Renaissance-era technique that sees it split into two 'competing' formations *(cori battenti)*. The architecture is perfectly suited to this stereophonic sound, turning the basilica itself into an instrument. In my opinion, Cappella Marciana performs the most interesting music on normal, non-festive Sundays. This might mean works by Andrea Gabrieli, Giovanni Pierluigi da Palestrina, Baldassare Galuppi or Antonio Lotti. You might even hear contemporary works composed by the choir's current director, Marco Germani.

⚲ EATING IN SAN MARCO: OUR PICKS

MAP p676

Rosticceria Gislon: Historic, canteen-style joint famous for deep-fried street food, including croquettes and deep-fried mozzarella. *9am-9.30pm* €

Ai Mercanti: Top chefs and sommeliers dine here for the modern, produce-driven dishes and artisanal wines. *1-2pm & 7-10pm Tue-Sat* €€

Rossopomodoro: Neapolitan chain serving decent pizzas, pasta dishes and grazing platters in upbeat, modern digs. *11.30am-11.30pm* €€

Chat Qui Rit: Refined, creative cooking celebrating top-tier Italian produce and subtle Asian accents. *noon-3pm & 6-10pm Tue-Sat* €€€

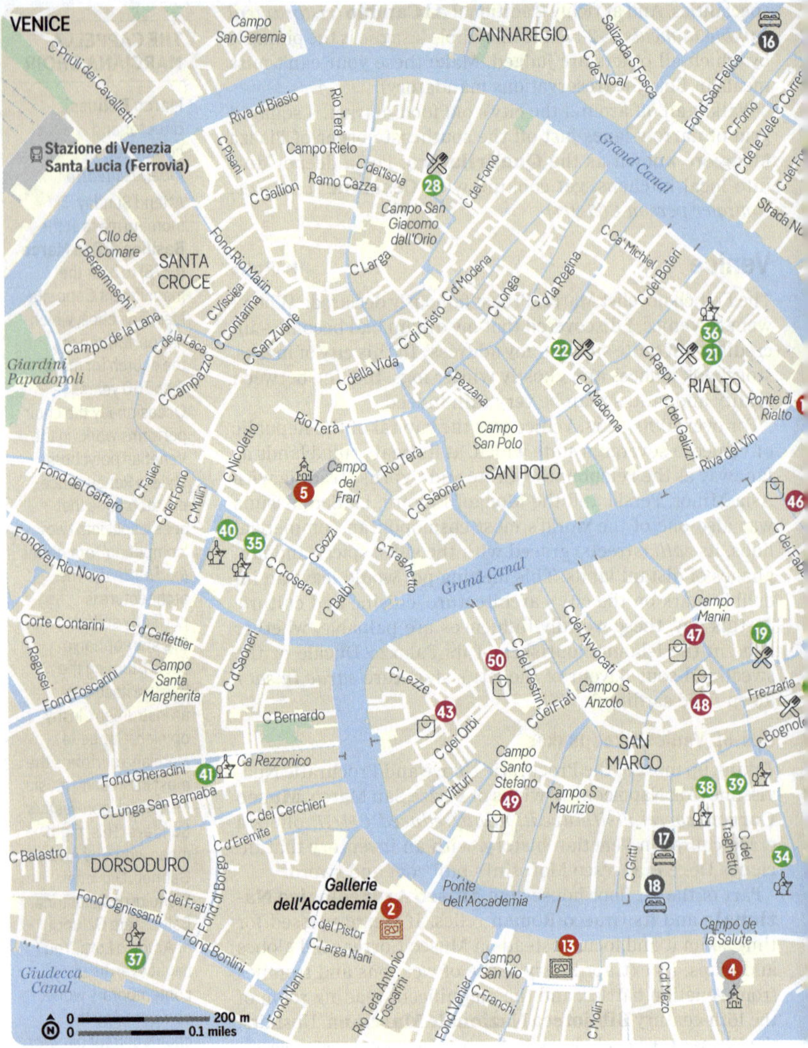

VENICE

CANNAREGIO

Campo San Geremia

C Priuli dei Cavalletti

Salizada S Fosca

C de Noal

Fond San Felice

C Forno

C de le Valle

C dei Fr

Strada Nu

Grand Canal

Riva di Biasio

Rio Terà

Campo Rielo

C dell'Isola

C del Forno

📡 **Stazione di Venezia Santa Lucia (Ferrovia)**

C Pisani

Ramo Cazza

C Gallion

28

Campo San Giacomo dall'Orio

SANTA CROCE

Cllo de C Comare

C Bergamaschi

Fond Rio Marin

C Viscata

C Contarina

C Larga

C di Cristo

C d Modena

C Longa

C de la Regina

Ca' Michiel

C dei Botteri

Fond Minotto

Giardini Papadopoli

C Campasio

C dela Laca

C San Zuane

C della Vida

C Piezzan

22

C d Madonna

C Raspi

36
21

RIALTO

Ponte di Rialto

1

C dela Lana

Rio Terà

C Nicoletto

Campo dei Frari

Rio Terà

Campo San Polo

SAN POLO

C dei Galizzi

Riva del Vin

Fond dei Tolentini

Fond del Gaffaro

C Fiubera

C dei Forno

C Mulin

5

C d Saoneri

C del Traghetto

46

Fondcl Rio Novo

40
35

C Crosera

C Gozzi

C Balbi

Grand Canal

Campo Manin

47
19

Corte Contarini

C d Ceffettier

C dei Saoneri

C Lezze

50

C dei Pestrin

C dei Frati

Campo S Anzolo

48

Frezzaria

C Raguseo

Campo Santa Margherita

C Bernardo

43

C dei Orbi

SAN MARCO

C Bognolo

Fond Gherdini

41

Ca' Rezzonico

C Vitturi

Campo Santo Stefano

49

Campo S Maurizio

38
39

C del Traghetto

C Lunga San Barnaba

C dei Cerchieri

C Gritti

17

34

DORSODURO

C d Eremite

C Balastro

Gallerie dell'Accademia
2

18

C Gritti

Fond Ognissanti

C dei Frati

Fond di Borgo

C del Pistor

Ponte dell'Accademia

Fond Bonlini

C Larga Nani

13

4

37

Rio Terà Antonio Foscarini

Campo San Vio

C d Mezzo

Giudecca Canal

C dei Franchi

Campo de la Salute

C Molin

0 ——— 200 m

0 ——— 0.1 miles

N

676

30 Rossopomodoro	**37** Experimental Cocktail Club	**43** Chiarastella Cattana	● **INFORMATION**
31 Rosticceria Gislon	**38** Il Caravellino	**44** De Biasi	**53** Ateneo San Basso Left Luggage Office
32 Trattoria al Gatto Nero	**39** Library Bar at Nolinski Venezia	**45** Fornace Mian	
33 Venissa Osteria	**40** Malvasia all'Adriatico Mar	**46** Giuliana Longo	
● **DRINKING & NIGHTLIFE**	**41** Osteria ai Pugni	**47** Libreria Linea d'Acqua	
34 Arts Bar	● **SHOPPING**	**48** Merchant of Venice	
see 18 Bar Longhi	**42** Cesare Toffolo	**49** Piedàterre	
35 Café Noir		**50** Rubelli	
36 Cantina Do Mori		**51** Venini	
		52 Wave Murano Glass	

TOP EXPERIENCE

Basilica di San Marco

In a city packed with architectural wonders, nothing trumps the Basilica di San Marco for sheer spectacle. In 828 CE, wily Venetian merchants allegedly smuggled St Mark's corpse out of Egypt in a barrel of pork fat to avoid inspection by Muslim authorities. Venice built a basilica around its stolen saint in keeping with the city's own sense of supreme self-importance.

PAOLO GALLO/SHUTTERSTOCK

TOP TIPS

● Dress modestly, covering knees and shoulders.

● Arrive early to avoid queues or purchase 'Skip the Line' tickets online; leave large bags at **Ateneo San Basso Left Luggage**.

● The **Campanile** *(adult/under 7yr €10/free)* offers 360-degree lagoon views, but book 'Skip the Line' tickets in high season.

PRACTICALITIES

● basilicasanmarco.it
● admission from €3
● 9.30am-5.15pm, museum & loggia only 9am-2pm Sun

Unmissable Highlights

Church authorities in Rome disapproved of Venice's self-glorification, but the city defiantly created a private chapel for its Doge that outshone the official cathedral. After the original St Mark's burned, the basilica was rebuilt twice, with the current incarnation completed in 1094.

Its facade ripples like a wave, with five portals capped by mosaics and arches, and four bronze horses prancing above the central doorway. Enter beneath the ornate triple arch of porphyry columns and reliefs from the 13th to 14th centuries. The oldest mosaic (1270) sits above the far-left portal, showing St Mark's stolen body arriving here.

Inside, 8500 sq metres of mosaics – many with 24-carat gold leaf – glitter with divine light. The narthex holds the oldest mosaics of apostles with the Madonna, standing sentry by the main door for more than 950 years.

Treasures abound: the **Pala d'Oro** *(€5)*, studded with 2000 gems; the **Tesoro** *(€3)* with Crusader booty, a Byzantine chalice and Archangel Michael icon; and the **Museo** *(€7)*, with close-ups of the mosaics and piazza views from the Loggia dei Cavalli. The most unforgettable experience? An **After Hours tour** *(walksofitaly.com; from €139)*, which includes the crypt.

continued from p675

The Doge's palace

For over seven centuries, Venice's spectacular **Palazzo Ducale** *(palazzoducale.visitmuve.it; adult/reduced incl Museo Correr from €25/13)* was the city's seat of government, enduring storms, fires, conspiracies – and even Casanova, who famously escaped the attic prison. The site likely became the Doge's residence in the 10th century, but the current palace began taking shape around 1340. The 1443 **Porta della Carta**, facing the Piazzetta, welcomed dignitaries into the **colonnaded courtyard**. Today, entry is from the waterfront side of the building, which leads into its colonnaded courtyard. From it, the **Scala d'Oro** leads to Palladio's **Sala delle Quattro Porte**, while the **Sala Consiglio dei Dieci** is where Venice's star chamber plotted under a Veronese ceiling. The vast **Grand Council Chamber**, with Tintoretto's gigantic *Paradise,* once hosted elections and ducal audiences, while the **Armoury** displays weapons and fragments of frescoes. Cross the **Bridge of Sighs** to the eerie **Prigioni Nove**, complete with graffitied cells.

The worthy, 60-minute **Secret Itineraries Tour** *(adult/reduced €32/20)* uncovers the **Pozzi** wells, top-secret **Chancellery**, and the **Piombi** attic prison where Casanova was imprisoned in 1756. Book both standard entry tickets and Secret Itinerary Tours online in advance to avoid queues.

Ponder Titian's masterpiece

Built for the Franciscans in the 14th and 15th centuries, the **Basilica di Santa Maria Gloriosa dei Frari** *(basilicadei frari.it; adult/reduced €5/2)* has none of the flying buttresses, pinnacles and gargoyles typical of international Gothic – but its vaulted ceilings and broad, triple-nave, Latin-cross floor plan give this minor basilica a grandeur befitting the masterpieces it contains.

Its undisputed star is Titian's restored 1518 altarpiece *Assunta* (Assumption), one of Italy's greatest Renaissance artworks and also the world's largest wood-panel painting.

The church harbours works by other Venetian greats as well, among them Bellini and Donatello, not to mention a rare Monks' Choir area dating from 1468. Among the numerous monumental tombs is that of Antonio Canova, designed by the sculptor himself and home to his heart.

Cross the Rialto at dawn

The best time to experience Venice's world-famous **Ponte di Rialto** is early in the morning (before 8.15am). Uncluttered

VENICE FROM THE WATER

Steven Moore, TV presenter, *Antiques Roadshow* judge. @mrstevenmoore
Some visitors think gondola rides are tacky, but they're actually a fabulous experience. Many gondoliers know Venice intimately, so instead of asking them to sing you 'O Sole Mio', ask them to point out any interesting details about the buildings. Golden hour, when the sun is beginning to set, is especially magical. Evening rides are also wonderful: look up and you might catch a glimpse of a chandelier or a ceiling fresco.
If you've got an hour to kill, take the *vaporetto* up or down the Grand Canal. From tip to toe it's around 40 minutes. I prefer the number 2 *vaporetto* over the 1: it's generally quieter and has less stops.

🍸 **DRINKING IN SAN MARCO: OUR PICKS** ───── MAP p676

Bar Longhi: Superlative martinis and bellinis in sumptuous surrounds on the Grand Canal. Expensive but magical. *11am-1am*

Il Caravellino: Historic restaurant bar with handsome wood panelling, leather armchairs and classic drinks. *8.30am-11pm*

Library Bar at Nolinski Venezia: Posh hideaway, with floor-to-ceiling bookshelves, Simon Buret ceiling art and creative libations. *5pm-12.30am*

Arts Bar: Cocktail den inside the St Regis Hotel serving clever libations inspired by Venetian artworks and architecture. *6.30pm-12.30am Tue-Sat*

GUGGENHEIM

Karole PB Vail,
Director Peggy
Guggenheim
Collection,
granddaughter of
Peggy Guggenheim.
When visiting the
Peggy Guggenheim
Collection, get up
close to the paintings
to appreciate their
superb execution.
Note the thickness
of the paint in
Jackson Pollock's
Alchemy and the
meticulousness of
Leonora Carrington's
*Oink (They Shall
Behold Thine Eyes)*.
Joan Miró's wonderful
Dutch *Interior II* is
a bit of a riff on Jan
Steen's 17th-century
painting *The Dancing
Lesson*, but Miró
made it all his own in
a very entertaining,
surreal way. I also
love the work of Yves
Tanguy, who painted
surreal, dreamlike
landscapes. The
collection is very
rich in sculpture;
look for Jean Arp's
Head and Shell, the
first sculpture Peggy
Guggenheim bought.

Ponte di Rialto (p679), Venice

by tourists and awnings, you'll be able to fully appreciate its elegant Renaissance lines and the superb view from its balustraded decks. Below you, the city prepares for another busy day: sharply dressed commuters spill out of *vaporetti* (small passenger ferries) and delivery workers unload restaurant supplies from bobbing boats. Costing 250,000 gold ducats and completed in 1592, the Istrian-stone bridge is the work of Antonio da Ponte, whose nephew Antonio Contino would go on to design San Marco's Bridge of Sighs.

Admire Venetian greats

Tracing the development of Venetian art from the 14th to 19th centuries, the unmissable **Gallerie dell'Accademia** *(gallerie accademia.it; adult/reduced €15/2)* contains more murderous intrigue, forbidden romance and shameless politicking than the most outrageous Venetian parties. Room 5 harbours Giovanni Bellini's sublime *Madonna and Child between Saints Catherine and Mary Magdalene* while Room 8 claims two Giorgione masterpieces: *Old Woman* and *The Tempest*. Even more commanding is Paolo Veronese's monumental *Feast in the House of Levi* in Room 10, condemned by Inquisition leaders for depicting dogs, drunkards, dwarves, Muslims and

 EATING IN SAN POLO & SANTA CROCE: OUR PICKS — MAP p676

All'Arco: Epicureans relish All'Arco's market-fresh seafood *cicchetti* (Venetian tapas) and in-the-know wines by the glass. *10am-2.30pm* €

Cantina Do Mori: Venice's oldest *bacaro* (bar), with interesting pan-Italian wines and tasty *cicchetti* and cheeses. *8am-7.30pm Mon-Sat* €

Osteria La Zucca: Daily changing menu of delicious vegetarian and meat dishes; book ahead. *noon-2.30pm & 7-10.30pm Mon-Sat* €€

Antiche Carampane: Book ahead for market-driven Venetian classics. Near Ponte de le Tette. *12.30-2.30pm & 7.30-10pm Tue-Sat* €€€

Reformation-minded Germans cavorting with apostles. Another highlight is Gentile Bellini's recently restored *Miracle of the Reliquary of the Cross at San Lorenzo Bridge* in Room 20. Allow at least 1½ hours for a visit, and avoid high-season queues by arriving at opening time or after 4pm.

Picasso, Pollock and Peggy

Set aside a couple of hours for the **Peggy Guggenheim Collection** (*guggenheim-venice.it; adult/reduced €16/9*), one of Italy's finest modern-art museums. Occupying an unfinished 18th-century Grand Canal *palazzo*, it was once home to American arts doyenne Peggy Guggenheim.

Works on display rotate, but look out for early works by Picasso and Mondrian – among them Picasso's *A Poet* (1911) and Mondrian's *Ocean 5* (1915) – as well as Magritte's enigmatic *Empire of Light* (1953–54). Another highlight: *Alchemy* (1947), one of Jackson Pollock's first revolutionary 'poured' paintings. A spirited advocate for contemporary Italian art, Guggenheim also influenced the reappraisal of artists such as Umberto Boccioni, Giacomo Balla and Giorgio de Chirico.

The gallery's **Nasher Sculpture Garden** includes works by Henry Moore, Alberto Giacometti and Isamu Noguchi.

Ponder a mystical basilica

Sitting on over a million tree trunks at the mouth of the Grand Canal, Baldassare Longhena's **Basilica di Santa Maria della Salute** (*basilicasalutevenezia.it; church free, sacristy adult/reduced €6/4*) is the Senate's *grazie* to the Madonna for saving the city from the plague of 1630–31. Inside, the lines of the building converge beneath the dome to form a vortex on the inlaid marble floors: esoteric types believe that the central black dot radiates healing energy. The **sacristy** houses Titian's self-portrait in the guise of St Matthew and Tintoretto's made-to-measure *Wedding Feast of Cana*. For a divine view, climb the basilica's iconic **dome** (*adult/reduced €8/6*).

Observe master glassblowers

The interlinked islands of **Murano** have been synonymous with glassmaking since the 13th century, and despite being extremely touristy, some of its furnaces offer fascinating glass-blowing demonstrations. Among these is certified traditional furnace **Wave Murano Glass** (*wavemuranoglass.com*), where you can watch the blowers from the entry to the factory for free, join an in-depth tour (€29 for 45 minutes) or take a two-hour beginners' course (€245).

MURANO'S BEST IN GLASS

Venini: Even if you don't have the cash to buy a Venini, pop by to see Murano glass at its finest.

De Biasi: These certified Murano artisans design their own jewellery, picture frames, bottle stoppers and even chopsticks.

Cesare Toffolo: Mind-boggling miniatures are the trademark here, along with featherlight drinking glasses and glossy black candlesticks.

Fornace Mian: Shuffle past the typical Murano kitsch and you'll find one of the best ranges of classic stemware on the islands.

Wave Murano Glass: This team of young artisans offers a modern take on ancient traditions.

 DRINKING IN DORSODURO: OUR PICKS ⸻ MAP p676

Malvasia all'Adriatico Mar: Waterside spot offering natural, small-scale wines from the Adriatic region. *5-10pm Mon & Tue, from 11am Wed-Sun*	**Osteria ai Pugni:** Hefty selection of wines by the glass plus *aperitivo*-friendly nibbles by Ponte dei Pugni. *10am-10.30pm Mon-Sat*	**Experimental Cocktail Club:** Seriously curated cocktail menus at the Zattare's old Adriatic Naval Company. *6.30pm-1am Sun, Mon & Thu, to 2am Fri & Sat*	**Café Noir:** Gritty, friendly, boho-spirited bar with a long list of cocktails and a faithful student following. *7am-2am*

VINE REVIVAL

If you were ever invited to dinner with the Doge, chances are you would have been served dorona, a local varietal that was golden hued and highly prized.

Venice's devastating 1966 flood was thought to have wiped out the remaining dorona vines, meaning the wine of the Doges was lost for ever. That is, until 2002 when winemaker Gianluca Bisol stumbled across golden grapes growing on Torcello. He subsequently tracked down another 88 vines and used them to revive an ancient vineyard enclosed by medieval walls on Mazzorbo.

Venissa now sells bottles of the liquid gold in handblown Murano glass bottles embossed with gold leaf. Tours and tastings are available.

You'll need about an hour to explore the excellent **Museo del Vetro** (*museovetro.visitmuve.it; adult/reduced €10/7.50*), which recounts the backstory of glassmaking.

A short walk away is the remarkable, 12th-century **Basilica dei Santi Maria e Donato** (*adult/reduced €3.50/1.50*), lavished with intricate mosaics.

See where Venice began

Torcello is one of the lagoon's most tranquil islands. But 1500 years ago, it was a different story. The first lagoon island to have been settled, it was once the site of a major city, with nine churches, two abbeys and its own bishop. The Byzantine-Romanesque **Basilica di Santa Maria Assunta** (*adult/child €6/5*) served as his cathedral. The oldest parts of the building date from 639, making it by far the oldest church on the lagoon.

Inside, grab an audio guide to decode the basilica's astonishing 12th-century mosaics, and make time for the **Museo di Torcello** (*adult/reduced €3/1.50*) across the square, which outlines the island's history.

Combine your Torcello trip with Burano, and avoid Mondays when the museum is closed.

Slow the pace

Famed for its lace and technicolour buildings, **Burano** has become a popular destination for social-media hacks seeking a bright backdrop for posing purposes. After you've snapped a trillion photos of the multihued houses of the outer canals, inevitably you'll find yourself on bustling **Piazza Baldassare Galuppi**.

Here, call inside the 16th-century **Chiesa di San Martino Vescovo** (*parrocchiadiburano.weebly.com; admission free*) to see Giambattista Tiepolo's 1725 *La Crocifissione* and the *Madonna di Kazan*, a 19th-century Russian icon considered a masterpiece of enamelwork.

Across the square, give yourself an hour to explore the **Museo del Merletto** (*museomerletto.visitmuve.it; adult/reduced €5/3.50*), which tells the story of Burano's revered lace industry.

From Burano, a bridge reaches tiny **Mazzorbo**, perfect for a mind-clearing walk or a feast at vine-flanked **Venissa Osteria** (*venissa.it*).

 EATING ON MURANO: OUR PICKS ──────────────── MAP p676

Panificio Pasticceria Marangon: Grab a morning pastry from this local bakery. *6.30am-1pm Mon-Sat, plus 5-7pm Mon, Tue & Thu-Sat* €

Osteria Ai Bisatei: Glassblowers come here for plates of fried fish, seafood risotto and *spaghetti vongole*. *11.30am-2.30pm Thu-Tue* €

Osteria al Duomo: Dishes up bowls of pasta and excellent pizza within a walled garden. *noon-2.30pm & 6.30-9pm Fri-Wed* €€

Osteria Acquastanca: The best restaurant on Murano serves mainly seafood dishes. *noon-3pm Mon-Sat, plus 7-9.30pm Mon & Fri* €€€

Florence & Tuscany

ICONIC LANDMARKS | RENAISSANCE ART | MEDIEVAL TOWNSCAPES

Stretching along the Tyrrhenian Sea below Liguria and Emilia-Romagna, Tuscany beckons with its wealth of historic sites scattered on the changing landscapes that slope down from the Apennines to the coast. Fortified palaces and ancient *case-torri,* the tower houses erected by wealthy pre-Renaissance families, define skylines, as do the stone-built bell towers of Gothic and Romanesque churches continuously visited by long-distance pilgrims for nearly a millennium.

The region's capital and undisputed headliner is Florence (Firenze), cradle of the Renaissance and home to an embarrassing wealth of cultural riches (even by Italy's inimitable standards). While it's easy enough to stay put in Florence, Tuscany's cypress-lined countryside rewards the curious. Of all the region's hilltop towns, few match Siena, where winding medieval streets lead to an extraordinary cathedral and storybook square. Closer to the coast, scholarly Pisa beckons with more than just its vertically challenged tower.

☑ **TOP TIP**

Summers can be scorching hot in Florence. If you're climbing the Duomo, Giotto's Campanile or the Torre di Arnolfo, keep in mind that hundreds of narrow steps await. People have fainted in the past – avoid the middle of the day when booking your tickets.

Florence

MAP p686

Few cities are so compact in size or so packed with extraordinary art and architectural masterpieces at every turn. The

 GETTING AROUND

Frequent high-speed trains connect Florence to other major Italian cities, including Rome, Bologna and Milan. High-speed and *regionale* (regional) trains connect Florence to Pisa, while a reasonably extensive regional bus network includes *corse rapide* (express services) between Florence and Siena. Other bus routes in Tuscany can involve long trips.

Florence itself is small and best navigated on foot; most major sights are within easy walking distance. Nonresident traffic is banned from the historic centre, and parking is an absolute headache and best avoided. Trams run between Florence Airport and the city's main train station, Firenze Santa Maria Novella.

urban fabric of this small city, on the banks of the Arno river in northeastern Tuscany, has hardly changed since the Renaissance and its narrow cobbled streets are a cinematic feast of elegant 15th- and 16th-century *palazzi,* medieval candlelit chapels, fresco-decorated churches, marble basilicas and world-class art museums brimming with paintings and sculptures by Botticcelli, Michelangelo et al. Unsurprisingly, the entire city centre is a UNESCO World Heritage Site.

Florence's centre of power

For over 700 years, **Palazzo Vecchio** has housed Florence's government, and it's still home to the mayor's office today. Built in 1299 above a Roman theatre, the fortress-like palace was designed by Arnolfo di Cambio and later expanded by the Medici.

Buy a **ticket** *(bigliettimusei.comune.fi.it; adult/reduced €12.50/10)* to see the vast Salone dei Cinquecento, begun in 1494 under preacher Savonarola and later transformed by Vasari with grand scenes of Florentine victories and a ceiling celebrating Cosimo I de' Medici.

Snoop around the private quarters, including Duchess Eleonora di Toledo's chapel by Bronzino and the Sala delle Udienze, awash with frescoes by Furio Camillo. Also, don't miss

Salone dei Cinquecento, Palazzo Vecchio, Florence

Donatello's *Judith and Holofernes* and Ghirlandaio's *Apoteosi di San Zanobi*. The **Secret Passages tour** *(musefirenze.it/en/attivita/percorsi-segreti; €5)* reveals Francesco I's hidden Studiolo of rare and curious treasures.

Cross the Ponte Vecchio

Built in 1345, Florence's **Ponte Vecchio** is one the city's best-known symbols, both because of its unusual architecture and its convoluted past. Originally, the bridge was mainly populated by *beccai* (butchers), but in 1593 Grand Duke Ferdinando I, who could not stand the smell of meat and the in-salubrious state of the market, evicted all businesses involved in 'vile arts', allowing only goldsmiths and jewellers to trade on the bridge. The 48 jewellery stores perched on the bridge survived the 1944 bombing of the city – all other bridges in central Florence were destroyed – and the major flood that hit the city in 1966.

Feast on masterpieces

The **Galleria degli Uffizi** *(uffizi.it; adult/reduced €25/2)* is one of the world's greatest museums, home to masterpieces from Giotto to Caravaggio. Commissioned in 1560 by Cosimo I

continued on p688

THE 1993 BOMBING OF THE UFFIZI

In 2021 the 4.4m-tall **Albero della Pace** (Peace Tree) – a bronze olive tree created by sculptor Andrea Roggi – was placed in Via dei Georgofili, behind the Uffizi, to commemorate one of the darkest days in Italy's recent history. In the early hours of 27 May 1993, a car bomb exploded, killing five people and injuring 48. Besides the loss of human life, the detonation devastated the Torre dei Pulci housing the Accademia dei Georgofili and the Uffizi. The bomb had been placed in a parked car and detonated by remote control by the Mafia, which had escalated its tactics in response to the tightening of prison laws for those involved in organised crime.

Beloved eatery near Dante's museum.

 EATING IN DUOMO & SIGNORIA: OUR PICKS   MAP p686

Osteria Nuvoli: People spill onto the sidewalk with vino in hand, or enjoy authentic Tuscan fare at a table in the cellar. *8am-9.30pm Mon-Sat* €

I Buongustai: The sisters running this historic *trattoria* on Via dei Cerchi serve homemade Tuscan pastas. *noon-3.30pm Mon-Sat* €

Da' Vinattieri: Traditional Florentine street food, with 18 different fillings for your *schiacciata* (flat bread) – or try the Florentine tripe. *11.30am-7.30pm Mon-Sat* €

Maledetti Toscani: The 'cursed Tuscans' are far from blasphemous when it comes to food – enjoy one of their rustic sandwiches on the go. *8.30am-7pm Mon-Sat, 10am-5pm Sun* €

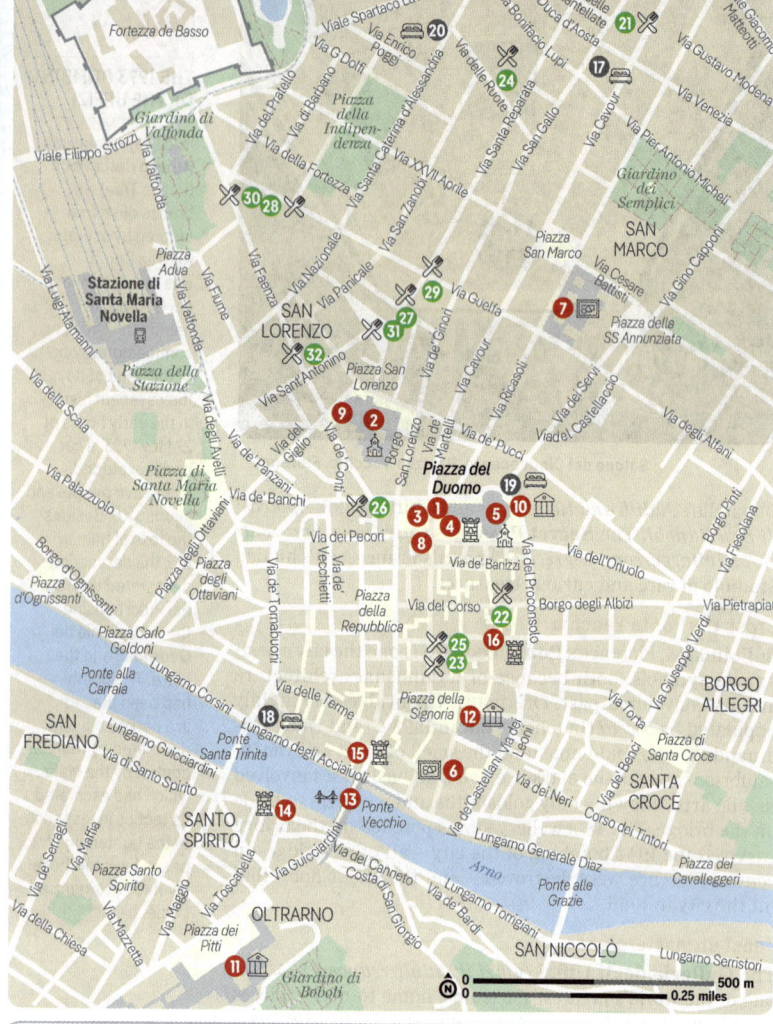

FLORENCE

HIGHLIGHTS
1 Piazza del Duomo

SIGHTS
2 Basilica di San Lorenzo
3 Battistero di San Giovanni
4 Campanile di Giotto
5 Cattedrale di Santa Maria del Fiore
6 Galleria degli Uffizi
7 Galleria dell'Accademia

8 Loggia del Bigallo
9 Museo delle Cappelle Medicee
10 Museo dell'Opera del Duomo
11 Palazzo Pitti
12 Palazzo Vecchio
13 Ponte Vecchio
14 Torre de' Barbadori
15 Torre degli Amidei
16 Torre della Castagna

SLEEPING
17 Antica Dimora Johlea
18 Antica Torre di Via Tornabuoni 1
19 Palazzo Niccolini al Duomo
20 Plus Hostel

EATING
21 Antica Trattoria da Tito
22 Da' Vinattieri
23 I Buongustai

24 Il Vegetariano
25 Maledetti Toscani
26 Osteria Nuvoli
27 Osteria Pepò
28 Osteria Vecchio Cancello
29 Ristorante Cafaggi
30 Trattoria Guelfa
31 Trattoria Mario
32 Trattoria Palle d'Oro

Piazza del Duomo

Nearly six centuries have passed since Filippo Brunelleschi completed the cupola topping the Cattedrale di Santa Maria del Fiore, providing Florence with an architectural landmark that would be revered for centuries. But the octagonal dome is only the most visible of the many treasures on Piazza del Duomo, where Gothic and Renaissance masters left an indelible mark on the city's identity.

Cattedrale di Santa Maria del Fiore

Designed by Arnolfo di Cambio and consecrated in 1436, the **Cattedrale di Santa Maria del Fiore** is crowned by Brunelleschi's revolutionary dome, inspired by Rome's Pantheon. Highlights include Ghiberti's stained-glass windows, a vast marble floor by Pollaiolo, and Vasari and Zuccari's *Last Judgement* fresco, best admired while climbing the 463 steps to the cupola's rooftop. The current neo-Gothic facade was added in the 19th century.

Giotto's Campanile

The 85m-tall bell tower of Santa Maria del Fiore was initiated by Giotto in 1334 and completed by Andrea Pisano and Francesco Talenti after Pisano died in 1337. The **Campanile di Giotto** encloses a narrow 414-step staircase leading to the panoramic platform Talenti added in 1359.

Battistero di San Giovanni

A prime example of Florentine Romanesque architecture, the piazza's octagonal **baptistery** was consecrated in 1059. Andrea Pisano and Lorenzo Ghiberti created its monumental bronze doors. Inside, stunning 13th-century mosaics are being restored and are viewable on scaffolding **tours** (*duomo.firenze.it; €65*).

Museo dell'Opera del Duomo

Many original sculptures from Piazza del Duomo now reside in the **Museo dell'Opera del Duomo**. Highlights include baptistery doors by Pisano and Ghiberti, and a reproduction of Arnolfo di Cambio's 1296 facade.

TOP TIPS

● The cathedral's ground floor is free, but a ticket is required for the cupola.

● Three passes are available: Ghiberti, Giotto and the all-inclusive Brunelleschi. Purchase online in advance.

● Before leaving Piazza del Duomo through Via dei Calzaiuoli take a moment to admire the 1358 Gothic **Loggia del Bigallo**.

PRACTICALITIES

● duomo.firenze.it
● adult/reduced from €15/5 ● hours vary

continued from p685

BELOW THE DUOMO

What is commonly referred to as the 'crypt' was in fact a welcome centre for pilgrims travelling along the ancient Via Francigena, the 3000km medieval route between Canterbury and Rome. Pilgrims would descend into the rooms below the cathedral to admire the vivid 13th-century cycle of biblical frescoes decorating the walls – well-earned spiritual wonder and respite to weary, faith-filled travellers. Hidden for centuries beneath layers of history, the rooms were only rediscovered in 1999, revealing a breathtaking visual narrative of faith and artistry. The frescoes' vibrant colours remain remarkably intact, their preservation owed to the absence of sunlight and humidity. Today they stand as an essential piece of the city's rich medieval heritage.

and designed by Vasari, the U-shaped palace once housed government offices before becoming a gallery under Francesco I. Admire its symmetrical facade from Piazza della Signoria before ascending to the 2nd floor via the Scalone Granducale. Highlights include Botticelli's *Nascita di Venere* (1485), the octagonal Tribuna degli Uffizi, and Michelangelo's *Tondo Doni* (1504–06), his only existing panel painting.

Don't miss the restored **Terrazzo delle Carte Geografiche**, covered in handpainted 16th-century maps. Later, encounter Leonardo, Raphael, and Roman sculptures in the **Sala della Niobe**. On the 1st floor, the Collezione degli Autoritratti showcases 250 self-portraits, while the final stretch includes Caravaggio's chilling *Giuditta che Decapita Oloferne* (1620). Book tickets in advance online.

Where the powerful prayed

Built over a 4th-century church, the **Basilica di San Lorenzo** (*sanlorenzofirenze.it; adult €9*) became the Medici family church in the 15th century. In 1425, Cosimo the Elder commissioned Brunelleschi's elegant redesign; his tomb now lies in the crypt-turned-museum, Museo del Tesoro di San Lorenzo. Nearly a century later, Pope Leone X, son of Lorenzo the Magnificent, asked Michelangelo to revamp the facade – but the Carrara-marble plan was never realised, leaving the exterior bare. Inside, *pietra serena* columns frame masterpieces like Filippo Lippi's *Annunciazione Martelli* (1440), Rosso Fiorentino's *Sposalizio della Vergine* (1523) and Donatello's sculpted pulpits (1460). Brunelleschi's *Sagrestia Vecchia* (Old Sacristy), left of the altar, is a highlight, decorated with Donatello's sculptural details. Before exiting, look up to the **Tribuna delle Reliquie** above the main portal, designed by Michelangelo.

Mingle with the Medicis

Matching their opulent palaces, the Medicis' final resting place is a grandiose masterpiece. Enter the **Museo delle Cappelle Medicee** (*bargellomusei.it/musei/cappelle-medicee; adult €9*) from the rear end of the Basilica di San Lorenzo in Piazza di Madonna degli Aldobrandini to find yourself under the 59m-high cupola of the Cappella dei Principi, where the Cosimo I, Francesco I and Cosimo III tombs are surrounded by the city's Florentine mosaic, or *commesso*. Continue to the **Sagrestia Nuova**, the marble hall designed by Michelangelo, where Lorenzo the Magnificent and his brother Giuliano are

Cooking up Tuscan classics for over a century.

 EATING IN SAN LORENZO & SAN MARCO: OUR PICKS

| **Trattoria Guelfa:** Select a first and second course from the hand-written menu that changes daily. *noon-2.45pm & 7-10.45pm* € | **Trattoria Mario:** Bustling *trattoria* serving authentic Tuscan cuisine. No reservations. *noon-3pm Mon-Sat, 7.30-10pm Thu & Fri* € | **Il Vegetariano:** Vegetarian dishes, freshly made savoury cakes and a variety of teas. *12.30-2.30pm Mon-Fri, 7.30-10.30pm Mon-Sun* € | **Antica Trattoria da Tito:** The walls are covered in scrawled messages from past customers testifying to its popularity. Book ahead. *12.30-3pm & 7-11pm Mon-Sat* €€ |

TODAMO/SHUTTERSTOCK

Michelangelo's *David*, Galleria dell'Accademia

buried. This smaller room, built between 1520 and 1534, is adorned with monumental sculptures whose details are elevated by two carefully constructed sources of natural light, which Michelangelo viewed as an essential element of his design.

Make a date with David

Michelangelo's iconic *David* is one of hundreds of artworks at the **Galleria dell'Accademia** *(galleriaaccademiafirenze. it; adult/reduced €16/2)*, from 13th-century gilded panels to Bartolini's neoclassical busts. Originally a Medici drawing academy (1563), it became a public museum in 1784. At the heart of the Sala del Colosso stands Giambologna's dynamic plaster *Ratto delle Sabine* (1581), surrounded with works by Lippi, Perugino and Botticelli. Before reaching *David,* pause at Michelangelo's four intentionally unfinished *Prigioni* (1519–34), marble figures straining to escape their stone prisons. Waiting at the end of the gallery is *David* (1504) himself, a 5m marble icon of freedom and beauty sculpted by Michelangelo at just 29. Book tickets on the website (there's a €4 reservation fee). Entry is free on the first Sunday of the month, but expect queues.

MAP p686

FLORENCE'S TOWER HOUSES

The stone-built *case-torri* (tower houses) that dot Florence's heart are a fascinating architectural remnant of the Middle Ages. These residential structures rise above the city's red rooftops, taking you back to an era when powerful families erected hermetic homes to protect themselves from enemy attacks and show off their wealth. The towers generally had a rectangular or square base and could have up to six or seven storeys. About 50 *case-torri* still stand. The best-preserved ones are the **Torre della Castagna**, the **Torre degli Amidei** and the **Torre de' Barbadori**. You can even sleep in one – the hotel **Antica Torre di Via Tornabuoni 1**, offering spectacular 360-degree views over the city from its crenellated rooftop.

Trattoria Palle D'Oro: Ideal lunch break, with simple Tuscan dishes. *noon-3pm & 7-10.30pm* €

Ristorante Cafaggi: Local favourite offering changing seasonal classics in an old-school atmosphere. *12.30-3pm & 7-10pm Mon-Sat* €

Osteria Pepó: Book ahead to secure a spot at this popular place serving generous portions of pastas and meats. *noon-2.30pm & 7-10.30pm* €€

Osteria Vecchio Cancello: This quirkily decorated *osteria* is known for its calm atmosphere and its steaks. *noon-2pm & 7-10pm Wed-Mon* €€

THE MEDICIS' BALLS

As you stroll through San Lorenzo, you'll inevitably spot the Medicis' emblem hanging on many of the neighbourhood's buildings. The shield adorned with six or seven spheres continues to loom over Palazzo Medici Riccardi, the Biblioteca Medicea Laurenziana and the ceiling of the Basilica di San Lorenzo. No one knows exactly what the balls of the Medicis' emblem mean. One hypothesis suggests that they represent the marks left by the Mugello Giant on the shield of Averardo, an ancestor of the Florentine rulers. A more worldly take on the story says that the spheres are simply coins, linking the family with their banking activities.

Trawl treasures at the Pitti

Dominating its namesake piazza, stately **Palazzo Pitti** *(uffizi .it/en/pitti-palace; adult €16)* became the Medici residence in 1549 and was later expanded by court architect Bartolomeo Ammannati. Start in the Galleria Palatina to explore the Sala di Ulisse, with works by Raphael and Vasari, then continue to the Sala dell'Iliade, where paintings by Andrea del Sarto surround Bartolini's *La Carità* under a Homeric ceiling. In the Sala di Apollo, meet Cosimo I's court jester Morgante, painted nude by Bronzino. Upstairs, the Galleria d'Arte Moderna showcases neoclassical sculptures by Canova, as well as Romantic and Macchiaioli works. Don't miss the Museo della Moda e del Costume, tracing Italian fashion from Eleonora di Toledo to Prada. Back on the ground floor, the dazzling Sala di Giovanni da San Giovanni, frescoed in 1635, celebrates a Medici wedding with trompe l'oeil splendour.

Siena

MAP p691

Unlike other major medieval powers, Siena could not rely on access to rivers or seas for transport and trade. Still, the city, nestled on three hills, flourished during the 13th century, developing a political system that would guarantee a period of peace prolonged enough to allow the development of one of Italy's most influential universities and one of Europe's richest art collections. Traces of this legacy are still visible today, starting from the architecture of the enchanting Piazza del Campo, the city's main square, to the Duomo, one of Tuscany's most impressive cathedrals.

Explore a theatrical square

Siena's shell-shaped **Piazza del Campo** has been the city's civic and political heart since the 12th century. Its transformation began with the 13th-century construction of the Gothic Palazzo Pubblico. Strict urban planning laws ensured architectural harmony, with double- or triple-arched windows and no balconies. The square, divided into nine segments, hosts December's **Mercato del Campo** *(mercatonelcampo.it)* and, most famously, the Palio horse race (p692). A 19th-century copy of Jacopo della Quercia's **Fonte Gaia** (1419) stands at its northern edge. Originally topped with a Venus statue, the fountain was altered after the Black Death, when religious authorities blamed pagan imagery for the plague. The statue's remains were reportedly buried in Florentine lands to wish the enemy an equal misfortune.

Art for the powerful

Flanked by the 88m **Torre del Mangia**, Siena's iconic **Palazzo Pubblico** was built between 1288 and 1342 as the seat of the Government of the Nine. Today, it houses the extraordinary **Museo Civico** *(museocivico.comune.siena.it),* showcasing centuries of Sienese art. Highlights include Martino Bartolomeo's *Sixteen Virtues* fresco and Spinello Aretino's *Storie di Alessandro III* in the Sala di Balìa, and Simone

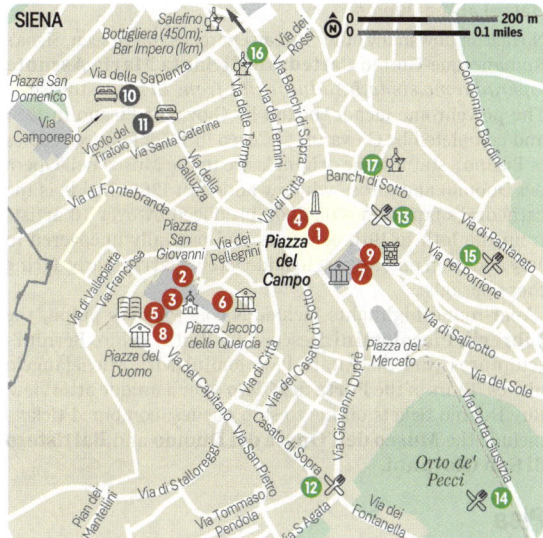

SIENA

Salefino
Bottigliera (450m);
Bar Impero (1km)

Piazza San Domenico

Piazza
San Giovanni

Piazza del Campo

Piazza Jacopo della Quercia

Piazza del Duomo

Piazza del Mercato

Orto de' Pecci

HIGHLIGHTS
1 Piazza del Campo

SIGHTS
2 Battistero di San Giovanni
3 Cattedrale di Santa Maria Assunta
4 Fonte Gaia
see 6 Museo Civico
5 Museo dell'Opera Metropolitana

6 Palazzo Pubblico
7 Porta del Cielo
8 Torre del Mangia

ACTIVITIES
9 Libreria Piccolomini

SLEEPING
10 Albergo Bernini
11 Hotel Alma Domus

EATING
12 La Taverna di San Giuseppe

13 Osteria Le Logge
14 Ristorante All'Orto de' Pecci
15 Ristorante Gallo Nero

DRINKING & NIGHTLIFE
16 Gastronomia Morbidi
17 Trefilari Wine Bar

MICHELANGELO'S DRAWING ROOM

In 1975 a series of wall drawings was discovered behind a layer of plaster in a storage room below the New Sacristy of the **Cappelle Medicee** (p688). The sketches were attributed to Michelangelo, who's believed to have hidden in this room in 1530, fearing retaliation from Pope Clement VII, a member of the Medici family, due to work done for the republican government during the brief period when the Medici were ousted from Florence. Fifty years after the discovery, Michelangelo's drawing room has opened to the public for the first time. A test run of guided tours was held in 2024 – tickets were sold out immediately and new dates have yet to be announced. Keep an eye on bargellomusei. beniculturali.it for updates.

Martini's *Maestà* (1312) in the Sala del Mappamondo. The star attraction is Ambrogio Lorenzetti's *Buon Governo* fresco cycle (1337–39) in the Sala della Pace, a powerful allegory of good government in city and rural life. And if the message wasn't clear enough, opposite the fresco you can see the *Effetti del Cattivo Governo,* the effects of a bad government.

 EATING IN SIENA: OUR PICKS ———— MAP p691

Ristorante Gallo Nero: Named after the black rooster icon of Chianti, Gallo Nero is worth visiting for its truffle *pappardelle* alone. *noon-2.30pm Thu-Sat, 7-9.30pm Mon-Sat* €€

Ristorante All'Orto de' Pecci: Behind the Torre del Mangia, this garden-restaurant is run by a co-op serving seasonal dishes made from ingredients grown on-site. *12.30-2.30pm & 7.30-10.30pm Tue-Sun* €€

La Taverna di San Giuseppe: Prepare for a Tuscan-flavours overload in this historic spot inside a 12th-century building with an Etruscan foundation. *noon-2.30pm & 7-9.30pm Mon-Sat* €€€

Osteria Le Logge: This Sienese institution breathes tradition from every pore, starting from the in-house underground cellar. *noon-2.30pm & 7-10.15pm Mon-Sat* €€€

SIENA'S PALIO: A HEARTFELT HORSE RACE

Piazza del Campo has been the heart of Siena since the Middle Ages. Today it remains the focal point during the **Palio**, a traditional horse race held on 2 July and 16 August, where Siena's *contrade* (districts) compete to win the *drappellone*, a painting displayed in the winning district's museum. Leading up to the race, centuries-old rituals are observed, including neighbourhood decorations, horse assignments, open-air dinners and horse blessings in local churches. Originating from 1633 Assumption celebrations, the Palio involves a historical parade, jockeys in traditional costumes and three laps around the sand-covered piazza. The event is deeply rooted in local culture – this is not a tourist attraction but a heartfelt celebration for all communities involved.

Marvel at the Duomo

No matter how many other Tuscan churches you've seen, Siena's Romanesque-Gothic **Cattedrale di Santa Maria Assunta** (*operaduomo.siena.it; adult/child from €14/3*) astonishes. The polychrome facade, begun by Giovanni Pisano in 1287 and completed by Giovanni di Cecco in 1376, features copies of Pisano's statues (the originals are in the Museo dell'Opera del Duomo) and a rose window added in 1288. Inside is the cathedral's famed mosaic floor, produced by over 40 artists from the 14th to 19th centuries and partially uncovered in July and from mid-August to mid-October (arrive early during these periods).

Year-round highlights include Nicola Pisano's pulpit, the **Libreria Piccolomini** frescoed by Pinturicchio, Bernini's sculptures, and the Altare Piccolomini with Michelangelo niches. Tours of the **Porta del Cielo** offer a unique attic view. Buy Duomo tickets online to skip queues; combined tickets include the **Museo dell'Opera del Duomo** and **Battistero di San Giovanni**.

Pisa

Once a maritime power to rival Genoa and Venice, modern Pisa is best known for an architectural project gone terribly wrong. But the world-famous Leaning Tower is just one of many noteworthy sights in this compelling city. Education has fuelled the local economy since the 1400s, and students from across Italy compete for places in its elite university. This endows the centre of town with a vibrant cafe and bar scene, balancing an enviable portfolio of well-maintained Romanesque buildings, Gothic churches and Renaissance piazzas with a lively street life dominated by locals rather than tourists.

Piazza dei Miracoli's sights

Piazza dei Miracoli is far more than the **Leaning Tower**, though its 251 steps and iconic tilt remain a must-see. Completed in 1370 but only stabilised in the late 20th century, the *torre pendente* is a medieval marvel. The adjacent **Duomo di Pisa**, built from 1063 with a dome added in 1380, incorporates materials looted during Pisa's Sicilian campaign, while the **Museo dell'Opera del Duomo** houses sculptures by Nicola and Giovanni Pisano and Bonanno Pisano's bronze Porta di San Ranieri. The piazza's **Battistero di San Giovanni** is the world's largest baptistery and home to Nicola Pisano's Carrara marble pulpit. Make time also for **Camposanto cemetery** to

 DRINKING IN SIENA: OUR PICKS — MAP p691

Salefino Bottiglieria: An extension of the homonymous restaurant, this natural-wine-focused *enoteca* is an ideal spot for discovering new labels. *6pm-1am Mon-Sat*

Bar Impero: Excellent cocktails are served under the tall, vaulted ceilings of this historic bar near Porta Camollia. *7am-midnight*

Trefilari Wine Bar: Get the evening going with a couple of glasses of wine sourced from small regional producers. *4pm-2am Tue-Thu, 2pm-2am Fri-Sun*

Gastronomia Morbidi: The artisanal products displayed at this deli-bar will make your mouth water. *9am-7.30pm Mon, 8am-8pm Tue-Thu, to 9pm Fri, to 7.30pm Sat, to 3pm Sun*

ZEVANA/SHUTTERSTOCK

Duomo di Pisa and the Leaning Tower, Pisa

view Buffalmacco's impressive fresco *Il Trionfo della Morte,* and for the **Museo delle Sinopie**, to eye-up rare preparatory sketches for Renaissance frescoes.

Five centuries of Tuscan art

Despite housing one of Italy's most valuable collections of medieval art, the **Museo Nazionale di San Matteo** *(adult/ reduced €5/2)* doesn't receive much attention from visitors. The precious collection of paintings and sculptures produced between the 12th and 16th centuries includes works by Masaccio, Beato Angelico, Benozzo Gozzoli, Nicola and Giovanni Pisano, Donatello and Michelozzo. It's contained in a former Benedictine convent founded in the 11th century overlooking the Arno.

SOLVING THE TILT

After its completion in 1370, Pisa's bell tower continued to slowly tilt southward for over six centuries, defying gravity and baffling architects through the ages. Only in the 1990s did engineers finally find a solution to stabilise its fragile foundation, through a pioneering technique known as 'controlled sub-excavation', which involved the careful removal of small quantities of soil from beneath the north side of the structure. Over the past three decades the tower has straightened by as much as 4cm, and is now tilted by 'only' 3.97° – and, remarkably, it's now considered as stable as it has ever been, secure for generations of future visitors to take a dubious photo of themselves pretending to prop it up.

 EATING IN PISA: OUR PICKS

Numeroundici: No reservations, no frills. Order at the counter, sit at a wooden table and enjoy one of the daily specials. *noon-10pm Mon-Fri, from 7pm Sat* €

Trattoria Sant'Omobono: Walk past the market stalls into this *trattoria* that seems sustained by a Corinthian column in the middle of the room. *12.30-2.30pm & 7.30-10pm* €€

Osteria di Culegna: With exquisite ravioli and a wide selection of meaty mains, this family-run *osteria* offers up authentic Tuscan flavours. *12.30-2.30pm & 7.30-10pm* €€

Trattoria da Stelio: Stelio has spent most of his life serving loyal returning customers after half a century of cooking simple, traditional classics. *noon-3pm Mon-Fri* €€

Naples & the Amalfi Coast

STREET LIFE | ARCHAEOLOGY | SPECTACULAR COASTLINES

 TOP TIP

The popularity of Naples' Quartieri Spagnoli has seen holiday accommodation proliferate in recent years, making housing increasingly scarce or too expensive for residents. Consider staying in an adjacent neighbourhood and then heading in for meals or experiences. It really helps.

If you picture Italy, much of it is likely infused with the lore of Campania. Perhaps it's the holy chaos of Naples, Vespas buzzing down ancient alleys while women hang laundry above, chatting animatedly with neighbours. Or the glittering island of Capri, playground of the rich, powerful and artistic for millennia. Then, you might be conjuring the plunging seascapes of the Amalfi Coast: vertical towns crossed by lemon-coated zigzag alleys that seem to rise straight out of the Mediterranean. Yes, any one of these things might well be on your mood board. The good news? It's all real, all waiting for you. Of course, the reason it will feel familiar is because much of it has been discovered already, so prepare yourself for high-season crowds. But there's plenty left to explore and still more than a few corners that will seem like a delicious secret. No matter where you go, there will be magic.

Naples
MAP p696

Italians sometimes joke that there's Italy and then there's Napoli – so singular is its character, so potent its historical legacy. And yet so few visitors are prepared for its uniqueness and capacity to surprise.

Its story begins with the Greek colony of Neapolis, founded in 474 BCE. Norman, Spanish and Bourbon rulers made

---

GETTING AROUND

Frequent high-speed trains connect Naples to Rome and other major Italian cities. Circumvesuviana trains connect Naples to Herculaneum, Pompeii and Sorrento.

Frequent ferries connect Naples to its bay islands, including Capri, where buses traverse the island. Ferries sail between Capri and Sorrento, while the extensive SITA bus network covers the Amalfi Coast. In Naples itself, the dense city centre is best explored by foot, though use a little more caution in crowded places and at night. Mass transport – buses, funiculars, the metro – is essential for making it up to hilltop areas like Capodimonte and Vomero. Driving in Naples is unnecessary and highly discouraged, as is driving along the Amalfi Coast in high season.

NAPLES & THE AMALFI COAST

NAPLES

Inset CAPODIMONTE

9

Parco di Capodimonte

7

LA SANITÀ

0 ____ 500 m
0 ____ 0.25 miles

MATERDEI

15

Calata Fontanelle

Via Santa Teresa degli Scalzi

LA SANITÀ

Salita Stella

Piazza Cavour

10

Via Miracoli

Via dei Vergini

Via Foria

Via Cesare Rosaroli

Via Carbonara

🏛 **MANN**

1

Via Salvator Rosa

Via S Guiseppe dei Nudi   Piazza Museo Nazionale

Via Tommasi

Via Enrico Pessina

Via Duomo

Via Anticaglia

6

13

8

Via della Zite

CENTRO STORICO

Via SS Filippo e Giacomo

4

VOMERO

Via Annibale Caccavello

3

Via F Palizzi

Salita Pontecorvo

Salita Tarsia

Via G Brombeis

Stazione Cumana di Montesanto

Piazza Dante

Via del Sole

Via San Sebastiano

2

Via Atri Via Nilo

Via Benedetto Croce

Via Mezzocannone

14

Via B Caposso

Via Montesanto

Piazza del Gesù Nuovo

5

TOLEDO

Via Toledo

Via Pasquale Scura

Corso Vittorio Emanuele

QUARTIERI SPAGNOLI

Vico della Tofa

Vico d'Afflitto

Vico P Gallupi

Piazza Carita

Via Montecalvario

Via A Diaz

12

Via A Depretis

BORGO OREFICI

Via Alcide De Gasperi

Via Cristoforo Colombo

Calata Porta di Massa

17

Via S Tommaso d'Aquino

Via Icoronata

16

Calata Porta di Massa Ferry Terminal

Porto Immacolatella

CHIAIA

Via dei Mille

Via G G Filangieri

19

18

Via G Nicotera

Via Nardones

Via Correri

Vico Verdi

Piazza Trieste e Trento

Piazza del Municipio

Parco Castello

Piazza del Plebiscito

Bay of Naples (Golfo di Napoli)

Via C Poerio

Riviera di Chiaia

Villa Comunale

Via G Arcoleo

Via Partenope (Lungomare)

PIZZOFALCONE

Monte Echia

Via Santa Lucia

Via Nazario Sauro

Porto di Santa Lucia

11

Via Lucilio

N 0 ____ 500 m
0 ____ 0.25 miles

⭐ **HIGHLIGHTS**

1 MANN

🔴 **SIGHTS**

2 Cappella Sansevero
3 Certosa e Museo di San Martino
4 Chiesa e Chiostro di San Gregorio Armeno

5 Complesso Monumentale di Santa Chiara
6 Duomo di Napoli
7 Museo di Capodimonte
8 Pio Monte della Misericordia
9 Real Bosco di Capodimonte

⚫ **SLEEPING**

10 Atelier Inès
11 Grand Hotel Vesuvio

🟢 **EATING**

12 Aria Restaurant
13 Januarius
14 La Locanda Gesù Vecchio

15 Pizzeria Starita

🟢 **DRINKING & NIGHTLIFE**

16 Astronomia Bar Segreto
17 Bar Mexico
18 Chandelier
19 Enoteca Belledonne

Naples wealthy, leaving behind architectural splendours like the imposing Castel Sant'Elmo and the Palazzo Reale. Today, it's a deliciously layered, always surprising beast – gritty yet aristocratic, unrelenting yet deeply humane, a maze of glittering ballrooms and bellowing street life.

Indeed, Naples is exactly what you expect while being not what you expect at all.

Witness a miracle

San Gennaro's blood – reputedly saved by a devotee after his rather gruesome death in 305 – has become famous for its miraculous liquefaction on the first Saturday in May, 19 September and 16 December. On these days, thousands flock to the **Duomo di Napoli** *(free)* to witness this miraculous event. Whether it's truly the blood of San Gennaro (or whether it's blood at all) is impossible to say: the Catholic Church prohibits anyone from opening the two hermetically sealed ampoules. Besides, it hardly matters. Those who gather do so out of reverence for their city as much as for their saint.

On any day, the Duomo is worth a visit for its artistic treasures, among them a breathtakingly frescoed **Chapel of San Gennaro**.

Wander the Museo Archeologico Nazionale di Napoli

The largest museum in central Naples, **MANN** *(mann-napoli.it; adult/reduced €20/2; closed Tue)* is also one of Italy's most important archaeological repositories. Its vast collection of Greek and Roman antiquities includes the monumental Farnese Bull, priceless Roman bronzes, and exquisite mosaics recovered from the ruins of Herculaneum and Pompeii. MANN also houses the second-largest collection of Egyptian artefacts in the country, spanning seven rooms and six centuries. Then there's the museum's blush-inducing Secret Room, home to over 250 pieces of erotica (gathered mainly from excavations at Pompeii and Herculaneum) that once titillated the Bourbon monarchy.

Escape to a hilltop palace and wood

The Royal Palace of Capodimonte began life in 1738 when Charles III originally planned to build himself a hunting lodge on the hill above Naples but pivoted to a palace that could accommodate both his expanding court and the priceless art he'd inherited from his mother, Elisabetta Farnese.

That palace is now the **Museo di Capodimonte** *(capodimonte.cultura.gov.it; adult/under 18 €15/free)*, whose magnificent

BEST SACRED ART IN THE CENTRE

Cappella Sansevero: Houses the iconic *Cristo Velato* statue, whose realistic marble folds and delicate contours have attracted admirers for centuries. *(museosansevero.it; adult/reduced €12/8)*

Pio Monte della Misericordia: Contains Caravaggio's *Sette Opere della Misericordia. (piomontedellamisericordia.it; €10)*

Chiesa e Chiostro di San Gregorio Armeno: The frescoes of San Gregorio Armeno here are among the best examples of Luca Giordano's intricate work in central Naples. *(free)*

Complesso Monumentale di Santa Chiara: An explosion of colourful majolica tilework set over 72 octagonal columns that connect to similarly decorated benches framing a lush private garden. *(Chiostro di Santa Chiara; monastero disantachiara.it; adult/reduced €7/5)*

EATING IN NAPLES: OUR PICKS — MAP p696

Pizzeria Starita: A constant contender for best in the city, and even if it's franchised, it's still stellar. *noon-3.30pm & 7pm-midnight Tue-Sun* €€

La Locanda Gesù Vecchio: Traditional recipes, local ingredients and a broad selection of wines. *2-3.30pm & 7-11pm Tue-Sun* €€

Aria Restaurant: This intimate Michelin-star restaurant elevates Neapolitan street food. *7.30-11pm Mon-Sat* €€€

Januarius: The cuisine is classical Neapolitan with down-to-earth products, but the fresco ceilings are out of this world. *1-3pm & 7.30-11pm Wed-Mon* €€€

collection includes a Caravaggio in situ, where it was meant to be, as well as contemporary works from artists like Mimmo Paladino and Umberto Manzo.

Done, get some fresh air at the **Real Bosco di Capodimonte**, the palace's 124-hectare former royal forest.

Explore a panoramic charterhouse

The paradoxical density and splendour of central Naples is hard to grasp when you're amid it, so spend a few hours surveying it from the hilltop **Certosa e Museo di San Martino** (*adult/reduced €6/2*). Originally a Carthusian monastery built between 1325 and 1368, it's now home to priceless frescoes and paintings by Neapolitan baroque masters such as Jusepe de Ribera and Cosimo Fanzago. The cloisters here are among the most beautiful in Italy, adorned and altered over the centuries by some of the country's finest artists, most importantly architect Giovanni Antonio Dosio in the 16th century and baroque sculptor Cosimo Fanzago a century later.

Herculaneum

Head back to 79 CE

The same eruption that destroyed Pompeii in 79 CE buried **Herculaneum** (*coopculture.it/en/poi/archaeological-park-of-Herculaneum*) under a volcanic mudslide. This site is more manageable than Pompeii and has an incredible array of artefacts. Among the highlights is the **Casa dei Cervi**, a two-storey villa that belonged to a noble family with a twisted sense of humour: cross the courtyard to see marble deer attacked by dogs and a drunkenly inappropriate Hercules. The **Casa Sannitica**, built in the 2nd century BCE by the Samnites, is a portal into Herculaneum's pre-Roman past, with wooden lattice fences, an impluvium and a fresco of the rape of Europa, while the vaulted rooms of **L'Antica Spiaggia**, likely port warehouses, became a refuge during the eruption. Equally intriguing is the **Terme Suburbane**, featuring intricate mosaics, and the **Casa del Tramezzo di Legno**, which preserves a folding wooden screen and bedframe.

Capri

Encounter the magical Blue Grotto

The world-famous **Grotta Azzurra** (Blue Grotto) is a spectacular natural phenomenon, although – fair warning – the tourist crush and breakneck pace of the experience may taint

HELP KEEP COMMUNITIES ALIVE

Naples' Quartieri Spagnoli has been synonymous with social decline for many years. However, thanks to the grassroots work of cultural associations, artists and residents, the neighbourhood has become a unique heritage site, a place that welcomes visitors with pride. Yet many people are forced to live on meagre incomes, and life remains difficult. It often means that they adapt in creative ways, and this might look charming to the outside eye. But these are real people living real lives – something to keep in mind when visiting. If you want to take a picture of someone or their home, ask first. If they say no, don't take it personally. The difference between gawking and engaging begins with our approach to delicate situations.

DRINKING IN NAPLES: OUR PICKS — MAP p696

Bar Mexico: This 1960s relic in Piazza Garibaldi serves a thick, sugary rocket fuel that will remind you why you're here. *5.30am-8pm Mon-Sat*

Astronomia Bar Segreto: A speakeasy that'll take a moment to find but is worth the search for its inspired drinks and service. *8pm-2am Thu-Tue*

Enoteca Belledonne: Stellar wine bar with a great selection of finger foods and a cosy setting. *hours vary*

Chandelier: You'd best reserve a table. Your reward is incredible drinks and abundant snacks. *8am-3pm*

TOP EXPERIENCE

Pompeii

The once-thriving city of Pompeii was buried under a layer of lapilli (burning fragments of pumice stone) by the eruption of Vesuvius in 79 CE. The result is a remarkably well-preserved slice of ancient life, where visitors can walk down Roman streets and snoop around millennia-old houses, temples, shops, cafes, amphitheatres and a brothel.

Top Sights

The Romans were nothing if not entertainers, and the 20,000-seat **Anfiteatro** (Amphitheatre) at the park's eastern end is proof of their love for the stage.

Pompeii's main piazza, the **Foro**, was the seat of religious, commercial and political life. It's best to end your day here because even when it's not summer the sun can be punishing.

The restored 90-room **Villa dei Misteri** dates to the 2nd century BCE. The Dionysiac frieze spans the walls of the large dining room and is one of the biggest and most arresting paintings from the ancient world.

The site of **Insula dei Casti Amanti** was first uncovered in 1912 and has since been discovered to include a room decorated with mythological figures, charcoal drawings made by children in a service courtyard, and an entrance hall where the skeletons of two eruption victims were found. You can watch the process of bringing Pompeii to life, as well as an innovative effort to bring photovoltaic panels onto the site, which was designed as part of the Pompeii for All initiative and has access for travellers with disabilities.

TOP TIPS

● Always enter the park via the less-crowded Amphitheatre entrance. Crowds are thickest in the morning; take the afternoon to explore.

● You should only buy your tickets directly through the Pompeii website.

● The excellent audio guides are multilingual.

PRACTICALITIES

● pompeiisites.org
● adult/reduced from €18/2 ● 9am-7pm Apr-Oct, to 5pm Nov-Mar

HERCULANEUM'S FRESCOES & MOSAICS

Pompeii may have more frescoes and mosaics, but Herculaneum is no slouch in the art department. Check them out in these fascinating dwellings and temples.

Casa dello Scheletro: Spectacular *lararium* (shrine) inlaid with impossibly tiny mosaic tiles.

Casa di Nettuno e Anfitrite: Intricate and vivid mosaic depicting Neptune and Aphrodite.

Colegio degli Augustali: Frescoes of Hercules fighting the good fight.

Casa dell'Atrio a Mosaico: This sea-view villa's floor is entirely covered in floral and geometric mosaics.

Casa del Gran Portale: Beautiful brick lintel entrance, and fascinating wall decorations of birds and bizarre designs.

RUI VALE SOUSA/SHUTTERSTOCK

your buzz. The grotto opens at 9am, but try to get here as early as possible to (slightly) shorten your wait. A ticket to the grotto costs €18 for a five-minute tour; duck as the gondolier ushers the boat inside, lest you crack your head open on the rock. Inside, the waters glow electric blue and the gondoliers serenade you with Neapolitan classics.

Ride a heavenly chairlift

From **Anacapri**'s Piazza Vittoria, the chairlift **Seggiovia del Monte Solaro** *(montesolarocapri.it; one way/return €11/14)* whisks riders up to **Monte Solaro**, Capri's highest peak. The 13-minute 589m ride up provides unforgettable views of terraced vineyards, white houses and lemon groves, with the Gulf of Naples and the Amalfi Coast winking in the distance.

Vertigo? You can also get to the top on foot by following Via Axel Munthe to Via Salita per il Solaro. Go right, then look for the iron crucifix marking La Crocetta pass. A left turn will take you to the hermitage of **Santa Maria a Cetrella**; turning right will get you to the summit. The hike takes about an hour each way.

 EATING & DRINKING NEAR POMPEII: OUR PICKS

Melius: Gourmet deli-restaurant offering dishes made with local ingredients such as Graniano pasta or anchovies from Cetara. *9am-2pm Tue-Sun, 5.30-10pm Tue-Sat €€*

Zi'Caterina: Spacious old-school restaurant that looks touristy but serves delicious traditional southern Italian food. *noon-midnight €€*

La Bettola del Gusto: Highly innovative Italian food such as seared-octopus couscous, made with proudly artisanal ingredients. *12.30-3pm & 7.30-11pm Tue-Thu & Sun, to midnight Fri & Sat €€*

Na' Pasta: Excellent pastas and a magical parmigiana makes the tight seating entirely worth it, especially after a few glasses of local wine. *12.15-7pm Tue-Sat, to 8pm Sun €€*

Seggiovia del Monte Solaro, Capri

Live it up in Capri Town

Capri Town's beauty is iconic. It's no wonder. Its white-washed labyrinthine streets – with their tiled courtyards and hand-painted ceramic street signs, shaded by purple blooms – are the ultimate Italian island dreamscape.

Your first port of call is **Piazza Umberto I**, called La Piazzetta by locals. It's perfect for people-watching, though your nosiness will cost you – an espresso can set you back €8. Wander side streets like **Via Le Botteghe**, peppered with luxe boutiques and restaurants. In Via Vittorio Emanuele, a queue leads to **Gelateria Buonocore**, famous for its freshly pressed waffle cones. Continue on to **Via Camerelle**, Capri's bougainvillea-strung haute couture street.

Escape to the gardens

For a break from Capri Town's bustling centre, escape to the tranquil **Giardini di Augusto** and nearby **Certosa di San Giacomo**. Built in 1371, the *certosa* (Carthusian monastery) houses 17th-century frescoes in its church and revolving modern-art exhibits. Meanwhile, the Giardini di Augusto

SEA MONSTERS & MERMAIDS

Capri's most iconic natural sight is undoubtedly the **Faraglioni** rock formation. The Faraglioni is formed by three stacked crags just off the island's coast: the 109m-high Saetta; Stella with its 60m-long central cavity; and Scopolo, home of the blue lizard, native only to Capri. Here swimmers revel and lovers kiss for luck as they sail through Stella's cavity. They must not know the legends.

The Faraglioni, like many of Campania's natural phenomena, are linked to Greek myth. Homer believed they were boulders hurled at Ulysses by the cyclops Polyphemus. Virgil thought they were the legendary home of murderous mermaids, waiting to lure sailors to death. Squint a little. Don't they look like a sea monster?

 EATING ON CAPRI: OUR PICKS

Salumeria da Aldo: A well-stocked Marina Grande minimart with a delicatessen where you can get a freshly made *panino* (sandwich). *7am-9pm* €

Pescheria Le Botteghe: Fish market with a raw bar and restaurant serving fishburgers and seafood pastas. *8am-3pm & 7-11pm, to 1pm Mon* €€€

Gennaro Amitrano: Michelin-star seafood restaurant at Marina Piccola, with elegant farm-to-table fare. *12.30-2.30pm & 7.30-10.30pm* €€€

La Capannina: A family-run traditional restaurant (established 1931) for dinner or drinks. Book ahead. *12.15-3pm & 7.15-11.30pm* €€€

DPVUE IMAGES/SHUTTERSTOCK

THE BEST BEACHES ON CAPRI

Bagni di Tiberio: Take a *gozzetto* (dinghy) to this chic pebble beach (entry €20), once Emperor Tiberius' bathing grounds – next to the ruins of one of his villas.

Marina Grande Beach: Free beach popular with day-trippers for its proximity to the port; large, boisterous stretch of pebbles and *lidos* (stretches of sand) with lots of families.

Marina Piccola: Petite (free) pebble beach with views of the Faraglioni and water that's always warm and still. Enjoy lunch and snacks at the various *lidos*.

Isole Faraglioni: This cliff 'beach' and diving point is stunning, but its beach clubs Da Luigi and La Fontelina are reservation only. Shuttle-boat service.

Spiaggia del Faro (Anacapri): Luscious cliff beach with views of the historic lighthouse; enjoy light lunches and *aperitivi* at the beach's *lidos*. Spectacular sunsets.

Bagni Regina Giovanna, Amalfi Coast

rewards with soaring views of Marina Piccola and the Faraglioni. Time your visit for the spring bloom for a particularly beautiful experience. Just outside the gardens, you'll find the entrance to **Via Krupp**, a 1.5km paved hairpin path leading down to **Marina Piccola** and a refreshing dip in the sea (the bus will take you back up).

Amalfi Coast

If you're looking for a secret corner of paradise, you're 1000 years too late to the Amalfi Coast. But who cares? It remains transformatively beautiful. Stretching 50km along the southern side of the Sorrentine Peninsula, the UNESCO-protected Costiera Amalfitana is a postcard-perfect vision of shimmering blue water fringed by vertiginous cliffs on which cling whitewashed and pastel-hued villages and terraced lemon groves. You won't be able to see it all, and you'll ruin your time trying. But choose wisely and you'll find yourself grinning like a fool at your luck.

Go beyond the souvenirs

Sorrento's historic centre offers much more than kitschy souvenirs. At the edge of town lies haunting **Il Vallone dei**

DRINKING ON CAPRI: OUR PICKS

| **Giardino Mediterraneo:** Chic outdoor cocktail lounge in a historic lemon grove. Enjoy tranquil views and lemon cocktails. *10am-midnight, to 8pm Sun & Mon* | **Bianca by La Palma Hotel:** Super luxe cocktail lounge in the new La Palma hotel, with bespoke cocktails, a restaurant and a rooftop view. 'Island chic' dress code. *7pm-1am* | **Taverna Anema e Core:** Bar with live music, DJ sets and a full menu of cocktails on Via Sella Orta. No dress code. A Capri institution. *11pm-4.30am* | **Hangout Capri:** Capri Town gastropub serving steaks plus classic and inventive cocktails in a cool, relaxed atmosphere. *11.30am-4pm & 6.30pm-2am* |

Mulini and its ruins of ancient wheat mills. A short walk away, **Piazza Tasso** is the city's convivial living room. From here, follow Via Luigi de Maio to the **Chiesa and Chiostro di San Francesco**, where pagan, Roman and medieval architecture make an evocative backdrop for art exhibitions. Make a stop at the nearby **Sedile Dominova**, a fresco-covered 14th-century nook that once served as a place for nobles to congregate, and check out the tiny **Chiesa dei Santi Felice e Baccolo**, home to *intarsio* (inlaid wood) master Giuseppe Rocco.

Swim like a queen

When Queen Giovanna II of Anjou-Durazzo wanted to escape the 14th-century bustle, she came to the dazzling natural pools beside a vast Roman villa outside Sorrento. Known today as **Bagni Regina Giovanna**, they can get crowded in summer but they're free, almost surreal in beauty, and worth the hike. Spend half a day and picnic at the ruins of the Pollio Felice villa above the pools. To reach them, take Via Capo from Sorrento to Traversa Punta Capo. Stop at the *alimentari* (deli) for a sandwich and water, then continue down the Traversa until it becomes a footpath that leads to a steep staircase.

Take to the sea

The best way to enjoy **Positano** may be from the sea, but ferries and group tours can be crowded and private tours can be exorbitant. Family-run **Bluestar Positano** (*bluestar positano.it*) offers a range of tours for every budget and timeframe. Early-bird and sunset tours offer a 1½-hour ride around the coast. The best part? Many of the boats are traditional wooden *gozze*.

The boat ride to **Adolfo** (*daadolfo.com*) might be short, but this throwback beach club and restaurant is one of the greatest reminders of how life used to be in Positano. You can only make reservations by telephone, and their distinctive boat is the only ride available from Positano town. Make sure you reserve sunloungers as well as lunch.

Hike the Path of the Gods

In the 1980s hikers christened an ancient, panoramic shepherd's trail the **Sentiero degli Dei** (Path of the Gods). Stretching 6km each way, it is indeed heavenly – running from Agerola (Bomerano) to Nocelle above Positano, and taking three to five hours to tackle. It's moderately challenging, with several route options; the most popular is Bomerano to Nocelle (mostly downhill), reachable by bus from Amalfi.

SONGS OF SORRENTO

It's not just the Sirens who composed intoxicating odes to Sorrento. Throughout the years some of Italy's most famous songs have been written in or about the city. 'Torna a Surriento', composed in 1894 by the De Curtis brothers, is one of the most famous examples of the *canzone napoletana* and has been recorded by singers all over the world. There are few songs so well known (and heartbreaking) to Italians as Lucio Dalla's 'Caruso', a tribute to the great opera singer and his lover. Indeed, the Bologna-born Dalla is considered by many to be an honorary citizen of the town, in honour of the song.

EATING & DRINKING IN AMALFI: OUR PICKS

Pasticceria Pansa: More than just morning coffee and *cornetti* (croissants), with plenty of non-alcoholic options. *7.30am-11pm* €

Trattoria dei Cartari: Head towards the paper museum for a locals-approved meal with the freshest catch in town. *noon-3.30pm & 7-10.30pm Tue-Sun* €€

Donna Stella: Pizzeria in an atmospheric lemon grove that serves delicious pizza plus salads. *11am-4pm & 5.30-10pm Wed-Mon* €€

Ristorante La Caravella: Michelin-starred restaurant with tasting menus featuring local specialities. *noon-2pm & 7-10pm Wed-Mon* €€€

BEST AMALFI SHOPPING

Dalla Carta alla Cartolina: Magical paper shop with art exhibits, near the famous Museo della Carta. Drop postcards in a mailbox and see its beautiful story come to life.

JP Boutique: Signature Amalfi designs, gauzy fabrics and unique accessories from an Amalfi-born artist and illustrator with a flair for the dramatic.

L'Altra Costiera: The best place in Amalfi for locally sourced ceramics from up-and-coming and established artists, many from Vietri sul Mare.

La Scuderia del Duca: Tucked behind the Terminal restaurant at the port, this place is full of great antiques and funky paper crafts that make excellent gifts.

Continue to Positano or return by public transport. The trail is well signposted, but consider getting a guide to explain the surrounding area and make sure you're OK. Also, wear good shoes, carry water, a windbreaker and prepare for crowds. With care, it's an unforgettable experience.

Dig deeper in Amalfi

Amalfi has always been a central point on the coast, and it remains so today. Pass through the vaulted arches to Piazza Duomo, dotted with historic coffee bars and dominated by the Arabic-Norman **Cattedrale di Sant'Andrea**.

The town centre was constructed in the 10th and 11th centuries, when Amalfi was a powerful maritime republic and the natural landscape lent itself to a fortification in the hills. Neighbourhoods followed suit and almost disappear into the stone, so sticking to the main drags means you'll likely miss them. So wander just a bit and you'll find yourself in a very local world of covered walkways and ancient alleys.

Find romance in Ravello

High above the coast, **Villa Rufolo**, just off Ravello's Piazza Duomo, was founded in the 13th century. In its 700 years, it's been the residence of King Robert of Anjou and several popes. Its history is evident in the 14th-century entrance tower, Gothic gateway, Moorish courtyard and 19th-century cascading gardens and lavish sitting rooms with sweeping Gulf views. It's not hard to see how it inspired Wagner in the second act of his opera *Parsifal*.

A 10-minute walk away is **Villa Cimbrone** and its gasp-inducing Terrace of Infinity, 280m above sea level. Both villas are swank hotels. If you're looking for somewhere to splash out, you could do worse. Otherwise, sip at Villa Cimbrone's **Grotto di Eva** garden bar.

DRINKING IN POSITANO: OUR PICKS

Franco's Bar: It would be criminal not to try to get here, even though the prices might magically swallow your wallet. *5pm–midnight*	**Il San Pietro di Positano:** You can't get much higher up and you won't get much more dramatic; worth the hike and the prices. *Apr–Oct*	**Fly:** Come on, when's the last time you had it large? Start here and continue below at Music on the Rocks. *6pm–2am*	**Bar Internazionale:** The closest you'll get to no frills in town, with locals stopping in for their own *aperitivo. 7am–11pm Thu–Tue*

Sicily

GRAECO-ROMAN RUINS | GOLDEN MOSAICS | STREET MARKETS

Everything about the Mediterranean's largest island is extreme, from the beauty of its rugged landscape to its hybrid cuisine and flamboyant architecture. Sicily is intense, ancient and contradictory, and every corner reveals the same incongruous mash-up of old and new, chaos and calm.

Now an autonomous region in Italy, the island was hotly contested for centuries – the ancient Greeks, Carthaginians and Romans all fell into its devilishly handsome lair. Later rule by Byzantines, Saracens, Normans, Germans, Angevins and Spanish blessed Sicily with artistic and architectural riches that remain star attractions.

The rich Sicilian kitchen, crafted from multiple cuisines, only intensifies the sensory feast. Island produce – sun-spun capers and cherry tomatoes, olives, creamy almonds and pistachios, pomegranates, wild saffron, farm-churned ricotta, shellfish, tuna and swordfish – has been the magic ingredient ever since Bacchus planted vines near Taormina and the Greek god of blacksmiths fired up his forge inside Mt Etna. Come curious. Come hungry.

☑ **TOP TIP**

Late spring and early autumn are ideal times to visit Sicily; temperatures are warm but not extreme, prices are lower and crowds much more manageable than they are in July and August.

 GETTING AROUND

Regular car-passenger ferries cross the Strait of Messina from the Italian mainland to Sicily. Once on the island a flurry of high-speed hydrofoils and slower *traghetti* (ferries) sail to Sicily's offshore Aeolian and Egadi islands. Boats run year-round, with reduced schedules in winter.

Driving in traffic-busy Palermo and Catania is a headache, but motoring along the coast and inland is pleasurable and scenic. The A18 and A20 *autostrade* (motorways) are toll roads. Away from towns, electric-vehicle charging stations are scarce. Trains and buses link Ionian coastal cities; buses offer faster links than trains between Palermo and Catania. Private operator **Ferrovia Circumetnea** *(circumetnea.it)* runs trains around Mt Etna villages. Island-wide, Sunday services are limited.

Palermo

Nearly 3000 years old, Palermo was conquered by the Arabs in 831 CE and, when the Normans invaded in 1072, Roger I (1031–1101) made the old Greek port the seat of his enlightened 'kingdom of the sun', encouraging resident Arabs, Byzantines, Greeks and Italians to remain.

Contemporary Palermo is stitched from rebellion, bravery, squalor and solidarity. It's a place where roving street vendors sell *pani ca meusa* (Sicilian bread roll stuffed with sautéed beef spleen) from hand-pushed carts, and locals chat in Italian, Albanian and Arabic. Be inquisitive. Peek into every citrus-filled cloister, cherub-spun chapel or trash-strewn back alley. You'll be astonished by what you find.

Royal tombs and a rooftop walk

The 13th-century **Cattedrale di Palermo** *(cattedrale.pal ermo.it; adult/child €12/6)* is a larger-than-life example of Sicily's unique Arab-Norman architectural style. Its interior safeguards royal Norman tombs containing two of Sicily's greatest rulers – Roger II and Frederick II of Hohenstaufen.

Save the best for last: the cinematic spiral up 110 steep stone steps to the cathedral's expansive roof terraces (open until

ELESI/SHUTTERSTOCK

Cappella Palatina, Palermo

DARE-TO-TRY STIGGHIOLA

At quick glance it looks like an ordinary sausage. It's not. Introduced to the city by the Greeks 2000 years ago, Palermo's beloved *stigghiola* sees veal, lamb or goat intestines wrapped around a spring onion or leek, seasoned with parsley and flamed to a crisp on a charcoal- or wood-fired grill. It's deemed both a delicacy and an icon of Palermo's sizzling street-food scene.

Several market stalls and *trattorie* or fast-food joints with street kitchens at Palermo's oldest street market – **Mercato di Ballarò** – grill *stigghiola* on home barbecues in the street. The snack is always served chopped in chunks, salted and doled out on a plastic plate with a wedge of lime.

midnight once-weekly in summer), with an unmatched city panorama. Visit at the end of the day to savour the setting sun recasting the city in spectacular pink.

Save cents with a **combined ticket** *(adult/child €15/8)* covering the cathedral (the tombs, crypt, apse, treasury and rooftop) and 15th- to 18th-century art in the neighbouring **Museo Diocesana di Palermo**.

Explore an Arab-Norman wonder

Norman Sicily's cultural complexity is beautifully evoked at Palermo's star attraction: **Cappella Palatina**, awash in gold mosaics from 1130. It's squirrelled away like a jewel inside **Palazzo dei Normanni** *(federicosecondo.org; adult/child €19/11)*, built by conquering Arabs in the 9th century.

Wind up the stone staircase in the 17th-century Maqueda courtyard to the 2nd floor, where treasures include the Hall of Viceroys, lit up in Murano glass; the Hall of Mosaics, decorated with secular mosaics; and the soaring square tower of the Hall of Winds.

Visit Friday to Monday when the Royal Apartments are also open, and cover up – short skirts, shorts and bare shoulders are forbidden in the chapel.

EATING & DRINKING IN PALERMO: OUR PICKS

Da Mimì di Guglielmo Damiano: Locals claim this Il Capo icon fries up the city's finest arancini (stuffed rice balls). *7.15am-10pm Mon-Sat, from 10am Sun* €

Moltivolti: You'll be hard-pushed to find a cooler co-working space, cafe, kitchen cooking up world cuisine (vegan included) and late-night bar. *9am-midnight* €

Ciccio in Pentola: Creative fish and seafood dishes paired with excellent service make this elegant *ristorante* a local foodie favourite. *noon-3.30pm & 7-11pm* €€

Gagini: Experience gourmet heaven at the contemporary kitchen of Italian-Brazilian chef Mauricio Zillo – Palermo's only Michelin-starred address. *12.30-2.30pm Wed-Sun, 7.30-10pm Tue-Sun* €€€

BEST SHOPPING: SLOW DESIGN ON VIA VITTORIO EMANUELE

Angela Tripi: Teeny terracotta *presepi* (crib figurines) in a 15th-century *palazzo* courtyard at Via Vittorio Emanuele 452.

Naná Aristova Jewels: Sicilian volcanoes inspire the contemporary jewellery by a Siberia-born Palermo-adopted jeweller at No 314.

Barbisio: Palermo's spiffiest hat shop at No 286 is a 1949 vintage. Buy a Sicilian *còppola* (flat cap).

Sicilia Inspired: Modern art, including drawings in Etna lava pigments, at No 292.

Rogato: 'Bags with history' are crafted from recycled materials at this boutique at No 130.

La Cittàcotte di Vincenzo Vizzari: Purchase a terracotta miniature of a Palermo church, palace or orange tree; No 120.

LIUB SHTEIN/SHUTTERSTOCK

Fontana dell'Amenano, Catania

Sunset drinks at the Fountain of Shame

So scandalised were Sicilian churchgoers by the flagrant nudity of cheek-baring nymphs and frolicking river gods on Piazza Pretoria's monumental **Fontana Pretoria** that they dubbed it Fontana della Vergogna (Fountain of Shame). Designed by Florentine sculptor Francesco Camilliani between 1554 and 1555 for the Tuscan villa of Don Pedro di Toledo, it was bought by Palermo in 1573 in a bid to outshine Messina's newly crafted Fontana di Orione.

The play of light on the nudes posing in the fountain's tiered basins is theatrical any time of day – and never the same twice. Come sunset, enjoy it from above over alfresco drinks at rooftop bar **Le Terrazze del Sole** *(6pm-midnight Mar-Oct).*

Catania

The days when travellers avoided Sicily's second-largest city are long gone. Despite first-glance chaos and scruffiness, Catania has magnetic pull, brimming with youthful energy and earthy spirit. A smart base for Ionian coast trips or Mt Etna climbs, it delivers both convenience and intrigue.

UNESCO-listed, Catania rose from two disasters: Etna's 1669 lava flow and the 1693 earthquake that killed 12,000. baroque

 DRINKING IN PALERMO: OUR PICKS

Altrove Bar: Italian craft beer, cocktails and killer margaritas lure a local crowd to this hip bar on Via Discesa dei Giudici. *5.30pm-1.30am Mon, to 2am Tue-Thu, 10am-1am Fri-Sun*

Tatum Art: Jazz lovers enjoy the intimacy of this small venue; reserve tables online. In summer concerts shift to seaside Mondello. *7pm-1am Tue-Sat, to midnight Sun*

Malox Cult: Don't miss the house Negroni (mixing Bulldog gin with Cinzano 1757 and Bèrto Bitter) at this cult bar with terrace on Piazzetta della Canna. *5.30pm-2am*

Botanico: Late-night music and cocktails down an alley festooned with greenery and street art. *6.30pm-2am Tue-Sun*

palazzi and churches, designed by Giovanni Vaccarini, sprouted from volcanic rock. Roman ruins sit beneath ornate facades, street art enlivens bohemian alleys, and *pasta alla Norma* (pasta with eggplant and ricotta) is served in ancient lava tubes – urban discovery here is intoxicating and richly layered.

Trawl a mouthwatering market

Tables groan under the weight of all manner of sea life at Catania's open-air fish market, **La Pescheria** *(closed Sun)*. Visit early morning – it opens at 7am and is being hosed down by 1pm. Access to the market, through a passageway by the side of gushing **Fontana dell'Amenano** (1867) on Piazza del Duomo, only adds to the theatre.

Grab a pew at **Scirocco Sicilian Fish Lab** *(sciroccolab.com),* with a terrace overlooking the market on Piazza Alonzo di Benedetto, and enjoy the show over a paper cone of battered fish or deep-fried Etna pasta in cuttlefish-ink sauce. For fish without bones, order *cartoccio di mare senza spine.*

Delve into Catania's spiritual and social heart

Begin with *paste di mandorla* (almond sweets) at **Prestipino**, its contrasting white limestone and black volcanic-sand plaster typical of Catania's baroque architecture. Energised, explore the showpiece **Cattedrale di Sant'Agata**, final resting place of Catanian composer Vincenzo Bellini (1801–35).

The 360-degree panorama from the rooftop terraces of **Museo Diocesano** *(museodiocesanocatania.com; terrace €3, adult/child museum €7/4, with Roman baths €10/6)* is a perfect introduction to Catania. The museum's star attraction is a jewel-drenched, silver reliquary bust of Catania's patron saint Agata. Nearby is Piazza del Duomo's **Fontana dell'Elefante** (1736), a smiling black-lava elephant from Roman times, surmounted by an Egyptian obelisk.

Give in to Sicilian baroque

If you only have time for just one church, make it **Chiesa di San Benedetto** *(monasterosanbenedettocatania.it; adult/child €6/4; open Tue, Fri & Sat).* Sweeping up the monumental staircase of angels into the 18th-century church, nothing prepares you for its sumptuous interior of white stucco, coloured marble, the rare jasper altar with gold inlays and graphic ceiling frescoes painted between 1726 and 1729 by Messina artist Giovanni Tuccari. His depiction of St Agatha

BEST ROOFTOP CLIMBS

Chiesa Badia di Sant'Agata: Enjoy a 360-degree city panorama from the church's terrace.

Monastero dei Benedettini di San Nicolò l'Arena: Climb 141 steps up to the church roof in the monastery complex on Piazza Dante.

Chiesa di San Giuliano: There are heavenly views from this 18th-century jewel climax with 34 dizzying steps across a cupola to its crowning iron crucifix. A must.

Museo Diocesano: Admire black-stone Via Etnea marching north to Mt Etna from rooftops above Piazza del Duomo.

Ostello degli Elefanti: Only Catania could have its city hostel in a 17th-century *palazzo* with rooftop bar, open to all.

EATING IN CATANIA: OUR PICKS

Nuova Trattoria del Forestiero: Wholesome, no-frills fare including a superlative *pasta alla Norma* typical to Catania. *1-3.30pm & 6.30-10.30pm Tue-Sun* €	**Mè Cumpari Turiddu:** Small producers and Slow Food sensibilities underpin the sophisticated, classically inspired dishes at this vintage-styled place. *noon-2.30pm Sat & Sun, 7-10.30pm daily* €€	**Canni e Pisci:** Fashionable, contemporary meat and fish restaurant, with pavement terrace next to Palazzo Biscari. *1-3pm Sun, 8-11.30pm Tue-Sun* €€	**Coria:** Ultimate modern Sicilian epicurean treat: five- to eight-course tasting menus between moody art works by Etna painter Nunzio Fisichella. *12.30-2.30pm & 7.30-10pm Tue-Sat* €€€

BEST STREET-FOOD BITES

Coppa di frittura di paranza: Traditional paper *coppa* or cone (*cartoccio* on some menus) of battered, deep-fried fish and seafood, usually squid, shrimps, anchovies, mullet and cuttlefish – served with lemon or lime to squeeze on top.

Sardine a beccafico: Stuffed and fried sardines.

Panelle di ceci: Deep-fried chickpea fritters, sometimes spiced with fennel seeds. Best devoured as an *aperitivo* with an Ionian coast craft beer: Birra Messina is a favourite.

Polpo arristo o bollito: Fried or boiled octopus.

Caponata con spada: Cold, sweet-and-sour Sicilian stew of aubergine, onion, pepper and celery with swordfish; *con polpo* mixes in octopus.

VADYM LAVRA/SHUTTERSTOCK

being tortured, in a lunette above the altar, is a masterpiece. Visit at noon when the ferocious ringing of church bells adds unparalleled drama to the frescoes.

Taormina

Yes, it's unashamedly touristy and expensive, but Taormina merits a day or two at least. After all, it's one of Sicily's most popular summer destinations for good reason, with an ancient amphitheatre, superb people-watching and hypnotic vistas in spades – all from the town's spectacular perch on the side of a seaside mountain.

Founded in the 4th century BCE, Taormina prospered under the Greek ruler Gelon II and later under the Romans, but fell into quiet obscurity until its 18th-century comeback as a Grand Tour playground for wealthy aristos.

A fashionable hike and *passeggiata*

Outside sweltering July and August, hilltop Taormina is best explored on foot. Walk up from seaside **Mazzarò** (or ride the cable car), from where 700-plus steps (2.2km, 45 to 60 minutes) zigzag from Via Nazionale (SS114), opposite the staircase to Isola Bella. Plunge through 19th-century city gate **Porta Messina** and follow **Corso Umberto I**, past the crenellated,

DRINKING IN CATANIA: OUR PICKS

Vermut: Vermouth, vino, *salumi* (charcuterie) and 20-plus versions of the ubiquitous spritz keep this budget-friendly hot spot pumping. *11am-2am*

Bohème Mixology Bar: Intimate cocktail den decked out in mismatched furniture, gilded mirrors and the odd gramophone. Creative syrups made from scratch. *6pm-2am*

Black Sheep Beer Store: Craft beer and cocktail bar with stupendous burgers oozing creativity and artisan produce. *7pm-1am Tue-Sun*

Razmataz: Sip wine with bohemians under a huge tree on a village-esque square off Via Etnea. *noon-1am Mon-Sat*

Teatro Greco, Taormina

BEST BEACHES AROUND TAORMINA

Isola Bella: Small, chic, pebble beach in Mazzarò, linked to the Isola Bella nature reserve by a shingle isthmus.

Spiaggia di Mazzarò: Shingle beach in Mazzarò. Rent boats here, and bag a table for an unforgettable seafood lunch at peerless *trattoria* Il Barcaiolo.

Baie delle Sirene: Cut down hidden steps by Mazzarò's Atlantis Bay hotel to access tiny Mermaid's Bay, dotted with rocky islets. Snorkelling heaven.

Spiaggia di Spisone: Shingle-sand beach with a free public section and private beach clubs, a 10-minute walk from Mazzarò.

Spiaggia di Mazzeo: The sandiest option, 3km north of Lido Mazzarò.

Arab-influenced **Palazzo Corvaja** (now the tourist office) and baroque **Chiesa di Santa Caterina d'Alessandria**.

Grab a filled-on-the-spot *cannolo* (pastry shell with a sweet filling of ricotta or custard) at **Pasticceria Gelateria D'Amore** to enjoy on Piazza IX Aprile, then continue west through 12th-century clock tower **Torre dell'Orologio** into Piazza del Duomo. End in soothing **Villa Comunale**, the public gardens that are open until midnight in summer.

Showtime at an ancient theatre

Suspended between sea and sky, Taormina's **Teatro Greco** (*parconaxostaormina.com; adult/child €14/7),* built in the 3rd century BCE, is the world's most dramatically situated Greek theatre. Bag a ticket for an evening summer concert and enjoy the thrilling double act: opera, dance or theatre on stage and – if you're lucky – an erupting Etna beyond. Outside of performances, visit early morning to dodge the worst of the high-season crowds.

Syracuse

More than any other city, Syracuse (Siracusa) encapsulates Sicily's timeless beauty. Ancient Greek ruins rise out of lush

EATING IN TAORMINA: OUR PICKS

Bam Bar: Traditional *granita* served in a ceramic-tiled interior, with terrace seating. Go for a seasonal fruity flavour – lemon, fig, melon or peach. *7.30am-10.30pm €*

Gustibus: Six-table bistro adjoining a gourmet grocery, with a menu venerating Sicilian cheese, salami and fresh produce. End with a glass of Limonetna (lemon liqueur). *noon-10.30pm €€*

Tischi Toschi: Chocolatey *caponata* (sweet-and-sour aubergine stew), wild-fennel 'meatballs' and rosemary-infused liqueur. *1-2pm Fri-Sun, 7-10pm daily, shorter hours winter €€*

Osteria RossoDiVino: The day's catch, seasonal produce and wine by independent producers in a romantic, candlelit courtyard. *noon-2.30pm & 7-10.30pm Wed-Mon €€€*

citrus orchards, cafe tables fill baroque piazzas, and honey-hued medieval side streets tango to the sea. In its heyday this was the largest city in the ancient world, bigger than Athens and Corinth.

Its 'once upon a time' begins in 734 BCE, when Corinthian colonists landed on the beautiful island of Ortygia (Ortigia), setting up the mainland city four years later. Almost three millennia on, the ruins of that city constitute one of Sicily's greatest archaeological sites, with cathedral-like caves and an amphitheatre hosting magical evening performances.

Walk the island's perimeter

Count less than an hour (longer with stops) to walk the perimeter of **Ortygia**; its sea-facing terraced houses and labyrinthine alleyways are what a Syracuse visit is all about.

Drink in views of the mainland from **Forte San Giovannello**, part of the island's 16th-century fortification system. Walk to **Forte Vigliena** – watch waves crash against the crenellated fort walls and take a dip with the locals. On the island's southern tip, visit 13th-century **Castello Maniace** *(adult/reduced €6/3)*, a stone fortress built for Emperor Frederick II and host to July's electronic-music festival **Ortigia Music**.

Continue along the western shore to **Fonte Aretusa**, a spring turned pretty pond. End on the pedestrian jetty – magic at sunset.

Kick back on a showpiece square

Soak up the city's warm cream and ochre palette on vast **Piazza del Duomo**, with a sweep of golden-stone *palazzi* that could be spun from sunlight. Along the side of the **Duomo** *(adult/child €2/1)*, spot thick Doric columns incorporated into the cathedral's structure.

Next door, 17th-century **Palazzo Arcivescovile** safeguards a library with rare 13th-century manuscripts and **Chiesa di Santa Lucia alla Badia**, a nuns' parlour with a beautiful blue majolica floor. Allow time for people-watching over a spritz at **Gran Caffè del Duomo** or a cone filled with pistachio, lemon or chocolate ricotta cream from hole-in-the-wall **I Cannoli del Re**.

Go Greek at the ruins

It's wild to think you can sit in the theatre where playwright Aeschylus watched his tragedies unfold. Hewn in the rocky hillside in the 5th century BCE and rebuilt two centuries

GOLDEN AGE

After its founding by Corinthian colonists in 734 BCE, Syracuse flourished, becoming a rich commercial town and regional powerhouse. Victory over the Carthaginians at the Battle of Himera (480 BCE) paved the way for a golden age: art and culture thrived, and the city's tyrannical kings commissioned impressive public buildings.

The finest intellectuals of the age flocked to Syracuse, cultivating the sophisticated urban culture that was to see the birth of comic Greek theatre. Syracuse's independence abruptly came to an end in 211 BCE when invading Romans breached the city's defences, devised by Archimedes, and took control. Under Roman rule Syracuse remained Sicily's capital but the city's glory days were over. Decline set in.

 EATING IN SYRACUSE: OUR PICKS

Divino Mare: Graze on Roman-style artichokes, oysters, cured meats and cheese at this wine bar by the market. *noon-3pm & 6-11.30pm Tue-Sat* €

A Putia delle Cose Buone: Creative home-style dishes brimming with local seafood, veggies etc; generous portions and a lovely atmosphere. *noon-11pm Wed-Mon* €€

Cortile Santo Spirito: Fine dining in a 17th-century *palazzo* on Ortygia's southern tip, with plant-based, seafood and meat tasting menus. *12.30-3.30pm & 7.30-10pm Tue-Sun* €€€

Don Camillo: Sterling service and innovative Sicilian cuisine in a refined setting; a Slow Food gourmand must. *1-2.30pm & 8-10.30pm Mon-Sat* €€€

Castello Maniace, Syracuse

later, Syracuse's **Teatro Greco** remains one of Sicily's most prestigious theatres, and watching a summertime play here is unforgettable.

Pre-performance, ramble around ancient Greek Syracuse in **Parco Archeologico della Neapolis** *(parchiarcheologici .regione.sicilia.it/siracusa-eloro-villa-tellaro-akrai; adult/ child €17/free, incl Museo Archeologico €18)*. Scan the QR code at the ticket booth for a map marked with three walking itineraries, 45 to 90 minutes long.

End at the **Museo Archeologico Paolo Orsi** *(adult/child €10/free, incl Parco Archeologico €18)*, a one-stop shop covering Syracuse's ancient backstory.

BEST SWIM SPOTS

Solarium Forte Vigliena: Metal stairs lead to rocks below, next to Forte Vigliena. Limited space, deep water.

Spiaggia Diane nel Forte: In summer a wooden platform by the rocks to Forte Vigliena creates this seasonal urban beach.

Spiaggia di Cala Rossa: Small crescent of sandy beach near Ortygia's southeastern tip – always packed.

Solarium Zefiro: Below Fonte Aretusa, a private 'beach' with sunloungers and parasols (reserve online), music and drinks on a wooden platform. Come dusk, it morphs into a sunset lounge bar. *zefirosolarium.it*

Solarium Zen: Private *lido* and late-night lounge bar, with loungers on terraces and decks between rocks, in new-town Syracuse. *instagram. com/zensiracusa*

DRINKING IN SYRACUSE: OUR PICKS

La Barca: Sip Negronis aboard a boat at Ortygia's marina, with occasional film screenings on deck, live music and excursions out to sea. *4pm–midnight Tue–Thu, 5pm–1am Fri & Sat*

Mi Ka Tù: Views of sundown's fireball sun slipping into the sea stun at this stylish wine-bar terrace on bar-lined Via Castello Maniace. *noon– midnight*

Cortile Verga: Enjoy drinks and chilled music in an 18th-century courtyard at one of Ortygia's top cocktail bars. *5.30pm– 12.30am*

Ortigia Mare Escursioni: Admire the sunset from sea with an *aperitivo in barca* ('evening drinks afloat'); book excursions at the seasonal stand on Ponte Umbertino. *hours vary*

Places We Love to Stay

€ Budget €€ Midrange €€€ Top End

Rome
MAP p652

Night and Day € On narrow, historical Via Rasella, a short walk from Trevi Fountain, is this simple, laid-back hostel-style guesthouse.

Navona Essence €€ On a quiet backstreet near Campo de' Fiori in the *centro storico,* this snug boutique hotel is well placed for pretty much everywhere.

Palazzo Scanderbeg €€€ Located in a 15th-century *palazzo* around the corner from the Trevi Fountain, with comfortable and elegant rooms.

Cinque Terre

Hotel Gianni Franzi €€ Smallish rooms loaded with an atmospheric mix of antique furniture and simple traditional architecture in Vernazza. Spectacular breakfasts served on a shared terrace.

Hotel Porto Roca €€€ On a vantage point high above Monterosso with the SVA trail running right past, this 43-room hotel is the pinnacle of luxury in Cinque Terre.

Turin

Combo Torino € A modern and bright hostel with a Japanese-inspired feel and beautiful communal spaces.

Palazzo Chiablese €€ Nestled in a little alleyway just off the Palazzo Reale, this B&B features beautifully decorated rooms halfway between the contemporary and the antique.

Milan
MAP p668

Maison Borella €€ Overlooking the Naviglio Grande, this charming canal-side hotel with an inner courtyard has appealing rooms with parquet floors and exposed-beam ceilings.

Spadari al Duomo €€€ Milan's original design hotel, with its stylish rooms like miniature galleries showcasing the work of emerging artists.

Lago di Como

Hotel Borgo Antico €€ Hits all the right notes, with attractive rooms, helpful staff, ample breakfasts and a quiet location a 10-minute walk from the centre of Como (town).

Miralago €€ A delightful B&B in Pescallo (a 10-minute walk from Bellagio's centre), Miralago has bright, attractive rooms and a small garden.

Verona

Corte delle Pigne €€ Set around a quiet internal courtyard, this tiny three-room B&B is two short blocks from Piazza dei Signori.

Due Torri Hotel €€€ This former Della Scala palace exudes luxury, with velvet-clad sofas, tapestry-clad walls and burnished antiques.

Bologna

Dopa Hostel € Stylish hostel featuring recycled design touches, classy tiled bathrooms and a great communal kitchen.

Bologna nel Cuore €€ Intimate and immaculate lineup of rooms and apartments run by friendly art historian Maria; divine breakfasts.

Venice
MAP p676

3749 Ponte Chiodo € A charming little B&B in Cannaregio with period furnishings, canal views and a private front garden. It's a short walk from superb neighbourhood wine bars.

Giò & Giò €€ A classic hideaway in San Marco, with floor-to-ceiling silk draperies, subtle rococo flourishes and heirloom furniture pieces. Angle for a room overlooking the gondola stop.

Gritti Palace €€€ High-end perfection, set in a 1525 Doge's palace on the Grand Canal and lavished with rare marble, Rubelli silk damask, precious artworks and antiques.

Florence
MAP p686

Plus Hostel € This mega-hostel on Via Santa Caterina d'Alessandria has a rooftop pool and an Irish pub on the opposite side of the street. What else do you need?

Antica Dimora Johlea €€ With precious silks curtains, canopy beds and perfect Duomo views from the rooftop terrace, this high-end boutique hotel is a relaxing retreat steps from the Galleria dell'Accademia.

Palazzo Niccolini al Duomo €€€ With unchallenged views of the Duomo, this 16th-century residence takes you back to an era of golden frames, frescoed walls and hand-carved furniture.

Siena
MAP p691

Hotel Alma Domus € Set by the ancient Santuario of Santa Caterina, this budget-friendly hotel is housed in a 14th-century building.

Albergo Bernini €€ With only 10 rooms, this family-run hotel at the northern end of the city centre makes for a cosy stay with beautiful terrace views.

Pisa

B&B Camilla €€ No detail goes unchecked in this lovely family-run B&B located a short walk from charming Borgo Stretto.

Rinascimento B&B €€€ The medieval *case-torre* exterior hides a modern boutique hotel that tastefully blends the old with the new.

Naples

MAP p696

Atelier Inès €€ An art gallery, a showroom and a jewellery boutique with six bespoke rooms and suites, this is a showstopper.

Grand Hotel Vesuvio €€€ Live the good life with expensive views, and don't worry too much about the celebrity guests.

Capri

Villa dei Fiori B&B €€ Spartan yet cosy island B&B in a tranquil garden with beautiful gulf

views, just off Capri Town's busy main drag.

Grand Hotel Quisisana €€€ Just steps from Capri Town's *piazzetta,* the historic Grand Hotel Quisisana has defined island opulence since 1845.

Sorrento & the Amalfi Coast

Palazzo Martinelli €€ What a find: a sleek boutique hotel in the heart of Sorrento's *centro storico* with five-star services.

DieciSedici €€ Chic rooms in a quiet corner of Amalfi that will make you feel like you've won. You have.

Hotel Palazzo Murat €€€ Of all the heavy hitters in Positano, this is the one to spend on – if only for the lush gardens.

Palermo

B&B Sant'Agostino €€ A stunning family-run guesthouse in an artist's house with original frescoes and a secret garden, plus bike rental, massages and cooking classes.

Grand Hotel et des Palmes €€€ Palermo's most historic pad, in the biz since 1874, is dazzling after a multi-million-euro restoration.

Catania

B&B Foro € Fabulous kitchenette-clad rooms, some with a balcony, open onto a sky garden strewn with flower pots at this clandestine guesthouse, home to artists Anna and Antonia.

Habitat €€ Sleek design, with a striking communal lounge and breakfast room, in a 19th-century factory turned boutique hotel, located footsteps from Teatro Massimo.

Taormina

La Pensione Svizzera €€ Enjoy the vintage elegance of Grand Tour days at this family-run 1920s hotel, a salmon-pink mansion with stone lions and sea vistas.

Hotel Villa Belvedere €€€ One of Taormina's original grand hotels, 1902 Villa Belvedere is distinguished and supremely comfortable, with five-star views, gardens and service.

Syracuse

Alla Giudecca €€ A 6th-century ancient Jewish ritual bath gurgles beneath this 15th-century patrician's house with a gorgeous courtyard in Ortygia's historic Jewish quarter.

Henry's House €€€ Sea views don't get bolder or better than at this waterfront 17th-century Ortygia *palazzo,* restored by an antique collector. The rooftop terrace is to die for.

A. LAENGAUER/SHUTTERSTOCK

La Pensione Svizzera, Taormina

Practicalities

DRESS CODE

When visiting churches in Italy, it's important to cover your shoulders, torso and thighs out of respect for local customs. Similarly, when dining in restaurants, dress smartly and avoid wearing beach attire. Italians generally frown upon overly casual clothing in these settings, so thoughtful attire is expected and appreciated.

SMPOLY/SHUTTERSTOCK

LGBTIQ+ TRAVELLERS

Rome, Milan, Turin, Bologna, Florence, Naples, Palermo and Catania are all gay-friendly cities, as are the coastal holiday resorts of Capri and Taormina. Major cities and some smaller centres host Pride parades in June and July. Head to *gay.it* for LGBTIQ+ news.

HEALTH

MedInAction (*medinaction.com*) provides English-speaking medical assistance, including house calls, prescriptions, referrals to English-speaking hospitals/clinics and online consultations. It also offers direct billing with many private insurance companies. Its app conveniently locates doctors near you.

ACCESSIBLE TRAVEL

Italy isn't easy for travellers with disabilities. Cobblestone streets are difficult for wheelchair users, and many buildings have no lift. The situation is similar for hearing- and vision-impaired travellers. However, a culture of inclusion is growing.

OPENING TIMES

Banks 8.30am–1.30pm and 2.45–4.30pm Monday to Friday
Bars & cafes 7.30am–8pm, sometimes to 1am or 2am
Restaurants Noon–3pm and 7.30–11pm
Shops 9am–1pm and 3.30–7.30pm (or 4–8pm)

SCAMS & THEFT

Petty theft can be an issue – pickpockets are active in touristy areas and on crowded public transport. Ticket touts can also be a problem at major sites, such as Rome's Colosseum. Watch out for people asking for signatures/donations in the street if they don't have appropriate ID. Report theft to police within 24 hours and ask for a statement.

PUBLIC HOLIDAYS

Many businesses close for at least part of the month, particularly around Ferragosto on 15 August.
New Year's Day 1 January
Epiphany 6 January
Easter Monday March/April
Liberation Day 25 April
Labour Day 1 May
Republic Day 2 June
Ferragosto 15 August
All Saints' Day 1 November
Feast of the Immaculate Conception 8 December
Christmas 25 December
St Stephen's Day 26 December

Language

English is not as widely spoken in Italy as it is in some other European nations. Of course, in the main tourist destinations you can get by, but in the countryside and more remote areas you'll find a few basic phrases come in very handy, particularly when speaking to older folk.

Basics

Good morning. Buongiorno.
Good evening. Buonasera.
Good night. Buonanotte.
Hello/hi. Ciao. (informal)
Goodbye. Arrivederci.
Yes please. Si grazie.
No thanks. No grazie.
Please. Per favore.
Thanks very much. Grazie mille.
Lovely to meet you. Piacere.
Excuse me. Mi scusi/Scusa. (formal/informal)
How are you? Come sta/stai? (formal/informal)
I'm well, thanks. Sto bene, grazie.
I'm unwell. Sto male.
Do you speak English? Wo parla/parli inglese? (formal/informal)
I don't speak Italian. Non parlo italiano.
I don't understand Non capisco.
How much does it cost? Quanto costa?
Where's the bathroom? Dove si trova il bagno?
The bill, please. Il conto, per favore.

Directions

Where's (the station)? Dov'è (la stazione)?
What's the address? Qual'è l'indirizzo?
Could you please write it down? Può scriverlo, per favore?

Can you show me (on the map)? Può mostrarmi (sulla pianta)?

Signs

Aperto/a Open
Chiuso/a Closed
Informazione Information
Bagno WC/Toilets
Prohibito/a Prohibited
Uscita Exit

Emergencies

Help! Aiuto!
Leave me alone! Lasciami in pace!
Call ...! Chiami ...!
    a doctor un medico
    the police la polizia

Menu Decoder

Piatto del giorno Dish of the day
Antipasto A hot or cold appetiser
Primo First course
Secondo Second course
Contorno Side dish
Pane Bread
Dolce Dessert
Frutta Fruit
Carta dei vini Wine list
Nostra produzione Made in-house
Senza glutine Gluten-free
Latticini Dairy products

NUMBERS

1	uno
2	due
3	quattro
4	cinque
5	sei
6	sette
7	saba
8	otto
9	nove
10	dieci
20	venti
50	cinquanta
100	cento
500	cinquecento
1000	mille
2000	duemila

MARKUS MAINKA/SHUTTERSTOCK

Fiumicino Airport

Arriving

A plethora of airlines link Italy with the rest of continental Europe and the world, including the country's flagship carrier, ITA Airways *(ita-airways.com)* and a number of low-cost European airlines. Alternatively, there are excellent rail and bus connections, especially to destinations in northern Italy, while car and passenger ferries serve Italian ports from across the Mediterranean.

By Air
Italy's main intercontinental airports are Rome's **Fiumicino Airport** (officially Leonardo da Vinci; *adr.it/fiumicino*) and Milan's **Aeroporto Malpensa** *(milanomalpensa-airport. com).* Venice's **Marco Polo Airport** *(veneziaairport.it),* **Naples International Airport** *(Capodichino; aeroportodi napoli.it),* **Catania– Fontanarossa Airport** *(aeroporto.catania.it)* and **Palermo Airport** *(Falcone– Borsellino; aeroportodi palermo.it)* have a handful of intercontinental flights.

By Train
Regular trains link Italy with France, Switzerland, Austria, Germany and Slovenia. Rail is often cheaper, more comfortable and greener than flying short distances, though air remains faster for those travelling longer distances from the UK, Spain and northern Europe.

MONEY
Currency: Euro (€)

CREDIT CARDS
Major credit cards are widely accepted (Amex less so). Businesses are now obliged by law to accept digital payments, although exceptions persist, particularly in the south, when paying for small items in coffee shops, cheap restaurants and pizzerias or small shops.

TAXES & REFUNDS
A 22% value-added tax known as IVA (Imposta sul Valore Aggiunta) is included in the price of most goods and services. Non-EU residents who spend more than €70.01 in one store (displaying a 'Tax Free' sign) at a single time can claim a refund when leaving the EU. See *taxrefund.it* for more information.

TIPPING
Generally speaking, Italians rarely tip and tips are never expected in Italy. In restaurants the *coperto* (cover) is included in the bill and includes service. Tips aren't expected in taxis, and only tourists who don't know better tip in hotels. Tips also aren't expected in bars, although some people leave small change.

Getting Around

Italy's long profile lends itself to high-speed train travel, which is well priced, efficient and perfect for hopping between major cities. The rail network works in conjunction with an efficient regionalised bus network. Major cities also have good public transport networks, making the need for a car redundant. That said, having your own wheels is the best way to properly explore the countryside.

Urban Transport
Cities have extensive bus, tram and metro networks – and in Venice, *vaporetti* (passenger ferries). Contactless payments by credit/debit card are prevalent on buses and trams. Validate tickets or risk fines. Most cities offer good-value travel cards. Bike- and scooter-sharing schemes are widespread.

GIVAGA/SHUTTERSTOCK

Car Hire
Prebooking cars online is cheaper, and opting for a smaller model makes parking easier. Renters must be aged 21-plus. **Automobile Club d'Italia** *(aci.it)* is a good resource. Take photos and videos of the car's condition – some rental agencies are notorious for 'finding' damage.

 TAXI

Taxi/Rideshare
City taxi ranks are widespread. Alternatively, phone for a radio taxi or use an app like **WeTaxi** *(wetaxi.it)*, **FreeNow** *(free-now.com)* or **ItTaxi** *(ittaxi. it)*. Radio/app taxi meters start running from their departure point. Uber Black is available in Rome, Milan, Bologna, Turin, Catania and Palermo.

DRIVING ESSENTIALS

Drive on the right

 30   130

Speed limits: 30–50km/h (urban areas), 90–110km/h (secondary roads), 130km/h (motorways)

0.05
Blood-alcohol limit: 0.05% (zero for drivers under 21 and those who've held a licence for less than three years)

Tolls & ZTLs
Motorway tolls are expensive. Pick up a ticket at the entry barrier and pay (by cash or card) as you exit. Most historic centres are Limited Traffic Zones (ZTLs), and can only be entered with a permit. Check with your hotel before arrival.

Train & Bus
Train travel is best between major cities and along the coast. Buses are better in rural areas. Buy train tickets on official sites: **Trenitalia** *(trenitalia.com)*, **Italo** *(italotreno.com)* and **Trenord** *(trenord.it)*. Tip: Italo often runs when Trenitalia strikes.

For places to stay
in Kosovo, see
p728

JESS KRAFT/SHUTTERSTOCK

Above: Sinan Pasha Mosque (p726), Prizren; Right: Prizren Fortress (p726)

Curated by
Anthony Ham

Kosovo

A YOUNG AND BEAUTIFUL NATION

Witness history being written in this excited new nation filled with Ottoman history, marvellous medieval monasteries, breathtaking hiking trails and spirited locals.

Many who've never been to Kosovo will warn you not to visit. That's their loss. Europe's newest country has the energy of an excited teenager, both curious and aspirational, and (aside from some parts of the north) it's perfectly safe to visit. Walk the capital Pristina's pedestrian boulevards with young locals who have a glimmer in their eye when talking about their new nation. See an ancient fortress, mosques and churches in Prizren's charming Old Town. Visit fresco-filled Serbian Orthodox monasteries and hike the Peaks of the Balkans, one of Europe's most buzzworthy trails.

Kosovo declared independence from Serbia in 2008, and while it has been diplomatically recognised by the majority of countries, there are still many – notably Serbia, Russia and Spain – that see its borders as a dotted line. Memories of the 1998–99 war that killed more than 13,000 and displaced hundreds of thousands remains top of mind, and, close to the northern border, ethnic Serbs and NATO forces – which intervened to protect Kosovo's Albanian majority during the war and maintain a peacekeeping force – eye each other warily. Yet Kosovo is ready to grow into adulthood. See in real time how this once traditional society is modernising, learn about its heart-wrenching history and wander its serene mountains. And go now before this off-the-beaten-track destination sees the same crowds as its neighbours.

MARKETA1982/SHUTTERSTOCK

THE MAIN AREAS

PRISTINA	PRIZREN	GJAKOVA	PEJA
Maturing capital city. **p724**	Historic cultural core. **p726**	Balkan bazaars and mosques. **p727**	Spectacular monasteries. **p727**

Find Your Way

Kosovo is small at under 11,000 sq km. If you're not on a tight schedule and don't mind some walking, taking the bus is a no-brainer. A car, as always, will give you more control.

Gjakova, p727

Between Prizren and Peja, this fascinating provincial town has one of the oldest, longest bazaars in the Balkans, as well as mosques and nearby wine country.

Pristina, p724

Spend a day or two wandering around and people-watching from the bars, cafes and restaurants in this young capital city.

Peja, p727

Popular as a gateway for hikes into the nearby mountains, Peja also grants access to Orthodox monasteries from the Middle Ages.

BUS

Buses in Kosovo are frequent and most sites are centralised around the three main cities, so you can easily save money and avoid chaotic traffic by taking public transport.

CAR

A vehicle lets you go off the beaten track and provides more mobility if doing day hikes in the mountains. Just do yourself a favour and park your car in the cities, as urban driving can be a nightmare.

Prizren, p726

There's so much history packed into this little Old Town, including a fortress, mosques, churches and artisanal shops.

Gračanica Monastery (p725)

Plan Your Time

Kosovo is small and contains few attractions. It's easy enough to get around, and certainly worth spending a week to explore before crossing into nearby Western Balkans countries.

Three Days to Travel Around

● Spend a day enjoying Kosovo's capital, **Pristina** (p724) and getting a taste for traditional cooking. Visit the Serbian Orthodox **Visoki Dečani Monastery** (p727) for superb medieval frescoes, then head to cultural capital **Prizren** (p726) to explore and watch the sunset from its fortress. Return to Pristina via 14th-century **Gračanica Monastery** (p725).

An Active Week

● Enjoy **Pristina** (p724)), then visit **Gračanica Monastery** (p725). Next, head for historic **Prizren** (p726): sacred buildings, a mountaintop fortress with exceptional views and fine filigree jewellery. **Gjakova** (p727) has a fabulous bazaar and one of Kosovo's most beautiful mosques. To round out your trip, visit **Visoki Dečani Monastery** (p727) and **Patriarchate of Peć** (p727) in Peja.

SEASONAL HIGHLIGHTS

SPRING
Cash in on lower prices and avoid the summer heat and crowds. With mild weather, it's a fine time to visit.

SUMMER
Explore Kosovo and attend Prizren Fest (p724) or DokuFest (p724)) in Prizren. Potentially Europe's quietest high season.

AUTUMN
Great weather for hiking the Accursed Mountains along the transnational Peaks of the Balkans Trail. Autumn colours.

WINTER
Snowshoe or ski Kosovo's untouched slopes (especially the Shar Mountains). Warm up with a red from the Rahovec wine region.

Pristina & Around

KOSOVAR CUISINE | HISTORIC ARCHITECTURE | MEDIEVAL MONASTERIES

Places

Pristina p724
Prizren p726
Gjakova p727
Peja p727

☑ TOP TIP

Summer is a good time to be in Prizren, with events like **Prizren Fest** *(prizrenfest. com)* in July. In early August, the city hosts Kosovo's biggest film festival: the **DokuFest International Documentary and Short Film Festival** *(dokufest.com)*.

Most Kosovo journeys begin in Europe's newest capital, which is full of optimism and potential. Pristina doesn't have many attractions, but has an appealing and unpretentious charm. Prizren, Kosovo's second city, is more noticeably historic. Where else can you photograph a fortress, a mosque and an Orthodox church all in the same frame? Climb to the fortress and take in the views, shop for fine filigree jewellery and join locals for a meal along the river or at a cafe near the old-town fountain. Gjakova (Đakovica in Serbian) is an appealing small city about halfway between Prizren and Peja. It's a relaxed place in the Kosovar heartland and is famous for the Ottoman Čaršija e Madhe, one of the longest bazaars in the Balkans. Save time to visit the remarkable monasteries around Peja.

Pristina

Get a taste of local culture

Pristina, Europe's newest capital, is like the Balkans 20 years ago and it holds fast to its culinary traditions more than most Balkan cities. For a great local *qebabtore* (kebab place), try family-run **Gjakova e Vjetër** *(facebook.com/gjakovaevjeter);* it's been around longer than most locals can remember. Tucked behind shops off Rr Johan V Hahn, **Babaghanoush** has pretty *meze* platters of Mediterranean dips along with lentil patties

---

 GETTING AROUND

Up to three buses hourly run between Prizren and Pristina (two hours), with less frequent but still regular services to/from Peja (1½ to two hours), Skopje in North Macedonia (three hours) and Tirana in Albania (three hours). From Gjakova's small bus station, there are

regular buses to Pristina (1½ hours), Prizren (one hour) and Peja (one hour).

Each of these places has an old town at its core and is best explored on foot. If you rent a car, parking can cost as little as €12 for 24 hours.

PRISTINA

KOSOVO FOOD

In Kosovo, most culinary traditions are often indistinguishable from those of Albania. Most prominent is stewed and grilled meat or fish. *Kos* (goat's-cheese yoghurt) is eaten alone or with almost anything. Other highlights include Turkish kebabs, *gjuveç* (baked meat and vegetables), *fli* (flaky pastry pie served with honey) and *tavë* (meat baked with cheese and egg). Turkish influences are also strong, with *byrek* (pastry with cheese or meat). The local beer is Peja (from the town of the same name), a *boza* (fermented drink) is a local speciality, and Vranac is red wine from the Rahovec (Orahovac) region of Kosovo. Pristina has the greatest variety, and the possibility of finding vegetarians dishes is growing, though still largely restricted to the capital.

and falafel balls. For dinner, try *tavë:* clay pots filled with meat, veggies or dairy and served straight from the oven.

Liburnia *(facebook.com/Liburnia)* is a great dinner option, with homemade bread to die for, folk music, and tangled vines and flowers cascading from the roof beams. Expect traditional Albanian mountain cooking with staples such as slow-cooked goat and steaming casseroles.

Also excellent, **Renaissance**, a seasonal organic restaurant south of Pristina's centre, has no menu – just a delicious three-course meal, including local wine and *rakija* (fruit brandy).

See Serbian Orthodox frescoes

Around 10km southeast of downtown Pristina, the Serbian enclave community of **Gračanica** is home to the Serbian Orthodox **Gračanica Monastery** *(entry €3)*. Built in 1321 by King Stefan Milutin, the UNESCO World Heritage five-dome church is filled with gorgeous frescoes depicting biblical scenes. There are 4000 faces in the church, which, as local legend has it, were painted by Greek artists in under 20 seconds each.

To get here, take the regional bus towards Gjilan from Pristina's **Plepat Bus Terminal** and get off near Gračanica Park.

THE KOSOVO WAR IN A NUTSHELL

In 1989, Kosovo's autonomy within Yugoslavia was suspended by Slobodan Milošević. Ethnic Albanian leaders declared independence from Serbia in 1990. Ethnic conflict heightened and the Kosovo Liberation Army (KLA) formed in 1996. In March 1999, a US-backed plan to return Kosovo's autonomy was rejected by Serbia, which moved to empty the province of its non-Serbian population. After Serbia refused to desist, NATO unleashed a bombing campaign on 24 March 1999. Nearly 850,000 Kosovo Albanians fled to Albania and Macedonia, telling of mass killings and forced expulsions. In June Milošević agreed to withdraw troops, air strikes ceased, the KLA disarmed and the NATO-led Kosovo Force (KFOR) took over. Independence followed in 2008.

Learn about Kosovo's history

To discover where modern Kosovo came from, spend some time in the **Museum of Kosovo** (*entry free*). The story begins with the Bronze Age (3300 BCE to 1200 BCE), where the standout piece is a large stone relief of an intricately carved Dardanian funeral procession.

Upstairs is the story of Kosovo's struggle for independence, which was declared in 2008. And don't miss the superb annex, the **Emin Gjiku Ethnographic Museum** (*entry free*), which occupies two Ottoman-era houses encircled by a charming walled garden.

Prizren

Hike to a spectacular fortress

Picturesque Prizren, 86km southwest of Pristina, is Kosovo's most appealing town to visit and has long been a hub for various cultures, sitting as it does halfway between Constantinople (İstanbul) and Rome.

From Prizren's Old Town, it's a strenuous 15-minute hike-climb along the road that leads past an Orthodox church to **Prizren Fortress** (*entry free*). The fortress has been much modified throughout the centuries; what you see today dates to the 18th century. When you reach the summit, take in glorious views of Prizren, encircled by mountains.

Allow time to wander the castle's dark tunnels and clamber along its stone walls, then head around the back of the castle to the lovely, tree-lined paved trail down to the river.

Visit the most beautiful mosque in Prizren

Like many Kosovo towns, Prizren has some superb mosques, none more so than **Sinan Pasha Mosque** (*entry free*), which towers over the main thoroughfare through the Old Town. Dating back to 1615, the style is unmistakably Ottoman. The mosque's impressive dome, slender minaret and colonnaded facade form a fabulous sight from the street. Venture inside (except during prayer times) to admire the detailed frescoes.

Remove your shoes before entering; women should wear a headscarf.

Shop for traditional jewellery

In the 15th and 18th centuries, Prizren was known throughout the Ottoman Empire for filigree – the delicate art of silver threading. Back then, filigree techniques were used to

 EATING IN PRIZREN & GJAKOVA: OUR PICKS

| **Te Syla 'Al Hambra':** Around since the 1960s, unpretentious Te Syla in Prizren does some of Kosovo's best kebabs. It's that simple. *7am-11pm* € | **Restaurant Marashi:** Riverside, beside a majestic old sycamore tree in Prizren. Traditional Albanian dishes share the menu with steaks cooked on hot stones. *8am-11pm* €€ | **Čaršija e Jupave:** Hotel restaurant serves cold cuts, *tavë Elbasan* (lamb in yogurt and garlic) and *tavë Gjakova* (veal with tomatoes and vegetables). *11am-11pm* €€ | **Hani i Haraçisë:** This former *caravanserai* (inn) in Gjakova is great for traditional dishes like veal *tavë* (hotpot). *8am-midnight* €€ |

decorate the handles of curved pistols and rifles, quite apart from traditional costume jewellery for locals. Today, the art form continues in jewellery shops found near the fountain in the historic centre and across the bridge on **Rr Adem Jashari**.

By providing an outlet for the work of a new generation of young artisans, tourism is helping to revive a centuries-old tradition that was in danger of disappearing.

Gjakova

Explore markets & the mosque bazaar

Around 89km southwest of the capital, Gjakova's Great or Grand Bazaar, the **Čaršija e Madhe**, was first laid out in the 15th century, when Kosovo lived under the rule of the Ottoman Empire. This makes it Kosovo's oldest surviving bazaar by quite a margin. And although it has been much modified through subsequent centuries, it's not difficult to imagine the bazaar during Ottoman times, particularly when the melodic Islamic call to prayer echoes through it.

The utterly superb **Hadum Mosque** *(entry free)* is one of the most beautiful in the Balkans. It is widely considered to be a classic example of early Islamic architecture in the region. The slender stone minaret suggests great antiquity, but it is a faithful replica of the original structure that was felled during the Kosovo War: the original mosque was built late in the 16th century. Inside, exquisite tile work and stone features encircle the prayer hall beneath the 13.5m-diameter dome with an extraordinarily intricate collection of floral motifs, geometric patterns, sweeping arabesques, and inscriptions or verses from the Quran.

Peja

Marvellous medieval monasteries

On the outskirts of Peja, 85km west of Pristina, the **Patriarchate of Peć** *(entry free, audio guide €2)* a UNESCO World Heritage medieval monastery, was historically used to crown kings. The Serbian Orthodox monastery dates back to the 1230s and includes a captivating cavernous church covered in vivid frescoes. Try to visit around 5pm to hear the sung prayers and chants of the elderly, black-clad nuns. With the last shafts of sunlight catching some of the frescoes, it's a haunting experience that evokes the Middle Ages.

South of Peja, don't miss the **Visoki Dečani Monastery** *(decani.org; entry free)*, which was built by Serbian King Stefan Dečanski in the early 14th century. On the outskirts of the town of Desan, the onyx-and-breccia-stone building features 10,000 painted figures, including the only medieval fresco of Jesus carrying a sword (meant to chop sins, not enemies in battle). The frescoes here are in the best condition of any frescoes that adorn Kosovo's monasteries. Before leaving, stop by the shop to grab a bottle of wine and cheese produced by the monastery's 25 resident monks.

You will need to bring your passport or ID card to gain entry to both monasteries.

KOSOVO'S HUMAN MOSAIC

According to the 2024 census, the population of Kosovo was 1.59 million; 92% are Albanian. Although the census put the number of Serbs at 1.5% of the population, the census excluded Serbian enclaves in the country's north, while many Serbs elsewhere in the country boycotted the census. Most estimates suggest that between 6% and 8% of people in Kosovo are Serbian, and most of these live in 10 protected enclaves (or exclaves, depending who you ask). Other ethnic minorities include Bosniak, Gorani, Roma, Turkish, Ashkali and Egyptian. The main religious groups are Muslim (mostly Albanians), Serbian Orthodox and Roman Catholic.

Places We Love to Stay

€ Budget €€ Midrange €€€ Top End

Pristina

MAP p725

White Tree Hostel € Cool backpacker hostel run by well-travelled owners; it feels more like an Albanian beach resort than a downtown Pristina bolthole.

Grand Boutique Hotel €€ Family home turned 10-room hotel with a walnut-tree-shaded garden, farm-fresh breakfasts and free bottle of wine.

Hotel Prima €€ Intimate, family-run and quiet, this is one of the best sleeps in Pristina. Count on high-standard rooms and friendly service.

Swiss Diamond Hotel €€€ This five-star international hotel has opulent rooms with classic luxury decor and facilities.

Prizren

Driza's House € This excellent budget place has well-equipped dorms, is quieter than many hostels, and breakfast is a great place to meet travellers.

Ura Hostel € Clean, modern hostel with air-con, a big hangout area and terrific location in the historic centre.

Hotel Prizreni €€ A pleasant combination of traditional and modern, with 12 small-but-stylish rooms and a perfect location.

Guri i Kuq Hotel & Vila €€€ With the ambience of a mountain lodge, this place has a fab restaurant, cosy wood-walled rooms and stunning views from its high perch.

Tiffany €€€ Cosy six-room boutique place with modern rooms, excellent bathrooms and flowerpots everywhere. There's an on-site restaurant.

Gjakova

Happy Hotel €€ Newish hotel rooms in a restored 300-year-old building. Some rooms have balconies overlooking the bazaar and there's a patisserie downstairs.

Hotel Čaršija e Jupave €€ Wooden beams, artworks on the walls, colourful decor, massage showers and great service. There's a memorable in-house restaurant as well, and free underground parking.

Peja

Stone Bridge Hotel € Modern hotel with 10 white-and-grey rooms and plush mattresses, smack in the heart of Peja.

Dukagjini Hotel €€ Peja buzzes around this 1951 stone-built hotel with small but grandly decorated rooms, a pool and a hot tub; 1st-floor rooms have huge terraces overlooking the square.

Hotel Kulla e Zenel Beut €€ An Ottoman-era stone-and-wood building with modern rooms and a fantastic restaurant.

Doa Boutique Hotel €€€ North of the Old Town and occupying a handsome villa, the Doa has rooms with wooden floors and Persian carpets, great bathrooms and a lovely vine-shaded garden.

TRABANTOS/SHUTTERSTOCK

Dukagjini Hotel

Practicalities

Time Zone
Kosovo runs on Central European Time (GMT/UTC plus one hour). The 24-hour clock is used, as is Daylight Saving Time, with clocks going forward the last Sunday in October, and back the last Sunday in March.

Tourist Information
Despite its growing tourism industry, Kosovo has few tourist centres, and nothing in Pristina. Tour operators and hotels often take up the slack, with extensive local information on everything from transport to attractions.

Smoking
One-third of the adult population (and half of adult men) smoke in Kosovo. While cafe terraces are filled with chain-smoking locals, there's a smoking ban for enclosed public spaces, so most venues are smoke-free inside.

Mobile Phones
Coverage is excellent throughout the country, and it's easy to obtain a SIM card with data for as little as €10; simply bring your passport to one of the offices of the mobile-phone providers. At the time of writing, Kosovo was still rolling out its 5G network; MTS Ipko and Vala are the local carriers.

COLORMAKER/SHUTTERSTOCK

Prizren (p726)

Opening Hours
Banks 8am–5pm Monday to Friday, to 2pm Saturday
Bars 8am–11pm
Clubs 8pm–3am Thursday to Saturday
Shops 8am–6pm Monday to Friday, to 3pm Saturday
Restaurants 8am–midnight

Etiquette
Kosovo is a generally conservative country, with complex rules of etiquette; however, these rarely affect travellers. Eat and drink plentifully of whatever is given to you whenever it is given. In rural areas, local women don't normally shake hands with strangers. And always dress modestly and generally cover up when visiting mosques or Serbian monasteries.

Public Holidays
Note that traditional Islamic and Orthodox Christian holidays are also observed, including Ramadan and Orthodox Easter.
New Year's Day 1 January
Independence Day 17 February
Kosovo Constitution Day 9 April
Labour Day 1 May
Europe Day 9 May

Language

In Albanian – also understood in Kosovo and North Macedonia – *ew* is pronounced as 'ee' with rounded lips, *uh* as the 'a' in 'ago', *dh* as the 'th' in 'that', *dz* as the 'ds' in 'adds', and *zh* as the 's' in 'pleasure'. Also, *ll* and *rr* are pronounced stronger than when they are written as single letters.

Basics

Hello. Tungjatjeta. *toon·dya·tye·ta*
Goodbye. Mirupafshim.
mee·roo·paf·sheem
Yes. Po. *po*
No. Jo. *yo*
Please. Ju lutem. *yoo loo·tem*
Thank you. Faleminderit.
fa·le·meen·de·reet
What's your name? Si quheni?
see choo·he·nee
My name is ... Unë quhem ...
oo·nuh choo·hem ...
Do you speak English?
A flisni anglisht?
a flees·nee ang·leesht
I don't understand.
Unë nuk kuptoj.
oo·nuh nook koop·toy

Emergencies

Help! Ndihmë! *ndeeh·muh*
Go away! Ik! *eek*
I'm ill. Jam i/e sëmurë. (m/f)
yam ee/e suh·moo·ruh

Call the doctor/police! Thirrni
doktorin/policinë! *theerr·nee
dok·to·reen/po·lee·tsee·nuh*

Eating & Drinking

What would you recommend?
Çfarë më rekomandoni? *chfa·ruh
muh re·ko·man·do·nee*
I'll have... Dua... *doo·a*
Cheers! Gëzuar! *guh·zoo·ar*
I'd like the bill/menu, please. Më
sillni faturën/menunë, ju lutem.
*muh seell·nee fa·too·ruhn/
me·noo·nuh yoo loo·tem*

Shopping & Services

I'm looking for ...
Po kërkoj për ... *po kuhr·koy puhr ...*
How much is it? Sa kushton?
sa koosh·ton
Cheers! Gëzuar! *guh·zoo·ar*
That's too expensive.
Është shumë shtrenjtë.
uhsh·tuh shoo·muh shtreny·tuh

NUMBERS

1
një *nyuh*

2
dy *dew*

3
tre *tre*

4
katër *ka·tuhr*

5
pesë *pe·suh*

6
gjashtë *dyash·tuh*

7
shtatë *shta·tuh*

8
tetë *te·tuh*

9
nëntë *nuhn·tuh*

10
dhjetë *dhye·tuh*

English & Other Tourist Languages

While most people dealing with tourists on a daily basis speak English extremely well, that's not true of the entire population. English is taught in schools, but the older generations are more likely to know some German, Russian or, along the coast, Italian.

FROM LEFT: YU XICHAO/SHUTTERSTOCK, JOHNER IMAGES/GETTY IMAGES

Pristina International Airport

Arriving & Getting Around

Entering Kosovo is generally a breeze, with welcoming and bureaucracy-free immigration and customs. Visitors from many countries do not need a visa to stay in Kosovo for fewer than 90 days.

By Air
Pristina International Airport is 18km from the centre of Pristina. At the time of writing, flights could not enter through Serbian airspace. Airlines include Wizz, Austrian and Swiss.

By Land
Kosovo has open land borders with Montenegro, Albania, North Macedonia and Serbia (open only inbound to Kosovo). Be sure to forewarn police and obtain a cross-border permit if hiking across borders.

Entering from Serbia
To travel between Serbia and Kosovo, you'll need to enter Kosovo from Serbia first. If you arrived here via Albania or North Macedonia and want to visit Serbia, you will need to go via a third country.

Car Hire
Driving here can be erratic, though roads are generally good. Never drive after dark, when headlights seem to be optional. High speed is also a concern. Pristina has car-hire options from the main companies (Europcar and Avis), as well as less expensive local companies. Not all car-rental companies elsewhere in Europe will allow you to take your vehicle into Kosovo. Always ask when booking.

MONEY
Currency: Euro (€)

CASH
Kosovo has been allowed to use the euro as legal tender since 2002, despite not being a member of the EU or eurozone. Virtually everyone prefers cash, with cards rarely (if increasingly) accepted. Bring an emergency supply of euros.

ATMS
You'll receive euros at ATMs. Some ATMs will ask you whether you accept or decline the ATM's conversion rate – always decline (and/ or choose euros) for a lower fee/better rate.

CREDIT CARDS
Paying with credit cards is still rare at restaurants or accommodation, although it's becoming more widespread.

TIPPING
Tipping isn't expected in Kosovo, though you can round up or give up to 10% if you appreciated the service.

731

Curated by
Leonid Ragozin

Latvia

DUNES AND BALTIC FORESTS

Where a stunning coastline meets an elegant capital city
and clear lakes sparkle amid mysterious forests.

Latvia is a country of blues and greens: its blues reflect the changing hues of the sea and inland lakes, while its greens come in the soothing shades of the forest canopy that covers the hinterland. That's from afar. A closer look reveals ever more colours: the golden radiance of sand dunes and luxuriant beaches; the brownish hue of peat bogs sprinkled with cranberry red. The pastel tones of its capital's art nouveau district; the hardened black timber and grey boulders that form the walls of the old barns dotting the countryside.

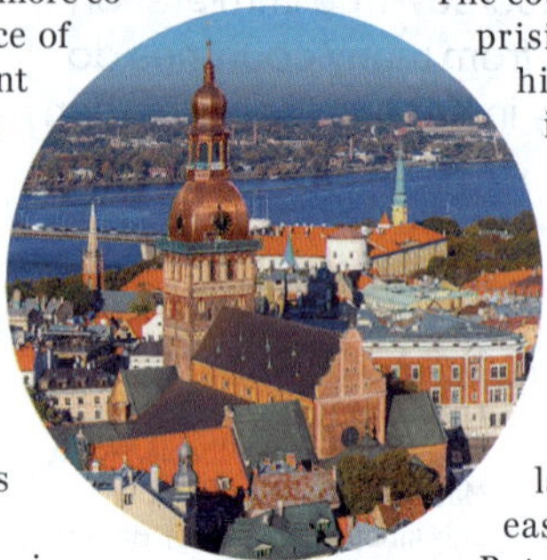

Latvia is defined by the juxtaposition of its capital, Rīga, with the rest of the country. Latvia's only large city, Rīga is where a whopping 52% of the country's population lives. This is one of the highest ratios of city-to-countryside dwellers in Europe. It's a fantastically cosy and welcoming place that doesn't fall over itself in order to please, but displays many quiet, understated charms.

The country beyond Rīga is surprisingly diverse, with four historical regions presenting an intriguing interplay of distinct landscapes and idiosyncratic towns: agricultural Kurzeme in the west, hilly and forested Vidzeme in the north, history-rich Zemgale in the south and the lakelands of Latgale in the east.

But the real treasure is the coastline – 500km of stunning beaches and pine-covered dunes that line the Gulf of Rīga and beyond, stretching all the way to the open sea in the west.

KAVALENKAVAVOLHA/GETTY IMAGES

THE MAIN AREAS

RĪGA	GULF OF RĪGA	GUAJA NATIONAL PARK	KURZEME & ZEMGALE
The national capital. **p736**	Endless dunes and beaches. **p740**	Latvia's Switzerland, or so they say. **p743**	Maritime and Baltic German vibes. **p745**

For places to stay in Latvia, see p747

VIESTURS JUGS/SHUTTERSTOCK

Left: Rīga (p736); Above: Gauja National Park (p743)

Find Your Way

No matter what direction you're headed, Latvia can be crossed in a few hours. This is an easy country to get around.

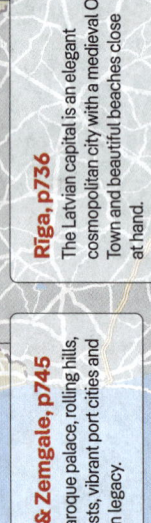

Gauja National Park, p743

Latvia's outdoor playground, where a quiet river meanders through forested hills.

BUS & TRAIN

Latvia has an extensive network of bus routes designed to reach most small villages and even standalone farmsteads. The train network is limited to suburban destinations near Rīga and select destinations around the country.

CAR

A car provides travellers with more flexibility. The road network is generally good, although there are almost no real motorways.

Gulf of Rīga, p740

Almost 300km of mostly uninterrupted beaches lined with pine-covered dunes.

Kurzeme & Zemgale, p745

A beautiful baroque palace, rolling hills, maritime forests, vibrant port cities and Baltic German legacy.

Rīga, p736

The Latvian capital is an elegant cosmopolitan city with a medieval Old Town and beautiful beaches close at hand.

ESTONIA

Vijandi · Tartu · Põlva

Valga · Tõrva · Ape · Alūksne · Balvi

Rūjiena · Valka · Smiltene · Gulbene

Limbaži · Valmiera · Cēsis Castle · Jaunpiebalga · Madona · Ludza

Vidzeme Coast · Salacgrīva · Saulkrasti

Gulf of Rīga · Baltā Kāpa · Gauja National Park · Sigulda · Turaida Museum Reserve · Teiči Nature Reserve · Lubāna · Varakļāni · Rēzekne · Malta · Gauja Rāzna National Park · Daugava River · Krāslava · Aglona · Daugavpils · Ilūkste · Zarasai

Koknese · Jēkabpils · Aknīste

Salaspils · Rīgas Doms · RĪGA · St Peter's Church · Rīga Central Market · Lielvārde · Bauska · Jaunjelgava · Jelgava · Kupiškis · LITHUANIA

Kolka · Roja · Dundaga · Mērsrags · Lake Engure · Kandava · Saldus · Mazeikiai

Oviši · Ventspils · Ugāle · Kuldīga · Ventas Rumba · Jūrkalne · Naval Church of St Nicholas · Liepāja

Baltic Sea

BELARUS

100 km
50 miles

Rīga's Old Town (p736)

Plan Your Time

Latvia is a compact country with a lot to offer, so it's possible to pack plenty of activities into a limited amount of time.

Pressed for Time

● If you only have a few days, base yourself in the capital, **Rīga** (p736), and take in as much of it as you can, from the Old Town with its spired churches and museums to the art nouveau buildings of the Jugendstil quarter. Make sure you allocate at least half a day for a trip to the seaside in **Jūrmala** (p740) or **Saulkrasti** (p742).

Five Days or More

● With more time, start with **Rīga** (p736), then venture to **Kuldīga** (p746) to admire the famous waterfall. Proceed to the lively port city of **Liepāja** (p746) for a healthy dose of seaside fun. Back in Rīga, make a dash for **Rundāle Palace** (p745) near Bauska, from where you can continue on to Lithuania.

SEASONAL HIGHLIGHTS

SPRING	**SUMMER**	**AUTUMN**	**WINTER**
Days get longer and the whole country is in bloom. Storks begin to return from their African holiday.	The entire nation repairs to the coastal dunes, forested lakes or the countryside.	It's getting dark again, but the national holiday season is in full swing and Rīga is decked out with light installations.	There's finally enough snow for cross-country skiing in Rīga or downhill skiing in Sigulda.

Rīga

HISTORY | JUGENDSTIL | LAID-BACK AMBIENCE

GETTING AROUND

Rīga's airport is served by bus 22. To avoid taxi scams, it's safer to use Bolt and wait for your ride in the 2nd-floor arrivals hall. Trams, buses and trolleybuses (rigassatiksme.lv) are essential if venturing beyond the city centre. Buses and trolleybuses may have the same number but run on different routes. Fares are paid with e-talons. Buy and refill them at Narvesen convenience stores or vending machines aboard newer trams. A single 90-minute journey costs €1.50 including transfers, but you need to validate your ticket again if changing transport.

☑ TOP TIP

There are no must-sees in Rīga – just go with the flow and do your thing. Sip coffee, visit Gothic churches and museums, shop for fresh produce at the markets and amble from one friendly bar to another when night falls.

Rīga is an independent and slightly mysterious place. It's always elegantly dressed despite its modest income and it keeps its house in good order. Riga has seen a lot, but won't tell you everything.

The city's architectural styles are what remains of her former overlords. The tall spires and cobbled streets of the Old Town (Vecrīga) are the legacy of Baltic German and Swedish rulers. The art nouveau facades in the centre hark back to the Russian Empire. Gloomy apartment blocks on the outskirts are the remnants of the Soviet footprint.

Having re-emerged as the capital of independent Latvia three decades ago, Rīga continues to add tasteful, history-conscious modern architecture, yet maintains a homey look. The border with the countryside, coastal dunes and pristine woods is blurred, with furry visitors occasionally venturing into town and wild mushrooms on sale at farmers markets.

Rīga's Cradle

See the city's beginnings

In 1201, the crusading bishop Albert von Buxhoeveden resolved to build a city on the site of an old marketplace at the mouth of the Daugava River. The spot he chose is now called **Jāņa sēta** (St John's courtyard). This is where the chronicled history of Rīga begins, which makes this enclosure, guarded by a partly reconstructed 13th-century wall, the best point to begin your exploration of Rīga's Old Town, also known as Vecrīga.

Once inside, note the curving lines above the red-brick gates – they are said to depict the back of the donkey that carried Jesus into Jerusalem. The gist of it is, 'follow Christ'. The courtyard bears the name of the adjacent **St John's Church** (janabaznica.lv), a 13th- to 19th-century amalgam of Gothic and baroque styles. It was first mentioned when the citizens installed catapults on the roof and successfully drove back attacking Livonian knights. Walk through Jāņa sēta into a square dominated by the needle-shaped **St Peter's Church** (svpetera.lv; entry adult/student/child €9/7/3).

RĪGA

Kronvalda parks

Esplanāde

Kronvalda parks

Vērmanesdārzs

Pils laukums

Rīgas Doms

St Peter's Church

Daugava River

Rīga Central Market

Hotel Vantis Riverside (1.9km)

Hotel Vantis Riverside (1.9km)

500 m
0.25 miles

WHERE TO EAT IN CENTRAL RĪGA: OUR PICKS

★ HIGHLIGHTS
1 Rīga Central Market
2 Rīgas Doms
3 St Peter's Church
4 Stūra Māja

● SIGHTS
5 Jāņa sēta
6 Janis Rozentāls &
  Rūdolfs Blaumanis
  Museum

7 Latvian Architecture
  Museum
see 6 Rīga Art Nouveau
  Centre
8 Rīga History &
  Navigation Museum
9 St John's Church
see 7 Three Brothers

● SLEEPING
10 Cinnamon Sally
11 Edvards

12 Grand Poet
13 Hestia Hotel Jugend
14 Hotel Bergs
15 Hotel Justus
16 Naughty Squirrel
17 Neiburgs

● EATING
18 3 Pavaru
19 Babo
20 Buberts
21 BURZMA

22 Milda
23 Silķītes un Dillītes
24 Zivju Lete

● DRINKING &
NIGHTLIFE
25 Čē
26 Kalve
27 Kaņepes Kultūras
  Centrs
28 Miit
29 Piana Vyshnia

Buberts: Away from the crowds, Buberts serves meat and fish dishes of variable provenance accompanied by craft beer. Good for breakfast. *8am-10pm* €

Zivju Lete: Contemporary cafe with bare-brick walls, wooden floors and date-friendly tables. Think fish and chips and towering seafood platters. *noon-10pm* €€

Silķītes un Dillītes: By the fish hall at the Central Market, this scallop-sized cafe combines superb seafood with draft beer. Try the herring with cottage cheese. *9am-5pm* €

Babo: Sleek Georgian place serving all you'd expect – *khachapuri* (cheese pastries), *khinkali* (dumplings) – but with a touch of chic. Great wines. *noon-11pm* €€

BITTER DELIGHT

What's your poison, Rīga? Apparently, it's a herbal liqueur known as Rīga Black Balsam. This thick black drink has an unforgettable, heart-wrenchingly bitter taste. Why? Well, it was originally a medicinal tonic and medicine is not supposed to be sweet. At least, not in 1752, when pharmacist Abraham Kunze concocted the recipe. So how do people make it more palatable? The traditional way is to mix it with hot blackcurrant juice, a concoction you'll find in many bars in Rīga. Others add it to coffee, tea or – an excellent combination – ice cream. That said, some people drink it on the rocks. Care to join them?

SERGED25/SHUTTERSTOCK

Three Brothers

The centrepiece of Rīga's skyline, this Gothic tower has been here since 1209, making it one of the oldest medieval buildings in the Baltics. Its soaring spire, added in the 17th century, is adorned with a golden-coloured weathercock, also a symbol of Rīga.

Local History at Dome Square

Meet by the cathedral

In joy or grief, in celebration or protest, or simply to stock up on Christmas gifts, the people of Rīga flock to the Old Town's main square: a cobblestoned space in front of the enormous **Rīgas Doms** (*doms.lv; entry adult/child €5/3*), the country's most prominent cathedral. Founded in 1211 as the seat of the Rīga diocese, the architecture is a mixture of styles spanning the 13th to the 18th centuries: Romanesque, Gothic and baroque, with the trademark Hanseatic feature of glazed black bricks. At the back of the cathedral, the **Rīga History & Navigation Museum** (*rigamuz.lv; entry adult/student/child €10/6/3*), founded in 1773, presents the sweep of local history from the Bronze Age all the way up to WWII.

Nearby, three old stone houses, dubbed the **Three Brothers**, form a photogenic row and exemplify Old Rīga's diverse collection of architectural styles. No 17 is over 600 years old, making it the oldest dwelling in town. The middle one (17th century) houses the **Latvian Architecture Museum** (*archmuseum.lv; free*).

WHERE TO EAT AND DRINK IN THE OLD TOWN: OUR PICKS

3 Pavaru: Stellar chefs run this jazzy culinary show, with improvisation and seasonal freshness at the heart of the menu. *5-11pm* €€€

Milda: Deep dive into Baltic gastronomy: creatively reinvented Latvian and Lithuanian staples and a chatty chef who won a nod from Michelin. *noon-11pm* €€

BURZMA: The food court at the top of the Galerija Centrs shopping mall combines stylish eateries and sweeping views of the Old Town. *10am-11pm* €

Piana Vyshnia: A transplant from Lviv in Ukraine, this perpetually heaving place celebrates *vyshnevka* – a sweet cherry liquor ubiquitous in Eastern Europe. *11am-3am*

Game of Fancy

Explore the Jugendstil quarter

Rīga entered the 20th century as the sixth-largest city in the Russian Empire, and was also rapidly expanding under ambitious mayor George Armitstead, a native Rigan of British origin. In 1901 the city celebrated its 700th anniversary by inaugurating a new street, Alberta iela, built in the revolutionary Jugendstil (art nouveau) style. Today, this street runs through the heart of the Jugendstil quarter, erected during a period of rapid development and social optimism. The architect responsible for many of the buildings was Mikhail Eisenstein, who happened to be the father of filmmaker Sergei Eisenstein (of *Battleship Potemkin* fame). See the full range of his talents in five adjoining buildings, from Nos 2a to 8. **Rīga Art Nouveau Centre** *(jugendstilsriga.lv)* is inside the house architect Konstantīns Pēkšēns built for himself, incorporating images of plants and animals characteristic of Latvia into ornamental reliefs. In the same entrance, surmount the wonderfully lavish stairwell to the 5th floor to find the **Janis Rozentāls & Rūdolfs Blaumanis Museum** *(memorialiemuzeji. lv; entry adult/concession €2/1)*, the former dwelling of a famous painter and his equally famous writer friend.

The KGB's Shadow

Notorious HQ of the secret police

Ominously located on a 17th-century execution site, the fin-de-siècle building known as **Stūra Māja** *(Corner House; okupacias muzejs.lv; guided tour adult/concession €15/9)* is remembered by generations of Latvians as the headquarters of the Soviet secret police. Arbitrary arrests, torture, executions – it all happened here. The museum can only be visited on a guided tour. There are five English-language tours daily, between 11am and 4pm.

Make Trade not War

The city's main market

In what might be the world's most large-scale act of 'beating swords into ploughshares', several German-built WWI zeppelin hangars were brought into the city in the 1920s and converted into pavilions for **Riga Central Market** *(centraltirgus.lv)*. Today, it's a landmark and a place where friends bump into each other while shopping for smoked fish, forest mushrooms, fruit, homemade bread... you name it. Most of the action happens outside; the hangars are now mostly food courts.

 WHERE TO DRINK IN CENTRAL RĪGA: OUR PICKS

Čē: Scruffy and cavernous, with anarchic outdoor seating – the ultimate bohemian haunt with a good choice of draft and bottled beer. *4pm-1am*	**Kaņepes Kultūras Centrs:** Old music school converted into a beer garden, presided over by a giant green lion on the roof. Essential concert venue. *4pm-late*	**Kalve:** For local connoisseurs, this tiny joint in Baznīcas iela is the place for a morning cup. The filter coffee 'day's brew' is especially good. *8am-6pm*	**Miit:** A sociable place that serves a mean coffee as well as vegetarian lunches and desserts. *8am-8pm*

Gulf of Rīga

Gulf of Rīga

PERFECT BEACHES | DUNE WALKS | JET-SET VIBES

Places

Jūrmala p740
Northern Coast p741

 TOP TIP

In any season, you can get off at Bulduri, walk towards the beach and join the promenading crowds headed in the direction of Majori.

On the map, Latvia's gulf resembles a pair of open jaws. The water in this inner sea is even less salty than the Baltic, while Estonia's islands shelter it from serious storms. The coast on both sides of Rīga is an almost uninterrupted stretch of exquisite sand and romantic pine-covered dunes. Sitting on a massive sandbar formed by the Lielupe River, Jūrmala is Rīga's backyard beach and what passes for Latvia's golden mile, a playground for jet-setters and minigarchs from the east (the Russian language still prevails here). This strip of wealthy suburbia squeezed between the river, the railway line and the sea stretches for 32km. North of Rīga, the dune-dominated terrain is less developed and even more beautiful. Suburban trains run in both directions, making beach hopping easy. The Jūrtaka hiking trail runs along the coast; cycling is also a great way to get around.

Jūrmala
Stroll the strand

The **beach** in Jūrmala doubles as Latvia's longest and flashiest promenade. The white sand is hard-packed and ideal for walking or making sand castles. Come here in any season and you'll see strolling urbanites, cyclists or even skiers gliding along the seafront when there's enough snow. In winter,

GETTING AROUND

From Rīga, hop on a frequent train to head in either direction along the gulf. Trains with the destinations Dubulti, Sloka or Tukums serve stations in Jūrmala. Trains heading to Skulte, Saulkrasti or Carnikava serve the northern coast.

In addition to the railway line that runs through Jūrmala, there's a local bus network that connects railway stations and villages beyond Jūrmala. Saulkrasti municipality runs a similar, albeit smaller, network.

Jūrmala is convenient for bicycles, which you can rent at Velopark *(velopark.lv)* in Bulduri, or you can cycle all the way from Rīga.

TRABANTOS/SHUTTERSTOCK

Jomas iela

you'll still spot the occasional desperado dipping into the icy water. Few developments have encroached on the bluffs behind the sand, leaving the beach largely unspoiled with only the odd cafe here and there. Jūrmala's oldest area near the Dzintari, Majori and Dubulti stations resembles Prussian resorts on the German Baltic coast, its skyline dominated by elegant timber-framed villas, some of which have intricate wood-carved decor. The heart of the action is the 1km-long pedestrian street, **Jomas iela**, which runs between Majori and Dzintari stations.

Northern Coast

Pick your beach

While most visitors flock to Jūrmala, the beaches north of Rīga are markedly quieter, wilder and more visually attractive – with pristine white sand and a faint whiff of resin carried by the wind from the pine-covered dunes. The train line runs just beyond the resort area of Saulkrasti, with stops every couple of kilometres, which makes it convenient not just for lazing by the sea but also for walking chosen stretches of the **Jūrtaka coastal trail** *(baltictrails.eu)*.

JŪRMALA TRAIN STATIONS

When arriving in Jūrmala by train, where to alight is a matter of taste. Here are some tips to help you decide.

Bulduri: A quieter part of Jūrmala, with restaurants and a short promenade leading to the sea.

Dzintari: Somewhat set back from the sea, but close to a park and convenient for its namesake concert hall.

Majori: This station has a picture-perfect setting and is in the centre of the action.

Dubulti: Has an art gallery inside the station and glimpses of old Jūrmala nearby.

Asari: Another beautiful station and a 10-minute walk from an unspoilt stretch of beach.

THE GUIDE

LATVIA GULF OF RĪGA

 WHERE TO EAT IN THE GULF OF RĪGA: OUR PICKS

36.Line: Relocated to Dubulti, this is Jūrmala's prime dining location with seafood and a grill. You might spot the occasional ex-Soviet celebrity. *1-10pm €€€*

Kinza House: Jūrmala is full of Caucasian restaurants; this is the best for Georgian cuisine. Gorge on *khachapuri* and *khinkali* if you can get a seat. *noon-10pm €€*

Bitīte: Good for a quick coffee or hearty breakfast. The elevated terrace is a prime vantage point overlooking Jūrmala's pedestrian Jomas St. *8.30am-9pm €*

Abra: A family cafe by the dunes in Saulkrasti, serving Latvian *karbonādes* (pork chops) and standard East European fare. *11am-4pm Fri, 24hr Sat & Sun €*

741

JOYCAYM/SHUTTERSTOCK

Baltā Kāpa

Vecāķi is the first train station by the beach north of the Daugava River. It feels like a low-key Jūrmala with large old villas and a few cafes along the main promenade. At **Kalngale** station, an atmospheric promenade runs through a darkly beautiful coniferous forest to a white-sand beach. In **Garciems**, a boardwalk follows a beautiful little river seasonally dammed by beavers.

Saulkrasti's dune of perfection

Get off at Pabaži station and walk 1.3km to **Baltā Kāpa** (White Dune), a viewpoint on top of a high cliff, where a fertile, forest river streams through the white sands on its last stretch before reaching the sea. This is one of the most enchanting places along the entire Latvian coast, and the wooden walkway along the 18m-high cliffs affords sweeping views of the Gulf of Rīga. The **Sunset Trail** (Saulrieta taka) runs to the centre of **Saulkrasti**, where you'll find an artfully designed beach with a cluster of restaurants. An additional perk is the deep water near the seafront, which makes for better swimming than elsewhere.

Gauja National Park

HIKING | RAFTING | CASTLES

Gauja National Park encompasses an enchanting landscape of forested hills that guard the meandering white ribbon of the Gauja River. Providing vertical dimension to a lowland country, these hills – unironically referred to as 'Latvian Switzerland' – draw hikers, rafters (it's not quite white water) and downhill skiers. There's even a bobsled track and a facility imitating zero gravity that's accessible to the public. But the main pull is the quiet, unpretentious beauty of this area – especially in autumn, when the hills are ablaze in yellow and bright red. Gauja Valley is Latvia's top outdoors destination, with Sigulda serving as its hub, but it also comprises medieval castles and charming little towns, as well as various historical monuments, entertainment parks and old mansions, known as *muižas*, which have been converted into hotels. Most of these attractions are located along the Mežtaka (Forest Trail) route.

Places

Sigulda p743
Cēsis p744
Līgatne p744

☑ TOP TIP

Start your exploration of Gauja National Park at the excellent Tourist Information Office at the train and bus station. It's stocked with walking maps and is the place to find out about daily events and tours.

Sigulda

A scenic river valley

Sigulda is a manifestation of what Latvians regard as an ideal life and aesthetic perfection. The town is a sprawling area of

GETTING AROUND

The most memorable way to traverse Gauja National Park is by hiking or cycling the Mežtaka trail. But to reach the trailhead, you'll need to take a combination of train and buses. Cēsis lies on the same train line as Sigulda and is also served by buses from Rīga, via Sigulda. Līgatne's train station is located by the main road leading to Estonia and Russia, 8km from the town centre. There are a few direct daily buses to Cēsis. Otherwise, catch a local bus to

Augšlīgatne on the main highway and proceed from there.

Sigulda's attractions are spread out. The place is a cyclist's paradise, with several rental shops around town, including Veloriba by the train station. Bus 3112 connects Sigulda and Turaida, with eight to nine services a day. Bolt is widely available.

Many local attractions are deep in the woods, accessible only by car, bicycle or a long hike.

FOREST TREKS

The trans-Baltic Forest Trail, known as **Mežtaka** *(baltictrails. eu)* in Latvia, follows the course of the Gauja River through the national park. The trail leaves from a key road junction near Gauja village and runs all the way to Valmiera. This is one of the most beautiful legs of the entire route. Stages tend to be fairly long, ranging from 19km to 26km, with limited options for bailing mid-route. If you only want to hike one section, choose between the Sigulda–Līgatne or Līgatne–Cēsis stages. Factor in extra time for the Līgatne nature trails if you choose the former.

large private homes surrounded by manicured grass and apple orchards, with plenty of space for lonely walks and bicycle rides through the magnificent valley of the Gauja River. A quintessential Sigulda experience is to cross the Gauja Valley, enjoying terrific views in all directions, in a cute **cable car** *(siguldaadventures.com; €19 return)* that departs from a precipice in the centre of town. This takes you to the **Krimulda Manor** *(krimuldamuiza.lv)* on the other side of the valley.

Explore the Turaida castle

Turaida *(turaida-muzejs.lv; entry adult/concession €8/from €2)* means 'God's Garden' in ancient Livonian and this green knoll capped with a castle is indeed an enchanting place. The red-brick edifice with its tall cylindrical tower was built in 1214 on the site of a Liv stronghold and reconstructed in the 1980s. A museum inside the castle's 15th-century granary offers an interesting account of the Livonian state from 1319 to 1561; additional exhibitions can be viewed in the 42m-high Donjon Tower and the castle's western and southern towers. Turaida is across the river from Sigulda and served by frequent buses from the railway station.

Cēsis

A stunning Livonian town

The Livonian knights who were responsible for founding Wenden (which became Cēsis seven centuries later) must have had a romantic side. The remarkable **Cēsis Castle** *(cesupils.lv; entry adult/concession €12/8)* is actually two castles in one, forming a single museum. The moody dark-stone towers belong to the restored old castle. You're handed a candle lamp at the start of your visit, making your exploration of the dark ruins suitably atmospheric. Back in town, make sure you visit the 13th-century **St John's Church** *(cesusirds.lv)*, where armour-clad Livonian knights prayed and buried their dead.

Līgatne

A chef's shack

Many of us dream of owning a little countryside house with a garden, and celebrity chefs are no exception. But only the latter would turn their home into a Michelin restaurant. Ēriks Dreibants based his brainchild, **Pavāru Māja** *(pavarumaja.lv)*, in an old maternity home that's surrounded by a garden where most of his ingredients are grown. Opt for a four-course lunch (€59) or an eight-course dinner (€99); book online.

 WHERE TO EAT IN GAUJA NATIONAL PARK: OUR PICKS

Jāņa Tirgus: This modern market hall is mostly a food court with a quality pizzeria in the middle. But you can also shop for produce here. *10am-8pm* €€

Doma Kafejnīca: Enjoy wraps, burgers, stir-fries and heavenly fruit-filled desserts in an enchanted garden. *11am-8pm Tue-Sun* €

Cēsu Maize: This artisanal bakery is always warm and redolent with the aroma of freshly baked bread. Owners can talk you through old recipes. *10am-6pm* €

HE Vanadziņš: High-end Nordic cuisine in a charming courtyard in the heart of Cēsis. *5-10pm Thu-Fri, noon-8pm Sat & Sun* €€€

Kurzeme & Zemgale

OPULENT PALACE | WATERFALLS | BEACHES

Western Latvia, known as Kurzeme, is surrounded by the sea on two sides. The milder climate here is more conducive to agriculture, unlike the forested north and east. It's a land of rolling hills, rapeseed fields that bloom in spring and storks' nests that preside over every village. This area was under Baltic German influence for almost 700 years – a story that culminated in the 17th century when the Duchy of Courland briefly turned itself into a mini-empire with overseas possessions in Africa and the Caribbean. What remains today are quaint Prussian-style towns and the castles and palaces of the Baltic German nobility. This ambience spills into the more forested southern part of Latvia, known as Zemgale. Typically lumped together with Kurzeme, these two regions share much of the same history.

Places

Rundāle p745
Kuldīga p746
Liepāja p746

☑ TOP TIP

For a full Karosta prison experience in Lijepāja, you can 'get arrested' and spend the night in prison. Conditions vary from semi-authentic to prison chic. For an additional donation, you can also arrange your escape.

Rundāle Palace

The abode of an adventurist

Built as a grand residence for the duke of Courland, Ernst Johann Biron, the magnificent **Rundāle Palace** *(rundale.net; entry including gardens adult/student/child €17/10.50/5.50)* is a monument to 18th-century aristocratic ostentatiousness and rural Latvia's architectural highlight. It was designed by Italian baroque genius Bartolomeo Rastrelli, who is best known for the Winter Palace in St Petersburg. About 40 of the

GETTING AROUND

Kuldīga, Liepāja and Bauska (for Rundāle Palace) are all served by frequent buses from Rīga's central station. Additionally, there's at least one train a day between Rīga and Llepāja. Four buses a day run between Kuldīga and Liepāja, making it easy to visit both on the same trip.

Local buses connect Bauska's bus station to Rundāle Palace roughly hourly. You don't need local transport in Kuldīga. In Liepāja, the adjacent train and bus stations are connected to the centre by the tram line. Tickets can be bought from the driver, but only with a card.

HISTORY OF KURZEME

The historical region in Latvia's west takes its name from the Curonians, a medieval Baltic group who also lent their name to the Curonian spit in Lithuania. The German crusaders of the Livonian Order subjugated them in the 13th century and continued to rule the region up until the Russian Revolution of 1917. When the Livonian Order collapsed in the 16th century, its last master Gotthard von Kettler set up the Duchy of Courland. The duchy was a disobedient vassal of the Polish-Lithuanian Commonwealth, and as the latter was increasingly consumed by the Russians, it drifted in that direction as well. It played an outsized role in St Petersburg politics for a few decades before being formally annexed by Russia in 1795.

palace's 138 rooms are open to visitors, as are the wonderful formal gardens, inspired by those at Versailles. Biron was the lover of Anna Ioanovna, the empress of Russia from 1730 to 1740, and a notorious adventurist in Russia. Rundāle Palace is 12km east of Bauska in Zemgale.

Kuldīga

A humble Niagara Falls

A newcomer to the UNESCO heritage list, charming Kuldīga – formerly known as Goldingen – has a Grimm Brothers' vibe and a striking setting above what is allegedly the widest waterfall in Europe, **Ventas Rumba**. This description might be a truth-stretcher – not in terms of width (249m), but in calling a human-sized drop in the riverbed a waterfall. Still, it's a truly awe-inspiring sight when seen from above. A zigzagging ribbon of white water runs across the Venta River, the banks overflowing with lush greenery. A stunning 19th-century red-brick bridge is a few hundred metres away. The deep lagoon is a favourite place for swimming and the location of the city beach.

Liepāja

Harbour fun and ghosts of the past

Liepāja is the type of city where you'll want to hum an uplifting tune as you stroll around the harbour and Old Town. The stunning white-sand **Blue Flag Beach** plays no small part in achieving this effect, as does the colourful harbour that serves as the city's prime nightlife spot. Old trees, manicured flower beds, water features, elegant walkways and cycling trails make the 3km-long **Seaside Park** the very definition of an urban oasis.

But this is also a place ridden with the ghosts of the past. The former navy garrison district of Karosta is located across the canal from central Liepāja. Its most striking landmark is the magnificent Russian Orthodox **Naval Church of St Nicholas**, whose massive golden cupola rises above drab Soviet-era *khruschevka* apartment blocks.

Also spooky is the beating heart of Karosta's tourism industry: the **Karosta Prison** *(karosta.lv; entry adult/student €8/5)*. Not exactly a Gulag, it was used by all political regimes throughout history as a detention centre for disobedient sailors. Conditions were torturous, as you'll be able to attest following a guided tour of the dark prison cells covered in Russian-language graffiti.

 WHERE TO EAT AND DRINK IN KULDĪGA & LIEPĀJA: OUR PICKS

Bārs Didro: Fantastic food and cocktails in a Kuldīga bar run by professional philosophers who also hold occasional intellectual discussions. *6-9pm Wed-Sat* €€

Celms maize: This artisanal bakery in Kuldīga serves fantastic breakfast sets and omelettes, all accompanied by freshly baked bread. *8am-4pm* €

MO Liepāja: Hard to define in culinary or geographic terms, this place is all about fresh, diverse ingredients. Great value for a Michelin spot. *noon-11pm Tue-Sun* €€

Spīķeris 53: Imaginative Baltic fish meals and craft beer inside an old warehouse. Outdoor tables face Liepāja's harbour. *4-10pm* €€

Places We Love to Stay

€ Budget €€ Midrange €€€ Top End

Rīga

MAP p737

Cinnamon Sally € This hostel is relentless in its efforts to create a homey and sociable atmosphere. By the train station.

Naughty Squirrel € Backpacker Old Town star with homey dorms and a ritual shot of booze at check-in.

Hotel Justus €€ A tidy upper-floor hotel, with angled ceilings in the rooms following the roofline. In the Old Town.

Edvards €€ Room design matches the laconic no-nonsense elegance of this house, built in 1890, in the heart of things in central Rīga.

Hestia Hotel Jugend €€ Convenient for the Jugendstil quarter, this hotel is artfully designed with brightly coloured rooms and comfy beds.

Hotel Vantis Riverside €€ On rustic Kīpsala Island facing the passenger port terminal, come here for another perspective on Rīga. Airy rooms with lots of sun and modern amenities.

Neiburgs €€€ Occupying one of Rīga's finest art nouveau buildings, Neiburgs blends historic details with contemporary touches.

Hotel Bergs €€€ A refurbished 19th-century building embellished with a Scandi-sleek extension, the 37 spacious rooms at the Hotel Bergs embody the term 'luxury'.

Grand Poet €€€ It doesn't get any plusher than these park-facing rooms with fine retro touches. The location couldn't be more central.

Gulf of Rīga

Parus Boutique Hotel €€ One of the Prussian-style villas that defines Jūrmala. Has 12 traditionally decorated rooms.

Pine Resort €€ Located on a quiet plot well off Rīgas iela, this small hotel is close to the best beach in Saulkrasti.

Hotel Jūrmala Spa €€€ The rooms in this towering black behemoth are on the small side, but they look brand new. Some come with sweeping sea views.

Sigulda

Mazais Līvkalns €€ No place is more romantically rustic than this idyllic retreat at the forest's edge.

Hotel Sigulda €€ The oldest hotel in Sigulda, built by Kropotkin. Charming facade, but rooms are fairly bland.

Spa Hotel Ezeri €€€ A luxurious spa complex that has fairly simple rooms with contemporary decor.

Cēsis

Glūdas Grava €€ Five studios with glassy front walls and individual entrances in a renovated brick garage.

Kārlamūiža €€ In the village of Kārļi, this former aristocratic manor has been reborn as a gentrified country hotel.

Villa Santa Hotel €€ Three 19th-century wooden buildings have been transformed into a lovely hotel deep in the woods.

Kuldīga

Jēkaba Sēta € This typical Latvian inn, complete with a pub, has standard-looking rooms with wooden furniture.

2 Baloži € Perched above a stream, this wooden house has Scandinavian-style rooms.

Hotel Metropole €€ Kuldīga's main hotel features a modern pale-colour palette and spacious rooms overlooking the Town Hall Square.

Noliktava No 5 €€ An astonishingly stylish place that fuses post-industrial and modern Nordic with elements of Soviet nostalgia. The name refers to Kūldiga's Soviet-era petrol station.

Virkas Muiža €€ This beautiful manor house with an ornate wooden front terrace has plush rustic-styled rooms with wood-dominated interiors.

Liepāja

Fontaine Valhalla Hotel € Inexpensive, brightly decorated rooms with shared bathrooms in a cosy wooden building near the harbour.

Hotel Roze €€ Stylish and comfortable, this pale-blue wooden villa has spacious rooms, each uniquely decorated.

Seven Sisters €€ Comfy self-check-in rooms in a quiet, village-like part of central Liepāja. Common kitchen, garden and plenty of parking spaces.

Promenade Hotel €€€ The poshest hotel in Kurzeme occupies an enormous grain warehouse facing the harbour.

Practicalities

LGBTIQ+ Travellers
Latvia is generally quite tolerant. At the time of writing, its president, Edgars Rinkēvičs, was the first openly gay national leader in Europe. Same-sex civil unions were recognised in 2024. But conservative anti-LGBTIQ+ forces are strong and casual homophobia is not uncommon.

Health
If you spend time in Latvia's dunes or forests in between May and July, getting bit by a tick is not a question of if but when. Consider getting an encephalitis jab (done long in advance) and watch out for Lyme disease.

Smoking
Smoking is widespread, but it is forbidden in restaurants (except terraces), parks, public transport stops and most other public places, as well as in the presence of a child or pregnant woman. House committees often ban smoking inside flats. Rental apartments are normally non-smoking zones.

Visas
Latvia is part of the EU and the Schengen zone, which means the vast majority of Western travellers don't need visas for visits up to 90 days. There was a virtual ban on visas for Russian and Belarusian citizens at the time of writing.

LN TEAM/SHUTTERSTOCK

Turaida castle (p744), Sigulda

Opening Hours
Banks 9am–6pm Monday to Friday
Government offices 8am–4pm Monday to Friday
Shops Supermarkets are typically open from 8am until 10pm or 11pm. Other shops close earlier, especially in the countryside.

Language
Latvian is one of two living Baltic languages and one of the most ancient Indo-European language groups.
Hello. Sveiks. *svayks*
Goodbye. Atā. *a·taa*
Thank you. Paldies. *pal·deas*
Yes. Jā. *yaa*
No. Nē. *nair*

Public Holidays
New Year's Day 1 January
Easter Sunday March/April
Labour and Convocation of the Constituent Assembly of Latvia Day 1 May
Declaration of Latvian Independence Day 4 May
Midsummer Day 23 June
St John's Day 24 June
Proclamation of the Republic of Latvia 18 November
Christmas 24–26 December
New Year's Eve 31 December

FROM LEFT: IBRAHIM ALKAN/SHUTTERSTOCK, JOHNER IMAGES/GETTY IMAGES

Bus, Rīga (p736)

Arriving & Getting Around

The majority of visitors enter Latvia either via Rīga International Airport or by bus from Estonia or Lithuania. Intercity buses are the dominant mode of domestic transportation; trains also serve some crucial routes.

Arriving by Air

Rīga International Airport is a well-run operation. Car hire and a cash machine are located in the arrivals hall. Taxis wait at the entrance, but it's better to use Bolt to avoid scams.

Getting Around by Bus

The bus network in the countryside is organised in such a way that you're never far from the nearest stop. Check schedules and fares at *autoosta.lv* or *1188.lv*, or use the Mobilly app.

Arriving by Bus

Buses from Tallinn, Vilnius and Kaunas arrive at Rīga International Bus Station in the heart of the city. The main streets can be reached by buses 3 and 21.

Other Transport

Trains are particularly useful for Jūrmala and the northern beaches. Other lines connect to destinations in Gauja National Park and Latgale. There are also daily trains to Liepāja. Car hire is available, but most locals use rideshare services like Bolt and CityBee. Latvia is criss-crossed by bicycle and hiking paths like the Baltic Coastal Trail (Jūrtaka) and Forest Trail (Meztaka).

MONEY
Currency: Euro (€)

CREDIT CARDS & CASH

You'll rarely need to pay in cash in Latvia, except at the market or when leaving a tip. ATMs are ubiquitous. Visa and MasterCard are universally accepted, American Express and UnionPay less so.

DIGITAL PAYMENTS

Most terminals around the country accept digital payments either through your phone or watch. The Mobilly app is great for buying all kinds of transportation tickets.

TIPPING

Tipping isn't really expected, but it's customary to leave a 10% tip if you're happy with restaurant service or to drop some coins into the tip jar at bars and coffee shops.

For places to stay in Lithuania, see p767

SUN CLOCK – © KLAUDIJUS PUDYMAS, SCULPTOR, ASTA SABONYTE/SHUTTERSTOCK

Above: Parnidis Dune (p763), Nida; Right: Hill of Crosses (p761), Šiauliai

Lithuania

UNSPOILED NATURE MEETS MILLENNIAL HISTORY

Traverse coastal dunes, lake-dotted forests and vibrant cities, and admire intricate woodcarvings in the Baltics' most creative country.

A sliver of land flanked by pine forest and covered with giant sand dunes jutting into the Baltic Sea, the largest of the three Baltic states is also the most beguiling. It has ancient forests teeming with wildlife, hundreds of lakes and a coastline strung with white-sand beaches, all of which make it irresistibly appealing to fresh-air fiends. Tranquil roads bisect the rolling countryside and its timeless villages, providing ideal terrain for touring cyclists and unhurried road-trippers.

Though Lithuania traded paganism for Catholicism long ago, pagan-style wooden grave markers still dot its cemeteries, while other traces of its past shine through in Lithuania's age-old craft of woodcarving and folk-metal music. More agrarian than its neighbours, Lithuania is also more homogeneous, and became even more so when the majority of its Jewish population was wiped out during the Holocaust.

Its two main cities are distinct in character: Vilnius beckons with baroque finery, cobbled streets and a multitude of churches, while creative Kaunas bristles with gorgeous interwar architecture and pays homage to basketball – the nation's passion. Lithuania's charms are many and varied: where else can you visit a nuclear power plant, explore genteel country manors, dine on exceptional seasonal cuisine and – above all – immerse yourself in the unspoilt nature of this land, to which the national identity is so deeply tied?

THE MAIN AREAS

VILNIUS & EASTERN LITHUANIA
The capital, castles and forest.
p754

KAUNAS, CENTRAL & SOUTHERN LITHUANIA
Architecture and museums, spas and unique sights. **p759**

CURONIAN SPIT & WESTERN LITHUANIA
From dunes and beaches to pine forests and a castle. **p763**

Find Your Way

Lithuania is easy to navigate on public transport, though cars are useful for reaching remote attractions. The country's flatness encourages cycling, and the seasonal boats connect the Curonian Spit to the Curonian Lagoon.

CAR

Driving is best for remote destinations. Parking in labyrinthine Old Town is tricky. In major cities Bolt and Spark offer car rentals by the minute or hour. Winter tyres are compulsory mid-November through March.

BUS & TRAIN

An extensive bus network links major cities and smaller towns. Trains are useful for travel between Vilnius and Kaunas or Vilnius and Klaipėda. Download the Autobusų Bilietai and LTG Link apps.

Vilnius & Eastern Lithuania, p754

Lithuania's capital is also the gateway to Trakai Island Castle and Aukštaitija National Park.

Kaunas, Central & Southern Lithuania, p759

Kaunas beckons with quirky museums while Šiauliai's Hill of Crosses, Druskininkai's spas and Panevėžys' art are all within easy reach.

Curonian Spit & Western Lithuania, p763

Hike up giant sand dunes, cycle forest trails, sun yourself on Baltic beaches and explore a centuries-old castle.

DANGEBURE/SHUTTERSTOCK

Palace of the Grand Dukes of Lithuania (p756), Vilnius

Plan Your Time

Hit Vilnius and Kaunas, then spend several days hiking and cycling the Curonian Spit and/or Aukštaitija. Palanga's beaches, Druskininkai's spas and Šiauliai's pilgrimage site are nice extras.

If You Only Do One Thing

● Focus your energy on **Vilnius** (p754) and the cobbled Old Town. Then visit **Gediminas Castle** (p756), the **Palace of the Grand Dukes of Lithuania** (p756) and the **Museum of Occupations and Freedom Fights** (p756). Other museums include the **National Art Gallery** (p757) and **Museum of Culture and Identity of Lithuanian Jews** (p757).

If You Have More Time

● Visit the **Curonian Spit** (p763), walk or cycle its long-distance trails and hike up giant sand dunes. Visit **Trakai Island Castle** (p758), and day-trip to **Aukštaitija National Park** (p758). Or haunt **Kaunas** (p759) and its UNESCO-recognised modernist architecture, **Art Deco Museum** (p760), **Amsterdam School Museum** (p760), **KGB Atomic Bunker** (p761) and **MK Čiurlionis Museum of Art** (p761).

SEASONAL HIGHLIGHTS

SPRING
Late spring is excellent for hiking in national parks. Temperatures are mild and days are long.

SUMMER
Lithuania is loveliest in summer when days are long and the Baltic Sea beaches beckon.

AUTUMN
Autumn colours and fewer visitors make this an ideal time for the long-distance Baltic Coastal Trail or Forest Trail.

WINTER
Wintry cities blanketed in snow can be magic. Don't miss the Christmas markets in Vilnius and Kaunas.

Vilnius & Eastern Lithuania

HISTORY | DINING | NATURE

Places

Vilnius p754

Trakai p758

Aukštaitija National Park p758

TOP TIP

Planning on intensive sightseeing? Download the **Vilnius Pass** (*govilnius. lt; €37/47/56 per 24/48/72 hours*), which grants free/discounted access to numerous museums. To arrange an English-language guided hike or kayak trip in Aukštaitija National Park, contact Visaginas-based **LitWild** (*litwildtravel.com*).

Lithuania's dreamy, compact capital celebrated its 700th birthday in 2023 and has a marvellously intact Old Town. It's rare in that locals actually live here, and its cobbled streets lined with weather-worn buildings testify to centuries of turbulent history. Today, these same buildings burst forth with independent boutiques, restaurants and lively cafes and bars.

Vilnius doesn't hide its scars and imperfections. The former 'Jerusalem of the north' lost 150,000 of its Jewish community in WWII. The baroque, Gothic and Renaissance churches of the city's historic heart sit alongside Holocaust museums, former ghetto remnants, preserved KGB torture chambers and buildings left derelict by decades of neglect. Yet optimism perseveres.

An easy day trip from Vilnius, tiny Trakai beguiles with its castle in the middle of a lake. East of Vilnius, Aukštaitija National Park beckons with its dense forest, plentiful lakes, small villages, and hiking and cycling trails.

Vilnius

Vilnius' mighty cathedral

Occupying a spot originally dedicated to the worship of Perkūnas, the Lithuanian thunder god, the neoclassical **Vilnius Cathedral** (*katedra.lt*) with its freestanding **belfry**

🧭 GETTING AROUND

Much of the compact Old Town is pedestrian. Hire bicycles at CycloCity stations or from Velotakas (*velotakas.lt*). Download the Bolt app for electric scooters and rideshares.

Buses and trolleybuses run from 5am to midnight. Download the Trafi app to purchase bus tickets (€1). The train and bus stations serve all major destinations around Lithuania, including Trakai (20 minutes). Aukštaitija National Park's main town, Ignalina, is well connected to Vilnius by daily buses (two hours) and trains (eight daily, 1½ to 1¾ hours); trains have cycle racks.

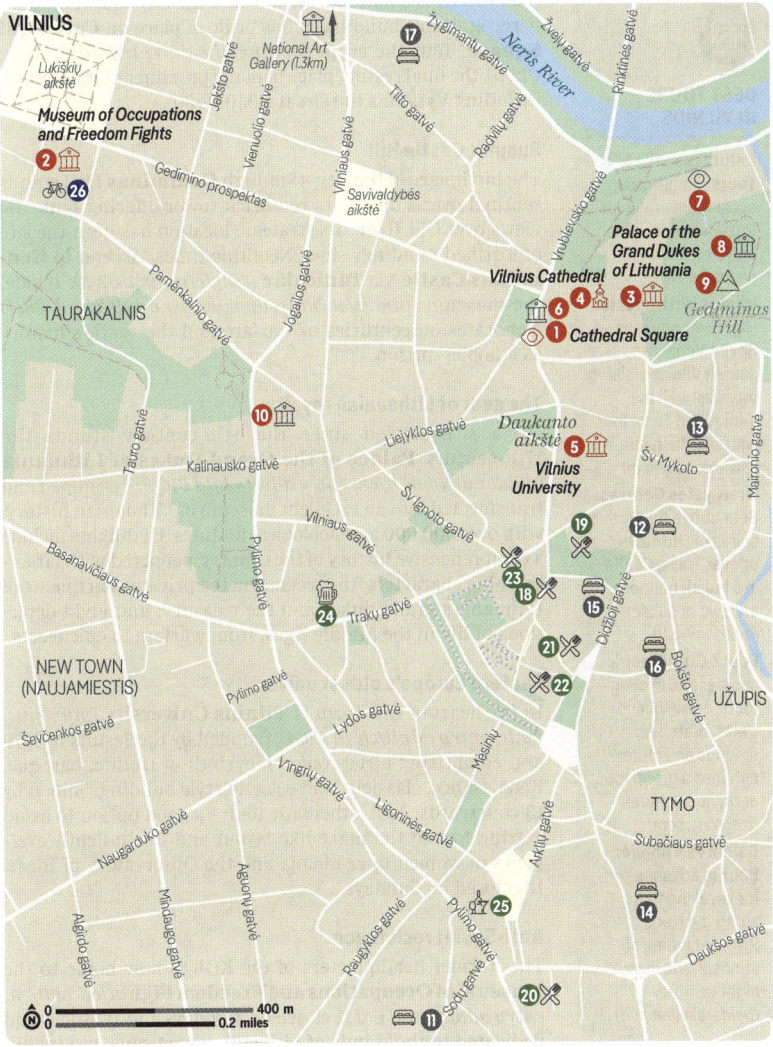

VILNIUS

Lukiškių aikštė

National Art Gallery (1.3km)

Museum of Occupations and Freedom Fights

Gedimino prospektas

Neris River

TAURAKALNIS

Palace of the Grand Dukes of Lithuania

Vilnius Cathedral

Cathedral Square

Gediminas Hill

Daukanto aikštė

Vilnius University

Šv Mykolo

NEW TOWN (NAUJAMIESTIS)

Traku gatvė

UŽUPIS

TYMO

0   400 m
0   0.2 miles

BEST TOURS IN VILNIUS

Velotakas Bike & Tours: Small-group cycle tours of Vilnius' top landmarks, plus bicycles for hire. *(velotakas.lt)*

Vilnius With Locals: Highly recommended Soviet Vilnius and Jewish Vilnius walking tours, as well the Vilnius Old Town tour with snacks. *(vilnius-uswithlocals.com)*

Oreivystés Centras: Soar above the Gothic spires of Old Town or over Trakai Castle in a hot air balloon at dawn or sunset. *(ballooning.lt)*

Feel Z City: Electric scooter and cycling tours, artsy Vilnius walks, craft beer tastings and more, either as a group tour or private venture. *(feelzcity.com)*

Baidares Vilniujé: Book in advance for kayaking tours along the Neris River, including an atmospheric dusk/night venture. *(baidaresvilniuje.lt)*

(bell tower) is a national symbol and the city's most instantly recognisable building. It has pride of place on **Cathedral Square**. Tour the crypt *(bpmuziejus.lt; entry adult/child €12/6)*, the final resting place of many prominent Lithuanians, including Vytautas the Great (1350–1430).

Summit Castle Hill

The birthplace of the city, 48m-high **Gediminas Hill** stands sentinel over Vilnius, its red-brick tower offering fantastic views over Old Town. Its strategic location has been the site of fortified buildings since Neolithic times. Ascend to **Gediminas Castle** via **funicular** *(single/return €2/3)*. Inside, the museum *(lnm.lt/en/museums; entry adult/child €8/4)* elaborates on centuries of warfare and the castle's history as a nobles' prison.

The seat of Lithuanian royalty

On a site settled since the 4th century stands the 17th-century **Palace of the Grand Dukes of Lithuania** *(valdovurumai.lt/en; entry adult/child €16/8)*, revamped and transformed into an excellent museum of Lithuanian history, with over 300,000 archaeological findings. Highlights include a comprehensive history of the country, peppered with larger-than-life characters; the reconstructed private apartments of Lithuania's grand dukes and the treasury; and vivid depictions of life in the Middle Ages, from warfare to epic feasts.

Eastern Europe's oldest university

In the heart of Old Town is **Vilnius University** *(muziejus. vu.lt; entry adult/child €8/4)*, founded by the Jesuits in 1579 and comprising a red-roofed labyrinth of Gothic, baroque, Renaissance, classicist and eclectic-style buildings joined by 13 courtyards. Join a thematic tour – a good option to avoid getting lost in the maze-like layout and for in-depth overviews of women in academia and the Observatory of Ideas. It's closed on Sundays.

Anti-Soviet resistance

This former headquarters of the KGB is now home to the **Museum of Occupations and Freedom Fights** *(olkm.lt/en; entry adult/child €6/3)*, closed on Mondays and Tuesdays and dedicated to thousands of Lithuanian partisans and intelligentsia who were murdered, imprisoned or deported by the Soviet Union from WWII until the 1960s. Backlit photographs,

EATING IN VILNIUS: OUR PICKS

Lokys: Game roasts are the main event at this 'hunter's restaurant' inside vaulted 16th-century merchant's cellars. *noon-midnight €€*	**Ertlio Namas:** Tasting menus of re-created centuries-old recipes (roe-deer sausage with pumpkin pudding) come with elaborate backstories. *5-11pm Mon-Sat €€€*	**Halès Turgus:** Traditional produce stalls mingle with en vogue eateries at the pungent 1906 food market. *7am-6pm Mon-Fri, to 3pm Sat €*	**Maurizio's Italian Food:** Chequered tablecloths, bonhomie and excellent Neapolitan-style pizza baked in a wood-fired oven. *noon-10pm Sun-Thu, to 11pm Fri & Sat €€*

Gediminas Castle

wooden annexes and a disorienting layout sharpen the impact of past horrors outlined in graphic detail. The basement prison cells are particularly unsettling, from the padded one to the cell once partially filled with icy water.

A window into the Litvak world

The excellent **Museum of Culture and Identity of Lithuanian Jews** *(jmuseum.lt; entry adult/child €6/3)* lets you explore Litvak (Lithuanian Jewish) history, culture, traditions and daily life through a mixture of written sources, films, interactive displays, photography and evocative Vilnius cityscapes by Lithuania's most prominent 20th-century Jewish painter, Rafael Chwoles. Learn about the achievements of world-famous Litvaks and delve into Litvak literature, music and visual arts. It's closed on Mondays.

The biggest repository of Lithuanian modern art

The vast **National Art Gallery** *(ndg.lt/en.aspx; entry adult/child €8/4),* closed on Mondays, is the country's most comprehensive collection of Lithuanian art from the 20th and 21st centuries. Arranged chronologically across 12 halls according to specific themes such as 'Crisis and rebellion', 'Women artists from interwar Vilnius' and 'At the crossroads of the epochs', it charts the story of a country striving towards its own artistic identity – under foreign occupation and as an independent country.

 EATING & DRINKING IN VILNIUS: OUR PICKS

14Horses: Use your hands to tackle beef tartare with fermented strawberries and pancakes with smoked eel on the four-course tasting menus. *5-11pm Tue-Sat €€*	**Nineteen18:** Industrial-style decor and a 10-course menu that may include chicken caramel, mushroom dumplings and desserts involving ants. *6-11pm Tue-Sat €€€*	**Alaus Biblioteka:** Sip your Lithuanian seasonal brew, surrounded by books, at this friendly bar with rotating craft beers on tap and by the bottle. *5pm-midnight*	**Apoteka Bar:** Reimagined mixology classics and autumn-in-a-glass originals, served beneath heavy wooden beams. *6pm-midnight Sun, Wed & Thu, to 2am Fri & Sat*

ASTA.SABONYTE/SHUTTERSTOCK

Trakai Island Castle

A Brief History of Vilnius' Jews

For centuries, Vilnius flourished as a centre for Jewish culture, with 60,000 Litvaks (Lithuanian Jews) making up almost half of the population. When the Germans invaded the Soviet Union in 1941, Vilnius fell within days. The Small Ghetto was established north of Vokiečių gatvė and destroyed 46 days later, its 11,000 inhabitants killed between 6 September and 20 October 1941 at Paneriai. The Large Ghetto was created in September 1941 south of Vokiečių gatvė to hold workers valuable to the German war effort. It was liquidated in September 1943, with 26,000 Jews perishing at Paneriai, and 10,000 shipped to concentration camps. Only 6000 Vilnius Jews survived the war.

Trakai

Visit Trakai Island Castle

Sitting on a 2km-long peninsula, attractive Trakai was appointed by Grand Duke Gediminas as Lithuania's capital in the early 14th century. Take the bridge to the **Trakai Island Castle** *(trakaimuziejus.lt; entry adult/child €12/6)* – Lithuania's most photogenic redoubt. Its labyrinthine museum covers the history of the town and the castle, and the setting is worth the day trip from Vilnius.

Aukštaitija National Park

Lithuania's oldest national park

Encompassing dense forest, lakes and wildlife, **Aukštaitija National Park** is the perfect place to enjoy hiking, cycling, swimming, canoeing and paddleboarding. In Palūšė, 8km west of the main town of Ignalina, rent canoes, paddleboards and bikes from **Tiki Tours** *(info.tikitours.lt)*. Several of the hiking trails (3.5 to 22km) and cycle loops (25 to 110km) start in Palūšė, taking in the park's tiny settlements and attractions, including Ginučiai's 19th-century watermill and the Ancient Beekeeping Museum near Stripeikiai.

Kaunas, Central & Southern Lithuania

ARCHITECTURE | MUSEUMS | QUIRKY SIGHTS

Sitting at the confluence of the Nemunas and Neris Rivers, Lithuania's second city Kaunas served a two-decade stint as the country's capital after Poland annexed Vilnius in the interwar period. It then became the centre of anti-Soviet dissent when Lithuania was forcibly incorporated into the USSR. Brimming with innovations in art, design and AI, the former European Capital of Culture (2022) is also the home of Lithuanian basketball, and its clutch of excellent museums rivals those in Vilnius.

Kaunas is divided into two halves. The cobbled Old Town has a medieval castle, handsome square and numerous restaurants and churches, while New Town, bisected by the tree- and restaurant-lined Laisvės alėja, features the lion's share of museums, as well as attractive art deco architecture.

North of Kaunas, Šiauliai draws visitors from afar with its unique pilgrimage site; Panevėžys features a superb contemporary art museum. South of Kaunas, Druskininkai entices with its spas and Soviet statuary.

Places

Kaunas p760
Šiauliai p761
Panevėžys p761
Druskininkai p762

☑ TOP TIP

If you're interested in modernist architecture, book tours of the **Amsterdam School Museum** and/or **Art Deco Museum** in advance. Ditto the **KGB Atomic Bunker** if you're into Soviet memorabilia. Basketball fans: catch a **BC Žalgiris** game in season (Oct–Apr).

GETTING AROUND

Old Town and New Town are walkable and a 10-minute stroll from one another. Hire a bicycle or Bolt e-scooter from multiple pickup points.

Buses and trolleybuses *(kvt.lt)* run from 5am to 11pm and are handy for reaching outlying attractions. Bus 29G runs hourly to the airport 10km north of the city centre; bus tickets from the driver cost €1.

There are numerous daily trains to Vilnius (one to 1½ hours), plus frequent buses to many destinations.

Kaunas

Two re-created apartment museums

Between 2016 and 2021, two young businessmen acquired two apartments from the interwar era, painstakingly restored them and opened them up to private tours. At the **Art Deco Museum** *(artdecomuziejus.lt/en; tours €25)*, the 'experiential' small-group excursion feels like an intimate, time-travelling visit to a friend's home. Find out how the Lithuanian well-to-do lived in the interwar period, sit on satin chairs, sip sparkling wine, learn the purposes of unusual furnishings and cutlery, and gain an appreciation for a world that vanished with Soviet occupation.

A few blocks away, at the **Amsterdam School Museum** *(amsterdamomokyklosmuziejus.lt/en; tours €25)*, the guide demonstrates clever compartments in cabinets, a hidden sideboard in the bedroom and other secret features. You then return to the lounge to learn of the fates of the bon vivant Jewish owner and the other Jewish occupants of the building during the war.

A stroll through Kaunas

Take a stroll around Kaunas' cobbled Old Town, beginning with the **Town Hall Square**, lined with 15th- and 16th-century German merchants' houses and centred on the 17th-century former **Town Hall**. Detour to the magnificent **House of Perkūnas**, a 15th-century merchant's residence, then walk north to the remains of the 14th-century **Kaunas Castle**, a bastion against Teutonic attacks around which the town originally grew. Pass by the red-brick 16th-century **Sts Peter & Paul Cathedral**, then follow the pedestrianised Vilniaus gatvė to the 1826 neo-baroque, interwar **Presidential Palace of Lithuania**. Finally, take New Town's pedestrianised Laisvės alėja to neo-Byzantine **St Michael's Cathedral** (1895) at its eastern end.

The art of MK Čiurlionis

One of Lithuania's oldest and grandest galleries, the **MK Čiurlionis Museum of Art** *(ciurlionis.lt; entry adult/child €10/5)* is the place to acquaint yourself with the paintings of Mikalojus Konstantinas Čiurlionis (1875–1911), arguably the country's greatest modernist artist and composer. Besides the permanent collection of his dreamlike landscapes, themed temporary exhibitions juxtapose his works against contemporary art, while conceptual VR journeys take you deep inside Čiurlionis' paintings. It's closed on Mondays.

Back in the USSR

Enter this former 1960s factory in western Kaunas to find yourself surrounded by busts of Lenin and communist banners. Your guide then ushers you into a Soviet-era atomic shelter designed to protect factory workers from radiation in case of nuclear war. **KGB Atomic Bunker Museum** *(atominis bunkeris.lt, tours by prior arrangement €15)* is a labour of love: an ever-growing private collection of objects from the USSR and beyond. Highlights include the re-created KGB interrogation office with its torture chair, ingenious KGB murder weapons and the gas mask room.

Šiauliai

An unusual pilgrimage site

Some 10km north of Šiauliai is the **Hill of Crosses**, covered in thousands of crosses that symbolise defiance, hope and compassion. Take your time wandering past the rows, taking in fine examples of ironwork, traditional Lithuanian *koplyt-stulpis* (wooden carvings topped with a roof) and magnificent sculptures of the Sorrowful Christ (Rūpintojėlis) – planted in tribute to 9/11 or Covid-19 victims, Ukrainian civilians killed by Russian missiles and a number of other personal reasons.

Panevėžys

Icon-O-Stasys

In central Panevėžys, the minimalist four-storey **Stasys Museum** *(stasysmuseum.com/en; entry adult/child €8/4)* is a fitting tribute to the celebrated local artist Stasys Eidrigevičius. The inaugural Icon-O-Stasys exhibition is an engrossing retrospective of Stasys' artistic endeavours, from his minimalist one-line drawings and the dreamlike world of his *Ex Libris* sketches to surreal photography and the wonderful mask series, *Sorrows*. It's closed on Mondays.

HISTORY OF THE HILL OF CROSSES

Some claim that the Hill of Crosses was created by the bereaved families of warriors killed in battle. Pagan traditions tell of sacred fires being lit here, long before the first crosses appeared (allegedly in the 14th century), multiplying after every uprising against the Russian tsars. Although planting a cross during Soviet times was an arrestable offence, pilgrims continued to commemorate those killed or deported to Siberia. In 1961, the Red Army destroyed the 2000-odd crosses and dug ditches at the hill's base, but overnight more crosses appeared. In 1972, they were destroyed after the immolation of a Kaunas student. Upon Lithuania's independence in 1991, the hill comprised over 40,000 crosses, which have multiplied tenfold since.

 EATING & DRINKING IN KAUNAS: OUR PICKS

Bernelių Užeiga: Munch on herring, meaty stews, beetroot soup and dumplings amid stuffed animal heads and rustic decor. *11am-10pm Sun-Thu, to 11pm Fri & Sat €*	**Avilys:** Wash down Lithuanian standards or beer snacks with pints of mead or unfiltered house beer in an atmospheric stone cellar. *noon-midnight €€*	**Uoksas:** Chef Artūras Naidenko crafts tasting menus from sustainable, seasonal ingredients from around the Baltic. *6-10pm Tue-Fri, 3-11pm Sat €€*	**Genys Taproom:** A heavy-rock soundtrack, outdoor terrace and 10 Kaunas-brewed beers on tap. *5pm-2am Mon-Fri, noon-2am Sat & Sun*

THE ARCHITECTURE OF OPTIMISM

Between 1919 and 1939, when the Polish annexation of Vilnius made Kaunas Lithuania's capital, the city underwent rapid urbanisation. This resulted in the construction of over 1500 buildings in modernist styles, from art deco, neoclassicism and traditionalism to functionalism and the Amsterdam School. Standout examples include the historicist Romuva Cinema with a glass turret (1940) at Laisvės alėja 54; the monumental Church of the Resurrection (1934); the art deco Jewish Bank (1925) at Laisvės alėja 106; and the Fire Station (1932) at Kanto gatvė 1 – a curved building with a concave facade and twin towers. In 2023, 44 buildings in Kaunas' New Town and Žaliakalnis (Green Hill) were granted European Heritage status.

TARTEZY/SHUTTERSTOCK

Grūtas Park

Druskininkai

A Baltic spa day

Experience the genteel spa town of Druskininkai, renowned for centuries for the healing properties of its mineral-rich waters, by drinking said waters at the riverside **Biuvetė**. Then opt for healing mud and mineral-water soaks at the **Medical SPA Eglės Sanatorija**, herbal and vertical baths at **Mana Sleep & Spa**, or mud baths, volcanic stone treatments, salt-room sessions and Charcot's showers at the **Grand Spa Lietuva**.

Graveyard of Soviet statuary

Some 8km east of the spa town of Druskininkai, **Grūtas Park** (*grutoparkas.lt; entry adult/child €15/9*) pays black-humoured homage to a dark period of Lithuania's history. Wander along forested trails flanked by barbed wire, watchtowers and a moat past multiple Lenins, Stalins, prominent Lithuanian communists and freedom fighters.

EATING IN IN ŠIAULIAI, PANEVĖŽYS & DRUSKININKAI: OUR PICKS

Bleu de Frenkel: Chanterelle soup, Manhattan pizza and cheesecake presented in a dining room in Šiauliai. *11am-10pm Sun-Thu, to 11pm Fri & Sat* €€

Galerija XX: Updated takes on Lithuanian classics, an appealing outdoor terrace and good cheesecake make this a firm Panevėžys favourite. *10am-11pm* €€

Sicilia: Druskininkai's top spot delivers wood-fired pizza and vaguely Italian-style fish and seafood with aplomb. *10am-11pm Sun-Thu, to 11pm Fri & Sat* €€

Bukhara: *Plov* and *shashlik* (grilled meat skewers) are standouts at this carpet-clad Uzbek restaurant in Druskininkai. *noon-10pm Sun-Thu, to 11pm Fri & Sat* €€

Curonian Spit & Western Lithuania

OUTDOOR ADVENTURE | BEACHES | CASTLE

According to legend, the sea goddess Neringa created the long sliver of land that juts out into the Baltic Sea, forming a protected harbour for local fishers. Its natural origins are no less enchanting. The Curonian Spit (Kuršių Nerija) was formed around 5000 years ago and today it's the youngest part of Lithuania: a mile across, 98km long and split almost evenly between Lithuania and Russia. Its dense birch and pine forests, crisscrossed by cycling trails and home to part of the long-distance Baltic Coastal Trail, shelter elks, wild boars and roe deer, while its extraordinary, wind-sculpted giant sand dunes have earned it the nickname 'Lithuania's Sahara'. Stay in one of four picturesque fishing villages – Nida, Juodkrantė, Pervalka or Preila – to explore.

Back on the mainland, Klaipėda (formerly Prussia's Memel) is the gateway to the Spit with a fantastic castle museum. Further north, Palanga is a quintessential Baltic beach resort; both have excellent dining scenes.

☑ TOP TIP

The Spit is particularly busy during the summer season (mid-June to end of August) and accommodation prices are high, particularly in Nida; book weeks in advance. Outside of peak season, many restaurants and bars shut down.

Nida
Lithuania's Sahara

Towering over the Curonian village of Nida, the 52m-high **Parnidis Dune** is simultaneously mighty and fragile – a

---

 GETTING AROUND

A passenger ferry connects Klaipėda's Old Ferry Port and the Spit. Car ferries run from Klaipėda's New Ferry Port.

A 50km bicycle trail runs between Nida and Smiltynė; rent bikes in Nida and Juodkrantė. Buses travelling to Nida via Juodkrantė stop in Preila and Pervalka in summer. Buses from Nida to Kaunas and Vilnius stop in all four villages year-round.

From Klaipėda, trains run to Vilnius (4¼ hours, four daily) via Šiauliai (1¾ hours). Intercity bus destinations include Kaunas, Vilnius, Nida and Šiauliai. Half-hourly buses (25 minutes) connect Klaipėda and Palanga.

NERINGA'S SHIFTING SANDS

Neringa's distinctive landscapes and unique marine, archaeological and cultural heritage are under threat both from human impact and natural forces (the wind and tides). Intensive logging and the resulting deforestation in the 17th and 18th centuries destabilised the sand dunes, which began to move towards the Curonian Lagoon, burying the oldest villages – some relocated several times, trying to outpace the shifting sands.

In 1768, an international commission set about replanting the forests in a bid to anchor the dunes, and there are constant efforts to prevent erosion today using brushwood hedges. But the sands are still moving, at least 1m a year, so it's more important than ever to stick to designated trails.

delicate landscape of mountain pines, meadows and fine blonde sand speckled with purple searocket flowers. A 1700m-long path winds its way along Nida's waterfront through pine forest and then up a steep flight of stairs to a series of boardwalks and viewpoints. At the summit, 'Lithuania's Sahara' – a grand panorama of sand dunes, scrubland and forest – unfolds all the way to the Russian border, a mere 4km away.

Amber creations through the ages

At Nida's state-of-the-art, subtly lit **Mizgiris Amber Museum** *(ambergallery.lt; entry adult/child €12/6),* a dramatic documentary reconstruction plays out on the undulating screen, explaining how amber is created, extracted and processed. Peer at insects suspended within golden depths and peruse chunks of unprocessed amber, millennia-old anthropomorphic figurines, amulets from ancient graves and the Perkūnas (Thunder) Stone – the world's largest piece of amber, weighing 3.8kg. Then venture upstairs to view amber transformed into unusual jewellery and off-the-wall creations by Lithuania's amber masters.

Hike the Baltic Coastal Trail

One of the most scenic stretches of the long-distance **Baltic Coastal Trail** *(baltictrails.eu/en/coastal),* which runs for 1322km from Lithuania's Nida to Tallinn, Estonia, is the 18km-long day hike from Nida to Pervalka. Follow it around Bulvikis Cape, through pine forest, past coastal reeds and birdlife, and around Preilos Bay and its small sandy beach. In Preila, ascend Preilos Hill (57m) for spectacular views of the Curonian Lagoon. Passing another small sandy beach in Karvaiciu Bay, skirt Pervalkos Cape before finding yourself in one-street Pervalka. Press on through pine woods to Zirgu ragas (Horse Cape) for fantastic vistas of the huge Dead Dunes in the distance.

Adrenaline adventures

In summer, take to the waters of the Curonian Lagoon on an SUP or canoe, rented from Nida operator **Irklakojis** *(irklakojis.lt; €10 per hour).* Alternatively, join one of their paddleboarding tours or a 'blokarting' safari (windsurfing on land) along the beach that stretches along the Baltic side of the Curonian Spit. Alternatively, head for **Neringos Sporto Mokykla** to learn flyboarding *(€20 per hour)* or wingfoiling *(€60 per hour).* Winter adrenaline thrills include ice-blokarting.

 EATING ON THE CURONIAN SPIT: OUR PICKS

Tik Pas Joną: Select mackerel, carp or eel from the smoking rack, then wash it down with *gira* or beer on tap in Nida. Takeaway available. *11am-10pm* €€

Sena Sodyba: Cold beetroot soup, dumplings and platefuls of grilled meat with all the trimmings, served in a garden setting in Nida. *noon-9pm* €

Juodkrantės Šašlykinė: The wonderfully marinated grilled pork and chicken *shashlik* hit your palate just right at this casual spot in Juodkrantė. *noon-10pm* €

Žvejonė: Chow down on grilled halibut, eel soup and other fish specialities at this waterfront Juodkrantė restaurant. *noon-10pm* €€

TRABANTOS/SHUTTERSTOCK

Witches' Hill

Juodkrantė

Among the witches

Follow the Raganų Kalnas sign into the old-growth forest in Juodkrantė to a coven of wooden sculptures that's taken shape along a woodland trail up **Witches' Hill** since 1979. The figures represent various characters from regional folklore, from knights, devils and dwarves to Neringa the sea goddess, a witch with a lopsided bosom and an intricately carved Lucifer peering through the Gates of Hell.

Klaipėda

City defences, Prussian-style

Founded by the Teutonic Order in the 13th century, the moat-protected **Klaipėda Castle** *(mlimuziejus.lt; entry adult/ child €7/3.50)* was revamped in 2021. The high-tech museum inside its restored curtainwalls and tunnels tells the story of Klaipėda from its origins to post-Soviet independence, with presentations enhanced by clever interactive elements. In a separate tunnel, the bunker-like **Museum 39/45** captures Lithuania's suffering during WWII with its tense background music, wartime paraphernalia and digital displays. The castle is closed on Mondays.

 EATING IN KLAIPĖDA & PALANGA: OUR PICKS

Stora Antis: This atmospheric 19th-century cellar elevates classic Lithuanian fare (baked duck, bean soup, pan-fried plaice) to haute-cuisine heights. *6–11pm Fri & Sat* €€

Etno Dvaras: Rustic Lithuanian mini-chain serves potato pancakes, roast meat with horseradish, soups and homemade *gira*. *11.30am–11pm Sun-Thu, noon–1am Fri & Sat* €

Žuvinė: Dine on zander with beetroot cream, smoked eel or halibut with black lentils in an interior straight out of *Architects' Digest*. *11am–10pm Sun-Thu, to midnight Fri & Sat* €€

Restoranas 1925: Committed to dairy fats and filling dumplings, this handsome timbered tavern has been catering to hungry crowds since 1925. *11am–11pm Thu-Sun* €

765

LIFE'S A BEACH IN NERINGA

A 50km-broad sweep of white sand that's so fine it squeaks underfoot, the Neringa beach spans the length of the Baltic side of the Spit. Dune-backed and pine-scented, it's divided into sections. The beach sections nearest to Nida, Juodkrantė, Preila and Pervalka are separated into mixed, women only (clothing is optional on women-only and nudist stretches) and pet-friendly sections and marked accordingly. Changing booths, steps down to the beach and volleyball courts are de rigueur. The Blue Flag beaches in Nida and Juodkrantė come with lifeguard stations, Nida's beach is wheelchair-accessible and the waters are shallow and hugely popular with families. Outside the designated beaches, you have vast stretches of sand entirely to yourself.

STUDIO MDF/SHUTTERSTOCK

Palanga beach

Palanga

A beach holiday, Lithuanian style

Stroll Palanga's pedestrianised, pine-fringed **Basanavičiaus gatvė** for a full-on sensory assault of beeping arcade machines, bungee trampolines, merry-go-rounds, bumper cars, portrait artists, restaurants and beer gardens. The smells of pine, candy floss and popcorn fill the air as buskers serenade passers-by and beachgoers queue up for ice cream. At the western end you'll find Palanga's 18km-long, white-sand **beach**, reachable via wooden boardwalks that lead through the forest and over the dunes and are punctuated with beach bars. The atmosphere is relaxed and welcoming, and lazy days of sunbathing and swimming beckon.

Discover the Amber Museum

Housed inside a 19th-century neoclassical palace, built by Count Feliksas Tyszkiewicz in 1897 at the heart of Palanga's Botanical Park, Palanga's fantastic **Amber Museum** (*lndm.lt/pgm; entry adult/child €8/4*) is home to 30,000 pieces of 'Baltic gold'. The exhibits take visitors through all aspects of amber, from its formation and collection to its use in human adornment, from Neolithic times to the present day. Don't miss terrific temporary exhibitions of leading Lithuanian jewellery designers. It's closed on Mondays.

Places We Love to Stay

€ Budget €€ Midrange €€€ Top End

Vilnius
MAP p755

Jimmy Jumps House € Movie nights, pub crawls, tank-driving tours and free waffles at this centrally located party hostel.

25 Hours Hostel € Arty loft dorms, snug doubles, women-only digs, guest kitchen and fantastic Gates of Dawn location.

Bernardinų B&B €€ Baroque flourishes and original frescoes make each room unique at this family-owned B&B within an 18th-century townhouse.

Domus Maria €€ This austere guesthouse inside a former 17th-century monastery features spacious rooms, some with Gates of Dawn views.

The Joseph €€ Original brick walls and heavy wooden beams highlight contemporary art in seven individually styled rooms in this 19th-century building.

Artagonist €€€ Stylish art-filled rooms, a giant wall mural and glass dome await at this 19th-century merchant house.

Hotel Pacai €€€ Slumber beneath timber beams amid centuries-old statuary at this restored 17th-century palace with gourmet restaurants.

Aukštaitija National Park

Tiki Inn € Polynesia-themed lakeside inn in Palūšė, with a terrace for sunset watching, hot tubs, sauna, free water-sports equipment and spartan rooms.

Lake & Library Hotel €€ Ignalina's lovely boutique hotel, with individually curated rooms overlooking Gavys Lake, a beach and volleyball court. Excellent breakfast.

Kaunas
MAP p760

Monk's Bunk Kaunas € Backpackers trade travel stories at Kaunas' well-equipped original hostel; spacious dorms and a knowledgeable host.

Villa Kaunensis € Spartan rooms with high ceilings overlooking Old Town square; the guest kitchen is a boon.

Moxy €€ Instagrammable bar and sleek, minimalist rooms await at this trendy New Town spot.

Daugirdas Hotel €€ At this handsome Old Town boutique hotel, 16th-century stonework and timber beams come with heated floors and jacuzzis.

HOF Hotel €€ Super-central yet quiet New Town location, helpful staff, business-style rooms and apartments with balconies.

Šiauliai

Juro Guest House € Spotless guesthouse located a short stroll away from most museums; super-helpful owner.

Šaulys Hotel €€ Šiauliai's swankiest choice has plush rooms in understated greys, a 1950s-style restaurant and English-speaking staff.

Panevėžys

Conviva Hotel €€ Tall ceilings, crimson carpets, sizeable rooms and a central location off the main square.

Hotel Romantic €€€ A converted old mill with Panevėžys' plushest rooms and an excellent restaurant terrace overlooking the park.

Druskininkai

Art Hotel €€ Wooden mansion comprising spacious studios in soothing blues and whites, with bold contemporary art and high-beamed family apartments.

Aqua Hotel €€ Perfect for a family stay, this three-star hotel is part of the vast Aqua Park complex; good breakfast buffet.

Curonian Spit

Sodyba Nidoje € Five spotless ensuite rooms in a central traditional wooden house in Nida, with kitchen access and picnic tables in the garden.

Miško Namas €€ Nab a room with a balcony or kitchenette at this immaculate Nida guesthouse with a library and garden.

Vila Flora €€ Central 19th-century timber villa in Juodkrantė, with split-level rooms.

Klaipėda

Preliudija € Minimalist, modern rooms await at this handsome mid-19th-century guesthouse in the heart of Old Town.

Michaelson Boutique Hotel €€ Atmospheric 18th-century warehouse comes with updated wood-beamed rooms in sleek greys and creams overlooking the Danė River.

Palanga

Vila Ramybė € Individually styled pastel-hued rooms (some with terraces) on a quiet street.

Life Balance Spa Hotel €€€ A spa and floor-to-ceiling windows are the perks at this glass-and-chrome stunner in a pine grove.

Practicalities

LGBTIQ+ Travellers

Lithuania is one of EU's lowest-ranked countries for LGBTIQ+ rights: homosexuality is decriminalised but same-sex marriage is banned and social attitudes are conservative. Vilnius, Kaunas and Klaipėda have small gay scenes. The National LGBT Rights Organization (*lgl.lt*) is a useful resource for travellers.

Kaunas (p760)

Electricity

Lithuania's electricity supply is 230V and plugs are mostly of the European two-round-pin variety. Travelers from outside Europe usually need an adapter.

Opening Hours

Banks 9am–5pm Monday to Friday
Government offices 8am–5pm Monday to Friday
Post offices 9am–7pm Monday to Friday, 9am to 2pm Saturday
Restaurants noon–11pm
Shops 9am–7pm Monday to Saturday; some open Sunday

Language

Symbols on vowels in written Lithuanian indicate they are pronounced as long sounds.
Hello. Sveiki. svay·ki
Goodbye. Viso gero. vi·so ge·ro
Excuse me. Atleiskite. at·lays·ki·te
Please. Prašau. pra·show
Thank you. Ačiū. aa·choo
Yes. Taip. taip
No. Ne. ne
I don't understand. Aš nesuprantu. ash ne·su·pran·tu
Cheers! Į sveikatą! ee svay·kaa·taa

Smoking

It's prohibited to smoke in restaurants and other enclosed public spaces (including bus stops) in Lithuania, as well as outdoor cafe and bar terraces. The same rules apply to vaping.

Visas

Visas are not required for citizens of the EU, USA, Canada, Japan, New Zealand, Australia or the UK for visits up to 90 days. From late 2025 onwards, non-EU visitors may need to apply for an ETIAS visa waiver in advance in order to be allowed to enter the Schengen area. Visit migracija.lt for further information.

Public Holidays

New Year's Day 1 January
Independence Day 16 February
Lithuanian Independence Restoration Day 11 March
Easter Sunday & Monday March/April
International Labour Day 1 May
Feast of St John (Midsummer) 24 June
Statehood Day 6 July
Assumption of Blessed Virgin 15 August
All Saints' Day 1 November
Christmas (Kalėdos) 25 and 26 December

FROM LEFT: HENK VRIESELAAR/SHUTTERSTOCK, JOHNER IMAGES/GETTY IMAGES

Arriving & Getting Around

There are a variety of ways to get to Lithuania, including flights to its two main airports (Vilnius and Kaunas), two international ferry services, and train and bus services from across Europe.

Arriving by Air
Lithuania's two main airports are in Vilnius and Kaunas. Palanga Airport receives seasonal summer flights. Vilnius Airport is connected to central Vilnius by train and bus. Ryanair hub Kaunas is served by buses.

Arriving by Bus, Train & Boat
Eurolines and Lux Express buses connect Vilnius and Kaunas to Europe. A daily train links Kraków and Warsaw with Tallinn and Riga via Kaunas and Vilnius. Ferries from Kiel (Germany) and Karlshamn (Sweden) dock in Klaipėda.

MONEY
Currency: Euro (€)

CASH & CARD
Multilingual ATMs are ubiquitous in cities and towns; even villages are likely to have one. Carry cash for small purchases (museums, bus tickets, market produce).

DIGITAL PAYMENTS
Digital payments are the norm at most businesses, particularly in bigger towns and cities. In rural destinations it's a good idea to carry cash.

TIPPING
Tipping 10% in restaurants is the norm; even if paying by card, tip with cash. In hotels, tipping is restricted to top-end establishments. Taxi drivers don't expect a tip; round up the fare for assistance with baggage.

Driving Essentials
Lithuanian roads are in good condition; car hire is offered in all major cities. Spark *(spark.lt)* is the electric carshare service. Winter tyres are compulsory from mid-November through March. Blood alcohol limit is 0.4g/L.

Getting Around
Lithuania's national bus network links all major cities and smaller towns. Buy tickets using the Autobusų Bilietai *(autobusubilietai.lt)* website or app. Larger cities and towns are well covered by public transport. LTG trains *(ltglink.lt)* are comfortable and cheap; handy routes include Vilnius to Kaunas, Vilnius to Klaipėda via Šiauliai, and Vilnius to Ignalina.

Curated by
Owen Morton

Moldova

UNDERGROUND WINE LABYRINTHS AND SOVIET MEMORABILIA

Visitors to Moldova love its cosmopolitan capital and excellent wine, as well as its quirky, Soviet-tinged breakaway state.

Wedged between Romania and Ukraine, Moldova is for the most part culturally Romanian but spent the latter half of the 20th century as part of the Soviet Union. Its road to independence was rocky, with a short civil war eventually leading to the establishment of the breakaway state of Transnistria, and political crises and corruption defining the 1990s and early 2000s. Since 2009, however, the country has begun to steer a path towards EU membership. And now, thanks to the expansion of budget airlines, it's seen an increase in travellers looking to discover a less-heralded destination.

It's easy to see the country's appeal: the capital, Chişinău, is a lively city and convenient base for trips to the further-flung areas. And anyone with a passing interest in wine should pay a visit to one of Moldova's wine cellars: the most impressive are Milestii Mici and Cricova, both of which comprise hundreds of kilometres of limestone tunnels. Further north, Soroca offers insight into small-town Moldova. To the south, Căuşeni's colourful frescoes delight admirers of Byzantine-style church art.

But it's fair to say that Moldova is most famed for Transnistria, a breakaway state where the Soviet Union lives on. Blocky architecture, concrete monuments, extensive use of the hammer-and-sickle motif and statues of Lenin standing proudly in front of brutalist government offices provide the rare opportunity to travel back in time to the USSR.

MAZUR TRAVEL/SHUTTERSTOCK

THE MAIN AREAS

For places to stay in Moldova, see p785

TRABANTOS/SHUTTERSTOCK

Left: Wine cellar, Cricova (p779); Above: St Mary's Church (p780), Orheiul Vechi

Find Your Way

Moldova is a relatively small country. The capital Chişinău is centrally located; it makes sense to base yourself here and explore the outlying sights on day trips.

BUS

There are good bus and minibus connections throughout Moldova, starting at the three bus stations in Chişinău. The tourist office can provide up-to-date information on which bus station serves which destination.

CAR

Driving in Moldova is easy, and offers the opportunity to see the country at your own pace. Roads are well maintained, driving standards are relatively high, parking is easy and there's rarely much traffic.

Transnistria, p782

A breakaway self-declared country, Transnistria evokes the long-gone days of the USSR.

Soroca, p781

The northern riverside town of Soroca is centred around a medieval castle.

Orheiul Vechi, p779

The country's top archaeological site contains ruins from every era of Moldovan history.

Chişinău, p774

Moldova's friendly capital is home to several diverting museums, as well as attractive parks and the finest restaurants and bars in the country.

UKRAINE

ROMANIA

Black Sea

Mogyliv-Podilsky
Yampil
Ocnita
Briceni
Stânca
Costeşti
Făleşti
Iaşi
Vastui
Bârlad
Tecuci

Camenca
Soroca
Floreşti
Bălţi
Ungheni
Călăraşi
Cricova
Hânceşti
Cimişlia
Comrat
Cahul
Vulcăneşti

Rîbniţa
Orhei
Orheiul Vechi
Dubăsari
Grigoriopol
CHIŞINĂU
Bendery
Căuşeni
Basarabeasca

Tiraspol

Palanca

Odesa

Dniester
Nistru (Dniestr)
Prut

0   40 km
0   20 miles

LEONID ANDRONOV/SHUTTERSTOCK

Arc de Triomphe (p774), Chişinău

Plan Your Time

Moldova's relatively small size means you can get a good sense of the country over a long weekend, but giving yourself extra time will allow you to dig deeper.

A Weekend in Chişinău

● Spend day one exploring **Chişinău** (p774): wander its parks and grand avenues, visit the museums and enjoy a stop in a cafe. On day two, take a day trip: either head to **Bender** (p782) for a surreal sense of return to the USSR or join a tour at **Milestii Mici** (p778) to enjoy a subterranean trip through Moldova's wine industry.

A Week to Explore

● With a week, you can take in most of Moldova's highlights. After visiting **Chişinău** (p774), **Bender** (p782)) and **Milestii Mici** (p778), head north to the country's foremost archaeological site, **Orheiul Vechi** (p779), and continue on to the riverside town of **Soroca** (p781) for an overnight stay. Or visit the gorgeous Byzantine-style frescoes in Căuşeni's **Church of the Assumption** (p784).

SEASONAL HIGHLIGHTS

SPRING

Milder temperatures make this a great time to spend a weekend in the city.

SUMMER

The country comes alive with bustling pavement cafes in towns and colourful countryside wildflowers.

AUTUMN

Early September is the grape harvest season: this is the perfect time to enjoy a wine-focused visit.

WINTER

It's dark and cold in winter, but if you catch a sunny day, the country is gorgeous under a blanket of snow.

Chișinău

SOVIET ARCHITECTURE | PAVEMENT CAFES | GREEN PARKS

GETTING AROUND

Although Chișinău is a reasonably large city, travellers will probably want to stick to the central area, which is very walkable: it's mostly flat, and the streets are laid out in a grid pattern that makes it easy to navigate. Minibuses and trolleybuses ply the route along the central Ştefan cel Mare Boulevard, and you may also need them to reach the north or south bus stations (route 9 goes to both). Taxis are easy to flag down and inexpensive. If you're driving, parking is free almost everywhere except around Cathedral Park.

☑ TOP TIP

Chișinău's friendly and helpful tourist office, just southeast of Cathedral Park, has plenty of information on things to do around the entire country. Their bus timetables tell you which of the three bus stations you need to reach your destination.

From its origins as a small medieval village, Chișinău grew into a city after Moldova became part of the Russian Empire in the 19th century. Largely flattened in WWII, it was rebuilt in classic Soviet style, with wide avenues, concrete apartment blocks and socialist-realist monuments. It went through a rough patch after independence, but has now emerged as a welcoming, cosmopolitan city with a lively pavement cafe culture (in summer, at least), diverting museums and excellent restaurants, bars and hotels. Although there may not be any traditional must-see attractions here, Chișinău is an extremely pleasant place and you could find yourself spending more time here than you expected.

Enjoy Chișinău's Central Green Space

Explore Cathedral Park

Any exploration of Chișinău should begin in **Cathedral Park**, which is centred around the city's cathedral, a vast, white domed beast with a separate bell tower. Southwest of the cathedral is Chișinău's very own **Arc de Triomphe**, erected in 1870 to celebrate Russia's victory over the Ottoman Empire. In summer, the park is a popular gathering spot.

Delve into Moldova's Past

Tread the palatial halls of the National History Museum

To get an introduction to Moldova's past, head to the **National History Museum** (*nationalmuseum.md; entry 50MDL; closed Mon*). Don't miss the remarkable hoard of ancient Greek armour found at Olănești – the bronze Attican helmet with carved panthers on the sides is especially fine – after which there's a wealth of exhibits from the 19th and 20th centuries. Finally, in the basement, there's an unflinching exhibition exploring the Gulag system and the crimes of the Soviet regime.

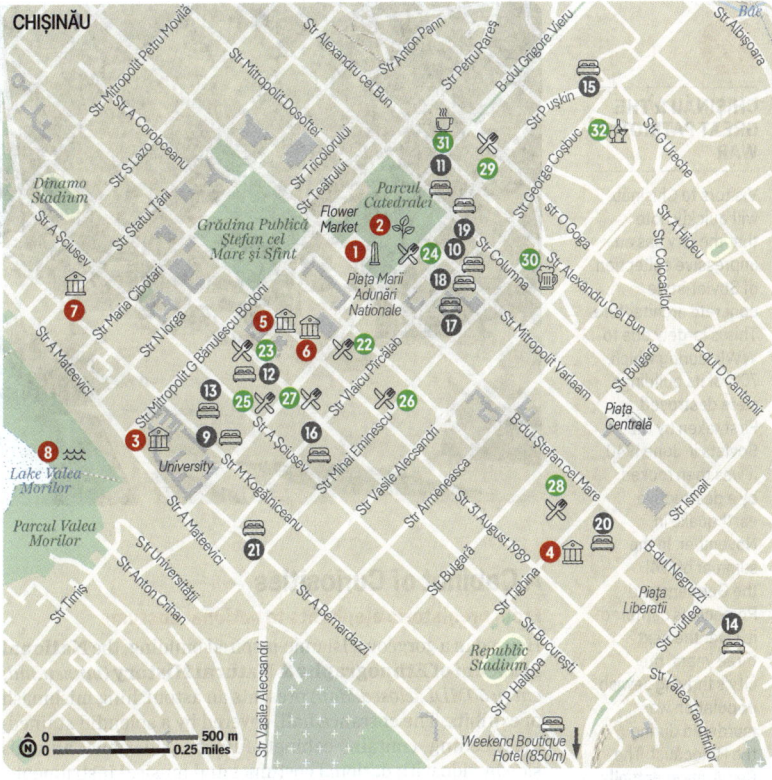

CHIŞINĂU

An Introduction to Moldovan Art

Explore the grandiose Fine Arts Museum

Art lovers should head straight to the **National Museum of Art** *(mnam.md; entry 50MDL; closed Mon)*. The ground floor is home to contemporary sculpture, early-20th-century portraiture, and religious icons, while upstairs you'll find more recent works. Mihau Grecu and Valentina Rusu-Ciobani – Moldova's most celebrated 20th-century artists – are well represented here. Rusu-Ciobani's *Friendship* is particularly fun, depicting a crowd of people sporting delightful 1970s clothing and hairstyles.

CHIȘINĂU & THE GREAT PATRIOTIC WAR

Visitors to Chișinău will quickly note that the city has an impressive collection of Soviet-style concrete architecture. This is largely due to WWII, during which 70% of its buildings were destroyed. First taken by the Soviets in June 1940, it was then rocked by a destructive earthquake in November. In the summer of 1941 the Germans and Romanians captured it. Over the next three years, the city's thriving Jewish population was murdered during the Holocaust. The Red Army eventually retook the city in August 1944. The city's **Military History Museum** (*entry 50MDL*) offers an engaging look at these events, though note that the exhibits do not shy away from the horrors of war.

A Cabinet of Curiosities

From prehistoric elephants to national costume

Housed in a gorgeous, Islamic-inspired building, the **National Museum of Ethnography & Natural History** (*muzeu.md; entry 50MDL; closed Mon*) presents an astonishing mishmash of exhibits. The entrance hall, covered by a splendid stained-glass ceiling, contains cabinets full of taxidermied animals side by side with national costumes and musical instruments. Other impressive displays include a detailed topographic model of Moldova and an enormous fossil skeleton of a deinotherium (a type of prehistoric elephant).

Lenin at the Lake

Take a stroll in Valea Morilor Park

Another of Chișinău's attractive green spaces, the **Valea Morilor Park** is centred around a large lake. You'll likely enter the park near the Graeco-Roman rotunda, from which you can descend the Cascades, an ornate staircase that passes pleasant fountains and colourful flower beds. At the bottom, head to your right to circumnavigate the lake – keep your eyes

 DRINKING IN CHIȘINĂU: OUR PICKS

Alt Ceva: Popular craft-beer pub with an industrial vibe and old-school cartoons playing on a big screen. *4pm-2am Mon-Thu, to 4am Fri & Sat, to midnight Sun*

Crème de la Crème: Chișinău's best people-watching spot, on the corner of the pedestrian Str Eugen Doga. *7.30am-9.30pm Mon-Fri, 8am-10pm Sat & Sun*

Marlène: Fabulously decadent cocktail bar that evokes the 1920s. Settle into the velvet chairs and enjoy the jazzy soundtrack. *4-11pm Mon-Fri, to midnight Sat & Sun*

Via Wine Bar: This wine bar is a short walk from Cathedral Park, with a well-selected list of Moldovan wines. *10am-10pm Mon-Fri, from noon Sat & Sun*

TRABANTOS/SHUTTERSTOCK

Valea Morilor Park

FROM MEDIEVAL VILLAGE TO MODERN CITY

Chișinău isn't a particularly old place: the first known mention dates from 1436, when it was an insignificant village in the Principality of Moldavia. Its growth into a city took place in the 19th century, after it became a part of the Russian Empire in 1812.

Following the Russian Revolution, it became the capital of the short-lived Moldavian Democratic Republic; 20 years later, the city was almost entirely destroyed in World War II. During the Soviet years, Chișinău became the capital of the Moldavian SSR and subsequently the capital of independent Moldova in 1991.

open for the tiny golden sculpture of the Little Prince, which sits atop one of the fence posts. At the west end of the park, Lenin hunters can veer to the right to reach the Madison Park events venue, outside which stands a statue of old Vladimir.

Close to the park is the defiantly old-school **City History Museum** (*facebook.com/muzeul.chisinaului; entry 50MDL; closed Mon*), housed in a gorgeous 19th-century water tower. Its cabinets full of dusty artefacts and photographs tell the story of Chișinău's history from its origins through to 1991, at which point history abruptly stops. The room covering the later Soviet period, with its delightfully retro tape players and DJ decks, is particularly diverting.

 EATING IN CHIȘINĂU: OUR PICKS

Black Rabbit Gastro Burrow: Smart restaurant with a stylish industrial feel, serving modern European dishes and decent veggie options. *10am–midnight* €€

Fuior: Upmarket, central restaurant with a contemporary Moldovan menu: try the carp fillet with polenta or the braised lamb with carrot cream. *11am–11pm* €€€

Taifas: Atmospheric restaurant serving traditional Romanian dishes, often accompanied by folk-music performances. *11am–10pm Mon–Sat, to 9pm Sun* €€

Wine Gogh: Stylish basement restaurant with a meaty menu and Van Gogh–inspired decor. *11am–10pm Mon, 11am–11pm Tue–Fri, noon–11pm Sat & Sun* €€

Eli-Pili: Eclectically decorated place with an extensive menu of light meals such as pancakes and dumplings. It's also a lively bar by night. *9am–2am* €

Little Napoli: Chișinău's best pizza restaurant has a wood-fired oven, cosy dining room and pavement seating for summer evenings. *11am–10pm* €€

Sincer: Popular modern cafe offering healthy breakfast and lunch choices, including soups, salads and sandwiches. *8am–9pm* €

Tbilisi: This garden restaurant has a menu of Georgian cuisine: *khachapuri* cheese breads, hearty stews and *khinkali* dumplings. *11am–11pm Mon–Sat, 11am–10pm Sun* €€

Beyond Chişinău

GETTING AROUND

The majority of destinations throughout the country can be reached by bus from one of Chişinău's three bus stations; if in doubt, the tourist office can tell you which station you need. If you're self-driving, the country is easy to navigate, with well-maintained roads originating in the capital and plenty of helpful signposting.

A number of Moldova's highlights can be found outside Chişinău, where the sights take in the full span of the country's history. The Orheiul Vechi archaeological site is one of Moldova's top outings, its ruins spread along an attractive river valley. In the northern town of Soroca, you'll find a splendid fortress. To the east, meanwhile, is the breakaway republic of Transnistria, in which the spirit of the USSR lingers on. Closer to Chişinău, meanwhile, are the wineries of Milestii Mici and Cricova, which produce some of the country's best wines and occupy remarkable underground labyrinths of limestone tunnels. These two destinations are perfect for a day of wine tasting.

Milestii Mici

TIME FROM CHIŞINĂU: **30MIN**

Marvel at the world's largest wine collection

Just 14km south of Chişinău is the massive **Milestii Mici** wine producer and cellar *(milestii-mici.md; tours from 350MDL)*. Buggies convey visitors from the beautiful gardens – complete with fountains dispensing wine-coloured water (red and white) – into chilly subterranean tunnels. Originally a limestone mine, the 200km of tunnels here are a consistent 12°C to 14°C year-round – ideal for wine storage, for which the passages have been used since 1968.

The tour's highlight is a visit to the remarkable labyrinth that is the bottle-storage chamber, which is listed in the Guinness World Records as the world's largest wine collection, comprising 1.5 million bottles. You'll also see the hidden room where 50,000 of the winery's most valuable bottles were stashed to escape destruction under Gorbachev's 1985 prohibition law, before emerging through some enjoyably Indiana Jones-esque secret doors into the tasting room. Inevitably, there's also a wine bar in the garden. It's the perfect spot for a cheap glass or two.

Cricova

TIME FROM CHIȘINĂU: **30MIN** /

Limestone tunnels and celebrity wine storage

The **Cricova Wine Cellars** (*cricova.md; tours from 600MDL*) are an easy 15km north of Chișinău and offer a similar cellar tour in another former limestone mine. Stop first in an underground cinema for a somewhat excitable film about the history of wine in general and at Cricova in particular. Afterward, you'll visit the sparkling wine–production plant and have a look around the wine-storage chamber where famous personalities ranging from Angela Merkel to Michelle Yeoh keep their wines. Not on display is the sizeable portion of Herman Göring's wine collection, seized by the USSR at the end of WWII and now stored here. The final stop is in the grandiose complex of tasting rooms. The nautically themed one is the most impressive, if a little inexplicable.

Orheiul Vechi

TIME FROM CHIȘINĂU: **1HR** /

Moldova's most important archaeological site

Spread around the village of **Butuceni** (and not, confusingly, the namesake town of Orhei) is the archaeological site of **Orheiul Vechi** (*orheiulvechi.com; entry free*). In this striking

☑ TOP TIP

Most places can be reached as a day trip from Chișinău, though Soroca is far enough away that an overnight stay is advisable, unless you're on a very tight timeframe.

779

STEPHEN THE GREAT

Among the most celebrated figures in Moldovan history is Ştefan cel Mare (Stephen the Great), the 15th-century ruler of Moldavia, a principality that covered present-day Moldova and a substantial chunk of northeast Romania. His reign lasted nearly 50 years, during which time he successfully defended his territory against Ottomans, Hungarians, Wallachians and Poles, and is credited with the establishment of many churches, including some of the famous painted monasteries in Romania's Suceava County. After his death he became a national hero, inspiring Romanian and Moldovan nationalism throughout the 19th and 20th centuries. Look for him on every denomination of the lei banknote.

Soroca Fortress

river valley and on the ridge above it, you'll find remnants of almost all periods of the country's history. Begin your visit at the archaeological museum, where you can check out a well-presented collection of interesting artefacts found at the site, suggesting settlement here dating back to at least 3500 BCE. Exhibits include pottery, daggers and an awful lot of skeletons.

Walk up the road into the village of Butuceni where the main sites are located. Call in at the **ethnographic museum** – a small dwelling done up as a 19th-century homestead – then head uphill via the stairs, aiming for the gold-domed roof of **St Mary's Church**. The church stands at the centre of what was once an ancient fortress that occupied this strategic spot, commanding fine views of the river valley on either side. It's worth taking a walk beyond the church along the ridge to enjoy those views. About five minutes on, the surefooted can descend a rough but marked path on the ridge's north side to reach the **Bosie cave monastery**, an extensive collection of cells and chambers hewn into the cliff. Don't miss the medieval Slavonic inscription adorning the doorway of the easternmost cave.

 ## EATING AROUND ORHEIUL VECHI

Eco-Resort Butuceni: Attractively rustic place neaer the Ethnographic Museum, with a slightly touristy menu of traditional cuisine. *10am-10pm* €€

Inspir: Small snack hut ideal for relaxing in a deckchair or hammock with a coffee or ice cream. On the opposite side of the valley from Butuceni. *10am-8pm* €

Moara Veche: For a light lunch, this hole-in-the-wall in the village is perfect: the menu includes paninis and pastries, and the coffee is good. *10am-6pm Wed-Sun* €

Villa Etníca: In the centre of the village is this hotel-restaurant, with a good menu of decent Moldovan meals. *noon-10pm* €€

Returning the other way along the ridge, the bell tower marks the entrance to tiny **Pestera cave monastery**, less extensive than Bosie but considerably easier to access. It's also of interest as it's still in use as an active church filled with icons, candles and incense.

Elsewhere in the valley lie scattered ruins from various eras, including the remains of a mosque and a church, and the fairly sizeable Turkish bathhouse down by the river. A reasonably well-marked walking trail links all the spots of interest. You can pick up a map at the museum or car park booth. Expect to spend from several hours to a full day here.

Tipova
TIME FROM CHIȘINĂU: 1½HR 🚗 / 🚌

Clerics in the caves

One of Moldova's more unusual religious establishments, the **Tipova Monastery** *(entry 10MDL)* is hollowed into the limestone cliffs on the west bank of the Dnister River, about 100km north of Chișinău. From the parking area, walk to the right of the modern yellow church, following a track towards the cliff edge, where you'll find rough stone steps leading down to the ticket booth. From here you can enter the monastery to the right, which dates back at least as far as 1700. Some chambers are just bare rock, some remain in use as a church or simple shrines, and others have been converted into an informative museum. If you take the path to the left from the ticket booth, you'll find older and simpler cave monastery complexes, including one in which legend claims King Stephen the Great married one of his wives.

Soroca
TIME FROM CHIȘINĂU: 2¼HRS 🚗 / 🚌

Views from castle ramparts

For an enjoyable day trip to one of Moldova's smaller cities, head to Soroca, which has a pair of distinctive attractions. The principal draw is the splendid **Soroca Fortress** *(facebook .com/cetatesoroca; entry 30MDL; closed Mon & Tue)*, which sits down by the Dnister River and is marvellously picturesque, with five witch-hat turrets. Inside, the doors off the central courtyard lead to rooms with museum displays of limited interest; more enticing is the chance to climb onto the ramparts and enjoy views over the town and river.

Elsewhere, from a small car park just south of town, you can ascend the 647 steps to the somewhat phallic **Candle of Gratitude** *(entry free)*, an immense finger of concrete

MOLDOVA & THE VINE

Moldova's winemaking tradition may extend as far back as 2800 BCE, though it seems the region first became known for its wine in the late medieval period under the reign of Stephen the Great. By 1914, it was the principal winemaking region of the Russian Empire, a position it retained while part of the USSR. The vineyards suffered a setback during the 1980s following Gorbachev's campaign against alcohol, but since independence the industry has flourished anew, exporting its wine primarily to the EU. The country produces both red and white varieties, though the reds are arguably better. Those from the Purcari Winery are particularly celebrated.

🍴 EATING IN SOROCA

Coffee In: Just next to the fortress, this simple little place is handy for a pick-me-up coffee and pastry. *7.30am-11.30pm* €

Dulcinella: Have a sweet tooth? Make a beeline for Dulcinella. There's a delightful selection of cakes and pastries, washed down by good strong coffee. *8am-8pm* €

La Faleza: Soroca's best restaurant has a delicious menu that's primarily Asian, but also stretches to steak, pizza and pasta. *10am-10pm Tue-Sun, from noon Mon* €€

Salat: On Soroca's central square, Salat offers an extensive budget menu, with options ranging from soups and salads to steaks and sushi. *10am-10pm* €

standing atop a hill. It houses an uninteresting chapel, and is primarily worth a visit for the splendid views over town and the Dnister River, with western Ukraine on the other side.

THE STRUVE GEODETIC ARC

In 1816, the Russian scientist Friedrich von Struve began a series of triangulations to calculate the exact size and shape of the Earth, a project that took him nearly 40 years to complete. His 34 calculations were made at various points across Norway, Sweden and what was then the Russian Empire, stretching from Hammerfest to Stara Nekrasivka on the Ukrainian–Romanian border. His work was of enough significance that the sites were inscribed on the UNESCO World Heritage list in 2005. One of the calculations was taken in Rudi, 40km west of Soroca. Marked by an obelisk, it's Moldova's only UNESCO site.

Transnistria

TIME FROM CHIȘINĂU: 1¼HR 🚌 / 🚆

Moldova is perhaps best known for being home to the breakaway state of **Transnistria**, a self-governing, self-declared independent country that occupies the territory east of the Dnister River. Infamous for its apparent refusal to accept the fall of the Soviet Union, Transnistria retains a unique vibe, with statues of Lenin, eternal flames and blocky monuments galore.

With the exception of the town of **Bender**, the UK FCDO advises against travelling to the territory of Transnistria, owing to the region being outside the control of the Moldovan government. That said, many travellers visit the area trouble-free: there are numerous tour operators – including **PMR Tours** (pmr-tours.com) and **Young Pioneers** (youngpioneertours.com) – who can arrange trips. It's also easy to visit independently by taking the frequent buses from Chișinău. Even self-driving into the territory presents no problems. The main pitfall to be wary of is the territory's name: it prefers the Russian-language Pridnestrovie, even to the extent of declaring that using the term Transnistria is illegal.

There are entry points to Transnistria on all the main roads into Bender. You'll need your passport, and though entry is technically free, be prepared to pay a fee of between €5 and €10. If you're driving, you'll also need to wait while forms are filled out authorising your entry. The process rarely takes longer than half an hour. Once you're in, you'll need some money: Transnistria has its own currency, the **Transnistrian ruble**. You can exchange dollars or euros at all banks. Payment by card is sometimes possible, but don't rely on it.

Most visitors to Transnistria head straight to the capital, Tiraspol. Here, on the main Pokrovskaya St is Transnistria's most iconic sight: a vast statue of Lenin, his coat billowing in the revolutionary breeze, standing in front of the parliament building. Opposite is the town's historical museum (closed for renovation at the time of writing) adjacent to an avenue of remembrance for the Great Patriotic War and the 1990s separatist conflict. A gold-domed chapel, an eternal flame and a tank on a pedestal complete the ensemble.

Bender

TIME FROM CHIȘINĂU: 1HR 🚌 / 🚆

From castles to communism

Bender is the gateway to the breakaway republic of Transnistria, but its principal attraction is its 15th-century **fortress** (bendery-fortress.com, 25 rubles), which sits in the centre of a slightly Disneyish park and has been given a sympathetic restoration and is crowned with turrets. There are two small museums inside: the Historical Museum presents the story of Bender alongside some interesting artefacts and enjoyable

MOLDOVA'S BEST SOVIET MEMORABILIA

Mosaics, Chișinău: There are numerous Soviet mosaics dotted around the city; the best takes up an entire wall in the central bus station.

The Circus, Chișinău: This vast circular arena features a pair of juggling figures cast in bronze above the entrance.

Palatul Municipal de Cultură, Bălți: On the side of this building is a splendid Soviet bas-relief depicting arts and culture.

Bender: Central Bender is a Soviet open-air museum, with statues of Lenin, bas-reliefs and grandiose monuments galore.

Comrat: Down in the autonomous region of Gagauzia, Lenin is still live and kicking. Head to the central government building to find the statue.

Lenin statue, Comrat

GAGARIN IURII/SHUTTERSTOCK

Bender fortress (p782)

FROM TAJIKISTAN TO THE MOON

To learn more about Moldova's experience before and during WWII, read Robert Frimtzis' memoir *From Tajikistan to the Moon*. Born to Jewish parents in Bălți in 1930, Frimtzis and his family were forced to flee the Nazi occupation when he was just 11 – a journey that took them from Moldova all the way to Central Asia. From there, Frimtzis was able to immigrate to America where he earned a master's degree from Columbia University and then worked on the developing space programme. The early chapters of his book tell the story of his childhood in Bălți and the terrifying reality of the advance of the German army.

models and dioramas, while the Museum of Torture is distastefully lurid. The real joy of the fortress is walking the ramparts and taking in the views from the observation tower over the main entrance.

The fortress is about a kilometre north of the centre, which itself is worth exploring for its Soviet time-capsule vibe. Start by walking south down the river through **October Park**, past the blocky concrete *Monument to Soviet Power*, until you reach the derelict port building – note its golden ship bas-relief. Head west from here to the **Palace of Culture** and check out its impressive mosaics, before wandering into the town centre along Lenin St. It won't be long before you find **Komsomol Park**, which has the requisite Lenin statue opposite the monumental Gorky cinema: pop your head inside for a glimpse of its ornate lobby.

Căușeni

TIME FROM CHIȘINĂU: 1¼ HR

Admire Byzantine-style frescoes

The straggly southern town of Căușeni is worth visiting for its **Church of the Assumption** *(entry 4 MDL),* which dates to around the 17th century. A squat building, it looks unimpressive from outside, but the interior is a riot of colour: every surface, including the ceiling, is bedecked with Byzantine-style frescoes depicting stories from the New Testament. Although there are similar churches in northern Romania, this one is unique for Moldova. The frescoes date from about 1760, and have been restored by a team of Moldovan and Romanian experts.

 EATING IN BENDER: OUR PICKS

Canteen CCCP: Get back in the USSR in this splendid self-service canteen, adorned with Soviet memorabilia aplenty. *8am-8pm* €

Georgia: Serves all the Caucasian classics: *khinkali* dumplings, *khachapuri* cheese bread and delicious grilled meats. *10am-midnight* €€€

La Vida: Central and popular restaurant with an extensive menu of international choices, ranging from pizza and pasta to sushi. *10am-1am* €€

Slavny Pekar: Pleasant bakery outside the Palace of Culture, with great pastries and desserts, and good strong coffee. *8am-8pm* €

Places We Love to Stay

€ Budget €€ Midrange €€€ Top End

Chișinău

MAP p775

Amazing Ionika Hostel € This chilled place is Chișinău's best hostel, with mixed dorms and private rooms available. It also arranges tours of the city and the rest of the country. Book ahead – it's popular.

Hotel Chișinău € For an authentic Soviet experience, try the Hotel Chișinău, a splendid (if slightly decaying) enormity on United Nations Sq.

City Park Hotel € Smart and modern rooms in one of the best locations in town, just north of Cathedral Park. Nab a room on the seventh floor for excellent views. Breakfast not included.

TA Collection Hotel € Smart and modern hotel with 45 clean, quiet rooms in a convenient central courtyard just off the Bulevardul Ștefan cel Mare.

Tapok Hostel € If Ionika Hostel is full, Tapok makes a worthy second choice. It's clean and friendly, and has a reasonably handy location.

Weekend Boutique Hotel € A little out of the centre, this quirky hotel (with artworks on the exterior of the building) has over-the-top decor and the unusual opportunity to rent a goldfish for the night.

Bristol Central Park €€ With an enviable position just down from Cathedral Park, the rooms at the Bristol have slightly faded glamour exuding early 20th-century charm. Book in advance: walk-in rates are just silly.

Glass Cube €€ Modern and attractively priced place with the eponymous glass-cube architectural feature helping it stand out from the crowd. Coffee and tea, but no breakfast available.

Komilfo Hotel €€ 1970s retro-kitsch is the name of the game here: brown carpets, gold-yellow wallpaper and green-tiled bathrooms. Style aside, it's spotless and comfortable.

Lion's Hotel €€ Stylish rooms in a handy spot on a quiet street, a short walk from the central parks. Breakfast, served on the top-floor terrace, is good.

Gregory Hotel €€€ Attractive boutique hotel with plush rooms equipped with stylish wooden furniture and balconies with city views. Good buffet breakfast and smooth service make it worth the splurge.

Nobil Boutique Luxury Hotel €€€ In a shiny glass tower with a delightfully bling lobby, Nobil's rooms are actually reasonably restrained and tasteful. The 7th-floor restaurant and bar offers decent city views, and there's also a good spa.

Radisson Blu Leogrand Hotel €€€ Chișinău's well-located Radisson has a gorgeous lobby with stained-glass ceiling and wine-themed murals. The rooms are predictably swish and comfy, and there's the requisite spa, gym, casino and wine shop.

Richmond €€€ Modern hotel near the central parks, with stylish rooms and a pleasant covered-terrace wine bar.

Cricova

Curtea Domneasca € Attractively rustic hotel on the east edge of Cricova; it's an easy walk to the winery. Beds are comfy, the welcome is warm and the breakfast is good.

Giowine €€ The most upmarket place to stay in Cricova, Giowine has smart rooms, a swimming pool, a sauna and a good restaurant.

Soroca

Central Hotel € True to its name, the Central Hotel is just off Soroca's main square. It won't be winning many awards, but it's cheap, clean and a perfectly decent place to lay your head.

Hotel Europa 1928 € Hotel complex 10 minute's walk south of the main square, with simple but clean rooms, a swimming pool and an unexpected pirate ship–themed decking area on the river bank.

Bender

Stary Bastion €€ Bender's smartest hotel by far, this hotel-restaurant-spa complex in the castle park is decorated in a ridiculously opulent style. It can be noisy, though, with parties and karaoke overnight.

Practicalities

LGBTIQ+ Travellers

Although same-sex activity is not illegal, LGBTIQ+ travellers may encounter intolerant attitudes. Same-sex partners are not legally recognised. In Transnistria, same-sex activity is legal, but in 2024 the government announced laws banning 'propaganda for non-traditional sexual relations'.

Crime

Moldova is a generally safe destination, though you should watch out for pickpocketing and bag snatching in Chișinău. Possession, use and smuggling of illegal drugs will likely result in lengthy jail sentences.

Natural Disasters

Minor tremors are not uncommon in Moldova, though earthquakes are rare. The last significant earthquake affecting the country was in 1986, measuring 7.1 on the Richter scale; similar quakes occurred in 1977 and 1940.

Visas

Citizens of the UK, EU, US, Canada, Australia, New Zealand and others can enter Moldova without a visa. South Africa is a notable exception. If you need a visa, you can apply for one online at mfa.gov.md/en. If you're visiting Transnistria you'll need to get an entry permit; this is most easily arranged at the border upon arrival.

DAN MORAR/SHUTTERSTOCK

Orthodox Easter celebration, Chișinău (p774)

Opening Hours

Cafes and restaurants in Moldova tend to open in the late morning and stay open until the late evening, while bars usually open from mid-afternoon. Standard shop hours are 9am to 6pm. Museums and tourist attractions are sometimes closed on Monday.

Language

Romanian is the official language of Moldova.

Hello. Bună ziua. boo-nuh zee-wa
Goodbye. La revedere. la re-ve-de-re
Excuse me. Scuzaţi-mă. skoo-za-tsee-muh
Please. Vă rog. vuh rog
Thank you. Mulţumesc. mool-tsoo-mesk
Yes. Da. da
No. Nu. noo
Do you speak English? Vorbiţi engleza? vor-bee-tsee-gle-za

Public Holidays

New Year's Day 1 January
Orthodox Christmas 7–8 January
Orthodox Easter April/May
Victory Day 9 May
Children's Day 1 June
Independence Day 27 August
Romanian Language Day 31 August
Christmas Day 25 December
Although not a public holiday, the celebrations for **National Wine Day** (first weekend in October) are worth attending.

Bus, Chișinău (p774)

Arriving & Getting Around

Most travellers arrive in Moldova by air. Chișinău's Eugen Doga Airport is 13km southeast of the city centre, with frequent bus connections into town. Taxis are easy to flag and cost around 150 MDL.

Overland Arrivals & Departures

Daily trains run from Bucharest and Iași in Romania to Chișinău. International bus links (eg FlixBus) run direct to Bucharest, Budapest, Bratislava, Brno and even a few places that don't begin with B.

Transnistria

If you're travelling to Transnistria by bus, you'll need to head to Chișinău's slightly chaotic central bus station. There's a small kiosk outside next to Croissant & Coffee that can sell you a ticket.

Buses

The best way to get around Moldova is by bus. You can go everywhere from Chișinău, though you need to know which of the three bus stations to use. Ask at the tourist office.

Car Hire

Driving in Moldova is easy: the roads are in good condition, signs are clear and there's rarely much traffic outside of Chișinău. Parking is generally free, even in Chișinău. Car-hire companies can be found at the airport. Police stops are infrequent and easy: show your documents and they'll wave you on. If an oncoming car flashes its headlights, it's most likely a warning that there are police ahead.

MONEY
Currency: Moldovan Lei (MDL)

CASH
While most places in Moldova take cards, you may need cash for smaller payments in museums and historic sites, especially outside Chișinău. ATMs are common and there's rarely any problem getting change, even if you pay with large notes.

CARD & DIGITAL PAYMENTS
An increasing number of places in Moldova take card and digital payments, in particular hotels and restaurants. Both Visa and Mastercard are commonly accepted.

TRANSNISTRIAN RUBLES
If you plan on visiting Transnistria, know that you'll need a different currency. The Transnistrian ruble is the only accepted legal tender inside the breakaway republic, and the only place to get it is in a Transnistrian bank. Bring dollars, euros or lei to exchange.

For places to stay
in Montenegro,
see p798

© DIDIER MARTI/GETTY IMAGES

Above: Kotor (p793); Right: Lake Skadar National Park (p796)

Curated by
Peter Dragicevich

Montenegro

MOUNTAINS, COAST AND ANCIENT TOWNS

With so much natural beauty squeezed into such a small area, Montenegro is a miniature marvel.

Montenegro may be one of Europe's newest and smallest nations, but it pushes well above its weight in the desired destinations stakes. A large reason for this is the extravagant beauty of its compact coastline. Nowhere is this more pronounced than in the extraordinarily picturesque Bay of Kotor, where the enclosing mountains dip their feet directly into crystalline waters.

Every summer tens of thousands descend on Montenegro's tiny Adriatic Coast, cramming the beaches and packing into the walled towns scattered along its length. When the crowds get to be too much, it's easy to escape to the mountains. In less than an hour you can be hiking along wild trails, tasting wine in remote villages or kayaking through the water lilies on vast Lake Skadar. Push a little further and there's rafting, canyoning and skiing, and even wilder corners to explore.

Montenegro's often painful position on the dividing lines of civilisations has bequeathed it a diverse and fascinating set of historic remnants. You'll find Illyrian ruins, Greek cemeteries, Roman mosaics, Byzantine frescoes, Serbian monasteries, Venetian palaces, Ottoman mosques, Austrian forts and lots of zany Yugoslav-era hotels and monuments.

Combine that with a Mediterranean climate and lots of delicious things to eat and drink, and you'll begin to see why this wee nation has such an outsized reputation.

CHRISTOPHER MOSWITZER/SHUTTERSTOCK

THE MAIN AREAS

COASTAL MONTENEGRO
Walled towns set alongside clear waters. **p792**

INLAND MONTENEGRO
Mountains, lakes and monasteries. **p795**

Find Your Way

Less than 300km from tip to toe, Montenegro is as compact as they come. A wall of mountains separates the coast from the interior, but the regions are well connected by highways.

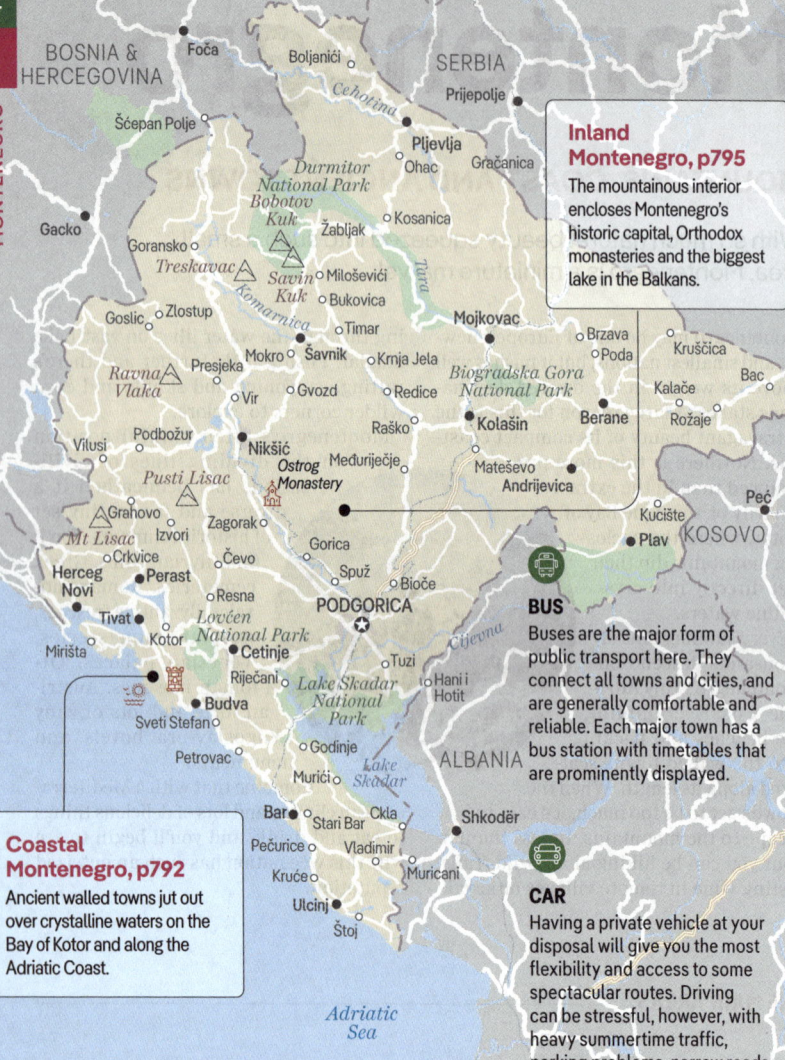

Inland Montenegro, p795

The mountainous interior encloses Montenegro's historic capital, Orthodox monasteries and the biggest lake in the Balkans.

BUS

Buses are the major form of public transport here. They connect all towns and cities, and are generally comfortable and reliable. Each major town has a bus station with timetables that are prominently displayed.

CAR

Having a private vehicle at your disposal will give you the most flexibility and access to some spectacular routes. Driving can be stressful, however, with heavy summertime traffic, parking problems, narrow roads and daredevil drivers.

Coastal Montenegro, p792

Ancient walled towns jut out over crystalline waters on the Bay of Kotor and along the Adriatic Coast.

BOSNIA & HERCEGOVINA

SERBIA

KOSOVO

ALBANIA

Adriatic Sea

Foča
Boljanići
Prijepolje
Šćepan Polje
Pljevlja
Ohac
Gračanica
Gacko
Durmitor National Park
Bobotov Kuk
Žabljak
Kosanica
Goransko
Treskavac
Miloševići
Bukovica
Goslić
Zlostup
Timar
Mojkovac
Brzava
Poda
Kruščica
Ravna Vlaka
Presjeka
Mokro
Šavnik
Krnja Jela
Biogradska Gora National Park
Kalače
Bac
Vir
Gvozd
Redice
Kolašin
Berane
Rožaje
Vilusi
Podbožur
Nikšić
Raško
Međuriječje
Matešević
Andrijevica
Kučište
Peć
Pusti Lisac
Ostrog Monastery
Grahovo
Izvori
Zagorak
Gorica
Spuž
Bioče
Plav
Mt Lisac
Crkvice
Čevo
PODGORICA
Herceg Novi
Perast
Resna
Lovćen National Park
Tuzi
Tivat
Kotor
Cetinje
Hani i Hotit
Mirišta
Riječani
Lake Skadar National Park
Budva
Sveti Stefan
Godinje
Muriči
Lake Skadar
Petrovac
Bar
Stari Bar
Ckla
Shkodër
Pečurice
Vladimir
Kruće
Muricani
Ulcinj
Štoj
Vranovo
Savin Kuk
Komarnica
Cehotina
Tara
Cijevna

0 50 km
N
0 25 miles

TRIFF/SHUTTERSTOCK

River Gate (p794), Kotor

Plan Your Time

Don't be fooled by its size: you could easily spend weeks exploring Montenegro and not be bored – especially if you factor in time for hiking and lying on the beach.

Just One Day

● Make the walled town of **Kotor** (p793) your priority. Get lost in the maze of lanes, call into whichever churches you stumble across and stop to pat the cats. In the late afternoon, head to **Perast** (p792) and take the five-minute boat ride to **Gospa od Škrpjela** (p792). Afterwards, stroll along the waterfront to watch the sunset before sitting down to a seafood feast.

Five Day Full Monty

● Split your first day between **Perast** (p792) and **Kotor** (p793). On day two take the serpentine road up through **Lovćen National Park** (p796) to **Cetinje** (p795), stopping at the **Njegoš Mausoleum** (p796) along the way. Visit **Ostrog Monastery** (p797) on day three, then backtrack to **Lake Skadar** (p796). Spend the following morning on the lake, then drop down to **Budva** (p794).

SEASONAL HIGHLIGHTS

SPRING
Coastal tourism bursts back to life at Easter. April is a lovely time to visit, although the water will still be chilly.

SUMMER
Peak season, with high temperatures and large crowds. On the plus side there's lots going on, including festivals in Perast and Kotor.

AUTUMN
A wonderful time to visit. The waters are still warm but the crowds have thinned out. Great weather for hiking.

WINTER
Snow falls on the mountains; the coast shuts down. Kotor celebrates Carnival in the lead up to Lent (usually late winter).

Coastal Montenegro

WALLED TOWNS | BEACHES | MEDIEVAL BUILDINGS

Places

GETTING AROUND

Regular buses connect the major towns of the coast, all of which have centrally located stations with timetables displayed prominently. In busy times, be prepared for traffic snarls. Vehicle ferries head across the narrow strait at the centre of the Bay of Kotor every 20 minutes (half-hourly after midnight). The journey only takes about five minutes; expect queues in summer.

☑ TOP TIP

While you're driving along the coast, keep an eye out for the various monasteries. All of them welcome visitors, as long as you're respectful and demurely dressed (no bare shoulders or above-the-knee shorts or skirts).

It's hard to avoid superlatives when talking about Montenegro's coast. Simply put, this is one of the world's great beauty spots. To the north is the fjord-like Bay of Kotor (Boka Kotorska), where majestic mountains rise precipitously from slate-grey waters. Driving around the bay, the views are never short of gorgeous.

Next up is the Budva Riviera, the part of the Adriatic Coast that roughly coincides with the area that remained under Venetian rule when the Ottoman Empire pushed north in the 16th century. Despite mammoth hotel developments marring prime spots, it remains strikingly beautiful.

As you head south you'll start to see the minarets of mosques rising from ethnic Albanian villages, culminating in the Muslim-majority town of Ulcinj. South of Ulcinj, a near-constant stretch of beach extends from the Milena Canal all the way to the Albanian border, broken only by the two arms of the Bojana River.

Perast

TIME FROM KOTOR: **20MIN** 🚐

Once a rich and powerful Venetian maritime hub – churning out ships and sea captains in quantities completely disproportionate to its diminutive size – petite Perast has learned to be content with merely being gorgeous. Despite having just one main street, this small town boasts 16 churches and 17 formerly grand palazzi.

Take a boat to Gospa od Škrpjela

Capped by a 17th-century stone church with a sky-blue dome, **Gospa od Škrpjela** *(Our Lady of the Rocks; church & museum €3)* is one of a pair of picturesque islets sitting just off Perast. It was artificially created around a crag where, on 22 July 1452, an icon of the Madonna and Child was found. Every year on that date, locals row over with stones to continue the task of the island's creation in a festival known as Fašinada.

Try to visit the island early or late in the day, as the church and adjoining museum (full of nautical knick-knacks and votive

GIVAGA/SHUTTERSTOCK

Perast

KOTOR THROUGH TIME

It's thought that an ancient Illyrian fortress once stood where St John's Castle is now. However, Kotor first entered the historical record in 168 BCE as the Roman town Acruvium, which survived until the 5th-century Ostrogoth invasion. After the Slavs arrived, Kotor developed as a city-state. During the Middle Ages, it passed through periods of Byzantine, Bulgarian, Serbian, Hungarian and Bosnian suzerainty before the Venetians eventually got the upper hand in 1420. The city owes much of its present look to nearly 400 years of Venetian rule, when it was known as Cattaro. In 1813 it joined briefly with Montenegro for the first time, but the Great Powers handed it to Austria, who held it until WWI.

paintings) can get uncomfortably crowded. In summer, boats line up on the Perast waterfront to ferry people there and back; off season, you may need to ask around. The larger boats operated by **Dado** *(shiptravel-dado.me; return €5)* are a good option as they depart roughly every 10 minutes, allowing you to stay on the island as long as you like. The smaller boats wait on the island for a predetermined time. Be sure to shop around as prices can range from €5 to €10 per person for the return voyage.

Kotor

TIME FROM BUDVA: **35MIN** 🚐

Wedged between brooding mountains and a moody corner of the bay, achingly atmospheric Kotor (pronounced '*koh-tor*') is perfectly at one with its setting. Hemmed in by walls snaking improbably up the surrounding slopes, the town is a medieval maze of churches, cafe-strewn squares and Venetian palaces. It's a place where the past coexists with the present, where lines of laundry flutter from wrought-iron balconies and hundreds of cats loll in marble laneways. Come nightfall, the illuminated city walls glow as serenely as a halo. Behind the bulwarks, the streets buzz with bars and live music.

Climb Kotor's city walls

The **Kotor City Walls** *(entry €15)* are the town's defining feature; a system of defensive ramparts and fortifications that arc up the mountain to a height of 260m above sea level. It's a hard,

 EATING IN KOTOR: OUR PICKS

Taraca Resto Bar: Tucked alongside the river, with an international menu, vegetarian and vegan options, and Yugoslav memorabilia on the walls. *8am-11pm* €€

Platanus: Popular cafe and pizzeria in Dobrota, with excellent service and a good breakfast selection, including eggs, croissants and porridge. *7am-1am* €€

Marenda Grill House: Aged steaks and traditional grills, including massive mixed platters for sharing, near the roundabout in Škaljari. *7am-11pm* €€€

Galion: Kotor's fanciest restaurant serves upmarket modern cuisine (especially seafood) in a romantic waterfront setting by the marina. *noon-11pm* €€€

BUDVA'S BEST BEACHES

Slovenska Plaža: Budva's heaving main beach stretches out for 1.6km. In summer, the promenade morphs into a bustling strip of fast-food outlets, bars and market stalls.

Pizana Beach: A marginally less chaotic small beach just to the north of the Old Town.

Ričardova Glava: 'Richard's Head' is a pretty little beach with the town walls as its backdrop, immediately south of the Old Town.

Mogren Beach: Beautiful, double-bayed Mogren is Budva's best beach. You can hardly see any buildings when you're lying on the fine pebbles here – a rare treat for the Budva Riviera.

Jaz Beach: The blue waters and broad sands of Jaz lie just off the highway, west of Budva.

Budva beach

shadeless slog to the top, and there's a hefty admission charge, but the views are glorious. When tackling the walls in summer, avoid the heat of the day and bring plenty of water with you.

The main entry point is near the **River Gate**. From here, there are 1350 steps and 1200m of path ahead of you. At a solid pace, it takes around 45 minutes to reach **St John's Castle** at the very top, built in the 15th century on the site of an ancient fortress.

Budva

TIME FROM CETINJE: **30MIN**

Budva is a place where history and beach culture collide. It's a photogenic walled town with ancient provenance, anchored on one end by a long sweep of beach that's jam-packed with thousands of holidaymakers in summer. Spreading back from the beach and gradually making its way up the surrounding slopes is a chaotic jumble of hotels and apartment blocks, with bigger, flashier ones being built all the time.

Explore the Old Town

Budva's Old Town has been settled for at least 2500 years, with the Venetians ruling the roost for nearly 400 of them. Within its 15th-century walls, it's as if time stopped in the Renaissance, and overdevelopment is but a troubling rumour. Hidden within the marbled lanes is the **Budva Museum** *(entry €3),* which does a great job of condensing the town's story into a concise narrative.

 EATING IN BUDVA: OUR PICKS

Konoba Bocun: Friendly little locals' tavern tucked away in a residential street, serving breakfast, sandwiches and traditional grills. *noon-8pm Mon-Sat* €€

Coco Bar, Food & Sea: Local-centric beach restaurant, and for good reason. Epic people watching, gorgeous views, beach playground for kids. *8am-11pm* €€

Konoba Portun: Charismatic Mićko doesn't believe in freezers – dishes at this stone-walled Stari Grad seafooder are determined by the daily catch. *2-11pm* €€€

Piano Nobile: Upmarket steak and burger bar in a beautiful Venetian building, spilling onto a little square. *1pm-1am* €€€

RUSLAN HARUTYUNOV/SHUTTERSTOCK

Inland Montenegro

MOUNTAINS | NATIONAL PARKS | HISTORIC CITIES

Away from the coast, nearly all of Montenegro is mountains, punctuated only by the occasional mirror-like lake and deep river canyon. The main exceptions to this are the plains around the nation's capital, Podgorica, spreading south to vast Lake Skadar.

Montenegro's statehood and cultural identity sprang from the slopes of Mt Lovćen, the mighty massif rising up above Kotor and Budva. It's here that the nation's origin story was formed – that of an indomitable warrior people holding strong while all around others fell to the Ottomans. The mountain's slopes of black beech trees give it a moody complexion, which bequeathed the nation its name: Crna Gora or 'Black Mountain' ('Monte Negro' in Italian).

The region's mountainous terrain lends itself to a large variety of outdoor pursuits, especially in its five national parks. But arguably the biggest thrill of all is to be found by simply driving around and enjoying the views.

Cetinje

TIME FROM BUDVA: **30MIN**

The capital of Montenegro until it was subsumed into the first incarnation of Yugoslavia in 1918, Cetinje (pronounced '*tse-tee-njeh*') is a refined, low-rise, pedestrian-friendly city filled with parks and elegant early-20th-century buildings. It sits in an idyllic green basin within the Lovćen massif, with craggy karstic peaks visible on every horizon.

With a population of 14,500, Cetinje is more like a large town than a city, but has more than its fair share of museums and galleries. Podgorica may be the nation's administrative capital, but Cetinje is the cultural capital.

Visit the royal palace

If you prefer to learn about history and culture by osmosis while poking around royal palaces and other heritage buildings, the **National Museum of Montenegro** (*Narodni muzej*

Places

GETTING AROUND

Podgorica is Montenegro's main transport hub, with good bus connections to all of its cities and major towns. A train line between Serbia and the coast stops at both Podgorica and Lake Skadar. Having a car will give you far more flexibility to explore the mountainous north, but be aware that some routes become snowbound in winter.

☑ TOP TIP

If you're planning to visit a few national parks, buy the annual pass *(€14; nparkovi. me/sections/1/online-tickets)*. Aside from Lovćen and Lake Skadar there are three parks in the north and east of the country.

Crne Gore; narodnimuzej.me; combined ticket adult/child €20/10) is for you.

The main attraction is the **Museum of King Nikola** *(adult/child €8/4)*. This maroon-coloured palace on the main square was built in 1871 and, while grand, it still manages to feel like the kind of place that a family could live in.

Lovćen National Park TIME FROM CETINJE: **10MIN**

Nature, views and architecture

Lovćen National Park *(nparkovi.me; entry €3)* is a 62-sq-km expanse taking in the peak of Mt Lovćen (1749m) and large tracts of forest crisscrossed with hiking paths and mountain-biking trails.

The park's cultural and architectural highlight is the **Njegoš Mausoleum** *(Njegošev mauzolej; narodnimuzej.me; entry adult/child €8/4),* which sits atop the massif's second-highest peak (1657m). Inside, under a golden mosaic canopy, a 28-tonne statue of national hero Petar II Petrović Njegoš rests in the wings of an eagle, carved from a single block of black granite by Ivan Meštrović.

Lovćen is more easily reached from Cetinje, but there's also an extraordinary 7km serpentine road connecting it to Kotor via 25 hairpin turns. The drive is thrilling and unsettling in equal measure, especially if you meet a large vehicle coming in the opposite direction.

Lake Skadar National Park TIME FROM CETINJE: **30MIN**

Birds, islands and water lilies

Shared between Montenegro and Albania, Lake Skadar is the largest lake in the Balkans. On the Montenegrin side, an area of 400 sq km was declared a national park in 1983, protecting one of the richest habitats for birdlife in Europe.

There's no better way to experience the lake than aboard a boat or kayak. The options are many and varied, depending on which kind of craft you prefer, your interests (birdwatching, island monasteries, ruined fortresses), where you launch from and the season. Whichever trip you choose, the scenery is guaranteed to be gorgeous.

It's easy to arrange a tour or hire a kayak from stalls in Virpazar, Vranjina and Rijeka Crnojevića. All of these are in the upper reaches of the lake, which is where you'll see the most water lilies. Recommended operators include **Golden Frog**

 EATING IN CETINJE: OUR PICKS

Polastičara Tara kod Sulja: Diner serving delicious *burek* (savoury pies) and sweet pastries. *7am-6pm Mon-Sat, to noon Sun, reduced hrs Nov-Apr* €

Verige: Food is prepared the traditional way, over wood and charcoal, in this hospitable roadside *pečenjara* (roastery). Cash only. *8am-11pm* €€

Kole: It serves omelettes and pasta, but the artery-clogging local specialities, served in giant portions, are the thing to try here. *7am-11pm* €€

Nacionalni Restoran Belveder: Traditional restaurant near Lipa Cave serving *ispod sača*–style meats (cooked under a dome covered with embers). *10am-10pm Easter-Nov* €€

Lake Skadar National Park

(*skadarlakecruise.com*), **Boat Milica** (*boatmilica.com*) and **Kingfisher** (*skadarlakeboatcruise.com*).

Undiscovered Montenegro (*undiscoveredmontenegro. com*) specialises in multi-day active itineraries, including kayaking and birdwatching cruises.

Ostrog Monastery

TIME FROM CETINJE: 1½HR

Montenegro's most revered religious site

There's something strangely affecting about **Ostrog Monastery** (*Manastir Ostrog; manastirostrog.com*). The setting is certainly part of it, positioned 900m above the verdant Zeta Valley and visible for miles around. Founded in 1665 within caves in a cliff face, the gleaming white **Upper Monastery** (*Gornji manastir*) gives the impression that it has grown out of the very rock.

Pilgrims queue to visit a tiny fresco-covered cave church that houses the fabric-wrapped remains of St Basil of Ostrog (Sv Vasilije Ostroški), the Serbian Orthodox bishop from Hercegovina who founded the monastery. Respectful tourists are welcome to join them.

PANORAMIC ROADS

You could argue that most of Montenegro's roads qualify for the title of 'panoramic route', but the National Tourist Organisation has officially designated four such routes and supported them with road signs, brochures and, for two of them (Durmitor and Korita), on-the-road audio guides. The 76km **Durmitorski prsten** (Durmitor Ring; route 2) circles through the mountains from Žabljak, visiting villages that are completely cut off by snow for months on end. It's well worth taking the suggested detour to Ćurevac (1625m) for exceptional Tara Canyon views. The other routes are the 800km **Kruna Crne Gore** (Crown of Montenegro; route 1), the 283km **More i visine** (Sea and Heights; route 3) and the 65km **Krug oko Korita** (Circuit around Korita; route 4).

 EATING AROUND LAKE SKADAR: OUR PICKS

Poslednja Luka Fr:iendly spot above the Crnojević River offering a short but delicious menu of lake fish and other local produce. *11am-8pm Tue-Sun* €

Stari Most: Freshwater fish experts (especially eel, trout and carp), located on Rijeka Crnojevića's riverside promenade. *11am-7pm* €€

Konoba Demidžana: Upmarket restaurant by the water in Virpazar showcasing traditional fish dishes and grilled meat. *8am-11pm* €€

Restoran Jezero: By the park office in Vranjina, serving tasty freshwater fish dishes and meaty grills on a lovely lakeside terrace. *8am-10pm* €€

Places We Love to Stay

€ Budget €€ Midrange €€€ Top End

Perast

Apartments Gudco €€
Two spacious, stone-walled apartments above a centuries-old family house. They're not flash but they have laundry facilities, dishwashers and million-dollar views.

Hotel Conte €€€ Not so much a regular hotel as a series of deluxe apartments in neighbouring heritage buildings.

Kotor

Montenegro Hostel 4U €
Buzzy party hostel in Dobrota with fun-loving staff who somehow manage to keep the place clean.

Old Town Hostel €€
Sympathetic renovations have converted this 13th-century palazzo into one of the best hostels in the country. Private rooms available.

Apartments Wine House €€
Cosy stone-walled apartments (three studios, one two-bedroom) offering a warm welcome in the heart of the Old Town.

Vila Panonija €€ Old stone house in Dobrota converted into a pleasant little hotel – or is it a large guesthouse?

Palazzo Radomiri €€€ A honey-coloured early-18th-century palazzo on the Dobrota waterfront transformed into a first-rate boutique hotel.

Hotel Astoria €€€ The decor straddles the line between fantastic and fantastical, but the rooms are luxurious and the Old Town location can't be beaten.

Hotel Vardar €€€ This lovely Old Town hotel is elegantly furnished with modern decor, offering glamour without the kitschy glitz.

Budva

Freedom Hostel € Beloved, sociable hostel with a small courtyard and tidy little rooms scattered between three buildings.

Sailor House €€ Centuries-old Stari Grad house with welcoming hosts, nicely decorated bedrooms and a guest kitchen.

Stella di Mare €€ Friendly staff, tidy rooms with balconies, and far more reasonable rates (doubles from €85) than neighbouring Bečići resorts.

Hotel Kadmo €€€ Hotel in a quieter block near the bus station, with spacious rooms, roof terrace and pool.

Hotel Budva €€€ Elegant hotel with a spa centre, a swimming pool and a waterfront location that's tough to beat.

Villa M Palace €€€ There's a seductive glamour to this modern block of luxurious apartments near the Stari Grad.

Cetinje

Hotel Dapčević € This unpretentious, family-run hotel is a short stroll from all of the sights. Rooms are spacious, clean and comfortable.

Casa Calda € A cluster of attractive and thoughtfully equipped apartments set behind a family home with a large lawn.

La Vecchia Casa € This period house captures the essence of old Cetinje. There's a tranquil rear garden and the rooms are full of antiques.

Gradska Cetinje €€€ The fanciest option in Cetinje is this new hotel occupying a converted mansion next to King Nikola's Palace.

Lake Skadar National Park

Villa Miela Lake Retreat €€
A beautifully restored and stylishly furnished traditional house near Virpazar, with a pool, a communal kitchen and tranquil views.

Hotel De'Andros €€€ Right in the heart of Virpazar, this recent remodelling of a Yugoslav-era hotel has sacrificed period features for comfort and contemporary style.

Ostrog Monastery

Ostrog Monastery Guesthouse € This simple guesthouse near Ostrog's Lower Monastery offers tidy single-sex dorm rooms. It's designed for pilgrims; expect to be woken early.

Hotel Sokoline €€€ Perched near Ostrog Monastery, this roadside hotel has upmarket rooms, extraordinary views and a rooftop restaurant.

Practicalities

LGBTIQ+ Travellers
Montenegrin society is conservative, and life for local LGBTIQ+ people can be extremely difficult. That said, travellers are unlikely to encounter problems, but only if they're willing and able to be reasonably discreet.

Accessible Travel
There are few provisions for travellers with disabilities in Montenegro. The mobility-impaired will find the cobbled lanes and steps challenging. It's common in Montenegro for cars to park on footpaths (presuming there is a footpath), making things exceptionally difficult for wheelchair users.

Smoking
Smoking is banned in most indoor public spaces, although not everyone follows the rule. The ban includes public transport, hotel lobbies, restaurants, bars and clubs, but not casinos. Smoking on the terraces of bars and restaurants is allowed, and smoke inevitably wafts inside.

Health
Travel insurance isn't legally required to visit Montenegro, but it is strongly advised. Tap water is generally drinkable, but there can sometimes be problems in summer. If you're unsure, ask.

KIRK FISHER/SHUTTERSTOCK

Clock tower, Kotor (p793)

Opening Hours
You'll soon realise that most Montenegrins have an extremely flexible approach to opening hours, and these can vary throughout the year, especially in tourist areas. Most shops close on Sunday. Some museums close on Monday, or for the whole weekend in winter.

Safe Travel
Safety standards can be lax in Montenegro, and tourists have died in avoidable rafting, ziplining and jet-ski accidents. Be wary when booking activities – cheapest isn't always best. When choosing an operator, ask around and check online reviews. When rafting, make sure you're given a functioning helmet and life jacket. Don't go canyoning in bad weather.

Bars, Cafes & Restaurants
In cafes and bars, take a seat and wait to be served. Whether you're in a restaurant or a bar, keep note of your waiter, as they're responsible for taking all your orders and settling the bill. When the waiter delivers your order, they'll drop the *račun* (bill) into a little glass on the table.

Language

The official language of Montenegro is Montenegrin, but other languages used in the country include Albanian, Bosnian, Croatian and Serbian.

Basics

Hello. Zdravo. *zdra*·vo
Goodbye. Doviđenja. do·vi·*je*·nya
Yes. Da. da
No. Ne. ne
Please. Molim. *mo*·leem
Thank you. Hvala. *hva*·la
Excuse me. Oprostite. o·*pro*·stee·te
Sorry. Žao mi je. *zha*·o mee ye
What's your name?
Kako se zovete /zoveš? (pol/inf)
ka·ko se zo·ve·te/zo·vesh

My name is ... Zovem se ...
zo·vem se...

Do you speak English? Govorite
li engleski? go·vo·ree·te lee
en·gle·skee

I don't understand. Ne razumijem.
ne ra·*zoo*·mee·yem

Directions

Where's...? Gdje je...? gdye ye...
What's the address?
Koja je adresa? *ko*·ya ye a·*dre*·sa
Can you show me (on the map)?
Možete li da mi pokažete (na mapi)?
mo·zhe·te lee da mee *po*·ka·zhe·te
(na *ma*·pee)

Signs

Ulaz Entrance
Izlaz Exit
Toaleti/WC Toilets
Muški Men
Ženski Women
Otvoreno Open
Zatvoreno Closed
Zabranjeno Prohibited

Time

What time is it? Koliko je sati?
ko·*lee*·ko ye *sa*·tee
It's (10) o'clock. (Deset) je sati.
(*de*·set) ye *sa*·tee
Half past (10). (Deset) i po.
(*de*·set) ee po
morning jutro *yoo*·tro
afternoon poslijepodne
po·slee·ye·*pod*·ne
evening veče *ve*·che
yesterday juče *yoo*·che
today danas *da*·nas
tomorrow sutra *soo*·tra

Emergencies

Help! Upomoć! *oo*·po·moch
Leave me alone! Ostavite me na
miru! o·sta·vee·te me na *mee*·roo
I'm ill. Ja sam bolestan/bolesna.
(m/f) ya sam *bo*·le·stan/*bo*·le·sna
Call a doctor! Zovite ljekara!
zo·vee·te lye·*ka*·ra
Call the police! Zovite policiju!
zo·vee·te po·*lee*·tsee·yoo

Eating & Drinking

What would you recommend?
Šta biste preporučili? shta *bee*·ste
pre·po·*roo*·chee·lee
That was delicious.
To je bilo izvrsno. to ye *bee*·lo
eez·vr·sno
Please bring the menu/bill.
Molim vas donesite jelovnik/
račun. *mo*·leem vas do·*ne*·see·te
ye·lov·neek/*ra*·choon

NUMBERS

1
jedan
ye·dan

2
dva *dva*

3
tri *tree*

4
četiri
che·tee·ree

5
pet *pet*

6
šest *shest*

7
sedam
se·dam

8
osam *o*·sam

9
devet *de*·vet

10
deset *de*·set

Road above Bay of Kotor (p793)

MONEY
Currency: Euro (€)

CREDIT CARDS & DIGITAL PAYMENTS
Credit cards are widely accepted, but not always at cafes, bars, kiosks and museums. Places that accept credit cards are also likely to accept digital payments. Don't rely on either as your only option.

CASH
It pays to have coins and small notes when paying for coffee and small purchases. ATMs dispense large notes.

TIPPING
Tipping isn't expected but is appreciated. In cafes, bars and taxis, round up to the nearest euro. For guides and waiters, leave up to 10% (in cash), but only if you're completely satisfied with the service. If not, don't feel obliged to leave anything. Tipping in hotels is unusual.

Arriving & Getting Around

Montenegro has two international airports – Tivat and Podgorica – and a de facto third in Croatia (Dubrovnik Airport), just 17km from the border. Ferries arrive from Italy and Croatia in summer.

Buses
The local bus network is extensive and reliable. Intercity buses are usually comfortable and air-conditioned. Stations display the bus timetables prominently, and staff are on hand to help out. Visit *busticket4.me* for timetables and tickets.

Parking
Many municipalities have replaced meters with app-based payment, which makes things tricky if you don't have a phone with internet connection. However, most towns also have designated parking lots where you can pay in cash.

Car Hire
Cars can be hired from airports and larger towns. Cowboy operators are rife. If the online price seems cheap, expect to be hit with a hefty insurance surcharge. Take photos of any pre-existing damage.

Entry Points
Montenegro has land borders with Croatia, Bosnia and Hercegovina, Serbia, Kosovo and Albania. At the crossing you'll need to present your vehicle registration documents and a locally valid insurance policy such as a European Green Card. Check that your policy covers Montenegro. Tivat and Podgorica airports are small and facilities are limited, but both have free wi-fi, ATMs, taxi stands and rental-car desks.

For places to stay in Netherlands, see p825

OLENA ZN/SHUTTERSTOCK

Above: Utrecht (p820); Right: Windmill, Kinderdijk (p816)

Curated by
Barbara Woolsey

Netherlands

CYCLING, CANALS AND DUTCH COURAGE

The old Dutch expression 'Just act normal – that's crazy enough' perfectly encapsulates travelling in the Netherlands. In these parts, the best pleasures are often simple and free.

Grounding, carefree moments are the highlight of Netherlands travel. Gone are the days of 'Golden Age' maximalism; today's Dutch culture is all about enjoying life's little things.

There's no end to the simple pleasures that can be savoured here, from activities (hiking parks and forests, picnicking along shorelines) to open-air sightseeing. The richest moments are most freely given on the Netherlands' 32,000km cycling network spanning multiple gears – from exploring long-distance 'cycling motorways' to leisurely pedal-pushing along canals. Across fabulously pancake-flat, scenic landscapes, urban centres become delightfully rural. Dykes, canals, rivers and coastal shore all beckon for discovery. As the Dutch like to say, 'cycling is freedom'.

Tradition and innovation intertwine across centuries-old windmills, tulip fields and visionary contemporary architecture. From Amsterdam to Delft and over to Den Haag, cities mean open-air museums featuring sculptures, street art and settings immortalised on Dutch Masters' canvasses (of course, the art legacy of Rembrandt, Vermeer, Van Gogh and Mondrian make traditional sightseeing in museums mighty fine, too). Some two-thirds of the Netherlands is agricultural across beautiful rainbow fields of crocuses, daffodils, hyacinths and tulips that burst into flower from March until May. The kaleidoscope of colour is nothing short of psychedelic, making anyone a believer that wanderlust is not about destinations but the journey itself.

LOIS GOBE/SHUTTERSTOCK

THE MAIN AREAS

AMSTERDAM
Seventeenth-century tradition, inspiring innovation. **p808**

SOUTH HOLLAND
Smaller cities, quirky and quaint. **p815**

UTRECHT
Canal-side cafes and boutiques. **p819**

MAASTRICHT
Roman history and pub-hopping. **p822**

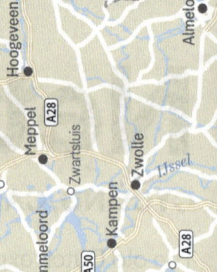

BICYCLE

Dedicated bike routes go virtually everywhere – in fact, most Dutch towns are blanketed with nicely paved paths. The Netherlands' extremely bicycle-friendly culture includes abundant parking facilities and two-wheeler train compartments. Most destinations are usually only a one- to two-hour route from each other.

TRAIN

Dutch trains are efficient, fast and comfortable. Service is frequent and regular across domestic destinations – sometimes five or six times an hour. It's an excellent system and possibly all you'll need to get yourself (and even your bicycle) anywhere in the country.

CAR

Dutch freeways are extensive but congestion-prone. Those around Amsterdam are especially known for rush-hour jams. Smaller roads are well maintained, but wide bike lanes, speed bumps and frequent construction can make driving less than fun.

Amsterdam, p808

On every traveller's bucket list with good reason, the Dutch capital has more canals than Venice and world-class museums immortalising artists from Rembrandt to Van Gogh.

Find Your Way

The Netherlands is compact and well connected. The journey from Groningen (the northernmost major city) to Maastricht (southernmost) is about 300km and only takes 3½ hours by high-speed train or car (traffic depending).

Utrecht, p819
Known for unique two-storey canals, Utrecht vaunts Amsterdam vibes minus crowds. Explore cavernous bars in medieval warehouses and the subterranean archaeology.

Maastricht, p822
Brimming with joie de vivre, the Netherlands' second-oldest yet least Dutch city has Roman and Romanesque heritage, tunnels and – yes – hills.

South Holland, p815
Smaller cities (including Rotterdam and Den Haag) promise offbeat architecture, canvass-worthy canals and peaceful palaces in close succession.

805

Plan Your Time

There are no domestic flights within the Netherlands, but you'll find out quickly that doesn't matter – most cross-country journeys are so short, you'll be in a new city before the next mealtime.

TONYV3112/SHUTTERSTOCK

Rijksmuseum (p809), Amsterdam

Around the Capital in Three Days

● Spend your first day in **Amsterdam** (p808) wandering around the city, starting on the historic Dam square and admiring the **Royal Palace** (p814), then strolling the **Medieval Centre** (p814).

● On the second day, hit **Rembrandthuis** (p814) before viewing the artist's masterpiece *The Night Watch* at the **Rijksmuseum** (p809). The unmissable **Van Gogh Museum** (p809) is nearby. Visit the **Anne Frank Huis** (p812), take a **canal cruise** (p813) and settle into a cosy canal-side **bruin café** (p813).

● Ease into the final day's hours cycling around **Vondelpark** (p809). Afterwards, grab lunch at **De Hallen** (p809). Shop along the **Negen Straatjes** (p814), then cross the IJ and go up **A'DAM Tower** (p812) for sundown.

SEASONAL HIGHLIGHTS

Any time is prime to visit – and it probably isn't even during tulip season. An eclectic, countrywide calendar of events delivers lively vibes year-round.

JANUARY
On **Nationale Tulpendag** (National Tulip Day; third Saturday of January; p809), tulip season kicks off in Amsterdam with some 200,000 tulips bursting on Museumplein.

MARCH
If the weather complies, you can get a jump-start on **bulbfield viewing** in March, and since it's still off-peak season, you won't have to fight the crowds to enjoy them.

APRIL
Dutch festival season kicks off on **King's Day** (27 April) with the biggest – and possibly the best – cross-country street party in Europe.

A Week of Greatest Hits

● In a week, you can cover the Netherlands' most iconic sightseeing. The 'hit list' starts with a couple of days in the capital **Amsterdam** (p808), where you can enjoy the world-class museums, cycle around Vondelpark and hang out in cosy cafes.

● Next, move on to **Den Haag** (p816), the seat of Dutch government, and make day trips to **Delft** (p818), Vermeer's hometown, and the world's largest flower garden in **Lisse** (p818) when the season's right.

● Spend the remaining couple of days based in **Rotterdam** (p815) to explore modern architecture and urban port living. Ride a waterbus to see windmills on a day trip to **Kinderdijk** (p816).

Cities Circuit in a Week

● Amsterdam may be the Netherlands' famous city, but spend a week discovering pint-sized urban centres by train and you'll probably find a new favourite. For starters, spend two days in **Amsterdam** (p808) powering through world-class museums and historic neighbourhoods.

● Then it's onwards to **Utrecht** (p819), an even better canal city, where you can discover medieval and Roman history. The next morning, head to **Den Haag** (p816) and explore **Mauritshuis** (p816).

● Board a train to nearby **Rotterdam** (p815) for street art and modern architecture, then continue in the same day (or the next) to **Maastricht** (p822). Here, big-city energy (only a sixth of Amsterdam's size) spans sophisticated dining and student-friendly nightlife.

MAY	JUNE	AUGUST	DECEMBER
On the second Saturday (and Sunday) in May, 600 **windmills** around the country unfurl their sails and welcome the public inside. Look for windmills flying a blue pennant.	Summer peak season promises long days and good weather. Dutch living goes outdoors, from **bicycle rides** to canal-side patio gatherings.	In late August, Maastricht's central square hosts the 'largest open-air restaurant in the world' during the **Preuvenemint** (p822) food festival.	Winter magic blankets the Netherlands (as, some years, does snow), **ice-skating** rinks set up in open spaces, and **Christmas markets** sparkle.

Amsterdam

HISTORIC CANALS | WORLD-CLASS MUSEUMS | ECLECTIC SHOPPING

☑ TOP TIP

If you'll be taking public transport often, the Amsterdam Travel Card and Amsterdam & Region Travel Ticket *(gvb.nl)* can save euros. Buying tickets at machines you'll pay €1.50 surcharge per paper ticket. Contactless checking in/out by card or phone (fixed rate charged as one transaction daily; no registration required) is wiser.

Canals lined by tilting gabled buildings are the backdrop for Amsterdam's treasure-packed museums, vintage shops and hyper-creative drinking, dining and design scenes. Amsterdam's canal-woven core is laced by atmospheric narrow lanes. You never know what you'll find: a tiny hidden garden; a boutique selling Dutch-designed homewares and fashion; a jewel-box-like *jenever* (Dutch gin) distillery; a flower stall filled with tulips in a rainbow of hues; an old monastery turned classical-music venue; or an ultra-niche sustainable restaurant or one reinventing age-old Dutch classics. Fringing the centre, postindustrial buildings in up-and-coming neighbourhoods house endless creative enterprises.

You can't walk a kilometre without bumping into a masterpiece. The Van Gogh Museum has the world's largest collection by the tortured artist. A few blocks away, Vermeer, Rembrandt and more star at the glorious Rijksmuseum. After exploring museums, there's no better spot to relax than Amsterdam's abounding *bruin cafés* (traditional pubs).

◈ GETTING AROUND

Navigating Amsterdam's central canal ring, it helps to remember that the major canals all run in a horseshoe-shaped loop, in alphabetical order. (The only exception is the Singel Canal forming the innermost ring.)

Cycling offers a relaxing and sustainable way to access parks and less touristy neighbourhoods. Bike-hire shops are everywhere (around €15 per day). Ride on redasphalt bike lanes, not pedestrian footpaths.

Amsterdam's public transport is run by GVB. Download its app for a journey planner *(9292.nl)* and live transport updates including crowd estimates. Most public transport routes converge at Amsterdam Centraal Station, including ferries to Noord.

Metro is mostly used by suburban commuters though line M52 conveniently runs from Amsterdam Noord via Centraal Station, Dam, the Southern Canal Ring and De Pijp.

Vondelpark & the South

Amsterdam's 'backyard'

Vondelpark's *(hetvondelpark.net)* 47 hectares of lawns, roses, sculptures, fountains, ponds and winding paths are made for sunny days. On the northern side, cafes, restaurants, shops and bars line Overtoom and surrounding streets, blending into the up-and-coming Oud West area; luxury boutiques and eateries grace leafy streets to the south.

World-renowned art museum

Resembling a castle, the **Rijksmuseum** *(rijksmuseum.nl; adult/child €25/free),* one of the world's most magnificent museums, fittingly showcases the Netherlands' richest collection of art. Masterpieces by the nation's greatest talent, such as Rembrandt (including *The Night Watch*), Vermeer *(The Milkmaid)* and Van Gogh *(Self-Portrait;* 1889), are displayed alongside some 8000 other treasures across 1.5km of gallery space.

Hang out at Museumplein

Amsterdam's most famous museums – the Rijksmuseum, Van Gogh Museum and **Stedelijk Museum** *(stedelijk.nl; adult/child €22.50/free)* – cluster around **Museumplein**, a vast public square where picnics abound in warm weather. Additional recreational facilities include a playground, skatepark and seasonal ice rink. Markets, concerts, festivals and more happen year-round.

World's greatest Van Gogh collection

The world-famous **Van Gogh Museum** *(vangoghmuseum. nl; adult/child €24/free, audio guide €3.75/2)* still manages to feel personal and intimate. The extensive collection of 200 paintings and 500 drawings by Vincent and contemporaries, including Gauguin and Monet, also holds over 800 handwritten letters, mainly between Vincent and his brother, as well as with Gauguin and Émile Bernard. Hear recordings at multiple listening stations.

Food and cultural hub

Cavernous red-brick sheds for servicing trams are now home to a food hall and cultural complex electrifying the Oud-West area north of Vondelpark. **De Hallen** *(dehallen-amsterdam. nl)* incorporates sustainable Dutch design boutiques, galleries, a cinema and the skylit **Foodhallen** *(foodhallen.nl).*

continued on p812

BEST MUSEUMPLEIN FESTIVITIES

Nationale Tulpendag: National Tulip Day (the third Saturday in January) sees Museumplein carpeted with 200,000 tulips, with a *dweilorkest* (traditional brass band) and a free pick-your-own bouquet.

Bevrijdingsdag: Dancing takes place on Liberation Day (5 May) as it did after Amsterdam's WWII liberation.

Keti Koti: Following the commemoration in Oosterpark, the 1863 abolition of slavery in Suriname and the Netherlands Antilles is vibrantly celebrated on 1 July.

Christmas Markets: Museumplein turns into a magical village with craft stalls and mulled wine from mid- to late December.

New Year's Eve: On 31 December, family-friendly electric fireworks at 6.45pm are followed by major celebrations from 10.30pm to the Netherlands' biggest fireworks display.

 EATING IN VONDELPARK, OUD-WEST & OUD-ZUID: CLASSIC DUTCH

Visque Winkel:	**Friet Boutique:**	**Lunchroom Grannies:**	**Hap Hmm:** Comfort food
Fishmonger with ready-to-eat *kibbeling* (fried fish pieces), smoked eel and herring. *noon-6pm Mon, 8am-6pm Tue-Fri, 9am-5pm Sat* €	Deep-fried goodness: crispy fries (with sauces), *bitterballen* (meat croquettes) and cheese-filled *krokketten*. *noon-10pm* €	Dutch breakfast favourites and lunch options including *limburgse stoof* (beef stew). *9am-5pm Wed-Sun* €	since 1935, from meatballs to chicken casserole, schnitzel, and pancakes or rhubarb pudding. *5-9.15pm Mon-Fri* €€

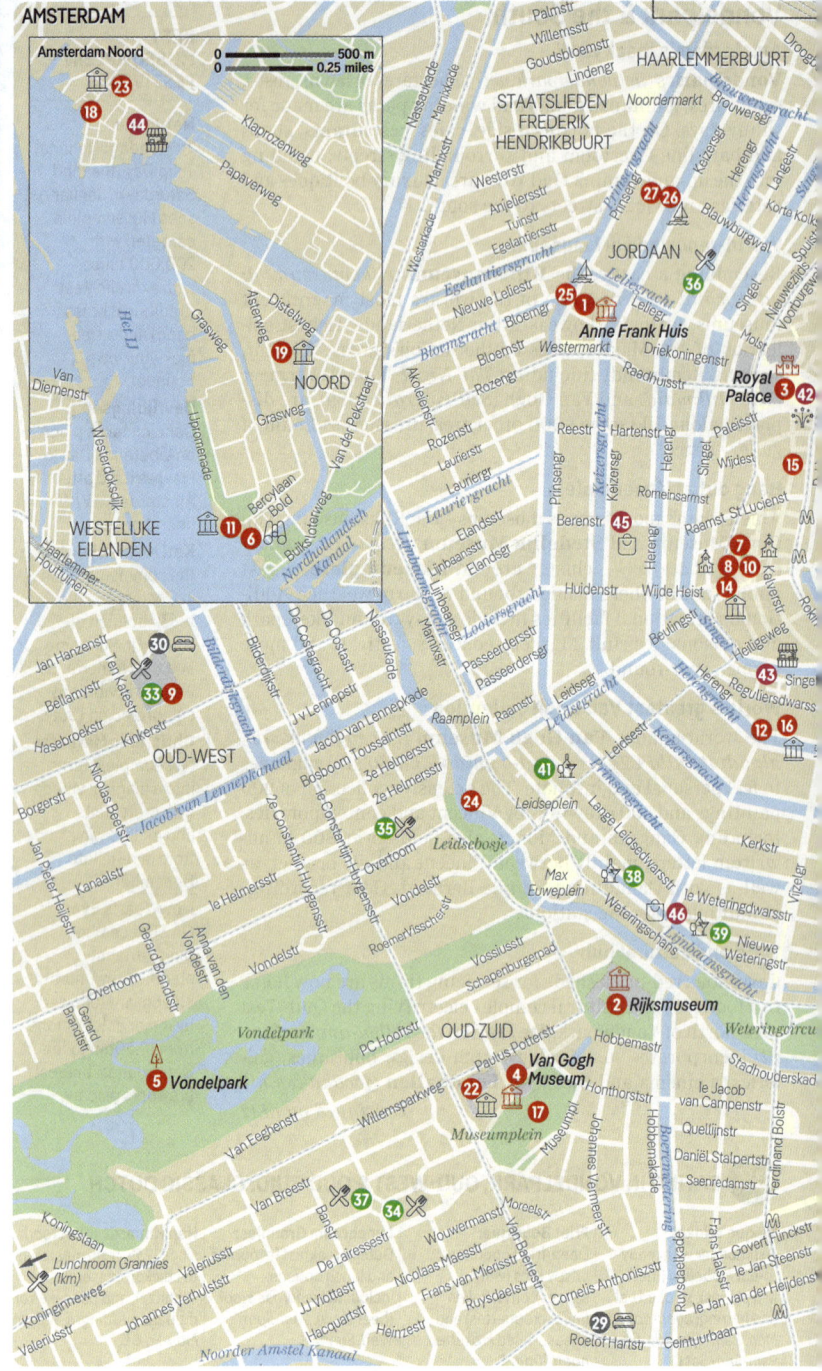

AMSTERDAM

Amsterdam Noord

0   500 m
0   0.25 miles

Het IJ

NOORD

WESTELIJKE
EILANDEN

HAARLEMMERBUURT

STAATSLIEDEN
FREDERIK
HENDRIKBUURT

Noordermarkt

JORDAAN

Anne Frank Huis
Westermarkt

Royal
Palace

OUD-WEST

Leidseplein

Leidsebosje

Max
Euweplein

Rijksmuseum

OUD ZUID

Van Gogh
Museum

Vondelpark

Museumplein

Lunchroom Grannies
(1km)

Noorder Amstel Kanaal

See Amsterdam Noord Inset

HIGHLIGHTS
1. Anne Frank Huis
2. Rijksmuseum
3. Royal Palace
4. Van Gogh Museum
5. Vondelpark

SIGHTS
6. A'DAM Tower
7. Begijnhof
8. Begijnhof Kapel
9. De Hallen
10. Engelse Kerk
11. Eye Filmmuseum
12. Golden Bend
13. H'ART
14. Houten Huis
15. Kalverstraat
16. Kattenkabinet
17. Museumplein
18. NDSM
19. NXT Museum
20. Oude Kerk
21. Rembrandthuis
22. Stedelijk Museum
23. Straat

ACTIVITIES
24. Kayak in Amsterdam
25. KINboat
26. Pure Boats
27. Those Dam Boat Guys

SLEEPING
28. art'otel amsterdam
29. College Hotel
30. Hotel De Hallen
31. Hotel The Exchange
32. St Christopher's at the Winston

EATING
33. Foodhallen
34. Friet Boutique
35. Hap Hmm
36. Miss G's Brunch Boat
37. Visque Winkel

DRINKING & NIGHTLIFE
38. Café de Spuyt
39. Café de Wetering
40. Café Schiller
41. Eijlders

ENTERTAINMENT
42. Nationale Tulpendag

SHOPPING
43. Bloemenmarkt
44. IJ Hallen
45. Negen Straatjes
46. Spiegelkwartier

continued from p809

Foodhallen's airy, open-plan communal dining area holds vendors cooking everything from Mumbai street food to Dutch meatballs.

Western Canal Ring, Jordaan & the West

Diary of a young girl

The **Anne Frank Huis** (*annefrank.org; adult/child €16/7, incl introductory program €23/14*) is a heartbreaking and profoundly significant place. This is where young Jewish girl Anne kept a diary while she and her family lived in hiding from the Nazis until they were betrayed and deported. Beyond the bookcase, entering the annexe's stark former living quarters steps back into 1942. Anne's pictures of Hollywood stars and Dutch royals remain on her bedroom walls. The museum also displays Anne's original red-checked diary.

Tickets must be pre-purchased online well in advance.

Amsterdam Noord

Algorithmic beauty

NXT Museum (*nxtmuseum.com; adult/child from €19.50/13.50*) is a media-art nirvana where technology electrifies creative expression. Across the 1400-sq-metre warehouse space, immersive exhibitions explore technology themes shaping the digital future. From robotics to facial recognition, displays represent collaborations between artists, scientists, sound engineers and coders.

Colossal urban canvases

Follow Noord's graffiti murals into the world's largest museum for street art, **Straat** (*straatmuseum.com; adult/child €19.50/free*). More than 150 works created on-site are spread across an 8000-sq-metre converted warehouse. Poke around art and historical info beside artists spraying and stringing up new installations. Guided tours and graffiti workshops are available.

Sky-high swings

The imposing waterfront **A'DAM Tower** (*adamlookout.com; lookout adult/child €16.50/10.50*), once corporate offices, is now an entertainment extravaganza. On its 100m-high rooftop, there's a 360-degree viewing platform and giant six-person swing – Europe's highest (*€7.50 per person*). On other levels, find a swish panoramic bar, a revolving restaurant and an excellent basement nightclub.

Motion pictures in focus

In a flying-saucer-shaped building, **Eye Filmmuseum** (*eye film.nl; exhibitions adult/child €21/free*) takes you deep into the magic of motion pictures. The permanent exhibition, 'What Is Film?', includes displays of early cameras and interactive elements with green screens and animation. Catch a classic or blockbuster in state-of-the-art cinemas (separate ticket); showings sometimes have a live music accompaniment.

'SEARCH & RESCUE' AREA

Separated from Amsterdam by the IJ River, Noord can feel a world away from the city centre's canals and crooked buildings. Gone are the days of geographic divide, when Noord was a largely industrial entity for maritime workers. Today, it's Amsterdam's fastest-growing neighbourhood, with housing and construction expected to double the residential landscape by 2050.

Noord's maritime heritage dates back to the 1600s. When shipbuilding declined in the 1980s, industrial landscapes were marooned. Squatters and artists salvaged derelict warehouses; fast forward 20 years and Noord is the 'place to be'. What the area continues to lose in quaint waterfront, it makes up for in edgy excitement. Still, you don't have to go far upstream to reach the countryside.

NDSM

Shipyard, squatters and street art

The **NDSM** *(ndsm.nl; free)* former shipbuilding yard fell into disuse from the 1980s before squatters arrived. Today, it has numerous cool waterside restaurants, striking architecture, a hangar full of artists' studios and the monthly **IJ Hallen** flea market (Europe's largest).

Oosterpark & East of the Amstel

Revisiting colonial footsteps

The Dutch slave trade, understanding cultural appropriation, and returning stolen artefacts back to Indonesia – at the **Wereldmuseum Amsterdam** *(amsterdam.wereldmuseum. nl; adult/child €18/7.50)*, themes around race, ethnicity and identity are explored. The permanent exhibition 'Our Colonial Inheritance' is a profound, comprehensive inspection of Dutch colonial legacy and part of the ethnographic museum's greater vision to address its past.

Southern Canal Ring

Strolling the Flower Market

The famous **Bloemenmarkt** (Flower Market), established in 1860, was where vendors sailed up the Amstel for blooming business. The market is no longer floating (now on piles), but you'll find real tulips here in season and bulbs sold year-round.

BEST CANAL CRUISES AROUND THE WEST

Pure Boats: Boutique operator with beautiful small boats; options include daytime 'highlights' trips (with apple pie) or enchanting evening trips (with cheese platters).

Those Dam Boat Guys: Laid-back trips lasting 90 minutes come with entertaining, irreverent commentary; BYO refreshments.

Miss G's Brunch Boat: Combines 90-minute weekend cruises with brunches, beats and Bloody Marys.

KINboat: Solar-powered boats depart from KINboat's Prinsengracht dock, with drinks (like hot chocolate or mulled wine) and snacks sold on board.

Kayak in Amsterdam: Get even closer to the water on guided paddling excursions, including a one-hour Around Jordaan tour passing landmarks like the Westerkerk.

 DRINKING IN THE SOUTHERN CANAL RING: BRUIN CAFÉS

Café de Spuyt: Mellow stop amid the hubbub off Leidseplein, with a menu of 150-plus Dutch and Belgian beers. *4pm-3am Mon-Thu, 3pm-4am Fri & Sat*

Café de Wetering: Sip or snack in an interior that wouldn't look out of place in a Vermeer painting. *4pm-1am Mon-Thu, to 3am Fri, 3pm-2am Sat, to 1am Sun*

Café Schiller: Sit down among portraits of Dutch actors and cabaret artists, painted by the former owner. *3pm-1am Mon-Thu, 12.30pm-3am Fri & Sat, to 1am Sun*

Eijlders: A WWII-era meeting place for artists who resisted toeing the Nazis' cultural line. It gets noisier at night. *4.30pm-1am Mon-Thu, noon-2am Fri & Sat, to 1am Sun*

BEST SHOPPING AREAS

Negen Straatjes:
A grid of nine little streets packed with tiny, specialised boutiques. Numerous fashion designers have flagship stores here.

Kalverstraat:
Shoppers work themselves up to fever pitch over the latest sales at high-street chain stores here. Budget snack shops abound.

Spiegelkwartier:
The 'art and antiques' district is packed with bitty contemporary galleries and vintage shops for treasure hunting.

Haarlemmerbuurt:
Long thoroughfare lined with independent food and fashion boutiques with an increasingly sustainable focus.

IJ Hallen: Europe's largest flea market is held monthly over a weekend. Over 750 stalls offer everything from vinyl to vintage clothing.

Around the Golden Bend

The **Golden Bend** (Gouden Bocht), a 500m stretch of 17th-century buildings, is a UNESCO World Heritage Site. Buildings are now private businesses; the eccentric **Kattenkabinet** (*kattenkabinet.nl; adult/child €12.50/free),* a feline-art museum, is publicly accessible.

Amsterdam's resilient H'ART

Once the satellite home of St Petersburg's State Hermitage Museum, this art museum rebranded as **H'ART** (*hartmus eum.nl; adult/child €38.50/free)* in the wake of the Russian invasion of Ukraine. Changing temporary exhibitions are loaned from prestigious partner institutions such as the Smithsonian and British Museum.

Nieuwmarkt

Rembrandt's former home and studio

In the 1606 canal house where Rembrandt once lived and worked, **Rembrandthuis** (*rembrandthuis.nl; adult/child €21.50/8)* makes for an insightful visit. Multimedia-guided visits go from kitchen to a showroom of paintings and sculptures. Rembrandt's painting studio is a serious highlight.

Medieval Centre & Red Light District

Amsterdam's oldest church

Beside the Red Light District, you'll find Amsterdam's **Oude Kerk** (*Old Church; oudekerk.nl; adult/child €13.50/3.50).* Worn tombstones set in the church's floor mark numerous famous Amsterdammers, including Rembrandt's wife, Saskia van Uylenburgh. Services, concerts and contemporary art exhibitions take place here. Climb the 164 steps on a guided tour up the 67m-high church tower for sweeping roofline views.

Religious and residential courtyard sanctuary

The 14th-century **Begijnhof** (*begijnhofkapelamsterdam.nl; free),* an enclosed former convent, comprises tiny houses and postage-stamp gardens in a scenic courtyard. The grounds keep the 1671-built **Begijnhof Kapel** (*begijnhofkapelam sterdam.nl),* the medieval **Engelse Kerk** (*erc.amsterdam)* and **Houten Huis** (the country's oldest preserved wooden house). As this is a residential area, loud talking and mobile phone noises are frowned upon.

A resplendent palace

Located on the historic Dam square, the **Royal Palace** (*paleis amsterdam.nl; adult/child €10/free)* began life as a glorified town hall. Napoleon's brother moved in during the French occupation, and now the Dutch king performs ceremonial duties here. Book online to ensure it's not closed for a royal event.

South Holland

URBAN ART | ARCHITECTURE | MARITIME CULTURE

Home to two of the Netherlands' major cities – Rotterdam and Den Haag – and many of its most traditionally pretty and historic towns, Zuid-Holland (South Holland) deserves kudos. Despite the region's popularity, its small urban centres keep true to their authentic flair and sincere hospitality.

Traversing from coast to midland, South Holland features vibrant landscapes and local life, pedalling past windmills (Kinderdijk), tulip-stuffed fields (Lisse), stately palaces (Den Haag) and masterpiece-worthy canals (Delft). Rotterdam, the second-largest Dutch city and home to Europe's largest port, moonlights as an open-air gallery. Crazily angled cube houses, pop art protruding from office buildings and lots of naughty sculptures accentuate modern architecture and urban art, transforming the city after WWII destruction. As you cycle between canal-crossed cities (distances are short, usually an hour or two), you get to know a multipack of memorable settings and landmarks from charming and quaint to wonderfully eccentric. South Holland's mixed bag is anything but ordinary.

☑ **TOP TIP**

Taking photos of South Holland's harbours is essential, but do so mindfully. The decks of beautiful historic barges may seem inviting, but some are residents' doorsteps. Before you strike a pose, observe signs saying 'Private. No entry unless invited'. Respect the folks living on them by knocking and asking first.

Rotterdam

Chock-a-block buildings

Perched high above the roads and intricately intertwined, Rotterdam's **Overblaak (Blaakse Bos) Development** comprises 38 vibrantly coloured residences and two 'super cubes'.

 GETTING AROUND

South Holland is easy to navigate. Visiting its cities on two wheels is a wonderful experience. The longest regional distance between cities – Gouda to Lisse – is only 35km. The cities, especially smaller centres like Lisse and Gouda, are a breeze for exploring on foot. Similarly, Rotterdam and Den Haag are so compact you might never need public transport if you have a bicycle – but train and bus networks are highly efficient and convenient.

All cubes are privately owned except for the **Kijk-Kubus Museumwoning** *(Cube House Museum; kubuswoning.nl; adult/child €3.50/1.50).*

Upside-down foodie world

Opened in 2014, Rotterdam's **Markthal** *(markthal.nl)* is an architectural masterpiece, and also the city's favourite foodie hub. The extraordinary horseshoe-shaped building has a 40m-high curving arch covered in a Sistine Chapel–like mural of fruit and veg. Dotted between avocados and grapes, tiny windows reveal 230 diversely sized apartments and offices. Down below, dozens of vendors plate up Spanish *pinchos* (tapas), Greek souvlaki, Asian bowls, dumplings and many more delicacies.

'Backstage' arts museum

Museum Boijmans van Beuningen *(boijmans.nl; adult/child €20/free)* is one of the Netherlands' most famous art institutions. While the museum's main exhibition is closed, its depot offers a unique gallery experience. The world's first open-access art storage facility showcases the museum's repository, including priceless works displayed against white grates and protective barriers. Guided tours are available.

Gouda

Beyond the dairy

Gouda's fame is mostly weighed in dairy blocks, but the cheese doesn't stand alone. The historic centre, close to the train station, has a cheesy staged market full of costumed mongers and maidens; it's a nice stroll for quaint medieval architecture. **Museum Gouda** *(museumgouda.nl; adult/child €16/free)* houses artefacts and artworks in a medieval hospital building, and the former cheese-weighing house **Goudse Waag** *(goudsewaag.nl)* is also worth a look.

Kinderdijk

Windmills and waterways

UNESCO World Heritage Site **Kinderdijk** *(kinderdijk.com; adult/child €19.50/8)* is a beautiful polder (area of dried land) landscape where 19 historic windmills rise like sentinels. A pumping station has been repurposed as a visitor centre. There's a dual pedestrian and bicycle path between the canals, and boat cruises are also available.

Den Haag

MAP p817

Famous paintings and pop culture

Offering a wonderful introduction to Dutch and Flemish art, the splendid **Mauritshuis** *(mauritshuis.nl; adult/child €20/free)* displays an 800-strong collection of paintings mainly created between the 15th and 18th centuries. Several masterpieces displayed here are pop-culture icons, including Vermeer's *Girl with a Pearl Earring* and Fabritius' *The Goldfinch,* as well as Van der Weyden's *The Lamentation of Christ* and Rembrandt's *The Anatomy Lesson of Dr Nicolaes Tulp.*

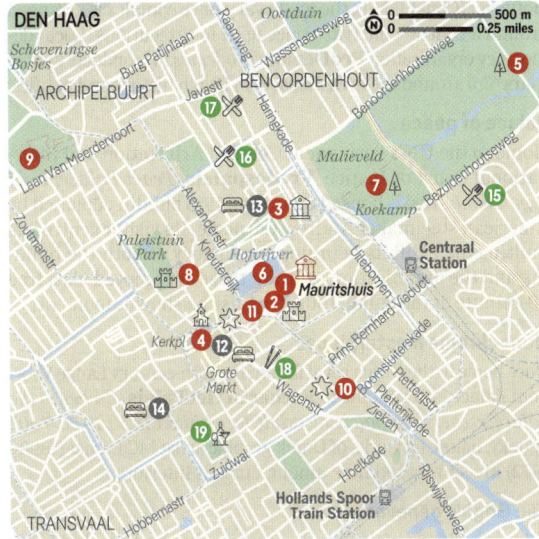

HIGHLIGHTS
1 Mauritshuis

SIGHTS
2 Binnenhof
3 Escher in Het Paleis
4 Grote Kerk
5 Haagse Bos
6 Hofvijver
7 Koekamp

8 Paleis Noordeinde
9 Vredespaleis

ACTIVITIES
10 De Ooievaart
11 ProDemos

SLEEPING
12 Collector Hotel
13 Hotel des Indes
14 Will & Tate City Stay

EATING
15 Baardman
16 Dekxels
17 Fouquet
18 Little V

DRINKING & NIGHTLIFE
19 Van Kleef

BEST OF DEN HAAG'S OUTDOORS

Postgezelboom: Across from Paleis Noordeinde, this gigantic horse-chestnut tree is a tranquil central space. Palace foundations were removed to continue its century-long growth.

Haagse Toren: Go up the medieval bell tower of Grote Kerk for amazing panoramas.

Hofvijver: Scenic public pondside seating. Stroll waterside Lange Vijverberg; sometimes, there's a market.

Paleistuin: Behind Paleis Noordeinde, this 20-hectare urban park is a flowery paradise.

De Ooievaart: See Den Haag's most interesting sights from a waterborne perspective during a canal cruise.

Urban national park

Unveiled in 2024, **Koekamp** is the perfect city park. Ponds, pathside canals and a deer enclosure create countryside vibes in the heart of the city centre. Koekamp is a green gateway to the adjacent **Haagse Bos** (Hague Forest). Here, 100 hectares of ancient woodlands have excellent cycling paths, wildlife and towering, shady trees. Together, both areas comprise the new national park, **Hollandse Duinen** (*nationaalparkhollandseduinen.nl*).

Palace of politics

Home to both houses of the Dutch government, the **Binnenhof** is one of Den Haag's most beautiful settings. Overlooking the

 EATING IN DEN HAAG: OUR PICKS ———————— MAP p817

Little V: Trendy Vietnamese restaurant decked to the nines in Dutch *kabinet* (cabinet of curiosities) style. *noon-10.30pm Tue-Thu, to 11pm Fri & Sat €€*

Dekxels: Asian small plates with Mediterranean twists. The well-priced wine list trawls the globe. *5-10pm Sun-Thu, to 11pm Fri & Sat €€*

Fouquet: Multicourse market-fresh daily menus in an elegant restaurant with impressive service. *11am-6pm Wed, Sat & Sun, to 1.30pm Thu & Fri €€*

Baardman: Beautiful, minimalist bistro with a Mediterranean-inspired menu. Mains swim in decadent sauces. *11am-11pm Tue-Sat €€*

Hofvijver (Court Pond), the medieval palace complex is arranged around a central courtyard once used for executions. Local democracy organisation **ProDemos** *(prodemos.nl)* conducts guided tours *(€6)* around the area focused on Dutch history and politics.

Palace of peace

Home to the UN's Permanent Court of Arbitration and International Court of Justice, **Vredespaleis** *(Peace Palace; vredespaleis.nl; free)* is housed in a grand 1913 building donated by American steelmaker Andrew Carnegie. Its visitor centre has multimedia exhibits detailing the history of both the building and the organisations within; these are enjoyed via a free 30-minute audio-guide tour. ID must be shown upon entry.

Monochrome masterpieces

Once home to the Dutch royal family, the 18th-century Lange Voorhout Palace is now home to **Escher in Het Paleis** *(Escher in the Palace; escherinhetpaleis.nl; adult/teen/child €13.50/10.50/7.50).* Spooky, haunting works of Dutch graphic artist MC Escher (1898–1972) are showcased here among opulent interiors.

Van Gogh's *genever*

Allegedly, Van Gogh found creativity in the barrels of this *genever* (Dutch gin) distiller. **Van Kleef** *(museumvankleef.nl; tastings Sat & Sun €26.50),* Den Haag's only surviving *genever* producer, offers an introduction to *genever* at its former production site. Displayed artefacts include *drankorgels* ('liquor organs'), barrels tapped by patrons, and Den Haag's first telephone book – drinkers (maybe even Vincent himself) dialled '1' for the distillery's 'moonshine hotline'.

Lisse

Seven million flower bulbs

Keukenhof Gardens *(keukenhof.nl; adult/child €20/9; round-trip shuttle bus from Amsterdam €32),* the world's biggest tulip show, hosts over a million annual visitors during the short bloom season (March to May). A springtime trip (preferably April) is a Netherlands' highlight.

Delft

Vermeer's legacy and famous porcelain

Delft's canals are worth aimlessly exploring – the scenery here feels much more quaint and laid-back than in Amsterdam. Delft remains remarkably unchanged since Johannes Vermeer painted *View of Delft* (c 1660–61) as a heartfelt expression of his birthplace. **Vermeer Centrum Delft** *(vermeerdelft.nl; adult/child €12/free)* provides insights into his life and work here.

Delft's **Markt**, one of Europe's oldest squares, has the impressive **Nieuwe Kerk** *(New Church; oudeennieuwekerkdelft.nl; adult/child €8.50/4).* The 109m-high church tower (steps only) promises panoramic views. Also on the square, shop authentic Delftware at the **outlet store** of the most famous Dutch porcelain manufactory. The independent boutique **De Blauwe Tulp** *(blue tulip.nl)* also paints and sells Delftware in a nearby studio-shop.

Utrecht

HIGHEST BELFRY | CRUISING CANALS | BUZZY PUBS

Petite but packing a punch, Utrecht Province has a fine selection of evocative castles and green nature. Utrecht city is a cultural hub in its own right, loaded with entertainment, great museums and throngs of young people. It's hard not to fall in love with one of the Netherlands' oldest urban centres and, for centuries, its religious heart. Historic Utrecht is also the Netherlands' top university city, with some 70,000 students in term time and a plethora of fun bars and cafes to match. Its 'waterline' location on what was then a major course of the Rhine was both blessing and curse, as two fabulous out-of-town archaeology museums explain. Visually, the city's central axis is the soaring Domtoren (belfry), especially at night when cloaked in imaginatively creative illuminations.

The Stormy Void

Roman remains and an invisible nave

Domtoren *(domtoren.nl)* is the city's iconic belfry tower and, at 112m, the Netherlands' tallest. It forms a visual axis for viewings in any direction. Hour-long guided **belfry tours** *(adult/child €14.50/8.50)* climb steps to the highest accessible point (95m).

Across the square is the **Domkerk** *(St Martin's Cathedral; domkerk.nl; entry by donation)*. If you think its shape seems odd, that's because only half the original size remains. Beneath the **Domplein** square, the fascinating archaeological site of **DOMunder** *(domunder.nl; tour adult/child €14.50/10)* goes

---

 GETTING AROUND

Utrecht's small historic core is a 10-minute walk from Utrecht Centraal station via the Hoog Catharijne shopping mall. Some buses stop centrally at Neude (p821); others depart from the station's west side. Trams access P&R sites where you'd be wise to leave a car. Diesel cars are banned altogether from the centre.

Het Zwarte Fietsenplan *(black-bikes.com)* hires out bicycles (from €18/72 per day/week). Subterranean bike-parking garages are free for stays of under 24 hours.

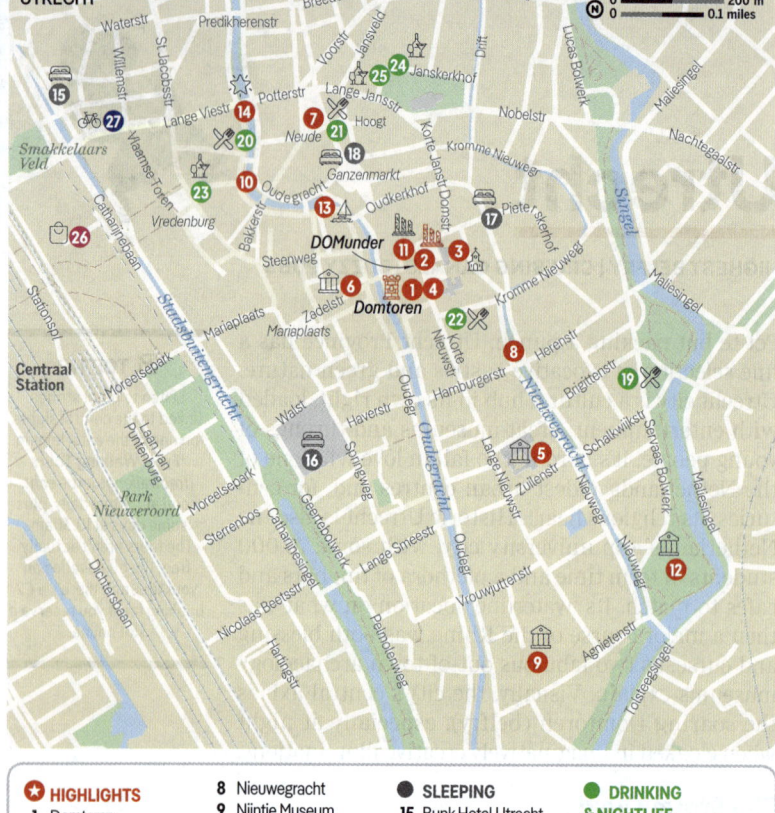

UTRECHT

back to the Roman period; lantern-lit tours reveal 2000 years of artefacts left lying where they were found.

Romanesque history is also explored on a visit to **Paleis Lofen** (*paleislofen.nl; adult/child €12.50/10*). The 12th-century residence for Holy Roman Emperors is partly built from recycled Roman wall-stone.

Double-Decker Canals

Kelders and canoes

The city's two most charming canals – buzzy **Oudegracht** and peaceful **Nieuwegracht** – cut right through the historic

Nieuwegracht

quarter. Both are unusual for their double-decker towpaths. Before Amsterdam was of any importance, Utrecht was a major river-trading hub, and merchants offloaded goods into *kelders* (storerooms) at water level. Roadways built above create the canals' special appearance. Glide canal waters on a kayak, canoe (several providers) or **pedal boat** *(stromma. com).* **Schuttevaer Canal Tours** *(schuttevaer.com; adult/child from €17.50/12.50)* runs two loop routes several times daily.

Party Time

Weekends in Utrecht

On warm evenings, the restaurants on the twin-level canal sides are full to bursting around Bakkerbrug by about 6pm. Groups of friends fill the terraces of **Neude** and Stadhuisplein, which stay rammed until well after midnight. A gaggle of cafes in Domplein's northwest corner are popular party starters. By midnight, many have drifted to Janskerkhof, where **Jans Bar** *(dejansbar.nl)* and **Hofman** *(hofman-utrecht.nl)* become clubs for dancing until 4am. Another small knot of bars on Drieharingstraat feeds the merry into **Club Poema** *(clubpoema.nl),* a popular student nightclub.

GREAT UTRECHT MUSEUMS

Museum Speelklok: A former church full of self-playing organs, musical boxes and assorted mechanised noise-makers from the 18th century onwards. *(museum speelklok.nl)*

Museum Catharijneconvent: Medieval religious art in a Gothic former convent complex. *(catharijneconvent.nl)*

Sonnenborgh Museum & Observatory: A 19th-century observatory on the city ramparts. *(sonnenborgh.nl)*

Nijntje Museum: Aimed at preschool-age children, this interactive museum is based on the cartoon characters created by local artist Dick Bruna (1927–2017), notably Nintje, known in English as Miffy. *(nijntjemuseum.nl)*

The savoury grilled veggie bowl has great flavours and textures.

 EATING IN UTRECHT: OUR PICKS

Zala's: Low-key yet gourmet multicourse surprise dinners at fair prices in a classy historic-house setting. *6pm-1am Wed-Sun* €€	**Stadskasteel Oudaen:** Restaurant, grand cafe and microbrewery in a 13th-century 'troubadour's castle'. *11am-late* €€	**Heron:** Turns 100% locally sourced fare into seasonal and imaginative dinners. *6-8pm Tue-Sat* €€€	**Vegitalian:** Two very different rooms for small-plate vegetarian dishes designed to share. *8.30am-10pm* €

Maastricht

ROMANESQUE CHURCHES | TUNNELS | FEASTING

GETTING AROUND

The train station and bus station are across the river from the old centre in the Wyck district. Bus 4 links the stations and Vrijthof.

When taking a train, check in/out using the correct pillar: yellow is for NS trains, blue for private Arriva services. International buses to Hasselt (Belgium) and Aachen (Germany) leave from the station's west side. Long-distance Flixbus services and Flibco buses to Charleroi Airport use the International bus stop, east of the rail tracks.

☑ TOP TIP

The concerts of André Rieu's Strauss Orchestra put intense pressure on Maastricht hotel beds for much of July. If you're not here for the waltzes, avoid the city at that time because there's no room at the inn.

Highly attractive Maastricht has Roman roots as a fort that guarded the Maas (Meuse) River crossing between Cologne and Gaul. It retains religious and historical buildings aplenty and brings a Burgundian sophistication to its dining and a bacchanalian delight to its drinking culture. People here are seen as irreverent by the standards of the Dutch, who struggle to follow 'Mestreechs', the impenetrable local dialect.

The fact that the city is Dutch at all is because of military commander Bernardus Dibbets, who in 1830 refused to accept an ultimatum to let Maastricht become part of Belgium. The city withstood a siege and, for nine years, was a disconnected exclave before the Netherlands reclaimed connecting land (the 'Limburg appendix'). It remains hemmed in on three sides by Belgium and Germany, perhaps explaining why Maastricht was chosen for the signing of the February 1992 treaty that paved the way for the EU and the euro as a common currency.

Saints & Sinners

History and revelry on the Vrijthof

The **Vrijthof** is Maastricht's finest square, with many attractive facades, pollarded plane trees, a grand **theatre** (theater aanhetvrijthof.nl) and the small **Fotomuseum Aan Het Vrijthof** (fotomuseumaanhetvrijthof.nl; adult/child €14/7).

During **Carnaval** in February or March, the clog-footed *Mooswief* (Cabbage Woman) is hoisted here at 12.11pm on the Sunday before Lent, and the open-air finale party on Tuesday night is again on Vrijthof. For much of July, local-born waltz king André Rieu fills the square with wildly popular orchestral concerts of light classical music. In late August, the square becomes one vast dinner party during **Preuvenemint** *(preu venemint.nl)*, the Netherlands' biggest food festival.

HIGHLIGHTS	4 St Janskerk	● EATING	● ENTERTAINMENT
1 St Servaasbasiliek	● SLEEPING	8 Bouchon d'en Face	12 Theater aan het Vrijthof
2 Vrijthof	5 Green Elephant	9 Café Sjiek	● TRANSPORT
● SIGHTS	6 Kruiserenhotel	10 Pitology	13 Bus Station
3 Fotomuseum Aan Het	7 Zenden	11 Witloof	14 International Bus Stop
Vrijthof			15 Train Station

At calmer times, come to enjoy the square's cafe-terraces or to survey its gaggle of towers. Painted ox-blood red to prevent erosion, the tower of Protestant **St Janskerk** *(stjanskerk maastricht.nl; adult/child €4/2)* can be climbed for godly city views. Next door, the Romanesque **St Servaasbasiliek** *(sintservaas.nl; adult/child €7/free)* is a basilica museum built over the tomb of Armenian-born bishop St Servatius. His skull is encased in an eerily human-looking gilt reliquary.

Getting Deep

Don't wander off underground

Over the centuries, some 230km of quarry tunnels were dug into the hills south of Maastricht; about 80km still exist.

🍴 EATING IN MAASTRICHT: OUR PICKS

Pitology: Grand mansion turned mellow stop for hot Greek wraps; of 15 varieties, five are veggie. Linden-shaded terrace. *noon-9pm Wed-Mon* €

Witloof: Classic Belgian dining: great mussels, rabbit with wine sauce and ham-wrapped chicory. What a beer cellar! *5.30-9.30pm Wed-Sun* €€

Bouchon d'en Face: Old-world place for traditional French cooking, with a good-value set menu. *5.30-10pm daily & noon-4pm Fri & Sat* €€

Café Sjiek: The place to go for *zuurflees* (sour horsemeat stew). Summer tables on the grass opposite. *5-9.30pm Wed-Mon* €€

DAY TRIPS FROM MAASTRICHT

Valkenburg: Gently quaint tourist town with forested hills, a castle ruin and a Pierre Cuypers replica of some Roman catacombs in an old limestone mine.

Netherlands American Cemetery & Memorial: Thought-provokingly vast WWII cemetery behind a white chapel-monolith, 9km southeast of Maastricht.

Roermond: Hometown of architect Pierre Cuypers, whose former home and workshop form a fascinating museum, the Cuypershuis. Munsterkerk and Sint-Christoffelkathedraal are fine churches restored after WWII.

Thorn: Picturesque village that was once the smallest principality of the Holy Roman Empire – and run by women. Almost every house is painted white and has been since the 1790s.

KIM WILLEMS/SHUTTERSTOCK

Moosweif (Cabbage Woman), Carnaval (p822)

Various tours run by **Maastricht Underground** *(explore maastricht.nl/en/maastricht-underground; tours adult/child from €11.75/9.25)* visit different sections uncovering charcoal murals linked to the tunnels' creation, Napoleonic history and hiding populations during WWII bombardments. One daily **North Caves** tour includes a visit to the 'secret' vaults in which a trove of the nation's art treasures (including Rembrandt's *The Night Watch*) was squirrelled away for three war years. Another is a once top-secret **NATO War Command**. The **Zonneberg Caves** are wide enough to visit by scooter!

Places We Love to Stay

€ Budget €€ Midrange €€€ Top End

Amsterdam   MAP p810

St Christopher's at the Winston € Rock 'n' roll rooms, a busy nightclub with live bands nightly, a bar and restaurant, a beer garden and a smoking deck downstairs. En-suite dorms are designed by artists (some are kinda out-there).

Hotel De Hallen €€ Housed in a former tram depot, this designer hotel has 58 industrial-chic rooms and six loft-style apartments, plus cool art and sculptures in its lobby, lounge areas, restaurant, bar and wraparound terrace.

Hotel The Exchange €€ Eye-popping rooms designed by students from the Amsterdam Fashion Institute. Rooms range from one- to five-star (with concept-driven designs); all have en-suite bathrooms.

College Hotel €€€ Originally a 19th-century school, the impressive-looking College Hotel has 40 stylish rooms you'd never think were former classrooms. It's a celebrity favourite situated 1km from Museumplein.

art'otel amsterdam €€€ Rooms have original artwork and there's a basement public gallery with changing exhibitions; the lobby features a fireplace and library. Located directly opposite Centraal Station.

Rotterdam

CitizenM € A new-generation hostel encompassing modern capsule-like rooms and super-stylish common spaces and coworking areas.

King Kong Hostel € Hip hostel in Rotterdam's party precinct, with female and mixed-sex dorms and great facilities including laundry and communal kitchen.

SS Rotterdam € On a retired 1950s ocean liner, pint-sized cabins restored with kitschy decor are fun (at least, for a couple of nights). The water-taxi station here is convenient.

Pincoffs €€ In an 1879-built customs house, Rotterdam's only truly boutique hotel has generations-spanning art and cosy comfort.

Den Haag   MAP p817

Will & Tate City Stay € Boutique hostel mixing dorms (including one for women only) and a few private rooms – all adorned with different murals. Close to Paard and the Grote Markt.

Collector Hotel €€ Central hotel fully delivering on old-world charm. Elegant decor extends into a lovely Renaissance courtyard.

Hotel des Indes €€€ Built as a residence in 1858, and a luxury hotel since 1881, this is Den Haag's sleekest accommodation.

Delft

Casa Julia € Boutique B&B in a 1920s building. Stylish, comfy and conveniently located rooms, though small, are well-priced.

Hotel Arsenaal €€€ Delft's classiest address, a former artillery warehouse transformed into stylish modern rooms.

Utrecht   MAP p820

Bunk Hotel Utrecht € Luxurious hostel with curtained pod-capsules, digital lockers and towels included, set in a stylishly converted church that's part bar-cafe and part occasional music venue.

Hotel Beijers €€ Beautifully appointed 17th-century mansion with period fittings tucked away in a quiet street a stone's throw from the belfry.

Mother Goose Hotel €€ Highly personable staff add to the considerable appeal of this sensitively reworked 13th-century mansion. The nightlife square right outside can get noisy.

Grand Hotel Karel V €€€ Five-star luxury in a converted historic hospital and former monastery that was visited by Holy Roman Emperor Charles (Karel) V in 1543.

Maastricht   MAP p823

Green Elephant € Choose a 'tiny dream house' to pay hostel prices but receive a degree of privacy in a keypad-lockable box-room with air-con.

Zenden €€ Boutique rooms spread over three city-centre houses, giving a bleached sense of otherworldliness, which is either stylish or antiseptic depending on your taste.

Kruisherenhotel €€€ A 1483 monastery complex converted into a design-statement hotel. Each room is unique, and some are a little small, but the overall ambience is a delight.

Château Neercanne €€€ Majestic 17th-century castle with baroque gardens, a cellar event room, Michelin-star restaurant and five-star luxury suites, 5km south of the centre.

Practicalities

SMOKING

Smoking any substance in bars or restaurants (not coffee shops) is illegal. Since 2024, supermarkets cannot sell tobacco, restricting sales to speciality shops. The government aims for a smoke-free future, with a ban on tobacco sales in shops and supermarkets from 2032.

SAMIRA KAFALA/LONELY PLANET

PUBLIC TOILETS

Public toilets are uncommon, apart from Amsterdam's so-called 'pee curls' (freestanding public urinals) in high-traffic areas. Plan to duck into cafes, pubs or shops (ask first!). Standard fee is €1.

HEALTH

Over-the-counter medications like aspirin are available in pharmacies and supermarkets (which sometimes have their own pharmacies too). Pharmacies and drugstores are widely available in cities and towns. For prescription medications, you'll generally need to get one by visiting a local healthcare provider. Pharmacies only fill medications; they don't write them.

TIPPING

With the demise of cash, it's now normal in restaurants for the credit card terminal to offer guests a choice of tip amounts: 5% is fine, 10% generous. Rounding up your taxi fare is common.

OPENING HOURS

Banks 9am–4pm Monday to Friday
Cafes/Bars Noon–1am Sunday to Thursday, to 3am Friday and Saturday
Museums 10am–5pm daily, some close Monday
Restaurants Lunch 11am–2.30pm, dinner 6–10pm
Shops 10am or noon–6pm Tuesday to Friday, 10am–5pm Saturday and Sunday, 1–5pm Monday (if at all)
Supermarkets 8am–8pm

BIKE SAFETY

In the Netherlands, letting faster riders pass is an important part of cycling etiquette, especially on busy bike paths. Avoid accidents by staying left, signalling when turning or slowing and ringing your bell before overtaking.

PUBLIC HOLIDAYS

Most museums adopt Sunday hours on public holidays (except Christmas and New Year).
Remembrance Day (4 May) is often a day off.
New Year's Day 1 January
Good Friday Before Easter
Easter March/April

Easter Monday Following Easter Sunday
King's Day 27 April
Ascension Day 40th day after Easter Sunday
Whit Sunday/Monday 50th day after Easter Sunday/Monday
Christmas Day 25 December

Language

The pronunciation of Dutch is fairly straightforward. If you read our pronunciation guides as if they were English, you'll be understood just fine. Note that öy is pronounced as the 'er y' (without the 'r') in 'her year', and kh is a throaty sound, similar to the 'ch' in the Scottish loch.

Basics

Hello. Dag./Hallo. *dakh/ha·loh*
Goodbye. Dag. *dakh*
Yes. Ja. *yaa*
No. Nee. *ney*
Please. Alstublieft/Alsjeblieft. (pol/inf) *al·stew·bleeft/a·shuh·bleeft*
Thank you. Dank u/je. (pol/inf) *dangk ew/yuh*
Excuse me. Excuseer mij. *eks·kew·zeyr mey*
How are you? Hoe gaat het met u/jou? (pol/inf) *hoo khaat huht met ew/yaw*
Fine. And you? Goed. En met u/jou? (pol/inf) *khoot en met ew/yaw*
Do you speak English? Spreekt u Engels? *spreykt ew eng·uhls*
I don't understand. Ik begrijp het niet. *ik buh·khreyp huht neet*

Directions

Where's the ...? Waar is ...? *waar is ...*
How far is it? Hoe ver is het? *hoo ver is huht*
What's the address? Wat is het adres? *wat is huht a·dres*
Can you show me (on the map)? Kunt u het mij tonen (op de kaart)? *kunt ew huht mey toh·nuhn (op duh kaart)*
A ticket to ..., please. Een kaartje naar ..., graag. *uhn kaar·chuh naar ... khraakh*

Please take me to ... Breng me alstublieft naar ... *breng muh al·stew·bleeft naar ...*
Does it stop at ...? Stopt het in ...? *stopt huht in ...*
I'd like to get off at ... Ik wil graag in ... uitstappen. *ik wil khraak in ... öyt·sta·puhn*
Can we get there by bike? Kunnen we er met de fiets heen? *ku·nuhn wuh uhr met duh feets heyn*

Time

What time is it? Hoe laat is het? *hoo laat is huht*
It's (10) o'clock. Het is (tien) uur. *huht is (teen) ewr*
Half past (10). Half (elf). *half (elf)* (lit: half eleven)
Morning 's ochtends *sokh·tuhns*
Afternoon 's middags *smi·dakhs*
Evening 's avonds *saa·vonts*
Yesterday gisteren *khis·tuh·ruhn*
Today vandaag *van·daakh*
Tomorrow morgen *mor·khuhn*

Emergencies

Help! Help! *help*
Call a doctor! Bel een dokter! *bel uhn dok·tuhr*
Call the police! Bel de politie! *bel duh poh·leet·see*
I'm sick. Ik ben ziek. *ik ben zeek*
I'm lost. Ik ben verdwaald. *ik ben vuhr·dwaalt*
Where are the toilets? Waar zijn de toiletten? *waar zeyn duh twa·le·tuhn*

NUMBERS

1	één *eyn*
2	twee *twey*
3	drie *dree*
4	vier *veer*
5	vijf *veyf*
6	zes *zes*
7	zeven *zey·vuhn*
8	acht *akht*
9	negen *ney·khuhn*
10	tien *teen*

NIGEL WIGGINS/SHUTTERSTOCK

Schiphol International Airport

Arriving

Located near Amsterdam, Schiphol International Airport – the Netherlands' main airport and the second-busiest in the EU – is serviced by most major airlines. Frequent high-speed trains from the airport's connecting station will have you in Amsterdam in under 20 minutes, Rotterdam and Utrecht in half an hour and Den Haag in just over an hour.

By Land
High-speed trains and a plethora of international buses connect the Netherlands with neighbouring countries. Arriving by car, train or bus is straightforward, with few to no border controls coming from Schengen neighbours. Local trains enter the Netherlands from Belgium and Germany.

By Sea
Several companies operate car/passenger ferries and train-ferry-train packages between the Netherlands and the UK. Routes include Harwich to Hoek van Holland, Hull to Europoort (Rotterdam) and Newcastle to IJmuiden (near Amsterdam). Reservations are essential for cars in high season.

MONEY

Currency: Euro (€)

CONTACTLESS PAYMENT

Increasingly, businesses such as trendier cafes and restaurants in Amsterdam accept digital payments (including credit cards) only. Make sure your credit card or mobile phone are set up for 'tap to pay'.

PAYING FOR PUBLIC TRANSPORT

Tap payments are the most convenient means of purchasing NS (nationwide) and GVB (Amsterdam) public transport tickets. Using OVpay, simply check in and out at the turnstiles into stations or wagons – just tap your contactless debit or credit card or phone on the card reader. Journeys are billed as a single transaction at the end of each day.

MISSED-CHECKOUT FARES

Remember to check in on each ride (each new transport leg in a single journey) by tapping your card to the reader. Tap again on exiting to check out. Failing to do so, you'll be charged a 'missed checkout' or 'incomplete journey' fare (up to €25 for NS transport; up to €5 for GVB transport).

Getting Around

Compact size, flat terrain and excellent rail infrastructure make the Netherlands one of Europe's easiest countries to get around. Train services are frequent and high-speed sprinters keep distances short; regional and national service is well integrated. Local and long-distance cycling paths straightforwardly connect cities and countryside. Endless day-tripping possibilities, whether to neighbouring cities or further out, are standard across Dutch destinations.

Commuting Peak Times
The Netherlands is a nation of commuters. Many citizens live in one city (say, Haarlem) and work in another (such as Amsterdam). Cycling long-distance trails or hopping on sprinter trains is a daily routine – plan travel times accordingly for rush-hour crowds.

DMITRY RUKHLENKO/SHUTTERSTOCK

Cycling
Approximately 35,000km of bike routes across the country make for joyful *fiets* (bicycle) adventures. Routes across cities – and between them – fabulously connect coasts and borders. Most cities are only a one- to two-hour cycling journey from the next.

Train
Trains are frequent and serve domestic destinations at regular intervals, sometimes five or six times an hour. First-class tickets usually aren't worth the extra cost. Consider them, though, during busy periods when seats in 2nd class might be overbooked.

LF Routes
Landelijke fietsroutes (long-distance routes), or LF routes, are the Dutch 'Ventura Highway'. Some are mapped by sightseeing themes across coast, midland and historical attractions. Go your own way, whatever that may be, via the LF app's excellent route planner *(nederlandfietsland.nl)*.

Driving & Rideshare
Peak-time traffic congestion and roadworks make driving a pain. Locals rely on trains and bicycles for every situation apart from missing the last train (midnight to 6am). In this case, taking an Uber from Amsterdam to Rotterdam isn't even uncommon.

DRIVING ESSENTIALS

Drive on the right

 50 120

Speed limits range from 50km/h (cities) to 120km/h (freeways)

0.05

Blood alcohol limit is 0.05%

Curated by
Anthony Ham

North Macedonia

WILD NATURE, ANCIENT HISTORY

North Macedonia is a Balkan treasure, a little-known world
of medieval monasteries, historic towns and stirring natural
beauty.

North Macedonia may be small but it's rich in glorious scenery and cultural heritage. This is a realm that has always stood at the crossroads of history and in the path of invading armies. The result is part Balkan and part Mediterranean, with strong traces of Greek, Roman and Ottoman legacies.

Glittering Lake Ohrid and its historic namesake town have etched out a place for North Macedonia on the tourist map, but travel further and you'll find dramatic mountains with blissfully quiet walking trails, lakes and riding opportunities. The national parks of Mavrovo, Galičica and Pelister are cultivating some excellent cultural and culinary tourism initiatives; these gorgeous regions are little explored, so if you want to get off the beaten track in Europe, this is the place.

Although North Macedonia has a small core of excellent places to stay, traditional restaurants serving fresh food, and professional local tour operators, tourism infrastructure isn't always what it could be. But therein, too, lies part of the country's charm: at times, exploring North Macedonia can feel like a magical DIY adventure.

Throw in some enchanted Ottoman old towns, superb Orthodox monasteries, stunning hiking trails, some Roman ruins and one of Europe's least-known wine regions, and North Macedonia may just be the finest Balkan sensation waiting to be discovered.

COLORMAKER/SHUTTERSTOCK

THE MAIN AREAS

SKOPJE & AROUND
Historic bazaar
and modernist
architecture. **p834**

LAKE OHRID
Ancient lake, ancient
villages. **p834**

**MAVROVO
NATIONAL PARK**
Magnificent
monasteries, pretty
villages, blissful hikes.
p837

BITOLA
Medieval town and
gateway to the wild.
p837

For places to stay in North Macedonia, see p838

TU XA NOI/GETTY IMAGES

Left: Skopje Old Town (p835); Above: Church of Sveti Jovan (p836) and Lake Ohrid

Find Your Way

Take the time to discover compact North Macedonia's cities, towns, traditional villages and, especially, its beautiful national parks, mountains and lakes. Outdoors lovers will find plenty to keep them occupied.

Mavrovo National Park, p837

Meet the monks at grand Sveti Jovan Bigorski Monastery in the hills of the national park.

Skopje & Around, p834

Dive into the capital's historic Čaršija (old Ottoman bazaar), then seek out modernist architecture and riverside monuments.

Lake Ohrid, p834

Discover the vastness and mystery of this seductive lake and explore Ohrid's distinctive old quarter up to clifftop Church of Sveti Jovan.

Bitola, p837

Immerse yourself in a North Macedonian provincial town, with a Čaršija and the country's premier Roman ruins.

CAR

You don't need a car to get around Skopje and Ohrid Town, but renting one is best for discovering the rest of North Macedonia, especially if you want to reach villages and outdoor-activities spots.

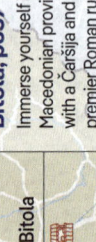

BUS

If you're not in a hurry, buses can get you between most cities and towns. Skopje serves the majority of domestic destinations. During summer and on Sundays (when most locals travel), prebook for Ohrid.

KOSOVO

SERBIA

GREECE

ALBANIA

SKOPJE

Bitola

Lake Ohrid

Mavrovo National Park

0 50 km
0 25 miles

ATOSAN/SHUTTERSTOCK

Mavrovo National Park (p837)

Plan Your Time

North Macedonia has plenty of possibilities if you like alfresco fun mixed in with historical towns. You'll need a few days to really savour the activities and dig into the history of the country.

One Week to Explore

● Spend a couple of days in **Skopje** (p834), then head straight to **Ohrid Town** (p834) to swim in the lake, stroll waterside villages and explore frescoed medieval churches at **Sveti Naum Monastery** (p836). Don't miss **Mavrovo National Park** (p837) for mountain hiking and local food. Finish at **Lake Prespa** (p837) and the ruins on the island of **Golem Grad** (p837).

More Than a Week

● Having enjoyed **Skopje** (p834), **Ohrid Town** (p834), **Lake Ohrid** (p834) and **Lake Prespa** (p837), stop in **Bitola** (p837), with its Ottoman quarter and ancient ruins, and discover North Macedonia at its historic and least touristy best. Next, visit **Mavrovo National Park** (p837) and stay in historic villages while you hike, ride and (in winter) ski your way through the park.

SEASONAL HIGHLIGHTS

SPRING

March can be cold and Orthodox Easter sees lots of local travellers. Temperatures warm up in May; attractions remain quiet.

SUMMER

Summers are for swimming in Lake Ohrid and mountain hiking. July and August have lots of festivals, but are overcrowded.

AUTUMN

September has fewer crowds and festivals. Hiking trails close in October. November is really cold.

WINTER

Mini high season in December and January. Carnival (Vevčani) and skiing (Mavrovo) are popular. It's bitterly cold at altitude.

Skopje & Around

HISTORIC TOWNS | MAGICAL LAKE | SCENIC LANDSCAPES

Places

Lake Ohrid p834

Mavrovo National Park p837

Bitola p837

 TOP TIP

For the best views of Skopje, take the cable car to **Mt Vodno** – a 10-minute journey during which you'll get to see the entire sprawl of the city. Take the 'Millennium Cross' special bus or a taxi from Skopje's **bus station** to the cable-car station.

Skopje is one of the most intriguing capitals in the Balkans. It combines an easygoing atmosphere, plenty of charm and tasty local cuisine with stirring architecture and rich history. Its Ottoman- and Byzantine-era sights are focused around the city's delightful Čaršija, bordered by the 15th-century Kameni Most (Stone Bridge) and Tvrdina Kale Fortress. Beyond the capital, the mysterious Lake Ohrid is a wonderfully seductive sight and among the most magical places in the Balkans. Mirror-like and dazzling on sunny days, it's a beautiful place, especially in and around the ancient town of Ohrid, with its cobbled streets, distinctive architecture and lakefront bars. East of Ohrid, Galičica National Park has mountain villages and Magaro Peak, which can be climbed. The gorges, pine forests, karst fields and waterfalls of Mavrovo National Park, North Macedonia's largest, offer a wonderful change of pace for visitors, while Bitola could just be North Macedonia's most enchanting old town.

Lake Ohrid

Explore the old quarter

Alongside its serene lake, **Ohrid Town's old quarter** cascades down steep streets, dotted with beautiful churches and offering sweeping views from the heights. Car Samoil St is lined

---

GETTING AROUND

Skopje International Airport (21km east of the city centre) is a minor hub with direct air services to regional cities and beyond. Shuttle buses with **Vardar Express** (*vardarexpress. com*) run between it and the city. Driving is generally hassle-free; the main worries are poor signage and finding somewhere to park. You'll need a car to reach small villages like Vevčani. Otherwise, buses connect Skopje with Ohrid Town (from where buses run along the lakeshore), Mavrovo and Bitola.

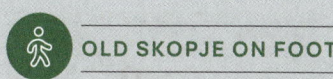

OLD SKOPJE ON FOOT

Walk from the river, through the Old Town and up to the fortress, passing museums and architectural gems; allow a day if you visit every museum.

START	END	LENGTH
Ploštad Makedonija	Tvrdina Kale Fortress	2km; 2hr

Begin south of the river, in ❶ **Ploštad Makedonija** (Macedonia Sq), the centrepiece of Skopje's audacious nation-building-through-architecture project. From the square, cross the ❷ **Stone Bridge**, then turn right (southeast) to the ❸ **Archaeological Museum of Macedonia**, a huge pile of Italianate-styled marble. Returning northwest, the ❹ **Museum of the Macedonian Struggle for Statehood & Independence** is fascinating for its subtlety-free propaganda. Much better is the mirrored-glass ❺ **Holocaust Memorial Center for the Jews of Macedonia**, commemorating North Macedonia's all-but-lost Sephardic Jewish culture. A short walk northeast brings you to the 19th-century Macedonian Orthodox ❻ **Sveti Dimitrija Church**. Across the

road, the ❼ **National Gallery of Macedonia** occupies the Daut Pasha Amam (1473), once the largest Turkish baths beyond İstanbul and a magical setting for the mainly modern art from across the country. The Old Town, the Čaršija, begins north across Bul Goce Delčev. Make for the ❽ **Čifte Amam**, which houses temporary exhibitions, and then the partially submerged ❾ **Sveti Spas Church**. Above the Old Town, the ❿ **Museum of North Macedonia** inhabits a concrete brutalist structure. Almost across the street, the ⓫ **Mustafa Pasha Mosque** dates back to 1492 and has a delightful rose garden. Continue the climb to the walk's literal high point, the 6th-century ⓬ **Tvrdina Kale Fortress**, for great views over the city.

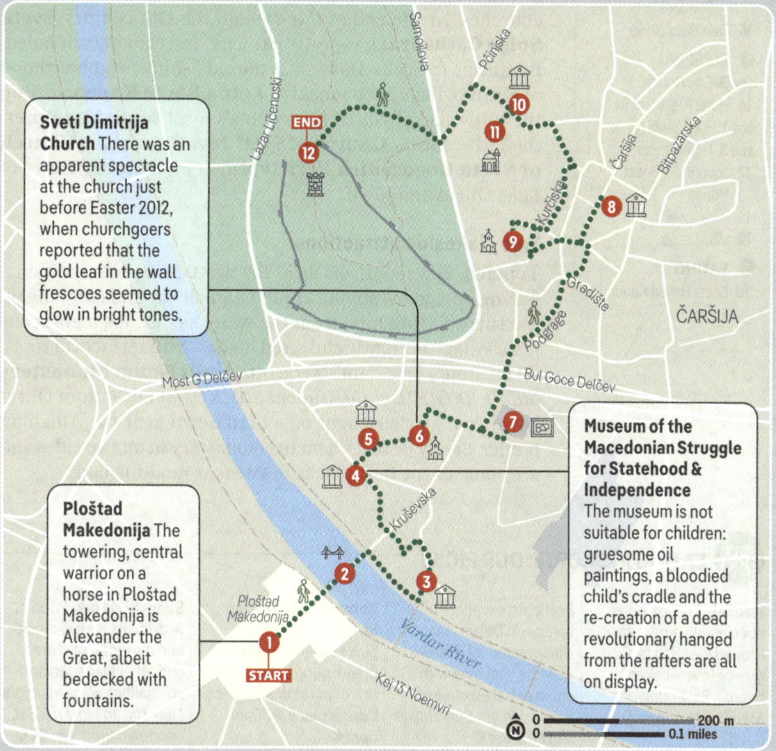

Sveti Dimitrija Church There was an apparent spectacle at the church just before Easter 2012, when churchgoers reported that the gold leaf in the wall frescoes seemed to glow in bright tones.

Ploštad Makedonija The towering, central warrior on a horse in Ploštad Makedonija is Alexander the Great, albeit bedecked with fountains.

Museum of the Macedonian Struggle for Statehood & Independence The museum is not suitable for children: gruesome oil paintings, a bloodied child's cradle and the re-creation of a dead revolutionary hanged from the rafters are all on display.

ČARŠIJA

Vardar River

0   200 m
0   0.1 miles

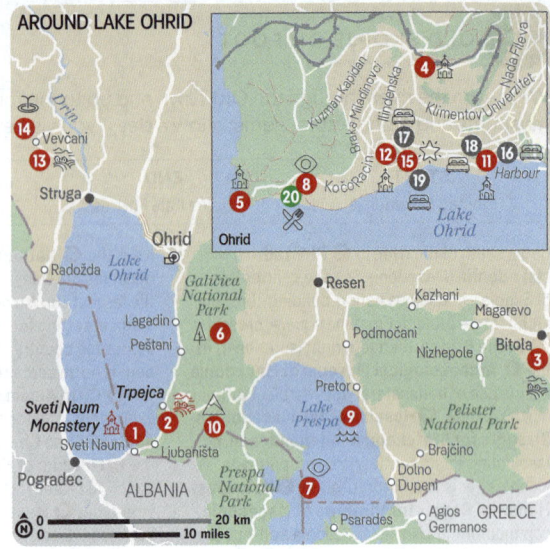

AROUND LAKE OHRID

with beautiful traditional architecture, as well as frescoed **Sveta Bogorodica Bolnička** and **Sveti Nikola Bolnički** churches. At the end of Car Samoil, the 11th-century **Sveta Sofija Cathedral** has pretty gardens, and elaborate, if faded, Byzantine frescoes. Don't miss the old fishing neighbourhood of **Kaneo**, including a meal at **Letna Bavča Kaneo**, or – up the hill – one of North Macedonia's most scenic structures, the 13th-century **Church of Sveti Jovan**. From the **Church of Sveta Bogorodica Perivlepta**, enjoy magical views of Lake Ohrid and town.

Enjoy lakeside attractions

Trpejca, 21km south of Ohrid Town, is Ohrid's last traditional fishing village. Wrapping around a small bay and climbing up the surrounding hills from the water's edge, it's a gorgeous little village of tightly clustered houses with terracotta roofs.

The stone, brick and terracotta **Sveti Naum Monastery** (*adult 100MKD, child/student 30MKD*), 8km south of Ohrid Town, is a glorious sight on a bluff down near the Albanian border. Sandy beaches hem the monastery in on two sides and are some of the best places to swim around the lake.

 EATING IN SKOPJE: OUR PICKS

Nadžak: Lots of local specialities, from *skara* (grilled meat) to *tavče gravče* (oven-baked beans). *9am-midnight Sun-Thu, to 1am Fri & Sat* €

Barik: An excellent little taverna in Debar Maalo, with great local dishes – try the veal liver with onion or baked cheese. *8am-midnight Sun-Thu, to 1am Fri & Sat* €

Kebapčilnica Destan: Skopje's best kebabs, plus seasoned grilled bread, peppers and a little raw onion at this classic Čaršija place. *9.30am-11pm* €

Skopski Merak: Popular with locals for live music and the menu of *skara* and other Macedonian specialities. *9am-midnight Mon-Thu, to 1am Fri & Sat, noon-midnight Sun* €€€

High above the northwestern corner of Lake Ohrid is one of the loveliest villages anywhere in North Macedonia. Ninth-century **Vevčani**, 28km from Ohrid Town, is one of the oldest villages in the country. Locals love it for its cool mountain air in summer, its traditional restaurants and **Vevčani Springs** *(adult/child 30/15MKD)* that writhe and burble through the forest at the top of the village.

Galičica National Park

A wild lake and magical island

The rippling, rock-crested massif of **Galičica National Park** *(galicica.org.mk/en)* separates Lakes Ohrid and Prespa and is home to **Magaro Peak** (2254m). You can dedicate half a day to hiking Magaro, a moderate, 8km loop hike (around four hours in total). From the top you'll get spectacular views of both lakes.

After your descent, cool off by swimming at **Lake Prespa**, and spend a day visiting the island of **Golem Grad**, Lake Prespa's star attraction, with ruins dating back as far as the 4th century. The only way to book a trip to Golem Grad is through **Villa Prespa Hotel** *(villaprespa.com)*. Visits take place from June to October, and start at around €80 per person.

Mavrovo National Park

Hike, ski or ride the trails

The largest of North Macedonia's four national parks, **Mavrovo National Park** *(npmavrovo.org.mk/en; free)* is rich in lakes, forests and vertiginous canyons. You can stay at the **Sveti Jovan Bigorski Monastery** (p838), and choose from 20 different hiking trails, which range from 1.7km (45 minutes) to 27km (five to eight hours). The excellent national park website has a brief description and elevation chart for each hike. Our favourite path is the 5.5km trail that connects Galičnik and Janče. **Shar Outdoors** *(sharoutdoors.com)* can arrange a guide.

Zare Lazarevski Ski Centre *(skimavrovo.com; day ticket 1300MKD),* North Macedonia's top ski resort, is hugely popular with locals and with skiers from across the Balkans.

Sherpa Horse Riding *(horseriding.com.mk; per person from €40)* arranges lovely excursions around Mavrovo. Rides range from 2½ hours to seven days through mountain valleys and traditional villages.

Bitola

Visit the bazaar

Crumbling and colourful 18th- and 19th-century townhouses, coupled with an authentic, workaday Čaršija, make **Bitola** worth a few days of your time. In its 19th-century Ottoman heyday, Bitola's **Stara Čaršija** was one of the finest in the Balkans. More than just a market, it was a regional centre of artisan traditions, with more 3000 shops and workshops crammed into Bitola's bazaar. That number may have fallen to closer to 70, but the same spirit lingers.

TOURS IN NORTH MACEDONIA

Free Pass Ohrid: Tailored tours to Galičica National Park, wine touring around Tikveš, boat trips and paragliding around Lake Ohrid. *(freepassohrid.mk)*

Bicycle MK: Guided day tours in Skopje, plus North Macedonia–wide adventures. All equipment is provided. *(bicycle.mk)*

Macedonia Experience: Horse riding, bike riding, community tourism forays into Mavrovo National Park, wine tasting and Ohrid excursions, all from a Skopje base. *(macedonia experience.com)*

Macedonia Travel: Large Skopje agency. Day trips to Canyon Matka and Ohrid, and off-the-beaten-track destinations. *(macedoniatravel. com)*

Balojani Tourist Services: Bitola-based operator: guided hiking, biking, gastronomy, wildlife-watching tours countrywide.

Places We Love to Stay

€ Budget €€ Midrange €€€ Top End

Skopje

Urban Hostel & Apartments €
A converted residential house with a sociable front garden, close to the main train station.

Hotel Senigallia €€ Once a boat, now a hotel with rooms that evoke classic semi-luxurious cabins, Hotel Senigallia has a great location and lots of character.

Hotel Solun €€€ Just off the main square, this stylish, beautifully designed place has modern and elegantly decorated rooms.

Hotel City Park €€€ Fresh rooms, modern and bright, some with balconies; the location is excellent, opposite the City Park.

Lake Ohrid   MAP p836

Villa Jovan € This utterly charming restoration of an 1856 mansion has nine rooms in the heart of the Old Town, with suitably creaky floors and wooden beams, and a cosy atmosphere.

Villa Lucija € Deep in the Old Town, and right on the lakefront with a riverside terrace, Lucija has warmly decorated, breezy rooms with lake-view balconies.

Hotel Sveti Naum € On the grounds of the Sveti Naum Monastery, some of this hotel's rooms have lovely lake views.

Jovanovic Guest House €€ This Old Town property has two studio apartments; the top-floor apartment's balcony has one of the best views in town, over the lake and Sveta Sofija Cathedral.

Hotel Aleksandrija €€ Rooms here vary from old-fashioned retro to slick designer; many of the latter have lake views from their big balconies.

Mavrovo National Park

Baba i Dede € Charming Galičnik guesthouse with a restaurant serving traditional homemade food.

Sveti Jovan Bigorski Monastery € For a unique experience, bed down in this famous monastery. It's more comfortable than you might expect, and while you might share a room, it's a soulful experience.

Hotel Tutto €€ This eco-hotel with a great restaurant has supremely comfortable rooms; the ones at the front have fine views from their balconies.

Bitola

Hotel Teatar € One of the loveliest hotels in the country; the sensitive design keeps true to the image of a traditional Ottoman house.

City House € This family-run mini-hotel has terrific rooms and a couple of apartments just off Širok Sokak; excellent breakfasts and an atrium cafe are further highlights.

IGOR PANEVSKI/SHUTTERSTOCK

Sveti Jovan Bigorski Monastery

Practicalities

Mobile Phones

If using a mobile (cell) phone, buying a local SIM card (from as little as €10, including data) is good for longer stays. Coverage is generally excellent throughout the country. North Macedonia uses the GSM phone system, which means that American CDMA phones won't work here.

Time Zone

North Macedonia runs on Central European Time: one hour ahead of GMT. For Daylight Saving Time, clocks go forward on the last Sunday in October, and back on the last Sunday in March.

Smoking

North Macedonia generally follows EU regulations banning smoking inside public places, but the rules are casually broken in many restaurants, bars and hotels. Around half (48.4%) of adult North Macedonians smoke.

Etiquette

North Macedonians are usually warm and welcoming, but socially conservative. Most are either Orthodox Christian or Muslim and neither religion deems it appropriate for women to bare much flesh; be aware that if you're a woman and wearing skimpy clothing you will get stared at. In churches and mosques, both men and women should cover their knees and shoulders.

FILIP P/SHUTTERSTOCK

Trpejca (p836)

Opening Hours

Banks 7am–5pm Monday to Friday
Cafes & Restaurants 8am–midnight
Museums Many close on Mondays
Shops 9am–6pm

Public Holidays

New Year's Day 1 January
Orthodox Christmas 7 January
Orthodox Easter Week March/April/May
Labour Day 1 May
Saints Cyril and Methodius Day 24 May
Ilinden Day 2 August
Independence Day 8 September
Revolution Day 11 October
St Clement of Ohrid Day 8 December

Language

Macedonian is written using the Cyrillic alphabet. Note that *dz* is pronounced as the 'ds' in 'adds', *zh* as the 's' in 'pleasure', and *r* is rolled.

Basics

Hello. Здраво. *zdra·vo*

Goodbye. До гледање. *do gle·da·nye*

Yes. Да. *da*

No. Не. *ne*

Please. Молам. *mo·lam*

Thank you. Благодарам. *bla·go·da·ram*

Excuse me. Извините. *iz·vee·nee·te*

Sorry. Простете. *pros·te·te*

What's your name?
Како се викате/викаш?
ka·ko se vi·ka·te/vi·kash

My name is ... Jас се викам ... *yas se vi·kam ...*

Do you speak English?
Зборувате ли англиски? *zbo·ru·va·te li an·glis·ki*

I don't understand.
Jас не разбирам. *yas ne raz·bi·ram*

Emergencies

Help! Помош! *po·mosh*

Go away! Одете си! *o·de·te si*

I'm lost. Се загубив. *se za·gu·biv*

I'm ill. Jас сум болен/болна. (m/f)
yas sum bo·len/bol·na

Eating & Drinking

What would you recommend?
Што препорачувате вие?
shto pre·po·ra·chu·va·te vi·e

Cheers! На здравје! *na zdrav·ye*

I'd like the bill/menu please.
Ве молам сметката/мени.
ve mo·lam smet·ka·ta/me·ni

Waxing Cyrillical

The following list shows the letters of the Macedonian and Serbian/Montenegrin Cyrillic alphabets. The letters are common to all languages unless otherwise specified.

Cyrillic	Sound	Pronunciation	Cyrillic	Sound	Pronunciation
А а	a	short as the 'u' in 'cut' long as in 'father'	Љ љ	ly	as the 'lli' in 'million'
			М м	m	as in 'mat'
Б б	b	as in 'but'	Н н	n	as in 'not'
В в	v	as in 'van'	Њ њ	ny	as the 'ny' in 'canyon'
Г г	g	as in 'go'	О о	o	short as in 'hot' long as in 'for'
Д д	d	as in 'dog'			
Ѓ ѓ	j	as in 'judge' (Macedonian only)	П п	p	as in 'pick'
			Р р	r	as in 'rub' (but rolled)
Ђ ђ	j	as in 'judge' (Serbian/Montenegrin only)	С с	s	as in 'sing'
			Т т	t	as in 'ten'
			Ќ ќ	ch	as in 'check' (Macedonian only)
Е е	e	short as in 'bet' long as in 'there'			
Ж ж	zh	as the 's' in 'measure'	Ћ ћ	ch	as in 'check' (Serbian/Montenegrin only)
З з	z	as in 'zoo'			
Ѕ ѕ	dz	as the 'ds' in 'suds' (Macedonian only)	У у	u	as in 'rule'
			Ф ф	f	as in 'fan'
И и	i	short as in 'bit' long as in 'marine'	Х х	h	as in 'hot'
			Ц ц	ts	as in 'tsar'
Ј ј	y	as in 'young'	Ч ч	ch	as in 'check'
К к	k	as in 'kind'	Џ џ	j	as in 'judge'
Л л	l	as in 'lamp'	Ш ш	sh	as in 'shop'

Skopje airport

Arriving & Getting Around

Skopje and Ohrid are well connected to other Balkan tourist hubs as well as wider international destinations. See the website Airports of Macedonia *(airports.com.mk)* for information about flights to/from North Macedonia.

By Air
Skopje is the only international airport in North Macedonia for flights from the rest of Europe. Budget airlines have improved its modest number of connections, and it's now linked pretty well to major European cities.

Driving Essentials
Drive on the right side of the road. The speed limits are 120km/h on motorways, 80km/h on open roads, and 50–60km/h in towns. Seatbelt and headlight use (even during the day) is compulsory, if not universally observed.

By Land
Buses connect Skopje or Ohrid with Pristina, Tirana, Sofia, Belgrade, Thessaloniki and other cities in neighbouring countries. From Skopje it's also possible to get to Ljubljana, İstanbul and Zagreb.

Visas
Entering North Macedonia is usually hassle-free. Citizens of any of the former Yugoslav republics, Australia, Canada, the EU, Iceland, Israel, New Zealand, Norway, Switzerland, Türkiye and the USA, and many other countries, can stay for three months without needing a visa. Check the website of the **Ministry of Foreign Affairs** *(mfa.gov.mk)* if unsure of your status. Your passport must have at least six months' validity when entering the country.

MONEY
Currency: Denar (MKD)

CASH & ATMS
Most tourist businesses, including lower to midrange hotels, only accept cash. North Macedonia's national currency may be the denar, but many tourist-related costs (eg tours and hotels) are quoted in euros. It usually works out better if you pay for smaller expenses in denars. ATMs are widespread in major towns, but surprisingly hard to find around Lake Ohrid, except in Ohrid Town itself.

CREDIT CARDS
Credit cards can often be used in larger cities (especially in hotels and restaurants), but don't rely on them outside Skopje.

TIPPING
North Macedonia doesn't have a tipping culture except at upmarket restaurants, where 10% is the norm.

For places to stay in Norway, see p864

XANNESIACX84/SHUTTERSTOCK

Above: Lofoten (p856); Right: Bryggen (p849), Bergen

Curated by
Anthony Ham

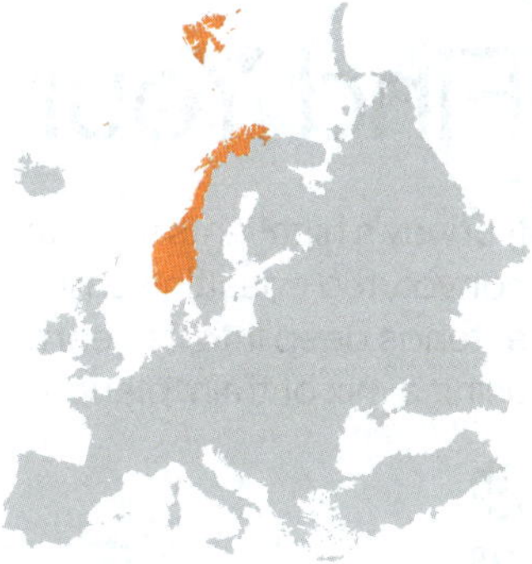

Norway

LANDSCAPES, ARTS, ACTIVITIES AND ARCHITECTURE

With its quietly confident cities, pristine wilderness and astonishing natural phenomena, Norway will steal your breath many times over.

Dramatic fjords violently gouged by glaciers; barren mountain ranges bejewelled by pure, glistening lakes; vast swaths of evergreen forest, and pristine, snow-laden wilderness – Norway's incomparable landscapes have been millions of years in the making, but it only takes seconds to fall in love. Norway's raw, unyielding beauty is simply staggering – it's certainly a candidate for Europe's most beautiful country – and the possibilities to experience it up close are endless. Norwegians love to explore their own country and join them you should, whether hiking, cycling, rafting or kayaking in summer, or snowshoeing, skiing and chasing the ephemeral aurora borealis (northern lights) in winter.

The country's urban landscapes, too, will grab your attention. Capital Oslo is no longer under the radar and is evolving at pace, with trailblazing architects erecting stunning structures befitting the nationally important cultural offerings within. Seemingly not even the quaintest island village is without a visionary attraction now, from cutting-edge contemporary art venues to minimalistic, luxury mountain lodges. And those landscapes, from the fjords to Lofoten, are an unfolding panorama of unrelenting magnificence. The pull of this country – whether to delve into its Viking roots, experience the unparalleled freedom of the outdoors or simply soak up the vibe of a neighbourhood cafe – remains as potent as ever. A once-in-a-lifetime destination it may be, but few visitors will leave Norway without longing to return.

LASSE JOHANSSON/SHUTTERSTOCK

THE MAIN AREAS

OSLO	**BERGEN**	**SOGNEFJORDEN**	**LOFOTEN**	**TROMSØ**
The culture capital. **p846**	Hanseatic history. **p849**	A spectacular 203km-long adventure. **p852**	Tolkein-worthy landscapes and fishing villages. **p856**	Northern lights and whale-watching. **p860**

Find Your Way

Norway's highlights span the length of its convoluted coastline and the excitement extends deep into its heart. You'll get around using a mix of train, plane, car and even boat.

CAR

Roads are excellent but often winding, speed limits are low, and ferries and tunnels defeat formidable mountains and oceans. Distances can be deceptive and getting anywhere can take longer than you expect, especially in summer.

TRAIN & BUS

Trains run as far north as Bodø. They're reliable, comfortable and many routes are unforgettably scenic. Long-distance buses are the primary option for public transport in the north, and there's an extensive network countrywide.

Tromsø, p860
An ideal location for aurora-spotting, the 'Gateway to the Arctic' is a lively introduction to the wild natural wonders beyond, with polar-themed museums and spirited nightlife.

Lofoten, p856
This jagged string of islands tugs at the soul with its fishing villages set against a backdrop of serrated peaks, at once intimidating and achingly beautiful.

Sognefjorden, p852
It's one of Norway's most popular natural attractions, but you can still find a quiet slice of paradise along the world's second-longest fjord.

Bergen, p849
The surrounding hills and fjords call to be explored, while Hanseatic history lingers at Bryggen and the culinary landscape spans homely bites and Michelin plaudits.

Oslo, p846
Norway's capital has a growing cache of world-class museums and architectural masterpieces, an exciting alternative vibe and a self-assured cuisine scene.

Knivskjelodden
(71°11'08"N)

Nordkapp
Honningsvåg · Kjøllefjord Østhavet
Revsbotn · Båtsfjord
Hasvik · Hammerfest
Lopphavet · Vadsø
Ringvassøy · Alta · Kirkenes
Tromsø
Ishavskatedralen · Fjellheimen · Karasjok
Andenes · Skibotn
Vesterålen · Finnsnes
Vestvågøy · Harstad
Lofotr Viking · Svolværgeita
Museum
Værøy Å
Røsthavet · Fauske
Vedøya · Bodø
Ørnes
Mo i Rana
Sandnessjøen
Brønnøysund
Namsos · Grong
Steinkjer
Trondheim
Kristiansund
Stadhavet
Ålesund · Molde
Romsdalen
Florø · Urnes Stave
Førde · Church
Sognefjorden · Flåmsbana · Lillehammer
Voss · Railway
Bergen · Myrdal · Hamar · Elverum
Fløibanen Funicular · Odda · Kongsvinger
Leirvik · Oslo
Stavanger · Drammen · Oslo Opera House
Tønsberg · Moss
Skien · Larvik · Fredrikstad
Arendal
Flekkefjord
Mandal
Kristiansand
Skagerrak

SWEDEN

DENMARK

NORTH SEA

0   200 km
0   100 miles

Oslo Opera House (p846)

Plan Your Time

Even on a short break in Norway you can combine natural beauty with stylish city life. Getting from place to place can take time, but the rewards that await along the way are exceptional.

Pressed for Time

● Absorb the artistic and architectural masterworks of **Oslo** (p846) as well as **Oslo Opera House** (p846) for Oslofjord views. After a couple of days, take the glorious railway to **Bergen** (p849), where you can wander the historic wooden alleyways of **Bryggen** (p849), feast on seafood, and ride the **funicular** (p851) up Mt Fløyen for superb city views.

Ten Days in Norway

● Begin in **Oslo** (p846), then catch the train to Myrdal and hop on the vintage-style, steep-as-steep **Flåmsbana Railway** (p853) to Flåm. Float down spectacular **Nærøyfjord** (p854) before heading to **Bergen** (p849) via Gudvangen. Fly to Bodø, rent a car and catch the ferry to **Lofoten** (p856) – allow three days to drive from one end to the other and back again.

SEASONAL HIGHLIGHTS

SPRING
The weather starts to warm and days lengthen. On **Constitution Day** (17 May), Norwegians gather in national dress for parades.

SUMMER
Mild summers draw crowds for **hiking**, **biking** and picnicking in nature. A full calendar of **festivals** fills long summer days.

AUTUMN
September can be fine, with fewer crowds. By November, **whale-watching tours** are at their peak in the waters near Tromsø.

WINTER
Winter reveals the **aurora borealis'** light show. Enjoy **Arctic adventures** by snowmobile, sled dog and reindeer around Tromsø.

Oslo

MAJOR MUSEUMS | COOL NEIGHBOURHOODS | MODERN ARCHITECTURE

GETTING AROUND

Oslo Gardermoen International Airport is Norway's international gateway. It's 35km northeast of the city but well connected to the Oslo S central station by express and suburban trains. In the city, when you can't travel on foot, the best option is the T-Bane, the metro rail network that passes through Nationaltheatret, Stortinget and Jernbanetorget stations. For Bygdøy and its museums, ferries sail from Rådhusbrygge Quay. For elsewhere around Oslofjord, it's Vippetangen Quay.

☑ TOP TIP

With so many museums to visit, the **Oslo Pass** *(visitoslo.com)* is a wise investment. It covers most museums and public transport, and entitles you to restaurant and tour discounts. Buy it online or at a tourist office.

Watch this space: Oslo is the next focal point of Scandi cool. Long derided as lacking the effortless designer cachet of Stockholm, Copenhagen or Helsinki, Oslo has gone quietly about its business, building architectural showpieces and creating a dazzling portfolio of museums that's already the region's best. It's only now that the rest of the world is starting to take notice, and Oslo is increasingly seen as a leading candidate for the title of Scandinavia's capital of the arts. But as Norway's capital city, Oslo does more than represent the nation's cultural showpiece. It also serves as a touchstone for the new Norway, one that is hip and multicultural and takes a slightly alternative slant on life. Nowhere is that more evident than in Grünerløkka, a once down-at-heel neighbourhood that has become one of Northern Europe's most happening city experiences.

An Iceberg-Like City Icon

Admire the Oslo Opera House

They take architecture seriously in Oslo, and the showpiece of this passion is **Oslo Opera House** *(operaen.no; tours adult/child 150/85kr)*. Opened in 2008, the building marked a fundamental shift in the city's orientation, bringing the former docks into play and opening up the city centre to the water in a transformative way. The opera house evokes a glacier or an iceberg floating in the inner reaches of Oslofjord. Climb to the roof for fine views, step back and contemplate its daring simplicity from across the water, and step inside to enjoy the curvaceous interior swathed in pine. For the full experience, join a guided tour and book tickets for an opera.

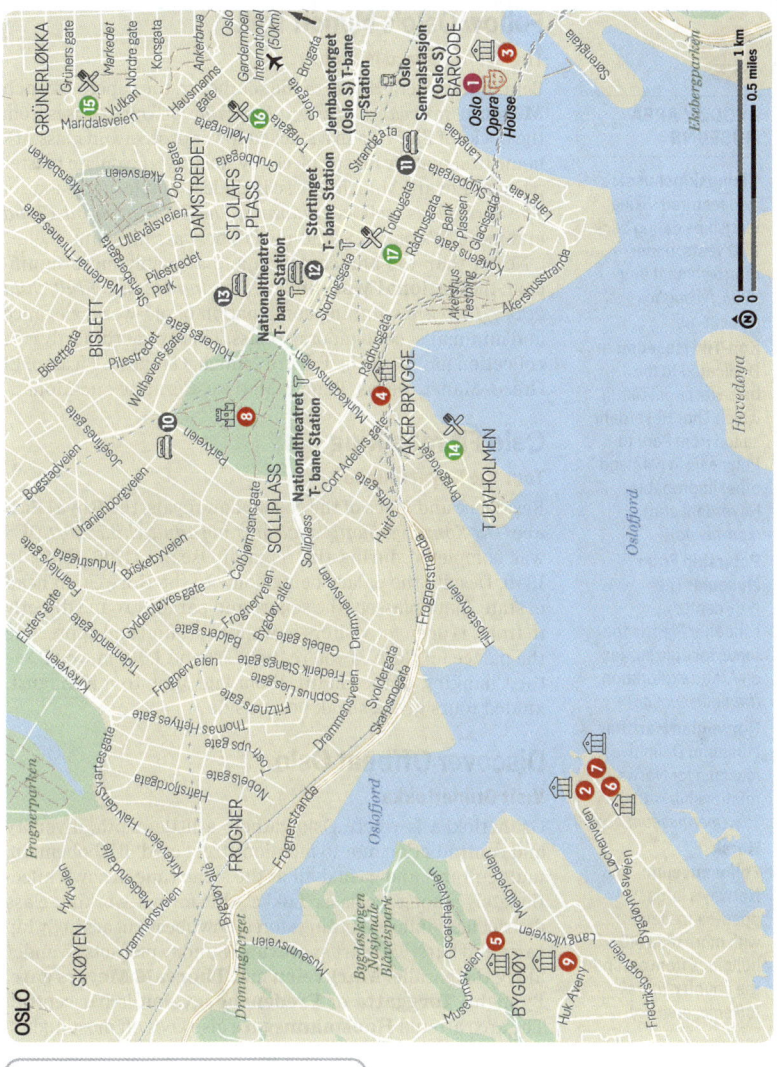

OSLO

★ **HIGHLIGHTS**

1 Oslo Opera House

● **SIGHTS**

2 Kon-Tiki Museum
3 Munch Museum
4 National Museum
5 Norsk Folkemuseum
6 Norwegian Maritime Museum
7 Polarship Fram Museum
8 Royal Palace
9 Vikingskipshuset

● **SLEEPING**

10 Camillas Hus
11 Citybox Oslo
12 Karl Johan Hotel
13 Smarthotel Oslo

● **EATING**

14 Lofoten Fiskerestaurant
15 Mathallen Oslo
16 Oslo Street Food
17 Sentralen Restaurant

BYGDØY AREA MUSEUMS

Vikingskipshuset: Two restored Viking longships dating back 1100 years; under refurbishment until 2026. *(vikingtids museet.no)*

Kon-Tiki Museum: Dedicated to the balsa raft Kon-Tiki, in which Thor Heyerdahl sailed from Peru to Polynesia in 1947, and other improbable Heyerdahl craft. *(kon-tiki.no)*

Polarship Fram Museum: The 19th-century schooner *Fram* is the focus for epic stories on Arctic exploration. *(frammuseum.no)*

Norwegian Maritime Museum: Definitive museum for Norway's relationship with the sea. *(marmuseum.no)*

Norsk Folkemuseum: Norway's largest open-air museum, with more than 140 buildings from around the country. *(norsk folkemuseum.no)*

Follow Oslo's Munch Trail

The art of Edvard Munch

Behind the Opera House to the southeast, the superb **Munch Museum** *(munchmuseet.no; adult/child 180kr/free)* rises from the docks of Bjørvika in a stacked tower of steel and glass. It's home to signature masterpieces by Norway's favourite master painter, Edvard Munch. These include a couple of versions of *The Scream*, as well as *Madonna*, *The Seine at Saint-Cloud* and more. It's one of Scandinavia's best art museums.

Newer than the Munchmuseet and arguably more significant, the **National Museum** *(nasjonalmuseet.no; adult/child 200kr/free)* is a stunning combination of old-world elegance and minimalist contemporary glass. This extraordinarily rich collection has works by Edvard Munch, Gauguin, Picasso, El Greco, Manet, Degas, Renoir, Matisse, Cézanne and Monet.

Oslo Fit for a King

Tour the Royal Palace

Residence and office of the Norwegian royals, the **Royal Palace** *(Det Kongelige Slott; royalcourt.no; adult/child 220/110kr)* was completed during the reign of Oscar I (1799–1859), in 1849. Despite the palace being home to the Norwegian head of state, Slottsplassen (the square and parade ground directly in front) is open for visitors to wander around and appreciate the palace up close. If you're there around 1.30pm, you'll see the Changing of the Guard. From late June to mid-August, guided tours give a sneak peek inside.

Discover Offbeat Oslo

Visit Grünerløkka

Grünerløkka is where Oslo gathers a little depth, diversity and contradiction, not to mention street cred. It's bohemian, multicultural and casual all at the same time. Known affectionately among locals as 'Løkka', this former working-class district has vintage-clothing stores, downbeat but achingly hip cafes and bars, edgy art spaces and Sunday markets. Wander along the parallel **Markveien** and **Thorvald Meyers gate**. By night, **Torggatta** or **Fredensborgveien** is bar central. The area around **Hausmannsgate** also goes off most nights.

 EATING IN OSLO: OUR PICKS

Oslo Street Food: Nothing screams new Oslo quite like this; dozens of food trucks plus DJs. *11am-11pm Mon-Thu, to 3am Fri & Sat, noon-10pm Sun €€*

Sentralen Restaurant: New Nordic fusion in casual surrounds at reasonable prices. *7.30am-8pm Mon-Fri, 11am-5pm Sat & Sun €€*

Mathallen Oslo: Market delis and cool cafes at a market and culinary venue celebrating small-scale producers. *10am-8pm Tue-Sat, 11am-6pm Sun €€*

Lofoten Fiskerestaurant: Perfectly presented seafood in an elegant setting. *11.30am-10pm Mon-Fri, noon-10pm Sat, 1-9pm Sun €€€*

Bergen

HISTORIC BUILDINGS | SCENIC BEAUTY | URBAN CHARM

Bergen ranks among Scandinavia's most beautiful cities. Surrounded by seven hills and seven fjords, the city has gorgeous wooden architecture that radiates from its compact historic centre. With medieval Bryggen as its centrepiece, the area around Bergen's inner harbour hums with people, energy and a feel-good atmosphere that draws return visitors from across Europe and further afield. The city is also known for its excellent culinary scene, it has its own musical soundtrack, and the hills that surround it are crisscrossed with cable cars and hiking trails.

You could easily spend a week in Bergen getting to know its charms and hidden corners. In this sense, Bergen is a worthy destination in its own right. At the same time, it is Norway's premier gateway to the country's fjords. Yes, Bergen really does have it all.

Bryggen & Harbour Life

A medieval port

Bergen's old city wharf, UNESCO World Heritage–listed **Bryggen**, has been the city's beating heart since the Middle Ages. Running along the eastern shore of Vågen Harbour (*bryggen* translates as 'wharf'), it remains a superb collection of colourfully painted wooden, rough-plank buildings leaning at precarious angles. Behind the facades, shoulder-width openings lead invitingly into dark corridors lined with artisan workshops and small boutiques, where the floorboards and leaning wooden walls creak as they would on an old sailing ship.

Highlights include the **Hanseatic Museum** (*hanseatiske museum.museumvest.no; incl Schøtstuene adult/child 150kr/ free),* which is closed until 2026, and **Schøtstuene** (*hanseatiske museum.museumvest.no; incl Hanseatic Museum adult/child 150kr/free),* a set of former assembly rooms. The 12th-century **Mariakirken** (*St Mary's Church; adult/child 95kr/free)* is Bergen's oldest building, with twin towers, a Romanesque entrance and a splendid baroque pulpit. Also stop by **Bryggens Museum** (*bymuseet.no; adult/child 170kr/free)* for a glimpse of what life and work were like here centuries ago.

GETTING AROUND

Most Bergen attractions can be reached on foot; boat, funicular and cable car cover the rest. From the **airport**, the Bybane light rail is best (when buying a ticket from the machines at the airport on the light-rail platform, you just need a Zone 1 ticket). Few hotels have their own car parks, and the city-centre public car parks routinely charge over 300kr per 24 hours. The 24-hour Bygarasjen next to the bus terminal has the cheapest parking (200kr).

☑ **TOP TIP**

If you'll be in Bergen for a few days and want to cram in as much as possible, **Bergen Card** *(visitbergen. com)* is a good option. It entitles you to free or discounted entry to museums, public transport, tours, the Fløibanen funicular and concerts.

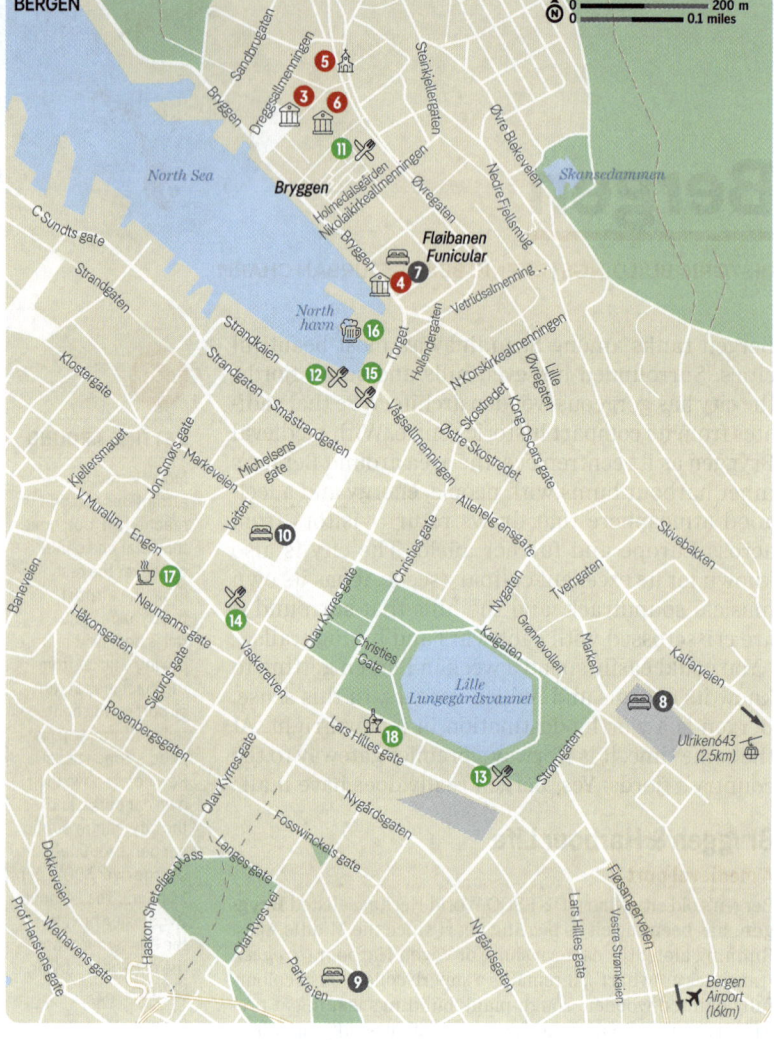

BERGEN

HIGHLIGHTS
1 Bryggen
2 Fløibanen Funicular

SIGHTS
3 Bryggens Museum
4 Hanseatic Museum
5 Mariakirken
6 Schøtstuene

SLEEPING
7 Det Hanseatiske Hotel
8 Grand Hotel Terminus
9 Hotel Park
10 Thon Hotel Bristol

EATING
11 Bryggen Tracteursted
12 Fisketorget Mathallen

13 Lysverket
14 Pingvinen
15 Torget Fish Market

DRINKING & NIGHTLIFE
16 Bryggeriet
17 Café Opera
18 Landmark
see 8 Terminus Bar

View from Above

Bergen's best panoramas

Take **Fløibanen** *(floyen.no; adult/child from 130/65kr),* a 26-degree funicular that ambles from the city centre, up a pretty, forested hillside dotted with whitewashed wooden homes, all the way to the summit of **Mt Fløyen** (320m). From the viewing platform, Bergen unfurls into the fjords. Walking tracks fan out from the top.

Mt Ulriken (643m) is twice the height of Fløyen and every bit as beautiful. The **Ulriken643** cable car *(ulriken643.no; adult one-way/return 230/395kr, child 110/160kr)* speeds in just seven minutes to the top, which has a superb panorama over the city, fjords and mountains. There's also a zip line.

Culinary Bergen

Norway's foodie capital

At **Pingvinen** *(pingvinen.no),* locals come for the meals their parents and grandparents used to cook. These might include *kjøttkaker* (meatballs with mushy peas and lingonberries), *plukkfisk* (cod with mashed potatoes, bacon and flatbread) or *lapskaus* (salted-lamb stew). **Torget Fish Market** has casual red tents on the harbourfront, where it serves ready-to-eat salmon, calamari, fish and chips, prawn baguettes and seafood salads. Far slicker, **Fisketorget Mathallen** has permanent stands, each with its own menu, from sit-down meals to traditional, creamy bowls of fish soup, oysters and caviar.

One of Norway's best eat streets, **Marken** runs from the train station to just in from the harbour and is filled with multicultural options and fun cafes. Historic Bryggen dining rooms don't come any more authentic than **Bryggen Tracteursted** *(bryggentracteursted.no).* For New Nordic cooking, plan a meal at **Lysverket** *(lysverket.no).*

BRYGGEN HISTORY

During the 12th and 13th centuries, Bergen was Norway's capital and a leading member of the Hanseatic League, whose member cities controlled northern European trade. Bryggen was the city's economic engine. In the 14th century, several *stuer* (trading firms) shared each of the wooden buildings that rose two or three stories above the wharf. The buildings combined business premises with living quarters and warehouses. Each building had a crane for loading and unloading ships, as well as a *schøtstue* (large assembly room) where merchants met and ate. These days, Bryggen's 58 buildings (some say 61) cover 13,000 sq metres (just 25% of the original). Most date from after the great fire of 1702.

 DRINKING IN BERGEN: OUR PICKS

Terminus Bar: Wood-panelled whisky den in Grand Hotel Terminus with more than 500 peaty tastes, including antique bottles. *5pm-midnight*	**Café Opera:** Bergen mainstay – cocktails, craft beer, folk music. *11am-11.30pm Mon-Wed, to 1.30am Thu-Sat, noon-11.30pm Sun*	**Bryggeriet:** Microbrewery overlooking the harbour; creative beers, mostly brewed in the Germanic tradition. *4-10pm Tue-Thu, 6-10.30pm Fri & Sat*	**Landmark:** Arthouse daytime cafe featuring 1930s Norwegian design, and a live-performance space for Bergen's best club events. *cafe 11am-5pm*

Sognefjorden

FANTASTIC FJORDS | STAVE CHURCHES | PICTURESQUE VILLAGES

GETTING AROUND

Getting to, around and then away from Sognefjorden involves a combination of road, train and boat. This being Norway, most connections run like clockwork. Where roads run into mountains, there are tunnels. Where they hit water, there are bridges or, more often, vehicle ferries. The main road through the Aurlandsfjord and Nærøyfjord arms of Sognefjorden is the E16, which connects Oslo with Bergen on Norway's west coast.

☑ TOP TIP

The fabulous year-round **Norway in a Nutshell** (fjordtours.com) tours, taken in whole or in part, combine the Bergen or Oslo train to Myrdal, the Flåmsbana line to Flåm, a cruise along Nærøyfjord to Gudvangen, a bus to Voss, and a final leg to Bergen or Oslo by train.

If you only have time to visit one Norwegian fjord, make it Sognefjorden, at 203km the world's second-longest fjord. The views here are simply extraordinary, an elemental combination of vertiginous rock, winter snow and ice, and waters that take on every shade of blue. Add some achingly pretty fjord-side villages and the iconic, near-vertical Flåmsbana Railway, and it's little wonder that the Sognefjorden arms of Nærøyfjord and Aurlandsfjord are very popular with visitors.

But opportunities to escape the crowds and find your own little corner of this paradise are many, whether you're cycling up and over the mountains or kayaking with the seals. And for every pretty but busy village and traveller hub like Flåm or Aurland, there's an Undredal or Otternes that feels like a fjord-side village unchanged by time, and that many travellers miss altogether because they're so busy admiring the view.

Look Down in Wonder

High above Aurlandsfjord

Deep, narrow Aurlandsfjord runs for 29 glorious kilometres, branching away from the main Sognefjorden in a water-filled chasm barely 2km wide in places.

The 45km, summer-only **Aurlandsfjellet** (*nasjonaleturist veger.no*) – or Snøvegen (the Snow Rd), as it's known locally – is among the most dramatic mountain roads in a country of many. This sinuous, narrow route climbs from sea level to the desolate, boulder-strewn high plateau that separates Aurland and Lærdalsøyri (Lærdal) and then back down again. Along the way, you can stop at **Stegastein**, an observation point that juts out above the abyss 630m above Aurlandsfjord. Even if you don't travel the full Aurlandsfjellet road, you can still reach Stegastein along a winding 8km road from Aurland.

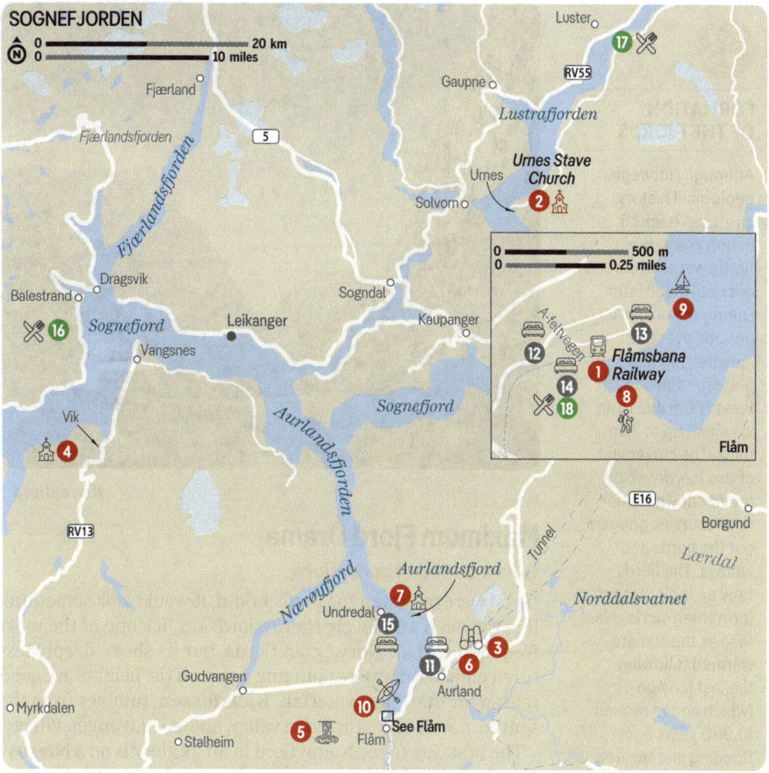

SOGNEFJORDEN

Luster

Fjærland

Fjærlandsfjorden

RV55

Gaupne

Lustrafjorden

Urnes Stave Church

Urnes

Solvorn

Fjærlandsfjorden

Dragsvik

Balestrand

Sogndal

Sognefjord

Leikanger

Kaupanger

Vangsnes

Vik

Aurlandsfjorden

Sognefjord

A-felvegen

Flåmsbana Railway

Flåm

E16

RV13

Borgund

Tunnel

Lærdal

Nærøyfjord

Aurlandsfjord

Norddalsvatnet

Undredal

Gudvangen

Myrkdalen

Aurland

See Flåm

Stalheim

Flåm

★ HIGHLIGHTS
1 Flåmsbana Railway
2 Urnes Stave Church

● SIGHTS
3 Aurlandsfjellet
4 Hopperstad Stave Church

5 Kjelsfossen
6 Stegastein
7 Undredal Church

● ACTIVITIES
8 Flåm to Aurland Walking Path
9 Nærøyfjord Cruise
10 Njord Kayak Centre

● SLEEPING
11 Aurland Fjordhotell
12 Flåm Camping & Hostel
13 Flåmsbrygga
14 Fretheim Hotel
15 Undredal Gjestehus
see 11 Vangsgaarden Gjestgiveri

● EATING
16 Ciderhuset
17 Lustrabui
18 Restaurant Arven

● DRINKING & NIGHTLIFE
see 13 Ægir Bryggeri

The **Flåmsbana Railway** (*one way/return adult from 440/630kr, child from 220/315kr*) is a 20km-long engineering wonder that hauls itself up 866m of altitude gain through 20 tunnels. At a gradient of 1:18, it's one of the world's steepest railway lines. The vintage-style train takes 45 minutes to climb to **Myrdal**, atop the bleak, treeless Hardangervidda plateau, passing deep ravines and thundering waterfalls along the way. The railway links in both timetable and location to the dramatic Oslo–Bergen railway, which wonderfully increases your options for onward travel.

FORMATION OF THE FJORDS

Although Norwegian geological history stretches back 1.8 billion years, the fjords were not carved out until much later. During the glacial periods over this time, elevated highland plateaus subsided at least 700m due to an ice sheet up to 2km thick. The movement of this ice, driven by gravity down former river courses, gouged out the fjords and valleys. The fjords took on their present form when sea levels rose as the climate warmed following the last Ice Age (which ended around 10,000 years ago), flooding into the new valleys left behind by melting and retreating glaciers. Sea levels may have risen by as much as 100m, creating fjords whose waters can seem impossibly deep.

MEDITERRANEAN/GETTY IMAGES

Nærøyfjord

Maximum Fjord Drama

Take a boat on Nærøyfjord

If you were to design the perfect fjord, it would look something like the deep and lovely Nærøyfjord. Yes, it's one of the most frequented of all Norwegian fjords, but its sheer, deeply textured cliffs with waters plunging down off the heights are good reason for that. One waterfall, **Kjelsfossen**, tumbles from the southern wall of Nærøydalen valley, above Gudvangen village.

The best way to see Nærøyfjord in all its glory is on a **Nærøyfjord cruise** *(thefjords.no; per person from 550kr),* which usually means taking one of the regular summer-only boats from Flåm to Gudvangen. Get up on the top deck, where you'll be able to appreciate the scale but also zero in on the detail.

Find Your Own Fjord Corner

Escape the crowds in Undredal

Undredal is one of the loveliest, quietest villages in all of Norway's fjord country. Most boats make a stop here, but few passengers disembark. If you drive the narrow mountain road down to Undredal off the Flåm–Gudvangen road, you may have this charming little place to yourself. Turn off the

EATING & DRINKING AROUND SOGNEFJORDEN: OUR PICKS

Lustrabui: Sourdough, *skillingsbollar* (sweet buns) and espresso at one of western Norway's best bakeries; in Skjolden. *7am-5pm Mon-Fri, to 3pm Sat* €

Ciderhuset: On a fruit farm, Balestrand's Cider House has tours, tastings and meals in a greenhouse restaurant. *noon-10pm late Jun–mid Aug* €€

Ægir Bryggeri: Craft beer and Norwegian comfort food amid flagstones and sheepskins in Flåm. *noon-10pm May-Sep, from 6pm Oct-Dec, from 5pm Jan-Apr* €€€

Restaurant Arven: Upstairs in Flåm's Fretheim Hotel; local ingredients and seasonal produce with surprising twists. *6.30-9.30pm* €€€

engine, park the car and walk. Better still, stay overnight: there's magic in the air as darkness falls and silence descends. Try the local Undredal goat's cheese (available at the jetty or in one of the village cheese shops), then climb to the cute-as-a-postcard 12th-century **Undredal Church** *(adult/child 50kr/free),* mainland Scandinavia's smallest still-operational house of worship.

From Flåm's **Njord Kayak Centre** *(seakayaknorway.com; tours from 825kr, rental from 745kr)* you can get out on the water and let the quiet lapping of paddles replace the sometimes over-bright bonhomie of the captains on the boat tours. All signs of mass tourism evaporate, too, along the 12km-long, fjord-side **Flåm to Aurland Walking Path**.

Medieval Houses of Worship

Sognefjorden's stave churches

If Norway's stave churches and other medieval religious buildings have captured your imagination, Sognefjorden offers an especially rich portfolio.

Established in the 12th century alongside the major overland trade route between eastern and western Norway, **Borgund Stave Church** *(stavechurch.com/en/borgund; adult/child 130/90kr)* now lies around 30km southeast of Lærdalsøyri along the E16. It has a wonderfully simple and darkly suggestive interior, a superb hand-carved altar and Norway's only extant free-standing medieval wooden bell tower.

Along sinuous fjord-hugging roads to the north, overlooking Lustrafjord, UNESCO World Heritage–listed **Urnes Stave Church** *(stavechurch.com/en/urnes; adult/child 150/100kr)* is Borgund's rival as Sognefjord's most impressive church. Dating from 1170 and built on the site of a previous chapel, Urnes is one of Norway's oldest church. Apart from its special location, it's defined by intricate wooden carvings, including exquisite vines and mythic creatures, and it looks like a forgotten set from *Lord of the Rings*.

Way out to the west, a long drive and the odd ferry crossing away, Vik is home to **Hopperstad Stave Church** *(stavechurch .com/hopperstad-stave-church; adult/child 110/80kr),* which feels like it was handcrafted by medieval artisans and then pieced together; it consists of 2000 different parts and was built around 1130.

NORWAY'S STAVE CHURCHES

Seemingly conceived by a whimsical, childlike imagination, the stave church is an ingenious adaptation to Norway's unique local conditions. Originally dating from the late Viking era, these ornately worked houses of worship are among the oldest surviving wooden buildings on Earth, albeit heavily restored. Named for their vertical supporting posts, these churches are also distinguished by detailed carved designs and dragon-headed gables resembling the prows of classic Viking ships. Of the 500 to 600 that were originally built, only about 20 of the 28 that remain retain many of their original components.

Lofoten

DRAMATIC LANDSCAPES | PRETTY VILLAGES | FABULOUS HIKES

GETTING AROUND

Svolvær is the main transport hub, with links to Bodø or Skutvik via ferries and express boats plus flights from its small airport. A car allows you to see more of the islands. Bus routes connect Svolvær to Kabelvåg, Henningsvær and points along the islands right down to Å, but services are sporadic, especially in winter. Download the Billett Nordland app to buy tickets. Buses don't always coincide with ferries arriving at Moskenes from Bodø; book onward transport in advance.

☑ TOP TIP

For something really special, plan to be here when the midnight sun bathes Lofoten in perpetual daylight (28 May to 14 July), or the polar night when the northern lights are always a possibility (5 December to 7 January).

Welcome to one of the most beautiful places on Earth. From the moment you first sight them across the water, Lofoten Islands' craggy silhouettes seem too beautiful to be true. Like some mythical Tolkienesque natural fortress, the impossibly high mountains rise steeply from the shore like a series of mirages.

Steeped in the fishing traditions of Norway's storied coastal communities, the Lofoten isn't just about astonishing natural grandeur. Clinging to the narrow shore and deep valleys are some of Norway's most beautiful hamlets, with Viking histories, hiking trails and a pretty harbour lined with colourful wooden buildings and great racks of cod, salted and dried, that lend a strange beauty to many already-spectacular scenes. And although the views are sometimes obscured by the dark storms of the Atlantic, Lofoten never loses its drama or its wild beauty. Spend as long here as you possibly can.

Norway's most Scenic Arrival

Take a slow boat to Lofoten

You could drive to the Lofoten Islands, but everyone should take the boat at least once – the approach by water is one of the most beautiful you can imagine. On a clear day, the islands seem impossibly high and jagged, as if they're an apparition of a Norwegian Atlantis with spires and ramparts rising from the ocean itself. It's one of the great boat journeys in Europe.

There are three main routes from the mainland to Lofoten. From **Bodø**, there's a foot-passenger express ferry to Svolvær (3½ hours), or a car ferry to Moskenes (3½ hours) via Røst and Værøy. Another option is the summer-only **Skutvik–Svolvær car ferry** (2½ hours). And, of course, the **Hurtigruten coastal ferry** passes through Lofoten on its daily journeys, stopping at Bodø, Stamsund, Svolvær and Sortland (Vesterålen).

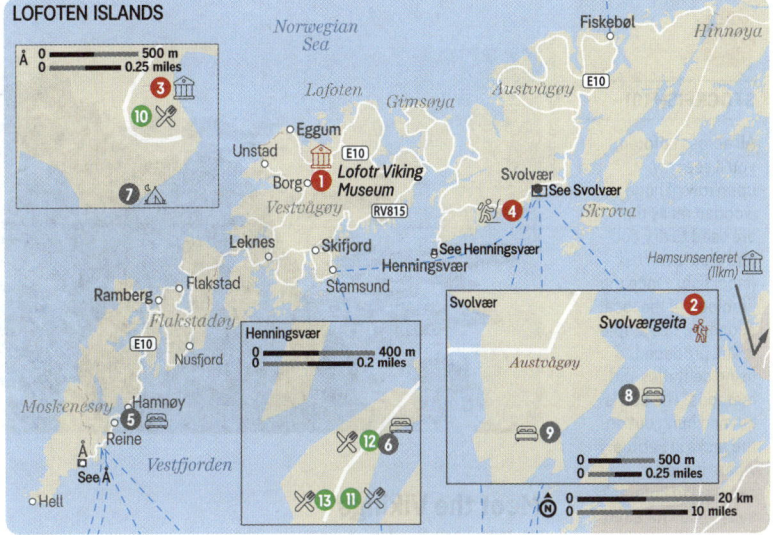

LOFOTEN ISLANDS

HIGHLIGHTS
1 Lofotr Viking Museum
2 Svolværgeita

SIGHTS
3 Lofoten Tørrfiskmuseum

ACTIVITIES
4 Northern Alpine Guides

SLEEPING
5 Eliassen Rorbuer
6 Henningsvær Bryggehotel

7 Moskenesstraumen Camping
8 Svinøya Rorbuer
9 Thon Hotel Lofoten

EATING
10 Bakeri

see 8 Børsen
11 Fiskekrogen
12 Klatre Kafeen
13 Lofotomat

Village Vistas

Classic Lofoten views

The scenes of *rorbuer* (fishers' cabins) clustered around rocky shorelines, with boats bobbing on the water, is the quintessential picture of the Lofoten Islands.

On Austvågøy, happening **Henningsvær** isn't just a pretty face, though it's certainly that too. Arranged more or less in a 'U' around its long, narrow harbour, the village tumbles with stylish boutiques and coffee shops. Beyond the harbour lies what could be the most picturesque football ground in the world.

On Flakstadøy, **Nusfjord** is another, albeit very different, Lofoten treasure. Sheltered from the sea and tucked away in the lee of high hills, nearly 40 oxblood-red wooden buildings – *rorbuer*, a cod-liver-oil factory, an old sawmill – encircle Nusfjord's tiny harbour. At the closed southwestern end of the harbour, climb the rocky slope for the classic Nusfjord vantage point.

Meanwhile, on Moskenesøy, a particular vista of **Reine** from the E10, with perfectly photogenic peaks beyond, is so arresting that there's a car park to enable safe stopping. And at the southernmost tip of Mosekesøy, **Å** (sometimes written as Å i Lofoten) is the kind of place that postcards were made for.

STOCKFISH 101

All across Lofoten, you'll see row upon row of huge wooden racks that are used to dry cod and create *tørrfisk* (stockfish). Once the lifeblood of the local economy, this staple is still produced using centuries-old methods. The cod is cut and hung out on the racks in February, where it's left exposed to Lofoten's salty winds for almost four months until May, when it's taken indoors to mature for a further two or three months before being sorted according to quality for various markets.

See what all the fuss is about at Svolvær's **Børsen**, an adapted stockfish warehouse turned fine-dining restaurant with stockfish on the menu. **Lofotomat**, in Henningsvær, is another fine option. In Å, there's the **Lofoten Tørrfiskmuseum**.

WHATAFOTO/SHUTTERSTOCK

Meet the Vikings

Visit the Viking Museum

Sitting just off the E10, 14km from Leknes on Vesvågøy, the **Lofotr Viking Museum** *(lofotr.no; adult/child from 200/150kr)* will transport you back a whole millennium to the height of the Viking age. The museum is the result of the unexpected discovery of an 83m-long chieftain's longhouse in 1981 at nearby Borg, the largest of its kind ever to be found in Scandinavia.

Wander through the exhibition in the main museum building to learn about the discovery and to see some of the astonishing treasures and artefacts unearthed along with the building, including gold-foil amulets, jewellery and ceramics. Then step inside the replica longhouse, where costumed interpreters re-create Viking life.

Scale Svolværgeita

Look down on Lofoten's capital

If Lofoten's soaring backdrop inspires you to get high, consider **Svolværgeita** (355m). Nicknamed 'The Goat' because its two granite spires resemble a goat's horns, Svolværgeita is visible from all over Svolvær and the view from up top adorns every second postcard on sale in town. In summer, you can enjoy the view yourself, as long as you have a head for heights and half a day to dedicate to the experience.

 EATING AROUND LOFOTEN: OUR PICKS

Bakeri: Unmissable historic village bakery in Å; divine *kanelsnurr* (cinnamon scrolls). *9am-3pm mid-May–Aug, varies rest of year* €

Klatre Kafeen: A few tables over the water in Henningsvær for shrimp sandwiches and codfish soup. *11am-1am Sun-Thu, to 2.30am Fri & Sat* €€

Børsen: Svolvær's top table in an atmospheric spot on Svinøya; try Lofoten stockfish. *11.30am-3.30pm mid-Jun–mid-Aug & 6-10pm year-round* €€€

Fiskekrogen: Elegant Henningsvær restaurant serving hearty seafood soup; delicately presented options. *noon-10pm Jun-Aug, varies Sep-May* €€€

Svolværgeita

We strongly recommend taking a guide; try Kabelvåg-based **Northern Alpine Guides** *(alpineguides.no)*. If you decide to go it alone, walk northeast along the E10 towards Narvik. After passing the marina, turn left on Nyveien, then double back on Øvreværveien, then left on Blåtindveien. The trailhead is just beyond the kids' basketball court. We can't recommend that you leap between the two spires, but that doesn't stop people from ignoring this advice.

For even better views, you could climb beyond Svolværgeita for another 30 minutes to the summit of **Fløya** (590m).

Trek a Remote Headland

Hike from Unstad to Eggum

The road off the E10 to Unstad is quiet, meandering along a gentle rise, past white wooden homes above the tranquil fjord waters. Both **Unstad** and **Eggum** are tiny settlements that crouch along Lofoten's western Atlantic shore, unprotected from offshore winds. It's a mostly flat trail (two hours, 9km one way), save for a slightly tricky section where you may want to use the metal chain handrail to keep your balance. The views are wild and windswept, winding past several headlands, a solitary lighthouse, superb seascapes and the ruins of a fortress by the ocean.

KNUT HAMSUN

If you take the ferry from Skutvik to Svolvær (and even if you don't), make sure you visit the **Hamsunsenteret** *(hamsunsenteret. no)*, around halfway between the E6 and Skutvik, along the Rv81. Daringly designed, the centre commemorates the life of Knut Hamsun, who won the Nobel Prize for Literature in 1920 and was both a literary giant and a controversial figure, thanks to his support for Nazi Germany. The centre covers both topics in a stunning series of unflinching displays. Hamsun moved to Hamarøy with his family at age three and later returned for a number of his working years as a writer.

Tromsø

WINTER ACTIVITIES | SUMMER ACTIVITIES | ARCTIC LIFE

GETTING AROUND

Prostneset is the main hub for buses, ferries and express boats. Tromsø's airport is the flight hub for Norway's north, with routes between Oslo and Svalbard, Alta and beyond. There's an airport shuttle bus to/from the city centre; local buses 40 and 42 also head that way for less than half the price, though space can be tight. Buses 20, 24 and 26 travel over Tromsøbrua towards the Arctic Cathedral; the 26 continues to Fjellheisen.

☑ **TOP TIP**

For those eager to see the northern lights, the **Fjellheisen** cable car is a must. At 421m above sea level, it has dazzling views over Tromsø. Head up after 6pm and check *norway-lights.com* for up-to-date forecasts.

Self-styled as Norway's 'Gateway to the Arctic', Tromsø is a small city with a big personality: unashamedly fun and alive with possibilities for Arctic-themed enjoyment. It's located 400km north of the Arctic Circle and lies on the east of Tromsøya, which is linked to Tromsdalen on the mainland by an arched bridge, Tromsøbrua.

By day there are landmark sights to explore, from an imposing modern church to fascinating museums telling tales of polar endeavour. By night, the city centre buzzes as locals and visitors alike make the most of lively music venues, historic pubs and excellent restaurants. Inky fjords and mountains topped with year-round snow set the stage for outdoor activities, and you can try them all here. Long summer days promise long summer hikes, while winter tempts with chances to glimpse the aurora borealis.

Tromsdalen's Heavenly Heights

Arctic cathedral and Fjellheisen cable car

Walk over 1km-long Tromsøbrua to reach **Ishavskatedralen** *(Arctic Cathedral; ishavskatedralen.no; adult/child 80kr/ free)*. The 35m-high triangular face of Tromsdalen Church (as it's officially known) reaches skywards, while the 11 ice-white, aluminium-coated concrete segments suggest glacial crevices.

Afterwards, head to **Fjellheisen** *(fjellheisen.no; adult/ child return 495/240kr, 295kr return after 5pm)*, just under 1km from the church via Turistvegen and Anton Jakobsens veg, for panoramic views of Tromsø and the mountaintops beyond. The gondola ride takes just four minutes. To return, bypass the gondola and descend via the 1200 stone steps known as Sherpatrappa (Sherpa Steps), named for the team of Nepalese Sherpa who laid them.

TROMSØ

Ishavskatedralen (1.2km);
Fjellheisen (2.2km)
Søndre Tollbugate

Wandering
Owl Tours
(500m)

Skolegata
Bispegata
Vestregata
Stranckesmuget
Stortorget
Hansgata

Stortorget
Harbour

Grønnegata

Sentrumstangenten

Parkgata

Kongsbakken

Kongsparken

Vestregata

Skolegata

Fr Langes gate

Skolegata

Storgata

Kaigata

Kirkegata

Kaigata

Killengrens gate

Bankgata

Richard
Withs pass

Grønnegata

Storgata

Strandskillet

Strandgata

Petersborggata

Parkgata

Dr Ikes gate

Fiskegata

Peder Hansens gate

Museugata

Strandvegen

Peder Hansens gate

Samuel Arnesens gate

Tromsøsundet

N 0 ——————— 200 m
   0 ——————— 0.1 miles

ACTIVITIES
1 Brim Explorer
2 Macks Ølbryggeri
3 Tromsø
  Villmarkssenter

SLEEPING
4 Clarion Hotel Aurora
5 Scandic Ishavshotel

EATING
6 Bardus Bistro
7 Emma's
  Drømmekjøkken
8 Fiskekompaniet
9 Risø Mat og Kaffebar

DRINKING
  & NIGHTLIFE
see 2 Ølhallen

A Taste of Brewing History

Take the brewery tour

Mack has been synonymous with beer in northern Norway since Ludwig Markus Mack founded its Tromsø brewery in 1877. Join a tour inside the original **Macks Ølbryggeri** *(mack.no; tours 230kr)* – now home to a microbrewery – to learn about the company's fortunes and foibles before tasting the goods and seeing small-batch brewing in action. Tours leave from Kjeller 5, next door to **Ølhallen** *(olhallen. no)*, which is Tromsø's oldest pub. It's well worth a pit stop after the tour.

BEST TROMSØ TOUR OPERATORS

Active Tromsø: Hiking, dogsledding, glacier walks, sea kayaking. *(activetromso.no)*

Brim Explorer: Ethical whale-watching encounters with minimal impact on the whales. *(brimexplorer.com)*

Tromsø Friluftsenter: Summer sightseeing, boat trips, winter trips to Sámi camps, humpback-whale and orca safaris. *(tromso-friluftsenter.no)*

Tromsø Villmarks-senter: Winter dogsledding, summer trekking, glacier hiking, sea kayaking, seal and seabird safaris. *(villmarks senter.no)*

Wandering Owl Tours: Guided hikes, wilderness sauna trip, scenic drives; in winter, aurora borealis photography workshops. *(wanderingowl.com)*

ROBERTO MOIOLA/SYSAWORLD/GETTY IMAGES

Winter Magic

Northern lights, dogsledding and whales

Witnessing the aurora borealis – the shapeshifting columns of milky white, green and mauve lights undulating and flickering high overhead – is an unforgettable experience. Tromsø sits right under the aurora belt, making it an ideal place to begin your hunt for the lights. Other winter possibilities around Tromsø include cross-country skiing, Sámi cultural visits, reindeer herding, snowshoe safaris, ice fishing and snow-mobiling. But our favourite is to venture out into the wilderness on a dogsledding expedition.

From November to January (and sometimes into February), you'll have a good chance of spotting humpback whales and orcas on a boat tour from the city harbour, whether by RIB boat, yacht or 'silent' catamaran. Trips can be up to eight hours long, but most of that time will be travelling to/from the area and searching for the whales, so bring warm clothes.

Dogsledding near Tromsø

Get Active in Summer

Enjoy endless summer days

Summer activities in the Tromsø hinterland include hiking, fishing, visits to Sámi camps, food-centric excursions, boat sightseeing and sea kayaking. Trips to scenic locations to see the midnight sun and general sightseeing trips are widely available. Wildlife enthusiasts can also go looking for seabirds and seals.

For something even more unforgettable, try the midnight-sun horseback-riding excursions with **Nordre Hestnes Gård** *(nordre-hestnes-gaard.no; per hr 750kr).*

 EATING IN TROMSØ: OUR PICKS

Risø Mat og Kaffebar:
The original Strandgata cafe has artisan coffee, cinnamon buns, soup and *smørbrød. 7.30am-5pm Mon-Fri, from 9am Sat €*

Emma's Drømmekjøkken:
Down-to-earth Norwegian cuisine (braised reindeer, baked *klippfisk). 11am-10pm Mon-Fri, from noon Sat €€*

Bardus Bistro:
Inviting, retro nook with top service and a changing menu of locally sourced produce such as reindeer. *noon-10pm Tue-Sat €€€*

Fiskekompaniet:
Contemporary seafood place with the freshest fruits of the sea; imaginative flavours. Enter via Killengreens gate. *4-10pm €€€*

Places We Love to Stay

€ Budget   €€ Midrange   €€€ Top End

Oslo
MAP p847

Citybox Oslo € How budget hotels should be done, with spacious rooms and boutique-chic communal spaces.

Smarthotel Oslo €€ Near to Slottsparken with no-frills, compact rooms offset by a large, vintage-inspired guest lounge.

Camillas Hus €€€ Boutique hotel with seven sumptuously decorated rooms in the former home of writer Camilla Collett.

Karl Johan Hotel €€€ A city-centre retreat with neutral grey decor and a bountiful breakfast served in a light-filled atrium.

Bergen
MAP p850

Thon Hotel Bristol €€ Bright modern hotel on Bergen's main square, close to restaurants, shopping and attractions.

Det Hanseatiske Hotel €€€ Housed in original Bryggen timber buildings, with period architecture and luxe contemporary fittings.

Grand Hotel Terminus €€€ Fine old hotel dating from 1928. Opposite the train station, it harks back to the heyday of rail travel.

Hotel Park €€€ Two 19th-century houses packed with curios and antiques comprise this family-run treasure.

Sognefjorden
MAP p853

Flåm Camping & Hostel € One of Sognefjorden's best campsites, with hostel accommodation, cabins and grassy camping areas.

Undredal Gjestehus €€ Charming little B&B and the ideal base for its namesake enchanted waterside hamlet.

Vangsgaarden Gjestgiveri €€ Whitewashed Aurland guesthouse with sweet, simple rooms behind an 18th-century facade, plus fjordside cabins.

Flåmsbrygga €€€ Beside the dock in Flåm, with balconies, superb fjord views, and an excellent pub and restaurant.

Aurland Fjordhotell €€€ Swathed in white wood and topped with a gabled roof, this summer-only hotel has motel-style rooms.

Fretheim Hotel €€€ In an 1870s building, handsome Fretheim has a mix of historic and contemporary rooms.

Lofoten
MAP p857

Moskenesstraumen Camping € This wonderful clifftop campground, just south of Å, has flat, grassy pitches between the rocks and cabins.

Eliassen Rorbuer €€ A terrific collection of 26 *rorbuer* (fishing huts) in Hamnøy, close to Reine, with refurbished interiors; some have great views.

Svinøya Rorbuer €€€ This collection of contemporary and traditional *rorbuer* across Svinøyabrua is some of Lofoten's best.

Thon Hotel Lofoten €€€ Encased in glass, this stylish harbourside hotel has fabulous views from the upper floors and binoculars in every room.

Henningsvær Bryggehotel €€€ A top-notch heritage hotel overlooking the harbour, with cosy rooms and classy soft-grey decor.

Tromsø
MAP p861

Clarion Hotel Aurora €€ This stylish waterside hotel, poking towards the sea like the prow of a ship, is superb.

Scandic Ishavshotel €€€ The architecture here evokes an ocean-going vessel with sleek, smart rooms in oranges and slate-greys.

MAURITIUS IMAGES GMBH/ALAMY

Eliassen Rorbuer, Lofoten (p856)

Practicalities

Tourist Information
Visit Norway *(visitnorway.com)*, the official tourist information service, has a wealth of information. Nearly every city and town has its own tourist office, and most tourist offices in reasonably sized towns or major tourist areas publish comprehensive booklets giving the complete, up-to-date low-down on their town and the surrounding area.

RONTAV/SHUTTERSTOCK

Visas
EU nationals don't need a visa for Norway. Those from the UK, US, Canada, New Zealand and Australia can stay for up to 90 days in any six months. From late 2026, they will need an ETIAS travel authorisation.

Public Holidays
New Year's Day 1 January
Maundy Thursday March/April
Good Friday March/April
Easter Monday March/April
Labour Day 1 May

Constitution Day 17 May
Ascension Day May/June, 40th day after Easter
Whit Monday May/June, eighth Monday after Easter
Christmas Day 25 December
Boxing Day 26 December

Time
Norway shares the same time zone as most of Western Europe. Daylight saving starts on the last Sunday in March and finishes on the last Sunday in October.

Opening Hours
Banks 9am–4pm Monday to Friday
Bars 6pm–3am
Restaurants noon–3pm and 6–11pm
Shops 10am–5pm Monday to Saturday
Supermarkets 7am–11pm Monday to Friday, to 10pm Saturday

Smoking
Smoking and vaping are forbidden in enclosed public spaces, including most hotels, restaurants and bars. Very occasionally, a hotel may have a small number of rooms where smoking is permitted.

Etiquette
• Norwegians are a pretty friendly and relaxed lot, and the behaviour expected of visitors is broadly similar to other liberal-minded Western European countries.
• Some smaller rural communities tend to be more conservative when it comes to matters of dress in particular.
• Loud behaviour is rarely welcome, especially in rural areas.

Language

Norway has two official written language forms: Bokmål, used below, and Nynorsk. They are very similar, and every Norwegian learns both at school.

Basics

Hello. Goddag. *goo-dahg*
Goodbye. Ha det. *hah-day*
Yes. Ja. *yah*
No. Nei. *nai*
Please. Vær så snill. *varr shoo snil*
Thank you. Takk. *tahk*
Excuse me. Unnskyld. *un-shül*
Sorry. Beklager. *beh-klah-gehrr*
What's your name? Hva heter du? *vah hay-tehrr du*
My name is ... Jeg heter ... *yai hay-tehrr*
Do you speak English? Snakker du engelsk? *snah-kehrr du ehng-ehlsk*
I don't understand. Jeg forstår ikke. *yay for-stohrr i-keh*

Directions

Where's ...? Hvor er ...? *voor arr*
Which way is ...? Hvilken retning er ...? *vil-kehn reht-ning arr*
How do I get to ...? Hvordan kommer jeg til ...? *voor-dahn ko-mehrr yai til*
Can you show me (on the map)? Kan du vise meg (på kartet)? *kahn du vee-seh mai (poh kahrr-teh)*

Signs

Ankomst Arrivals
Avgang Departures
WC/Toaletter Toilet
Gjestgiveri/Pensjonat Guesthouse
Kamping/Leirplass Camping ground
Ledig Vacancy
Vandrerhjem Youth hostel

Time

What time is it? Hva er klokka? *vah arr klo-kah?*
It's ... Klokka er ... *klo-kah arr*
Half past (9). Halv ti. *hahl too*
morning formiddag *forr-mi-dahg*
afternoon ettermiddag *eh-tehrr-mi-dahg*
evening kveld *kvehl*
yesterday i går *i-gor-rr*
today i dag *ee-dahg*
tomorrow i morgen *ee-mor-rrn*

Emergencies

Help! Hjelp! *yehlp*
Go away! Forsvinn! *foh-shvin*
I'm ill. Jeg er syk. *yai arr sük*
Call ...! Ring...! *rring*
    a doctor en lege *ehn lay-geh*
    the police politiet *poo-li-tee-eh*

Eating & Drinking

What would you recommend? Hva anbefaler du? *vah ahn-beh-fah-lehrr doo*
Cheers! Skål! *skohl!*
That was delicious. Det var nydelig. *Day vahrr nü-deh-lee*

NUMBERS

1
en *ehn*

2
to *too*

3
tre *trray*

4
fire *fee-rreh*

5
fem *fehm*

6
seks *sehks*

7
sju/syv *shu/süv*

8
åtte *oh-teh*

9
ni *nee*

10
ti *tee*

Oslo Gardermoen airport

Arriving & Getting Around

Oslo Gardermoen is Norway's largest airport. There are direct flights from many European cities to Bergen and Tromsø too. Oslo airport is connected to the city centre by public trains, buses and an airport express train.

Discounted Tickets
On most regional train services operated by **Vy** *(vy.no)*, the earlier you book, the cheaper the ticket will be. A limited number of Lavpris (low-fare) tickets are allocated to each service, so try to book ahead.

Domestic Flights
If your time is limited, flying can be a good option. **SAS** *(flysas. com)* and **Norwegian** *(norwegian. com)* have extensive domestic networks. **Widerøe** *(wideroe.no)* services smaller cities.

Hiring a Car
Most cars in Norway have automatic transmission, with an increasing number of hybrid and electric vehicles (EVs). Find EV charging stations at *ladestasjoner.no*.

Road Conditions
Norway's roads are excellent, with tunnels and efficient car ferries helping to smooth your way around the country's challenging terrain. All but smaller mountain roads remain open during winter.

MONEY
Currency: Norwegian krone (kr or NOK)

CREDIT CARDS
Norway is well on its way to becoming a cashless society – you'll find the vast majority of transactions these days are made by card, although most places still accept cash. Visa, Eurocard, MasterCard, Diners Club and American Express cards are widely accepted.

ATMS
'Minibanks' (the Norwegian name for ATMs) are widespread and most accept major credit cards as well as Cirrus, Visa Electron and/ or Plus bankcards. Check your bank's fees for international withdrawals and transactions.

TIPPING
Although a tip will always be appreciated in Norway, it's never expected and is usually reserved for stellar service. If you choose to tip, around 5% to 10% is standard.

For places to stay
in Poland, see
p894

CINEMATOGRAPHER/SHUTTERSTOCK

Above: Old Town Market Square , Warsaw (p875); Right:Złota Brama, Gdańsk (p890)

Curated by
Marc Di Duca

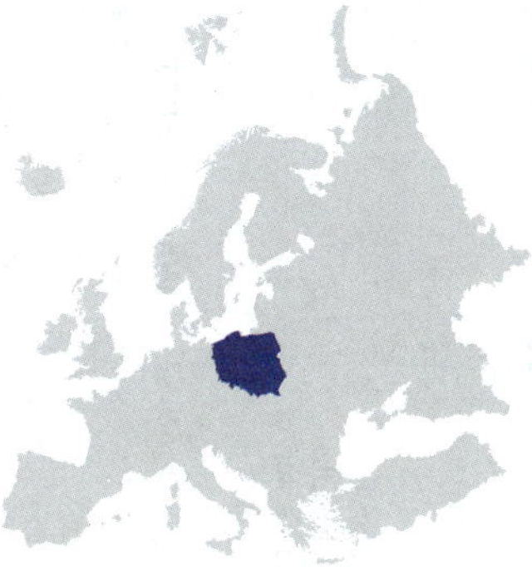

Poland

A WARM, WELCOMING AND RESILIENT NATION

Poland is all about history: its millennium-long tale is set against centuries of European power struggles and features a cast of millions.

If you were to put together a list of countries with 'most eventful pasts', Poland would be high up in the rankings. The Slavic nation has spent centuries at the pointy end of history, grappling with war, invasion and meddling neighbours. 'Poland has not yet perished' goes the rather pessimistic first line of the national anthem, and indeed, no Russian tsar or German dictator ever managed to suppress the Poles' strong sense of nationhood and cultural identity.

In fact, Poland is thriving. The country's economic revival from one of the world's poorest nations, where petrol and food were once rationed, to a modern, vibrant economy has been remarkable. Its cities are modernising, its infrastructure is expanding and it occupies a strategic, central location within the EU and NATO. As a result, bustling Warsaw and Kraków exude a sophisticated energy that's a heady mix of old and new.

Away from the cities, Poland is geographically diverse, from its northern beaches to the long chain of mountains on its southern border. In between, towns and cities are dotted with ruined castles, market squares and medieval churches.

Although prices have skyrocketed in recent years, Poland is still good value. And as the Poles continue to reconcile their distinctive national identity with their location at the heart of a troubled Europe, it's become a fascinating time to visit.

LIYA_BLUMESSER/SHUTTERSTOCK

THE MAIN AREAS

WARSAW
Nation's capital with bags of history. **p872**

KRAKÓW
Poland's best-preserved city. **p878**

WESTERN POLAND
Vibrant, off-the-beaten-path destination. **p885**

POMERANIA
Beaches, castles and 20th-century history. **p889**

Find Your Way

Poland is big: it's the ninth-largest country in Europe. Journey times can be longer than you expected, but infrastructure is improving. Apart from the southern mountains, the country is largely flat.

TRAIN

Rail is the most convenient way to travel. The network is relatively cheap and there are some high-speed rail services. Some of the old tracks and rolling stock remain in service, however.

AIR

Domestic flights are operated by LOT with a hub in Warsaw. There are few direct flights between other cities. Flying can save you hours on the trains.

Pomerania, p889

The capital of the north is Gdańsk, where you'll find great museums, the country's best beaches and the story of the Solidarity movement.

Warsaw, p872

An intriguing mix of royal palaces, communist-era architecture and compelling museums. Low-key and refreshingly few tourists.

Western Poland, p885

Two of Poland's most happening cities are Poznań and Wrocław. The first is a confident business centre; the second is a student town.

Kraków, p878

Explore museums that unravel the city's complicated history and enjoy Poland's most sophisticated dining and entertainment.

SEGOYA/SHUTTERSTOCK

Market square, Kraków (p878)

Plan Your Time

Poland could easily fill up a month of travels, so choose your destinations carefully to create an itinerary that's best suited to your availability.

Pressed for Time

● If you can only visit one place in Poland, then it should be **Kraków** (p878), Poland's tourist epicentre – it's a bit like Prague but with a more authentically Eastern European feel. There are museums galore as well as lots of Jewish and WWII heritage; when the sightseeing is over, there are many excellent, cosy taverns to retreat to.

A Week in Poland

● Start in **Kraków** (p878) with its royal sights, Jewish culture and WWII heritage, before taking a train to **Warsaw** (p872) to climb the PKiN Tower, feast in milk bars and ramble through royal gardens and palaces. From there, hop aboard a short flight to **Gdańsk** (p889), where beaches and museums dedicated to amber, WWII and the Solidarity trade union await.

SEASONAL HIGHLIGHTS

SPRING

The first flowers appear on the plains, but in April the sleet is still falling by the Baltic.

SUMMER

Poland can surprise with sweltering temperatures and high humidity. Ideal for Baltic beach days.

AUTUMN

The forests of southern and eastern Poland put on a fiery show and the cities are at their busiest.

WINTER

Snow can fall everywhere in Poland, but it's heaviest in the mountains. Sub-zero temps prevail for months.

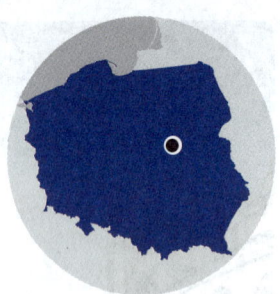

Warsaw

MUSEUMS | ARCHITECTURE | HISTORY

☑ TOP TIP

On the right bank of the Vistula, the Praga neighbourhood has two beaches: Rusałka is near the zoo and has views of the Old Town skyline; Poniatówka is near the National Stadium and Saska Kępa. Borrow deck chairs, towels and other beach gear for free in summer.

By the end of 1945, the Polish capital of Warsaw lay in ruins. Rebuilding began almost immediately and it's a process that continues to this day. You'll encounter restored baroque, Gothic, neoclassical and Renaissance buildings in the Old and New Towns; gems of the post-WWII socialist-realist period, such as the grandiose Palace of Culture & Science; and innovative 21st-century revamps of old factories and other industrial sites.

Original fragments and treasures from Poland's turbulent past are preserved in a superb selection of museums. The exhibitions at the huge Warsaw Rising Museum, the even bigger POLIN Museum of the History of Polish Jews and the intriguingly curated Museum of Warsaw leave no stone unturned.

This is also a city blessed with plenty of greenery. Enjoy the parklands at Wilanów, aptly described as Poland's Versailles, and stroll the shady paths of Łazienki Park to encounter petite royal palaces and an ornamental lake.

Take a Tour of the Royal Castle

History rebuilt

Warsaw's **Royal Castle** *(zamek-krolewski.pl; entry adult/ concession 60/45zł)* began life in the 14th century as a wooden stronghold and evolved into one of Europe's most splendid

---

⊙ GETTING AROUND

Warsaw Chopin Airport *(lotnisko-chopina. pl)*, 9km south of the city centre, has frequent buses and less-frequent trains to central Warsaw (30 minutes). From **Warsaw Modlin Airport** *(modlinairport.pl)* 39km north of the city, there's a bus connection to central Warsaw (one hour). Two efficient train lines provide access across much of Warsaw, but the distance between stations can be long. Local trains can also be used for crossing the city, most handily between the two sides of the Vistula River. Warsaw's extensive network of buses and trams is the fastest way to get around. Bolt and Uber are best for taxis.

WARSAW

POLIN Museum of the History of Polish Jews (550m)

Krasiński Gardens

MURANÓW

Royal Castle

Tunnel

Tunnel

Rynek Mariensztacki

Ratusz Arsenal

Plac Bankowy

Browery Warszawskie (1km)

Ogród Saski

Ogród Prezydencki

Skwer ks. Jana Twardowskiego

Skwer S. Jankowskiego Agatona

Park Kazimierzowski

Park Praski

Vistula River

SRÓDMIEŚCIE PÓŁNOCNE

Warsaw Rising Museum (1.5km)

Plac Grzybowski

Świętokrzyska

Nowy Świat-Uniwersytet

Warszawa Powiśle Train Station

Eatery Trad (420m)

Palace of Culture & Science

Centrum

SRÓDMIEŚCIE

Action Park 'Burza' (4km)

Wilanów Palace (9km), Łazienki Park (2km)

0 — 500 m
0 — 0.25 miles

⭐ **HIGHLIGHTS**
1 Palace of Culture & Science
2 Royal Castle

🔴 **SIGHTS**
3 Barbican
4 Dung Hill Terrace
5 Heritage Interpretation Centre
6 Jan Kiliński Monument
7 Little Insurgent Monument
8 Mazovia
9 Mosaic House
10 Museum of Artistic and Precision Crafts
11 Museum of Warsaw
12 Old Town Market Square
13 Sigismund's Column
14 St John the Baptist Cathedral

⚫ **SLEEPING**
15 Castle Inn
16 Chopin Boutique B&B
17 Hotel Bristol
18 Oki Doki Hostel Old Town
19 PURO Warsaw Downtown
20 Safestay Warsaw Old Town

🟢 **EATING**
21 Bez Gwiazdek

22 Enoteca
23 Kulturalna
24 Między Nami
see 18 Mon Nom
25 Oma
26 SAM Powiśle
27 Sambal
28 Syrena Irena
29 Żyto

🔴 **SHOPPING**
30 Dom Sztuki Lodowej
31 Lapidarium
32 Polish Poster Gallery

REBUILDING WARSAW

Around 70% of Warsaw was destroyed during WWII. After 1945, this presented an opportunity for a wholesale reimagining of public spaces so that more parks and modern housing estates could be created. But not everything was swept away. Rubble was reused so that original bricks and other decorative elements could be incorporated – to learn more about this visit the **Heritage Interpretation Centre** in the Old Town and **Action Park 'Burza'**. By 1953 much of the Old Town and the Royal Route had been meticulously reconstructed, although it wouldn't be until 1984 that the **Royal Castle** (p872) would be complete. The enormous efforts of Varsovians were acknowledged in 1980 when UNESCO inscribed the Old Town on its World Heritage list.

palaces. For a time the Polish parliament met here. The original building was destroyed during WWII; what you see today is a post-war rebuild.

The interiors have been restored to their heyday in the 17th and 18th centuries. The magnificent **Great Assembly Hall**, with dazzling gilded stucco and golden columns, has an enormous ceiling painting, a re-creation of *The Disentanglement of Chaos* by Marcello Bacciarelli.

The **National Hall** is hung with six huge canvases depicting pivotal scenes from Polish history. The **Marble Room** has trompe l'oeil paintwork and portraits of Polish kings. The 22 paintings in the **Canaletto Room** were used as a reference during the reconstruction of Warsaw's historic buildings.

In the **Crown Prince's Rooms** are epic-scale paintings by Jan Matejko, including *The Constitution of 3 May 1791* and *Stefan Batory at Pskov*.

Learn about Poland's Jewish Past

A millennium of Jewish history

Housed in a huge chunk of contemporary architecture, the **POLIN Museum of the History of Polish Jews** (*polin.pl; entry adult/concession main exhibit 45/35zł*) documents over 1000 years of Polish Jewish history. The extensive multimedia exhibition includes accounts of the earliest Jewish traders in the region through waves of mass migration, progress, pogroms, WWII and the Holocaust, right up to contemporary times. Allow a minimum of two hours for your visit.

Room after room examines every aspect of Jewish life, starting with the Jews' arrival in central Europe a millennium ago and ending with a film featuring local Jews talking about their contemporary lives. Obviously, the build-up to WWII and the Holocaust receive much attention.

Warsaw's Best Views

Top dog on the skyline

Seven decades after its 1955 debut, this 237m-tall, 3288-room colossus continues to dominate central Warsaw. A 'gift of friendship' from the Soviet Union, the **Palace of Culture & Science** (*pkin.pl; viewing terrace adult/concession 28/23zł*), or PKiN, remains one of the Warsaw's tallest and most iconic buildings. The highlight is the view from the 30th-floor viewing terrace, accessed via a superfast lift.

 EATING IN OLD TOWN & NEW TOWN: OUR PICKS

Mon Nom: Lovely bistro, with potted plants and quirky art on the walls; a great breakfast or lunch spot. *9am-10pm Mon-Fri, to 11pm Sat & Sun* €€

Sambal: Indonesian restaurant serving authentic dishes such as *rendang padang*, a beef and coconut milk stew. *noon-9pm Tue-Fri & Sun, to 10pm Sat* €€

Żyto: Facing New Town Square, this Ukrainian restaurant serves hearty bowls of borscht and other regional dishes. *noon-10pm* €€

Enoteca Classy choice overlooking attractive New Town Square; good for Polish and Italian food or a simple glass of wine. *noon-10pm* €€€

MONUMENTS OF THE OLD TOWN

If you know where to look, you'll find fascinating historical and artistic monuments dotted around the Old Town.

START	END	LENGTH
Castle Square	Museum of Artistic and Precision Crafts	1.5km; 1-2hr

Spend a moment in Castle Sq, overlooked by the 22m 1 **Sigismund's Column**, and consider that in 1945 all around you would have been rubble. Walk along ul Świętojańska to 2 **St John the Baptist Cathedral**, Warsaw's mother church. Continue ahead to the 3 **Old Town Market Square**. The picturesque square's central statue is the symbol of the city: Syrenka, the fierce mermaid brandishing a sword. Head inside the 4 **Museum of Warsaw** to see the original statue.

Exit the square along ul Celna – look through a gate to see the bas relief 5 **Mazovia** created in 1966 by sculptor Edmund Majkowski. Nearby, in 6 **Dung Hill Terrace** overlooking the Vistula, is the *Strong Man* statue. Continue along ul Brzozowa to the stout fortress walls that partly encircle the Old Town. Look out to the New Town beyond, where you can see a striking socialist-realist 7 **mosaic** covering the side of one building.

Check out the stalls of craftspeople and artists in the 8 **Barbican** before continuing around the fortress to find the poignant 9 **Little Insurgent Monument**. Further along the walls is the 10 **Jan Kiliński Monument** and a clock with copper and gold-leaf zodiac signs on the side of the 11 **Museum of Artistic and Precision Crafts**.

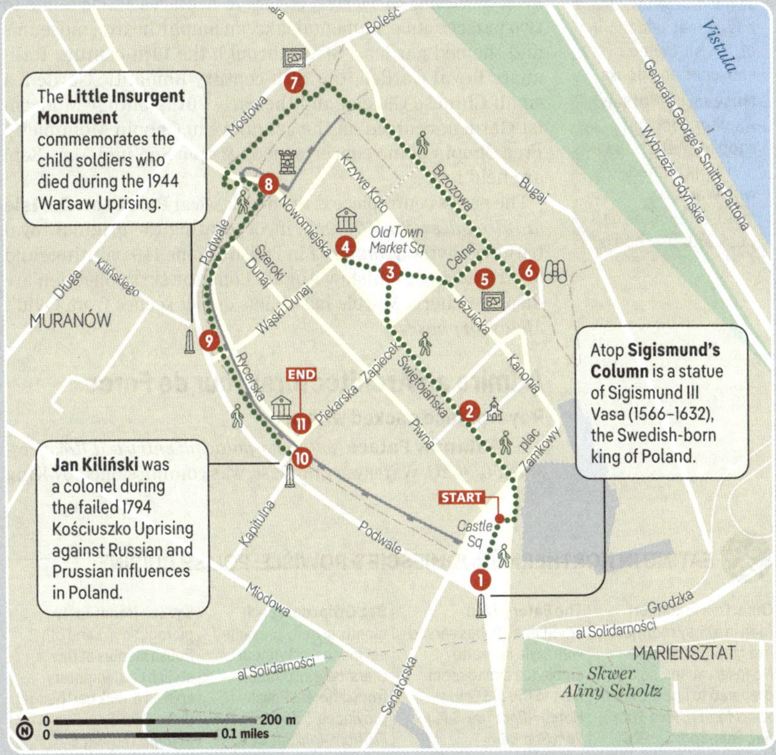
The **Little Insurgent Monument** commemorates the child soldiers who died during the 1944 Warsaw Uprising.
Atop **Sigismund's Column** is a statue of Sigismund III Vasa (1566–1632), the Swedish-born king of Poland.
Jan Kiliński was a colonel during the failed 1794 Kościuszko Uprising against Russian and Prussian influences in Poland.
Boleść
Mostowa
Vistula
Generała George'a Smitha Pattona
Wybrzeże Gdyńskie
Bugaj
Brzozowa
Krzywe Koło
Nowomiejska
Old Town Market Sq
Celna
Podwale
Szeroki Dunaj
Wąski Dunaj
Długa
Kilińskiego
MURANÓW
Jezuicka
Kanonia
Świętojańska
Zapiecek
Piekarska
Rycerska
END
Piwna
plac Zamkowy
START
Castle Sq
Kapitulna
Podwale
Miodowa
Grodzka
al Solidarności
MARIENSZTAT
Skwer Aliny Scholtz
al Solidarności
Senatorska
0 200 m
0 0.1 miles

BEST SHOPPING

Dom Sztuki Lodowej: Good examples of pottery, Christmas baubles and crafts, from painted wood carvings to traditional costumes.

Lapidarium: Antiques and curios, including jewellery, folk and religious art, vintage postcards and photos.

Polish Poster Gallery: Stocks a good range of locally produced poster art, both originals and cheaper new prints.

POLIN Museum of the History of Polish Jews: The gift shop has a great selection of Jewish-themed souvenirs and books.

Museum of Warsaw: Another good gift shop for T-shirts and bags printed with Warsaw's mermaid symbol, plus postcards and books.

A Doomed Resistance
Warsaw in WWII

A former tram power station houses the **Warsaw Rising Museum** *(1944.pl; entry adult/concession 35/30zł)*, which covers in forensic detail Warsaw's heroic, doomed uprising against the German occupation in 1944. It's an immersive, dark and at times claustrophobic experience that evokes the horror of the times and the courage of the fighters.

The ground-floor exhibition begins with the division of Poland between Nazi Germany and the Soviet Union in 1939 and moves through the major events of WWII. An elevator then takes you to the mezzanine (2nd floor) and the start of the uprising in 1944 with day-by-day displays.

A life-size reproduction of the B-24J Liberator heavy bomber, used to drop supplies for insurgents, fills much of the ground-floor Liberator Hall. Here you can also watch newsreel films shot during the uprising, as well as a six-minute 3D film that re-creates the view from a flight over the devastated city in 1945.

Leafy Royal Grounds
Take a walk in Łazienki Park

Once a royal hunting ground, **Łazienki Park** *(lazienki-krolewskie.pl; entry free)* covers 76 hectares and is home to two palaces, an ornamental lake, an amphitheatre, museums and themed gardens. Stroll through the 18th-century Italianate Royal Garden, the 19th-century Romantic Garden, a small Chinese Garden and the early 20th-century Modernist Garden, centred on the art nouveau Chopin Monument. Free Chopin piano concerts (noon & 4pm Sun mid-May–Sep) are held here.

The park's centrepiece is the neoclassical **Palace on the Isle** *(adult/concession 60/30zł)*, incorporating the original royal bathing pavilion *(łazienki* in Polish). Some 140 paintings and art from King Stanisław August Poniatowski's collection are displayed here. Marble bas-reliefs depict scenes from Ovid's *Metamorphoses*.

Admire an Architectural Tour de Force
Royal palace packed with art

The **Wilanów Palace** *(wilanow-palac.pl; entry adult/concession 50/30zł)*, Warsaw's grandest, was commissioned by King

EATING IN NORTHERN ŚRÓDMIEŚCIE & POWIŚLE: POLISH CUISINE

Oma: Delish comfort food in a cosy room just like grandma's house. No reservations, so be prepared to line up. *noon-9pm Mon-Fri, 9am-9pm Sat, 9am-8pm Sun* €€

The Eatery Trad: Traditional dishes served with style in a retro ambience dining room next to the old Lotos Hotel. *1-11pm Tue-Sat, to 9pm Sun* €€

Bez Gwiazdek: Each month, artfully presented set menus at 'Without Stars' take inspiration from different Polish provinces. *5.30-10pm Tue-Fri, from 4pm Sat* €€€

Syrena Irena: Tasty pierogi, soups and other Polish staples at this stylish contemporary spin on a 'milk bar' budget diner. *11am-8pm Sun-Wed, to 10pm Thu-Sat* €

CINEMATOGRAPHER/SHUTTERSTOCK

Łazienki Park

WARSAW FIGHTS BACK

Every year on 19 April at noon and 1 August at 5pm sirens sound across Warsaw and people fall silent. This is in remembrance of the beginning, respectively, of the **Ghetto Uprising** (lasting 29 days) and **Warsaw Uprising** (lasting 63 days) in 1943 and 1944, and of those who fought bravely against the city's Nazi German occupiers.

In 1944, insurgents took control of large parts of Warsaw by creating barricades from ripped-up paving slabs and using the sewers as underground communication lines. Sadly, the hoped-for support from the Allies and the Soviets failed to arrive, even though the Red Army was camped just outside Warsaw. In both uprisings, well over 250,000 Poles lost their lives.

Jan III Sobieski in 1677. It changed hands several times over the centuries, with each new owner adding a bit of baroque here and a touch of neoclassical there. Miraculously, Wilanów survived WWII almost unscathed, and many of its furnishings and art were retrieved and reinstalled after the war.

The route through the palace involves some doubling back, but there are attendants to show the way. The tour starts with the **Princess Marshall Lubomirska's Apartments**, an immaculately restored salon dating from the late 18th century and including the magnificent Chinese and Hunting Rooms.

The **White Hall**, the palace's largest room, is hung with portraits of successive owners of Wilanów; the stairs here lead to the **Potocki Art Gallery**, displaying works of art gathered by the Potocki family, owners of Wilanów from 1799 to 1821.

Enveloping the palace is a splendid 45-hectare **park** *(adult/ concession 10/5zł)*, where the landscaping ranges from a fragrant lily and rose garden to the Orangery, dotted with contemporary sculptures.

 EATING IN NORTHERN ŚRÓDMIEŚCIE & POWIŚLE: CASUAL SPOTS

SAM Powiśle: Relaxed bakery, cafe and deli with dishes made from organic produce. *8am-8pm* €€

Między Nami: Vibey cafe-bar serves delicious open sandwiches for breakfast. *4pm-midnight Mon, 10am-midnight Tue-Thu, 10am-1am Fri & Sat, 10am-8pm Sun* €€

Kulturalna: Great spot for something tasty in a spacious hall off the main lobby of the Teatr Dramatyczny in PKiN. *noon-midnight Sun-Thu, to 2am Fri & Sat* €€

Browary Warszawskie: Drink craft beer brewed on site and dig into culinary treats either from the brewery or the food hall. *noon-10pm Sun-Thu, to midnight Fri & Sat* €€

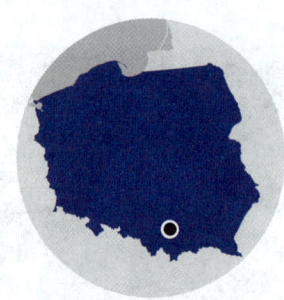

Kraków

HISTORY | ARCHITECTURE | CULTURE

☑ **TOP TIP**

Head to one of Kraków's communist-era bars *mleczny* (milk bars) for a trip down nostalgia lane to the 1980s and a wallet-friendly canteen meal of omelettes, pierogi, soup, mashed potatoes and other belly-fillers. Due to the increasing cost of living, they've seen a resurgence recently.

The southern metropolis of Kraków is the former capital of Poland and one of the finest medieval cities in all of Europe. The most quintessentially Polish destination, it's a place steeped in legends of dragons and kings. Its thousand years of history kicked off with plundering Tatar hordes and continued on through multiple royal dynasties, the waxing and waning of empires, the unfurling of Europe-wide trade routes in the Middle Ages, the decline that followed after the Polish capital was moved to Warsaw in the 16th century, the terror of the Nazi regime during WWII and decades of communist repression – all followed by its rejuvenation as a tourist magnet. Kraków's turbulent history bequeathed it layers of architecture, which survived WWII largely intact. And while the Holocaust casts a long shadow, Jewish culture is enjoying a renaissance in the rejuvenated Kazimierz district.

A Medieval Marketplace Unveiled

Explore an interactive subterranean museum

When Kraków's market square was undergoing renovations around two decades ago, the remains of the original millennium-old marketplace were found beneath the Cloth Hall. They have since been transformed into **Rynek Underground** *(muzeumkrakowa.pl; entry adult/child 25/17zł),* a subterranean 'Middle Ages meets the 21st century' experience.

🧭 **GETTING AROUND**

Trains and buses run from the airport to the central Kraków Główny train station and the adjacent bus station every 30 minutes (20 minutes, 4am to midnight). Thirty-minute taxi rides to the city centre cost 80 to 100zł with Kraków Airport Taxis and 40 to 75zł with Uber or Bolt.

The best way to explore the grid-like neighbourhoods is on foot. Kraków's integrated tram and bus system runs from 5am to 11pm, with less frequent night services after 11pm. Purchase tickets via the Jakdojade app or at the machines at tram stops and validate them on board.

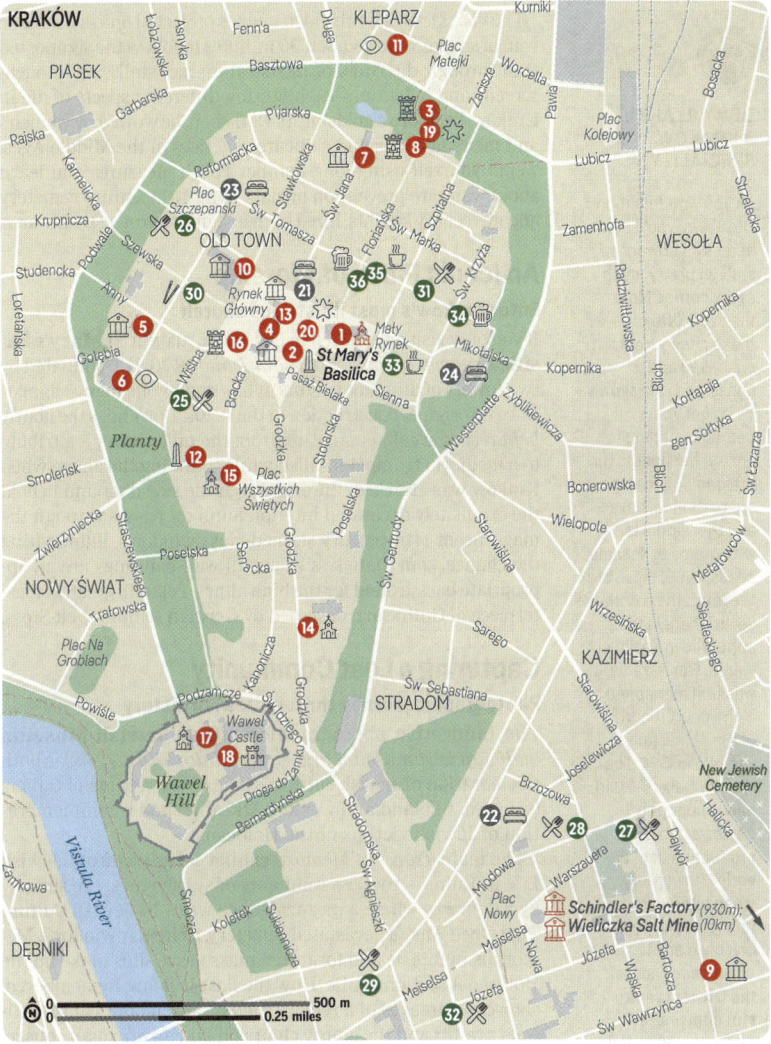

KRAKÓW

OBWARZANKI: A KRAKÓW SPECIALITY

As you wander around Old Town, you'll come across an *obwarzanki* stall on pretty much every corner. More than 200,000 of these chewy treats are baked and consumed in Kraków daily; get yours before lunchtime to ensure freshness. The braided dough rings are parboiled, baked and then sprinkled with poppy or sesame seeds – yup, these are the forefathers of the Jewish bagels that appeared in Kazimierz in 1610. *Obwarzanki* was first mentioned in the court records of King Ladislaus II Jagiello in 1394. The Kraków Bakers' Guild had a monopoly on *obwarzanek* production until the early 17th century, when rules were relaxed. Anyone can bake an *obwarzanek* now at the **Obwarzanek Museum** (*muzeu-mobwarzanka.com*), including you.

The visit kicks off with video images projected onto a dramatic wall of smoke. Give yourself 90 minutes to follow the signposted trail through the ruins of medieval market stalls, with touchscreens and holograms highlighting different aspects of life in Kraków. Peer into a goldsmith's workshop, be wowed by women's and men's fashions and skincare practices in the Middle Ages, weigh yourself using long-defunct Polish measures and learn about 'vampire prevention burials' at an 11th-century cemetery and mercenary knights, hired by merchants to protect their wares.

An Iconic Place of Worship

Enter Kraków's most illustrious church

If you only visit one church in Old Town, make it **St Mary's Basilica** (*mariacki.com; entry adult/child 18/10zł*). Dominated by two towers of different heights, it has undergone many changes since its original construction in the 1220s. Don't miss the hourly *hejnał* (bugle call) emanating from the taller tower – a tribute to a medieval trumpeter killed while sounding the alarm when Kraków was attacked. Enter through the side door and behold the exquisitely decorated interior. Sunlight passes through the magnificent 14th-century stained-glass windows, illuminating the chancel. Jan Matejko's colourful wall paintings are an appropriate background for the high altar – Poland's greatest masterpiece of Gothic art, designed by German sculptor Veit Stoss.

Capturing a Lost Community

Photographic journey through Jewish history

The innovative photographic **Galicia Jewish Museum** (*galiciajewishmuseum.org; entry adult/child 35/25zł*) is both a celebration of Jewish culture in the former region of Galicia (southeast Poland and western Ukraine) and a commemoration of Jewish victims of the Holocaust.

The main *Traces of Memory* exhibit takes you from 'Jewish Life in Ruins' – roofless remnants of synagogues, the shadow by a doorway where a mezuzah once was – to 'Jewish Culture That Once Was' (a devastated cemetery, a circular window). Memorials in forests and forgotten mass grave sites make up the Holocaust section, while 'How the Past Is Being Remembered' showcases images of a reconstructed slave labour camp, anti-Nazi graffiti and the empty chairs on Podgórze's main square. At the end, there's a hopeful note in the form of 'Revival of Jewish Life': images of Festival of Jewish Culture concerts and young Jews partaking in the March of the Living.

EATING IN OLD TOWN: BUDGET BITES

Antler Poutine & Burger: This tongue-in-cheek Canadian burger joint also dishes up poutine (fries smothered in gravy and melted cheese). *noon-10pm* €

Milkbar Tomasza: A modern take on a traditional Polish *bar mleczny*, where panini sit proudly beside pierogi. *8am-6pm Mon-Sat, from 9am Sun* €

Kuku Taiwanese: Bowls of Taiwanese curry, dumplings with chilli sauce and sesame soup noodles are served with maximum efficiency. *11.30am-9.30pm* €

Charlotte Chleb i Wino: Warsaw restaurant outpost, known for croissants, croque monsieurs and sandwiches, along with French wine and coffee. *7am-midnight* €

Wawel Royal Castle

On any given day, Wawel Royal Castle – Poland's answer to Buckingham Palace and Westminster Abbey – teems with visitors. Its glorious mishmash of Romanesque, Renaissance and Gothic architecture – the product of conquests, fashion and multiple royal dynasties – plus glittering treasures, looming towers and verdant grounds demonstrates why Kraków is a world-class city.

Wawel Cathedral

The Royal Castle

In centuries past, the ground-floor **State Rooms** were where royals received guests, held court and entertained. Pass through the vast, individually styled halls, liberally sprinkled with oil paintings and 16th-century Flemish tapestries, including the ostentatious Throne Room.

The **Royal Private Apartments** are the 1st-floor bedchambers, with modestly proportioned beds that feature carved four-poster frames. The Renaissance furnishings of King Sigismund the Old, the painted ceiling beams of the royal guest room and the tiny bejewelled 'Hen's Foot' (Queen Jadwiga's chapel) in the 14th-century Belvedere Tower stand out.

Below, vaulted Gothic rooms hold the **Treasury's** sceptres and orbs, gold goblets, royal banners, textiles and exotic objects acquired by King Sigismund III.

Wawel Cathedral

Built on the orders of Władysław the Short (1306–33), the first king to be crowned here, the current incarnation of **Wawel Cathedral** (1364) is actually the third, with the 1020 CE original and its successor having burned down. Arguably the most important building in Poland, the cathedral has hosted the coronation of virtually every Polish king and queen. Poland's monarchs occupy tombs in the cathedral and the royal crypt.

TOP TIPS

● Book your visit to Wawel Royal Castle in advance.

● You can visit the castle grounds free of charge.

● You can either book tickets to Wawel Royal Castle's separate attractions or get a day pass that covers everything.

● Entry to Wawel Cathedral must be purchased separately.

PRACTICALITIES

● wawel.krakow.pl/en

● adult/child from 49/37zł

● 10am-4pm Mon, 9am-5pm Tue-Sun

PODGÓRZE'S UNLIKELY HERO

Podgórze was home to at least two prominent Gentiles who risked their lives to save Jews during the Holocaust. The best known is Oskar Schindler, the heavy-drinking profiteer and anti-hero, whose story was told to millions through Thomas Keneally's book *Schindler's Ark* (1982) and Steven Spielberg's *Schindler's List* (1993).

Schindler originally saved the lives of Jews because he needed their cheap labour at his enamelware factory, and he used his connections and paid bribes in order to keep his employees from being shipped off to concentration camps. As is movingly quoted at the end of Spielberg's film, in reference to a passage in the Talmud, 'Whoever saves one life, saves the world entire'.

KANUMAN/GETTY IMAGES

Wieliczka Salt Mine

Learn about Schindler & the Polish Resistance

Museum of German occupation

Covering the German occupation of Kraków during WWII, the interactive **Schindler's Factory** (*muzeumkrakowa.pl/en; entry adult/child 40/35zł*) – one of Kraków's most popular museums – is housed in the former enamel factory of Oskar Schindler, the Nazi industrialist immortalised in Steven Spielberg's 1993 film *Schindler's List*.

The 30-minute introductory film showcases ordinary Cracovians telling their (often horrific) stories of life under German occupation. You then pass through labyrinthine rooms, each revolving around a specific theme. Sepia photographs, original radio and video footage, period objects, multimedia installations and individual stories of the city's residents immerse you in the unsettling prewar years and the first days of the war. Move on to the German repression of the city's Jewish residents and members of the Polish resistance, and the outright horror of the deportations to the death camps.

Though abandoned after WWII, Oskar Schindler's former office survived intact. The room's centrepiece is a symbolic Survivors' Ark – a giant translucent cube filled made of thousands of enamel pots, similar to the ones made by Schindler's employees.

 EATING IN KAZIMIERZ: OUR PICKS

Karakter: Whole-animal dishes like tripe and sweetbreads, plus conventional offerings for the offal-averse. Three-course lunch (63zł) is a steal. *1-11pm* €€

Pierwszy Stopień: While the dishes at this plant-bedecked spot lean carnivore, the pearl barley kashotto with white asparagus is a thing of beauty. *1-10pm* €€

Kropka Kraków: Modern Polish joint with globally-tinged dishes (pierogi with Korean-style sauce) and natural wines. *4-10pm Tue-Fri, from 1pm Sat & Sun* €€

Dawno Temu Na Kazimierzu: Atmospheric Jewish-themed restaurant shows off hearty variations of lamb and duck in a tiny candlelit space. *10am-11pm* €€

Delve Deep into the Wieliczka Salt Mine
Three hundred kilometres of salt

Some 14km southeast of Kraków, the UNESCO-listed **Wieliczka Salt Mine** *(wieliczka-saltmine.com; entry adult/child 156/124zł)* has been welcoming tourists since 1722 and today is one of the area's most popular attractions. It's a subterranean labyrinth of tunnels and chambers – a whopping 300km distributed over nine levels, the deepest being 327m underground – dug out by miners over the centuries right up until 1996. A small part is open to the public via two guided tours: the **Tourist Route** and the **Miners' Route**. Highlights of the Tourist Route include the 17th-century Chapel of St Kinga, a subterranean church measuring 54m by 18m by 12m, and the enormous Stanisław Staszic Chamber, which measures 36m in height and has hosted a subterranean bungee jump and even an underground balloon flight.

The immersive three-hour Miners' Route gives you a deep appreciation for the demanding and perilous profession. Visitors dress in grey miners' coveralls and hard hats and are given a headlamp and emergency respirator. You then make your way through narrow workmanlike passages.

It is cool in the tunnels so bring a sweater. Buy tickets online in advance, particularly for the English-language tours, which sell out.

The Horror of Auschwitz-Birkenau
The Nazis' most infamous concentration camp

Many visitors combine a stay in Kraków with a visit to the **Auschwitz-Birkenau Memorial & Museum** *(auschwitz.org)*. Some 1.1 million people – mostly Jews – died at Auschwitz-Birkenau between 1941 and 1945: they were gassed, worked to death and mistreated. The scale of the place and the scope of the horror can be overwhelming. It is not a place to bring children.

Both sections of the camp – Auschwitz I and the much larger outlying Birkenau (Auschwitz II) – have been preserved and are open to visitors free of charge. It's essential to visit both to appreciate the extent and the inhumanity of the place.

Oświęcim (the Polish name for Auschwitz) has frequent train services from Kraków (65 to 100 minutes). Local buses run constantly between the station and the Auschwitz I entrance. Or you can walk the 1.5km in about 20 minutes. Frequent buses also link Auschwitz I with Birkenau; the walk is 3km.

KRAKÓW'S BEST TOURS

Free Walking Tour: Old Town tours depart four times daily from March to October (less frequently November to February). *(freewalkingtour.com)*

Kraków Pub Crawl: Classic drinking tour visits four venues and starts out from the Main Market Square. *(krawlthroughkrakow.com)*

Delicious Poland: Superb foodie tours of Kazimierz that involve sampling typical Polish food and drink until you're fit to burst. *(deliciouspoland.com)*

Jarden Tourist Agency: Personalised Jewish-themed tours, including two- and three-hour walking tours of Kraków's Kazimierz and Podgórze. *(jarden.pl)*

Cracow City Tours: Decent range of walking and bus tours, including a popular four-hour coach tour and excursions to the Wieliczka Salt Mine and Auschwitz-Birkenau. *(cracowcitytours.pl)*

 DRINKING IN OLD TOWN: OUR PICKS

Pożegnanie z Afryką: Burlap sacks full of coffee, earth-coloured decor and nicely brewed espresso define this *Out of Africa*-themed coffee shop. *10am-8pm*

Bonobo: Linger over an espresso, cake or a glass of red wine at this well-stocked travel bookshop. *noon-11pm Mon-Fri, from 3pm Sat & Sun*

House of Beer: Sink into a leather sofa and choose from 21 draught beers and over 200 bottles from Poland, Germany, Lithuania and Belgium. *2pm-midnight*

Viva La Pinta: Award-winning microbrewery pouring a range of craft beers in a courtyard garden. Popular in summer. *4pm-midnight Sun-Thu, to 2am Fri & Sat*

THE ROUTE OF KINGS & QUEENS

This walk through the Old Town's cobbled streets follows the 400-year-old coronation route of Poland's kings and queens.

START	END	LENGTH
Florian Gate	Wawel Royal Castle	1.6km; 2½hr

Start at ❶ **Florian Gate**, the most important of Kraków's eight medieval gates. Together with the 15th-century ❷ **Barbican** – an impenetrable defence tower that withstood several sieges – the gate forms the City Defence Walls museum. Detour along ul Pijarska to ❸ **Czartoryski Palace**, then continue down ul Florianska to ❹ **St Mary's Basilica** (p880). Try to be here on the hour to hear the bugle call. Walk past the ❺ **monument to Adam Mickiewicz** (Poland's greatest literary hero) before cutting through the bustling ❻ **Cloth Hall**, a medieval shopping arcade in the middle of Rynek Główny, Europe's largest medieval town square. Head to its northwest corner to visit the ❼ **Historical**

Museum of Kraków inside the 17th-century Krzysztofory Palace. Proceed to the 14th-century ❽ **Town Hall Tower** for lofty Old Town views. Head to ul Jagiellonska and pass by ❾ **Collegium Maius**, followed by the neo-Gothic ❿ **Collegium Novum** (1873–87), then cut through the park that encircles Old Town to pass the ⓫ **Bishop's Palace** where former Pope John Paul II made appearances at the 'Papal Window'. Walk past ⓬ **St Francis' Basilica** and turn right onto busy ul Grodzka. You'll pass ⓭ **St Andrew's Church** – an 11th-century Romanesque fortress church – before turning down the cobbled ul Kanonicza that leads to ⓮ **Wawel Royal Castle** (p881).

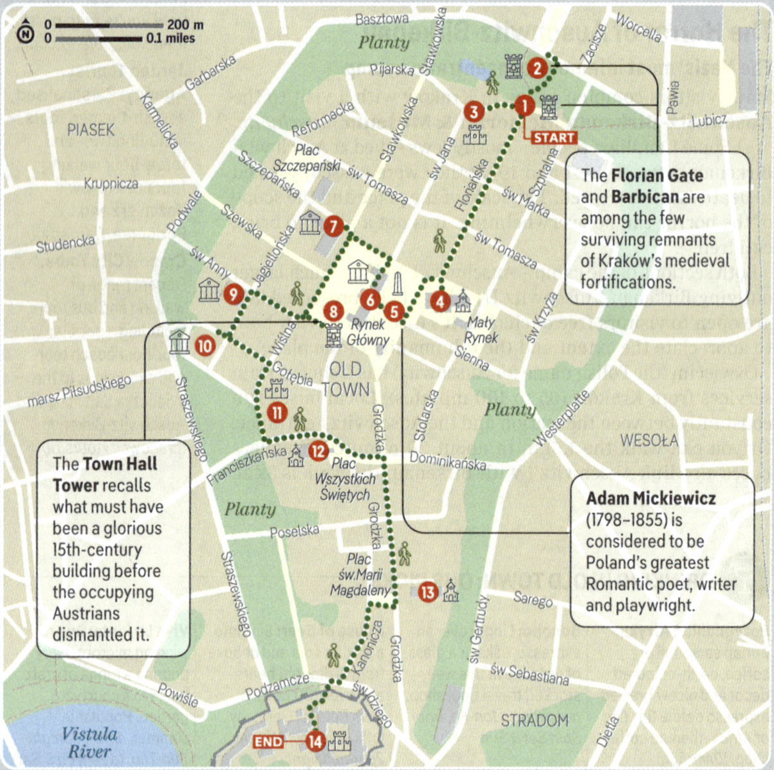

The **Florian Gate** and **Barbican** are among the few surviving remnants of Kraków's medieval fortifications.

The **Town Hall Tower** recalls what must have been a glorious 15th-century building before the occupying Austrians dismantled it.

Adam Mickiewicz (1798–1855) is considered to be Poland's greatest Romantic poet, writer and playwright.

Map features: Basztowa, Planty, Pijarska, Sławkowska, Zacisze, Worcella, Pawia, Lubicz, Reformacka, Plac Szczepański, sw Tomasza, sw Jana, sw Marka, sw Tomasza, sw Krzyza, Mały Rynek, Sienna, Rynek Główny, OLD TOWN, Planty, WESOŁA, Golębia, Stolarska, Dominikańska, Plac Wszystkich Świętych, Planty, Poselska, Plac św.Marii Magdaleny, Sarego, sw Gertrudy, STRADOM, sw Sebastiana, Dietla, Powiśle, Podzamcze, sw.Idziego, Kanonicza, Grodzka, Stradomska, Vistula River, Piasek, Karmelicka, Garbarska, Krupnicza, Studencka, Podwale, Szewska, Jagiellonska, sw Anny, Wiślna, marsz Piłsudskiego, Straszewskiego, Franciszkańska

0 — 200 m
0 — 0.1 miles

Western Poland

ARCHITECTURE | HISTORY | NIGHTLIFE

The western Polish cities of Wrocław and Poznań are worthwhile stop-offs on a wider Poland tour. Slightly off the trodden path from Poland's main attractions, these two cities have a lot to offer travellers who make the effort to reach them.

Wrocław is the capital of Silesia and Poland's fourth-largest city, and its 12 islands, 130 bridges and verdant riverside parks on the Odra River are idyllic. The beautifully preserved ecclesiastic district on Cathedral Island is a treat for lovers of Gothic architecture.

Poznań's city centre buzzes and hums as locals head to its many restaurants, pubs and clubs. The city has bags of heritage, from medieval times to the mid-20th century, when Poznań rebelled in a big way against communist rule.

Wrocław

Everyone loves Wrocław (vrots-wahf) and it's easy to see why. The capital of Lower Silesia is a more manageable version of Kraków, with similar culture and entertainment offerings, plus an appealing character all its own.

Visit the old Town Hall

Poznań's Renaissance town hall, topped with a 61m-high tower, instantly attracts attention. Its graceful form replaced a 13th-century Gothic structure, which burned down in the early 16th century. Every day at noon two metal goats appear through a pair of small doors above the clock and butt their horns together 12 times, in deference to an old legend. These days, the town hall is home to the city's Historical Museum.

Wrocław's toughest climb and best view

Of the many towers you can climb in Wrocław, the most difficult – but most rewarding – is the 91m-high tower of the

Places

Wrocław p885
Poznań p886

GETTING AROUND

Wrocław is 3½ hours from Warsaw and three hours from Kraków by train. The city has an efficient network of trams and buses *(MPK; mpk. wroc.pl)* covering the city centre and suburbs; however, almost everything is within easy walking distance of the Rynek.

Poznań is relatively compact and the major museums are centrally located. The tram network is useful, but not all stops sell tickets.

☑ **TOP TIP**

Wrocław's helpful tourist office is centrally located at Rynek 14 and is open daily.

HERE COME THE DWARFS

Across Wrocław, you may (literally!) stumble upon **tiny bronze dwarfs** horse-riding, bellringing, singing, sleeping and much more. Measuring up to 30cm, the dwarfs pop up everywhere. Indeed, by 2025, there were more than 1100 and more continue to appear. The tourist office distributes a popular 'Find the Dwarf' map. There are also apps and a Dwarfs Festival in September, with a big weekend of games, culture and fun.

Wrocław's dwarf obsession began with Orange Alternative, a 1980s dissident group that used ridicule as a weapon during the humour-free days of communism. It painted pictures of orange-capped *krasnale* (dwarfs) on places where the authorities had painted over anti-government graffiti – cleverly drawing attention to the critical messages.

14th-century **Church of St Elizabeth** (*Kościół Św Elżbiety; elzbieta.archidiecezja.wroc.pl; tower adult/child 17/11zł*), reached via a narrow set of 304 steps. What awaits is arguably the most expansive panorama in the city. Back on the ground, the 14th-century Gothic basilica has a triple nave reaching 30m and is lined by medieval chapels.

Wander the most evocative quarter

Cathedral Island (Ostrów Tumski) – which actually became connected to the mainland in the 19th century – was the cradle of Wrocław. It was here that the Ślężanie, a tribe of West Slavs, constructed their stronghold in the 7th or 8th century. In 1000, Wrocław's first church was built here.

The centrepiece of Cathedral Island, the **Cathedral of St John the Baptist** (*Archikatedra Św Jana Chrzciciela; katedra.wroclaw.pl; chapels & tower adult/child 35/25zł*) is a three-aisled Gothic basilica built between the 13th and 16th centuries with three beautiful **baroque chapels**. For views, climb 40 steps and a lift will then whisk you to the top of the 91m-high **tower**.

A wonder all around

A grand spectacle in its day, the **Racławice Panorama** (*Panorama Racławicka; mnwr.pl; entry adult/child 50/35zł*) still impresses. A giant cyclorama wrapped around the internal walls of a rotunda depicts the battle for Polish independence. It took place at Racławice, 40km northeast of Kraków, on 4 April 1794 between the Polish army and Russian troops. The Poles won, but it was all for nought: months later, the nationwide insurrection was crushed by the tsarist army and Poland ceased to exist as a nation until WWI.

Savouring the art of old

The **National Museum** (*Muzeum Narodowe; mnwr.pl; entry adult/child 20/15zł*) is a trove of fine art from across the ages, including medieval sculpture, Silesian paintings, ceramics, silverware and furnishings from the 16th to 19th centuries. The collection covers most of Poland's big names; be prepared for moody portraits and massive battle scenes.

Poznań

Poznań was founded in the 9th century on Ostrów Tumski (Cathedral Island) during the reign of Duke Mieszko I, Poland's first ruler, and became the seat of power along with Gniezno.

EATING IN WROCŁAW: TOP CHOICES

Restauracja Lwia Brama: Top-flight restaurant serves modern Polish fare in an inviting medieval cellar on Cathedral Island. Refined service. *noon-10pm* €€€

Baba: Much lauded upscale yet homestyle Polish bistro helmed by top chef Beata Śniechowska. Always buzzy, with a surprising local wine list. *4-8pm* €€€

Le Gosse Restauracja: Popular neighbourhood bistro with refined air aided by white tablecloths; it does a smashing breakfast. *9am-11pm* €€

Restauracja Wrocławska: Specialises in Silesian fare and great beer. Hearty dishes include seasoned pork, beef, mushroom and potato dishes. *noon-10pm* €€

Poznań Cathedral

In the Second Partition of Poland in 1793, the city fell under Prussian occupation and was later renamed Posen, a period that ended with the Wielkopolska Uprising in 1918. But the city is also famous for another rebellion: the massive June 1956 Uprising that led to calls for political change.

Explore Cathedral Island and Śródka

Located east of the Old Town across the Warta River, **Ostrów Tumski** (Cathedral Island) is where Poznań was founded. The original 9th-century settlement was gradually transformed into an oval stronghold surrounded by wood-and-earth ramparts, with an early stone palace. Mieszko I added a cathedral and further fortifications, and by the end of the 10th century, Poznań was the most powerful stronghold in the country. The best way to appreciate the double-towered Gothic **Poznań Cathedral** (*Katedra Poznańska; katedra.archpoznan.pl; entry free*), its architecture and its historical background is by picking up an audio guide from the nearby **Porta Posnania Interactive Heritage Centre** (*Porta Poznania ICHOT; bramapoznania.pl; entry adult/child 28/22zł*).

POZNAŃ'S FESTIVAL CALENDAR

Blues Express: Summer odyssey of blues concerts at train stations, starting in Poznań. (*bluesexpress.pl*)

Old Jazz Festival: Mid-September, with local and international jazz performers. (*oldjazzfestival.pl*)

Malta Festival Poznań: Late June, with alternative theatre and other arts. (*malta-festival.pl*)

St Martin's Day: On 11 November, with a parade from the Church of St Martin (Kościół św Marcina) to the Imperial Palace (Zamek).

Enter Enea Music Festival: Open-air jazz concerts in late May/June at Jezioro Strzeszyńskie, a lake 12km north of town. (*entereneafestival.pl*)

BitterSweet Festival: Top international music acts, held in Citadel Park in September. (*bittersweetfestival.pl*)

 DRINKING IN POZNAŃ'S CENTRE: OUR PICKS

SARP Social Club: Wednesday night jam sessions are a highlight at this bar, often with a jazz-funk flavour. *11-1am Tue-Thu & Sun, from 4pm Mon, 11-3am Fri & Sat*	**Dragon Social Club:** Eclectic pub and music venue with a relaxed vibe for a diverse, alternative crowd. *noon-1am Mon-Wed & Sun, to 3am Thu-Sat*	**Blue Note Jazz Club:** Opens for gigs; not all of them are jazz. Check the website at bluenote. poznan.pl. *hours vary*	**Brovaria:** Microbrewery serving its own Pilsner, honey, dark, wheat and seasonal beers. Also has a restaurant and hotel. *noon-11pm Mon-Sat, 11am-8pm Sun*

LONGFIN MEDIA/SHUTTERSTOCK

Monument to the Victims of June 1956

The June 1956 Uprising in Poznań

The June 1956 industrial strike in Poznań was the first mass protest in the Soviet Bloc, erupting just three years after Stalin's death. It originated in the city's largest industrial plant, the Cegielski Metalworks (then named after Stalin), when workers demanded a refund on an unfairly charged tax. A strike ensued, escalating into a full-scale protest when 100,000 people – one-quarter of Poznań's population at the time – gathered on Plac Mickiewicza, demanding 'bread and freedom' and improved working conditions. Ignored by city officials, an angry crowd stormed police headquarters and the Communist Party building, releasing 257 prisoners from jail. The uprising deteriorated into bloodshed after tanks and troops were brought in. Seventy-six people died and many more were wounded or arrested in this little-known struggle. Today, it is depicted at the **Museum of Poznań June 1956** (*Muzeum Poznańskiego Czerwca 1956; wmn.poznan. pl; entry adult/child 15/10zł*). The small museum is located downstairs in a neo-Romanesque castle, where you can take a fascinating step back into the events. English descriptions are limited. Across the road is the evocative **Monument to the Victims of June 1956**.

 EATING IN POZNAŃ'S CENTRE: OUR PICKS

Pyra Bar: Lots of potato dishes, some of which are vegetarian and gluten-free. Or just hang out with a drink. *11am-9pm Sun-Thu, to 11pm Fri & Sat* €

Republika Róż by Andrzej Gołąbek: Menu of hearty, well-prepared Polish mains. Excellent soups, salads and burgers, too. *noon-10pm Tue-Sat, to 8pm Sun* €€

Fromażeria: Acclaimed restaurant with a cheese-tasting menu, combining Polish and French traditions. *5-10.30pm Mon-Thu, to midnight Fri & Sat, 2-10pm Sun* €€€

MUGA: Seasonal international dishes in this long-standing gourmet favourite, with an affiliated Casa de Vinos wine bar. *5-10pm Tue-Sat* €€€

Pomerania

CASTLES | HISTORY | BEACHES

History, amber, beaches and red bricks have shaped Poland's breezy northern province, one of Poland's most engaging regions.

Cream-hued beaches shelving into the nippy Baltic Sea, wind-crafted dunes vivid against leaden skies, stern red-brick churches and castles erected by a medieval order of pious knights and silenced shipyards that once seethed with anti-communist tumult – this is Pomerania, Poland's north, a land of many faces.

The epicentre of Pomerania is Gdańsk, northern Poland's metropolis, a rapidly modernising city with a photogenic historic centre. Like most of the region, Gdańsk has changed hands many times over the centuries, each invader bequeathing a layer of architecture and culture for today's visitors to enjoy.

South of Gdańsk, top billing goes to Malbork Castle, once the mothership of the Teutonic knights and still the world's largest brick building.

Places

Gdańsk p889
Malbork p892

☑ TOP TIP

Buy amber at Gdańsk's Amber Museum, Mariacka St and the amber market in the Foregate at the western end of Długa St.

Gdańsk

Follow the Royal Way

Lined by the city's grandest facades, Gdańsk's **Royal Way** was the route Polish kings traditionally paraded down during their periodic visits. Of Poland's three Royal Ways (Warsaw, Kraków and Gdańsk), Gdańsk's is the shortest at just 500m long.

 GETTING AROUND

Gdańsk has a comprehensive public transport network that's cheap and easy to use. Buses, trams and the SKM train service run to every corner of the city and beyond. Single tickets cost just 4.80zł, and a 24-hour pass is 22zł. The website of the public transport company *(ztm.gda.pl)* has a useful journey planner. This flat city can also be seen by bike and shared scooters. That said, the best way to see the old historical centre is on foot. Trains run regularly from Gdańsk to Malbork.

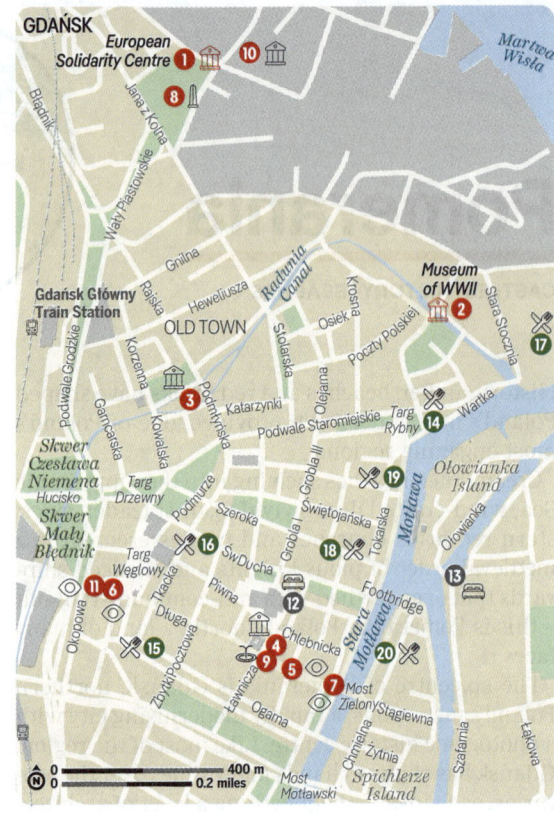

★ HIGHLIGHTS
1 European Solidarity Centre
2 Museum of WWII

● SIGHTS
3 Amber Museum
4 Artus Court Museum
5 Długi Targ
6 Foregate
7 Green Gate
8 Monument to the Fallen Shipyard Workers
9 Neptune Fountain
10 Sala BHP
11 Upland Gate

● SLEEPING
12 Gotyk House
13 Hotel Podewils

● EATING
14 Kubicki
15 Pomelo Bistro Bar
16 Restauracja Gdańska
17 Restauracja Motlava
18 Restauracja Pod Łososiem
19 Tawerna Dominikańska
20 TYGLE

Starting at the western end, turn your back on rumbling Okopowa to face the **Upland Gate** (Brama Wyżynna), the traditional entry point for kings dating from 1574. It now houses the Pomerania Regional Tourist Office. A few steps east rises the **Foregate**, a large 15th-century construction that has served as an execution site, a jail, the city's amber museum and now an amber market. Just beyond the Foregate's hefty doors stands the 17th-century **Złota Brama** (Golden Gate), a triumphal arch. On the other side extends **ul Długa** (Long St) with its many rebuilt townhouse gables.

After 325m, ul Długa suddenly widens out into **Długi Targ**, Gdańsk's showpiece square. On your left gurgles the famous **Neptune Fountain**, behind which lurks the **Artus Court Museum**, part of the Historical Museum of Gdańsk. Also on the right, near the western end of the square, is the city's modest tourist office. Blocking the way to the riverfront is the Royal Way's exit, the 16th-century **Green Gate** (Brama Zielona). Meant as a residence for the king (who never stayed there), it once housed the office of Lech Wałęsa, leader of Poland's first independent trade union and Nobel Peace Prize winner, when he was president. It is now home to the National Museum's photographic exhibition.

Tour Gdańsk's must-see museum

Opened in 2016, the **Museum of WWII** *(muzeum1939.pl; entry adult/concession 32/22zł)* is a bold addition to the northern end of Gdańsk's waterfront. A must-visit attraction, it traces the fate of Poland during the world's greatest conflict, focusing on human suffering. Few leave unmoved. The museum covers 5000 sq m, so a minimum of three hours is needed to do the main exhibit justice.

Opened by local lad and Polish prime minister Donald Tusk in 2017, the museum occupies one of Gdańsk's most striking buildings. Outside, all you can see is a wedge of glass and steel, like a missile that has wedged itself into the earth without exploding. Most of the structure that houses the main exhibition is a bunkerish, brutalist grey concrete block, 14m underground.

The museum is divided chronologically into three sections with 18 individual spaces. The first section examines the causes of the war, tracing the rise of Hitler, the Nazis and other totalitarian regimes after WWI. Section two largely deals with the human suffering caused during WWII, from concentration camp prisoners and the persecuted Polish intelligentsia to soldiers on the front line and those subjected to forced labour. The third and final section looks at how WWII ended and its impact on Europe after 1945. The museum is free on Tuesdays.

A glimpse into prehistory at the Amber Museum

Gdańsk's **Amber Museum** *(muzeumgdansk.pl; entry adult/child 37/26zł)* has become an unmissable attraction since it opened in 2020. It's housed in dramatic style within the massive red-brick hulk of the Great Mill, a medieval structure that has long since ground its last grains.

The interior of the Great Mill has been blacked out to enhance the glow of the nuggets, blobs and small boulders of prehistoric tree sap that seem to be illuminated from within. The lower floor looks at amber in its natural form, with slabs containing insects and plants (inclusions) and lumps in all shapes, sizes and colours, as well as lots of information on how amber is formed and why there is so much of the stuff in the Baltic. The upper floor explores what people have used amber for over the millennia: from medicine to tools to crucifixes, chess sets and furniture. For those in the market for Baltic gold, the best is saved for last in the shape of a large amber jewellery shop.

TOP SOUVENIRS

Amber: Milky white, treacle gold and liver red hunks of fossilised resin wash up on Baltic beaches after winter storms.

Goldwasser: Spice-infused liqueur with flakes of 22-karat gold has been distilled in Gdańsk since 1598. Yes, you can drink it!

Kashubian handicrafts: The region south of Gdańsk produces some distinctively Slavic handicrafts, such as ceramics and linen.

Solidarność memorabilia: A Lech Wałęsa moustache, a 1980s pin badge or just about anything bearing the famous Solidarność logo: memorabilia celebrating the famous trade union makes for a unique souvenir.

Jopenbier: Made by the PG4 microbrewey near the train station, this is Gdańsk's traditional beer.

EATING IN GDAŃSK: BEST LOCAL FOOD

Pomelo Bistro Bar: Using ingredients from mostly local suppliers, the menu at this eclectic, colourful place features Kashubian dishes. *9am-10pm €€*

Restauracja Motlava: Almost gourmet versions of Polish and Kashubian dishes in an understated dining environment. *noon-10pm €€*

TYGLE: Finely crafted local dishes populate the refreshingly brief menu at this well-run restaurant with an upmarket feel. *9am-9pm Mon-Sun €€*

Stacja Food Hall: In the Galeria Metropolitana mall, this food hall has hard-to-find Kashubian options. *noon-10pm Mon-Thu, to midnight Fri & Sat, to 9pm Sun €*

GDAŃSK TOURIST CARD

The Gdańsk Tourist Card *(kartaturysty. visitgdansk.com)* grants free entry to many of the city's attractions, including the Amber Museum, the National Maritime Museum and the Historical Museum of Gdańsk, as well as discounts to other attractions and restaurants. The slightly over-complicated card comes in two versions: Explorer and Premium Explorer, the difference being that Premium gives you access to more attractions while the simple Explorer card is more focused on families. You also have the option of adding public transport tickets to your package. Cards are valid for 24/48/72 hours *(65/75/85zł)* and are available from the city's municipal tourist offices or online. Download the card to your phone to save 5zł.

Solidarity at the shipyard

North of the city centre, Gdańsk's former shipyard played a major role in bringing an end to communism in Eastern Europe. Led by shipyard electrician Lech Wałęsa, it was here that dockers punched a hole in the communist monolith, the resulting cracks spreading to the Berlin Wall and the Iron Curtain.

The first structure you'll see at the shipyard is the striking **Monument to the Fallen Shipyard Workers**, which commemorates those killed in the riots of 1970. This was the first monument in a communist country to commemorate the ideology's own victims.

Though the vast majority of production facilities have been cleared away, the original Lenin shipyard gates have been left untouched, the huge 'STOCZNIA GDAŃSKA' sign a great selfie spot.

The main attraction in the shipyard area is the excellent **European Solidarity Centre** *(ecs.gda.pl; entry adult/child 35/30zł)*, housed in a purposefully ugly example of 21st-century architecture. Its rusty steel plates were designed to evoke ships under construction. The extensive permanent exhibition examines Poland's post-war fight for freedom, from the Gdańsk shipyard strikes of the 1970s to the round-table negotiations of the late 1980s and beyond. The displays blend state-of-the-art multimedia with actual artefacts. Don't miss it.

A short stroll through the now-landscaped former shipyard brings you to the **Sala BHP**, the shipyard's former Health and Safety Building. This is where the dock workers' 21 demands were famously signed off; it has been left exactly as it was then.

Malbork

Visit the world's largest red-brick castle

Malbork Castle *(zamek.malbork.pl; entry adult/concession 80/60zł)* is the largest in Poland – and indeed in Europe. This massive, UNESCO-listed, red-brick complex on the banks of the Nogat River was begun by the Teutonic Knights in the 13th century and served as the order's headquarters for almost 150 years.

Visits are by a self-guided audio tour that ushers you through the complex at a resonable pace. First up is the **Middle Castle** where the Grand Masters' Palace sports grand interiors, including the kitchen with its 6m-wide fireplace and the Great Refectory, the largest chamber in the castle. Opposite is an excellent amber museum, a highlight of the tour. The prescribed route then continues to **St Anne's Chapel**, where 12 of the Grand Masters are buried.

 EATING IN GDAŃSK: BEST TRADITIONAL RESTAURANTS

Restauracja Gdańska: Hearty traditional dishes amid antiques and model ships at Gdańsk's most famous restaurant. *noon-10pm* €€€

Restauracja Pod Łososiem: Founded in 1598 and famous for its fish dishes, this is one of Gdańsk's most highly regarded restaurants. *9am-9pm* €€€

Kubicki: Top Gdańsk restaurant dating from more than a century ago. It serves 100% local dishes. *1-10pm* €€€

Tawerna Dominikańska: Popular with tourists and locals, this contemporary restaurant by the river serves well-presented local favourites. *10am-1am* €€

Malbork Castle

Next comes the **High Castle** with its spectacular arcaded courtyard. This was the monastic part of the castle, where monks would sit in session in the Chapter House before heading for the refectory. The mock-up of the monks' medieval kitchen is an aromatic affair with nary a potato or tomato in sight.

One of the most striking interiors is **St Mary's Church**, accessed through a beautiful Gothic doorway known as the Golden Gate. Damaged during the bombardment of 1945, renovation ended in 2016 with the walls left as bare brick – a powerful reminder of the Red Army shells.

History of Malbork Castle

This immense castle took shape in stages. First came the so-called High Castle, the formidable central bastion begun around 1276. When Malbork became the Teutonic Knights' capital in 1309, the fortress expanded. The Middle Castle was built to the side of the high one, followed by the Lower Castle. The whole complex was encircled by three rings of defensive walls. The Polish army seized Malbork in 1457 during the Thirteen Years' War when the military power of the knights started to erode. Malbork then became the residence of Polish kings visiting Pomerania. After the First Partition in 1772, the Prussians turned it into barracks. Despite sustaining serious damage during WWII, the entire complex has been rebuilt.

Places We Love to Stay

€ Budget €€ Midrange €€€ Top End

Warsaw   MAP p873

Oki Doki Hostel Old Town € Prime-location hostel with pleasant dorms and private rooms, a well-equipped kitchen and inviting social spaces.

Safestay Warsaw Old Town € Large and lively hostel with comfy beds, clean bathrooms, well-equipped kitchens, a choice of dorms (some women only) and private rooms, and a friendly on-site bar.

Castle Inn €€ Overlooking Castle Sq, this creatively designed 'art hotel' has quirkily themed rooms, including Jungle, Orient Express and Comic Book.

Chopin Boutique B&B €€ Vintage furniture lends each room a unique vibe. Superb breakfast buffet, free bicycles and nightly Chopin recitals. Also pet friendly.

PURO Warsaw Center €€ Polish brand of Scandi-style design hotels has a winner with its brand-new, perfectly located property. The Loreta bar has great skyline views.

Hotel Bristol €€€ Warsaw's most historic address where VIPs and celebs have stayed throughout the decades. Its neoclassical facade conceals original art nouveau features.

Kraków   MAP p879

Globetrotter Guest House € Spacious, wallet-friendly private rooms (singles, doubles and quads) in a quiet Old Town corner. Has tea/coffee facilities,

laundry service and guest fridge.

Dream Hostel € A mixture of 5-bed dorms and private en-suites with lime-green accents in a handy central location. A sound Kazimierz choice; the guest kitchen is a bonus.

PURO Kráków Kazimierz €€ Stylish rooms, spot-on technology, a well-equipped gym and all-day brasserie attract millennial professionals.

Hotel Gródek €€ A tranquil cul-de-sac location, rooftop terrace overlooking the Old Town and a library with a cosy bar are perks at this intimate boutique hotel with individually-designed rooms.

Bonerowski Palace €€€ Luxe 14th-century palace featuring Europe's largest Swarovski chandelier, medieval portals and restored polychrome decor; the 16 antique-furnished rooms and suites come with marble bathrooms.

Wrocław

Babel Hostel € Close to the train station, pleasant budget accommodation, dorms and private rooms in renovated apartment rooms with pretty decor. Funky common room.

Wrocław Patio €€ Spread behind the Victorian facades of two adjoining tenements overlooking the Church of St Elizabeth and connected by a sunny courtyard. Has comfortable rooms in many styles.

Hotel Monopol €€€ Top hotel holds 120 luxurious rooms behind an elaborately sculpted facade. Bonuses include a panoramic rooftop restaurant and bar, pool, sauna and a breakfast buffet.

Poznań

Hotel Stare Miasto €€ Good value choice featuring a tastefully chandeliered foyer and spacious breakfast room. Bright, decent-sized rooms with some cheaper smaller singles.

Hotel Altus Poznań €€ Old Town high-rise hotel on Święty Marcin with stylish rooms and great views from the upper floors.

Puro Poznań Stare Miasto €€€ Central location, underground car park, designer decor, comfortable lobby, helpful staff and sharply styled bedrooms flooded with light.

Gdańsk   MAP p890

Camping Nr 218 Stogi € Gdańsk's best-known campsite at Stogi Beach. Good facilities, but it gets overcrowded in July and August.

Hotel Podewils €€€ Vintage guestrooms, elegant period furniture, carpet bags of old-world charm and an unrivalled view of the Old Town across the Motława River.

Gotyk House €€€ Gothic-themed guesthouse squeezed into Gdańsk's oldest building. Has a wonderful location next to St Mary's Church.

Practicalities

LGBTIQ+ Travellers
Poland isn't a place that welcomes overt displays of LGBTIQ+ sexual orientation. Since 1990, this deeply religious country has found LGBTIQ+ rights tough to handle. The populist Law and Justice Party openly encourages anti-gay sentiments.

Health
Poland has a good healthcare system. Urban hospitals are on par with Western Europe, but in rural areas this may not be the case. You'll need an EHIC (European Health Insurance Card) to access care for free. A UK GHIC (Global Health Insurance Card) will get you free emergency treatment.

Electricity
Polish current works on 230V/50Hz. Almost all sockets in Poland are the modern European two-prong type. If travelling from outside Europe you'll need an adapter.

Smoking
Poland has had a comprehensive smoking ban since 2010, and lighting up is prohibited in all public places. However, because of the relatively high number of smokers in the country, many ignore this rule, especially at public transport stations. Cheaper hotel rooms in Poland can still have a bit of a stale cigarette smell.

BBA PHOTOGRAPHY/SHUTTERSTOCK

Old Town Market Square (p875), Warsaw

Opening Hours
Banks 9am–5pm Monday to Friday, to 1pm Saturday
Offices 8am–4pm Monday to Friday
Post Offices 8am–8pm Monday to Friday, to 1pm Saturday
Restaurants 11am–11pm
Shops 8am–6pm Monday to Friday, 10am–8pm Saturday
Supermarkets 7am–10pm Monday to Saturday

Visas
Poland is part of the Schengen Area. Visitors from the UK, USA, Australia, New Zealand, Canada, Japan and many other countries do not need visas. Most visa-free nations outside the EU can stay for a maximum of 90 days out of 180.

Public Holidays
New Year's Day 1 January
Epiphany 6 January
Easter Sunday & Monday March/April
Labour Day 1 May
Constitution Day 3 May
Pentecost Sunday 7th Sunday after Easter
Corpus Christi 9th Thursday after Easter
Assumption Day 15 August
All Saints' Day 1 November
Independence Day 11 November
Christmas 25 and 26 December

Language

Polish vowels are generally pronounced short. Nasal vowels are pronounced as though you're trying to force the air through your nose, and are indicated with n or m following the vowel. Note that ow is pronounced as in 'how', kh as the 'ch' in the Scottish loch, and zh as the 's' in 'pleasure'. Also, r is rolled in Polish and the apostrophe (') indicates a slight y sound.

Basics

Hello. Cześć. *cheshch*
Goodbye. Do widzenia. *do vee·dze·nya*
Excuse me. Przepraszam. *ps·he·pra·sham*
Sorry. Przepraszam. *pshe·pra·sham*
Please. Proszę. *pro·she*
Thank you. Dziękuję. *jyen·koo·ye*
Yes. Tak. *tak*
No. Nie. *nye*
What's your name?
Jak się pan/pani nazywa? (m/f pol) *yak shye pan/pa·nee na·zi·va*
My name is ...
Nazywam się ... *na·zi·vam shye ...*
Do you speak English? Czy pan/pani mówi *chi pan/pa·nee moo·vee* po angielsku? (m/f) *po an·gyel·skoo*
I don't understand.
Nie rozumiem. *nye ro·zoo·myem*

Transport

boat łódź *wooj*
bus autobus *ow·to·boos*
plane samolot *sa·mo·lot*
train pociąg *po·chonk*
One ... ticket Proszę bilet *pro·she bee·let* **(to Katowice),** ... (do Katowic) ... *(do ka·to·veets)* **please.**
one-way w jedną stronę *v yed·nom stro·ne*
return powrotny *po·vro·tni*

Emergencies

Help! Na pomoc! *na po·mots*

Go away! Odejdź! *o·deyj*
Call the doctor/police!
Zadzwoń po lekarza/policję! *zad·zvon' po le·ka·zha/po·lee·tsye*
I'm lost. Zgubiłem/Zgubiłam się. (m/f) *zgoo·bee·wem/zgoo·bee·wam shye*
I'm ill. Jestem chory/a. (m/f) *yes·tem kho·ri/a*
Where are the toilets?
Gdzie są toalety? *gjye som to·a·le·ti*

Eating & Drinking

What would you recommend? Co by pan polecił? (m)/Co by pani poleciła? (f) *tso bi pan po·le·cheew/tso bi pa·nee po·le·chee·wa*
Do you have vegetarian food? Czy jest żywność wegetariańska? *chi yest zhiv·noshch ve·ge·tar·yan'·ska*
I'd like the ..., please. Proszę o rachunek/jadłospis *pro·she o ra·k·hoo·nek/. ya·dwo·spees*
I'll have ... Proszę ... *pro·she ...*
Cheers! Na zdrowie! *na zdro·vye*

Shopping & Services

I'm looking for ... Szukam ... *shoo·kam*
How much is it? Ile to kosztuje? *ee·le to kosh·too·ye*
That's too expensive. To jest za drogie. *to yest za dro·gye*
market targ *tark*
post office urząd pocztowy *oo·zhond poch·to·vi*
tourist office biuro turystyczne *by·oo·ro too·ris·tich·ne*

NUMBERS

1
jeden *ye·den*

2
dwa *dva*

3
trzy *tshi*

4
cztery *chte·ri*

5
pięć *pyench*

6
sześć *sheshch*

7
siedem *shye·dem*

8
osiem *o·shyem*

9
dziewięć *jye·vyench*

10
dziesięć *jye·shence*

Tram, Kraków (p878)

Arriving & Getting Around

Poland may be Eastern Europe's best served country by air, with flights from across the continent and overseas. Improving transport infrastructure means getting around is not the trial it once was.

City Transport
All Polish cities and large towns have bus, tram and even metro services that are cheap and efficient. Download the relevant transport app on your smartphone to avoid hassling with tickets.

Polish Trains
PKP (Polskie Koleje Państwowe; pkp.pl) is the main train operator. The system is undergoing extensive modernisation with new tracks and stations coming online every week. PKP also runs trains to other European cities.

Driving Essentials
Drive on the right and have headlights switched on day and night, year-round. The blood alcohol limit is 0.2g/L. Road conditions are improving, but watch out for bad surfaces and potholes in rural areas.

Arriving by Air
With over 20 million passengers annually, Warsaw's Chopin Airport (WAW) is the busiest in the country. Ryanair has its own airport: Modlin (WMI), 40km north of the capital. Kraków (KRK) and Gdańsk (GDN) also have busy airports with domestic and international connections. There are flights to Poland from around the world, including North America, the Middle East and Asia.

MONEY
Currency: Złoty (zł)

CASH VERSUS CARDS
Even a mobile coffee machine on the back of a bike might take a credit or debit card. However, always carry some cash just in case.

EUROS
The common currency is not likely to make an appearance any time soon, but you can still pay with euros at major tourist sights and most city hotels, and even some restaurants.

ATMS
ATMs are ubiquitous in cities and towns, but villages rarely have one. Stick to banks and avoid free-standing Euronet ATMs in shops, which give a much poorer rate of exchange than other ATMs and charge a fee.

Curated by
Joana Taborda

Portugal

A LAND SHAPED BY THE ATLANTIC

A coastline brimming with beaches and seafood, vineyards spread across terraced hills, creative cities warm people welcome you to Portugal.

Portugal's story is one of looking both outwards and inwards. There were times when navigators set sail to colonise other lands, times when the country shut itself to the world, marked by a dictatorship that lasted nearly 50 years, and times when the doors opened to all craving a slice of year-round sunshine, quality surf and a slow-living lifestyle. Tourism drives the Portuguese economy today, and it's easy to see why this Atlantic-facing nation has become so popular in recent years.

Some are drawn to Lisbon's golden light, cast over the capital's hills and cobblestone streets. Others prefer the allure of Porto, with its dreamy riverside promenade, Port wine cellars and endless tile facades. Some head straight to the coast, to bask on the shores of the Algarve or chase the waves along the wild west coast. Few brave inland, to witness ancient villages, meet the people tending the fields of oaks, olives and vines, or simply disconnect and gaze at the stars. But that's the beauty of Portugal – you get to choose. One day, you could be toasting the sunset at one of Lisbon's numerous viewpoints and rooftops, the the next, hopping on a train from Porto to the Douro Valley for a wine tasting, or driving along the Costa Vicentina, stopping for a seafood feast wherever you feel like. Around here, it's all about going with the flow.

APROPOS IMAGES/SHUTTERSTOCK

THE MAIN AREAS

LISBON
The cool and laid-back capital.
p904

PORTO
Romantic city to sip Port wine.
p911

FARO & THE ALGARVE
Beaches, seafood and coastal trails.
p916

COIMBRA
Home to Portugal's oldest university. **p921**

ÉVORA & THE ALENTEJO
Ancient crafts, vineyards and rural flavours.
p926

For places to stay in Portugal, see p930

CAIO PEDERNEIRAS/SHUTTERSTOCK

Left: Douro Valley wine (p915); Above: Praia do Camilo (p920), Lagos

Find Your Way

Standing strong on Europe's western border, where the land meets the Atlantic, Portugal's coastline stretches for 560km, but just beyond the dramatic sandy shores lie rugged mountains, schist villages and rolling vineyards.

Porto, p911

Porto captivates with its artistic vibe and riverside setting. Taste the world's best ports or follow the Rio Douro east to discover vineyards and ancient towns.

Coimbra, p921

Home to Portugal's oldest university, Coimbra is perhaps the most visited place in the Beiras, a region of high-lands, schist villages and river beaches.

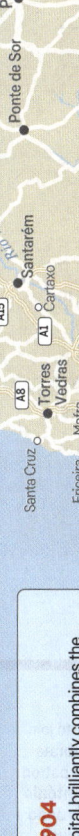

CAR

A car will give you more freedom to explore different regions in a single trip, from beach-hopping along the coastline to touring hidden vineyards, hilltop villages and natural parks.

TRAIN

Portugal's railway system, **Comboios de Portugal** (*cp. pt*), mostly covers the west and south coast, but some areas like the Douro Valley and cities like Évora and Coimbra can also be accessed by train.

BUS

If you're not planning on driving, buses are a great alternative, especially if you want to veer off the coast. **Rede Expressos** (*rede-expressos.pt*) and **FlixBus** (*flixbus. pt*) operate regular trips between major cities and smaller towns.

Lisbon, p904

Portugal's capital brilliantly combines the past and the future, with historic monuments alongside creative districts. Its surroundings house romantic palaces and beaches.

Évora & the Alentejo, p926

It's all about slowing down in the Alentejo. Start in Évora, before driving off to explore wineries, meet local artisans or take on the wild coastline.

Faro & the Algarve, p916

Every summer, people flock to the Algarve for a beach holiday. Those flying in will land in Faro, but it's worth venturing further to find other shores, wildlife and seafood.

Map labels: Portalegre, Arronches, Badajoz, Elvas, Ponte de Sor, Estremoz, Redondo, Reguengos de Monsaraz, Mora, Montemor-o-Novo, **A6**, Templo Romano, Évora, Vidigueira, Moura, Serpa, Beja, Rio Guadiana, Mértola, SPAIN, Huelva, Lepe, Ayamonte, Vila Real de Santo António, **A22**, Tavira, Olhão, Sé, Igreja da Misericórdia, Faro, São Brás de Alportel, Quarteira, Loulé, São Bartolomeu de Messines, **A2**, Albufeira, **A22**, Castelo de Silves, Silves, Monchique, Portimão, Lagos, Sagres, Atlantic Ocean, Castro Verde, Almodôvar, Ourique, Odemira, Aljustrel, Santiago do Cacém, **A2**, Alcácer do Sal, Grândola, Sines, Comporta, Setúbal, Sé de Lisboa, Almada, Barreiro, Caruche, Coruche, Santarém, Cartaxo, Rio Tejo, **A15**, Alverca do Ribatejo, **A1**, Torres Vedras, **A8**, Óbidos, Santa Cruz, Ericeira, Mafra, Sintra, Cascais, LISBON, Castelo de São Jorge, Museu Nacional de Arte Antiga

901

Plan Your Time

Portugal is compact enough to explore in a couple of days, but there are plenty of places to linger, too, if you decide to stay for a while. To skip the crowds, come in the shoulder seasons.

MAZUR TRAVEL/SHUTTERSTOCK

Mosteiro dos Jerónimos (p904), Lisbon

A Capital Roundup

● Begin your trip in **Lisbon** (p904), taking in the capital's sights. Choose between historic monuments including the **Mosteiro dos Jerónimos** (p904) or modern art hubs such as the **Fundação Calouste Gulbenkian** (p907), but don't miss a chance to sample a *pastel de nata* (custard tart) at a local **pastelaria** (p906).

● As the sun sets, head to the riverside or brave the hills to capture the pink-hued skies from one of the city's numerous *miradouros* (viewpoints; p906) before settling down for a **fado show** (p907).

● A day or two later, end the trip in style by hopping on a train to the city's outskirts, opting between **Sintra**'s (p908) romantic palaces and the urban beaches of **Cascais** (p908).

SEASONAL HIGHLIGHTS

Summers are the busiest here, and there are plenty of beaches, but spring and autumn can be just as nice for wine tasting, hikes and quirky folk festivals.

FEBRUARY

Portugal's **Carnaval** features much merrymaking. Places such as Loulé and Torres Vedras have the largest parades, but villages like Podence have quirkier ancient rites, with devilish-looking characters taking over their streets.

MAY

University students in Coimbra celebrate graduation with a bang by throwing a nine-day-long street party for **Queima das Fitas** (p921).

JUNE

Lisbon and Porto join forces to celebrate their respective patron saints, **Santo António** (p904) and **São João** (p911), while music festivals kick off across the country.

A Week of Highlights

● When you feel like you've seen it all in Lisbon, take the train or bus to **Coimbra** (p921), where students roam the streets in black capes. Visit the country's oldest university, **Universidade de Coimbra** (p922), wander between **monasteries** (p921) and, if you can, stick around to hear the city's **unique fado style** (p923).

● Then continue north on the railway towards **Aveiro** (p924). Art Nouveau buildings line this city's canals, which can be explored on a *moliceiro* boat.

● End your trip in **Porto** (p911), admiring tile facades, touring Port wine cellars along the river, and tucking into a hearty forkful of *francesinha* sandwich. Take a short day trip to the **Douro Valley** (p915), then return to Porto to fly back home.

Slow-Paced Adventure

● From Lisbon, travel down south, following the west coast. Stop at **Vila Nova de Milfontes** (p929) for a swim or a surf lesson, before continuing towards **Lagos** (p919), a small town in the Algarve famous for its caves and award-winning beaches. Then drive east to **Faro** (p916), taking time to explore its surroundings, which include the **Parque Natural da Ria Formosa** (p917), a haven for flamingos and dolphins.

● Next, head to **Mértola** (p929), a riverside town where Islamic ruins stand alongside a medieval castle. Spend an evening around **Barragem de Alqueva** (p927), swimming in river beaches, sipping wine and gazing at the stars, before making your way to **Évora** (p926), home to a Roman temple and an eerie bone chapel. The city is less than two hours from the capital, making it easy to close the loop.

AUGUST

The Minho's most spectacular festival, **Romaria de Nossa Senhora d'Agonia** (p915) in Viana do Castelo, brings fireworks and lively parades with people dressed in folk costumes or sporting giant papier-mâché heads.

SEPTEMBER

The **grape harvest** begins, and the country's major wine regions, the Douro Valley and the Alentejo, offer plenty of opportunities to get in on the action.

NOVEMBER

The smell of roasted chestnuts lingers in the air as the rainy days start to creep in. Marvão celebrates with a **chestnut festival** (p926), and around Vidigueira, *vinho de talha* is poured during the **Amphora Wine Day** (p926).

DECEMBER

With **Christmas** around the corner, towns light up with holiday decorations, and Óbidos' castle becomes even more magical. Fireworks usher in the new year and snow begins to fall around Serra da Estrela.

Lisbon

ANCIENT HISTORY | MAGICAL SUNSETS | CREATIVE EDGE

GETTING AROUND

You can explore most of Lisbon on foot, but be ready to encounter a number of hills (some of which you can skip by tram or funicular). The metro *(metrolisboa.pt)* links the city's main districts, with buses *(carrismetropolitana.pt)* covering the remaining outskirts, so there's no need for a car. Trains *(cp.pt)* whisk you up to the coast, and ferries *(ttsl.pt)* cover the river districts. Cycling is best in flatter areas like Belém and Parque das Nações.

☑ TOP TIP

From film festivals and book fairs to art exhibits and outdoor concerts, Lisbon is a living cultural hub. June is the busiest month, with locals hitting the streets to celebrate **Santo António**. The whole city is in party mode, with the highlight being the evening of 13 June.

Lisbon may look effortlessly charming today, with its photo-worthy tiled facades, viewpoints scattered across its hills, and flaky custard tarts that melt in the mouth. But it wasn't always like this. The Portuguese capital has seen the rise and fall of empires like the Romans and the Moors, withstood a tragic earthquake that ravaged much of its city centre, and suffered a dictatorship that shook people to their core. It's an emotional backlash that's still heard in the lyrics of fado, the city's traditional melancholic song. However popular Lisbon has become, its roots remain humble. This is a city where past and future coexist, artisans share space with young, up-and-coming designers, and the remaining century-old *pastelarias* (pastry and cake shops) are joined by modern fine-dining halls. In Lisbon, simple pleasures like witnessing the sunset are always worthy of a toast.

A City of Layers

Uncover 2500-plus years of history

As one of the oldest cities in Europe, Lisbon has been through a lot. For a quick history recap, visit **Lisboa Story Centre** *(lisboastorycentre.pt; adult/child €7.50/3.50)*. If you'd rather see what's left today, head to Alfama to find the ruins of a 1st-century-CE outdoor theatre at the **Museu do Teatro Romano** *(ruins free, museum €3)*, before wandering through the district's narrow lanes leading to **Sé de Lisboa** *(sedelisboa.pt; adult/child €7/5)*, a church built in 1150 on the site of a mosque and restored in the 1930s, or hike to **Castelo de São Jorge** *(castelodesaojorge.pt; adult/child €15/free)*, a partly restored mid-11th-century fortress with superb views over the city.

Then jump forward to the 1600s, when Portugal was at the height of its colonial rule, erecting monumental buildings like the **Mosteiro dos Jerónimos** *(museusemonumentos.pt; adult/child €18/free)* and **Torre de Belém** (closed for renovations at the time of writing), now UNESCO-listed sites. But perhaps the most memorable event in Lisbon's history is

LISBON

★ HIGHLIGHTS
1 Castelo de São Jorge
2 Sé de Lisboa

● SIGHTS
3 Convento do Carmo & Museu Arqueológico
4 Largo das Portas do Sol
5 Lisboa Story Centre
6 Miradouro da Graça
7 Miradouro de Santa Catarina
8 Mosteiro dos Jerónimos
9 Museu de Arte Contemporânea MAC/CCB
10 Museu de Arte, Arquitetura e Tecnologia (MAAT)
11 Museu do Fado
12 Museu do Teatro Romano
13 Pink Street
14 Quake
15 Torre de Belém

● SLEEPING
16 Home Lisbon Hostel
17 Patio São Vicente Guest Houses

● EATING
18 Canalha
19 Confeitaria Nacional
20 É Um Restaurante
21 Manteigaria
22 O Trevo
23 Pastéis de Belém
24 Tasca Zé dos Cornos

● DRINKING & NIGHTLIFE
25 Finalmente

● ENTERTAINMENT
26 O Corrido

● SHOPPING
27 Casa Pereira da Conceição
28 Chapelaria Azevedo Rua
29 Livraria Bertrand
30 Luvaria Ulisses
31 Manteigaria Silva

RIDING LISBON'S TRAMS WITH MINIMAL IMPACT

Carris' yellow trams are ubiquitous in Lisbon's historic centre. Riding them has become such a must-do that travellers often mistake them for tourist rides. **28E** is the most popular, but it's also the locals' only public transport for getting across town from Alfama. Hop on the 28E outside the rush hour or later in the evening – the route is just as enchanting at nightfall. If your time to travel around is tight, look for alternatives – same experience, but slightly different itineraries. Tram **12E** travels to and from Martim Moniz via Alfama's viewpoints and the Sé cathedral, while tram **25E** connects Praça da Figueira to Campo de Ourique (Prazeres) via Cais do Sodré and Santos.

Pastéis de Belém

the Great Earthquake of 1755. Feel the earth shake beneath you again in the immersive room at **Quake** *(lisbonquake. com; adult/child €29/21),* or stand beneath the roofless Gothic church, **Convento do Carmo** *(museuarqueologicodocarmo.pt; adult/child €7/free)* for a quiet reminder of that shocking day.

Sweet Tooth, Much?

Pastries and sweet liquor

Even in the alternative Lisbon of Yorgos Lanthimos' film *Poor Things,* eating a *pastel de nata* (custard tart) is a must-have experience. **Pastéis de Belém** *(pasteisdebelem.pt)* has held the original (and very secret) recipe since its creation in 1837 by monks at Mosteiro dos Jerónimos. But modern versions like **Manteigaria** *(manteigaria.com)* are a close contender. For a bigger sweet spread, hit the city's famous *pastelarias* like **Pastelaria Versailles** *(grupoversailles.pt)* or **Confeitaria Nacional** *(confeitarianacional.com).* And if you want a post-meal tipple, don't miss the *ginjinha* (sour-cherry liqueur) bars around Rossio.

A View to Remember

Capture Lisbon's magical sunsets

More than a lookout, *miradouros* are Lisbon's official gathering spots. Just before the sun sets, you'll see people flock to **Miradouro de Santa Catarina** near Bairro Alto to toast the day away or up to **Miradouro da Graça** (reached via a funicular) for a drink at the neighbourhood's kiosk. Meanwhile, Alfama's viewpoints are more like photo-ops, with **Largo das Portas do Sol** earning you that typical postcard view of terracotta roofs backed by the shimmering Rio Tejo while tram 28 whisks past on the opposite side.

Painting the Town Red
Popular nightlife districts

Kick off your night out in Lisbon at **Bairro Alto**, the city's party district. Space is tight, so you'll most likely wind up standing outside with a drink in hand, hopping from door to door. Alternatively, head to **Cais do Sodré**, where you'll find the infamous **Pink Street** (officially Rua Nova do Carvalho), flanked by several bars, and hit the remaining clubs here or around **Cais do Gás**. If you're looking for a drag show, try **Finalmente** *(finalmenteclub.com; daily shows 3am)* near Príncipe Real – the city's first gay nightclub, open since 1976.

The Calling of Fado
Learn about Portugal's popular urban song

Fado's roots run deep in Lisbon's old quarters, Alfama and Mouraria. This sorrowful music genre went from working-class entertainment to a famous world-music genre in what feels like a heartbeat. Learn about its nuanced history at the **Museu do Fado** *(museudofado.pt; adult/child €5/free)*, catch a live show at **O Corrido** *(ocorrido.com)* or watch the queen of fado, Amália Rodrigues (1920–99), resurrected on stage at **Ah Amália** *(ah-amalia.pt; adult/child €20/17)* through a life-size hologram.

Where Art Lives On
Ancient crafts and modern-art hubs

You could spend a whole day hopping between the city's endless art spaces, from the classic **Museu Nacional de Arte Antiga** *(museudearteantiga.pt; adult/child €10/free)*, holding Hieronymus Bosch's *Temptations of St Anthony*, to Belém's contemporary-focused museums, including the **MAC/CCB** *(ccb.pt/macccb; adult/child €15/12)*, with a permanent 20th-century collection, and the **MAAT** *(maat.pt; adult/child €15/free)*, with rotating art-meets-tech exhibits.

Street art thrives in districts like **Graça** and **Marvila**, but also underground across the city's metro stations. Contemporary architecture stands out in places like the **Fundação Calouste Gulbenkian** *(gulbenkian.pt; adult/child from €8/free)*, home to two art museums and a beloved free urban park.

LISBON'S BEST HISTORIC SHOPS

Chapelaria Azevedo Rua: The oldest hat-maker in Portugal, in business since 1886.

Luvaria Ulisses: This shop sells custom-made gloves at Rua do Carmo. Its tiny space welcomes one client at a time.

Casa Pereira da Conceição: Go for the decor and architecture, stay for the scent of freshly ground coffee. For both connoisseurs and first-timers.

Livraria Bertrand: The world's oldest in-business bookshop, in Rua Garrett since 1773, is a must-stop for bookworms and history buffs.

Manteigaria Silva: A family-owned grocery shop and one of the top places to buy *bacalhau* (salted cod) and other delicacies.

 EATING IN LISBON: OUR PICKS

É um Restaurante: A project by Crescer, this casual fine-dining restaurant trains and hires unhoused people. *12.30-3pm & 7-10pm Tue-Sat* €€

Tasca Zé dos Cornos: Family-owned Portuguese *tasca* (tavern), where space is tight and sharing tables is the norm. Walk-ins only. *noon-4pm Tue-Sat* €

Canalha: Award-winning chef João Rodrigues mixes the homely environment of a traditional *tasca* with a modern-cuisine menu. *12.30-11pm* €€

O Trevo: Home to Lisbon's (allegedly) best *bifana* (pork sandwich), this corner spot has a mix of tourists and regulars. *7am-10pm Mon-Sat* €

Beyond Lisbon

Travel beyond the capital and you'll stumble upon picturesque coastal towns, World Heritage–listed monasteries and medieval villages.

Places

Cascais p908
Sintra p908
Setúbal p909

Set off on a day trip or pack up for a week-long adventure across Lisbon's outskirts. You could hit the Portuguese Riviera, a trio of coastal towns to the west of the city stretching from Estoril and Cascais to Sintra, where pristine golden beaches meet romantic palaces less than an hour away. Alternatively, head south across the Rio Tejo to find wilder sandy stretches, hiking trails and wildlife-spotting opportunities, or venture further north where ancient Knights Templar routes and world-famous pilgrimage spots merge with modern surfing hubs, including Nazaré with its record-breaking waves. Whichever direction you choose, you're bound to find something that will captivate you.

Cascais

TIME FROM LISBON: **40MIN**

Seaside promenade, beaches and gelato

Portuguese royalty set the trend of holidaying in Cascais long ago. Today, this coastal town remains pretty posh with its seaside manors (some turned into hotels), and curated museums clustered around the **Bairro dos Museus** *(bairrodosmuseus. cascais.pt; from €5, 24hr pass €15),* the museum quarter. It's the last stop on the train line from Cais do Sodré, with a string of beaches to choose from.

Hot summer days call for ice cream at **Santini** *(santini.pt),* before riding the seaside promenade towards the dramatic cliff formation of **Boca do Inferno** (Mouth of Hell). You can rent electric scooters or bikes at the **Mobi Cascais** *(mobi.cascais .pt/geral/quiosques-mobicascais)* kiosk inside the train station. If you stick around for lunch, Rua Afonso Sanches (aka **Rua Amarela**) has a stretch of restaurants to pick from.

Sintra

TIME FROM LISBON: **40MIN**

Romantic monuments and misty trails

Most of Sintra's romantic palaces and the top-of-the-hill Moorish castle are shrouded in urban legends and ghost stories. A guided full-moon hike with **O Caminheiro de Sintra** *(mig uelboim.com; from €14)* reveals the town's mystical charm. If, however, you're here at daylight, you have time to wander through its monuments.

GETTING AROUND

Trains whisk you from Lisbon's Cais do Sodré station to Estoril and Cascais, and from Rossio station to Sintra. Check **Comboios de Portugal** *(cp.pt)* for schedules. Tomar can also be reached by rail via Santa Apolónia. For places around Setúbal, you're best off getting a bus from Sete Rios station run by **Carris Metropolitana** *(carrismetropolitana. pt)* or **Rede Expressos** *(rede-expressos.pt).*

TRABANTOS/SHUTTERSTOCK

Palácio Nacional da Pena, Sintra

From Sintra's train station, follow the trail along Volta do Duche towards **Palácio Nacional de Sintra** *(parquesdesintra.pt; adult/child €13/10)*. Visit this former royal palace recognised by its striking conical chimneys, then stop by **Casa Piriquita** *(piriquita.pt)* for a mandatory pastry – the pillow-shaped *travesseiros,* filled with egg and almond cream, are the speciality – and finish with a tour around **Quinta da Regaleira** *(regaleira.pt; adult/child €15/10),* a neo-Manueline villa and gardens where a 27m initiation well draws the crowds. Alternatively, tick off the big-hitters, the **Palácio Nacional da Pena** *(adult/child €20/18),* which looks straight out of a fairy tale with its bright yellow walls emerging from the mountains, and the 10th-century **Castelo dos Mouros** *(adult/child €12/10),* with battlements high enough to take in the whole town. You can reach both via bus 434 or by hailing a taxi/tuk-tuk from the station to the top of the hill. Buy tickets at *bilheteira.parquesdesintra.pt.*

Setúbal

TIME FROM LISBON: 1HR

Market feasts, dolphins and sandy shores

The greasy aroma of *choco frito* (deep-fried cuttlefish), Setúbal's signature dish, lingers through the streets at lunchtime. Many restaurants pick their fresh catch from **Mercado do Livramento** *(mornings only, closed Mon),* where you can also stock up on the region's creamy cheese and sweet Moscatel wine. A small estuary surrounds the city, where you can spot dolphins (boat trips depart from the marina). Further west is **Serra da Arrábida**, home to paradisiacal beaches and numerous mountain trails *(arrabidatrails.com).*

BEST BEACHES NEAR LISBON

Praia do Meco: Between Sesimbra and Costa da Caparica, this beach comes with a separate nudist area.

Praia da Adraga: A secluded beach on Sintra's coast with its own seafood restaurant.

Praia Tróia-Mar: Take the ferry from Setúbal to Tróia to reach this sandy stretch.

Portinho da Arrábida: Crystal-clear waters, a quiet bay and nearby restaurants make this one of Arrábida's best beaches.

Praia da Foz do Arelho: A lagoon meets the sea at this beach near Óbidos, popular with families and windsurfers.

Praia de Carcavelos: Surfers love this beach along the Cascais line.

Praia da Morena: There's sand as far as the eye can see at this Costa da Caparica favourite.

EATING AROUND LISBON: BEST SEAFOOD

Azenhas do Mar: Restaurant perched above Azenhas do Mar saltwater pool, with plenty of seafood dishes and local wines. *12.30-10pm* €€	**Casa Santiago:** Busy restaurant famous for Setúbal's signature dish, *choco frito. 11.30am-3pm & 6-9.45pm Mon-Sat* €€	**Casa Mateus:** Restaurant in the centre of Sesimbra for seafood aficionados. Make reservations. *12.30-3pm & 7-10pm Tue-Sun (dinner only Tue)* €€	**Taberna do Ganhão:** Go for the appetisers with a cold beer and look out on lovely Prainha beach in Baleal. *3-10pm Mon-Sat* €€

DRIVING AROUND ESTREMADURA & RIBATEJO

Take on medieval castles, sacred landmarks and a surfing hot spot on this road trip around Estremadura and Ribatejo.

START	END	LENGTH
Óbidos	Tomar	127km; 5 hours

Drive along the west coast, beginning in the medieval town of ❶ **Óbidos**, where bookshops take over every corner and sour-cherry liqueur is poured in a chocolate cup. While Rua Direita gets all the traction, especially during festive seasons, it's worth climbing up the battlements to look over the maze of whitewashed houses.

Continue to ❷ **Nazaré**, where surfers have broken records riding waves up to 30m high at Praia do Norte. Watch it all from Forte de São Miguel Arcanjo in winter, or stick to the shore at Praia da Nazaré, where fish sellers showcase racks of dried fish and octopus.

Heading inland, you'll encounter three sacred landmarks. The ❸ **Mosteiro de Alcobaça**,

the stage of one of Portugal's most tragic love stories, is followed by the ❹ **Mosteiro da Batalha**, which steals the show with its stained-glass windows and intricate Gothic facade. Then comes ❺ **Fátima**, home to one of the world's largest Christian shrines. The huge Santuário de Fátima draws thousands of pilgrims on 13 May and 13 October, with celebrations of the apparitions of Our Lady.

End the trip in ❻ **Tomar**, following in the footsteps of the Knights Templar. The Convento de Cristo is the main attraction, with its striking mix of Gothic and Renaissance elements, but there's also a medieval synagogue, a quirky matchbox museum and forest trails to explore.

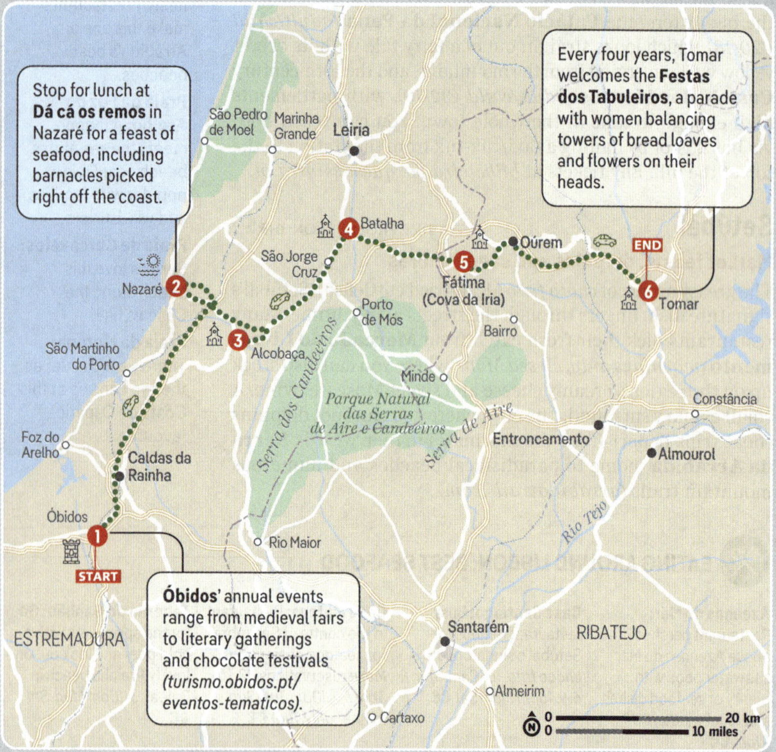

Stop for lunch at **Dá cá os remos** in Nazaré for a feast of seafood, including barnacles picked right off the coast.

Every four years, Tomar welcomes the **Festas dos Tabuleiros**, a parade with women balancing towers of bread loaves and flowers on their heads.

Óbidos' annual events range from medieval fairs to literary gatherings and chocolate festivals (*turismo.obidos.pt/eventos-tematicos*).

São Pedro de Moel · Marinha Grande · Leiria · São Jorge Cruz · ❹ Batalha · Óurem · END · Nazaré ❷ · ❸ Alcobaça · ❺ Fátima (Cova da Iria) · Porto de Mós · ❻ Tomar · São Martinho do Porto · Bairro · Foz do Arelho · Caldas da Rainha · Minde · Constância · Parque Natural das Serras de Aire e Candeeiros · Entroncamento · Almourol · Óbidos · ❶ START · Rio Maior · Serra dos Candeeiros · Serra de Aire · Rio Tejo · ESTREMADURA · Santarém · RIBATEJO · Almeirim · Cartaxo

N | 0 — 20 km | 0 — 10 miles

Porto

PORT WINE | ARTISTIC ROOTS | HEARTY CUISINE

Porto is the city that gave Portugal its name and so much more. Its proximity to the river and the ocean made it an attractive place for various peoples to settle, including Celts, Iberians, Romans and Moors. The city grew from the ancient Morro da Sé hilltop neighbourhood to the riverfront district of Ribeira and expanded in multiple waves. By the 19th century, Porto had become a hub for the liberal movement, stuck in a brotherly dispute between Dom Miguel (absolutist) and Dom Pedro IV (liberalist). Eventually, liberalism won, earning Porto the nickname of 'Invicta' (Invincible), which is still thrown about today. This northern city has since forged its own artistic expression and architecture. Locals are known for their distinct accent and hospitality, and for not mincing their words. The University of Porto, among the largest in the country, contributes to perpetually renewing the city's youthful and rebellious spirit.

Hunting for Tiles

Capture Porto's iconic *azulejos*

With its eye-popping blue-and-white tiled facades, Porto makes the perfect backdrop for a photoshoot. The best part is that it's free: stand in front of the **Capela das Almas** with its 16,000-tile facade or step into **São Bento train station** to witness Portugal's history told in a series of panels.

Design lovers can pop into the **Banco de Materiais** *(museu doporto.pt; free; closed Mon),* a pioneering project responsible for safeguarding elements of Porto's architecture, like its iconic *azulejos* (tiles). Or try painting your own by joining a workshop at **Gazete Azulejos** *(gazeteazulejos.com; €38).*

A Trip Back in Time

Explore the city's major historic sites

Wandering through **Cais da Ribeira**, a UNESCO-listed district, you'll encounter some of Porto's oldest sights. Start with

GETTING AROUND

Walking is the best way to get around the city centre, though there are several steep hills. From Porto airport, the metro *(metrodoporto.pt)* goes straight into the city centre. If you're arriving by bus or train, you'll likely end up at the Campanhã station. From there, it's a short metro or taxi ride to the city centre. Trams take you along parts of the coast; buses connect you to the outskirts, like Serralves. Both are run by **STCP** *(stcp.pt).*

☑ **TOP TIP**

Once a year, Porto celebrates its patron saint, **São João**, by throwing a big party on the evening of 23 June. Locals set up impromptu barbecues outside, paper lamps are launched into the skies, and everyone dances to their favourite tunes, hitting passersby with a squeaky plastic hammer until the midnight fireworks.

a visit to the 12th-century Romanesque cathedral **Sé do Porto** *(church free, cloister & treasury adult/child €3/free)*, then make your way to the **Igreja de São Francisco** *(ordemsaofrancisco porto.pt; adult/child €10/3)*, a church hiding a spectacular baroque interior with carved gilded altarpieces. Next door is the **Palácio da Bolsa** *(palaciodabolsa.com; adult/child €14/free)*, where 18kg of gold leaf covers a neo-Moorish-style room. More baroque gems include the **Igreja dos Clérigos** *(free)* with its gilded altar and the adjoining 76m-high **tower** *(torredosclerigos.pt; adult/child €10/free)*. While you're here, you might as well pop into **Livraria Lello** *(livrarialello.pt; €10)*, one of Portugal's most beautiful bookshops.

Francesinha

Mad for Port & Francesinha

Dive into Porto's culinary obsessions

Porto's most famous delicacy, beyond the namesake Port wine, is the *francesinha*. Some call it a sandwich, but really, it's a knife-and-fork job to tuck into the multiple layers of meat squished inside slices of bread drenched with melted cheese and a thick tomato sauce. Try it at **Café Santiago** *(cafesantiago.pt)* or head to **Kind Kitchen** *(kindkitchen.pt)* for a vegan version.

If you want to sip that sweet fortified wine, go across the Douro to Vila Nova de Gaia, where you'll find a row of cellars offering regular tours. **Porto Augusto's** *(portoaugustos.pt; €15)* does a quick 20-minute rundown of Port styles, **Niepoort** *(niepoort.pt; from €45)* offers more exclusive tastings, and **Churchill's 1982 Garden Bar** *(drinkchurchills.com)* has the perfect views to pair with a glass of Port tonic.

PORTO'S BEST ART SPACES

Museu Nacional Soares dos Reis: Portugal's first public art museum, featuring a mix of sculptures, ceramics, paintings and antique furniture.

Centro Português de Fotografia: This free museum housed in a former political prison displays old cameras and stages temporary photo exhibits.

Rua de Miguel Bombarda: Art galleries line this street in the Cedofeita district.

Casa da Música: Concert hall with an irregular polyhedron structure designed by Dutch architect Rem Koolhaas; guided tours on Monday, Wednesday and Friday.

Serralves: See contemporary art shows in this large estate featuring an Art Deco building, a sculpture park and a museum envisioned by architect Siza Vieira.

 EATING IN PORTO: OUR PICKS

Flor dos Congregados: The smell of roasted pork tenderloin will lure you into this cosy tavern. *7-10pm Mon-Wed, noon-3pm & 7-10pm Thu-Sat* €€

Taberna Folias do Baco: Douro winery set up in Porto to showcase its natural wines paired with delish snacks. *6pm-midnight Thu-Mon* €€

Borboleta: Escape from the city bustle to the terrace of this veggie-friendly restaurant. *noon-4pm & 7-11pm Wed-Fri, noon-11pm Sat & Sun* €€

Yeatman: Chef Ricardo Costa's two-Michelin-star restaurant at the Yeatman resort in Vila Nova de Gaia. *seating at 6.30pm, 7.30pm & 8.30pm Tue-Sat* €€€

Beyond Porto

Terraced vineyards rising above the Douro, lush natural parks and ancient folk rituals await a short hop from Porto.

Places

Braga p914
Guimarães p914
Viana do Castelo p915
Douro Valley p915
Bragança p915

You can spend days lingering in Porto, posing against tile facades and drinking Port tonics at sunset, but there's a whole world to see just outside the city. A train whisks you through the middle of the Douro Valley, where vineyards grow in steep terraces, to the heart of medieval towns like Guimarães, the country's first official capital, and up the coast, where windswept beaches await in Viana do Castelo. Driving further inland, you'll reach the likes of Gerês, home to waterfalls and lush hiking trails, and the region of Trás-os-Montes, where you can still witness ancient carnivals like the Caretos de Podence, wander through remote villages and occasionally hear a different tongue, influenced by its proximity to neighbouring Spain.

GETTING AROUND

Trains *(cp.pt)* run along the coast towards Viana do Castelo and into the Douro Valley with stops at Régua and Pinhão. Guimarães and Braga are also accessible by rail; the latter is a great base to explore Gerês. While buses take you close to this national park, a car will give you more freedom to reach its wilder sections. Driving is also the best way to cover Trás-os-Montes.

Braga

TIME FROM PORTO: 1HR

A sanctuary of churches and coffee

When Holy Week comes around, Braga becomes a magnet for pilgrims. After all, the city has the biggest church collection in Portugal. Even if you're not a devotee, it's worth visiting the **Santuário do Bom Jesus do Monte** *(bomjesus. pt),* a striking baroque sanctuary sitting atop 500-plus stairs (take a funicular). The city also has a laid-back coffee culture. From the century-old **Café A Brasileira** *(abrasileirabraga. pt)* to the bookshop cafe of **Centésima Página** *(centesima. com),* there are plenty of spots to hunker down with a brew – or switch things up with a local craft beer from **Letraria** *(cervejaletra.pt).*

Guimarães

TIME FROM PORTO: 1HR

Meet Portugal's medieval core

Guimarães was the country's first official capital. Today, this UNESCO-listed medieval town still feels kind of frozen in time with its maze of stone houses and a crenellated **castle** looming on a hill. The **Paço dos Duques de Bragança** *(pacodosduques.gov.pt; adult/child €8/free incl castle)* offers a glimpse of what would have been a rich royal residence, complete with Flemish tapestries, porcelain and antique furniture. Later, splurge on modern fine dining at **A Cozinha** *(restauranteacozinha.pt)* or **Le Babachris** *(lebabachris.com),* or kick back at **Taberna Trovador** *(tabernatrovador.eatbu. com)* with wine and a round of *petiscos* (tapas).

Viana do Castelo

TIME FROM PORTO: 1HR

Pilgrimage sites and folk parades

Head north along the coast and you'll reach Viana do Castelo, a city of fishers, sailors and surfers. Every summer, they share their sandy shores with the thousands of visitors who come to partake in pilgrimages like the **Romaria de Nossa Senhora d'Agonia** *(festasdagonia.com)* in August. In the backdrop of nearly every photo of the city is the iconic neo-Byzantine church **Santuário do Sagrado Coração de Jesus** *(templosantaluzia.org).* Drive or hike up the hill, or take the **Elevador de Santa Luzia** *(adult/child €2/1).*

Douro Valley

TIME FROM PORTO: 2½HR 🚂, 1½HR 🚗

Scenic journeys and terraced vineyards

There are many ways to reach the Douro Valley, including aboard a steam train or driving along the N222. Its steeply terraced vineyards are a sight to behold, whether you're sailing the river on a quiet **solar boat** *(daurum.pt; from €15)* or enjoying the views from a *quinta* (estate) over a glass of wine. A visit to the **Museu do Douro** *(museudodouro.pt; adult/child €8/free)* in **Peso da Régua** is a must if you want to learn more about the history of the region, or you can picture the wine's journey through the tiles at **Pinhão**'s **railway station**. There are outstanding viewpoints here like **Miradouro Casal de Loivos**.

To see a different side of the Douro, head east to **Parque Arqueológico do Vale do Côa** *(arte-coa.pt; tours from €16),* to discover Europe's largest open-air gallery of Palaeolithic rock art on a hike or kayak trip.

Bragança

TIME FROM PORTO: 3HR 🚌, 2HR 🚗

Medieval walls and carnival masks

Strategically located to deter any curious Spaniard, Bragança's 12th-century **Cidadela** still stands strong today. Step inside its medieval walls to find the **Domus Municipalis**, a rare Romanesque building, the original **Castelo de Bragança** *(castelo-braganca.pt; adult/child €3/free),* and the **Museu Ibérico da Máscara e do Traje** *(museudamascara.cm-braganca.pt; adult/child €1.21/free),* where you can spot a collection of folk-style masks worn in festivals like the **Podence carnival** in February.

THE HEART OF VIANA

The Heart of Viana is a symbolic heart-shaped design found in jewellery, on clothes and in decoration that has come to represent the city of Viana do Castelo – and even the Minho – itself. The heart's history dates back to the 18th century, when Queen D Maria I, thankful for the birth of her male child, asked for a golden heart to be made in worship to the Sacred Heart of Jesus. The jewellery version is made using the traditional, labour-intensive *filigrana* process, where tiny chains and threads of gold are woven and then melted together to create intricate patterns. Check them out in the Gold Room at the **Museu do Traje** (Clothing Museum) or purchase your own in town.

Faro & the Algarve

WILDLIFE | BEACHES | SEAFOOD FEASTS

☑ **TOP TIP**

Consider the Vamus bus tourist pass, including the inter-city Aerobus (from €35 online) or CP Trains Algarve Pass (from €21.90 in ticket offices) if you're planning multiple trips or to travel the Algarve's breadth.

Flourishing as Roman Ossónoba, remembered as the Moors' last stronghold and conquered by King Afonso III in 1249, Faro doesn't lack historical credentials. Yet for many visitors to the Algarve, Faro is little more than a fleeting glimpse through a plane window before being whisked further along the coast. Stick around, though, and you'll find a majestic cathedral, marina-facing rooftop bars and an estuary abounding with wildlife and island beaches.

Doubling as a city and a district, Faro is the best year-round base to explore the Algarve. Whether you're heading east to Tavira, where churches meet oyster farms, to the big resorts in the west including Albufeira, or inland, where small towns like Loulé are proud of their ancient crafts, sweet delicacies and wine heritage, you can reach every part of the region from Faro in little more than an hour.

Faro

Ancient sites and ferry rides

Meander through Faro's old town by passing through **Arco da Vila**, a neoclassical gate. Inside, surrounded by orange trees, you'll find the cathedral, **Sé** *(adult/child €5/free)*, whose bell tower has sweeping views of Ria Formosa. Outside the medieval walls, 18th-century **Igreja de Nossa Senhora do Carmo** *(€2)* hides a creepy yet bewitching chapel built with over 1000 exhumed skulls and bones of Carmelite monks. A

 GETTING AROUND

Faro Airport is under 20 minutes from the centre; taxis are usually plentiful. Próximo, Faro's main bus operator, has regular services on line 16 *(€2.80)* between the beach, airport and city centre; buy tickets onboard. Vamus' Aerobus links towns to the west (bus-stop ticket machine). Faro train station, Próximo's bus terminal and the Vamus/long-distance bus station are clustered near the walkable city centre. A large free car park at Largo de São Francisco backs the old town's walls.

loop back brings you to the marina, where you can hop on a
ferry *(adult/child from €2.35/1.15 one way)* to **Praia de Faro**,
the city's main beach.

Parque Natural da Ria Formosa

An island haven

Encompassing flamingo-visited salt pans, birdlife-rich wet-
lands, swirling inlets and a handful of barrier islands, the
Parque Natural da Ria Formosa *(icnf.pt)* is phenomenal.
Accessible from Faro, Olhão and Tavira, this nature reserve

is best explored by boat. Ferries take you to the island's sandy beaches in Barreta (aka Deserta), Culatra, Armona, Tavira and Cabanas. Dolphin pods can also be spotted across the waters, with tours led by marine biologists like **Ocean Vibes** (*ocean vibesalgarve.com; €55*). For birdwatching, join solar-boat tours with **Lands** (*lands.pt; from €45*) or follow the 2.5km trail through the protected area of **Quinta de Marim** (*icnf. pt; €3*). The salt pans are birdlife havens too, and some are still used for salt production, including **Salinas do Grelha** (*salinasdogrelha.pt; from €9*), where you can float in a mini Dead Sea between May and October.

Loulé

The artisan town

A 30-minute drive west from Faro takes you to Loulé, where you can wander around artisan workshops like **Casa da Empreita**, specialised in palm weaving, or watch *cataplanas* (cooking pots) being hammered at the **Oficina de Caldeireiros**. If you fancy learning the crafts yourself, sign up for a workshop with **Loulé Criativo** (*loulecriativo.pt*). Other attractions include the **Banhos Islâmicos de Loulé** (*museudeloule.pt; free*), the only (known) example of Islamic baths in Portugal, and the **Mercado Municipal**, with its striking arched Moorish doorways and red onion-dome towers. The town comes alive during the carnival in February or March and **Festival MED** (*festivalmed.cm-loule.pt*), a celebration of world music in June.

Albufeira

The soul of the party

As one of the Algarve's most developed resort towns, Albufeira has everything you can imagine: all-inclusive hotels, vast sandy stretches and a busy nightlife strip. But there are ways to escape the crowds. Veer off the old town to find wilder beaches like **Praia dos Arrifes** and **Praia da Galé**, hire a kayak or SUP to reach secret coves with **Albufeira Surf Sup** (*albufeirasurfsup.com; from €35*), or dive underwater with **Easy Divers** (*easydivers.pt; €100*) to discover the **EDP Art Reef**, an artificial-reef-cum-art-gallery filled with sculptures by Portuguese artist Vhils. And if you do decide to have that nightcap on the Strip, there are quieter options like **Connection** (*connectiongaybar.com*), Albufeira's main gay bar, or the tree-shaded cocktail garden at **Libertos** (*liber tosclub.com*) – before midnight, at least.

COSTA VICENTINA

Ocean-shaved sheer cliffs, footprint-free sands, dune-blotted beaches and surf-pounded shores are only a fragment of Algarve's windswept west coast known as Costa Vicentina. Stretching from Burgau to Odeceixe's regional-border-slicing Ribeira de Seixe, this protected landscape is also a prime spot for hiking. The Rota Vicentina's (*rotavicentina.com*) **Fishermen's Trail** stretches for 227km and has eight one-day sections between Odeceixe and Lagos. All are excellent day hikes, but the final leg between Luz and Lagos is the easiest both in intensity and for public transport. Following a well-marked track, the route ambles atop **Rocha Negra**, a volcanic and sandstone cliff packed with fossils and traces of the Middle Cretaceous period.

EATING IN THE ALGARVE: OUR PICKS

O Recife: Long-standing *churrasqueira* (grill restaurant) in Faro serving chicken piri-piri by the half or whole. *noon-3pm & 7-10pm Thu-Tue €*

A Sereia: Atop Sagres' fish market with a window looking down at the catch arriving, seafood doesn't get fresher. *noon-6pm Mon-Fri €*

Tasca do Kiko: Behind Lagos' boatyard, this tucked-away tapas restaurant has sharing plates crammed with flavour. *12.30-3pm & 6-10pm Mon-Sat €€*

Windmill: Splurge on the three-course Mediterranean menu served inside this romantic windmill in Albufeira. Reservations required. *6.30-10pm €€€*

Castelo de Silves

Silves

Among vineyards and citrus trails

At Silves' hulking sandstone **castle** *(cm-silves.pt; €2.80)*, do as Moorish kings would have done centuries ago: peer through the crenellated russet walls and survey the citrus-scented scene. Sweet oranges can be picked here from November until August in farms such as **Quinta de Santo Estevão** *(quinta-santo-estevao.pt; from €15)*. Almond trees are also part of the landscape, with the dried fruit making its way to traditional treats like *doce fino* (almond sweets) sold at **Doçaria do Sul** *(docariadosul.pt)*. The surrounding vines, first planted by the Phoenicians, invite you for a wine tasting in estates like **Morgado do Quintão** *(morgadodoquintao.pt; from €42.50)* or **Quinta dos Santos** *(quintadossantos.com; from €45)*. Every August, you can travel to another era during **Silves' Medieval Fair** *(feiramedievaldesilves.pt)*.

Lagos

Chasing caves, dolphins and sunsets

In the 15th century, caravels embarked from Lagos on colonising missions and returned with enslaved Africans, giving

BEST REGIONAL SEAFOOD DISHES

Cataplana: Arguably the Algarve's most distinctive dish, this seafood stew is cooked in a special pan shaped like a clam.

Conquilhas à Algarvia: *Conquilhas* are small clams pulled from the sand at low tide, cooked with garlic, coriander, lemon and oil.

Arroz de lingueirão: *Arroz de marisco* (seafood rice stew) is plentiful, but this traditional razor-clam version takes top billing.

Muxama: This salt-cured tuna speciality is a delicious, hard-to-find appetiser.

Xerém de conquilhas: Moorish-influenced cornflour dish comparable to porridge; Olhão's clam recipe is most celebrated.

Sardinhas assadas: Charcoal-grilled, salt-seasoned sardines are a summer favourite, especially during celebrations.

Kayaking, Lagos

rise to Europe's first slave market. Today, boats depart from Lagos' marina seeking dolphins and caves rather than discoveries. Kayaks offer even better access with tours like **Kayak Explorers** *(lagoskayakexplores.com; €35),* often including a stop for snorkelling. And when the crimson sun sinks into the deep blue beyond, there's no better place to be than the wave-chiselled headland of **Ponta da Piedade**. There are also plenty of beaches around, from sweeping **Meia Praia**, a popular kitesurfing spot, to pocket-sized **Praia do Camilo** and **Praia de Porto de Mós**, favoured among surfers.

Coimbra

REGAL LEGACY | GRANDIOSE ARCHITECTURE | UNIVERSITY CULTURE

Located along the Rio Mondego (Portugal's longest river at 234km), Coimbra is one of Portugal's most ancient and important cities. Formerly known as Aeminium, back when the town was a centre for Roman commerce, Coimbra went on to become a capital city and residence of the royal family after Dom Afonso Henriques declared himself king. Later, the city found itself at the heart of the Portuguese Renaissance, where baroque art and architecture thrived during the 16th and 17th centuries – the famous Joanina Library is a prime example. Coimbra has no greater claim to fame, however, than its UNESCO-listed university, one of the oldest and most prestigious in the world. The intellectual culture, which has prevailed in the city since the mid-1500s, gave a start to a number of Portugal's best-known literary, music, artistic and scientific geniuses across the decades – and continues to do so to this day.

Sacred Art

Religious sites old and new

Coimbra is one of Portugal's intellectual epicentres, and much of its history began in monasteries like the **Mosteiro de Santa Cruz** *(church free, sacristy, chapter house & cloisters €4)*. This 12th-century Manueline structure was once home to the country's most renowned medieval schools. Come to see the 4000-pipe organ and marvel at the tile paintings and elaborate cloister. On the west bank of the river are the 14th-century **Mosteiro de Santa Clara-a-Velha** *(adult/child €4/ free),* founded by the saintly Queen Isabel and left in ruins after frequent flooding, and the 17th-century **Mosteiro de Santa Clara-a-Nova** *(adult/child €6/3),* built nearby to replace it as a tribute to the queen. Near the university is the **Sé Velha** *(€2.50),* the only Romanesque cathedral still standing in the country, although it's more reminiscent of a small castle than a church, with some clear Islamic influences. A bit further

GETTING AROUND

The city is easily explored on foot, but the old town has some steep hills. On the public bus system, the electric blue line connects the city's upper and lower parts, while the Linha do Botânico goes past the Botanical Garden. You can also opt for the tourist Coimbra Yellow Bus; newspaper kiosks sell daily and single-use tickets. Long-distance trains arrive at Coimbra-B station, while short-distance trains arrive at Coimbra-A station near the city centre.

☑ TOP TIP

For a true feel of the city, visit while the university is in session – much of the city's atmosphere is thanks to the student population. If you're into *festas* (parties), plan your trip for **Queima das Fitas** in May or **Festas das Latas** in October.

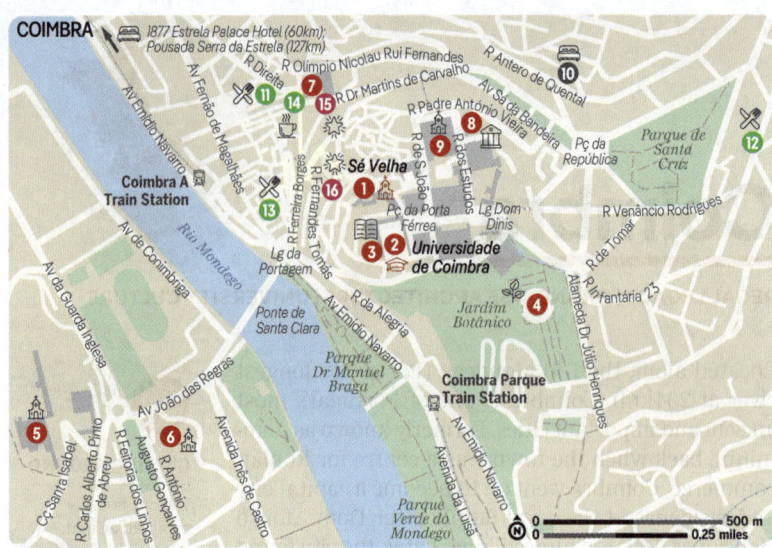

away is the **Sé Nova** *(€1),* a 16th-century baroque and neoclassical cathedral that was originally the city's Jesuit College.

A City of Students

Tour Portugal's oldest university

Founded in 1290, the **Universidade de Coimbra** *(visit.uc.pt; adult/child €16.50/free)* is among the oldest universities in the world. While the university got its start in Lisbon, the faculty was moved to Coimbra in 1537 to the grounds of the former royal palace, now a UNESCO World Heritage Site still occupied by the university. The former **Throne Room** is now the Great Hall of Acts, featuring 17th-century *azulejo* walls

 EATING & DRINKING IN COIMBRA: OUR PICKS

Café Santa Cruz: A Coimbra institution, set in a 1264 chapel, perfect for a drink and a pastry and afternoon fado. *8am-midnight Mon-Sat, to 8pm Sun* €

Zé Manel dos Ossos: Tiny *tasca* serving local cuisine in a room wallpapered in hand-written notes. *12.30-3pm & 8-10.30pm Mon-Fri* €

No Tacho: This family-run *tasca* with traditional dishes is a favourite among locals. *7.30-10pm Mon & Tue, 12.30-3pm & 7.30-10pm Wed-Sun* €€

O Palco: Top-tier eatery where everything served is produced within 100km of Coimbra. *12.30-3pm & 7-10pm* €€€

Biblioteca Joanina, Universidade de Coimbra

A MUSICAL LEGACY

Lisbon may claim the origins of fado, but Coimbra also has its own version of this soulful music genre, called *fado de estudante* (student fado). Sung by groups of students dressed in their black capes, the lyrics are typically more hopeful than the *lisboeta* style, covering love, longing and their beloved university, while the guitar is tuned lower to better fit the outdoors where these performances often take place. But if you want to catch a regular session, check out **àCapella** *(acapella.com.pt)* or **Fado ao Centro** *(fadoaocentro.com).* Some say it was Coimbra's student wear that inspired the Hogwarts look in JK Rowling's *Harry Potter* series.

and gargoyle motifs on the wooden ceiling. The **Armoury** that once stored the weapons of the Academic Royal Guard is now primarily used for academic ceremonies. And the king's private quarters were used as the private examination hall until the age of the Enlightenment.

Tickets also give you access to the **Museu da Ciência**, housing the country's oldest collection of Portuguese natural history and antique scientific instruments; and the **Biblioteca Joanina**, one of the most beautiful baroque libraries in the world, with 60,000 books dating back as far as the 16th century. The library itself is designed to preserve the works, with 2m-thick walls, oak shelves and two resident colonies of bats 'employed' to eat insects that could potentially damage the pages. When you're done exploring the interiors, rest up at the 13-hectare **Jardim Botânico** located nearby.

Beyond Coimbra

Mountain peaks, ancient cities and lost villages make up the landscape around the Beiras' largest city.

The area around Coimbra is exceptionally varied, so there's a perfect city side trip for every taste. A short train ride takes you to Aveiro, a city of canals, Art Nouveau buildings and sweet delicacies – plus a few beaches not far away. Head inland to find Viseu, where Renaissance art lives on in museums and churches. The city also marks the start of Portugal's longest cycling lane. And if it's the mountains you crave for, drive off to Serra da Estrela, where you can try anything from skiing and hiking to swimming in river beaches, depending on the season. Wool factories and delicate sheep's-milk cheese are also part of the region's appeal.

Aveiro

TIME FROM COIMBRA: **30MIN**

Canals, dunes and sweet treats

The canals that run through the historic heart of Aveiro have earned it the nickname of 'Portuguese Venice'. Take a ride on the colourful *moliceiro* boats – once used to collect a type of seaweed called *moliço* and now a tourist attraction – past Art Nouveau buildings, salt flats and lagoons. Tours from the **Cais dos Moliceiros** typically run 45 minutes to an hour. Aveiro is equally known for its freshly caught oysters – try them at **Ostraveiro** (*ostraveiro.com*) – and *ovos moles,* a sweet delicacy combining egg yolk and sugar wrapped in wafer-like cases with sea motifs. **Confeitaria Peixinho** (*loja.confeitaria peixinho.pt*) has been dishing out boxes of these since 1856.

With a bit more time, you can tour the ceramic factory at **Museu Vista Alegre** (*vistaalegre.com; adult/child €6/free);* venture further to **Costa Nova**, a beach enclave famous for its row of colourful striped cottages; or hike along the dunes of **São Jacinto** nature reserve, a great place to spot the pink flamingo.

Viseu

TIME FROM COIMBRA: **1½HR**

Historic sites and Renaissance art

Like many great cities, Viseu's story starts with a hero. The city was once the home of Viriato, the chief of the Lusitani tribe, who valiantly defended his people during the Roman invasion. While he lost the battle, the town's Romanisation

GETTING AROUND

Trains or buses link Coimbra to Aveiro, while Viseu is accessible by bus only. To reach Serra da Estrela, it's best to rent a car or spend a day in Viseu or Castelo Branco before hopping on a bus to Covilhã, one of the park's gateways. The journey can vary from 2½ to three hours.

Moliceiro **boats, Aveiro**

VILLAGE NETWORKS

The **Aldeias Históricas de Portugal** *(aldeias historicasdeportugal. com)*, or Historic Villages of Portugal, is a network of small towns in the Beiras region joined together in a tourism and development project for their unique cultural patrimony. The majority of the villages are fortified, situated on high ground and have a history dating back to at least the Roman period. Among the highlights are Monsanto, Belmonte, Linhares da Beira and Piódão villages. Meanwhile, the **Aldeias do Xisto** *(aldeiasdoxisto.pt)*, or Schist Villages, joins together 27 villages built of schist across the Serra do Açor, Zêzere and Tejo-Ocreza regions. This ecotourism initiative allows an immersion into local living, along with access to myriad hiking and mountain-biking trails, regional cuisine, river beaches and more. **Cerdeira** stands out for its creative community.

brought fast development, turning it into an important economic centre. The city's centrepiece today is the **Sé de Viseu**, the 12th-century cathedral sitting imposingly in Viseu's main square, sporting a Romanesque-Gothic portal and a vaulted Manueline ceiling. Next to it, in the old bishop's palace, is the **Museu Nacional Grão Vasco** *(museunacionalgraovasco.gov. pt; adult/child €10/free)*, where you can admire paintings by Portuguese Renaissance artist Vasco Fernandes (c 1475–1542), better known as Grão Vasco.

A countryside cycle

After exploring the city centre, set off on a cycling adventure by following the **Ecopista do Dão**, a 49km trail that connects Santa Comba Dão and Viseu. Rent bikes from **Abelenda Bike Rental** *(quintadoriodao.com; from €14.50)* and look out for the Rio Nagozela beach and the Rio Paiva valley along the way.

Serra da Estrela

TIME FROM COIMBRA: 2½HR

Winter sports and river beaches

Some 65 million years ago, the Eurasian and African tectonic plates collided, creating the Serra da Estrela, the tallest mountain range in continental Portugal; its highest point is **Torre** at 1993m. When the Portuguese want to see snow, this is where they go. The ski (sledging) season runs from December to April, although your best chances for consistent snowfall are in January and February. Hiking is also popular, with paths like the **Passadiços do Mondego** *(passadic osdomondego.pt)*, a 12km route following the Rio Mondego. Summer is ideal for a swim in the river, with beaches like **Praia Fluvial de Loriga** and **Poço da Broca da Barriosa**, as well as **Cascata do Poço do Inferno** (more famous for the waterfalls and a popular spot for canyoning).

Évora & the Alentejo

RURAL HEARTLAND | STARGAZING | ANCIENT CRAFTS

GETTING AROUND

Évora is easily accessible from Lisbon by bus and rail. Once there, you can cover the city centre on foot. Surrounding towns like Estremoz can be reached by bus with **Rede Expressos** *(rede-expressos.pt),* while other places may require two transfers. Having a car can help shorten the distances, and most towns offer free parking.

✅ **TOP TIP**

Summer can be scorching hot, but it's also the time of many festivals. September and October are harvest seasons for grapes and olives, while November is reserved for chestnut and *talha* wine tastings, around Marvão's **chestnut festival** and Vidigueira's **Amphora Wine Day**. Check *visitalentejo.pt* for other popular annual events.

Three rivers flow through the Alentejo, Portugal's largest region: the Tejo, the Sado and the Guadiana. At the heart of their confluence is Évora. The city's strategic position has made it a coveted spot for communities since prehistoric times. The Neolithic people erected menhirs and dolmens across Évora's hills, the Romans built roads and introduced winemaking, while the medieval palaces recall a time when the city was a retreat for the Portuguese crown. It's these historical chapters that have made Évora a UNESCO World Heritage Site. From here, you can set off on endless adventures, taking in the starry skies around Alqueva Lake, the beaches along the coast or the castles dotted across the mountains up north. Take your time to soak in the oak-covered landscape, savour the wine, cheese and black pork, and watch artisans carefully craft textiles, ceramics and all things cork.

Évora

The historic gateway to Alentejo

Évora's iconic site is the **Templo Romano**, a ruined Roman temple dating back to the 1st century BCE, featuring imposing Corinthian columns capped with Estremoz marble. From here, you can access a number of sites: **Convento dos Lóios** *(adult/child €5/free; closed Mon & Tue),* a striking 15th-century church adorned with blue-and-white tiles; **Paço de São Miguel** *(free; open weekends only),* a former palace filled with stunning fresco ceilings; and **Museu Nacional Frei Manuel do Cenáculo** *(museusemonumentos.pt; adult/child €10/free; closed Mon),* displaying the archaeological artefacts uncovered near this ancient city. The striking Gothic cathedral, **Sé** *(evoracathedral.com; adult/child €5/free),* offers incredible views from its rooftop, while the **Igreja de São Francisco** *(https://igrejadesaofrancisco.pt; adult/child €6/free)* has an eerie chapel covered with thousands of bones.

ÉVORA & THE ALENTEJO

Sertã · Fátima · Tomar · Abrantes · Nisa · Castelo de Vide · Serra de São Mamede · Caldas da Rainha · Gavião · Portalegre · Alburquerque · Santarém · Crato · Cartaxo · Almeirim · Ponte de Sor · Arronches · Torres Vedras · Coruche · Mora · Estremoz · Elvas · Badajoz · Borba · Olivenza · LISBON · Vendas Novas · Montemor-o-Novo · Redondo · Évora · Montijo · Setúbal · Reguengos de Monsaraz · SPAIN · Comporta · Alcácer do Sal · Portel · Barragem de Alqueva · Atlantic Ocean · Grândola · Ferreira do Alentejo · Vidigueira · Moura · Santiago do Cacém · Beja · Sines · Serpa · Cercal · Aljustrel · Rosal de la Frontera · Ourique · Castro Verde · Mértola · Odemira · Almodôvar · Villanueva de los Castillejos · São Teotónio · Alcoutim · Gibraleón · Silves · São Bartolomeu de Messines · Ayamonte · Lepe · Huelva

Estremoz

Hunting for art and souvenirs

Travel 40 minutes northeast to Estremoz on a Saturday morning to catch the **weekly market**. The free car park fills up quickly as vendors gather around the surrounding streets to sell anything from fresh produce to leather goods and cork items. From here, it's a short walk to the **Museu Berardo Estremoz** *(museuberardoestremoz.pt; adult/child €3.50/free)*, which holds one of Portugal's largest private tile collections. The nearby **Museu Municipal** *(cm-estremoz.pt; adult/child €1.50/free)* traces the origins of Estremoz' UNESCO-listed ceramic figurines known as *bonecos de Estremoz,* while the **Centro Interpretativo do Boneco de Estremoz** *(€1.50)* focuses on more modern interpretations.

Barragem de Alqueva

River beaches, boat rides and stargazing

When it opened in 2002, Barragem de Alqueva changed Alentejo's landscape forever, creating Europe's largest artificial lake.

THE GUIDE

PORTUGAL ÉVORA & THE ALENTEJO

THE ALENTEJO CRAFTS

Portugal is famous for its handmade crafts, some of which are produced in the heart of Alentejo. Arraiolos, Mértola and Reguengos de Monsaraz are known for their intricate rugs and blankets. In **Portalegre**, weavers have become masters in turning paintings into stunning hand-woven tapestries, which can be admired at the **Museu da Tapeçaria de Portalegre Guy Fino** *(cm-portalegre. pt)*. Lost crafts like *chocalos* (metal rattles) are produced near **Viana do Alentejo**. For ceramics, head to **São Pedro do Corval**, the country's largest ceramic hub – it seems every door here leads to a ceramic workshop. And if you're just sticking around Évora, don't miss **O Cesto** *(ocesto.com. pt)*, which sells a mix of pottery and cork-based souvenirs.

AROXOPT/SHUTTERSTOCK

Marvão

Just one hour south of Évora, the area has endless draws. Take in the immense landscape from medieval villages like **Monsaraz**, hop on a boat or kayak from **Centro Naútico de Monsaraz** *(sem-fim.com/centro-nautico; from €15)*, or dip your toes in idyllic river beaches (with temperatures reaching up to 30°C) like **Praia Fluvial da Amieira** or **Praia de Azenhas d'El Rei**. At night, your eyes will inevitably turn to the stars. The lack of light pollution has made this area one of Europe's first Starlight Tourism Destinations. Two observatories provide regular stargazing sessions *(from €20)*: the **Observatório do Lago Alqueva** *(olagoalqueva.pt)* and the **Dark Sky Alqueva** *(darkskyalqueva.com)*.

Comporta to Zambujeira do Mar
Surf, beaches and coastal trails

If you miss the sight of the sea, travel west to find a coast sprinkled with secluded beaches and fishing towns. **Praia da Comporta** is the closest to Évora, and its shores can

EATING IN THE ALENTEJO: OUR PICKS

PREC: This food hub in Mértola doubles as a shop and restaurant serving top-notch vegetarian meals. *9am-4pm Mon-Fri* €

Taberna Sal Grosso: Choose from a range of tasty *petiscos* on the chalkboard of this lively Évora tavern. *noon-3.30pm & 7-10.30pm Thu-Mon* €€

Venda Azul: Waiters rush between tables with trays of Alentejo pork at this friendly restaurant in Estremoz. *noon-3pm & 7-10pm Tue-Sat* €€

Fago: A creative seasonal menu and local *ginjinha* await within Marvão's castle walls. *7.30-11pm Thu-Sat, 12.30-3pm Sat & Sun* €€€

be explored barefoot or on a horse with **Cavalos na Areia** *(cavalosnaareia.com; from €70)*. Further down, the nature reserve of **Santo André** is a prime spot for birdwatching, **Porto Covo** is famous for its small coves, while **Praia do Malhão** near **Vila Nova de Milfontes** is ideal for beginner surfers. **SurfMilfontes** *(surfmilfontes.pt; from €50)* offers lessons and vacation packages with accommodation. And if you feel like escaping the crowds, the beaches of **Almograve** and **Zambujeira do Mar** are great alternatives. You can also explore the entire coastline in one fell swoop by hiking the **Fishermen's Trail** (p918).

Serra de São Mamede
Tracking medieval gems
Most people think of the Alentejo as a region of dry flatlands. But head north, and you'll encounter the mountains of Serra de São Mamede. Here, nature thrives, with lush fields lining the roads with oak, ash and chestnut trees, the fruit of which is melded into local sweets. History is visible in the remains of medieval strongholds like **Marvão**, with its striking castle clinging to a rocky ridge, and **Castelo de Vide**, where a synagogue recalls the town's former Jewish community. The old train tracks that once connected the two villages have been converted into the **Rail Bike Marvão** *(railbikemarvao.com; from €25)* route, allowing visitors to pedal through the middle of the mountains, while **Caballos Marvão** *(caballosmarvao. com; from €30)* takes you across on a horse.

Mértola
The Museum Village
Just before the Alentejo meets the Algarve, you'll pass through a sea of whitewashed villages, rural farms and vineyards. Occasionally, you'll hear the sound of *cante alentejano,* the region's polyphonic song, echoing through old taverns. Among the highlights is riverside Mértola, nicknamed the Museum Village after the network of free museums *(museudemerto la.pt)* spread across town, including a Roman house and the remains of an Islamic neighbourhood.

BEST ALENTEJO WINERIES

Fitapreta: António Maçanita and Alexandra Leroy are reinstating forgotten grape varieties at this innovative winery on Évora's outskirts.

Quinta do Quetzal: Whether you're standing outside or atop the panoramic terrace, you can expect fine views of sloping vineyards.

Herdade do Cebolal: After a tour of his family's vineyards, Luís will produce an assortment of cheeses and charcuteries, all showcasing local producers.

Herdade do Esporão: Wine and olive-oil tastings come together at this Reguengos de Monsaraz winery that houses Alentejo's only Michelin-star restaurant.

Herdade dos Outeiros Altos: With sustainable agriculture practices, this Estremoz winery strives to use indigenous varieties for its organic wines – some aged in *talhas* (clay amphorae).

Places We Love to Stay

€ Budget €€ Midrange €€€ Top End

Lisbon & Around

MAP p905

Home Lisbon Hostel € One of the city's oldest hostels, this affordable option in the heart of Baixa was rated the best in the world for four years straight.

Patio São Vicente Guest Houses €€ Refurbished, independent cottage houses in Alfama with a private interior courtyard.

Chalet Saudade €€ This classic 19th-century manor in Sintra's historic centre has been transformed into a vintage guesthouse.

Wine & Books Hotel €€€ Culture-driven five-star hotel in Belém near Mosteiro dos Jerónimos. One for bookworms and wine lovers.

Porto

MAP p912

Passenger Hostel € Dorms and private rooms above the iconic São Bento train station.

Mo House €€ Tastefully decorated guesthouse that provides breakfast and a kitchenette to cook your own meals.

Yeatman €€€ A two-Michelin-star restaurant and a spa make this one of the most luxurious options in Vila Nova de Gaia.

Douro Valley & Minho

Hostel Douro Backpackers € Owners Pedro and Sara will tell you everything you need to know about Pinhão while handing you a glass of wine on arrival.

Pousada Caniçada-Gerês €€ Exceptionally comfortable, modern guesthouse with mesmerising mountain views and an inviting pool for summer visits.

Ventozelo Hotel & Quinta €€€ Splurge a little and stay amid the vineyards of this estate near São João da Pesqueira.

Feel Viana €€€ Overlooking Praia do Cabedelo, this hotel features sustainably built luxury cabins, good food and a spa to make up for the Minho's unpredictable weather.

Faro & the Algarve

Olive Hostel € Laid-back dorms and private rooms in Lagos with colourful decor, welcoming hosts and a sociable terrace.

São Paulo Boutique Hotel €€€ Five soothing suites, with a peaceful private patio and small pool, make this converted historic home in Tavira a central bolthole.

Vila Origens €€€ Set in Albufeira's old town, this luxurious, Moorish-inspired, adult-only hotel is personality-packed with patterns, tiles and cabanas around the inviting pool.

3HB Faro €€€ Modern, comfortable and upscale, this Faro hideaway has an indulgent spa, rooftop pool and quality restaurant.

Coimbra & Around

MAP p922

AQ 188 Guest House €€ Renovated historical home turned guesthouse with light-filled spaces, comfy beds and an inviting back patio, near the university.

Pousada Serra da Estrela €€ This classic, mountain hotel has been fully modernised, and while its pool and restaurant are great, the views are the winner.

1877 Estrela Palace Hotel €€€ This elegant, carefully restored palace in Aveiro has nice modern decor, rooftop canal views and excellent staff.

Évora & the Alentejo

Heaven Inn Évora Hostel € Choose between a double room with a terrace or shared dorms at this friendly hostel with a cosy lounge facing the Igreja de São Francisco.

Três Marias €€ Between Vila Nova de Milfontes and Porto Covo is this serene country house with 15 rooms, a swimming pool and sauna; also offers bike rentals.

Montimerso Skyscape €€€ Sleep under the starry skies at this sustainable property on the outskirts of Monsaraz. Cycling and hiking trails take you along the lake.

Hotel Albergaria do Calvário €€€ Custom-made wool headboards, exposed stone walls and old millstones dot this central Évora hotel with 22 rooms and an apartment with a fully equipped kitchen.

Practicalities

TRAVEL INSURANCE

Insurance is not mandatory to travel to Portugal, but it's good to have. Consider one that covers flight cancellation and medical care. EU travellers can apply for the European Health Insurance Card (GHIC for UK residents) that covers emergency medical treatment free of charge.

ELECTRICITY

Portugal uses 230V/50Hz European-style plugs with two round pins. Don't forget to pack an adaptor if travelling from outside the region.

VISAS

EU nationals don't need a visa for any length of stay. Visitors from the UK, Canada, the US, Australia and New Zealand can stay for up to 90 days in any six months without a visa.

WILDFIRES

Emerging heatwaves, lack of rain and neglected rural lands have all contributed to the rise of wildfires in Portugal. Check the latest report on wildfire risk at IPMA *(ipma.pt/en/riscoincendio/rcm.pt)* to avoid getting caught off guard.

K I PHOTOGRAPHY/SHUTTERSTOCK

LGBTIQ+ TRAVELLERS

In 2025, Portugal ranked fourth in the Spartacus Gay Travel Index of the world's best LGBTIQ+ friendly countries. For a country that has spent decades under a dictatorship, liberal ideals are something of a novelty, and negative attitudes may prevail outside the big cities.

OPENING HOURS

Banks 8.30am–3pm Monday to Friday
Bars 7pm–2am
Cafes 9am–7pm
Clubs 11pm–4am Thursday to Saturday
Museums 10am–6pm Tuesday to Sunday
Restaurants noon–3pm and 7–10pm
Shopping malls 10am–10pm
Shops 9.30am–noon and 2–7pm Monday to Friday, 10am–1pm Saturday

PUBLIC HOLIDAYS

New Year's Day 1 January
Carnaval Tuesday February/March
Good Friday March/April
Liberty Day 25 April
Labour Day 1 May
Corpus Christi May/June
Portugal Day (Camões and Communities Day) 10 June
Feast of the Assumption 15 August
Republic Day 5 October
All Saints' Day 1 November
Independence Day 1 December
Feast of the Immaculate Conception 8 December
Christmas Day 25 December

Language

Portuguese comes from the Romance language family and is closely related to Spanish, French and Italian. It's descended from the colloquial Latin spoken by Roman soldiers.

Basics

Hello. Olá. *o-laa*
Goodbye. Adeus. *a-de-oosh*
Yes. Sim. *seeng*
No. Não. *nowng*
Please. Por favor. *poor fa-vor*
Thank you. Obrigado/a (m/f). *o-bree-gaa-doo/a*
Excuse me. Faz favor! *faash fa-vor*
Sorry. Desculpe. *desh-kool-pe*
What's your name? Qual é o seu nome? *kwaal e oo se-oo no-me*
My name is … O meu nome é … *oo me-oo no-me e …*
Do you speak English? Fala inglês? *faa-la eeng-glesh*
I (don't) understand. (Não) Entendo. *(nowng) eng-teng-doo*

Directions

Where's the …? Onde é …? *ong-de e …*
Could you please write it down? Podia escrever isso, por favor? *poo-dee-ashkre-ver ee-soo poor fa-vor*
Can you show me (on the map)? Pode-me mostrar (no mapa)? *po-de-me moosh-traar (noo maa-pa)*

Signs

Entrada/Saída Entrance/Exit
Aberto/Fechado Open/Closed
Há Vaga Rooms Available
Não Há Vaga No Vacancies
Informação Information
Esquadra da Polícia Police Station
Proibido Prohibited
Casa de Banho Toilets
Homens Men
Mulheres Women
Quente/Frio Hot/Cold

Time

What time is it? Que horas são? *kee o-rash sowng*
It's (10) o'clock. São (dez) horas. *sowng (desh) o-rash*
Half past (10). (Dez) e meia. *(desh) e may-a*
in the morning. da manhã. *da ma-nyang*
in the afternoon. da tarde. *da taar-de*
in the evening. da noite. *da noy-te*
yesterday. ontem. *ong-teng*
tomorrow. amanhã. *aa-ma-nyang*

Emergencies

Help! Socorro! *soo-ko-rroo*
Go away! Vá-se embora! *vaa-se eng-bo-ra*
Call …! Chame …! *shaa-me …*
　　a doctor. um médico. *oong me-dee-koo*
　　the police. a polícia *a poo-lee-sya*

NUMBERS

1
um *oong*
2
dois *doysh*
3
três *tresh*
4
quatro *kwaa-troo*
5
cinco *seeng-koo*
6
seis *saysh*
7
sete *se-te*
8
oito *oy too*
9
nove *no ve*
10
dez *desh*

RADU BERCAN/SHUTTERSTOCK

Gare do Oriente train station, Lisbon

Arriving & Getting Around

Lisbon is the country's main entry point. Domestic and international flights arrive at Terminal 1. Terminal 2 is used by low-cost carriers for departing flights. It's also possible to fly directly to Porto or Faro.

City Sightseeing
While you can explore Porto and Lisbon on foot, the metro system makes it easier to travel between districts. Lisbon has a handful of accessible stations, but Porto is better equipped as most platforms are lower.

Watch the Cobblestones
Rainy days can make Portugal's famous stone pavements pretty slippery, so watch your step. If you're travelling with kids, bring a light pram with thicker wheels and pack a baby carrier just in case.

Hitting the Road
Buses and trains take you on a slow journey around the country, but renting a car is ideal for setting off at your own pace. Most cars are manual; automatic transmission cars are typically more expensive.

Driving Essentials
The Portuguese drive on the right. Paid-toll *autoestradas* (motorways) and high-traffic secondary roads (IPs and ICs) are generally in good condition. Smaller, toll-free roads (N or EN) are usually narrow and curvy in mountainous areas, and poorly lit at night. The speed limit is 50km/h in urban areas, 90km/h on secondary roads and 120km/h on motorways.

MONEY
Currency: Euro (€)

CARDS & DIGITAL PAYMENTS
Most hotels and smarter restaurants accept credit cards; smaller guesthouses and some *tascas* might not. Restaurants will usually display a sign outside with the cards they accept. Tap-and-pay is becoming ubiquitous, though some places may only accept Portuguese cards or require a minimum payment.

CASH
Always carry a bit of cash and loose change with you. You might need it for that coffee and *pastel de nata* later on.

TIPPING
While it's not mandatory, some places have started to include a tipping charge. If there's no prior notice, 10% is usually fine, but few Portuguese ever leave more than a round-up to the nearest euro.

PANDO HALL/GETTY IMAGES

Curated by
Mark Baker

Romania

RURAL CHARM, UNSPOILT NATURE, ENERGETIC CITIES

One of Europe's last undiscovered bastions, Romania has an appealing blend of modern cities and timeless villages, pitched amid forests and soaring mountains.

Beautiful and beguiling, Romania's rural landscape remains relatively untouched by the country's urban evolution. It's a land of aesthetically stirring hand-ploughed fields, sheep-instigated traffic jams and lots of homemade plum brandy – or *țuică* as it's known locally.

Many visitors focus their attention on Transylvania, with its eye-catching natural beauty and medieval legacy of fortified Saxon towns like Brașov and Sighișoara. Bram Stoker's fictional *Dracula* added a darker, more mystical cast to the forests and mountain passes, and towering Bran Castle appears straight out of central casting as an imaginary setting for this Victorian melodrama. Across the Carpathian chain, the UNESCO-listed painted monasteries dot the northern province of Bucovina. The country's fiery, 16th-century origin story – forged in conflict with the then-expanding Ottoman Empire – is colourfully illustrated on the facades of the churches here.

Further east, the Danube Delta, where the mighty Danube River empties into the Black Sea, remains a pristine nature reserve that's home to more than 300 species of birds, including many rare varieties. It's an ideal spot for birders, of course, but with miles of marshland and empty beaches, the delta appeals to nature lovers of all stripes. Energetic cities, including Brașov, Sibiu and especially Bucharest, have excellent hotels and restaurants as well as loads of culture – both the highbrow and lowbrow variety. Together, they showcase Romania as a rapidly evolving European country.

NATALIA SOKOLOVSKA/SHUTTERSTOCK

THE MAIN AREAS

BUCHAREST
Romania's bustling capital never sleeps.
p938

TRANSYLVANIA
Saxon folkways and gorgeous scenery.
p944

BUCOVINA MONASTERIES
Riveting history told through colourful frescoes. **p950**

THE DANUBE DELTA
Coastal wildlife and pristine nature. **p953**

For places to stay in Romania, see p956

MO WU/SHUTTERSTOCK

Left: Bucharest Old Town (p943); Above: Bran Castle (p945), Transylvania

Find Your Way

Romania is a deceptively large country, divided by the Carpathian Mountains. Trains and buses are viable modes for getting around, but travel can be slow. Hiring a car gives you options, but highways can be crowded.

TRAIN

Trains are handy for travel from Bucharest north to Brașov and Sighișoara, but less practical for Transylvania's smaller towns and villages. Trains also link Bucharest with Suceava, a handy jumping-off spot for the Bucovina monasteries.

BUSES & FERRIES

Buses run between nearly every Romanian town and city, though navigating timetables can be tricky. Much of the Danube Delta is closed to car traffic; travel by passenger ferry or water taxi from Tulcea instead.

Bucovina Monasteries, p950

Rugged mountains and forests form an epic backdrop to magnificent monasteries and churches.

The Danube Delta, p953

Natural serenity of delta waterways, plus age-old cultural histories and hidden beaches.

Bucharest, p938

Romania's capital has left communism behind and is charging ahead with urban regeneration and culinary and cultural offerings.

Transylvania, p944

Picturesque peaks, brawny castles and fortified churches stand watch over timeless towns and rustic hideaways.

UKRAINE

MOLDOVA

Chernivtsi

Rădăuți
Voroneț
Suceava

Iași

Piatra-Neamț
Bacău

Vaslui

Bistrița

Târgu Mureș

Sighișoara
Citadel

Cluj-Napoca

Sibiu
St Mary's Evangelical Church

Sebeș

Deva

Oradea

Arad

Timișoara

Caransebeș
Mehadia

SERBIA

Szeged

HUNGARY

Carpathian Mountains

Olt

Brașov
Bran Castle
Sinaia

Făgăraș Mountains

Târgu Jiu

Craiova

Orșova

Ploiești

Pitești

Buzău

Brăila

Galați

Babadag
Hârșova

Tulcea

Sulina

Histria

Constanța

Mangalia
Negru Vodă

Călărași

Giurgiu

BULGARIA

Danube

BUCHAREST
Romanian Athenaeum
Palace of Parliament
Spring Palace

Black Sea

Ialomița

Mureș

Siret

0   100 km
0   50 miles

DRAGOS ASAFTEI/SHUTTERSTOCK

Calea Victoriei (p938), Bucharest

Plan Your Time

Distances are large, particularly in Transylvania. Organise your time according to your interests and plan transport carefully.

Bucharest City Break

● Tour the vast **Palace of Parliament** (p939). Pair this with a stop at the **Spring Palace** (p939), the opulent former-Ceauşescu residence. Stroll on **Calea Victoriei** (p938) for a look at 'Little Paris'. Enjoy a drink in idyllic **Sera Eden** (p943) and a promenade in **Cişmigiu Garden** (p943). Sip coffee in the **Old Town** (p943) and sample new Romanian cuisine at a spot like **KAIAMO** (p939).

A Week to Spare

● Spend a day ambling around **Bucharest** (p938), then take a train to **Braşov** (p944) – Transylvania's main event – for castles, activities and beer at street-side cafes. Spend a day in the medieval citadel of **Sighişoara** (p946). Carry on to **Sibiu** (p947) or switch it up with a tour of the painted monasteries in **Bucovina** (p950), before returning to the capital.

SEASONAL HIGHLIGHTS

SPRING
Budding trees mark spring's arrival, especially in the capital city. May is particularly busy in Bucharest, with multiple festivals.

SUMMER
July and August are hot and crowded everywhere. Beat the heat by heading into the mountains.

AUTUMN
The cultural calendar is rolling in Bucharest with the biannual **George Enescu International Festival** of classical music.

WINTER
Ski season is in full swing in Transylvania; Christmas holidays add cheer. Sibiu and the surrounding villages are particularly festive.

Bucharest

URBAN ENERGY | HISTORY | MUSEUMS

GETTING AROUND

Bucharest is a big city, and you'll quickly hit your 10,000 steps. The metro reaches most places visitors want to go, but you'll still find yourself walking quite a bit from the stations to your destination. Rideshares like Uber and Bolt are plentiful and reasonably priced; this is the preferred way to get around for residents. The public transport network includes buses and trams, but these are more for daily commuters and less practical for visitors.

☑ **TOP TIP**

Bucharest truly shines when it comes to outdoor garden bars and cafes. After a long day of hitting the pavement, repair to one of these hidden oases to relax over a glass of wine or fresh-made lemonade. We've listed some of our favourites (p943).

Bucharest has changed considerably since communism fell in 1989, bringing an end to 40 years of darkness and isolation. Centuries-old Byzantine churches stand alongside French-built belle-époque palaces (which once prompted the nickname 'Little Paris'), accompanied by a buzzing cafe culture. The Palace of Parliament that former dictator Nicolae Ceaușescu defiantly imposed on the city still looms large. It's certainly worth a visit, but look past this controversial building and instead get lost in historic side streets where late 19th- and early 20th-century manors abound, with garden bars often tucked behind. The museum scene is excellent and new Romanian cuisine is worthy of the Michelin-star limelight.

Amble through Little Paris

Neoclassical and beaux-arts buildings

Any visit to Bucharest begins with a walk along elegant **Calea Victoriei**, the capital's main thoroughfare. The early 20th century was Bucharest's most prosperous era, and during the reign of Carol I, the first king of Romania, large neoclassical buildings and beaux-arts palaces sprang up; by the end of the 1930s, the city had acquired the moniker Little Paris.

The **Equestrian Statue of Carol I** propped up in front of the Central University Library makes for a nice introduction to the capital's past, sitting right next to the site of events from the 1989 Revolution that ended the communist regime. Facing it is the former Royal Palace, today housing the **National Museum of Art** (*Muzeul Național de Artă; mnar.ro; entry adult/senior/student 32/16/8 lei*).

Nearby is the emblematic **Romanian Athenaeum** (*Ateneul Român; filarmonicaenescu.ro/en; entry 15 lei*), a classical music venue that can be visited outside rehearsals and performances. From May to early October, the street has a festival-like atmosphere on weekends and is pedestrian-only during 'Open Streets'., a new initiative when major roads are closed to traffic, turning the city centre into a pedestrian-only space

Palace of Parliament

BUCHAREST'S ORIGINS

Originally certified as a royal residence in 1459 during Vlad Țepeș' rule of Wallachia, the ruins of Bucharest's **Old Princely Court** date from the 15th century. Directly across from the ruins is **Hanu' lui Manuc**, the oldest inn in town and known for its restaurant serving Romanian food. **Old Princely Court Church** is Bucharest's oldest church (16th century); it's a revered place of worship where hundreds of pilgrims arrive on Tuesdays to pray to the relics of St Anthony the Great. Street names such as Covaci (blacksmiths), Șelari (saddle makers) and Blănari (furriers) tell the story of occupations practiced centuries ago. Str Lipscani is the biggest, named after the city of Leipzig (many of the traders at the time brought their wares from there).

Follow the Dictator's Trail

Visit a traumatic mega-palace

A must-see highlight for many, the gigantic and exorbitant **Palace of Parliament** *(cic.cdep.ro; entry adult/student tour 60/30 lei)* was commissioned by dictator Nicolae Ceaușescu in 1984, during a period of economic hardship. It's the world's second-largest administrative building after the Pentagon. For locals, it's also a painful reminder of Ceaușescu's traumatic ambitions. Today, the eclectic-style building houses the Romanian Parliament and the **National Museum of Contemporary Art** *(mnac.ro; entry adult/senior/student 32/16/8 lei)*. Even so, much of it remains unused. Of the 1100 rooms, only 400 are finished. Visits are by guided tour only, reserved in advance by telephone *(+0733-558-102)*. Don't forget your passport.

Follow up with a visit to the **Spring Palace** *(Palatul Primăverii; casaceausescu.ro; entry adult/concession 75/65 lei)*, the former residence of Ceaușescu, his wife Elena and their three kids. At a time when the population was facing daily power cuts, food rationing and limited heating during long winters, this gilded mansion with a private cinema, decadent spa and peacocks roaming about in the garden stands in glaring contrast. Book online for guided tours.

 EATING IN BUCHAREST: BEST FOR NEW ROMANIAN CUISINE

KAIAMO: Theatrically set, experimental Romanian cuisine by chef Radu Ionescu-Fehér. A 50 Best Discovery restaurant close to Herăstrău. *6pm-11pm Tue-Sat* €€€

NOUA. Bucătărie Românească: Chef Alex Petricean's signature tasting menu 'Romania on a plate' is served in seven acts. *6pm-9pm Wed-Sat* €€€

Noua B.A.R: More casual, equally fascinating universe of Romanian dishes with a twist, and brunch-like tantalising treats. *hours vary* €€

KANÉ: Farm-to-table at its best with contemporary Romanian creativity in a historic building brought back to life. *6.30pm-11pm Wed-Sat* €€€

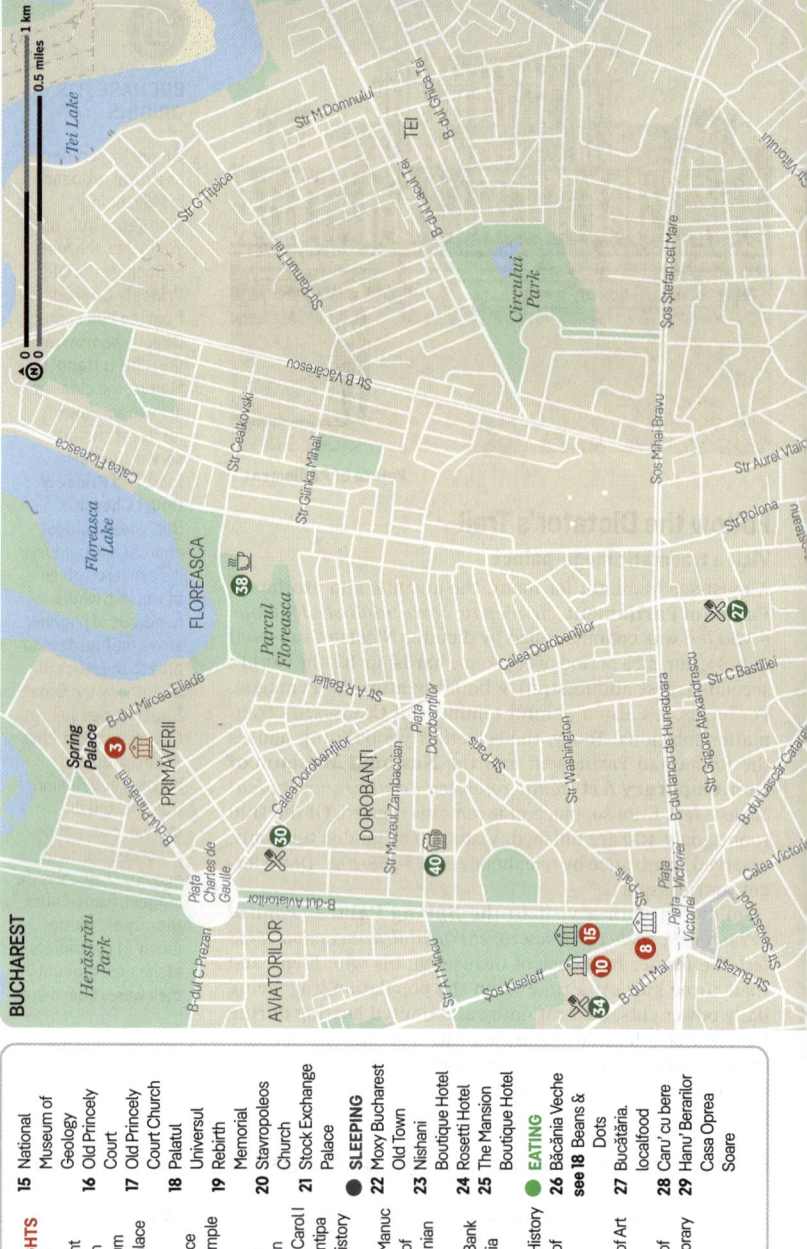

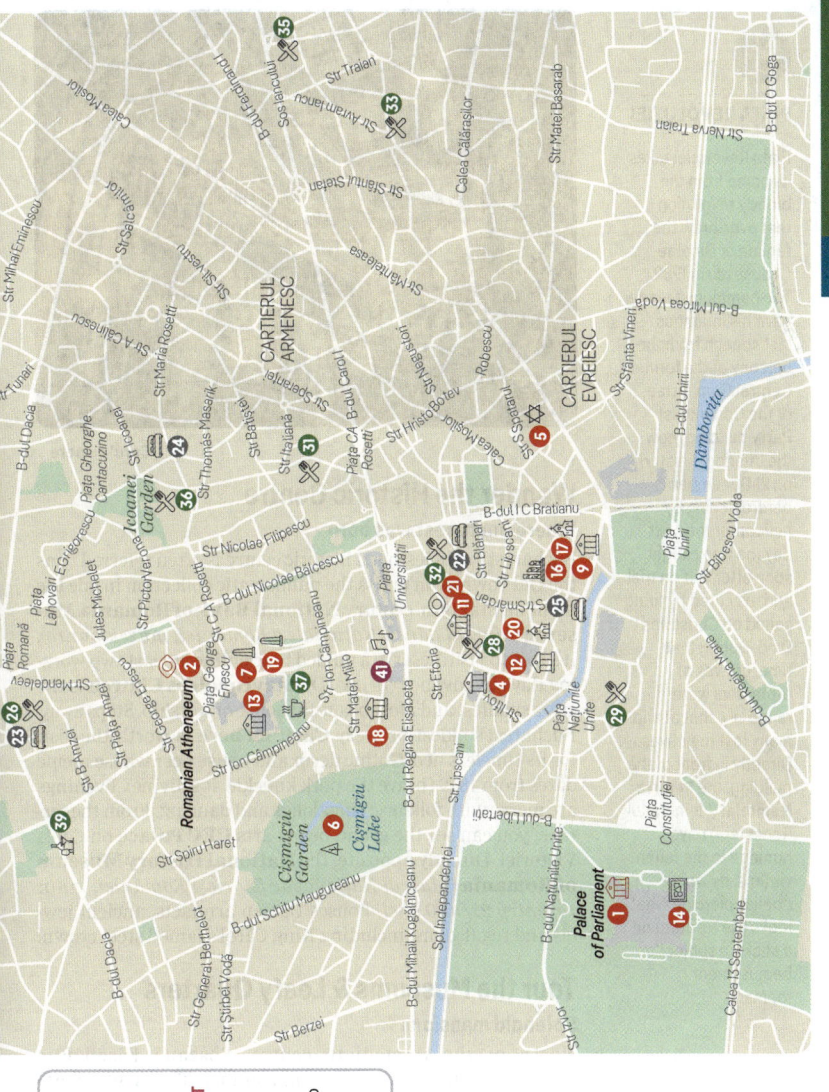

30 KAJAMO
31 KANÉ
32 La Vita e Velo
33 Mosafir
34 Noua B.A.R
35 NOUA Bucătărie
Românească
36 Sera Eden

● DRINKING &
NIGHTLIFE
see 18 ApolloIII
37 Artichoke Social
House
see 18 FIX Me a
drink

38 Grădina
Floreasca
39 Grădina
Monteoru
40 Mercato
Comunale

● ENTERTAINMENT
41 Control Club

● SHOPPING
see 22 Circa 1703-
3071
see 22 ESHTE Shop
& Café

PIAȚA REVOLUȚIEI

Piața Revoluției takes its name from the bloody revolution that overthrew the regime of Nicolae Ceaușescu in 1989. The communist leader gave his infamous last speech from the balcony of the former Central Committee of the Communist Party building (now the Interior Ministry) on 21 December before fleeing by helicopter the next day (he was caught soon after, put on trial and executed by firing squad on Christmas Day). During that time, crowds of protestors were randomly shot at and many lost their lives. Directly in front of the building, the **Rebirth Memorial** (Memorialul Renașterii) pays homage to the fallen victims, its white obelisk piercing what looks like a potato on a stick – a subject of bemusement for many.

SAXANAD/SHUTTERSTOCK

Caru' cu bere

Wander the Historic Centre
Where Bucharest was born

Bucharest's cobblestoned historic centre is often referred to as the Old Town. Don't miss the numismatic collection inside the monumental 19th-century **National Bank of Romania Museum** *(Muzeul Băncii Naționale a României; muzeu.bnr.ro)*. It's free to visit; reserve a guided tour online at least two working days in advance (bring ID). **Stavropoleos Church** is the city's smallest and most beautiful house of worship. Steps away, Bucharest's oldest brewery **Caru' cu bere** is worth the visit for its timeless neo-Gothic decor and house beer whose recipe dates from 1879 (brave the pork knuckle, it's divine). Evenings are merry with folkloric singalongs and dancing. From the terrace, you can see the grand beaux-arts **CEC Palace** on Calea Victoriei. Directly opposite, the **National History Museum of Romania** *(Muzeul Național de Istorie a României; mnir. ro; entry 22/10/0.5 lei)* houses Dacian artefacts, ancient jewels and regal gems, including King Carol's famed steel crown.

Tour the Museums & Leafy Quarters
Splendid mansions

North of the immediate centre, Șoseaua Kiseleff is home to Bucharest's best museums. The wide tree-lined boulevard starts with kid-favourite **Grigore**

 EATING IN BUCHAREST: BEST FOR ROMANIAN FOOD

Băcănia Veche: The go-to place for authentic meals in Piața Romană. Artisanal delicacies and a cosy, dim-lit garden. *noon-10pm Mon-Sun* €€

Hanu' Berarilor Casa Oprea Soare: Interwar-inspired menu and historic brewery in a splendid neo-Romanian manor near Piața Unirii. *8am-midnight Mon-Sun* €€

Bucătăria.localfood: Where Millennials go for comfort food. Unfussy menu and playful locale, just off Piața Romană. Reserve. *1-10pm Wed, noon-10pm Thu-Sun* €€

Mosafir: Charming bistro in a heritage building, combining bistronomy with Romanian cuisine, focusing on local, seasonal ingredients. *1-10pm Wed-Sun* €€

Antipa Natural History Museum (*Muzeul de Istorie Naturală Grigore Antipa; antipa.ro; entry adult/senior/student 32/16/8 lei*). The **Museum of the Romanian Peasant** (*Muzeul Țăranului Român; muzeultaranuluiroman.ro; entry adult/senior/student 20/10/5 lei*) is a classic for its collection of peasant costumes, religious icons and folkloric bits and bobs, with a gift shop and restaurant on-site. In an extraordinary early 20th-century building, the **National Museum of Geology** (*Muzeul Național de Geologie; geology.ro; entry adult/student/senior 15/10/5 lei*) is less visited, but highly worthwhile.

Hang Out in Cișmigiu
Energetic quarter and beautiful city park

With its cluster of bars, shops and galleries, the Cișmigiu district has become a designated 'Creative Quarter'. It's also home to **Cișmigiu Garden**, the oldest public park in town. Walking past the Art Nouveau Hotel Cișmigiu, you soon find yourself by **Palatul Universul**, a former printing house brought back to life as a culture hub. Inside, **FIX Me a drink** serves botanical cocktails, while **Apollo111** runs a great bar and hosts disco nights. Also worth checking out is the buzzing **Beans & Dots** speciality coffee store.

Down the block, **Control Club** is an undisputed favourite for live indie and electronic music concerts. The leafy garden terrace is open all year long. For a chilled spot to mingle, sip a craft beer or coffee, head to artsy **Artichoke Social House**.

Bucharest's Emerging Old Town
Perfect spot for people-watching

The Old Town made a dramatic U-turn a decade ago and turned into a party hotspot. Amid heritage sites and Byzantine-like churches, a mismatch of mass tourism and shops coexists. Certain streets are paving their own way. For example, at the intersection of Doamnei with Str Ion Ghica, presided over by the imposing **Stock Exchange Palace**, a design/coffee hub is shaping new grounds. Local architects have joined forces in a manifesto of sorts, converting the area into a vibrant, here-to-stay community.

Start by people-watching on the buzzing sidewalk of **La Vita e Velo**, a bike shop and cafe that is as enticing as its good looks suggest. Across the street in Ghica House is **ESHTE Shop & Café**, a creative space fostering Romanian artisans and contemporary designers, with exclusive items found only here. Entering the courtyard next door, long-enduring **Circa 1703-3071** is a vintage-seeker's dream; an eclectic shop opened by an architect who's passionate about antiques.

JEWISH BUCHAREST

Bucharest's Jewish quarter was once home to a vibrant community during the interwar period of the 20th century – some 70,000 people, representing 11% of the city's population, lived here. The majority of the neighbourhood was destroyed during the 1980s to make room for the enormous Palace of Parliament. A handful of monuments survived. A replica of Leopoldstädter Tempel (Vienna's largest synagogue, destroyed in 1938), the red-brick **Choral Temple** (*entry 10 lei*) is a stunning example. In the area, several residential buildings remain. The most remarkable is the legacy of Marcel Iancu, a Romanian-Israeli architect who was the brain behind Bucharest's modernist architecture. One example is the Solly Gold building, found at B-dul Hristo Botev 34.

 DRINKING IN BUCHAREST: BEST GARDEN BARS

| **Sera Eden:** Part greenhouse, part botanical sanctuary, this posh garden cafe lies behind a historical villa. *noon-11pm Mon-Fri, 10-11pm Sat & Sun* | **Grădina Monteoru:** Urban garden turned party hotspot on the site of Casa Monteoru, one of Netflix's *Wednesday* locations. *5pm-2am Mon-Fri, noon-2am Sat & Sun* | **Mercato Comunale:** Food trucks and local craft beer in a hip, relaxed garden with a playground and stage for live events. *hours vary* | **Grădina Floreasca:** Stylish alfresco cafe by the pool, set in Floreasca Park. Hosts occasional jazz evenings. *10am-midnight Mon-Sun* |

Transylvania

MOUNTAINS | MYSTERY | HISTORY

Places

GETTING AROUND

Slow-moving but reliable train services connect Bucharest with major towns and cities in Transylvania. The national rail service, CFR *(cfr.ro)*, has a passenger timetable on its website. That said, a car is essential for getting to smaller towns and villages, monasteries and trailheads. Note that in summer, the region's highways, particularly the stretch over the Carpathians from Bucharest to Braşov, get very crowded.

☑ TOP TIP

Transylvania covers a big area. Cities are linked by crowded highways and trains. If time is limited, it's best to focus on one or two cities or regions rather than trying to take in the entire province.

After a century of being name-checked in literature and cinema, the word 'Transylvania' now enjoys worldwide recognition. The mere mention conjures a vivid landscape of mountains, castles, spooky moonlight and at least one well-known count with a wicked overbite. Unexplained puncture wounds notwithstanding, Transylvania is all those things and more. A melange of architecture and chic sidewalk cafes enliven the towns of Braşov, Sighişoara and Sibiu.

Braşov & Around

TIME FROM BUCHAREST: **3HR**

Gothic spires, medieval gateways, Soviet blocks and a huge Hollywood-style sign: Brasov's skyline is instantly compelling. A number of medieval watchtowers still glower over the town. Between them sparkle baroque buildings and churches, while easy-going cafes line main square Piaţa Sfatului. Visible from here is forested Mt Tâmpa, sporting 'Brasov' in huge white letters.

Find your bearings on the main square

Any visit must begin with the city's beautiful, sweeping main square, **Piaţa Sfatului**, the envy of many Romanian towns and cities. At the centre of the square (actually an overgrown triangle) stands the **Council's House** (Casa Sfatului), from 1420, topped by the Trumpeter's Tower, in which the town councillors would meet. These days, the building is home to the small local history museum; you can still hear the trumpeters play from the tower every day at 6pm, or at noon on weekends. Pedestrianised Str Republicii trails off from here and is stuffed with more bars, cafes and ice cream joints.

Visit the Black Church

The **Black Church** (*Biserica Neagră; bisericaneagra.ro; entry adult/concession 25/20 lei*) may be Braşov's only true 'must see'. The church dates from the late 14th century and is the country's largest Gothic church (the bell tower stands 65m high). It got its name from its charred appearance following the Great Fire of 1689. Despite the crowds, the interior feels hushed and peaceful. The acoustics are helped by the 16th- to

Piaţa Sfatului, Braşov

19th-century Anatolian rugs that are draped across the interior; these were once placed on pews reserved for church donors.

Climb the medieval town walls

Large parts of Braşov's fortification system from the Middle Ages are still standing. Raised in stages between 1400 and 1650, the walls and towers were built in anticipation of attacks by the Turks. Seven bastions were built at the most exposed points, each one defended by a guild whose members tolled their bastion bell. The most popular spot to see the old walls is along the fortification's western section, which parallels a stream and pedestrianised Str După Ziduri. A good access point is 200m south of the Black Church. Above here, on the hillside, are two watchtowers – the **Black Tower** (Turnul Negru) and **White Tower** (Turnul Alb) Despite the names, both are brownish in colour. It's possible to climb to the towers for dramatic views, but be forewarned: the going is steep. Two impressive gates into the walled city, the 19th-century **Schei Gate** (Poarta Schei) and the 16th-century **Catherine's Gate** (Poarta Ecaterinei), were part of the old fortification system.

Venture out to Bran Castle and Râşnov Fortress

Thanks to Bram Stoker's novel *Dracula*, **Bran Castle** *(Castelul Bran; bran-castle.com; entry adult/senior/student 90/60/50 lei)*

WHERE TO EAT IN BRAŞOV: OUR PICKS

| La Ceaun Michael Weiss: Focused on Romanian food. There's a section of cauldron and slow-cooked dishes, including *bulz* (roasted polenta). *noon-10pm €€* | Am Rosenanger: A German-flavoured restaurant that serves Saxon and other Transylvanian specialities, such as spätzle noodles with paprika. *noon-10pm €€* | Bistro de l'Arte: This two-decades-old bistro still turns out some of the city's most inventive cooking. *noon-11pm €€* | La Birou: Elaborate and delicious breakfasts with plenty of fresh vegetables and other healthy ingredients. *8am-4pm €* |

FROM BRAȘOV WITH LOVE

Between 1950 and 1960, when Romania still considered itself Moscow's buddy, Brașov was officially named 'Stalin City'. Stalin's rule tampered with much more than the the town's name: forced industrialisation yanked thousands of rural workers from the countryside and plonked them down in the city in an attempt to crank the totalitarian motor of industry. One of the first displays of public opposition to the Nicolae Ceaușescu government flared up here in 1987. Thousands of disgruntled workers took to the streets demanding basic foodstuffs. Ceaușescu called in the troops and quashed the uprising, though it paved the way for protests across Romania that would topple the regime two years later.

EUGENE LOZOVSKI/SHUTTERSTOCK

Viscri fortified church

is arguably Romania's best-known tourist attraction – though connections to Stoker's fictional vampire or the historical Wallachian prince, Vlad Țepeș, are thin. That said, your first glimpse of this spectacular fortress-castle, rising above the town on a rocky promontory, will take your breath away. Teutonic knights first built a wooden fortress at this strategic location between Wallachia and Transylvania in the 13th century. For centuries the castle was controlled by Brașov's Saxons, and then fell into the hands of Romania's ruling monarchy after WWI. Commonly paired with Bran Castle on day trips from Brașov, nearby **Râșnov Fortress** *(Cetatea Râșnov; celatea-rasnov.ro)* roosts precariously on a rocky hilltop. It was built by Teutonic knights to guard against Tatar and Turkish invasions. Walk up to the fortress from the village or take a lift *(round trip adult/child 30/20 lei)*.

Sighișoara & Around   TIME FROM BRAȘOV: 2HR 🚗

Saxon settlers first started coming to Sighișoara (Schässburg in German) as early as the 12th century, by invitation of the then-ruling Hungarian kings. The magnificent fortress town they built welcomes visitors to the present day. Indeed, so resplendent are Sighișoara's pastel-coloured buildings, stony lanes and medieval towers, you'll rub your eyes in disbelief. During the Middle Ages, the booming commercial centre supported

WHERE TO EAT IN SIGHIȘOARA: OUR PICKS

Mimoza: In a lovely setting on a cobbled street, Mimoza has an eclectic menu that includes Romanian and Thai dishes as well as pizza. *9am-midnight* €€

Joseph T: Arguably Sighișoara's best restaurant. Romanian and international dishes, plus very good steaks. *7.30am-10.30am, 5pm-midnight* €€

Geurgius Krauss: A fancy establishment in a beautiful citadel setting with Art Deco interiors. Romanian and pan-European dishes. *7.30am-midnight* €€€

Alex Bakery: A little bakery selling delicious *plăcintă* (fried pastries) with all kinds of fillings, both fruity and meaty. We loved the plum-filled ones. *7.30am-10pm* €

more than a dozen traditional guilds, and towers still honour trades like 'Tinsmiths' and 'Tailors'. If Sighişoara doesn't sate your thirst for medieval splendour, it'll make a great jumping-off point to explore Saxon villages such as Viscri and Biertan.

Visit Sighişoara's citadel

From the moment you arrive, you'll want to scramble up to Sighişoara's towering medieval **citadel**. There are several ways to access the citadel; the main stairway starts north of the main square, Piaţa Hermann Oberth. The highlight is the glorious **Clock Tower**, whose multicoloured-tiled roof glitters like the scales of a dragon. The tower was built in the 14th century and expanded 200 years later. It contains Sighişoara's wonderfully old-school history **museum** *(muzet.ro; entry adult/student 20/5 lei)*, looking like a curio shop filled with centuries-old furniture and household items filling up cramped rooms at different levels. Climb to the top of the tower where you can have a close look at the clock mechanism and wooden figurine. Above it all is an observation platform providing a 360-degree panorama of red-tiled roofs and surrounding mountains.

Find idyllic Transylvanian towns

About 40km southeast of Sighişoara, the village of **Viscri**, with a medieval fortification system and flanked by bucolic meadows, epitomises the romance of rural Transylvania. Britain's King Charles, in his days as Prince Charles, put the town on the tourism map decades ago, and it's fair to say the place has never looked better. The only sounds you'll hear (aside from other visitors) are the rattle of horse-drawn carts and the clank of a blacksmith's workshop. The highlight is the medieval **fortified church** *(adult/concession 20/10 lei)*. Its splendidly restored whitewashed walls and tiled roof, in their day, represented a feat of medieval engineering. Rising sharply above a huddle of Saxon-style buildings, the **fortified church** *(entry 20 lei)* at **Biertan**, 30km southwest of Sighişoara, is a poetic sight. Its late Gothic church, ringed by concentric walls and flanked by soaring buttresses, is among the most impressive in Transylvania.

Sibiu
TIME FROM BRAŞOV: 2½HR

Sibiu is awash in aristocratic elegance. Noble Saxon history emanates from every Art Nouveau facade and gold-embossed church, all parked elegantly around graceful squares. Renowned composers Strauss, Brahms and Liszt all played here during the 19th century, and Sibiu has stayed at the forefront of Romania's cultural scene. Houses with distinctive eyelid-shaped windows (imagine a benign Amityville Horror House) watch a cast of artists and buskers on the street below. Cafes and bars inhabit brick-walled cellars and luminously decorated attics.

Stroll expansive Piaţa Mare

Strolling is the best way to take in Sibiu's highlights. Start out at **Piaţa Mare** (Large Square). This enormous square was laid out in the 14th century as a market and later used for public executions. It's dominated by the **Roman Catholic Cathedral**

DUBIOUS DRACULA LINKS

Bram Stoker poached the name for his fictional character Dracula from the annals of medieval Wallachian history. But it was the Romanian-born American historian Radu Florescu who linked Dracula to Vlad Ţepeş, a real historical figure. His father, Vlad II, was the first to call himself 'Dracul' (dragon), thus founding the Drăculeşti dynasty. Florescu made his assertions not in a scientific paper, but in a series of pop-history books that were propelled to fame by US TV networks. He was the one who claimed that Vlad Ţepeş was born in Sighişoara, even pointing at a specific house in the fortress that now contains one of several Dracula-themed funhouses. There is no historical evidence to back this up.

THE 'VIA TRANSILVANICA' HIKING TRAIL

An amazing feat of cooperative efforts, the Via Transilvanica hiking trail *(viatransilvanica.com)* traverses Romania from Bucovina to Banat via the whole of Transylvania. It's divided into eight large sections, all with Latin names pointing to the history of corresponding regions. In Transylvania's northeast, the Terra Siculorum section runs through the mainly Hungarian Székely Land via Praid and Sovata. The Terra Saxonum section goes through Viscri, Saschiz, Sighişoara, Criş, Malancrav, Biertan and onwards to Mediaş. Beyond the latter it connects to Terra Dacica which passes through Alba Iulia. A separate branch, Terra Borza Tectonica, branches off south towards Braşov. The entire route is well-marked and complemented with a dedicated smartphone app with guides in several languages.

(Biserica Romano-Catolică Sfânta Treime), built in baroque style between 1726 and 1738. The interior gleams with gold decoration and bright frescoes. The **Brukenthal Palace** *(Palatul Brukenthal; brukenthalmuseum.ro; entry adult/senior/student 50/25/12.5 lei)*, at Piaţa Mare 5, is the most important building. It once served as the residence of Transylvanian governor Samuel von Brukenthal (1721–1803) and now exhibits European art from the 15th to 18th centuries. The most valuable works include a 16th-century painting by the German Renaissance master Lucas Cranach the Elder and one of the Flemish painter Pieter Brueghel's busy winter landscapes – but the interior is the main attraction. Not far from Piaţa Mare, the **History Museum** *(Muzeul de Istorie; brukenthalmuseum.ro; entry adult/senior/student 36/18/9 lei)* goes deep into the town's origins, with illuminating exhibitions about the Saxon guilds and local handicrafts.

Move on to Piaţa Mică

After sprawling Piaţa Mare, **Piaţa Mică** (Small Square) immediately feels homier and more manageable. The square is lined with decent restaurants and cafes. Make a note to return at night, when the lighting gives the place a fairy-tale feel. The **Bridge of Lies** (Podul Minciunilor), an innocent-looking 19th-century iron bridge at the square's northern end, is filled with legend. Depending on whom you ask, the name stems either from the dishonest merchants who once did business here or young lovers swearing their undying affection (or virginity). If you tell a lie while standing on it, it's supposed to creak.

Don't miss Piaţa Huet

Tiny **Piaţa Huet**, to the west of Piaţa Mică, is dominated by the city's pride and joy: **St Mary's Evangelical Church** (Catedrala Evanghelică Sfânta Maria). Sibiu's Gothic centrepiece rises more than 73m over the Old Town. Don't miss climbing the tower (200 steps) for the city's best panorama. While inside, marvel at ghoulish stone skeletons, 17th-century tombs and the largest organ in Romania, all framed by a magnificent arched ceiling. Built in stages from the mid-1300s to 1520, the church was planted atop the site of an older 12th-century sanctuary.

See the ASTRA ethnographic museum

The **ASTRA National Museum Complex** *(muzeulastra.ro; entry adult/student 35/9 lei)*, 5km south of Sibiu, claims to be both Romania's and Europe's largest outdoor ethnographic

WHERE TO EAT IN SAXON LAND: OUR PICKS

Taverna Antika: A quaint garden under the castle wall in Biertan. Aptly for a Saxon village, the food is mostly sausages and pork knuckles. *noon-10pm* €€

Unglerus Medieval Restaurant: In Biertan, Unglerus has satisfying goulash, fried trout and a standout wine cellar. *9am-10pm* €€

Cafe & Artizanat: Shady courtyard cafe in Viscri that's an ideal lunch spot, with daily local specials. *noon-7.30pm Tue-Sun* €€

Hanul Greweln: A welcoming inn in the town of Mediaş, with a crowd-pleasing selection of pasta and meat dishes. *10am-10pm* €€

FABIANIRWIN/SHUTTERSTOCK

ASTRA National Museum Complex

museum: it covers a whopping 96 hectares. Even if ethnography or folkways are not your thing, it's worth spending a few hours here to marvel at the diversity of people who have lived and thrived in the territory of modern-day Romania. The heart of the museum is the immense open-air exhibition space, where churches, water mills, inns, forges, wineries, farmhouses and traditional homes have been lovingly reconstructed to show off the ingenuity of traditional cultures.

From Roman village to Saxon centre

Sibiu traces its roots to Roman times, when it was known as Cibinium. The city rose to its peak influence during the Saxon period, when its 19 guilds were protected by sturdy city walls with 39 towers and four bastions. The Habsburgs ruled Transylvania from here between 1692 and 1791 and again from 1849 to 1867, when Sibiu served as the seat of the Austrian governors. In the late years (1987–89) of the Nicolae Ceaușescu dictatorship, Sibiu was home to Ceaușescu's son and heir-apparent, Nicu. The city is also the birthplace of former Romanian president Klaus Iohannis, who served as city mayor until 2014, when he succeeded Traian Băsescu as president.

 WHERE TO EAT IN SIBIU: OUR PICKS

Crama Sibiul Vechi: Sibiu's most evocative restaurant, with Romanian fare such as cheese croquettes, meatballs and peasant's stew with polenta. *noon-10pm* €€

Weinkeller: Romantic alleyway behind St Mary's Evangelical Cathedral, featuring traditional Romanian mains and Transylvania wines. *6pm-11pm* €€

Kulinarium: The best of several restaurants lining Piața Mică, serving smoky Austrian sausages, spinach soup with quail eggs, trout with wild rice and more. *noon-11pm* €€

Pardon Cafe & Bistro: Delightful hideaway by the city walls that's happily cluttered with antiques. Outdoor seating looks towards the watchtowers. *9am-11pm* €€

Bucovina Monasteries

HISTORY | ARCHITECTURE | NATURAL BEAUTY

GETTING AROUND

Public transport is thin on the ground in Bucovina and this is one place where it really pays off to have a car. The monasteries are located roughly 20km to 30km from one another, and guesthouses and restaurants are spread throughout the region. An alternative to driving would be to book a guided day tour, with transport included (p952). The nearby city of Suceava makes a good base for exploring the monasteries. It's home to some decent hotels and it's also where many of the regional tour operators are based.

North and west of the city of Suceava, in the northern province of Bucovina, a half-dozen beautifully frescoed monasteries (*romaniatourism.com/painted -monasteries.html; admission per monastery 10 lei*) number among Romania's leading attractions. These UNESCO-protected monasteries are not simply works of art in their own right, but are deeply tied to the rule of 15th-century Moldavian leader Ştefan cel Mare and the region's cultural and religious struggle against the Ottoman Empire – indeed, to the origins of Romania itself. The setting, amid forested hills and tiny villages, couldn't be lovelier.

Arbore Monastery

A tiny but lovely church

Arbore Monastery (Mănăstirea Arbore), in the village of Arbore, receives a fraction of the visitors and hence feels more private and special. The small scale allows you to study the paintings up close to appreciate the skill and techniques involved. The monastery dates from 1503 and was the brainchild of local nobleman Luca Arbore. It took just five months to build but four decades to paint. The tiny interior consists of just three chambers: the chamber nearest the altar has a well-preserved votive painting (on the facing wall) of Arbore and his family offering the church to God. The tombs of Arbore and his family sit in another chamber. The interior is in the process of long-term restoration and may be closed during your visit.

Humor Monastery

A fortress surrounded by ramparts

Founded by Chancellor Theodor Bubuiog under Moldavian Prince Petru Rareş, **Humor Monastery** (Mănăstirea Humor), built in 1530, is surrounded by ramparts, with a three-level brick-and-wood lookout tower. The narrow walls enclosing the last stretch of stairway were designed so that defending soldiers could kill attacking Turks one by one. Humor's

predominantly red-and-brown exterior frescoes (1535) are divided topically. On the southern wall's left-hand side the Virgin Mary is commemorated; on the right, St Nicholas' life and miracles are captured. Other features to look for include a badly faded depiction of the 1453 siege of Constantinople, with a parable depicting the prodigal son's return.

Moldoviţa Monastery

See Prince Rareş' surviving throne

Built in 1532, **Moldoviţa Monastery** (Mănăstirea Moldoviţa) occupies a fortified quadrangular enclosure with tower, gates and well-tended lawns. The central painted church has been partly restored and features impressive frescoes from 1537. The southern exterior wall depicts the 626 CE siege of Constantinople under a combined Persian-Avar attack. The besiegers are depicted in Turkish dress – keeping parishioners concentrated on the then-contemporary foe. Inside the sanctuary, on a wall facing the carved iconostasis, a pious Prince Petru Rareş offers the church to Christ. The monastery's museum displays Rareş' original throne.

☑ TOP TIP

Visitors are expected to act and dress respectfully. In practice, this means you should cover your legs and shoulders. These rules are often waived on hot days. If you turn up in shorts, cover yourself with one of the capes hanging near the entrance.

 EATING NEAR THE PAINTED MONASTERIES: OUR PICKS

Antique: Unexpectedly elegant restaurant in Rădăuţi. It's worth a special trip – the chefs aim for something higher than traditional cooking. *11am-11pm* €€€

Popasul Domnesc: This beautiful, modern resort In Voroneţ has an excellent restaurant with a terrace overlooking the monastery. Reserve. *11am-10pm* €€

Casa Humor: West of Gura Humorului, offering delicious traditional food, local cheese and a memorable version of the classic dessert *papanaşi* (pastry). *noon-10pm* €€

Popas Turistic Bucovina: Perfect spot to grab a well-prepared lunch of traditional Bucovinian cooking near the Suceviţa Monastery. *10am-9.30pm* €€

BEST TOURS FOR SEEING THE MONASTERIES

The monasteries are scattered over a wide area, which entails a lot of driving. Instead of driving yourself, join a guided tour for both convenience and added historical context. Here are some of our favourite tours:

Explore Bucovina: Group tours of the Painted Monasteries as well as customised trips. *(explorebucovina.com)*

Hello Bucovina: Wide variety of tours, including day trips to the Painted Monasteries and other regional sights. *(hellobucovina.com)*

Painted Monasteries of Bucovina: Knowledgeable guided tours led by local Sorin Fodor. *(paintedmonasteries.ro)*

DENNY VAN DER VAART/SHUTTERSTOCK

Suceviţa Monastery

Suceviţa Monastery
Bucovina's largest painted monastery

Suceviţa Monastery (Mănăstirea Suceviţa), built from 1582 to 1601, is the largest Bucovina monastery. It's perhaps best known for its exterior fresco *The Ladder of Virtues*, with its 32 steps to heaven, near the main entry. It exhorts priests to righteous behaviour and to avoid the unfortunate fate of the clerics depicted tumbling from the ladder due to their sins. The church's tomb room contains the coffins of monastery founders Simion and Ieremia Movilă. The continuity of the Old and New Testaments is emphasised on the southern exterior wall, where a tree grows from the reclining figure of Jesse, flanked by ancient Greek philosophers. The Virgin, depicted as a Byzantine princess, stands nearby, with angels holding a red veil over her head.

Voroneţ Monastery
Church with a famous blue hue

Built in just three months and three weeks by Ştefan cel Mare following a key 1488 victory over the Turks, **Voroneţ Monastery** (Mănăstirea Voroneţ) is widely considered the masterpiece of the bunch. It's the only painted monastery that has an internationally recognised colour associated with it. 'Voroneţ Blue', a vibrant cerulean hue created from lapis lazuli and other ingredients, is prominent in its frescoes. A 2011 fresco restoration in the entryway revealed the incredible quality of these paintings even more clearly. The wondrous size, scope and detail of *The Last Judgement*, which fills the entire exterior western wall, has earned near-universal accolades as being the most marvellous of the Bucovina frescoes.

The Danube Delta

NATURE | WILDLIFE | BEACHES

The sprawling Danube Delta features a fantastic, tangled network of ever-eroding canals, riverbeds and wetlands. Come here to discover remote fishing villages, miles of reed-lined water channels, stretches of deserted coast and one of the world's great sanctuaries for migrating birds. The region's main port, Tulcea, is a natural jumping-off point for moving deeper into the delta. The city has a pleasant riverside promenade with pretty views out over the Danube. In warm weather, the promenade is lined with private boat operators offering a variety of excursions on slow boats and speedboats. Two Black Sea coastal towns, Sulina and Sfântu Gheorghe, have excellent pensions, restaurants and beaches, yet retain a remote, cut-off feel. Both make good bases for exploring the delta's hidden channels and quaint fishing villages.

> ☑ **TOP TIP**
>
> Tulcea's **Tourism Information Centre** *(romaniatourism.com/ danube-delta.html)* has maps and can also help plan boat trips.

Hire a Boat to Explore the Delta

Ride the waves through the wetlands

From May to September, Tulcea's riverside promenade is lined with private boat operators, all offering a similar mix of guided excursions (from two to eight hours) into the delta. Highlights include **Mila 23**, a sleepy fishing village north of the delta's Sulina channel. Longer tours carry on to the wonderfully preserved village of **Letea**, known for its wild horses, and then on to **Sulina**, along the delta's central channel. Prices

---

 GETTING AROUND

Tulcea is easy to reach by bus. The bus station is located at the western end of the promenade near the passenger-ferry terminal and within walking distance of hotels and restaurants. To access destinations within the delta, the state-run ferry operator **Navrom** *(navromdelta.ro)* operates year-round passenger ferries that depart from the port at the western end of the promenade. Buy tickets on the Navrom website or in person at the Navrom Terminal. Alternatively, more expensive water taxis run from the promenade to popular spots within the delta, like Sulina and Sfântu Gheorghe.

THE DANUBE DELTA: A EUROPEAN TREASURE

After passing through several countries and absorbing countless lesser waterways, the Danube River empties into the Black Sea south of the Ukrainian border. The Danube Delta is one of the country's leading attractions. At Tulcea, the river splits into three separate channels: the Chilia, Sulina and Sfântu Gheorghe, creating a constantly evolving 4187-sq-km wetland of marshes, floating reed islets and sandbars. The region provides sanctuary for 300 species of bird and 160 species of fish. Reed marshes cover 1563 sq km, constituting one of the largest single expanses of reed beds in the world. The delta is a haven for wildlife lovers, birdwatchers, fishers and anyone wanting to get away from it all for a few days.

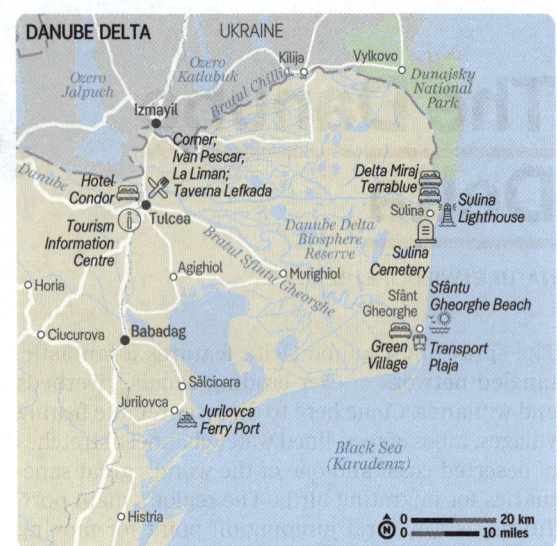

are standard across operators. Shorter trips start at around 120 lei per person, with longer journeys costing up to 200 or 300 lei per person. Excursions typically leave between 8am and 11am. Wear a hat and pack plenty of sunscreen.

Discover Sulina's Fascinating History

Coastal town and former HQ

The tiny Black Sea coastal town of Sulina, on the eastern end of the central Sulina channel and about 65km east of Tulcea by ferry, has the same beautiful beaches and opportunities for exploring the delta as other villages, but has a richer history than most. In the mid-19th century, tiny Sulina served as the headquarters of one of the world's earliest multinational organisations: the European Commission of the Danube. Learn about Sulina's rich cultural diversity at the **Sulina Lighthouse** *(icemtl.ro; entry adult/child 20/10 lei)*, the headquarters of the commission. Maybe the best place to get a feel for the seaport in its heyday is the remarkable **Sulina Cemetery** *(discover-sulina.com; entry free)*, where the various faiths and nationalities still rub shoulders, so to speak, in a tiny, harmonious setting. Don't miss the row of

EATING IN TULCEA: OUR PICKS

Ivan Pescar: Excellent traditional fish soup, as well as grilled fish and various stews and seafood concoctions. *noon-10pm* €€

La Liman: The best option close to Tulcea's passenger ferry port. Decent local specialities, plus plenty of fish offerings. *8am-11pm* €€

The Corner: Convenient location across from the Central Eco-Tourism Museum of the Danube Delta makes it a lifesaver for a drink or pizza. *8am-11pm* €

Taverna Lefkada: Family-run and more intimate than most restaurants along Tulcea's port. Greek slant, with nice yogurt-based desserts. *Tue-Sun noon-9pm* €€

fallen British sailors from the 19th century, laid to rest just in front of the cemetery's small chapel. Not far from here, find the grave of a pirate, identified by the trademark skull and crossbones. Sulina Beach, just beyond the cemetery, is a clean, tranquil spot to swim in the Black Sea.

Relax at Sleepy Sfântu Gheorghe

Beautiful, isolated delta town

There's not much to do in tiny Sfântu Gheorghe, at the eastern edge of the southern Sfântu Gheorghe channel, and that's precisely the point. The only way to get here is by boat (100km east of Tulcea by ferry), which keeps the crowds away. Take your pick between lazing on the beautifully pristine **Sfântu Gheorghe Beach** or exploring the waterways on a private boat trip, negotiated with a local fisherman. The beach is 4km east of the town centre. Walk 40 minutes or take the **Transport Plaja** *(5 lei)*, a tractor-hauled transport wagon that leaves the village every 20 minutes from June to September.

Find an Isolated Beach at Gura Portiței

Arguably Romania's best Black Sea beach

The low-key resort at **Gura Portiței**, 50km south of Tulcea, occupies a perilously thin strip of sand that separates the coastal lakes of Golovița and Razim from the wider Black Sea. The main attraction is the long beach and clean water for swimming. Many visitors opt to bed down at a quaint fisherman's house in the coastal village of Jurilovca and head to the **Jurilovca Ferry Port** for the 30-minute ride *(one-way 50 lei)* or private boat *(one-way 40 lei)* across the lake.

Places We Love to Stay

€ Budget €€ Midrange €€€ Top End

Bucharest   MAP p940

Rosetti Hotel €€ Boutique aparthotel grafts contemporary design onto a historic, early 20th-century villa. A block south of Grădina Icoanei.

Nishani Boutique Hotel €€ This newly appointed boutique hotel near Piața Romană has a great mix of modern design and traditional elements. Serves Aromanian cuisine.

Moxy Bucharest Old Town €€ Hip hotel with playful design and a state-of-the-art video wall. Comfortable rooms, great breakfast and communal workspace.

The Mansion Boutique Hotel €€ Stylish hotel right in the middle of the action on pedestrian Str Franceză. Each room has a unique theme.

Transylvania

Brașov

Secret Boutique Hostel € Newish hostel that's close to the action yet quiet, with spotless, well-appointed six- and eight-bed dorms.

Belfort €€ Clean, bright midrange hotel above the city and just below Mt Tâmpa. Some rooms have mountain views.

Schuster Boarding House €€€ Luxuriously reconstructed townhouse with a glorious rooftop terrace. Easy walking distance from the central square.

Sighișoara

Central Park €€ Unexpectedly opulent hotel with artwork, European antiques and chandeliers sparkling above a grand stairway.

Joseph Hayn Apartments €€ If you had a Transylvanian Saxon grandma, this would be her apartment. Filled with mid-20th-century ambience, complete with a vinyl player in some of the rooms.

Casa Savri €€ Outstanding citadel guesthouse with an ideal mix of modern amenities and traditional Saxon decor and furnishings.

Sibiu

B13 € Popular, well-run hostel with a great central location on the main pedestrian street.

Art Hotel €€ Handsome boutique, perfectly situated in the trendy Lower Town just minutes from the main sights.

Rosen Villa Sibiu €€ High-end guesthouse in a quiet residential neighbourhood, within walking distance of the train and bus stations.

Bucovina Monasteries   MAP p951

Acasă în Bucovina €€ Upscale farmhouse lodging southeast of the town of Gura Humorului. Horse-and-buggy rides will be a treat for kids. Excellent restaurant.

Casa Verde €€ Traditional Voroneț guesthouse with friendly owners; the setting is a five-minute walk from the monastery.

La Roată €€ Collection of detached guesthouses 500m west of the Gura Humorului town centre. Has spacious rooms, beautiful views and kid-friendly attractions like a playground and table tennis.

MyContinental €€ Ideal three-star option in central Suceava, offering excellent value, an outdoor terrace for breakfast and a central location within walking distance of the main square.

Hotel Sonnenhof €€€ Fancy four-star place in Suceava, located 3km outside of town along the Târgu Neamț road. Has an excellent in-house restaurant and relaxing, high-end breakfasts.

Danube Delta   MAP p954

Hotel Condor €€ Modern high-rise in Tulcea. Opened in 2023 and still has that clean 'new car' smell. Good central location, 200m from the promenade.

Terrablue €€ Spotless modern pension in Sulina, with two outdoor pools and a small terrace on the river. Located in a rural area 2km west of the port area. Arrange transport directly with the pension.

Delta Miraj €€ Homey hotel/pension located 3km west of Sulina's port. Has a lovely riverside terrace for relaxing and a popular outdoor pool. Arrange transport in advance from Sulina port.

Green Village €€€ Four-star resort has the best facilities in Sfântu Gheorghe. Accommodation is in bungalows with thatched roofs designed to harmonise with the delta setting.

Practicalities

LGBTIQ+ Travellers
Romania is a conservative society and LGBTIQ+ attitudes are generally negative. Progress has been made in protecting the rights of LGBTIQ+ individuals, but same-sex partnerships are not recognised. Bucharest has a large gay community and attitudes tend to be more tolerant in larger cities.

Safe Travel
Romania is a safe country and travellers needn't worry about taking any special precautions. That said, small-scale theft, scams and pickpockets can still be a problem. Always lock car doors and watch wallets and purses in crowded areas. Never change money on the black market; this is always a scam.

Accessible Travel
Romania is not yet well-equipped for people with disabilities, though there has been noticeable improvement in recent years. Stairs and uneven footpaths will pose challenges, and ramps and accessible toilets are few and far between. Newer hotels and international chains should be equipped to handle guests with special needs. Always ask when booking.

Toilets
There are few public toilets and those that do exist are often not clean. Use better facilities at restaurants and fast-food chains, hotels or highway petrol stations when you have the chance.

MO WU/SHUTTERSTOCK

Sighişoara (p946)

Opening Hours
Banks 9am–5pm Monday to Friday
Museums 10am–5pm
Offices 8am–5pm Monday to Friday
Post Offices 8am–7pm Monday to Friday
Restaurants 9am–11pm
Shops 9am–6pm Monday to Friday, to 2pm Saturday

Insurance
Insurance is not required when travelling to Romania, but it is recommended. Consider purchasing comprehensive insurance that covers both medical care and flight cancellations. EU residents can get a free European Health Insurance Card (EHIC), which covers emergency medical treatments without charge.

Public Holidays
Many public holidays correspond with important events on the Orthodox calendar.
New Year 1 and 2 January
Orthodox Easter Monday April/May
Labour Day 1 May
Pentecost May/June, 50 days after Easter Sunday
Assumption of Mary 15 August
Feast of St Andrew 30 November
Romanian National Day 1 December
Christmas Day 25 December
Boxing Day 26 December

Language

Note that ew is pronounced as 'ee' with rounded lips, oh as the 'o' in 'note', ow as in 'how', uh as the 'a' in 'ago', and zh as the 's' in 'pleasure'. The apostrophe (') indicates a very short, unstressed i (almost silent).

Basics

Hello. Bună ziua. *boo·nuh zee·wa*
Goodbye. La revedere. *la re·ve·de·re*
Excuse me. Scuzaţi-mă. *skoo·za·tsee·muh*
Sorry. Îmi pare rău. *ewm' pa·re ruh·oo*
Please. Vă rog. *vuh rog*
Thank you. Mulţumesc. *mool·t·soo·mesk*
Yes. Da. *da*
No. Nu. *noo*
What's your name? Cum vă numiţi? *koom vuh noo·meets'*
My name is ... Numele meu este ... *noo·me·le me·oo yes·te ...*
Do you speak English? Vorbiţi engleza? *vor·beets' en·gle·za*
I don't understand. Eu nu înţeleg. *ye·oo noo ewn·tse·leg*

Transport

boat vapor *va·por*
bus autobuz *ow·to·booz*
plane avion *a·vyon*
train tren *tren*
One ... ticket (to Cluj), please. Un bilet (până la Cluj), vă rog *oon bee·let ... (pew·nuh la kloozh) vuh rog*
one-way dus *doos*
return dus-întors *doos ewn·tors*

Emergencies

Help! Ajutor! *a·zhoo·tor*
Go away! Pleacă! *ple·a·kuh*
Call the ...! Chemaţi ...! *ke·mats' ...*
  doctor un doctor *oon dok·tor*
  police poliţia *po·lee·tsya*
I'm lost. M-am rătăcit. *mam ruh·tuh·cheet*

I'm ill. Mă simt rău. *muh seemt ruh·oo*
Where are the toilets? Unde este o toaletă? *oon·de yes·te o to·a·le·tuh*

Eating & Drinking

What would you recommend? Ce recomandaţi? *che re·ko·man·dats'*
Do you have vegetarian food? Aveţi mâncare vegetariană? *a·ve·tsi mewn·ka·re ve·je·ta·rya·nuh*
I'll have ... Aş dori ... *ash do·ree ...*
Cheers! Noroc! *no·rok*
I'd like the Vă rog, aş dori..., *vuh rog ash ... do·ree ...* **please.**
  bill nota de plată *no·ta de pla·tuh*
  menu meniul *me·nee·ool*

Shopping & Services

I'm looking for ... Caut ... *kowt ...*
How much is it? Cât costă? *kewt kos·tuh*
That's too expensive. E prea scump. *ye pre·a skoomp*
market piaţă *pya·tsuh*
post office poşta *posh·ta*
tourist office biroul de informaţii turistice *bee·ro·ool de een·for·ma·tsee too·rees·tee·che*

Accommodation

campsite teren de camping *te·ren de kem·peeng*
guesthouse pensiune *pen·syoo·ne*
hotel hotel *ho·tel*
youth hostel hostel *hos·tel*
Do you have a ... room? Aveţi o cameră ...? *a·vets' o ka·me·ruh ...*
  single de o persoană *de o per·so·a·nuh*
  double dublă *doo·bluh*

NUMBERS	
1	**unu** *oo·noo*
2	**doi** *doy*
3	**trei** *trey*
4	**patru** *pa·troo*
5	**cinci** *cheemcj'*
6	**şase** *sha·se*
7	**şapte** *shap·te*
8	**opt** *opt*
9	**nouă** *no·wuh*
10	**zece** *ze·che*

FROM LEFT: RADU BERCAN/SHUTTERSTOCK, POPESCU - VALCEANU MARIUS/SHUTTERSTOCK

Subway train, Bucharest (p938)

Arriving & Getting Around

Bucharest's **Henri Coandă International Airport**, 16km north of the capital, is the primary point of entry for most travellers. Other cities with major airports include Cluj, Sibiu, Iași and Timișoara.

Trains & Buses

Trains are slow but reliable for travelling between large cities. Most services are run by the national rail company Căile Ferate Române *(CFR; cfrcalatori. ro)*. Buses and smaller maxi-taxis go nearly everywhere, but the system can be confusing.

Visas

Romania is part of the EU's common border Schengen zone. EU nationals don't need a visa. Those from the US, Canada, UK, Australia and New Zealand can stay for up to 90 days in any six months.

Road Conditions

Romanian roads are crowded and often in poor condition. The country has limited stretches of four-lane motorway; most travel will be along two-lane national highways. When calculating journey times, figure on 50km per hour.

Parking

Cars offer more flexibility than trains or buses and are essential for visiting out-of-the-way attractions, like monasteries and trailheads. Note that parking can be tight to non-existent in cities. When booking accommodation always ask about parking facilities; it's usually best to pay extra for parking rather than search for a spot on your own.

MONEY

Currency: Romanian Leu (Lei)

CHANGING MONEY

The best place to exchange money is an ATM. You can also change money at private exchange booths *(casa de schimb),* but be wary of commission charges and ask how many lei you will receive before handing over your bills. You may need to show a passport to change money.

CARD PAYMENTS

International credit and debit cards, as well as contactless payment options, are widely accepted at hotels, restaurants and shops. In rural or isolated areas, where ATMs are limited, you'll need to carry some cash.

TIPPING

Tip 10% for good service in restaurants. Round up taxi fare to the nearest lei. Tip the cleaning staff 5 to 10 lei per night in hotels.

Russia is currently considered **unsafe to visit**

**Above: Statue of Tsar Alexander II and Cathedral of Christ the Saviour;
Right: Red Square and St Basil's Cathedral**

Curated by
Leonid Ragazin

Russia

THE WORLD'S LARGEST COUNTRY AT WAR

Russia's all-out attack on Ukraine creates serious risks for Western travellers.

In 2014, Russia annexed Crimea, beginning what was initially a low-intensity conflict with Ukraine. At the time, it was still safe to visit this massive, diverse and fascinating country. But that all changed in February 2022, when a full-scale invasion of Ukraine turned Russia into a no-go zone – at least for the nationals of major Western countries. In the wake of the invasion, hundreds of thousands fled Russia: this included most of the political opposition, independent journalists and regular citizens. People left partly for moral reasons, and partly out of fear of harsh and arbitrary new laws that criminalise any criticism of the war and the Russian military, which could lead to lengthy prison sentences.

Russia spans 11 time zones, and a flight from Moscow to Vladivostok in the far east takes over eight hours. Unsurprisingly, this enormous territory, occupying one-third of the Eurasian landmass, encompasses a plethora of climatic zones and landscapes, from the Arctic tundra and taiga boreal forest in Siberia to hot steppes, semi-deserts and lush subtropics in the Caucasus. It has its share of iconic travel destinations: St Petersburg, Moscow's Kremlin and Red Square, the gorgeous Baikal – the planet's oldest and deepest lake – as well as the volcanic Kamchatka Peninsula, filled with bears and geysers.

That said, the Asian part of Russian beyond the Ural Mountains – larger and more resource-rich – is mostly uninhabitable due to its severe climate. This explains why nearly 80% of Russians live in the country's European part, which is referred to as 'Central Russia' despite it being in the west. East of the Urals, meanwhile, is an archipelago of population centres stretching along the Trans-Siberian railway, which runs along the southern edge of Siberia towards Vladivostok – an epic journey that was once a major drawcard for travellers.

Russia Today

On the face of it, life in Russia feels largely unchanged by the war with Ukraine. Even as the West imposed harsh sanctions, increased defence production spurred a mini economic boom. Moscow, St Petersburg and other large cities are flourishing. For many people the war seems far away from their daily life, despite the occasional Ukrainian drone strike. As for frontline casualties, the people who have suffered the most are those from the most destitute classes and the peripheral regions. The middle-class majority in large population centres has been largely unaffected.

The government excels in pinpoint repression by targeting only a few while instilling fear in millions. Posting a Ukrainian flag on social media, openly criticising the war or expressing support for the opposition (branded as 'extremists' under the Russian law) are all actions that may result in a harsh prison sentence. But the goal of such policies is not imprisonment: it is to drive dissidents out of the country. The number of political prisoners was under 1700 at the time of writing.

At press time, the conflict in Ukraine was at a crossroads. US President Donald Trump was pushing for peace, but a failure to achieve a ceasefire could result in a greater escalation.

History

Russia only emerged in its current nation-state form, with ethnically defined borders and an 80% ethnic Russian population, in 1991. The country's previous incarnations, all encompassing different geographical realms, have become highly politicised in the wake of the Russo-Ukrainian conflict.

The Kyivan Rus and the Tatar-Mongol Yoke

The semi-legendary 9th-century Viking warrior Rurik, a leader of the Rus tribe, established a dynasty that was initially based in Novgorod. The Rus would dominate the emerging Russian state for the next 600 years. Rurik's successor Prince Oleg moved the capital to Kyiv, starting a polity that became known as Kyivan Rus.

Kyivan princes imported Orthodox Christianity and the Cyrillic alphabet from the Byzantines. They also began colonising Finno-Ugric and Baltic tribal lands to the northeast, founding a trading post called Moscow, first mentioned in 1147.

Kyiv's dominance ended when Batu Khaan of the Golden Horde sacked the city in 1240 and conquered most other Russian principalities, ushering in a period known as the Tatar-Mongol Yoke. The Horde didn't meddle in local affairs, ruling instead via vassal Russian princes. In a political context requiring shrewd diplomatic skills, Moscow gradually emerged as the centre of power. The Grand Prince Dmitry defeated the Mongols in the battle of Kulikovo Pole in 1380, although the vassalage formally lasted for another hundred years.

Moscow tsardom

Ivan III, the first Moscow ruler to be called tsar (from Caesar), became known as 'the collector of Russian lands' following his

WHY IS VISITING RUSSIA DANGEROUS?

In 2025, entering Russia was not difficult for most passport holders, but there are good reasons why Western governments warn against visiting in unequivocal terms.

Western visitors have occasionally been arrested on dubious charges and then wind up languishing in prison, often for years, before eventually being swapped for Russian prisoners. Foreigners can also be prosecuted under Russia's harsh legislation, which punishes any criticism of the war in Ukraine or support of the opposition on social media. Russia also maintains a long list of 'undesirable organisations', which includes major Western NGOs like Amnesty International. An affiliation with any of these undesirables is considered a crime. Finally, there is the war itself. Ukraine has demonstrated a capacity to carry out strikes on Russian territory. In 2024, its kamikaze drones hit targets deep inside Russia. At the moment, one needs a pressing reason to travel to Russia and a clear-eyed view of the potential risks. Your government will have little leverage if you wind up in jail.

The map shows the western region of Russia and surrounding countries with the following labelled locations:

SWEDEN, Murmansk, *Barents Sea*, Naryan Mar, Salekhard, FINLAND, *White Sea*, Arkhangelsk, Khanty Mansiysk, Petrozavodsk, *Lake Onega*, Syktyvkar, *Baltic Sea*, TALLINN, St Petersburg, Vologda, Tyumen, ESTONIA, Pskov, Veliky Novgorod, Kirov, Perm, Yekaterinburg, LATVIA, RĪGA, Yaroslavl, Kostroma, Kurgan, Kaliningrad, LITHUANIA, Tver, Ivanovo, Yoshkar Ola, Chelyabinsk, VILNIUS, Smolensk, MOSCOW, Vladimir, Nizhny Novgorod, Kazan, Ufa, WARSAW, MINSK, Kaluga, Ryazan, Ulyanovsk, POLAND, BELARUS, Bryansk, Tula, Saransk, Samara, Oryol, Lipetsk, Penza, Orenburg, KYIV, Kursk, Tambov, Saratov, Belgorod, Voronezh, UKRAINE, *Don*, Volgograd, KAZAKHSTAN, *Aral Sea*, ROMANIA, CHIŞINĂU, Rostov-on-Don, BUCHAREST, *Crimea*, Krasnodar, Elista, Astrakhan, *Black Sea*, Stavropol, UZBEKISTAN, BULGARIA, Cherkessk, Grozny, *Caspian Sea*, Nalchik, Makhachkala

1000 km
500 miles

subjugation of rival city-states. Moscow's consolidation of power morphed into imperial expansion under Ivan IV (known as Ivan the Terrible in the West), who sacked the remnants of the Golden Horde on the Volga and turned it into Russia's main river.

The end of the Rurik dynasty in 1598 precipitated a period known as the Smuta (Troubles). The Poles seized Moscow in 1610, but the invasion united Russia and a popular militia ousted them in 1612. The following year, the enthronement of 16-year-old Mikhail Romanov began a dynasty that would rule until 1917.

The Russian Empire

At the beginning of the 18th century, the young tsar Peter the Great undertook sweeping Western reforms that transformed Russia into a major European power. He defeated Sweden in the Great Northern War and built a new imperial capital, St Petersburg. In the late 18th century, the German-born Catherine the Great conquered swathes of land in what is now Ukraine; the enslavement of peasants reached its peak during the same period.

Napoleon invaded Russia in 1812 – the French imperator's biggest blunder. Despite capturing Moscow, he was driven out of the country and the Russian army marched all the way to

FAST FACTS

Capital Moscow

Population 143 million

Area 17,098,246 sq km

Official language Russian

Time zone GMT+2 through GMT+12

Currency Ruble

MOSCOW: AN INSIDER'S VIEW

Moscow resident **Yekaterina** reflects on life in the city during the war.

In the summer of 2025, Moscow feels excessively gorgeous and mellow. Gardens and flowerbeds are in bloom everywhere. Electric buses run on time and are extremely quiet. Roughly six new metro stations are opened every year. Food couriers in the streets mingle with hip-looking youngsters. There has been a never-ending succession of public events: a corgi parade, a triathlon, a flea market, a cinema festival. Also padel – everyone is playing padel this year. After a game of padel, we go to an open-air terrace for brunch or a glass of wine, despite the chilly weather. We talk about the interminable renovations in the Moscow streets, which annoys everyone. This is one subject that's okay to discuss openly – unlike the war, drone attacks and the increasingly absurd bans on saying or doing all sorts of things. The noise from asphalt pavers disrupts the conversation, but people say: 'We can put up with it'. Whatever they mean by that.

GARY LATHAM/LONELY PLANET

Lenin bust

Paris. Returning officers brought back new subversive social ideas and the failed 1825 uprising of idealistic aristocrats, known as the Decembrists, inspired revolutionary movement.

Tsar Alexander II abolished serfdom in 1861 and launched progressive reforms of the courts and local government. But revolutionaries assassinated him in 1881, ushering in a reactionary period.

The Soviet period

The last of the Romanovs, Nicholas II, lost a war with Japan and suppressed a nationwide uprising in 1905. By dragging Russia into WWI, he precipitated a democratic revolution and the abolition of the monarchy in February 1917. In October of the same year, the Bolsheviks, under Marxist Vladimir Lenin, seized power in a coup and defeated other political factions in the ensuing civil war. A new multinational state, the Soviet Union, was created in 1922, with a Russian republic, the RSFSR, as its largest constituent part.

Communist rule brought about rapid industrialisation and urbanisation as well as a reign of terror under Joseph Stalin in the 1930s. Hundreds of thousands were executed, millions languished in Gulag labour camps or died in artificial famines and forced deportations.

This was followed by an even greater catastrophe when Nazi Germany invaded the USSR in June 1941. Soviet losses in WWII were an estimated 25 to 27 million people, of which around half were from the RSFSR. The war's most decisive battles – Stalingrad, Kursk and the siege of Leningrad – took place in the territory of today's Russia, and Soviet troops seized Berlin in May 1945.

Stalin's death in 1953 brought about a transition from mass terror to a period of liberalisation under Nikita Khrushchev. Prone to bewildering eccentricity, he was deposed in 1966. His successor Leonid Brezhnev oversaw a detente in relations with the US, but the Soviet economy was becoming increasingly dysfunctional and uncompetitive.

Brezhnev's politburo made the fateful mistake of invading Afghanistan in 1979 – a move that drained the USSR's already scarce economic resources. Brezhnev died in 1982 as a much-ridiculed gerontocrat. The reform-minded Mikhail Gorbachev came to power in 1984, opening the final chapter in Soviet history.

Gorbachev launched political and economic reforms collectively branded as *perestroika* (reconstruction), which soon spun out of control. Mass rallies in Moscow demanded democratic change while the mishandled economy rapidly deteriorated.

In 1989, the Soviet Bloc in Eastern Europe collapsed, while Boris Yeltsin emerged as the pro-democracy leader of the RSFSR and Gorbachev's nemesis. The climax came in August 1991, when party hardliners staged a military coup and arrested Gorbachev at his dacha in Crimea. Yeltsin led a successful resistance and rallied millions to defend democracy, thus sidelining Gorbachev for good. At the end of 1991, together with the leaders of Ukraine and Belarus, Yeltsin abolished the USSR and sent the newly emerged Russian national state on its own precarious journey.

Post-Soviet period

Yeltsin also launched 'shock therapy' reforms that caused hyperinflation and instantly drove millions into abject poverty. The period of democratic rule in the 1990s is remembered by Russians as a time of institutional degradation, a bloody war in Chechnya, uncontrolled crime, rampant corruption and national humiliation.

As the 20th century drew to a close, what people wanted most of all was a semblance of stability. And this came through Yeltsin's chosen successor, Vladimir Putin. The former KGB officer began his rule in late 1999 by subjugating Chechnya. He also appointed a technocratic government that implemented prudent fiscal policies and undertook long-delayed institutional reforms. Simultaneously, he tightened the state's grip on the media and the political system at large.

Putin was still flirting with democracy when he stepped down in favour of his faithful ally Dmitry Medvedev in 2008. But he ran for presidency again in 2012, a decision that precipitated the Bolotnaya protests in Moscow. These protests saw rising star Alexey Navalny emerge as the leader of the opposition.

Meanwhile, relations with the US-led West were deteriorating following NATO's 2008 decision to expand to Ukraine and Georgia. A short-lived war with the latter flared up a few months later. In 2014, Putin responded to Ukraine's Maidan revolution by annexing Crimea and launching an armed conflict in the east of Ukraine.

This low-intensity conflict changed in 2022, when Putin order an all-out invasion of Ukraine in a dramatic move that changed European history. With all eyes on the invasion, he also managed to get rid of Navalny, who survived a near-lethal poisoning in 2020 but died in prison the following year.

RUSSIA OUTSIDE RUSSIA

Visits to Russia might be problematic for both moral and security reasons, but obtaining firsthand knowledge from Russians about their culture has never been easier. The lion's share of educated Russian elite fled the country in the wake of the all-out invasion in Ukraine. Estimates put the scope of emigration between 500,000 and 1 million people. This mass flight went in many directions, with numerous opposition activists, journalists and cultural figures ending up in the EU, especially in cities such as Berlin, Rīga and Vilnius. Major diasporas were also formed in Georgia, Armenia, Serbia and Montenegro. Some went as far as Buenos Aires. The result is that some of the most prominent Russian performers or writers can only be seen in the West. Celebrities like Boris Grebenshchikov ('Russia's Bob Dylan'), famous rock bands like DDT and B2, and Gen Z stars like Monetochka tour the world without ever returning to Russia. If you happen to be interested in Russian culture, keep an eye out for them in your hometown.

Curated by
Brana Vladisavljević

Serbia

DIVERSITY OFF THE BEATEN PATH

History galore, festive spirit and a medley of landscapes and cultures all define this little-visited country in the heart of the Balkans.

A sense of history permeates Serbia. The nation's fate has been shaped by its position on Europe's crossroads ever since the Slavs' arrival in the Balkans. Some would say sheer *inat* – a trait of proud defiance – steered it through epic tribulations and triumphs alike, from the centuries of Turkish and Habsburg dominance to victories in two world wars and the boom and bust of Yugoslavia.

Byzantine, Ottoman, Austro-Hungarian and socialist modernist architectural styles compete across Serbia in a visual timeline of its turbulent past. The 20th century left swathes of communist-era concrete atop a multicultural urban mosaic: between the art nouveau of Subotica and minaret-studded Novi Pazar, medieval Orthodox monasteries and Belgrade's brutalist showpieces, the contrasts couldn't be more pronounced. The diversity is equally apparent in Serbia's great outdoors. Vojvodina's sunflower-covered lowlands rise through the forested hills of Šumadija towards the edges of the Dinaric and Carpathian mountain ranges, while enormous river gorges, ancient karst caves and peculiar rock formations punctuate the country's remote corners. These distinctive landscapes remain the habitats of endangered wildlife species including brown bears and griffon vultures.

Still, it's the social dynamism that stays with you. Trumpet-blasting festivals and *rakija* (fruit brandy)-making prowess are vital manifestations of Serbian élan, as much as the country's sporting successes and acclaimed arts inherited from Yugoslav days.

BRANKO JOVANOVIĆ/SHUTTERSTOCK

THE MAIN AREAS

BELGRADE	**NOVI SAD**	**TARA NATIONAL PARK**	**ĐERDAP NATIONAL PARK**
Spirited metropolis in constant transition. **p970**	Multicultural hub on the Danube. **p975**	Mountain scenery, outdoor action, wildlife. **p977**	Iron Gates gorge and medieval fortresses. **p979**

For places to stay in Serbia, see p980

TRABANTOS SHUTTERSTOCK

Right: Kalemegdan Fortress (p970), Belgrade; Above: Golubac Fortress (p979)

Find Your Way

Serbia's main places of interest to travellers are fairly spread out in all directions from the capital, but extensive public transport and good motorways make exploring the country pretty straightforward.

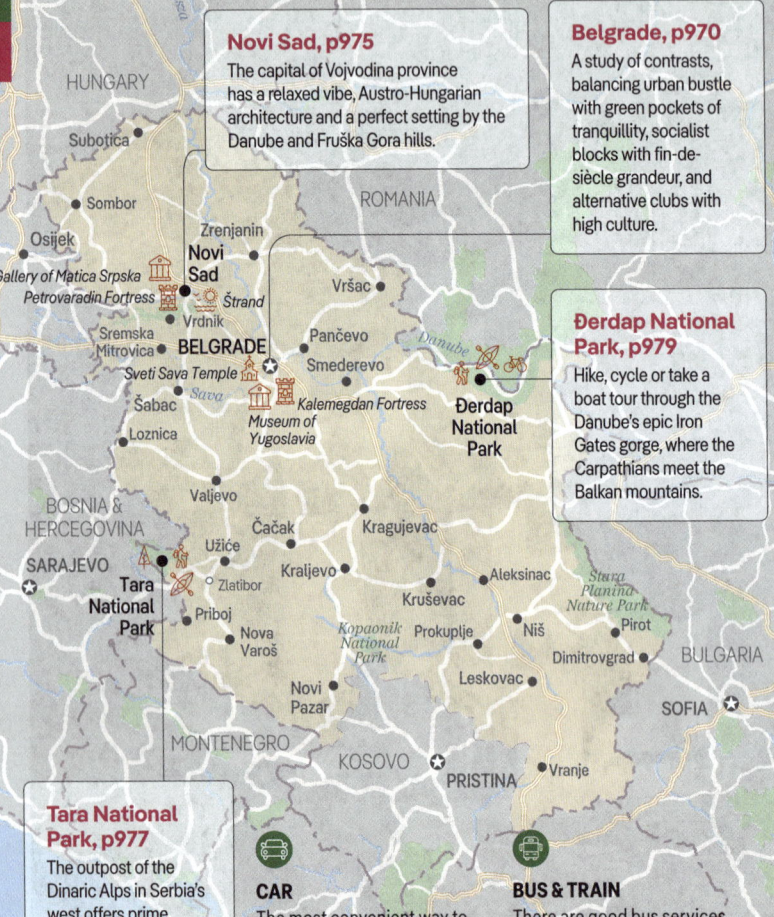

Novi Sad, p975
The capital of Vojvodina province has a relaxed vibe, Austro-Hungarian architecture and a perfect setting by the Danube and Fruška Gora hills.

Belgrade, p970
A study of contrasts, balancing urban bustle with green pockets of tranquillity, socialist blocks with fin-de-siècle grandeur, and alternative clubs with high culture.

Đerdap National Park, p979
Hike, cycle or take a boat tour through the Danube's epic Iron Gates gorge, where the Carpathians meet the Balkan mountains.

Tara National Park, p977
The outpost of the Dinaric Alps in Serbia's west offers prime panoramas as well as excellent hiking, biking, kayaking and rafting.

CAR
The most convenient way to get around, especially for rural and more remote areas (though note that minor roads can be in poor condition). Various car hire companies have offices at Belgrade airport.

BUS & TRAIN
There are good bus services between major towns and national parks. In more rural areas connections can be sporadic; check ahead for return times. A high-speed train connects Belgrade and Novi Sad.

HUNGARY
Subotica
Sombor
Osijek
Gallery of Matica Srpska
Petrovaradin Fortress
Sremska Mitrovica
Šabac
Loznica
ROMANIA
Zrenjanin
Novi Sad
Štrand
Vrdnik
Vršac
Pančevo
Smederevo
BELGRADE
Sveti Sava Temple
Sava
Kalemegdan Fortress
Museum of Yugoslavia
Danube
Đerdap National Park
BOSNIA & HERCEGOVINA
SARAJEVO
Tara National Park
Užice
Zlatibor
Priboj
Nova Varoš
Valjevo
Čačak
Kraljevo
Kragujevac
Aleksinac
Kruševac
Kopaonik National Park
Prokuplje
Niš
Novi Pazar
Leskovac
Stara Planina Nature Park
Pirot
Dimitrovgrad
BULGARIA
SOFIA
MONTENEGRO
KOSOVO
PRISTINA
Vranje
Adriatic Sea

0   100 km
0   50 miles

NENAD NEDOMACKY/SHUTTERSTOCK

Petrovaradin Fortress (p976), Novi Sad

Plan Your Time

There's more than big-city Belgrade to keep travellers engaged. Novi Sad has a relaxed vibe and cultural sights while national parks provide plenty of opportunity for outdoor adventures.

A Long Weekend

● Devote your stay in **Belgrade** (p970) to exploring its historical, epicurean and outdoor highlights. Learn about its past at **Kalemegdan Fortress** (p970) and the **Museum of Yugoslavia** (p971), sample new Balkan cuisine and traditional *kafana* (cafe or tavern) fare, and enjoy the city's **clubbing** (p974) scene. In summer, have a swim on **Ada Ciganlija** (p972) or take in the views over Belgrade from **Mt Avala** (p972).

A Week to Explore

● From Belgrade, catch the train to **Novi Sad** (p975) for a day in this Habsburg-flavoured town, touring its galleries and the **Petrovaradin Fortress** (p976) or chilling out on **Štrand** (p977) beach. Outdoor adventures await south of Belgrade. Two national parks, **Tara** (p977) in the west and **Đerdap** (p979) in the east, offer hikes, bike rides and boat trips on the Drina and Danube Rivers.

SEASONAL HIGHLIGHTS

SPRING

The pleasant weather is ideal for hiking or biking in the national parks. Belgrade's cultural and sports calendar is packed.

SUMMER

Summers are scorching; river kayaking or rafting is a great way to cool off. Major music festivals take place countrywide.

AUTUMN

The wine harvest brings festivals – the perfect time for wine tasting, ideally along with farmstead dining in Vojvodina province.

WINTER

Hit the slopes in Serbia's ski resorts. Snowshoeing along the mountain trails is a great way to escape the après-ski crowds.

969

Belgrade

YUGO-NOSTALGIA | CREATIVITY | NIGHTLIFE

GETTING AROUND

From the airport, bus 72 goes to the central Zeleni Venac stop, A1 minibus runs to the main bus station and Slavija Sq, and bus 600 goes to the train station. If catching a taxi, head to the ticket machines in the arrivals hall to get a receipt (the fare is fixed according to zones). Belgrade's public transport (free since 2025) includes buses, trolleybuses and trams; tram 2 is a circular route around Stari Grad. Local ridesharing apps include CarGo and Yandex.

☑ TOP TIP

Stari Grad (Old Town) is loosely defined by pedestrian Knez Mihailova, central Republic Sq and Terazije thoroughfare. Other key areas include Dorćol (to the east from Kalemegdan Fortress), Vračar (around the Sveti Sava Temple) and Zemun (across the rivers from Stari Grad).

Belgrade is full of contradictions. Seemingly its only constant is the urban bustle – with a controversial waterfront development the latest addition to an ever-evolving skyline – but the sunsets on Kalemegdan's ramparts remain as serene as they would have been when the Celts first settled on the promontory above the Sava and Danube Rivers. Its Ottoman conquerors, battling over the city with Austria-Hungary, called it Dar-ul-Jihad (House of Wars); yet it arose from the ashes countless times over two millennia and came to be a cradle of progress during its Yugoslav heyday. Its Serbian name, Beograd, translates as 'White City', although its fin-de-siècle mansions and communist-era monoliths sport many shades of grey.

Belgrade is both a microcosm of Serbia (just stroll any of its green markets) and a world apart. Its history is bewildering, its nightlife enviable and its spirit – from theatre stages to basketball courts, from street art to cocktail bars – is the reason to keep coming back.

A Crash Course in Belgrade's History

Tracing the White City's past

Although repeatedly destroyed and rebuilt over the centuries, Belgrade has significant relics of its tumultuous past.

The White City's ground zero is **Kalemegdan Fortress** *(beogradskatvrdjava.co.rs; fortress grounds free, audio guide with map 300RSD)*, first settled by the Celts and expanded by the Romans; much of what stands today is the product of 18th-century Austro-Hungarian and Ottoman reconstructions. Get an audio guide at the souvenir shop and look for attractions including the **Big Gunpowder Magazine** (housing Roman sarcophagi and tombstones), lonesome **Nebojša Tower** (a Turkish-era dungeon), the spooky **Roman Well** (actually built by the Austrians), ivy-swathed **Ružica Church** (a former garrison chapel) and the symbol of Belgrade, the **Victor Monument** by Ivan Meštrović.

One of the world's largest Orthodox basilicas, the neo-Byzantine **Sveti Sava Temple** *(hramsvetogsave.rs)* in Vračar

BELGRADE

holds special historical significance. On this spot the Ottomans burnt the relics of St Sava, the founder of the Serbian Orthodox Church. Ponder the scale of the project, completed after almost a century. Inside, the glittering mosaics (including the 1248-sq-metre mosaic adorning the cupola) are astonishing. Over in Zemun, **Gardoš Tower** (*adult/child 300/200RSD*) was erected in 1896 to mark the millennium of Hungarian statehood and has wonderful Danube views. Mosey around this baroque neighbourhood – Austria-Hungary's border town for nearly two centuries – to appreciate its quaint atmosphere.

Serbia's capital has a particular Yugo-nostalgic appeal. The **Museum of Yugoslavia** (*muzej-jugoslavije.org; entry adult/*

Yugotour: Mini road trip through the Yugoslav era in the iconic Zastava car, taking in the socialist modernist architecture of New Belgrade. *(yugotour. com)*

Food & Culture Tour Belgrade: Get introduced to Serbian cuisine and customs with passionate local foodies. *(foodtour belgrade.com)*

Belgrade Art Tours: Explore independent art galleries and the White City's subculture, including its thriving street art. *(belgradearttours. com)*

iBikeBelgrade: A great way to enjoy the city: these cycling tours go everywhere, from Ada Ciganlija to Zemun. *(ibikebelgrade.com)*

No Fat No Stress: Kayaking tours that take you out on the Danube to secluded Beljarica wetlands, aka 'Belgrade's Amazonia'. *(facebook .com/nofatnostress)*

child 600/300RSD) is ex-Yu history HQ and it's attached to the 'House of Flowers' mausoleum of Marshal Tito, the former socialist federation's lifelong president; free guided tours in English take place on Saturdays. Among many fascinating exhibits are the Relay of Youth batons carried across Yugoslavia for Tito's birthdays and unique gifts from foreign dignitaries.

The Culture Map of Belgrade

Tour the capital's top museums

The stately home of the **National Museum** *(narodnimuzej.rs; entry adult/child 300/150RSD, Sun free)* has archaeological treasures – with a special focus on the prehistoric cultures of Vinča and Lepenski Vir plus the Roman era – and galleries filled with Serbian masterpieces. Observe the development of the nation's artistic expression from Romanticist Đura Jakšić to surrealist Milena Pavlović-Barili.

The beehive-like modernist building of the **Museum of Contemporary Art** *(msub.org.rs; entry adult/child 600/300RSD)*, surrounded by a sculpture garden, stages exhibitions from its trove of 20th-century art such as video performances by Belgrade native Marina Abramović and graphic production by the Yugoslav avant-garde Zenitism movement. Release your inner nerd with some sci-fi-ish interactive elements at the **Nikola Tesla Museum** *(tesla-museum.org; Serbian/English tours 400/800RSD, cash only)*. On display are some of the great scientist's inventions and tools, as well as personal items and the sphere-shaped urn containing Tesla's ashes. Guided tours (on the hour) last 45 minutes.

Green Belgrade

Find oases in the Big Smoke

While Kalemegdan Park is Belgrade's central outdoor sprawl, there are plenty of nature havens around the city.

An easy escape from the urban buzz (16km from central Belgrade), **Mt Avala** is a favourite with cyclists. Take in the panoramic vista over Belgrade, the plains of Vojvodina and Šumadija's hills from the observation platform of the tallest **tower** in the Balkans (204.5m) *(avalskitoranj.rs; entry adult/child 400/200RSD)*.

Come summertime, Belgraders flock to the pebbly lakeside beach on **Ada Ciganlija** *(adaciganlija.rs)*, a verdant island – now attached to the riverbank – on the Sava River. The beach has carried the Blue Flag designation since 2012. There are two main bicycle rental locations: near the roundabout after you cross the embankment and by the big car park on the southern side of the lake.

 EATING IN BELGRADE: OUR PICKS

Dva Jelena: Renowned old-school *kafana* (tavern), established in 1832; sample national classics like *Karađorđeva šnicla* (*kajmak*-stuffed escalope). *10am-1am €€*

Iva New Balkan Cuisine: Head chef Vanja Puškar reinvents local gastronomy in a fusion of flavours and organic ingredients. *9am-midnight Mon-Sat, to 11pm Sun €€*

Ambar: Set in trendy Beton Hala, Ambar is popular for its small-plate takes on Balkan staples and a long craft *rakija* (fruit brandy) list. *hours vary €€€*

Šaran: Sample the daily catch turned into delicacies like the 'Smederevo-style' pike at Zemun's best fish restaurant. *4pm-1am Tue & Wed, 1pm-1am Thu-Sun €€€*

BELGRADE'S TOP FESTIVALS

Belgrade Dance Festival: See the world's major dance troupes – from Akram Khan Company to Compañía Nacional de Danza – in March and April.

Mikser Festival: Belgrade's creative side is in the spotlight in May, with a programme of music, design, sustainable development and quirky innovation.

Belgrade Summer Festival: Sample innovative music, dance, theatre and visual arts around the city in July and August.

Bitef: Week-long showcase of experimental and traditional European theatre in September, launched in 1967.

October Salon: Prestigious biennial exhibition of contemporary visual arts, featuring local and international artists, in September and October.

BEST SHOPPING IN BELGRADE

Belgrade Design District: Small boutiques showcase emerging local fashion designers, jewellers, artists and designers.

Bombondžija Bosiljčić: Handmade sweets – a tradition handed down for three generations – including *ratluk* (Turkish delight).

Parfimerija Sava: Old-world perfumery (established in 1954), with unique hand-mixed scents and vintage bottles.

Yugovinyl: Fantastic record store, with about 20,000 albums in all possible genres and a big focus on Yugo-era new wave.

Ivko: Famous women's fashion label with colourful knitwear inspired by Serbian folk motifs.

Rakia Shop: *Rakija* in a range of flavours, plus delicacies like *ajvar* (red-pepper spread) and *slatko* (fruit preserve).

Silosi, Belgrade Marina

The Night Is Young

Go clubbing in the White City

Belgrade has a reputation as one of the global party cities – indeed, its clubs stay thumping till the early hours.

Dorćol's repurposed industrial spaces are now hubs of alternative culture and nightlife. The clubs and bars sharing the address of **Cetinjska 15** – the ramshackle grounds of a former brewery – are the go-to destination for indie music, craft beer, vegan bites, LGBTIQ+ parties and lots more. Over at Belgrade Marina, **Silosi** *(silosi.rs)* is a brutalist complex of four giant silos covered with striking murals, hosting festivals, art exhibitions, DJs and other happenings; it has stunning sunsets, too.

A number of venues have firmly positioned Belgrade on Europe's clubbing map. **Barutana** *(facebook.com/barutanabeograd)* is a summer club in the former **gunpowder magazine** on Kalemegdan Fortress, hosting legendary open-air raves. **Klub 20/44** *(facebook.com/klub2044)* draws an alternative crowd and top electronica DJs; until recently a cult *splav* (river barge) on the Sava, it has started a new chapter on land. At **Drugstore** *(drugstorebeograd.com),* another stalwart of Belgrade's underground scene, you can party to techno sounds in a former slaughterhouse.

DRINKING IN BELGRADE: OUR PICKS

Druid Bar: Speakeasy-evoking nook with vinyl music, impeccably dressed bartenders and skilfully mixed cocktails. *5pm-midnight Sun-Thu, to 1am Fri & Sat*	**Lenja Buba:** The small cocktail bar at Belgrade Urban Distillery serves top concoctions – including *rakija*-based ones, naturally. Cash only. *5pm-midnight*	**Krafter:** Sample rotating Serbian craft-beer choices on draught at this industrial-chic venue on a leafy pavement. *9am-midnight Sun-Thu, to 1am Fri & Sat*	**Wine Art Bar:** Enjoy a glass of Serbian vino at the wonderful rooftop terrace on an atmospheric Dorćol corner. *noon-midnight Sun-Thu, to 1am Fri & Sat*

Beyond Belgrade

OUTDOOR ADVENTURE | HISTORY | RURAL LIFE

North of the capital is Novi Sad, a Habsburg-flavoured cultural hub. To the south, two scenic national parks provide outdoor adventures galore.

While much younger than Belgrade, Novi Sad is no ordinary second city. The capital of Vojvodina province was a stronghold of national culture in the Habsburg-ruled north; in recent times, its formidable fortress played host to the legendary EXIT music festival. Other draws are its venerable museums and galleries, one of Serbia's best beaches and a thriving bicycle culture.

Rich legacies of times past abound in southern Serbia – from brooding Ottoman-era forts along the Danube to sacred Orthodox monasteries cradled in green valleys. Out west, Tara National Park makes a scenic stage for hiking, biking, kayaking and rafting. In the east, the mighty Danube substitutes Serbia's lack of coastline with its widest and deepest stretches in Đerdap National Park.

Novi Sad

TIME FROM BELGRADE: **36MIN** 🚆

The capital of culture

It's no accident that in 2022 Novi Sad became the first non-EU city to carry the prestigious title of European Capital of Culture. To appreciate the significance of this creative hub, tour its esteemed museums and galleries.

Trace the province's past from the earliest days at the **Museum of Vojvodina** *(muzejvojvodine.org.rs; entry adult/child 300/200RSD)* to understand its multi-ethnic character, and stroll through an early 20th-century urban landscape for a glimpse into the trades of the epoch.

The **Gallery of Matica Srpska** *(galerijamaticesrpske.rs; entry adult/child 400/200RSD, Fri free)* displays centuries of masterpieces, from Byzantine icons to modernist paintings by the likes of Vojvodina's own Sava Šumanović. Curator-led themed tours on weekends cost 1200RSD.

Places

Novi Sad p975
Tara National Park p977
Đerdap National Park p979

GETTING AROUND

The high-speed train between Belgrade and Novi Sad runs frequently and takes 36 minutes.

The gateway to Tara National Park is Bajina Bašta, which has good bus connections with Belgrade; from Bajina Bašta, buses go to Mitrovac, Kaluđerske Bare and Perućac within the park.

The scenic Đerdap Hwy (State Rd 34) winds its way along the Danube through Đerdap National Park; sporadic buses connect Kladovo, Donji Milanovac and Golubac with Belgrade.

NOVI SAD

Fish i Zeleniš
Project 72
Hotel Veliki
Café Veliki
Miloša Bajića
Masarikova
Jovana Subotića
Laze Telečkog
Museum of Vojvodina
Pavla Papa
Trg M.
Slobode
Mladene
Šafarikova
NS Bike
Bulevar Mihaila Pupina
Varadin Bridge
Varad Inn
Jevrejska
Narodnih Heroja
Petra Drapšina
Platona
Petrovaradin Fortress
Gallery of Matica Srpska
Stražilovska
Stevana Musića
Kej Žrtava Racije
Leopold I
Sonje Marinković
City Museum of Novi Sad
Maksima Gorkog
Bulevar Cara Lazara
Bulevar Cara Lazara
Dunav (Danube River)
Gogoljeva
Bulevar Oslobođenja
Jirečekova
Frushkogorska
Sunčani Kej
Šekspirova
Limanski Park
Jasmin A Maslina
Bulevar Despota Stefana
Kineska Četvrt
Štrand
Sunčani Kej
Liberty Bridge
Kamenički Put
Fisherman's Island
Dunavski Rafting
N   0   400 m
     0   0.2 miles

The Habsburgs' bastion

Towering over the river on a 40m-high volcanic slab, **Petrovaradin Fortress** is one of Europe's biggest fortresses and one of its best preserved. Constructed using slave labour between 1692 and 1780, its dungeons have held notable prisoners including Karađorđe (founder of Serbia's royal dynasty) and Yugoslav president Tito. Check out the iconic 'drunken' clock tower: the size of the minute and hour hands are reversed so far-flung fisherfolk can tell the time.

For a unique perspective on Petrovaradin, the **City Museum of Novi Sad** (*museumns.rs; entry adult/child 400/200RSD*) has insight into the citadel's history and organises tours in

 EATING IN NOVI SAD: OUR PICKS

Café Veliki: A must for its foodie overview of Vojvodina, from goulash to *gomboce* (plum-stuffed dumplings). *8am-11pm Sun-Thu, to midnight Fri & Sat* €€

Project 72: Smart bistro with inventive small plates (like oxtail with celery puree) based on organic produce and a strong Serbian wine list. *noon-11pm* €€

Fish i Zeleniš: Charming Mediterranean-inspired nook serving vegetarian and pescatarian meals from locally sourced ingredients. *noon-11pm* €€

Jasmin A Maslina: In a refined setting bathed in light, the focus is on seasonal produce; the creative menu changes quarterly. *noon-11pm Tue-Sun* €€€

English *(1300RSD)* of a fraction of its 16km and four levels of creepy-but-cool *katakombe* (underground tunnels).

For 25 years, the fortress has been filled with thousands of revellers each July during **EXIT Festival** *(exitfest.org)*.

A day by the Danube

Novi Sad's **Štrand** *(entry 70RSD)* is a 700m-long sandy beach that is thronged with bars and stalls come summertime. When the tide is low, you can cross over from its western end to the small **Fisherman's Island**. Technically a peninsula, it's a wonderful spot for a picnic or lazy stroll.

Dunavski Rafting *(dunavskirafting.com; 2 people per hr 300RSD)* rents out canoes and kayaks for paddling around Fisherman's Island. Novi Sad's stretch of the Danube Cycling Path, along **Sunčani Kej** (Sunny Quay), makes for pleasant pedalling. **NS Bike** *(per day 170RSD)* rents out bicycles.

Tara National Park

TIME FROM BELGRADE: 3HR

Go wild in the Dinaric Alps

Some of Serbia's most impressive scenery is found within the 250-sq-km **Tara National Park** *(nptara.rs),* set along the Bosnian border. With densely forested slopes and the dramatic Drina River canyon, this easternmost outpost of the Dinaric Alps is a true outdoor playground. A wide range of adventures is organised by **Republik Tours** *(republiktours.com),* and if you prefer to go solo, the visitor centres at Perućac and Mitrovac have maps and rent out kayaks and bikes.

Cutting through steep limestone cliffs, the emerald Drina creates a stunning background for water-based activities. **Tara Tours** *(taratours.rs; entry adult/child rafting 1000/500RSD, cruise 3000/1500RSD)* has rafting for beginners and full-day boat cruises. Contact **Green Bear** *(greenbear.rs; three-hour tours per person €40)* for stand-up paddleboarding from Vrelo waterfall to the remarkable 'Little House on the Drina'. The placid **Perućac** and **Zaovine** Lakes are popular kayaking spots.

Hikers are in for a treat along Tara's 30 marked trails; see the park website for maps. For easy treks, nine official lookouts provide stupendous views – **Banjska Stena** (1065m), 6km from Mitrovac, overlooks Perućac Lake, while **Crnjeskovo** (980m), 3km from Kaluđerske Bare, rises above Rača Gorge. Also crisscrossing the park are major mountain-biking routes. **Visoka Tara** is a 26km loop along forest and gravel paths, starting and ending at Šljivovica village. **Carska Tara** is a 42km trail from Kaluđerske Bare to Perućac, on a combination of macadam and asphalt.

VILLAGE LIFE

Bački Monoštor: Watch horseshoe and fishing-net makers at work in the heart of Gornje Podunavlje nature reserve, aka 'the Amazon of Europe'.

Kovačica: Village in Vojvodina famous for its naïve art; **Kovačica Naïve Art Gallery** has rotating exhibitions and paintings for sale.

Guča: Home of the boisterous **Guča Festival**, featuring a competition of *trubači* (trumpeters) from across Serbia since 1961.

Sirogojno: On the slopes of Zlatibor mountain, this **open-air museum** with wooden cottages is a snapshot of 19th-century rural life.

Gostuša: Remote 'stone village' on Stara Planina (Old Mountain); its houses are covered from base to roof with plates made of local stone.

EATING AROUND TARA: OUR PICKS

Tarsko Jezero: At Zaovine Lake, classic local dishes come with stunning views; get the *duvan čvarci* (shredded pork cracklings) appetiser. *9am-8pm* €€

Tarvil: A novelty for Tara, this modern Zaovine spot with panoramic views adds Cuban cusine and vegetarian choices to the Balkan staples. *9am-10pm* €€

Viskonti: Mećavnik resort's stylish restaurant, with books and wine bottles lining a long wall, serves pastas and pizzas plus national cuisine. *7am-11pm* €€

Studenac: Terrace views of the 'Little House on the Drina' in Bajina Bašta; go for the trout or *pljeskavica* (spicy hamburger). *7am-11pm Mon-Sat, from 8am Sun* €€

SPAS & WINERIES

Vrnjačka Banja: Serbia's premier spa destination, with landscaped parkland, heritage villas and plenty of wellness treatments on offer.

Sokobanja: Framed by mountains, this spa town has a working Ottoman-era **hammam** (with men's and women's pools).

Negotin region: Negotin's **Rajac** and **Rogljevo** villages feature bucolic 19th-century *pimnice* (wine cellars) made of stone.

Župa wine region: Rustic 19th-century *poljane* (winegrowers' lodges) are preserved across Župa. **Ivanović Winery** is the region's most famous.

Fruška Gora wineries: Just outside Novi Sad, Fruška Gora hills are home to small, family-owned vineyards. **Kovačević Winery** is one of the oldest.

Wine celler, Rogljevo
DMZ001/SHUTTERSTOCK

Đerdap National Park

TIME FROM BELGRADE: **2HR**

Adventure along the Danube

Serbia's largest national park and its first UNESCO Global Geopark, the 637-sq-km **Đerdap** *(npdjerdap.rs; entry to protected areas 290RSD)* is where the Carpathian and Balkan mountain ranges meet; it's increasingly a contender for outdoor adventures with Tara in the west. **Nature Travel Office** *(naturetraveloffice.com)* runs multi-activity group tours around the park.

The limestone cliffs of the Iron Gates gorge soar for 100km along the Danube, which reaches its narrowest and deepest points here – a fantastic setting for activities on the water. **Wild Serbia** *(wildserbia.com; tours €69)* organises full-day Đerdap kayaking tours with transport from Belgrade. Alternatively, see the Iron Gates highlights by speedboat from Tekija (one hour) with **Đerdap Boat Tours** *(djerdapboat tours.com; 1500RSD)* or take a two-hour trip through the gorge with **Golubac from a Boat** *(golubacizbrodica.rs; adult/child 1500/750RSD)*.

With signposted paths and lookouts, the park provides rewarding hikes; register with the visitor centre in Donji Milanovac *(office@npdjerdap.rs)* before setting off. There are nine marked trails, of which two 7km paths lead from Đerdap Hwy to the peaks of Mt Miroč: **Veliki Štrbac** (768m), overlooking the narrowest part of the Iron Gates, and **Mali Štrbac** (626m), with views of the gigantic Decebalus rock sculpture across the Danube.

The international **EuroVelo 6** cycling path hugs the Danube for 110km through the park. For those without their own wheels, **ACE Adventure** *(ace-adventurecentre.com; tours €270)* has two-day cycling tours along the river between Ram and Golubac fortresses.

MEDIEVAL MONASTERIES & FORTRESSES

Studenica: UNESCO-listed monastery established in 1196, Studenica has the acclaimed *Life of Virgin Mary* fresco cycle.

Sopoćani: Romanesque monastery built by King Stefan Uroš I in 1265. Its frescoes are prime examples of medieval art.

Manasija: Protected by massive walls with 11 towers, this 15th-century monastery is known for the *Holy Warriors* fresco.

Golubac: Fourteenth-century fortress with nine towers, set on a rocky promontory at the entrance to the Danube's Iron Gates gorge.

Maglič: Guardian of the Ibar valley since the 13th century, Maglič fortress has fantastic views over central Serbia's green hills.

 EATING AROUND ĐERDAP: OUR PICKS

Nana: Modern place in Golubac offering Mediterranean-inspired pastas, risottos, burgers and salads in addition to standard local fare. *8am-10pm* €€

Jezero: Try delicacies like grilled Miroč cheese at this Kladovo tavern with a timber-framed interior. *8am-midnight Mon-Fri, from 10am Sat & Sun* €€

Lepenska Ribica: Typical checkered-tablecloths *kafana* in Donji Milanovac serving hearty grub from fish soup to *roštilj* (grilled meats). *9am-10pm* €€

Restoran Dinčić: At Silver Lake, settle in on the rounded terrace facing a lush garden for a leisurely meal of freshwater fish specialities. *8am-11pm* €€

Places We Love to Stay

€ Budget **€€** Midrange **€€€** Top End

Belgrade

MAP p970

El Diablo Hostel € Lovely small hostel set in a townhouse right next to Skadarlija, with dorms plus two private rooms, and super-welcoming staff.

Hostel Bongo € Unbeatable location in a passage off Terazije. Scandi minimalist style with bright colours, sweet garden terrace and experienced staff.

Arka Barka € Bobbing off Ušće Park, this 'floating house' has dorms and rooms with hand-painted walls, plus free bike and scooter use and fresh river breezes.

Smokvica B&B €€ Rustic-chic B&B in a whitewashed 19th-century mansion in Dorćol; rooms have vaulted ceilings, hardwood floors and supersonic showers.

Savamala Bed & Breakfast €€ Cool B&B located in 1908 building in Savamala quarter, offering 11 rooms furnished in mid-century modern style.

Dominic Smart Luxury Suites €€ With four equally convenient locations across Stari Grad, these elegant and spacious suites are an excellent midrange option.

Hotel Moskva €€€ A Secession-style icon on Terazije, the 123-room Moskva is laden with old-world glamour; past guests include Albert Einstein and Indira Gandhi.

Mama Shelter €€€ The whimsical design hotel, a skip from Kalemegdan Park, attracts millennials with fun rooms and fab sunset views from its large rooftop restaurant.

Square Nine €€€ The work of Brazilian architect Isay Weinfeld, just off Knez Mihailova; luxury rooms have limestone bathrooms and there's a rooftop Japanese restaurant.

Novi Sad

MAP p976

Varad Inn € Hostel with a lovely garden cafe, set in a baroque-style building from 1714 in Petrovaradin's Lower Town; rooms with private bathrooms.

Hotel Veliki €€ Convenient central location just off pedestrian Zmaj Jovina, huge comfortable rooms and a hip restaurant representing Vojvodinian cuisine.

Leopold I €€€ Luxury hotel set atop Petrovaradin Fortress, with both baroque-style and modern rooms; the two restaurant terraces have great Danube views.

Tara National Park

Hotel Tara €€ A great option at Kaluđerske Bare, this hotel built of stone and wood has a warm atmosphere, 18 spacious rooms and a restaurant.

Vila Drina €€ Convenient for activities around Perućac Lake, with 15 rooms in pleasing pastel tones; the stately building is next to a small waterfall.

Mećavnik Resort €€€ A cluster of small rural houses in Drvengrad movie-set village, featuring smart units with wood details and folk-design touches.

Đerdap National Park

Zeleni Zaliv €€ Unwind in wood-and-clay cabins in Poreč Bay, just outside Donji Milanovac; slow-food dining on demand, plus kayaks and paddleboards for rent.

Vila Dunavski Raj €€ Family-owned B&B secluded in a pine forest near Golubac, serving tasty organic breakfasts. Large balconies for chilling out on.

Eko Farma Kladovo €€ These tidy bungalows on the outskirts of Kladovo are great for families; optional buffet-style meals, bike rental and on-site animal farm.

Leopold I

Practicalities

LGBTIQ+ Travellers
As evidenced by the furore over Belgrade's early Pride parades (chronicled in the 2011 comedy *Parada*), life is not all rainbows for the LGBTIQ+ community in Serbia. Discretion is advised. Check out prajd.rs for the latest news.

Health
Serbia has a reciprocal healthcare agreement with many EU states; this covers most emergency medical care except for emergency repatriation. Excellent, affordable healthcare is readily available in the cities – Serbia is a dental-tourism destination for those in the know. For minor illnesses, chemists can give advice and sell over-the-counter medication.

Etiquette
Greetings usually involve three kisses on the cheeks.
Dress conservatively if visiting monasteries, and walk backwards out of a church.
Make eye contact during toasts. The person who initiated the drinks will insist on paying.

Smoking
Smoking is banned in enclosed areas such as offices, shops, hotels and public transport. However, it's still largely permitted in restaurants and bars, where enforced nonsmoking sections are a rarity. It's usually pointless asking someone to put out their cigarette in these establishments.

MARK PELF/SHUTTERSTOCK ©

Ada Ciganlija beach (p972)

Opening Hours
Banks 9am–5pm Monday to Friday
Bars 11am–midnight (later on weekends)
Restaurants 8am–midnight
Shops 8am–7pm Monday to Saturday

Visas
Tourist visas for stays of up to 90 days aren't required for citizens of the EU, UK, USA, Australia, New Zealand and Canada. Officially, visitors must register with the police. Hotels will do this for you, but if you're staying in private accommodation, you should register within 24 hours of arrival. This is rarely enforced, but a lack of registration confirmation upon leaving Serbia could result in a fine.

Public Holidays
New Year 1 and 2 January
Orthodox Christmas 7 January
Statehood Day 15 and 16 February
Orthodox Easter April/May
Labour Day 1 and 2 May
Armistice Day 11 November

Language

The official language is Serbian and the official writing system uses both the Roman and Cyrillic alphabets.

Basics

Hello. Zdravo/Здраво *zdra·vo*
Goodbye. Doviđenja/Довиђења *do-vee-dje-nya*
Yes. Da/Да *da*
No. Ne/Не *ne*
Please. Molim/Молим *mo·lim*
Thank you. Hvala/Хвала *hva·la*
Excuse me. Izvinite/Извините *iz·vee·nee·te*
Sorry. Žao mi je/Жао ми је *zha·o mi ye*

What's your name?
Kako se zovete/zoveš? (pol/inf)
Како се зовете/зовеш?
ka·ko se zo·ve·te/zo·vesh

My name is ...
Zovem se .../Зовем се ... *zo·vem se*

Do you speak English?
Govorite/Govoriš li engleski? (pol/inf)
Говорите/Говориш ли енглески?
go·vo·ri·te/go·vo·rish li en·gle·ski

I don't understand.
Ne razumem./Не разумем.
ne ra·zu·mem

Shopping & Services

I'm looking for...
Tražim .../Тражим...
tra·zhim

How much is it?
Koliko košta ...?/Колико кошта ...? *ko·li·ko kosh·ta*

That's too expensive.
To je preskupo./То је прескупо.
to ye pre·sku·po

Emergencies

Help! Upomoć!/Упомоћ! *u·po·moch*

Go away! Idite!/Идите! *i·di·te*

Call ...! Zovite ...!/Зовите ... ! *zo·vi·te*

  a doctor lekara/лекара *le·ka·ra*
  the police policiju/полицију. *po·li·tsi·yu*

I'm lost.
Izgubljen/Izgubljena sam. (m/f)
Изгубљен/Изгубљена сам. (m/f)
iz·gub·lyen/iz·gub·lyena sam

I'm ill.
Ja sam bolestan/bolesna. (m/f)
Ја сам болестан/болесна. (m/f)
ya sam bo·le·stan/bo·le·sna

Eating & Drinking

What would you recommend?
Šta biste preporučili?
Шта бисте препоручили?
shta bi·ste pre·po·ru·chi·li

Do you have vegetarian food?
Da li imate vegetarijanski obrok?
Да ли имате вегетаријански оброк?
da li i·ma·te ve·ge·ta·ri·yan·ski o·brok

Cheers! Živeli!/Живели! *zhi·ve·li*

I'd like the bill/menu please.
Mogu li dobiti račun/jelovnik, molim?
Могу ли добити рачун/јеловник, молим?
mo·gu li do·bi·ti ra·chun/ye·lov·nik mo·lim

NUMBERS

1	**jedan/један** *ye·dan*
2	**dva/два** *dva*
3	**tri/три** *tri*
4	**četiri четири** *che·ti·ri*
5	**pet/пет** *pet*
6	**šest/шест** *shest*
7	**sedam/седам** *se·dam*
8	**osam/осам** *o·sam*
9	**devet/девет** *de·vet*
10	**deset/десет** *de·set*

Nikola Tesla Airport, Belgrade

Arriving & Getting Around

Belgrade airport receives most international flights. With extensive bus services countrywide and good main roads, it's easy to get around. For flexibility and convenience to reach remote and rural destinations, it's best to hire a car.

Arriving by Air
Belgrade's **Nikola Tesla Airport** is the country's main entry point. The national carrier is Air Serbia. **Niš Constantine the Great Airport** is small and serviced by Wizz Air, Ryanair, Turkish Airways and Air Serbia.

Taxi/Rideshare
Taxis can be flagged down or ordered; make sure the meter is turned on. Not many taxis accept credit card payments. Belgrade's rideshare app is CarGo; there's also Yandex but no Uber. For long-distance carpooling, use the BlaBlaCar app.

Buses
There are good long-distance bus connections. Major cities have public bus systems. In Belgrade, public transport (including buses, trolleybuses and trams) is free since 2025. In Novi Sad, buy single-ride tickets from the driver.

Driving Essentials
Belgrade airport has major car rental offices. Petrol stations are easy to find around the country. Street parking in all bigger towns is regulated by zones/hours; tickets can often be paid only via SMS (in Serbian). The speed limit is 50km/h in towns, 80km/h outside towns, 100km/h on expressways and 130km/h on motorways. You must drive with short headlights on, even in the daytime.

MONEY
Currency: Serbian Dinar (RSD)

CASH
ATMs and exchange offices are easy to find in towns and cities; cash is still indispensable in villages and remote areas. Have some cash on hand for markets, newsstands, taxi rides and public transport, as well as for admission fees.

CREDIT CARDS
Major debit and credit cards, particularly Visa and MasterCard, are accepted by hotels, restaurants, shops, petrol stations and when booking tours. Not many taxis accept card payments; specify when booking if you need to pay by card.

TIPPING
Tips in restaurants or for tour guides are not obligatory, but 10% is a good idea for satisfactory service and always appreciated; it's also customary to round up the taxi fare.

For places to stay
in Slovakia, see
p1001

BEATRICAB/SHUTTERSTOCK

Above: Lomnický štít (p998), Tatranská Lomnica; Right: Blue Church (p992), Bratislava

Curated by
Luke Waterson

Slovakia

MAJESTIC MOUNTAINS, CASTLES AND MEDIEVAL MARVELS

Close to tourist hotspots Vienna and Budapest, Slovakia will always be beautifully off-piste. This is its allure: ornate historic architecture and astounding mountainous terrain that remains perennially crowd free.

Nature defines Slovakia. The capital Bratislava has an Old Town full of arresting medieval and baroque buildings, but the forest-swaddled hills looming just behind it dominate the proceedings. These soon swoop into the serrated summits of the High Tatras, Europe's smallest alpine mountain range, yet still home to many of Eastern Europe's loftiest peaks and the Carpathians' very highest. Then there's the east's gorge-gouged national park Slovenský Raj; UNESCO-listed, cave-riddled Slovenský kras; and another UNESCO spectacle, the primeval beech forests of the Carpathians. In the south, the Danube River frames the landscape.

Consequently, the culture here is of a back-to-nature, down-to-earth sort: hiking, cross-country skiing, alfresco fire-pit grill-ups, overnight sojourns in middle-of-nowhere mountain houses, traditional costumed dances and brightly hued wooden architecture all showcase the countryside's extraordinarily vivid folklore.

Tradition is not lost here, as it can be in more urbanised nations. Surrounded by busier destinations like Austria (west), Czechia (northwest) and Hungary (south), this under-the-radar country may not receive the attention it deserves. But if you dig entire districts, villages and towns of seamlessly preserved medieval buildings, if you're entranced by the world's densest concentration of castles, if you yearn for thick forests and jagged mountains and prefer these places to be untrammeled and peaceful, Slovakia should be your next adventure.

KAYO/SHUTTERSTOCK

THE MAIN AREAS

BRATISLAVA
Slovakia's capital and castle-dotted surroundings. **p988**

WESTERN SLOVAKIA
More castles and national parks. **p994**

HIGH TATRAS & EASTERN SLOVAKIA
Mountains and medieval townscapes. **p997**

Find Your Way

Slovakia's centre-of-Europe location extends from Austria and Czechia in the west, Hungary in the south, Poland in the north and Ukraine in the east.

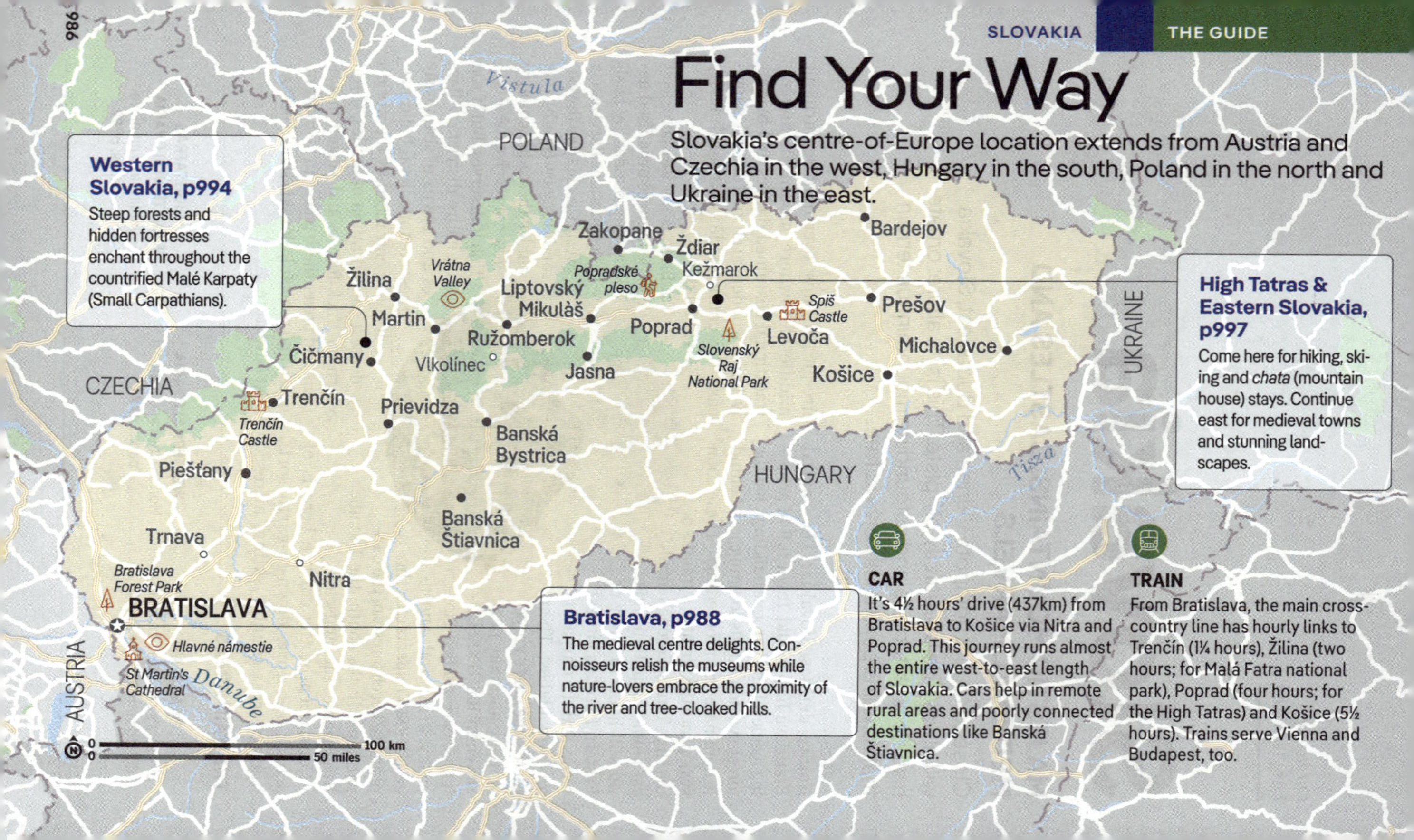

High Tatras & Eastern Slovakia, p997

Come here for hiking, skiing and *chata* (mountain house) stays. Continue east for medieval towns and stunning landscapes.

TRAIN

From Bratislava, the main cross-country line has hourly links to Trenčín (1¾ hours), Žilina (two hours; for Malá Fatra national park), Poprad (four hours; for the High Tatras) and Košice (5½ hours). Trains serve Vienna and Budapest, too.

CAR

It's 4½ hours' drive (437km) from Bratislava to Košice via Nitra and Poprad. This journey runs almost the entire west-to-east length of Slovakia. Cars help in remote rural areas and poorly connected destinations like Banská Štiavnica.

Bratislava, p988

The medieval centre delights. Connoisseurs relish the museums while nature-lovers embrace the proximity of the river and tree-cloaked hills.

Western Slovakia, p994

Steep forests and hidden fortresses enchant throughout the countrified Malé Karpaty (Small Carpathians).

POLAND

UKRAINE

HUNGARY

CZECHIA

AUSTRIA

Vistula

Danube

Bardejov
Prešov
Michalovce
Košice
Levoča
Spiš Castle
Kežmarok
Ždiar
Zakopane
Poprad
Slovenský Raj National Park
Popradské pleso
Liptovský Mikuláš
Jasná
Ružomberok
Banská Bystrica
Banská Štiavnica
Vlkolínec
Vrátna Valley
Martin
Prievidza
Žilina
Čičmany
Trenčín
Trenčín Castle
Nitra
Piešťany
Trnava
BRATISLAVA
Bratislava Forest Park
Hlavné námestie
St Martin's Cathedral

0   50 miles
0   100 km

Hlavné námestie (p988), Bratislava

Plan Your Time

One week is sufficient for Slovakia's highlights. Use Bratislava or Košice as your base: the former for culture, the latter for mountain scenery.

A Weekend Break

● Begin in **Bratislava's** comely medieval Old Town, discovering knockout square **Hlavné námestie** (p988) and **Bratislava Castle** (p991) for city views. Visit some cafes: Bratislava's are special. Take an afternoon picnic to hilly **Bratislava Forest Park** (p992). On day two, head to icons like the **Blue Church** (p992), **City History Museum** (p989) or a half-day exploration of castle **Hrad Devín** (p994).

A Week or More

● Spend two to three days in Bratislava, and don't miss the **Danubiana Meulensteen Art Museum** (p992) and the fortress **Červený Kameň** (p995). Tour **Trenčín Castle** (p995), then proceed to Poprad to explore the **High Tatras** (p997) for two days. Wander medieval gems **Levoča** (p1000) and **Bardejov** (p1000), and finish in dignified Košice, arranged around **St Elizabeth's Cathedral** (p1000).

SEASONAL HIGHLIGHTS

SPRING
Bratislava City Days enlivens the capital with street performances and openings of normally off-limits city spaces.

SUMMER
Bratislava Cultural Summer delivers two months of music. In July, check music fest Pohoda (Trenčín) or Východná Folk Festival (High Tatras).

AUTUMN
Western Slovak towns and the Tokaj wine region near Košice celebrate grape harvest; Pezinok has the biggest wine festival.

WINTER
Bratislava's **Christmas Markets** (p990), which begin in late November, brighten the city centre.

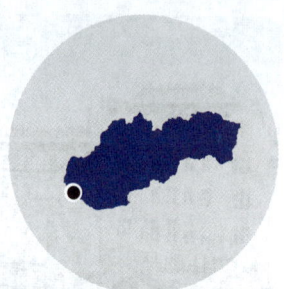

Bratislava

ARCHITECTURE | CAFES | COUNTRYSIDE EXCURSIONS

GETTING AROUND

Walking around the Old Town is best, though wheelchairs and prams may struggle with the cobbled streets. Trolleybuses run from Hlavná stanica train station to the Old Town and Koliba for Bratislava Forest Park. Take buses from Most SNP bus station to Hrad Devín or Danubiana Meulensteen Art Museum. Trains (from Hlavná stanica) or buses (from main bus station Mlynské nivy) link the capital with Western Slovakia. Seasonal boats connect Bratislava and Devín.

☑ **TOP TIP**

Bratislava's Old Town invites you to linger, but don't limit your time to just this area: Bratislava Forest Park, Danubiana Meulensteen Art Museum and stupendous castles like those at Devín are all a part of Bratislava's rich tapestry.

Bratislava is an ideal mid-sized city, big enough to have a swag bag of internationally significant sights yet sporting a centre small enough to stroll. Abutting dramatic nature – its suburbs ascend into the lonely foothills of the Malé Karpaty (Small Carpathians) and its Old Town brushes the Danube – it's also well-connected to major cities like Vienna, Budapest and Prague.

At the centre of Europe, Bratislava has always been prone to invasions. It fell to Roman, Hungarian and Austrian invaders, was briefly incorporated in early Slavic states, and spent time as a socialist country following WWII. This historical hotchpotch explains a cityscape that interweaves a stone castle built by the Slavic Great Moravian people, medieval Hungarian burghers' houses and baroque palaces, and some startling Soviet brutalism.

Yet, as you unwind in an elegant cafe-bar in the lively Old Town, with live music reverberating nearby, you'll likely opine that Bratislava – upheaval aside – has had the last laugh.

Meander the Old Town
Bratislava's iconic medieval heart

No matter how often you visit Bratislava, acquainting yourself with the city on foot always works wonders. Enter the Staré mesto (Old Town) through the only surviving city gate from Bratislava's 13th-century walls, **Michael's Gate** *(Michalská brána; muzeumbratislava.sk; adult/child €6/4)*. Buy tickets in nearby **Red Crayfish Pharmacy** and climb the small baroque tower for stunning panoramas. Afterwards, walk cobbled Michalská, Biela and Františkánske námestie to **Hlavné námestie**, the city's main square and the showcase for some of its most beloved historic buildings.

Among the architectural set-pieces, the standout is **Stará radnica** (Old Town Hall), a 14th-century clocktower-crested

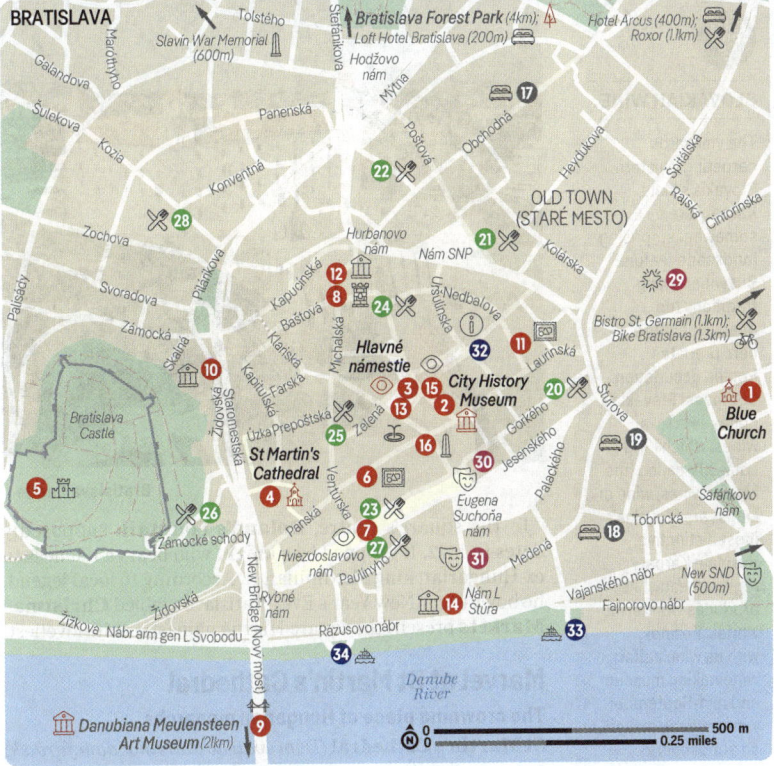

BRATISLAVA

complex that's among Slovakia's oldest standing structures. This encompasses the excellent **City History Museum** (*Múzeum mesta Bratislavy; muzeumbratislava.sk; adult/child €8/4*) charting Bratislava's importance down the ages, from its role as monarchical crowning place to its guilds and crafts. Tickets include entry to the Apponyiho Palace, prime Bratislava views from the tower and a ground-floor exhibition on local viticulture (tastings cost extra).

SLOVAKIAN WINE

The vineyards carpeting Western Slovakia's Malé Karpaty are a somewhat surprising landscape feature. But winemaking traditions run deep: viticulture here predates Roman occupation. Southeast Slovakia's honey-like Tokaj wines, which King Louis XIV called 'the king of wines, wine of kings', are Slovakia's most distinctive; the Malé Karpaty region, meanwhile, produces wonderful whites. Pezinok, with its wine cellars, winemaking museum and mid-September wine festival, makes an atmospheric spot to sample the local wines. Malá Tŕňa, southeast of Košice, is the Tokaj region hub. Several Bratislava bars and the City History Museum – which has an expert-selected collection featuring any year's 100 best wines – are the capital's best places to partake.

SAIKO3P/SHUTTERSTOCK

Bratislava Castle

In the square's centre, **Roland's Fountain** supposedly dates to 1572. It's topped by a knight who bears a likeness to ex-Hungarian king Maximilian II. According to local legend, he bows every New Year's Eve. Bratislava's fabled **Christmas Markets** present the square Hlavné námestie at its loveliest.

Marvel at St Martin's Cathedral

The crowning place of Hungarian monarchs

St Martin's Cathedral (*Dóm svätého Martina, dom.fara.sk; entry free*), with its terracotta roof and white walls sheering to an 85m-high spire, has a colourful history: it was the coronation place for 19 Hungarian kings and queens between 1563 and 1830, a time when Ottoman invasions made the previous monarch-making spot (Székesfehérvár) too dangerous. The interior of this 14th- and 15th-century Gothic sanctuary also has four chapels, a horseback statue of St Martin, extensive crypts and stained-glass windows to hold you in thrall.

Boat Trips along the Danube

Bratislava by water

Bratislava is the fourth-biggest city on the EU's longest river and Danube boat trips, conveniently departing from the Staré

EATING IN BRATISLAVA: CAFES AND SNACKS

Black.: Coffee roasters concentrate on the exquisite coffee here, also tempting with cakes and vegan sandwiches. *9am-6pm €*

Emil: In the Mirbach Palace, Emil serves coffee and light bites in its vaulted interior and courtyard. *10am-10pm Tue-Sat, to 8pm Sun, to 6pm Mon €*

Bistro St Germain: This chic eatery concocts breakfasts, three-tier sandwiches, burgers and wraps. *11am-11pm Mon & Tue, from 8am Wed-Sat, 8am-9pm Sun €*

Soupa: Friendly to wallets, dietary restrictions and the environment, veggie- and vegan-friendly Soupa is a stalwart choice. *8am-6pm Mon-Fri €*

mesto's southern edge east of Most SNP, are a fun way to appreciate the city and its fetching surrounds. Trips with **LOD** *(lod.sk)* head upriver to Hrad Devín (p994), a crag-top castle on the Slovakia–Austria border *(€24 return; daily Apr-Sep, weekends Oct & Nov)*, and along Bratislava's stretch of the Danube *(€15 return; daily Apr-Sep)* to catch optimal Old Town vistas. **Twin City Liner** *(twincityliner.com; from €25 one-way; 1½ hours)* runs boats upriver to Vienna, also passing Hrad Devín and Donau-Auen National Park's tranquil forested riverbanks.

Climb to Bratislava Castle

A fortified settlement from the beginning

The capital's dominant landmark is the huge four-turreted **Bratislava Castle** *(snm.sk; grounds free, museum adult/child €14/7)*, standing on its own hilltop across the ring road west of the Staré mesto. The 9th-century remnants of the original Great Moravian castle are still on display and the 13th-century **Crown Tower** can be climbed for bird's-eye views. The current castle's white walls and terracotta roofs were mostly achieved in the 1760s under renowned Habsburg monarch Maria Theresa. Today, the Renaissance- and rococo-styled fortress can be explored through its **Museum of History**, which provides an overview of Slovakia from medieval times onward and serves as an access point to the castle's interior, including the Crown Tower. But the free-of-charge **grounds** are the highlight: the **baroque gardens** and zigzagging pathways afford beautiful views of the Danube-wrapped Staré mesto.

Stroll along the Hviezdoslavovo námestie

Home to performing arts and quirky statues

Long tree-lined **Hviezdoslavovo námestie** *(free)* is probably the most appealing city square for lingering. At the eastern end are the historic building of the 1886-built **Slovak National Theatre** (closed for repairs, with shows currently at the **New SND**, just southeast of the Staré mesto) and Reduta Palace housing the **Slovak Philharmonic** *(filharmonia.sk; tickets from €16)*. Prefer quirky to queen-like? Check much-loved statue **Watcher** *(Čumil; visitbratislava.com; free)*, a statue of a worker emerging from a manhole. It's north of the square along Rybárska brana.

INDEPENDENCE STRUGGLES

Short-lived Slavic kingdoms Samo's Empire (c 631–c 658 CE) and Great Moravia (c 833–c 927 CE) both encompassed parts of Slovakia. But Slovak history has largely taken place under the jurisdiction of foreign powers, in particular the Hungarians, who controlled Slovakia between 895 CE and 1918. After WWI, a temporary Slovak Socialist Republic was created in the southeast before Slovakia was incorporated into Czechoslovakia. Then came German (WWII) and Soviet (1947–91) control. Only in 1993, after the Velvet Divorce brought separation from Czechia, did Slovakia become permanently independent. Bratislava's Námestie SNP is the cradle of Slovak independence: this was where crowds gathered during the run-up to the fall of communism.

EATING IN BRATISLAVA: BEST RESTAURANTS

Modrá Hviezda: The 'Blue Star' specialises in glamorous Slovak dishes, like venison with caramel-cognac sauce. *5.30-10pm Wed-Fri, noon-10pm Sat & Sun* €€€

Bratislava Flagship: Popular intro to Slovak cuisine in a vault-roofed former theatre. *11am-10pm Mon-Thu, 11am-11pm Fri, noon-11pm Sat, noon-10pm Sun* €€

Gatto Matto: Out-of-this-world pizza is the driving force of this Italian restaurant within a smart townhouse near St Martin's Cathedral. *11am-10pm* €€

Roxor: The journey to this standout near Račianské mýto park 2km north of the Staré mesto is repaid by Bratislava's best burger experience. *11am-9pm* €€

Hike Around Bratislava Forest Park
Explore the Small Carpathians

The **Malé Karpaty** (Small Carpathians) forested massif sweeps northeast across Western Slovakia to Slovakia's best national parks in the Carpathians proper. Bratislava's northern suburbs rise into the foothills through **Bratislava Forest Park** *(visitbratislava.com; free)*. Amid these hilly, thickly wooded footpaths and biking trails is the **Kamzík TV mast** *(veza.sk; observation deck €7)*, its revolving restaurant and viewpoint marking the park's high point. From Hlavná stanica, take bus 145 or trolleybus 44 to final stop Koliba: Kamzík is then a 1.75km walk.

Bratislava's Blue Church
The city's prettiest building

Dedicated to St Elisabeth of Hungary, the early 20th-century **Blue Church** *(modrykostol.fara.sk; free)* is a powder-blue-and-cream vision. The edifice is an art nouveau masterpiece, from its undulating arches to cupola-crested clocktower tip (36.8m). See the website for its limited opening hours.

From Contemporary Art to White-Water Rafting
Danube-based delights in Čunovo

Countrified suburb Čunovo has two top-tier Bratislava attractions right on the Danube – although each is likely to attract a different type of person. The main draw is Slovakia's most spectacular art gallery. Atop a gorgeous river promontory, the **Danubiana Meulensteen Art Museum** *(danubiana. sk; adult/child €12/6)* impresses with its waterside location and outdoor sculpture garden. Inside, floor-to-ceiling gallery windows overlooking the Danube are the eye-catching accompaniment to contemporary art displays, including works by groundbreaking Slovak artists like Rudolf Sikora and Miroslav Cipár.

Practically adjacent to the museum is the world-class watersports complex **Divoka Voda** *(divokavoda.sk)*, its two churning channels offering Class II to IV rapids for instructor-guided white-water rafting *(from €35 per 1½ hours)* and kayaking *(from €10 per hour)*.

To get here, take bus 91 from Most SNP bus station to end-of-the-line Čunovo and walk (3km). Alternatively, hire bikes from **Bike Bratislava** *(bikebratislava.sk; €25 per day)* and cycle from the Staré mesto (19km via riverside cycleways).

Oddball Tours of the Soviet Era
Take in the city's brutalist landmarks

Slovakia was where the Eastern Bloc once met the West, and Soviet-era builders consequently made bold brutalist statements along the frontier in Bratislava. Most striking in the Staré mesto is **Most SNP** *(u-f-o.sk; adult €9.90)*, a

Slavín War Memorial

BEST MUSEUMS & GALLERIES

Bratislava City Gallery: The best bit about this nationally important art collection, spread across the Mirbach and Pálffy Palaces, is Pálffy Palace's 'Passage' exhibit featuring 15,000 books, arranged around mirrors, which creates the illusion of peering into a never-ending library.

Slovak National Gallery: Engaging riverside art space hosting the city centre's best contemporary art exhibits.

Museum of Jewish Culture: Compelling museum located in the city's former Jewish quarter, which was largely destroyed during the construction of the Bratislava ring road.

Nedbalka Gallery: Focuses on displays of 20th-century Slovak art and sculpture, impressively arranged around an atrium.

bridge outlandishly crowned by a 95m-high bar-restaurant and flying saucer-shaped observation deck. It rises above the ring road where it crosses the Danube. Across the bridge to the south is the super suburb **Petržalka**, Europe's largest Soviet-era housing estate.

Another exceptional viewpoint is the **Slavín War Memorial** *(visitbratislava.com; free)*, northwest of the Staré mesto on Slavín Hill. The monument, topped by a swastika-crushing soldier, honours the Soviet soldiers who died liberating Bratislava from German forces in 1945; it was built between 1957 and 1960.

Visit these and many other Soviet-era landmarks with the fun offbeat tours run by **Authentic Slovakia** *(authentic slovakia.com; per person in normal/Soviet-era vehicle €35/55)*.

 DRINKING IN BRATISLAVA: BEST BARS

KC Dunaj: Alternative cultural centre with a rooftop bar and eclectic performances from live music to comedy. *4pm-1am Thu-Sat, to midnight Sun-Wed*

Bratislavský Meštiansky Pivovar: This brewery serves its own beers along with traditional Slovak dishes. *11am-11pm Tue-Sat, to 10pm Sun & Mon*

Cafe Verne: Mingle with locals to sample buzzing Bratislava nightlife in this boho spot. *9am-midnight Mon-Thu, 9am-1am Fri, 10am-1am Sat, 10am-midnight Sun*

Sky Bar & Restaurant: Drinks, especially cocktails, and Spanish-influenced cuisine with stunning Staré mesto views. *5pm-midnight Tue-Sat*

Western Slovakia

CASTLES | ANCIENT MINING TOWN | NATIONAL PARK

Places

 TOP TIP

A great way to explore Western Slovakia is on foot in the Malé Karpaty hills. The beautiful 102km Štefánikova Magistrála trail runs across the region from Hrad Devín at the Slovakia–Austria border to Bradlo. The path is named after Slovak WWI hero Milan Štefánik.

Western Slovakia is an outdoor playground of bedazzling, forest-cloaked and castle-flanked mountains that increase in magnitude as they approach the peaks of the High Tatras to the east. And best of all? It's easily visited on day trips from Bratislava. In addition to splendid strongholds, like those at Devín, Červený Kameň and Trenčín, there's also the enchanting UNESCO-listed medieval mining settlement of Banská Štiavnica in the south and an explosion of greenery in the folklore-rich Malá Fatra National Park further east. The latter was once the stomping ground of Slovakia's real-life Robin Hood: Juraj Jánošík, a 17th-century bandit-turned-hero, and the topography befits that of an outlaw's lair, with bulky mountains tumbling into concealed forested ravines. Meanwhile, the Malé Karpaty (Small Carpathians) range of hills ramparts the region's north, presiding over the homonymous wine region that yield much of the country's best vino.

Devín

TIME FROM BRATISLAVA: **25MIN**

Embattled borderland bastions

Bratislava's suburbs stretch to the Austrian border, where clifftop castle **Hrad Devín** (*hraddevin.mmb.sk; €8*) guards the Danube's confluence with the Morava. First built in stone in the 13th century, it contains an archaeological exhibition

---

GETTING AROUND

Regular trains head northeast from Bratislava to Trenčín (1¼ hours) and Žilina (two hours), the jumping-off point for Malá Fatra National Park. Buses connect Bratislava to the important castles of Devín, Červený Kameň and Bojnice. Buses are also best from Bratislava to Banská Štiavnica, though there are fewer services. And don't discount walking. Picturesque pathways, including the long-distance Štefánikova Magistrála, thread the entire region through its lovely forested hills.

Trenčín Castle

CASTLES AND CRACKING VIEWPOINTS

Hrad Bojnice: This spellbinding, still-furnished turreted affair is the most fairy-tale-like fortress. It's 60km southeast of Trenčín and 177km northeast of Bratislava.

Hrad Beckov: A whopping fortress presiding over the Váh River valley from a 60m-high crag; 20km southwest of Trenčín.

Hrad Červený Kameň: Above Častá, 37km northeast of Bratislava, this furnished 16th-century castle stands out amid the green Malé Karpaty slopes.

Vrátna Valley: Climb by cable car through Malá Fatra National Park to access ridge hikes at 1500m.

Čičmany: This village, a 1¼-hour bus ride southwest of Žilina, is a cherished vestige of Slovak folklore.

Kalvaria: The best panoramas of Banská Štiavnica come from the baroque chapel complex.

showcasing site finds from Neolithic times onwards and stages summertime events from kid-friendly medieval games to DJ sessions. Bus 29 links Devín to Bratislava's Most SNP bus station. Boats (p991) run here too.

Trenčín
TIME FROM BRATISLAVA: 1¼HR

Castle-topped medieval treasure

Trenčín, the 2026 European Capital of Culture, is a dashing, richly historic city built around a beguiling square. The cityscape's climax is cragtop **Trenčín Castle** *(muzeumtn.sk; adult/child €9/4, with tour €12/5)*, its storied walls dating to the 11th century. A famous Roman inscription from 179 CE on the cliff beneath the castle can be glimpsed from the Hotel Elizabeth.

Banská Štiavnica
TIME FROM BRATISLAVA: 3½HR

Magical mining tour

Sparkling like the silver once found in its hills, this UNESCO-listed 13th-century mining town is a trove of riches. Top sights include burghers' houses from the 16th to 18th century, the

---

🍴 EATING BEYOND BRATISLAVA: OUR PICKS

La Piazetta: Suave space in castle-crowned Trenčí n for some of Slovakia's finest Italian cuisine. *11am-10pm Mon-Thu, to 11pm Fri, noon-10pm Sat* €€

Gurmánsky Grob: Brilliant spot with an inviting garden 20km northeast of Bratislava. Sample traditional Slovak oven-roasted goose. *11am-10pm* €€

Terchovská Koliba Diery: Scenic restaurant near Terchová's Horné Diery gorge evokes a romanticised shepherd's hut, with traditional Slovak fare. *10am-9.30pm* €€

Elizabeth Cukráreň & Kaviareň: Pamper yourself in Piešt'any, then enjoy coffee, cake or local wine at this elegant spa complex. *9am-9pm* €

JAROMOND/SHUTTERSTOCK

Malá Fatra National Park

astounding hillside chapel complex **Kalvária** *(kalvaria.org; free)* and the dignified centrepiece **Old Castle** *(muzeumbs. sk; adult/child €8/4)*. Delve into the centuries-old mining heritage at the **Open-Air Mining Museum** *(muzeumbs.sk; adult/child €14/7)* 2km west of town, where 90-minute guided tours explore old mine passageways. Buses from Bratislava change at Zvolen; trains take longer.

Malá Fatra National Park

TIME FROM BRATISLAVA: 3HR 🚆 + 🚌

Folklore, gorges and mountain magic

This tantalising 226-sq-km mountainous swathe is greener and less visited than the High Tatras. Yet it contains some serious summits, including high point **Velký Kriváň** (1708m), plus extensive hiking trails and a beautiful ski area.

Northern village Terchová makes the best base. It's crested by the **Juraj Jánošík Statue**, which honours the local folk hero and outlaw, whose birth and exploits in these parts imbue the peaks with added mystique. The must-do hike is **Horné Diery** *(slovakia.com; free)* a precipitous waterfall-splashed gorge reached via a three-hour out-and-back trail with ladder-and-chain sections. Access it from Hotel Diery, 2km east of Terchová. A photogenic road south of Terchová rises to Vrátna Výťah and the **Vratna Valley ski area** *(vratna.sk; day pass €25)*. Take **Vrátna Cable Car** *(€21 return)* for a spectacular 15-minute ascent to the Snilovské saddle (1524m) below Chleb Peak. Ski slopes (Dec-Mar) and more hiking trails beckon up top.

Buses connect Terchová to Žilina (45 minutes) and Vrátna Výťah (15 minutes).

High Tatras & Eastern Slovakia

MOUNTAINS | OUTDOOR ADVENTURE | MEDIEVAL TOWNS

Welcome to the 1.5-mile-high club: the jagged peaks of the High Tatras (Vysoké Tatry) have some 25 summits that surpass 2400m. These are Slovakia's highest mountains and some of the highest in Eastern Europe as well. The encompassing Tatras National Park (Tatranský národný park), accessed from Poprad by mountain railway, cable car and hiking trails, is Slovakia's top outdoor destination. It's home to skiing, phenomenal hiking – including the famous 72km-long Tatranská Magistrála, a rugged hike that traverses the whole range – and more eclectic activities such as dogsledding, river trips, bear-spotting and overnighting in high-altitude huts.

But don't forget to lower your gaze from the snowy summits and turn further east. Slovakia's second city Košice and a surfeit of UNESCO World Heritage Sites – from medieval towns Levoča and Bardejov to ornate wooden churches and cave-ridden karst – will make your moments in Eastern Slovakia as eye-catching as they are esoteric.

Places

Poprad p997

Tatranská Lomnica p997

Starý Smokovec p998

Štrbské Pleso p998

Košice p1000

☑ TOP TIP

There is a great deal to see in this relatively small region. Love mountain scenery? Stick to the High Tatras for drama, Slovenský Raj for beauty or Slovenský kras for off-piste karst. Culture? Košice. History? Košice with journeys out to Levoča, Bardejov and around.

High Tatras

Head to the mountain resorts

If you crave proximity to the raw power of the mountains without sacrificing a cent of comfort, the High Tatras resorts are for you. **Tatranská Lomnica** is on the eastern side, the

---

 GETTING AROUND

The dependable Bratislava–Košice train line serves Poprad, Spišská Nová Ves (change for buses to Levoča and Slovenský Raj National Park), Presov (change for trains to Bardejov) and Košice, where you can get buses to the likes of caving hotspot Slovenský kras and the Tokaj wine region. The Tatras Electric Railway links Poprad to outdoor activity bases in the High Tatras, with cable cars ascending further into the mountains.

HIGH TATRAS DAY HIKES

These are our favourite High Tatras day hikes, easily accessed via public transport.

Ždiar to Vel'ké Biele Pleso (4½hr): Climb from winsome Ždiar to the mountain tarn where the Tatranská Magistrala multi-day trail begins.

Štrbské Pleso to Popradské Pleso (1½hr): Link two alpine lakes, then replenish calories at Horské Hotel Popradské Pleso at trail's end.

Hrebienok & Studeny Potok Circuit (1½hr): Forest loop from the funicular top station passes by delightful waterfalls.

Štrbské Pleso to Kriváň (7hr): Out-and-back trek from Slovakia's prettiest mountain lake to its prettiest peak Kriváň (2494m).

Smokovec resorts of Starý (Old), Novy (New), Horný (High) and Dolný (Low) Smokovec are in the middle, and Štrbské pleso is to the west.

From **Tatranská Lomnica**, Slovakia's most hair-raising cable car ascends to **Lomnický štít** (*vt.sk; adult/child return to Skalnaté pleso €32/24, return Skalnaté pleso–Lomnický štít €59/51*), the nation's second-highest summit at 2634m. Take a six-seat chairlift to Štart, then the gondola to **Skalnaté Pleso** (*vt.sk; free*), a winter sports area and hiking trailhead beside a lake, which is poised infinity pool–style on the mountainside. A vertigo-inducing cable car then soars an additional 855m in under nine minutes to the mountaintop. Timeslots can sell out quickly; you get 50 minutes on the summit to take pictures and enjoy refreshments in the cafe. **Ski Resort Tatranská Lomnica** (*vt.sk; day pass €55/41*) has some dramatic pistes: the black run from Lomnické sedlo is Slovakia's steepest.

In the Smokovec area, the 19th-century resort **Starý Smokovec** makes the most atmospheric base. Learn how to climb the toughest summits and other extreme activities with the **Mountain Guide Society** (*tatraguide.sk; tours €400-500*). You can also climb to **Hrebienok**, complete with restaurant, gallery and trailheads, for some thrilling and demanding hikes. Access is via the **Hrebienok Funicular** (*vt.sk; return adult/child €15/12*).

The most dazzling resort, however, is **Štrbské Pleso**, set around a divine forest lake. Lakeside lodges here provide the High Tatras' best places to stay. Take out a **row boat** (*strbskepleso.sk; €23 per 40 minutes*), walk around the lake, or dine along its shores. The best hike is the 1½-hour climb through forest to wild-feeling **Popradské pleso** lake, from where bigger peaks rise up.

All resort areas are connected by mountain railway to Poprad.

Off-piste thrills

Ready for some outdoor adventure? Sign up for an excursion run by **Adventoura** (*adventoura.eu; per person from €130*). Search the High Tatras for brown bears on a bear-watching tour (Jun-Oct), try dog-sledding in winter or go rafting down the Dunajec River gorge in summer. Both white-water rafts and traditional wooden rafts are available.

Hut-to-hut hikes

If you've ever trekked in the Alps, then you're likely familiar with the hut-to-hut system that enables hikers to spend multiple nights in the backcountry without having to pitch a tent. Slovakia's mountain

EATING IN THE HIGH TATRAS: OUR PICKS

Vino & Tapas: In Poprad, this brick-walled place creates food art with great wine pairings. *11am-2.30pm & 6-9.30pm Tue-Fri, 6-9.30pm Sat* €€€

Felka Café & Brew Bar: Probably the High Tatras' best barista coffee, bagels and cakes, on the road to Poprad Airport. *8am-6pm Mon-Fri, from 9am Sat & Sun* €

Koliba Patria: On the Strbské pleso lakeshore, Slovak mountain dishes, like deer goulash or sheep's cheese dumplings, are exemplary. *11.30am-9pm* €€

Humno Tatry: Lively chalet-style restaurant, cocktail bar and club, by the Tatranská Lomnica cable-car base station. *11am-10pm Sun-Thu, to 3am Fri & Sat* €€

MACIEJ PAWLIK/SHUTTERSTOCK

Štrbské pleso

ranges, including the High Tatras, have a similar network of mountain huts: this is the best way to experience the country's mountainous terrain. For a small fee, you can stay in the beautiful *chaty* (mountain huts) situated strategically across the range. The four-day traverse on the well-signposted **Tatranská Magistrala** trail, from Vel'ke biele pleso (east) to Podbanské (west), is a phenomenal hut-to-hut experience. Our favourite overnight huts? Lakeside **Chata pri zelenom plese** (p1001) *(chataprizelenomplese.sk)* is a 30-minute hike from the trailhead, and wood-ensconced **Zamkovského chata** *(zamka.sk)* is perfect for night two. Accommodation is basic but dinner and breakfast are usually available and the mountain panoramas are unbeatable. Figure on €50 for a bed, breakfast and dinner, or €18 for just a bed.

Eastern Slovakia

Central Europe's greatest fortress

UNESCO-listed masterwork **Spiš Castle** *(Spišský hrad; spissky hrad.com; adult/child €8/4)* is one of Europe's largest fortifications. The 12th-century stronghold sprawls for four hectares through bulwarks and bulky defensive walls over a hilltop 1km east of village Spišské Podhradie. Views from the fortifications are fantastic and far-reaching. In summer, **night tours** *(adult/child €10/8)* are atmospheric, crowd-beating ways to explore this prodigious ruin. From Poprad, it's an hour-long bus ride east to Spišské Podhradie's main square; the entrance to the castle, clearly visible from here, is 850m southeast.

Gorgeous hikes in Slovenský Raj

Discerning outdoor-lovers routinely cite **Slovenský Raj National Park** *(Slovak Paradise; npsr.sk; free)* and its forests, cliffs, ravines and waterfalls as harbouring the country's finest hiking. The standout stretch departs from **Podlesok**: it's a two-hour ascent up a precipitous ladder- and technical-assist

UNMISSABLE UNESCO SITES

Levoča: This town, 40 minutes by bus from Poprad, is festooned with Gothic-Renaissance buildings like the Church of St Jacob, which has a wondrous altar.

Bardejov: Dazzlingly intact Middle Ages trading hub of bewitching, steep-roofed buildings. It's 1¾ hours north of Košice by train.

Hervartov Church: Finest of the nine wooden churches of the Slovak Carpathians, representing the crossroads between Roman Catholic and Greek Orthodox faiths. It's 19km southwest of Bardejov.

Poloniny National Park: Forested expanse that's part of UNESCO's Ancient and Primeval Beech Forests of the Carpathians. Access from Runina, 122km northeast of Košice.

trail through **Suchá Belá Gorge**. Return via Kláštorisko, and descend to the Hornád River and riverbank paths to return to Podlesok. Altogether, it's a five-hour loop. From Hrabušice, 2km northeast of Podlesok, buses (or a 5km walk) reach Spišský Štvrtok and mainline trains.

Visit Košice, Slovakia's second city

Košice is Eastern Slovakia's biggest city, with a nexus of culture and historic architecture along **Hlavné námestie**. This long plaza of flower-bedecked gardens and cafes is in the running for the hotly contested title of 'Slovakia's prettiest town square'. The main feature is Slovakia's largest church, **St Elizabeth's Cathedral** *(domsvalzbety.sk; free, tower adult/child €3/2)*, with gaudily elaborate roof decorations: climb the north tower's 160 stone steps for the city centre's finest views. Also on the square is Slovakia's first musical water feature, the **Singing Fountain** *(visitkosice.org; free)* and, two blocks east, the quaint thoroughfare of workshops known as **Hrnčiarska** *(visitkosice.org; free)*, which showcase centuries-old trades such as blacksmithing and herbal medicine.

Go underground in Slovenský kras

Rožnava, 50 minutes by train from Košice, is the stop-off for delving into **Slovenský Kras National Park**, which comprises the Slovakian part of one of Europe's greatest cave systems. Of the many cavernous marvels, **Domica Cave** *(ssj. sk; tour adult/child €10/5)*, one hour southwest of Rožnava by train and bus, is the largest, with tours that include an underground boat ride. The extraordinary **Dobšinská Ice Cave** *(ssj.sk; tour adult/child €12/6)*, packed with ice and enthralling speleothems (mineral deposits), is one hour north by bus.

EATING IN KOŠICE: OUR PICKS

San Domenico Caffe: Trailblazer for vegan food in Košice, with first-rate cakes a block off the main square. *7.30am-7.30pm Mon-Sat, from 9am Sun* €	**Republika Východu:** Superb bistro offering everything from fruit-and-granola bowls to succulent beef cheeks. *8am-10pm Mon-Thu, to 11pm Fri & Sat, to 8pm Sun* €	**Pub u Kohúta:** Atmospheric pub serving hearty Slovak fare alongside Hrnčiarska's traditional crafts workshops. *11am-2pm & 4-11pm Mon-Fri, noon-midnight Sat* €	**Slávia:** Art nouveau diamond with a glass-roofed restaurant on the main square and a Slovak-international menu. *8am-11pm Mon-Fri, 9am-11pm Sat, 9am-10pm Sun* €€€

Places We Love to Stay

€ Budget €€ Midrange €€€ Top End

Bratislava   MAP p989

CHORS Like a Hotel € Hostel or hotel? The small-but-smart 'capsule rooms' at this well-appointed place start cheap. Even the dorms are comprised of separate private cabins. Round-the-clock bar and all-you-can-eat breakfasts (€8).

Loft Hotel Bratislava €€ Retro industrial chic is the theme in the Loft's sleek 111 rooms, perfectly complementing the cool on-site brewery-restaurant Fabrika.

Hotel Arcus €€ Outside of the centre, near gorgeous Medická záhrada, these relaxed middleweight digs have high-ceilinged rooms either with balcony or overlooking the serene garden.

Marrol's Boutique Hotel €€€ The capital's most sophisticated accommodation is this neo-baroque boutique choice with an elegant restaurant, spa and fitness centre.

Roset Boutique Hotel €€€ With an art nouveau exterior, these generous, minimalist apartments on the Staré mesto's edge are both practical (safes; kitchenettes) and luxurious (towelling robes; turn-down service).

Hotel pri Mlyne €€€ Take the bus from Bratislava's Lamač train station to Lozorno (25 minutes) to reach this romantic oasis with a spa and landscaped grounds. Countryside peace and city proximity.

Pezinok

Palace Art Hotel €€€ Elegant, park-enfolded 800-year-old chateau in the wine town of Pezinok, with two beautiful restaurants.

Piešťany

Ensana Thermia Palace €€€ Flanked by gardens and resplendent with art nouveau design, this palatial complex is *the* place to experience Piešťany's fabled spa culture.

Trenčín

Hotel Elizabeth €€ Yellow-and-cream art nouveau beauty below Trenčín Castle crag that's a visitor attraction itself. Trenčín's Roman inscription, carved in 179 CE, can be seen from its terrace.

Banská Štiavnica

Divná Pani Luxury Gallery Rooms €€€ Plush, idiosyncratic central Banská Štiavnica burgher house. Each room is an art gallery; the cafe is a statue-dotted library.

Malá Fatra National Park

Hotel Diery €€ Whitewashed apartments and rooms have a wellness area, *koliba* (rustic Slovak restaurant) and, right outside, the trailhead for Malá Fatra's breathtaking Horné Diery gorge.

High Tatras

Chata pri zelenom plese € Our pick for a *chata* (mountain hut) stay: superlative High Tatras ridge views from the cosy bar-restaurant alongside Zelené pleso lake, a tough two-hour hike from the Skalnaté pleso cable-car station.

Horský Hotel Popradské Pleso € Epitomises Slovakia's 'Horský Hotel' tradition: basic but beautifully located hotels in remote mountain locales. This lake-fronting place has a restaurant and outdoor sauna/hot tub. It's a 90-minute hike up from Štrbské pleso.

Ginger Monkey Hostel € The High Tatras' eastern flanks, the Belá Tatras, have charming Ždiar as their base, and this brightly painted, wood-built hostel is the village's most atmospheric lodging.

Grand Hotel Kempinski €€€ The best address at the best High Tatras resort: lovely lakeside Štrbské pleso. Outstanding mountain luxury from the bathtubs and minibars in the rooms to the chandelier-hung pool. Exquisite peak-dotted panoramas.

Košice

Penzión Slovakia €€ The 11 rooms above the Rosta steakhouse, a stone's throw from Košice's main square, each represent a different Slovak city.

Ecohotel Dália €€ Excellent 37-room, lower-middle-range choice several blocks from the main square. Among Slovakia's first ecohotels.

Levoča

Hotel U Leva €€ Fronting Slovakia's most magnificent medieval townscape: Levoča's lovely main square. Rooms exude warm-hued colours and substantial polished wood. There's a prepossessing vaulted restaurant.

Practicalities

Tourist Information
Slovak Tourist Board *(slovakia. travel/en)* Slovakia's official tourist resource online.
Tourist Information Centre *(visitbratislava.com)* Bratislava's helpful main tourist office, near Hlavné námestie.
Visit Košice Infopoint *(visitkosice. org/en)* Košice's tourist office, on the main square Hlavné námestie.

Health & Safe Travel
The biggest risks in Slovakia come in the great outdoors. Bears reside in mountainous areas: stick to marked paths. Mountain exploration comes with other dangers: avalanches, rapidly changing weather and, of course, tumbling over sheer rock faces. Seek advice before attempting mountain hikes.

Etiquette
Greetings Start conversations politely: Slovaks are initially quite formal, but soon open up.
Privacy Respect personal space and don't ask intrusive questions until you get to know someone better.
Clothing Never wear revealing clothing in a church; always take off your shoes when entering someone's home.

Electricity
Type E sockets are most common here: two round holes plus the earth pin.

SHEVCHENKO ANDREY/SHUTTERSTOCK

Tatranská Lomnica (p998)

Opening Hours
Banks 8am–5pm Monday to Friday
Restaurants 11am–10pm
Museums 9am–4pm Tuesday to Sunday
Cable cars 9am–4pm

Entry & Exit Formalities
Slovakia is in the Schengen area, an EU territory that allows Schengen citizens, and many others, free movement across internal borders without checks. Non-EU passports should still have an expiry date of ideally six months or longer after the visitor's intended departure date. Most visitors don't need visas for stays of under 90 days.

Language
Hello. Ahoj.
Good morning. Dobré ráno.
Good day. Dobrý deň.
Good evening. Dobré večer.
Goodnight. Dobrú noc.
How are you? Ako sa maté (formal), Ako sa maš (informal)
Cheers! Na zdravie!
Bon apetit. Dobru chut.'
Do you understand? Rozumiete? (formal), Rozumieš? (informal)
I understand/don't understand. Rozumiem/Nerozumiem.
Do you speak English? Hovorité po anglicky?
Excuse me! Prepáčte!

Bratislava–Košice train (p997)

Arriving & Getting Around

The main visitor entry point is Bratislava's MR Štefánik Airport, which serves many European destinations. Getting around Slovakia is a breeze via its superb, regular and punctual train and bus network.

MONEY
Currency: Euro (€)

CASH OR CARD?
There are ATMs that accept international cards in nearly all towns and cities, and even many villages. Most hotels, restaurants and attractions countrywide take card payments. Nevertheless, carry cash as a back-up for purchases at markets, museum tickets and even accommodation in remoter locations – scenarios in which paying with a card may be impossible.

TIPPING
Slovaks don't tip consistently. However, tipping of up to 10% for main restaurant meals is becoming increasingly common in tourist hubs like Bratislava. Rounding up restaurant bills and taxi fares at least one or two euros as a minimum is common practice.

Arriving by Air
Besides Bratislava airport, there's a well-connected airport in Košice. Vienna (one hours' drive from Bratislava) has more flight options, especially for destinations outside Europe.

Arriving by Train
Bratislava makes a handy cross-Europe rail stop, with trains throughout the day regularly arriving from Vienna (one hour), Budapest (2¼ hours) and Prague (4¼ hours).

Arriving by Boat
The most stylish way to arrive is via boat along the Danube. Boats ply the Vienna–Bratislava route at least once daily from March to November, and less frequently in winter.

Getting Around
Within Slovakia, trains are best. From Bratislava, major destinations include Trenčín (change for some of Western Slovakia's best castles), Žilina (for Malá Fatra National Park), Poprad (for connections to the High Tatras, plus other places like Levoča), Prešov (for Bardejov) and Košice. Buses will get you to all other places.

Curated by
Mark Baker

Slovenia

RELAXING TOWNS AND PRISTINE NATURE

Living proof that the best things really do come in small packages.

From the soaring peaks of the Julian Alps and the subterranean magic of the Postojna and Škocjan caves, to the sparkling emerald-green lakes and rivers and the short but sweet coastline along the Adriatic Sea, tiny Slovenia – with a surface area of just 20,000 sq km and a population of two million people – really does have it all. A welcoming mix of climates brings warm Mediterranean breezes up to the foothills of the Alps, where it can snow even in summer. And with more than half of its total surface still covered in forest, Slovenia does more than simply claim it's 'green', it really is one of the greenest countries on earth.

The country is first and foremost an outdoor destination. The list of activities on offer is endless, with the most popular pursuits being skiing, hiking and, increasingly, cycling. Fast rivers like the Soča cry out to be rafted and there are ample chances to try out more niche activities like horse riding, ballooning, caving and canyoning.

But don't sleep on Ljubljana. Slovenia's capital is a culturally rich city that values sustainability over unfettered growth. Enlivened by native-son Jože Plečnik's buildings and beautification projects and a pretty riverside location, Ljubljana is worth a couple of days of pleasant rambling. See the castle, museum-hop and enjoy Slovenia's best cafes and restaurants.

UNAPHOTO.COM/SHUTTERSTOCK

THE MAIN AREAS

LJUBLJANA
Slovenia's green, livable – and fun – capital city. **p1008**

LAKE BLED & JULIAN ALPS
Mountain peaks, perfect lakes and blue-green rivers. **p1014**

SLOVENIAN KARST & COAST
Stunning caves and a romantic Adriatic port city. **p1016**

For places to stay in Slovenia, see p1018

NOSOVA ELIZAVETA/SHUTTERSTOCK

Left: Franciscan Church of the Annunciation (p1012), Ljubljana;
Above: Bled Island (p1014), Lake Bled

Find Your Way

The best of Slovenia includes sightseeing in Ljubljana, the highlights of the lakes and peaks of the Julian Alps, and the country's unique karst and coast region.

TRAINS & BUSES

Public transport is good and you won't necessarily need a car to get around. Trains and buses can take you to all the places covered here. We've noted, where appropriate, whether train or bus is the better option.

CAR

Cars are practical for moving around the country quickly. That said, don't use your own vehicle to get around Ljubljana. The centre is largely closed to car traffic, and walking and cycling are much more practical.

Ljubljana, p1008

Enjoy low-stress strolling around Slovenia's immediately charming capital city.

Slovenian Karst & Coast, p1016

Mix incredible caving with the sea breezes, sunsets and seafood along the Adriatic Coast.

Lake Bled & Julian Alps, p1014.

Take in the beauty of Lake Bled and then swim or paddle at Lake Bohinj and Bovec.

HUNGARY

Hodoš
Murska
Sobota
Beltinci

AUSTRIA

Klagenfurt

Maribor

Dravograd
Slovenj
Gradec
Ravne na
Koroškem
Velenje
Celje
Žalec
Krško

Kranjska
Gora
Jesenice
Bled Castle
Bled
Lake Bled
Bled
Island
Škofja
Loka
Kamnik
Domžale
Trbovlje
Hrastnik
Zagorje
ob Savi
Litija
Trebnje
Novo
Mesto

Mt Triglav

Lake
Bohinj
Most na Soči

LJUBLJANA

Vrhnika
Grosuplje
Ivančna
Gorica
Ribnica

Sava

Nova
Gorica
Idrija
Logatec
Cerknica
Postojna
Kočevje

Ajdovščina
Postojna
Cave
Divača
Pivka
Ilirska
Bistrica

Lipica
Lokev
Škocjan
Caves

Trieste
Koper
Izola

Tartinijev Trg
Piran

Adriatic
Sea

ITALY

CROATIA

40 km
20 miles

Triple Bridge (p1012), Ljubljana

Plan Your Time

Two to three days is sufficient for the major sights in Ljubljana. You can cover the country's highlights in a week.

A Weekend in Ljubljana

● Explore **Ljubljana Castle** (p1008), then wind through the tiny squares of the **Old Town** (p1010). Admire **Prešernov trg** (p1012) and take in the perplexing geometry of Jože Plečnik's **Triple Bridge** (p1012). Wander through the **Central Market** (p1010) or float down the Ljubljanica River in a **historic boat** (p1013). Spend day two touring Plečnik's **National & University Library** (p1013) or the **City Museum of Ljubljana** (p1013).

A Week's Sightseeing

● Begin in Ljubljana before heading up to Bled to see one of the world's prettiest **lakes** (p1014). Check out the equally beautiful **Lake Bohinj** (p1015) and then raft the rapids of the **Soča River** (p1015). Head south to see two of Europe's most impressive caves: **Postojna** (p1016) and **Škocjan** (p1017). Finish up at the breathtaking port of **Piran** (p1017).

SEASONAL HIGHLIGHTS

SPRING
Expect sunshine, warm temps and wildflowers in Alpine valleys. It's still too cold to swim in the Adriatic.

SUMMER
Coastal resorts like Piran fill to the brim. Lakes Bohinj and Bled are warm enough to swim in.

AUTUMN
Mountain air grows cooler and swimming winds down. Resorts like Bled and Bohinj hold their last big shindigs.

WINTER
It's ski season in the Julian Alps. Carnival celebrations are held around the country in February or early March.

Ljubljana

CITY FUN | MUSEUMS | ARCHITECTURE

GETTING AROUND

Central Ljubljana is closed to motor-vehicle traffic, so take public transport or walk, which is a delight. The main promenade follows the Ljubljanica River and is lined by restaurants and cafes. Ljubljana is also ideal for cyclists, and there are bike lanes and special traffic lights everywhere. Hire bikes from the popular **BicikeLJ** *(bicikelj. si)* bicycle-sharing system for a nominal fee. From April through October, the Slovenian Tourist Information Centre rents bikes and hands out bike maps.

☑ **TOP TIP**

Start at the **Ljubljana Tourist Information Centre**, where the enthusiastic staff dispense information, maps and useful literature. They can help book accommodation and also offer a range of interesting city tours.

Throughout history, Ljubljana (loo-BLI-ah-nuh) has always retained the relaxed ambience of a small town, rather than a sprawling metropolis. This is a feeling that continues to this day: Slovenia's capital is one of Europe's greenest and most liveable urban spaces. Car traffic is restricted in the centre, leaving the leafy banks of the emerald-green Ljubljanica River, which flows through the city's heart, free for pedestrians and cyclists to enjoy. In summer, cafes set up terrace seating along the river. Slovenia's master of minimalist design, Jože Plečnik, graced the capital with beautiful bridges and buildings, as well as dozens of classical design elements such as pillars, pyramids and obelisks, which exist solely to make the city even prettier. Attractive cities are often described as 'jewel boxes', but here the name really fits.

Castle Hill

Ljubljana's stately castle has stood guard over the town since medieval times (12th century) and grew in importance in the 15th century under the Habsburg monarchy as a bulwark against Ottoman encroachment. These days, it's the first port of call for visitors wanting to know more about the origins of the city or simply to have some fun.

Explore Ljubljana Castle

Hike or ride a **funicular** up to lofty **Ljubljana Castle** *(ljubljanskigrad.si)*. There's tons of fun things to do up here, including many activities designed for families and small children. If you don't have much time or don't want to spend much money, the grounds are free to enter. Note, however, you'll have to pay to see the historic chambers, including the castle **Watchtower** and the **Chapel of St George**, and to visit the **Virtual Castle**, **Slovenian History Exhibition** and **Museum of Puppetry**. See the various options and admissions packages in the sidebar (p1010).

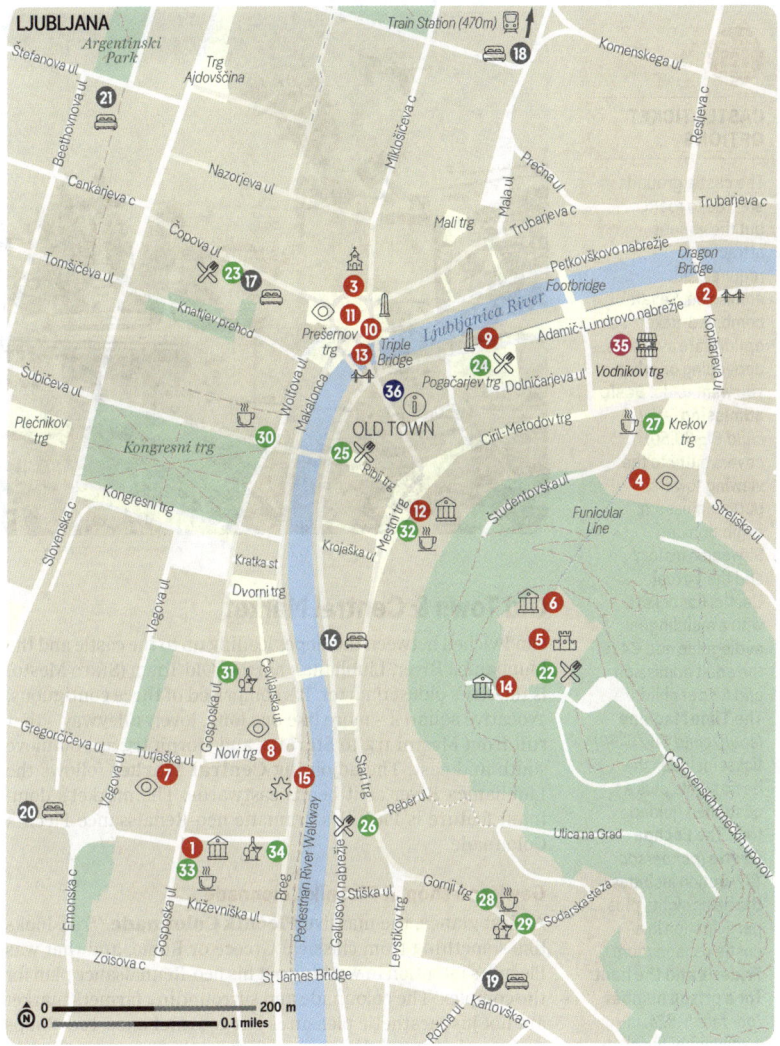

SIGHTS

see 14	Chapel of St George
1	City Museum of Ljubljana
2	Dragon Bridge
3	Franciscan Church of the Annunciation
4	Funicular Lower Station
5	Ljubljana Castle
6	Museum of Puppetry
7	National & University Library
8	Novi Trg
9	Plečnik Colonnade
10	Prešeren Monument
11	Prešernov Trg
see 14	Slovenian History Exhibition
12	Town Hall
13	Triple Bridge
see 5	Virtual Castle
14	Watchtower

ACTIVITIES

15	Barka Ljubljanica

SLEEPING

16	Ad Hoc Hostel
17	AS Boutique Hotel
18	City Hotel Ljubljana
19	Hotel Bloom
20	Hotel Mrak
21	Urban Boutique Hotel

EATING

22	Gostilna na Gradu
23	JAZ by Ana Roš
24	Odprta Kuhna
25	Pop's Place
26	Vino & Ribe

DRINKING & NIGHTLIFE

27	Cafe Čokl
28	Črno Zrno Specialty Coffee
29	Ferdinand
30	Kavarna Zvezda
31	Kolibri
32	Pritličje
33	Stow Cafe
34	Wine Bar Šuklje

SHOPPING

35	Central Market

INFORMATION

36	Ljubljana Tourist Information Centre

CASTLE TICKET OPTIONS

The castle grounds are free to roam, but the various attractions require paid admission. Several combined-ticket options are available, depending on what you want to do. **Basic admission** *(adult/ child €15/10.50)* covers entry to the viewing towers, puppet museum, exhibition on Slovenian history and the Virtual Castle. For tickets with a multilingual audioguide add €4 to the adult admission and €3 per child. The **Time Machine** *(adult/child €19/13.50)* ticket includes the basic sights plus a costumed guided tour. The **Escape Castle** *(per person €19)* option includes the basic sights plus participation in a castle escape room. **Friderik and the hunt for a prison number** *(per family €24)* is a scavenger hunt designed for families with young children.

Old Town & Central Market

Sandwiched between the slopes leading up to the castle and the Ljubljanica River, Ljubljana's narrow Old Town (Staro Mesto) is the city's oldest quarter. It's comprised of three contiguous, evocative squares – more like one long, lovely alleyway – that run from Mestni trg to Stari trg and Gornji trg as you move south and east. The adjoining **Central Market** follows the Ljubljanica River as it bends eastwards. The market's dominant feature is Plečnik's dramatic neo-Renaissance Plečnik Colonnade.

Gawk and shop at Plečnik Colonnade

At first glance, the massive **Plečnik Colonnade** *(free)* looks like something from classical Greece or Rome, and that was Plečnik's intention in working out his neo-Rennaisance plan for the complex. The colonnade and surrounding farmers market are not just aesthetic pleasures but gourmet ones, too. Shops and stands around the square sell everything from meats and cheeses to fresh fruit and veg – this is a great place to stock up on provisions. Most vendors open from 6am to 6pm on weekdays, with shorter hours on Saturday. Pogačarjev trg serves as

BEST FOR EATING IN LJUBLJANA: OUR PICKS

Gostilna Na Gradu: Treat yourself to Slovenian specialities at Ljubljana Castle at this Michelin Bib Gourmand winner. *noon-10pm Mon-Sat, to 5pm Sun* €€

Pop's Place: Centrally located craft beer and burger bar that's become a must-visit. Avoid traditional meal times: it gets busy. *noon-midnight* €€

JAZ by Ana Roš: Michelin-starred chef Ana Roš brings her inventive dishes using locally sourced ingredients to Ljubljana at prices that won't break the bank. *noon-midnight Mon-Sat* €€€

Vino & Ribe: This unassuming spot in the Old Town has a small but excellent menu of grilled fish, fried fish, sardines and carafes of house wine. *noon-10pm* €€

Dragon Bridge

the setting for the weekly popular food fair **Odprta Kuhna** ('Open Kitchen') held on Fridays from March to October.

Look inside Ljubljana's Town Hall

Walk inside the city's striking Gothic **Town Hall** *(visit ljubljana.com; free),* the seat of the city's government since the late 15th century, to find a late Renaissance courtyard, arcaded on three levels, where theatrical performances once took place. Look above the south portal leading to a second courtyard to see a unique relief map of medieval Ljubljana as the city appeared in the second half of the 17th century.

Snap a photo of Dragon Bridge

The much-loved **Dragon Bridge**, topped with four scary-looking dragons, one on each corner, and adorned with 16 smaller dragons, is prime Instagram territory. Indeed, it's fair to say that if you don't take a shot of one of those dragons, well, then you haven't actually been to Slovenia. Aside from dragon imagery, the bridge, built in Viennese Secession (art nouveau) style in 1901, is regarded as one of the most beautiful bridges of this particular style ever built.

DRAGON OBSESSIONS

With those scary-looking dragons on Dragon Bridge and a dragon prominent on the city's coat of arms, many visitors assume Ljubljana's dragon obsession goes back centuries. While dragon symbols have been floating around since medieval times, the city's fling with dragons is a relatively modern affair. Just before the turn of the 20th century, a wily mayor named Ivan Hribar apparently persuaded the authorities in Vienna that Ljubljana needed a new crossing over the Ljubljanica and submitted plans for a 'Jubilee Bridge' to mark 50 years of Franz Joseph's reign. The early designs for what's today Dragon Bridge envisaged winged lions, but these were swapped out at the last minute for dragons. The rest is history.

BEST COFFEE IN LJUBLJANA: OUR PICKS

Cafe Čokl: This fair-trade place near the foot of the castle's funicular station roasts its java in-house; see the chalkboard for daily specials. *7am-6pm*

Kavarna Zvezda: Possibly the best cakes in Ljubljana, with pride of place going to the *gibanica* (layer cake of poppy seeds, walnut and curd cheese). *8am-9pm Mon-Sat, 10am-8pm Sun*

Stow Cafe: Fresh-roasted speciality coffee in the Ljubljana City Museum. Tell the museum ticket office you're going to the cafe to avoid the admission fee. *10am-6pm Tue-Sun*

Črno Zrno Specialty Coffee: In the Old Town, light-roasted coffee from Colombia as well as special 45-minute guided tastings (per person from €25). *11am-3.30pm Mon-Sat*

STEPH COUVRETTE/SHUTTERSTOCK

Prešernov Trg & Center

Tiny **Prešernov trg** serves as the centrepiece of Ljubljana's wonderful architectural aesthetic. The square, a public space of understated elegance, serves not only as the link between Center (the modern part of the city) and the historic Old Town but also as a favourite meet-up point. Taking pride of place is the **Prešeren Monument**, erected in honour of Slovenia's greatest poet, France Prešeren (1800–49).

Contemplate the Triple Bridge

The **Triple Bridge** *(free)* runs south from Prešernov trg to the Old Town. When it was built as a single span in 1842 it was nothing spectacular, but between 1929 and 1932 superstar architect Jože Plečnik added the two pedestrian side bridges and furnished all three with stone balustrades and lamps. The name was changed and, almost a century later, the bridge was added to the UNESCO World Heritage list, along with several sites recognised as 'Plečnik's Ljubljana'.

Explore the Franciscan Church

The 17th-century salmon-pink **Franciscan Church of the Annunciation** *(marijino-oznanjenje.si; entry €3)*, could well

 BEST FOR DRINKS IN LJUBLJANA: OUR PICKS

Kolibri: Sip exquisitely crafted cocktails in a cosy nook on a hidden corner in Center. *7pm-midnight*	**Ferdinand:** Great cocktails, craft beers and cosy outdoor seating on a quiet stretch of the Old Town. *9am-midnight*	**Wine Bar Šuklje:** Welcoming wine bar for sampling highly rated wines from Bela Krajina in southeastern Slovenia. *9am-11pm*	**Pritličje:** By day, a popular cafe with convenient sidewalk terrace. By night, a lively bar and cultural centre. *9am-1am Sun-Wed, to 3am Thu-Sat*

Ljubljanica River

CITY PLANNER EXTRAORDINAIRE

Few architects have had as great an impact on their hometown as Jože Plečnik. Born in Ljubljana in 1872, Plečnik was educated in Graz and studied under architect Otto Wagner in Vienna. From 1911 he spent a decade in Prague teaching and helping renovate Prague Castle. Plečnik's list of Ljubljana creations is endless: from the National and University Library and colonnaded Central Market to the cemetery at Žale, where you can see his own simple headstone. He was also a city planner, and redesigned the banks of the Ljubljanica River, including the Triple Bridge, and Tivoli Park. His eclecticism alienated him from mainstream modern architecture during his lifetime, and he was relatively unknown outside his home country when he died in 1957.

be the unofficial symbol of the city, and is just as striking inside as it on the outside. Enter through a small door to the left of the main entrance to find a riot of baroque design inside.

Learn about Roman-era Ljubljana

The excellent **City Museum of Ljubljana** *(mgml.si; adult/child €8/6)* is strong on Ljubljana's Roman origins as the colony of 'Emona'. The museum highlights a reconstructed street that once linked the eastern gates of Emona to the Ljubljanica as well as a collection of well-preserved classical artefacts.

Tour Plečnik's masterpiece library

Among all the buildings the architect and urban planner Jože Plečnik designed for Ljubljana, the working **National & University Library** *(nuk.uni-lj.si; adult/child €5/free)* is widely considered his masterpiece. Art historians contend this is where the great man aligned his designs and materials with the larger purpose of the building itself: the acquisition of knowledge. The **Main Reading Room** sports huge glass walls and stunning lamps, which were also designed by Plečnik. The library is open to visitors from 10am to 6pm Monday to Friday and 2.30pm to 6pm on Saturday.

Sail the Ljubljanica River

Sailing along the Ljubljanica River is a relaxing and fun way to take in the city. Several companies run tours, but only the creatively named **Barka Ljubljanica** *(Ljubljanica Boat; barka-ljubljanica.si; tours adult/child €15/7)* operates a wooden vessel. It's 10m long and carries up to 48 people on a 50-minute tour. Boats depart hourly from the Breg embankment, just below **Novi trg**.

Lake Bled & Julian Alps

OUTDOOR ADVENTURE | BLISSFUL VIEWS | HISTORIC CASTLES

Places

☑ TOP TIP

Time your visit to avoid the summer high season (July and August) when tour buses descend upon the lake and camper vans clog the narrow streets. Winter snow can make roads impassable in these parts. Vršič Pass closes most years from November to April.

The Julian Alps region is the Slovenia of tourist posters: mountain peaks, mirror-like lakes and blue-green rivers. Prepare to be charmed by Lake Bled (with an island and a castle!) and surprised by Lake Bohinj (how does Bled score all that attention when down the road is Bohinj?). The lofty peak of Mt Triglav, at the centre of a national park of the same name, may dazzle you enough to prompt an ascent.

Lake Bled

TIME FROM LJUBLJANA: 1HR 🚌

With its bluish-green lake, handsome church on an islet, a medieval castle clinging to a rocky cliff and some of the highest peaks of the Julian Alps as a backdrop, Bled has become Slovenia's most popular resort. It attracts everyone from honeymooners to backpackers, who come for the romantic setting, hiking, biking, water sports and canyoning.

Take in the castle, lake and island

Lake Bled is best explored on foot and by boat. Three footpaths signposted 'Grad' lead to **Bled Castle** *(blejski-grad. si; entry to castle & museum €17)* and if you start around the **Blejsko Srce** (Heart of Bled) it should take you between 15 and 25 minutes. Magical, tiny **Bled Island** sits in the middle of the lake and is just as picturesque up close. Board one of the *pletna* (a wooden boat that resembles a Venetian gondola) at **Gondolas Mlino** *(round trip €18)* for a short ride that feels like a time machine. Once you arrive, climb the 99 stairs into the **Church of the Assumption** *(blejskiotok.si; €12)*.

 GETTING AROUND

Bus connections from Ljubljana to Bled and Bohinj are frequent and cheap. Buses are also good for moving between places within the region. Both lake areas are compact and walkable. The area is committed to sustainable travel so drivers can stow their cars and hit the foot or bike paths to move around. The Soča Valley is spread out and easiest to explore by car.

Lake Bohinj

TIME FROM LJUBLJANA: 1½HR

Lake Bohinj may lack Bled's glamour, but it's less crowded and in many ways more authentic. It's an ideal summer holiday destination. People come primarily to swim in the crystal-clear water, and to enjoy leisurely cycling and walking trails as well as outdoor pursuits like kayaking and horse riding. It's 26km southwest of Bled.

Go swimming, boating and paddleboarding

Lake Bohinj's chilly waters warm to a swimmable 22°C in July and August. You can enter the water from any point on shore, though the decent small beaches on both the northern and southern shores are most convenient. Some beaches on the northern shore are reserved for naturists. Adventure outfitters around the lake rent kayaks, canoes and SUP boards and provide guides for hiking and mountaineering. In winter you can go skiing, snowshoeing and ice climbing. We've listed our favourite excursions in the sidebar.

Soča Valley

TIME FROM LJUBLJANA: 2HR

The Soča Valley, particularly the arresting blue-green colour of the Soča River, is just as stunning as you've heard, and neither photos nor written descriptions do it justice. It's worth exploring slowly, from the frothy rapids to the placid streams. Thrill-seekers flock to the town of Bovec for outdoor fun.

Whitewater rafting on the Soča

Whitewater rafting on the Soča River is one of the most thrilling adventures Slovenia offers. Several outfitters run trips down the river from bases around Bovec. **Nature's Ways** (*econaturesways.com*) runs guided white-water rafting and canyoning adventures for small groups, with an emphasis on minimal environmental impact. And lots of screaming, of course. **Soča Rafting** (*socarafting.si*) was the first rafting company in Slovenia and is still at the top of its game, offering novelties such as hydrospeed, where you glide along the river and might get mistaken for a fish. For something different, **Adrenalin Park Bovec** (*ziplineslovenia.si*) features more than 3km of ziplines over the Julian Alps. They also rent e-bikes, scooters and kayaks.

BEST OF BOHINJ OUTDOORS

Savica Waterfall: An easy(ish) stroll through lush forest leads to one of Slovenia's most magnificent waterfalls.

Mostnica Gorge: Spend the day listening to the sounds of the forest as you follow wooded paths towards a heavenly valley.

Hike & Bike: Organises nighttime walks by lantern around the lake and guided forest therapy meditation sessions.

Electric Boat Tours: Operates throughout the year between Ribčev Laz and Ukanc; there's no better way to take in the lake.

Vogel Ski Centre: The 22km of runs make this a top skiing destination. It's 1540m above the lake's southwestern corner and accessible by cable car from Ukanc.

BEST FOR EATING IN BLED & BOHINJ: OUR PICKS

Park Restaurant & Cafe: The creator of Bled's trademark *kremšnita* (cream cake) recipe is still the best, according to almost everyone. *11am-10pm* €€

Bled Castle Restaurant: Recognised as one of the top sustainable restaurants in Europe, this elegant dining room overlooks Lake Bled. *noon-10pm* €€

Hotel Bohinj: The chic hotel restaurant near Lake Bohinj is open for lunch, snacks and dinner, with a wide range of main courses and desserts. *noon-10pm* €€

Majer'ca: Modern Alpine cuisine near Lake Bohinj, with multi-course tasting menus you can design yourself. *4-10pm Mon-Fri, 1-9pm Sat & Sun* €€

Slovenian Karst & Coast

CAVES | ADRIATIC SUNSETS | SEAFOOD

Places

Postojna Cave p1016
Piran p1017

☑ TOP TIP

Parking is tight along Slovenia's coast, particularly in Piran. Work out parking in advance with your hotel. For Piran, parking is only available at Garage Fornače, outside the Old Town. Shuttle buses (5am to 1am) connect the parking area and town centre.

The Karst region is a limestone plateau stretching from the Gulf of Trieste to the Vipava Valley. Rivers, ponds and lakes can disappear and then resurface in the Karst's porous limestone, often resulting in underground caverns like the fabulous caves at Postojna and Škocjan. To the southwest, Slovenia's short Adriatic Sea coastline (just 47km) features clean beaches, boats for rent and delicious seafood, with the highlight being the port of Piran.

Postojna Cave

TIME FROM LJUBLJANA: 1HR

The jaw-dropping Postojna Cave system, a series of caverns, halls and passages, extends underground for some 24km and is two million years old. Visits are by 1½-hour guided tours, with much of the distance covered by electric train. Note the cave has a constant temperature of 8°C to 10°C, so a warm jacket and decent shoes are advised.

Tour a subterranean wonderland

Stepping through the entrance of **Postojna Cave** (*postojnska-jama.eu; adult/student/child in high season €32.90/25.90/19.50; tours hourly 9am-6pm, daily Jul & Aug, fewer departures rest of year*) takes you from the clear light of the Mediterranean hinterland and into the darkness and then, as your eyes adjust, into another world. Few places in Slovenia have the power to dazzle quite like this. Guided tours unveil 5km of the expansive cave. Entering the **Great Mountain** cavern feels like stepping into the secret den of a James Bond villain or some kind of Hollywood special effects scene. From there, you pass through dry galleries adorned with delicate stalactites, needle-shaped formations and even translucent 'curtains'.

◎ GETTING AROUND

Postojna lies 53km southwest of Ljubljana and is connected to the capital by regular buses and trains. Buses running between Ljubljana and the coast stop at Divača, from where a bus continues on to the Škocjan Caves. That said, a car is more practical for reaching these caves. Regular buses travel between Ljubljana and Piran. Once in town, the port area is small and walkable. Note that cars are restricted in Piran's Old Town.

See more jaw-dropping beauty at Škocjan Caves

The immense complex of **Škocjan Caves** *(park-skocjanske-jame.si; guided tour adult/concession/child €18/14/9)*, just 20km southwest of Postojna, is – for many travellers – a rival to Postojna Cave for the title of Slovenia's best cave experience. The Škocjan cave system was formed by the Reka River, which carves its way through a gorge beneath Škocjan village and then vanishes into the Dead Lake. Two-hour guided tours begin at 500m-long **Silent Cave**, which is filled with beautiful stalactites, stalagmites and flowstones that resemble snowdrifts. Silent Cave ends at the **Great Hall**, 120m wide and 30m high – it's a fantasy world of exotic dripstones, deposits and mighty stalagmites.

Piran

TIME FROM LJUBLJANA: **2HR**

Clustered in a tight huddle of stone and terracotta on a narrowing peninsula in the northern Adriatic, Piran (Pirano in Italian) sparkles as the crown jewel of Slovenia's 47km coastline. Wander the twisty alleyways of the impeccably preserved Old Town with its Venetian Gothic architecture, climb to the summit for a gorgeous church, medieval walls and incredible views, or just chill in the elegant main square, Tartinijev trg.

Stroll the centre of a lovely port

Most explorations of Piran begin in the graceful, oval-shaped, pastel-hued **Tartinijev trg**. The 'square' is named after Giuseppe Tartini (1692–1770), an 18th-century composer, violinist and Piran's favourite native son. A **statue** honours the great man in the centre of the square; his birthplace, **Tartini House** *(facebook.com/casatartini; entry free)*, hosts cultural events and exhibitions. Next door is the cute 1818 **Church of St Peter** with its twin Doric columns. Other highlights to enjoy from the outside include the grand **Court House** and the porticoed 19th-century **Municipal Hall**, home to the helpful **tourist information centre** at the western end of the square.

BEST SUNSET SPOTS IN PIRAN

Piran Town Walls: Soak in the amazing views from the preserved medieval walls high up above town.

Boat Harbour: Pick any vantage point along the coastal boardwalk, but this one is glorious in the late afternoon.

Hotel Piran Rooftop: The rooftop bar of Piran's iconic hotel is the classiest place in town for a sundowner.

Bell Tower: It may close just before sunset, but there are great views here; watch the spectacle over town from just outside the door.

Strunjan Landscape Park: About an hour's walk along the coast from Piran, this trail takes you up on 80m-high cliffs with amazing views.

 BEST FOR EATING IN PIRAN: OUR PICKS

Fritolin Pri Cantini: First choice of the places on Trg 1 Maja and a classic Old Town experience: order calamari under a cosy grape-wine canopy. *11am-9pm* €	**Sarajevo 84:** Order a plate of beans and some *čevapčiči* (spicy meatballs of beef or pork) with Bosnian bread and you'll be set for the day. *10am-10pm* €	**Restaurant Neptune:** Try delicious dondoli clams (sea truffles) and other top-notch seafood and pasta at this old-school joint. *noon-3pm & 6-10pm Wed-Mon* €€	**Stara Gostilna:** The home kitchen of young Michelin-starred chef Kristian Zule features lobster ravioli, perfect seafood and a huge wine list. *6am-midnight Mon-Sat* €€€

Places We Love to Stay

€ Budget €€ Midrange €€€ Top End

Ljubljana

MAP p1009

Prešernov Trg

City Hotel Ljubljana €€ Good-value, central high-rise with clean rooms. It's a short walk from the train and bus stations and has an excellent breakfast buffet and a welcoming reception. Book ahead as it's popular in season.

AS Boutique Hotel €€€ Step inside a hidden courtyard just steps from Pre   šernov trg to find this upscale boutique, tastefully decorated with stunning contemporary art and a fashionable mid-century feel. Some rooms offer castle views.

Old Town

AdHoc Hostel € Well-situated, efficiently run hostel right on the Ljubljanica River has brightly painted, airy dorms and several private doubles. Good choice for hitting the coffee bars and restaurants along the riverbank.

Hotel Bloom €€ Lovely boutique below Gornji trg features eye-catching art deco styling and 10 newly refurbished rooms, with lovely hardwood floors and tasteful furnishings. Enjoy your breakfast or an evening drink in the hidden back garden.

Center

Urban Boutique Hotel €€ Great-value, upscale three-star with quiet, high-standard rooms and an excellent breakfast that features lots of locally sourced items and made-to-order eggs. The Center location is close to the sights, yet removed from the noise of busy Slovenska cesta.

Hotel Mrak €€ Cosy, family-run hotel with 35 refurbished rooms set in an older building. Almost opposite the Križanke on Trg Francoske Revolucije, it's ideally located for culture vultures. The back courtyard is lovely for breakfast in nice weather.

Bled

Old Parish House €€ The former property of the Parish Church of St Martin has been transformed into a welcoming guesthouse with timber beams, hardwood floors and chic finishes.

Hotel Triglav Bled €€€ An historic facade hides modern touches and lakeside views, plus a fine restaurant that makes coming home after a day on the water a true pleasure.

Lake Bohinj

Boutique Hotel Majer'ca €€ Scandi cool rooms in Stara Fuzina with views of the mountains and private saunas for the lucky few who snag the suites.

Hotel Bohinj €€ Equal parts sumptuous and wacky, this restored lodge spares no expense spoiling its guests while maintaining a true soul. Ask about the nightclub.

Postojna

Lipizzaner Lodge €€ Pleasant rural guesthouse run by a Welsh-Finnish couple with brilliant local expertise. You'll feel enveloped in the local countryside, but still close to everything.

Hotel Jama €€€ Literally atop Postojna Cave, this huge socialist-era hotel was renovated and turned into luxury lodging with great views; pay extra for a front-facing room.

Piran

Hostel Adriatic Piran € Offering dorms and rooms of varying sizes, this is one of the only budget options in Piran. Rooms are plain but nicely looked after. Shared bathrooms.

Guesthouse Rosemary €€ Tucked away in the back streets but within walking distance of everything, Rosemary has polished wooden floorboards, wrought-iron furnishings and great reviews from travellers.

PachaMama €€€ Built by travellers for travellers, this excellent guesthouse sits just off Tartinijev trg and has 12 fresh rooms, decorated with timber and lots of travel photography.

Practicalities

LGBTIQ+ Travellers
Slovenia is a largely tolerant destination and members of the LGBTIQ+ community are unlikely to face any overt forms of discrimination. Ljubljana is especially welcoming and same-sex couples holding hands on the street, for example, are unlikely to attract even a passing glance.

Health
Slovenia is a safe country, and travellers needn't worry about taking any special precautions. Tap water is safe to drink and of very good quality. Like much of Central Europe, Slovenia's forests and grasslands are filled with ticks. On hikes or treks, use repellent and cover up exposed skin.

Toilets
Public toilets, especially in Ljubljana, are plentiful and relatively easy to find. Unlike in many European countries, toilets are often free of charge. Authorities are working to make toilets accessible for travellers with disabilities.

Insurance
Consider a policy that covers flight cancellations and medical care. Alternatively, or additionally, EU travellers can apply for the European Health Insurance Card (EHIC) that covers emergency medical treatment outside their home country free of charge.

ALESSANDRO ZAPPALORTO/SHUTTERSTOCK

Tartinijev trg (p1017), Piran

Opening Hours
Banks 8.30am–12.30pm & 2pm–5pm Monday to Friday
Pubs 11am–midnight Sunday to Thursday, to 2am Friday & Saturday
Restaurants 11am–10pm
Shops 8am–7pm Monday to Friday, to 1pm Saturday

Accessible Travel
Slovenia is reasonably accessible for travellers with disabilities. Facilities include public telephones with amplifiers, pedestrian crossings with beepers, Braille on maps at bus stops, sloped pavements, ramps in government buildings and reserved parking spaces.

Ljubljana is largely wheelchair-accessible. The centre is mostly flat; pavements have kerb cuts. Most buses are equipped with lifts. Old Town's cobblestone streets are a challenge.

Public Holidays
New Year's 1 and 2 January
Prešeren Day (Culture Day) 8 February
Easter & Easter Monday March/April
Insurrection Day 27 April
Labour Day 1 and 2 May
National Day 25 June
Assumption Day 15 August
Reformation Day 31 October
All Saints' Day 1 November
Christmas Day 25 December
Independence Day 26 December

Language

Slovene belongs to the South Slavic language family, along with Croatian and Serbian (although it is much closer to Croatia's northwestern and coastal dialects). It also shares some features with the more distant West Slavic languages through contact with a dialect of Slovak. Although most Slovene adults speak at least one foreign language, often English, German or Italian, any effort on your part to speak the local tongue will be rewarded.

Basics

Hello. Zdravo. *zdra·vo*
Goodbye. Na svidenje. *na svee·den·ye*
Excuse me. Dovolite. *do·vo·lee·te*
Sorry. Oprostite. *op·ros·tee·te*
Please. Prosim. *pro·seem*
Thank you. Hvala. *hva·la*
You're welcome. Ni za kaj. *nee za kai*
Yes. Da. *da*
No. Ne. *ne*
What's your name? Kako vam/ti je ime? (pol/inf) *ka·ko vam/tee ye ee·me*
My name is ... Ime mi je ... *ee·me mee ye ...*
Do you speak English? Ali govorite angleško? *a·lee go·vo·ree·te ang·lesh·ko*
I don't understand. Ne razumem. *ne ra·zoo·mem*

Directions

Where's the ...? Kje je ...? *kye ye ...*
What's the address? Na katerem naslovu je? *na ka·te·rem nas·lo·voo ye*
Can you show me (on the map)? Mi lahko pokažete (na zemljevidu)? *mee lah·ko po·ka·zhe·te (na zem·lye·vee·doo)*
How do I get to ...? Kako pridem do ...? *ka·ko pree·dem do ...*
Is it near/far? Ali je blizu/daleč? *a·lee ye blee·zoo/da·lech*
(Go) Straight ahead. (Pojdite) Naravnost naprej. *(poy·dee·te) na·rav·nost na·prey*

Time

What time is it? Koliko je ura? *ko·lee·ko ye oo·ra*
It's (one) o'clock. Ura je (ena). *oo·ra ye (e·na)*
half past seven pol osem *pol o·sem* (literally 'half eight')
in the morning zjutraj *zyoot·rai*
in the evening zvečer *zve·cher*
yesterday včeraj *vche·rai*
today danes *da·nes*
tomorrow jutri *yoo·tree*

Emergencies

Help! Na pomoč! *na po·moch*
Go away! Pojdite stran! *poy·dee·te stran*
I'm lost. Izgubil/Izgubila sem se. (m/f) *eez·goo·beew/ eez·goo·bee·la sem se*
Where are the toilets? Kje je stranišče? *kye ye stra·neesh·che*
I'm ill. Bolan/Bolna sem. (m/f) *bo·lan/boh·na sem*
Call ... Pokličite ...! *pok·lee·chee·te*
  a doctor zdravnika *zdrav·nee·ka*
  the police policijo *po·lee·tsee·yo*

Eating & Drinking

What would you recommend? Kaj priporočate? *kai pree·po·ro·cha·te*
Cheers! Na zdravje! *na zdrav·ye*
I'd like the ..., Želim ..., *zhe·leem ...*
please. prosim. *pro·seem*
  bill račun *ra·choon*
  menu jedilni list *ye·deel·nee leest*

NUMBERS

1	**en** *en*
2	**dva** *dva*
3	**trije** *tree·ye*
4	**štirje** *shtee·rye*
5	**pet** *pet*
6	**šest** *shest*
7	**sedem** *se·dem*
8	**osem** *o·sem*
9	**devet** *de·vet*
10	**deset** *de·set*

Ljubljana Airport

Arriving & Getting Around

Ljubljana Airport is the country's only international airport. The airport is 27km north of the city and well connected by taxi or shuttle bus. Slovenia is thoroughly integrated into European rail and bus networks.

Public Transport in Ljubljana
Central Ljubljana is walkable but use buses to reach outlying neighbourhoods. Buses operate from 5am to 10.30pm (fare €1.30). Pay fares with a contactless debit card or purchase a magnetic 'Urbana' card.

Driving
Before driving in Slovenia, purchase an **e-vignette** online *(evinjeta.dars.si)*, required to drive on major highways. Vignettes can also be purchased at petrol stations near the border. The price is €16/32 per week/month.

Driving Essentials
Drive on the right.
The speed limit is 50km/h in urban areas, 90km/h on secondary roads and 130km/h on motorways.
Blood-alcohol limit is 0.05%.

Long-Haul Train & Bus Travel
Train and bus routes cover the entire country. Trains are generally more useful for covering longer distances, such as from Ljubljana to Maribor. Buses are more useful for shorter distances and on select routes, such as from Ljubljana to Lake Bled or to Piran. Trains and buses depart from the **Ljubljana Train Station**.

MONEY
Currency: Euro (€)

CHANGING MONEY
ATMs are ubiquitous and offer better rates for changing money than private exchange booths. That said, many banks, post offices, tourist offices and exchange bureaus do change money. Banks usually charge a commission of 1%. Other agencies charge 3%.

CARD & DIGITAL PAYMENTS
Paying with credit or debit cards is common around the country and often preferable to cash. The only exceptions might be smaller shops in outlying areas. Ticket machines in Ljubljana's buses now also accept card payments.

TIPPING
Hotels Gratuity for cleaning at your discretion.**Pubs** Not expected unless table service provided. **Restaurants** 10% for decent service.**Taxis** Round up fare to nearest euro.

For places to stay in Spain, see p1084

SAIKO3P/SHUTTERSTOCK

Above: Donostia-San Sebastián (p1059); Right: Park Güell (p1046), Barcelona

THE MAIN AREAS

MADRID
The elegant Spanish capital.
p1028

BARCELONA
Catalonia's boundless Mediterranean-side capital.
p1043

NORTHERN SPAIN
Surf-whipped coast, buzzing cities, majestic mountains.
p1057

Curated by
Isabella Noble

Spain

A SOULFUL, SUNNY, FIESTA-LOVING LAND

Passionate, sophisticated and devoted to living the good life, Spain is at once a stereotype come to life and a country more diverse than you ever imagined.

One of the globe's most-loved travel destinations, Spain proudly combines entrancingly diverse landscapes with bold cultural, arts and gastronomy scenes. Its cities march to their own beguiling beats with cutting-edge architecture spanning the centuries, unrivalled nightlife that goes on until the early hours, and neighbourhood plazas that burst with energetic tapas bars. At the same time, ancient villages – often spectacularly located on hilltops – serve as beautiful signposts to old Spain while often also breaking new ground.

Spain's landscapes stir the soul, from the jagged Pyrenees and the wildly beautiful cliffs of the Atlantic northwest to the charming Mediterranean *calas* (coves) and pine forests. Vast expanses of the country are protected as national parks and nature reserves, where emblematic wildlife prowls the hills and valleys.

Above all, Spain lives very much in the present and every day here is something to celebrate. Perhaps you'll sense it along a crowded after-midnight street when all the world has come out to play. Or maybe that moment will come when a flamenco performer touches something deep in your soul. A sunset stroll along a flour-soft strand as the Mediterranean glows on the horizon could well be the time. And Spain's world of food counts among Europe's finest, whether you're lingering over a *café con leche* with a morning *tostada* or diving into an innovative multicourse tasting menu. Whenever it happens, you'll nod in recognition: this is Spain.

JEFF WHYTE/SHUTTERSTOCK

TRAIN

Spain's excellent railways will have you zipping between cities in no time, with expansive views to enjoy along the way. **Renfe** (renfe.com) is the national operator.

CAR

Beyond the big cities, hit the road with your own wheels for the chance to weave past offbeat villages, explore wild natural parks, road-trip into the hills and discover secluded pockets of coastline.

Northern Spain, p1057

Colourful fishing towns, beautifully green valleys and surf-pounded beaches mingle with mountainous majesty, arts-rich cities and Camino de Santiago heritage.

BUS & FERRY

Buses are often the easiest way to reach smaller destinations without driving. There are few places buses don't go in Spain, but plan ahead and factor in flexibility to accommodate local schedules. Ferries zip to/between the Balearics plus smaller places like Galicia's Illas Cíes.

Madrid, p1028

The Spanish capital is one of Europe's liveliest, friendliest and most engaging cities. Come for the show-stopping galleries and architecture, stay for the buzzing *barrios* (districts), festivals and nightlife.

Seville, p1073

Andalucía's fun-packed capital is the gateway to fiery flamenco, timeworn white villages, historical cities, fabulous food and beaches both wild and classic.

0   200 km
0   100 miles

Find Your Way

Extending almost 1000km from north to south, Spain is one of Europe's largest countries. It's also hugely varied, with regions showcasing distinctive cultures, identities and even languages. Major hubs are well connected; more offbeat destinations reward those who make the effort.

THE GUIDE

SPAIN

Barcelona, p1043

In this unstoppable, richly multicultural city, centuries of Catalan culture and tradition meet creative new energy, Modernista architecture, dazzling museums and a superb food scene.

Balearic Islands, p1068

Beautiful beaches draw sun-seekers to the seductive Balearics, where turquoise waves wash onto golden-white shores. But there's much more to discover.

Valencia & Around, p1064

Sunny Valencia ranks among Spain's most captivating cities, with Roman ruins, divine dining, regenerated green spaces and an exquisite surrounding coastline.

Plan Your Time

Spain is a richly varied country that rewards slow explorations and (many) repeat visits. The country is a year-round delight, though fewer crowds and usually pleasant weather make shoulder season the sweet spot.

RICHIE CHAN/SHUTTERSTOCK

La Sagrada Família (p1043), Barcelona

A Long Weekend

● With just a few days to play with, you'll want to hit Spain's two major cities (linked by high-speed train). You're bound to dine and drink well the entire time.

● Head straight for **Barcelona** (p1043) to take in the Mediterranean air on arrival, before digging into Modernista masterpieces like Gaudí's **La Sagrada Família** (p1043) and **Casa Batlló** (p1046) and picking from an array of top-tier museums. Also spend time simply wandering between neighbourhoods, stopping for coffee or vermouth on the plazas.

● Next, hop on the train to reach the Spanish capital **Madrid** (p1028) in under three hours. A couple of days allows time for the **Palacio Real** (p1029) and a major gallery or two (perhaps the **Museo del Prado**, (p1034), as well as a taste of Madrid's famous nightlife, **El Rastro** (p1033) market and some flamenco.

SEASONAL HIGHLIGHTS

Summer and spring bring town *ferias* (fairs), but even in winter there's plenty of fun, from flamenco fiestas to ancient cultural events.

FEBRUARY
Riotous Carnaval celebrations light up winter. Sunny Cádiz hosts Spain's most famous **Carnaval** (p1080), rivalled only by Tenerife in the Canaries. Badajoz, Sitges, Ciudad Rodrigo and the Balearics also go mad for Carnaval.

MARCH
Teams of local artists create giant papier-mâché sculptures for Valencia's unmissable **Las Fallas de San José**, which involves street parties, fireworks, concerts, cooking competitions and, finally, the burning of the *fallas* (statues).

APRIL
A more sombre celebration takes over during **Semana Santa** (Holy Week), which sees elaborate *pasos* (holy figures) paraded. It's big everywhere, but especially in Seville (p1075), Málaga, Lorca, Cuenca, Zamora and Ávila. Sometimes falls in March.

Ten Days to Travel Around

● A slightly longer trip allows you to combine Barcelona and Madrid with another major city, while still freeing up the odd day for adventures further afield. Follow the long-weekend itinerary, then pick from heading south to the Andalucian capital **Seville** (p1073; 2¾ hours by train from Madrid) or zipping southeast to lovely **Valencia** (p1064) on Spain's east coast (two hours by train).

● In Seville, wander the **Gothic cathedral** (p1075) and take in the Islamic-Christian wonders of the **Real Alcázar** (p1075), perhaps with a side trip to Córdoba to see the spectacular **Mezquita** (p1078) or to Granada for the unmatched **Alhambra** (p1081). In Valencia, spend a couple of days wandering the markets, biking to the beach and exploring **La Albufera**'s (p1067) waterways. There's wonderful food at every turn on this itinerary, too.

With More Time

● If you're lucky enough to have an extra week (or a few) in Spain, or if you've visited before, pick one of its less obvious regions. Exploring at a slow pace means time for dipping into tiny villages, seeking out secret coves and lingering over lunches.

● Northern Spain is a road-tripping treat. Take in one of Europe's most dramatic coastlines on a spin west from **San Sebastián** (p1059), with stops in **Bilbao** (p1058), for the don't-miss **Guggenheim** (p1058); the **Picos de Europa** (p1060), for astonishing mountain hiking; and **Santiago de Compostela** (p1061), home to the spectacular, ancient **cathedral** (p1061) marking the main end of the Camino de Santiago. Alternatively, combine Catalonia's **Costa Brava** (p1054) with the Pyrenees, or meander through Castilla y León's cities, like **Salamanca** (p1038).

MAY	JUNE	AUGUST	SEPTEMBER
Madrid's festival calendar is jam-packed, and the major **Fiestas de San Isidro** (p1029) celebrates the city's patron saint with parades, live music, *chotis* dancing and all-night fun.	Spain's major pilgrimage sees up to a million devotees join the **Romería del Rocío** (p1077) in Andalucía on Pentecost (Whitsunday) weekend; it's sometimes in May. June/July is also the time for **Pride celebrations** in Madrid (p1035), Barcelona and beyond.	Visit in August or, depending on regions, September for the start of the **vendimia** (grape harvest). From sherry-making Jerez to famous La Rioja and Galicia's *albariño* bodegas (p1063), many wine regions throw a big fiesta.	Barcelona puts on a mesmerising show of Catalan culture in honour of one of the city's two patron saints during the **Festes de La Mercè** (p1047) – from *castells* (human towers) to *correfocs* (fire-running).

Madrid

OUTSTANDING MUSEUMS | GASTRONOMY SCENE | NIGHTLIFE CULTURE

No one can agree on what exactly the phrase *de Madrid al cielo* (from Madrid to the skies) means. Most likely, the meaning is akin to 'the sky's the limit', a feeling many visitors get waking up to Madrid's crisp mornings. Ask any *madrileño* and they'll proudly tell you it's the best city in the world. They have good reason for this – Madrid has some of the world's best art museums, two enormous parks in its centre, and Europe's largest palace.

But it's the friendliness of its citizens that really makes Spain's capital stand out. This inclusivity has also given Madrid a reputation as one of the world's most LGBTIQ+ friendly cities. *Madrileños* love a good party and Pride is among many fiestas that shake the city till the wee hours. And when the sun rises again in the clear blue sky and the mountain air rushes in from the sierra, the possibilities for the day ahead seem limitless.

 TOP TIP

Grabbing a table on a plaza and watching *barrio* life roll by is one of Madrid's great joys. End your day with sunset and Sierra de Guadarrama panoramas from the viewpoint near **Templo de Debod**, an actual Egyptian temple. Many top museums have specific free-admission days; check ahead.

Madrid's Historic Heart

Soak up the grand Plaza Mayor

Plaza Mayor sits at the heart of what locals call 'Madrid de los Austrias', which refers to the period of Habsburg rule. From 1619 to 1700, this was the beating commercial and cultural

---

⊘ GETTING AROUND

Central Madrid is mostly flat, compact and walkable, though Lavapiés, Malasaña and Calle de las Huertas are steep. Puerta del Sol is a great place to orient yourself.

You can access just about anywhere within central Madrid by the extremely efficient and cheap metro *(metromadrid.es)*. If you're travelling the long main road that runs from Atocha station to the Prado, it's easier to take the bus. Try to avoid the roads during rush hour between 6pm and 8pm.

From Terminal 4 at Madrid's Barajas airport, the *cercanías* (local train) to central Atocha station takes 29 minutes *(renfe.com)*. From other terminals, you can take the slightly faster metro to Nuevos Ministerios and change or take the bus to Atocha. A taxi from Barajas airport to central Madrid costs €30.

Fiestas de San Isidro

heart of the city. It still retains its original character with centennial shops located under stone arcades. Five floors up with 377 balconies, this handsome arena was completed in 1619 under head architect Juan Gómez de Mora. While three major fires have ravaged the square – the last in 1790 destroying three-quarters of the space – Juan de Villanueva's reconstruction remained mostly faithful to the original design.

The square is still a major venue for festivities, including the **Fiestas de San Isidro** in mid-May. While it's fun to people-watch at one of the many *terrazas,* you'll pay more for the location. Just north of the square, 1894-founded landmark **Chocolatería de San Ginés** *(chocolateriasangines. com)* serves some of Madrid's finest chocolate and churros, 24 hours a day.

A Royal Palace & Other Treasures

Exploring the Palacio Real and Galería de las Colecciones Reales

A testament to the enormous wealth of Spain's royal family, the **Palacio Real** *(patrimonionacional.es; adult/child €20/13)* is the largest in Europe at 135,000 sq metres. Home to the succeeding Bourbon dynasty, it's a vast baroque Christmas

continued on p1032

MADRID WALKING TOURS

GuruWalk: Platform that recommends curated free walking tours around Madrid's neighbourhoods. *(guruwalk.com)*

Madrid Museum Tours: Tours by licensed art historian Hernan Satt, tailored for art and history lovers and enriched with historical tidbits. *(madridmuseumtours. com)*

Devour Tours: Discover Madrid's fabulous food scene on a neighbourhood walk taking in tapas bars, vermouth spots and local markets. *(devourtours.com)*

Cuadros de la Calle: This free tour takes you around Lavapiés and La Latina to see their best street murals and graffiti. Book through GuruWalk.

La Cara Oculta de Madrid: A macabre-themed free tour explores Madrid's blood-soaked hotspots, from Inquisition tribunals to crime scenes. *(tourstilla.com)*

EATING AROUND PLAZA MAYOR: OUR PICKS

La Campana: Perhaps the most famous place for *bocadillos de calamares* (squid sandwiches) in Madrid; the queue generally moves quickly. *10am-11pm Tue-Sun* €

Rollo Ocho: Eat Spanish seasonal fare outdoors on a cobbled *terraza* with gorgeous views of Madrid's viaduct. *6pm-2am Mon-Thu, from 12.30pm Fri-Sun* €€

Taberna La Bola: Much-loved bastion of traditional Madrid famed for its *cocido* (meat-and-chickpea) stew. Always busy and very noisy! *1-4pm Sun-Wed, noon-9.30pm Thu-Sat* €€

Mercado de San Miguel: A 19th-century market turned gastronomic hub, with faves like La Casa del Bacalao. *10am-midnight Sun-Thu, to 1am Fri & Sat* €€

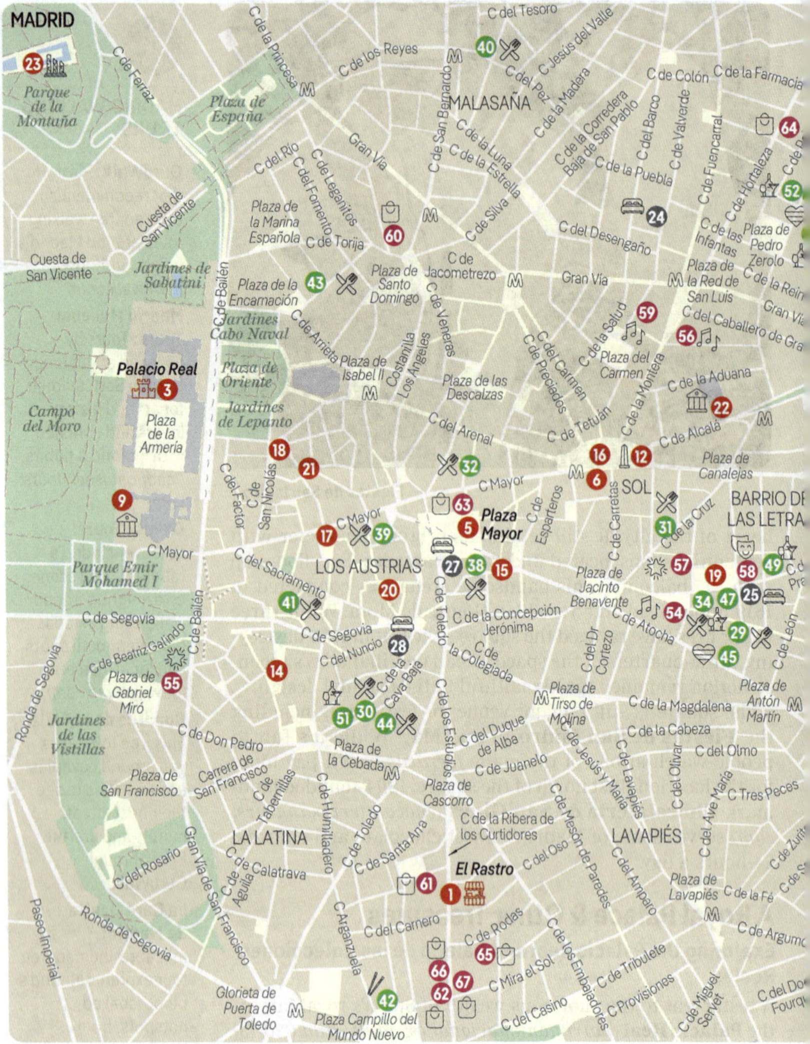

MADRID

MALASAÑA

BARRIO DE LAS LETRAS

Palacio Real

Plaza de la Armería

LOS AUSTRIAS

LAVAPIÉS

LA LATINA

El Rastro

Plaza Mayor

SOL

Parque de la Montaña

Parque Emir Mohamed I

Campo del Moro

Jardines de Sabatini

Jardines de Lepanto

Jardines Cabo Naval

Jardines de las Vistillas

★ **HIGHLIGHTS**
1 El Rastro
2 Museo del Prado
3 Palacio Real
4 Parque del Buen Retiro
5 Plaza Mayor

● **SIGHTS**
6 Casa de Correos
7 Centro de Arte Reina Sofía

8 Estanque Grande
9 Galería de las Colecciones Reales
10 Monument to Alfonso XII
11 Museo Thyssen-Bornemisza
12 Oso y Madroño Statue
13 Palacio de Cristal
14 Plaza de la Paja
15 Plaza de la Provincia

16 Plaza de la Puerta del Sol
17 Plaza de la Villa
18 Plaza de Ramales
19 Plaza de Santa Ana
20 Plaza del Conde de Barajas
21 Plazuela de Santiago
22 Real Academia de Bellas Artes de San Fernando

23 Templo de Debod

● **SLEEPING**
24 Hostal La Zona
25 Hotel Alicia
26 Only YOU Atocha
27 Pestaña Plaza Mayor
28 Posada del Dragón

● **EATING**
29 Casa Alberto
30 Casa Lucio

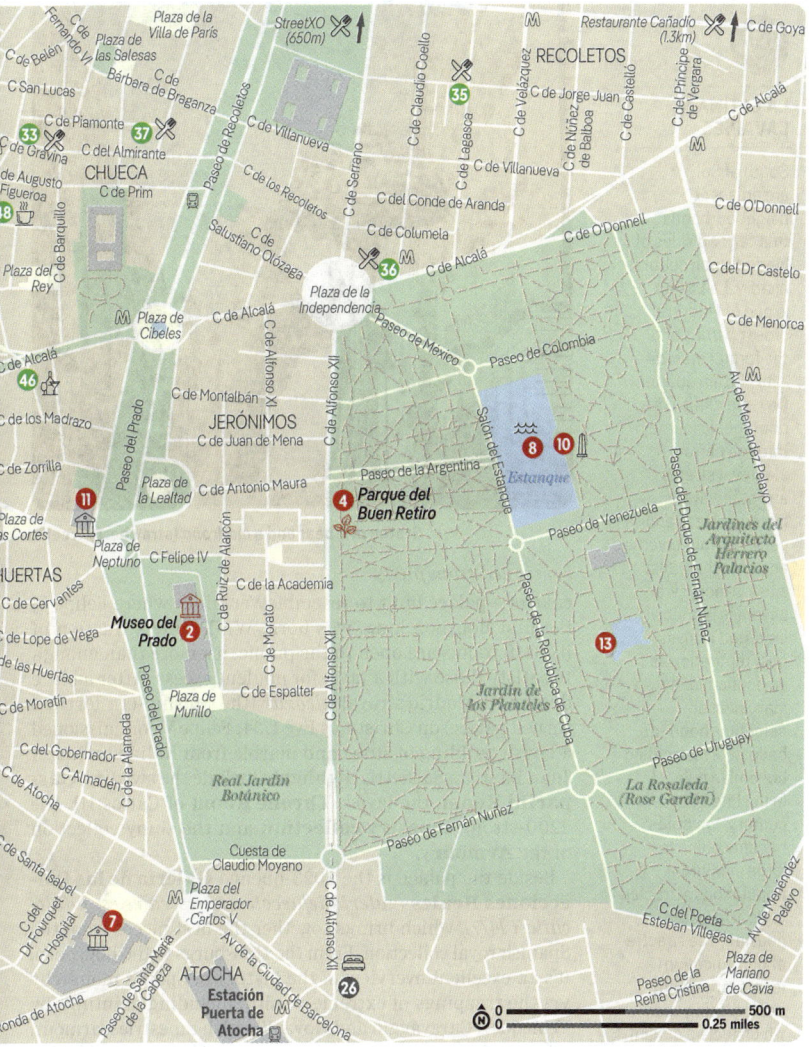

LA LATINA & LAVAPIÉS

South of Sol are adjacent neighbourhoods that tell two sides of Madrid's rich cultural history. **La Latina** is one of Madrid's oldest *barrios* and the former *morería* – its Muslim quarter. Day and night, it's a photogenic journey through narrow medieval streets and stairways, historic plazas and centuries-old taverns and churches. Just a few streets away, Lavapiés has slowly emerged from its past reputation as an economically marginalised neighbourhood to become a fascinating bohemian hub. In the late 20th century, **Lavapiés** became home to large immigrant populations attracted to its affordable housing. The spectre of gentrification looms larger with each passing year, which fuels a defiant community spirit and a progressive arts and culture scene.

Statue of a bear and a madroño (strawberry tree)

continued from p1029

cake of a palace built to resemble Versailles where Felipe V, the first Bourbon king, was born. While only a fraction of its 3418 rooms are open to the public, it's more than enough to satisfy those with a taste for opulent excess. After a blaze destroyed Madrid's royal *alcázar* (the Muslim-era fortress turned palace) on Christmas Eve 1734, Felipe V commissioned a lavish building of stone and marble from Italian architect Juan Bautista Sachetti. Highlights include the swirling **Gasparini Room**, the lavish **Throne Room** of Carlos III, the 2200-strong **tapestry collection** and the shiny collection of the **Armoury**.

Beside the palace is the 2023-opened **Galería de las Colecciones Reales** *(galeriadelascoleccionesreales.es; adult/child €14/7)*, which brings together the best pieces from the Spanish royal collection. From the Habsburgs to the Bourbons, it's an excellent overview of the history of Spain's monarchy via the trappings of extreme wealth, including paintings by Velázquez, Caravaggio and Goya, Flemish tapestries, armour, fabulous furniture and ornate carriages. Also here is a section of the city's original 9th-century wall, built by Mohamed I of Córdoba to protect the kingdom of Al-Andalus from Christian

 EATING & DRINKING IN LA LATINA & LAVAPIÉS: OUR PICKS

Casa Lucio: Iconic Spanish restaurant on Cava Baja known for oxtail and hearty stews. Ask for its dish of the day. *1-4pm & 8.30-11.30pm €€*

Trèsde: Cava Alta star partnering with sustainable producers. Seasonal Mediterranean menu and wine pairing. *1.30-3.30pm & 6.30-10.30pm €€*

Shibari Sushi & Grill: Manchego chef Jordan makes excellent Japanese fare, to go with selected wines from local bodegas. *1-4pm & 8-11pm Wed-Sat, 1-4pm Sun €€*

Taberna El Tempranillo: Outstanding *vinoteca* (wine cellar) on Cava Baja, with an entire wall of excellent wines, and Spanish tapas. *8pm-midnight Mon, 1-4pm & 8pm-midnight Tue-Sun*

ALEXANDRA LANDE/SHUTTERSTOCK

invaders. A combined ticket *(adult/child €24/12)* covers both attractions.

A Four-Centuries-Old Flea Market

Shopping at El Rastro

Every Sunday and on public holidays, Madrid's oldest and largest flea market sets up along La Latina's Plaza de Cascorro, Calle de la Ribera de los Curtidores and Ronda de Toledo. Open from 9am to 3pm, vibrant **El Rastro** features a labyrinth of open-air stalls peddling clothes, souvenirs, handicrafts, antiques and every bric-a-brac under the sun. Come earlier to experience the frenetic atmosphere, or kick back with a cold *caña* (small draught beer) in one of the historic taverns surrounding the market. Several vendors only accept *efectivo* (cash). Start at the top from La Latina metro and work your way down.

Stroll in Spain's Epicentre

Puerta del Sol to Plaza de Santa Ana

Sol, Santa Ana and Huertas are the boisterous heart of Madrid, tightly packed with fabulous shopping, eating and entertainment options. Begin in the **Puerta del Sol**, the official centre point of Spain and a perennially busy crossroads. Now a gracious pedestrianised hemisphere of elegant facades, in Madrid's earliest days this was the eastern gate of the city. The **Casa de Correos** houses the regional government of the Comunidad de Madrid and was built as the city's main post office in 1768. Facing it from the rooftops opposite is the towering **Tío Pepe** sign, long a city landmark. Look out for the **statue of a bear** nuzzling a *madroño* (strawberry tree) at the plaza's eastern end; this is the official symbol of Madrid. Right nearby is the **Real Academia de Bellas Artes de San Fernando** *(realacademiabellasartessanfernando. com; adult/child €10/free; closed Mon)*, which has works by Goya, Rubens and Zurbarán.

From here, move over to **Plaza de Santa Ana** in Huertas, where the streets tumble down the hillside to the east. A delightful confluence of elegant architecture and irresistible energy, the square presides over the upper reaches of the Barrio de las Letras. Dating from 1810, it became a focal point for intellectual life. A statue of poet and playwright Federico García Lorca stands right by the **Teatro Español** *(teatroesp anol.es),* where Lorca had his biggest theatrical success with

 EATING & DRINKING IN HUERTAS: OUR PICKS

Casa Toni: One of Madrid's best old-school Spanish bars. Specialities include cuttlefish, gazpacho and offal. *12.30-4pm & 7.30-11.30pm Wed-Mon* €

Casa Alberto: Atmospheric old tavern, where Cervantes is believed to have written *Don Quijote. noon-11pm Tue-Sat, to 4pm Sun* €€

Azotea del Círculo: Order a cocktail, then lie down on the cushions and admire the vista from this fabulous rooftop terrace. *10am-2am*

Salmón Gurú: One of Madrid's best cocktail maestros, Diego Cabrera, serves masterful drinks at this excellent space. *6pm-late*

FLAMENCO & LIVE MUSIC

Café Central: Renowned Art Deco bar where you'll hear everything from Latin jazz and fusion to tango and classical jazz.

Tablao Flamenco 1911: Previously known as Villa Rosa, this well-regarded flamenco venue featured in Almodóvar's *Tacones lejanos* (High Heels).

Sala El Sol: Madrid institutions don't come any more beloved than this terrific venue for rock, pop, techno, funk and soul.

Corral de la Morería: One of Madrid's most renowned flamenco *tablaos*, with over 60 years of history and top-tier performances.

Wurlitzer Ballroom: Just off Gran Vía, this small but consistently good venue is a real indie music gem – a haven for late-night music fans.

Yerma in 1934. Stop at 1904-opened **Cervecería Alemana** *(cerveceriaalemana.com),* one of Ernest Hemingway's haunts, or at **El Lateral** *(lateral.com)* for creative tapas.

Golden Triangle of Art
Take in Paseo del Prado's splendid galleries

Acting as the city's cultural hub and green oasis, Paseo del Prado (with its three top-tier art museums) and the leafy Parque del Buen Retiro were granted World Heritage status in 2021. The best time to visit the Prado, Thyssen-Bornemisza and Reina Sofía galleries is straight after opening or in the last hour before closing, when it's typically quieter. The Paseo del Arte pass (€32.80) includes admission to all three galleries.

The **Museo del Prado** *(museodelprado.es; adult/child €15/free)* is one of the world's most dazzling art galleries. From the medieval to early modern, its vast collection of European paintings includes big draws such as Rubens, El Greco, Bruegel, Dürer, Bosch and Rembrandt. But it's the Spanish masters that really steal the show – Velázquez' enigmatic *Las meninas* and Goya's chilling *Pinturas negras* herald the dawn of modern art. Other unmissable highlights include Titian's *Emperor Carlos V on Horseback,* Rubens' *The Three Graces,* El Greco's *Nobleman,* and the shimmering light of Joaquín Sorolla. While the work of female artists is almost completely absent, one notable exception is Sofonisba Anguissola's portrait of Felipe II.

Baron Thyssen-Bornemisza's collection has occupied a mansion set back from the Paseo del Prado since 1992. Featuring Dürer, Caravaggio, Degas and Roy Lichtenstein among its many treasures, the **Museo Thyssen-Bornemisza** *(museothyssen.org; adult/child €14/free)* will satisfy the most fickle of art connoisseurs. Works are (mostly) arranged top-down in chronological order. Look for standouts such as Dalí's *Dream Caused by the Flight of a Bee Around a Pomegranate,* Caravaggio's *Portrait of Saint Catherine of Alexandria,* Degas' *Swaying Dancer,* Francis Bacon's *George Dyer in a Mirror,* Dürer's *Jesus Among the Doctors,* Picasso's *Harlequin with a Mirror* and Edward Hopper's *Hotel Room.* Don't miss the Baroness' Collection, which includes works by Canaletto, Van Gogh, Gauguin, Toulouse-Lautrec, O'Keeffe, Matisse and Munch.

The third star of Madrid's 'golden triangle of art', the **Centro de Arte Reina Sofía** *(museoreinasofia.es; adult/child €12/free)* is home to a modern collection mainly focusing on Spanish artists, with figures such as Dalí, Miró and Picasso

---

 EATING IN SALAMANCA: OUR PICKS

El Perro y La Galleta: Chic, cosy spot across from Retiro park, with Spanish and American breakfasts plus homemade pastries and desserts. *hours vary* €€

El Paraguas: Asturian dishes like bean stew or fried veal with ham and cheese, in an elegant setting with a patio for streetside dining. *12.30pm-2am* €€€

Restaurante Cañadío: Cantabrian restaurant with *pintxos* (Basque tapas) bar that opens before dinner service, and outdoor seating. *hours vary* €€

StreetXO: Fiery, edgy younger sibling of Madrid's famous Michelin-starred restaurant, DiverXO, led by Spanish chef Dabiz Muñoz. *noon-midnight* €€€

DUO IMAGES/SHUTTERSTOCK

Palacio de Cristal, Parque del Buen Retiro

MADRID SQUARES

Plaza de la Villa: In the heart of the city, this was Madrid's main square in medieval times and still has some of the oldest architecture.

Plaza del Conde de Barajas: Charming square near Calle Mayor. Unless the Sunday art market is on, it's a relatively serene spot.

Plaza de Ramales: Near the Palacio Real, here you can rest in peace – just like Velázquez, whose bones are scattered somewhere nearby!

Plaza de la Provincia: Just off Plaza Mayor, its lovely fountain depicts the evolution of Madrid's coat of arms.

Plazuela de Santiago: A starting point for the Camino de Santiago, so you might see eager pilgrims outside the church.

Plaza de la Paja: One of Madrid's oldest and prettiest squares, in La Latina.

looming large. Its star attraction is indisputably *Guernica*. A harrowing reflection on the atrocities committed during the Spanish Civil War, Picasso's masterpiece stuns crowds to this day.

Madrid's Beloved Green Lung

Relaxing in El Retiro

Once the exclusive preserve of kings, the **Parque del Buen Retiro** is now open for everyone to enjoy its vast grounds. The park is particularly lovely in summer, when it acts as a green oasis for the city's heat-frazzled population, and in autumn when its trees put on a beautiful burnished display.

The oldest surviving part is the large **Estanque Grande**, where visitors can hire rowboats and admire the huge **monument to Alfonso XII** on the east side of the lake. The beautiful cast-iron and glass **Palacio de Cristal** was built to house flora and fauna for the 1887 Philippines exhibition, and its curved glass roof was a marvel of engineering at the time. It's now an annexe of the Reina Sofía museum and regularly hosts modern art exhibitions along with the nearby Palacio Velázquez.

Join the Festivities at Madrid Orgullo

The largest Pride festival in Europe

On the weekend following International Pride Day, the city rolls out the red carpet to welcome LGBTIQ+ tourists from all over the world for Europe's largest Pride festival, **Madrid Orgullo** *(madridorgullo.com),* held annually in July. In earlier years, bars were allowed to set up impromptu discos outside, but now outdoor music is restricted to Plaza de Pedro

MALASAÑA & CHUECA

There's no question that Malasaña and Chueca are where the party's at. The bohemian hangout and LGBTIQ+ quarter lie side by side, bisected by Calle de Fuencarral, with the boundary between the two becoming ever more fuzzy. All this is a little exhausting for locals, who have complained about the constant noise and high rents. The noise has been a problem ever since *la movida madrileña* got underway in Malasaña in the early 1980s following the transition to democracy. In a reaction against years of repression, a group of artists, who dubbed themselves *raros* (weirdos), were keen to break with tradition. The most famous figures to emerge from this scene are film director Pedro Almodóvar and singer Alaska.

UNAI HUIZI PHOTOGRAPHY/SHUTTERSTOCK

Madrid Orgullo parade (p1035)

Zerolo, Plaza del Rey, Plaza de Callao and Plaza de España. Saturday's **parade**, which runs down Paseo del Prado and Paseo de Recoletos, tends to be heaving. You can avoid the worst of the crowds by taking the *cercanías* (local train) to Recoletos and viewing it from there. Another event not to be missed is the **Carrera de Tacones** (High Heels Race) down Calle de Pelayo; if you want to take part, email *carrerataco nespelayo@gmail.com*.

At any time of year, tap into Madrid's LGBTIQ+ scene at the outstanding **Librería Berkana** *(libreriaberkana.com)* bookshop and at beloved nightlife venues like **Why Not?**, **YOU&ME**, **Axel Hotel Sky Bar** *(axelhotels.com)* and **Studio 54** *(studio54madrid.com)*.

 EATING & DRINKING IN MALASAÑA & CHUECA: OUR PICKS

Hermanas Arce: Clean Nordic lines, home-cooked food, incredible desserts and beautiful breakfasts. *9am-4pm Mon-Fri* €€

El Cisne Azul: Renowned for seasonal produce used in innovative dishes incorporating wild mushrooms. *1-4pm & 8-11.30pm Tue-Sat, 1-4.30pm Sun* €€

Pez Tortilla: Usually packed out with customers clamouring for its superior Spanish omelette and craft beers. *noon-midnight* €

Diurno: One of the most important hubs of *barrio* life in Chueca. It's always full with a fun local crowd relaxing amid the greenery. *hours vary*

Beyond Madrid

Sparkling cities, monumental cathedrals, quiet trails and vast natural expanses await in the *comunidades autónomas* surrounding the capital.

Endless historical, cultural, natural and culinary riches tempt visitors to Spain's great, rolling centre. Stretching across the Iberian Peninsula's interior plateau, Castilla y León is home to historic cities that were already mighty two millennia ago when the Romans ruled Hispania. Within easy reach of Madrid, the Castilian jewels of Salamanca, Segovia, Ávila, León, Burgos and Astorga draw plenty of visitors (especially at weekends), but their buzzing old towns retain a timeless beauty. West of Madrid, little-visited Extremadura is a journey into the heart of old Spain, with the beautifully preserved cities of Mérida, Cáceres and Trujillo. Closer to the capital lie the palatial monastery of San Lorenzo de El Escorial and the 2000-year-old imperial city of Toledo.

Places

San Lorenzo de El Escorial p1037

Toledo p1038

Salamanca p1038

Segovia & Ávila p1039

Burgos, León & Astorga p1041

Cáceres & Mérida p1041

San Lorenzo de El Escorial TIME FROM MADRID: 1HR 🚆

A royal residence

Around 50km northwest of Madrid, in the Sierra de Guadarrama, the monumental World Heritage–listed **Real Monasterio de San Lorenzo de El Escorial** (*patrimonionacional. es; adult/child €14/7*) is among the Comunidad de Madrid's most worthwhile excursions. Filled with art and surrounded by glorious gardens, King Felipe II's 16th-century home is both a royal residence and mausoleum. The complex was designed by architect Juan Bautista de Toledo; after his death, Juan de Herrera, a towering figure of the Spanish Renaissance, oversaw its completion. Among endless highlights is the 17th-century **Panteón de los Reyes** (Crypt of the Kings), where almost all Spain's monarchs since Carlos I are interred. Felipe II's marble-and-gold-trimmed coffin lies in the royal crypt. The bright **Salas Capitulares** (Chapter Houses), whose ceilings are richly frescoed, contain a treasure chest of works by El Greco, Titian, Tintoretto, José de Ribera and Hieronymus Bosch (known as El Bosco to Spaniards).

The complex closes on Mondays, though the gardens open every day. For a pause, enjoy a picnic in the gardens or head towards pretty Calle Floridablanca, where standouts include grilled or roasted meats at **Restaurante Charolés** (*charoles restaurante.com*).

GETTING AROUND

This sprawling area is ideal for exploring by car, combining walkable cities with wide-open countryside and villages. That said, most major cities and towns in Castilla y León, Castilla-La Mancha and the Comunidad de Madrid have good **Renfe** (*renfe.com*) train links, making for easy day/ overnight trips from the capital. Regular buses fill the gaps. For Extremadura, trains link Madrid and Cáceres, with bus options for other destinations.

EL GRECO IN TOLEDO

Doménikos Theotokópoulos, better known by his Spanish nickname El Greco, moved to Toledo in 1577. Toledo has immortalised his art, with many large commissions gracing its churches.

Iglesia de Santo Tomé: Home to El Greco's 1585 masterpiece *El entierro del Conde de Orgaz.*

Museo del Greco: Impressive collection of El Greco's works from the 16th and 17th centuries.

Museo de Santa Cruz: Formerly a hospital and orphanage, it exhibits several of El Greco's paintings.

Convento de Santo Domingo El Antiguo: El Greco's final resting place houses his earliest canvases created in Toledo.

Mirador del Valle: Spectacular viewpoint portrayed by El Greco's famous masterpiece *Vista de Toledo.*

Toledo

TIME FROM MADRID: **50MIN** 🚆

City of three cultures

Spain's capital until 1561, Toledo has lived through many incarnations since it was first conquered by the Romans in 193 BCE. After the fall of the Roman Empire, it successively became the capital of the Visigothic kingdom, a stronghold of the Córdoba Emirate, and the seat of power of the Holy Roman Emperor and King of Spain, Charles V. Vestiges of a multilayered past give this UNESCO-listed fortified city its unique character today – a rich cultural fusion of Moorish, Christian and Jewish influences, earning it the nickname 'The City of Three Cultures'.

Begin at the **Catedral de Toledo** (*catedralprimada.es; adult/child €12/6*), Toledo's architectural magnum opus featuring lavishly carved baroque chapels, massive murals and intricate frescoes. Its cloister retains some Mudéjar-style elements, hinting at its previous incarnation as a mosque. Make your way to the 14th-century **Sinagoga del Tránsito** (*cultura.gob.es; adult/child €3/free*), with painstakingly detailed carved walls blending seamlessly with Mudéjar design. The whitewashed **Sinagoga de Santa María La Blanca** (*turismo.toledo.es; €4*) could easily be mistaken for a mosque with its horseshoe-shaped Mudéjar arches and ornate carvings. The nearby 15th-century **Monasterio de San Juan de los Reyes** (*toledomonumental.com; adult/child €4/3*), with elaborately carved marble altars, was built by the Catholic Monarchs Isabel and Fernando to be their final resting place. A 10-minute stroll brings you to the **Iglesia de San Román** (*closed Mon*). Finish at the **Mezquita del Cristo de la Luz** (*toledomonumental.com; adult/child €4/3*), constructed in 999 and later transformed into a church.

Salamanca

TIME FROM MADRID: **1¾–2¼HR** 🚆

Plazas, cathedrals and architecture

There are few places where such a wealth of architectural treasures have been packed into such a small area as in Salamanca. What's often described as Spain's most perfect square is actually an 'irregular quadrilateral', but in simple terms Salamanca's **Plaza Mayor** is absolute perfection. For almost three centuries it has served more like the auditorium of a grand opera house than an administrative centre (and occasional bullring). When the lights go on at dusk, it's worthy of a standing ovation.

 EATING & DRINKING IN TOLEDO: OUR PICKS

La Malquerida de la Trinidad: Known for its good breakfast menu and traditional dishes. *10am-1.30am Sun-Thu, to 2.30am Fri & Sat* €€

Bar Ludeña: Charming tavern founded in 1955; its star dish is *carcamusas* (pork stew). *11am-4pm Mon-Sat & 8-11pm Thu-Sat, noon-4pm Sun* €

Bar Santa Fe: No-frills tapas bar near Plaza de Zocodover, with a wide selection of traditional local fare. *7am-midnight* €

Restaurante La Clandestina: Traditional tapas and game with a modern twist, on a tree-shaded terrace. *1-3.45pm Wed-Sun, 8pm-midnight Tue-Sun* €

Plaza Mayor, Salamanca

Guided-tour groups passing among this city's historical riches invariably pause to try to spot the fabled 'lucky' frog on the ornate 16th-century facade of the 1218-founded **Universidad de Salamanca** *(usal.es; adult/child €10/free)*, just 500m southwest of Plaza Mayor. But a stroll through one of the world's great temples of academia is an insight into what made Salamanca great.

Immediately east of the university, Salamanca's two majestic cathedrals can get crowded but, at opening time (10am), savvy visitors who make a beeline directly for the **Catedral Vieja** *(catedralsalamanca.org; adult/child €10/7)* tend to have the luxury of soaking up 900 years of history in almost complete solitude. Then backtrack to begin the tour 'from the beginning' in the **Catedral Nueva** (dating back a mere five centuries!).

Segovia & Ávila

TIME FROM MADRID: 30-90MIN

Segovia's fairy tale palace and Roman aqueduct

Segovia's whimsical **Alcázar** *(alcazardesegovia.com; adult/child €10/8)* is said to have inspired Walt Disney's design of the *Sleeping Beauty* castle. Built on Roman foundations and taking its name from the Arabic *al qasr* (fortress), it dates back to the 12th century. With its steeply pitched roofs, like witches' hats, and crenellated battlements, the Alcázar is one

SIERRA DE GREDOS

The great granite slabs of the Sierra de Gredos, rising like whale-backs 150km west of Madrid, are spectacular hiking terrain. Mountain villages are seeing a resurgence after years of accelerating depopulation, as *madrileño* hikers awaken to the fact that this spectacular wilderness lies within day-tripping distance (a scenic two-hour drive from the capital). We love it here in summer when the highlands, rising to 2592m, bring a respite from the soaring temperatures down below. It's gorgeous in winter too, when the peaks are sifted with snow and wild ibex descend by their hundreds into the valleys. Then comes spring – the best season of all – when the meltwater booms down the hillsides in crystal cascades and the cliffs are laced with waterfalls.

EATING IN SALAMANCA: BEST TAPAS

Bambú Tapas y Brasa: *Pincho moruno* (steak skewer) and the award-winning truffled duck-egg are major crowd-pullers. *1-3.30pm & 8-11.30pm Wed-Sun* €€€

Cuzco Bodega: Tiny spot popular for great wine and irresistible tapas (including mini-burgers). It's often standing room only. *1-4pm Tue-Sat & 8-11.30pm Mon-Sat* €€

El Bardo Centro: Hearty tapas stews are what this backstreet favourite is all about. Also popular for the *menú del día* (daily set menu). *10am-5pm & 7-11.30pm* €€

Bar La Fragua: Amazing value for money. A speciality is the ever-changing *cazuela del día* (stew of the day). *8am-noon & 4pm-midnight* €

CAMINO CULTURE

Bisected by the ancient Via de la Plata trade route and the **Camino Francés**, the area around Astorga and León is excellent hiking country. The classic Camino Francés has been pounded by a millennia of boot prints. Almost halfway between Astorga and Ponferrada, **Cruz de Ferro** (Iron Cross), at 1504m above sea level, is the highest point on the Camino Francés. Less famously, Astorga is also the northern extreme of the Via de la Plata.

You don't have to be a dedicated pilgrim to experience the Camino. For something truly memorable, consider spending a day (or two) tackling the mountain passes between Astorga and Ponferrada (a total of about 52km). Breathtaking scenery, pilgrimage camaraderie and hearty local food are all part of the experience.

SCSTOCK/SHUTTERSTOCK

Acueducto, Segovia

of Spain's instantly recognisable national treasures. From the parade ground outside, it's a spectacular sight, but cross the drawbridge over the moat to enter a magical realm that surpasses any movie.

The mind-boggling spectacle of 24,000 blocks of airborne granite that makes up Segovia's **Acueducto** (Roman aqueduct) is impossible to appreciate at a single glance. Fortunately, there are several ways to view the 165 looping arches that constitute one of the finest feats of 1st-century Roman engineering. Our favourite is to climb the steps to the northern end of the main set of arches. The aqueduct is at its best when the setting sun throws looping shadows across Plaza Oriental.

While in town, don't miss the Gothic gem that is Segovia's hilltop **cathedral** (catedralsegovia.es; adult/child €4/3), best known for its rare collection of tapestries.

Patrolling Ávila's city walls

Ávila rises from the plains like a monumental granite island, with convents, churches and mansions barely daring to peek above the cliff-like battlements. Broken only by nine main gates, these **murallas** (muralladeavila.com; adult/child €8/5) are among the best-preserved medieval ramparts in the world. Climb up from **Puerta del Alcázar** (10am–8pm) for a swallow's-eye view of the city as you walk 1km around the top of

EATING IN SEGOVIA & ÁVILA: OUR PICKS

Mesón de Cándido: In a 300-year-old building, the same family has been serving Segovia's best *cochinillo* (suckling pig) for generations. *1-4.30pm & 8-11pm* €€

Casa Duque: Founded in 1895, this historical tavern is known for its garlic soup, roast kid and *cochinillo. 12.30-11pm* €€€

Pastelería Muñoz Iselma: Family-run Ávila business producing delicious almond slices known as Jesuitas. *9.30am-2pm & 4-8pm Mon-Fri, 9.30am-8pm Sat & Sun* €

La Bruja: A rustic wood-beam dining room serving all the Ávila specialities, along with Argentine-style charcoal grilled steak. *1-4.45pm & 8-11.30pm* €€

the battlements to exit near one of the city's 88 watchtowers at **Puerta del Carmen**. For a fuller appreciation, you can walk around the outside from here, enjoying incredible views over the plains and the Sierra de Gredos as you circle the southern ramparts to **Mirador de Ávila** (at the southeastern corner).

Burgos, León & Astorga

TIME FROM MADRID: 2¼–4HR

A tale of three cathedrals

One of Spain's finest Gothic gems awaits discovery in Burgos, 250km north of Madrid. Step into the city's spectacular 13th-century **Catedral** *(catedraldeburgos.es; adult/child €10/2)* and see the tomb of Rodrigo Díaz (aka El Cid), one of Spain's greatest national heroes. He died in 1099 but his legend reached a crescendo about a century later with the epic poem *Cantar de Mío Cid* ('Song of My Cid').

West from Burgos, León has made an art form out of its plazas. On Plaza de la Regla, the **Catedral de León** *(leon. es; adult/child €6/free)* dazzles in Gothic splendour and the glint from 125 stained-glass windows.

Equally evocative is the **Catedral de Astorga** *(catedralastorga.com; adult/child €10/8)*, 45km further west from León. It's one of the most important religious sites on the Camino Francés pilgrim route, with three spectacular towers like rocket-ships tethered together with stone bridges and flying buttresses. A visit includes a free virtual-reality tour in which you have the incredibly realistic sensation of flying through the building.

Cáceres & Mérida

TIME FROM MADRID: 3HR

Strolling through a magical old city

One of the thrilling cities of Extremadura, Cáceres is defined by its glowing, UNESCO-listed **Ciudad Monumental** *(turismocaceres.org)*, which has survived almost intact from its 16th-century period of splendour. Signs of the city's flourishing Jewish and Muslim periods create a harmonious mix with its more recent Catholic past and present – so picturesque it has starred in big-screen productions like *Game of Thrones*.

From **Plaza Mayor**, hemmed by elegant houses with elaborate Renaissance facades, a stairway leads underneath the **Arco de la Estrella** arch to the superb Renaissance-style **Plaza de Santa María** and the Gothic **Concatedral de Santa María de Cáceres** *(concatedralcaceres.com; adult/child €7/5)*.

FLAVOURS OF CASTILLA Y LEÓN

Castilla y León has 26 Denominaciones de Origen (DO), and many of these marks of gastronomic distinction hail from southern pastures. Salamanca's Morucha beef, Ávila's Negra Ibérica cow and Guijuelo's *jamón* (ham) are all prized nationally. Distinct dishes from Salamanca include *farinato* (a lard, bread and flour sausage flavoured with paprika, anise and brandy) and *hornazo* (a pork pie with chorizo and boiled eggs). While meat dominates the cuisine, flat green lentils from La Armuña and seven varieties of bean from Ávila are staples in stews. *Segovianos* take *cochinillo* (suckling pig) seriously; traditionally it should be slow-roasted in a clay pot. For something sweet, try the cylindrical *bollo maimón* and egg-yolk *yemas de Santa Teresa*.

 EATING IN BURGOS & ASTORGA: OUR PICKS

El Patio: A huge local favourite (but rarely frequented by tourists), this large Astorga bar fills up quickly with tapas-eaters at weekends. *8am–1am Fri-Tue* €€

La Quinta del Monje: Popular for tapas, including *morcilla* (the blood sausage for which Burgos is so famous). *hours vary* €

La Lorencita: A perennial old-Burgos favourite and prize-winner for the regional Tapas y Pincho awards in 2020. *noon-midnight Tue-Sat, to 5pm Sun* €€€

Café Pasaje: Overlooking Astorga's Plaza España, with tables heaped with Maragato meat and vegetables, this place is hard to beat. *8am–11pm* €€

EXTREMADURA JEWELS

Many regional highlights are easily visited en route to/from Cáceres or Mérida.

Trujillo: Dazzling small city, with ancient walls, a hilltop 13th-century castle and a monumental Plaza Mayor.

Parque Nacional de Monfragüe: A dramatic, hilly 180-sq-km paradise for birdwatchers and other nature lovers, just north of Cáceres.

Guadalupe: The UNESCO World Heritage Site of Real Monasterio de Santa María de Guadalupe is Spain's most important monastery.

Medellín: Around 40km northeast of Mérida, little-known Medellín was a major town in Roman times and has its own beautiful Roman Theatre.

Valle de la Vera: One of the remotest parts of Spain, home to small hamlets and delightful hill and mountain country.

ROBALITO/SHUTTERSTOCK

Templo de Diana, Mérida

Stroll the street to Plaza de los Golfines, and then to **Plaza de San Mateo**, with the **church** of the same name. Follow the unmissable white towers to the imposing **Iglesia de San Francisco Javier**. Continue to the **Judería Vieja**, in the Barrio de San Antonio, the old Jewish district.

Fans of contemporary art will also want to dip into the **Museo de Arte Contemporáneo Helga de Alvear** (museo helgadealvear.com; free; closed Mon).

Echoes of Roman times

Born Augusta Emerita, once the capital of the Roman province of Lusitania, today Mérida's spectacular ruins lie sprinkled around town. Admission to most sites is by combined ticket (adult/child €17.50/8.50).

At the very heart of Mérida lies an unusual plaza with the **Templo de Diana**, an original ancient Roman temple, flanked by modern buildings. Among many other highlights is the spectacular, 60-arch **Puente Romano** (Roman Bridge) on the broad Río Guadiana. But the main event is Mérida's **Teatro Romano** (teatroromanomerida.com). One of the world's best-preserved Roman theatres, it was built around 15 BCE by the will of Marcus Vipsanius Agrippa, Augustus' right-hand man, to seat 6000 spectators – and still hosts summer performances. Before entering, visit the superb **Museo Nacional de Arte Romano** (turismomerida.org; adult/child €3/free; closed Mon) next door.

 EATING IN CÁCERES & MÉRIDA: OUR PICKS

La Cacharrería: Exclusive and cosy, taking classic Cáceres cuisine and making it even more refined. *2-3.30pm & 8.30pm-midnight Thu-Mon* €€

Tapería 8a Arte: Popular with a young Cáceres crowd for its wide array of local tapas and gluten-free and vegan options. *noon-11.30pm Thu-Tue* €

La Carbonería Restaurante: Perfect place in Mérida for those serious about their meat, with a delicious tapas bar next door. *hours vary* €€

Agallas Gastro & Food: Trendy Mérida restaurant with extravagant dishes and great quality/price ratio. *1-5pm & 8.15pm-midnight Tue-Sat* €

Barcelona

ART & ARCHITECTURE | CATALAN CULTURE | FOOD-AND-DRINK SCENE

Catalonia's capital is one of Europe's most desirable cities – a sunny, Mediterranean-hugging hub that breezily combines its rich cultural traditions with a forward-thinking, environmentally aware attitude.

During Barcelona's medieval Golden Age, great churches and mansions were built across the Ciutat Vella (Old City), shaping today's Barri Gòtic, La Ribera and El Raval neighbourhoods, where creative tapas and vermouth bars and boundary-pushing galleries now sit between centuries-old walls. Then came the industrial boom, with areas like El Poblenou, Gràcia and Sants taking centre stage, and the creation of an entirely new district, L'Eixample, where otherworldly Modernista buildings still command attention. Ever since the late 19th century, the city has been breaking ground in art and style as well as architecture.

Barcelona has experienced an astonishing boom since hosting the 1992 Olympics. With tourism now a key part of the local economy, the city is pushing forward ambitious plans to balance the needs of local residents and the tourism industry.

> ☑ **TOP TIP**
>
> Barri Gòtic and La Ribera (especially El Born) are the busiest, most overtouristed neighbourhoods. Head out early to explore, book museum tickets ahead and keep an eye on belongings. Gràcia, Sant Antoni and Poble Sec have few 'official' sights, but offer wonderful restaurants and bars. For wheelchair-accessible tours, see *disabledaccessibletravel. com*.

Gaudí Galore

Best of the Modernista architect

Dominating Barcelona's skyline, Antoni Gaudí's **La Sagrada Família** (*sagradafamilia.org; adult/child €26/free*) continued on p1046

 GETTING AROUND

Much of Barcelona is flat and walkable. The city has over 250km of bike lanes; bike-hire outlets are everywhere *(€12 per day).*

The excellent TMB metro system has eight lines; buy a 10-journey **T-Casual pass** *(tmb. cat; €12.55)*. The main exceptions are Tibidabo/

Collserola (funicular or train) and Montjuïc (funicular, bus and cable car).

For the airport, the frequent, 24-hour **Aerobús** *(aerobusbarcelona.es; €7.45)* takes 30 to 40 minutes; alternatively, take a taxi (around €30), train (R2 Nord line) or metro (L9 Sud).

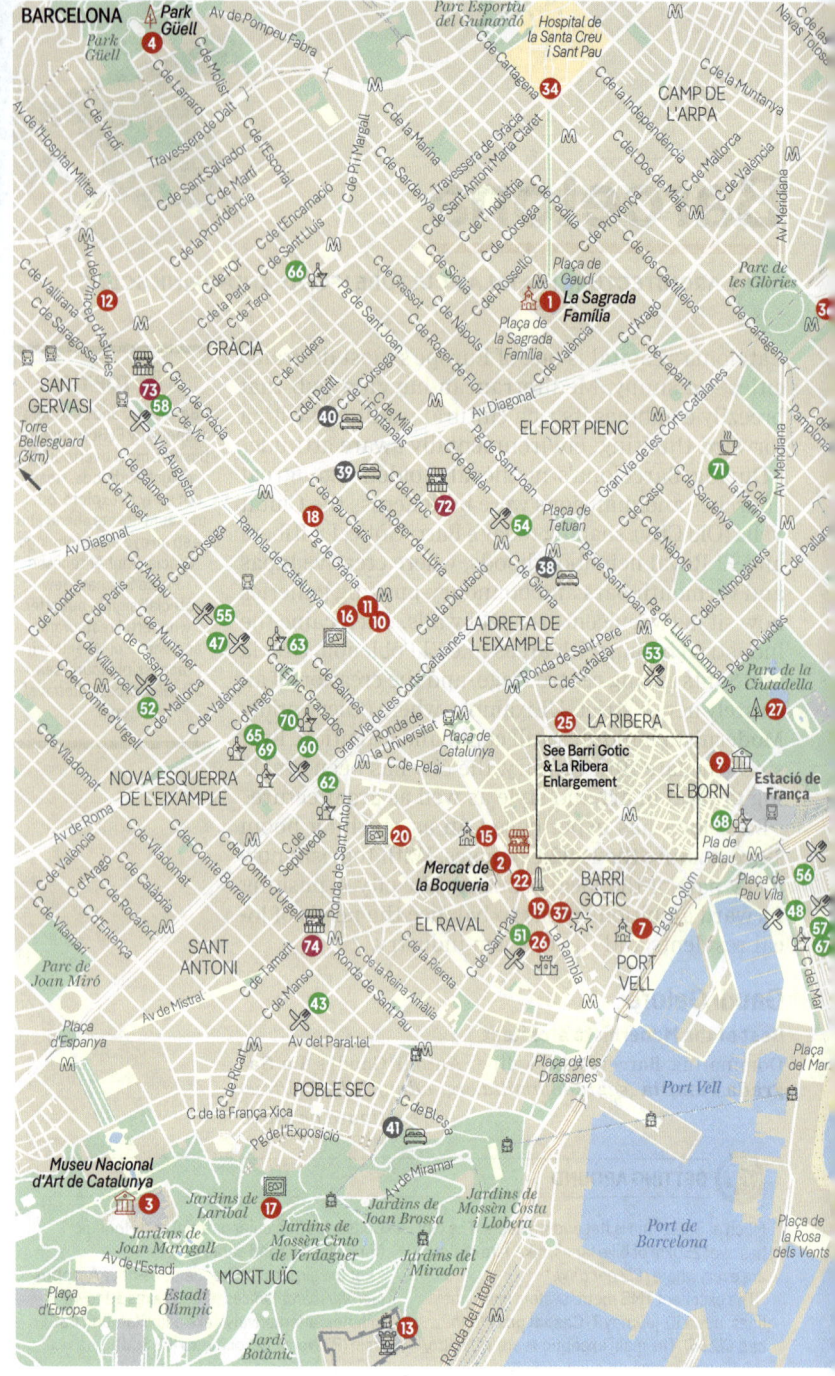

BARCELONA

Park Güell

Park Güell

SANT GERVASI

Torre Bellesguard (3km)

GRÀCIA

SANT GERVASI

Parc Esportiu del Guinardó

Hospital de la Santa Creu i Sant Pau

CAMP DE L'ARPA

La Sagrada Família

Plaça de Gaudí

Plaça de la Sagrada Família

Parc de les Glòries

EL FORT PIENC

LA DRETA DE L'EIXAMPLE

Plaça de Tetuan

NOVA ESQUERRA DE L'EIXAMPLE

Ronda de Sant Pere

LA RIBERA

Parc de la Ciutadella

See Barri Gòtic & La Ribera Enlargement

EL BORN

Estació de França

Plaça de Catalunya

SANT ANTONI

EL RAVAL

Mercat de la Boqueria

BARRI GÒTIC

PORT VELL

Plaça de Pau Vila

Parc de Joan Miró

Plaça d'Espanya

POBLE SEC

Plaça de les Drassanes

Port Vell

Port de Barcelona

Plaça del Mar

Museu Nacional d'Art de Catalunya

Jardins de Laribal

Jardins de Joan Brossa

Jardins de Mossèn Costa i Llobera

Plaça de la Rosa dels Vents

Jardins de Joan Maragall

Jardins de Mossèn Cinto de Verdaguer

Jardins del Mirador

MONTJUÏC

Plaça d'Europa

Estadi Olímpic

Jardí Botànic

⭐ **HIGHLIGHTS**
1 La Sagrada Família
2 Mercat de la Boqueria
3 Museu Nacional d'Art de Catalunya
4 Park Güell
5 Platja de la Barceloneta

🔴 **SIGHTS**
6 Ajuntament
7 Basílica de la Mercè
8 Basílica de Santa Maria del Mar
9 Born Centre de Cultura i Memòria
10 Casa Amatller
11 Casa Batlló
12 Casa Vicens
13 Castell de Montjuïc
14 Catedral de Barcelona
15 Església de Betlem
16 Fundació Antoni Tàpies
17 Fundació Joan Miró
18 La Pedrera
19 La Rambla
20 MACBA
21 Moco Museum
22 Mosaïc de Miró
23 Museu Picasso
24 Palau de la Generalitat
25 Palau de la Música Catalana
26 Palau Güell
27 Parc de la Ciutadella
28 Plaça de Sant Felip Neri
29 Platja de la Mar Bella
30 Platja de la Nova Icària
31 Platja de la Nova Mar Bella
32 Platja del Bogatell
33 Rambla del Poblenou
34 Recinte Modernista de Sant Pau
35 Temple d'August
36 Torre Glòries

🔴 **ACTIVITIES**
37 Runner Bean Tours

⚫ **SLEEPING**
38 Casa Bonay
39 Casa Mathilda
40 Generator Barcelona
41 Hotel Brummell
42 Hotel Neri

🟢 **EATING**
43 Bar Calders
44 Bar del Pla
45 Bar Mono
46 Bar Pimentel
47 Besta
48 Bodega la Peninsular
49 Buriti
50 Can Fisher
51 Cañete
52 Disfrutar
53 Fismuler
54 Funky Bakers Eatery
55 Gresca
56 Jai-Ca
57 La Cova Fumada
58 La Pubilla
59 Little Fern Café
60 Mont Bar
61 Xiringuito Escribà

🟢 **DRINKING & NIGHTLIFE**
62 Candy Darling
63 Carita Bonita
64 El Xampanyet
65 La Chapelle
66 La Vermuteria del Tano
67 La Violeta
68 Paradiso
69 Punto BCN
70 Sky Bar
71 Three Marks

🔴 **SHOPPING**
72 Mercat de la Concepció
73 Mercat de la Llibertat
74 Mercat de Sant Antoni
75 Mercat de Santa Caterina

continued from p1043

MODERNISME HIGHLIGHTS

Casa Vicens: A UNESCO-listed masterpiece, Gaudí's first commission was built between 1883 and 1885 in Gràcia.

Palau Güell: In El Raval, the palatial home Gaudí designed for his patron Eusebi Güell is one of the world's first Art Nouveau buildings.

Palau de la Música Catalana: Built between 1905 and 1908 by Lluís Domènech i Montaner, this 2146-seat concert hall still hosts music.

Torre Bellesguard: Dating back to medieval times, this lesser-known Gothic-Modernista building was transformed by Gaudí in the early 1900s.

Casa Amatller: Josep Puig i Cadafalch's marvel combines Gothic, Romanesque and Dutch urban architecture.

Recinte Modernista de Sant Pau: A UNESCO-protected Domènech i Montaner wonder, created as a hospital between 1902 and 1930.

stops everyone in their tracks. Despite the crowds, this is an unmissable, UNESCO-listed Barcelona highlight. The main construction is due to be completed in 2026. After taking over from original architect Francisco de Paula del Villar y Lozano in 1883, Gaudí (who is buried in the neo-Gothic **crypt**) spent 43 years of his life on the basilica. Above the main building there will eventually be 18 **towers**, some of them already open to visitors. The spectacularly sculpted **Façana del Naixement** (Nativity Facade) is the oldest of the basilica's three monumental facades; the 2018-completed **Façana de la Passió** (Passion Facade), depicting Christ's last days and death, is largely the recent work of the late sculptor Josep Maria Subirachs. Within, extraordinary leaning pillars evoke a natural forest.

On Passeig de Gràcia, the elegant boulevard that bisects L'Eixample, **Casa Batlló** (*casabatllo.es; adult/child €29/free*) is one of Barcelona's most beautiful and curious buildings. Created between 1904 and 1906, this is Gaudí at his fantastical best, from the playful facade with its bulging bone-like balconies and purple-blue *trencadís* tilework to the ground-breaking experiments in light and architectural form. The showstopper is the endlessly mesmerising rooftop.

Neighbouring Casa Milà is better known as **La Pedrera** (*lapedrera.com; adult/child €29/free*), or the Quarry, because of its wave-like grey-stone facade. In the top tier of Gaudí's achievements, this madcap masterpiece with 33 balconies was built between 1905 and 1910 as a combined apartment and office block.

At UNESCO-listed **Park Güell** (*parkguell.barcelona; adult/child €18/13.50*), just north of Gràcia, Gaudí turned his imagination to landscape gardening, creating an ingenious interplay between architecture and the natural world. Visiting the park's trail-laced northern part (*zona forestal*) is free. Best views? From 182m-high **Turó de les Tres Creus**, in the southwest corner.

For all Gaudí sights, book tickets ahead and arrive early or just before closing to beat the crowds. Guided tours are highly recommended.

Glowing Spires & Ancient Squares

Taste Ciutat Vella's long past

Sitting on the foundations of Roman Barcino, the Barri Gòtic is the oldest part of Barcelona and still the hub for festivities

EATING AROUND EL POBLENOU: OUR PICKS

Can Fisher: On Bogatell, reliably good seafood and a chic decor make this a good pick for a paella. *12.30-11pm Mon-Fri, from 10am Sat & Sun €€*

Little Fern Café: Expect a line on weekend mornings at this cafe beloved for its fresh aesthetic, granola bowls and avocado toasts. *9am-4pm €*

Xiringuito Escribà: An open-plan beach bar for digging into a classic, seafood or surf-and-turf paella or *fideuà* (paella-like fish and seafood noodle dish). *noon-10.30pm €€€*

Buriti: Get your morning energy jolt at this Brazilian restaurant with a healthy menu that delights both vegans and meat-eaters. *hours vary €*

Park Güell

BARCELONA'S MARKETS

In the 19th century, many *mercats* (markets) were redesigned by local architects. Today, stalls mingle with bars.

Mercat de la Boqueria: Famous, historic, busy, known for tapas bars such as El Quim.

Mercat de la Llibertat: Modernista hub of Gràcia life covered in 1893. Great tapas at Hermòs Bar de Peix.

Mercat de Santa Caterina: Designed by boundary-pushing architects Enric Miralles and Benedetta Tagliabue. Don't miss Bar Joan.

Mercat de Sant Antoni: Restored 1882 Modernista marvel anchoring Sant Antoni. Home to legendary Bar Pinotxo.

Mercat de la Concepció: Created in 1888 by Antoni Rovira i Trias. Popular for 24-hour flower shop Flores Navarro.

such as **Festes de la Mercè** in September. Extending northeast from the Barri Gòtic, La Ribera grew from the 10th century and became Barcelona's medieval commercial epicentre. Just east, palm-dotted **Parc de la Ciutadella** is central Barcelona's beloved green haven, created for the 1888 Universal Exposition on the site of the much-hated, long-demolished Ciutadella fortress (which had been built after the War of the Spanish Succession).

With its elaborate spires and neo-Gothic facade, the **Catedral de Barcelona** *(catedralbcn.org; adult/child €16/8)* rises in the heart of the Barri Gòtic, preserving a sacred crypt and a cloister that echoes with the honking of 13 white geese. Much of the building dates from the 13th and 14th centuries. Just across Via Laietana, La Ribera's harmonious **Basílica de Santa Maria del Mar** *(santamariadelmarbarcelona.org; adult/child from €5/free)* is Barcelona's most magnificent Catalan Gothic church, built between 1329 and 1382. Climb to the rooftop of either temple for exquisite views.

 EATING & DRINKING IN CIUTAT VELLA & SANT ANTONI: OUR PICKS

El Xampanyet: A legend of Barcelona's *cava* (sparkling wine) scene; arrive early for delicious tapas (tangy anchovies, gooey tortilla). *hours vary*	**Bar Mono:** Polished gastropub with all the classic tapas to check off your list, plus a good vegetarian menu. *11am–midnight Mon-Fri, to 1am Sat & Sun* €€	**Bar del Pla:** El Born favourite specialising in natural wines and creative tapas such as wasabi mushrooms. *noon–11pm* €€	**Bar Pimentel:** Understated tapas bar for *cava*, vermouth and wine; bites include tortilla and squid with lime mayo. *1-11pm Sun-Thu, to 11.30pm Fri & Sat* €€
Fismuler: El Bulli–trained chefs lead this innovative favourite where market menus change daily and wines are glorious. *hours vary* €€€	**Paradiso:** Named the globe's greatest bar in 2022 by The World's 50 Best Bars; try the mezcal-fuelled Cloud. *5pm-3am*	**Cañete:** Upmarket stylish bar for tapas and sharing plates like spicy octopus, oxtail stew and plump anchovies. *1pm-midnight Mon-Sat* €€	**Bar Calders:** Lively Sant Antoni bar for wines and vermouth paired with modern tapas from wraps and hummus to nachos. *hours vary* €

BEST GUIDED TOURS

Spanish Civil War Tours by Nick Lloyd: Historian-led tour of 1930s Barcelona, giving context to a complicated history. *(thespanishcivilwar. com)*

Barcelona Architecture Walks: Led by practising architects and architecture professors, including a Gaudí stroll. *(barcelona rchitecturewalks.com)*

Devour: Excellent food-focused tours supporting small businesses and local producers. *(devourtours.com)*

Runner Bean: Free daily tours led by knowledgeable guides. Bookings required; tips expected. *(runnerbean tours.com)*

Hidden City Tours: Social enterprise that trains guides who have been homeless; routes show a different side to modern-day Barcelona. *(hiddencity tours.com)*

Platja de la Barceloneta

The **Plaça de Sant Jaume** is home to the **Palau de la Generalitat** and the **Ajuntament** (City Hall). Remnants of Roman Barcino can still be seen at the **Temple d'August** *(free)*, near pretty **Plaça de Sant Felip Neri**.

Strolling La Rambla

Barcelona's most famous boulevard

Ancient **La Rambla** connects Plaça de Catalunya to the waterfront, flanked by the Barri Gòtic and El Raval. Once the site of a stream outside the city walls, today it's undoubtedly busy and touristed, but look closely and you'll find centuries of Barcelona history. With five sections, you'll hear it referred to as Las Ramblas (Les Rambles in Catalan). Highlights include the **Església de Betlem**, a church built in the late 17th and 18th centuries; the colourful **Mosaic de Miró**; and the famed **Mercat de la Boqueria** (p1047). Visit early and keep an eye on belongings.

 EATING & DRINKING IN L'EIXAMPLE & GRÀCIA: OUR PICKS

Gresca: At Gresca's open-plan kitchen, chef Rafa Peña reinvents seasonal produce alongside natural wines. *hours vary* €€

Besta: Exquisite menus blend Catalan and Galician flavours, mostly with a seafood focus (vegetarian options on request). *hours vary* €€

Disfrutar: Boundary-pushing, three-Michelin-star venue led by chefs Mateu Casañas, Oriol Castro and Eduard Xatruch. *12.45-2pm & 7.45-9pm Mon-Fri* €€€

Mont Bar: Bistro-style Michelin-starred restaurant with superb wines and next-level cooking using seasonal, organic produce. *1-2pm & 7-10pm Tue-Sat* €€€

Funky Bakers Eatery: Stylish cafe-deli for Barcelona-roasted coffee, delicious babkas, creative brunches and seasonal dishes. *hours vary* €€

Three Marks: Best coffee in town? Head to this speciality roastery in the Fort Pienc area and sit on the terrace. *8am-4pm Mon-Fri, 9.30am-5pm Sat & Sun*

La Pubilla: Alexis Peñalver's Gràcia kitchen has Catalan-style breakfasts and market-fresh menus. *9am-noon, 1-3.30pm & 8pm-midnight Tue-Sat* €€

La Vermuteria del Tano: Long-running favourite with decorative barrels, Perucchi vermouth and traditional conserves. *9am-9pm Tue- Fri, noon-4pm Sat & Sun*

For a more local-life experience, head to **Rambla del Poblenou** or L'Eixample's **Rambla de Catalunya**.

World of Picasso
Delve into the artist's early years

Five medieval palace-mansions on La Ribera's Carrer de Montcada create a striking setting for the **Museu Picasso** *(museupicassobcn.cat; adult/child €14/free)*. But what makes this landmark gallery truly impressive is its showcase of Málaga-born Pablo Picasso's formative years. The first two rooms display early oil paintings and sketches, including the famous *Portrait of Aunt Pepa,* done in 1896 in Málaga when Picasso was just 15. Room 3 houses one of the museum's star pieces, the enormous *Science and Charity,* from 1987. Subsequent rooms showcase the famous Blue Period (including *Woman with a Bonnet* from 1901, in room 8). In rooms 12 to 14, Picasso's 1957 series of renditions of Velázquez' 1656 masterpiece *Las meninas* dazzles among arches.

Fans of contemporary art will also enjoy the next-door **Moco Museum** *(mocomuseum.com; adult/child €17/14),* L'Eixample's **Fundació Antoni Tàpies** *(museutapies.org; adult/child €12/free)* and El Raval's groundbreaking **MACBA** *(macba.cat; adult/child €11/free).* The great-value **Articket Barcelona** *(articketbcn.org; €38)* covers six major galleries. Most museums close Monday.

Waterfront Fun
From beaches to cutting-edge architecture

Barcelona's waterfront stretches from the Port Vell marina near Montjüic to the concrete sprawl of Parc del Fòrum. **Barceloneta** is a grid-like former fisherfolk's neighbourhood engineered in the 18th century, and is renowned for its tapas bars, like **Jai-Ca** *(barjaica.com),* **La Cova Fumada**, **La Violeta** and **Bodega La Peninsular**.

To the northeast, sprawling **El Poblenou** is a former industrial area that has become one of the city's most fashionable hubs, home to the sky-high **Torre Glòries** *(miradortorreglories.com; adult/child €18/free).* The best way to enjoy this area is by joining the runners, walkers, cyclists, paddleboarders, rollerbladers and beach-goers. The Poblenou-area beaches of **Nova Icària**, **Bogatell**, **Mar Bella** and **Nova Mar Bella** have a more relaxed feel than busy, central **Platja de la Barceloneta**.

Go Dancing in the Gaixample
Heart of Barcelona's LGBTIQ+ scene

Over in Esquerra de L'Eixample, the grid between Aragó, Gran Via, Balmes and Comte Urgell streets is popularly known as the 'Gaixample'. With its many bars, clubs, restaurants, bookshops and rainbow flags, this is the epicentre of Barcelona's LGBTIQ+ scene. Popular nightspots include **Punto BCN** for drinks and drag shows, and relaxed **La Chapelle**.

VERMOUTH HOUR

First brought to Spain from Italy in the mid-19th century, vermouth has experienced a dazzling revival in Barcelona over the last decade. Based on red or white wine, the drink is infused with botanicals and fortified with brandy. The best places serve it over ice with an olive and a thin slice of orange. It's ideally enjoyed with friends around midday, especially on weekends – *l'hora del vermut*. Vermouth is always accompanied by light snacks, such as salty crisps or a few tapas (anchovies, croquettes, *patates braves*). To *fer el vermut* (do a vermouth), choose from a wealth of *vermuterias* (vermouth bars), though most Barcelona bars now serve it. The Gràcia and Sant Antoni districts are particularly known for their vermouth-hour scenes.

FESTES DE LA MERCÈ

Held around 24 September, the **Festes de la Mercè** is Barcelona's greatest annual celebration. Honouring one of the city's two patron saints, festivities involve four days of concerts, dancing and street theatre. Much of the fun centres on the Barri Gòtic, particularly the **Basílica de la Mercè** *(basilicadelamerce. com)*, Plaça de Sant Jaume, Via Laietana, La Rambla and the cathedral. But La Mercè is celebrated all over town. In La Ribera, the **Born Centre de Cultura i Memòria** *(barcelona. cat)* hosts displays and parades of fantastical Catalan creatures, while **Parc de la Ciutadella** (p1047) has food markets and live music. Cultural highlights include *castells* (human towers), *gegants* (papier-mâché giants), *sardana* (folk dance) and *correfoc* (fire-running).

COLORMAKER/SHUTTERSTOCK

Museu Nacional d'Art de Catalunya

Weekends-only **Carita Bonita** is a hub for Barcelona's lesbian community. **Candy Darling** has drag shows and a cultural focus, while rooftop cocktails await at Axel Hotel's **Sky Bar** *(axelhotels.com)*. In late June or early July, Barcelona hosts its packed two-week **Pride** *(pridebarcelona.org)* festival, with a Pride march on the Saturday.

Museums on the Mountain

Explore Montjuïc's terrific galleries

Rising up behind Poble Sec, pine-covered Montjuïc (173m) hosts some of Barcelona's finest museums, pretty gardens and an ancient hilltop **castle**. The spectacular neobaroque Palau Nacional, housing the **Museu Nacional d'Art de Catalunya** *(museunacional.cat; adult/child €12/free)*, was built for the 1929 World Exhibition. Its vast collection of mostly Catalan art spans the early Middle Ages to the early 20th century. The high point is the extraordinary Romanesque frescoes, including the 12th-century *Christ in Majesty* (Sala 7) and *Virgin Mary and Christ Child* (Sala 9), both rescued from churches in northern Catalonia.

The nearby, light-flooded **Fundació Joan Miró** *(fmirobcn. org; adult/child €15/free)* is home to the world's greatest collection of artworks by the Catalan surrealist Joan Miró, and was designed by Miró's friend, the Catalan architect Josep Lluís Sert. Standouts include the huge 1979 tapestry of the *Fundació* and *Man and Woman in Front of a Pile of Excrement* (1935).

Beyond Barcelona

Uncover Catalonia's shimmering shores, dive into ancient cities or escape into some of the country's loveliest mountain terrain.

Barcelona's urban sprawl gives way to Catalonia's beloved coastlines. Just beyond Barcelona, Sitges has long been one of Spain's liveliest LGBTIQ+ friendly destinations, with beaches, parties and festivals year-round. On the central Costa Daurada, Tarragona was the first city to be settled by the Romans on the Iberian Peninsula. Northeast from Barcelona, the Costa Brava is one of the most dazzling parts of Spain's long shoreline, with culture-rich Girona awaiting just inland. If you only visit one place on the Costa Brava, Cadaqués – former home of Salvador Dalí – is the quintessential whitewashed village. Heading west into Aragón, the regional capital Zaragoza combines entrancing monuments with a great tapas scene. North of it all, the majestic Spanish Pyrenees straddle Catalonia, Aragón, Navarra and the Basque Country.

Places

Montserrat p1051

Sitges p1052

Tarragona p1052

Cadaqués & the Costa Brava p1054

Zaragoza p1054

The Spanish Pyrenees p1055

Montserrat
TIME FROM BARCELONA: 1½HR

Monastic mountain majesty

Attracting millions of visitors every year, Montserrat is Catalonia's most emblematic mountain. It's home to a historic mountain-side monastery and an ethereal natural landscape where curvaceous rock columns transform into sharp needle-like peaks at a distance, inspiring the Catalan name that translates as 'serrated mountain'.

Founded in 1025, the Benedictine **Monestir de Montserrat** *(montserratvisita.com; adult/child €20/10)* has been drawing pilgrims for centuries to see the icon of **La Moreneta** (the 'Little Brown One' or 'Black Virgin'), a wooden figure of the Virgin Mary prominently displayed at the centre of the

---

 GETTING AROUND

Sitges has excellent *rodalies* (commuter train) connections to Barcelona *(rodalies.gencat. cat)*. Tarragona and Zaragoza are linked to Barcelona and beyond by **Renfe** *(renfe.com)* trains. For the Costa Brava and the Pyrenees, it pays to have your own wheels, or use local buses (some routes only operate seasonally).

Some places restrict private-vehicle access during high season. For Montserrat, take the **FGC** *(fgc.cat)* R5 train from central Barcelona, then change to the Aeri cable car *(aeridemontserrat.com)* or Cremallera rack railway *(cremallerademontserrat.cat)*.

THE CATALAN LANGUAGE

Prepare to be viciously side-eyed if you get caught calling Catalan a dialect of Spanish. Although it is a Romance language similar to both Spanish and French – you'll find that some words, such as *hola* and *merci* respectively, are identical – Catalan is distinct and spoken by over four million native speakers. Catalan is not only spoken in Catalonia, but also in parts of Valencia, the Balearic Islands, and even as far away as the Italian city of Alghero in Sardinia, which was colonised by the Catalans in the Middle Ages. Although most people in Catalonia are likely to speak Spanish as well, trying out a Catalan phrase here and there is usually appreciated.

altar. Despite the large tourist complex with shops, restaurants and museums, this is still a working monastery. With careful timing, you might catch a performance by the Escolania de Montserrat, one of the oldest boys' choirs in Europe.

Beyond the monastery complex, Montserrat is a natural park with many inspiring walking trails, including summiting the mountain (1236m) on the 10.3km **Sant Jeroni Loop**.

Sites

TIME FROM BARCELONA: **35MIN**

A festive beach town

A popular day-trip escape from Barcelona, lively Sitges has a crop of beautiful beaches and a glitzy nightlife scene. Listen to the bells of the **Església de Sant Bartomeu i Santa Tecla** ring out as you lounge on the main strip of sandy beaches, or explore a little further up the coast to clothing-optional **Platja dels Balmins**.

Historically LGBTIQ+ friendly, Sitges traces its clubbing scene back to the 1980s. Catch the two largest celebrations of colour and love during Carnival in late February/early March or June's Pride parade.

Sitges also has a delightful, buzzy historic centre. Learn about one of the leading artists of Modernisme, Santiago Rusiñol, at the **Museu del Cau Ferrat** and the ornate **Palau de Maricel** *(museusdesitges.cat; adult/child €12/free);* they are closed on Mondays.

Tarragona

TIME FROM BARCELONA: **1–2HR**

Roman relics

Formerly known as Tárraco, Tarragona spent hundreds of years as the region's Roman capital. Today, well-preserved remnants of the ancient city are found throughout the old town of this vibrant, modern hub. A joint ticket *(tarragona.cat; adult/child €15/free)* offers access to all the major sites, which individually cost €5. Enter the history museum at **Torre de les Monges** and soon you'll be peering out over the **Circ Romà**, a partial preservation of a much larger chariot course. The museum continues underground, finishing at the **Torre del Pretori**, where you can climb to the top for a spectacular view of the sea-facing **Amfiteatre de Tarragona**, built in the 2nd century for up to 15,000 spectators.

Romans aside, the **Catedral de Tarragona** *(catedraldetarragona.com; adult/child €12/8.50)* is one of the largest in Catalonia and features a blend of Gothic and Romanesque styles.

EATING IN GIRONA: OUR PICKS

Rocambolesc: Ice-cream shop with special flavours and fun popsicles; from the family of El Celler de Can Roca. *10.30am-11pm Sun-Thu, to midnight Fri & Sat* €

L'Argadà: Catalan steakhouse, where seasonal *calçots* (spring onions) are served in a traditional roof tile. *1.30-3.30pm & 8-10.30pm Mon-Sat, 1.30-3.30pm Sun* €€

Café Le Bistrot: Tables romantically arranged on the steps of Sant Domènec; book ahead. *1-4pm & 7.30pm-midnight Mon-Sat, 1-4pm Sun* €€

El Celler de Can Roca: World-famous and recognised for dramatic plating and gourmet cooking techniques. *12.30-9.30pm Wed-Sat, from 7.30pm Tue* €€€

GIRONA ARCHAEOLOGICAL WALK

Despite the contemporary city that surrounds it, Girona's old quarter maintains its medieval charm.

START	END	LENGTH
Museu d'Historia dels Jueus	Café Le Bistrot	2km; one hour

Just north of the Pont de Sant Agustí, you'll find the ❶ **Museu d'Historia dels Jueus**, located in a 13th-century Jewish home. Turn right on Carrer Sant Llorenç and walk up to a medieval fountain, ❷ **Font dels Lledoners**. Turn left through the plaza towards the steps of the Gothic-baroque ❸ **Catedral de Girona**, home to the *Tapestry of Creation* from the 11th or 12th century.

Trot down for a better look and go through the gate towards the ❹ **Basílica de Sant Feliu**. Take a right to pass the 12th-century ❺ **Banys Àrabs**. At the end of this road, find the ❻ **Plaça dels Jurats** and ❼ **Monestir de Sant Pere de Galligants**, which houses lovely cloisters and the

archaeology museum. Climbing up the Passeig de la Reina Joana, follow the archaeological path to reach the ❽ **Jardins dels Alemanys** and access the ❾ **Muralles de Girona** for the walk along the walls, passing the towers of Gironella and Sant Domènc.

Descend the walls at Torre del General Peralta Bastion and continue until you pass the ❿ **Convent de Sant Domènec de Girona**. A huge convent founded in 1253, it now belongs to the university. Turn left on the Pujada de Sant Domènec and walk towards the picturesque stairs, where you might snag a table at ⓫ **Café Le Bistrot** (p1052).

The **Museu d'Història de Girona**, housed within an 18th-century cloister, provides context about Girona through the ages.

Next to the cathedral, the **Museu d'Art de Girona** has a sprawling collection, from religious Romanesque artworks to Modernisme.

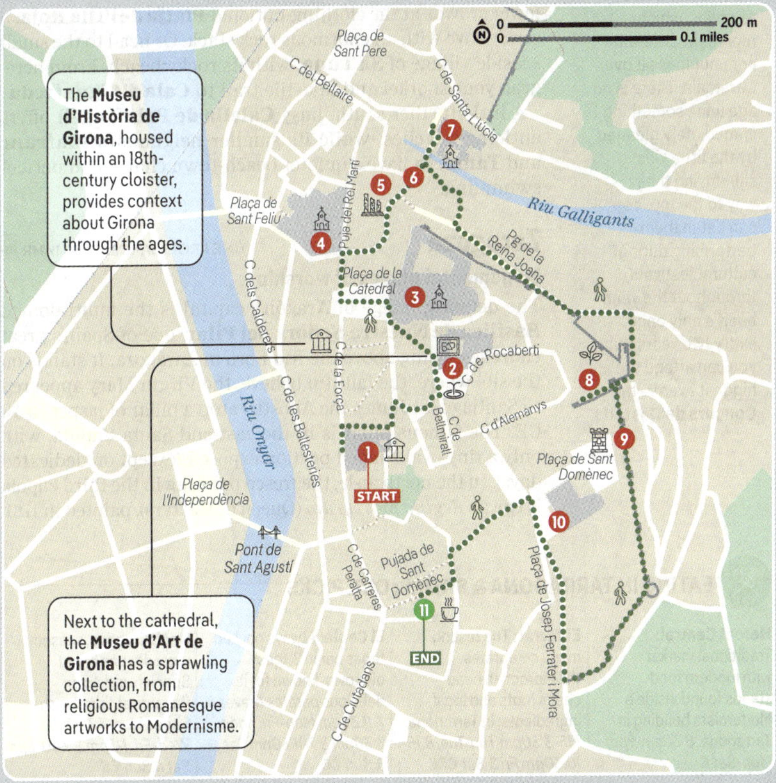

Cadaqués & the Costa Brava

TIME FROM BARCELONA (CADAQUÉS): 2¼HR

Winds of Cap de Creus

Just north of Cadaqués, the **Parc Natural de Cap de Creus** (*parcsnaturals.gencat.cat*) is defined by its dry and weather-worn rocky landscape, filled with jagged and uncanny shapes that inspired the controversial surrealist artist Salvador Dalí throughout his life. Today it's a protected park with many marked walking paths, including an 8km route that you can follow from Cadaqués to the 19th-century lighthouse – **Far Cap de Creus** – at Spain's most eastern point. Venture to swimming spots **Cala Culip** and **Cala Jugadora**. During certain times of year, park roads close to vehicles, and a SARFA bus service (*moventis.es*) is offered from Cadaqués and the Corral d'en Morell car park.

Beach-hopping around Begur

Another of the Costa Brava's loveliest pockets is the cliff-edged shoreline around the charming town of **Begur**, 60km south of Cadaqués. The ruins of the 16th-century **Castell de Begur** provide one of the most majestic views of the Costa Brava; on clear days you can even see the Pyrenees. **Platja de Sa Riera** has plenty of sand to go around, but there are fewer crowds at the clothing-optional **Platja de l'Illa Roja**, a sandy cove with an enormous rock stack. Or head to the small seaside village of **Sa Tuna**, with its rocky beach. From here, grab your snorkel and take the trail to **Cala d'Aiguafreda**.

A little further south, busy **Calella de Palafrugell** offers enticing beaches, while its smaller neighbours **Llafranc** and **Tamariu** have a quieter beach-town charm and perfect swimming.

Zaragoza

TIME FROM BARCELONA: 1½HR

Monumental places of worship

The defining image of Aragón's capital is the multi-domed **Basílica de Nuestra Señora del Pilar**, one of Spain's great churches, rising above the Río Ebro in Zaragoza. It stands on the site where, the faithful believe, the Virgin Mary appeared to Santiago (St James the Apostle) atop a pillar of jasper in 40 CE. The famous pillar is in the east-end Santa Capilla, with only a tiny oval-shaped portion exposed (except on dedicated days). In the north aisle, the fresco painting in the third cupola is Goya's *Regina Martyrum* (Queen of Martyrs), painted in 1781.

EATING IN TARRAGONA & SITGES: OUR PICKS

Mercat Central: Traditional market with modern food stands found inside a Modernista building in Tarragona. *8.30am-9pm Mon-Sat €*

El Terrat: The tasting menu celebrates the Moroccan head chef's roots and local ingredients; in Tarragona. *1.15-3.30pm Thu-Tue, 8.15-10.30pm Fri & Sat €€€*

El Cable: Always packed tapas bar in Sitges' old town, known for its delicious *patates braves*. *7-11.30pm Mon-Fri, noon-3.30pm & 7-11.30pm Sat & Sun €€*

NeM: Creative, season-rooted tapas blend Spanish and Asian flavours at this stylish Sitges fave. *7.30-11pm Wed-Fri, 1-5pm & 7.30-11pm Sat & Sun €€*

SINCLAIR_JVZ/SHUTTERSTOCK

La Seo, Zaragoza

Goya's earlier *Adoración del Nombre del Dios* adorns the ceiling of the choir at the church's far east end. Goya's work can also be seen at the **Museo Goya** *(museogoya.fundacionibercaja.es)* and the **Museo de Zaragoza** *(turismodearagon.com),* both slated to reopen in 2026 following renovations.

Though overshadowed in scale by the basilica, Zaragoza's **La Seo** cathedral is arguably a finer work of Christian architecture. Built between the 12th and 17th centuries, it stands on the site of Islamic Zaragoza's main mosque. A joint ticket covers both churches *(catedraldezaragoza.es; adut/child €10/free).*

High point of Islamic architecture

The dour castle-like exterior gives no hint of the ornate decorative joys within the **Aljafería** *(turismodearagon.com; adult/child €7/free).* Built as a fortified palace for Zaragoza's Islamic rulers in the 11th century, it passed into Christian hands in 1118, and in the 1490s the Reyes Católicos (Catholic Monarchs), Fernando and Isabel, tacked on their own palace. Wandering through its exquisitely sculpted courtyards and delicate interwoven archways, you can get a sense of the pomp and majesty of both the Islamic court and its Christian successors.

The Spanish Pyrenees TIME FROM BARCELONA: **3–4HR** 🚗

Mountain hikes and other adventures

Some of Spain's most dramatic mountain country awaits in the Pyrenees, which spill over into France north of Zaragoza

THE COSTA BRAVA & DALÍ

Teatre-Museu Dalí: Topped by larger-than-life eggs, Dalí's theatre-museum opened in 1974 and is a centrepiece of the artist's hometown, Figueres.

Casa Museu Dalí: Just outside Cadaqués, the artist's labyrinthine house in Portlligat is unlike any historic home you've seen before, including his former workshop.

Cap de Creus: Dalí's painting *The Great Masturbator* mimics the shape of one of the cape's strangest rocks, located in Cala Culleró.

Castell Gala Dalí: Dalí's wife Gala is buried at the 14th-century castle he gifted to her, located between Girona and Palafrugell.

Expo Dalí: Small gallery in Cadaqués that showcases the artist's original prints.

 EATING IN CADAQUÉS & BEGUR: OUR PICKS

Compartir: Try the multicourse tasting menu from El Bulli alums for Catalan flavours made to share in Cadaqués. *1-3pm & 8-10pm Tue-Sat* €€€

Havana: Begur's Cuban connection results in authentic Caribbean flavours. *1-3.30pm & 7-10.30pm Thu-Mon, 7-10.30pm Wed* €€

Es Baluard: A family-run Cadaqués restaurant by the sea for traditional Catalan feasts and paella. *1-3.30pm & 8-10pm Wed-Sun, 1-3.30pm Mon* €€€

Lua: This cosy spot in Cadaqués serves Mediterranean and Asian fusion food like curry-covered pork meatballs. *1-3.30pm & 8-10.30pm* €€

ILLIA SHVEDOV/SHUTTERSTOCK

Parc Nacional d'Aigüestortes i Estany de Sant Maurici

and Barcelona. Every corner of these undeveloped mountains is breathtaking in its majesty and inspiring in its beauty. Two pristine national parks provide the scenic high, with innumerable great walking trails and other adventure-activity opportunities.

In the north of Aragón, the 156-sq-km **Parque Nacional de Ordesa y Monte Perdido** (*miteco.gob.es*) encompasses limestone peaks, plunging canyons, thick forests, meadow pastures, rivers, waterfalls and turquoise mountain lakes. The park's **Valle de Ordesa** is one of the most spectacular canyons in Europe, with multiple walking routes including a classic 9km trail (one way).

Over in Catalonia's north, the 405-sq-km **Parc Nacional d'Aigüestortes i Estany de Sant Maurici** (*parcsnaturals. gencat.cat*) is rife with well-marked trails, welcoming *refugis* (huts) and impressive scenery at every turn. With over 200 lakes, overlooked by 3000m-high mountain peaks, the beauty of this glacier-carved realm feels downright cinematic. A standout hike (15.5km) is crossing the park in one day from Espot to Boí, connecting the Estany Llong and Estany d'Amitges routes through the **Portarró d'Espot** (2423m) pass. This area and its surrounds are also home to some of Spain's most popular ski slopes.

 EATING IN ZARAGOZA: OUR PICKS

La Clandestina: Stylish bistro known for its brunch (with *cava*), tasty vegetarian creations and great cheesecake. *hours vary* €€

Restaurante Palomeque: Rich, original Spanish dishes in a cosy dining room or streetside. *11am–midnight Mon–Fri, noon–6pm Sat* €€€

Bodegas Almau: All manner of tapas (anchovies a speciality), and hundreds of wine bottles at a 150-year-old bar. *11am–4pm & 7pm–midnight* €

Taberna Doña Casta: Join the crowds for tasty croquettes and *huevos rotos* (fried eggs with potatoes). *7pm–1am Tue, noon–4.30pm & 7pm–1am Wed–Sun* €

Northern Spain

DRAMATIC SCENERY | CULTURE-PACKED CITIES | GASTRONOMY

Often lyrically talked about as 'Green Spain', the northern stretch of the country feels a world away, with its rugged cliffs, verdant countryside, stone-built villages and wild surf beaches fronting the Bay of Biscay or the wide-open Atlantic. Each region has its own distinctive identity and, in most cases, language, and the culture-rich main cities are as enthralling as the quiet hills.

In the Basque Country, cows and sheep graze in valleys between lofty mountains, rocky coves are battered by furious Atlantic swells, while the cities buzz with art, gastronomy and nightlife. Many Basque people see their identity as strongly tied to the region they call Euskadi (País Vasco in Spanish), which officially includes the provinces of Vizcaya (and its capital Bilbao), Gipuzkoa (and its capital Donostia-San Sebastián) and Álava (and its capital Vitoria-Gasteiz). However, many Basques consider Euskal Herria ('the land of Basque speakers') to more broadly include Navarra and three provinces in southern France.

To the west, the autonomous region of Cantabria and the Principality of Asturias stretch just a little over 300km along the Bay of Biscay, yet encompass a dramatically beautiful world of Atlantic-whipped shores giving way to the snowcapped, adventure-laced Picos de Europa mountains. Galicia, Spain's northwest

☑ TOP TIP

Across the region, many shops (and some tourism activities) close for lunch during the 'siesta hours' (between about 2.30pm and 5pm). For budget-conscious dining, take advantage of *menús del día* (rarely served in evenings). Summer can be busy along Spain's northern coast; beaches are less packed in spring and autumn.

 GETTING AROUND

The north is well connected by air. Major towns have good bus and train connections; the narrow-gauge Renfe Cercanías Ancho Métrico *(renfe.com)* rattles across the north. For more remote destinations, hire a car or plan ahead to align with limited public transport services.

Many travellers explore this region on foot, taking advantage of local trails including the Camino del Norte variant of the Camino de Santiago. The main cities have enjoyably walkable old towns.

NORTHERN SPAIN

corner, combines the pilgrim magnet of Santiago de Compostela with a dramatic, wave-battered coastline.

Bilbao

Once defined by its steelworks and shipbuilding industries, Bilbao has seen a remarkable journey of regeneration since the 1990s. The staggering architecture, venerable dining scene, fascinating museums and endlessly creative cultural arena make Bilbao the most exciting urban centre in the Basque Country.

Arty Bilbao

The gleaming, titanium-clad **Museo Guggenheim Bilbao** (*guggenheim-bilbao.eus; adult/child €18/free*), on the banks of the Ría del Nervión, is the city's most striking building. Filled with pieces by some of the world's best contemporary artists, this extraordinary Frank Gehry–designed landmark is reason alone to visit Bilbao. Start your visit in the central atrium, a light-filled space in which the interior architecture can be admired. From here, three floors of galleries emerge, linked by staircases, catwalks and lifts. Check ahead for what's currently on show and any thrilling temporary exhibitions.

 EATING IN BILBAO: OUR PICKS

La Viña del Ensanche: Mouthwatering morsels include ham, seared mackerel and crispy asparagus tempura. *10am-10.30pm Tue-Fri, from 1pm Sat* €

El Globo: Outstanding *pintxos* (labelled in English) that showcase the great bounty of the Basque countryside. *hours vary* €

Gure Toki: Many consider this Bilbao's best *pintxos*. Try mini pastry parcels filled with stir-fried veg and prawns. *10am-11pm Thu-Tue* €

Mina Restaurante: Serious creativity is on the tasting menu at this riverside restaurant, which some critics call Bilbao's best. *2-3pm & 9-10pm Wed-Sun* €€€

Exterior works to seek out include Louise Bourgeois' spider-like *Maman* and Anish Kapoor's *Tall Tree & the Eye,* both by the river; and Jeff Koons' *Puppy,* a 12m-tall Highland terrier made up of thousands of flowers.

But Bilbao's art scene extends beyond the Guggenheim. Don't miss the **Museo de Bellas Artes** (*bilbaomuseoa.eus; free),* which houses works by Murillo, El Greco and Goya. For a glimpse into the city's contemporary art scene, pop into riverside gallery **Uribitarte40** (*bilbaoarte.eus),* avant-garde Basque-focused **Sala Rekalde** (*salarekalde.bizkaia.net*) and **Azkuna Zentroa** (the Alhóndiga), a former wine-storage warehouse turned cultural centre (*azkunazentroa.eus*).

Donostia-San Sebastián

Officially named in both Basque (Donostia) and Spanish (San Sebastián), Donostia-San Sebastián is a city that celebrates the art of eating. Just as good as the food is San Sebastián's glamorous beachside setting. Little wonder, then, that over-tourism is a growing concern for locals. In 2023, mayor Eneko Goia announced a ban on the construction of new hotels to combat high visitor numbers.

Beach life

The crescent-shaped **Playa de la Concha** (and its westerly extension **Playa de Ondarreta**) is largely sheltered from Atlantic swells. Swim out to floating diving platforms or join in a volleyball match on the sand. At the eastern end of the beach, there are accessible hot showers, changing rooms and lockers and an accessible ramp down to the sand. From June to September, a free assisted bathing service is available.

Opposite Playa de la Concha is **Isla de Santa Clara**. In summer, **Motoras de la Isla** (*motorasdelaisla.com; €5)* runs boat trips to the island from the fishing port. You can also paddle to Santa Clara by SUP or kayak; rent them at **Club Deportivo Fortuna** (*cdfortunake.com; from €13 per hr).*

Fronting the Gros district, **Playa de la Zurriola** is the city's other beachy jewel, known for its surf waves (often beginner-friendly) and buzzing local scene. Don't miss **Mundaka**,

PAMPLONA

The Navarran capital of Pamplona (Iruña in Basque) combines a rich history and well-preserved old town with a youthful vibe and buzzing bar scene. It's easy to get a sense of Pamplona's past by wandering the cobbled streets, following the path of pilgrims walking the Camino de Santiago. At **Cafe Iruña,** you might expect former regular Ernest Hemingway to swing through the doors at any moment. But far from being caught up in the events of bygone years, Pamplona is a city that feels alive. Its most famous festivity is the raucous bull-running festival of **San Fermín**; it's important to note that the running of the bulls itself can be bloody and animal rights activists condemn its cruelty. There is a growing anti-bullfighting movement in many parts of Spain.

 EATING IN DONOSTIA-SAN SEBASTIÁN: PINTXOS & MICHELIN STARS

Bar Borda Berri: Perennially popular, old-school *pintxo* bar that lives up to the hype. *12.30-3.30pm Wed-Sat & 7.30-10.30pm Tue-Fri* €	**Paco Bueno:** This no-frills bar is the place to go for piping-hot battered prawns; order them at the counter. *11am-3pm* €	**La Viña:** Try the famous baked cheesecake, prepared daily and left to stand on shelves by the bar. *10.30am-4pm & 7-11pm Tue-Sun* €	**Ganbara:** This *pintxo* bar is highly regarded for its delectable plates and snacks; good wine list, too. *12.30-3.30pm & 7-11pm Tue-Sat* €
Txepetxa: Anchovies with various accompaniments are the house speciality at this traditional local bar. *noon-3pm & 7-11pm Tue-Sat* €	**Arzak:** Chefs draw on thousands of ingredients to create new dishes in 'the lab' at one of the world's best restaurants. *1.15-3.15pm & 8.45-10.30pm Tue-Sat* €€€	**Akelañe:** Three-Michelin-starred restaurant serving Basque nouvelle cuisine; located in the suburb of Igueldo. *1-2.30pm & 8.30-9.30pm Tue-Sat* €€€	**Martín Berasategui:** Chef Martín Berasategui takes a scientific approach at this triple-starred temple to food. *1-2.15pm Wed-Sun, 8.30-9.30pm Thu-Sat* €€€

100km west en route to Bilbao and a big name in the surf world due to its famous left-hand barrel; rent gear or book a lesson with **Mundaka Surf Shop** *(mundakasurfshop.com; rental from €10).*

Santillana del Mar

Just inland from the Bay of Biscay on Cantabria's western coast, Santillana del Mar is one of Spain's loveliest towns. Even high-season crowds seem to do little to diminish the charm of its cobbled lanes and plazas or its palaces and mansions built with wealth from South America.

Stepping into the past

Spain's most important prehistoric site, just outside Santillana del Mar, was discovered by an amateur archaeologist and his eight-year-old daughter in 1879. Magnificent **Altamira** *(cultura.gob.es; adult/child €3/free; closed Mon)* stands as a testament to the fact that humankind (extremely artistic humans at that) have called this area home for at least 35,500 years. The wonderfully executed animals (mostly created around 18,500 years ago) continue to thrill modern viewers with their artistic beauty as they gallop – sometimes larger than life-size – across the walls. Bison are curved cleverly across the rippled ceiling of the cave so that their muscles and contours are often revealed almost in three dimensions. It's unfortunate (if understandable) that the originals are under protection – viewed only occasionally by experts – but the incredibly realistic and interactive museum mock-up of the cave complex offers an unexpectedly fascinating experience.

Picos de Europa

Compact but dramatically varied, the 674-sq-km **Parque Nacional Picos de Europa** *(parquenacionalpicoseuropa.es)* is one of the favourite haunts for Spanish mountain enthusiasts. The park's three 2000m limestone massifs straddle the provinces of Cantabria, Asturias and Castilla y León. The pretty hill town of **Potes**, in the Cantabrian foothills of the Picos, and **Cangas de Onís** on the Asturian side make ideal bases.

Hiking the Picos

There are over 40 well-marked hiking routes across the Picos suited to all levels of energy, fitness and enthusiasm. Be prepared for squalls and carry waterproofs, warm gear, sunblock and a hat. Busy even on a winter's weekend, the **Ruta del Cares** is so popular it's often referred to as 'Spain's favourite hike'. Rich in flora and fauna and with fine mountain views, the 11km (one-way) route between **Poncebos** in Asturias and **Caín** in Castilla y León is an adventure, threading along ledges, passing through tunnels and crossing bridges in a gorge high above the Río Cares. The track is generally hiked from north to south.

The 753m-long **Teleférico de Fuente Dé** *(telefericodefuentede.com; adult/child from €13/6)* has been carrying visitors from **Fuente Dé** village (near Potes) to the top of the Picos

EATING PINTXOS

Grazing on *pintxos* (Basque tapas) is the best way to sample San Sebastián's famously good food. The city's best-known *pintxo* bars are in the Parte Vieja, along Calle 31 de Agosto and near Plaza de la Constitución. Inside the bars, the counters are piled high with small plates of *pintxos*, such as prawn or salmon mousse on a sliver of bread, skewers of squid or octopus, quail eggs, mushrooms and foie gras. Most bars also offer made-to-order hot *pintxos*, which are listed on a board behind the bar. Order your *pintxos* from the bartender and eat them wherever there's space (often standing up). Locals tend to have just one *pintxo* per bar before moving on to the next. Many bars are known for their house speciality.

Altamira museum, Santillana del Mar

JAMES JACKMAN/LONELY PLANET

for more than 50 years. Weather permitting, you can hike down from an altitude of 1853m. The ride up to the cafe on the summit takes just four minutes but you should allow three to four hours for the 15km hike back down the slopes. If you opt to avoid the full walk back down, there are several (flatter) routes crisscrossing the higher peaks.

Santiago de Compostela

The destination of half a million people who follow the Camino de Santiago pilgrim trails every year, Santiago de Compostela is one of Spain's most beautiful cities and arguably the one where the aura of past centuries lives on strongest. It is also a thriving modern regional capital, with one of Spain's top universities.

Marvel at Santiago's cathedral

Entering magnificent **Praza do Obradoiro** for the first time, you'll stop dead in your tracks, just as many thousands of pilgrims do every year, eyes magnetised by the soaring Churrigueresque facade of the **Catedral de Santiago de Compostela** *(catedraldesantiago.es),* believed to house the tomb of Santiago (St James) the Apostle. Today's cathedral is one of Europe's architectural and historical highlights, and features a mix of an original Romanesque structure, constructed between 1075 and 1211, and later Gothic and baroque flourishes.

Inside, the **Altar Mayor** (High Altar) is a fantastically elaborate Churrigueresque confection with a statue of Santiago at its centre. The ambulatory (walkway) round behind the Altar Mayor passes the inside of the **Puerta Santa** (Holy Door), which opens only in holy years, and brings you round to a flight of steps descending to a view of the large 19th-century silver casket that contains, we're assured, Santiago's remains. Re-emerging, you can climb stairs up behind the Santiago statue, embrace him and make a wish.

CATHEDRAL TIPS

At 7am, the Santiago cathedral is practically empty, even in peak summer months.

Entry to the Pórtico de la Gloria, Cubiertas (roof) and Museo Catedral is by ticket. Advance bookings, at least two weeks ahead for July and August, are essential for the first two.

Guided night tours (sometimes in English) are a treat. You'll enjoy stunning views from the Tribune, an upper-level balcony. Tickets *(€25)* go on sale 15 days ahead.

The popular **rooftop tour** *(adult/child €15/12)* provides a close-up look at the towers and their decorative adornments, plus tremendous city views. Be ready to climb over 150 steps.

The permanent collection of the **Museo Catedral** *(adult/child €7/free)* contains a sizeable section of Maestro Mateo's original carved-stone choir.

Pórtico de la Gloria, Catedral de Santiago de Compostela (p1061)

TOLOBALAGUER.COM/SHUTTERSTOCK

The cathedral's artistic high point, at the west end of the nave, the **Pórtico de la Gloria** features 200 Romanesque sculptures by Maestro Mateo, who was given charge of the cathedral-building programme in the late 12th century.

Prazas, museums and markets

At the northern end of Praza do Obradoiro, the **Hostal dos Reis Católicos** *(paradores.es)* was built in the 16th century as a pilgrim hostel by order of the Reyes Católicos. Today it's a *parador* (luxurious state-owned hotel), open for self-guided tours.

Opposite the cathedral, the elegant 18th-century **Pazo de Raxoi** is now Santiago's city hall. Head a few steps north to **Praza das Praterías** (Silversmiths' Square), centred on the 1825 **Fuente de los Caballos** and the excellent **Museo das Peregrinacións** *(museoperegrinacions.xunta.gal; free)*, which is closed on Mondays.

A bustling hub of Santiago life, the **Mercado de Abastos** *(closed Sun)* comprises 300-odd stalls piled high with fresh produce from Galicia's farms and coasts. Popular bars and restaurants line the street outside; inside, **Nave 5 Abastos** (Aisle 5) is set with long tables where you can sit down for well-priced meals cooked up in adjacent stalls.

 EATING IN SANTIAGO DE COMPOSTELA: OUR PICKS

O Gato Negro: Old-school tavern (since 1922) with market-fresh seafood, empanadas and more. Be ready to eat standing. *12.30-3pm & 7.30-11pm Tue-Sat* €€

Café-Jardin Costa Vella: The garden cafe is a delightful breakfast spot. Also does light local-produce tapas, cakes and wines. *8am-12.30pm & 4.30-10.30pm* €

A Moa: Great mix of Galician and worldly fare in street-level wine bar, stone-walled restaurant and verdant garden. *1.30-3.45pm & 9-11pm Tue-Sat, 1.30-3.45pm Sun* €€

Abastos 2.0: Seafood dishes at marketside outdoor tables; daily-changing €50 *menú* at the indoor 'Barra' (reservations required). *noon-3.30pm & 8-11pm Mon-Sat* €€€

Cabo Fisterra & Around

Once believed by Europeans to be the western limit of the world, hilly, heather-clad Cabo Fisterra (Cape Finisterre) extends into the Atlantic 3km south of the fishing port Fisterra on Galicia's dramatic Costa da Morte. The cape is the final destination for particularly enthusiastic Camino de Santiago pilgrims who push on for an extra 89km from Santiago de Compostela – and for those who walk the Camiño dos Faros along the Costa da Morte.

End-of-the-world lighthouse

Despite the crowds, **Cabo Fisterra** remains a wonderfully panoramic and atmospheric spot, topped by a squat 19th-century lighthouse, the **Faro de Fisterra**. Some who reach it on foot follow a tradition of burning worn-out old boots and socks on the rocks just below the lighthouse. The easiest and quickest way to walk from Fisterra to Cabo Fisterra is simply to head 3km along the AC445 road to the lighthouse, with the panoramas expanding as you go. Other, even more scenic paths lead here too, including over the top of **Monte do Facho** (242m), the promontory's highest point.

Walking the Camiño dos Faros

You can definitely enjoy the Costa da Morte pottering around by car, bicycle or motorbike, but you'll get the most intimate connection with its diverse scenes and moods by exploring on foot. A superb, often challenging, long-distance path, the **Camiño dos Faros** (*Lighthouse Way; caminodosfaros.com*) traces the whole coastline from Malpica de Bergantiños to Cabo Fisterra. Its eight stages are marked only in the Malpica-to-Fisterra direction (with small green arrows and paint blobs). Arguably most spectacular are Stage 7 (Muxía to Praia de Nemiña, 25km) and Stage 8 (Praia de Nemiña to Cabo Fisterra, 27km). Some people walk the whole trail in one trip; others do day walks. Expect sun, wind and rain: beware of fog rolling rapidly in, and avoid precipitous cliffs on gusty days.

NORTHERN WINES

Best known among characterful Galician wines are the fruity *albariño* whites from the Rías Baixas DO. Many good reds come from the native *mencía* grape, and in recent years winemakers have revived Galician grapes including *godello* (whites), *brancellao* and *merenzao* (reds). Produced using Hondarrabi Zuri grapes, Basque *txakoli* is a fresh, crisp, dry and slightly sparkling white wine that goes well with seafood or *pintxos* on sunny days. Wine aficionados the world over know the wines of La Rioja, where vines have been cultivated since Roman times. Cantabria, Asturias and the Basque Country are famous for their ciders, poured from up high for maximum fizz. Wineries across the north are open for tours and tastings; it's best to book. The *vendimia* (grape harvest) starts in August.

 EATING ON THE COSTA DA MORTE: OUR PICKS

O Pirata, Fisterra: The freshest of fish and seafood, traditionally prepared, at good prices and overlooking the harbour. *noon-5pm Tue-Sun* €	**Etel & Pan, Fisterra** Friendly cafe doing excellent burgers, *bocadillos* and salads, with plentiful vegetarian options. *noon-3.30pm & 7-10.30pm Fri-Tue* €	**Casa Fontequeiroso, Nemiña** Superb dinners based around traditional Galician recipes at a small rural hotel (p1084). Non-guests should call first. *7-9pm* €€	**Lonxa d'Alvaro, Muxía** Fish *a la brasa* (char-grilled), seafood-stuffed *filloas* (crêpes) and lobster rice are the stars here. *hours vary* €€€

Valencia & Around

OTHERWORLDLY ARCHITECTURE | ELEGANT MARKETS | UPBEAT BEACHES

GETTING AROUND

Most of Valencia's sights are within easy reach of the main plaza and others are a short cycle or tram ride away. Taxis are affordable, costing around €10 from the centre to the beach. Bikes (around €15 per day) are a lovely way to explore the city. **Valenbisi** *(valenbisi. es)* is the city's bike scheme; a weekly ticket costs €13. While many parts of the surrounding Valencia region (including La Albufera) are easy to explore with public transport, hiring a car is useful.

☑ TOP TIP

Want to pack in a lot of sights? The **Valencia Tourist Card** *(€17/24/30 per 24/48/72 hr)* offers unlimited travel, discounts and a glass of wine at El Corte Inglés. Buy it from tourist information offices or access *visitvalencia.com* for 10% off.

With fun beaches, culture-packed cities and a fierce culinary heritage, Spain's east coast has an extraordinary feel-good factor. In recent years, the Valencia region has embraced urban regeneration, forward-thinking events and gorgeous green spaces (often guided by sustainability), attracting a new wave of visitors.

Over 2000 years of history have carved Valencia's warren-like old-town, from the Romans who founded it to the 20th-century architects who flexed their creativity. Ancient ruins have been painstakingly preserved, but the city isn't stuck in the past. Russafa is the creatives' *barrio,* with cool cafes, hidden galleries and brilliant restaurants; the seaside has a fresh feel with lively *chiringuitos* (snack bars). Further south, rewilding projects revive the dunes and ecosystems of La Albufera. Throw in a 9km-long park with bike routes, wildflowers and lemon trees, and it's clear Valencia is snapping at the heels of its Catalan neighbour. Among the city's many festivities, few rival the famous Las Fallas, held amid thundering pyrotechnics each March.

Taste Local Delicacies

Valencia's splendid Central Market

A feast of Valencia-grown produce awaits within the **Mercat Central** *(mercadocentralvalencia.es; closed on Sun),* a Valencian Art Nouveau–style market in the centre of Ciutat Vella. Inside, domed glass ceilings preside over pyramids of olives, fish and veg straight from the fields. A great way to get a taste for its buzzing, still-local atmosphere is by sipping a refreshing *horchata* (typical Valencian sugary cold drink made from tiger nuts) at the bar at **La Huertana**. Don't forget the *fartón,* an iced bun for dunking. **Les Tomates de Javier** sells the best Valencian tomatoes, **Retrogusto** *(retrogustocoffeemates.com)* brews cracking coffee, and **Solaz** sells cheesecake made by the

VALENCIA

0 —— 500 m
0 —— 0.25 miles

Túria Ⓜ

Jardín del Túria

Puente de las Artes

Puente de San José

C de Blanquerías

Pont de la Fusta

Jardines del Real (Los Viveros)

C/Albacraya

C de General Elio

Av Menéndez y Pelai

Puente Ademuz

Paseo de la Pechina

Av de Corona

C de Na Jordana

Plaza de los Fueros

C de Sagunto

C de San Pío V

Paseo de la Ciudadela

C de la Alameda

Playa de la Patacona (5km)

Jardín de las Hespérides

Jardín Botánico

C de Guillem de Castro

C de Corona

BARRIO DEL CARMEN

C de Caballeros

Plaza de la Virgen

Puente del Real

Playa de la Malva-rosa

10 **23**

C del N

Gran Vía Fernando el Católico

C de Quart

C de Murillo

Catedral de Valencia **1**

18

C de San Pío V

Alameda Ⓜ

Pl de la Ciudadela

C de León

C de Azcárraga

16

4 **Mercado Central**

Plaza de la Reina

11

Plaza de Tetuán

Jardín del Túria Ⓜ

3

C de Juan de Austria

Plaza de Juan de Villarrasa

15

CIUTAT VELLA

C de la Paz

Plaza Alfonso el Magnánimo

Puente de las Flores

Àngel Guimerà Ⓜ

C de Guillem Sorolla

C del Hospital

C Linterna

C de San Vicente Mártir

C d'Oriste

C de Salvà

20

C de Colón

C de Sorní

Colón Ⓜ

C de Gabriel Miró

Gran Vía Ramón y Cajal

C de Guillem de Castro

Plaza San Agustín

Plaza del Ayuntamiento

L'EIXAMPLE

See inset (800m)

C de Ángel Guimerà

C de Calixto III

Av Pérez Galdós

Xàtiva Ⓜ

C de Colón

C de Cirilo Amorós

C Martí

C d'Alacant

C Joaquín Costa

C de Dénia

Gran Vía del Marqués del Turia

C Reino de Valencia

Inset

See main map (800m)

Jardín del Túria

Av Baleares

Av de Francia

Av de Menorca

8

7

21

C Pelayo

C Bailén

Estación del Norte

2 **6**

Ciutat de les Arts i les Ciències

Puente de l'Assut d'Or

5

Túria

0 —— 500 m

Ⓜ **Bailén**

C de Cádiz

C de Dénia

14

13

19

Av Reino de Valencia

C del Pintor Salvador Abril

C Dr Sarmí

C General Urrutia

RUSSAFA

Jesús Ⓜ

C de San Vicente Mártir

C de Puerto Rico

12

C Literato Azorín

C Sueca

C Cuba

17

C Centelles

Av Peris y Valero

Estación Joaquín Sorolla

22

C de San Vicente Mártir

Parque Central

Av Dr Waksman

Av Ausiàs March

Ⓜ **Patraix**

9

Mirador El Pujol (14km);
La Devesa (17km);
Bon Aire (19km);
Paseos en Barca El Perro (19km);
Cova Tallada (109km);
Cala Blanca (114km);
Cala del Portixol (118km);
Cala de Dins (119km)

VALENCIA POTTERY STUDIOS

Valencia has an ancient ceramics heritage, and modern artisans are throwing bold new shapes.

Cuit: Make your own mug in this chic Russafa studio to pick up the next month, or buy one readymade. *(cuit.es)*

Ana Illueca: The un-trendy area near Cabanyal is the unlikely home of this whip-smart pottery studio. *(anaillueca. com)*

Plou Estudi: Geometric shapes with pops of blue and yellow line shelves in this studio and shop.

Escuela Fictile: Japanese pottery has a huge influence on Macarena's pieces, found in her peaceful workshop.

Konlakalma: Katrin makes asymmetric vases and fluid sculptures using coil and slab building techniques. *(konlakalma.com)*

ROB TILLEY/GETTY IMAGES

Ciutat de les Arts i les Ciències

team of Ricard Camarena, owner of the two-Michelin-starred Ricard Camarena restaurant.

Find the Holy Grail
Spot a relic from 100 BCE

An impossible task? Not according to the **Catedral de Valencia** *(catedraldevalencia.es; adult/child €10/6)*. Inside Valencia's Gothic cathedral is an agate goblet dating from 100 BCE. Dazzling gold handles and a base embellished with pearls, rubies and emeralds were added in the medieval era. But at just 17cm tall it's easy to miss: head towards the hushed 14th-century **Capilla del Santo Cáliz**. Constructed between the 13th and 15th centuries, the cathedral features splendid star vaulting and Renaissance-style frescoes above the main altar. A stomp up 207 spiral steps to the **bell tower** *(adult/child €3/free)* is thrilling.

A Wondrous Complex
Dive into Santiago Calatrava's masterpiece

Establishing Valencia as a beacon of contemporary architecture, the astonishing **Ciutat de les Arts i les Ciències** *(cac.es)* is mostly the work of Valencian architect Santiago Calatrava.

 EATING IN RUSSAFA: OUR PICKS

Maipi: Old-school *taberna* serving whatever's fresh from the market, like sweet prawns or artichokes with *jamón*. *1.30–4pm & 8.30–11pm Mon–Fri* €

La Cantina de Ruzafa: Wholesome canteen famous for its stewed bull sandwich topped with fried eggs. *9.30am–5pm Mon–Thu, from 9am Fri* €

Amor Amargo: Cosy Art Nouveau interiors with ambitious cooking – the nine-hour ribs are heavenly. *noon–12.30am Tue–Sun, from 7pm Mon* €€

2 Estaciones: Meticulous food with seasonality at its core. The weekday *menú express* is fantastic value. *1.30–3.30pm & 8.30–10.30pm Wed–Sat* €€€

The architecture is a marvel in itself; a walk through the complex that occupies a vast swathe of the old Túria riverbed won't cost you a penny.

Calatrava balanced mighty, organic architecture by using ceramic mosaic tiles called *trencadís*. They're perhaps most striking on **Palau de les Arts**, an ultramodern performing-arts complex with four auditoriums. Tours run several times daily *(adult/child €18/14)*. To the south, the unblinking eye of the **Hemisfèric** houses an IMAX cinema with a 900-sq-metre screen. Across an expanse of water, **Museu de les Ciències** *(adult/child €9.40/7.20)* stretches out like a giant whale skeleton, housing an interactive science museum. Next up, resembling a huge purple mussel, the **CaixaForum** stages interesting exhibitions on diverse themes.

Bike to the Beach
Explore Valencia's loveliest gardens

Valencia's best park is found in an old riverbed that was diverted due to flooding. Snaking through the city for over 9km, **Jardín del Túria** is a delight to explore by bike. Inaugurated in 1986, today the riverbed is a haven of baobab and palm trees frequented by chattering parakeets and songbirds. On a leisurely route of around 12km (one way), it's possible to cycle all the way to pretty **Playa de la Patacona**, with its seafront restaurants and *chiringuitos*. Pick up wheels at **Valencia Bikes** *(valenciabikes.com; €15 per day)*, close to the Túria metro.

Boating & Bird-Spotting
Cruise La Albufera's waters

Just 15km south of Valencia proper, glorious La Albufera is the birthplace of paella, with much of the area protected by the peaceful **Parque Natural de la Albufera**. People have fished the freshwater lake here since prehistoric times, and the rice paddies have been around since at least the 15th century. This rice is used in the best paellas – try one at **Bon Aire** *(restaurantebonaire.com)* in **El Palmar**. A handful of boat trips join the local fisherfolk who use flat-bottomed boats and nets to harvest fish and eels from the shallow waters. Jaime, a La Albufera local, offers insightful trips with **Paseos en Barca El Pero** *(paseosenbarcaelpero.es; from €70)*. Sunsets are spectacular: book Jaime's sunset cruise or head to **Mirador El Pujol**.

SWIMMING SPOTS BEYOND VALENCIA

Around Xàbia: Cala del Portixol is famed as the most beautiful on the coastline. Cala Blanca and Cala de Dins are fairy-tale coves, accessible only by foot.

Dénia: Dénia's coastline has lots of little surprises. Swim in shimmering waters outside Cova Tallada, an artificial cave best accessed by kayak.

Fuente de los Baños: In the mountains around Montanejos, these emerald pools fed by hot springs are a dreamy wild-swimming spot.

Altea: Hilltop, whitewashed Altea, set between two protected natural parks, has lofty viewpoints, pebble beaches and turquoise waters.

La Devesa: Part of La Albufera's natural regeneration, La Devesa is accessed only by foot along a path bordered by rosemary and pines.

 EATING IN CIUTAT VELLA: OUR PICKS

Ostras Pedrín: Join a cool crowd out to get tipsy on *cava* and feast on a sea of oysters. *11am-midnight Mon-Sat, to 4pm Sun* €

La Samorra: Traditional tapas in a tiled *taberna*. Don't miss the *figatells* (meatballs). *7.30pm-midnight Wed-Sat, 12.30-5pm Thu-Sat, noon-5pm Sun* €€

Central Bar: Informal tapas bar among the fruit stalls of Mercat Central, with unbeatable cheesecake. *9am-3pm Mon-Thu, to 3.30pm Fri & Sat* €€

Forastera Restaurant: Dreamy dinner-date spot with a market-fresh tasting menu and wines from small artisanal producers. *hours vary Thu-Mon* €€€

Balearic Islands

DREAM BEACHES | SOARING MOUNTAINS | CHARMING VILLAGES

☑ TOP TIP

In recent years, Mallorca and the other Balearics have suffered from growing overtourism concerns. Sidestep the summer crowds by visiting in shoulder season or winter. For Easter and summer, book well in advance. The opening hours provided here are for summer. Beyond Palma de Mallorca, many venues reduce hours or close in the off-season.

Etymologists may wrangle over the origins of their name, but there's no disputing the seductive magic of the Balearic Islands, clustered in the western Mediterranean off the east coast of Spain. Each of the four principal islands has its unique cultural identity, with a dialect related to Catalan, and own vibe.

Mallorca lives up to the social-media-worthy images of sun-warmed ochre buildings, scarlet bougainvillea in soulful hill towns and long beaches with aquamarine seas, but is also deeply enhanced by a contemporary outlook and rich culture. For Miró, it was the pure light. For hikers and cyclists, it's the Serra de Tramuntana's limestone spires. Foodies will love the markets and, of course, the chefs – inspired as much by their Mallorcan forebears as by contemporary Mediterranean cuisine. Meanwhile, beyond the built-up resorts, coves and white-sand bays rim the shoreline.

Menorca, the quieter pair to Mallorca, remains largely undeveloped, with brilliant, pristine beaches, megalithic ruins, two fascinating main towns (eastern Anglo-Spanish Maó and western mazelike Ciutadella) and dry stone walls crossing pastures. Ibiza's party-hard spirit draws crowds in summer, who relax on its beaches and hidden coves, and fill its somnolent, sunbaked white villages. Ibiza's part-

GETTING AROUND

Mallorca, Ibiza and Menorca have airports. Ferries (see *ferryhopper.com*) connect Alcúdia (Mallorca) with Ciutadella (Menorca) and Palma (Mallorca) with Ibiza Town; they also run to/from mainland destinations including Barcelona, Dénia and Valencia. Smaller ferries run between Ibiza and Formentera (30 minutes).

Car hire spikes seasonally so book well ahead, or use reliable local buses. Mallorca's **Ferrocarril de Sóller** *(trendesoller.com)* vintage train is a highlight. Well-marked cycling and walking paths crisscross the islands.

BALEARIC ISLANDS

ner (together, they are called the Pityuses or Pine Islands) Formentera, is pure bliss, with astonishing beaches and protected reserves.

Mallorca

History and art in the Mallorcan capital

Palma de Mallorca (universally shortened to Palma) is a stunner. Rising in sand-coloured stone from the broad still waters of the Badia de Palma, the city has been home to Christian Reconquistadors, Moors, Romans and, way back, the Talayotic people. All Palma visits begin best at the magnificent, waterfront **Catedral de Mallorca** *(catedraldemallorca.org; adult/child €10/free),* called 'La Seu'. Although the foundations went up in the 12th century on the site of the central mosque, most of the structure is predominantly Gothic. Continue your history lesson with the **Palau de l'Almudaina** *(patrimon ionacional.es; adult/child €7/4),* an Islamic fort converted into a royal residence in the 13th century, and the Moorish **Banys Àrabs** *(€3.50).*

Built with flair and innovation into the shell of the Renaissance-era seaward fortifications on the southwest side of Palma's old town, contemporary art gallery **Es Baluard** *(esbaluard.org; adult/child €6/free; closed Mon)* is one of the finest on the islands. Art lovers will want to make the pilgrimage to the wonderful hilltop compound and still-standing studios of Catalan artist Joan Miró, the **Fundació Pilar I Joan Miró** *(miromal lorca.com; adult/child €10/free; closed Mon).*

Off-the-beaten-track strands and coves

Mallorca's beaches are legendary. In the northeast, a 10km drive from castle-topped **Artà** through the mountainous

MALLORCA'S VILLAGES

Pollença: Attractive old quarter, historic religious sites, good food and easy beach or mountain access.

Artà & Capdepera: Each has superb medieval architecture overlooked by a walled, hilltop fortress.

Deià: Famous honey-coloured home to artists, writers (visit Casa Robert Graves) and musicians.

Biniaraix & Fornalutx: Walk from Sóller to these stone mountain villages blooming in subtropical flowers.

Banyalbufar: Moorish terraces with vineyards step to the sea.

Caimari & Campanet: Eat like royalty in foothill gateways to the Serra de Tramuntana.

HIKING THE SERRA DE TRAMUNTANA

Hikers come from far and wide for Mallorca's mix of soaring mountain peaks and cove-cracked coastline. You can hike year-round, though the best months are March to May and late September to October. Hiking UNESCO Reserve **Serra de Tramuntana** often involves some aspect of **Ruta de Pedra en Sec** (Dry Stone Route; GR221) – a 140km, 10-day hike between Sant Elm and Pollença. Well-marked and with accommodation at the end of each stage, this is a superb way to experience Mallorca far from the tourist crowds. A couple of favourite portions include the moderate Deià to Sóller hike (10km; four hours) and the famous **Camí de s'Arxiduc** (Path of the Archduke), a 13km circular route from Valldemossa.

woodland of Parc Natural de la Península de Llevant will bring you to wide, sandy **Cala Torta** (sometimes you have to walk down). Small, sheltered bays, **Cala Mitjana** and **Cala Estreta** (the latter is stone) are accessible down a rough track in the mountains. You can walk to them all from **Cala Mesquida** (about an hour to Estreta). Walk further north for **Cala Matzoc**. Often empty, this sandy beach is a timeless vision of Mediterranean coastline.

In the southeast, most beaches are fjord-like indents with sheets of white sand lapped by soft minty-blue waters. Just north of busy **Cales de Mallorca**, a walking trail leads several kilometres through woodland to a series of four pristine coves: **Cala Bota**, **Cala Virgili**, **Cala Pilota**, and just north, the best of the lot: **Cala Magraner**.

On the west coast, a Mallorcan highlight is to walk from a mountain village to its coastal *cala* (cove). Hardly a secret, but divine all the same, is the steep 2.5km (one-way) walk from Deià to **Cala Deià**, with famous restaurant **Ca's Patró March**.

Popular southern beaches include **Platja des Trenc**, **Cala Pi**, **Caló des Moro** and **Cala Mondragó**, but explore further and the aqua waters unfurl. **Platja d'Almunia** and **Platja de Ses Roquetes** are connected by a hiking trail. At **Cala Llombards**, a beach-hut bar, palm-leaf-shaded loungers and a ladder into the sea constitute the extent of human intervention.

Menorca

Menorca's dreamy beaches

Menorca's paper-white sands and jewel-blue waters are some of the Med's best, and authorities have taken measures to preserve their natural beauty. You'll usually need your own wheels to reach them (arrive early!), and then you often park and walk the final 1km to 3km. The loveliest beaches are strung along the south coast. Menorca's less-developed north coast is rugged and rocky, perforated with small, scenic coves.

Along with teeny **Cala Macarelleta**, the pair of exquisite horseshoe bays, **Cala Macarella** and **Cala Turqueta**, 13.5km southwest of Ciutadella, get very busy in summer for their bleach-blonde sands, unbelievably turquoise waters and cliffs cloaked in pines and holm oaks. It's a lovely 2km clifftop walk between the two via **Cala des Talaier** (accessible only on foot). Twin white-sand beaches of Banyuls and Bellavista make up **Platges de Son Saura**, 12km southeast of Ciutadella.

You'll be rewarded for the effort it takes to reach some of the island's quietest and most beautiful beaches, halfway along

EATING & DRINKING IN PALMA DE MALLORCA: OUR PICKS

El Perrito: Santa Catalina quarter's brunch mainstay: bagels, homemade cakes, fresh juices and hearty specials. *8am-4pm Mon-Sat, to 3.30pm Sun €*

La Rosa Vermuteria: Start your evening with a *vermut* (vermouth) and local-inspired tapas at this stylish spot. *noon-midnight €€*

El Camino: Stylish tapas bar: coffered ceilings, mosaic tiles and marble bar for watching your tasty bites prepared. *1-3.45pm & 6-10.45pm Tue-Sat €€*

DINS Santi Taura: Traditional Mallorcan cooking with a twist in this adults-only Michelin-star restaurant. *hours vary Tue-Sat €€€*

Cala Macarelleta, Menorca

HIKING MENORCA

Mystery-shrouded **Camí de Cavalls** (Path of Horses) loops 186km around the entire length of Menorca's coast. Connecting watchtowers, cannons and fortresses, it's believed to have been built in the 13th or 14th century to enable horseback patrols along the coastline and protect the island from sea invasions.

After years spent buried under scrub, the trail has been cleared and turned into a public footpath (GR223). It takes between seven and 10 days to hike, or you can do one of the 20 stages (5km to 14km each; outfitters can drop you off). Accommodation isn't always available at the end of each stage, meaning careful preplanning is required (see *camidecavalls.com*).

the southern coast. From **Sant Tomàs**, take the footpath west via **Platja Binigaus** to sublime **Cala Escorxada**, which has luminous waters, white sands and zero development. Continue west and you'll reach tiny **Cala Fustam**, which is a favourite of naturists. **Cala Mitjana** is most easily reached (1.5km) from **Cala Galdana** resort.

Ibiza & Formentera

Walking World-Heritage Dalt Vila

The heart and soul of the island, **Ibiza Town** (Eivissa) is a vivacious and elegant capital with a UNESCO World Heritage–listed fortified old quarter called **Dalt Vila** *(ibiza.travel)* set against a spectacular natural harbour. Its seven colossal, floodlit 16th-century bastions are visible from across southern Ibiza. Dalt Vila is tranquil and atmospheric, with many of its cobbled lanes accessible only on foot.

Enter via the **Portal de Ses Taules** gateway, just in from **Passeig Marítim** and behind neoclassical market **Mercat Vell**. All lanes lead steeply to **Castell d'Eivissa**, a walled district of historical buildings constructed over a 1000-year period, and **Catedral de Santa Maria de les Neus** on the summit. Sunset is gorgeous. Don't miss the wonderful **Museu d'Art**

EATING IN CIUTADELLA & MAÓ: OUR PICKS

Mercat de Peix: Tapas and *pintxos* bars fill this 1920s fish market, next to Maó's town market in the church cloisters. *11am-11pm Mon-Sat* €

Arjau Mao: Traditional Menorcan dishes and paella centring seafood and lobster, served portside. *1-3.30pm Thu-Mon* €€€

Pinzell: Contemporary remake of Mediterranean classics in Ciutadella. The squid stuffed with walnuts is exquisite. *1-3.30pm & 8-11.30pm Wed-Mon* €€

Pez Limón: Bold and unexpected culinary creations are the hallmark of this cosy Ciutadella tapas bar. *8-10.30pm Mon-Fri, 1-3pm & 8-10.30pm Sat* €€

IBIZA'S TOP CLUBS

Amnesia, Sant Rafel: Ibiza's most influential club, where DJ Alfredo pioneered Balearic Beat. *(amnesia.es)*

Hï Ibiza, Platja d'en Bossa: In 2022 and 2023, *DJ Magazine's* 'world's best club' with marquee DJ residencies. *(hiibiza.com)*

Pacha, Ibiza Town: Ibiza's original mega-club: multilevel dance floor, Funky Room for soul and disco. *(pacha.com)*

Ushuaïa, Platja d'en Bossa: Glitzy pool parties at Ibiza's hottest daytime club. *(theushuaiaexperience.com)*

DC 10, near the airport: Underground vibe and music-savvy crowd. *(dc10ibiza.com)*

Carrer de la Verge, Ibiza Town: Ibiza's main LGBTIQ+ village, with around 20 bars and clubs.

[UNVRS], Sant Rafel: World's largest club (formerly Privilege), regularly hosting thousands of clubbers. *(unvrs.com)*

TOLOBALAGUER.COM/SHUTTERSTOCK

Trucador Peninsula, Formentera

Contemporani d'Eivissa *(eivissa.es/mace; free),* housed in an 18th-century armoury.

Formentera's brilliant beaches

With sugar-white sands and perfectly clear turquoise water, the astonishing beauty of Formentera's pencil-slim **Trucador Peninsula** rivals that of the world's most glorious beaches. Walk or cycle along glittering **Ses Salines** (saltpans) to reach dirt tracks winding through steep sand dunes and emerge on the west side of this narrow sliver at dreamy **Platja Illetes**. On the peninsula's east coast (just a few steps away) is equally gorgeous **Platja Llevant**. The beaches get packed, but they're still an essential Formentera experience. The Trucador Peninsula is part of the **Parc Natural de Ses Salines** *(car/motorcycle €6/4).* Bring water, food and supplies.

The island's entire southern arc is necklaced with sandy alabaster bays lapped by aqua-tinted waters, known collectively as **Platja de Migjorn**. The best bits are at the southeastern end, around **Platja es Arenals**.

EATING & DRINKING IN IBIZA TOWN: OUR PICKS

Can Costa: Reasonably priced grilled meats and paella make this a popular go-to in the Old Port. *1-3.30pm & 8-11pm Mon-Fri* €

La Barra de la Bientirada Ibiza: Hearty Spanish-fusion dishes in central Ibiza Town. Save room for killer cheesecake. *noon-midnight* €€

Bar Es Cafetí: Bar with eclectic decor in Dalt Vila, perfect for a pit stop with cocktails and finger foods. *10am-6pm Mon-Fri, noon-6pm Sat, to 4pm Sun*

Petit Vermut Eivissa: Cheerful vermouth, *apéro* and cocktails with tapas in a casual corner spot in the Old Port area. *4.30pm-late*

Seville

HERITAGE SITES | ARCHITECTURE | DINING

The Andalucian capital and jewel in the southern region's cultural crown, Seville is a luminous, romantic city. Its unique blend of artistic influences (Moorish, Jewish, Christian and Romani) infuses every detail from its magnificent Mudéjar architecture to the sultry notes of the flamenco guitar. This is a city built to explore on foot: a pleasant mesh of narrow cobbled streets and jaunty plazas, invigorated by the debonair nightlife that spills from tapas bars and bodegas.

Once-mighty civilisations, including the Romans, the Moors and the Reyes Católicos of the Spanish empire have left indelible marks on Seville, layered across the urban space. Countless generations of homebred *sevillanos* have treated Seville with reverence. As a result, the city's well-heeled past endures into the present, through impeccably preserved churches, aristocratic palaces, picturesque streets scented with orange blossom, and UNESCO-listed landmarks such as the imposing Gothic cathedral. Seville's fiestas are legendary, from the energetic Feria de Abril to more sombre Semana Santa.

☑ **TOP TIP**

Book tickets for the cathedral or the Real Alcázar as early as possible, but avoid visiting them on the same day (there's too much to take in). Admission is at a set time and can sell out days in advance. The cathedral is often closed for religious events and holidays.

A Royal Spectacle

Palaces, courtyards and gardens of the Real Alcázar

Since the 10th century, Moorish rulers and Spanish monarchs presided over their kingdoms from the exquisitely decorated

 GETTING AROUND

Much of Seville is best explored on foot, with sights clustered close together. For more spread-out attractions, rent bicycles from docking stations (Sevici app) or **Surf the City** (*surfthecity.es),* along with electric scooters.

An electric tram line connects the San Sebastián bus station to the central Plaza Nueva. The main Plaza de Armas bus station serves major destinations across Andalucía. High-speed trains run from Sevilla Santa Justa. Buses link Sevilla Santa Justa train station to central Seville.

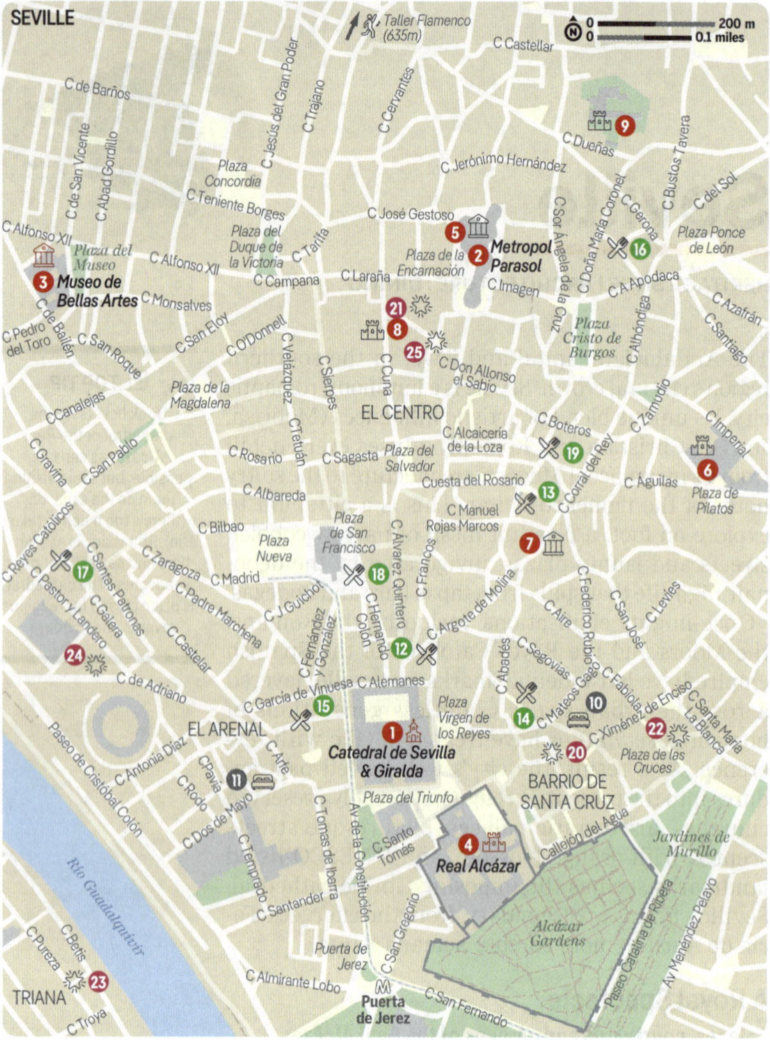

SEVILLE

Taller Flamenco (635m)

C Castellar

0 — 200 m
0 — 0.1 miles

C de Barños

C de San Vicente

C de Jesús del Gran Poder

C Trajano

C Cervantes

C Jerónimo Hernández

C Dueñas **9**

C Bustos Tavera

C del Sol

C Abad Gordillo

Plaza Concordia

C Teniente Borges

C Tarifa

C José Gestoso

C Sor Ángela de la Cruz

C Doña María Coronel

C Gerona

Plaza Ponce de León

3 **Museo de Bellas Artes**

Plaza del Museo

C Alfonso XII

C Alfonso XII

Plaza del Duque de la Victoria

C Campana

C Laraña

Plaza de la Encarnación

5

2 **Metropol Parasol**

C Imagen

C A Apodaca

C Azafrán

C Pedro del Toro

C de Bailén

C San Roque

C Monsalves

C San Eloy

O'Donnell

C Velázquez

C Cuna

21 **8**

25

C Don Alfonso el Sabio

Plaza Cristo de Burgos

C Alhóndiga

C Santiago

C Canalejas

Plaza de la Magdalena

C Sierpes

EL CENTRO

C Alcaicería de la Loza

19 C Boteros

C Corral del Rey

C Zamudio

C Imperial

6

C Gravina

C San Pablo

C Rosario

C Tetuán

C Sagasta

Plaza del Salvador

Cuesta del Rosario

13 C Manuel Rojas Marcos

C Águilas

Plaza de Pilatos

C Reyes Católicos

C Albareda

C Bilbao

Plaza de San Francisco

C Álvarez Quintero

7

C Santas Patronas **17**

C Zaragoza

C Madrid

Plaza Nueva

18

C J Guichot

C Francos

C Argote de Molina

C Aire

C Federico Rubio

C San José

C Levíes

24

C Galera

C Pastor y Landero

C Padre Marchena

C Castelar

C de Adriano

C Hernando Colón

C Fernández y González

12

C Abades

C Segovias

C Mateos Gago

14 **10**

C Fabiola

C Ximénez de Enciso

C Santa María La Blanca

22

EL ARENAL

C García de Vinuesa

C Atemanes

15

Plaza Virgen de los Reyes

Plaza de las Cruces

20

BARRIO DE SANTA CRUZ

C Antonia Díaz

C Pavia

C Dos de Mayo

11

C Arfe

C Tomás de Ibarra

1

Catedral de Sevilla & Giralda

Plaza del Triunfo

Callejón del Agua

Jardines de Murillo

Paseo de Cristóbal Colón

Río Guadalquivir

C Temprado

C Santander

C Santo Tomás

C San Gregorio

4 **Real Alcázar**

Alcázar Gardens

Paseo Catalina de Ribera

Av Menéndez Pelayo

TRIANA

C Betis

C Pureza

23

C Troya

C Almirante Lobo

Puerta de Jerez

C San Fernando

Puerta de Jerez

⭐ **HIGHLIGHTS**
1 Catedral de Sevilla & Giralda
2 Metropol Parasol
3 Museo de Bellas Artes
4 Real Alcázar

🔴 **SIGHTS**
5 Antiquarium
6 Casa de Pilatos

7 Museo del Baile Flamenco
8 Palacio de la Condesa de Lebrija
9 Palacio de Las Dueñas

⚫ **SLEEPING**
10 Casa del Poeta
11 La Banda

🟢 **EATING**
12 Antigua Taberna de Las Escobas
13 Bar Alfalfa
14 Bodega Santa Cruz
15 Casa Morales
16 El Rinconcillo
17 La Brunilda
18 Mamarracha
19 PETRA

🔴 **ENTERTAINMENT**
20 Casa de la Guitarra
21 Casa de la Memoria
22 La Casa del Flamenco
23 Pura Esencia
24 Tablao Flamenco Andalusí
25 Teatro Flamenco Sevilla

Real Alcázar *(alcazarsevilla.org; adult/child €15.50/free)*, tearing down, augmenting and rebuilding sections of the labyrinthine complex.

The finest building overlooking the Patio de la Montería (Hunting Party's Courtyard) is the **Palacio de Don Pedro**. Built for King Pedro I (1350–69) with the help of Moorish Granada's finest artisans, it has an exquisite Mudéjar-style interior. Highlights include the golden-tiled dome ceiling of the Cuarto del Príncipe (Prince's Suite), and the spectacular Salón de Embajadores (Hall of the Ambassadors), originally Pedro I's throne room.

At the heart of this palace is the sublime central courtyard, the **Patio de las Doncellas** (Maidens' Courtyard). The sunken garden at its core, framed by carved arches, plasterwork and tiling, was uncovered by archaeologists in 2004. The Palacio Gótico (Gothic Palace), much remodelled for Carlos I in the 16th century, is now known as the **Salones de Carlos V**. The **Jardines de los Reales Alcázares** (Royal Alcazar Gardens) offer shaded paths between mazes of myrtle, fish-filled ponds and lofty palm trees.

Seville's Monumental Gothic Treasure

Tour the cathedral

When Castilian king Fernando III captured Seville from the Almohad dynasty in 1248, he ordered that the 12th-century great mosque be converted into a church. Flying buttresses, gargoyles and lavish ornamentation decorate the exterior of the world's largest Gothic building, Seville's **cathedral** *(cated raldesevilla.es; adult/child €13/free),* officially known as the Catedral de Santa María de la Sede.

The visitor entrance is through the horseshoe arched door-way, **Puerta del Lagarto**. On your left, a gentle ramp swirls up through the **Giralda**, a former minaret repurposed as the cathedral's bell tower, with expansive views over Seville. The often-closed **Capilla Real** contains royal tombs, including the remains of Fernando III in a silver urn. Enter the series of rooms to your left to admire major art treasures, including

SEMANA SANTA IN SEVILLE

Seville puts on one of Spain's most elaborate manifestations of Christian Holy Week. From Palm Sunday to Easter Sunday, hooded *nazarenos* (penitents) carry huge *pasos* (floats holding revered statues, such as La Macarena) through the streets in ghostly solemnity. Parades lead from their home churches to the cathedral, often in the early evening. The *nazarenos* are members of the city's 50 *hermandades* or *cofradías* (religious brotherhoods, some of which include women), dressed in white robes with pointed conical hoods. The highlight of Semana Santa is La Madrugá in the early hours of Good Friday, when several of the city's most venerated statues make their appearances.

 EATING IN SEVILLE: OUR PICKS

Casa Morales: Family-run tapas bar notable for its sherry, *albóndigas* (meatballs) and croquettes. *noon-4pm & 8pm-midnight Mon-Sat, noon-4pm Sun* €€

Bodega Santa Cruz: The slow-cooked *montadito de pringá* (tender meats and sausage served on crusty bread) is a highlight. *8am-midnight* €

Antigua Taberna de Las Escobas: Seville's oldest tavern, around since 1386. Luminaries from Cervantes to Lord Byron have dined here. *noon-11pm* €€

La Brunilda: Enter through blue doors to a modern interior with inventive tapas, including an excellent mushroom risotto. *1.30-4.30pm & 8.30-11.30pm* €€€

Mamarracha: Trendy tapas place, with eclectic fare like *alcachofa a la brasa* (grilled artichokes). *1-5pm & 8pm-midnight Mon-Thu, 1pm-12.30am Fri-Sun* €€€

Bar Alfalfa: Snug bar with tasty tapas, including *salmorejo* (cold, tomato-based soup), overlooked by hundreds of dusty bottles. *9am-midnight* €€

El Rinconcillo: Purveyors of libations and tapas since 1670. Tabs are chalked onto the wood in front of you at the end. *1-5.30pm & 8pm-midnight Wed-Mon* €€€

PETRA: Inventive takes on popular tapas (meat, vegetarian and vegan). The gourmet experience isn't priced as such. *12.30-11.30pm Mon-Sat* €€

a Goya in the Sacristía de los Cálices, a Zurbarán in the Sacristía Mayor, and Murillo's shining *La inmaculada* in the Sala Capitular.

Hugging the exterior wall, the four figures carrying an ornately carved catafalque mark the **Tomb of Columbus**. It contains the famed voyager's remains, something which DNA testing in 2006 upheld as fact.

The Palaces of Barrio de Santa Cruz
Sumptuous mansions in the former Jewish quarter

The **Palacio de la Condesa de Lebrija** *(palaciodelebrija. com; adult/child €14/6)* condenses each of Seville's golden ages beneath one roof. Built in the Mudéjar-Renaissance style, its central courtyards are flanked by intricate plasterwork arches, *azulejos* and wide stairways. Head northeast to the bougainvillea-covered 15th-century **Palacio de las Dueñas** *(lasduenas.es; adult/child €14/10)*, residence of the late Duchess of Alba. It was also the birthplace of poet Antonio Machado. Further south lies the **Casa de Pilatos** *(fundacionmedinaceli. org; adult/child €12/free)*, with an exquisite *artesonado* (ceiling of interlaced beams).

From Ancient to Modern at Las Setas
Admire Museo Antiquarium and Metropol Parasol

Some of the best views of the cathedral come from atop one of Seville's more modern constructs. Officially called the **Metropol Parasol** *(setasdesevilla.com; adult/child €16/free)*, Las Setas (giant wooden mushrooms) straddle the broad Plaza de la Encarnación. Equally fascinating is the **Antiquarium** *(sevilla.org; adult/child €2/free; closed Mon)* beneath Las Setas: the ruins of Colonia Julia Romula Hispalis, the Roman iteration of Seville, date to around 40 CE.

Treasures of the Museo de Bellas Artes
Artistic masterpieces in a convent

The delightful mannerist palace housing Seville's **Museo de Bellas Artes** *(museosdeandalucia.es; EU/non-EU citizen free/€1.50)* exhibits 15th- to 20th-century artworks, but it's the Golden Age masterpieces that make this one of Spain's top art museums. Sala V contains the most impressive paintings, including Murillo's *Inmaculada concepción*. Highlights elsewhere include Zurbarán's *Cristo crucificado* (Sala VI and another in Sala X), El Greco's portrait of his son (Sala II), Velázquez' *Cabeza de apóstol* (Sala IV) and Goya's *Don José Duaso* (Sala XI).

Beyond Seville

Architectural wonders in some of Spain's oldest cities, evocative hill villages, glorious protected parks and a breathtaking coastline await around Andalucía.

With its wild Atlantic coastline and beloved Mediterranean shores, Andalucía evokes many of Spain's greatest calling cards. Much of this sunny, soulful region has passed through Phoenician, Greek, Carthaginian, Roman and Visigothic hands. It also tells the subsequent Al-Andalus story of the melding of three cultures – Moorish, Christian and Jewish – traceable in the ancient neighbourhoods of Córdoba, Granada, Cádiz and even Málaga, as well as the regional capital Seville. The buzzy coast and culture-packed cities give way to a mountainous interior filled with olive groves and pine forests, while sprawling nature reserves dot the countryside. Wander enchanting *pueblos blancos* (white towns) in the evening golden light, or glimpse Granada's Alhambra outlined against the snow-tipped Sierra Nevada, and you'll witness time standing still.

Parque Nacional de Doñana

TIME FROM SEVILLE (EL ROCÍO): 1HR

Lynx-spotting and exceptional birdwatching

The World Heritage–listed **Parque Nacional de Doñana** *(mite co.gob.es),* spread around the Río Guadalquivir delta, forms one of Europe's most extensive wetland areas, which is a haven for around 10,000 flamingos and over 500,000 other wintering birds. At this 601-sq-km park southeast of Huelva, together with the bordering Parque Natural de Doñana (which is under less strict protection), endangered creatures such as the Iberian lynx and Spanish imperial eagle have bounced back from the brink under close conservation. Visits to the national park are via accredited agency only, usually by 4WD; Seville-based **Doñana Wings** *(donanawings.com)* and **Naturanda** *(naturanda. com)* are recommended, as are local operators **Doñana Nature** *(donana-nature.com),* **Discovering Doñana** *(discovering donana.com)* and **Doñana Reservas** *(donanareservas.com).* If you're lucky, you have a good chance of spotting a lynx and her cubs in the mid-to late-summer months.

The main national park hub is the evocative Huelva province village of **El Rocío**, also known as the destination for Spain's greatest pilgrimage, the **Romería del Rocío** in May/

Places

GETTING AROUND

Córdoba, Málaga, Cádiz and Granada have efficient rail links *(renfe.com),* including with Seville. The best way to enjoy them is on foot; apart from Granada (which has some hilly neighbourhoods), they're largely flat, compact cities. Málaga and Cádiz are ideal for cycling, too, with plenty of bike-hire options. Further afield, it's best to hire a car. Buses reach most destinations, with companies such as **Alsa** *(alsa.es),* but services are limited and often reduced on weekends.

June. It's also possible to access Doñana from Sanlúcar de Barrameda in neighbouring Cádiz province.

Córdoba

TIME FROM SEVILLE: **50MIN**

A wonder of Islamic architecture

Jewel of the Moorish Caliphate when it was the Grand Mosque of Córdoba, and later one of Spain's great cathedrals, the **Mezquita** *(mezquita-catedraldecordoba.es; adult/child €13/ free)* is one of the world's most magnificent buildings. Free to access, the **Patio de los Naranjos** is the courtyard entrance to the Mezquita filled with palms, orange trees and ornate fountains, and overlooked by the 54m-high **Torre Campanario** (Bell Tower), which requires a separate ticket. Inside the Mezquita, a forest of arches stacks into the distance. It would have been a truly vast mosque upon its final enlargement in 994. The arches, resting on 856 columns (there were originally 1293), are striped strawberries-and-cream, mimicking the date palms of northern Africa.

At the southern wall is the building's pinnacle of Islamic-era decoration, the *maksura* (royal prayer enclosure). The geometric decoration of the arches and skylit domes are at their most lavish here. On the back wall is the *mihrab,* the decorative prayer niche facing Mecca, added along with the *maksura* during the extensions ordered by Al-Hakim II in the 960s. The gold mosaic cubes around its portal were created by a master sculptor from Byzantium. The construction of the current **Capilla Mayor** (main altar) and *coro* (choir) in the heart of the Mezquita began during the reign of Carlos I (1516–56) and was completed in 1766, with plateresque, Gothic, baroque and Renaissance motifs all at play.

Córdoba's other historical treasures include atmospheric **La Judería** (the Jewish quarter), the 14th-century **Alcázar de los Reyes Cristianos** *(cultura.cordoba.es; adult/child €7/free; closed Mon)* palace-fortress and the UNESCO-listed ruins of **Medina Azahara** *(museosdeandalucia.es; EU/non-EU citizen free/€1.50),* the palace-city just outside town built in the 10th century on the orders of Abd ar-Rahman III.

Cádiz

TIME FROM SEVILLE: **1¾HR**

Exploring Cádiz' buzzing *barrios*

Founded as Gadir by the Phoenicians in 1100 BCE, sultry Cádiz is Europe's oldest continuously inhabited settlement.

BLOOMING WONDERS

Among Córdoba's loveliest features are its famous flower-filled patios. In summer, Córdoba becomes a furnace, hence the millennia-old Roman and Moorish tradition of building houses with inner courtyards to facilitate airflow. Some courtyards are open to the public year-round, including the grand **Palacio de Viana** *(palaciodeviana.com);* others only during the **Fiesta de los Patios de Córdoba** (the first two weeks in May). Participating courtyard owners welcome visitors into their inner sanctums, where you can admire hanging plant pots, creeper-clad walls, fountains, quirky patio furnishings and exuberant flower arrangements. A great place to get started is the San Basilio (aka Alcázar Viejo) neighbourhood to the north and west of the Alcázar.

Runs great cooking classes and food tours too.

 EATING & DRINKING IN CÓRDOBA: OUR PICKS

Nuur: Paco Morales gives centuries-old recipes such as pistachio soup the modern treatment; two Michelin stars. *1.30-6pm & 8.30-11.30pm Thu-Sat* €€€

Casa Pepe de la Judería: Around since 1920, Pepe's serves classic tapas such as *berenjenas con miel* (aubergines in honey). *1-4pm & 8pm-midnight* €€

Garum 2.1: Award-winning spot for imaginative takes on Cordoban dishes, like *salmorejo* with jelly sherry cubes. *1-4pm & 8pm-midnight Mon, Tue & Thu-Sat* €€

Jugo Vinos Vivos: Facing a tiny square and fountain, Jugo is all about live wines, sourced directly from small Andalucian producers. *hours vary*

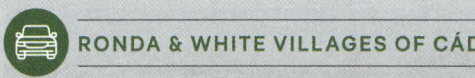

RONDA & WHITE VILLAGES OF CÁDIZ

Andalucía's white villages and olive-tree-covered countryside are just as magical as the famed cities, especially around Ronda and Sierra de Grazalema.

START	END	LENGTH
Ronda	Arcos de la Frontera	140km; 1–2 days

Built astride a huge gash in the mountains carved out by the Río Guadalevín, **❶ Ronda** is a large *pueblo blanco* with a dramatic history. Soak it all up from the grand 1793 Puente Nuevo. Drive 20km north to **❷ Setenil de las Bodegas**, where buildings (homes, restaurants) are curled into cave-like streets beneath the ledges of the Río Trejo.

Zip 35km west, crossing from Málaga province into Cádiz province, to reach **❸ Zahara de la Sierra**. This fortified hill village of red-tiled white houses clusters beneath a ruined 12th-century Moorish castle, all overlooking a turquoise reservoir. From here, the sinuous CA9104 climbs high to the Puerto de las Palomas pass (1357m) before swooping down to **❹ Grazalema**, a

beautiful wool-producing village with sloping cobbled streets and delightful rural hotels for overnight stops.

Heading 20km southwest, travel along the A374 through cheese-making Villaluenga del Rosario (the province's loftiest village) to **❺ Benaocaz**, a former Moorish settlement and the jumping-off point for hiking the 3.3km Calzada Romana (an old Roman road to Ubrique). By car, it's just 7km downhill along corkscrew turns to leather-manufacturing **❻ Ubrique**, backed by the knife-edge Cruz de Tajo. A 40km spin northwest drops you in **❼ Arcos de la Frontera**, a cragtop beauty of a *pueblo blanco* whose origins predate the Romans.

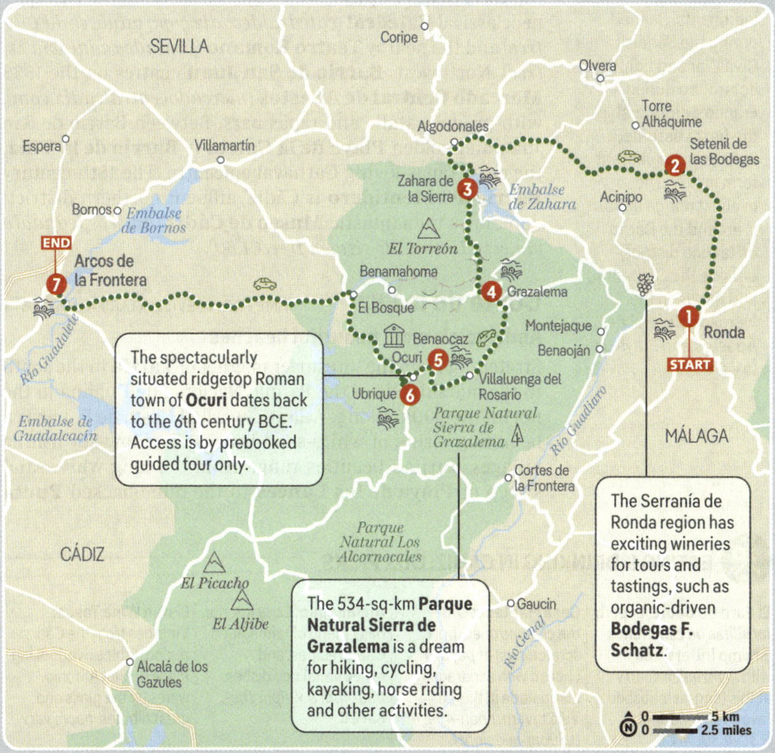

The spectacularly situated ridgetop Roman town of **Ocuri** dates back to the 6th century BCE. Access is by prebooked guided tour only.

The Serranía de Ronda region has exciting wineries for tours and tastings, such as organic-driven **Bodegas F. Schatz**.

The 534-sq-km **Parque Natural Sierra de Grazalema** is a dream for hiking, cycling, kayaking, horse riding and other activities.

CARNAVAL

If you're in Cádiz before Easter (in February or March, depending on the Easter dates), you'll be joining the *gaditanos* for Carnaval – Spain's biggest, liveliest, 10-day singing, dancing and drinking street party, complete with float parades, street food, fireworks and over 300 *murgas* (bands). Carnaval dates back to the 15th century, when costumed revelry was brought by homesick Genoese merchants. Banned during the Spanish Civil War and tightly controlled during Franco's dictatorship, the fiesta assumed its present exuberant form in 1977. The liveliest *murga* action is around the Barrio de la Viña district, outside the Cathedral, and between the Mercado Central de Abastos and Playa de la Caleta.

Generalife, Granada

The best way to dig into this appealing port city is by wandering its distinctive *barrios*. The **Barrio de Santa María** is the old Roma quarter, home to flamenco-world icon **La Perla** *(perladecadiz.com);* check for shows. Oldest of all is the **Barrio del Pópulo**, which spreads around the baroque-neoclassical **Catedral** *(catedraldecadiz.com; adult/child €10/ free)* and the nearby **Teatro Romano** *(juntadeandalucia.es; free)*. Northwest, **Barrio de San Juan** centres on the 1838 **Mercado Central de Abastos** *(mercadocentralcadiz.com)*, with produce stalls and tapas bars. Between Barrio de San Juan and golden **Playa de la Caleta** is **Barrio de la Viña**, the city's tapas-loving Carnaval epicentre. The 18th-century **Barrio del Mentidero** is Cádiz' affluent northern district; don't miss the fantastic **Museo de Cádiz** *(museosdeandalu cia.es; EU/non-EU citizen free/€1.50)*.

Costa de la Luz   TIME FROM SEVILLE (TARIFA): 2¼HR 🚗

Andalucía's most beautiful beaches

Stretching from the kitesurfer magnet of **Tarifa** in the south to the marshlands of the Parque Nacional de Doñana in the north, the 200km-long, Atlantic-washed Costa de la Luz is a beguiling string of white-sand beaches and low-key fishing villages. Tarifa's beauties range from the long white-sand sweep of **Playa de los Lances** to the dune-backed **Punta**

 EATING & DRINKING IN CÁDIZ: OUR PICKS

El Faro de Cádiz: Superb *tortillitas de camarones* (shrimp fritters) pair with *manzanilla* sherry at this long-established favourite. *1-4.30pm & 8.30-11.30pm €€*

Casa Manteca: Order the *chicharrones* (pork scratchings) or *payoyo* cheese with asparagus marmalade in this La Viña tavern. *noon-4pm & 8.30pm-midnight €*

Almanaque: Cosy interior, daily menu of reimagined Cádiz recipes, and exceptional rice dishes. *1.30-4pm & 9-11pm Tue-Sat €€*

Listán Wine Tasca: Vintages from the Cádiz region, tables overlooking Plaza de San Antonio, wines by the glass and great nibbles. *hours vary*

Paloma and spectacular **Playa de Bolonia** with its 30m-high dune. North from Bolonia are the laid-back beach towns of **Zahara de los Atunes** and **Los Caños de Meca**, with long white-sand strands dotted with *chiringuitos* and surf schools. **El Palmar** has some of Andalucía's best surf waves and its own beach-bar scene, a quick hop away from **Vejer de la Frontera**, one of Andalucía's most exquisite *pueblos blancos*. Just north, seafront **Conil de la Frontera** is renowned for its many beaches, from the family-friendly strand of **Playa La Fontanilla** to the seven sheltered, nudist-friendly coves of **Calas de Poniente**. Pick your strand, bring a beach umbrella and join the fun.

Granada & Around

TIME FROM SEVILLE: 2½HR 🚗 + 🚌

The magical Alhambra

One of the most architecturally perfect buildings in existence, the Moorish palace-fortress of **Alhambra** *(alhambra-patronato.es)* sits high above Granada; its name derives from the Arabic *al-qala'a al-hamra* (the Red Castle). The 9th-century Alhambra was transformed during the 13th and 14th centuries by Granada's Nasrid rulers into the magnificent royal residence you see today.

Its walls carved with elegant Arabic inscriptions, the remarkable **Palacios Nazaríes** complex was originally divided into three parts: the Mexuar, Serallo and Harem. At the heart of the Serallo, where sultans conducted negotiations with Christian emissaries, is the **Patio de los Arrayanes**, named after the myrtle hedges around its rectangular pool and surrounded by marble-columned arcades. To the north, the Sala de la Barca, with a copy of its original cedar ceiling, leads into the **Salón de los Embajadores** – the largest, most striking chamber, with a domed marquetry ceiling symbolising the seven heavens of Islam. Continue to the **Patio de los Leones**, centred on an 11th-century fountain channelling water through the mouths of 12 marble lions.

The **Generalife**, the Nasrid rulers' summer estate, takes its name from the Arabic *jinan al-'arif,* meaning 'the overseer's gardens'. The Patio de la Acequia features immaculately tended gardens, while the Escalera del Agua is a marvel, with water channels running down stone balustrades.

Albayzín: Granada's UNESCO-listed old quarter

The cobbled alleyways, whitewashed mansions and scenic plazas of the UNESCO-listed Albayzín, Granada's old Moorish

ALHAMBRA TIPS

General tickets *(€22)* cover all areas; Gardens, Generalife and Alcazaba tickets *(€12)* exclude Palacios Nazaríes.

Access to Palacios Nazaríes is limited to 300 visitors every half-hour; book time-slot tickets as far in advance as possible.

Alhambra by night is a special experience: book Night Visit Palacios Nazaríes *(€12.70)* year-round or Night Visit Gardens & Generalife *(€8.50)* in April, May, September, October and November.

Bring ID that matches the name on your ticket – authorities are cracking down on scalpers buying up day tickets and reselling them to ticketless visitors by the gate.

🍴 EATING IN TARIFA & VEJER DE LA FRONTERA: OUR PICKS

El Jardín del Califa: Romantic Vejer spot with a creative Moroccan–Middle Eastern menu and Cádiz province vintages. Book ahead! *1-4pm & 7.30-11pm* €€

El Francés: At the standing-room-only bar or terrace tables in Tarifa, munch on classics with a twist. Also runs Silos 19. *12.30pm-midnight Fri-Tue* €€

El Lola: Stylish flamenco-themed tapas bar in old-town Tarifa, with dishes including seasonal *almadraba* tuna. *1-4.30pm & 7pm-midnight* €€

La Judería: Tucked away in a Vejer alleyway, this spot dazzles with its stellar rice dishes and goat's-cheese cheesecake with honey. *hours vary* €€

CABO DE GATA

Beach lovers dazzled by the Costa de la Luz are equally likely to fall for magical Cabo de Gata. At the opposite end of Andalucía (around two hours' drive from Granada), this wild stretch of the Almería coast is protected as the spectacular 340-sq-km **Parque Natural de Cabo de Gata-Níjar**, featuring some of Spain's most pristine, least crowded white-sand beaches, excellent scuba diving and other water sports, and a dramatic Mediterranean coastline ripe for exploration on foot or by bike. Between small, laid-back villages – like Rodalquilar, Las Negras, Pozo del Fraile and San José – trails weave across a desert-like volcanic landscape, taking in remote lighthouses, wind-battered capes and hidden-away coves that require a little more effort to reach.

quarter, occupy a hill facing the Alhambra. Allow a full day to explore, before dropping back down to the **Catedral de Granada** *(catedraldegranada.com; adult/child €7/free)*, housing the tombs of the Reyes Católicos.

Off Carrera del Darro, the Albayzín's **Baños Árabes El Bañuelo** *(alhambra-patronato.es; €8.50)* is a well-preserved 11th-century Moorish public bath complex. Nearby, occupying the 16th-century Casa de Castril, the **Museo Arqueológico** *(museosdeandalucia.es; EU/non-EU citizen free/€1.50)* houses regional artefacts, from Palaeolithic to late Moorish times. Dominating the Plaza del Salvador near the top of the Albayzín, the 16th-century **Colegiata del Salvador** church was built atop a former mosque. A short wander southwest brings you to the **Mirador San Nicolás**, the famous viewpoint for sunset shots of the Alhambra silhouetted against the Sierra Nevada.

Hike into the Sierra Nevada

The 862-sq-km **Parque Nacional Sierra Nevada** *(miteco.gob.es)* – Spain's largest national park – is home to 2100 of Spain's 7000 plant species, as well as Andalucía's largest ibex population (around 15,000). It's also where you'll find **Mulhacén** (3479m), the highest point in mainland Spain. Ample day hikes (many doable from Granada) and multiday trails beckon walkers and mountaineers. The lower southern reaches – **Las Alpujarras** – and their dramatic valleys, dotted with age-old *pueblos blancos,* lend themselves beautifully to road-tripping and walking. The best months for hiking are April to mid-June and mid-September to early November for Las Alpujarras, while summer is good for the high Sierra Nevada. Along with summiting Mulhacén, highlights include walks around the three villages in the Barranco del Poqueira – Pampaneira, Bubión and Capileira – and lofty, *jamón*-making Trevélez. **Nevadensis** *(nevadensis.com)* can organise guided hikes.

Málaga

TIME FROM SEVILLE: 2¼ 🚗 + 🚌

City of artists

Begin your exploration of Málaga's artistic side at the **Museo Picasso Málaga** *(museopicassomalaga.org; adult/child €13/free)*, a must-visit in the city of the artist's birth. Among 200-plus works, highlights include a painting of Picasso's sister Lola, done when he was only 13, *Portrait of Paulo with White Hat* and *Olga Khokhlova with Mantilla*. The nearby **Museo**

 EATING & DRINKING IN GRANADA: OUR PICKS

Damasqueros: The tasting menu may feature aubergines with sardines and miso or veal sweetbreads. *1-3.30pm & 8.30-10.30pm Mon-Sat, 1-3.30pm Sun* €€€

Casa de Vinos La Brujidera: Wood-panelled bar with a superb wine cellar; most wines are available by the glass. *hours vary*

Taberna La Tana: Realejo favourite, serving over 500 Spanish wines alongside platters of cold cuts and other bites. *12.30-4pm & 8.30pm-midnight*

Bar Provincias: Old-school spot (around since 1945) perfect for people-watching as you munch on fried fish and seafood bites. *1-11.30pm*

ADIANY MONTELO/SHUTTERSTOCK

Parque Nacional Sierra Nevada

Casa Natal de Picasso (*museocasanatalpicasso.malaga.eu; adult/child €3/free*) is located in the house where the artist was born.

Continue on to the **Museo Carmen Thyssen** (*carmenthyssenmalaga.org; adult/child €12/free*), housed in an elegant 16th-century palace in the heart of the city's former Moorish quarter. A short walk away lies the **Museo de Málaga** (*museosdeandalucia.es; EU/non-EU citizen free/€1.50*), in the Palacio de la Aduana, which combines the former Museo Bellas Artes and the Museo Arqueológico.

As you pass through the neighbourhood of **Soho**, look for murals by the likes of Dean Stockton (D*Face), Shepard Fairey (OBEY) and ROA. Many museums close Monday.

MÁLAGA'S MULTICULTURAL HISTORY

Teatro Romano: Roman theatre built during the reign of Augustus in the 1st century CE and working up until the 3rd century.

Alcazaba: A winding pathway takes you through Arabic-style arched doorways, peaceful gardens and geometric-tiled courtyards at the city's 11th-century Moorish palatial fortress.

Castillo de Gibralfaro: Another vestige of Málaga's Moorish past, rising high above the city – you can hike up in 30 minutes.

Catedral de la Encarnación de Málaga: The colossal cathedral stands right in the centre of the city. Construction began in the 16th century on the site of a former mosque.

EATING & DRINKING IN MÁLAGA: OUR PICKS

Bodegas El Pimpi: In front of the Alcazaba, this fun bar has leafy courtyards, wine cellars and cosy rooms. The 'tunnel' is best for tapas. *noon-2am* €€

La Tranca: Elbow your way into this old-fashioned bar with vermouth and classic Andalucian tapas like tortilla and olives. *noon-1am* €

La Cosmo: Sleek modern dining by chef Dani Carnero. Try duck breast with barbecue sauce. *1.30-3.30pm & 8-11.30pm Mon-Sat* €€

Antigua Casa de Guardia: Old-school wine bar where muscatel and Pedro Ximénez are served straight from the barrel. *hours vary*

Places We Love to Stay

€ Budget €€ Midrange €€€ Top End

Madrid MAP p1030

Hostal La Zona € This stylish *hostal* has clean, bright rooms and breakfast is until noon.

Only YOU Atocha €€ Not only stylish but also sustainable, eschewing single-use plastics and offering electric-car charging.

Hotel Alicia €€ One of the landmark properties of the designer Room Mate chain, overlooking Plaza de Santa Ana.

Posada del Dragón €€ Remodelled La Latina inn with modern interiors retaining its traditional *corrala* courtyard.

Pestaña Plaza Mayor €€€ This sought-after address has been renovated with exposed brick, velvet walls and rooftop pool.

Toledo, Cáceres & Salamanca

Áurea Toledo €€ Five-star hotel spread across four historic courtyard houses with artefacts.

Hospes Palacio de San Esteban €€ In a 16th-century former Salamanca convent, with garden and pool.

Parador de Cáceres €€€ This old-town conglomeration of 14th-century Gothic palaces has stylish rooms.

Barcelona MAP p1044

Generator Barcelona € The switched-on Generator chain runs this large, social Gràcia hostel.

Hotel Brummell €€ In Poble Sec, this 20-room boutique hotel has an urban garden with a pool.

Casa Mathilda €€ Beautiful 1920s Eixample Dreta building converted into a 14-room boutique hideaway.

Casa Bonay €€€ A creatively restored 1896 Eixample building houses one of Barcelona's best boutique-design hotels.

Hotel Neri €€€ Two historic palaces merged to become this impeccable 22-room Relais & Chateaux property.

Costa Brava, Tarragona & Zaragoza

Tramuntana Hotel €€ Adults-only 11-room boutique hotel tucked away in old-town Cadaqués.

H10 Imperial Tarraco €€ Incredible views and a rooftop pool for recharging in Tarragona.

Hotel Sauce €€ Welcoming, family-run hotel in Zaragoza with fresh, cheerful rooms.

Bilbao & San Sebastián

Pensión Aida €€ Guests are made to feel welcome at this pensión with bright rooms.

Miró Hotel €€€ Opposite the Guggenheim, this contemporary design hotel charms art lovers.

Picos de Europa & Galicia

Hotel Costa Vella €€ Tranquil rooms, super-helpful staff and a lovely garden cafe overlooking Santiago.

Casa Fontequeiroso €€ Welcoming small hotel in deep Costa da Morte countryside, with superb home-cooked meals.

Valencia MAP p1065

Casa Clarita €€ Joyful interiors with colourful, chic murals by local artist Jaime Hayon.

YOURS €€€ Minimal design hotel scented with hand-poured candles. Plunge pool is heaven in summer.

Balearic Islands

Can Fuster, Sant Joan de Labritja €€€ Restored, eight-room, 150-year-old Ibizan farmhouse with pool.

Hotel Basilica, Palma de Mallorca €€€ Tear yourself away from your understated room for the rooftop pool with cathedral views.

Hotel Nou Sant Antoni, Ciutadella €€€ Spectacular Menorca boutique hotel in the heart of the old town.

Seville & Costa de la Luz MAP p1074

La Banda € Perennial Seville favourite for its stunning rooftop terrace, sociable ethos and evening events.

La Casa del Califa €€ North Africa–inspired rooms and fab restaurant in a 16th-century building in Vejer de la Frontera.

Casa del Poeta €€€ Deep in Seville's Barrio de Santa Cruz, stay at this restored 17th-century mansion.

Córdoba, Granada & Málaga

Patio del Posadero €€ Traditional Córdoba-Moorish touches and boutique design in a 15th-century property.

Hotel Casa 1800 Granada €€ Old-world coffered ceilings, contemporary rooms and beautiful courtyard within a 16th-century Granada building.

Hotel Boutique Teatro Romano €€ Light, contemporary rooms with views of Málaga's Roman theatre and Alcazaba.

Practicalities

HEATWAVES & WILDFIRES

In recent years, Spain has been experiencing increasingly intense heatwaves. Devastating wildfires and serious droughts often accompany them. If you're caught up in any of these, follow guidance from local authorities. Common restrictions during droughts might include beach showers and public fountains being switched off and bans on refilling swimming pools.

DANIEL FERRER PAEZ/SHUTTERSTOCK

SMOKING

Smoking is banned in enclosed public spaces, near hospitals and on over 660 beaches. Legislation to ban smoking on bar/restaurant terraces was in the works at the time of writing. Cannabis has been decriminalised for personal use, in small quantities.

LGBTIQ+ TRAVELLERS

In 2024, Spain ranked joint first place on the Spartacus Gay Travel Index of LGBTIQ+ friendly countries. It was the fourth country in the world to legalise same-sex marriage (in 2005), along with same-sex adoption. The 2023 Ley Trans brought groundbreaking legislation around rights for trans people. Spain's LGBTIQ+ hubs are Madrid, Barcelona, Sitges and Gran Canaria, though you'll find lively scenes countrywide.

TIPPING ETIQUETTE

Though tipping isn't obligatory, it's definitely appreciated. In restaurants, 5% to 10% (more common) is appropriate; for bars/cafes, people sometimes leave loose change. If paying by card, ask to add the tip to the bill total.

OPENING HOURS

Opening times vary seasonally and are typically more reduced in winter and/or peak summer months.
Banks 8.30am–2pm Monday to Friday
Cafes 7am–late
Bars Varies; often 6pm–late
Restaurants 1pm–4pm and 8.30pm–11pm or midnight
Shops 10am–2pm and 5pm–8pm Monday to Saturday

TOURISM TAX & PRIVATE RENTALS

Spain has experienced a surge in private short-term tourist rentals (especially apartments) in recent years, which many people link to growing overtourism issues. If booking one, check it's legally licensed. Some destinations also apply a tourism tax, usually added to accommodation bills.

PUBLIC HOLIDAYS

National holidays:
New Year's Day 1 January
Good Friday March/ April
Labour Day 1 May
Feast of the Assumption 15 August
Fiesta Nacional de España 12 October
All Saints' Day 1 November

Constitution Day 6 December
Christmas 25 December
Other common holidays:
Three Kings' Day 6 January
Maundy Thursday March/ April
Corpus Christi June
Feast of the Immaculate Conception 8 December

Language

English is quite widely spoken, especially in larger cities and popular tourist areas, but less so in rural villages and among older Spaniards. Spanish (Castilian) is the national language; Catalan, Galician and Basque are co-official regional languages. Learning a few words of the local language goes a long way.

Basics

Hello. Hola. *o·la*
Goodbye. Adiós. *Adiós*
Yes. Sí. *see*
No. No. *no*
Please. Por favor. *por fa·vor*
Thank you (very much). (Muchas) Gracias. *(moo·chos) gra·thyas*
Excuse me. Perdón. *per·don*
Sorry. Lo siento. *lo syen·to*
What's your name? ¿Cómo se llama usted? *ko·mo se lya·ma oo·ste*
My name is ... Me llamo ... *me lya·mo ...*
Do you speak English? ¿Habla inglés? *a·bla een·gles*
I don't understand. No entiendo. *no en·tyen·do*

Signs

Abierto Open
Cerrado Closed
Entrada Entrance
Hombres Men
Mujeres Women
Prohibido Prohibited
Salida Exit
Servicios/Aseos Toilets

Time

What time is it? ¿Qué hora es? *ke o·ra es*

It's (10) o'clock. Son (las diez). *son (las dyeth)*
It's half past (one). Es (la una) y media. *es (la oo·na) ee me·dya*
yesterday ayer *a·yer*
today hoy *oy*
tomorrow mañana *ma·nya·na*

Emergencies

Help! ¡Socorro! *so·ko·ro*
Go away! ¡Vete! *ve·te*
Call the police! ¡Llame a la policía! *lya·me a la po·lee·thee·a*
Call a doctor! ¡Llame a un médico! *lya·me a oon me·dee·ko*

Menu Decoder

Menú del día Set lunch menu
Menú degustación Tasting menu
Tapas Small, savoury dishes
Pintxos Basque-style tapas, usually on bread
Ración or media ración Full-plate or half-plate portion of tapas
Marisco Seafood
Carne de cerdo Pork
Carne de vaca Beef
Pollo Chicken
Vegetariano Vegetarian
Vegano Vegan
Sin gluten Gluten-free

NUMBERS	
1	uno
2	dos
3	tres
4	cuatro
5	cinco
6	seis
7	siete
8	ocho
9	nueve
10	diez
20	veinte
50	cincuenta
100	cien

MAKSIM SAFANIUK/SHUTTERSTOCK

AVE train

Arriving & Getting Around

Spain's public transport is among Europe's best, with a fast and super-modern train system, an extensive domestic air network, a well-maintained road network, and buses that connect villages in the country's most remote corners.

Major Points of Entry
Most international travellers arrive into Madrid or Barcelona, though Málaga, Valencia, Mallorca, Ibiza, Alicante and the Canaries also have busy airports, particularly for hops within Europe. Transport to/from airports is usually efficient.

Train
Renfe *(renfe.com)* is the national train system that runs most services in Spain, including the high-speed AVE trains. Private operators such as **Iryo** *(iryo.eu)* and **Ouigo** *(ouigo. com)* offer alternatives, often at lower prices. Most cities have local trains called *cercanías* (*rodalies* in Catalonia).

Bus
Most buses are geared towards local residents, which means weekend services are generally more limited. Tickets can often be booked online in advance, though for more remote routes you may need to pay in cash.

Car & Taxi
To rent a car in Spain, you must have a licence, be aged 21 or over and, in most cases, have a credit card (few places accept debit cards). Rates and availability vary enormously by season – book as far ahead as possible. Taxis are readily available in the big cities and main tourist destinations. Note that Uber doesn't operate in some places, though rideshare company **Cabify** *(cabify.com)* often fills the gap.

PANDO HALL/GETTY IMAGES

MONEY

Currency: Euro (€)

CARD & DIGITAL PAYMENT
All major credit and debit cards are widely accepted (including contactless payments and Apple/Google Pay), though some places don't take Amex. There's sometimes a minimum spend and splitting bills isn't always an option. You may still occasionally need cash for small shops, flea markets, buses and tipping.

HOW TO SAVE A FEW EUROS
Many destinations offer tourist passes covering major sights at a discount, available at tourist offices, online or at the sights. Museums often have dedicated free-access days. Most sights offer discounted tickets for students, children and people over 65. Accommodation-wise, cut costs by skipping peak season (July/August and Easter) and weekends. Take advantage of lunchtime restaurant deals.

Curated by
Anthony Ham

Sweden

FUTURISTIC CITIES, PLACID ARCHIPELAGOS AND THE ARCTIC

Sweden is a Nordic dream date, offering wild landscapes illuminated by the aurora borealis, archipelagos for island-hopping, and cutting-edge urban fashion, food and design.

The best thing about Sweden is its untamed nature. Whether you're sailing across an archipelago or trekking along Lappland's long-distance trails, the sense of space, solitude and freedom is matched by few corners of Europe. So go pitch a tent by a Baltic beach or ride a husky sled beneath the eerie glow of the northern lights.

Sweden's cities don't let the side down, either. Urban residents clearly got the memo to 'look sharp', while the prevalence of irresistible furnishings, textiles and lighting in cafes, restaurants and Swedish homes is nothing short of enviable. Yet Swedish style is rarely ostentatious: form and function are tightly linked in a society that reveres moderation, simplicity and practicality.

And there's more to Sweden than contemporary design. The countryside is dotted with ancient rune stones, while huge stone-ship settings and burial mounds recall long-gone kings and chiefs. Across the country, walled medieval cities, seaside fortresses, turreted palaces and revealing museums attest to Sweden's long and complex history. Also part of Sweden's backstory are the Sámi, Europe's only indigenous people, who arrived in Sweden's north millennia ago and domesticated its reindeer. Lappland's wilderness is the best place to gain insight into this oft-overlooked part of the country's cultural tapestry, whether you dig into 'slow food' at a Sámi restaurant or spend a night or two in a Sámi reindeer camp.

TRABANTOS/SHUTTERSTOCK

THE MAIN AREAS

STOCKHOLM	**UPPSALA**	**GOTHENBURG**	**MALMÖ**	**KIRUNA & THE ARCTIC**
Illustrious capital on the water. **p1092**	University town; ancient burial mounds. **p1097**	Sweden's bustling second city. **p1101**	Modern city with futuristic architecture. **p1104**	Quirky gateway town to the Arctic. **p1107**

For places to stay in Sweden, see p1110

Left: Stockholm (p1092); Above: Malmö (p1104)

Find Your Way

Sweden is huge, with a sparsely populated northern half. The public transport is excellent, with train networks and reliable buses connecting the main population centres. Some ferry/boat services are seasonal.

BUS & CAR

Buses connect most towns, though services to remoter small towns and to Lappland trailheads are few. Having a car gives you the greatest flexibility. Winter tyres are required from December to April.

TRAIN

The super-scenic Inlandsbanan operates daily between June and late August from Östersund all the way north to Gällivare. Year-round trains connect Gävle on the Bothnian Coast and Östersund, plus Åre and Trondheim, Norway.

Kiruna & the Arctic, p1107

This quirky Arctic mining town welcomes you to the nearby Icehotel and the Abisko wilderness, alternately lit by the midnight sun and the northern lights.

Uppsala, p1097

One of Sweden's oldest cities, with a buzzy ambience surrounding its university; gateway to the impressive ancient burial ground of Gamla Uppsala.

Gothenburg, p1101

Sweden's second city is replete with shopping, adventurous dining and thought-provoking museums, and features Scandinavia's biggest fun park.

Stockholm, p1092

Flanked by a forested archipelago, Sweden's capital dazzles with its world-class museums, striking setting, cutting-edge design and superb restaurants.

Malmö, p1104

There's plenty to keep even the most exacting visitor satisfied in Sweden's third city, from cultural venues and contemporary architecture to an exciting culinary scene.

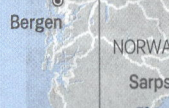

0   400 km
0   200 miles

NOWACZYK/SHUTTERSTOCK

Dogsledding near Kiruna (p1107)

Plan Your Time

Given the large distances between places and extreme contrasts between summer and winter, organise your time according to your passions and plan ahead (trains, ferries, flights).

A Long Weekend

● Focus on multifaceted **Stockholm** (p1092), touring the **Kungliga Slottet** (p1092) and walking the cobbled streets of **Gamla Stan** (p1096). Art lovers shouldn't miss Skeppsholmen island, home to the exceptional **Moderna Museet** (p1094). Check out Sweden's most famous sunken warship at the superb **Vasamuseet** (p1095), before enjoying the bars in **Södermalm** (p1094).

A Week to Spare

● Devote a couple of days to **Stockholm** (p1092), a couple more to **Gothenburg** (p1101) or **Uppsala** (p1097), then fly north to the quirky mining town of **Kiruna** (p1107), beyond the Arctic Circle. Take in some of the Arctic activities on offer, and enjoy it all beneath the midnight sun or the northern lights – what you see and do will depend on the season.

SEASONAL HIGHLIGHTS

SPRING
Days are getting longer and there's **skiing**, **husky-sledding** and **snowmobiling** in Lappland.

SUMMER
The **hiking season** begins in June, with daylight almost around the clock. Attractions and hiking trails are full in July and August.

AUTUMN
From early September everything's quieter; **hiking** conditions can be ideal. By October, days shorten and temperatures drop steadily.

WINTER
The **Icehotel** (p1108) opens in December. Stockholm, Gothenburg and other cities wow with **Christmas markets** and festivities.

Stockholm

HISTORICAL ARCHITECTURE | LOCAL CUISINE | SWEDISH CULTURE

GETTING AROUND

From **Arlanda Airport**, frequent express trains *(arlandaexpress.com)*, buses *(flygbussarna. se)* and taxis run to central Stockholm. **Stockholm Skavsta Airport** is connected to the city by direct buses. Stockholm's tunnelbana (metro), local train lines *(pendeltåg)*, buses and trams extend to many parts of the city. Download the **SL app** *(sl.se)* to buy e-tickets. City ferries connect Gröna Lund Tivoli on Djurgården with Skeppsholmen and Slussen. SL tickets are valid for these ferries, but not for archipelago ferries (buy tickets on board).

☑ **TOP TIP**

Walking is the best way to get around Stockholm. Pick a neighbourhood according to your interests, taking the tunnelbana (metro) and then exploring on foot.

Sweden's capital is rich in style and cultural assets. Beguiling Gamla Stan, the city's oldest district, features a royal palace, gabled buildings and razor-thin cobblestone streets. To the south, formerly working-class Södermalm is one of the city's coolest neighbourhoods. West, the islands of Djurgården and Skeppsholmen harbour everything from Viking treasures and an ill-fated warship to Abba memorabilia and contemporary art.

Norrmalm is the city's modern commercial centre. East of Norrmalm, glitzy Östermalm is home to celebrity hangouts and luxe boutiques. Further east still are the Ladugårdsgärdet parklands, where you'll find more great museums and a superb sculpture garden.

Given the bounty drawn from Stockholm's surrounding waters, fields and forests, it's not surprising that food is a serious passion here. Whatever the global culinary trend, Stockholm is on it. Swedish classics are equally revered, and traditions are both faithfully adhered to and cleverly tweaked by Stockholm's forward-thinking chefs.

The Royal Family's Residence

Explore the Royal Palace and Armoury

Built on the ruins of medieval Tre Kronor castle, the 608-room **Kungliga Slottet** *(theroyalpalace.se; adult/child from 180/90kr)* at the heart of Gamla Stan is still used for its original purpose. Highlights of the royal apartments open to the public include the glittering Karl XI Gallery, inspired by Versailles' Hall of Mirrors, and Queen Kristina's silver throne in the Hall of State. Don't miss the Changing of the Guard in the outer courtyard.

Accessed off Slottsbacken, in the lofty vaults of the palace, the interactive, kid-friendly **Livrustkammaren** *(Royal Armoury; livrustkammaren.se; adult/child 150kr/free)* is also a gem.

A Celebration of Laureates

Meet the Nobel Prize recipients

Small but fascinating, the **Nobelmuseet** (*nobelprizemuseum. se; adult/child 140kr/free*) has a wealth of touch-screen info, personal items gifted by Nobel Prize winners, and 36 short films that include interviews with laureates including Ernest Hemingway and Martin Luther King.

BUMBLE DEE/SHUTTERSTOCK

Vasamuseet

**STORIES
OF A SHIP**

The *Vasa* was raised
from the Stockholm
seabed in 1961
and painstakingly
reassembled. A
17-minute film at the
Vasamuseet sheds
light on the salvage
operation and the
vessel's conservation,
then a 25-minute
guided tour provides
more context.
The fascinating
bottom-floor
exhibition uses
modern forensic
science to re-create
the faces and life
stories of the ill-fated
passengers

Dazzling Contemporary Art
Stockholm's modern-art maverick

In Skeppsholmen, the **Moderna Museet** *(modernamuseet.
se; adult/child 150kr/free)* has an outstanding permanent collection of 140,000 artworks, including key pieces by the most
prominent 20th- and 21st-century artists. The likes of Dalí,
Matisse and Warhol are represented; also look out for works
by Scandinavians such as Hilma af Klint, Öyvind Fahlström
and Vera Nilsson.

Södermalm's Hip 'Hoods
SoFo vs Hornstull

Debate rages over which is Södermalm island's trendiest district.
First up is **SoFo** (short for 'south of Folkungagatan'). At Nytor-
get garden square, you'll find pioneering grocery and restaurant
UrbanDeli *(urbandeli.se)* and Michelin pick **Bar Agrikultur**
(baragrikultur.com), specialising in small plates of seasonal
produce and craft gins. Nearby retailers include **Grandpa**
(grandpastore.com/se) for cool fashions, vintage treasure-trove
Söders Retro & Design and **6/5/4** *(654.se)* for surfboards
and hip outdoors clothing.

Then there's **Hornstull** at the western end of the island.
On weekends between April and September, locals flock to
its secondhand market, **Hornstulls Marknad** *(hornstulls
marknad.se)* on the waterfront. Year-round pleasures include
Debaser Strand *(debaser.se)*, a Mexican restaurant, bar,
nightclub and live-music venue, or **Bitza** *(bitzahornstull.
com)* for Palestinian-style pizza and spicy shakshuka eggs
for weekend brunch.

Home Cooking & Beer
Classic Södermalm alehouses

Södermalm is home to some of Stockholm's most atmospheric pubs. **Blå Dörren** *(bla-dorren.se)* in Slussen occupies the site of a 17th-century tavern. Vaulted ceilings and timber panelling set the scene for Swedish classics such as elk meatballs with lingonberries. Mural-clad **Pelikan** *(pelikan.se)* is the place to enjoy classic *husmanskost* (home cooking) – roasted reindeer, Västerbotten cheese pie, Arctic char, herring – and there's a hefty list of aquavit. Dating from 1908, **Kvarnen** *(kvarnen.com)* is an old-school Hammarby football-fan hangout. Come early for a pint at this handsome beer hall hung with large artwork.

A 17th-Century Warship Reborn
Remarkable naval museum

Vasa, the flagship of Gustav II Adolf, set off from Stockholm on its maiden voyage on 10 August 1628. Unfortunately, being slightly too tall and slightly too narrow, it tipped over in a gust of wind and sank to the bottom of Saltsjön. Yet what you see before you in Djurgården's purpose-built star museum, the **Vasamuseet** *(vasamuseet.se; adult/child 150kr/free)*, is 98% the very same vessel.

Thank You for the Music
ABBA memorabilia

There's much joy to be had at **ABBA: The Museum** *(abba themuseum.com; adult/child from 239/100kr)*, Djurgården's celebration of the demigods of Swedish pop. The story of how Benny, Björn, Frida and Agnetha conquered the world is told through memorabilia and interactivity, including classic music videos, outlandish costumes and spangly, star-shaped guitars. If that 1970s phone goes 'ring, ring', pick it up to have a chat with one of the band members.

Norrmalm's Old Market Square
Food hall and flea-market finds

A market square since the 17th century, cobbled **Hötorget** is flanked to the west by the old PUB department store (now the Haymarket by Scandic hotel) where Greta Garbo worked before becoming a movie star. On the south side is **Hötorgshallen**, a multicultural food hall selling everything from sushi and local candies to fragrant teas. Squeeze into galley-themed dining nook **Kajsas Fiskrestaurang** for a huge bowl of *fisksoppa* (fish stew).

BEST FOR SWEDISH DESIGN

Åhléns: Central department store that's especially good for Swedish-made housewares, bedding and other items to bring home as gifts.

DesignTorget: Affordable Nordic design for the home and yourself from a small Swedish chain that supports new creatives.

Iris Hantverk: Impeccably made woodwork, linens, textiles, candlesticks, handmade soaps, glassware and crafting books.

Mall of Scandinavia: Home to some of the best-known Swedish and international brands, including Björn Borg, Naturkompaniet and J Lindeberg.

Svenssons: Homewares that have the occasional pan-Nordic items, but it's mostly about Swedish style.

 EATING IN GAMLA STAN & SÖDERMALM: OUR PICKS

Kryp In: Book ahead for this cosy Gamla Stan restaurant that wows with creative takes on traditional Swedish dishes. *5-11pm Tue-Sun* €€

Meatballs for the People: Swedish comfort food in Södermalm, including meatballs for vegans. *11am-11pm Sun-Thu, to midnight Fri & Sat* €€

Chaikhana: Come for afternoon-tea spreads and tea-tasting events at this delightful teahouse. *11am-7pm Wed-Fri, noon-6pm Sat & Sun* €€

Celeste: Choose between the set menu or the award-winning seasonal bar menu. Bar bites also available. *5pm-1am Thu-Sun* €€€

A WALK AROUND GAMLA STAN

Stroll through the heart of old Stockholm, taking in magical architecture and old-world charm, seemingly unchanged since medieval times.

START	END	LENGTH
Gamla Stan metro	Gamla Stan metro	2.5km; 1hr

From ❶ **Gamla Stan metro**, head north on Munkbroleden to ornate 17th-century palace ❷ **Riddarhuset**. Swedish nobility once gathered here to govern the country. The statue is of Axel Oxenstierna (1583–1654), an adviser to Queen Christina. Continue on Mynttorget and turn down the main shopping street, ❸ **Västerlånggatan**. Zigzag up to quieter Prästgatan, turn left up the hill on Spektens gränd and right at the junction to ❹ **Stortorget**, Gamla Stan's beautiful main square and location of the 1520 Stockholm Bloodbath. It's tourist central with vividly coloured antique buildings, souvenir shops and cafes. The cobbled square's grandest building is the former Stock Exchange,

now the ❺ **Nobelmuseet** (p1093). Continue on ❻ **Köpmangatan**, browsing the shops, to the triangular 'square' at its end. The ❼ **St George & the Dragon statue** on a plinth is a 1912 bronze replica of Berndt Notke's 15th-century wooden original in Storkyrkan cathedral. Head right and continue on Österlånggatan to ❽ **Järntorget**. On this pretty square, a Gamla Stan feature since the 14th century, is bakery-cafe ❾ **Sundbergs Konditori**, serving coffee from a copper samovar since 1785. Turn back onto Västerlånggatan; on the right is ❿ **Mårten Trötzigs Gränd**, steep steps connecting to Prästgatan. Follow this street to Tyska brinken, turn left and go back downhill to Gamla Stan station.

If you're near **Kungliga Slottet** around noon, you'll catch the impressive Changing of the Guard, with its fanfare and marching band.

During the Stockholm Bloodbath of 1520, Danish King Christian II tricked, trapped and beheaded 82 rebellious Swedes on **Stortorget**. One of the victims had a son, Gustav Ericsson Vasa, who became Sweden's king on 6 June 1523, now Sweden's national day.

0 — 200 m
0 — 0.1 miles

Stallbron

Slottskajen

Kungliga slottet

Mynttgatan

Storkyrkobrinken

Riddarhus-torget

Riddarholms-bron

RIDDAR-HOLMEN

Lilla Nygatan

Stora Nygatan

Kåkbrinken

Schönfeldts Gränd

Munkbrogatan

Munkbroleden

Gamla Stan

START/END ❶

Riddar-fjärden

Centralbron

Västerlånggatan

Trångsund

❺

❹

Källargränd

Skomakaregatan

Svartmangatan

Köpmangatan

❻

❼

Brunnsgränd

Kindstugatan

Sjöbergsgatan

Sankt Hoparegränd

Ferkens Gränd

Skeppsbron

Österlånggatan

Packhusgränd

Prästgatan

Västerlånggatan

Tyska Brinken

❿

❾

❽

Tullgränd

Järntorgs-gatan

Södra Bankogränd

Tjärhovs-gränd

Uppsala

GREAT FOOD | TOP MUSEUMS | MEDIEVAL HISTORY

Home to Scandinavia's oldest university (founded in 1471), Uppsala is no stranger to the buzz emitted when students crowd the room. Budding scholars account for 50,000 of Uppsala's total population (242,000), earning it the nickname 'the City of Eternal Youth' and solidifying Uppsala's reputation as a cradle of culture and nightlife, which manifests itself most strikingly in the sheer number of boho-spirited cafes and bars. But Uppsala's been around since the 3rd century CE, and remnants of the past are on full display at Gamla Uppsala (Old Uppsala), a few kilometres north of the city. Back in the 6th century, this fascinating archaeological site was a flourishing religious centre where human sacrifices were made, in addition to serving as a burial ground. Its sheer scale reveals the magnitude of the religious, economic and political power that was once centred on one of Sweden's oldest cities.

Legends of Old Uppsala

Ancient burial mounds

Gamla Uppsala, 4km north of Uppsala, lends itself easily to myths and legends. Start with the **Gamla Uppsala Museum** *(upplandsmuseet.se; adult/child 150kr/free)*, which contains finds from the site. Gamla Uppsala's three biggest mounds – **Östhögen** (East Mound), **Mitthögen** (Middle Mound) and **Västhögen** (West Mound) – immediately seize your attention. Legend has it they contain the pre-Viking kings Aun, Egil and Adils, who appear in the epic poem *Beowulf* and Icelandic historian Snorre Sturlason's *Ynglingsaga*. After exploring the mounds, pop over to the adjacent 12th-century **Gamla Uppsala Kyrka** to admire the extraordinary detail of an 11th-century rune stone incorporated into the church's exterior in the 1800s. Afterwards, down a glass of mead at **Odinsborg** *(odinsborg.nu)*, which has been serving the fermented honey elixir, now in Viking horns, since the 1890s.

GETTING AROUND

Uppsala is wonderfully walkable; the train and bus stations are conveniently central. If you arrive by car, most hotels are central and have parking garages (around 250kr per 24 hours). The historic quarter is best explored on foot, but bicycles are also popular; **Ski Total Cykel** is a central place for rental. **Upplands Lokaltrafik** *(ul.se)* runs public transport within the city and county. Bus 2 for Gamla Uppsala leaves from Stora Torget in central Uppsala.

☑ **TOP TIP**

Don't miss the opportunity to meet the hottest guy in Uppsala: **Jona**! This half-man, half-fish bronze statue stands by the river on Östra Ågatan.

UPPSALA

House of Curios

A weird and wonderful collection

The delightfully weird and well-organised **Museum Gustavianum** *(uu.se/gustavianum; adult/child 150kr/free)* is Uppsala's best museum. It inhabits Uppsala University's oldest standing structure (built between 1622 and 1625), topped by a restored sundial, and houses an eccentric collection of preserved oddities and cultural quirks. It really is Uppsala's cabinet of curiosities, a destination museum harbouring everything from Egyptian mummies and dried sea creatures to Viking helmets and Celsius' very own thermometer.

But nothing matches the fascinating 17th-century **Augsburg Art Cabinet**, a rotating curio with 1000 ingenious trinkets, or the 17th-century **anatomical theatre** where executed criminals and other unfortunates were dissected in full view of 200 spectators.

Climb Uppsala's Summit

Castle roof vistas

The view from **Uppsala Slott** *(visituppsalaslott.se; adult/child 150/75kr)*, the castle that rises on the highest hill above central Uppsala, is partially blocked by the surrounding trees. The solution? Climb onto the roof! Run by **Go Adventure** *(goadventure.se)*, the climb is a wonderful way to see the castle, beginning with a climb up the elaborate interior staircase and out onto the castle roof. It's not for those who suffer from vertigo!

Uppsala Nights

Try the local home brews

Students congregate in bars and cafes along **Sankt Larsgatan** (a block or two southwest of the river), **Sankt Olofsgatan** (near the university) and **Drottninggatan** (near the Domkyrka).

Craft-beer fans should direct themselves to Uppsala's beloved **Bryggeriet Ångkvarn** *(bryggerietangkvarn.se)*, a low-key option with prime riverside seating on Östra Ågatan, started by a devout home brewer. Hopheads should head to **DomCraft** *(domcraft.se)*, the space at the back of the Domkyrka.

WHO WAS CARL LINNAEUS?

As you might expect in a town with one of Europe's oldest universities, the legacy of Uppsala's greatest minds echoes down through the centuries, and none more so than that of Carl Linnaeus (1707–78). After studying in Uppsala, Linnaeus returned in 1741 as a professor of medicine and botany. Known as the 'father of modern taxonomy', Linnaeus basically designed the system, still used today, of naming or classifying plants, animals and other organisms in his 1735 book, *Systema Naturae*. The revised 10th edition, published in 1758, described 4400 animal species and 7700 plant species. Linnaeus also published *Philosophia Botanica* (1751) on how to maintain a botanical garden, as brought to life at Uppsala's Linneträdgården (p1100).

EATING & DRINKING IN UPPSALA: OUR PICKS

Klostergatan 5: Centrally located, candlelit, creative Nordic bistro that feels like a neighbourhood find. Reserve ahead. *5pm–midnight Tue-Sat €€*

Hambergs i Skytteanska Trädgården: Summer outpost of Uppsala's favourite seafood table. *11.30am-10pm Tue-Sat mid-May–Sep €€*

Bryggeriet Ångkvarn: Prime riverside seating on Östra Ågatan. Fans of maltier craft beers will be at home here. *3pm-midnight Tue-Sat*

DomCraft: The cathedral's former religious school offers local and European-wide brews from 20 taps. *5-11pm Mon-Thu, 4pm-1am Fri & Sat*

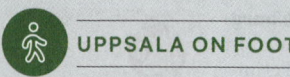

UPPSALA ON FOOT

Walk among the gardens and along cobblestone streets to sample Uppsala's fascinating history and imagine yourself in medieval times.

START	END	LENGTH
Stora Torget	Uppsala Slott	2.8km; 1hr

From the main square, **1 Stora Torget**, head northwest on Svartbäcksgatan, passing the Anders Celsius statue. **2 Linnéträdgården** is Sweden's oldest botanical garden (1655), rebuilt to the 18th-century design of taxonomist Carl Linnaeus. Cross the Fyris on the charming 1846 iron bridge **3 Järnbron**; an info board recounts its history. One block west, pop into **4 Ofvandahls Hovkonditori**, Uppsala's oldest coffee shop. University Park, on Sankt Olofsgatan, shelters nine **5 Uppland Rune Stones** peppered about like granite soldiers from the Viking Age or a graveyard from *Lord of the Rings*. The most famous is 11th-century No 489, known as the Woman's Stone. Uppsala's imposing **6 Domkyrka** – Scandinavia's largest cathedral – looms 100m east. It hosted centuries of Swedish coronations until 1719 and is the final resting place of kings, queens and scientists. Map nerds and rare-book fiends will appreciate the exhibition to the left of the university library entry, **7 Carolina Rediviva Bibliotek**. It displays the astonishing *Carta Marina* and *Codex Argentus* (520 CE), the most complete document written in the Gothic language. It's a short slog uphill to pink **8 Uppsala Slott** (p1099), built for Gustav Vasa in the 1550s and rebuilt in 1757 after a fire. The interior is open to group tours only, but the Uppsala Konstmuseum displays modern art within the castle walls.

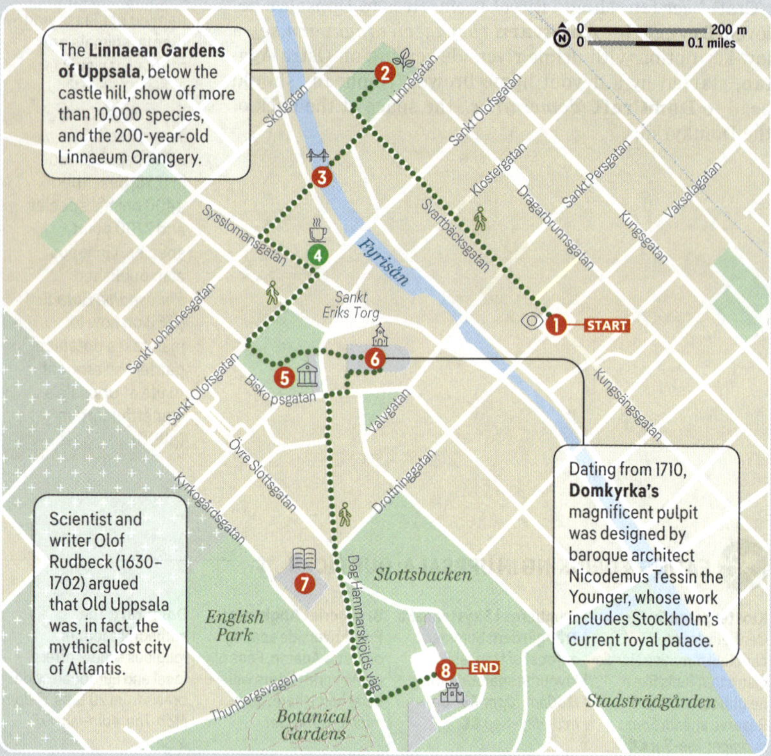

The **Linnaean Gardens of Uppsala**, below the castle hill, show off more than 10,000 species, and the 200-year-old Linnaeum Orangery.

Scientist and writer Olof Rudbeck (1630–1702) argued that Old Uppsala was, in fact, the mythical lost city of Atlantis.

Dating from 1710, **Domkyrka's** magnificent pulpit was designed by baroque architect Nicodemus Tessin the Younger, whose work includes Stockholm's current royal palace.

Gothenburg

WORLD-CLASS MUSEUMS | FAMILY-FRIENDLY CITY | NATURE ESCAPES

With over 600,000 inhabitants, Sweden's second city is arguably its most engaging: a heady mix of stimulating museums, quirky shops, funfair hair-raisers and nautical heritage. It may be a cliché, but this understated city really does have something for everyone, from the boxy motors at the Volvo Museum and Viking ships at the Stadmuseet, to Scandinavian fashion at the Nordstan mall and picnicking in the Slottsskogsparken. Families, too, have plenty to enjoy, including the Universeum (often declared Sweden's top kids' attraction), the terrifying rides at Liseberg Park and a continuous supply of ice cream to savour on beaches up and down the coast. This is also a place that likes to get active: the city hosts the world's largest half-marathon and there are endless possibilities for sea kayaking to uninhabited islands – just the thing after all those XXL Gothenburg cinnamon buns!

Hip, Offbeat 'Hoods

Distinctive neighbourhood duo

Two fascinating, former working-class districts of Gothenburg sit south of the original 17th-century core. **Haga** *(haga shopping.se)* is a low-rise grid of timber-clad houses centred on the shopping street of Haga Nygatan. Once the haunt of sailors, dockers, prostitutes and street urchins, the neighbourhood is now populated by artists and 30-something professionals. An unexpected highlight is the **Hagabadet** *(hagabadet.se),* originally a bathhouse built for the poor and now a spa with Roman baths.

With its tall, ornate, 19th-century tenement blocks, wide avenues and intriguing indie shops, **Linné** is the best place for nightlife, its streets lined with restaurants, bars and cafes inside converted warehouses and factories.

GETTING AROUND

Västtrafik *(vasttrafik. se)* runs the comprehensive public transport network (buses, trams and ferries) in and around Gothenburg. Be aware that some services do not run at weekends. If you are only visiting the leisure quarter and the city centre, you may not need public transport at all. Cycling is another way of getting around swiftly. The city is well set up for cycling, with dedicated lanes almost everywhere. For bicycle rental, try **Cykelkungen**.

GOTHENBURG

⭐ HIGHLIGHTS
1 Konstmuseum

🔴 SIGHTS
2 Haga District
3 Linné District
4 Stadsmuseum
5 Universeum
6 Världskulturmuseet

🔴 ACTIVITIES
7 Hagabadet

⚫ SLEEPING
8 Avalon
9 Dorsia Hotel
10 Hotel Vanilla
11 STF Göteborg City

🟢 EATING
12 28+
13 Brogyllen
14 Koka

🔴 ENTERTAINMENT
15 Liseberg

☑ TOP TIP

The best way to reach Gothenburg from Landvetter Airport (27km west of the city) is on the **Flygbussarna** (flygbussarna.se) airport bus, running hourly. A taxi to the centre costs around 550kr.

Nordic & Dutch Masters

A day at the art museum

The city is full of excellent museums, but when it comes to art, top status goes to the **Konstmuseum** (goteborgskonst museum.se; adult/child 70kr/free). The real highlights begin on the top two floors – the Renaissance collection includes works by Cranach and Veronese, and there's a whole room of Rembrandts. Scandinavian masters such as Bruno Liljefors, Edvard Munch, Anders Zorn and Carl Larsson have pride of place in the Fürstenburg Galleries. Also look out for the superb sculpture hall.

Family Fun in Gothenburg

Theme park and more

Liseberg *(liseberg.se; day pass from 500kr)* is Scandinavia's largest amusement park and the city's most popular attraction. Rides include a 116m-tall free-fall tower and longest dive coaster.

Kids love **Universeum** *(universeum.se; adult/child 225/175kr)*, where visitors explore a humid rainforest and interactive exhibitions on nanotechnology, space travel and mixing music. Parts of the permanent exhibition at the **Världskulturmuseet** *(Museum of World Culture; varldskultur museet.se; adult/child 150kr/free)* were designed by children.

At the **Stadsmuseum** *(goteborgsstadsmuseum.se; adult/child 70kr/free)*, young visitors can ride a typical blue-and-white tram, climb the city towers and explore the *Äskekärrskeppet*, Sweden's only original Viking vessel.

The Wonderful World of Volvo

Visit a car-industry icon

When it comes to Swedish brands, car manufacturer Volvo is rivalled only by IKEA in terms of global reach. The **World of Volvo** *(worldofvolvo.com; adult/child from 200/120kr)* presents the manufacturer's productions chronologically, from the curvaceous limousines of the 1930s to the famously boxy models of the 1980s. Highlights include the original P1800 coupe that Roger Moore drove in UK television series *The Saint*. Take tram 5 or 10 to Eketrägatan, then bus 32 to Arendals Skans.

GOTHENBURG PASS

Gothenburg's **City Pass** *(gocity.com)* includes entry to the vast majority of the city's attractions, discounted and free city tours and, for a bit more, unlimited access to the public transport system. As with any discount card, the question is always: is it worth it? In summer, it certainly is, especially if you plan on hitting most of the museums and taking a couple of tours. But in winter, with non-museum attractions closed, it's going to be hard to get your money's worth: you'd be better off paying admission at the individual sights. Also, note that the pass doesn't cover the pricier attractions in the city, such as Liseberg or World of Volvo.

 EATING IN GOTHENBURG: OUR PICKS

Brogyllen: Many consider this long-established cafe the best purveyors of cinnamon buns. *7am-7pm Mon-Fri, 8am-6pm Sat & Sun* €

FeskarBrittas Kro: Stylish barge restaurant selling fish dishes made with ingredients straight from the fish auction. *hours vary* €€

28+: French-Swedish fusion cuisine served at an upmarket cellar restaurant for over 30 years. *6pm-1am Tue-Sat* €€€

Koka: Elegant restaurant showcasing modern Swedish cuisine. No meat, only seafood and vegetarian dishes. *6pm-midnight Tue-Sat* €€€

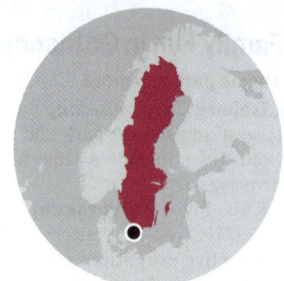

Malmö

21ST-CENTURY ARCHITECTURE | SWEDISH CUSINE | MUSEUMS

GETTING AROUND

A compact city centre and well-maintained bike paths and pavements mean that Malmö is best explored on foot or by bicycle. The local bike-rental scheme Malmö by Bike is easy to use, with stations across the city. Alternatively, bikes and scooters can be rented at **Travelshop** (*travelshop.se*) on Centralplan in front of Centralstation. If you need to use the (expensive) local buses, download the Skånetrafiken app to buy a ticket and look up timetables and routes.

Over the past two decades, the establishment of Malmö University and construction of the Öresund Bridge have totally reinvigorated Sweden's fastest-growing metropolis, linking it with Copenhagen and, by extension, the rest of Europe. Malmö is now home to thriving biotech, IT and design sectors. Many other industries (IKEA among them) are moving their headquarters here, lured by the city's mild weather, youthful and diverse population, focus on innovation and proximity to the Continent.

All of this makes Malmö a great destination to visit. Respect for the city's rich architectural heritage goes hand-in-hand with socially progressive and sustainable urban planning, making exploration of the city centre and surrounding neighbourhoods highly rewarding. So too is immersion in the local cultural and food scenes, among the most impressive in Sweden, which reflect the fact that the local population is drawn from almost every nationality on Earth.

Malmö's Historic Core
Cobbled streetscapes and heritage buildings

Locals flock to the cobbled streets of **Gamla Staden** (Old Town) to socialise and shop. It incorporates three historic market squares – **Stortorget** (the town square), **Lilla Torget** (the little square) and large Gustav Adofs Torg. Dating from 1590, pretty Lilla Torget is the epicentre of Malmö's eating and drinking scene, with plenty of outdoor seating in its bars and bistros.

The oldest half-timbered house in the city is **Thottska Huset** (1558) on the corner of Östergatan and Humlegatan, while other notable examples include the buildings in **St Gertrud Quarter**, a courtyard complex at Östergatan 7B.

☑ **TOP TIP**

Accommodation-wise, the harbour district is a good choice in summer due to its proximity to the beach and its many outdoor eateries.

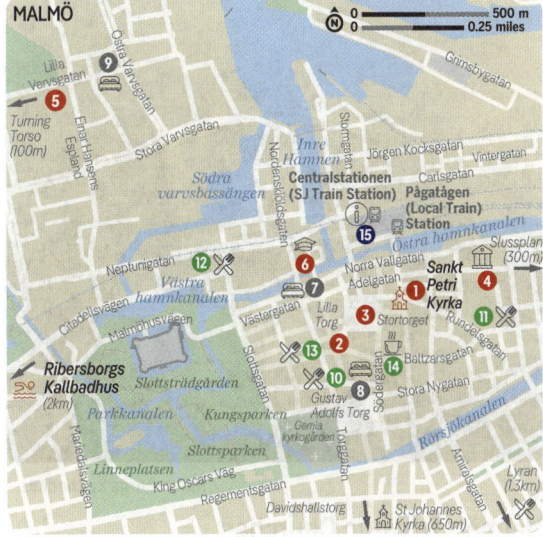

MALMÖ

Medieval Roots, Futuristic Vision

Malmö's contemporary architecture

Malmö's most recognisable building was designed by Spanish architect Santiago Calatrava. Known as the **Turning Torso** (2005), this mixed-use twisting residential tower in the **Västra Hamnen** (Western Harbour) was originally conceived as a free-standing sculpture.

More recent notable buildings include the 2015 aluminium-and-glass **World Maritime University**, overlooking the canal near Centralstation, and **Malmö Saluhall** (food hall).

In Västra Hamnen, the 2013-built **Slussplan** mixed-tenure project is an exercise in regenerative architecture, while low-slung 2018 **Marint Kunskapscenter i Malmö** faces Ribersborgs beach.

Straddling the strait between Denmark and Sweden, **Öresundsbron** is Europe's longest road and rail bridge, and its most visually striking one.

Dining with a Difference

Delicious food and a culinary experiment

Its owners describe **Kollektivkrogen** *(kollektivkrogen.se)* as 'our living room away from home' and are particularly proud of their restaurant's unusual business model. It's a collective enterprise, funded by a group of 50 locals, each committing to working two shifts per month in the restaurant. Expect friendly service and innovative riffs on seasonal traditional dishes, with a focus on local ingredients.

THE HANSEATIC LEAGUE

Visitors to Malmö inevitably comment on the number of handsome 15th- and 16th-century brick buildings in Gamla Staden and wonder how they came to be built. The answer lies in the history of the Hanseatic League, a medieval maritime confederation of merchant guilds, market towns and city states in Central and Northern Europe. Membership of the league brought with it tax-free agreements, cooperative security arrangements, diplomatic networks and other privileges. As a major player in Europe's herring trade, Malmö was welcomed into the league as a *kontore* (foreign trading post) from the 15th century. Its merchants grew rich as a result, building grand homes and warehouses to demonstrate their mercantile success.

WIRESTOCK CREATORS/SHUTTERSTOCK

Ribersborgs Kallbadhus

Malmö's Historic Churches

Gothic and art nouveau grandeur

In the Middle Ages, the profits from Malmö's lucrative herring trade funded the Gothic-style, 14th-century **Sankt Petri Kyrka** *(svenskakyrkan.se/malmo)*. Don't miss the huge 17th-century carved oak altarpiece and the medieval murals in the Krämarkapellet (Merchants Chapel). Opened in 1907, the Evangelical Lutheran **St Johannes Kyrka** (St John's Church) in Triangeln is a magnificent showcase of art nouveau architecture and design.

Sand, Sea & Saunas

Relax at Malmö's favourite beach

In summer, most locals can be found in one spot: **Ribersborgs Stranden**. The heritage-listed **Ribersborgs Kallbadhus** *(ribersborgskallbadhus.se)*, a cold bathhouse that has been a Malmö institution since 1898, sits at the end of one of the beach piers. Everyone goes nude in the pools and saunas.

 EATING & DRINKING IN MALMÖ: OUR PICKS

Lilla Kafferosteriet: Freshly roasted coffee and delectable cinnamon buns in a 17th-century house. *8am-6pm Mon-Fri, from 10am Sat & Sun* €

Johan P: This old-school Mälmo institution is known for its fresh-off-the-boat seafood. *11.30pm-9pm Mon-Sat, to 3pm Sun* €€€

Lyran: The chefs at this restaurant in Möllevången use the best local produce in their Swedish tapas tasting menu. *5-11pm Tue-Sat* €€€

Vollmers: This intimate, two-Michelin-star restaurant offers a fixed multicourse menu and wine pairings. *6-11.30pm Wed-Sat* €€€

Kiruna & the Arctic

ARCTIC LANDSCAPES | OUTDOOR ACTIVITIES | SÁMI CULTURE

Bathed in the clear Arctic light, surrounded by bleakly beautiful wilderness, and sitting atop one of the world's largest iron mines, Kiruna is one of the more fascinating places in northern Sweden. The mine has been the city's lifeblood since the 1880s. And yet, thanks to the mine, Kiruna is sinking and it's being relocated – en masse, brick by brick – a few kilometres to the east.

Beyond Kiruna, Sweden's far north is the Arctic in all its magic, and Kiruna's hinterland in particular is a world of pristine Arctic wilderness and home to the Sámi. Come for the northern lights, or aurora borealis, the greatest spectacle on the planet: Abisko is renowned as the best place to see the lights anywhere, but keep an eye on the heavens wherever you happen to be when darkness falls. In winter, go dogsledding through snowbound forests, and sleep amidst ice sculpture in the Icehotel.

Kiruna

Tour a moving town

Kiruna is a town on the move, with a fascinating story to tell. One of the more challenging structures to move was the early 20th-century **Kiruna Kyrka**, looking like a huge Sámi *kåta* (hut) – this major logistical task was accomplished flawlessly over two days in August 2025. With it, the new town centre is already shaping up with excellent services and some striking architecture.

To learn more, join the 2½-hour **A City in Motion** tour run by the **tourist office** *(kirunalapland.se)*. The three-hour **Stejk Kiruna City Tour** *(stejk.se/kiruna-city-tour)* gives an entertaining overview of the community, finishing with stir-fried moose and reindeer at the **Stejk** food truck and teepee.

Go deep underground

The giant slag heaps marking the above-ground part of the **LKAB Iron-Ore Mine** *(kirunalapland.se; adult/child 400/300kr)* – responsible for producing an astonishing

Places

GETTING AROUND

Kiruna is fairly spread out, so rent a car or be prepared to walk. **Kiruna Airport** has several daily flights from Stockholm. The airport bus meets flights; it loops through town stopping by the tourist office. Daily trains run to Narvik (Norway) via Abisko, with overnight services to Stockholm. **Länstrafiken Norrbotten** *(lanstrafiken norrbotten.se)* runs buses in northern Lappland, while **Länstrafiken Västerbotten** *(tabussen.nu/ lanstrafiken)* covers southern parts. Outside peak season bus services are practically nonexistent.

THE MOVING TOWN

It's not that long ago that you'd wake in Kiruna at 1.30am to find that the ground was shaking. Hundreds of metres below Kiruna's old city centre, dynamite was being detonated. It happened at night to take advantage of the fact that few employees were underground at the time, rather than the 800 who work in the mine during the day.

More than a century of shaking has taken its toll: old Kiruna is on the verge of collapsing into the mine, hence the building of the new city 3km east of the present one. Taking place in stages over 25 years, wooden buildings, including the Sámi-hut-like church, are being moved to the new town wholesale. Sadly, some handsome old stone buildings will have to be demolished.

80% of the world's iron ore – dominate the city. Each day, 68 wagons carrying 100,000 tonnes of iron ore head west to Narvik to be shipped around the world. Departing daily from the tourist office, three-hour tours take you into the mine's subterranean depths, through tunnels and past machines hundreds of metres below the Earth's surface.

Jukkasjärvi

Sleep in the Icehotel

From a humble start in 1989 as a small igloo by the Torne River in Jukkasjärvi, 20km east of Kiruna, the **Icehotel** *(icehotel. com)* has grown into a legendary snow-and-ice edifice that's re-created anew every winter, its rooms filled with ice sculpture.

In the 'cold accommodation' reception, there are heated bathrooms and sauna. You leave your possessions in your locker overnight and retire to your ice bed, topped with a thick mattress covered in reindeer hides. You're provided with sleeping bags guaranteed to keep you warm despite the -5°C temperature inside the rooms (outside it can be -40°C). Come morning, you are revived with hot lingonberry juice, followed by a spell in the sauna.

The Icehotel is seasonal, opening from mid-December to April.

Learn about Sámi culture

The outdoor Sámi museum **Nutti Sámi Siida** *(nutti.se; adult/child 180/90kr)* has *lávvu* and goahti tents, *njalla* (storehouses on poles to keep food safe) and other mainstays of nomadic life. Hand-feed reindeer, buy duodji (handicrafts) and enjoy Sámi fare at **Restaurant Ovttas** *(nutti.se/restaurant)*, inside a traditional Sámi structure.

Next to the museum-restaurant complex, **Jukkasjärvi Kyrka** is one of Lappland's oldest churches (1608).

Go dogsledding in winter

In the pale blue winter half-light of the forest, there is little noise. That is, apart from the panting of the dogs, the coarse scrape of the sled across the ice, and the crunch of heavy boots in the snow. And then there's the quiet thrill of standing tall behind the sled, in perpetual motion, as the dogs pull and guide you through forests and across frozen lakes. In Jukkasjärvi, **Nutti Sámi Siida** *(nutti.se)* can make the arrangements for a dogsledding excursion or longer expedition out in the surrounding country. Another option in Kalixfors, 20 minutes south from Kiruna, is **Kiruna Husky** *(kirunahusky.com)*.

 EATING & DRINKING IN KIRUNA & THE ARCTIC

Annis Grill: Wildly popular option at the southern entrance to Kiruna's new town, serving Thai dishes and Swedish meatballs. *9.30am-9pm €*	**Camp Ripan Restaurang:** Home-cooking, splurge-worthy seasonal dishes and tasting menus near Kiruna. Book ahead. *noon-2pm & 5-9.30pm €€€*	**Restaurant Ovttas:** Innovative Sámi cooking at Jukkasjärvi's museum; try the seawood caviar taco or reindeer tenderloin. *10am-3.30pm & 5-8.30pm €€*	**Icebar:** Drink vodka- and gin-based cocktails from ice glasses while sitting on designer ice chairs beneath ice chandeliers in Jukkasjärvi. *10am-5pm*

NOWACZYK/SHUTTERSTOCK

Icehotel, Jukkasjärvi

Puoltsa

See the Arctic from horseback

Based in tiny Puoltsa, 32km southwest of Kiruna, **Ofelaš** (*ofelas.se*) is a terrific, Nature's Best–certified Sámi outfitter that arranges trekking on hardy and handsome Icelandic horses. They can cater to all levels of experience and budget, from short rides for beginners into the nearby hills and along the lakeshore, to longer expeditions (which can be combined with a Sámi food experience).

Abisko

Look for the northern lights

Abisko (Ábeskovvu in Sámi), 94km northwest of Kiruna, is the gateway to 75-sq-km Abisko National Park. Thanks to a unique local microclimate known as the 'blue hole' (which has to do with Arctic winds colliding with Sweden's northern mountains), it has the driest climate in Sweden, with the most clear nights of any aurora-borealis-viewing destination.

Across the highway from the **STF Abisko Turiststation** (*abisko.nu*), a chairlift takes you up Mt Nuolja (1164m) to the **Aurora Sky Station** (*auroraskystation.se*). In summer from up here, you get wonderful views of the surrounding wilderness, bathed in the pearlescent light of the midnight sun from the deck of the Panorama Café. In winter, if you're lucky, you'll see the northern lights in all their eerie, haunting glory.

Learn to photograph the aurora borealis with STF Abisko–based **Lights Over Lapland** (*lightsoverlapland.com*).

JOKKMOKK'S WINTER MARKET

On the first weekend in February, tens of thousands of Sámi travel to Jokkmokk from all over Scandinavia for the Jokkmokk Winter Market – the oldest and largest of its kind. It's the most exciting (and coldest!) time to be in Jokkmokk, with temperatures as low as -40°C! The event has been going strong since 1605, when King Karl IX decreed that markets should be set up in Lappland to increase taxes, spread Christianity and exert greater control over the nomadic Sámi. Reindeer races and handicraft stalls take centre stage. The Winter Market is preceded by the smaller Historical Market, with several days of folk music, plays, cinematography, photography exhibitions and food-tasting sessions.

☑ TOP TIP

Visit Kiruna at its liveliest during the late-January **Snöfestivalen** (*snofestivalen.com*) – a festival of snow sculpting that draws snow and ice artists from all over and involves Sámi reindeer-sled racing.

Places We Love to Stay

€ Budget   €€ Midrange   €€€ Top End

Stockholm
MAP p1093

Vandrarhem af Chapman & Skeppsholmen € Storied vessel anchored in a superb location off Skeppsholmen. The hostel's common areas are on dry land.

Långholmen Hotell & Vandrarhem €€ Former prison on tiny Långholmen island, now a pleasant hostel/hotel near trendy Hornstull on Södermalm.

Backstage Hotel €€ Chic party pad, adjacent to the Abba Museum. Fans will adore the Abba Gold suite.

First Hotel Reisen €€€ Stockholm's oldest hotel in Gamla Stan has an impressive waterfront location. Rooms sport classic Scandi style.

Uppsala
MAP p1098

Foundry Hotel Apartments € Slick, fully equipped apartments occupy a converted industrial foundry (1898).

Grand Hotell Hörnan €€ At this historic 1907 family-run hotel on the Fyris, rooms have soaring ceilings, a gorgeous riverside setting and high-class everything.

Elite Hotel Academia €€ Sleek, high-end hotel in a stunning glass tower. Rooms have understated charm, with designer fittings, but it's the excellent service that you'll love.

Gothenburg
MAP p1102

STF Göteborg City € Super-central, big and with lots of traveller-friendly facilities, this youth hostel has all en suite rooms.

Hotel Vanilla €€ The restrained furnishings and immaculate bathrooms give the welcome feeling of staying in a Swedish home.

Dorsia Hotel €€€ Richly textured and deliciously flamboyant hotel with stylish touches and opulent breakfasts.

Avalon €€€ For those who want to surround themselves with aptly Nordic design, this superb hotel has it in spades, and there's a busy cocktail bar.

Malmö
MAP p1105

More Hotel Västra Hamnen €€ North of the city centre and offering studios, apartments and a harbour location, this is a good choice for families with children.

Hotel Noble House €€ Steps from the bustle of Gustav Adolfs torg, this Best Western property has colourful communal spaces and beige-themed, cosy bedrooms.

Hotel Duxiana €€€ In Gamla Staden, this stylish boutique option has a chic bistro and ultra-comfortable beds.

Kiruna & the Arctic

Abisko.net € Backpacker hostel in Abisko with doubles and dorms, spread over two buildings, with kitchens and sauna. Husky-sledding tours arranged.

Hotel Arctic Eden €€ Sámi-inspired design, spa, indoor pool, excellent restaurant and certified Sámi handicrafts await you in Kiruna.

Scandic Kiruna €€ Curvaceous business-style hotel in new Kiruna, with plush rooms, Skybar and lofty sauna with a view.

Abisko Mountain Lodge €€€ Plush mountain lodge with stylish rooms and cabins, sauna and on-site Brasserie Fjällköket serving seasonal cuisine.

VIKTORISHKY/SHUTTERSTOCK

Avalon, Gothenburg

Practicalities

Tourist Information

Most towns in Sweden have centrally located tourist offices *(turistbyrå)* providing free street plans and information on accommodation, attractions, activities and transport. Most are open long hours daily in summer; from mid-August to mid-June some close down while others have reduced hours.

Midsummer's Day celebration

NATALIA BOHREN/SHUTTERSTOCK

Visas

EU nationals don't need a visa. Those from the UK, Canada, New Zealand, the US and Australia can stay for up to 90 days in any six months; from late 2026 they'll need an ETIAS travel authorisation.

Public Holidays
New Year's Day 1 January
Epiphany 6 January
Good Friday, Easter Sunday and Easter Monday March/April
Labour Day 1 May
Ascension Day May/June

Whit Sunday and Monday Late May or early June
Midsummer's Day Saturday between 19 and 25 June
All Saints' Day Saturday, late October or early November
Christmas Day 25 December
Boxing Day 26 December

Time

Sweden is one hour ahead of GMT/UTC, like most of Western Europe. It also uses daylight saving time: the clocks go forward an hour on the last Sunday in March and back an hour on the last Sunday in October.

Opening Hours
Banks 9.30am–3pm Monday to Friday, some city branches until 5pm or 6pm
Bars and pubs 11am or noon to 1am or 2am
Government offices 9am–5pm Monday to Friday
Restaurants 11am–2pm and 5–10pm, some close on Sunday or Monday
Shops 9am–6pm Monday to Saturday, until 4pm Sunday

Smoking

Smoking is banned in restaurants, bars and most public spaces. Smoking rates are low: less than 13% of adults in Sweden smoke.

Etiquette

• Sweden is a polite society but not a casually chatty one – strangers typically won't make idle conversation while waiting in queues, and attempts to do so may be greeted with confusion.
• Making small talk on public transport is taboo. Once the ice is broken, Swedes are helpful and happy to show off their English.

Language

As a member of the Germanic language family, Swedish shares common roots with English and German. However, the closest relatives of Swedish are, of course, the other Scandinavian languages, Danish and Norwegian.

Basics

Hello. Hej. *hey*

Goodbye. Hej då./Adjö. *hey daw/ aa·yeu*

Yes. Ja. *yaa*

No. Nej. *ney*

Please. Tack. *tak*

Thank you (very much). Tack (så mycket). *tak (saw mew·ke)*

You're welcome. Varsågod. *var·sha·gohd*

Excuse me. Ursäkta mig. *oor·shek·ta mey*

Sorry. Förlåt. *feur·lawt*

How are you? Hur mår du? *hoor mawr doo*

Fine, thanks. And you? Bra, tack. Och dig? *braa tak o dey*

What's your name? Vad heter du? *vaad hey·ter doo*

My name is ... Jag heter ... *yaa hey·ter ...*

Do you speak English? Talar du engelska? *taa·lar doo eng·el·ska*

I don't understand. Jag förstår inte. *yaa feur·shtawr in·te*

Directions

Where's the ...? Var ligger ...? *var li·ger ...*

What's the address? Vilken adress är det? *vil·ken a·dres air de*

Can you show me (on the map)? Kan du visa mig (på kartan)? *kan doo vee·sa mey? (paw kar·tan)*

How far is it? Hur långt är det? *hoor lawngt air de*

How do I get there? Hur kommer man dit? *hoor ko·mar man deet*

Time

What time is it? Hur mycket är klockan? *hur mew·ke air klo·kan*

It's (two) o'clock. Klockan är (två). *klo·kan air (tvaw)*

Half past (one). Halv (två). (lit: half two) *halv (tvaw)*

At what time ...? Hur dags ...? *hur daks*

At (10) o'clock. Klockan (tio). *klo·kan (tee·oh)*

in the morning på förmiddagen *paw feur·mi·daa·gen*

in the afternoon på eftermiddagen *paw ef·ter·mi·daa·gen*

yesterday igår *ee·gawr*

tomorrow imorgon *ee·mor·ron*

Emergencies

Help! Hjälp! *yelp*

Go away! Försvinn! *feur·shvin*

Call ...! Ring ...! *ring ...*

    a doctor efter en doktor *ef·ter en dok·tor*

    the police polisen *poh·lee·sen*

It's an emergency! Det är ett nödsituation! *de air et neud·si·too·a·fhohn*

Eating & Drinking

What would you recommend? Vad skulle ni rekommendera? *vaad sku·le nee re·ko·men·dey·ra*

What's the local speciality? Vad är den lokala specialiteten? *vaad air deyn loh·kaa·la spe·si·a·li·tey·ten*

Do you have vegetarian food? Har ni vegetarisk mat? *har nee ve·ge·taa·risk maat*

Cheers! Skål! *skawl*

NUMBERS

1
ett *et*

2
två *tvaw*

3
tre *trey*

4
fyra *few·ra*

5
fem *fem*

6
sex *seks*

7
sju *fhoo*

8
åtta *o·ta*

9
nio *nee·oh*

10
tio *tee·oh*

Bicycle rental, Stockholm (p1092)

Arriving & Getting Around

Stockholm is the primary point of entry for most travellers visiting Sweden. The main airport, Arlanda, is about 40km from the city centre. Most international flights depart from Terminal 5.

Taxi

Airport taxis are expensive, especially in Stockholm, where major companies offer a fixed fare from the airport to the city centre. Always ask your driver in advance if your destination is covered by the city-centre rate.

Hiring a Car

You can hire a car from the age of 18 in Sweden, as long as you have held a licence for at least a year, although some companies limit rental options or add a surcharge for drivers aged under 25.

Bicycle

Cycle paths are extensive and well marked. Most cities have public rental networks (often electric bikes). **Cykelfrämjandet** *(cykelframjandet.se)* has maps of scenic trails. You can take bicycles for free on most trains and buses.

Road Conditions

Roads are well maintained in Sweden. Drivers tend to obey traffic rules. Roads can be snowy and icy during winter. Studded tyres are a legal requirement between December and March.

MONEY

Currency:
Krona (kr or SEK)

A CASHLESS COUNTRY?

Cash is definitely not king in Sweden. The country has one of Europe's most cashless economies, thanks to strong investment in digital payment technologies long before the COVID pandemic. As a result, many shops, restaurants, hotels and tourist attractions have stopped accepting cash. There are few instances where you might need some.

CREDIT & DEBIT CARDS

Hotels, cafes and restaurants accept international debit and credit cards (not all accept Amex). Many stores support contactless payments and Apple Pay.

CONTACTLESS TRAVEL

Public transport tickets must be bought in advance, at stations or using local apps. Contactless debit cards can be used as tickets in Stockholm.

For places to stay in Switzerland, see p1135

SAIKO3P/SHUTTERSTOCK

Above: Matterhorn (p1129) & Zermatt (p1128); Right: Eiger Express (p1130), Wetterhorn & Grindelwald

Curated by
Nicola Williams

Switzerland

ALPINE TRADITION, OUTDOOR ACTION AND URBAN FUN

The Swiss don't do half measures: chocolate-box villages of film-set ilk, once-in-a-lifetime rail journeys, untamed nature off the charts...

No other place inspires exploration quite like Switzerland, a small country in western Europe that gave the world melt-in-the-mouth chocolate, cyberspace and an overdose of godlike landscapes. Where else can you follow flower trails around glittering lakes, cross glacial ice roped to a guide and corkscrew up vertiginous alpine passes like James Bond – all in one weekend?

How incredible and intoxicating it all is. But this is Sonderfall Schweiz ('special-case Switzerland'), a privileged neutral country, proudly idiosyncratic, insular and unique. Its four official languages alone speak volumes. French is spoken in Suisse Romande in the west, in Geneva and all around its lake, and in most of the split-personality canton of Valais. Moving east, Germanic Switzerland baffles with Swiss-German in avant-garde Swiss capital Bern; in the flush of art-rich cities north; and across the Swiss Alps, from extreme-sports hub Interlaken in the Bernese Oberland to the glitterati-infused ski slopes of ritzy St Moritz in Graubünden. It is here, shouldering up to Austria and Italy in the country's southeast, that you might get to hear Romansh – Switzerland's fourth national language few have ever heard of (or heard). This is where the mountains get really wild – if you want to tiptoe off-grid, the protected Swiss National Park is the sweet spot. Then there is Ticino, a charismatic pocket of Italian-speaking exuberance and dolce vita in the hot south.

Sheer variety alone has you spellbound in Switzerland.

AARONCHENPS2/SHUTTERSTOCK

THE MAIN AREAS

GENEVA
Lakeside living and belle époque romance.
p1118

NORTHERN SWITZERLAND
World-class art in culture-rich cities.
p1123

THE SWISS ALPS
Bucket-list vistas and outdoor adventure.
p1127

TICINO
The country's 'dolce' Italianate soul.
p1132

Find Your Way

Switzerland's ravishing landscapes inspire immediate action – grab boots, leap on board, toot bike bell and let spirits rip. However you choose to get around, the going is typically smooth and the scenery is XXL magnificent.

TRAIN, BUS, BOAT & CABLE CAR

Swiss trains, buses and paddle steamers on lakes all run like clockwork and connect seamlessly with mountain railways and cable cars. Transport is pricey – consider carefully the numerous discount-giving travel cards and tickets that are available.

CAR & MOTORCYCLE

A car is not essential, but can be useful for unearthing the country's nooks, crannies and most rural folds. Navigating steep relentless switchbacks is part of the joy of a summer road trip across high mountain passes in the Alps; check if open on *alpen-paesse.ch*.

Northern Switzerland, p1123

Feel the edgy urban pulse of the country's Germanic roots in a flush of northern cities, from one of Europe's least-known capitals to wealthy, hard-working and increasingly hip Zürich.

Ticino, p1132

Switzerland meets Italy: feast on pizza, gelato and a rich dose of dolce vita (the 'sweet life') in this Italian-speaking Swiss land of lakes, palm trees and more hours of sunshine than anywhere else in the country.

The Swiss Alps, p1127

Soul-soaring mountain peaks, glacier, lakes and gorges stitch together this extraordinary swathe of the country, where the bulk of the action kicks off outside. Summer- or winter- sports fiends, this is your 'hood.

Geneva, p1118

Meet French-speaking Switzerland. 'Big bang' secrets, beachside DJs and chocolate-box old towns: Lake Geneva's eponymous town and its belle epoque shores delight and surprise.

50 km
25 miles

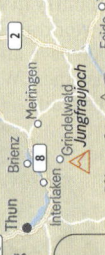

Jet d'Eau (p1118) and Lake Geneva, Geneva

Plan Your Time

Despite the gravity-defying geographical terrain at times, Switzerland distances are manageable, variety is within easy reach and pretty much everything runs with clockwork precision and efficiency.

A Quick Taster

● Spend a day in Francophone **Geneva** (p1118), enjoying old-town flanerie and a lake swim. Venture east along Lake Geneva by rail or paddle steamer, stopping in art-rich **Lausanne** (p1121) or music-mad **Montreux** (p1121). Cross the famous *Röstigraben* (Switzerland's linguistic, cultural divide) to capital city **Bern** (p1123). End on the Swiss-Italian Riviera (p1134).

A Week in the Mountains

● Use metropolis **Zürich** (p1125) as a stepping stone to **Grindelwald** (p1130) for alpine scenery on skis or afoot, and take a ride of a lifetime up **Jungfraujoch** (p1130). Consider a pit stop in **Lucerne** (p1130), epitome of graceful lake living. Zip to **St Moritz** (p1131) for more alpine action, then loop east into Italian Switzerland in medieval **Bellinzona** (p1132).

SEASONAL HIGHLIGHTS

SPRING
Warm days: cafe terraces unfurl, flowers bloom along lake promenades, lake cruises spring into action.

SUMMER
Ski lifts open for hikers and mountain bikers, and high mountain passes are snow-free. Time to swim in lakes.

AUTUMN
Toast September's grape harvest at wine festivals. Ticino goes chestnut crazy. Mountain resorts hibernate in October.

WINTER
Carve through powder and scoff cheese fondue in an alpine resort. Ski season is mid-December to early April.

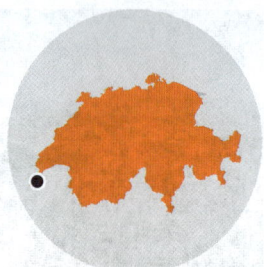

Geneva

CULTURE AND CHOCOLATE | OLD-TOWN FLANERIE | URBAN BEACHES

GETTING AROUND

Geneva is walkable, but **TPG** *(tpg.ch)* buses, trams and shuttle boats save tired legs; buy tickets *(three-stop single/hr/day Chf2/3/10)* at stops or on the TPG+ app.

Hotel guests receive a free **Geneva Transport Card**, covering unlimited public transport – also included in the **Geneva City Pass** *(geneve. com; Chf30/40/50 for 24/48/72hr)*. Rent a bike via the **Donkey Republic** *(donkey. bike)* app.

☑ TOP TIP

To meet *chocolatiers* and taste their creations, buy a **Choco Pass** *(adult/ child Chf30/6)* at Geneva **tourist office** *(geneva.ch)* inside the train station or online; Chf1 goes towards Switzerland's climate protection/sustainable tourism. The 24-hour pass covers nine chocolate shops, Monday to Saturday.

French-speaking Geneva (Genève) is a rare breed. Glinting in the sun with the wealth of luxury jewellers, chocolate shops and investment banks, its flawless, glossy veneer can feel impenetrable. But meander away from the manicured lakeshore – into less touristy neighbourhoods like grungier Pâquis, village-like Carouge or along the postindustrial Rhône – and a rougher-cut diamond emerges, quietly humming with attitude.

A place of international diplomacy ever since persecuted Protestants from France sought refuge here during the Reformation in the 16th century, Geneva is home to 200-odd international and nongovernmental organisations, including the UN, World Health Organization and International Committee of the Red Cross. Getting a soaking on the pier beneath its emblematic Jet d'Eau pencil fountain, a 1951 rendition of the plume of water that shot into the sky for 15 minutes each Sunday to release pressure at the city's water station, is a rite of passage.

Feel Geneva's Antique Heartbeat

Explore the old town

Head to Gothic **Cathédrale St-Pierre** *(concerts-cathedrale. ch; towers adult/child Chf10/5)* and spiral up its towers to enjoy lake and old-town views. Next door at the **Musée International de la Réforme** *(musee-reforme.ch; adult/child Chf13/6)*, closed Monday, learn how Geneva became a safe haven for Protestant refugees persecuted for their faith during the 16th-century Reformation. Uphill on **Grand-Rue**, philosopher Jean-Jacques Rousseau (1712–78) was born at the **Maison de Rousseau et de la Literature** *(m-r-l.ch/; adult/child Chf7/5)*. End on **Place du Bourg-de-Four**, Roman forum, medieval-fair host and modern-day cafe-terrace hub.

GENEVA

Old Town

R de la Madeleine
R de Rive
R Jean-Calvin
R Verdaine
Terrasse
Agrippa
d'Aubigné
Pl du Bourg-
de-Four
Parc des
Bastions

0   200 m
0   0.1 miles

Av de Ferney
Av de la Paix
Pl des
Nations
Av de France
R de Lausanne
R de Montbrillant
Parc de
la Perle
du Lac
R de la Croix-Rouge

Av Giuseppe Motta
R de Vermont
R du Grand Pré
Parc des
Cropettes
Gare de
Cornavin
R de la Servette
CERN
(6.5km);
Science Gateway
(6.5km)
R Voltaire
R de Lausanne
R Butini
Q Wilson
R du Môle
R de Monthoux
R des Alpes
Pl de
Cornavin
R du Mont-Blanc
Lake
Geneva

Q Gustave-Ador

TCS Camping
Genève-Vésenaz
(3.3km)

Jet d'Eau
Q du Seujet
Rhône
Q des Bergues
R du Rhône
Pl de la
Fusterie
R du Stand
Jardin
Anglais
R des Eaux-Vives
R de Montchoisy
Parc La
Grange

Av Pictet de Rochemont

See Old Town
Enlargement
OLD
TOWN
Pl
Neuve
R de la Croix-Rouge
Bd Georges Favon
Plaine de
Plainpalais
Parc des
Bastions
Bd des Philosophes
Bd Helvétique
Rte de Chêne
Rte de Malagnou

0   1 km
0   0.5 miles

⭐ **HIGHLIGHTS**
1 Jet d'Eau

🔴 **SIGHTS**
2 Cathédrale St-Pierre
3 Conservatoire et Jardin
  Botaniques
4 Grand-Rue
5 Horloge Fleurie

6 Maison de Rousseau et
  de la Literature
7 Musée International de
  la Réforme
8 Parc de la Perle du Lac
9 Place du Bourg-de-Four
10 Plage des Eaux-Vives
11 Quai du Mont Blanc

🔴 **ACTIVITIES**
12 Baby Plage
13 Bains des Pâquis
14 Bains du Jet d'Eau
15 Genève Plage
16 Quai de Cologny

⚫ **SLEEPING**
17 Hôtel Bel'Esperance

🟢 **EATING**
18 Bistrot des Halles
19 Buvette des Bains
20 Chez Ma Cousine
21 El Catrín

🔵 **INFORMATION**
22 Tourist Office

Venerate Mont Blanc

A waterfront walk along Quai du Mont Blanc

Satellites ensure Geneva's **Horloge Fleurie** (Flower Clock) next to **Pont du Mont Blanc** keeps perfect time, with the world's longest second hand (2.5m) and 6500 flowers. Across the bridge, views of Mont Blanc (4805m) encrust **Quai du Mont Blanc**. Promenade along the lakeshore to **Parc de la Perle du Lac**, where outdoor films are screened in summer (*cinetransat.ch; free*). North again, the **Conservatoire et Jardin Botaniques** (*cjbg.ch; free*) showcases 11,000 species from around the world.

BEST LAKESIDE SWIM SPOTS

Genève Plage: May to September, this 1930s swimming-pool complex buzzes. *(geneve-plage.ch; adult/child Chf7/3.50)*

Bains des Pâquis: Vintage lake-water pool with retro vibe; sunrise concerts and full-moon swims in summer, saunas and lake dips in winter. *(aubp.ch; adult/child Chf2/1; extras Chf15–22)*

Bains du Jet d'Eau: Two small sleek pools in front of the Jet d'Eau, with lifeguards and snack bar. *(adult/child Chf2/1; Tue-Sun Jul-mid-Sep)*

Plage des Eaux-Vives: Human-made shingle beach with coffee trucks, showers, accessible ramps and family-friendly **Baby Plage** *(plagepublique deseauxvives.ge.ch; free).*

Quai de Cologny: Lounge on a ring-shaped wooden platform, suspended above the water.

DETAN BARIC/ALAMY

CERN

Science Fest

Unravel the universe at CERN

Fathoming out particles that make up matter is what physicists at the European Organization for Nuclear Research or **CERN** do. This is where British scientist Tim Berners Lee invented the World Wide Web in 1989. **Science Gateway** *(visit.cern; free with online advance reservation)* shines light on CERN's incredulous work with science shows, films and exhibitions. Take tram 18 from Gare de Cornavin.

 EATING IN GENEVA: GOOD-VALUE DINING

Buvette des Bains: Grab breakfast, salads, oysters and a superlative cheese fondue at Bains des Pâquis' trendy, no-frills buvette (snack bar). *7am-10.30pm* €

Chez Ma Cousine: Generous portions of chicken, potatoes and salad at the old town's much-loved rotisserie. *11am-11.30pm Mon-Sat, to 10.30pm Sun* €

Bistrot des Halles: Join locals at the zinc bar for *côte de boeuf* (steak), calf kidneys and other bistro classics in the covered market. *7.30-7pm Mon-Fri, 6am-4pm Sat* €€

El Catrín: Authentic tacos and party vibe at this fun-loving Mexican hangout near the station. *6-11.30pm Wed, noon-2pm & 6-11.30pm Thu-Sun* €€

Beyond Geneva

Gem villages, vineyards and castles bead the mythical northern shore of Europe's largest alpine lake.

Heading out of urban Geneva, join dots along the lakeshore between medieval villages, bijou pleasure ports and grassy 'beaches' cradling pebbly shores and summer bars. Rivalling Geneva in the dining and nightlife stakes is Lausanne (Switzerland's fourth-largest city), with an Olympian pedigree and vistas that pack a punch. A city of steps, its *escaliers* (staircases) link the hilltop old town and EPFL campus (Europe's version of Boston's MIT, where bold young scientists are engineering future brilliance) with belle époque beauty by the water. Continuing east, Lavaux vineyards so steep they are UNESCO-listed waltz along the shore to jazzy Montreux and the lake's emblematic château. Bicycle, e-bike or train, sailboat, vintage steamer or stand-up paddle: pick your means and level up with the local outdoor-action set.

Places

Lausanne p1121
Montreux p1121
Gruyères p1122

Lausanne

TIME FROM GENEVA: **45MIN**

Meet the watch at the cathedral

Atop Lausanne's steeply pitched, medieval Old Town, **Cathédrale de Notre Dame** *(cathedrale-lausanne.ch; belfry adult/child €5/2)* might lack the lightness of French Gothic buildings, but its 'backstage' encounters thrill. Visit after dark when you can accompany the *guet* (nightwatch) – floppy black hat, candlelit lantern – on his nightly climb up 153 steps to his lookout and spartan bunk room atop the 79m-tall **Tour du Beffroi** (Belfry Tower). In keeping with a medieval tradition dating to 1405, the nightwatchman (or, since 2021, a female *guette*) calls out the hours into the night from 10pm to 2am.

Aim for a full moon or a night around midsummer when starlit views of the city laid out at your feet glow gold. To join *le guet/guette* at 10pm, you must call their 'office' (+41 21 312 74 91) to reserve for the following day.

Montreux

TIME FROM GENEVA: **65MIN**

Follow a trail of flowers to Château de Chillon

Art, music and natural beauty collide in Montreux, 30km southeast of Lausanne. The elegant lakeside town has been a magnet for artists and celebrities since the 19th century. Pink Floyd, David Bowie, Elton John and Ella Fitzgerald have all played at

GETTING AROUND

Regular SBB trains trundle along the lake from Geneva and Lausanne to Montreux and beyond. CGN steamers from Lausanne (1¾ hours) and Montreux (15 minutes) dock right in front of Château de Chillon.

Use Lausanne's metro, buses and trolleybuses to tackle city hills. Hotel guests get a free **Lausanne Transport Card** covering transport; otherwise buy tickets on the TL app *(t-l.ch)*. Cut sightseeing costs with a **Lausanne City Pass** *(1/2/3 days Chf30/40/50)*, also covering transport.

BEST LAUSANNE MUSEUMS

Olympic Museum:
Sprint against Usain Bolt at this museum. Stacks of interactive exhibits for all ages.

Plateforme 10:
Modern art in a trio of museums in an architecturally striking complex by Lausanne train station.

Collection de l'Art Brut: The world's original collection of Art Brut – subversive, 'raw art' by artists with no formal training – inside an 18th-century château.

Fondation de l'Hermitage:
A 19th-century mansion with art exhibitions, gardens and a family-friendly cafe-bistro.

Palais de Rumine:
Archaeology, geology and money museums inside the palace (1891–1906) where the treaty finalising the break-up of the Ottoman Empire after WWI was signed.

MARISA ESTIVILL/SHUTTERSTOCK

Château de Gruyères, Gruyères

Montreux's world-famous music festival, an annual fixture since 1967. Poking around the recording studio where rock band Queen recorded several albums at **Queen: The Studio Experience** (*mercuryphoenixtrust.org/studioexperience; free*) is a tearjerker.

Soak up summer splendour along the **Chemin Fleuri**. The Flower Path unfurls along the waterfront for 2.5km to Switzerland's best-preserved medieval fortress **Château de Chillon** (*chillon.ch; adult/child Chf15/7*). Spellbinding floral displays are positively tropical, and views of alpine mountain peaks across the water in France are Disney movie stuff. In odd years during summer's **Biennale Montreux** (*biennale.ch; Aug–Nov*), sculptures by Swiss sculptors dot the lake path.

Gruyères

TIME FROM GENEVA: **90MIN** 🚗

On the trail of cheesemakers

A classic day trip for Genevans, this tiny chocolate-box village seduces with cobbled streets, flower-strewn wooden houses and 13th-century **Château de Gruyères** (*chateau-gruyeres.ch; adult/child Chf13/5*). Come summer weekends, you might catch alpenhorn players in the streets. But cheese is the cherry on the cake – AOP Gruyère, to be precise. Get up close to the production process at two very different dairies: industrial **La Maison du Gruyère** (*lamaisondugruyere.ch, adult/family Chf8/12*) next to Gruyères train station, and 17th-century rustic wooden chalet **Fromagerie d'Alpage de Moléson** (*moleson.ch; adult/child Chf5/3*), 5km south, where cheesemaker François still heats the milk each morning in a cauldron over a wood fire and presses curds by hand into the moulds. Book at both to bag a spot.

 EATING & DRINKING IN LAUSANNE: OUR PICKS

Jetée de la Compagnie: Yoga, DJ sets, sunrise concerts at a 'beach' bar in an industrial container with tables by the water. *10am-midnight, from 9am Sun*

Great Escape: Grungy club-like interior and tree-shaded terrace above Place de Riponne. *10am-1am Mon-Thu, to 2am Fri, 11am-2am Sat, noon-1am Sun*

Le Barbare: Lausanne's best hot chocolate, plus superlative coffee, lunch and brunch year-round. *9am-midnight Tue & Wed, to 1am Thu-Sat, 10am-6pm Sun* €€

Café de l'Evêché: Dip into a traditional cheese fondue, laced with beer, in this old-school cafe by the cathedral. *7am-midnight Mon-Fri, from 11.30am Sat & Sun* €€

Northern Switzerland

ART AND ARCHITECTURE | CITIES | URBAN SWIMMING

Cradled by different beauty from the archetypal soaring mountains and alpine valleys, the Swiss Plateau in the north is Swisser than Swiss. Glacial meltwaters from the Bernese Alps trickle into the Aare River, a perfect ribbon of turquoise that wraps itself around Bern, the laid-back city few realise is Switzerland's capital. The holey cheese that couldn't be more Swiss if it tried hails from the surrounding Emmental countryside, as beautiful as Bern's cobbled picture-book Altstadt is enchanting.

Further north, velvety fields and rolling hills frame urban Basel. Nowhere is Switzerland's Franco-Germanic roots quite so apparent as in this multicultural powerhouse of a city, where Switzerland meets France and Germany at the heart of the Rhine confluence.

The metropolis vibes max out in Zürich, the country's hardworking financial centre which, being Swiss, softens the urban blow with a dreamy lake location and oversized nature right on its doorstep: the Rheinfall waterfall, mirrorlike Lake Constance, those whopping Swiss Alps on the horizon...

☑ **TOP TIP**

August is the month for Zürich's **Street Parade** *(streetparade.com/en)*, a techno celebration that has firmly become one of Europe's largest and wildest street parties. Join 800,000 revellers dancing to live music and DJ sets at one of eight stages and 29 'love mobiles'.

Bern

Bern will sweep you off your feet with its riverside location, World Heritage–listed **Altstadt** (Old Town), phenomenal art and views of snow-frosted Alps on the horizon. Catch bears,

GETTING AROUND

Efficient SBB trains link all the main towns and cities; a car is only needed if you want to meander completely off the urban beaten track. Bern, Basel and Zürich are all a delight to explore on foot; buses, trams and local trains cover longer distances (download public-transport apps at *bernmobil.ch, bvb.ch* and *svv.ch* respectively). Free or inexpensive bicycle-rental schemes make cycling fun – all three cities are part of the **PubliBike** *(publibike.ch)* bike-sharing scheme.

a golden cockerel, jester and god of time Chronos twirling four minutes before the hour on Bern's historical **Zytglogge** clock tower.

Soak up Swiss art in technicolour

Take in Switzerland's answer to the Guggenheim. Rising like three rippling waves above farmland just outside town, Renzo Piano's striking **Zentrum Paul Klee** *(zpk.org; adult/child Chf20/7)* is a tribute to the visionary Swiss-German artist, born near Bern in 1879. Rotating exhibitions draw on a 4000-strong collection of Klee's colour-charged, music-inspired works, showcasing his prodigious career, from expressionism to Cubism and surrealism. Bus 12 runs from Bahnhof to the museum.

Swim down the Aare

Drifting past the historic landmarks of the Altstadt or dipping with locals during their lunch break in the city's shockingly cold turquoise water is a rite of passage. Providing you're an experienced swimmer, try the classic route: hike 2km upstream from **Marzili Pools** to **Camping Eichholz**, then drift back with the current to Marzili's brilliant (and free) lido to swim laps, sunbathe, play volleyball or grab an ice cream. The views of the domed **Bundeshaus** and the **Münster**'s medieval spire are spot on.

Basel

Basel draws culture fiends from far and wide with its exciting art museums, nightlife and cute Altstadt (Old Town) anchored by its colourful **Rathaus** and 13th-century Münster. One-third of its urban population being non-Swiss today assures a continuing international flavour.

Meet art masters at Basel's 'big three'

Basel's cultural scene is its biggest drawcard, with the **Kunstmuseum Basel** *(kunstmuseumbasel.ch; adult/child Chf30/12)* showcasing a world-class collection spread across three buildings in the heart of the city. Switzerland's largest collection of public art spans masters from the 15th century to present day.

Attack contemporary art next at the wacky **Museum Jean Tinguely** *(tinguely.ch; adult/child Chf18/free)*, designed by Ticino architect Mario Botta. Arrive by ferry from the **Münster** (cathedral) or cross Mittlere Brücke (Middle Bridge) and walk east. The museum is above a pebble beach, pleasant for swimming or floating downstream with a *Wickelfisch* (sold at the tourist office) back to Mittlere Brücke.

HOW SWISS CHEESE GETS ITS HOLES

Named for its birthplace in the Emme River valley, 15 minutes by train from Bern, Switzerland's Emmentaler cheese has a proud history dating back to the Middle Ages. Copycat cheesemakers around the world have appropriated the Emmental name, but only authentic Emmentaler Switzerland AOC conforms to the original production technique, using raw milk from grass-fed cows, cellar-ripened in giant wheels for at least 120 days.

Emmentaler's famous holes, known as 'eyes', result from the release of carbon-dioxide bubbles by bacteria during the ageing process. The larger the holes, the longer the cheese has matured, and the more pronounced its flavour.

EATING & DRINKING IN BERN: OUR PICKS

Altes Tramdepot: Cavernous tram hall pairing schnitzel and *Bauernrösti* (fried potatoes topped with an egg) with microbrews. *11am-12.30am* €€

Kornhauskeller: Dine beneath vaulted frescoed arches at this cellar restaurant championing Mediterranean cuisine. *11.30am-11.30pm Mon-Sat, to 10pm Sun* €€

On Tap: Atmospheric vaulted cellar with 12 craft beers on tap and more by the bottle. Pair with antipasti. *4-11.30pm Mon-Wed, to 12.30am Thu-Sat*

Abflugbar: Slick, stylish, speakeasy-style cellar bar with knockout cocktails. Try the basil smash. *7.30pm-12.30am Wed-Sun*

Rathaus, Basel

Final calling card is **Fondation Beyeler** *(fondationbeyeler.ch; adult/under 25 Chf25/free)*, in a light-filled, open-plan building by Italian architect Renzo Piano. Exhibitions rotate 19th- and 20th-century works and ethnographic art from Africa, Alaska and Oceania.

Zürich

MAP p1124

With a gorgeous location at the meeting of the Limmat River and Zürichsee, Zürich is hip and culturally ambitious, too. Pair old-world lanes in the cathedral-pinned Old Town with postindustrial edge in the artsy Züri-West 'hood. May to mid-September, swim at a lake- or riverside *badi* (lido) and enjoy a lake cruise.

Gen up on Swiss history

Celebrate national history and culture at the **Landesmuseum Zürich** *(landesmuseum.ch; adult/child Chf10/free)*. Elaborately carved and painted sleds, traditional costumes, reconstructed historical rooms and more are beautifully presented at the main branch of the Swiss National Museum. Find exhibits on archaeology, and Zürich's history and national identity. The gift shop has one of the city's best choice of souvenirs.

 EATING & DRINKING IN ZÜRICH: OUR PICKS ——— MAP p1124

Haus Hiltl: A buffet of meatless delights or dine formally upstairs at the world's oldest vegetarian restaurant (1898). *7am-10pm Mon-Fri, 8am-11pm Sat, 10am-10pm Sun* €

Old Inn: Homemade pastrami and other delicacies in antique-style gastropub in art nouveau building. *11.30am-2pm Mon-Fri, 6pm-midnight Tue-Sat* €€

Frau Gerolds Garten: A focal point of the city's alfresco summer drinking scene, in Züri-West. This is one of Europe's best grownup playgrounds. *hours vary*

Clouds: Survey the city from the heady heights of this sophisticated bar on the 35th floor of the Prime Tower. *5pm-midnight Wed & Thu, to 1am Fri & Sat, noon-8pm Sun*

BEST ZÜRICH CHOCOLATE SHOPPING

Lindt Home of Chocolate: Buy Lindt at factory prices at this educational experience with showpiece 9m chocolate fountain.

Café Sprüngli: Try pralines, Luxemburgerli macarons and Grand Cru Absolu, a chocolate made only with cocoa beans and cocoa pulp, at this historic cafe from 1836.

Max Chocolatier: Stylishly packaged bars, truffles and pralines, made with 100% natural ingredients.

Berg und Tal: Artisan grocery stocking several brands of locally produced bean-to-bar chocolate, including Taucherli and Garçoa.

La Flor: Specialising in single-origin bars made from sustainably grown cacao sourced directly from farmers.

★ HIGHLIGHTS	● EATING	8 Frau Gerolds Garten
1 Kunsthaus - Moser Building	3 Café Sprüngli	● SHOPPING
● SIGHTS	4 Haus Hiltl	9 Berg & Tal
2 Landesmuseum Zürich	5 Old Inn	10 Freitag
	6 Restaurant Markthalle	11 Im Viadukt
	● DRINKING & NIGHTLIFE	12 La Flor
	7 Clouds	13 Max Chocolatier

Admire great art at the Kunsthaus

Explore Switzerland's largest art collection at the superlative **Kunsthaus** (*kunsthaus.ch; adult/child Chf24/free*) museum, where thought-provoking exhibits span two main buildings, linked by an underground tunnel with an Ólafur Elíasson sculptural artwork on its ceiling. Seek out its unparalleled collection of the works by titans of the Swiss art world, including Augusto and Alberto Giacometti and Ferdinand Hodler.

Feel the pulse of Züri-West

Züri-West's **Im Viadukt** (*im-viadukt.ch*) is a trendy shopping and dining complex beneath old stone railway bridges. Stroll the viaduct's three blocks between Limmatstrasse and Geroldstrasse to see what catches your eye. Grab breakfast or dinner at **Restaurant Markthalle** (*restaurant-markthalle. ch*). Inside a stack of shipping containers, **Freitag** (*freitag.ch*) sells colourful wallets and bags of all shapes and sizes made from recycled truck tarps.

The Swiss Alps

OUTDOOR SPORTS | INCREDIBLE SCENERY | PRISTINE PEACE

You have every right to feel petite in the Swiss Alps. Stretching from the canton of Valais above the Rhône Valley in the west to Graubünden in the east, they cut, slice and dice more than half of Switzerland into an astonishing outdoor playground of cloud-shredding snowy peaks, thunderous gorges, ice-blue glaciers and lakes – all ripe for summer hiking and winter skiing.

Switzerland's invisible *Röstigraben* (linguistic and cultural border) kicks in just beyond the French-speaking town of Verbier, where starlets sip cocktails and farmers craft AOP Raclette cheese. Arriving in Zermatt, tongues wag in Swiss-German as everyone stares, transfixed, at the famous Matterhorn. Moving north, the Bernese Oberland – shaped by a godlike hand – is another diva forcing visitors to constantly peer up in wonder. Whether flirting with mountaineering on a *via ferrata*, scaling new heights atop Jungfraujoch or thrilling out on Interlaken whitewater, be prepared to experience nature in overdrive.

Verbier

Ritzy Verbier is the diamond of the Valaisian Alps: small and expensive, it draws accomplished winter skiers and summer-time mountain bikers. This French-speaking 'place to be' is an easy train from Geneva and its international airport to Verbier's valley station **Le Châble**, from where cable cars glide to the top.

Fly high on a Mont Fort sunrise

Watching the sun rise over pink peaks at dawn from **Mont Fort** (3330m) is a goosebump moment. If a 4.25am cable-car departure and Chf89 price tag (covering breakfast and all-day cable-car travel) is too extreme, ride a later bubble up to **Les Ruinettes** (2191m) and beyond to Mont Fort *(Chf22 with a free summertime VIP Pass, incl in hotel accommodation Jun-Oct)* from the **Médran cable-car station** on Verbier's main street. Harness the daredevil in you for the descent:

GETTING AROUND

There are excellent SBB train services from the rest of Switzerland to mountain resorts such as car-free Zermatt and Interlaken; funiculars often cover the final leg up to resorts. Cable cars typically close for servicing in late April and late October.

If you are driving in winter, carry snow chains or use winter tyres. In early and late summer, check if mountain passes are open (signs at the bottom of access roads usually say so).

☑ **TOP TIP**

Remember the *Glacier Express* and other panoramic lines are mountain trains: last-minute cancellations due to blocked lines by snow or rockfall happen (your reserved journey still takes place, but on regular lines).

at 100km/h on the 1.4km-long **Mont 4 Zipline** *(adult/child over 8 Chf45/20)*. The bird's-eye view over the Tortin Glacier is of once-in-a-lifetime experience.

Mountain-bike in an alpine playground

Ski-celeb Verbier morphs into bike central in summer. Whether you're tearing down the mountainside as a family on chunky *trottinettes* (hairnet and helmet included in fat-tyre scooter rental; from eight years) from the top of the Savoleyres or Les Ruinettes cable cars, or tackling technical jumps with expert mountain bikers in a dedicated bike park, there is something to suit most abilities. June to mid-October, mountain bikers can transport wheels on the Médran cable car and La Chaux Express chairlift from Les Ruinettes to access 19km of down-hill descents in **Verbier Bike Park** *(verbierbikepark.ch; day pass adult/child Chf55/28, with VIP Pass Chf28/14).*

Zermatt

Nothing prepares you for that first intoxicating glimpse of car-free Zermatt's peak rising majestically above the town and ski slopes. Step off the train and a puff cloud invariably

 DRINKING IN VERBIER: BEST APRÈS-SKI

Ice Cube: Summer or winter, watch paragliders paint rainbows in the sky from this slope-side 'cube' at Les Ruinettes. *9am-4.15pm Jun-Sep & Dec-Apr*

Le Rouge: Swoosh off the blue Le Rouge piste and into The Red for drinks, 'funky fondue' soirées and resident DJs spinning dance tunes. *noon-midnight*

Pub Mont Fort: Downtown's après-ski heavyweight: live music, DJ sets, terrace and pub grub (apricot chicken wings, fries in melted cheese). *3pm-2am*

Farinet: Less intimidating than other bars, the downtown lounge bar with sun terrace hosts a happy hour and live bands nightly in season. *3pm-2am*

clings to the 4478m hooked summit, making the sudden pop-up brilliance of a cloudless Matterhorn all the more wondrous.

Summit 3883m and glide into Italy

Admire ice sculptures in a palace 15m deep in a glacier, whoosh down ice slides and snow-tube atop **Klein Matterhorn** (3883m), accessed from Zermatt town by three cable cars culminating with the **Matterhorn Glacier Paradise** (*matterhornparadise.ch; adult/child return Chf125/62.50*), the world's highest-altitude 3S cable car. The view of 14 glaciers and 35 other peaks over 4000m at the top is beyond breathtaking.

Assuming it's a bluebird day, hop aboard the 1.6km-long **Matterhorn Alpine Crossing** (*matterhornalpinecrossing. com; adult single/return from Zermatt Chf156/240*) for a spellbinding cable-car journey over a spectacular glacial world of ice – and across the world's highest alpine border crossing – to Testa Grigia (3458m) in Cervinia, Italy.

Ride Europe's highest cogwheel railway

The Matterhorn dominates the scenic ride aboard the **Gornergratbahn** (*gornergrat.ch; adult/child return summer Chf132/66, winter Chf96/48*) – an 1898 vintage – from Zermatt to **Gornergrat** (3089m). Larch forests and the Vispa River melt into snowfields as the train staggers up gradients of up to 20% for 9.4km. Alight at the top to a hypnotic panorama of the Gornergrat glacier, Monte Rosa massif and Switzerland's highest peak, Dufourspitze (Dufour Peak; 4634m). Toast your good fortune on the sun-blazed terrace of **Kulmhotel Gornergrat** (*gornergrat-kulm.ch*).

Interlaken

Victorian-era glamour meets big mountains in Interlaken, which thrills with just about every heart-pumping alpine sport. Squished between the glacier-fed lakes of Thun and Brienz, this is the springboard to the Alps' fabled Jungfrau Region.

Hook up with a guide

Capped by the pearly white peaks of Eiger, Mönch and Jungfrau, this petite alpine town is second only to Queenstown, New Zealand, when it comes to extreme sports. **Outdoor Interlaken** (*outdoor.ch*) is a one-stop adventure shop for pretty much every buzz-inducing activity imaginable: tandem paragliding or skydiving, bungee jumping from a mountain gondola above a dazzling alpine lake, whitewater rafting and canyon swinging between gorge walls at speeds of 120km/h.

THE GLACIER EXPRESS

Gorging on cinematic shots of peaks, lakes, racing whitewater and other natural landscapes is what a day aboard the bucket-list **Glacier Express** (*glacierexpress.ch; single 1st/2nd class Chf159/272, plus reservation fee Chf49*) is about. Pulled by steam engine when it first puffed out of Zermatt in 1930, the iconic red train traverses 91 tunnels and 291 bridges on its slow journey to St Moritz (p1131). Creeping along at 10km/h at times, the average speed on its 290km-long journey is just 42km/h. On the final leg between Chur and St Moritz, the six-arch, 65m-high Landwasser Viaduct on the UNESCO World Heritage–listed Albula railway line razzle-dazzles.

EATING IN ZERMATT: OUR PICKS

Stefanie's Crêperie: Perfect crepes with sweet or savoury (cheese fondue with cherry brandy!) toppings. *1-7pm Mon & Tue, 11.30am-9.30pm Wed-Sun* €

Blatten: Follow a knowing crowd to this small family-run chalet cafe and prized lunch address, in Zermatt's peaceful Blatten hamlet since 1850. *10am-6pm* €

Zum See: Tuck into a cracking rösti and other top-drawer grassroots dishes at this centuries-old chalet in the Zum See hamlet. *8.30am-5pm* €€

Potato: With produce sourced within 99km and ceiling lamps crafted from wooden veg crates, you don't get more local – or brilliantly creative. *6-11pm Mon-Sat* €€€

**MORE MYTHICAL
TRAIN RIDES**

Bernina Express:
Plunge through 55
tunnels and across
196 bridges on
this 156km journey
through the Engadine,
from Chur to Tirano
(four hours) aboard
panoramic coaches
(tickets.rhb.ch).

**Golden Pass
Express:** Variable-
gauge bogies mean
the journey between
Interlaken and
Montreux on Lake
Geneva can be done
in a single 3½-hour
trip *(gpx.swiss).*

Centovalli Railway:
Narrow-gauge line
linking Locarno with
Domodossola (Italy)
in 1¾ hours *(vigezzina
centovalli.com).*

**Gotthard Panorama
Express:** Five-hour
journey mixes a cruise
across Lake Lucerne
with a train through
ravines and past
mighty St Gotthard
mountain range to
Bellinzona and Lugano
*(gotthard-panorama-
express.ch).*

Grindelwald

Skiers and hikers cottoned onto the charms of this mountain resort in the late 19th century. The geranium-studded chalets, verdant pastures and Oscar-worthy backdrop (the Eiger's north face, glinting tongues of Oberer, crown-like peak of Wetterhorn) are as tantalising as ever.

Eternal ice at Europe's highest train station

Brave the crowds on the once-in-a-lifetime trip to Jungfraujoch, Europe's highest train station, at 3454m. From Grindelwald, the **Eiger Express** *(jungfrau.ch; round trip adult/child Chf97.80/20)* wings you up to Eigergletscher station, where you switch to the Jungfrau Railway up to UNESCO World Heritage–listed **Jungfraujoch** *(jungfrau.ch; round trip from Grindelwald adult/child Chf201/20).* The summit is always snow white. From the Sphinx observation deck, spot the **Aletsch Glacier.** Grindelwald's **Outdoor Mountaineering School** *(outdoor.ch; 2-day hike Chf395)* organises summer roped hikes on the 23km-long sea of ice with a guide.

Pick up speed at First

Rising above Grindelwald, the 2184m summit of First gets hearts thumping with up-close views of Eiger's ferocious north face and the 4078m fang of Schreckhorn from **First Cliff Walk by Tissot** *(jungfrau.ch; free),* a gravity-defying lookout platform jutting 45m into the void.

Less than an hour's walk from the First cable-car top station unveils the the calm sapphire waters of **Bachalpsee.** In winter, there's great powder for snowboarding and free-skiing. From **Faulhorn** (2681m), sledge 15km down to Grindelwald on the world's longest sledge run.

Lucerne

Lounging lakeside on the Swiss Alps' northernmost fringe, Lucerne (Luzern in German) has been on the map since the 13th century when merchants crossing the **St Gotthard Pass** traded their wares here. Mountains of myth ring its cobalt lake; Goethe, Queen Victoria, Wagner and more all waxed lyrical about the medieval Old Town.

Devour frescoes, fountains and medieval towers

Using the 14th-century covered wooden footbridge **Kapellbrücke,** cross the Reuss River into Lucerne's perfectly preserved **Altstadt.** Minutes from the train station, this warren

 EATING IN GRINDELWALD: OUR PICKS

Cafe 3692: Grindelwald ingredients in tasty specials at this quirky, woodsy hut. Or try alpine teas with pastries. *9am-11pm Fri & Sat, to 6pm Sun* €

Stallbeizli-Heuboden: Fondue heaven at this mountain hut in a converted barn with summer terrace. *noon-10pm Tue-Sat, to 8pm Sun* €€

Glacier Fine Dining: Feast on foraged flowers, herbs and berries. Or Graubünden salmon marinated in gin made from Eiger glacier water. *6-11pm Thu-Mon* €€€

Airtime: In nearby Lauterbrunnen, chill over breakfast, gourmet sandwiches, coffee with cake and Staubbach beer. *9am-5pm Fri-Mon* €

Reuss River and Kapellbrücke, Lucerne

of cobbled streets hides ornate fountains and frescoes illustrating city history and culture. Fill your water bottle at the colourful **Fritschibrunnen** on Kapellplatz, admire painted facades on **Hirschenplatz**, and nod to the stone fountain on historic market square **Weinmarkt**. End by the river to confront roof panels depicting the Dance of Death on 15th-century covered timber bridge **Spreuerbrücke** (1408).

St Moritz

Switzerland's cradle of alpine tourism, St Moritz has been luring royals, celebrities and moneyed wannabes since 1864. With its aquamarine lake, emerald forests and aloof mountains, the town looks a million dollars. Beyond the glamour, vast swathes of the surrounding Graubünden region are remote and ripe for exploring.

Dare to try extreme bobsledding and tobogganing

For buzz, try careering headfirst down glass-smooth ice at 135km/h on St Moritz's **Olympic Bob Run** *(olympia-bobrun. ch; bobsleigh guest ride Chf269)*. Handcrafted from natural ice in Celerina near St Moritz, this 1722m-long ice channel is the world's oldest bobsleigh run, dating from 1904. Or torpedo headfirst down the **Cresta Run** *(cresta-run.com; 1st 5 rides Chf700)*, a tobogganing course created by British visitors in 1885. In a lying down position, you use a rake on special boots to brake and steer at speeds of up to 140km/h.

BEST LUCERNE MUSEUMS

Verkehrshaus: Switzerland's most visited museum, the interactive Swiss Museum of Transport is a family-must. *(verkehrshaus.ch)*

Sammlung Rosengart: View works by Paul Klee, Monet, Cézanne, Matisse and more in this world-class modern-art collection. *(rosengart.ch)*

Kunstmuseum Luzern: A hot spot for Swiss and international art. *(kunstmuseum luzern.ch)*

Zivilschutzanlage Sonnenberg: Tour a 1976 underground bunker large enough to accommodate 2000 people during the Cold War. *(unterir disch-ueberleben.ch)*

Bourbaki Panorama: Admire a huge circular painting by 19th-century Swiss artist Edouard Castres. *(bourbaki panorama.ch)*

 DRINKING AROUND LAKE LUCERNE: IDYLLIC SPOTS

| **Rigi Kulm Hotel:** Modern incarnation of Switzerland's oldest mountain hotel has superlative views from Rigi's peak. *9am-4.30pm Mon-Fri, 8.30am-5pm Sat & Sun* | **Restaurant Seerose:** The shady lakeside terrace makes this a tempting spot for a post-hike spritz or beer in Weggis. *noon-10pm* | **Bürgenstock Resort:** If you're feeling flush, take the boat and funicular up to this luxury resort for a cocktail in its Lakeview Bar. *10am-midnight Sun-Thu, to 1am Fri & Sat* | **Seehotel Waldstätterhof:** The lakeside terrace of this Brunnen hotel is ideal for an aperitif or dinner as the sun sets. *11.30am-2pm & 6.30-10pm* |

Ticino

ITALIAN DOLCE VITA | LAKES | HISTORY

GETTING AROUND

Geography dictates how you can explore this southern tip of Switzerland. A car allows you to go deep into its least-ventured folds – the steep switchbacks won't be to the taste of uncertain drivers. SBB trains connect towns with the rest of Switzerland and nearby Milan in Italy. Boats join the dots year-round between towns and villages on Lago Maggiore *(navigazionelaghi.it)* and Lago di Lugano *(lagolugano.ch)*.

☑ **TOP TIP**

Locarno is the eastern terminus of the historic **Centovalli Railway** *(vigezzinacentovalli.com)*, which trundles in slow motion through burrows via 34 tunnels and across 83 bridges to Domodossola in Italy. Dramatic alpine vistas are nonstop and mesmerising.

The Swiss Alps make their final descent into Italy's sunny plains in Ticino, Switzerland's only entirely Italian-speaking canton where glaciers meet palm trees and Swiss efficiency fuses with Italian flair. Here, on the country's southern tip, olive trees and palms ring alpine lakes. Narrow, twisting valleys sport stone-built villages little changed in two centuries. Gone are the fondue and rösti – think pasta, risotto and polenta instead. Mediterranean winter means sunny days and snow-free lakeshores. In August's sizzling heat, dine in a grotto – a traditional rural dining venue, in a cool shady spot. Earthy autumn ushers in September's grape harvest and Castagnata in October when local chestnuts are picked and celebrated in every guise.

At the heart of the canton rises Bellinzona, Ticino's head-turning capital and a UNESCO World Heritage site, with its fortified ramparts and medieval magic. Venturing south, the tranquil lake waters of Lugano and Locarno on the shared-with-Italy shores of Lago Maggiore quietly seduce.

Ticino's Medieval Capital

Fortress-hop in Bellinzona

Begin at Bellinzona's mighty **Castelgrande** *(fortezzabellinzona.ch; adult/concession Chf28/18)*, with towers and ramparts free to scramble round. The defensive walls that barrel out for 450m to the west afford top-drawer panoramas of the town and mountains beyond. Continue up the other side of the valley to **Castello di Montebello**, with drawbridges, towers and archaeological exhibits. End with the long climb up switchbacks to **Castello di Sasso Corbaro**, perched high on a wooded hillside and exuding an austere beauty.

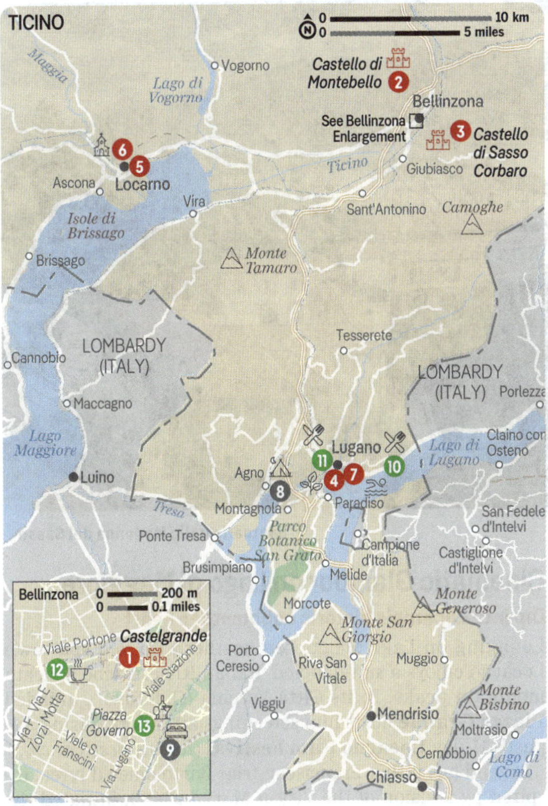

Map Legend

★ HIGHLIGHTS
1 Castelgrande
2 Castello di Montebello
3 Castello di Sasso Corbaro

● SIGHTS
4 Parco Ciani

5 Piazza Grande
6 Santuario della Madonna del Sasso

● ACTIVITIES
7 Lido di Lugano

● SLEEPING
8 Camping Lugano Lake

9 Ostello Montebello

● EATING
10 Le Bucce di Gandria
11 Staglio

● DRINKING & NIGHTLIFE
12 L'Arte del Caffè
13 Paprika Lounge Bar

PALMS, PARROTS & ICY PEAKS

Welcome to the 'Sunshine Capital of Switzerland'! With around 2300 hours of sunshine per year, Locarno is hands-down Switzerland's sunniest town. Thanks to its protected location on the northern rim of Lago Maggiore, ringed by mountains that block cold winds while retaining warmth, sunny days combine with a microclimate to create an almost Mediterranean environment. Palm trees, banana plants, olive trees and tropical flowers thrive in the mild climate here, as does the odd escaped pet parakeet that you occasionally see squawking in trees in city parks. Winter temperatures rarely drop below freezing here, in sharp contrast to Ticino's ice-bound valleys just a short drive away.

Savour the Difference on a Passeggiata

Chill out in Lugano

One of the joys of staying in Lugano is an evening stroll along the promenade, with palm trees and flowerbeds lacing the sparkling waters of Lago di Lugano. Inland, sculpture-dotted **Parco Ciani** is a gorgeous place for a gelato or picnic on a red bench. On hot days, swim in pools or from the sandy beach at **Lido di Lugano** (*lugano.ch; adult/child Chf11/7*). Meandering east, Piazza Manzoni anchors the old-world lanes and boutiques of the atmospheric **Old Town**.

TRABANTOS/SHUTTERSTOCK

Santuario della Madonna del Sasso

Cinematic Glamour on Lago di Maggiore

Dip into Locarno's historic cobblestone heart

Lounging on Lake Maggiore's northern tip, old spa town Locarno enjoys a sun-dappled 'Italian Riviera' vibe beneath mountain peaks. In its Città Vecchia (Old Town), arcaded **Piazza Grande** hosts film screenings after dark during August's 11-day **Locarno Film Festival** *(locarnofestival.ch)*.

Legend has it that Franciscan friar Bartolomeo d'Ivrea, inspired by a vision of the Virgin Mary in 1480, initiated the construction of **Santuario della Madonna del Sasso**, clinging to an outcrop in Locarno's Orselina suburb. To make the pilgrimage here, ride the Cardada **funicular** *(cardada.ch)* from just south of Locarno train station. Walk back down into town along the chapel-lined **Via Crucis** (Way of the Cross).

 EATING & DRINKING IN TICINO: OUR PICKS

Staglio: The best pizza slices in Lugano town that won't break the bank. Central location just back from the lakefront. *11am-9pm Mon-Thu, from noon Fri-Sun* €

Le Bucce di Gandria: In Gandria village above Lugano, feast on seasonal local flavours and sensational lake views. *7-10pm Thu-Sun, noon-2pm Sat & Sun* €€

Paprika Lounge Bar: Dive into inventive drinks and bites at this trendy spot in Bellinzona, perfect for a quick drink or lunch. *7am-10pm Mon-Fri, 8am-2pm Sat*

L'Arte del Caffè: This elegant cafe en route to Castelgrande is a great place for an Italian caffeine shot before the uphill castle hike. *8am-5.30pm Mon-Sat*

Places We Love to Stay

€ Budget €€ Midrange €€€ Top end

Geneva

MAP p1119

TCS Camping Genève-Vésenaz € Campsite with cabins, tent pitches and van park overlooking a grassy beach on Pointe à la Bise, 7km north from downtown Geneva.

Hôtel Bel'Esperance €€ Single to family rooms sleeping four add extra appeal to this reliable midrange hotel. The icing on the cake: a rooftop terrace for lake-drooling.

Lausanne

Lausanne Jeunotel € Smart hostel a stone's throw from the lake, a Roman archaeological dig and the International Olympic Committee's shiny HQ. Dorms sleep two to six.

Mad House € The 'it' address in lively Flon (actually part of Accor's Ibis Styles brand), with rooftop bar, street-art deco and cool rooms from the team behind MAD club.

Montreux

Auberge de Jeunesse Montreux € Roll out of your bunk and into the lake at this modern hostel, midway between Montreux and Château de Chillon.

Hôtel La Rouvenaz €€ This boutique hotel–restaurant across from Montreux lakefront, with a down-to-earth contemporary ambience, is startling good value.

Gruyères

Fleur de Lys € Modern comfort with antique touches in a 17th-century building, plus a decent restaurant with a hidden terrace out the back.

Hotel de Gruyères €€ Cosy, traditional lodgings near the village entrance and car parks, with views of the surrounding mountains.

Bern

Am Pavillon € A pleasingly converted late-19th-century townhouse near the Hauptbahnhof, with bags of art-nouveau charm.

Hotel Marthahaus €€ In a leafy neighbourhood, this sweet and simple guesthouse is crisply designed, quiet and sprinkled with modern art.

Verbier

Map Hostel € Go vintage in the old vicarage, down the hill in Vieux Verbier. Bunk rooms sleep two to six.

Ride Inn €€ 'Chalet-style' B&B with shared bathrooms and summer garden. The bike-mad hosts are a mine of local information.

Zermatt

Jaëgerhof Hotel € Consistently reliable, this functional but attractive hotel sports three-star singles, doubles, twins and family rooms. Copious breakfast buffet.

Hotel Plateau Rose € Another brilliant deal, up a small hill by the Matterhorn Glacier Paradise cable car. Matterhorn views from its back garden are the finest in town.

Interlaken

Backpacker's Villa Sonnenhof € This slick, ecofriendly chalet and art-nouveau villa has immaculate dorms, a relaxed lounge and a well-equipped kitchen.

Salzano Hotel & Spa €€ This intimate chalet hotel on Interlaken's fringes has a quiet spa, big mountain views and outstanding Italian cooking.

Grindelwald

Gletschergarten €€ Brimming with pine, warmth and family heirlooms, this sweet family-run chalet has gorgeous mountain views.

Valley Hostel €€ A great activity base, this chilled hostel in Lauterbrunnen has pine-panelled dorms and a garden with compelling waterfall views.

Lucerne

Capsule Hotel € One-person enclosed sleeping booths, or 'capsules', in multi-capsule rooms, with shared bathrooms. Clean, comfortable alternative to dorm beds.

Hotel Continental Park €€ By pretty Vögeligärtli park in the new town, with stylish rooms and a Ticino-inspired restaurant. Bike hire available.

Mürren & Jungfrau

Mönchsjochhütte € Share the dinner table and dorm with rock climbers at Switzerland's highest serviced hut. Sensational sunrise.

Ticino

MAP p1133

Ostello Montebello € Bellinzona's youth hostel occupies an enviable location between Castelgrande and Montebello. It has basic dorms and a large common room.

Camping Lugano Lake € One of four campsites clustered by Lake Lugano at the end of the runway of Lugano's small airport. High-standard facilities.

Practicalities

AARONCHENPS2/SHUTTERSTOCK

SAFE TRAVEL

Switzerland is very safe. Streets are well lit, and street crime and petty theft are uncommon. Check for ticks after a hike. As weather becomes increasingly fickle and extreme, a warming climate poses the greatest threat. Tap water is safe to drink; fill your bottle for free at fountains.

INSURANCE

If you're skiing, snowboarding or hiking, ensure your policy covers helicopter rescue and emergency repatriation.

Alternatively, summer or winter, when buying your lift pass online or in situ, most resorts offer optional insurance (usually Chf3 per day) covering emergency rescue off the mountain and medical care.

LGBTIQ+ TRAVELLERS

Switzerland is a tolerant country and reasonably progressive on LGBTIQ+ rights.

Zürich, Geneva, Lausanne, Bern and Lucerne have the liveliest LGBTIQ+ scenes. Pride kicks off on the snow in Verbier in April.

NATURAL DISASTERS

Download the Alert Swiss app or consult its website *(alert. swiss)* to receive national alerts, notifications, extreme weather warnings and information about a variety of hazards. The national service also issues relevant safety instructions.

LANGUAGES

German (p519), French (p449), Italian (p717) and Romansh are spoken in Switzerland.

ALPINE HAZARDS

Mountain risks include snowstorms, avalanches, landslides, flooding and thunderstorms. Keep up-to-date with *natural-hazards.ch*.

Summer or winter, alpine weather is notoriously fickle. Even in August it can feel like four seasons in a day, with sun, fog, storms and snow. Before heading into the mountains, check weather forecasts on *meteoswiss.admin.ch*. Subscribe to alerts for your specific location.

OPENING HOURS

Museums 10am–6pm; many close Monday or Tuesday and some stay open late Thursday
Restaurants noon–2.30pm and 6pm–9.30pm (7.30pm–10.30pm in French-speaking Switzerland and Ticino); closed one or two days per week.
Shops 10am–6pm Monday to Friday, to 4pm Saturday (6pm or later in French-speaking Switzerland).

PUBLIC HOLIDAYS

Some cantons observe other holidays and religious days, eg 2 January, Labour Day (1 May), Assumption (15 August) and All Saints' Day (1 November).
New Year's Day 1 January
Good Friday March/April

Easter Sunday and Monday March/April
Ascension 40th day after Easter
Whit Sunday and Monday Seventh week after Easter
Swiss National Day 1 August
Christmas Day 25 December
Boxing Day 26 December

Swiss International Air Lines

Arriving & Getting Around

Zürich Airport, 9km north of the city centre, and Geneva Airport, 4km northwest of the town centre, both have a mainline train station, with speedy trains into town plus regular public transport.

Arriving by Road
Bordering France, Germany, Austria, Liechtenstein and Italy, Switzerland is easily accessible by road. High alpine passes are snow-blocked and closed in winter (October to May/June). Roads signs for motorways are green.

Cycling & E-Biking
Well-signposted, scenic cycling routes spaghetti across the country; find cycling and mountain-biking pages on *schweizmobil.ch*. With SBB Rent-a-Bike *(rentabike.ch),* collect at one train station and return to another.

Driving Essentials
Drive on the right. Headlights must be turned on day and night. November to March, winter tyres are essential. Blood alcohol limit is 0.05%. To use motorways, pay an annual toll *(Chf40)* online at *vignette-schweiz.com*.

Trains, Buses & Cable Cars
Interconnected trains, boats, yellow PostBuses and cable cars have most of the country within easy, car-free reach. Consult routes and buy tickets on *swissrailways.com* and *travelswitzerland.com*. Download the SBB app *(sbb.ch)* for train timetables and tickets.

MONEY
Currency: Swiss franc (CHF or Chf)

CONTACTLESS PAYMENT
Almost every hotel, shop, restaurant, cafe, bar and business supports contactless payments and Apple Pay – there is no minimum payment amount.

CARDS & ATMS
Credit cards are widely accepted; EuroCard/MasterCard and Visa are the most popular. ATMs are widespread and accessible 24 hours.

CASH
Swiss francs are divided into 100 centimes (*Rappen* in German-speaking Switzerland). Many shops and small businesses don't accept large-denomination notes – 100, 200 and 1000 franc notes. Businesses throughout Switzerland accept cash payments in euros. Change will be given in Swiss francs at the rate of exchange calculated on the day.

Curated by
Virginia Maxwell

Türkiye

WHERE EUROPE AND ASIA MEET

Replete with stunning natural landscapes, dynamic cities and evocative remnants of ancient empires, Türkiye offers the perfect mix of cultural, leisure and adventure tourism.

Europe's second-largest country by both area and population is impressive by every measure. Mighty empires have cut a swathe through its territory over millennia, leaving cities, monuments and wonderfully diverse cultures in their wakes. These bequests enrich the lives of locals to this day, and make travelling here an extraordinarily rewarding experience.

Many visitors are drawn by the Aegean and Mediterranean coastlines with their sparkling turquoise-blue waters and sybaritic summer resorts, while others are lured by the quietly compelling landscapes, towns and outdoor attractions of inland Anatolia. Otherworldly destinations such as Cappadocia, home to fairy chimneys, cave dwellings and hot-air-balloon voyages, are deservedly famous, but it's often experiences in off-the-beaten-track villages that will prove most memorable, largely due to the warmth and generosity of locals.

Cities are also a major drawcard, most notably the capital in all but name, İstanbul. Its magnificent minaret-studded skyline, bustling medieval bazaars and world-class eating and drinking scene live up to their reputations and then some. Sailing the length of the storied Bosphorus Strait or boarding a ferry to cross between Europe and Asia are highlights, but so too is a deep dive into the city's thriving cultural scene with events galore. Time spent here – as well as in the extraordinary ancient cities of Ephesus, Hierapolis, Pergamum and Troy – is sure to be a highlight of every traveller's itinerary.

ESIN DENIZ/SHUTTERSTOCK

THE MAIN AREAS

İSTANBUL	**GALLIPOLI PENINSULA & TROY**	**ANCIENT CITIES**	**AEGEAN & MEDITERRANEAN COASTS**	**CAPPADOCIA & NEMRUT DAĞI NATIONAL PARK**
Magical city on the cusp of continents. **p1144**	History-laden sites of epic battles. **p1150**	Spectacularly sited Greek and Roman settlements. **p1154**	Popular seaside summer playgrounds. **p1158**	Extraordinary Anatolian landscapes. **p1160**

For places to stay in Türkiye, see p1163

NINA ZORINA/SHUTTERSTOCK

Left: Gallipoli (p1150); Above: Cappadocia (p1160)

0 — 200 km
0 — 100 miles

Gallipoli Peninsula & Troy, p1150
Two fabled battlefields: the coastal landscape where Turkish and Allied forces clashed in WWI, and the ruined ancient city over which the Trojan War was fought.

İstanbul, p1144
Home to major attractions such as Aya Sofya, Topkapı Palace and the Grand Bazaar, Türkiye's largest city has a stupendously beautiful setting and an exhilarating local lifestyle.

BULGARIA

Edirne

The Bosphorus

GREECE

İpsala

Topkapı Palace
İstanbul
Tekirdağ Çorlu
Keşan
Gallipoli Peninsula & Troy
Lâpseki
Çanakkale Epic Promotion Centre
Çanakkale
Museum of Troy

Grand Bazaar *Aya Sofya*
Sea of Marmara
Bandırma Bursa

Kocaeli (İzmit)
Adapazari Bolu

Uludağ (2543m)
Edremit Balıkesir Eskişehir
Ayvalık
Bergama
Bergama Acropolis
Manisa
Çeşme **İzmir**
Selçuk
Aydın Nazilli **Pamukkale**
Ephesus
Milas Yatağan
Bodrum
Bodrum Castle Akyaka
Marmaris
Fethiye

Cide İnebolu
Amasra Sinop
Zonguldak
Karabük Safranbolu Kastamonu
Ilgaz
Gerede
Çankırı Çorum
ANKARA
Kırıkkale Yozgat
Polatlı
Kütahya
Kırşehir

Afyon *Tuz Gölü (Salt Lake)*
Uşak
Göreme Open-Air Museum
Akşehir Nevşehir
Eğirdir Gölü *Beyşehir Gölü*
Aksaray **Göreme**
Cappadocia National Park
Odemis
Hierapolis
Burdur Isparta
Denizli
Ereğli
Muğla
Karaman Adana
Tarsus
Aegean & Mediterranean Coasts Antalya
Side Mersin (İçel)
Chimaera Kemer
Kalkan Çıralı Alanya
Ölüdeniz Beach & Lagoon Kaş Olympos
Silifke

Aegean Sea

Mediterranean Sea (Akdeniz)

Ancient Cities, p1154
Three of the ancient world's most extraordinary cities: Pergamum, Ephesus and Hierapolis, all within easy reach of the Aegean coast.

Aegean & Mediterranean Coasts, p1158
Türkiye's summer playground, where sun-spangled waters, sandy beaches and relaxing cruises on *gülets* (traditional wooden yachts) await.

Cappadocia & Nemrut Dağı National Park, p1160
Kick back in a cave hotel in Göreme, float over fairy chimneys in a hot-air balloon or climb to the summit of Nemrut Dağı.

Find Your Way

Türkiye's regions of Thrace and Marmara sit at the easternmost edge of Europe, bordered by the Bosphorus. East of this waterway, the Asian peninsula of Anadolu (Anatolia) is where the bulk of Türkiye's territory lies. İstanbul straddles both continents.

AIR

Scheduled flights between airports in over 50 cities and major towns are operated by **Turkish Airlines** (turkishairlines.com) and low-cost carriers **AJet** (ajet.com), **Pegasus** (flypgs.com) and **SunExpress** (sunexpress.com). Most fly via the hubs of İstanbul and Ankara. The busiest airports are in İstanbul, Antalya, Ankara and İzmir.

CAR

A network of well-maintained highways links most of the country. Car hire is easy to arrange; manuals are the default option though automatics are available. Be warned that distances can be great and that petrol is pricey. Hire cars usually have a tag that enables road tolls to be paid and charged to the driver automatically.

BUS

An extensive intercity bus network is a reliable and affordable means of getting around. Most bus companies offer free shuttles between city centres and otogars (bus stations) on their fringes. Reliable companies include **Flixbus** (flixbus.com.tr) and **Metro Turizm** (metroturizm. com.tr). Dolmuşes (local minibuses) service smaller destinations.

Plan Your Time

It's sensible to prioritise the country's major tourist drawcards – including İstanbul, Cappadocia, the archaeological sites of Ephesus and Hierapolis, and the Mediterranean coast – as they are relatively easy to access.

SUKSAMRAN1985/SHUTTERSTOCK

Travertines, Pamukkale (p1157)

Pressed for Time

● If your time is limited to less than a week, adopt 'less is more' as your mantra. Spend a couple of days in **İstanbul** (p1144), visiting its splendid mosques, palaces, museums, galleries and bazaars.

● Then fly to İzmir and take the İzban metro from the airport to Tepeköy, from where another line continues to the welcoming tourist town of Selçuk. This is located next to the country's number-one archaeological site, **Ephesus** (p1156).

● Next, take a bus to Denizli, from where taxis and minibuses travel the short distance to **Pamukkale** (p1157), home to the famous cascade of Travertines (terraced basins) upon which the ruins of the ancient spa city of Hierapolis perch. Return to İstanbul from Denizli Çardak Airport.

SEASONAL HIGHLIGHTS

Spring and autumn are particularly traveller-friendly, with reasonable crowds and accommodation prices. Summer is generally high season.

MARCH

Low-season prices apply to accommodation across the country and tourist sites are relatively uncrowded, making this a good time to visit.

APRIL

The annual commemoration of Allied soldiers killed in WWI on Gallipoli's battlefields is held on 25 April at **Anzac Cove** (**Anzac Koyu**; p1152).

MAY

Pleasantly mild weather across the country. Shoulder season prices apply everywhere except Cappadocia and İstanbul, where it's high season.

Ten Days Along the Coast

● After spending a few days in **İstanbul** (p1144), fly to İzmir and head straight to Selçuk to visit **Ephesus** (p1156).

● Next, drive or take a series of buses and dolmuşes south along the stunning Aegean and Mediterranean coasts, sampling the vibrant nightlife in **Bodrum** (p1158), taking a 'blue cruise' out of **Fethiye** (p1159), eating fresh seafood in **Kaş** (p1159), swimming at **Patara** (p1159) and **Kaputaş** (p1159) beaches and partying in the backpacking beach resort of **Olympos** (p1159) next to one of the best beaches in Türkiye.

● Fly out of the airport at nearby Antalya, which offers frequent connections to a wide range of destinations within Türkiye, Europe and the Gulf states.

Backpacker's Türkiye in Two Weeks

● This two-week itinerary follows a classic traveller's route. Start with four full days in **İstanbul** (p1144), spending three days in the Old City and Beyoğlu and one day sailing the length of the Bosphorus.

● Next, drive or take a bus to Çanakkale, from where you can visit **Troy** (p1153) and the **Gallipoli** (p1150) battlefields. From Çanakkale, head down the Aegean coast en route to Selçuk, where you can spend a day at **Ephesus** (p1156; don't miss the Terraced Houses) and perhaps explore some of the sites and villages nearby.

● Then fly from İzmir's Adnan Menderes Airport to Kayseri and make your way to the village of Göreme to stay in an atmosphere-laden cave hotel and explore the extraordinary and unique landscape of **Cappadocia** (p1160).

JUNE	AUGUST	SEPTEMBER	DECEMBER
Summer months are best for taking a **balloon ride** in Cappadocia or a **gület** (traditional wooden yacht) cruise on the Mediterranean coast.	Towns and resorts along the coast are inundated with sun-seeking Turks, making accommodation expensive and hard to source.	School holidays have finished, making this an excellent time to holiday on the Mediterranean coast, where the water remains warm.	Crowds flock to İstanbul to celebrate Christmas and New Year, but elsewhere many hotels and resorts close for the winter season.

İstanbul

HISTORICAL MONUMENTS | EATING & DRINKING | FERRY TRIPS

☑ TOP TIP

Plan your sightseeing around the weekly closures of major attractions. Topkapı Palace is closed on Tuesday, the Grand Bazaar is closed on Sunday and most mosques (including the Blue Mosque, Aya Sofya and the Süleymaniye) are closed to non-worshippers during prayer times and for parts of Friday (usually morning to mid-afternoon).

This magical meeting place of Asia and Europe has more top-drawer attractions than it has minarets (and that's a lot). And although some ancient cities are the sum of their monuments, İstanbul factors a lot more into the equation. You can admire Byzantine churches and Ottoman mosques in the morning, shop in bazaars and cutting-edge boutiques in the afternoon, and party in bars, taverns and clubs into the night. There's something here for every type of traveller.

Founded by Megarian colonists (who named it Byzantium), the ancient settlement was subsequently conquered by the Persians and Athenians before achieving independence. Then the Romans arrived, renaming it Constantinople and endowing it with monuments that still stand today. In 1204 Venetian soldiers of the Fourth Crusade took their turn at the helm, only to be replaced by the returning Byzantines, who ruled until the Ottomans stormed into town and stayed until the Republic was declared nearly five centuries later.

⊙ GETTING AROUND

The Old City enclaves of Sultanahmet and the Bazaar District, and Beyoğlu across the Galata Bridge, can be explored on foot or by using the excellent public transport system including trams, metro, ferries and buses. To travel, you'll need an İstanbulkart (rechargable transport card), which is good value and can be purchased from and recharged at machines at metro, funicular and tram stations and stops.

The major otogars (bus stations) in the city are Esenler Otogarı (aka Büyük İstanbul Otogarı) and Alibeyköy Otogarı. Intercity and international trains depart from Halkalı Garı. All three stations are located on the European side of the city.

ISTANBUL

Üsküdar – Harem Sahil Yolu

Beylerbeyi Palace (3km)

Kadıköy Çarşı (3.7km)

Şişhane

Sirkeci

HIGHLIGHTS
1 Aya Sofya
2 Grand Bazaar
3 Topkapı Palace

SIGHTS
4 Basilica Cistern
5 Blue Mosque
6 Dolmabahçe Palace
7 Hippodrome
8 Istanbul Modern
9 İstiklal Caddesi
10 Museum of Turkish & Islamic Arts
11 Süleymaniye Mosque

ACTIVITIES
12 Ayasofya Hürrem Sultan Hamamı
13 Cağaloğlu Hamamı
see 18 Çukurcuma Hamamı
14 Kılıç Ali Paşa Hamamı
15 Zeyrek Çinili Hamamı
18 Hamamhane

SLEEPING
16 Archeo
17 Cheers Hostel
19 Hostel Le Banc
20 Marmara Guesthouse
21 Second Home Hostel

EATING
22 Aheste
23 Antiochia
24 Bitlisi
see 18 Cuma
25 Cuppa
26 Hafız Mustafa
27 Hamdi Restaurant
28 Hayvore
29 Karaköy Güllüoğlu
30 KD Karadeniz Aile Pide ve Kebap Salonu

DRINKING
31 Bâb-ı Âli Kahvesi
32 Geyik
33 Mıkla
34 Mimar Sinan Teras Cafe
35 Şark Kahvesi

ENTERTAINMENT
36 Hodjapasha Cultural Centre

SHOPPING
37 Çarşamba Pazarı
38 Spice Bazaar
39 Tarlabaşı Pazarı

1145

BEST HAMAMS

Ayasofya Hürrem Sultan Hamamı: Dating from 1556, this hamam near Aya Sofya has separate baths for males and females.

Cağaloğlu Hamamı: Built in 1741, this is one of the most beautiful hamams in the city. Separate baths for men and women.

Zeyrek Çinili Hamamı: Painstakingly restored hamam dating from the early 16th century. The male and female *hararets* (steam rooms) are particularly beautiful.

Kılıç Ali Paşa Hamamı: Beautifully restored Karaköy hamam dating from 1580. It has one *hararet* that's open at different times for men and women.

Çukurcuma Hamamı: Modest neighbourhood hamam in Beyoğlu that functions as a mixed bath, with all clients using the space at the same time.

VLADYSLAV TRAVEL PHOTO/SHUTTERSTOCK

Mosaic, Aya Sofya

A Sublime Place of Worship

Admire exquisite Byzantine mosaics

There are many important monuments in İstanbul, but **Aya Sofya** *(muze.gen.tr/muze-detay/ayasofya; €25)* – commissioned by the great Byzantine emperor Justinian, consecrated as a church in 537, converted to a mosque by Mehmet the Conqueror in 1453, declared a museum by Atatürk in 1935 and converted back into a mosque in 2020 – surpasses the rest due to its innovative architectural form, rich history, religious importance and extraordinary beauty.

Only Turks and worshipping foreign-national Muslims can enter the prayer hall; other visitors are restricted to the upstairs galleries, which are home to a number of Byzantine-era mosaics. Note that when this book was researched, the mosaics and paintings on the dome were due to be covered and scaffolding was to be erected in the nave (main prayer hall) while stabilisation work in the building occurs. This means that views down to the nave from the gallery will be obscured for multiple years. The ticket office for non-Muslims is in Kabasakal Caddesi on the east side of the building.

 EATING IN İSTANBUL: BEST OLD CITY EATS

Bitlisli: Bustling eatery in Hocapaşa serving southeastern Anatolian food, including tasty kebaps and pides (Turkish-style pizzas). No alcohol. *11.30am-11pm* €

Hafız Mustafa: Sweets shop serving milk puddings, baklava and *künefe* in its upstairs tea salon in Sultanahmet. More branches across the city. *8am-2am* €

KD Karadeniz Aile Pide ve Kebap Salonu: Serving tasty pides, soups and kebaps, this joint is the best in the enclave off Divan Yolu. No alcohol. *10am-11pm* €

Hamdi Restaurant: The best-loved eatery in the Old City, this multi-floored restaurant serves excellent kebaps. *noon-midnight* €€

Adorning the City Skyline
İstanbul's iconic mosque

Officially known as Sultanahmet Camii (Sultanahmet Mosque), the **Blue Mosque** *(free)* is İstanbul's most photogenic building, with a wonderfully curvaceous exterior featuring a cascade of domes and six slender minarets. The interior is adorned with 21,000 blue İznik tiles that give the building its unofficial but commonly used name.

On the western side of the mosque is the **Hippodrome**, originally built by the Byzantine emperors as an arena for chariot races. On its edge is the **Museum of Turkish & Islamic Arts** *(muze.gen.tr/muze-detay/tiem; €17)*, housed in an Ottoman palace built in 1524 for İbrahim Paşa, grand vizier to Süleyman the Magnificent. It has a splendid collection of artefacts, including antique carpets displayed in a dedicated hall.

Showcase of Ottoman Life & Culture
Opulent gardens, palace and pavilions

Topkapı Palace *(muze.gen.tr/muze-detay/topkapi; TL2400)* is the subject of more colourful stories than most of the world's museums put together. Libidinous sultans, ambitious courtiers and beautiful concubines lived and worked here between the 15th and 19th centuries when it was the court of the Ottoman Empire.

Organised into four park-like areas, the palace comprises a multitude of opulent structures, including a sprawling Harem where the sultans and their families lived, ornately decorated pavilions for relaxation, handsome audience chambers where courtiers and foreign diplomats were received, a set of rooms where important religious relicts were safeguarded, and a Treasury where precious art and objects were stored.

İstanbul's Original Shopping Mall
Historic and atmospheric marketplace

The colourful and chaotic **Grand Bazaar** *(Kapalıçarşı; instagram/grandbazaarofistanbul; free)* has been the heart of the Old City for centuries. Starting as a small vaulted *bedesten* (warehouse) built on the order of Mehmet the Conqueror in 1461, it grew to cover a vast area as more than 60 lanes between the *bedesten*, neighbouring shops and *hans* (caravanserais) were roofed, and the market assumed the sprawling, labyrinthine form it retains today.

BEST İSTANBUL MARKETS & BAZAARS

Grand Bazaar: The most famous and historic bazaar in the city. A visit here is essential.

Kadıköy Çarşı: This market near the *iskele* (ferry dock) in the Asian suburb of Kadıköy has shops and street stands selling top-quality Turkish produce. Closed Sunday.

Çarşamba Pazarı: On Wednesday mornings, the streets northwest of the Fatih Mosque host a sprawling market with fresh produce and cheap clothing, footwear and homewares.

Spice Bazaar: Known the Mısır Çarşısı (Egyptian Market), this bazaar in Eminönü started trading in the 1660s and is known for its dried fruits, nuts, honey and spices.

Tarlabaşı Pazarı: Lively and cheap street market held on Sundays near Taksim.

 EATING IN İSTANBUL: BEST BEYOĞLU EATS

Karaköy Güllüoğlu: Exceptionally delicious baklava is on offer at this Karaköy institution. Good *burek* (filled pastry), too. *7.30am-1am Mon-Sat, from 8am Sun* €

Hayvore: Tasty dishes of the day and pide are on offer at this local favourite located in a side street off İstiklal Caddesi. *8.30am-11pm* €

Antiochia: This Asmalımescit stalwart gets our vote for serving the best kebaps in the city. *noon-midnight Mon-Fri, from 2pm Sat* €€

Aheste: Serving Modern Turkish cuisine, this stylish Asmalımescit restaurant offers tasting and à la carte menus with some vegetarian options. *6pm-midnight* €€€

The bazaar and surrounding streets host many cafes and cheap eateries open for lunch Monday to Saturday. The picks of these are **Şark Kahvesi**, a historic coffeehouse on Sipahi Sokak, and the fast-food stands on **Kılıççılar Sokak**, just outside the bazaar's Kılıççılar Gate.

The Pinnacle of Ottoman Architecture
Remarkably intact mosque complex

Commissioned by Süleyman I (known as 'the Magnificent'), the **Süleymaniye Mosque** *(free)* was the fourth imperial mosque built in İstanbul and it certainly lives up to its patron's nickname. Though not the largest of the imperial mosques, it's one of the grandest and most beautiful. When visiting, don't miss the panoramic terrace behind the mosque and the beautifully decorated *türbes* (tombs) of Süleyman and his wife Haseki Hürrem Sultan (Roxelana), which are located to the right of the main entrance.

The streets below the mosque are home to a number of rooftop cafes with spectacular views, the best of which are **Mimar Sinan Teras Cafe** and **Bâb-ı Âli Kahvesi**.

Watch the Dervishes Whirl
Sufi cultural performance

To witness the ancient art of Dervish whirling, head to the **Hodjapasha Cultural Centre** *(hodjapasha.com; adult/child US$41/23)*, a beautifully converted 550-year-old hamam in Sirkeci that stages cultural performances including a 60-minute 'Dervish Experience' at 7pm daily. The musical and dance elements of this Sufi performance symbolize stages on the path to accessing God. Photography is not allowed. Bookings are essential.

Party in Beyoğlu
Epicentre of dining and nightlife

Beyoğlu is where visitors and locals come in search of good cafes, restaurants, bars, live-music venues and clubs. Built around the major boulevard of **İstiklal Caddesi**, it incorporates a mix of bohemian shopping and residential districts such as Galata, Çukurcuma and Cihangir; bustling eating and drinking enclaves such as Asmalımescit; and historically rich pockets such as Karaköy, now home to boutiques, bars and cafes.

 EATING IN İSTANBUL: BEST BEYOĞLU CAFES & BARS

Cuppa: Cihangir cafe offering tempting pastries, wraps and *tosts* (toasted sandwiches) made with house-baked sourdough. *8am-5pm* €

Geyik: Pocket-sized Cihangir bar where the action usually spills out onto the street. Great cocktails. *4pm-2am*

Cuma: Laid-back foodie oasis in the heart of Çukurcuma serving good coffee and excellent, seasonally driven food. *noon-midnight* €€

Mikla: This swish summer-only bar on the rooftop of the Marmara Pera Hotel in Asmalımescit has a spectacular panoramic view. *6pm-2am Mon-Sat*

Popular bar strips and districts include Karaköy, Nevizade and Sofyalı Sokaks off İstiklal Caddesi and Akarsu Yokuşu in Cihangir. All are busiest on Friday, Saturday and Sunday nights.

To get to Beyoğlu from the Old City, take the tram (direction Kabataş). Alight at Karaköy for Galata, Tünel and Asmalımescit; at Tophane for Çukurcuma and Galatasaray; and at Kabataş for Cihangir and Taksim. Funiculars carry passengers up the steep slope to İstiklal Caddesi from both Karaköy and Kabataş.

Cutting-Edge Art & Architecture
Türkiye's most impressive art gallery

Housed in a spectacular Renzo Piano–designed building next to the Bosphorus, **İstanbul Modern** *(istanbulmodern.org; adult/concession TL750/470)* is home to an extensive collection of Turkish art that's showcased in a multi-roomed exhibition gallery. The museum also stages a constantly refreshed programme of expertly curated exhibitions by high-profile local and international artists. Facilities include a terrace restaurant with Bosphorus views and a design shop selling quality souvenirs and gifts.

Sail Along the Bosphorus
Admire waterside mansions and palaces

Linking the Sea of Marmara (Marmara Denizi) with the Black Sea (Karadeniz), the Bosphorus Strait is the geographical spine of the city, and also its greatest treasure. On one side is Europe, on the other Asia – both shores are lined with former fishing villages that have been transformed into ritzy residential suburbs. The water's edge is fringed with grandiose palaces that once housed sultans and their families, including **Dolmabahçe**, **Çırağan** and **Beylerbeyi**. There are also numerous *yalıs*, seafront mansions built by wealthy Ottomans and foreign embassies as summer retreats.

The easiest way to experience the Bosphorus is by boarding the morning **Uzun Boğaz Turu** *(Long Bosphorus Tour; sehirhatlari.istanbul; adult/child under 6yr TL640/free)* ferry that departs from Eminönü every day at 10.35am, cruising up the Bosphorus for two hours before arriving at Anadolu Kavağı at the mouth of the Black Sea, where it pauses for 2½ hours before returning to Eminönü at 4.40pm. During the break at Anadolu Kavağı, many passengers choose to walk up to the ruins of **Anadolu Kavağı Kalesi**, a medieval castle overlooking both the Black Sea and the Bosphorus.

BEST FERRY TRIPS

Taking a trip on one of İstanbul's ferries is a highlight of every visit. For routes and timetables, see *sehirhatlari.istanbul.*

Long Bosphorus Tour: Spot Ottoman and Byzantine monuments up and down the Bosphorus Strait.

Haliç Ferry Line: Cruise the length of the Haliç (Golden Horn) to visit important Ottoman monuments, shrines and mosques at Eyüpsultan.

Eminönü or Karaköy to Kadıköy: The classic Europe to Asia trip; make sure you visit the Çarşı (fresh-produce market) in Kadıköy.

Princes Islands: Known as the Adalar (Islands), these car-free settlements in the Sea of Marmara are popular weekend destinations for İstanbullus.

Eminönü or Karaköy to Üsküdar: A cross-continent trip to an ancient district studded with Ottoman-era mosques.

Gallipoli Peninsula & Troy

WWI BATTLEGROUNDS | ARCHAEOLOGY | SCENERY

☑ **TOP TIP**

Crowded House Tours (*crowdedhousegallipoli. com*) and **TJ's Tours** (*anzacgallipolitours.com*) offer early-morning minibus transfers from İstanbul including tours, with pickup at hotels in Sultanahmet and Taksim. They run daily tours of the north and south battlefields and the Troy archaeological site, and pick up participants in both Eceabat and Çanakkale.

The stunning landscapes on either side of the Dardenelles Strait have long histories as battlegrounds, the vestiges of which are preserved at Gallipoli and ancient Troy (Truva). To visit these storied sites, the small town of Eceabat on the Gallipoli Peninsula and the university city of Çanakkale across the strait make good bases. The latter is known for its attractive *kordon* (waterfront promenade).

Today, the Gallipoli (Gelibolu) Peninsula battlefields are protected landscapes covered in pine forests and fringed by idyllic beaches and coves. However, the bloody battles fought here in 1915 are still alive in Turkish and foreign memories. On Anzac Day (25 April), a dawn memorial service is held at North Beach. The Turkish victory is commemorated by Turks on 18 March each year.

The archaeological site of Troy is located approximately 30km southwest of Çanakkale. Its association with Homer's *Iliad* makes it one of Türkiye's most visited archaeological sites.

Moving Tributes to Fallen Soldiers

WWI battlefield sites and memorials

The battlefields of WWI's Gallipoli Campaign (known in Türkiye as the Battle of Çanakkale) are protected as part of the **Gallipoli Historical Area** (*canakkaletarihialan.gov.tr*).

 GETTING AROUND

Regular buses (five hours) connect İstanbul's Alibeyköy and Esenler otogars with Eceabat and Çanakkale.

The battlefields are best explored by car or on a tour; cars can be rented in Çanakkale and Eceabat. A 6.5km suspension bridge and a car ferry cross the Dardanelles Strait.

Dolmuşes to Troy (35 minutes) leave on the half-hour between 9.30am and 5pm from the northern end of the bridge over the Sarı River in Çanakkale. Ask to be let off at the Museum of Troy, from where it's a 750m walk to the archaeological site.

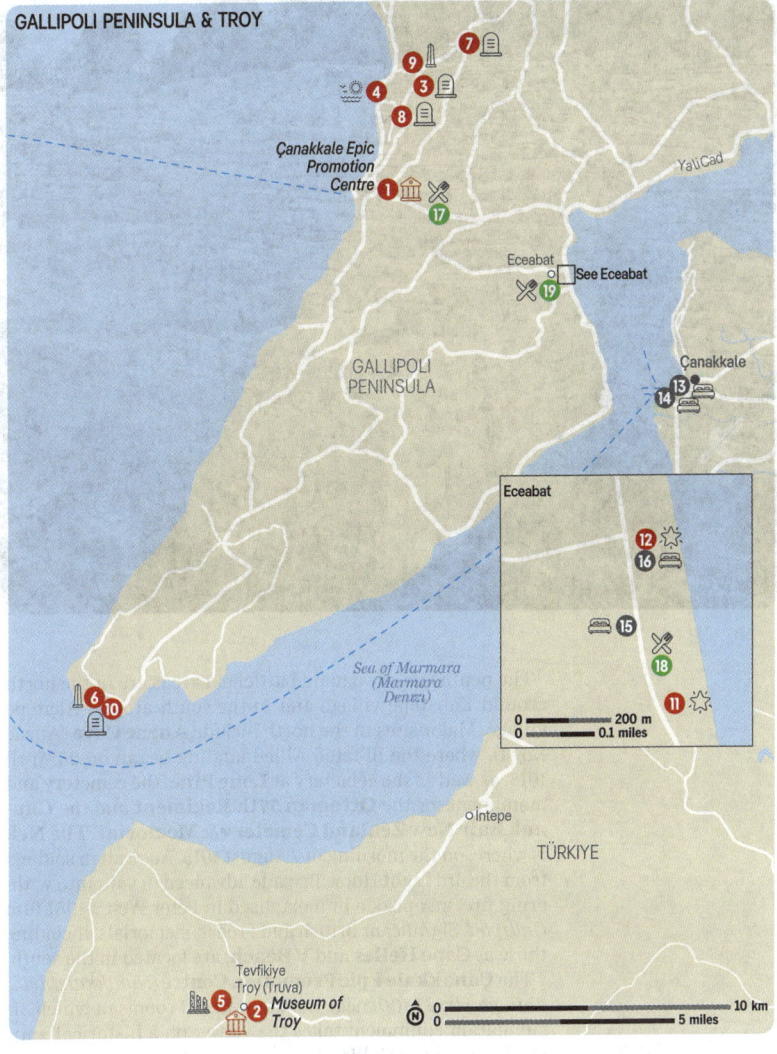

GALLIPOLI PENINSULA & TROY

Çanakkale Epic Promotion Centre

Eceabat See Eceabat

GALLIPOLI
PENINSULA

Çanakkale

Eceabat

Sea of Marmara
(Marmara
Denizi)

0   200 m
0   0.1 miles

İntepe

TÜRKIYE

Tevfikiye
Troy (Truva)
Museum of
Troy

0   10 km
0   5 miles

⭐ **HIGHLIGHTS**
1 Çanakkale Epic
   Promotion Centre
2 Museum of Troy

🔴 **SIGHTS**
3 57th Regiment
   Cemetery
4 Anzac Cove

5 Archaeological Site
   of Troy
6 Cape Helles British
   Memorial
7 Chunuk Bair New
   Zealand Cemetery
   & Memorial
8 Lone Pine Cemetery

9 The Nek
10 V Beach Cemetery

🔴 **ACTIVITIES**
11 Crowded House Tours
12 TJ's Tours

⚫ **SLEEPING**
13 Büyük Truva Hotel
14 Grand Anzac Hotel

15 Hotel Crowded House
16 TJ's Hotel

🟢 **EATING**
17 Doyuranlar Aile Çay
   ve Gözleme
18 Gözde Köfteci
see 13 Kısmet Balık Evi
19 Suvla

The peninsula's two main battlefield areas are in the north around Kabatepe village and in the south around Alçıtepe village. Major sites in the north include **Anzac Cove** (Anzac Koyu), where the ill-fated Allied landing began on 25 April 1915, as well as the cemetery at **Lone Pine**, the cemetery and monument for the **Ottoman 57th Regiment** and the **Chunuk Bair New Zealand Cemetery & Memorial**. **The Nek** is where, on the morning of 7 August 1915, Australian soldiers from the 3rd Light Horse Brigade advanced in vain into withering fire, an episode immortalised in Peter Weir's 1981 film *Gallipoli*. Significant British and French memorials, including those at **Cape Helles** and **V Beach**, are located in the south.

The **Çanakkale Epic Promotion Centre** (*canakkaletarihi alan.gov.tr; TL100*) near Kabatepe has 11 rooms in which 3D simulation equipment takes the viewer on a historical journey through the Gallipoli campaigns from a predominantly Turkish point of view.

EATING IN ECEABAT & ÇANAKKALE: OUR PICKS

Doyuranlar Aile Çay ve Gözleme: A tea garden on the road from Eceabat to Kabatepe. Combine the *gözleme* (stuffed flatbreads) and tea. *8am-6.30pm* €

Gözde Köfteci: Close to the sea in Eceabat, this restaurant is renowned for its meatballs. The lentil soup is delicious too. *5am-midnight* €€

Kısmet Balık Evi: A family-run business in Çanakkale that stands out for the freshness of its seafood. *10am-10pm* €€

Suvla: Eceabat winery with a tasting room, shop and wine bar serving simple modern twists on Turkish classics. *9am-10pm* €€€

LIU YU SHAN/SHUTTERSTOCK

Archaeological Site of Troy

Decipher Layers of History

Ruins of ancient Troy

Best known as the subject of Homer's epic poem *Iliad*, the Trojan War – if it actually happened – would have been only an eyeblink in the history of ancient Troy, which spans thousands of years. Its many cycles of destruction and reconstruction have been identified in 10 main archaeological layers excavated at the **Archaeological Site of Troy** *(muze.gov. tr; incl museum €27)* and named Troy 0 through to Troy IX.

Start your visit at the excellent **Museum of Troy** before moving on to the ruins. Follow the boardwalk to the right to reach the foundations of the east walls of Troy VI. Close your eyes and imagine a colossal wooden horse, a gift from the Greeks, passing through the sturdy sea-facing gate of the city walls. From here, continue north past the Temple of Athena, a Roman-era theatre and the palace complex of Troy II. The original trial trench established by German amateur archaeologist Heinrich Schliemann, is nearby, as is the Troy II Ramp, once a point of entry into ancient Troy.

HEINRICH SCHLIEMANN

Until the 19th century, many historians doubted whether ancient Troy had existed. However, one amateur German archaeologist, Heinrich Schliemann (1822–90), proved them wrong. In 1870 Schliemann uncovered the remains of a ruined city (the current-day archaeological site). He also unearthed a cache of gold artefacts that he named 'Priam's Treasure'.

During his hasty and destructive dig, Schliemann failed to appreciate that Troy was a series of settlements built one on top of the other over the course of about 2500 years. Furthermore, it was soon established that the treasures (which he smuggled out of the country and are now in Moscow's Pushkin Museum) were not from the time of Homer's Troy, but from the much earlier Troy II.

Ancient Cities

Bergama
(Pergamum) • Sındırgı
Gördes
Menemen Manisa Salihli Midikli
İzmit Kula
Selçuk • Tire Ödemiş
Şirince Nazilli Pamukkale
Söke Aydın
Yenihisar Karagol
(Didim) Yatağan
Milas Muğla

ARCHAEOLOGICAL SITES | MUSEUMS | NATURAL WONDERS

GETTING AROUND

Buses travel from both İstanbul and Çanakkale to destinations including Bergama, Ayvalık, İzmir, Selçuk and Denizli (for Pamukkale). Some of these services involve a change of bus in İzmir.

There are regular buses and dolmuşes between the İzmir otogar and Bergama, Selçuk and Pamukkale. The İzban metro departs from İzmir's city centre before stopping at the airport and continuing to Tepeköy, from where another line continues to Selçuk.

Dolmuşes connect Pamukkale with Laodicea and Denizli.

Türkiye is the proud possessor of 22 sites, structures and landscapes inscribed on UNESCO's World Heritage List, a number of which are the remnants of ancient cities located in the country's west. Three of these – the spectacular and well-preserved ruins of Pergamum, Ephesus and Hierapolis – are among the most visited sites in the country, featuring on many travel itineraries. Easy detours from the coast, all three are located close to towns with excellent tourist infrastructure including hostels, hotels, cafes and restaurants. Selçuk and Pamukkale are particularly well endowed in this respect, making them tempting spots for a few days of R&R during longer trips. Pamukkale also makes an excellent base for those keen to deviate from the well-travelled tourism route and explore the more isolated but equally spectacular sites of Laodicea, Afrodisias and Kibyra. Other sites – Xanthos and Letoön – are located on the Turquoise Coast but can be visited on a day trip.

Bergama

Evoke the splendour of ancient Pergamum

The laid-back market town of Bergama is the modern successor to the once-powerful ancient city of Pergamum. During Pergamum's heyday (between Alexander the Great and the Roman domination of Asia Minor), it was one of the Middle East's richest and most powerful small kingdoms. The **Acropolis** *(muze.gov.tr; €15)*, linked to the town by a cable car, retains structures including a magnificent amphitheatre and a columned temple dedicated to Trajan.

The fascinating **Asklepion** *(muze.gov.tr; €13)*, 2.5km uphill from town, was Pergamum's famed medical centre. Dedicated to Asclepius (the god of healing in Ancient Greece), it dates from the 4th century BCE.

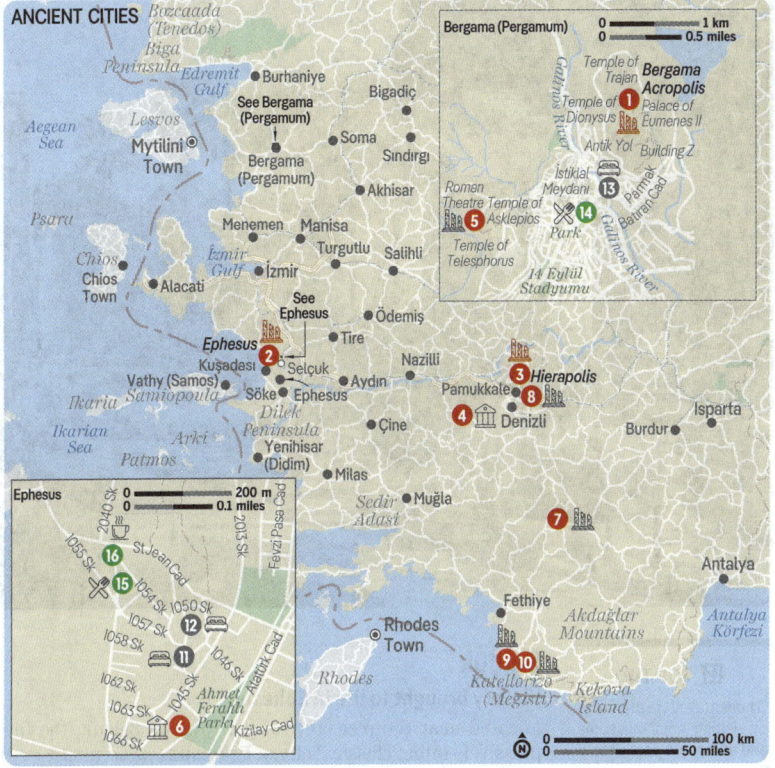

ANCIENT CITIES

★ HIGHLIGHTS
1 Bergama Acropolis
2 Ephesus
3 Hierapolis

● SIGHTS
4 Afrodisias
5 Asklepion
6 Ephesus Museum
7 Kibyra

8 Laodicea
9 Letoön
see 2 Terraced Houses
see 3 Travertines
10 Xanthos

● SLEEPING
11 Ayasoluk Hotel
see 3 Melrose House
12 Nilya Hotel

13 Odyssey Guesthouse
see 3 Venus Suite Hotel

● EATING
14 Altın Kepçe Bergama Köfte
15 Kybele Gastro
see 2 Selçuk Pidecisi

● DRINKING & NIGHTLIFE
16 Art House Cafe

TOP TIP

Those travellers planning on visiting major museums and archaeological sites in the country should consider purchasing a **MuseumPass Türkiye E-Card** *(muze. gov.tr/MuseumPass)* which gives access to most of the major sites covered in this chapter – including the three covered in this section – and can save users a considerable amount of money.

Selçuk

History brought to life in Ephesus

Located near the pleasant tourist town of Selçuk, the impressively intact classical city of **Ephesus** *(muze.gov.tr; €40)* has extensive structures including the ornate Library of Celsus, originally commissioned in the early 2nd century CE, an agora, a steep hillside theatre and an evocative row of seven Roman-era **Terraced Houses** *(additional €15)* featuring frescoes and mosaics. A stroll down the central Curetes Way, home to the Temple of Hadrian and the Hercules Gate, is like walking two millennia back in time.

Before visiting the site, pop into the **Ephesus Museum** *(muze.gov.tr; €10)*, located in Selçuk's town centre across from the otogar. Its standout exhibits are two marble statues of Artemis dating to the 1st and 2nd century CE.

Buy your Ephesus tickets at the museum to avoid queuing at the site. Minibuses from Selçuk's otogar run regularly to and from the site's Lower Gate.

EATING & DRINKING IN BERGAMA & SELÇUK: OUR PICKS

Altın Kepçe Bergama Köfte: Restaurant popular for Bergama's famous *patlıcan çiğırtması* (aubergine dish). *7am-6.30pm Mon-Sat* €

Selçuk Pidecisi: Cheerful spot for tasty pide (flatbreads with a range of toppings) near the Selçuk train station. *10am-10pm* €

Kybele Gastro: Fine dining in a beautiful Selçuk setting, with distinctive mezes and well-prepared meat dishes. *4pm-midnight Mon-Sat* €€

Art House Cafe: Colourful, rustic Selçuk joint serving coffee, tea, beer, wine and shisha. *2pm-1am*

EFIRED/SHUTTERSTOCK

Ephesus

Pamukkale

The ancient health resort of Hierapolis

Founded around 190 BCE by Eumenes II of Pergamum, the ancient spa city of **Hierapolis** *(muze.gov.tr; €30)* sits atop Pamukkale's extraordinary cascade of saucer-shaped **Travertines** (or terraced basins). Though abandoned after a devastating earthquake in 1334 CE, it retains much of the grand infrastructure built during its heyday and commands stunning views over the powder-white travertines and surrounding countryside.

The ruins are spread over a large area. Don't miss the Roman Theatre, Sanctuary of Apollo, Martyrium of St Philip the Apostle and Agora.

Most visitors enter the site via the South Gate, approximately 2.5km uphill by road from Pamukkale village. The Town (aka Lower) Gate is at the foot of the travertines. Many visitors choose to take advantage of the free transfers to the South Gate offered by pensions and hotels, and then walk down the travertines to the village.

MORE ANCIENT CITIES

Those travellers with their own transport may wish to visit the sites of other ancient cities in this part of Türkiye.

Laodicea: Very close to Pamukkale, this splendid site has ruins including a nymphaeum, a temple, two theatres and a basilica.

Afrodisias: Major structures include a stadium, a temple dedicated to Aphrodite and a marble council chamber. Don't miss the magnificent on-site museum.

Kibyra: Hellenistic, Roman and Byzantine-era structures include a stadium, a theatre, a basilica, an agora, an odeon, baths and a nymphaeum.

Xanthos: Ancient Lycia's capital city, with a fine Roman theatre and agora.

Letoön: Lycian site with temples dedicated to Apollo, Artemis and Leto.

Aegean & Mediterranean Coasts

BEACHES | CRUISES | PARTYING

Places

 ☑ TOP TIP

If planning to sign up for a 'blue cruise', make sure the boat has easily accessible lifeboats and lifejackets, that the captain and crew have a good command of English, and that meals are included. Also ask for an itinerary and check whether the weather and sailing conditions will accommodate it.

Stretching south from the point where the Dardanelles Strait meets the Aegean Sea, this part of the country offers extraordinary landscapes, ancient sites and a diverse array of outdoor activities. Turks flock here in summer, when the string of former fishing villages along the coast heave with holidaymakers.

Sitting at the meeting point of the Aegean and Mediterranean Seas, Bodrum is the quintessential 'Turkish Riviera' hot spot. Further south, Fethiye is a major hub for the famous *mavi yolculuk* ('blue cruise'), a multi-night cruise on a *gület*. These traditional Turkish wooden yachts offer experiences ranging from basic to luxurious but have one thing in common – they give passengers an unparalleled opportunity to soak up the beauty of the famed Turquoise Coast, which stretches between Fethiye and the southern city of Antalya. This is Türkiye at its most staggeringly beautiful: an endless azure sea lined with sandy beaches and backdropped by majestic mountains.

Bodrum

Türkiye's summer playground

The main attraction in Bodrum Town is a lively waterfront lined wall-to-wall with restaurants, cafes, boutiques and bars. There's also a 15th-century **sea castle** now housing the

---

⊙ GETTING AROUND

Flights from İstanbul arrive at **İzmir Adnan Menderes**, **Milas-Bodrum** and **Dalaman airports**. Regular buses connect the İzmir and Bodrum otogars; there are fewer services between Selçuk and Bodrum. Slow dolmuşes go around the peninsula.

From Fethiye, regular dolmuşes follow the coast to Antalya, stopping at Kalkan, Kaş and the Olympos turn-off. Dolmuşes also link Patara, Kalkan, Kaputaş and Kaş. In summer, direct buses via the inland route link Fethiye and Antalya as well as Fethiye and Kaş via Kalkan.

Bodrum Underwater Archaeology Museum *(muze.gov. tr; €20)*.

The best beaches on the peninsula are **Yahşi Plajı**, **Bitez Plajı**, **Kadıkalesi Halk Plajı**, **Küdür Halk Plajı** and **Akçabük Plajı**.

For a memorable evening, head to the waterfront restaurants in the former fishing village of **Gümüşlük**.

Fethiye

Sailing the Turquoise Coast

Tucked into the southern reaches of a broad bay scattered with dozens of pretty islands, the harbour town of Fethiye is known as a base for *gület* cruises, which are offered between April and October.

From Fethiye, boats usually call in at famous **Ölüdeniz beach** and stop at Kaş, Kalkan and/or the island of Kekova.

Fethiye-based cruise agencies that get consistently good reviews from readers include **Alaturka** *(alaturkacruises.com)*, **V-GO Yachting** *(bluecruisesturkey.com)* and **Before Lunch Cruises** *(beforelunch.com)*. Book well ahead.

Kaş & Kalkan

Float over a sunken city

The former fishing villages of Kalkan and Kaş on the Mediterranean coast are now summer resorts known for their eating and drinking scenes and their proximity to great beaches including **Patara** and **Kaputaş**.

Kaş is also known for its diving, with easily reached wrecks located relatively close to shore. Nearby, the island of **Kekova** is surrounded by the partly submerged ruins of the ancient city of Simena some 6m below the water. Known as the *batık şehir* (Sunken City), this can be explored from the water's surface in a sea-kayaking tour run by Kaş tour operators such as **Bougainville Travel** *(bougainville.com.tr)*, **Dragoman** *(dragoman-turkey.com)* and **Sea Kayak Türkiye** *(seakayak turkiye.com)*. Diving and swimming here are forbidden.

Olympos & Çıralı

Ghostly flames and a great beach

An important Lycian city in the 2nd century BCE, Olympos is more famous these days for being a backpacking beach resort with a party vibe. It's also home to one of the best **beaches** in the country. Nearby **Çıralı** is a holiday hamlet with dozens of family-friendly hotels and pensions. The ruins of **ancient Olympos** *(muze.gov.tr; €10)* are set inside a deep valley near Çıralı where you'll find that most enigmatic of classical icons: the eternal flame of the **Chimaera** *(Yanartaş; TL45)*. The best time to visit the latter is just before dusk.

TREEHOUSE ACCOMMODATION

The word 'treehouse' that is used to describe most of the accommodation in Olympos is a misnomer, given that few – if any – huts are actually up in the trees. Most are small, rustic wooden bungalows sometimes (but not always) slightly raised off the ground. Bathrooms are generally shared, though some bungalows have en-suite rooms. Not all treehouses have reliable locks, so store valuables at reception. And a cautionary note: be extra attentive to personal hygiene while staying at Olympos. In summer, especially, the large number of visitors can stretch the camps' capacity for proper waste disposal to the limit, so be vigilant about where and what you eat.

Cappadocia & Nemrut Dağı National Park

HIKING | HOT-AIR BALLOONING | ANCIENT RUINS

GETTING AROUND

Buses travel long distances to Göreme from İstanbul via Ankara, from İzmir and from Antalya; it's possible to fly into **Nevşehir Kapadokya Airport** from İstanbul or **Kayseri Erkilet Airport** from İstanbul, İzmir and Antalya. Dolmuşes service most of Cappadocia.

The closest airport to Nemrut Dağı is **Adıyaman**. To get to the park, hire a taxi for the day from Adıyaman or Malatya, or join a tour from Kahta, 30km east of Adıyaman, Malatya or Şanlıurfa.

☑ **TOP TIP**

The summit of Nemrut Dağı can be approached from either Adıyaman in the south or Malatya in the north. However, the route from Adıyaman includes numerous other ancient sites, making this the preferred option.

Cappadocia is famed for its strange towering rock formations known as fairy chimneys. Dotting the region's unique terrain, these were formed up to 12 million years ago by volcanic eruptions flinging ash across the landscape and are best viewed while enjoying the region's signature experience – a hot-air-balloon ride at sunrise. On the ground, rock-hewn churches covered in Byzantine frescoes are secreted into cliffs, villages are honeycombed out of hillsides and vast subterranean complexes where early Christians once hid are tunnelled under the ground.

Equally extraordinary is the landscape of Nemrut Dağı National Park in the country's southeast, where 2000 years ago a megalomaniac Commagene king erected his own memorial sanctuary on Nemrut Dağı (Mt Nemrut; 2150m). The fallen heads of the gigantic decorative statues of gods and kings that are found here are one of Türkiye's most remarkable sights.

Among the Fairy Chimneys
Cappadocia's iconic landscape

While there are a number of attractive villages and towns across Cappadocia that can be used as a base when exploring the region, the majority of travellers are drawn to the village of Göreme. This is where most of the balloon operators are based and where hikers can spend days exploring the spectacular nearby **Pigeon**, **Zemi**, **Red** and **Rose** valleys. The village is also blessed with a stunning array of boutique hotels, many of which have been converted from traditional cave dwellings.

The other ace up Göreme's sleeve is its **Open-Air Museum** (*muze.gov.tr; €20*), a collection of ancient rock-hewn churches on the edge of town, some of them featuring astoundingly colourful Byzantine-era frescoes. This is an astonishing site, only rivalled in Cappadocia by the area's two fascinating underground cities: **Derinkuyu** (*muze.gov.tr; €13*) and **Kaymaklı** (*muze.gov.tr; €13*).

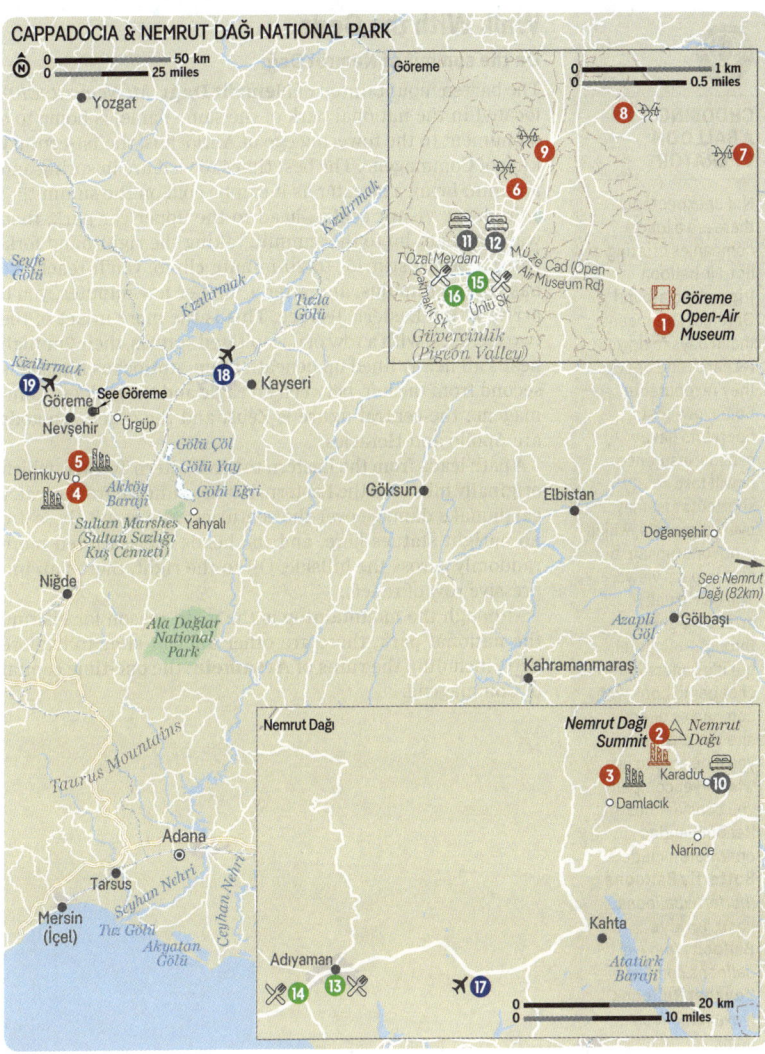

CAPPADOCIA & NEMRUT DAĞı NATIONAL PARK

Göreme

Göreme Open-Air Museum

Nemrut Dağı

Nemrut Dağı Summit

⭐ **HIGHLIGHTS**
1 Göreme Open-Air Museum
2 Nemrut Dağı Summit

🔴 **SIGHTS**
3 Arsameia
4 Derinkuyu Underground City
5 Kaymaklı Underground City

6 Pigeon Valley
7 Red Valley
8 Rose Valley
9 Zemi Valley

⚫ **SLEEPING**
10 Işık Pansiyon
11 Kismet
12 Köse Hostel

🟢 **EATING**
13 Adıyaman Kebap Salonu
14 Alim Sofrası
15 Fat Boys
16 Retro

🔵 **TRANSPORT**
17 Adıyaman Airport
18 Kayseri Erkilet Airport
19 Nevşehir Kapadokya Airport

Walk With the Gods

On the summit of Nemrüt Dağı

The barren mountaintop of **Nemrüt Dağı** *(Mt Nemrut; €10),* located in the national park of the same name, is home to a monument to the towering ego of Antiochus, the 1st-century king of Commagene. The best times to visit are in spring and autumn; bring a sweater as it can be cold on the summit.

From the visitor centre, head to the upper car park, then walk the path up to the summit, taking the right-hand fork. After a pretty stiff 15- to 20-minute climb, you'll reach the base of the tumulus, and after a further few minutes, you'll arrive at the Eastern Terrace. This is the more intact of the two terraces, with a row of decapitated statues, their 2m-high heads all neatly lined up beneath them. Antiochus himself is second from the left, between an eagle and the goddess Commagene; the central figure is Zeus, and the other two gods are Apollo and Heracles.

A path leads from the Eastern to the Western Terrace, which originally mirrored the Eastern, but has suffered from greater earthquake damage over the centuries: as a result there are no upright statues here, and the heads are scattered more randomly across the hillside. Off to the right, there's an impressive row of reliefs.

Although the mountaintop is the main reason for visiting the national park, there are other ancient sites to explore here, including the ruins of **Arsameia**, the one-time capital of Commagene.

CHOOSING A BALLOON OPERATOR

Not unexpectedly, there are a lot of companies offering hot-air-balloon trips in and around Göreme. This means that it pays to do your research and check they're reputable. Some low-cost operators have minimal insurance, or will take safety shortcuts and may overfill baskets, which is not only unsafe but also impairs views. You can usually arrange flights through your hotel, but it's generally cheaper to book with companies directly, and this ensures you'll be able to use whichever company you consider best. Recommended operators include **Butterfly Balloons** *(butterflyballoons. com),* **Turkiye Balloons** *(turkiye balloons.com)* and **Voyager Balloons** *(voyagerballoons. com).*

 EATING & DRINKING IN ADIYAMAN & GÖREME: OUR PICKS

Alim Sofrası: A no-frills but excellent Adıyaman kebap joint in the university district on the west side of town. *11am-11pm* €

Adıyaman Kebap Salonu: The name says it all. Good kebaps, too – the Adana kebab really doesn't hold back on the heat. *8.30am-8pm Mon-Sat* €

Fat Boys: This perennially popular place in Göreme has a good menu of tasty Turkish dishes and a well-stocked bar. *8am-midnight* €€

Retro: A friendly family-run place, with great views over Göreme from the terrace. *11am-11pm Mon-Sat* €€

# Places We Love to Stay

€ Budget   €€ Midrange   €€€ Top End

İstanbul   MAP p1145

Old City

Cheers € Excellent central location, a rooftop bar with panoramic view, and air-conditioned dorms and rooms.

Second Home Hostel € Friendly place in Hocapaşa near Eminönü. Basic dorms, entertainment programme and popular home-style dinners.

Marmara Guesthouse €€ Family-run pension offering a warm welcome, comfortable rooms, a rooftop terrace and delicious breakfast.

Beyoğlu

Archeo € Well-run hostel in supremely convenient Tophane. The ground-floor cafe is a popular hangout.

Hostel Le Banc € Galata hostel with a small roof terrace. Air-conditioned dorms have their own bathrooms, as do the private rooms.

Hamamhane €€ Well-run Çukurcuma hotel with rooms, studios and suites in two buildings.

Gallipoli Peninsula & Troy   MAP p1151

Eceabat

TJ's Hotel €€ Close to the ferry port, with clean rooms.

Hotel Crowded House €€ Also near the ferry port. Rooms are clean and spacious.

Çanakkale

Büyük Truva Hotel €€ Clean and comfortable hotel with sea views.

Grand Anzac Hotel €€ Very close to the clock tower, with exceptionally clean and large rooms.

Ancient Cities   MAP p1155

Bergama

Odyssey Guesthouse € There are superb views of the archaeological sites from the terrace of this friendly and well-run pension.

Selçuk

Nilya Hotel € Quaint, family-run accommodation with Ottoman-style decorations in a garden setting.

Ayasoluk Hotel €€ Serene, stylish lodgings with a fine restaurant (open to outside guests) and a pool.

Pamukkale

Venus Suite Hotel €€ Attractive rooms, free parking and a poolside restaurant are the draws at this excellent choice.

Melrose House €€ Guests here inevitably comment on the generous and tasty breakfasts. Facilities include a restaurant and a swimming pool.

Aegean & Mediterranean Coasts

Bodrum

Asmin Otel € Cheerful, small hotel with a pool near the main Bodrum bus station.

Merih Butik Hotel €€ Operated by a friendly and helpful Turkish-Australian couple, this delightful small guesthouse has comfortable rooms and a lovely courtyard.

Fethiye

El Camino Pub & Hostel € A fun, well-run hillside hostel with private rooms and four-bed dorms.

Orka Boutique Hotel €€ The 22 very central rooms here have swish contemporary styling; the choicest have small seafront balconies.

Kaş & Kalkan

Caretta Hotel €€ Cliffside hotel in Kalkan that's a perennial favourite for its swimming platforms and bright rooms with terraces.

Hideaway Hotel €€ Welcoming Kaş hotel with 23 large, airy rooms (most with balconies) and a roof terrace.

Olympos & Çıralı

Bayrams € Large Olympos operation with a lively bar and accommodation in small wooden cabins linked by narrow paths.

Hotel Canada €€ This beautiful place in Çıralı has 26 rooms in the main house as well as gardens filled with hammocks and bungalows.

Cappadocia & Nemrut Dağı National Park   MAP p1161

Göreme

Köse Hostel € This friendly, clean and centrally located hostel is a genuine bargain in a generally pricey town.

Kismet €€ Kismet's cave rooms are gorgeous and traditionally decorated, and the owner Faruk is hugely friendly and helpful.

Nemrut Dağı

Işık Pansiyon € On the slopes of Nemrut Dağı, providing friendly and comfortable accommodation and delicious meals. Can pick you up from Adıyaman or Kahta.

Practicalities

Visas

Although visas are not necessary for citizens of some countries (including the UK, the USA, New Zealand and many European nations), many others must obtain a visa before entering Türkiye. Check whether this is necessary at *mfa.gov.tr*. If you do need a visa, organise this electronically at *evisa.gov.tr*.

NURTEN ERDAL/SHUTTERSTOCK

Health

Türkiye has an extensive healthcare system. It's possible to receive services from public and private hospitals for a fee. Hospitals are available 24/7.

Public Holidays
New Year's Day 1 January
National Sovereignty & Children's Day 23 April
Labor & Solidarity Day 1 May
Commemoration of Atatürk, Youth & Sports Day 19 May

Democracy & National Unity Day 15 July
Victory Day 30 August
Republic Day 29 October
The dates of the major religious holidays of Ramazan, Şeker Bayramı and Kurban Bayramı vary according to the lunar calendar.

Smoking

Smoking is prohibited on public transport and in enclosed public spaces, including restaurants, cafes and shopping malls. Vaping is not illegal, but the sale or trade of vapes is.

LGBTIQ+ Travellers

Homosexuality isn't a criminal offence in Türkiye and people are legally permitted to change gender, but there are no laws protecting LGBTIQ+ people from discrimination, and violence towards them has been recorded, same-sex marriage isn't recognised and the dating app Grindr is banned. That said, same-sex couples will have no problem booking a double room in the major cities and tourism destinations.

Tap Water

Tap water is safe to drink, although it is heavily chlorinated; many locals prefer to drink bottled water.

Safe Travel

- Be aware of pickpockets on public transport and in bazaars.
- Female travellers, especially those travelling solo, should be on the lookout for possible drink spiking.
- Don't use or carry illegal drugs; penalties for drug offences include long prison sentences.
- Some dogs carry the potentially fatal rabies virus; if bitten, seek immediate medical attention.

Language

Turkish belongs to the Ural-Altaic language family. It's the official language of Türkiye and Northern Cyprus, and has more than 80 million speakers worldwide.

Basics

Hello. Merhaba. *mer*·ha·ba
Goodbye. Hoşçakal. hosh·*cha*·kal
Yes. Evet. e·*vet*
No. Hayır. *ha*·yuhr
Excuse me. Bakar mısınız. ba·*kar* muh·suh·*nuhz*
Sorry. Özür dilerim. er·*zewr* dee·*le*·reem
Please. Lütfen. *lewt*·fen
Thank you. Teşekkür ederim. te·shek·*kewr* e·*de*·reem
You're welcome. Bir şey değil. beer·*shay* de·*eel*
How are you? Nasılsınız? na·suhl·suh·nuhz
Fine, and you? İyiyim, ya siz? ee·*yee*·yeem ya seez
What's your name? Adınız nedir? a·duh·*nuhz* ne·deer
My name is ... Benim adım ... be·*neem* a·*duhm* ...
Do you speak English? İngilizce konuşuyor musunuz? een·gee·*leez*·je ko·noo·*shoo*·yor moo·soo·*nooz*
I understand. Anlıyorum. an·*luh*·yo·room
I don't understand. Anlamıyorum. an·*la*·muh·yo·room

Directions

Where is ...? ... nerede? ... *ne*·re·de
What's the address? Adresi nedir? ad·re·*see* ne·deer
Could you write it down, please? Lütfen yazar mısınız? *lewt*·fen ya·*zar* muh·suh·*nuhz*

Can you show me (on the map)? Bana (haritada) gösterebilir misiniz? ba·*na* (ha·ree·ta·*da*) gers·te·*re*·bee·leer mee·seen·*neez*
It's straight ahead. Tam karşıda. tam kar·shuh·*da*
at the traffic lights trafik ışıklarından tra·*feek* uh·shuhk·la·ruhn·*dan*

Signs

Açık Open
Bay Male
Bayan Female
Çıkış Exit
Giriş Entrance
Kapalı Closed
Sigara İçilmez No Smoking
Tuvaletler Toilets
Yasak Prohibited

Emergencies

Help! İmdat! *eem*·dat
I'm lost. Kayboldum. kai·bol·*doom*
Leave me alone! Git başımdan! *geet* ba·shuhm·*dan*
Call a doctor! Doktor çağırın! dok·*tor* cha·*uh*·ruhn
Call the police! Polis çağırın! po·*lees* cha·*uh*·ruhn
I'm ill. Hastayım. has·*ta*·yuhm
I'm allergic to (nuts). (Çerezlere) alerjim var. (che·rez·le·*re*) a·ler·*zheem* var

NUMBERS

1	**bir** beer
2	**iki** ee-*kee*
3	**üç** ewch
4	**dört** dert
5	**beş** besh
6	**altı** al-*tuh*
7	**yedi** ye-*dee*
8	**sekiz** se-*keez*
9	**dokuz** do-*kooz*
10	**on** on

Marmaris

Arriving

Most travellers arrive by air or boat. Türkiye has land borders with multiple countries but only the borders with Greece, Bulgaria and Georgia are easy to cross. The status of other land borders varies; check before using them. Note that foreign governments currently advise against travel to Iran, Iraq and Syria.

By Air

There are direct or connecting flights from many countries of the world to Türkiye's larger airports, including İstanbul, İstanbul Sabiha Gökçen, İzmir Adnan Menderes and Antalya.

By Boat

Ferry services operate from Greek islands (Chios, Kos, Kalymnos, Lesvos, Kastellorizo, Rhodes, Samos, Symi) and Northern Cyprus (Gazimağusa and Girne) to Türkiye (Ayvalık, Bodrum, Çeşme, Kaş, Kuşadası, Marmaris, Mersin, Taşucu); they are more frequent in summer.

MONEY

Currency:
Türk lirası (TL or ₺)

CREDIT CARDS

Since credit-card usage is very high all over the country, almost all restaurants, hotels and shopping points accept credit cards without any extra commission. ATMs belonging to different banks are found at airport arrival halls and across the country, from small towns to big cities.

EXCHANGING MONEY

The euro and US dollar are most easily converted into Turkish lira. Exchange your foreign currencies at a *döviz bürosu* (exchange office), which provides better rates and faster transactions than banks. Exchange offices usually don't charge commission; the offices in city areas usually offer better rates than those at the airports.

TIPPING

In some restaurants, *servis ücreti* (service charge), an additional fee of approximately 10%, is charged. If this doesn't apply, tipping is left to the customer's discretion.

Getting Around

Travelling within Türkiye is generally comfortable. Intercity and regional trains are less commonly used, although a high-speed train (YHT) currently operates between İstanbul, Eskişehir, İzmir, Ankara, Konya and Sivas. Buy tickets from train stations or the TCDD (bilet.tcdd.gov.tr) website and app.

Transport Cards
The big cities have efficient modern transport systems that can include tram, bus and metro. Rechargeable transport cards are necessary in cities including İstanbul (İstanbulkart; pictured), İzmir (İzmirim Kart) and Antalya (AntalyaKart). These are generally available at ticket machines in airports and metro stations.

ONAPALMTREE/SHUTTERSTOCK

Taxi/Rideshare
Ridesharing services including Uber, BiTaksi and iTaksi are available in İstanbul, and Uber also services most large cities. Travellers are less likely to encounter problems with overcharging if they opt for a rideshare rather than a taxi.

Road Conditions
In addition to the wide and high-quality intercity roads, there are also highways starting from the country's northwest and moving towards the west and south. Urban and town roads are mostly asphalt. There may be difficulties on the roads during the winter months due to heavy snowfall and rain.

Hiring a Car
Global car-rental companies have offices in airports and city centres. Renters must have a valid driver's license and credit card. Car-rental companies generally ask for drivers to be at least 21 years old.

Unwritten Rules of Traffic
Violating traffic rules and speed limits is common among locals, so be careful and avoid driving at night. Stay alert, as radar speed checks are frequent on intercity roads. Downtown car parks managed by municipalities, shopping malls and private companies are the best options for safe parking.

DRIVING ESSENTIALS

Drive on the right

130

Speed limit is 130km/h on major highways, 110km/h on smaller highways and 50km/h in built-up areas

0.05

Blood alcohol concentration limit is 0.05%

⚠

Ukraine is
currently
considered
unsafe to visit

Above and right: Kyiv

Curated by
Leonid Ragazin

Ukraine

A COUNTRY UNDER BRUTAL ATTACK

If you travel to any part of Ukraine, you will be risking your life.

All of Ukraine was an active war zone at the time of writing, following Russia's all-out invasion that began in February 2022. Artillery fire has flattened entire cities and towns along the frontlines in the east, while other parts of Ukraine – especially Kyiv and Odesa – are subject to constant drone and missile attacks. As of August 2025, almost 7 million people had left Ukraine due to the war. This is the equivalent of 17% of the country's pre-war population; most of those who have fled are women and children.

No matter how the war ultimately ends, it is already clear that Ukraine will emerge from the conflict as a vastly different country. At the time of writing, about one-fifth of Ukrainian territory was occupied by Russia, with tiny chunks of land being added every day as the Russian army slowly progresses

Crimea was one of Ukraine's main tourist destinations prior to its annexation in 2014. Following Russian annexation, visits to Crimea were technically still possible and even encouraged by Russia, but those who dared to go were considered to be in direct violation of Ukrainian laws.

The country's other attractions remain under Ukrainian control. These includes Kyiv, Ukraine's beautiful and ancient capital, the marvellously flamboyant port city of Odesa and elegant Lviv. Although visiting the country is not impossible, you need a legitimate work- or family-related reason to go. While many foreigners travel to Ukraine as aid workers and advisors, war tourism is unethical and a bad idea, as is any self-styled political activism, however well-intentioned. Peace talks initiated by US President Donald Trump had produced some hope for a ceasefire at the time for writing.

OLEKSANDR POPENKO/SHUTTERSTOCK

THE SCALE OF DESTRUCTION

Since the start of Russia's invasion, parts of Ukraine have experienced destruction on a massive scale. Even if the war ends soon, the mining region of Donbas and other frontline areas will be too dangerous to travel in for years because of the cluster ammunition and land mines that both sides have used. At the time of writing, the most devastated areas in Donbas – once a densely populated and urbanised industrial region – were on the Russian side of the frontline. Some cities, like Bakhmut, have been almost completely erased from the face of earth by heavy artillery. On the Ukrainian-controlled side, Kharkiv, the country's second-largest city, suffered most due to its proximity to the Russian border. Kyiv, Odesa and Dnipro have also been hit hard multiple times. Russian strikes have extended as far as Lviv and Mukachevo in the country's far west. Although civilian casualties have been comparatively low, key infrastructure will take years to rebuild.

Ukraine Today

At the time of writing, war defined every aspect of life in Ukraine. The invasion began with air raids and missile attacks on major Ukrainian cities in the wee hours of 24 February 2022. But the 'shock and awe' attack didn't lead to Ukraine's capitulation. Instead, over three and a half years later, the war is still ongoing.

Kyiv, Lviv, Odesa and other major Ukrainian cities have retained some semblance of normal life throughout the conflict, although night-time attacks have forced people to sleep in bomb shelters and upended their lives in multiple other ways, including blackouts and interruptions in the water supply.

Forced enlistment, often carried out using brutal or outright criminal methods, has compelled many men to stay at home for days on end. Others have risked their lives in order to escape, whether by traversing the Carpathian Mountains or swimming across the rivers on the border of the EU. While millions of women and children have gone on to start new lives in the West, most men remain in Ukraine as a result of the ban on travel for all men eligible for the draft (aged 25 to 55): the result is millions of separated or broken families. The brutal demographic and social realities of wartime Ukraine defy imagination.

The conflict had reached a crossroads at the time of writing, with the Trump-led US trying to bring both sides to the negotiating table. The potential success of these efforts remains an open question.

History

Kyiv is the cradle of Ukrainian, Russian and Belarusian nationhood. This has created a range of highly politicised interpretations, especially during times of armed conflict involving all three countries.

Kyivan Rus

In the 9th century, a Viking tribe known as the Rus founded the original East Slavic state. Tracing their roots to the semi-legendary Prince Rurik, the Vikings moved their capital from Novgorod, in today's Russia, to Kyiv in 879, establishing the polity known as Kyivan Rus and claiming control of the lucrative trade route between Constantinople and Northern Europe.

Kyivan Rus reached its pinnacle under the rule of Volodymyr the Great (978–1015), when it stretched from the Volga to the Danube and the Baltic. Volodymyr also established Orthodox Christianity as the pre-eminent religion. Internal feuds between rival princes and nomadic attacks from the east eventually led to the disintegration of the first state in East Slavic lands.

The Mongol Invasion

After the Mongol Golden Horde sacked Kyiv, the city was largely abandoned and the centre of power shifted to the northeastern Rostov-Suzdal principality, where Moscow would eventually come into being.

As the Golden Horde disintegrated in the 15th century, much of today's Ukraine turned into a zone permanently contested by the Crimean Khanate, one of the Horde's fragments, the fledgling Moscow tsardom and the emerging Polish-Lithuanian union. By the 1340s, the latter had taken control of the Galicia-Volynia principalities in the west of today's Ukraine, sending Lviv and the surrounding lands on a different trajectory than the rest of the Kyivan Rus.

The Cossacks

The power vacuum in the steppe on both sides of the Dnipro River was gradually filled by runaway serfs and outlaws who mixed with the remaining nomadic populations. These people became known as the Cossacks. The most famous group of Cossacks lived on the lower Dnipro, in a fortified island community called the Zaporizhya Sich.

Although they were officially under Polish-Lithuanian rule from 1569, the Cossacks often rebelled and remained staunchly Orthodox. In 1654 they formed their own so-called Hetmanate to assert the concept of Ukrainian self-determination. But the ensuing conflict only led to a change of overlords, from Polish to Russian, and attempts to rebel against Moscow failed miserably. In 1775 Catherine the Great ordered the destruction of the last Cossack stronghold.

FAST FACTS

Capital Kyiv
Population 41 million (pre-war estimate)
Area 603,628 sq km
Official language Ukrainian
Time zone GMT+3
Currency Hryvna (UAH)

KYIV AT WAR

Kyiv resident **Yury** reflects on life in the city during the war.

The war has lasted so long that it's hard to remember life without it. Many friends and relatives are at the front, some for more than three years now. Kyiv and Kharkiv, where my father and two shattered apartments remain, were hit especially hard. Nighttime missile and drone strikes are part of the routine. In the first years, there were blackouts and water cuts, but it's less common now. My wife and I got a corgi who we named Orlyk, after the author of the first Ukrainian constitution. But the dog refuses to go for evening walks: a couple of times there were explosions nearby and now he digs his paws in. Many people in Kyiv still go to bomb shelters. We don't. Life goes on: traffic jams in the downtown, small hopes, cognitive dissonance. Everyone wants peace, but no one wants to give away what is ours. I believe Ukraine will still surprise the world.

ANDREAS WOLOCHOW/SHUTTERSTOCK

Independence Monument, Kyiv

The Russian Empire

Under Russian rule, Ukraine saw an unprecedented economic boom as the empire expanded into the sparsely populated steppe east and south of Kyiv. Cossacks and Ukrainian and Russian peasants were the largest groups of colonists, followed by Jews, Germans, Greeks and Bulgarians, all of whom were invited by the crown to cultivate the phenomenally productive land, which soon became known as the 'breadbasket of Europe'.

In 1772, Prussia, Austria and Russia decided to carve up Poland. Under the resulting Partitions of Poland (1772–95), most of western Ukraine was handed to Russia, but the far west around Lviv went to the Habsburg Empire. The Ukrainian nationalist movement was born in Kyiv in the 1840s, but when the tsarist authorities there banned the Ukrainian language from official use in 1876, the movement's focus shifted to Austrian-controlled Lviv.

Soviet Rule

Following WWI and the collapse of the tsarist monarchy, Ukraine had a shot at independence, but the international community was unsupportive. In the aftermath of the Russian Civil War, most of today's Ukraine wound up as the Ukrainian Soviet Socialist Republic, founded in 1922. Swathes of today's western Ukraine, however, became part of the newly independent Poland.

In the first decades of the Soviet rule, the initial policy of 'Ukrainization', encouraging the expansion of Ukrainian language into political and cultural spheres, soon gave way to Stalin's terror and a man-made famine, known in Ukraine as the Holodomor, which today is sometimes described as a deliberate genocidal policy.

Ukraine's entire territory became one the main battlefields of WWII. Entire cities were levelled and some 6 to 8 million Ukrainians, at least 1.6 million of them Jews, were killed. In the post-war arrangement, western Ukraine remained firmly under Soviet control, with both the USSR and Poland conducting population swaps and suppressing Ukrainian nationalist resistance.

After the death of Stalin, Nikita Khrushchev, a self-styled Ukrainian, took the reins of the USSR and once again expanded Ukraine's territory by placing Crimea under its control. He was succeeded by the Ukrainian-born Leonid Brezhnev, but his rule was associated with Ukraine's increasing Russification.

The catastrophe at the Chornobyl nuclear power station in 1986 spurred the rise of Ukrainian nationalism. Ukraine proclaimed independence in the wake of the failed August 1991 coup in Moscow and sealed the decision in a referendum in December that same year.

Independence

The three and a half decades of Ukrainian independence were a roller-coaster that began with a deep economic crisis. Leonid Kuchma, a Soviet-style rocket-factory manager, came to power in July 1994 and stayed in place for 10 years. But growing discontent led to the peaceful Orange Revolution of 2004, which was triggered by accusations of electoral fraud in favour of Kuchma's perceived appointee, Viktor Yanukovych.

In the following years, the pro-Western Orange coalition failed miserably to eliminate corruption or improve the economy, and Yanukovych was elected president in 2010. While exacerbating corruption, Yanukovych tried to appease both the West and Moscow by simultaneously pursuing integration with EU and maintaining strong links with Russia. Ultimately, he had to make a choice and at the end of 2013 he made the fateful decision to embrace Russia. This precipitated the drama of the second Maidan revolution, which culminated in brutal fighting in the centre of Kyiv. Dozens of people were killed and Yanukovych eventually fled to Russia.

As pro-Maidan forces in Kyiv celebrated victory, Moscow responded by annexing Crimea and launching a stealthy annexation of the Donbas mining region with the help of local separatists. The new Ukrainian government sent in troops and an armed conflict ensued, with Moscow effectively commanding separatist forces and backing them up with regular troops. The first phase of the conflict was partially defused by the Minsk agreements of 2015, which left parts of the Donetsk and Luhansk regions under Russia's de facto control.

In the 2019 election, the first post-Maidan president Petro Poroshenko lost heavily to comedian Volodymyr Zelensky, who ran on the platform of mending relations with Russia. His talks with Putin in Paris resulted in a ceasefire, but Zelensky then changed tack at the beginning of 2021 by clamping down on Putin's key Ukrainian ally Viktor Medvedchuk and launching a campaign for NATO membership.

Putin responded by positioning Russian troops on the Ukrainian border in March 2021. This started a period of dangerous brinkmanship and mishandled diplomacy between Moscow, Kyiv and the West. Failing to change the Ukrainian stance, Putin ordered an all-out invasion 11 months later.

UKRAINIAN REFUGEES

Maybe a Ukrainian restaurant popped up in your neighbourhood in recent years. The reason for that is the war. In the wake of Russian aggression, about 7 million Ukrainians fled the country. Most went to the EU, although a sizeable share preferred Russia for reasons pertaining to family or politics. Since Ukraine has banned draft-eligible men from leaving the country, the vast majority of refugees are women and children. This has created a demographic time bomb and is additionally a massive resilience test for families. The longer the war goes on, the more rooted the refugees become in their adopted countries and the less chance there is that they will ever return. Ukrainian refugees are proverbially industrious. In countries that have been smart about licensing and language classes, like Czechia, they are giving back more to local economies than they are taking. They also tend to be proud ambassadors of Ukrainian culture and cuisine. Be sure to visit your nearest *borsch* station when you get a chance.

TOOLKIT

The chapters in this section cover the most important topics you'll need to know about in Europe. They're full of nuts-and-bolts information and valuable insights to help you understand and navigate Europe and get the most out of your trip.

Getting Around the Region
p1176

Accommodation
p1178

Family Travel
p1180

Health & Safe Travel
p1182

Women Travellers
p1184

Food, Drink & Nightlife
p1186

Responsible Travel
p1188

LGBTIQ+ Travellers
p1190

Accessible Travel
p1191

Nuts & Bolts
p1192

Hofbräuhaus (p487), Munich, Germany

Getting Around the Region

Much of Europe is brilliantly connected by road and plane, with some epic long-distance train routes. Ferries breeze across to the islands. Public transport varies wildly but is generally good in cities and towns, becoming sparser in rural regions.

TRAVEL COSTS

Car rental
from €30
per day

Petrol
approx €1.55
per litre

Train
Vienna–Budapest
from €52,
London–Paris
from £35

Metro ticket
€0.60 (Bucharest)
to €4.10 (Munich)

Car

Having your own wheels gives you flexibility and is the best way to reach remote places. That said, cars are often impractical in city centres, where traffic jams and parking issues can make it well worth using public transport instead. Some European cities, such as London, Milan and Stockholm, have implemented congestion charges.

Hiring a Car

Car hire gives you freedom to explore Europe's remotest corners. It's often cheaper to prebook a car than hire one on arrival. You'll generally find major car-hire companies at airports, including Sixt, Hertz and Enterprise. The minimum age for hiring cars ranges from 18 to 25 years. A valid licence issued at least one year prior is necessary. Make sure you have adequate insurance (minimum third-party liability). To cover damage to the car and reduce the excess, purchase additional collision damage waiver (CDW) insurance.

Air

To save money, travel off-season, avoiding mid-June to early September, Easter, Christmas and school holidays. Regardless of your destination, it's sometimes better to pick a recognised transport 'hub' as your initial port of entry, where high traffic volumes keep prices down. The busiest airports are London, Istanbul, Amsterdam, Madrid, Frankfurt and Paris.

DRIVING ESSENTIALS

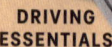

Drive on the right, apart from in the UK, Ireland, Malta, Cyprus and the Channel Islands

Speed limits are typically 50km/h in cities and 120km/h on motorways

All vehicle occupants must wear seatbelts

Bicycle Hire

Much of Europe is brilliant for cyclists and bike hire is prevalent. Many train stations have bike-rental counters and major cities (including London, Paris, Berlin and Amsterdam) have bike-sharing schemes. It's sometimes possible to return the bike at a different outlet so you don't have to retrace your route. Hostels are another good place for cheap bike hire.

Ferry

Ferries are a scenic way to explore Europe, whether you're crossing the English Channel to France or island-hopping around Greece. There may be reductions on off-peak and advance-purchase tickets. **Direct Ferries** *(directferries.co.uk)* is great for timetables, fares and ticket bookings. Lake and river ferry services operate in many countries, including Austria and Switzerland.

Border Crossings

Border formalities have been relaxed in most of the EU but still exist in all their original bureaucratic glory in the more far-flung parts of Eastern Europe.

In line with the Schengen Agreement, there are officially no passport controls at the borders between 29 European states, namely: Austria, Belgium, Bulgaria, Czechia, Croatia, Denmark, Estonia, Finland, France, Germany, Greece, Hungary, Iceland, Italy, Latvia, Liechtenstein, Lithuania, Luxembourg, Malta, the Netherlands, Norway, Poland, Portugal, Romania, Slovakia, Slovenia, Spain, Sweden and Switzerland. Sometimes, however, there are spot checks on trains crossing borders, so always have your passport. The UK was a nonsignatory to Schengen and thus maintains border controls over traffic from other EU countries (except Ireland, with which it shares an open border), although there is no customs control. The same goes for Ireland.

Cyprus is a prospective Schengen area member; for up-to-date details see *schengenvisainfo.com*.

Most borders in Eastern Europe can be crossed via train, where border guards board the train and go through compartments checking passengers' papers. It is rare to get hit up for bribes, but occasionally in Belarus or Moldova you may face a difficulty that can only be overcome with a 'fine'. Travelling between Türkiye and Bulgaria typically requires a change of trains and is subject to a lengthy border procedure.

Train

Comfortable, frequent and reliable, trains are *the* way to get around Europe; whole trips can be organised purely around rail travel (p48). France, Germany, Austria, the Low Countries and Switzerland score highly in quality and quantity of railways. Many state railways have websites publishing timetables and fares.

Train Info

Going by train? **Man in Seat 61** *(seat61.com)* is comprehensive, while **DB Bahn** *(bahn.de)* provides excellent schedule and fare information in English for trains across Europe.

RAIL PASSES

If you're covering lots of ground, a rail pass makes perfect sense. Compare point-to-point charges and rail passes beforehand to make sure you'll break even.

Interrail *(interrail.eu)* offers a Global Pass to European residents for unlimited rail travel through 33 European countries. Passes are valid for four, five or seven days in a month; 10 or 15 days in two months. Interrail also offers One Country passes, valid in the country of your choice for up to one month. The equivalent for residents of non-European countries are **Eurail** *(eurail.com)* passes; prices and benefits are the same.

National rail operators might offer their own passes, or at least a discount card, with substantial reductions on tickets purchased (eg the BahnCard in Germany or the Half-Fare Card in Switzerland).

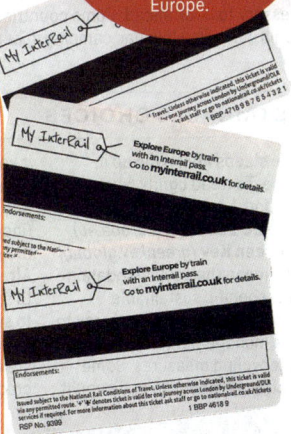

CAROLYN JENKINS/ALAMY

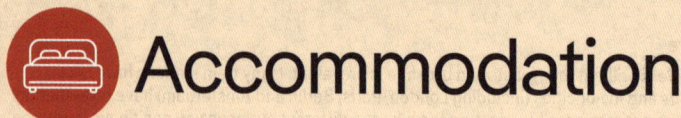

Accommodation

From boutique spa hotels in the Alps to villas by the Med, revamped caves to grand castle sleeps, bare-bones hostels to family-run B&Bs or cloud-grazing mountain huts, where you stay in Europe will form a huge part of your travel experience.

Hotels

From sweet-and-simple family places to ultra-luxe spa hotels, hotels in Europe vary wildly in style and price. Cheap digs around bus and train stations can be convenient for late-night or early-morning arrivals and departures, but check the room beforehand. Top-end boutique and design hotels continue to punch high. Look out for creative options set in old castles, monasteries, palaces or even former prisons.

Hostels

If you're on a budget, Europe's hostels are ideal. Those affiliated to **Hostelling International** *(HI; hihostels.com)* usually offer the cheapest secure roof over your head. You need to be a YHA or HI member to use them; non-members can stay by paying a few extra euros. Private hostels and backpacker digs have fewer rules, more self-catering kitchens and fewer large, noisy school groups. If you aren't happy to share mixed dorms, ask when you book.

B&Bs

Guesthouses (pension, *Gasthaus, chambre d'hôte* etc) and B&Bs offer greater comfort than hostels for a marginally higher price. Most are simple affairs, normally with shared bathrooms. B&Bs in the UK and Ireland often aren't really budget accommodation – even the most humble have midrange prices and there's a new generation of boutique B&Bs, which are pretty flash.

Camping

Camping in Europe is popular. Most campsites are some distance from city centres. See **Hipcamp** *(hipcamp.com)* for details on prime campsites across Europe. There's usually a charge per tent or site, per person and per vehicle. In busy areas and high seasons, it's sometimes necessary to book ahead. Some countries, such as Germany and Estonia, have free bivouac camping in beauty spots.

SUSTAINABLE CHOICES

Green sleeps are on the up in Europe. To tread lightly when travelling, keep your eyes peeled for the **EU Ecolabel** *(europa.eu)* and **Green Key** *(greenkey.global)*, which mean the accommodation meets specific sustainable criteria, from renewable energy to waste management, water saving and recycling measures. Some will offer an incentive or discount if you arrive by public transport. As a rule of thumb, camping and glamping sites, farmstays (including *agriturismi*) and mountain huts (of which the Alps has a vast network) tend to score highly when it comes to sustainability. An increasing number of hotels and B&Bs are also upping their green credentials.

CHEAP SLEEPS

Some university towns rent out their student accommodation during the holiday periods. This is a popular practice in France, the UK and many Eastern European countries. University accommodation is sometimes in single rooms (though more commonly in doubles or triples) and might have cooking facilities. For details, ask at individual universities, at student information offices or local tourist offices.

Online hospitality clubs, linking travellers with thousands of global residents who'll let you occupy their couch or spare room – and sometimes show you around town – for free, include:

Couchsurfing
(couchsurfing.com)

BeWelcome
(bewelcome.org)

5W
(womenwelcomewomen.org.uk)

Trusted Housesitters
(trustedhousesitters.com) Stay for free in exchange for pet sitting.

Check the rules of each organisation and the laws of each country. Always let friends and family know where you're staying and carry your mobile phone with you.

Wild Camping

Scandinavia and Scotland come up trumps if you prefer to head off into the wilds and camp where you please. Elsewhere, be aware of the rules. Camping is often illegal without the permission of the local authorities or landowners (don't be shy about asking; you might be pleasantly surprised). Some hikers still occasionally pitch their tent, and you'll usually get away with it if you have a small tent, are discreet, stay just one or two nights, decamp during the day and don't light a fire or leave rubbish.

HOW MUCH FOR A NIGHT IN A...

Hostel dorm bed
€15–40

Farmstay
€100–120

Campsite including tent
€15–30

Boutique hotel
from €100

Farmstays

Fresh eggs for breakfast, animals to pet, walking trails on the doorstep, meals brimming with homegrown produce – farmstays are a terrific (and often inexpensive) way to get a flavour of the land. Italy has a rich network of state-regulated *agriturismi*. Participating farms must grow at least one of their own crops. See *agriturismo.it* for details. Agritourism has since spread to the UK, France and other countries; see *farmstayplanet.com*.

Glamping

A step up in price from camping, glamping has soared in popularity across Europe and is a terrific way to slip back to nature without sacrificing creature comforts (we're talking proper beds, private toilets, even hot tubs). Green in every sense of the word, glamping sites vary wildly – from geodesic domes in nature reserves to luxe igloos for northern-lights spotting in the Arctic, treetop safari tents to converted horseboxes.

Hay Hotels

Fancy hitting the hay? In Switzerland, Austria and Germany, you can get back to nature by swapping a bed for a barn or a *Heuhotel* (hay hotel). Farmers provide cotton sheets (to avoid straw pricks) and woolly blankets for extra warmth, but you'll need your own sleeping bag and torch. For further details, visit **Schlafen im Stroh** (*myfarm.ch*).

Ramping Up the Romance

All over Europe you can stay in some incredible places if budget isn't an issue, with luxury hotels lodged in everything from castles to caves, lavishly converted abbeys, vineyards and sea-facing fortresses. These vary from country to country, but include **Romantik Hotels** (*romantikhotels. com*) in Austria, Switzerland, Germany and Italy, **château** (*bienvenueauchateau.com*) sleeps in France, Portugal's **pousadas** (*pousadas.pt*) and Spain's **paradores** (*paradores.es*).

Bookings

During peak holiday periods, particularly Easter, summer and Christmas – and year-round in popular cities like London, Paris and Rome – it's wise to book in advance. Most places can be reserved online and are usually cheaper through the hotel's own website.

Savings

Long-stay discounts are usually possible and hotel owners in southern Europe might be open to a little haggling. In many countries it's common for business hotels to slash their rates by up to 40% on Friday and Saturday nights.

Family Travel

Castles and palaces, caves and pirate coves, fantasy woodlands and villages that are pure Grimm fairy-tale stuff – Europe is kid heaven, especially if you look beyond the obvious and seek out the obscure.

Trip Planning

Plan ahead and select a few big-ticket items aimed specifically at kids, such as Disneyland Paris or Tivoli Gardens in Denmark. Don't write off the less obvious sights or smaller attractions. Many of Europe's art galleries and iconic monuments give out kids' activity books that lay out special interactive itineraries for children. Hit a festival. Many European festivals have a strong family bias and have been entertaining children for centuries, from Seville's Feria de Abril to France's Bastille Day.

Breastfeeding, Baby Food & Changing

Nappies (diapers) are widely available; baby-changing facilities vary from country to country but are generally pretty comprehensive. Baby formula and baby food are widely available in supermarkets and drugstores. However, brands differ – you might want to bring your own stash as backup. Most European countries have a pretty relaxed attitude to breastfeeding in public, although European women are less likely to breastfeed than women elsewhere.

Where to Stay

For a hassle-free first trip to Europe with kids in tow, choose destinations well geared towards families, where distances are short, public transport efficient and there's plenty of green space and/or playgrounds. Private apartment rentals can work out cheaper than hotels and give you greater flexibility in terms of mealtimes.

FAMILY TRAVEL ON A BUDGET

Saving money starts with picking the right accommodation. In hotels, cots for babies and tots are usually free of charge on request. For cheap rooms, many hostels have at least one family room.

Lunch specials and fixed-price menus in restaurants tend to be inexpensive. Street food in cities (from pizza to souvlaki) and picnics in the country and on the coast (raid local markets and supermarkets) can be great ways to economise.

Look out for free local guest cards, many of which reap excellent savings on activities. Kids under 12 (sometimes 18) often get free or reduced entry to sights and attractions.

Rental-car companies can arrange child and booster seats, which as a rule are obligatory for children aged 12 and under (measuring between 135cm and 150cm). Newer public transport is often accessible for buggies and prams. In many countries in Europe, children under six travel free on public transport, or half-price until 15 years (proof of age may be required). Keep an eye out for money-saving family passes.

Outdoor Action

Winging you from seaside cove to cow-bobbled pasture, fast-flowing river to mountaintop, Europe is brilliant for families wanting to embrace the great outdoors. Many destinations have gentle, well-marked, family-friendly hiking and cycling trails, some of which are accessible to buggies (strollers) and prams. Most tourist offices can point out family-friendly hikes – from llama walks to wildlife-spotting trails and coastal paths leading to hidden beaches. They can also advise about age-appropriate activities for adventurous kids, be it surfing lessons, rock climbing or white-water rafting. In winter, the Alps and Scandinavia are full-on winter wonderland stuff, with resorts offering ski lessons for children (generally aged four up), plus slope-side magic from snowshoeing to tobogganing, dogsledding and reindeer encounters.

Keep it Light

Bring a light pram that easily folds, with thicker wheels to deal with cobblestones, and pack a baby carrier.

Facilities

Lots of cities and towns across Europe are very green and feature parks with duck ponds and play areas where kids can let off steam. Many lakes have supervised beaches, with kids' splash areas, slides and games. Even cities have lidos with activities like table tennis, volleyball and slides.

Sights & Attractions

All over Europe, big-hitter museums and galleries have dedicated exhibitions, workshops, tours and activities for kids, so it's worth checking websites ahead to get an idea of what's on. Some also offer autism- and neurodivergent-friendly sessions.

ADMISSION

Children aged between five and 18 get heavily discounted (usually half-price) entry on sights, attractions and tours. Tots aged four and under nearly always go free.

EATING OUT & KIDS' CUISINE

Children are generally welcome in all but the most formal of restaurants in Europe, but check ahead.

Some restaurants offer kids' menus, which are usually deep-fried, child-pleasing favourites. Others will make a half (small) portion of adult meals.

Many family-friendly restaurants can provide high chairs or booster seats, but ask when booking. You might want to bring along your own bibs, wipes, cutlery, books and toys.

Mediterranean countries tend to make a real fuss of young children, from hair ruffling to extra sweets.

Attitudes relax the further south you go. In countries like Spain, Italy and Greece, expect to see local kids staying up late(ish) and eating at the same time as their parents. You're likely to see them playing in squares while parents are nearby having a drink.

From frites and crêpes in France to pizza and gelato in Italy and fish and chips in the UK, Europe has plenty of staples that appeal to little appetites.

Health & Safe Travel

Travelling in Europe is usually very safe. With comprehensive health care, political stability and generally low crime rates, you'd be unlucky to encounter any serious problems. The usual common-sense rules of getting the right insurance and stashing away valuables apply.

VACCINATIONS & INFECTIONS DISEASES

No jabs are necessary to visit Europe. However, the World Health Organization (WHO) recommends that all travellers be covered for diphtheria, tetanus, measles, mumps, rubella and polio, regardless of their destination. Since most vaccines don't produce immunity until at least two weeks after they're given, visit a physician at least six weeks before departure.

Health Insurance

To travel anywhere in Europe, you should secure adequate travel insurance. A good policy should include comprehensive health insurance including medical care and emergency evacuation. If you are engaging in risky sports (white-water rafting, paragliding, rock climbing, surfing, off-piste skiing and the like), you may need to pay for extra cover. Check the small print.

If you're an EU citizen or a citizen of Iceland, Liechtenstein, Norway or Switzerland, the free EHIC (European Health Insurance Card) covers you for most medical care in 32 European countries, including maternity care and care for chronic illnesses such as diabetes (though not for emergency repatriation). Offering the same benefits, the UK equivalent is the GHIC card. However, you will normally have to pay for medicine bought from pharmacies, even if prescribed, and perhaps for some tests and procedures. The EHIC and GHIC do not cover private medical consultations and treatment out of your home country; this includes nearly all dentists, and some of the better clinics and surgeries.

Non-EU citizens should find out if there is a reciprocal arrangement for free medical care between their country and the EU country they are visiting.

Tap Water

Tap water is generally safe to drink in Western Europe. However, bottled water is recommended in much of Eastern Europe and is a must in some countries where the giardia parasite can be a problem. Don't drink water from rivers or lakes as it may contain bacteria or viruses. In Greece, the water is often safe to drink but doesn't taste pleasant.

An increasing number of countries have free water fountains at train stations, airports and around major cities, so bring your own bottle.

WASPS & MOSQUITOES

Wasps can be pesky in midsummer but are only dangerous for those with an allergy. Mosquitoes can be a nuisance around rivers and lakes. Bring repellent.

FROM LEFT: PIXEL-SHOT/SHUTTERSTOCK, BANGKOK CLICK STUDIO/SHUTTERSTOCK

Availability & Cost of Health Care

Good health care is readily available in Western Europe, and for minor illnesses, pharmacists can give valuable advice and sell over-the-counter medication. They can also advise if you need specialised help. The standard of dental care is usually good.

While the situation in Eastern Europe has improved since the EU accession of many countries, quality medical care is not always readily available outside major cities. Embassies, consulates and five-star hotels can usually recommend doctors or clinics.

Condoms are widely available in Europe; however, emergency contraception may not be, so take the necessary precautions.

Resources

The **World Health Organization** *(who.int)* publishes the free online book *International Travel and Health,* which is revised annually. **MD Travel Health** *(mdtravelhealth. com)* provides up-to-date travel-health recommendations for every country.

It's usually a good idea to consult your government's website before departure, if one is available:

- **Australia** *(smartraveller.gov.au)*
- **Canada** *(health.canada.ca)*
- **UK** *(gov.uk/foreign-travel-advice)*
- **USA** *(cdc.gov/travel)*

Mountain Safety

Every year people die from landslides and avalanches in the Alps. Always check weather conditions before heading out; consider hiring a guide when skiing off-piste. Before going on challenging hikes, ensure you have the proper equipment and fitness. Inform someone at your hotel/guesthouse where you're going and when you intend to return.

EXPOSURE

One of the biggest risks with travelling in Europe is exposure to the elements. Summers in the south can be extremely hot, with temperatures soaring up to 40°C in countries like Italy and Greece. Seek shade from the midday sun, drink plenty of water to stay hydrated, wear sunblock and avoid overly exerting activities. At the other extreme, winters can be cold in the Alps and Scandinavia. Wear appropriate thermal clothing, check forecasts before planning activities and ideally go with a guide.

PICKPOCKETS & THIEVES

Pickpockets are most active in dense crowds, especially in busy train stations and on public transport during peak hours.

Don't store valuables in train-station lockers or luggage-storage counters. Be vigilant if someone offers to carry your luggage.

Don't leave valuables in your car, on train seats or in your room.

When going out, don't flaunt cameras, laptops or other expensive electronic goods.

Carry a small day pack, and consider using small zipper locks on your packs.

A money belt with your essentials (passport, cash, credit cards, airline tickets) is a good idea; carry a wallet with a day's worth of cash so you needn't delve into it in public.

Record your passport number and issue date or, even better, copy the relevant data pages. If you lose your passport, notify the police immediately and contact your nearest consulate.

Most scams involve distracting you – someone asking for directions or spilling something on you – while another person steals your wallet. Be alert in such situations.

Women Travellers

Travelling in Europe as a solo female traveller is a joy. Many cities and towns are small, walkable and safe. Countries topping gender-equality rankings include Sweden, the Netherlands, Denmark, Spain and Iceland, but with mindfulness, diligence and planning you shouldn't encounter problems elsewhere either.

Where to Stay

Where you stay matters. Book somewhere central and try to arrive during the daytime so you can easily get your bearings. For peace of mind, look out for hotels with 24-hour receptions (you might want to ask for an upper-floor room), hostels with women-only dorms and secure private rentals. Female-run and women-only hotels are also on the rise, so do your research.

What to Wear

Modest dress is required for visiting churches and mosques and may also help to deter unwanted male attention. When entering Orthodox churches, women need to cover their hair, so taking a scarf is a good idea.

Unwanted Attention

Women might attract unwanted attention in Türkiye, rural Spain and southern Italy, especially Sicily, where many men view whistling and catcalling as flattery. Intense staring is common. If ignoring unwanted male attention doesn't work, tell your interlocutor that you're waiting for your husband or boyfriend. If necessary, walk away. If you feel yourself being groped on a crowded bus or metro, be loud to draw attention to the incident. You can report incidents to the police, who are required to press charges.

Getting Around

Public transport is overall safe, but take greater care travelling in remote, quiet or poorly lit areas at night. Make sure taxis are registered or use a licensed ride-share app offering a women-only service such as Bolt and Uber. Hitchhiking alone is not recommended anywhere.

Common-Sense Precautions

In Europe, you should take all the usual precautions you would in any other part of the world. Walking alone at night is usually safe in well-lit, busy central areas. Avoid deserted streets and keep belongings close. Be aware of your surroundings and trust your gut – if it doesn't feel right, it probably isn't. Make a note of the local emergency number and keep your phone well charged.

Tell a Friend

Stay connected. Let friends or family know where you are going and when you'll be back. One of the easiest ways to do this is with the **Find My Friends** (find-myfriends.com) app, which allows them to track your location in real time.

GROUP TOURS

Part of the fun of solo female travel is getting to socialise with like-minded people. **Solo Female Travelers Club** (solofemaletravelers.club), **Intrepid Travel** (intrepidtravel.com), **Insight Vacations** (insightvacations.com) and **Travel Queen** (travel-queen.co.uk) offer carefully tailored women-only group tours and expeditions that provide an easy road in. Food tours, city walking tours, cookery classes and guided activities can also be great ways to connect. **GetYourGuide** (getyourguide.com) is a good starting point.

Food, Drink & Nightlife

When to Eat

Breakfast (7–10am) Substantial, with fruits, cereal, yoghurt, eggs, bread, pastries and plentiful coffee.

Lunch (noon–2pm) Usually soup or salad followed by a main course; sometimes a sandwich on the hoof.

Afternoon tea (3–4pm) The exception to not snacking between meals is this coffee-and-cake ritual.

Dinner (7–10pm) A two- or three-course meal; served later the further south you go.

Where to Eat

Cafes Bakery-cafes, coffee houses, organic delis and ice-cream parlours.

Patisseries French-style bakeries serving pastries and cakes.

Street food Market stalls and pop-up kitchens serve everything from pizza to pierogi.

Restaurants From cheap-and-cheerful to Michelin-starred, restaurants cover every cuisine imaginable.

Pubs From brewpubs to gastro pubs, often with beer gardens.

MENU DECODER

Aperitivo Italian happy hour, which can easily turn into a budget-friendly dinner. Some *aperitivi* include a buffet of antipasti, pasta salads and cold cuts for the price of a single drink.

Full English Britain's famous fry-up with sausage, bacon, egg and toast. In Scotland, expect tattie scones (potato bread), in Wales laverbread (seaweed).

Tapas Spanish small plates designed for sharing, which can be served hot or cold and combined to make a full meal of it. These might include *tortilla* (omelette), *jamón* (ham) or cheese.

Kaffee und Kuchen German afternoon ritual of coffee and fancy cakes. Also popular elsewhere.

Fondue At home in the Alps, this is a gooey feast of melted cheese served in a communal pot. Use a fork to dip in toasted bread.

HOW TO...

Eat in Restaurants

Reservations It's best to book at popular and top-end restaurants, especially in high season. Call a week ahead.

Menus English menus are not a given all over Europe, though you'll often find them in city hot spots. If in doubt, there's usually waitstaff who can translate.

Bon appétit Dining out with locals? It's polite to wish them *bon appétit* (or the equivalent) before digging in.

Water Asking for free tap water is not the done thing in many European countries (including Germany, Belgium and the Netherlands), especially in upmarket places.

Dress Smart casual in fancier establishments, where the locals dress up for dinner. In more relaxed places, jeans, sneakers and T-shirts are fine.

Tipping Check local customs. If service charge is included in the bill, you don't need to tip. Otherwise, around 10% is standard for good service. Some places allow you to add this with card payments, otherwise hand it to your server.

HOW MUCH FOR A...

Breakfast
€10–20

Cup of coffee
€1.50–5

Glass of wine
€2–10

Beer
€2–8

Sandwich
€5–12

Tapas dinner
€15–25

Fixed-price lunch
€15–30

Fine-dining tasting menu
€100–300

HOW TO... ### Know Which Cutlery to Use

Picture the scene: you arrive at a fancy restaurant and are shown to your table. Laid out is more silver cutlery than you would expect at a palace. Four forks. Two knives. Two spoons. There are four glasses, too.

So where to begin? The champagne flute is for a fizzy aperitif and the smaller, usually round glass is for water. The other two are wine glasses: large for red; smaller for white.

Your napkin (place on your lap) will be on a charger plate (a decorative underplate). The small plate (placed at around 11 o'clock with a butter knife on it) is for bread. The bigger plate is for salad. The largest plate is for your main, though a waiter is likely to bring this to you.

For cutlery, work from the outside in. The smallest fork on the right is for seafood. On the left, the smaller fork is for your starter; the larger for your main. Same goes for knives on the right. The spoon to the right is for your main. If you're having soup, steak or fish on the bone, a waiter will bring a new instrument to help you. Finally, the small spoon and fork at noon above your charger plate are for dessert.

Don't Switch

Unlike the American cut-and-switch cutlery handling, in Europe your fork stays in your left hand and your knife in your right when eating.

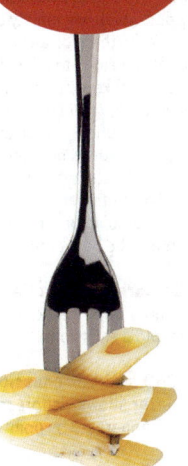

HOW TO SPEND A NIGHT AT A BRITISH PUB

In Britain, pubs – also known as boozers or taverns – are institutions akin (somewhat) to the church: a social spot and local community hub, with nearly always someone giving a sermon of some kind. Similarly, there are a few traditions to look out for. Here's how to go out for a pint (roughly 473.1mL of beer).

Pick a table and order a round Brits usually buy a 'round' of drinks, which means one person orders and pays for all the drinks, then someone else will do the same, and so on.

Queue at the bar The staff keeps track of who is next and it's impolite to order out of turn. When ordering, remember that a 'pint of beer' usually means an ale, an unfiltered beer served at room temperature. There are

plenty of good cask ales, but you might want to ask for a 'pint of lager' instead.

Adding to your 'round' There's no tipping, but you may also consider buying snacks such as crisps, nuts or pork scratchings to tear open and share with the table.

Say cheers! Charge your glasses together and proclaim 'cheers' before you begin drinking.

Last orders When a bell rings (usually at 10.50pm), that means last orders and you have 10 minutes to order a final drink. When it rings again at 11pm, that's 'time at the bar' and you can't order any more drinks. You then have 20 minutes to finish up and leave.

Responsible Travel

Climate Change & Travel

It's impossible to ignore the impact we have when travelling; Lonely Planet urges all travellers to engage with their travel carbon footprint, which will mainly come from air travel. While there often isn't an alternative, travellers can look to minimise the number of flights they take, opt for newer aircrafts and use cleaner ground transport, such as trains. One proposed solution—purchasing carbon offsets— unfortunately does not cancel out the impact of individual flights. While most destinations will depend on air travel for the foreseeable future, for now, pursuing ground-based travel where possible is the best course of action.

The **UN Carbon Offset Calculator** shows how flying impacts a household's emissions

The **ICAO's carbon emissions calculator** allows visitors to analyse the CO2 generated by point-to-point journeys

Go Vegan or Veggie

Plant-based food comes with a lower carbon footprint. Health-food shops and farmers' markets are good places to stock up on essentials, while many towns and cities now have vegetarian and vegan restaurants.

On the Rails

Rail travel is much greener than by car or plane, and much of Europe has high-speed, inexpensive trains. In Switzerland, SBB trains run entirely on renewable energy, while Austria's public transport network is on track to becoming carbon-neutral.

Airbnb

Many of Europe's greatest cities – from Florence to Amsterdam, Barcelona and Lisbon – have felt the backlash of Airbnb rentals as locals complain of being pushed out by rising rents. Consider staying in a hotel, hostel or family-run guesthouse instead.

Light pollution means that natural nighttime darkness is becoming increasingly rare. Switch off the lights and look up at the skies at one of Europe's **International Dark Sky Places** (*darksky.org*).

There's a red alert for Europe's glaciers. Dry, hot summers mean they're shrinking at unprecedented levels, from Switzerland's Aletsch to Italy's Ventina glacier. Many are predicted to disappear entirely by 2100 – or sooner.

Buy Local

Up your sustainable credentials by staying, eating and buying local. Swap the chains for independent B&Bs and guesthouses, pick up the freshest seasonal produce (including picnic treats) at farmers' markets and look for Slow Food label restaurants.

Dodge Peak Season

Beach and mountain resorts that are often swamped for a few months of the year, then deserted for the rest, are increasingly becoming things of the past. Think sustainably and visit in the low or shoulder seasons.

Find out about and volunteer for citizen-science projects from tree planting to bumblebee monitoring by visiting *earthwatch. org.uk* or *citizenscience.eu.*

Search for eco-savvy businesses implementing everything from renewable energy to water-saving measures with **Green Key** *(greenkey.global).*

Green Cities

Aiming for carbon neutrality by 2050, Amsterdam topped the 2024 Arcadis Sustainable Cities Index. The city scored highly for renewable energy, waste reduction, cycling infrastructure and electric public transport.

Overtourism

Responsible tourism means casting the net wider than the usual crowded hot spots. In peak season, eschew places like Dubrovnik, Rome, Paris, Santorini and Venice in favour of less visited destinations that are equally appealing.

Walk or Bike It

Want to lower your carbon footprint? Check out Europe's excellent network of walking and cycling trails, taking you from coast to peak, country to city. Many places offer bike-sharing schemes, making it a breeze to zip around town.

Refill en Route

Bring along your own refillable water bottle, cup and lunchbox to avoid unnecessary plastic and minimise waste. Train stations and airports often have free water fountains, and some restaurants and cafes will refill your bottle.

Low-Impact Activities

Skiing and artificial snow can cause erosion, disturb wildlife and increase emissions. Look for winter resorts diversifying their offer with low-impact activities like cross-country skiing, snowshoeing, winter hiking and tobogganing.

RESOURCES

greendestinations.org
Enthusiastic guide to sustainable travel.

greentraveller.co.uk
Low-carbon holidays and travel guides.

selectgreenhotels.com
Eco-friendly hotels in Europe, with organic food and renewable energy.

⭐ LGBTIQ+ Travellers

While the rainbow flag flies high in much of Europe, there's still some discrimination in staunchly conservative, Catholic pockets of the continent and Islamic regions. Countries like Britain, Spain, Portugal, Denmark, Belgium and Iceland have flourishing gay scenes. In less tolerant countries like Albania, Montenegro, Serbia and Türkiye, discretion is advised to avoid homophobic and transphobic hostility. Cities often feel more progressive than smaller towns.

Equality Act

In the UK, sexual orientation is a protected characteristic under the Equality Act 2010. This means LGBTIQ+ travellers are legally protected from discrimination as a consumer and when using public services. Many other countries in Europe have their own version of anti-discriminatory legislation, including the General Act on Equal Treatment in Germany and the Netherlands, Spain's Law 4/23, ensuring equality plans and anti-harassment protocols for LGBTIQ+ individuals, and Sweden's Discrimination Act and 2025 Legal Gender Recognition Act.

PRIDE EVENTS

Britain hosts more than 150 Pride events each year, including a colossal late June/early July bash in London *(prideinlondon.org)* and a massive two-dayer in Brighton *(brighton-pride.org)* each August. Other big-hitter Pride events across Europe include the mammoth **Madrid Orgullo** *(madridorgullo.com)*, attracting two million revellers, Berlin's party-loving **Christopher Street Day** *(pridefestival.berlin)* in July, Amsterdam's two-week-long **WorldPride** *(pride.amsterdam)* from late July to early August, and Nice's Pink Parade in late July.

The Rainbow Map

The **Ilga Europe Rainbow Map** *(rainbowmap.ilga-europe.org)* ranks 49 European countries on their legal and policy practices for LGBTI people, from 0% to 100%, and is searchable by country and category such as equality and non-discrimination, family, hate crime and speech, legal gender recognition and asylum.

SAME-SEX MARRIAGE

At the time of writing, 22 European countries had legalised same-sex marriage. These are Andorra, Austria, Belgium, Denmark, Estonia, Finland, France, Germany, Greece, Iceland, Ireland, Liechtenstein, Luxembourg, Malta, the Netherlands, Norway, Portugal, Slovenia, Spain, Sweden, Switzerland and the UK.

Summer Scene

In summer, the LGBTIQ+ scene often flicks to the sand, sea and party beats of islands in the Med. Top gay-friendly destinations include Mykonos and Lesbos in Greece, nightlife-mad Ibiza, Malta and the dune-flanked beaches of Gran Canaria.

RESOURCES

Gay Times *(gaytimes.com)* Online magazine covering fashion, culture, drag and music.

Trans Unite *(transunite.co.uk)* UK-wide network of transgender support groups, including online.

Rainbow Cities Network *(rainbowcities.com)* Global network for LGBTI equality.

Travelgay *(travelgay.com)* Travel guide covering clubs, bars, beaches, saunas and more.

Accessible Travel

Accessible travel remains a work in progress in Europe. Some historic spaces haven't been retrofitted to aid those in wheelchairs, but ramps and wheelchair-access lifts are more prevalent in newer buildings and at stations. Also, the list of wheelchair-accessible and autism-friendly stays is growing.

Passenger Assist

The railway networks in many countries offer mobility assistance for navigating a station or boarding a train. You'll usually need to call or book through an app at least 24 hours ahead.

Airports

Major airports can usually assist passengers with reduced mobility. Services range from barrier-free shopping to parking and transfers from terminal to plane. Notify your airline at least 48 hours before departure, and head to the Special Assistance desk in Arrivals.

Accommodation

Small guesthouses and B&Bs (especially those in historic buildings) are often unable to provide services for guests with reduced mobility. Larger, more expensive hotels (four-star or above, usually) have facilities tailored to travellers with disabilities.

GALLERIES & MUSEUMS

Accessibility is on the up at many galleries and museums in Europe, with ramps, lifts and well-spaced exhibitions. Some even have quiet times, ear defenders, sensory maps, Braille signs and audio description.

MAGIC KEYS

For travels in the UK, get a radar key, which unlocks thousands of public accessible toilets. For Europe, the Euro Key can be ordered through **CDF Darmstadt** (cbf-da.de), a German organisation for people with disabilities.

Cobbled Streets

Europe's historic city centres often have uneven cobblestones and narrow lanes that can be difficult to navigate for wheelchair users or the vision-impaired, particularly when crowded in the peak summer season.

Public Transport

Congested inner cities and archaic underground subway systems make Europe a tricky destination for people with mobility issues. However, newer trains tend to be good and buses often have low floors, ramps and lifts.

RESOURCES

AccessAble (accessable.co.uk) Detailed access information for thousands of venues across the UK and Ireland.

Accessible Europe (accessibleurope.com) Specialist European tours with van transport.

Society for Accessible Tourism & Hospitality (sath.org) Reams of information for travellers with disabilities.

Sage Traveling (sagetraveling.com) Great resource for finding accessible hotels in cities all over Europe.

Limitless Travel (limitlesstravel.org) Accessible holidays in Europe, from cruises to coach tours.

Sunflower Scheme

A discreet way to show that you have an invisible or unnoticeable disability is to wear a sunflower lanyard. This alerts staff at airports, on public transport and in museums and shops that you may require assistance. Visit hdsunflower.com for details.

Nuts & Bolts

VISAS

Citizens of the US, Canada, Australia, New Zealand and the UK currently need only a valid passport to enter nearly all countries in Europe, but check requirements before travelling as there are some exceptions. All visas have a 'use-by' date and you'll be refused entry afterwards. In some cases it's easier to get visas as you go along rather than arranging them all beforehand. In late 2026, the EU is introducing a new visa-waiver scheme called ETIAS. Citizens of visa-exempt countries will have to fill in an online application and pay €20 (free for those under 18 or over 70). The authorisation will be valid for three years.

Time

Nearly all of Europe, with several exceptions (Russia, Belarus, Iceland), observes daylight saving time on synchronised dates in late March (clocks go forward an hour) and late October (clocks go back an hour).

Europe is divided into four time zones. From west to east:

UTC (Britain, Ireland, Portugal, Iceland) GMT (GMT plus one hour in summer)

CET (the majority of European countries) GMT plus one hour (GMT plus two hours in summer)

EET (Greece, Türkiye, Bulgaria, Romania, Moldova, Ukraine, Belarus, Lithuania, Latvia, Estonia, Kaliningrad, Finland) GMT plus two hours (GMT plus three hours in summer)

MSK (Russia) GMT plus three hours

Internet Access

Internet access varies enormously across Europe. In most places you'll be able to find wi-fi (also called WLAN in some countries), although whether it's free varies greatly. Internet cafes are increasingly rare but not impossible to find.

OPENING HOURS

These vary from country to country, and can differ between cities and small villages, but generally:

Banks 9.30am to 3pm or 5pm Monday to Friday

Cafes 8am–11pm

Pubs and bars Noon–midnight; to 1am Friday and Saturday

Restaurants Lunch noon–2.30pm, dinner 6–10pm (later in cities)

Shops 9am–5.30pm (6pm in cities) Monday to Saturday, 10am–5pm Sunday; big-city convenience stores open 24/7

Electricity

Europe generally runs on 220V, 50Hz AC. The UK runs on 230/240V AC, and some old buildings in Italy and Spain have 125V. If your home country has a vastly different voltage, you'll need a transformer.

The UK and Ireland use three-pin square plugs. Most of Europe uses the 'europlug' with two round pins. Greece, Italy and Switzerland use a third round pin in a way that the two-pin plug usually fits. Buy an adapter at the airport.

ATMs

ATMs are ubiquitous in major towns and cities, but you should always have a back-up option. In remote areas ATMs are scarcer. Much of Europe uses a chip-and-pin system with a four-digit PIN.

Toilets

Many public toilets require a small fee either deposited in a box or given to the attendant. Availability of toilets varies. If you can't find one, simply drop into a hotel or restaurant and ask to use theirs, or make a nominal purchase at a cafe.

PUBLIC HOLIDAYS

Each country in Europe observes its own public holidays and national days, but widely celebrated ones include:

New Year's Day 1 January

Epiphany 6 January

Easter March/April

Labour Day 1 May

Whit Monday 6th Monday after Easter

Ascension Day 6th Thursday after Easter

Corpus Christi 2nd Thursday after Whitsunday

Assumption 15 August

All Saints' Day 1 November

Immaculate Conception 8 December

Christmas Day 25 December

St Stephen's Day 26 December

ETIQUETTE

Politeness goes a long way. Master enough of the local language to be able to say the basics, such as 'hello', 'please', 'thank you' and 'goodbye' when entering or leaving shops, cafes and restaurants.

In Italy, eat spaghetti with a fork, not a spoon, and never order coffee with your lunch or dinner.

Raise a toast by saying 'cheers' in the local language, clinking glasses and making eye contact.

Respect local customs. For instance, in Islamic countries you should avoid eating, drinking or smoking in public during Ramadan fasting hours.

Take your cue from locals in terms of dress. Beachwear is usually a no at restaurants and in cities.

Dress modestly at religious sites. Bring a shawl or wrap to cover shoulders in churches. In mosques and Orthodox churches, women should also cover their hair.

STORYBOOK

Our writers delve deep into different aspects of European life.

Parque Arqueológico do Vale do Côa (p915), Portugal

JOALACERDA/SHUTTERSTOCK

A HISTORY OF EUROPE IN
15 PLACES

From the rumblings of Crete's Minoan civilisation 5000 years ago to the modern day, Europe's history makes for gripping reading. Waves of invaders and explorers, Roman emperors, war-waging Vikings, dastardly kings and conquerors, power-hungry dictators, philosophical movers and shakers – it's an epoch-spanning, page-turning tale of success and failure, war and peace, horror and glory. By Kerry Walker

HISTORY IN EUROPE is palpable. Town and city, castle and palace, church and cathedral, remote standing stone and cross-strewn battleground – everywhere you go, you're confronted with the vestiges of the past. This little continent has played a disproportionately huge role in shaping world history.

Prehistory is etched out in rock art, standing stones and Neolithic chamber tombs, nodding to mysterious early civilisations. Skip forward a few millennia and temple-topped Ancient Greece is swirling in Homeric myth, with the Roman Empire hot at its heels. The Middle Ages brought Scandinavian Vikings in mighty longships, and a continent-wide frenzy of castle and palace building. The Renaissance ushered in a great revival of the sciences and arts, followed by the opulent architecture, literature and music of baroque.

The 20th century makes for more sobering reading: the brutality of two world wars is still felt at battlefields and concentration camps, and Soviet-led communism in Eastern Europe echoes at memorials and remnants of the Berlin Wall. The 21st century has also shaken the continent to its core, with economic and energy crises, farmers' protests, anti-immigration riots, spiralling living costs, COVID and, most recently, Russia's 2022 full-scale invasion of Ukraine, with the war raging on at the time of writing.

1. Parque Arqueológico do Vale do Côa, Portugal
SAVED FROM THE FLOOD

Côa has been called the largest open-air collection of Palaeolithic rock art in the world. Over 1200 carvings have been uncovered, some going back 22,000 years. The first discovery was in the early 1990s, as Portugal's biggest energy company was excavating the area. The prospect of flooding the valley and losing access to the carvings forever enraged the public and many international supporters. In 1995, a new government was elected and lost no time in cancelling the dam project. The Battle of Côa, as it became known, was a rare victory of heritage and culture.

For more on Parque Arqueológico do Vale do Côa, see p915.

2. Brú na Bóinne, Ireland
PREHISTORIC PASSAGE TOMBS

Located within a bend in the River Boyne in County Meath are the burial tombs of Newgrange, Knowth and Dowth, which date from around 3200 BCE. The remarkable complex is one of the most important

Neolithic sites in the world, and the ceremonial structures also contain a large collection of megalithic art. Newgrange's passage leads to a central chamber that directly aligns with the sunlight of the winter solstice, and it was a place of ritual. In 2020, analysis of the DNA of a man buried in Newgrange revealed that his parents were closely related, suggesting he could have been royal.

For more on Brú na Bóinne, see p620.

3. Stonehenge, England
ROLLING STONES

Britain's stone circles are a mysterious echo of its ancient past. Most famous of all is Stonehenge, the myth-laden ring on Salisbury Plain that has been drawing people to it for 5000 years. Why did these long-ago people build these structures? Was it to chart the movements of sun and moon? To honour the dead? To bury royalty? Hauling bluestones almost 200 miles across the country by sledge and sea, with each of the immense boulders weighing two to five tonnes, would have been an unimaginably arduous task.

For more on Stonehenge, see p188.

Brú na Bóinne (p620), Ireland

4. Knossos, Greece
MINOAN PALACE COMPLEX

The Palace of Knossos – the elaborate ruins and re-creations of the grand capital of Minoan Crete – is ripe for the imagination. The immense palace, courtyards, apartments and frescoes tell the tale of this powerful civilisation about which much has been found (including the Bronze Age port town of Akrotiri in Santorini) but about which much is still unknown. The Minoans developed the first written language (Linear A) and traded widely, and perhaps peacefully as none of their towns were fortified. The whole civilisation disappeared mysteriously, possibly related to fallout from Santorini's 16th-century-BCE volcanic explosion.

For more on Knossos, see p559.

5. Troy, Türkiye
STRAIGHT FROM THE HORSE'S MOUTH

The site of antiquity's most famous war, Troy is such a staple of mythology that it's sometimes surprising to learn it's a real place. Legends tell of the Trojan prince Paris' abduction of Helen of Sparta, and the subsequent Greek expedition to recover her, culminating in Odysseus' Trojan Horse trick. While this makes a fantastic yarn, it's likely to have only the vaguest resemblance to historical fact. It's true, though, that the ancient city of Troy was one of the largest in the Aegean region, but was totally destroyed around 1250 BCE. The surviving ruins may not be Türkiye's most impressive, but they are testament to one of the world's most powerful stories.

For more on Troy, see p1153.

6. Arena di Verona, Italy
IMPERIAL GRANDEUR

Following the assassination of Caesar in 44 BCE, Rome returned to civil war until Caesar's adopted son, Octavian, gained the upper hand. In 27 BCE, Octavian was acclaimed Augustus (meaning 'great') and the Senate conceded virtually unlimited power to him, ushering in the era of imperial rule. By the time Verona's extraordinary amphitheatre was completed in 30 CE, Augustus' stepson Tiberius ruled over an empire that stretched all the way to Palestine, where Jesus of Nazareth was just starting his public ministry. Verona was by then an important town, worthy of this grand arena, which predates Rome's mighty Colosseum by 50 years.

For more on Arena di Verona, see p673.

7. Nationalmuseet, Denmark

RAIDERS AND TRADERS, EXPLORERS AND MARINERS

The Vikings conjure up fearsome warriors in longboats, raiding and pillaging foreign lands. However, these Scandinavian seafarers were also successful farmers, traders, sailors and explorers. The Viking Age began when 'North Men' ransacked Lindisfarne Monastery on the coast of northeastern England in 793 CE, and went on to last about 250 years. During this time, opportunist raids evolved into organised conquests. Settlements were established in England, France, Iceland, Greenland and Newfoundland. Copenhagen's Nationalmuseet offers an unbeatable crash course in Viking history via its superb collection of weaponry, warships and rune stones.

For more on the Nationalmuseet, see p316.

8. Alhambra, Spain

A NASRID MARVEL

The sight of Granada's ochre-hued hilltop Alhambra backed by the snow-dusted peaks of the Sierra Nevada is one of Andalucía's most magical. Above all others, the Alhambra is Spain's great Moorish relic, a fantastical palace-fortress laced with fragrant gardens, interlocking patios and rushing water features, perfected under the Nasrid emirs, particularly Mohammed V. Though the first records of a fort here date from the 9th century, it's believed the original buildings on the Alhambra hill could have existed since Roman times. The celebrated Palacios Nazaríes (a highpoint in Islamic architecture) and elegant Generalife were created in the 14th century – this is the Alhambra roughly as we know it today.

For more on the Alhambra, see p1081.

9. Tower of London, England

JEWEL IN THE CROWN

When William the Conqueror had the White Tower built as the centrepiece of his London fortress during the 1066 Norman Conquest, it was the ultimate muscle-flexing symbol of pomp and power. With its riot of towers and battlements overlooking the Thames, the iconic tower gallivants through 1000 years of history. It has been a fortress, a royal residence, a treasury, a mint, an arsenal and a prison. The Crown Jewels (protected by the famous red-coated Yeoman Warders, or Beefeaters, and a flock of fabled ravens) dazzle with the world's biggest diamonds. And its walls whisper of murdered princes and beheaded queens.

For more on the Tower of London, see p175.

10. Hofburg, Austria

PALACE OF HABSBURG DREAMS

Imagine what you could do with unlimited riches and Austria's top architects at hand for 640 years, and you'll have the Vienna of the Habsburgs. The crown jewel is the Hofburg, HQ of the Habsburgs from 1273 to

Auschwitz-Birkenau Memorial & Museum (p883), Poland

DIRKVG/SHUTTERSTOCK

1918, with a flabbergasting stash of cultural and art treasures. The oldest section is the 13th-century Schweizerhof (Swiss Court-yard), named after the Swiss guards who protected its precincts. Feel the weight of the empire marvelling at the treasury's im-perial crowns and precious religious relics, the equine ballet of snow-white Lipizzaner stallions at the Spanische Hofreitschule and the chandelier-lit apartments fit for a rather fussy Empress Elisabeth.

For more on the Hofburg, see p80.

11. Bryggen, Norway
HANSEATIC HOT SPOT

For over 400 years, Bryggen, the warehouse complex in Bergen's sheltered harbour, was dominated by a tight-knit community of German merchants allied to the Hanseatic League. The League established its first of-fice here around 1360, importing grain and exporting dried fish, among other prod-ucts. By the 15th century, Dutch and En-glish competitors (and the Black Death, which killed 70% of Bergen's population) brought about the Hanseatic League's de-cline. But by the early 17th century, Ber-gen was the mercantile hub of Scandinavia again and Norway's most populous city, with 15,000 people. Bryggen remained a key trading centre until the League's of-fices finally closed in 1899.

For more on Bryggen, see p849.

12. Château de Versailles, France
SUN KING MEGALOMANIA

Louis XIV, better known as Le Roi Soleil (the Sun King), ascended the throne aged five. Bolstered by claims of divine right, he involved the kingdom of France in a series of costly wars with Holland, Austria and England. Taxation to refill the state coffers caused widespread poverty and vagrancy, but didn't stop Louis XIV from building the most extravagant palace on French soil at Versailles in 1663. The king forced his 6000 courtiers to compete with each other for royal favour, thus quashing the feuding ar-istocracy and creating the first centralised French state. The château razzle-dazzles with the French monarchy at the height of its glory.

For more on the Château de Versailles, see p396.

13. In Flanders Fields Museum, Belgium
LEST WE FORGET

Whole villages disappeared into the mud during WWI, where for several years sol-diers rotted in sodden trenches in Flanders fields. The whole course of WWI could have been very different if plucky Liège had not previously delayed German advances by 12 valuable days. Rebuilt from scratch follow-ing the war, the town of Ypres bears witness to the madness of war. The unmissable sight is In Flanders Fields Museum, which spells out the horrors of the Great War in artefacts from maps to military equipment.

For more on In Flanders Fields Museum, see p133.

14. Auschwitz-Birkenau Memorial & Museum, Poland
HOLOCAUST MEMORIAL

The first gassings at this death factory, also known as Oświęcim, 50km west of Kraków, took place as early as 1941. By the end of WWII, a least 1.1 million human be-ings had perished at this most notorious of concentration camps – mostly Jews, fol-lowed by Poles and Roma. Now a memorial museum, Auschwitz is not a tourist sight – it's a lesson in the horror and futility of war and the dangers of dictatorship out of control. Few remain unmoved by the lev-el of inhumanity they see here, and it's a place that illustrates the extreme brutal-ity of the mid-20th century.

For more on the Auschwitz-Birkenau Memorial & Museum, see p883.

15. Berlin Wall, Germany
COLD WAR SYMBOL

For 28 years, from 1961 to 1989, the Ber-lin Wall was the paramount symbol of the Cold War. A complete circuit, some 155km in circumference, it was built around West Berlin by the German Democratic Republic (GDR) to close off the route via which more than 3.5 million of its citizens had defect-ed to the West. The 'Fall of the Wall', offi-cially dated to 9 November 1989, was the culmination of a wave of events, including the waning of Soviet power in the Eastern Bloc countries, which led to the collapse of communism in Eastern Europe and the re-unification of Germany on 3 October 1990.

For more on the Berlin Wall, see p465.

EUROPE'S
TRANSHUMANCE

Ancient Europe was widely trodden by nomadic livestock herders and, in many places, it's a tradition that remains alive today. By Mark Eveleigh

IN 2023, EUROPE'S transhumance (seasonal migration of livestock) was inscribed on UNESCO's Intangible Cultural Heritage List. You'll find this ancient rural tradition taking place across Europe – although always on smaller scales than in historical times – from Spain in the west to Greece in the east. The economic boost that such events bring to communities helps convince young people to maintain rural traditions rather than abandon the villages to join swelling human migrations into the cities. Many are coming to understand that the grass isn't always greener on the other side of the fence.

Spain's Fiestas de la Trashumancia

Spain is just one of several countries where you can experience transhumance. Take a sightseeing trip to the Spanish capital in October, and you might be astounded to find your explorations of Madrid's historic centre brought to a standstill by an invasion of more than a thousand sheep.

The first warning comes with the clanking of heavy bells on the necks of the big goats that lead the migration. Shoppers, commuters and tourists cluster in doorways, as sheepdogs dash around their legs with single-minded alertness, ears cocked for the whistled orders of the shepherds.

Madrid's Fiesta de la Trashumancia (dates vary in October) has been celebrated since 1994 as part of the initiative to maintain migration routes that date back more than 750 years. In 1273, Alfonso X – known as Alfonso El Sabio ('The Wise') – issued a royal decree guaranteeing shepherds absolute freedom of movement, in perpetuity, through a nationwide network of migration trails that were henceforth to be known as *cañadas reales*. The establishment of these formal routes was designed to benefit the all-powerful Mesta organisation, a sort of brotherhood of wealthy sheep-owners who were the power behind Spain's monopoly in precious merino wool. Perhaps the most famous of all *cañadas reales* runs right along what is now Calle Mayor, in the heart of the country's capital, but many more of these ancient migration routes would already have been regularly trodden back in Roman times.

Astorga, in Castilla y León, also celebrates a Fiesta de la Trashumancia in October, and the village of Brieva de Cameros – which claims to be the last Riojan community to maintain the historic flocks – has a smaller festival in June. As with Madrid, these processions are now symbolic, but the Spanish government still maintains a network of livestock migration routes that

stretch thousands of kilometres across the country. Although long-distance droving is now a thing of the past, in Spain you'll still often see *pastores* (shepherds) grazing their flocks along *cañadas reales* in remote parts of Extremadura and Castilla y León.

Spain's Last True Nomadic Shepherds

In 2004, during an assignment for CNN, I joined three septuagenarian brothers – the last of Spain's true migrant shepherds – on a 250km trek. Together we drove the flock of 3000 merinos from the plains of southern Aragón to the appropriately named Monte Perdido (Lost Mountain) in the high Pyrenees. We trekked through the daylight hours and slept rough on the rocky ground at the edge of the flock. There's a mistaken belief that long-distance treks were cruel and that the modern alternative – transporting by vehicle – is less stressful.

'Only the bad shepherd rushes,' Aurelio Noguero, one of the brothers, told me as we rested one hot afternoon in the shade of a scraggy Spanish oak. 'The good shepherd travels slowly and allows his flock to arrive in good health.' While animals invariably lose weight during stressful truck or rail journeys, experts believe that sheep often gained more than 10kg during the slow, steady weeks of the *trashumancia*.

Two decades later, I hiked coast-to-coast across Spain (this time researching for my travel book *Vagabond: A Hiker's Homage to Rural Spain*) and followed part of the Cañada Real Zamorana as it headed northwards. That ancient trail still links with the Cañada Real Soriana Occidental, connecting Badajoz and the Portuguese borderlands with Spain's northern *meseta* (plateau). During my 1225km hike, I occasionally came across shepherds moving short distances between pastures – sometimes accompanied by intimidating mastiffs with the spiked collars designed to fend off Spain's growing population of wolves – but modern health regulations (combating the spread of foot-and-mouth disease, for example) now forbid the long-distance movement of livestock on foot.

The European transhumance isn't confined only to sheep, however. Each June, the Galician town of Sabucedo lures visitors by the hundreds for the festival known as A Rapa das Bestas (literally the 'shearing of the beasts'), when herds of feral horses are rounded up from the surrounding mountains. It's a typically dramatic Spanish tradition that dates back to the 16th century, providing an opportunity for manes and tails to be trimmed and for the annual health checks and branding (and, these days, micro-chipping).

Austria's Almabtrieb

In the Austrian Alps, autumn is the time for the cows to be brought home from the highland summer pastures to their cosy lowland barns. The festival known as the Almabtrieb sees the cows being adorned with elaborate headdresses and clanking cowbells. In the Alpine villages of Fügen, Gattererberg, Hart and Gerlos, the villagers dress in traditional Tracht costumes and party to the tune of *Volksmusik* (folk music) and hearty yodelling.

More than just the transfer of livestock, the Almabtrieb (taking place around September) was traditionally a thanksgiving, welcoming the herdsmen back from their seasonal exile high on the mountain slopes. The night before the homecoming, the herdsmen celebrated their final night on the mountain – known as Gru-Nacht in the Austrian Tirol. The celebrations continue (often fuelled by copious amounts of Krautinger, schnapps made from fermented turnips) after the return to the villages along the Wildschönau valley with feasting, dancing and a series of produce and craft markets that now draw visitors from far and wide.

Alpseeding in Switzerland

In the Swiss Alps (especially in the highlands south of Lucerne and Bern), an ancient tradition sees as many as 400,000 cattle and 200,000 sheep and goats descending from the slopes in August and September. The lead cows and the best dairy cows are often decorated with flower crowns known as *Tschäppl* that are crafted from branches and adorned with seasonal flowers such as chrysanthemums, dahlias and sunflowers. To the rural communities of the Swiss Alps, it remains a way of celebrating a fruitful summer. Visitors flock to the villages to join in festivities that invariably involve traditional costumes, highland music and huge amounts of first-class cheese that's a direct result of the rich highland grazing.

Known to ecologists as Alpseeding, such migrations have become an integral part of the natural cycle of these habitats over hundreds (in some cases thousands) of years – just like the Serengeti savannas would cease to exist without the passage of millions of wildebeest and zebras. In more recent years, traditional Swiss livestock has also been joined by growing herds of alpacas, imported from South America.

The Basque Country's Artzain

After sheep were introduced into the Basque Country from North Africa around 2500 BCE, they became so ingrained in the local way of life that the Euskera (Basque language) word for 'wealth' is *aberastasuna* (literally 'possession of herds'). A great part of the region's rich highland culture stems from legends of the tough wandering shepherds. Basque celebrations frequently feature *Joaldunak* (figures adorned in sheepskins and clanking copper goatbells, to drive away the evil spirits), and Basque parents continue to thrill their children with tales of the Basajaun (a sort of benevolent 'yeti' that helps injured shepherds and warns them of encroaching storms).

Today, the Basque region is divided into the French Pays Basque and the Spanish

THE ECONOMIC BOOST THAT SUCH EVENTS BRING TO COMMUNITIES HELPS CONVINCE YOUNG PEOPLE TO MAINTAIN RURAL TRADITIONS.

Swiss cow with *Tschäppl* (flower crown)
TRAVELKLUTZ/SHUTTERSTOCK

País Vasco and, until 1841 when customs laws were implemented between the two countries, Basque shepherds would drive herds – hundreds of thousands strong – between summer grazing on the high Pyrenees and sheltered winter valleys in the Basque lowlands. The *artzain* (shepherds) led incredibly spartan and solitary existences but they were usually paid for a season's work in sheep rather than cash, which eventually led to their independence as livestock owners in their own right.

In the 19th and 20th centuries, thousands of Basque sheepherders went to find work in Mexico, Chile and California. Some returned wealthy and built spectacular homes, which you can often recognise as you walk around Basque villages by the symbolic palm tree that was at once a status symbol and a souvenir of their travels.

Spanish shepherds, in particular, were in demand throughout the Americas (and even as far away as Australia) not only for their tireless dedication but also for the home-spun veterinary skills that kept the flocks healthy and disease-free even in the remotest and most inhospitable landscapes. Until recently, it was customary for a Spanish shepherd to castrate lambs by the simple procedure of biting the testicles off with their own teeth. The habit is said to survive even into the present time, although I'm very happy to say that it wasn't a skill that my septuagenarian travelling companions ever shared with me.

SCANDINAVIAN ARCHITECTURE
FOR PEOPLE & NATURE

There's something in Scandinavian architecture that makes visitors feel at home. Clean lines, wall-sized windows and pale timber define 'Scandi style', but beneath the aesthetic lies a deeper philosophy: design should improve everyday life. By Paula Hotti

ACROSS DENMARK, NORWAY, Sweden and Finland (considered together here, as part of the broader concept of Scandinavia), architecture has long been defined by a commitment to simplicity, light and the use of natural materials. While these characteristics make the style well known worldwide, they also reflect a style born out of necessity: adapting to the rugged landscapes, the soft and slanting (and at times borderline nonexistent) light and the harsh demands of the northern climes.

Underlining this aesthetic, you can also find the conviction that good design should not make everyday life only visually pleasing but also more functional. In short, beauty should go hand in hand with practicality.

The Roots of Northern Aesthetics

Today, Scandinavian architecture and design are more than a regional style. They stand for a way of life. Leaf through a book in a glass-walled library in Helsinki, step inside a minimalist hotel in Copenhagen or a museum flanked by Norwegian fjords, and you'll notice the same muted harmony of light and space, with an implicit feeling that everything has been placed where it should be. This is architecture with both design and comfort in mind.

But before we get ahead of ourselves, let's step back in time. The story of Scandinavian architecture begins centuries ago, in the rugged landscapes of the north. Early Scandinavian builders worked with what they had – that is, endless forests and ancient stone. Out of these, they crafted remarkable structures such as Norway's wooden stave churches – intricate examples of timber engineering that have stood for almost 900 years. Dotted in valleys and fjords, such as in the Sognefjorden region, these churches were built to endure the long, unforgiving winters.

Yet the Nordic countries didn't truly have a unified architectural identity until the beginning of the 20th century. Take Finland, for example. When the country fell under Russian rule and Helsinki was announced the capital of the autonomous Grand Duchy of Finland in 1812, it was decided that the sleepy seaside town needed a more dignified appearance. Enter Carl Ludvig Engel (1778–1840), a German architect dispatched from St Petersburg with a brief to give the city some gravitas.

From 1816 onwards, Engel transformed provincial Helsinki into a neoclassical capital, complete with a majestic Senate Square, pastel facades and boulevards worthy of the bourgeois who began to settle

there. The project took 24 years, during which Engel lived and worked in Helsinki and, according to rumours, never quite warmed to the place. Today, his creation – the cream-white Helsinki Cathedral with its turquoise dome rising above Senate Square – has become the city's most loved and recognised landmark.

Like many Nordic capitals in the 19th century, Helsinki sought to imitate continental grandeur with pillars, domes and other fashionable flourishes before forging its own architectural identity. But as the 20th century approached, a quiet rebellion began to simmer. Architects in the north began to question whether imitation really was the highest form of flattery. Partially out of this questioning emerged the National Romantic movement as an effort to find a style rooted in local traditions.

One of its champions was Martin Nyrop (1849–1921), the architect of Copenhagen's City Hall (opened in 1905). Unimpressed by the idea of mimicking other countries' architecture, Nyrop quipped: 'They don't build Danish churches in Italy.' Nyrop was inspired by Danish craft traditions and motifs that rose from the country's nature and identity. Building the City Hall took 13 years, and the result was architecture that felt at home in its own landscape.

From National Romanticism to Modernism

This evolving mindset found its fullest expression in modernism and functionalism, roughly from the 1910s and 1920s onward. Inspired by the continental Bauhaus and functionalism, Scandinavian architects embraced the idea that design should serve everyday life, and that beauty and practicality could go together. Yet, unlike the more industrial-style modern architecture of Central Europe, the Scandinavian approach never lost its human touch. It remained grounded in craftsmanship, natural materials and the soft northern light – the same three ingredients that had defined Scandinavian architecture from the start.

Walk the centre of any Nordic capital today, and you can still observe this evolution: the classical facades and pillars giving way to the more whimsical National Romantic style, to the flourishing lines of Jugendstil (or art nouveau) and, finally, to modernism. Jugendstil itself was largely a reaction to industrialism, a time of tension between the new opportunities created by evolving industries and the old traditions that people feared losing. It drew on romantic nationalism, mythology and the rediscovery of Nordic heritage.

By the 1920s, however, new ideas began to drift northward as Nordic architects conducted study trips to see groundbreaking buildings on the Continent. What they brought back was not just a style, but the entire philosophy of functionalism. Perhaps the most recognisable part of Scandinavian architecture today, this approach is defined by clean lines, natural materials and a desire to rethink how spaces can serve society and the people who inhabit them. Each Nordic country interpreted these ideas in its own distinctive way, giving modernism a local accent.

Regional Interpretations

In Denmark, the work of Arne Jacobsen (1902–1971) is a prime example. In Aarhus, the new town hall, opened in 1942 and designed by Jacobsen and Erik Møller (1909–2002), is a functionalist triumph: modern, yes, but also deeply rooted in Scandinavian tradition. Bright, open spaces and locally sourced materials – marble cladding from a Norwegian quarry – make the building feel both contemporary and unmistakably Scandinavian.

Meanwhile, in Finland, Alvar Aalto (1898–1976) ushered in the modern age of functionalism with a humanist sensibility. Aalto's buildings softened modernism's hard edges with warm materials, gentle curves and a deeply felt concern for how spaces actually feel to be lived in. Take the Paimio Sanatorium near the Finnish city of Turku. Here, Aalto and his first wife, the architect and designer Aino Aalto (1894–1949), created interiors that complement the building's architecture, making the sanatorium feel like a comforting space instead of a clinical hospital.

Both Aalto and Jacobsen carried their architectural ideals into everyday design, creating furniture and objects that unite function with beauty.

Sweden hosted one of the most defining moments in the story of Scandinavian architecture. At the 1930 Stockholm Exhibition, titled 'Housing, Transportation, Furnishing', architect Gunnar Asplund (1885–1940) presented functionalism not as a set of abstract rules, but as a tangible, lived experience. In light-filled pavilions and open spaces, visitors encountered a vision of modernism as a public symbol of progress and social idealism – a distinctly Nordic way of building houses and living in them.

In fact, throughout 20th-century Scandinavian architecture, light, simplicity and connection to nature remain constant. Expansive windows and uncluttered interiors are not just aesthetic choices but expressions of a philosophy that architecture should enhance human wellbeing and harmony with the environment. Take Jacobsen's Aarhus town hall as an example. Large windows not only let in light but also symbolise transparent decision-making. Wood, stone and glass dominate, creating a dialogue between indoors and out. It is minimalistic, yet it doesn't feel cold. Warmth appears in the curve of a door handle and the glow of a lamp.

Designing for People & Nature Today

Scandinavian architecture continues to evolve with imagination and environmental awareness. In Oslo, the Opera House by Snøhetta emerges from the harbour side like a glacier, its sloping roof providing both astounding acoustics and cool vistas to the fjord. In Copenhagen, the Bjarke Ingels Group (BIG) has reimagined what a power plant can be: CopenHill functions simultaneously as a ski slope, hiking trail and the world's tallest climbing wall.

In Helsinki, the recently commissioned Kumma Museum of Architecture and Design (set to open in 2030 and designed by JKMM Architects) promises to continue this tradition, using recycled bricks and other sustainable materials and techniques to create an environmentally conscientious building.

Travellers can best experience Scandinavian architecture in cultural spaces like Denmark's Louisiana Museum of Modern Art, where art and nature meet through glass walls, or Helsinki's Aalto Studio and House, which offer an intimate glimpse into the architect's world.

What makes Scandinavian architecture so intriguing is its ability to balance practicality with beauty and minimalism with warmth. It doesn't shout for attention but quietly invites you to step in and stay awhile. Whether you're exploring a centuries-old wooden stave church or taking in the city from the rooftop of a futuristic opera house, the same ideals shine through. These are buildings designed not just to be admired, but to be loved.

GOOD DESIGN SHOULD NOT MAKE EVERYDAY LIFE ONLY VISUALLY PLEASING BUT ALSO MORE FUNCTIONAL. BEAUTY SHOULD GO HAND IN HAND WITH PRACTICALITY.

Aarhus Rådhus (p326), Denmark

UWE ARANAS/SHUTTERSTOCK, BUILDING DESIGNED BY ARCHITECTS ARNE JACOBSEN AND ERIK MØLLER

FROM BAGUETTES TO VODKA

This whimsical tour is a lighthearted look at European stereotypes and how they've come about. By Anna Kaminski

CONSIDER EUROPE: A kaleidoscope of landscapes, cuisines, languages, cultures and quirks. When those outside the continent discuss specific countries and their inhabitants – and even when European citizens of a specific country discuss their neighbours – they often fall back on stereotypes. Some are affectionate exaggerations, others are outdated clichés, but most contain a grain of truth.

The Stiff-Upper-Lip Brits

The ability to remain unflappable in the face of danger is allegedly a core British trait, summed up by the WWII slogan, 'Keep calm and carry on.' It's synonymous with the 'stiff upper lip' (determination in the face of ad-

versity) – an 18th-century American expression that's come to be associated with the British bearing wartime privations without complaint. Whether this applies to today's Brits is up for debate, whereas the stereotype of Brits as world champions of politeness is spot-on. Orderly queueing is a national pastime, while 'sorry' must be the most overused word in the British lexicon, and a kneejerk reaction even if someone has just trodden on their foot. As for lengthy discussions of the weather, they can be attributed to the Brits' discomfort with 'personal' conversation topics such as individual earnings, political views or family relationships – all perfectly acceptable in other cultures.

The Romantic French

In the popular imagination, the French accent is the sexiest in the world, *français* is the lingua franca of *amour*, and Paris is the 'city of love' where beret-clad romantics with baguettes under their arms sip glasses of red wine in chichi cafes and share declarations of love on the Pont Neuf. The first two are entirely subjective, surely, and as for Paris being a particularly wondrous place to fall in love, those who arrive with such lofty expectations are bound to be disappointed by the realisation that Paris is like any other big city: with its own share of traffic snarls and other problems. Nonetheless, the stereotype owes itself to centuries of French literature celebrating love and art, descriptions of the city as ultra-romantic by the likes of Hemingway, and Hollywood movies such as *Midnight in Paris* and *French Kiss*.

The Punctual Germans

As the cliché goes, in Germany, if a train is scheduled to leave the station at 10.03am, it will depart not a second earlier or later. If a work meeting is due to last an hour, that's exactly how long it will be, and if you're a few minutes late, you're a social pariah. In reality, the punctuality of the Deutsche Bahn has taken a nosedive in recent years, with a third of long-distance trains being delayed as the overloaded railway network is in need of an update. The Industrial Revolution introduced strict time-keeping and structured schedules, and the Germans' appreciation of punctuality and a fondness for order and a rules-based society became ingrained in the national psyche because of the Prussian military tradition. My German friends say: 'Where you see *verboten* (forbidden), we see a framework of trust and predictability within which we have the freedom to be ourselves.'

The Sauna-Loving Finns

According to a pandemic joke, Finns were happy with the 2m social-distancing rule being lifted because they could go back to their normal 4m distance. Lack of emotional warmth and social awkwardness are likewise stereotypically associated with Finns; even neighbouring Estonians – also seen as reserved by outsiders – joke that they are gregarious social butterflies by comparison. Yet much is a matter of interpretation through a cultural lens: what's considered aloof by, say, Mediterranean standards, is seen as respectful in Nordic societies. Once you genuinely get to know individual Finns, you may find them to be warm and opinionated. Another stereotype is an abiding love of nature and a fondness for saunas, for both of which there is strong evidence. When you're sitting in a steamy wooden hut with strangers for long stretches without uttering a word, what's perceived as awkward elsewhere becomes an ability to comfortably sit in easy silence.

The Pasta-Munching Italians

Food dominates any cliches about Italians. In popular lore, all Italians eat pasta in copious amounts and their *nonna*'s recipe is the only 'authentic'. Things of little consequence are discussed at top volume, with emphatic gesticulation, and as everyone knows, unmarried Italians all live with their parents. In reality, while pasta is indeed widely consumed countrywide, with each region boasting its own varieties, it's less popular in the north than in the south. Italians do spend a lot of time arguing about recipes: given that food is central to Italian culture, the passion behind epicurean opinions is real. Compared with Northern Europe, the volume of Italian conversations may indeed seem loud, whereas strong attachment to family is an age-old social feature not limited to Italians: you'll find a similar devotion in other Mediterranean countries, and multi-generational families living under one roof may owe as much to economic insecurity as to blood ties.

The Vodka-Drinking Poles

Poland is often associated with vodka – in fact, the country produces some of the world's finest – so naturally, Poles are stereotyped as epic consumers of the tipple (typically while raising endless toasts at weddings and family gatherings). But while there are dedicated *wódka* bars popular with students in Kraków, Warsaw and other big cities, beer consumption has long overtaken vodka as Poland's favourite drink and Poles barely make it into the top 20 of Europe's biggest drinkers. It's true that Poland has long had a deeply ingrained hospitality culture, which historically demanded that visitors be greeted with food and shots of vodka – but the times, they are a-changin'.

INDEX

INDEX

A – B

Map Pages **000**

Map Pages **000**

Map Pages **000**

Map Pages **000**

Map Pages **000**

THIS BOOK

The 5th edition of Lonely Planet's Europe guidebook was curated by Kate Armstrong, Mark Baker, Joel Balsam, Cristian Bonetto, Marc Di Duca, Peter Dragicevich, Mark Eveleigh, Kata Fári, Anthony Ham, Paula Hotti, Anna Kaminski, Catherine Le Nevez, James March, Vesna Maric, Virginia Maxwell, Owen Morton, Anja Mutić, Isabella Noble, Leonid Ragozin, Anna Richards, Helena Smith, Joana Taborda, Brana Vladisavljevic, Kerry Walker, Luke Waterson, Nicola Williams, Barbara Woolsey and Angelo Zinna.

This guidebook was produced by the following:

Destination Editor
Shauna Daly

Coordinating Editors
Christopher Pitts, Brana Vladisavljevic

Production Editors
Amy Lysen, Kathryn Rowan, Jeremy Toynbee

Image Researchers
Dominic Allen, Norma Brewer, Dermot Hegarty

Cartographers
Valentina Kremenchutskaya, Daniela Machová, Anthony Phelan

Assisting Editors
Sofie Andersen, Imogen Bannister, Michelle Bennett, Liana Cafolla, Nigel Chin, Katie Connolly, Melanie Dankel, Helen Koehne, Anne Mulvaney, Karyn Noble, Holly Proctor, Fionnuala Twomey

Assisting Cartographers
Dorothy Davidson, Mark Griffiths, Jennifer Johnston, Chris Lee-Ack

Contributing Writers
Rudolf Abraham, Isabel Albiston, Hugh Francis Anderson, Eygló Svala Arnarsdóttir, Alexis Averbuck, Kat Barber, Olly Berry, Joe Bindloss, Caroline Bishop, Abigail Blasi, Federica Bocco, Jade Bremner, Shaun Busuttil, Jean-Bernard Carillet, Daniel James Clarke, Fionn Davenport, Natalia Diaz, Virginia DiGaetano, Jamie Ditaranto, Kathy Donaghy, Keith Drew, Mark Elliott, Becki Enright, İsmet Ersoy, Daniel Fahey, Steve Fallon, Mary Fitzpatrick, Esme Fox, Michael Frankel, Duncan Garwood, Benedetta Geddo, Kay Gillespie, Laurie Goodlad, Gemma Graham, Laura Hall, Jennifer Hattam, Anthony Haywood, Sandra Henriques, Annika Hipple, Rooksana Hossenally, Felicity Hughes, Sarah Irving, Ömercan Kaçar, Lauren Keith, Cyrena Lee, Daphné Leprince-Ringuet, Lucy Lovell, Emily Luxton, Marlene Marques, Chrissie McClatchie, Mike McEacheran, Hugh McNaughtan, Mélissa Monaco, Mary Nicklin, John Noble, Nanjala Nyabola, Thomas O'Malley, Stephanie Ong, Lorna Parkes, Ashley Parsons, Marisa Megan Paska, Samantha Priestley, Isabel Putinja, Kevin Raub, Joseph Reaney, Simon Richmond, Daniel Robinson, Madeleine Rothery, Eva Sandoval, Andrea Schulte-Peevers, Sarah Souli, Regis St Louis, Paul Stafford, Nicola Leigh Stewart, Monica Suma, Rowan Twine, Sara van Geloven, Ryan Ver Berkmoes, Tasmin Waby, Neil Wilson, Fabienne Fong Yan, Peter Yeung

Cover Researcher
Katelyn Perry

Thanks Daniel Bolger, Kate James, Darren O'Connell, Charlotte Orr, Saralinda Turner

Mapping data sources:
© Lonely Planet
© OpenStreetMap http://openstreetmap.org/copyright

MIX
Paper | Supporting responsible forestry
FSC™ C021741
www.fsc.org

Paper in this book is certified against the Forest Stewardship Council™ standards. FSC™ promotes environmentally responsible, socially beneficial and economically viable management of the world's forests.

Published by Lonely Planet Global Limited
CRN 554153
5th edition – Jun 2026
ISBN 978 1 83869 387 9
© Lonely Planet 2026
10 9 8 7 6 5 4 3 2 1
Printed in Malaysia